DERBY DIARIES

OPERA DIARIES

The Earl of Derby

THE DIARIES OF EDWARD HENRY STANLEY, 15th EARL OF DERBY (1826–93)

BETWEEN 1878 AND 1893

A SELECTION

Edited by

JOHN VINCENT

LEOPARD'S HEAD PRESS

2003
Published by
LEOPARD'S HEAD PRESS LIMITED
1–5 Broad Street, Oxford OX1 3AW

© The Earl of Derby (text)
John Vincent (additional matter)

ISBN 0 904920 45 3

British Library Cataloguing in Publication Data

Diaries of Edward Henry Stanley, 15th Earl of Derby
(1826-93)
A selection 1878-1893
(History)

Typeset by
Cambrian Typesetters, Frimley, Surrey
Printed by Halstan & Co. Ltd., 2-10 Plantation Road, Amersham, Buckinghamshire HP6 6HJ

To Pig and Pat

Contents

Acknowledgements

I would like to take this opportunity to thank all who have generously contributed to the gradual development of this volume. I appreciate the generosity of Lord Derby, owner of the diaries, in making them available. To Mrs Brenda Burgess, former Librarian at Knowsley, to her successor Mrs Askari, Keeper of the Collections, and to Mrs Naomi Evetts, of the Liverpool Record Office, custodian of the diaries today, I owe much for their professional guidance. For help on points of Victorian scholarship, I am indebted to Dr Andrew Jones and Dr John Pemble. Dr Nigel Brailey has generously shared his deep knowledge of Asian history. Professor John Powell and Mr W Patrick Jackson, CB, have been unstinting in their selfless encouragement and support throughout this long task, and without the guidance of that great friend of friendless books, Alan Bell, sometime Librarian of the London Library, this book might never have seen the light of day. For faultless preparation of a long and complex text, I am exceedingly fortunate in being able to thank Mrs Anne Merriman.

Publication on this scale would have been impossible without generous support from scholarly sources. I gratefully acknowledge the munificent assistance of the following: the Marc Fitch Fund, the Council of the Historic Society of Lancashire and Cheshire, and the Scouloudi Foundation in association with the Institute of Historical Research.

Preface

This is the fourth volume which I have extracted from the diaries of the 15th Earl of Derby and here my work on this archive ends. It would be wrong of me, however, not to make it clear at once that my labours have been confined to the diaries themselves (with occasional exceptions), and that Derby's official papers and personal correspondence in Liverpool Record Office should be regarded as a largely unexplored and potentially important source, not lightly to be neglected and in particular not to be disregarded by scholars just because of the publication of these various volumes of selections from the diaries.

Introduction

Edward Henry Stanley, fifteenth Earl of Derby (1826–93), was the elder son of the Lord Derby who was thrice prime minister and the longest serving party leader in modern British history. The fifteenth Earl was the only cabinet minister to serve under both Disraeli and Gladstone (and the only minister to watch both premiers falling asleep in cabinet while transacting important business). In a period when formal cabinet records were not kept, he had claims to be the fullest cabinet diarist, and perhaps the shrewdest political analyst too, of his time. For much of his public career he seemed, especially to non-political opinion, eminently fitted to be prime minister. That his handwriting was consistently legible, and his sentences clear, over the whole period for which his diaries extend, from 1849 to 1893, should only add to the regard in which historians hold him.

The Diaries

The diaries used in this edition are as described in the preceding volume.[1] They continue to be of foolscap size, with Derby writing almost a foolscap side on most days, and sometimes much more by overrunning on to adjacent pages. There were seasonal variations. At quiet times, on holiday, in summer and autumn, and at Christmas, there were many nearly blank pages. In each year, the first six months were busier than the second six months; Derby never neglected the London season. The diaries are in good condition, and apart from some idiosyncratic spellings of unusual proper names, present almost no difficulties to the reader.

The diaries themselves remain as before on deposit with the rest of the papers of the XIVth and XVth Earls of Derby in Liverpool Record Office. The catalogue reference for the papers of the XVth Earl is 920 DER (15). The Derby archives in Liverpool Record Office remain the property of the present Earl, and permission should be sought and acknowledged for any citations. Enquiries about any such matters should be made to the Keeper of Collections, c/o The Earl of Derby's Estate, The Estate Office, Knowsley, Prescot, Merseyside, L34 4AG (tel 0151-489-4437), while archival questions should be referred to The Archivist, Liverpool Record Office, Central Library, William Brown Street, Liverpool L3 8EW (tel 0151-233-5817).

This is the third and penultimate volume of the diaries, taken in chronological sequence, but the fourth in order of publication. No section now remains wholly unpublished. However, all volumes published are selections only, there being nowhere where the diaries are published in full over a considerable length of time. The partial exception is accounts of cabinet meetings, which are published unabridged.

The discovery of the diaries is a story in itself, but need not be repeated here.[2] It is enough to say that they are now readily accessible without prior appointment in Liverpool Record Office, where local arrangements for photocopying can be made. Since the Derby archives, whether papers or diaries, and *whether published or unpublished*, remain in private ownership, being the property of the present Earl, permission should be sought and acknowledged for any citations.

The papers of the 15th Earl were extensively weeded by him, and perhaps by his family and executors after his death, and in many respects may prove disappointing. Many leading correspondents are represented by only a few letters each. They form however an extensive collection, probably never fully explored and certainly by no means confined to the diaries; and they have not yet (2002) been fully catalogued, though an excellent draft catalogue is available on open shelves in the Record Office. A fuller catalogue is in course of preparation.

How contemporaneous were the diary entries? There is no exact answer, save that entries were nearly always written within 24 hours of the events described. (Accounts of cabinets appear to be based on notes actually taken in cabinet, for when meetings were sometimes held in more cramped conditions, the diarist records that contrary to his usual practice he has to depend on his memory.) Whether Derby habitually wrote on retiring, or early the following day, is hard to make out. Sometimes he wrote up his diary entry for the current day several times in the course of the day. Suffice to say that the only occasions when the diary lacked the hot breath of contemporaneity were when there was nothing at all going on, or when he was ill. (His entry for Christmas Day, for instance, was written on that day, as an escape from enjoyment.)

What did he read? He was inundated with pamphlets on public questions, and reading (and burning) these absorbed much time. Titles and topics are rarely noted. The same is true of books. Only occasionally does he record actual authors, as opposed to his haunting of London bookshops, his care for his library, his antiquarian collecting, and his roaming of the countryside, book in hand. What he did think worthy of specific mention were rather articles in the great periodicals of opinion, perhaps because they were well suited for reading to Lady Derby as her sight began to fail. Enough survives, however, to show a cultivated and serious, if not perhaps voracious, mind, with certain special interests; thus he was well versed in recent works on the interior of Africa in the years before he became Colonial Secretary, and he kept abreast of developments on the Far Left of political theory, including Henry George, Wallace, and Marx.

It seems plain that his sources of information were manifold. He saw the national press, whether hostile, friendly, or neutral, regularly, and had a clear picture of the current outlook of each paper. On occasion, and with proper distaste, he seems to have inspected the Scandalous Sixpennies, the gutter press of the late seventies.

A great peer like Derby had innumerable points of contact with national life. A regular attender at the House of Lords, he would meet there, or at least watch, other frontbenchers or cabinet members, many of them political intellectuals, some of them social intimates. Less regularly, but quite often, he would observe the debates in the House of Commons, though he did not mix socially with MPs there. He cultivated the national press, and was frequently visited informally by Lawson of the *Telegraph*. He had a good relationship with Russell, the editor of the Liverpool local paper.

He knew the leading medical men, the leading lawyers, the leading men of science, the leading men of letters, almost as a matter of routine. He gave interviews to Herbert Spencer and talked politics with Charles Darwin. He saw it as his duty to support statistics, or at least needy statisticians. Once a Cambridge Apostle, he partook of its adult counterpart among distinguished metropolitan intellectuals, known as The Club. He was also an active member of its more political counterpart, Grillions.

As to matters academic and cultural, he was a member of the supreme court regulating squabbles at the ancient universities, he was a weighty member of London University Senate, he nurtured Manchester University, and helped Liverpool University College get off the ground, while at the same time running the National Portrait Gallery and the British Museum. He inherited from his father a regional responsibility of great importance, for there remained a residue from the funds raised in the Sixties for the relief of the Cotton Famine. This sum became the Cotton Districts Convalescent Hospital Fund, producing hospitals at Southport and Buxton, and was administered with zeal by Derby and other Lancashire worthies.

As the landowner of a great urban, agricultural, and industrial estate, Derby had his finger on the pulse of all aspects of the Lancashire economy. His agents in the north, as well as his land agents and men of affairs in the south-east, were well qualified to give their own interpretations of where England was heading. He gleaned much from discussions with neighbours in Kent who were big figures in the City. As a leading figure in the Peabody Trust, he was de facto landlord to very large numbers of the London poor. As chairman of the Lancashire magistrates over nearly thirty years, he knew in detail how local government worked in a populous industrial country, where he had the constitutional roles of both uncrowned king and acting premier in pre-county council days. As chairman of the Liverpool bench for many decades, he devoted three or four days each quarter to dealing with the petty crime of the area. His knowledge of drink, Irishmen, and working-class violence was therefore extensive and peculiar.

In two respects his roots did not reach deep. He did not cultivate either the manufacturers or the military. True, he concerned himself with the local Volunteers, and tried to put the struggling local Rifle Association on its feet, but he did not hobnob with generals. It was not an area of life he wished to penetrate. As for the industrialists, while he allowed himself to stay in their houses when it was convenient for him to do so while on business, he does not seem to have felt under any obligation to entertain them at Knowsley. (Even key allies among mill owners like Hugh Mason seem never to have visited.) However, hospitality was extended en masse at huge garden parties to the smaller fry from the local Liverpool middle class, but not to individual millionaires across Lancashire. At heart, Derby still liked to think of Lancashire as a county of great families and their estates.

The great exception to Derby's omnivorous grasp of modern life was the Church. It was a complete blank on his map. He never knowingly spoke to a churchman, other than relations enjoying family livings. He never had a clergyman to dinner. Generous to dissenters, because aristocrats are generous to poor folk, he quite uncharacteristically turned down clerical applications, except where, as in the case of Liverpool Cathedral, he had particular local reasons for not wanting to look mean. And yet the aristocratic code took precedence even in this area of first principle – in the case of Bury church, he gave thousands to restore the church because a kinsman was parson.

Why this was, is not entirely easy to say. For a start, nothing is ever said of Lady Derby's churchmanship or religious practice, an odd omission, though she did once take Matthew Arnold to church at Knowsley. There is no hint of a shared outlook in the diaries. Derby's hostility to religion cannot entirely be put down to the row with Salisbury, for he was a marked sceptic much earlier than that. Something arose from utility; Derby simply felt strongly that religion was a waste of money, and that money should not be wasted. This view certainly went deep. Yet, though sighing for a religion-less world,

Derby did go to church, and not only for funerals, about which he took much trouble. In some years he attended his parish church several times, in other years not at all. Sometimes he attended at Christmas "to show myself to the people", but never at Easter; when in office, he studiously worked throughout Easter (thereby making subordinates work too.) He only attended church when resident at Knowsley, never when in Kent or London; religion was a Lancashire duty, thrown off when he became his real self away from his own county.

Charity however was another matter. Here we see Derby at his most meticulous and obsessive. Each day he was drowning in begging letters. They had first claim on his time, taking perhaps two hours a day. Almost nothing went unanswered. What had perhaps begun as a hobby turned into an industry. Applications poured in from as far away as Central Europe. No secretary ever assisted him. At Knowsley, the librarian had a small fund with which to act as almoner in the house and locally. Lady Margaret Cecil did good works in the village, but that was all. The diaries almost certainly fail to record the full extent of Derby's charities, while the payments named in this edition are only given as a small sample of those in the diaries.

Relative to Derby's total rental, most of the sums given are small, even tiny. Relative to Derby's disposable income, the sum spent on benefactions is rather large. Relative to what Derby spent on himself, benefactions loom very large. It is likely that the item for benefactions understates matters, payments to superannuated and injured staff and their relicts being probably charged to estate and household accounts rather than as the benefactions they in fact were. Perhaps Derby's greatest generosity was the hardest to express, namely the slice taken out of his working day by correspondence on mendicancy. It was clearly well known in the vicinity of Liverpool that anyone with a connexion however remote with the Derby interest, or with a good story to tell, would find Derby a soft touch. Word spread, hence the vital importance to Derby of the principle, not followed to the letter, that his charities were strictly confined to the county of Lancashire. Derby's standing in Liverpool, Lancashire, and perhaps even nationally to some extent, was based on the widespread popular picture of him as everyone's donor of last resort.

Knowsley itself, if not perhaps the remoter estates, was also, if not quite a charity, certainly something of a welfare state. Though not entirely a bed of roses, for the labour could be hard, and even, in the shooting season, dangerous, employees were exceptionally well treated. Derby provided model cottages in the village, pensions for servants and their widows, allowed widows to remain in estate properties "as a matter of course", paid for medical treatment by his own GP, and subsidised industrial life assurance (while dissolving the local but amateurish life assurance society set up by his father). In all respects except education, he provided for those under him; and education is but a partial exception, since he gave here and there to Lancashire village schools having claims on him, without, it would appear, concerning himself with primary education on his doorstep.

The diary, so meticulous in other matters, makes no mention of the tipping of servants, a matter probably of great importance to them. Tipping of the upper class young, on visits, birthdays, and festive occasions, is recorded, and was substantial. It was not beneath Derby's dignity, on the other hand, to know of misdemeanours downstairs; without himself seeing offending parties, he usually brought influence to bear in favour of leniency, except perhaps where drink was involved, just as in court he seems to have taken pride in the shortness of his (meticulously calculated) average sentence.

Derby's estate brought him the pleasure of daily administration. At Knowsley, he was always premier. His heads of departments there always formed a ministry. He liked his colleagues, and found many passing satisfactions. Visually Knowsley grew less neglected. His rent roll grew by the year. It proved immune to agricultural depression, unlike that of everyone else, including his Bedford in-laws. He could not entirely overlook the fact that he had succeeded financially where his father had failed. Such considerations led to mellowness. Windfall receipts from sales of land to railway companies led to more mellowness. And he had no needy or demanding family to provide for (though no lack of distant black sheep) which might diminish the pure unsullied pleasure to be derived from great wealth.

It was as well for Derby that land entailed the simple pleasures of administration. For to him, unlike his father, most country sports were as nothing. He rode, but only solitarily, and there were relatively few days of the year when he led shooting parties of his guests from Knowsley. It does not seem to have been a particularly pleasurable experience for him as he grew older, occurring as it did in the worst weather of the year, but it was the sort of thing one did.

Entirely different was Derby's deep and long-standing pleasure, almost erotic in intensity, in forestry, which after all was not the sort of thing one did, and not something one can imagine his father doing. Silviculture had since the early Sixties given him a domain of his own, or perhaps taken him out of the house and away from his father. What might have been harder to foresee was the way it grew into a passion for individual trees on the one hand, and a lust for scenic landscape on the other. In the background of his life in the Seventies and Eighties was the search for the perfect country estate, a search no whit diminished by his already possessing at Witley near Hindhead and Haslemere an estate meeting his exacting requirements. The deepest evocations of pleasure in the diaries relate to trees and forests.

★ ★ ★

To escape from the tedium of enjoyment was one of Derby's great purposes. In one direction he accomplished it by looking at remote estates that he never bought, by day trips to Hindhead, and by being his own head forester; in another direction he achieved it by administration. But what was administration? It was a curiously plural affair. It began before breakfast in his room, with attention to miscellaneous private business, to his diary, and to begging letters. It progressed to such few minutes as he could devote to the government of whichever of his houses he was living in, and in particular to the care of its library and its works of art. At Knowsley, it might include brief but decisive consultations with the heads of each of the main departments on the estate. Of encounters with indoor servants, or indeed of encounters with anyone before dinner, the diaries do not speak. We may perhaps assume that lunch, like breakfast, was normally solitary if indeed it took place at all.

Yet Derby often records complex impressions of what "people" were thinking. Who were these [always anonymous] "people"? The answer lies between those he walked back from the House of Lords with (Lowe particularly) and those he had lunch with at the Travellers'; these somehow constituted opinion. A third possibility, shown by some entries, is that there was a system whereby public figures, diplomatists and members of the opposite party especially, wrote to Lady Derby, in the sure knowledge that their views would reach Lord Derby, while still leaving it open to them to deny having been in touch.

Derby might thus reach the office somewhat after noon. By 4.30, he would be off again to the sitting of the House of Lords, which rarely took long. He was present both as departmental minister, answering occasional questions, and as cabinet spokesman, the latter being the weightier role. More present to his own mind very often was stopping the Upper House compassing its own downfall in some conflict with the Commons. On many days, the walk back to the office was the significant part of the day's attendance. When back at the office, he worked fast indeed, for he had a suburban rush hour train to catch, and all was timed to the nearest minute. Fortunately, the British Empire in its heyday was a part-time job which fitted well into perhaps 4 hours a day.

The secretary of state was perhaps less a minister than a personnel director. The one inescapable task he had was to fill posts, reputably if possible, but at any rate to fill them. He had to adjudicate when officials were involved in rows. He had to deal with requests for patronage, though political patronage at this time seems quiescent. He had to have some idea of the worthiness of the whole vast Colonial Service and to be civil to such of them as happened to pass through London. The London agents of the settler colonies had little business to transact, but it was all the more incumbent on the Colonial Secretary to pass his time giving them a sense of consequence. The personnel side of the Empire was enough to exhaust the energies of any minister and leave nothing over for policy in a broad sense, not least if as in Derby's case one aimed at perfect fairness.

★ ★ ★

When Derby resigned in spring 1878 he did so without a master plan. If he intended to become a senior Liberal politician, he did not confess it to his diary, nor convey it by his actions. For some weeks he genuinely expected war, which would have changed everything. Hence there was no immediate quarrel on resignation: civil talk with the Queen, small talk with Salisbury with no awkwardness, and apparent nervous kindliness from Disraeli. Only after peace was secured did Derby find battle lines drawn in domestic politics, in the course of the summer.

Sheer relief at being out of office is prominent in the 1878 diaries, but so is determination to take stock of the situation gradually and not to make any false move. His social circle ceased almost at once, and permanently, to include Conservatives, even colleagues of long standing like Cross. His hate mail abruptly ceased, he showed no sign of poor health, and he sought an interval of entire rest – a "state of pleasant idleness" which included taking up gymnastics at nearly 52 – "it is late for that sort of thing".

He showed little sign of resentment against those who had ousted him. He made hardly any accusations against the Borgias of Hatfield, still less against Disraeli. He set his face against either quarrelling openly with Disraeli, or accepting any favour from him. Though Disraeli was unpleasantly sharp about Derby in the House of Lords, Derby never broke with him socially, partly from good sense, partly from a deeply-felt real loyalty. Pallbearer at his funeral, Derby paid the pensions of Disraeli's servants, and was active in organising the erection of a statue to his memory.

Derby continued to meet Schouvaloff on a number of occasions[3] including having him to shoot at Knowsley[4]. He also met some, but not all, of the other diplomatists. He cultivated Lord Sefton, his Whig opposite number and neighbour in Lancashire, with whom he got on well, though Sefton was a very different sort of man. Derby admitted to his diary, rather daringly, that "franchise extension" was inevitable, thereby making himself eligible to join the Liberal mainstream – but on the other hand declined an invitation from Gladstone[5], not for the last time, to nearby Hawarden:

> "Gladstone is not popular with the Liberals... and his strong ecclesiastical bias prevents any great personal sympathy growing up between us."

For all that, Derby finished the year with an unexplained outburst (his only recorded one) of churchgoing[6]. This coincided with the confirmation that Lady Derby was suffering from cataract[7], a heavy blow. The inner Derby might sigh longingly for "a kind of property I have often desired & never possessed – a large tract of land in a picturesque county, away from towns", but Derby the politician was from late summer 1878 closely marking the turning of opinion against Disraeli from the high tide of "peace with honour". A clue to future intentions lay in his deciding to keep up an expensive private wire from Tonbridge to his remote Kent property at Fairhill. Likewise he gave his name to subscribe for the new Liverpool bishopric "which I rather dislike than otherwise; but... refusal would be ascribed to dislike to parting with money". He kept in touch with opinion: on his Swiss holiday in 1878 he read *The Times,* the *Pall Mall Gazette,* and the *Daily News.* He expressed support for Chamberlain's caucus system[8] while remaining enough of a high Whig to give vent to profound and irrational suspicions of the Crown whenever possible.

By 1879 his mood was less one of a retired minister enjoying his ease. "I am constantly busy when in London, & at times have the feeling of wanting leisure". He did not expect a Conservative defeat. "But the public mind continues in a conservative mood: there is no revival of democratic zeal, only a wish for better administration".[9] Derby was deeply committed against the two disastrous "little wars", the Afghan and the Zulu. The party he gave to which 800 were invited[10] should perhaps be seen as a political celebration of Isandhlwana. He announced his near-certainty about "the approaching bankruptcy of India"[11]; since this did not happen, it shows loss of nerve rather than prescience. Loss of nerve, too, may be found in the mention of Carnarvon, of all people, arguing for retaining in all South Africa only the harbour of Cape Town.[12].

On the lighter side, Derby noted some singular requests in his post[13], and furnished an astringent sketch of the late Lord Carlisle. He was pleased that Lancashire knew nothing of the agricultural distress so widely prevalent, and viewed with some complacency the hardship of his Bedford in-laws.

In the spring he referred with his usual objectivity to his own possible demise. Dr Drage, his Kensington doctor, had found a return of the symptoms of 1843. 'In that case *"bonsoir la compagnie"*'.[14] Perhaps the doctor erred, for we hear no more. but it reminds one that Derby lived in the daily expectation of the return of a fatal condition, even if the hints are few. In fact he was well enough. He "found the difficulty of hearing increases"[15] as well it might in a crowded Liverpool courtroom, but he could do a 5-hour walk with ease[16], and both at Knowsley and in Kentish lanes he governed from the saddle.

He cultivated those whom statesmen and great peers do well to cultivate. Of an appearance in society, he excused himself thus: "...it is good to show oneself in society now and then."[17]. Sending £10 to Mr Smith of Coalville, saviour of the gypsy children, he noted: "having subscribed more for appearance' sake than for any other reason."

When he went to church at Knowsley, there was again a hint of ulterior motive of the best kind: "Church in morning, not having been seen there, or indeed anywhere, for a long while by the village folks." When the weather was hard, Derby's interest in it was not meteorological but sociological, in its effect on the working class in the great towns and on unemployment; he could hardly see a snowflake without worrying about its impact on the whole social order.

His estate looked after its own. Derby paid life pensions to employees and to their widows[18], whether the employees were dead, injured, or simply past useful service. It went without question that they could keep their estate houses after ceasing employment. Medical care was provided free. Derby wound up the village insurance society founded by his father, which had run down, nudging employees to save instead with industrial assurance.[19] Derby and Lady Derby did some sick visiting themselves, though this was unusual.[20]

Politically, he remained in suspense and uncommitted. "Economy is again beginning to be in favour. . ."[21] ". . .in short the nation is coming to its senses". Yet though Jingo was dead, it was not yet clear what would replace him: "I see no signs of any other than a conservative feeling. . . what men want is peace, revival of trade, & security against ceaseless troubles: not organic change."[22] He did not see doom written on the landed aristocracy: "The leading opponents of the Corn Laws sincerely believed that their abolition would break down the landed aristocracy: which on the contrary is far stronger than it was before."[23]

He continued to see Schouvaloff.[24] He made a welcome new acquaintance in Dilke (who on a country walk professed to mistake Derby for a tramp.) He was as prudish as ever: "buy one of the new penny weeklies. . . find it full of the grossest indecency"[25], and as wearisomely meticulous, e.g. over his foreign holiday expenses in 1878 and 1879, calculated to the last franc, and even a visit to the dentist's, where thanks to laughing-gas "I was exactly 11 minutes in the house" before returning to his desk.

As a political neutral, he was in heavy demand from public bodies. The T.U.C., the Cooperative Congress, the Social Science Congress, the committee for Arctic exploration, and the St Helens bicycling club all demanded his patronage; in the end he confined himself to chairmanship of the Manchester Horticultural Society[26], to being a patron of Edward Lear, to playing the part of royalty in strenuous ceremonies at Southport,[27] and to supporting Lancashire vernacular literature.[28]

His meetings with Liberal leaders were few. He was sounded by Harcourt, an old personal friend, and he travelled up from Dover with Granville, whom rather oddly he suspected of being "rather radical in his ideas as to large landed estates"[29] Land, not tax, was the chief point on which he felt nervous about the Liberals. What Derby emphatically did not do was associate himself with either the Gladstonian court or the Liberal party machine.

Though at 53 he reflected "I have had good health. . .and a singularly happy home"[30], by the autumn of 1879 the diaries return to a more familiar mixture of dire warnings[31] about his health from Dr Drage, and the bad effect that Knowsley always had upon the health or spirits of Lady Derby even within a few weeks. It may not have helped that visits to Knowsley usually coincided with the shortening of daylight. Derby had involvements at Knowsley which meant much to him but which Lady Derby could not very well share – for instance the potentially rowdy tenants' dinners for all and sundry, ("many of the cottagers having brought friends with them, which I do not forbid"); and the repeated attacks of the Knowsley smell did nothing to lessen his longings for some rural paradise which never quite materialised. At no time however did he stop leafing through the pages of "Estates for Sale" in the hope of finding his idyll.

Though he remained prominent among the (uncommitted) great and the good up to the 1880 election, it is important to note how much he was taken by surprise by the course of events. He probably expected a Conservative victory in 1880, at least until very late in the day. Such a result would not have grated on his own "growing desire of ease". He was unimpressed by the Midlothian campaign, and expected a Granville ministry in the event of a Liberal victory. He did not sniff radicalism in the air:

". . .there is a singular absence of anything that can be called radicalism. I see no trace of the bitterness of class-feeling which certainly existed 30 years ago. . . The Liberal Programme is mild enough. . ."

And again:

". . .The new House will be decidedly Liberal, but I do not see that it will be democratic"[32]

As a collector of opinions, forecasts, reflections, and explanations, the diarist is highly valuable for putting the election weeks into day-by-day sequence without the distortions of hindsight.

Lady Derby emerged in the 1880 elections for the last time as a driving force in her own right, more Liberal, more committed, more partisan than her husband.

Derby did not foresee, any more than Gladstone, the explosion in Ireland. Though generous to the Irish Relief Fund, to which he sent £50 before the election, he thought "distress. . .wildly exaggerated."[33]

Though his Whig serenity was undisturbed by the new ministry – he thought Chamberlain's appointment to the Board of Trade, with admission to the cabinet, a good one[34] - he applied himself to taking out various kinds of reinsurance; thus he sent £21 to the Clerk Maxwell memorial fund –

"I subscribe with pleasure, for it is well to make friends among the scientific party. . ."[35]

Of a charitable exercise, Derby writes similarly:

". . .Wearisome as such ceremonies are, & an utter waste of time, they are necessary, if local popularity is to be maintained."[36]

And when Easter Day fell on 28 March 1880, which was almost the eve of poll, Derby overcame his scruples and went to church:

". . .(Easter Day). Show myself to the village in the accustomed manner."[37]

It was Harcourt, Derby's college friend and fellow-Apostle at Cambridge, who as the new Home Secretary took the first step to bringing Derby back into public life, by inviting him to chair a Royal Commission on City charities and companies, which over the centuries had become far too rich for any visible good that they did. This role well befitted Derby, for the need was to produce acceptable reforms while holding back an unjust radical onslaught on privilege. This was ultimately done to some effect, with benefits mainly in the field of education that are very much still with us today.

In politics, the diary for 1880 shows Derby closely following the ups and perhaps still more the downs of Gladstone's first year in office. His qualms about Gladstone are spelled out at length. "I can never feel sure what Gladstone will do next."[38] Despite his holding prestige as an abomination, Derby swallows whole the doctrine of military honour.[39] He accepts the presidency of a cooperative congress – "it serves to divert support from more revolutionary schemes."[40] Always, when doing the right and generous thing, he hints at the ulterior social motive. To his annual garden party at Knowsley, 260 persons were asked; why, or of what sort, is not clear,[41] except that Derby had no intention of lessening his hereditary influence. He could well afford to be expansive, his surplus for the year being £60,000[42], with rapidly growing Bootle now starting to replace Liverpool as the jewel in his crown.[43] His revised will of 1880 showed Derby's sense of how he held great wealth in trust. For his sister there was £12,000, for public bodies £20,000, for servants £10,000 (on a sliding scale according to years of service).

Though he had encountered signs of his mysterious life-threatening illness in 1880 – "some uncomfortable symptoms have reappeared. . . strict care in living will be necessary for some weeks" – by early 1881 he believed that "a certain indolence, mental & bodily, is the chief danger against which I have to guard."[44] On balance, his weight, regularly recorded, was slowly rising between 1878 and 1885. Politics did not stir him, there being (as he saw it) only one party: "the extraordinary display of changed public feeling at the elections has destroyed the official prospects of Conservatives for some time to come."[45]

What stirred Derby most in 1880 and 1881 was the need to avoid a clash between Lords and Commons. On this issue he exerted real powers of leadership, and with some effect. It was easier for him to do this because Gladstone and others led him to believe the 1881 Land Act was to be far more moderate than it actually was. It is a question whether Gladstone's utterances in early 1881 were not deliberate misinformation.[46] This belief in a high-minded peerage which adjudicated on public affairs meant Derby was necessarily severe on playboy peers like Hardwicke who let the side down.[47] Derby viewed the tendencies of the age not with alarm but with a certain complacency, telling his friend Lowe:

". . .that no sign had appeared either of reckless faction, or of democratic envy of the rich, or of class-feeling among the working section of the population. . ."[48]

Life between Midlothian and the 1884 Reform Act seemed as stable as it had ever been, with as little reason why it should ever change. Derby, as ever, industriously supported stability by diligent generosity: 15 guineas to the Arundel Society, saying "I hardly know what, nor care, but it is the right business to "patronise art" – though not, it would seem, music. To the widow of a murdered Irish peer, £20;[49] to Kent Opthalmic Hospital, £10[50]; to the children of his brother-in-law Col. West, £10 each as a tip[51]; to the O'Donoghue, a worthless Irish MP who lived by cadging, a "loan" of £100.[52] To his chief agent, Hale, he gave £200 to cover illness in his family. Tonbridge Free Library received £50[53], and the London Labourers' Society £100.[54] An estate carpenter was startled to get £42,[55] and the indigent Lord Winchilsea got £5 for his poems.[56] Lancaster Grammar School got £50,[57] and Liverpool medical students were found prizes.[58] In the same category of semi-charitable good works of a great landowner, one may include his purchase of £1,000 of shares in the new Mersey Railway.[59]

In 1880–82 Derby and Lady Derby were unwell. How unwell, is hard to say, for the relevant entries are few, and the stiff upper lip plays its usual part. That they were more unwell than in previous and subsequent years seems likely; the difficulty is to know how far it affected their decisions, especially about taking office. Derby's kidney trouble returned in 1881 but seems to have been kept under control.[60] A form of depression

returned – "the sensation which would be produced by the first information of impending misfortune. Business in which I can take an interest drives it off at once: especially if
transacted in company with other people. . .".[61] Lady Derby suffered perhaps more
severely. She was "brought . . . into a condition of gloom and depression which is painful
to witness. . . . And I watch any tendency in that direction with the more anxiety from
knowing the family predisposition."[62] Next summer he reported "her spirits depressed,
without any obvious cause for anxiety. This has happened to her before but, knowing the
family tendency to melancholy, I never see it without uneasiness."[63] Behind Derby's
characteristic understatement, one has to recall that the family had never ceased to be
haunted by the death of Lady Derby's eldest brother in a sudden fit of depression in
1873, and by the fact that two of her other brothers were sadly far from "all right". Derby,
with his peculiar terror of inherited insanity, was not the man to take such things lightly.

Lady Derby's depression might be conjecturally explained in any number of ways.
Increasing blindness, though not yet total, was the most obvious. The failure of political
ambition, as Derby trod water, was another. Others might relate it to shortening days and
the onset of winter. Yet again, some might note that it seemed to coincide with the final
return of Schouvaloff to Russia. But it would not be surprising if she had an overwhelm-
ing sense of defeat. Derby had his money and his estate management – what did Lady
Derby have?

Derby did indeed have his money. In 1880 he put by £80,000 out of current income
"which I never did before, nor probably shall again." This prosperity allowed him to avoid
bringing matters to a head with the emollient Hale as to whether to adopt a more rigor-
ous and parsimonious style of landlordism. Derby settled, in effect, to forego about
£20,000 p.a. for the sake of running the estate on an easy rein and the good will that
brought:

" . . . Hale understands the estate, and the people, and keeps all quiet, though he
certainly does not spare my pocket."[64]

Sales of land to railway companies, especially in Bury and Bootle, and sales of land for
building, provided the flow of exceptional and unforeseen income which featherbedded
Derby's Lancashire farmers, and meant that the Great Depression left him completely
untouched.

Derby after two years of Liberal government was no office-seeker and certainly no
Gladstonian. He would, it is true, have voted for the 1881 Irish Land Act had it come to
a vote, which it did not, but with interior reservations:

" . . . The whole transaction increases (if possible) the distrust I have long felt for
Gladstone, who is equally uncongenial to me as a high churchman and dévôt and
as an ardent democrat".[65]

Derby, at Knowsley, was not just a private sportsman, but the provider of sport (and
food) for his local community. Shooting meant bonding. "More than 100 lookers-on
walked with us";[66] "a great crowd of lads with us all day."[67]

Derby entered 1882 apparently well reconciled to his marginal position, the more so
perhaps as "I ought to have £50,000 surplus every year after all expenses paid."[68]
Knowsley itself he found "more agreeable to the eye than ever it was in my time, notwithstanding increase of smoke." Though "conscious of an increased disinclination to bodily
exertion"[69] and tending to put on weight, his health was "better at 55 than at 35." He

watched trade "which is reviving"[70] as closely as any merchant. It emerged that he was a non-smoker, albeit a reluctant one. His social life was full. During a stay of 8 weeks at Knowsley, "we have been almost perpetually occupied with receiving company. . . . I have seldom had less of a really idle time."[71] The guests however though members of Society came from the foothills rather than the peaks. The Derbys were outside the smart set, and their dinner party lists (space forbids inclusion of all 25 guests; the prosopography of the London season awaits its student) were mostly taken from the Whig second eleven. Derby was curiously unworried about his historical situation:-

> " . . . I do not believe that the aristocracy will recover lost power, or that the democracy can be anything but the governing class."[72]

His solicitude for the House of Lords took the form chiefly of an antique concern about the quality of its oratory. His reports on its debates are full and judicious, and may be unrivalled; they fill a gap in the printed sources. He covers opinion, mood, faction, audience, audibility, eccentricity, and much else that might well have perished. His generally low opinion of Salisbury's performances probably reflects reality rather than pique – Salisbury's unsure hold on his own party before 1885 was a central fact.

While toying with his own version of internal exile – he was attracted by a Fylde estate for sale "in a wild picturesque country"[73] – Lady Derby's health and spirits had worsened.

She was "again despondent about her eyes[74], and intended to discontinue her Swedish eye specialist, thinking he did her eyes no good[75]. A month later she "now thinks the weakness of her eyes incurable and increasing: habitual low spirits have returned upon her."[76] In high summer she found relief. ". . .On Hindhead she found that she could see better, which shows that nerves have much to do with her affliction of the eyes."[77] Looking back to the low spirits of the spring, Derby wrote in summer "This description was not exaggerated when written, but matters have mended since; it is only at intervals that these gloomy fits occur."[78] The vicissitudes continued. Though in September, at Knowsley, "her eyes. . .very much worse"[79], in November we find Lady Derby "well & happy at Paris."[80]

Derby's response was at once loyal, stoical, and morbid. Loyal, in that he put Lady Derby first; stoical, in that he steadfastly pursued work in hand, however tedious; and morbid, in that he felt the hand of death on his own shoulder. He set his mind to maintaining his local position, but with inner grumbling. ". . .About hospitals what is there new to be said?"[81] Agreeing to open a bazaar for a Liverpool hospital, he commented "a silly waste of time, but such things are not to be avoided if one lives in a populous district."[82] Visiting Bury, he noted, "Having been so little in the town, I am surprised not to be actually unpopular." After each visit he carefully noted the warmth of his reception there as compared to other places.[83] Called on to attend the opening of a new hospital building, Derby "gave an ambiguous answer . . . those frequently recurring ceremonies are a waste of life."[84] The work he really wished for was work which came to his desk: "though often tired of work when I have it to do, it is necessary to me, & when it is not to be had (as now) I suffer from the want of it."[85]

Duty of course did prevail. Derby did attend the Stanley Hospital bazaar in Liverpool;[86] he did lay the foundation stone of the new sessions house and banquet at the Adelphi;[87] he did steer the Boiler Explosion Bill through parliament in concert with the arch-radical Hugh Mason.[88]

This left him little time for his idea of senatorial leisure, such as reading Renan's new work on the Book of Solomon[89], lunch with Herbert Spencer to hear his strange ideas, writing his critique of John Bright[90], keeping abreast of the progressive thought of Wallace and Henry George[91], and reflecting that "I consider all over £200,000 a year super-fluity".[92]

The chores of a magnate, and the problem of a depressive wife, were engrossing his attention when destiny, in the form of a cabinet reshuffle consequent upon the Phoenix Park Murders, intervened. On 15 May 1882, Granville offered Derby the India Office; Derby declined, in a letter to Granville of 18 May, "ascribing my reasons to personal reasons exclusively. . . .They are entirely personal, and do not concern me alone." But an earlier entry of May 1882 partly contradicts this. Here Derby says he hopes the question of an offer will not arise, but of the three alternatives, "there is probably no one that would not injuriously affect my personal position." He was a politician in need of an excuse, and fortunate to have one in the form of Lady Derby's health and possible suicidal tendencies. What the compelling reasons were which led him to turn down India in May 1882 is hard to establish, dislike of Gladstone apart.

One possible reason is doubts about his own health. Derby was in an unusually morbid frame of mind in summer 1882: ". . .My 56th birthday: there will not be many more."[93] Something had evidently gone wrong in May, and he had been seeing his doctors:-

". . . Both Gorst and Drage think great care necessary to prevent aggravation of the kidney symptoms. I will take care, for it is stupid to die prematurely by one's own negligence; but the imagination does not easily realise the existence of disease where there is a total absence of pain or discomfort, or even weakness. I accept the medical opinion, but I do it by an effort of reason."[94]

The eventual cure was to see a third doctor, a Dr Garrod, who took a more hopeful view of the complaint; but Derby's comments support the argument that he had felt himself close to death.

". . . I left him with a more hopeful feeling as to my prospects of life, though it is a puzzle to myself how little I really care about the matter, one way or the other. Most of the things I wished to do are done, and I have no plan on hand in the success of which I feel any very lively interest. Only it seems like blundering & mismanagement to go off the stage before one's time."[95]

Ere long his mind turned back from mortality to chores, charities, the social order, and the role of the peerage. He agreed to be vice-president of the British Association for their Southport meeting; he invited them over to Knowsley for a bunfight, and was appalled by their want of manners. He decided vegetarianism would be "an immense saving to our poorer classes" and sent a fiver in anonymous support. He sighed earnestly at the enormous prices reached at the Duke of Hamilton's art sale, or rather its effect on social stability:

". . .The effect on the poorer part of the community cannot be good. To a man earning £50 a year it must seem monstrous that the year's wages of 80 labourers should go for what he would call a mere fancy. Every such display of wealth strengthens socialism."

Display of wealth or not, his Knowsley garden party was for 250 guests.[96] In his semi-royal Lancastrian role, Derby also attended that unique popular festival, the Preston

Guild, finding "my reception was quite extraordinarily warm, which is the more curious as I have never laid myself out for social popularity. . . .I had every reason to be satisfied with the feeling shown by the Preston people towards my family and myself."[97] His view was that he was maintaining a dynastic position, not pursuing a personal career; and hence it is all the more curious that he should ask, not for the first or last time, "How long will Knowsley be a possible residence for the family?"[98] and turn his thoughts to a Scottish estate. "There is something attractive in the idea of a valley 22 miles long."

But those were dreams. The reality, in autumn 1882, lay in cultivating the higher journalists – Lawson, Escott, Knowles, Morley, Reeve - ; in saving for a rainy day "I have as yet only £400,000 put by . . .[99]; in entertaining Matthew Arnold, who took Lady Derby to church, but failing to record his conversation[100]; and in dealing with servant problems, and sacking a cook[101]; in noting infirmities of sight and hearing. "I can seldom hear what passes in general conversation, at least not without effort" though "my deafness is not increasing"[102]; while his eyes were also a difficulty. "Troubled most of this day with aching eyes: result, I suppose, of railway travelling & reading in the carriage."[103] "When I remember how they gave way in 1856-7-8, I may be well content that they trouble me so little now. . ." "I have come to the resolution to spare my eyes more than has hitherto been my habit."[104] But, he added, he would never endure using glasses in reading. Infirmities such as these, normally of little consequence, could be relevant to a secretary of state such as Derby was about to become.

On 29 November Derby went to Granville and discussed again the question of joining the cabinet, certainly without pleasure or elation. "I left Ld G. feeling anxious & weary, & had much talk with M. as to acceptance or refusal." The next day he called again on Granville, "& settled the matter by saying that I was ready to accept the India Office." On the same afternoon Gladstone called, "very friendly and civil", but merely confirmed what Granville had said. Derby then went north for some time and sold £50,000 of land to the Midland Railway[105], returning only to find Gladstone in difficulties with the Queen over his cabinet reshuffle[106]. The result was that, not unwillingly, Derby took the Colonial Office, making it a favour to a harassed premier.

Derby's entry into his new post was unhurried. Appointed on 15 December, he was sworn in on 16 December, and then went to Knowsley for the Christmas duties of a territorial magnate. He did not visit his department, but he did read Hyndman on the coming proletarian revolution to Lady Derby.[107] To his surprise he learned that his estates came to nearly 80,000 acres, nearly 10,000 acres more than he had always believed.[108] At Christmas he (but probably not Lady Derby) ". . .showed myself at church, for decency."[109] As to his work, he was clear that "South Africa is the real difficulty", the rest of the empire presenting few problems.

Derby had quite recently given thought to imperial and especially African matters and had read serious works of travel. He had decided that the interior of Africa offered "very little or no material advantage"[110] and he had read General Gordon on Africa, commenting "he must be in command, & absolutely independent."[111] Nowhere either on taking office or later did Derby reflect in broad terms upon imperial policy or upon the empire as a unity, except to express his deep dislike of annexation. As to economic aspects of empire, they pass unmentioned, except as potential additions to the budget, a matter of which he was acutely conscious.

The diaries show that Derby as Colonial Secretary was technically far from idle, the main failing which public opinion came to see in him. He did not neglect his boxes. On the contrary, day after day he strained every nerve to complete all outstanding work in the day that it arose or reached him. He counted the boxes in and counted them out, never letting work accumulate. In terms of boxes per hour, he must have worked swiftly, making use of every spare minute. His view of a minister's role was that he was more bureaucrat than policymaker, more a model civil servant running a model civil service department than a politician. His officials gave exemplary support; his discussions with them were quite free of friction. They, like him, were University intellectuals, seasoned by colonial and administrative experience. Not once did Derby have to complain of a hitch in the civil service machine. The diaries show among other things the well-oiled perfection of the messenger service which circulated boxes to wherever a minister might be with relentless efficiency every day of the year, including Christmas and Easter. The Colonial Office administered 90% of the Empire with unfailing sagacity and faultless efficiency; its misfortune was that it was the remaining 10% – South Africa and the South Pacific – which excited press, parliament, and public.

Derby's empire was a hopeless miscellany. As he said, "it would not be easy to find in any office a greater diversity."[112] His lists of daily petty business give a good idea of this diversity.[113] It was the middling colonies, Malta and Mauritius, Trinidad and Hong Kong, Cyprus and Jamaica, which furnished the greater part of his routine. Each was self-contained, unrelated to any other imperial question, with internal intricacies that London had to grasp. None were much more than the accidental deposit of history. Derby's experience at the Colonial Office was of a random multiplicity of colonies, not of a great and orderly empire: in truth the idea of a deliberately acquired British Empire as we conceive it in retrospect, was barely palpable to the men who had charge of it at the time.

The accusations of dilatoriness flung at Derby can well appear objectively true and certainly in character but they take no account of context. Not only was he the victim of a short-lived manoeuvre by Bismarck intended to create a Franco-German colonial entente against England, but he was also the victim of ill-judged pressure from his leaders Granville and Gladstone – who were both, as it happened, his chief and perhaps only patrons in cabinet and party and therefore impossible to oppose.

Over New Guinea, Derby probably wished to act with all due speed, though without any enthusiasm. That however was not what the English or Australian publics saw. The difficulty was that Granville at the Foreign Office wished above all to appease Germany, partly on Egyptian grounds. Derby delayed any decisive action in order to meet Granville's wishes, and got roundly abused for it when procrastination led to German annexation. In the case of the South African coastline, the colleague who most inhibited action was the prime minister himself. What can a colonial secretary do, if his personal patron is a prime minister given to dramatic utterances in favour of German colonisation?

The year 1883, Derby's first full year at the Colonial Office, went well. The British Empire virtually ran itself. Even South Africa was quiet, Basuto and Zulu affairs unexpectedly settling themselves, and Boer expansionism not having come to a head. The cabinet too was tranquil. Gladstone was away in France on doctor's orders 17 January-2 March, and also on a cruise for three weeks in September, which removed a possible cause of turbulence. The opposition remained at sixes and sevens; ministers simply ignored such setbacks as a Commons defeat over Bradlaugh, and the collapse of their scheme for a second Suez Canal. The diary thus inclined to the apolitical – Derby twice declined invitations from Gladstone in the recess – and to careful balancing of private and public life:

Grouse and deer do not interest me; what does interest me is the possession of a large tract of picturesque wild country, capable of improvement and ornament by planting.[114]

My part has been quiet and even obscure, for colonial affairs have attracted little attention, & I do not know when official life has been to me so little of a burden.[115]

In the background we catch glimpses of the real Knowsley. Though, as Derby said, "my hours are so regular that a slight departure from them is felt", the Knowsley servants' ball kept him awake till 5 a.m.[116] (and did so without complaint); while, on the death of an old servant, a deputation from the Knowsley servants asked him to see that it was announced in the papers.[117]

Towards the end of the year the storm clouds suddenly came much closer. The massacre[118] of the Egyptian army under Hicks Pasha began a crisis on the Nile which was to be the main concern of ministers for the next year and a half. At the same time the cabinet began its discussions on the franchise bill, plunging at once into dissension over the Irish dimension of the Reform Bill and nearly losing Hartington in December 1883. In foreign affairs, Bismarck and France began to manoeuvre for a rapprochement whose outward expression would be colonial expansion at the expense of England (and thus of Derby's reputation). There is surprisingly little sign in the diaries that Derby understood what was afoot, or saw Franco-German colonial encroachments in terms of an attempted diplomatic revolution aimed at giving Germany security on the Rhine. A bumptious and irritable France[119] annoyed about English advances in Egypt was visible and comprehensible; a scheming Bismarck seeking reinsurance eluded his attention, as did the broader theme of the European partition of Africa. Derby maintained a complete mental unawareness of the "scramble for Africa" even as he was involved in a crucial phase of carrying it into reality in both southern and western Africa.

In retrospect it is strange to find Derby writing late in the year, at the time of the Berlin West Africa Conference:

I have really been more free during the last month, more master of leisure, than at any period of the year.[120]

Interpreted, this meant that Derby's love of duty and love of ease both led him to clear his desk rather than to press large policies. To a person of his temper it mattered greatly that he coped (and his health coped) once again with the burdens of office; the smear campaign of 1878 had used a supposed breakdown against him. It might not have been so, for he remained at heart a medical pessimist:

. . .But my life is precarious, & will probably not be long.[121]

A clean desk was the essence of his colonial policy:

. . .I have literally at this moment not a letter unanswered, nor a paper undealt with.[122]

The correspondence of his new department, to and from, was 40,000 annually, against 70,000 at the Foreign Office[123], which made it intrinsically more manageable, the more so as Derby increased the use of printing for departmental papers.

Derby was also relieved to find that his marked and unvarying distrust of Gladstone was scarcely justified, at least in 1883; 1884 was to be another matter entirely. Despite having so little to complain of departmentally, and despite being in so many ways a Gladstonian, the diary shows Derby dealing with Gladstone in business matters with a wariness and want of trust amounting almost to slyness.

The summer of 1883 established just how far ministers had lost control of parliament, how impossible it was to pass any local government reform legislation, and how nothing could be done without Irish approval – or, similarly, only those things could be done which offered handsome inducements to Parnell. The unproductiveness of 1883 set the scene for the Reform Act of 1884. Any flicker of rapprochement that may have existed in 1882 had died. In Derby's eyes, the Irish situation in 1883, though technically under control, was one of disastrous antagonism:

"I doubt if since the Union England and Ireland have ever been so wide apart."[124]

Derby had to look elsewhere in his official life for his pleasures, albeit negative ones. It meant much to him, in a Whiggish way, that he managed to block Prince Leopold's desire for a colonial governorship[125]. He also had the true mid-Victorian pleasure in blocking selfish business interests. Of his South African policy, he wrote:

The secret hope of every colonist is that large forces will be sent out from England. They will be disappointed so far as I am concerned.

Among miscellaneous matters for 1883 occur gifts of £50 to Bootle Cricket Club and £105 to a fire relief fund in Kingston, Jamaica.[126] The Peabody Trust charity for London artisan housing continued to flourish, with Derby its second-in-command; by this means he lodged by proxy 14,600 needy but respectable Londoners[127]. The Trust ran smoothly and required little attention. At Knowsley, signs of the old paternalist community lingered. Derby still in 1882 believed his total acreage was "something under 70,000", even fourteen years after inheriting it; he would in due course find out it was really over 80,000. Lady Margaret Cecil set up a sort of co-operative stores in the village, hardly an act of rebellion since Derby had long preached the co-operative gospel; and there seemed hardly a jarring note, but for the watchful presence of Harcourt's detectives from the moment Derby took office – a constant reminder if one were needed that Irishmen were organised to kill Englishmen.

Lamentable though Parliament's inability to legislate in 1882-83 was, it meant that ministers had less to do and less to quarrel over than formerly. A symbol of these quiet times was Derby complimenting Chamberlain on his Transvaal speech '. . .and he seemed pleased.' The relationship was between one man of the world and another. The enmities that followed in 1884 were related to the imminence of the election and should not be antedated as if they existed throughout the Gladstone ministry.

Was it a "cabinet of chums"? Not quite, but the atmosphere was friendly rather than otherwise. It was perhaps made friendlier by everybody's intolerance of Harcourt as an impossible blusterer. Derby himself had few aversions. He probably underrated Selborne whom he saw as both dull and unworldly. This reflected Derby's own allergy to High Churchmen. (But he also sneered at the Evangelical Shaftesbury on account of his godly manner.) He was cruel too about Carlingford, a fellow sceptic, the only colleague he derided repeatedly, partly as a Gladstonian toady, partly as a genuine believer in appeasement in Ireland. Carlingford to Derby was a symbol of the defeat of landlordism and the betrayal of property rights in Ireland, a matter on which he felt deeply, never holding that the 1881 Land Act was justifiable except on grounds of a revolutionary situation.

However insecure Derby felt about Ireland, he at least felt secure about the Empire. It was in 1883 that he began to invest in colonial loans instead of home rail debentures. He did so on a large scale, so that this amounted to a considerable gesture of confidence in the future of the white empire, particularly Australia. No question of financial impropriety or conflict of interest could possibly have been involved, nor were commercial profits in question. It is nevertheless the more interesting, since Derby had divested himself of Indian stock on the grounds of possible default a few years earlier, and never returned to it.

An important change took place in his social life in 1883. Lady Derby now declined all invitations on account of her eyes[128]. This did not obviously diminish Derby's social life, though he became assiduous in reading aloud to Lady Derby when in the country. It was not that Lady Derby was blind; but the hot and crowded rooms of the London season sorely tested her. If anything, the Derbys became closer as they communed over the higher thought of their day in their Kentish retreat; and the concerns of the British Empire had to be adjusted to fit the short space between the 4.30 sitting of the House of Lords, and an early train from Victoria to Bromley (outside the session, the 4.13 p.m. departure was a favourite.) This Pooterish existence owed everything to the railway network, which allowed Derby to live the life of a suburban commuter while having the social standing of a great Lancashire magnate, without having to go to Lancashire much.

Derby had perfected the art of being in two if not three places at once. In one and the same day he had found it was possible to be the lord of great estates at Knowsley, a busy official in central London, and at his ease in Kentish rural solitude. The convenience of the train service between Knowsley and Euston was such that a northern magnate residing in his own house could without difficulty now attend cabinets and deal with affairs in central London. Every minute was used to best advantage, but much turned on Knowsley being so near a busy north-south main line.

There was much that Derby and still more Lady Derby disliked about Knowsley – the polluted air, the smell, the constant entertaining, the lack of local society, the want of exercise and of beauty. Derby often considered selling and retreating to some remote picturesque spot, as far from an expanding Liverpool as possible. Yet on the other hand Derby did take a pleasure from his unquestioned masculine role at Knowsley. He was head of half a dozen departments, giving orders to all in turn, and having an easy command of the business of each. He was his own head agent. Each day brought decisions to be made, and he made them. He could not, it was true, control estate expenditure with the frugality[129] he would have liked, but in other departments like forestry and the library he was master. He did indeed improve Knowsley, bringing order out of muddle, and he could well be proud of a personal achievement which had conspicuously evaded his father.

Knowsley also supplied what Derby found, if not enjoyable, irresistible: duty. Duty summoned him to barren days at Quarter Sessions sentencing petty criminals. This meant that he knew more than any other leading figure of the ways of the drinking classes, who largely coincided with the urban immigrant Irish. Duty summoned him to continue the glorious charitable work of his father in the Cotton Famine, a residue of funds from that time being put to work building hospitals and convalescent homes at Southport and Buxton. By the same token, Derby was sent for to sort out the uncertain finances of horticultural societies, volunteer units (he showed no anti-military prejudice), and hospitals around Lancashire, but not, as he made very clear, outside his county. At the county boundary, personal duty ended, but small subscriptions took over. It was a tribute to Derby's regional standing that he was regarded as a senior figure no less in Manchester than in his own Liverpool.

It is hard to know how to convey the range of Derby's small subscriptions. Of course, they were indeed individually small; small in relation to total rental of £220,000, small in relation to annual savings of £80,000, small in relation even to total personal expenditure of perhaps £2,100. The question is whether they were seen as small by the lucky recipients.

Thus, taking the year 1879 as a sample, we find Boys' Refuge £10; Islington Industrial Home £10: victims of floods in Hungary £50: Newsvendors Institution £5: Meteorological Society £13: Birkbeck Institution £50; a cottage for a village schoolmaster; widows & orphans of soldiers killed in S. Africa £20; Cavendish Lab £100: Sailors' Aid Society £10: the distressed poet Martin Tupper £50; Newspaper Press Fund £4; National Training School for Cookery £5; memorial to Dr Farr of the Register Office £50; Irish Relief Fund, £50.

This eclectic range of sympathies explains why Derby was deluged with begging letters which took up much of each morning. Many were comic in their shameless absurdity or fraudulence. The record nevertheless insists that Derby was a diligent, industrious, and tireless giver outside his county. Inside Lancashire, giving was more a matter of paternal responsibility and helping in crisis. Consider the exceptionally hard winter of 1878-1879. Derby began by giving £100 to the Liverpool Central Relief Fund for free breakfasts for the poor.[130] Then, as the exceptional weather continued – "I remember no frost that has lasted so long" – [131]he gave £100 to the local relief fund in his town of Bury, £50 to aid distress in Bootle (in addition to £20 given before) and £1 each in New Year gifts to keepers and "more if they have had specially hard work."[132] Later came £20 in aid of distress at Ormskirk and it went without saying that he took the chair at a meeting in aid of local miners killed in a disaster.[133] Such actions were not so much charity as part of the aristocratic code by which the landlord looks after his own people whatever their misfortunes. His will of 1878, indeed, left those pictures and books he was free to leave to Liverpool, whose cricket club he also fostered.

The aristocratic principle even overrode his dislike of religion and parsons. We find Derby giving the enormous sum of £2,300 for rebuilding Bury church, partly because he was landlord there, partly because he was related by marriage to the parson, Canon Hornby. To Chester Cathedral he gave, most reluctantly, £200, groaning "it is a waste": the reason again seems to have been secular, that it was a Duke (Westminster) who was doing the fund-raising.

For Derby 1884 was a bumper year. The savings for the year were exactly £83,000, a record.[134] "Probably no family in England has grown so rapidly in material resources"[135], Derby reflected, not necessarily correctly. As Lancashire urbanised, so the nature of his estate had changed; it now consisted of 5,000 tenants, the majority of whom (3,000) were urban residents, while 2,000 were rural people, equally divided between farmers and labourers[136]. Derby's target was now to reach an income of £240,000, partly at least because it would divide three ways neatly between savings, expenses, and reinvestment in the estate. As the rental had risen from £31,881 in 1800, to £95,199 in 1850, to £216,000 in 1883, nothing seemed impossible.

As to Reform, Derby of course viewed it with dislike. On the other hand he wanted it to pass without the radicalising effects of a row, and with the House of Lords undamaged. His role was a very secondary one: he confined himself to correspondence about tactics with Granville, Harcourt, and Kimberley, and seems to have been totally surprised by the eventual settlement. The incidental details he gives of bargaining positions along the route are sometimes surprising even if second-hand.

The main business of the diary in the calendar year 1884 was the group dynamics of Gladstone's cabinet as it considered Egypt and the Soudan. This may be an oft-told tale, but Derby's picture is a particularly full and telling one. There is Gladstone "asleep for a considerable time" in a critical cabinet[137]; there are the carefully staged scenes by the premier[138]; there are the cabinets called at bizarrely short notice but for no particular object; there is the discussion by the cabinet of matters decided at previous meetings; there is the failure by Gladstone to sum up or draw conclusions from what became haphazard conversation; there was the way the War Minister, Hartington, regularly turned up twenty minutes late when there was a war on, in protest at always being over-ruled. In 1883 Derby had noted with relief and appreciation how unexpectedly undicta-torial Gladstone was in cabinet; in 1884 with equal reason he deplored the complete want of system and order in Gladstone's cabinets.

Derby reports in 1884 as never before on the proceedings of a cabinet of very able parliamentarians who collectively were unfit to govern. The extraordinary thing about General Gordon's death was that it already dominated cabinet business a twelvemonth before it occurred, and yet despite abundance of time, paralysis ensued. Derby was not directly concerned with Egyptian issues, since Egypt was not a colony, but his reporting of cabinet debate on the subject is fuller than on any other theme, as if he foresaw disas-ter. His only apology was the reminder that, universal hand-wringing notwithstanding, British forces had not suffered defeat; it was the Arabs who had in fact been thrashed. Khartoum was not really a repeat of Isandhlwana, Maiwand, or Majuba.

Derby did not expect the Scramble for Africa. He thought it a foolishness which had better be indulged and which it was probably politically impossible to stop. In any case, he was not thinking tropically in early 1884. "My colonial or departmental difficulties are just now few. . . . Australia is maturing the plan of confederation, & until that takes some definite shape the question of New Guinea need not be seriously dealt with."[139] If Derby had pulled off Australian confederation, as he well might, and would have liked, it would have been a notable feather in his cap, and much would have been forgiven him as regards tropical inactivity. Otherwise, he accepted his primary task was to patch up a settlement of the South African question – Basutos, Bechuanas, Boers, and Zulus. He recognised that as a simple matter of domestic politics the path of least resistance lay in accepting the idea of South Africa as "another India".[140] "I note as curious the unanimous feeling . . .against the Boers, & in favour of our extending our influence in S.Africa. . . . My personal sympathy with the new movement [imperialism] is not warm: but I have no scruple in recognising and accepting it. If England chooses to throw away a million or two on Bechuanas, Basutos, & such like, she is rich enough to afford the amusement: and in fact the state of opinion leaves little choice."[141]

Thus a deeply sceptical Lancashire magnate at a desk in Whitehall became the found-ing father of two African sovereignties, Botswana and Basutoland; and the upholder of fair settlements for the Transvaal and Zululand. But grand design there was none.

In the half-year January to June 1885 the Derby diary serves principally as confirmation and elaboration of material about cabinet discussions available elsewhere. The departmental or administrative aspect of Derby's life recedes almost entirely, and likewise there is little room for gossip or being a regional magnate. At one level, there is a chronological story: of how the crisis over the fall of Khartoum was steered seamlessly into the Penjdeh crisis and the threat of war with Russia, followed by the risk of a split in the cabinet for electioneering reasons. At another level, it is a story of how frequent and not ineffective meetings of the cabinet simply wore its members out to a point where they had lost the wish to continue in office, Gladstone excepted. Derby did not see matters as a case of Whigs v. Radicals:–

> "I do not see. . .a split of the Cabinet into two hostile parties: the situation is rather that every man has his own ideas, & no two of them are alike."[142]

In any case, "party politics are dead"[143]; what remained were insoluble but pressing real problems. Hartington's ambiguous status as an isolated dissident (most of the time), with a tendency to sulk, yet also the recognised heir apparent, made the idea of a coherent Whig faction impossible. The premier, with his way of "pronouncing more than once that these Arabs of the Soudan are fighting for their country and their freedom", and that "we have no right to meddle with them"[144] – while slaughtering them in quantity – was at least as isolated in the cabinet as Hartington. Few things in Gladstone's career were as adroit as his switch from the peace party in the Soudan to the war party in Afghanistan, leading a united cabinet, party, parliament, and country, and using the second war to extricate himself from the first.

These wars of 1885 that did not happen, enabled other matters to be seen in their proper proportions. Of European colonisation, Derby said loftily "the comparatively unimportant colonial troubles are settling themselves"[145]; of south Africa, he opined, correctly, "I do not believe in any permanent pacification"[146]; of imperialism generally, "I detest these annexations, but they are impossible to avoid."[147]

It was not the Colonial Office, but the Cabinet, that drove Derby to his eventual conclusion:-

> "But I sometimes think my temperament is too nervous for public affairs – that I take them too seriously. I am beginning to have had enough of official life, & doubt whether I shall continue it when the present Cabinet breaks up."[148]

Notes

1 *Selection*, n. 1

2 *Ibid.*, 2-4.

3 3 Apr., 12 Apr., 3 May, 23 May, 28 May, 27 Nov., 15 Dec. (twice), 16 Dec. 1878.

4 30 Dec.1878.

5 7 Sept. 1878.

6 13 Oct. 1878 ("Church, the first time since June"), 20 Oct., 27 Oct., 25 Dec. 1878, 5 Jan. 1879

7 Dec. 1878

8 6 Nov. 1878

9 29 Mar.1879

[10] 24 Mar.1879. In 1885 he sent out about 1100 invitations to his London house: 600 came (6 May 1885).

[11] 29 Mar. 1879.

[12] 26 Mar. 1879.

[13] 15 Mar., 28 Mar. 1879

[14] 3 Apr. 1879.

[15] 16 Jan. 1979.

[16] 11 Feb. 1879.

[17] 28 Feb 1879.

[18] 6 Jan.1879

[19] 16 Oct. 1879

[20] 11 Jan. 1880

[21] 9 Apr. 1879

[22] 15 Apr. 1879

[23] 5 Jan. 1879

[24] 5 Mar., 7 Mar., 30 Oct., 8 Nov. 1879

[25] 12 July 1879

[26] 19 Jan. 1880

[27] 18 Sept. 1879

[28] 22 Oct. 1879

[29] 3 Sept. 1879

[30] 21 July 1879

[31] 6 Oct. 1879

[32] 3 Apr. 1880

[33] 12 Jan. 1880

[34] 29 Apr. 1880

[35] 27 Apr. 1880

[36] 18 June 1880

[37] 28 Mar. 1880.

[38] 12 Sept. 1880

[39] 3 Sept. 1880

[40] 2 Oct. 1880

[41] 25 Sept. 1880

[42] 20 Sept. 1880

[43] 12 July 1880

[44] 1 Jan. 1881

[45] *ibid.*

[46] 8 Jan. 1881

[47] 28 Jan,. 1881

[48] 8 Jan.. 1881

[49] 5 Mar. 1881

[50] 7 Apr. 1881

[51] *ibid.*

[52] 8 Apr. 1881

[53] 5 Sept. 1881

[54] *ibid.*

[55] 12 Apr. 1879

[56] 22 Apr. 1879

[57] 31 Oct. 1881

[58] 4 Oct. 1881

[59] 5 Sept. 1881.

[60] 9 July 1881

[61] 24 Sept. 1881

[62] 1 Nov. 1880

[63] 2 Aug. 1881

[64] 18 Sept. 1881

[65] 10 aug. 1881

[66] 17 Dec. 1880

[67] 21 Dec. 1880

[68] 1 Jan. 1881

[69] 1 Jan. 1882

[70] *ibid.*

[71] 30 Jan. 1882

[72] 21 Jan. 1882

[73] 10 June 1882

[74] 23 Mar. 1882

[75] 26 Mar. 1882

[76] 23 Apr. 1882

[77] 19 July 1882

[78] Aug. 1882

[79] 19 Sept. 1882

[80] 3 Nov. 1882

[81] 24 Mar. 1882

[82] 29 Mar. 1882

[83] 25 Mar. 1882

[84] 29 Apr. 1882

[85] 6 Apr. 1882

[86] 29 May 1882

[87] 1 June 1882

[88] 22 May 1882. Derby seems to have been considered acceptable in progressive circles; a deputation asked him to attend the T.U.C. conference (3 May 1882), though he did not go.

[89] 14 May 1882

[90] 2 June 1882

[91] 3 June 1882

[92] 1 June 1882

[93] 21 July 1882

[94] 12 June 1882

[95] 3 Aug. 1882. Cf. 31 Aug. 1882. "Saw Drage, who. . .talks more cheerfully than he did." Derby made a new will in Aug. 1882.

[96] 16 Sept. 1882, 3–6pm.

[97] 8 Sept. 1882

[98] 11 Sept. 1882

[99] 29 Sept. 1882

[100] 1 Oct. 1882

[101] 22 Nov. 1882

[102] 18 Nov. 1882

[103] 29 Nov. 1882

[104] 30 Nov. 1882

[105] 12 Dec. 1882

[106] 15 Dec. 1882

[107] 18 Dec. 1882

[108] The new map of the estate showed it at "80,000 acres at least" (21 Sept. 1884).

[109] 25 Dec. 1882. Knowsley had its own chapel, then still in use. An American visitor noted, "Our evening was quiet, and we broke up early, as they always have a midnight service in the chapel on New Year's eve for the family and servants and any of the guests who like to attend. . . .The chapel was full, all the servants (including my French maid) and household. Lady Margaret [Cecil] . . . sat at the organ, and everybody, gardeners, keepers, coachmen, cooks, housemaids, joined in the singing. . .Lady Margaret and Lord Lionel stood at the head of the stairs and shook hands with all the guests and all the servants, wishing all a "Happy New Year". – Mary King Waddington, *Letters of a Diplomat's Wife 1883-1900,* (1903), p. 232.

[110] 15 May 1881

[111] 26 June 1881

[112] 20 Jan. 1883

[113] ibid.

[114] 18 Aug. 1883

[115] 26 Aug. 1883 (end of session retrospect).

[116] 30 Oct. 1883

[117] 19 Sept. 1883

[118] Nov. 1883

[119] 22 Nov. 1883

[120] 30 Nov. 1883

[121] 13 May 1883

[122] 18 July 1883

[123] 27 July 1883

[124] 25 Feb. 1883

[125] In the process launching Lansdowne on his public career.

[126] 24 Jan. 1883.

[127] 14 Feb. 1883.

[128] 1 July 1883

[129] Frugality was not part of the Knowsley way of life. A foreign visitor was amazed when a house-maid appeared in her bedroom at 9.30 "with an enormous tray and breakfast enough for a family – tea, beefsteaks, cold partridges, eggs, rolls, toast, potatoes, buns, and fruit – you never saw such a meal. She couldn't believe that I only wanted tea and toast and an egg. . ."

[130] 17 Dec. 1878.

[131] 26 Jan. 1879.

[132] 30 Jan. 1879.

[133] Derby subscribed £105.

[134] 1 Jan.1885.

[135] 1 Jan. 1884.

[136] 9 Jan. 1884

[137] 22 Oct. 1884

[138] E.g. over economy, 24 Jan.1884.

[139] 10 Feb. 1884.

[140] Mineral wealth appears never to have crossed his mind.

[141] 11 Feb. 1884

[142] 8 Jan.1885

[143] 11 Jan. 1885

[144] 23 Apr. 1885

[145] 8 Jan. 1885

[146] *ibid.*

[147] 9 Mar. 1885

[148] 15 Mar. 1885

1878

1 Apr. 1878: Answered the Queen's letter, with due respect and verbal gratitude (for she writes civilly) but carefully avoiding anything like a pledge not to oppose the war[1].

Wrote to Lord Beaconsfield, declining the Garter, assigning no reason: in truth my reasons are not such as it would be easy to give in a letter to the minister making such an offer.

In the first place, it is a kind of offer for which I care nothing: which gives me no added social or political importance: which is generally bestowed as a job or a bribe, and which leading statesmen have often refused (Peel, Melbourne, Disraeli himself). In the next, the acceptance of it would be considered by many people as binding me not to oppose the govt.: and, as I wish to keep my hands free as regards the threatened war, I will accept nothing that might be a restraint. Lastly, the offer (though probably in part due to real friendly feeling) is connected with the policy which will evidently be adopted in Downing St.: that of representing my secession as not due to any real divergence of ideas, but to ill-health and weariness of office on my part. Of the latter there has been enough: but it would not have influenced me if other reasons had been wanting.

It is announced that Salisbury is my successor; this was however settled some days ago: he takes P. Currie[2] as his private secretary, & keeps Barrington as précis writer.

Heard later in the evening that my brother has accepted the post of Sec. of State for War[3]; he writes to tell me so, but the news had come first from other quarters. It has affected me in a strange way, pleasantly & painfully, the latter feeling rather preponderating: on the one hand I am glad of his personal success, & still more so on account of the family, which maintains its parliamentary position: on the other hand is to be set the separation of our political lives, in the probable event of war taking place, & a party being formed for & against it. The appointment is I think a good one: to some extent it has been influenced by the wish to neutralise opposition on my part: but I don't know that the Premier could have done better. Hardy takes the India Office with a peerage[4]: the latter had been promised him when his claim to lead the H. of C. was waived[5] in favour of Northcote.

2 Apr. 1878: Disposed of six boxes, the last that will come from the office: but I have no feeling of regret that this business is ended. It may come again, but with my disposition – caring nothing for the show or appearance of power, and much for freedom in personal relations – I am sure that I am happier as a private man – so far as a great peer can be a private man. Eight years of Downing Street have paid my debt to the state, and Lady D., like myself, prefers a quieter existence. Nothing now troubles my peace except the prospect of an unpleasant debate on the reserves, for next week.

. . . Left for Windsor by 12.10 train from Paddington, went down with Richmond, Salisbury, Hardy, and F. Talk on the way with Salisbury about office arrangements. No awkwardness on either side. I gave up the seals, the Queen saying a few civil words, and my part was ended.

. . . Drove to F.O. . . . Left the office at 5.00, never, I hope, to return. I have been head of it for just 6½ years: longer than any one now living: Ld. Russell held it for 6 years 3 months, Granville and Malmesbury for shorter dates.

3 Apr. 1878: News that Adderley is to be made a peer[6], which is a job: for he has rendered no remarkable service, & has no great territorial position. In fact he is promoted in order to get him out of the way. Sandon[7] takes his place: a fairly good appointment.

. . . Application through Col. Champneys for help to the family of Adm. Stanley, who died lately, in debt, & leaving a large number of children. This I must consider, and perhaps arrange it through Lawrence[8]. The Adm. was a distant cousin, & I saw him only once in my life; still he is of my name & class.

. . . Schouvaloff called, and described with some humour his first interview with Salisbury: he told me also, which is important, that Austria which already has the promise of Bosnia and Herzegovina now asks more: but he did not know, or would not say, what it was. He expressed uneasiness at the effect which the circular just issued by Salisbury may have in Russia, thinking it will be taken there as a message of war.

News in the papers of the murder of Lord Leitrim[9], by his tenants. He was 72 years of age, a strange being, eccentric to the verge of madness, a kind landlord, but despotic. He was one of the chief sufferers by the Irish Land Act of 1870: for his estates, mostly wild and poor land and very extensive (over 90,000 acres) were let to small tenants at low rents: consequently the value of the tenants' interest was much greater than if they had been rented at their full value: and, as this interest is the measure of the compensation to be claimed on eviction, Lord Leitrim had to pay twice as much for every tenant removed as he would have done had he or his predecessors exercised their undoubted rights in a less liberal spirit. . . . I have never for one moment regretted the decision to which I came years ago, to break off all connection with Ireland: though it may be a question whether I ought not to replace the land sold by an equal area in England.

4 Apr. 1878: . . . Destroyed a number of private papers, & put away others, that were in Sanderson's[10] care since 1874.

Heard with pleasure a report that Sanderson is likely to receive a better appointment than he now has: a commissionership of Customs is talked of: but it is mere report. Northcote is anxious to get his services: and Salisbury, according to what is believed, equally anxious to get rid of him from a kind of jealousy both of him & Tenterden[11], dating from the days of the conference.

. . . Carnarvon called: talk over the situation: he low in spirits, and inclined to agree in what Granville told a deputation the other day, that any minister can involve the country in war, and that there is scarcely an instance of an opposition succeeding in averting one. He does not understand the complete change of opinion on Salisbury's part within a year: nor do I, except through female influence. Lady Salisbury has always, since Constantinople, desired to be at the F.O. and has not concealed the wish.

. . . Budget in H. of C. Northcote[12] puts 2d. more on to the income tax, & increases the tobacco duty, but does not touch spirits as was expected. The reason privately assigned is the fear of Irish obstruction if whisky were made dearer. . . . Of the £6,000,000 vote, over one half has been spent . . .

5 Apr. 1878: . . . Agreed, after communicating with Lawrence, to make a partial provision for Adm. Stanley's children – £50 a year for 10 years. Wrote in this sense to Col. Champneys.

Made notes for a speech, which will I hope be the last I shall deliver for some time. Rumours of an approaching dissolution, but they rest on no certain foundation. The F.O. much disquieted by a report that Sir H.D. Wolff[13] is to be under-secretary when Bourke[14] becomes Common Serjeant: a man who has been mixed up in a low class of city speculations, and is generally distrusted, so much so that Lord B. passed him over in 1874. He has of late made himself useful, I imagine, in various underhand ways.

. . . Heard with some pain of language held by C.S.[15] which I will not more specially note, as this mem. is sufficient for my recollection.

Much thought over the position of affairs, as regards party and family. . . . I will not act in haste, but the moment seems opportune[16], and certainly it will not be much in my line of business to defend the church establishment, which seems likely to be the next object of attack. . . . I do not know whether in the thoughts noted down above I am influenced in any degree by the violent hostility shown towards me by a section of the party, a hostility which was never entirely concealed, and of late has been displayed without disguise. It affects me to a certain extent: that is, it shows me clearly that between the ideas of that section and mine there is a radical opposition, hardly possible to be got over by any amount of good will, even if it existed. I am afraid I must add there is a good deal of evidence, though no absolutely certain proof, that in the attacks made upon me lately in the conservative press both Lord B. and Salisbury have taken part, so far at least as that they have approved and sanctioned them.

7 Apr. 1878: . . . Much and serious talk with M. as to the political future. The question is, can I as matters stand call myself a Conservative or not? In some respects by temperament and habit of mind I am one. Distrust of loud talk and heated partisanship, dislike to sudden and hasty changes, desire for administrative efficiency rather than for the assertion of any abstract principle of government are my characteristics, if I know myself: and these go rather with the conservative than with the revolutionary habit of thought. On the other hand, I cannot conceal from myself that in the administration of the last four years there has been, irrespective of the question of war, much to disappoint and little to satisfy me. No effective attempt has been made to restrain expenditure, which has continually increased. There has scarcely been even the wish to utilise a season of political calm for the purpose of pushing on social and administrative reforms. I doubt if any question of internal policy has been considered with half the care that was given to the Titles Bill and to the details of the P. of Wales's visit to India. The best that can be said of our internal administration is that it has done no particular harm: but for all purposes except that of carrying on routine duty it has been very useless. It has not been such an administration as that of Sir R. Peel in 1841–1846: nor as that of Pitt in his early days of peace. In the future the changes impending are county franchise: something in regard of the land laws: and, beyond that, the question of the church. As to the franchise I am satisfied that, whatever we may like or dislike, its extension is inevitable: and to engage in a useless opposition to it is undesirable. On the land laws my personal bias is in favour of keeping things as they are, but this will probably not be possible, and moderate changes may retard others of a more violent character. The church question is clearly not ripe, and does not seem likely to become so, except in the event of a general disruption within the establishment itself. On the whole I incline to keep quiet, watch events, take little part except where the question of war or peace is concerned, and hold myself unconnected with party ties. If, as is quite possible, Lord B. chooses to dissolve on the strength of his war policy, I shall be driven to separate myself openly and entirely from his supporters: but it will be better in that case to let the separation seem a matter of necessity rather than of choice.

In the papers, a singular trial, showing what modern manners are. A Mrs. Thistlethwaite is sued for debts amounting in all to several thousands, for dress and ornaments of various kinds. Her husband refuses to pay, and hence the action. She was one of what is called the *demi-monde*, married a man with £20,000 a year or more, then turned saint, and preaches and prays in a very edifying manner. Gladstone, Kinnaird[17], and other intensely respectable people are among her chief admirers. But sanctity does not seem to imply frugality, and the habits of earlier life survive in the married *dévoté*.

8 Apr. 1878: . . . Did not leave the house till it was time to go to the Lords. Walked there with Sanderson, nervous and uncomfortable enough. Found the house fuller than I have almost ever seen it: galleries crammed from end to end: as was also the space below the bar and that below the throne. Lord B. moved his address in a speech of an hour and a quarter: the first part of it was dull, for he recapitulated at length the contents of documents already published and familiar: the latter part was fine as a piece of declamatory rhetoric, though rather too stilted and theatrical for a severe taste: he was so vague that what he said might have meant anything or nothing, but it left the impression that he expected and did not deprecate a war. Granville followed, adroit and skilful as usual, carefully avoiding anything that might compromise him in the future: I came next, and had an advantage in having been personally alluded to by the Premier, which enabled me to interweave sentences of reply into what I had already prepared. I spoke three-quarters of an hour[18], very well listened to, the house not emptying at all, though it was past 8.00, and though nervous at first I managed to bring out all that I had to say with some force and effect. In short, I satisfied myself on the whole, and was the more pleased to do so because there can now be no more talk of my being incapacitated by health for business. Cairns followed, addressing a comparatively thin audience; Selborne replied on him; Carnarvon said a few words, not much to the purpose; Houghton delivered himself of a speech the end of which so far as I could understand it contradicted the beginning; indeed, he told us that his view of the case was one which nobody had taken yet. Argyll began well, but rather spoilt his speech by harping on his old theme: how the Turks had broken the treaty first, how all that had happened was their fault, & how we ought to have joined with Russia against them: as this theory is even less popular than it was last year, his argument fell flat. Salisbury closed the debate on the government side, attacking me, but not with any great bitterness: & evidently embarrassed in discussing the general question by the fear of saying more than would be prudent in his position. Kimberley said a few words: I walked home with Sefton[19]. During the evening I sat below the gangway, on the lowest bench, between Chelmsford[20] and Lord Verulam[21].

9 Apr. 1878: With Sanderson[22] to Brighton to see the Aquarium: which I have meant to do for years, and never have done. It is very well worth the trouble. . . . I had arranged this expedition purposely to get rid of the ideas of last night's debate, and so far it succeeded.

. . . From what I hear, it seems as if the debate of yesterday had made, & would make, a considerable impression. The Prime Minister has never yet in public disclosed his real mind so freely, & war is believed in as probable by many who till lately doubted. In the first instance it will most likely be popular; but in these days the temper of the people changes rapidly & it may not be long before they ask what they are fighting for. Anyway, my part is played, & I have earned the right to stand aloft and look on.

Read to M. after dinner, from Cowper's poem of *Retirement*, those passages which describe a statesman's release from office, his delight in his recovered freedom, the gradual growth of *ennui*, & his return to court. It is strange that they come back to me now, for I do not think I have read them since I was a boy at school, when Cowper was with me a favourite poet – I hardly know why.

10 Apr. 1878: This day 30 years I walked about London streets as a special constable[23], part of the time in the company of Prince Louis Napoleon. An odd recollection!

Lawrence called, bringing maps of an estate in Sussex, 4,600 acres. . . . It is in St. Leonards forest, a very picturesque part of the county as is said, & within 40 miles of London. I settle to go down & see it. . . . Lawrence half recommends the purchase, saying that to find an estate of such extent so near London is rare. The investment as regards interest will be a bad one; but it will give me a kind of property which I have often desired & never possessed – a large tract of land in a picturesque county, away from towns. Fairhill, Holwood, & Witley are not of the size to be called estates. On the other hand, the price will probably not be less than £180,000, and my projects of laying by money will have to be deferred.

. . . Noticed at the committee[24] that J. Manners[25] had a look as of extreme depression and melancholy: which made me think that a peaceable result of negociations is still possible. It is odd that, whereas during my last few weeks of office I was constantly receiving letters of abuse from the supporters of war, since retiring I have not had one that has been otherwise than complimentary and friendly.

11 Apr. 1878: . . . Letter from Mundella[26], in which he asks me to help him to answer an absurd charge made against me of having kept back the Russian terms of peace from my colleagues. I should hardly think it worth doing, but as the statement is in a Sheffield paper, & he wishes to reply to it, I will give him the necessary materials.

. . . Anonymous letters of advice seldom contain anything worth notice, but I have one today which is singular. The writer points out the evil effects of prosperity on the lower classes in making them disrespectful to their superiors, and generally in demoralising them, and he intimates that 'a good rattling war' would set all this right, and bring them again into a proper position of dependence. How much of the war-feeling among the upper class may be due to some such idea, vaguely entertained? or to what is the same feeling in a slightly different form, [due to] jealousy of wealth acquired by industry, when compared with the low pay of officers and government employés? . . .

12 Apr. 1878: . . . To an exhibition in Bond Street, to see Turner's[27] drawings: but the crowd & heat were too great for pleasure. I was moreover vexed to find that, liking art as well as I do, the power to discern exceptional merit in Turner was not in me. I could see that the drawings were good, but not that they were far above all others, as is thought, & no doubt truly. My incapacity in this respect is worth remembering, when I grow impatient (as it is difficult not to do) of foolish & ignorant judgement in political matters, which I have studied, & which the talkers have not.

Walk for exercise. Dined early, & to the Lyceum. It is years since I have been to a play, & I went expecting not to be interested, for increasing deafness causes me to lose much of the dialogue in ordinary conversation, and I expected the same here; but, having a box close to the stage, every word was audible, and I enjoyed & admired the acting of Irving[28], in an English adaptation of the French play of Louis XI. . . . The words were rant & rubbish, the other actors indifferent: but Irving's performance made it worth while to go. The Galloways[29] were with us, & Schou.[30] looked into the box.

Münster[31] called in the afternoon, & hinted at possible mediation by Bismarck: but he did not know whether it would be accepted by Russia or not. The basis of the negocia-tion appears to be that the English fleet shall go out of the sea of Marmora, & the Russian troops fall back to a certain distance from Constantinople. He gave few details, & I did not like to ask. He said that since the beginning of the week the war-feeling had greatly cooled down, which his diplomatic politeness ascribed to my speech: but Northcote's[32] increase of the income tax has probably more to do with the matter[33].

13 Apr. 1878: Letter from Bourke, in answer to one from me. He has missed the Common Serjeant's place, for which he was a candidate, the electors preferring Charley[34], the Conservative M.P. for Manchester: a strange choice, for he is a man of no ability, & of extreme opinions. Bourke had expressed an intention of retiring from the F.O. in any case, and I wrote to dissuade him earnestly from so doing: understanding that Drummond Wolff would be the successor, which would be a selection very injurious to the reputation of the office.

. . . Wolff is essentially an intriguer, mixed up with questionable city companies, and ill thought of: though nothing has ever been proved against him which should exclude him from society: he has got into favour with Salisbury or rather with Lady Salisbury, has made himself useful to them, and expects his reward. Bourke is not the most efficient of under-secretaries, but he is honest, willing, and can speak fairly well. To my great relief, he writes that he does not mean to resign.

14 Apr. 1878: . . . The papers are busy with my speech of Monday, which has altogether produced considerable effect, making some people very angry, and giving others much pleasure. Gladstone[35] told me on Wednesday night that he thought it had checked the war-feeling a good deal: I was glad to hear it, but suspect that Northcote's addition to income tax has had more to do with the result, and said so. One result is plain: it has put an end to talk of my having resigned from ill-health, failure of nerves[36], and so forth. There is no farther question of the reality of the differences that have divided me from the Cabinet. Personally, I believe myself to have gained by resignation: if I had stayed on, and war had either followed or been averted, the credit would have belonged to the Premier exclusively, and my position would have been that of a not very willing follower: as it is, I have gained the reputation of independence and moral courage, making no heav-ier sacrifice than that of giving up an office of which I had become thoroughly weary. But till the matter was settled, I have never even to myself admitted the influence of such personal considerations. – I will add though that, though I have none but friendly feel-ings for Disraeli, his personal character has affected my decision. Knowing him to be utterly without scruple, where political consequences are concerned, I have been (it may be) unduly prejudiced: certainly I have received with distrust propositions coming from him which would not perhaps have excited the same feeling had they proceeded from someone whom I knew to be a lover of peace. Salisbury's entire conversion to the war party is still to me unexplained. He was strongly opposed to the Crimean War which was much more intelligible and defensible. Cairns has shown himself to be more a popularity hunter than I had thought him: the rest merely follow their leader.

15 Apr. 1878: . . . The foreign situation seems unchanged: the newspapers are occupied chiefly, & not unreasonably, with an extraordinary debate in the H. of C. on Friday night[37]: Mr. O'Donnell[38], one of the obstructive Irish party, called attention, as he said, to improper steps taken by the govt. to detect the murderers of Ld Leitrim: this was his plea for raising the question of the murder: but he went into the subject of the murder itself, defending by implication the assassins, & hinting that the hatred felt by the peasantry towards their landlord was due to his using his power to corrupt their wives & daughters: not a very probable charge against a man of 72. Very foolishly, instead of answering these accusations, which would have been easy, other Irish M.P.s tried to suppress the debate by excluding reporters: a violent quarrel followed, & feeling rose so high that Gladstone, Lowe[39], & Hartington[40] were hooted & hissed in the lobby by members – a thing never done in my parliamentary experience. Northcote seems to have had no power over the House, & altogether the scene was discreditable. I am sometimes disposed to wonder whether there is not among a section of the so-called Conservatives a lurking jealousy of the power & predominance of parliament, such as might have been felt in the 17th century, & a consequent feeling of satisfaction when parliamentary proceedings become ridiculous. Obstruction when practised by three or four men, who rise on every possible occasion, can be dealt with by checking them: but where some five and twenty unite for the same purpose, & divide the work among them, there are no means of sufficiently proving the existence of a deliberate design to make mischief. Mere loquacity is not an offence of which parliament can take notice, & you cannot impute anything beyond loquacity.

Received 14 letters, an unusual number for one post: answered nearly all. Several were as usual to beg. . . . Read & walked much in the garden, which since the new walks were made gives room for exercise. This place[41] will never have the peculiar wildness & the picturesque charm which belongs to Holwood: but it is more entirely quiet & secluded, & the rides and drives all round more varied. At this time of year the garden-like richness of the surrounding county makes itself felt.

17 Apr. 1878: Set off with M. to see Bedgebury, B. Hope's[42] place, about 15 miles distant . . . The country on the way is pretty & pleasant: worth seeing, though hardly worth going far to see. . . . I also note with less pleasure the change produced by cessation of novelty: before living in Kent, & when I compared it with the less pure air & less abundant vegetation of Lancashire, I thought every part of this neighbourhood beautiful: now, after years of familiarity, I can still see that it is pretty, & enjoy it: but the pleasure produced is far less. – I have less reason to complain than anyone, having secured in Fairhill, Witley[43], & Holwood three of the best situations, in point of natural beauty, that are to be found in England: & all within two hours of St. James's Square.

18 Apr. 1878: . . . News in the papers that an expedition is to be sent from India, ostensibly to Malta: but I have little doubt that what is really contemplated is the occupation of some point on the Syrian coast, or an adjacent island, as decided in the Cabinet of 27

March. Wrote to Lawson on the subject, in guarded terms. Note that this project has been carefully kept back till parliament had separated for a month, so that no questions can be asked, or debate raised[44].

19 Apr. 1878: Walk in afternoon with M. planning new paths & planting to the north of the house.

20 Apr. 1878: . . . Letter from Post Office, asking if I wish to keep up the private wire from Tunbridge, for which a rent will be charged of £42. I consult with M. & we agree that it is worth retaining.

. . . Letter from Layard[45], compliments & farewell, which I answer.

21 Apr. 1878: . . . Walk alone & with M. – L. West[46] comes over from Knowle, the first time we have seen him since he went to B. Ayres.

22 Apr. 1878 (Easter Monday): London by the 8.49 train. . . . Working on letters & papers, of which a large heap awaited me. – Amused with a letter from the D. of Bedford[47]: I had referred to him an application to me to be a patron of a new theatre, finding the money: his name was mentioned as a proposed patron in the printed prospectus: he now asks to have it back that he may prosecute the parties.

Corrected a proof of my speech of the 8th – disagreeable trouble. . . . Luncheon at Travellers. By 5 p.m. train to Liverpool, Knowsley by 11, where found Sanderson.

23 Apr. 1878: . . . Drove into Kirkdale . . . Large attendance of magistrates at the sessions . . . Heavy calendar, 81 prisoners: the largest number I remember here.

24 Apr. 1878: Kirkdale again, sat from 10 to 5.30, having disposed of all but a few cases . . . One trial lasted between 3 & 4 hours. . . . Another trait of English manners: a decent sort of artisan, a printer, comes into a little fortune of £600 odd: he draws most of the money in notes & gold, & beginning at 8 a.m. passes the day in various public houses treating everybody who will drink with him. Naturally before the end of the day he is dead drunk, & is robbed. But what a notion of pleasure! & none of the witnesses seemed to think the proceeding other than ordinary & natural. I could not but make the old remark: that in 9 cases out of 10 drink was at the bottom of the mischief. It hardly ever happens that a sober man is robbed by a sober man: at least among the persons who come before these sessions. . . . In these 2 days I passed about 35 sentences, 7 years the longest, one day the shortest. They averaged 6 to 12 months.

25 Apr. 1878: Received last night a return from Moult[48] of the receipts & expenses of the year ending 1st July 1877. The total receipts are £185,938: against £183,653 in the preceding year, & £181,227 in the year before that. Thus the increase of £2,000 a year continues steadily, in the face of bad times. Compulsory deductions are £26,413 against £30,498 last year, & £33,581 in 1874–1875:

Household £25,000: the same last year, & £28,616 the year before
Estate £69,049 against £67,906 last year, & £55,449 the year before
Miscellaneous £25,632 against £21,993 last year, & £21,538 the year before
Total £146,094 against £145,397 last year, & £139,184 the year before

In the above account the expenditure on estates is thoroughly unsatisfactory, the more so as having been from the first excessive it continues to grow. The item of building alone is enormous, £39,000 & more. Law charges have been heavy, but that is not unreasonable, considering the quantity of railway work: the miscellaneous items are swelled by the cost of Keston & Fairhill[49]: but these are luxuries, & I do not grudge the price we pay for them. It is in Hale's[50] department that the waste, for such I must consider it, goes on: & seeing him today I spoke seriously, but in a friendly way, about it. I am not, however, sanguine of much good being done.

In all other respects I have no reason to find fault. The growth of income is more than I expected in the depressed state of trade, but Hale says that there is more demand than ever before for building land in Bootle & Kirkdale. Yet in Manchester it is alleged that things were never so bad, & we are threatened with a strike in the cotton industry which is to throw 120,000 people out of work. I do not understand what is really happening.

. . .With Sanderson & Broomfield[51] over most of the park. Well pleased with what has been done: every part . . . seems clean & in order. But on the whole I never saw Knowsley so free from eyesores of any kind. The rabbits are well kept down: and though a good deal of smell comes from St. Helens, neither Broomfield nor Harrison think that any damage has been done.

Moult tells me that in Manchester things are thought to be worse than ever: the trade to the east is lost, & there seems no prospect of its being recovered (I mean by the east the Turkish empire). In addition there is a great strike actually begun, & likely to go on: for the men seem inclined not to give way, & the masters care little whether they do or not, work as they allege being carried on at a loss. – Yet building continues, & both Hale and Moult agree that the demand for new houses in Bootle is greater than at any former time. I do not understand the situation.

26 Apr. 1878: Left Knowsley by early train: London 2.20: parted at Euston from Sanderson: St. J. Square, where busy with letters & papers till 4.40. Then by train to Fairhill. . . . Agree to give my name to support the new scheme of making a bishopric at Liverpool, which I care nothing for, & rather dislike than otherwise: but both parties have taken it up, & refusal would be ascribed to dislike to parting with money. The thing can do no particular harm, but I shall attend no meeting in its favour, nor do more than give what custom & my local position make necessary.

27 Apr. 1878: . . . Long early walk . . . nearly 3 hours brisk walking: glad to find I can do it without weariness. Walk later with M. . . .

Meet the tenant of Underriver Farm, an intelligent conversible sort of man, & some talk with him about the neighbours, crops, etc. He says he has land of his own, 130 acres . . . which he wants to sell: was I minded to make an offer? I said no, it was too far off from here, & not enough of it together: but why did he want to sell? He answered that he had 8 sons, wanted capital to set them up in business . . .

News in the papers that Hardy[52] is to be a peer by the title of Cranbrook: his elevation is fairly earned by political success, & is justified by his means: he has 5,000 acres in Kent, & over £20,000 a year, as is believed, from the Low Moor [iron] works & other investments. It was understood that he was to be raised to the peerage when the leadership devolved on Northcote, passing him over: at which he was much disappointed, but took it well. His style of speaking will be less effective in the Lords than in the place he has left: he is eloquent, passionate, & declamatory, but cannot argue, or debate with effect, unless he has first lashed himself into rage: rhetorical rage only, for both in business & society he is a good-natured & agreeable person.

28 Apr. 1878: . . .Wrote 14 letters & notes: mechanical work, which in official days was taken off my hands by Sanderson: but it is not amiss to have some employment of this kind, giving that sense of occasional compulsory labour which prevents a holiday from growing tedious.

. . . Letter from a German doctor, modestly asking me for a loan of £100. Pender[53] sends me a collection of letters by a Manchester editor who has created a strong sensation in the north by a clever pamphlet (included in this series) entitled *The Crown & The Cabinet*. It is a review of the last volume of the life of the Prince Consort, published nominally by Mr. T. Martin[54], really by the Queen, & in which is included an extraordinary correspondence between Albert & Baron Stockmar[55]. The subject of Stockmar's never-ceasing advice is the necessity of raising the position of the Crown, so that the Queen shall be really the head of the Cabinet, guiding & influencing its decisions. Albert entirely agrees & approves, & they unite in lamenting that English statesmen should not see the matter in the same light. The imprudence of publishing such letters at any time would be great: just now it is deadly serious, for the part which the Queen has taken in stirring up war is partly known, partly suspected, & the publication seems intended to call special notice to it. To make matters worse a number of the *Quarterly* has just appeared, containing the same high prerogative doctrine in equally unguarded terms: and this article will undoubtedly be ascribed to ministerial influence, though I do not suppose that any member of the government has had to do with it.

I have omitted to note the result of an election for Tamworth, vacated by the retirement of a Conservative, Mr. Hanbury[56]: the Liberal candidate won by nearly 2 to 1. This looks as if the war policy were unpopular: though it is fair to note that the Liberal was one of the Bass family[57], & beer was therefore on the side of peace.

The situation remains unchanged, so far as we know: the expedition from India either has sailed or is about to sail: & in a fortnight I presume that its object must be disclosed. Negociations continue, but not much hope is entertained of the result.

30 Apr. 1878: . . . A conference [is] about to be held in Birmingham in favour of peace . . . I decline to take any personal part: for though the object is one which I approve, & the language held is not likely to be of a decidedly party character, it would be scarcely decorous for a minister just retired from office to agitate in the provinces against the policy of his late colleagues.

The newspapers tell absolutely nothing that is new: the popular feeling as far as can be judged from them is curiously apathetic about the prospects of war. The danger has so long hovered over men's heads that they have got used to it, & hardly believe in its reality. Even with the help of this explanation, it is an odd state of things: enthusiasm in favour of war, though foolish, is intelligible, & vigorous opposition equally so: but the mass of the public in all classes seem content simply to take what comes, treating the matter as one beyond their power to deal with, & so best left alone.

. . . I find from 4 to 5 hours walking, such as I have had today, enough for my legs: which ought not to be, but 4 years of a sedentary life leave their effects for a time.

1 May 1878: . . . Went to Coutts, & there settled for the purchase of £40,000 railway debentures, giving 4 per cent: they will cost about £43,000, all expenses covered. I shall then have £180,000 nominal capital invested, worth at present rates about £190,000. The whole transaction did not occupy 15 minutes.

. . . Waited some time at Charing Cross . . . home[58]: by 4.12 train . . . Found Arthur C.[59] arrived: quite unaltered: his voice & laugh heard all over the house: he admits having done nothing yet but lose money by the farm, but feels sure that it will come right: in any case, his life is happy & harmless, & no other would have suited his disposition.

Revenue returns for the month show an improvement of nearly a million over last year: notwithstanding depressed trade, the prospect of war, & a strike in Lancashire imminent.

. . . Hornby, the parson of Bury[60], writes asking me to come over & fix a site for his new school: as to which he & Statter[61] cannot agree.

2 May 1878: Bright warm day: walk . . . suggesting improvements . . . well pleased on the whole. I resolve to plant apple and cherry trees largely in the meadows, wherever there is no view to intercept. They do no harm to pasture, increase the yield of the soil, & ornament the country in the absence of timber.

. . . Nothing new on either side, but things look as if there were less excitement than prevailed six weeks ago. *The Times*, which aims at representing exactly the state of middle-class feeling, writes in such a strain that it is impossible to make out its drift: evidently the editor does not see his way, & wishes in any event to have as few of his words to eat as possible. *Daily News* steadily against war, but rather too openly pro-Russian to make its advocacy effective. *Telegraph* pugnacious, but I think a little less so. *Post* & *Pall Mall* hot for fighting.

I have been pestered during the last few days with begging letters from Germany, & could not understand why: the explanation is in an article of some Vienna paper, which gives a probably altogether fabulous report of my income, which in Austrian florins must no doubt seem rather large.

3 May 1878: . . . Walk for exercise: for the first time since leaving office I felt something like depression of spirits, connected with the want of some occupation which I can feel to be of use. Yet my reason tells me that a holiday is not only a right after four years of incessant anxiety and labour, but in some sense a duty, as without it health and energy will suffer . . . Anyway, I am glad of our intended visit to Paris[62], little as in general I care for sights . . .

Saw Schouvaloff, who talked openly of the state of negociations: he seldom sees Salisbury, having construed something said by the latter as a prohibition to call without previous appointment. I think this is a misunderstanding, and said so. He is going back to his own country next week to see if there is any possibility of an understanding being come to: which he does not seem much to expect. The most encouraging feature of the matter is that S.[alisbury] has more than once repeated that he does not see what there is to fight about. – Münster sees M. and tells her of Salisbury's language: how he says that there is no need to consult the Cabinet, that they are not to be allowed to interfere in negociations. 'Beaconsfield and I can settle it all': and how he laughs at the Premier for his courtier-like ways of subservience to the Queen. Odd, if true, and probably there is some foundation for it: but diplomatists know how to suit their language to the persons they talk to, and no doubt Münster supposes that any dispraise of Salisbury will be welcome to us just now[63*].

4 May 1878: . . . Went by appointment to a photographer in Regent Street: one of the nuisances which must be endured, for the public will have its photographs of men known in public life &, if sittings are refused, fancy likenesses are substituted. . . . Write to decline the presidency of the Welsh Eisteddfod which is to meet this year at Birkenhead. . . .

5 May 1878: Up early, & with M. & Margaret to Charing Cross by 7.30: we were met there by Sanderson: talk with him, & we settle that he goes with his sister to Keston. . . . We reached Paris about 6, & took up our quarters in the D. of Bedford's house, which he has taken for a month.

. . . The P. of W. has taken an active part, & on Friday last delivered a speech in its praise & that of France, which has made him very popular here, & is equally disliked at Berlin. But he was right to say what he did.

. . . Much talk of arrangements to be made for the week, which M. enjoys thoroughly – I wish I could, but strange company gives me no pleasure to compensate for the feeling of embarrassment & restraint which it produces.

6 May 1878: . . . To the Exhibition[64] . . . The bigness of it is the most noticeable feature, all former exhibitions of all nations might have been put into its enclosure, & still left room. . . . Some eastern ivory, & enormous specimens of malachite from Russia, interested us most.

. . . Saw Lyons[65], & had ten minutes talk with him. He seemed fatigued, & complained of the amount of social duty imposed upon him – receptions & dinners every night, & a ball for the Prince[66] next week, the first he has given. The only thing he told me was that the determination of the French people to stand by their present form of govt. was showing itself more & more clearly as time went on – which I was glad to hear. He confirmed what I knew before, that France will observe absolute neutrality in eastern affairs.

Home, read & wrote. Ld Acton[67], Renan[68], & Ly Granville[69] came to dinner: Renan grown very old & fat since I met him at Madame Mohl's[70]. He talked with abundant energy, but chiefly on antiquarian & ecclesiastical subjects, to which Ld Acton drew the convn. Thence to the Opera which, never having seen, I was not sorry to visit for once. . . . the house is by far the finest thing in the nature of a theatre that I have ever seen, the interior one mass of marble & gilding.

7 May 1878: Walk early, alone, into & nearly round the Bois de Boulogne . . . . . . losing myself in the alleys, I walked for half an hour before meeting anyone to tell [me] the road. When I did, my informant was a workman employed in clearing the roads: he walked with me some way &, finding from what I said that he was speaking to an Englishman, asked whether we were going to war with Russia? He proved to be an old soldier, who had served in the Crimea & in Italy: he talked fluently & intelligently about his campaigns, the state of the army, etc. I suppose there are many English privates who would have as much intelligence, but they would hardly converse with the same ease & readiness. Home after a ramble of 2½ hours.

. . . We dined about 20 . . . The dinner was truly French: 3 out of 4 were talking at once before soup was taken away, & later the clatter of tongues became universal. I could hardly make out a word, which I ascribed to being deaf, but found that other Englishmen were in the same case. – Some talk with Taine[71] afterwards, but only of a complimentary kind.

8 May 1878: News from London. The H. of C. has discussed the bringing of Indian troops to Malta. Harcourt[72], Fawcett[73], & others making their comments & accusing Northcote of having deceived them by declaring that there was no change in policy, & withholding the knowledge of what was being done till after parliament had separated. That this was done purposely there can be no doubt: & it was a mistake, for why should a minister show distrust of an assembly in which he has a large majority? Intentional deception I do not think there has been, but Northcote lays himself open to that charge by carrying to excess his reasonable desire of conciliating all parties. No doubt has been expressed as to the troops really being intended for Malta, & it is possible that the fact may be so, & that the design of an occupation is suspended.

. . . Duc Decazes[74] called: we had some interesting conversation: he thought Austria would prefer to take the provinces & remain at peace, but if war broke out between Russia & England she would be forced into it somehow. He said the French reserve forces had been called out for the first time, the success had been remarkable: the official strength of the army including these was 1,200,000 men: but in practice it would be about 100,000 less. As to the internal condition of the country, he was despondent, saying that there was no govt., that power was really in the hands of irresponsible persons (he meant Gambetta) . . .

10 May 1878: Gladstone has delivered another speech[75] at Hawarden, fine & forcible, but apparently a little overdone, & less effective on that account. He assumes throughout that Ld Beaconsfield has wanted a war from the first, which I do not believe: the Premier only wants to do whatever will be most popular, & to satisfy his party. He talks moreover as if the business of the Indian troops, & the article in the *Quarterly*, taken together implied a design against parliamentary govt.: whereas the latter was probably not inspired by any member of the Cabinet, & the Indian affair, though it may be a mistake, is not grave enough to be made the ground of such an attack.

. . . Dined at the embassy, meeting Mr. & Mrs. Waddington[76], the minister for foreign affairs, & his wife: he (who was my contemporary, or a little my junior, at Cambridge) a thorough Englishman in appearance: short, placid, & sensible: he talks without the slightest French accent: they say that his French is equally pure from any admixture of English: we had no serious conversation: but I liked his manner & way of talking. Mrs. W. is American, lively, a little marked with the peculiarities of her country, but pleasant.

11 May 1878: . . . The Duke[77] [of Bedford] much impressed with the reckless outlay of the Paris municipality, & fears that the same thing will happen in London when the power of local taxation is put into the hands of a directly elected local board. – I hear both from Gavard[78] & Sheffield[79] that the municipal debt of Paris amounts to £180,000,000, an incredible sum, & just 18 times that of London . . .

. . . Heard with regret that Ld Stratford de Redcliffe[80] at 87 or 88 is reduced to absolute poverty: obliged to sell his pictures, his London house, and all that he can do without. It is believed that he put the whole of his savings into Turkish securities: a strange proceeding for one who knew Turkey as he did. His only son is dead, but there is a wife and several unmarried daughters.

12 May 1878: Left the Duke's house between 6 & 7, & by train to Calais. . . . London a little before 7. Found a vast heap of newspapers & pamphlets, but only a few letters, these having been regularly forwarded. So ends our little excursion, pleasant on the whole, but I feel the uselessness of going into foreign society, & should not do it at all but for M.'s pleasure. From growing hardness of hearing, & the rapid way in which the French talk, I cannot follow a conversation sufficiently to enjoy it.

. . . I was struck with the absence of apparent poverty or distress anywhere, & with the fact that nobody complained of what had been or was being done, though they might express alarm as to the future. The expenditure on Paris seems quite as great as during the Empire, & I believe this is with the present govt. a point of policy. . . . As to general politics, I picked up one or two facts. Everybody is for peace & against intervention in the Russian quarrel: so far all parties agree. There is an increasing confidence felt in the stability of the Republic: the storm of last year has cleared the air . . . Gambetta is the real master of the situation.

13 May 1878: See Sanderson who low in spirits & thinks himself ill, though he says Drage[81] can find nothing the matter. Talk with him about a place as commissioner of customs, there being a vacancy on the board. I had heard about this from Tenterden, & suggested to Sanderson to apply at once to Northcote, & to Tenterden to support his application. I would under other circs. have written to Northcote myself, but just now it would be inconsistent with the political attitude I have assumed, & probably would do no good.

. . . H. of Lds at 5 . . . but there was no business. In the lobby V. Harcourt met me, & said that it had been resolved to raise in both Houses the question of the moving of Indian troops to Malta without the sanction of parliament: he seemed confident that there could be no defence, all precedents were the other way. He said Ld Selborne[82] was to argue the question in the Lords. I observe that *The Times*, which declines to commit itself, but has of late rather supported the Cabinet than otherwise, now writes strongly against the concealment that has been practised.

Saw Lawson[83]: he thought the troops were really going to Malta now, though believing that such had not been the original intention. Nothing, he thought, could be known of the negociations till Schou. came back. Münster called: said in his judgment the chances of peace or war were equally balanced, it was impossible to guess at the result. Dined at home, & quiet evening.

14 May 1878: . . . With Sanderson to Witley . . . Talk with Sanderson about his prospects: I renewed an offer which I had made once before, to help him with the necessary means if he preferred to exchange into the diplomatic service, as he is evidently not inclined to return to his old post in the office. However, he seemed not disposed that way.

. . . to The Club for dinner . . . The Dean[84] & Dr. Smith[85] talked of the Lit. Fund dinner of last week: at which the so-called Stanley[86], the African discoverer, was present, got very drunk, & when called upon to return thanks attacked the chairman for something he had said, in a vulgar & violent fashion. He is evidently an unpleasant being, & one to be avoided.

News that old Ld Russell[87] is dying at last. He is 86, & has long been in a state nearly childish. Lacaita[88] saw him lately, & failed to elicit any answer that could be understood, as to passing events: whereon it occurred to him to talk about some place in Italy which the old man had visited in early youth, & in which he was known to have taken much interest (I believe on account of a love affair). Ld Russell burst into tears, and began to quote Italian poetry, which he did for some time. Lacaita told me this at dinner.

I note that a change has come over the newspapers: even the *Pall Mall*[89], which in its eagerness for war will hardly criticise anything done by the present Cabinet, warns Northcote that the secrecy observed about the Indian expedition will have to be explained. The only solution which occurs to me is that the troops were meant, in the first instance, to occupy some point on the Turkish coast: that their destination was afterwards changed (as Lawson thinks): but, as this cannot be avowed, some other excuse will have to be found. I do not, however, expect that much will come of the affair. . . . I find a general impression that he [Disraeli] is bent on exalting to the utmost her personal power, & on uniting Crown & people against the aristocracy. I cannot, however, say that I have seen any tendencies of this kind in him: though he is more of a courtier than I like or approve. He is supposed to hate the Whig aristocracy: but he has always been willing enough to join with any of them who would act with him. The difficulties have come from their side.

15 May 1878: Newdegate[90] called, nominally to talk over the business of the Indian troops, which he has criticised in the House: but he rambled on in such a way that I could make little of it: his chief topics being his distrust of Disraeli, and the confidence placed in him by my father. Carnarvon[91] came also, and we discussed the situation in a general way. I find him agreeing with me that there is nothing to be done with the Conservative party, and that no attempt at a reunion should be made: that it will be well to cultivate the Whigs, between whom and ourselves there are no substantial differences: but without a formal rupture from our present connections: and that no step should be taken in haste, lest we should seem to be acting under the influence of pique or resentment. I advised him to be ready to speak on Monday: but, if he spoke, not to make an elaborate attack only to give his opinion briefly. On the whole, I am inclined to think that he and I may act together better than I had expected: unless his High Church notions stand in the way.

In afternoon, talk with M. as to whether any overture should be made to C.S.[92*] of whose unfriendly language and conduct we have more evidence than enough. The problem to solve is, how to mark our sense of it without an actual rupture and without awkward explanations. On the whole we agree to leave matters where they are, to keep aloof, and to let any demand for explanations come from the other side.

16 May 1878: . . . At 11, went to the Cotton Districts Hospital fund[93] meeting at the Westminster Palace Hotel: met there Sefton, Winmarleigh[94], G. Ashworth, Birley, Maclure, Shuttleworth, & one or two more: we sat about $1\frac{1}{2}$ hours. Our capital is about £150,000, & on my notice £10,000 of it which had been lodged in Indian securities was withdrawn.

Winmarleigh & Ashworth both talk uneasily as to the strike in Lancashire, which has led to a good deal of ill feeling. In Blackburn there has been rioting, a house burnt, & troops sent from Preston: a sort of thing of which we have had no recent experience. Ashworth explains the matter by saying that the men have had their own way for years past, & the younger ones among them hardly understand that circs. may force them to give in. The co-operative societies are also failing in all directions, which I am sorry to hear. Ashworth also says that the Paris exhibition is unsatisfactory as regards machinery: we are beaten by several countries in what we thought our special department: but he has always been a croaker. Walk home with Winmarleigh: he talks about the Queen's book, the Albert-Stockmar correspondence, etc.: he says it has produced a profound impression in the north, & that we shall hear more of it.

. . . Talk of the D. of Bedford's affairs: it seems he has lately told M. what the amount of his rental is: £230,000 from land & houses, £30,000 from mines, in average years: I thought it had been more, for in one year he certainly received over £300,000. But his estate has been admirably managed, & is quite free of burdens.

17 May 1878: . . . Harcourt[95] called: some talk with him . . . . . . He talked of the P. of W.'s visit – said rather significantly that it had lasted long enough: that he had not been very civil to the President[96], whom he was disposed to treat as an inferior ('he remembers that he is the P. of Wales, & forgets that he is not in England') . . . He further mentioned that the P. talks Imperialism wherever he goes, and makes no secret of his wish to see the Republic subverted: which has done away the good effect of his late speech.

18 May 1878: . . . In afternoon, walk to South Kensington, for meeting of Nat. Portrait Gallery there: Hardinge, Scharf[97], Somers, B. Hope, & B. Cochrane the trustees present. Cochrane very noisy & silly, full of what he is going to do for the trust in parliament. . . . Stanhope presents us with a statue of his father, well enough executed, but not in the least like the man. On the way to Kensington, I went to see a picture by Millais, 'The Bride of Lammermoor', which is much talked of & admired.

19 May 1878: . . . Reading for the second time Taine's English literature . . . It is well done, & interesting in many respects: perhaps a severe critic might say that the author sets out with a certain preconceived idea of English character & adapts his conclusions to it.
. . . The chief event of the week has been a serious disturbance in Lancashire, caused by the reduction of wages in the cotton trade, & consequent strike of the men. Blackburn, Burnley, Accrington, Preston & other large towns have all been troubled with mobs, in one or two cases houses have been wrecked, in many, windows have been broken & other mischief done: troops have been sent from Preston: altogether the state of matters is unlike anything which has been known during the last 20 years. The explanation seems to be that, whereas in the American war every operative knew that the cause of his suffering lay beyond the reach of English hands to remove, in the present case the action of the masters is thought to be unreasonable. It is the supposed injustice, not the privation, that causes irritation: & the attacks on private property have been clearly made without previous concert, by unorganised bodies, generally consisting of lads & of the roughs of the neighbourhood, to whom any opportunity of rioting is welcome. No sign of socialist doctrines, or of deliberate determination to create terror, appears anywhere.

20 May 1878: Walk from Keston through Bromley & Lewisham, intending to walk in to London . . . the appearance even where the houses are good enough is squalid & mean. . . . New building appears to have ceased altogether: between Bromley & London I don't think a single house was to be seen in process of construction.
. . . In afternoon, answering letters: of which I receive more than ever before, on all possible subjects.
. . . To H. of Lords early: where debate on the question whether it is legal to bring Indian troops into a European colony without the previous sanction of parliament. It was determined by the Opposition not to raise any question of policy, but to argue the constitutional point only: this resolution was perhaps wise under the circs., but it made the debate uninteresting. Ld Selborne argued his case from precedents, clearly & fully, rather

too fully for debating purposes, for he spoke two hours, & his speech though instructive & lucid was not lively: as indeed from the nature of his argument it hardly could be. The reply, by Cairns[98], was equally long, & not more entertaining: he had prepared himself to argue a somewhat different point from that which Selborne laid stress on, & much of his reply was therefore beside the mark. . . . When Cairns sat down, it was near 9, & the House, at first fairly full, had emptied. Cardwell[99] said a few words, dull & little to the point. Carnarvon & I went away. Granville[100] & the Premier spoke briefly to a thin audience, but it was evidently felt to be a merely formal proceeding & not much was said on either side. Both Carnarvon & I resolved not to speak, unless anything had compelled us to it, & for the same reason: that we do not wish to seem factious or resentful. We walked home together.

He tells me that Carington[101], who is much with the P. of Wales, repeats a saying of the latter, to the effect that when he is King he means to be his own Foreign Minister. Not much importance should be attached to this foolish (perhaps drunken) talk of a foolish person: but it shows the tendency of royal minds at the present time. No such speech could have been made 20 years ago.

21 May 1878: Writing letters as usual: sent one applicant £5: refused another, who merely on the strength of his name being Stanley (for he does not claim relationship) asks me to take & furnish a house for him. One must have personal experience of the requests which people will make, else they would hardly be believed.

. . . Read with care a curious abstract, made in Manchester, of the blue book relative to land. I have had it by me for a year, but wanted leisure till now. The argument of the compiler is that, though the calculation which set down the landowners of England & Wales at 30,000, has proved absurdly wrong, since they are really upwards of a million; the error is more in form than in fact, since 30,000 owners do absolutely possess 27,000,000 acres out of 33,000,000, or 9/11ths of the whole. He makes out that the holders of less than one acre are in number 703,000 (omitting small figures): the holders of more than one, & less than a hundred acres, 227,000 nearly: making 930,000 out of 973,000, who collectively own less than 4,500,000 acres out of 33,000,000. Thus the remaining 43,000 owners hold seven-eighths of the soil; and a further calculation shows that 24,000 persons hold 26,000,000 acres collectively, or four-fifths of the whole. The results are ingeniously worked out, & no doubt accurate, though they do not touch the main fact that the number of small proprietors is greater than anybody had supposed.

22 May 1878: Settled about sending of pictures from Knowsley to Nottingham for an art exhibition there. Accepted the invitation to open a bazaar at Stanley park: the same thing that I did 7 years ago.

. . . Dined in the Middle Temple Hall . . . . . . as we left the Hall in procession, I had a very warm reception from the students. M. & Margaret dined with Carnarvon, & went on to the Palace ball. M. describes with some humour the awkwardness of Cross[102] & others, who hardly seemed to know whether to come up to her or not.

23 May 1878: London U. Senate, which I have not attended for a long while: the meeting was large, 20 present & Granville, Kimberley, Acton, Paget[103], Lubbock[104], etc.

. . . Schouvaloff has returned, and brings concessions which he thinks ought to be satisfactory, but he tells M. that he finds Salisbury in a less pacific mood than when he left

England . . . It is believed that the Queen, who till lately was hot for war, has taken fright . . . She will, however, be a difficulty to all her ministers in future. The present Premier has flattered her incessantly and grossly: always letting her think that it was for her to guide the Cabinet and govern the country. (He himself has told me as much, and that it was the only way of dealing with her.) She takes this kind of talk quite seriously, and is encouraged by her children and German relations. But as she knows nothing of what the world is thinking, and will not listen to any observation that makes against her feeling of the moment, her desire to interfere is not accompanied by any sound judgment as to what should be done.

24 May 1878: Sir W. Thomson[105] called on M. & showed her the new invention called phonograph which reproduces audibly and several times over words spoken into it . . . the voice a ridiculous squeak more like that of Punch than of a human being. . . .

25 May 1878: . . . Received a letter from a Mr. Stead[106], who induced me some weeks ago to revise my speech of 8 April, with a view to its being reprinted: he circulated it in a broadsheet, and now tells me that 360,000 copies have been sent out, and 40,000 more ordered: in all over 400,000: of these 30,000 have been circulated gratis, the rest sold in ordinary course. Manchester alone took 70,000: the large northern towns absorbed the greater part: Liverpool had very few: he says the effect has been considerable: and on Conservatives as well as Liberals. Froude told me the same thing some days ago.

26 May 1878: . . . A.D.[107] writes to me about C.S. – a good, friendly letter: but she does not know half the story. – I answered, explaining the matter, so as to make it clear that there is no irritation on our side, only needful precaution against future inconvenience.

28 May 1878: . . . Talk with Schou., who seems confident that a settlement will be come to, and is pleased in proportion. I gathered from him that both Kars and Batoum will be left in Russian hands; in fact that on the Armenian side they keep all they have got: but that *per contra* Bulgaria will be divided, and some concessions made as regards European Turkey. He spoke in general terms, as was natural, but was quite explicit as to Batoum. He told M. that Gortschakoff, who is past 80, an invalid, and but lately thought to be on his deathbed, is doing all he can to prevent a settlement, out of personal jealousy, though aware that failure must lead to a war. Bismarck is eager for a congress, and declares that it need not take a week. On the whole, the prospects are better than they have been yet. It is clear that in the English Cabinet the peace party has won the day: Salisbury has again gone round to it, the Premier is said to acquiesce, but there has been great opposition on the part of others – Cairns and Hicks Beach[108] are named as the dissentients, but as to this nothing certain can be known.

Talk with Goschen[109], interesting enough: his experience of poor law administration has created in his mind a strong apprehension of socialism: he says that in the H. of C., if anyone proposes anything supposed to be in the interest of the working class, no member dares vote against it, though many in their hearts may be convinced that it will do more harm than good: he instanced the Plimsoll[110] proposals: adding that the H. of C. would pass a bill knowing that its effect must be to crush the trade it deals with, rather than lie open to the imputation of rejecting a philanthropic measure.

. . . In what Goschen says of the socialistic tendency of much modern legislation, there is undoubtedly truth: and he is probably right in thinking that it will cause inconvenience: yet, if one had cared to argue the point, it might be contended on the other hand that in a country like ours, where the separation of classes is carried farther than elsewhere, where the rich are very rich, and the poor very poor, a more stringent enforcement of strict economical rules as against the working man would create so much discontent as to amount to danger. In other words, it is a choice of evils, and probably we have chosen the lesser evil of the two.

29 May 1878: Death of Ld Russell in the papers: it had been long expected. His mind had gradually failed, & it was a relief to his friends when he ceased to appear in the Lords. Strange to see how essentially ephemeral is the fame which political life brings. Lord Russell had been for 40 years an active & leading politician . . . yet since 1866, when he quitted office for the last time, he has been as much forgotten as if already dead & buried. It is equally strange that he, who had been twice prime minister, & on one occasion held the office for 5 years, felt, and did not conceal, deep disappointment at not being included in Gladstone's Cabinet of 1868. He wanted a nominal post, Lord Privy Seal or the like, that would have enabled him to have a voice in all that was proposed. Lord Melbourne had the same infirmity, in 1846–7, though at the time partly paralysed and unfit for business. I shall not attempt to sketch Lord Russell's character. Its merits & faults were on the surface. He was one of the most consistent of politicians: a Whig, to whom Tories were natural enemies, & radicals injudicious allies. That all the world should adopt Whig ideas was in his view the destiny of mankind, & the duty of every individual was to do whatever might be possible to bring about that result. A partisan by nature & lifelong habit, he had the faults of one: could be factious, & not too scrupulous: but whatever he might be guilty of in that respect was for the sake of his party & not for his own. In debate, notwithstanding his weak voice & puny appearance, he could be very effective, especially at the close of a long sitting, when he would sum up in a pointed, telling way, which never failed to produce its effect. He was at his worst in a prepared statement, or in opening a debate, when he would often be languid, feeble, & at times discursive. He had an odd ambition for literary fame, which was never gratified: his books are many, none very good ,most of them worthless. But literature was to him an amusement, & almost his only one. He went little into what is called society, & in later years at least reading & writing were his chief pleasures. To money he was wholly indifferent: the family believe him to have died in debt. . . .

31 May 1878: Death of Russell Gurney[111] announced: one of the most honest, independent, & respected of M.P.s. He was conservative in general politics, but had nothing of the high-church and high-prerogative tendencies of the present day. He resigned the recordership of London only a few months ago: & to the general surprise was refused the customary pension: without fault or reason assigned. It was a mean piece of economy . . .

    H. of C. adjourned suddenly, in consequence of the death of Wykeham Martin[112], member for Rochester, in the library. He had heart disease, & died in a few minutes without previous illness. No event of the same kind has occurred since Perceval[113] was shot, nearly 70 years ago.

    R. Bourke came to see me, yesterday I think; says he has been offered the governorship of N.S. Wales, which he refused, not liking to leave parliament: he relieved my mind

of one apprehension by saying that if he left F.O. his successor would not be Drummond
Wolff, but Plunket[114]: a good man, capable, & honest, by all reports.

1 June 1878: Learn . . . that Adm. Stanley[115], whose family I have lately helped, married
a farmer's daughter, & his children are in a corresponding rank of life.

B. Museum at 1.00 . . . . . . Walked back with Walpole[116], & talk on present events. I
find that he dislikes the warlike & expensive policy of the last few months nearly as much
as I do, & says a good many Conservatives are of the same opinion.

Travellers for luncheon: home: by 5.00 p.m. from Euston to Edgehill. Reach Knowsley
at 10.30, just 6 hours from door to door.

Reading on the way an interesting book by a Mr. Wilson[117], called *Resources of Modern
Countries* – originally a series of articles in Fraser. The writer comes to the conclusion that
all countries have of late been living beyond their means, & running deeper in debt than
their prospects will justify: . . . and that it is to the waste of capital that has already taken
place that the distress of the working class throughout the world is due. His conclusions
are too much in the pessimist sense for me to accept, especially as to the reckless way in
which English colonies have been in the habit of mortgaging their future, & the probability of their some day suspending payment. His view of Indian finance, too, is that
which I have long held: that insolvency there is only a question of time.

2 June 1878: . . . Wrote among others to Lord Granville, telling him what is the truth as
to the pending negociations and giving an opinion upon them. I pointed out that the
conditions on which we go into Congress are in effect a concession of nearly all that
Russia asks[118*] . . . I had no doubt, I said, that Lord G. would think as I did that the solution arrived at was more satisfactory than a war: but if we were to make these terms,
which Russia would have accepted at any time since the beginning of the discussion, what
was the object of our armaments? for what purpose had we spent six millions? and what
was there to show for it? My ostensible object in writing was to ask if Lord G. intended
to raise any discussion before Whitsuntide, or immediately after it.

3 June 1878: At 4.30 to Prescot, & thence by rail to Grange, for my aunt's funeral. At
Carnforth met F. Hopwood[119], going on the same errand. We travelled, dined, & passed
the evening together.

. . . Talk also of the new Liverpool bishopric, which F.H. evidently considers a job got
up by certain persons for purposes of their own: he says it is unpopular among the clergy
. . . But he speaks (I judge) as a friend of the present bishop[120], who naturally does not
like his see divided.

Note that this bishop's son, young Jacobson, lately in F.O. as a clerk, & whose retirement on account of debt & other scrapes I think I have noted in this journal, has gone
thoroughly to the bad. After detection in this country he was sent off to N. Zealand,
where he is now in gaol for obtaining money under false pretences.

4 June 1878: Drove over to Witherslack & waited at the Church . . . Only the family
attended . . . F.[121] could not come, which as matters stand is just as well. . . . O.
Penrhyn[122] read the service, & returned with us to St. Helens . . . Back by 2.40 train,
Knowsley about 5.40.

. . . It is announced that both Ld Beaconsfield & Salisbury attend the congress: an unusual proceeding, which to the Premier has the recommendation of being without precedent, & making people stare: but I suppose the real fact is that neither of them will trust the other alone. There has been some talk on the subject in parliament, but the question was not one to raise a serious debate upon, & the world in general is well satisfied with the prospect of peace.

5 June 1878: No news in the papers, but from the way they write it is clear that peace is thought certain: & there is a general feeling of relief: but the fear of war has never been as strong as might have been expected, considering how near we have been to it. To be sure, the Cyprus & Scanderoon[123] business is still a mystery.

It is singular that, while in Manchester the stagnation in trade & business is complete, building at Liverpool goes on steadily.

6 June 1878: Sent, through Lawrence, £25 to Mrs. H.S.[124] – who is dying as usual. The trouble with that family threatens to be endless. The eldest son is in N. Zealand, living chiefly on help from me, without character & without health: his daughter again is with the grandmother, has no means, no acquaintance, & has quarrelled with her nearest relatives, who might at least have given her a home. There are two others for whose education I am paying. Not one of them will ever do anything for themselves except beg, & that they do readily enough.

7 June 1878: . . . Talk with Nathan about the deer: he reckons them at 212 red deer and 220 fallow . . . I tell him the red deer must be kept up to 200, all above that figure he can dispose of as he sees opportunity.

. . . Another sample of odd requests: a lady, not known to me, writes from the West End that a young couple of her acquaintance would be much improved in health by a few months' tour on the Continent: would I object to pay their expenses? No reason is assigned for applying to me rather than to anybody else. I refuse, but civilly, having ceased to wonder at any kind of application.

8 June 1878: Hear . . . from Hale that the Cheshire Lines Co. are ready to pay me £75,000, I think the sum is. Wrote on this to Lawrence to give notice to Alexander that I will pay for Holwood[125] at the end of the year. Rain continued all day, heavily: the earth is saturated: a wetter season has not been known.

9 June 1878: Letter from Sir A. Gordon[126], from Fiji, enclosing one from the widow of consul Liardet[127], lately dead in Samoa. As usual, she wants a pension, saying she has nothing to live on. The consul had blundered in every possible way, & had been recalled for explanations. I send the correspondence to Tenterden, glad that I have nothing to do with it.

Church early to show myself to the people: Mary was taken ill & M. stayed at home with her. In afternoon, Mr. McCorquodale[128] and another called to ask me to take the chair at a meeting to get up a subscription for the families of the miners killed at Haydock. I agreed after some discussion.

. . . I was introduced today by Hale to Mr. Thompson[129] . . . he has lately been appointed my agent under Hale for the Fylde estates. We had no conversation to enable me to form any judgment of him.

Letter from Cross, asking me to be chairman of a commission to enquire into, & regulate, certain London charities, of which the collective income is alleged to exceed £100,000, & it is believed that of this by far the greater part goes to waste, there being in the City parishes no population requiring help, & the value of land having swelled bequests & gifts originally small to quite unintended proportions. I have deferred my answer for a day or two.

10 June 1878: . . . Set out with M. & Margaret for Liverpool, in heavy rain: we drove to the Town Hall, were received by the Mayor & Mayoress, & I attended a meeting of the Molyneux trustees, which lasted about half an hour. Then came luncheon, but happily no speeches: at 2.30 we drove slowly through the streets to Stanley Park, M. & I in the Mayor's carriage with him & the Mayoress. . . . We were very well received, cheered everywhere, & most warmly in the poorest & most squalid district – St. Ann's St., Scotland Road, etc. Strange & perplexing to me, but so it is. The crowd at Stanley Park was great, we were told 25,000 people in all had collected. . . . I made a short speech about the Stanley Hospital, the object for which the bazaar is held: we then bought all sorts of rubbish at the stalls, as is expected on such occasions: drove round the park, & so home.
    . . . The Molyneux trust, a meeting of which I attended for the first time, owes its existence to a curious accident. A Mrs. Molyneux, in 1727, left the sum of £500 in charity, chiefly for the benefit of seamen's widows: this sum was meant to be invested on landed security, but the trustees overstepped their powers, & bought land with it, which they had no right to do: the result is that the landed estate now returns £1,300 a year, & other investments £400 more: making £1,700 a year income, or, at the usual rate of 25 years' purchase, just 85 times the value of the original capital. . . . The money is divided among sailors' widows, in very small sums, none getting more than £6 a year . . .

11 June 1878: Another cold & wet day: more disagreeable weather can hardly be imagined.
    . . . Letters: one from the Bishop of Manchester[130] . . . He also suggests that I should write or say something to put an end to the strike: which I hardly see my way to do: unasked advice being seldom of use, and the offering it not at all in my line. There is another consideration, which I never see referred to in the press. Whatever may be the mischief done by strikes (and in the present case I am not clear that the workingmen have not some right on their side) they are a vent, an outlet, for a great deal of socialist, or at least anti-capitalist, feeling which in foreign countries does not evaporate so harmlessly: and I am not clear that, if this feeling found no escape in its present direction, it would not break out more dangerously in another.

12 June 1878: Into Liverpool to attend a meeting in aid of the widows & children of miners killed by the explosion at Haydock last week. . . . I gave £105, M. £25: no larger sum was promised by anyone except the owner & lessee of the collieries where the accident occurred. I took the chair, & opened the proceedings, speaking about 10 minutes. . . . The Bp spoke in a sensible manly way, which I liked: free from professional cant, & from exaggeration. . . . Home at 2.00 . . .
    . . . Walk in the park, in heavy rain, which has hardly ceased since Friday [7 June] . . .

13 June 1878: Death of the ex-king of Hanover[131] is announced: he was comparatively young, under 60: a dull, honest, obstinate man. Every decision that he took, small or great, was with him a matter of conscience, not to be revoked or even discussed. He has been more pitied than usually happens to dethroned kings, partly on account of his blindness from a child, partly because he lost his kingdom with little or no fault of his own. He might probably have made terms with the German govt., but that was not in his nature.

14 June 1878: . . . Lionel West[132] came in the evening: he brings copy of the *Globe*, containing the full text of agreement between the English and Russian governments, which can only have been obtained by some trick. . . . There is something comic in the accident happening just now, for Salisbury has signalised his entrance into office by adopting extraordinary precautions for the maintenance of secrecy, even keeping back confidential papers from Tenterden and the clerks, and deciphering his own telegrams, which was never done before by a Sec. of State. It will annoy the Premier, than whom no one is more inclined to be scrupulous, and even pedantic, in the observance of forms.

In point of public policy I do not see that the disclosure will do any particular harm: but it destroys much of the interest which would otherwise attach to the results of the Congress, since it is certain that what England & Russia mutually agree to accept or at least not to resist will be acquiesced in by other powers.

15 June 1878: M. wants me to buy Hollydale, which for that reason I suppose I shall: but it will be dear, £300 per acre.

Very lazy & drowsy all day, I don't know from what cause: tried gymnastics again, but could do very little: at nearly 52 it is late for that sort of thing.

16 June 1878: Church: collection for Haydock explosion, gave £2. Walk back with L. West. Walk with him in afternoon to Croxteth, & in Sefton's gardens & woods: but they are rough & out of order, not pleasant to see. Yet Sefton likes the place, & lives there a good deal: but I fancy he cares for little except the shooting.

. . . Reading a new series of Nassau Senior's[133] conversations. He is the real inventor of what is called the American practice of interviewing: conversing, that is, with some eminent or notorious person, putting down the substance of what passes, & showing it to the interlocutor as a guarantee of accuracy. Senior was careful & conscientious in taking this last precaution, & hence his reports may be relied upon as conveying truthfully the opinions of the individuals quoted: he lived much abroad &, from constantly making notes of what he heard, became a sort of authority. His journals were circulated in M.S. Several volumes of them have been in my hands. None are without interest: but, relating as they do almost exclusively to politics, they will not greatly attract the next generation. In the year 1900, few people will care to know what the Orleanists or Republicans of 1860 thought about the policy of Louis Napoleon, or the Italian war. Thiers is the statesman whose opinions are most largely set down in these last volumes: & a queer medley they are of shrewdness, vanity, & inveterate prejudice.

17 June 1878: Letters as usual: I don't know when I have had so many applications for all sorts of purposes, from all sorts of persons.

Much sensation appears to have been produced by the publication of the Anglo-Russian agreement, the authenticity of which is not now denied. It is a bitter disappointment to the war party, as well it may be. It in effect leaves untouched the substance of the San Stefano treaty, and gives the Russians all they ever wanted and more than they expected. Kars & Batoum remain to them: so does the piece of Bulgaria which they want. Bulgaria up to the Balkans is autonomic, and the district south of the Balkans is to be semi-autonomic, a separate state. This is the only real concession which Russia has made, not unimportant, but it is open to the criticism that the separation between the two districts may probably not last longer than that between Wallachia & Moldavia, and it has also the effect of leaving the northern part of Bulgaria more wholly under Russian power, than if the state had been made larger. As matters stand it will be another Servia.

18 June 1878: Wrote to Ld Granville on the situation. He has put a question which Richmond[134] refused to answer: Ld Grey[135] pressed it, but to no purpose. From the tone of the newspapers I gather that a profound sensation has been produced by the memorandum. The *Pall Mall* is furious, *Telegraph* cool & dissatisfied, *Standard* openly in mutiny. *D. News* satisfied, but asking reasonably enough what was the meaning of all these preparations, if we were to end by escaping on the Russian terms?

I note, as a singular comment on our warlike zeal of the last few months, that the militia reserves have been estimated on paper at 30,000 men. When the time of calling upon them drew near, it was found that only 25,000 were to be expected: the number actually coming forward has a little exceeded 23,000, & of these more than 2,000 have been rejected on medical grounds: so that we have hardly more than 2/3rds of the force supposed to be available. Is the case the same in other military departments?

19 June 1878: . . . Wrote to Carnarvon to dissuade him from making a move in the H. of Lords, which he seemed disposed to do, and had written in that sense to M. I tell him that we may have to appear as witnesses against the Cabinet but it ought to be as unwilling witnesses, and certainly we should not volunteer as accusers. I also advise him, if he does anything, to consult with Granville, and let the latter if possible take the initiative.

. . . Note that the strike in the Lancashire cotton-trade . . . has all but come to an end: the masters not caring whether their mills were open or closed, in the present state of trade, could afford to wait, & were determined to stand firm: consequently the men have for the most part given in. A cause which I never see referred to in the newspapers must be telling against the working class: emigration has practically ceased from the distress in America, & at the same time sanitary care has largely diminished the mortality. Consequently population is growing faster than it ever grew before: faster, probably, than capital. There is a constant influx of fresh hands wanting employment: & employment just now is not abundant. How will this affect the prospects of the artisans? & the political future of the country?

We have never yet seen how our present institutions will work in a time of general distress. I do not anticipate rioting or violence, as a rule, but I should expect to find many crude schemes for artificially stimulating production and consumption, taken up by the public, and supported in parliament by men who know better, but dare not offend their constituents.

20 June 1878: Drive with Hale to Bootle . . . walk over the land newly laid out for building, of which there is a good deal. Bootle is believed to have now over 20,000 inhabitants, and they increase in number rapidly. The houses chiefly in demand are small, fit for artisans &

clerks. We went over the unfinished docks – greater works than the Egyptian pyramids, in point of labour & cost: looked at the timber ships unloading: at the tunnel making under the canal: & at a new Welsh chapel, Wesleyan, I think, handsome both inside & outside. There is still a large mass of land unlet at the north end of the estate . . . I think an average might be taken at £1,400–£1,500 per acre, which would make the total value of the Liverpool estates something between £1,500,000 and £1,800,000. They give a little over £39,000 present rental, but I see my way to its reaching £50,000 before many years are over, & they may possibly touch £60,000 by the end of the century.

The reflection is often present to my mind – will all this immense material prosperity of Lancashire continue? It has sprung up in less than a century: will another hundred years see the end of it? And, if so, what will remain? The docks certainly: they are built as if for endless duration: a few public buildings here & there: but the hundreds of thousands of cheap ugly brick cottages, built in rows, & all alike, will have crumbled away: a few years of neglect is enough to destroy them and, being on the surface of the ground, not even the foundations will show. May not the same thing have happened to ancient cities, the remains of which puzzle us at the present day from their smallness when contrasted with what we read of their population & magnitude. No observer even notices the moment when decadence sets in: it is a gradual process, & only our modern system of perpetual census-taking, & measuring everything in figures, can make it visible. I fancy that in Cornwall, where the mines are being abandoned, & in South Wales, there is already an exodus, & that villages once crowded are standing empty. But I know less of this than I could wish, & must enquire further.

21 June 1878: Altogether an idle & rather wasted day, for I did nothing that I can call to mind beyond writing a few letters. I should already begin to doubt, as I used in old days, whether so inactive an existence was justifiable, but reason tells me that after 4 years of unusually laborious work an interval of entire rest is good: that without it any work which may come to me in the future is less likely to be effectively done.

22 June 1878: . . . With M. to Lathom[136] . . . the park & grounds are exactly as I remember them 40 years ago . . . the sight of Lathom left some melancholy impressions. Of all whom I knew there in childish days, not one remains except E.B.W. & Jessy W., both old, infirm, & separated from me by the accidents of life, though we are affectionate when we meet. At 52, nothing else is to be expected. I thought, too, much of my mother[137]: Lathom is the only place where she ever seemed to feel really at home, and in my youngest years I was often & long there with her.

23 June 1878: Yesterday at Lathom talk to the gardener about his hothouses, etc. He tells me that coal was a few years ago, during the prosperous times, at 19s. the ton delivered: it has now fallen back to something less than 6s. the ton. The difference is due to wild speculation when things looked well for business, & to stagnation now. . . . The relief of cheapened coal to consumers having small incomes must be great.

24 June 1878: . . . Saw a curious and amusing letter from F. Wellesley to his father. On his being presented to the Empress at Schönbrunn, she, who was going out riding herself, at once ordered a horse for him, and desired that he would follow her: she then took him to a sort of exercising ground that she has had made in the grounds, and tested his horsemanship by taking him over all sorts of fences and other leaps. He came off with credit, and was delighted with her cordiality: but it is an odd style of introduction for a diplomatist.

He likes Austrian society: says there is a frank kindness about both men & women, quite different from what he has been used to in Russia, where he never could trust the people he dealt with, or feel at home.

Much discussion in the papers of what is supposed to be passing in Congress, but nobody knows certainly. The general result of what is related is that there has been a crisis in the last few days (real or simulated) & that the matters in dispute have been settled by compromise. *The Times* is working hard to prove that the loss of Kars, Batoum, & all Bulgaria north of the Balkans will leave Turkey rather stronger than it was before! But the most serious question raised is that of a protectorate, in some form, of Asia Minor: which it seems to be thought that the Cabinet contemplate, though for my part I can hardly believe it.

25 June 1878: . . . Several other letters about charities . . . A fair sample is one from Cheltenham just received. A lady writes to say that she is out of health, that carriage exercise would be good for her, but is too expensive: will I send her £50 to enable her to hire carriages for the summer? Nothing about her family or antecedents, nor any reason given why I should be selected from the rest of mankind to supply her with comforts. The worst of these appeals is that they really destroy the pleasure of giving: what one has to spare is rather snatched out of one's hands than freely offered.

. . . Cleared off & destroyed a multitude of old letters.

26 June 1878: Seeing yesterday in the *Telegraph*[138] an article about the possible occupation[139] of Cyprus[140] which is evidently inspired, I wrote to Granville to call his attention to it. There is a general expectation that the Premier will not let the Congress end without some sensational proceeding of this kind. Others suggest that he will take up the Euphrates valley line, and support it by guarantee or state assistance in some form: a recklessly wasteful proceeding, but not on that account less likely to be adopted. A third more fanciful idea is that a protectorate of Palestine will be established, so that Jerusalem shall be virtually a British possession. To all these wild projects the public, as far as can be judged, listens with indifference, and some amusement: but it is curious to see how little desire there appears to be to influence the result one way or the other.

27 June 1878: Up early, & to Preston by 9.25 train from Edgehill. Heat & dust disagreeable: the weather being almost tropical. At Preston found a small attendance of magistrates, about 35: we sat over 12 hours: not much controversy about any part of our business . . . Walking back to the station, I was taken to see the new Conservative Club, in which I am a large shareholder: a good, handsome building, well lighted & ventilated.

. . . In parts of England the heat has ranged from 91° to 97° in the shade which for June is almost without precedent.

. . . Wrote to Sanderson, enclosing £200 for the quarter. . . .

29 June 1878: . . . Letter from Granville, on the unauthorised publication of the Russian agreement: the explanation of which is now known. A copyist of the name of Marvin[141] was called in to make a copy of this paper, by the Treaty Dept.: and it appears that he contrived to make or secure a copy for his own use, which he sold. The office is not a little amused: for, by way of ensuring absolute secrecy, Salisbury has refused to let the clerks know anything of what is going on, and has kept the papers in his own or Currie's[142] hands: consequently they are free from all possible suspicion and, having been hurt by what they consider undeserved mistrust, they openly rejoice over the failure of the new plan. It is in fact the extreme desire to keep these negociations from them that has caused the mischief: for, if copies were wanted in haste, and they were not to make them, nobody would be employed except the copyists, who as a rule are never allowed to touch any but mere routine documents.

1 July 1878: Receive monthly reports from Statter . . . land is beginning to let again, after long stagnation.

. . . Leave Knowsley at 10.15 . . . St. J. Square by 4.25.

I have passed the last month in great quiet & ease, & on the whole with pleasure: but the east winds of the last week have been a real drawback to enjoyment: they come loaded with vapours from the chemical works, & the smell cannot be kept out of the house, by night or day. The nuisance is increasing every year. In all other respects, I am well satisfied.

2 July 1878: Stopped at a shop in Audley St., attracted by the sight of some singular photographs. They were professedly those of ladies in fashionable society, & respectable: but the dress, attitude, & general style suggests 'demi-monde': being indeed hardly decent: one does not understand how respectable women can allow their likenesses to be publicly exhibited in such a way.

. . . Lawson called: not well pleased at the doings of the Congress, which might have been expected, but trying to put a good face on the matter. He says if Batoum can be saved, & the indemnity got rid of, the thing may still be a success: otherwise it will cause general disappointment. He suspected that we should annex Cyprus, but knew nothing certainly. Lady Salisbury, he said, has got hold of *The Times*, & is inspiring the editor, but often leads him wrong, from her inaccurate way of talking.

3 July 1878: Lawrence came early, & with him I prepared a new will: the last dating Jan. 1877, since which time I have a good deal more to dispose of.

I leave to Ly D. £20,000: Mary & Margaret, £10,000 each; Sanderson, £5,000; the three lads[143] £2,000 each: to my sister[144], whatever remains unpaid at my death of the £20,000 promised her: to charities & public institutions, £10,000 more. Some minor family legacies, in all about £90,000 bequeathed. I leave £80,000 as a fund to accumulate to pay off any remaining charges on Knowsley. To Ly D., Keston, or Holwood if I have it, for her life. These are the chief provisions. My brother is residuary legatee, which is only just, as regards personal property at Knowsley, rents, etc.

. . . Walk round Regents Park for exercise. Sanderson came to luncheon.

Dined Sir W. & Ly Harcourt's at their new house in Grafton St. Met Stanhopes[145], Beaumonts[146], Ly Skelmersdale[147], Granville, Beust[148], & others. Pleasant evening. Some talk after dinner with Granville on the situation. He tells me Carnarvon was anxious to raise a discussion, but was advised to keep quiet by Cardwell, whom he consulted. He thinks, and the impression is general, that there is a risk of the Congress breaking up on the question of Batoum[149]: the cession of which to Russia is unpopular with all parties . . . Granville asks what I think Lord B. would do, in the event of Russia refusing to give way? I answer that Lord B. does not really want a war: he has no military tastes or aptitudes: but that he looks upon every question from the point of view of personal and party popularity: and, that if the choice lay between concluding a peace which at home would be thought unsatisfactory, or making a war which would spread over Europe, I do not believe he would be withheld by any scruples from adopting the latter alternative.

4 July 1878: . . . By 4.30 train to Keston, where M. & I intend to pass our 8th wedding day.

Walk into & round the little adjoining place, Hollydale, which is for sale, 50 acres at £15,000 as I am told: examined it thoroughly: the house is old, patched up at various times, & bad: probably not worth repair: the grounds neglected, & want much clearing up, but pretty: some very fine trees, especially beech & lime: a lake which has run more than half dry: neglect visible everywhere, but something might be made of the ground. The chief object of possessing it would be to prevent the erection of villas close to Keston: it is an excellent site for that purpose. But to buy building land for the purpose of not building upon it is a costly amusement.

. . . The public institutions to which I have left bequests are as follows: London University, University College, and Trin. Coll. Cambridge, £2,000 each: Rugby School[150], the Royal Socy., the Royal Institution, the Literary Fund, & the Brompton Hospital, £1,000 each: all free of duty. But this is only a first list, & may be added to in future years, if I live.

Amused with a story told last night of a Mr. Langtry, the very stupid husband of a celebrated beauty, whose portrait is in every exhibition, and her photograph in every shop window. He is invited everywhere, and treated as a great personage on his wife's account. He is reported to have said 'that if he had known what a reception he should have in fashionable society – which he had always heard was very difficult to get into – he should not have married so soon, but gone into it as a bachelor, when he could have enjoyed himself more'.

5 July 1878: . . . After discussion with M. I agreed to buy Hollydale and wrote to Lawrence that I will offer the price asked – £15,000. It is not a good investment but, considering how Knowsley is surrounded by yearly increasing nuisances, I do not believe that my successors will blame me for securing to them, within easy distance of London, an extent of land sufficient to give the enjoyments of a country place, free of the annoyance of being overlooked & trespassed upon. I have now – Keston, 137 acres, Holwood 344, Hollydale 50, all touching, & in effect forming one property. Total 531 acres, & it will be further increased in a few years. If I can obtain the land lying east of Keston to the wood called 'Ninhams' and a few fields south-east of Holwood park, there will be a compact mass of about a square mile, enough for privacy & pleasure.

6 July 1878: . . . More odd applications: a Dutch lady writes to ask whether I will pay for the education of one of her children: and a German author, or journalist, wants to be supplied with materials for a pamphlet.

. . . The roads full of excursionists: who find pleasure in driving out, packed as tight as they can manage to be, in open vans, blowing horns & shouting: they then stop at a public house on the road, dine, drink, & come home rather noisier than they went. It is well that amusement can be found on these terms.

The newspapers all this week have been full of the Congress: no other subject attracts the least attention: & as far as can be judged the general feeling is one of not wholly reasonable disappointment. In truth the public mind has been in a childish state: at one moment elated & excited as if great successes had been achieved, at another disgusted as if all had failed: & in both cases equally without cause. The Bulgarian settlement, whatever may be its permanent value, put people in good humour: the cession of Bosnia & Herzegovina to Austria did not create much feeling on its own account, but it is known to have been part of the Russian plan, & is on that ground unpopular: besides that it seems inconsistent with the attitude which the British govt. has hitherto assumed. Batoum is in all mouths: why it should interest the public, who mostly don't know whether it is in the Black Sea or the Aegean, is not evident: but the press is for once unanimous, & if it be ceded the impression will be unfavourable. The indemnity question is not much discussed. The Greek claims are not wholly rejected, but philhellenes will not be well satisfied with the extent of territory added to Greece. The philo-Turks have more substantial reason for dissatisfaction, Turkey having lost two provinces in Europe, a slice of another, & Kars at least on the Asiatic side, if not Batoum also. Altogether it is plain that, if the Congress does not break up, the arrangements which it will make are not such as to satisfy anybody – perhaps not the worst thing that can be said of them.

The danger is lest Disraeli, who would prefer a tragical and signal disaster to a commonplace failure, should set on foot some new scheme, such as an Asiatic protectorate, or annexation of a Turkish island, which may set all Europe by the ears. If nothing of the kind is attempted, Russia will carry off the substantial advantages of the dispute, whatever she may have yielded in point of form. I do not blame our Cabinet for this, having thought from the first that there were only two alternatives, either to accept in the main the result of Russian successes, or to go to war: but the Premier at least is justly punished if the war spirit which he has done so much to rouse turns against him. But it may be that we have not yet heard the last word, and criticism is premature. . . .

8 July 1878: Batoum is announced as settled, the Russians retaining it, but as a free port, & with the fortifications dismantled. The *Telegraph* has an announcement, which seems authoritative, of Cyprus being occupied & of our having entered into a separate treaty with the Porte for the protection of Asiatic Turkey[151]. I reserve comment till we get more details. The other journals know nothing of these transactions.

Granville called to talk over the situation, but I could throw little light upon it. A hundred questions & doubts occur, which a few days must solve . . . Are we acting with the consent of the Congress or without it? Do we invite any other power to join in the new treaty of guarantee? Do we claim in regard of it any authority over the Porte, or are we to defend the Turks, & let them govern as they please? All those are points of the highest importance, but as to which we are quite in the dark.

. . . H. of Lds at 5.00 where, in answer to a question put by Granville, Richmond confirmed the story of the *Telegraph*: the same answer was given in both Houses: the general feeling appeared to be one of surprise & perplexity: at least it was so in the Lds: nobody has had time to make up his mind. . . .

10 July 1878: Saw Harcourt, the French ambassador[152], who called to talk about the

Congress arrangements: he professed to know nothing & to have heard nothing except what was in the papers: I could see that he was uneasy as to the possible effect to be produced in France: but that was a delicate subject, & I could not press him upon it. He says Münster is very angry, which if true is not so intelligible, for the scheme has an appearance of being suggested by Bismarck. He tells me (which indeed I have heard elsewhere) that there is much talk among our naval men as to the want of any good harbour in Cyprus, & as to the unhealthiness of the climate.

Carnarvon called, a good deal excited, and wishing me to take the lead of the opposition out of Granville's hands, which is nonsense, and I told him so as civilly as I could. He is afraid lest Granville should be too moderate, and does not see that violence would only play the game of the Cabinet. He left me, I think, cooler than he came, but hardly convinced.

. . . Read again in the last few days a good deal of the *Life* of Kingsley[153], published some two years ago: a book or rather a character which utterly perplexes me, by the contrast between the moral & intellectual qualities. Kingsley appears to have been one of the most unselfish, conscientious, & earnest reformers, in the real sense of the word, that have lived in our time: & his influence, founded on these characteristics, appears to have been considerable. One cannot read his letters without being impressed by them: but what he really believed, how he came to believe it, & by what process he created for himself a religion which was that of nobody else, is unexplained & I suppose inexplicable. Probably the combination of a strong imagination with a weak logical faculty made him what he was. To me the book is a puzzle, though an interesting one.

11 July 1878: . . . Gen. Peel[154] came to luncheon, much aged, but retaining his old spirits & humour. I was glad to see him again: he reminded me, not disagreeably, of old House of Commons scenes: though assuredly I would not go through that life again.

Wrote, after much consideration, to Talbot[155], asking him to tell my brother that I cannot support him in the event of a contest. I put it on the ground that the expected dissolution will turn on questions of foreign policy, as to which I am opposed to the Cabinet, and never more so than since the announcement of the last few days.

12 July 1878: Lawrence called with draft of my will, which I again carefully went over with him. I have left it in the main as it stood on the 3rd, but with modifications. I leave all pictures at Knowsley which may have been bought by me to the Corporation of Liverpool for their art gallery: those inherited of course remaining with the house & estate. I leave 3,000 volumes of the Knowsley library to my brother, the rest to Liverpool. I add one or two more legacies to public institutions. I made Ly D. co-executrix with my brother, & residuary legatee, but have first set aside for my brother all that in justice ought to belong to a successor . . . My plan of a large endowment for some national purpose is postponed, though not abandoned. I shall revert to it, if I do not give in my lifetime what I have to give for such uses: but the claims first to be satisfied are those of duty to family & connections: others may follow.

Saw Drage, chiefly to talk to him about M. who seems low & worried, Mary[156] having a return of her old complaint & requiring continual care. He thinks me in good health, which I hardly feel sure of myself, being nervous & anxious about public affairs: but that feeling will probably pass off.

13 July 1878: M. goes off early to see Mary, who is to go through an operation. . . . Worked on notes for a speech on the Turkish arrangement, though when it is to come off I don't know. By 12.30 train to Fairhill, Sackville[157] with us . . . The new rooms at Fairhill are partly furnished & habitable, though the walls are still bare, & more ornaments wanted. But on the whole the house is better than it seemed possible to make it when we bought the place, five years ago. . . .

16 July 1878: . . . Making notes for a speech, as to which I am embarrassed by the difficulty of compressing all that there is to say within the necessary limits.

Granville calls: says he intends to take the discussion at once on Thursday, fearing that people will go out of town if a day next week is fixed. He is also not anxious to divide in the Lords, & thinks that it will be easier to discuss the subject without dividing if the debate follows immediately on the First Minister's announcement. I tell him I shall be ready.

Received from my brother a letter, the answer to which I have delayed. In it he assures that nothing has been said by himself or his wife against me: which I quite believe as far as he is concerned, but not as to her.

. . . Ld B. & Salisbury returned to London, & had a great reception[158] arranged for them at Charing Cross.

17 July 1878: Day very hot: all morning at home, working on notes for a speech, the most difficult, I think, that I ever had to make . . .

Wrote to my brother, assuring him that I never believed anything had been said by him unfitting our mutual relations: offering farther verbal explanation if desired by him, but not otherwise: and leaving it clearly to be inferred that I do not equally accept the disclaimer given on behalf of his wife. In truth, I have evidence as to the way in which she has used her tongue, which makes it clear to me that she cannot be relied on: though I am quite willing to believe that there is more of mere gossip than of malice in the affair[159].

18 July 1878: Sleep rather disturbed: feeling very nervous and uncomfortable: revised notes of speech. . . . Day extremely hot, the hottest, they say, this year. I did not stir out till 4.30, when to the Lords: the House was very full as to the galleries, the bar, and the throne: fairly so as to the attendance of peers: but I have seen more present. Lord Beaconsfield spoke an hour and a half, very well, as he always does, from the rhetorical point of view, but feeble, I thought, in argument. He touched very lightly on the real difficulties of the case, Cyprus and the Asiatic guarantee: and dwelt, as I thought, at needless length on the arrangements as to the Turkish frontier in Europe: but probably he was anxious to conciliate the ultra Turcophiles, who have shown some inclination to be dissatisfied with the treaty. Granville followed him, less effective than he sometimes is . . . I spoke next, for about an hour[160], fairly to my own satisfaction. Salisbury answered me with extreme acrimony: contradicting what I had stated as to the Cabinet of the 27th of March in language so unusual that Granville called him to order, and I rose again to make a personal explanation.

19 July 1878: Received a note from Granville, & called upon him, he wishing to put some farther questions as to Cyprus.

. . . Granville called upon me in the afternoon, & talked over the possibility of farther explanations being asked as to Cyprus & the Indian expedition: I told him what I know, said that as a matter of course I should be ready to defend myself if attacked: but that I did not wish to volunteer any further statement. Though satisfied in the event of a wrangle that I can prove my case, the prospect of renewed personal discussion is disagreeable, & made me nervous & uncomfortable. Partly at Granville's suggestion, I wrote to Northcote. . . .

20 July 1878: Keston: too hot to walk early, sat or rambled in the shade with a book. Pender came over to luncheon, & suggested that we should join him in a cruise in the Levant, in November next: he is going out in one of the telegraph ships, which he seems to use as his private yacht.

Sanderson came, & he & I walked in Holwood. Walk with M. in Hollydale.

Letter from Granville about the Cyprus affair, which I could not answer, not having heard from Northcote.

Later, I received Northcote's answer to my letter of yesterday; he admits that the occupation of Cyprus was determined upon 'in principle': but, as I understand his explanation, not decided as a measure to be immediately executed. This is a point on which proof is impossible, in the confused way in which our Cabinet business was usually done: but in any case it is very different from the unqualified contradiction given by Salisbury.

Letter from the Queen, deprecating further discussion of the affair: and expressing disapproval of its having been discussed at all. She has forgotten her own permission to make the usual explanation of an outgoing minister, of which I shall remind her.

21 July 1878: Wrote briefly to Northcote. Sketched out on paper what I should say in the event of any farther debate on the Cyprus affair: which being done, my mind is at ease upon it.

Walk in Holwood with M. in afternoon. Read aloud some of the essays of Montaigne in English . . .

My 52nd birthday. It is a little more than thirty years since I began active public life by contesting Lancaster[161]: a little more than twenty years since I began to take a prominent part, by the passing of the India bill in 1858: and of those last twenty I have passed nearly eight in a Secretary of State's office. If I consulted present inclinations I should say that I had done with party politics – though not with public affairs in a national sense. But we are not our own masters, and events may force me back into the turmoil against my will. Meantime I shall enjoy rest with the feeling that it has been fairly earned.

22 July 1878: Unwell in the night, shivering, and feverish: but the sensation passed off. I slept again, and woke fairly fit for business, though very weak.

London by 10 o'clock train: letters, etc. Saw Sanderson and Granville, and told the latter of my decision not to stir in the matter of my statement of Thursday, and Salisbury's contradiction, unless it is raised again. I said at the time that I adhered to what I had asserted and, though confirmatory details might be given, absolute proof on either side is impossible. I showed him Northcote's letter, which is more than half an admission that I was right. . . .

25 July 1878: Much talk with M. as to a short tour in the Alps next month. We both liked the idea, but settled nothing. It is difficult, after so much excitement as that of the last two years, to settle down quietly in a country place without definite occupation: the reaction from past exertions tells on nerves & spirits. We both feel this, & hence our plan.

26 July 1878: H. of Lords at 5.00, where M. came also, there being a notice by Lord Rosebery[162] to call attention to the secret convention with Russia. He spoke well, making some telling points. Salisbury answered, for him, rather temperately, & on some points with effect, but it was impossible to get rid of the fact that the instructions intended for publicity would have conveyed a wholly incorrect impression of what had passed, but for the accidental publication of the secret agreement between England & Russia.

27 July 1878: Drage came: I shall not require to see him again, being now recovered, & I think whatever was amiss came chiefly of the hot weather.

B. Museum at 12.00 . . . the Duke [of Somerset][163] coming late, I was put in the chair. We sat 3 hours, which is a new thing for us to do . . .

. . . Keston by 4.30 train: pleasant cool evening, & walk: but M. in low spirits about her eyes, which she thinks are getting worse.

28 July 1878: . . . Turning over in my mind the expediency of settling in my lifetime some matters which I had relegated to my executors. I might leave a permanent memorial of myself at London University, etc., etc., by an expenditure of from £2,000 to £500 in each case for a prize, scholarship, or exhibition, to bear my name. The question is whether it is worth anticipating to that extent the general distribution of such means as I have which must take place at my death? On the one hand, is the advantage of the respect & thanks which one earns in that way: on the other, the additional trouble given by importunate applicants, whom the reports of a benefaction of any kind attract by thousands. I well remember that Peabody[164], the American, found it impossible to live in England after his gift of £100,000 had been announced. The begging letter writers hunted him down, stopped him in his walks, & forced themselves into his lodgings. He went abroad till the storm had abated.

29 July 1878: . . . Letter from Lord Winmarleigh, asking to be allowed to express in public his opinion as to my probable reunion with the Conservative party. He seems to have said something on the subject already & has been agitated by reports that I had joined the Liberals. I answer in vague terms, that it is hardly time to call upon me to give assurances as to my future political course: that at the end of a parliamentary session there can be no reason for my making any declaration: that whatever I do will not be done on impulse or in haste: that I cannot authorise him to say anything pointing to the probability of a reunion, but that I am free from any personal pledges or engagements. I add that in the event of a dissolution I cannot support my brother, & give the reason as I did to Talbot (v. diary, 11 July).

News in the papers that Lord Lorne[165] is appointed to succeed Lord Dufferin[166] as gov.-gen. of Canada. The selection is odd: for Lord L. has shown no sign of ability, & given some evidence to the contrary, by the publication of a good deal of the feeblest kind of verse. On the other hand, the colonists will be pleased by having a daughter of the Queen settled among them, & Ld L. may for aught I know to the contrary be fairly capable for the post. The choice is made evidently to please the Queen, & in pursuance of the new system which is to put the royal family as much as possible in positions of power. It is singular that the princess should care to go into what must be an uncongenial banishment: but the relations between her mother and her have not been agreeable of late years, & by exile she obtains more personal independence than she has ever before known.

In the *D. News*, an interesting article, showing that the effect of what are called 'bad times' on the general prosperity of England has been less than is commonly supposed. The writer takes for his standard of comparison the exceptionally prosperous year 1873: & he shows that pauperism has decreased since then in the ratio of nearly 1 in 6 (742,000 against 890,000): that savings banks deposits have increased from £61,500,000 to £73,000,000: & that the income assessed to income tax has risen from £513,000,000 to nearly £580,000,000.

30 July 1878: . . . Intended to go with Tenterden to make the usual declaration as to S.S.[167] in the court of exchequer, but find a note from him that he is wanted at Osborne[168] & cannot come.

31 July 1878: . . . In H. of C. last night, a fine speech[169] from Gladstone against the Berlin treaty, perhaps as powerful a summary as could be put together of all that there is to say of its demerits. The force of the argument was perhaps lessened by exaggeration on some points, but substantially I think what he said was true, though he dwelt more on the condition of the eastern Christians than I should have cared to do.

It is worth notice that Bourke has stated in express terms that our guarantee to defend Asiatic Turkey is dependent on good government being established in that country: which it evidently will not be unless we take it in hand. And that we seem to have no intention of doing: so that the engagement is likely to be altogether illusory. Better so, in the general interest: but it is not an altogether creditable state of things.

2 Aug. 1878: In H. of C. a powerful speech[170] from Lowe, directed entirely against the action of the Cabinet in straining the royal prerogative . . . His speech was the only one of any interest, the rest of the debate being dull. Carnarvon, having been referred to incidentally in a speech lately made by the Prime Minister, thought it necessary to come up to town & deliver an answer, or protest. He did it well enough, if the thing was worth doing at all, which I do not think it was. But in such matters a man must judge for himself. His disposition is towards a restless and fidgety activity: mine perhaps tends too much to letting things alone, especially where personal interests alone are concerned.

3 Aug. 1878: . . . See our courier Duruz, the same who went with us to Pau.

Saw Drage, more out of form than necessity. He much commends our going abroad[171] now, on account of M. whose health & nerves he thinks require a change: and indeed this was my chief reason.

With Tenterden . . . well pleased with his new dignity of K.C.B. but not so well, as I gather, with the altered arrangements of the office. In effect the system of transacting all confidential business with a private secretary, apart from the department, reduces the permanent officials to the position of clerks who are used & trusted only in matters of routine. But the inconveniences of this new plan are so great that it is pretty certain to be given up after a short time[172].

4 Aug. 1878: Read & finished the life of Diderot[173] by Morley, interesting as the only existing record of a man who has left a reputation probably deserved, but which rests on the effect produced by him on his contemporaries: for of the voluminous works of Diderot it is not likely that anything is now read, even in France. . . . It is impossible not to admire the strength of their convictions, & the zeal with which they gave their lives to propagate them. . . . The priest in our age figures as one of the guardians of property, & is accordingly tolerated by many who disbelieve in him: in the last century, rich men were frankly free thinkers, not supposing that they endangered their own position thereby, or not caring, comparatively, whether they did or no.

9 Aug. 1878: Left Geneva at 9.30 and posted to Chamonix . . . Chamonix is a town of hotels: doubled in size in the last 16 years.

11 Aug. 1878: No news in the papers . . . except that Northcote meets his deficiency by borrowing: repayment to be in five years: no new taxes. This is probably, all things considered, as good an arrangement as he could have made.

13 Aug. 1878: Of the papers I see here only *The Times, Pall Mall,* & *D. News:* I gather that the session is ending without any further serious criticism, but that there is a growing conviction that our Anglo-Turkish agreement is not seriously intended. It is argued that, if we are to take seriously the engagement to defend & to reform the Turkish empire in Asia, it is impracticable, & that we cannot therefore be bound to it: if on the other hand we are to take it as explained by Bourke: if we are only pledged to defend the Turks on condition of their governing well, the compact is merely illusory, since the condition upon which alone it becomes binding will never be fulfilled. In that case, it is argued, the sole use of it was to serve as an excuse for taking Cyprus, & as a set-off to those provisions of the Treaty of Berlin which have given to Russia three-fourths of what she claimed.

There is vague talk of an Anglo-German alliance, which would be quite in the Premier's line: nothing would please the court or the Tories more than a coalition, monarchical & dynastic in character, against republican France. But we know nothing of any such intention.

14 Aug. 1878: . . . Corrected the proofs for Hansard of my speech of 18 July[174], a tedious business, the report being inaccurate as usual, and in parts sheer nonsense.

16 Aug. 1878: Left Chamonix with regret, but we have seen all that can be seen without longer & harder expeditions than M. is fit for.

18 Aug. 1878: . . . Pleasant drive up the valley to Zermatt . . .

22 Aug. 1878: . . . Visp to Brig by rail . . . . . . found many letters, but none of interest: mine were chiefly to beg, or else about local business in Lancashire.

23 Aug. 1878: . . . Nothing has struck me more than the extraordinary way in which the alpine part of Switzerland is, so to speak, occupied & possessed by foreigners. Everywhere are hotels, many enormous, nearly all large & good . . . The whole population seems to live on the stranger. This fact alone ought to make one cautious in reasoning about the social condition of the Swiss peasantry . . . Note that since leaving the environs of Geneva I have not seen a single building answering to what we should call a private gentleman's house.

24 Aug. 1878: Left Andermatt early . . . I think the upper part of the lake of Lucerne, from Fluelen to Gersau, a country more agreeable to live in during summer than any known to me: & I catch myself indulging in foolish fancies of building a villa in some picturesque & convenient situation, near the lake, whence Lucerne would be accessible by steamer in one direction, & the mountains in another. . . . But this is M.'s first tour in the Alps, & naturally she wishes to see all that can be seen in the time available, & I wish to show it her. The boat, though large, was disagreeably crowded with English & American tourists.

29 Aug. 1878: Ride up in 2 hours to Mürren, a new place, at least new to me, & there at 5,000 feet above the sea find a considerable British colony. Two large hotels, crowds of English hanging about, a church building, *The Times* kept in the hotel we went to. Among the visitors was Newman Hall[175], who recognised me, & we had a little talk. . . .

1 Sept. 1878: Left Interlaken soon after 8.30, & drove with 4 horses to Thun . . . We adopted this way of travelling, though slower, having had enough of the crowding & discomfort of the railroad, & wishing to enjoy the journey quietly. . . . Drove on to Berne in the afternoon . . . Put up at the Bernerhof: excellent, as indeed all the Swiss hotels are that we have seen.

2 Sept. 1878: Walk early about the town with M. Sir H. Rumbold[176] calls, & we walk with him to the parliament house of Switzerland, a handsome building, neither too gorgeous nor unduly plain. See the room in which the federal parliament meets, large & convenient, but bad for hearing. Also the Cabinet room, where the 7 members sit each in an armchair, wide apart, so that there can be no easy conversation: a bad plan, if real business is to be done.

Leave in railway for Basle . . . So ends my 5th Swiss trip. I was in the Alps as a boy, I think in 1842: but it may have been 1841: again in 1850: with my brother in 1862: & at Lucerne in 1868. Each visit has been more enjoyed than the last: the only drawback being that I cannot now walk as in old days: yet even in this respect I do not know how much is real failure of muscular power, & how much more want of training.

3 Sept. 1878: Basle to Paris, 10 hours: nothing remarkable: we had a coupé, with sofa seats, so that M. could lie down. . . .

4 Sept. 1878: Left Hotel Bristol at 7.00: reach Calais at 1.00: London a little before 6.00. . . . Newspapers are full of an accident in the Thames: a river steamer, with 7 or 800 passengers on board, ran into last night by a screw-collier, & only a small number escaped[177]. This is the largest destruction of life that has taken place for years by any similar casualty.

. . . The uncertainty as to a dissolution in the autumn continues: contrary to the usual practice, which is to take some rest before speechmaking begins again, several ministers have been holding forth: Lord Sandon[178] & Cross at Liverpool, my brother at Barrow, etc. But this may be no more than a compliance with local pressure.

I have read but little in the last month, though having leisure enough for desultory reading. A book on Holland by an Italian, a memoir of the last days of Louis XV of France, a good account of Tyrol & the Tyrolese by an Englishman settled among them, Trollope's *Australia*[179], & a few novels have been nearly all that I have done in that line. But having gone for health, rest, & change of ideas, & found them, I do not consider the time wasted.

5 Sept. 1878: See the courier Duruz, his pay is £12 for the month, I make it £20, for his work has been very well done. The total cost of this tour has been £346 nearly, for 31 days: rather more than before, but we have travelled fast, & Swiss inns are expensive. It has answered its purpose well: M. is better in health & spirits than she has been for years: & I have been kept from thinking of political complications, past & future, as to which there is nothing to be done at the present moment, & which are therefore better allowed to rest. If ever we return to the Alps, I think the point to make for will be Grindelwald . . .

7 Sept. 1878: Send Mrs. Gladstone £20 for a charity, not very willingly, but she begs with such importunity that refusal is hardly civil. She takes the opportunity also to invite us to Hawarden: but I shall not go[180]. Gladstone is not popular with the Liberals, except with one section of them: he has shown so much heat and passion even where he was right in the main that his judgment is distrusted: and his strong ecclesiastical bias prevents any great personal sympathy growing up between us.

8 Sept. 1878: In a speech just delivered, Sir W. Lawson makes a good hit: he says that for the Prime Minister's phrase of 'peace with honour' he would substitute 'peace with honours': referring to the shower of decorations & promotions which has fallen on all concerned in the Berlin treaty.

One of the Austrian generals commanding in the newly annexed provinces, where the resistance is becoming serious, is reported to have said: 'We began by occupying Bosnia, & now it is Bosnia that occupies us.'

9 Sept. 1878: Hale writes that the Cheshire Lines Co. may be expected to pay in about 2 months: the amount over £76,000 besides interest . . . I shall still have left after paying for Hollydale £70,000 to do what I like with.

Holwood is unpaid for: but sales now being negociated will more than cover that. I think I shall endeavour to extend myself a little more round Witley. The idea of a Scotch estate has often tempted me: but how often should I see it in the year? And another house to keep up is not desirable. Failing that, two other ideas occur: one, to secure a large block of rough mountain land in Wales, where it is cheap, to try experiments in planting on a large scale: the other to buy in the New Forest, where the value is sure to rise, & where my successors may like to establish a cottage for occasional resort. This last notion has been in my head since I went through the Forest with M., three years ago, I think.

11 Sept. 1878: . . . To London . . . Sanderson calls . . . He tells me that the plan of working through a secret committee is practically given up, & that the office has returned to its former condition. State of things in Turkey not satisfactory: no power of keeping order, & throughout the mountain districts a condition of absolute anarchy. The Austrians too have met with more resistance than they expected, & have increased their army of occupation to an enormous force . . . Nothing settled as to the Greek boundary, nor as to reforms in Asia. Note that I saw yesterday a letter from Malet[181] to Ly D. giving a deplorable account of the state of things at Constantinople. The final settlement of Turkish affairs is still a long way off, if indeed they admit of one.

Call on A.D.[182] Hear much fashionable intelligence: the only item that interests me being the marriage of Ld Gerard's daughter to a Col. Oliphant, a ruined gambler, who lately had to leave England, until his friends could settle his debts at play. He has absolutely nothing, & Lord G. gives them £2,000 a year. The old man had set his heart on his daughter making a brilliant marriage, as he had on his son being distinguished in the fashionable world: the son[183] is a fool, who does nothing but squander money[184] & make himself ridiculous: & the daughter has thrown herself away. Such are the disappointments of social vanity: for which it is not easy to have much compassion. But Gerard[185] is a good neighbour & a worthy man, though not of the wisest sort: & I am sorry for him.

12 Sept. 1878: A colliery accident in S. Wales[186]: nearly 300 lives lost: the second casualty on a great scale within 8 days.

Death of Ly Egerton of Tatton[187]: a foolish good-natured woman, whose silly sayings used to amuse the London world. My father made her husband a peer: by which she lost precedence as the daughter of a marquess: though really pleased, she made a sort of grievance of this, saying that 'Lord Derby had taken away her honour'.

In the Manchester press, very gloomy forebodings as to trade . . . . . . the root of the mischief seems to be that foreigners, especially Americans, are now supplying themselves with goods which we used to produce. If this competition continues & increases, as appears probable, our growth in wealth will be checked, towns will not increase as they have done, & possibly may go back. Will this be an unmixed loss? I think not: the dirty squalid life of the Lancashire towns is not so attractive that one should wish it indefinitely extended: & it is the belief that prosperity will never fail that has encouraged & seemed to excuse the rampant extravagance of all classes. It may be, however, that the journalists & those whom they represent are unnecessarily alarmed: predictions of the approaching decline of English manufacturing have been abundant during the last 30 years, & they have never yet come true.

Walk to the sessions house[188] . . . Was elected as usual to the chair . . . About 60 magistrates present at first but, as always happens, they tailed off, & after nearly 4½ hours sitting we ended with less than a dozen. . . . The sitting was the longest I recollect. Asked about the debt of the county, & sinking fund, the working of which is not very clear: but it seems the debt amounts to about £200,000. It is paid off at the rate of £27,000 a year or thereabouts but, new debt being continually incurred, it does not much diminish on the whole.

Ashworth talked as dolefully about prospects as the Manchester papers: said he & some friends had been 'appalled' by what they saw at Paris: foreign made locomotives & other machinery as good as the best English work & far cheaper. He mentioned especially a remarkable specimen of a locomotive that had come from Norway – of all countries in the world. He says employers are thoroughly alarmed & the more so because the men refuse to recognise the existence of any problem.

14 Sept. 1878: Write many letters, all on matters of indifference, except one in answer to Granville. He has written evidently with the object of keeping up a political correspondence with me, and seeing what I have to say to the doings of the Cabinet. I answer in a frank friendly way, yet saying nothing that implies a promise of concerted action. If that is to come, it must come of itself, and not seem to be the result of deliberate calculation beforehand. And, though I hardly see how an ultimate union with the Liberals should not take place, I do not wish to pledge myself to one prematurely. In my letter, I agreed with him that finance was the weak point of the present policy, that expenditure had been reckless, that this should be dwelt upon: I said, with truth, that I knew too little of what is doing to judge whether our relations with France were in any danger or not: I threw cold water on the Greek grievance[189], on which he sounded me: but entirely agreed with him as to the dangers of what is being done in Afghanistan, while declining to condemn it absolutely without further acquaintance with the facts. I said that in my judgment Lytton[190] was not to be trusted, being excitable & fantastic: that the Anglo-Indian public is essentially military, & always ready for a war on any pretext: that the danger was there-fore real, but that I thought Hardy[191] less impetuous than would be thought from his style of speaking, and that he, Hardy, must know the dangerous state of Indian finance. I had always, at least for many years, thought bankruptcy a mere question of time as regards the Indian revenue, since we barely lived within our means there in the most quiet times, meeting every difficulty by borrowing. I thought Fawcett more nearly right in his views on that subject than any public man on either side, and invited attention to it. . . .

16 Sept. 1878: The De La Warrs[192] drive over to luncheon . . . she good-natured, but very silly: he agreeable, & his manners remind me more & more of his father.
    . . . Much conversation & correspondence in the family about a peerage which is said to have been offered to, & accepted by, Odo Russell[193]: it is a fair reward of his diplo-matic service, & may be taken by him without any sacrifice of political neutrality: but he has no means to support it, and a title will be only an encumbrance unless the Duke is prepared to endow it, which appears doubtful. There is some hitch somewhere, for the question remains unsettled, though it is more than a month since the offer was made.

17 Sept. 1878: Seeing an advertisement in the papers which evidently refers to Minard Castle (Pender's former place in Argyllshire)[194], I wrote to the agents for particulars. The trustees will soon have a large sum in hand; it cannot be expected that any successor of mine will profit by railway sales as I have done &, considering how completely Lancashire has ceased to be 'country' in the popular sense of the word, it is really to me a question whether I should not be doing better by those who come after me if I bought a place in the most picturesque part of the Highlands, than if I invested the money in ground rents, & thus added a few thousands to an income which is already as large as anyone need to have. In this I am thinking of others more than of myself, for the Scotch life of shooting on the moors does not interest me personally. Norway or Switzerland are better.
    . . . Drive with M. in afternoon to leave cards at Summer-hill: I had heard much of this place, which is often visited as a show from T. Wells: the sight rather disappointed me: the trees are good, not exceptionally old or large, the grass rich, & the ground pleasantly varied: but we saw no fern or underwood, & the absence of these from a park gives an air of monotony. It may be that I am unduly fastidious: for I seldom see an English park that does not seem to me a little dull. It may be that Scotch & foreign experiences suggest invidious comparisons.

18 Sept. 1878: Wrote again to Mr. Binney[195] on his scheme – the most notable point about which is that he sends me a sensible letter from Arch[196], the agitator, about working men's wages in the rural districts: in which he, Arch, points out that, unless there is special care exercised in buying the land, & also in choosing the tenants, the scheme is sure to fail. My view of it [is] that the experiment will be a good one to try: if there is a demand anywhere for land in small plots, it is right that steps should be taken to supply it: if not, it is well that a popular delusion should be exposed. Mr. Binney's answer on that point is of the vaguest character &, as far as it is yet possible to judge, I should doubt his plan leading to any result. I have told him that I will not give my name as a director (a thing I never do): but that if he satisfies me that it is a reality, & not merely a project, I have no objection to contribute.

20 Sept. 1878: Passed most of this day, as I have done several of late, in a state of pleasant idleness: reading much, writing a little, walking in my own grounds, & riding in the lanes. My conscience does not reproach me, for I have earned rest, & there is nothing special to be done; but I am surprised to find how much more congenial than formerly a life of inaction has become.

22 Sept. 1878: Walk by Downe & High Elms. More people about than in the Fairhill lanes. Met a bicycle going full 20 miles an hour, downhill. The roads in these parts are full of them. I see in the papers that not long ago a man rode on one from Bath to London & back in 24 hours. Will the fashion pass away like other fashions? It ought not, for a horse that costs only £5, & wants no food, ought to be of real use to poor men. But I suppose the art of managing these contrivances ought to be learnt early.

23 Sept. 1878: . . . Sanderson told M. that he had seen Salisbury's speech of 18 July as corrected[197] by him for Hansard[198], and that in the correction he had struck out or altered as much as he could the offensive parts. This is all right, though we shall never have much to say to one another again.

M. left for Scotland at a quarter before twelve: she was evidently from the first opposed to my going with her, & I did not press it. The case stands thus: Mary Galloway is in bad health, & naturally nervous about herself: her husband[199] thinks she makes too much of a small matter: & presses her to receive more company at Galloway House than she feels equal to: if M. & I had gone together, he would certainly have insisted on a party being made up to entertain us: whereas M. going alone will be allowed to be quiet with her daughter. I can see that she looks forward with no pleasure to the visit: instead it is obvious that the relations between the G.'s are becoming uncomfortable. He is kindhearted but stupid & obstinate in small matters: & the want of children – the fault of which rests with him – has not sweetened his temper. There was from the first no great affection on the wife's side, but its place is partly supplied by pride, a strong sense of duty, & the knowledge that her choice was deliberately made, without haste & without pressure from any quarter. But I know that visitors have left Galloway House impressed with the conviction that things were not going on there satisfactorily.

24 Sept. 1878: . . . Found in the house (Chevening) P. Stanhope[200] & his Russian wife, the latter enormously large & fat, rather good-looking, not much conversation . . . . . . Lawn tennis with Stanhope . . . The game was new to me, but it is easily learnt, up to a certain point.

25 Sept. 1878: News in the papers that Cairns is made an earl: a distinction which may have been fairly earned by his professional & political position, but which he would not have got but for his timely conversion as regards eastern matters.

New trouble preparing for England. The mission sent from India to the Afghan government has been refused admittance &, if the telegrams are correct, the refusal has been public & insulting. We are therefore probably involved in a second Afghan war, the issue of which is not doubtful, but the effects on Indian finance are likely to be disastrous. It is not clear to me that the intention of Ld Lytton has not been from the first to provoke a quarrel: at least to give the Ameer no choice except between war or submission. In any case, the war excitement is kept up, & attention is diverted from the weak points in the Berlin settlement, as well as from the unpleasant financial position in which this year's expenditure has left us.

. . . Stanhope got hold of a mask representing the Premier, & paraded in it, imitating the great man with a mock pomposity which tickled us.

26 Sept. 1878: Left Chevening . . . The Stanhopes are to come to us at Knowsley. . . . Our other journalist, Forbes[201], left abruptly yesterday, being under orders to start at once for India. He talks as well as he writes, saying much in few words. He showed me proofs of an article on Cyprus in the 19th century, which he thinks will make a sensation: it is the result of a recent visit, & condemns the occupation of the island as useless for any reasonable purpose, military or political. It is written with considerable art, for the position assumed by the writer is that of a disappointed supporter of the ministerial policy.

28 Sept. 1878: Rode early, but in so much rain that I came home wet through. Rode again in afternoon, to try Margaret's new horse, with which I am well pleased. It cost £250, & mine £200, but they are worth the money. I intend in future to take more & more to riding: it is the best form of exercise, less dull than a solitary walk &, though the Lancashire country is not interesting, yet within the park wall there is range enough, & now that the rabbits are gone the turf is not dangerous as it used to be. I think it was Abernethy[202] who said to a patient: 'Sir, walking is exercise for the legs, but riding is exercise for the guts.'

29 Sept. 1878: News of the death of Sir T. Biddulph[203]: whom I have often met at Balmoral, Windsor, & Osborne. He was a dull dry man, very silent, & seemed always as if weighed down by the monotony of his existence, which was certainly not a cheerful one: but he was respected, liked by those he had to do with, & in the army had the reputation of a good officer. The Queen I believe trusted him, but he was not thought to have influence over her.

1 Oct. 1878: Received . . . begging letters of all sorts: not less than 8 or 10 by a single post.

. . . Promise Lord F. Hervey[204] £25 for a workingmen's club somewhere in London.

Agree, at Statter's suggestion, to allow £20 a year for 4 years to one Dyson[205], a parson somewhere in Bury, who is trying to get help from the ecclesiastical commissioners. . . .

2 Oct. 1878: Sign deeds for purchase of Hollydale . . . M. returned from Scotland. . . . Read to her a short, but excellent article by Lowe in the *Fortnightly,* a review of the policy of 'Imperialism': which the author describes as the negation of justice, & the preference of appearance & show to reality. The argument is sound, though in some points, according to Lowe's custom, pressed too far. When there is so much talk of our future being like that of Holland, & of the necessity of extended empire to enable England to preserve its rank in the world, I wonder that the precedent of Spain has never been applied. Spain in the 18th century possessed an empire vaster than that of India: which yet did not save her from losing the rank of a great Power, or enable her to exercise the slightest influence on European affairs.

The *Pall Mall* follows up the hint given yesterday by the *D. News*, & points out Northcote & Salisbury as the two ministers supposed to be adverse to farther developments of a 'spirited foreign policy'.

Carnarvon has been making a non-political speech, on things in general, in which he expatiates at length on the necessity of truthfulness & plain dealing in public affairs. I think this utterance is a mistake for, whether so intended or not, what he has said is certain to be taken as a personal attack, though veiled, on the Premier: which, if he meant it, is in his position a piece of bad taste. He is clever, active, cultivated: but his activity has a look of fussiness: & he wants discretion.

3 Oct. 1878: Ride early, from 11.00 to 1.30. Walk with M. immediately after luncheon . . . Came in at 3.30 to receive Mr. & Mrs. Lecky . . . Take Lecky[206] out for a walk round the park. The Jerseys[207], Lowes, & Eustace Balfour[208] came later. The party settled down well together, & was pleasant.

. . . News in papers, failure of a Glasgow bank[209], with liabilities said to come to £10,000,000: much anxiety in consequence, & other failures are feared. The feeling of depression & insecurity is universal in the great towns, & increased by the unsatisfactory state of finance, doubly important when the cost of an Afghan war must be added to the bill already incurred.

Read an interesting article in the *19th Century* by a Mr. Hyndman, which he entitles 'The Bankruptcy of India'. His argument is that, during the last 20 years, years of peace & free from exceptional disaster, the people of Hindostan are steadily growing poorer . . . He ascribes this state of things to the increased weight of taxation, & to the enormous drain of capital caused by the debt (all held in England) . . . Probably many of the statements summed up above will be disputed, & there may be exaggeration in them: but one cannot read the paper without an increased sense of the difficulty of the situation: & coming at this time it is especially useful. . . .

5 Oct. 1878: Balances from Moult . . . Over £9,000 has been paid for expenses in Preston, the Fylde, & the north. Where it all goes to I cannot conceive, but while Hale remains anything like systematic economy is impossible. I have enough left to go on with, but not much to spare.

Ld & Ly Jersey left us: to our regret, they are both good company, & the addition to an acquaintance is satisfactory. They seemed, & I think were, pleased with their visit.

Shooting with Pilkington of Roby Hall[210] on the Roby beat . . . We killed 209 head, chiefly hares. Mr. P., his wife & daughter, dined with us.

Cabinet summoned for today, the first since the session.

Lowe instructs M. in the use of the new writing machine, to which he has taken. It is worked by an action like that of playing the pianoforte. I do not see that anything is gained in speed . . .

Talk of bicycles: Lowe says it is not unusual for young men to go out from London on a half holiday, 40 miles into the country & back, without much exertion or any fatigue.

6 Oct. 1878: News of the death of Sir F. Grant[211], which was expected: he was 75, & in bad health. He gave general satisfaction as president of the Academy, being a man of the world, & a man of business. He was much in society, a thorough gentleman & a pleasant companion. His speeches were few, short, & to the point: not eloquent, which indeed an imperfection in his speech would have made impossible, but free from pedantry or exaggeration. Those who understand art better than I pretend to do place him not in the first rank of his profession: but his portraits are life-like, and in that line at least he was the most popular painter of the day. It is expected that Leighton[212] will be his successor.

Some talk of the recent death of Ld Dysart[213], a strange being who lived to nearly 80, a recluse & a miser. He never left his house in London, a small one in some street off the Strand, saw no one, & did nothing except save money. That he has done to some purpose, having accumulated, as is said, £1,400,000[214], besides leaving a large inherited estate in land. He was believed to keep £200,000 always by him in banknotes – not an economical proceeding. He is succeeded by a grandson, a boy: the son was a madman, always in debt & trouble, & is happily dead.

7 Oct. 1878: All our guests . . . left us early. Lowe is excellent company in a house: always ready to talk & always worth hearing. Mrs. L. a drawback to the pleasure of her husband's company: vulgar, noisy, & garrulous to excess: provoking ridicule continually without being aware of it. Yet she draws well, & is neither ignorant nor stupid, though silly. Lecky & his wife are both agreeable. Of [Eustace] Balfour I saw little: like his brothers he has brains, cultivation, & weak health. He has set up in life as an architect.

. . . The result of the Cabinet of Saturday appears to be known. There is to be no immediate attack on Kabul: but demonstrations of military force along the frontier, the Quettah garrison to be reinforced, a valley leading into the mountains occupied, & probably the mouth of the Khyber as well. It is impossible to know absolutely what has passed: but I have scarcely any doubt but that the main arrangements were settled privately between the Prime Minister & the Governor General[215], that an Afghan war has been all along contemplated, that since the imperfect success at Berlin it has been pressed on in order to give the English public something new to think of, & that Northcote & the rest, now thoroughly alarmed (& not without cause) at the financial position, are holding back as far as they can.

The Glasgow failure, the increasing badness of trade, & the prospect of a deficit seem to be telling on the public mind &, as far as can be judged by the language of the newspapers, & by speeches reported in them, there is much more of despondency than of exultation in the general feeling.

8 Oct. 1878: Talk with Harcourt[216] as to the Afghan business: he shows me a letter from his military attaché, saying that our War Office treat the matter as serious: feeling sure that Shere Ali[217] has European advisers, from the nature of his movements. Gen. Baker[218], who is going out as military adviser (brother of the Pasha) speaks with uneasiness of the narrowness of the defiles, the difficulty of using artillery, & the resistance to be expected from the natives. Nothing, according to this gentleman's report, is to be done beyond preparation for next year.

Harcourt adds that the language officially held by Salisbury is that they do not consider the Russians as in any way responsible for what has passed. Lord Beaconsfield, who lately saw Harcourt, was more frank, saying that no doubt the affair was got up by Russia at the time when a general quarrel with us was expected, but that there is no reason to suppose that the Russians were now anxious to stir up a war, and in any case Russian action in the matter would be ignored. This is a sensible way of putting it, and no doubt represents the truth.

Letter from A. Russell[219] saying that his brother has finally resolved to decline the peerage: on which I wrote to congratulate him on both the offer & the refusal, but especially on the latter, explaining how it would have been considered as a mark of approval by him, & by the Russell family, of the general foreign policy of the Cabinet.

9 Oct. 1878: Received a letter from the Liverpool Institute, accepting my offer of £200, & proposing two plans for the disposal of it, one of which I accepted.

Received an invitation from the Liverpool Peace Society to attend & address a meeting, which I declined civilly. . . .

We had planned for tomorrow a visit to Liverpool, but Harcourt received an unexpected summons up to town, obliging him to leave us tomorrow early. He does not know the reason, but suspects that it has to do with Egypt. He is sore on that subject, & in plain terms accuses Salisbury of not having kept faith with him: the precise nature of the point in dispute I did not gather, but it appears that in Harcourt's view our govt. undertook not to sanction any arrangement giving Rivers Wilson[220] power in Egypt, without full communication with the French: this engagement he affirms that they have not kept, & he added that Waddington had used decided language in the matter.

Harcourt[221*] talks also a good deal about the P. of Wales, who he says is making himself unpopular in French society, partly by his needlessly open proclamation of Bonapartist sympathies, partly by considering himself above all social rules – a pretension which Parisians are not likely to admit. He invites himself and his friends everywhere not always with much regard to the convenience of those concerned – plays high, & is not as punctual in payment as the etiquette of gamblers requires. On the whole it is clear that Harcourt wishes his visits to Paris were shorter and fewer.

10 Oct. 1878: We meant to go shooting . . . but wind & rain were so violent that we gave it up. At home all morning, walk for exercise in afternoon.

. . . Letter from O. Russell in answer to mine: in which he characteristically ascribes his refusal of a peerage to his having heard through M. & his brother that my opinion was adverse. He can hardly expect me to swallow this ingenious flattery: but, whatever the motive, he was right in his decision. I imagine that the Duke's advice to accept, which seems to have been given, was either hasty or not sincere: & that he never meant to endow the title. At any rate, he has taken the other line now.

11 Oct. 1878: . . . News of a heavy failure in Manchester, caused by the Glasgow smash: general uneasiness & anxiety among persons concerned in business. Trade shows no sign of recovery, revenue is falling off, an Afghan war is now treated as a certainty, the difficulties at Constantinople continue: I do not think that for 20 years & more the prospect has been so unpleasant. But for the evidence before one's eyes it would be inconceivable that a part of the press – *Pall Mall, Standard,* & *M. Post* – is undisguisedly in favour of war with Russia, on the ground that Shere Ali is acting under Russian influence, & that this is an affront which we ought not to endure.

12 Oct. 1878: . . . I have not noticed . . .the death of a very old acquaintance & colleague – Lord Chelmsford[222]. He died at 84, after a life of more unbroken health & happiness than falls to the lot of most men. The son of a small West Indian proprietor, he served as a boy in the navy: then read law: not, as he told me, with the intention of practising, but in order to qualify for a magistrate's appointment in the West Indies. An earthquake, or the eruption of a volcano, I forget which, destroyed his father's estate, reduced the family to poverty, & raised him to the Chancellorship. It cannot be said that Ld Chelmsford was in the first rank as a politician, nor was he rated high as a lawyer: but he had fair ability, considerable industry, & thoroughly understood how to deal with a jury. A handsome figure, a pleasant manner, & a good voice, added to his success: he was known to be scrupulously honourable; judges trusted him, & competitors had no such stories to tell against him as (justly or unjustly) circulated in the case of Lyndhurst, Campbell, Kelly, & Westbury[223]. In the H. of C. he was an imperfect success: rather too long in his speeches, which moreover had no great point or power: but he never fell below a certain level of performance which, if not high, was respectable. In society he was a universal favourite: having high spirits, perfect good humour, & an unfailing stock of good stories. It was impossible to find a more agreeable companion: & it was noted of him that he made no enemies: whether from nature, policy, or principle, he avoided giving pain, & spoke ill of no one. He had in his professional life only two disappointments, one the long delay after he became a law officer (which he was in 1846) & before he reached the great prize of the Chancellorship: this was an accident of party politics, & left no sting behind: the other, which he felt acutely, was his supersession by Ld Cairns in the beginning of 1868. Yet the mortification which he did not disguise had no effect on his discharge of duty: to the last, so long as health served, he continued to serve on appeals with as steady industry as though his future had depended upon it.

His prosperity remained with him for, though he left little wealth, always spending freely what he made, all his sons turned out well: & two hold distinguished positions, one in command at the Cape, the other as one of the Lords Justices, nearly the highest post which a lawyer can fill.

13 Oct. 1878: Church, the first time since June.

In afternoon, walk with Hale . . . I arranged for 3 small plantations . . . The appearance of the ground near & beyond the village is greatly improved of late years . . . the look of roughness & neglect that I used to find fault with is gone. The cottages are nearly all restored or rebuilt: & have an air of neatness & substantial comfort which is satisfactory to see.

. . . Singular accident . . . at a Liverpool theatre – the Coliseum . . . somebody raised the cry of fire: down this staircase the crowd poured, till they fell over one another at the bottom, and 37 persons were smothered or crushed. . . .

17 Oct. 1878: Talk with Hale in the office: I agreed to pay £6,000 odd if necessary to buy up leases in Stanley St. . . . Sir U. Shuttleworth[224] offers 85 acres in Sowerby at £57.10s.

per acre, which Hale thinks excessive . . . & I decline the offer. Agreed to enfranchise certain copyholds in Newborough, etc. Agreed to give up the pew rents of Bootle church . . . I make no advantage of them as it is . . . Signed 6 leases . . . Desired Moult to send up £2,000 to my private account with Coutts.

Long conversation with Ld Halifax[225] on the Afghan question: he showed me a letter written by him to Granville, embodying the results of an interview with Ld Northbrook[226]. The results arrived at were, in substance, that there is no ground of quarrel with Russia on account of her interference in Afghanistan, inasmuch as the move was made when war seemed probable, & when Indian troops had been brought over to Europe: that as regards the Ameer it is impossible to decide how far he has been in the wrong as we do not know what passed between him & the Indian govt., nor what provocation he may have had: that it is necessary to take some step to bring him to terms, but that any considerable extension of territory is undesirable, or any permanent occupation of Afghan country. To these points I added two more – that in the event of a war the bulk of the expense should be borne by England, not by India: & that as far as possible it should be met by taxation, not by incurring debt.

Ride in afternoon.

Dr. Gorst[227] came to dinner.

18 Oct. 1878: Walk early in the park with Ld Halifax: much political talk. He is not less alarmed than I am by the state of Indian finances: refuses to believe in the possibility of much reduction in civil outlay, saying with truth that, as the civilisation of a country advances, govt. becomes more & more expensive: thinks something might be done to lessen military expenditure: & that the cost of the depots at home of regiments stationed in India might be transferred to the English exchequer. But he holds that we must be extremely careful not to give Indian creditors a supposed claim on England. Yet he admitted the extreme difficulty of our allowing India to become bankrupt. He blamed the increased cost of public works, & the plan of charging them on capital.

Talk of home affairs: the Queen: he agrees with me that, spoilt & flattered as she has been during the last 4 years, she will find no minister to her mind when Ld B. retires, & will probably give a great deal of trouble. Thinks the P. of W. quite as eager as his mother to extend her [sic] prerogative, but less dangerous, as he is not respected like her. Talk of the church establishment: he thinks it safe for a long while yet: that the ritualists though noisy are few: & that, when the burials question is settled, the dissenters will not know where to look for a grievance. Bright had said to him last year that , if disestablishment did not come soon, the position of the church would be unassailable.

. . . Capt. & Mrs. Burton[228] left us. He has made himself amusing & agreeable in general, especially to the men: she a little foolish, though clever, talks incessantly of her husband's doings & her own, makes herself a butt, but takes ridicule with perfect good humour. We did not know till after they were gone that there had been some unpleasantness between Capt. B. & Ld Halifax, the latter having as Indian minister refused something, I don't know what, which the former claimed as a right. Strong language was used, & the meeting cannot have been agreeable: but both parties had the good sense to keep their disagreements to themselves.

Vernon Harcourt & Ly Harcourt came. . . .

19 Oct. 1878: The Talbots[229] left us early: with good sense & discretion, neither said anything about public affairs, except in the vague way of common conversation: not a word passed as to F. & our mutual relations. I give Talbot credit for this reticence, which is not natural to him. Sefton, the Hopwoods, & Ld & Ly Halifax also left: Vernon Harcourt & his wife are now our only guests.

Walk with Harcourt[230] round great part of the park, and much talk on politics. He took much the same view as Lord Halifax on home matters: thought the demand for disestablishment of the church was growing weaker. Gladstone might take it up, but hardly any other leader: county franchise must be passed, and the burials question, but beyond that he did not see his way to a large programme, and did not think one necessary. He thought ill of the prospects of the Liberals as a party: even granting that they gained more than they expected at the next elections, they would still be in a minority: the Irish might possibly turn the scale, and turn out the govt., but they would not support a new one. The difficulty was personal: Gladstone would neither lead nor retire: the D. of Devonshire[231] was an old man, and his death withdrawing Hartington from the Commons would create great confusion. In fact there would be no leader, and he did not know what would follow. He talked of Lord Beaconsfield, with whom before the Eastern Question broke out he had come to be on friendly relations: thought him a Tory of the last century, not in the least a modern Conservative: his flattery of the Queen, and disposition to make the most of the prerogative, were consistent with his printed ideas: Bolingbroke would have taken the same line: he thought he, Disraeli, had an evident dislike of the system of parliamentary govt., though he had risen under it: he asked me whether I believed that Lord B. really wished for war, if he had had power to do as he pleased? I said I thought not – that Disraeli was above all things a party leader – that, if it had been necessary in order to keep his party together, he would have made war without hesitation – that he had aimed throughout at taking the line which seemed most likely to please the majority of Conservatives, but that war for its own sake was not an object to him. Harcourt seemed to agree in this view.

20 Oct. 1878: Church: walk in afternoon to Croxteth with Sir W. Harcourt, and a good deal more talk. I find his general tone very conservative, so much so that there is really no perceptible difference between his ideas and those of Northcote or Cross: he is for maintaining the church, for reducing taxes when possible rather than attempting to lessen the debt: he would shorten the period for which the settling of land is permitted, but disdains any idea of breaking up great estates: thinks parliamentary govt. cannot be worked successfully without an aristocracy: had not at first liked the notion of a reduced county franchise, but sees now that it is necessary: expects no particular result from it. In short, in all substantial matters his belief seems to be that we are doing very well as we are, and that large changes are neither necessary nor possible. If he represents Whig feeling, on what ground do the Whigs mean to appeal to the constituencies? They seem to think it enough to hold themselves ready for the chance of the present Cabinet becoming discredited in popular opinion. Harcourt dwells much on the want of leaders, the difficulty of replacing Hartington when the Duke dies: I don't know whether he wants the place for himself, but certainly he denies the fitness of anybody else. He tells me, to my surprise, that Roebuck[232], whom I knew to be as vain as a peacock, but thought honest, is unfavourably regarded in the House, being under strong suspicions of personal corruption. He has certainly been mixed up in questionable speculations with an undoubted rogue – one Lever[233]. And he is supposed to have received private help from two or three rich Conservatives (whom H. named) – of course on the implied condition of voting for the govt.

Talk, among a thousand other things, of great commercial men: Bass has told Harcourt that he sold beer to the yearly value of £2,250,000: making about 7½% profit: which would give him, or rather the firm, an income of £150,000. Talk of the D. of Devonshire, whose affairs Harcourt seems to know: he has £200,000 rental, exclusive of what he gets from Barrow, which in good years has been nearly £100,000 more.

21 Oct. 1878: Dull wettish morning: ride early . . .

Walk in afternoon with Harcourt. More talk on affairs: I am struck with his evident reluctance to move in any matter if he can help it. We spoke of the administration of London, as to which he thought the opposition of the City would be fatal to any bill: of local govt. in the counties, which he supposed the squires, jealous for the dignity of quarter sessions, would never allow to pass: & he dealt with two or three other questions in the same spirit.

In the papers, reports of sundry failures, & great uneasiness in the mercantile world. The loss by the Glasgow bank which lately broke is six millions, & a report on its management has ended in the disclosure of long continued fraud, & the arrest of the directors. No sign of improvement in any quarter: wages are falling, banks refusing accommodation, in short there is every sign of a bad winter. I hear also that landlords are getting alarmed, farms being thrown on their hands, & tenants impossible to be found.

. . . In the papers, two long speeches by Northcote[234] . . . they are in his ordinary style, sensible & inoffensive enough: he deals much with finance, defends the Cabinet from the imputation of waste, & argues that the public ought to be content because they are not paying as highly in proportion to wealth as they did 20 years ago. The argument does not seem conclusive, but it is not fair to judge these provincial utterances too severely. He took a hopeful line about revenue, seeming to imply, though he did not exactly say it, that he hoped to end the year without a deficit. He declared in plainer terms that Cyprus would cost little or nothing beyond its military expenses. He made it evident that personally he does not like the high-flown language of what is called imperialism, & does not wish to extend the empire: but nobody supposed that he did; the question is whether he will not be led or driven into measures that may lead to war, though contrary to his own judgment. About Afghanistan he was vague, which probably was unavoidable. On the whole, his speech will have done the ministry no particular good, but also no harm.

22 Oct. 1878: Walk early with Hale, taking Broomfield with us: we settled finally (1) a belt to be made along the wall of the park . . . (2) a piece of planting beside & behind the girls' school, (3) another piece beyond the boys' school, (4) a rough old pit . . . to be planted round, (5) .. a belt to be made outside the Huyton lodge . . .

Walk with Ld Winmarleigh in afternoon. Some talk about public & personal affairs. He expressed willingness to make up any difference between my brother & me. I told him, what is the truth, that I would as soon employ him as any man on such a business if need were but that, as nothing unpleasant had passed between us, there was no occasion for mediation. We talked of the political situation, he evidently inclined to be inquisitive, but restrained by delicacy – of which nobody has more – I thought it best to be reserved, & what I said was to the effect that, till I knew what the Cabinet meant to do, I could not judge what my attitude towards them would be. I did not conceal my opinion that there has been a good deal of underhand work on the part of the Premier, but I did not dwell on that, & took care to speak without any show of annoyance or resentment. Nothing passed as to personal relations with Cross, Northcote or others. We talked of Burials Bill, County Franchise, & the like, Ld W. as usual deprecating equally change on one hand, & resistance on the other. He believed the Cabinet would settle the burials question before a new election: hoped they would not let it stand over. Did not like the lowering of franchise in the counties: the farmers were very much afraid of it: but supposed it would have to be done some day.

23 Oct. 1878: . . . Talk with Mr. Biddulph – he is a banker & seems a sensible sort of man. He says there is more gloom & discouragement in 'business circles' than he has ever known: many people think English trade never will revive to its former prosperity, especially in the coal & iron industries . . . He does not, however, expect many failures, for too little has been doing of late to have made speculation possible. Note that I hear in various quarters of tenants throwing up their farms, & landowners being unable to replace them: not that this has happened to me anywhere that I know of.

24 Oct. 1878: . . . Northcote has been delivering a series of speeches in the Midland counties, remarkable only for their length & number: he has said nothing foolish, nor anything new: on the whole, they leave an impression of commonplace, perhaps hardly to be avoided: the chief thing noticed about them is the peculiarity of a minister in the midst of the recess, & with no election immediately impending, 'stumping the country' as if on an electioneering tour.

Smith[235] of the Admiralty & my brother are gone to Cyprus: which is curious, as a Cabinet is called for tomorrow, which will have to decide the question of peace or war with Afghanistan. Can it have been an object with the Premier to get them out of the way?

25 Oct. 1878: Shooting . . . Came home rather weary, which I ought not to be after only 6 hours of easy walking.

26 Oct. 1878: . . . To Southport . . . where the Convalescent Fund committee were to meet . . . On meeting we agreed to go straight to the hospital with which we are trying to negociate, & did so, examining it inside & outside minutely. Ashworth, Winmarleigh, the Mayor & I also went to the Children's Sanatorium, another institution with which we are trying to negociate . . . After discussion we referred the business of terms with both these societies to a committee . . . Here our business ended, but the Mayor had a luncheon for us at which about 40 persons were present. Winmarleigh & I had both to return thanks for our healths being drunk but, as reporters were not admitted, it mattered little what we said. . . . On leaving by the 5.40 train, I was cheered by a crowd, as also on going out of the hotel: but more of them insisted on shaking hands than was altogether pleasant.

27 Oct. 1878: Church: very fine clear day . . .

Short walk in afternoon.

The Cabinet on Friday [25th] appears to have been attended by 9 only out of its 13 members: two being on the Continent, one (J. Manners) in the gout, & one (Hicks Beach) at Gloucester. His not being recalled from thence, & the silence of the newspapers, seems to indicate that we are not to have an autumn session. . . .

29 Oct. 1878: M. went to open a girls' school, or college, near Liverpool, & returned not tired & pleased with her day.

Kirkdale at 11.00, sat till 5.45. Calendar exceptionally heavy, 110 cases. Magistrates present at opening, about 25: counsel 33. We disposed of 31 prisoners, nearly all pleading guilty. The longest sentence was 2 years, for a robbery with violence: the only case with anything new in it was one for an attempt to commit suicide, which I never before knew dealt with at sessions: I gave a merely nominal sentence – one day's imprisonment.

30 Oct. 1878: Kirkdale at 10.00, sat till near 6.00. Of this time nearly 6 hours were occupied in tracing the identity of a duck, which a respectable young innkeeper was accused of having stolen. He was acquitted, & quite justly, for the evidence was conflicting, & I believe he was really innocent: at any rate, nothing was proved.

. . . Came home very weary, from the long sitting, close air of the court, & fatigue increased by the difficulty I find in hearing the witnesses. This, however, is not new, nor do I think that my infirmity in that respect has increased.

31 Oct. 1878: Ly D. & Margaret[236] leave for Woburn.

Kirkdale at 10.00, where three trials . . . then an appeal case . . . When this case was over at 3.30, I made an excuse to leave, being in truth exhausted with three days sitting in air which is foul beyond endurance & makes me ill after a time. I am afraid I have grown less able to endure this particular form of nuisance not having been much exposed to it of late years.

Home, where arrears of letters, etc. Not very well, having had no exercise or air since Monday, which always disagrees with me.

E. Hornby of Bury has made a personal appeal to me to relieve him from embarrassment, he having gone beyond the means in his possession in the outlay on his new church. Having already given £2,000, I was not disposed to do more: but have promised £300 more. Note that his brother the Admiral[237] promised me £500 back which I lent him, but I have never seen it.

Dined alone, & early to bed.

1 Nov. 1878: Walk early with Hale . . . marked out the boundary of a small plantation or belt which I want to make this year if there is time . . . I find him willing to accept some help in the office, which he never was before, & I press this upon him. Talk of a plan which is on foot at Ormskirk for a coffee house, or temperance public house, to replace the beer-shop, which I tell him I will gladly encourage. Other matters were chiefly small details relating to individual cottages, pits to be planted round, corners filled up, & so forth.

See Barnes[238] about the shooting for Dec.. I am well pleased with the way he does his work.

See Broomfield[239], & give some last orders. I have settled that he need not come south, as he is full of business here.

See Latter[240], & arrange for an extension of the library in the rooms now adjoining it.

Monthly report from Statter, new rents are scarcely anything: he reports the state of trade as bad as it can be, & everybody tells the same story. The causes are not so easily ascertained. . . . on the whole I do not think any adequate solution has been found. . . . Meanwhile there are gainers as well as losers: cheap coal & cheap iron benefit one class if they injure another: & persons with small fixed incomes are undoubtedly more at their ease now than they were in the full swing of commercial prosperity, 5 years ago.

A second Cabinet has been held, summoned at short notice. The result seems to be that the Indian authorities, who now as always are pressing for instant war, have been checked, & a final message is to be sent to the Ameer before fighting begins. The Indian telegrams report extreme discontent among both civil & military at this decision: which helps to show what their feeling is in the matter, & how eagerly an occasion of quarrel has been sought. It is impossible to do more than guess at what has passed – I believe it to be something of this sort. Lytton must have had private instructions from the Premier to take up a policy of action & adventure on the frontier, reversing that of Lawrence & Northbrook. The Cabinet knew nothing of these orders & no doubt have been alarmed at the length to which matters have been pushed. They are trying to hold back the Gov. General, & very probably Disraeli, seeing how unpopular an Afghan war will be, is himself anxious to get out of the scrape. But that is not easily done. The *Telegraph* meanwhile keeps up its screams about the non-execution of the treaty of Berlin, & *The Times* writes on the same subject in a tone of alarm. But I have not made out what is the precise act, or omission, which is construed as a breach of faith. The Russian papers are hardly wiser than ours, talking of the treaty as already torn up, & saying everything which can create irritation here. Of course their articles are translated & reproduced in England. But the fever of last winter & spring has passed away, if I judge rightly: & the general uneasiness about trade & finance has a cooling influence on hot heads.

2 Nov. 1878: Left Knowsley at 8.30, reached St. J. Square at 2.40, where found M., & we went on by the 6.35 train to Keston.

There is in the *Nineteenth Century* a curious, but too hostile, article by a Mr. Dunckley[241] . . . The purport of his article is to ascribe to Disraeli a set purpose of extending the prerogative of the Crown at the expense of the constitution: with which object passages from his early novels are cited, side by side with some of the Stockmar letters which the Queen has indiscreetly published. There is certainly a good deal of evidence to show that he has always professed, and probably felt, dislike of the Whig oligarchy of the last century, and that the idea of defeating them, and the middle class also, which he dislikes still more, by a combination between the 'monarch and the multitude' has been a favourite one with him: but I do not believe that it has in practice governed his conduct. . . . He has used the Queen's name freely, more freely than is the custom in English politics: but he has used it where his own objects were concerned, and I do not believe that he would have stirred in the 'Empress question' but for her eagerness to get this new title. The new attack upon him, however, will in one respect improve his position. The English people had rather suppose that a statesman holds fantastic and impracticable ideas than that he holds none at all, and is guided merely by personal or party considerations: and the coincidence between the novels of 1840–1848 and the speeches and actions of 1878 indicates a greater degree of consistency than Disraeli has usually been credited with.

3 Nov. 1878: . . . Sanderson called, much to our satisfaction: short walk with him, & talk of current affairs. I do not gather that the Russians have so far done anything, or even threatened to do anything, in violation of the treaty: &, as they are not bound to evacuate

the provinces they hold till May next, it is early to speculate on the chances of their refusing to keep their word. . . . It appears that the Russians rest much on a sort of quibble,
that no definitive treaty of peace has been signed: that of San Stefano being only preliminary, and that of Berlin not a treaty of peace between Russia & Turkey, peace being
already made. So I understand Sanderson, but I cannot be sure of accuracy. He tells me
that in the City there is an idea that the worst is over, & that times are going to mend.
Also, that V. Lister[242] is in a bad way as to health: but he, Sanderson, does not expect any
advantage from the vacancy if it should occur, P. Currie being his senior, & having
Salisbury's entire confidence.

4 Nov. 1878: Much troubled with violent cold in the head, but not unwell with it. Rode
about 2 hours . . . Walk with M. later. . . . Read to M. [an article] by Gladstone called
'Electoral Facts'[243] in which he argues that the elections which have taken place on
vacancies since the beginning of 1876 show a complete change of opinion in the
constituencies. To most people it would seem that the data are hardly adequate, & that
too much stress is laid on small details. . . . The inference is obvious that what happened
in 1874 may probably happen again. – The municipal elections just come off, & which
are now always treated as party questions, . . . have ended rather in favour of the Liberals,
whose gains considerably exceed their losses, but the change is not so marked as to imply
a complete revulsion of opinion.

   There is trouble in a new quarter: a dispute between U.S. fishermen & the
Newfoundlanders[244] . . . has revived the interminable controversy as to fishing rights.
. . . All the American journals maintain that the compensation to Canada for loss of fishery rights, as awarded by arbitration, must not be paid till this question is settled. The
sum is about £1,000,000, if I remember right: & the Americans have long wanted an
excuse for escaping the payment. They have probably found one.

5 Nov. 1878: Still troubled with cold in the head, but less than yesterday.
   . . . There is just ended an extraordinary trial of strength – a six days' walking match,
at the Agricultural Hall. Several of the competitors accomplished more than 500 miles:
the winner did 521. Running or walking were equally allowed, and the men rested whenever they pleased. The distance, as above, is at the rate of nearly 87 miles for each 24
hours . . . The winner was not even countrybred, being a Cockney from Bethnal Green.
The taste for these displays is apparently increasing.
   . . . I extract from the newspapers the following notice of the amount of revenue drawn
in bad times from liquor & tobacco:
   Revenue from spirits, excise & customs together, £20,675,000: from malt, & sugar
used in brewing, together £8,247,000: from tobacco, £8,000,000: from licences for the
sale or manufacture of the above articles, £1,941,000 (figures below thousands omitted).
Add wine, £1,628,000: and we have a total of £40,500,000.
   These extraordinary figures point to various conclusions. The most satisfactory is that
a workingman, not liable to house tax or income tax, escapes almost tax free, if he chooses
to abstain from drink & smoking: in fact, he contributes nothing except about 20 per cent
on the cost of his tea or coffee: & so far he is probably better off than a man in the same
position anywhere else in the world. On the other hand it is a strange situation that our
revenue should depend to the extent of full one half on national habits which, carried to
the length they are, cannot be called otherwise than national vices: nor is it probably just

– though it is their own doing – that so large a proportion of the whole mass of taxation should come mainly out of the pockets of the poorer class.

6 Nov. 1878: . . . Read to M. an article[245] by Chamberlaine [sic] in the *Fortnightly* on the new plan of borough committees to regulate the choice of candidates & generally to direct local politics, which we have taken to call 'the caucus': that, however, being a misapplication of the American term. . . . The real opponents of the system are the local wire-pullers, who have got influence in election matters nobody knows how, & don't like to lose it: the leaders of little cliques, like the 'Permissive Bill' party, who object to sacrifice their special hobby in the interest of the entire party: and that large number of people who, though they accept the doctrine of self-government in the abstract, are not pleased to see it practically applied. Whether the change be good or bad, it is likely to become general. The advantages to a party of discipline & organisation are so great that once tried it will never be given up.

7 Nov. 1878: . . . Walk with M. in afternoon. Read to her afterwards, as is now my daily habit.

Answered a letter from the Arbitration Socy. at Manchester, declining to take the chair at their meeting. I gave as my reasons (1) that I could not with truth say that I thought the principle of arbitration applicable in all cases – e.g. I do not believe it would have been possible to arbitrate successfully in the late war between Russia & Turkey: and (2) that I could not speak on foreign affairs without criticising the conduct of my former colleagues, which I did not care to do except under an obligation of public duty . . .

8 Nov. 1878: . . . [In evening], heard from [Lord] Sackville [Cecil] that he has been sounded by [Arthur] Balfour as to his willingness to sit in the next parliament, with an intimation (of course from Salisbury, though not so stated) that a seat would be found for him. He had no hesitation in declining, but consulted M. as to whether he should suggest the substitution of either of his brothers for himself. This she advised him not to do, first because they neither care for the thing, nor would they be suited for the kind of life: next because their sitting in the H. of C. would only complicate family politics, which are confused enough already. He, Sackville, seems to have acquiesced, & probably the matter will drop.

Saw in the papers with real regret the death of a man whom I at one time knew well, & have never ceased to remember with a friendly interest – W.G. Clark[246], my 'coach' at Cambridge, later a tutor of his college, & public orator of the University. He was probably one of the three or four best scholars now living in England: but he was more than a scholar: for he had thought as well as read, talked brilliantly, & had considerable pretensions to wit.

9 Nov. 1878: . . . I have often noted of late, & never more than today, the constant increase of small gossiping newspapers, for the most part published weekly, which make scarcely a pretence to serious political opinion, but trust for their sale to scandal, personal sketches, trashy novels, & 'canards' of the most startling kind. *Vanity Fair* and *The World* were among the first: to which are now added *The Whitehall, Mayfair, London, Truth, Light, The Week, Coming Events, The Medley, Brief,* & others whose names I forget. They may not all exactly answer the description given above, but certainly it is true of the great majority. Their multiplication is perhaps not important: but in so far as it has any effect the effect is bad. They lower the tone of journalism: they take the place of a better class of journals: & they tend to create anew in the upper & middle classes that prejudice against the press which used to be strong 25 or 30 years ago, & which has only died out, if it has died out, in our day. It is noticeable that by their price, usually 6d., these publications clearly show themselves to be intended for the upper class of readers. I have not read much in any of them but, as far as I can judge, they are for the most part merely gossipy & foolish – not malignant: nor have I ever heard that 'blackmailing' flourishes as an institution in the journalism of London, as it notoriously used to do in New York, & I believe does in Paris to this day.

10 Nov. 1878: Violent rain & wind, that lasted all day . . .

The Premier's speech of last night at the Guildhall has been expected with unusual interest, & I opened the *Observer* with an uncomfortable doubt as to what it might contain. He has, however, been moderate, & I think safe. There is a flourish of trumpets towards the end about the imperial destinies of England, but it involves no attack on foreign governments, & is harmless. The language used about Afghanistan seems so vague that it may mean anything: while, as to the treaty of Berlin, he says in effect, though in a circuitous manner, that there is no reason for supposing that any power intends to break it. He goes on indeed to affirm that, if it is attacked, we ought to defend it with all our energy & all our resources: but those are words of course under the circumstances: & there is an entire absence of hostile or ambiguous references to Russia. On the whole I think it is a speech that will have relieved the minds of his colleagues, and done no harm. I should predict, however, that it will dissatisfy the more violent section of his followers. From all I can gather, the 'Jingo' feeling is abating, partly by mere effect of time, partly as a result of industrial depression. The prospect of having to pay for an Afghan war has done something in the same direction.

11 Nov. 1878: M. went over to luncheon at Frognal. Lord Sydney[247] talked much about the Court: said the Queen and Premier had both agreed in trying to get rid of Ponsonby[248], who is too Whig in his opinions for the new ideas that prevail there: but the plan fell through from the difficulty of finding anyone fairly competent for the place.

12 Nov. 1878: Lowe came to luncheon, riding over from Caterham, & returned in the dark. He talked of the Premier's speech: thought with me that it was more quiet than might have been expected, & would do no mischief: but dwelt on the entire omission of all mention of internal affairs. I do not think there is much in that criticism: what could Ld B., or anybody else, say about the state of trade or the prevailing depression that would be new or to the purpose? While on foreign affairs he really had something to tell. He talked also of the immorality of putting forward the rectification of our frontier as a reason for going to war with Afghanistan: & here I agree: but, though it may be the real reason, it has never been avowed as such.

. . . Report from A.D. (which I don't believe) that Hartington is to resign his post of leader, & Gladstone to return to it. That would mean, in the actual state of opinion, the break-up of the Whig party which was never less to be desired than now.

13 Nov. 1878: Wrote in answer to a fresh appeal from the D. of Westminster, promising

£200 for the restoration of Chester cathedral. I give this reluctantly, for it is a waste, but the Duke had a sort of half-promise from me before, which I could not well have evaded.

Day disagreeable, snow on ground, which soon melted, & drizzling rain. There have been heavy snow-storms in the north. Walk for exercise in afternoon . . .

Read to M. a striking article[249] in the *Westminster* of last July on the condition of the Indian peasants. The writer brings out forcibly – though not, as would appear, with any set purpose of doing so – the incidental disadvantages of a regularly organised administration applied to a community which has been accustomed to rough & ready methods. Under native rule, fear of violence, & occasional arbitrary interposition by the authorities, kept the village moneylender in check: now he is protected by an efficient police, secure as regards his person, & the courts enforce payment of his claims. As he lends at rates varying from 20 to 40 per cent, & the borrowers are habitually reckless, the land is fast passing into his hands: & the equal justice which we administer ends in the practical servitude of the peasantry, with no advantage to the state. I suspect that this is a grievance of which we shall hear more, & which will not be easy to deal with.

14 Nov. 1878: London by 10 o'clock train with M. Day wet & disagreeable.

To S. Kensington for . . . Nat. Portrait Gallery trustees: we met at 11.30 & sat an hour & a half. None was present except Ld Hardinge[250], B. Hope, Ld Ronald Gower[251], & Scharf . . . The collection is now really a fine one, & improves every year.

. . . Beust & Münster both called: talk with them over the state of foreign affairs.

Return to Keston by 6.35 train.

15 Nov. 1878: Wet unpleasant day, stayed at home till luncheon. M. went to visit Darwin[252] at Downe. Wrote many notes & letters. Walk in the wet for exercise.

Wrote to Moult to see if I can establish a private account with Heywood[253], for charities & donations only, so that these shall cease to be mixed up with my private expenditure.

Wrote to a Dr. Dunbar, a Scotchman, sending him £20. He asked me for some help to start a son in the world, writing in a sensible manly way, unlike such applicants in general, whose letters seldom impress one with a favourable view of human nature.

Wrote to Sanderson for a report of the Noxious Vapours Commission, lately issued, but which I have not seen. The reason for which it is wanted is that I have received a request from the Liverpool Town Council to introduce a deputation to the Local Govt. Board, to ask for more stringent action against these nuisances. This I have promised to do, the matter being one which concerns the whole neighbourhood, without distinction of class or party.

Münster told me yesterday that matters were looking better in the east: the Russian assurances being satisfactory: he thought there would be no great eagerness on the part of our govt. to press for withdrawal of the Russian troops: the country was in such a state that, if they were to withdraw at once, there would be no chance of order being kept. Nor was Constantinople in danger, since the whole Turkish army was massed in front of it, & the British fleet was ready to give support.

He spoke, with evident satisfaction, of the distressed state of the Austrian army of occupation: saying that there are no roads in Bosnia, that the necessary supplies have to be carried on the backs of animals, & that it is a question whether they will not be starved out before the end of winter. He thought the political consequences of the occupation could not be foreseen: already it had [set] Hungarian against German, & the union of the empire was threatened.

Beust's conversation ranged over a great variety of subjects &, as is not uncommon with him, was so desultory that I could not always follow the connection of ideas. He talked freely of his own transfer to Paris: from what he said to me & separately to M., I gathered that he has been in constant disagreement with Andrassy[254] during the last three years: Andrassy forbidding him absolutely to give any pledge of co-operation with England, & requiring that his assurances should be so vague as to admit of their being disallowed if necessary. Andrassy was well pleased by the opportunity given by the Berlin negociations, & by Ld Beaconsfield's evident dislike of Beust, to get rid of him from London: but he did not contemplate his transfer to any other post: the Emperor, however, interposed, & insisted on his having Paris: so he has gained the transfer which he long wished for, & that by the means of his personal enemy. – He made one remark which struck me, as to the folly of which Austria had been guilty, in dreading & discouraging the French Republic of 1848–1851, which had been in reality peaceable & conservative: whereas the elevation of L. Napoleon, which the Court of Vienna applauded, had cost them their Italian provinces, & indirectly caused the war of 1866.

Received in the afternoon a telegram from the committee just formed to oppose the Afghan war, asking my name for a memorial which they propose to address to the Prime Minister. I declined, not knowing the terms of the memorial, and preferring to wait till parliament meets before giving an opinion.

16 Nov. 1878: Ride early . . . Walk with M. later, & settle with her as to the places for some pines & cedars in the upper, or southern, part of the grounds.

. . . Lawrence sends me a letter from Mrs. H.E. Stanley[255], widow of the young man who married in India, & was killed by an accident. It is creditable to her. For the sake of giving her son a better education, she has engaged herself as a governess, devoting most of her income to his schooling. It is the only instance of good sense & principle that I have yet met with in that branch of the family. The letter was elicited by an enquiry from the trustees as to her means of living. They are, I presume, going to distribute the £12,000 paid by me this year among the family.

17 Nov. 1878: Dull dark day: whether from this cause, or because the Premier's Guildhall speech has revived interest in current politics, I have a return of that indescribable nervous sensation which I used to know so well when in office, and from which my father suffered during much of his life. I can only represent it as a sense of impending danger or calamity, without external cause of any kind. The feeling passed off before evening, I do not know why, any more than I know why it came.

. . . News from the Cape is unsatisfactory. Local troubles have been going on there for a long while, but they appeared to be in a fair way of settlement : by the last reports, however, it seems that the Zulu tribes are becoming hostile, & we seem to have on hand the necessity of providing for a Zulu war: which from the number & warlike habits of the race . . . is a serious matter. Northcote's position cannot be pleasant, for the revenue shows no elasticity, though the falling off has not been as great as from the state of trade many people expected.

18 Nov. 1878: Ride early . . . Short walk on the commons with M. in afternoon.

Mr. Norman[256] (aged 85) called with his daughter. He is the oldest resident, & next to Col. Lennard[257] the largest proprietor in this neighbourhood. He remembered having seen Pitt walking in his grounds & on the common, when a child (this could not have been later than 1801 – 77 years ago). He told us various details about the changes of hands through which land in these districts has passed: had seen it, he said, nearly all in the market, much of it several times over: but he had never known a single instance where land was bought by any person intending to cultivate it himself as a matter of profit. He says woodland does not pay here as it used, he supposes from the increased employment of iron. He speaks of the large extent of land which was under wood in his time, but has been grubbed, chiefly in order to plant fruit trees. (Note that the papers are full of reports of tenant farmers having to throw up their farms, of rents being reduced, & of arable being turned into grass, as requiring less labour.)

19 Nov. 1878: . . . To the Westminster Hotel, to meet a deputation from Lancashire & Cheshire on noxious vapours: the object being to press the Local Govt. Board to take action with a view to lessening the nuisances arising from alkali works, copper works, etc. I had agreed to introduce this deputation, & the meeting was in order to settle beforehand what we should say, & the order of the speakers. The Mayors of Liverpool & Warrington were there, Col. Blackburne[258], Sir R. Brooke[259], Mr. Warburton[260], etc. We had also a few strangers from other parts of the county where similar nuisances prevail. We sat about an hour in discussion: I in the chair. At 3.00 we went to Sclater-Booth[261]: I opened the case, speaking about 15 minutes: there were reporters present. We were about 30, I think, in all. The business lasted an hour. Home, & by 5.15 back to Keston.

In *The Times* of today, an odd article on my brother, praising his aptitude for business, very justly, and ending with the remark that it would be a pity if he were to leave an office for which his training particularly fits him. It is evident that the writer believes that for some reason he is to be removed elsewhere or to resign. But we know nothing more.

G. Villiers[262], Clarendon's brother, now in India with the Gov. General, has contrived, not for the first time, to get into trouble with a woman. The injured husband has made a scandal: V. has had to be sent up the country on some pretext of business, & it is not thought possible that he should keep his office. The family are vexed, for of the brothers he was the only one who promised to keep up the reputation it had in the last generation.

The papers are full of announced or expected reductions in wages, distress in various towns, failure of firms, etc. The depression in nearly all branches of industry is worse than it has been since the cotton famine, & more diffused. Everything points to a winter of scarcity & discontent.

20 Nov. 1878: . . . In the papers, a correspondence between Ld Lawrence & the Premier, in which the latter refuses the request of the Afghan committee that no action shall be taken until parliament meets, but promises that papers shall be published without delay. I do not think that, taking our constitutional practice as it is, any other answer could have been expected, or that Ld B. is to be blamed for sending it: but attention is being more & more called to the anomaly in leaving the uncontrolled power of making war or peace in the hands of the Crown. A minister may involve the country in war without its knowledge – disavowal of what he has done may be impossible without ridicule & discredit – yet there is no remedy: & the removal from office of the author of the proceeding may be nothing more than the anticipation by a year or two of what would have happened in the ordinary course of political vicissitudes. I shall be surprised if this subject is not a good deal dwelt upon at the coming election.

The agricultural labourers of Kent, especially of the district round Maidstone, have lately been threatened with a reduction of wages, in consequence of bad times: their Union has taken the opportunity of making a demonstration, & some hundreds of them yesterday paraded the streets, ending in a meeting at St. James's Hall: where they were told by Auberon Herbert[263] that the land ought to be theirs: with some other sentiments equally to the purpose. It seems likely that the Kentish landlords will have to reduce their rents: for many farms are going begging, & the low prices of the present year tell heavily against them.

In the north, Ld Londonderry[264] has closed one of his largest collieries, on the ground that he can no longer work it with advantage: he adds in his letter that he has 60,000 tons of coal on the bank for which he can find no sale.

21 Nov. 1878: Ride early, by Westerham, Downe, etc.

. . . Wrote to Coutts to withdraw my subscription for 1879 from the Conservative Registration Assocn.: a London agency, of which I know little, but to which I was asked to subscribe a few years ago. As I am not under local obligation to assist its promoters, the withdrawal has no necessary significance. But I must before long consider what shall be done in the more important case of the various associations for similar purposes established in Lancashire.

In *The Times* & other papers, a long despatch from the India office, summing up & vindicating the Afghan policy of the Cabinet. The previous despatches on which it is founded are soon to follow. I see the publication commented upon by some opposition journals as unusual, but this seems unduly fastidious criticism. In the absence of parliament, what other method exists of telling the public what is passing? . . .

22 Nov. 1878: The force prepared to act against the Afghans has crossed the frontier: but from the attitude of the Ameer war was known to be inevitable, & the actual declaration of it has produced no sensation. It may be a very small or a very serious affair. If reasonable terms are offered, and no check occurs, it is possible that he may make peace early in the spring, & without even the occupation of Kabul: if on the other hand he is driven to despair, or prefers destruction to submission – either of which things are possible – he may give infinite trouble before all is ended. The one thing certain is the financial effect which will be disastrous. Indian finance cannot bear a new burden &, though there is no doubt of English solvency, the moment is ill-chosen for new taxation, when trade & manufactures are in a worse condition than has been known for many years.

23 Nov. 1878: News in the papers that parliament is summoned for the 5th. This is quite right, & probably necessary under the Act of 1858. We wrote at once to put off our party invited for the 9th, till next week. . . .

24 Nov. 1878: . . . Letter from Granville: he says that the calling together of parliament is judicious: that the govt. will have a large majority: that they will make the most of some military successes, for the benefit of their followers, then throw over Lytton's policy. He adds that the accuracy of Cranbrook's summary of what has passed is much disputed. Northbrook especially complains of it, as misrepresenting what has passed by leaving out material circumstances, & there is to be a published correspondence on the subject. – Granville's letter reads to me as though he were not anxious to do or say more than he can help: but perhaps in this respect I do him injustice.

The fort of Ali Musjid, at the entrance of the Khyber, is taken with little loss, & it is supposed that the pass will be traversed without difficulty, when the force will rest at Jellalabad till spring. Another body is advancing in the direction of Kandahar.

In a book on the landed interest just published by Caird[265], the writer on farming subjects, is a curious abstract from the return of landowners made some years ago. According to this, the territory of the U.K. may be divided into 4 parts: the first quarter being held by 1,200 owners, with an average of 16,200 acres for each: the second quarter by 6,200 persons, holding an average of 3,150 acres apiece: the third quarter by 50,770 owners, with 380 acres apiece: the fourth by 261,830 persons, averaging 70 acres apiece. The 600 families of the peerage hold among them rather more than one-fifth of all land.

In the above calculations the holders of less than an acre are not included: they are more than twice as many as all the rest put together, but they collectively own less than 1/200th part of the land, & are in fact rather house-proprietors than anything else.

25 Nov. 1878: . . . Wrote to Granville, dwelling on the practical absurdity, for such it is, of parliament being called together when there is no option as to the course to be taken: for such is the case after a war has been begun. Supposing a parliamentary majority to declare the war unjust & unreasonable, they could not stop it: they might make the Cabinet responsible by turning it out, which is only anticipating by a little the inevitable fate of every ministry: but the mischief is done. It is idle to talk of England as a self-governed country, when the war-making & treaty-making power is exclusively in the hands of the executive. I said that I did not blame the present govt. for simply acting on precedent: but that I thought the whole subject wanted looking into. I also suggested that we ought not to let India pay the whole cost of the war: that England should contribute, & that by means of taxation, not by loan: which is justice & sound finance, while the effect of a heavy income tax, in bad times, will be to bring the public to its senses. . . .

26 Nov. 1878: . . . Read, write, make Afghan notes: but I cannot satisfy myself. It is not easy to know what has actually passed and, though I know nothing of what was doing or planning by Lytton in 1876–1877, yet as a member of the then Cabinet I am technically responsible, & cannot well join in criticism upon it[266].

27 Nov. 1878: With M. to London by 10.17 train from Tunbridge. Very wet day. See Drage, not having been quite well lately. See Sanderson, but talk mainly of his family affairs, which do not prosper, for he has still to keep his brother & brother's family, who can do nothing for themselves till business in the City gets a little better.

London U. Senate in afternoon . . . I took the chair.

Schouvaloff called, the first time that M. or I have seen him since the Berlin congress. He talked freely of affairs: told M. that his personal relations with the Premier and Salisbury had been so disagreeable that he would not stay beyond a few months: could not say whether he should succeed to Gortschakoff's place or not: thought there would be a powerful party against him: and the Emperor, though friendly whenever they met, had never forgotten, and never would entirely forget, the fact that his (Schou.'s) representations had induced him to sacrifice the triumph of a march into Constantinople. He told this to M., not to me, as an illustration of how little things – matters of form rather than of substance – impress royal minds. He partly explained his dislike to the English ministers by saying that, when the Anglo-Russian agreement came out, they had openly accused him of publishing it through the Russian embassy.

– About Afghanistan his language was that the Ameer was a more formidable enemy than we seemed to think him: having 40,000 regular troops, fairly disciplined, & well enough armed for mountain war, where the fighting is generally at short distances. He believed the Ameer counted on the frontier tribes, feeling sure that they would turn against the English at last, & harass their communications. He (Schou.) thought we had been unexpectedly fortunate so far, which he ascribed to the attack having been made before it was expected: but the difficulties would begin when we penetrated further into the country.

. . . He talked of the Berlin treaty: saying it would have no existence within a year or two. He disclaimed any intention on the part of Russia to break it, saying that the condition of Russian finance and internal administration was such that nothing would induce his govt. to go into a new war if it could be avoided. But the course of events would be too strong for diplomacy. Whenever the Russian troops retired, there would be a general rising of the people against the Sultan and, unless Europe agreed on a mixed occupation to maintain order, and preserve the Sultan's authority, the Turks would have no sufficient force to resist it. The Roumelians would never rest till they had secured the same advantages as the Bulgarians north of the Danube[267]: nothing except force would keep them apart.

Return to Fairhill by 5.35 train, arriving a little after 7.00. Day continues excessively wet.

28 Nov. 1878 (Thursday): Another wet & windy day: it has not once been fine since Sunday morning. . . . Wrote to congratulate Carnarvon on his marriage with Miss Howard of Greystoke[268] . . .

See also in the papers that Stanhope[269] has got the post vacated by Ld Chichester[270], of First Commissioner of Church Estates. It is an easy, not disagreeable, post, permanent, & well suited for him: as it gives him something to do; & an increase of income.

. . . In the papers, a long letter from the D. of Argyll[271], & a speech by Childers[272], both criticising severely the action of the govt. in Afghan matters: so that things look as if the debates of next week would be violent & bitter. Ld Cranbrook's despatch, published last week, is much complained of, as unfairly throwing blame on his predecessors, & as misrepresenting facts. Much is also made of a singular assertion of Salisbury, that there had been no change in Afghan policy: which certainly does not appear to be borne out by the facts. . . .

2 Dec. 1878: Saw Granville, and had with him half an hour's conversation. I asked whether it was intended to raise a general debate on the address, or to raise the question of the policy of the war by a separate and substantive resolution? He did not know, had come from a meeting of his friends, where I gather from what he said that there had been considerable difference of opinion: personally he inclined to moving something, in which I entirely agreed. We discussed the Blue Book in some detail. He said there was a general belief that parliament would be dissolved in January: though it is not easy to see why, as the state of Europe is unsettled, & with an Afghan war, & probably a South African war, on hand, there is nothing by which popularity can be gained, or on which a cry can be raised. But it may be that there would be more danger to the Cabinet in waiting till the result of last year's finance becomes known. . . . Granville told me that, of all who had taken part in the consultation, Gladstone was the most averse to decided measures in the H. of C. – that he wanted to ask for an estimate of the cost of the war, to move for certain letters omitted from the correspondence, and by these and other means to avoid a division on the main question[273]. Harcourt, whom I met later, confirmed this, saying in explanation that Gladstone could not bear to have it shown that there is so large a majority against him. A odd weakness, if true, but Harcourt does not love him.

3 Dec. 1878: Application from Mr. C.T. Stanley for a loan of £10, which I send to him. He always borrows from me small sums in this way, & repays them punctually: the only borrower known to me who does.

Saw Carnarvon, and discussed with him the question of the moment: but he had not read the papers, being more engaged with his coming marriage . . . Talk as to where we shall sit in the H. of Lords: I suggested the cross benches but he objected, saying that we should speak with more effect in condemnation of everything done by the govt. to which we may object if we speak from their side. . . . I cannot say that a reunion with the Conservatives seems to me probable. The party has pronounced against the old doctrine of non-intervention, to which I have adhered more than to any other political principle of the day: and to me the combination of a war-policy with high church and high prerogative is singularly objectionable.

Walk with M. to her oculist . . . I learnt in the afternoon that he is convinced there is a beginning of cataract, which was suspected before, but not certain. He is, however, of three eye-doctors whom she has consulted the only one who is clear on this point. The news was a shock to me more than to M. who expected it.

4 Dec. 1878: Granville called in the afternoon, bringing a copy of the speech. It is very short, very unpretending: altogether skilfully drawn up for its purpose. It speaks of the Afghan business as an expedition merely, not as a war: lays stress on the certainty that the treaty of Berlin will be executed: & on the friendly assurances received from all powers. This will be a bitter disappointment to the Jingos: who see in the Afghan imbroglio the elements of a future quarrel with Russia, & rejoice accordingly. The *Pall Mall* hints at the probability that we are to be surprised by a sudden announcement that the object of the war is accomplished – that Jellalabad will be held, the frontier advanced, & no attack made on Kabul.

. . . Read to M. . . . an interesting article in the *Fortnightly*[274], by Mr. L. Courtney, on the future migration of trade from this country, in consequence of the increasing dearness of coal & the increase of industrial enterprise elsewhere. The writer points to the decay of the tin & copper industries of Cornwall, & argues that our iron trade, at least, will go the same road. It is worth notice that Gladstone has propounded the same doctrine in a recent review. It seems, however, to me a doubtful one, for these reasons. We cannot foretell the future of industry: who in 1778 would have believed in the present extent of the cotton trade? We cannot say what may follow on the discovery of new sources of motive power, always possible. We cannot tell that improvements in navigation, such as we have seen in the last 30 years, may not make it possible to bring over American coal (which is inexhaustible) at rates not excessive. Much of our success has been owing to the superiority of English workmen: & there is no more reason now than before why we should lose that advantage. Nevertheless all such warnings are useful: for they tend to check exorbitant demands on the part of workmen, reckless speculation among capitalists, & extravagance in all classes. They may also lead us to pay more attention than we have to the really urgent question of lessening the weight of the debt.

5 Dec. 1878: Find . . . a note from Lord Grey[275], saying that he moves an amendment to the effect that war (whether just or not) should not have been made without the consent of parliament.

At 4.30 to the H. of Lds. with M. & Margaret: the house is fairly filled, especially the galleries. I think there were nearly as many there as in the house itself. Ravensworth[276] opened the session, speaking too long, over an hour, fairly well in parts, dull at other times, but on the whole he promises to be a bore, as his father was. Oddly enough in his position, he called attention to, & supplemented, the most remarkable omission in the speech from the throne, the absence of all notice of the prevailing distress. – Ld Inchiquin[277] followed, short, & mostly unheard. Granville's speech was in his best style, adroit, courteous, hitting hard, but using only smooth words. He brought up Cranbrook, furious at being accused of misrepresentation: his vindication of himself was delivered so much in earnest as to produce an impression of sincerity, but his explanation of the despatch objected to was confused & vague. Ld Grey spoke but in an empty house, & heavily, though the substance was good sense: Salisbury defended himself, Northbrook replied upon him, both vigorously, neither first rate: Ld Beaconsfield had sat to all appearance half asleep & looking very old & feeble, during the debate: but he roused himself to reply, & for a few minutes spoke with the force & energy of his former days. The substance of what he said was not much – rhetoric, not argument, but it served the purpose well enough. Granville made a short reply: we separated at 11.00[278].

I sat on the cross benches, against Carnarvon's renewed advice: but I cannot see the force of his reasoning, unless he supposes that we have a considerable Conservative following, which I do not believe. He sat on the ministerial side below the gangway, but so near me that we could communicate as if sitting side by side.

6 Dec. 1878 (Friday): . . . Granville called to show me the amendment which Halifax is to propose on Monday.

7 Dec. 1878: . . . Sanderson called: I went over with him the substance of what I propose to say on Monday, as to which he made some useful comments.

Keston with M. in afternoon, for a quiet Sunday.

Heard that the world of society is agitated by a report which has appeared in one of the gossiping newspapers, to the effect that a claimant is to come forward for the Bedford title & estates. The Duke[279] & his family know nothing of the story: & in all probability it is a mere invention. The late Duke[280] kept a mistress in early life, by whom I believe he had children: & as he never married (of which, however, his health is a sufficient explanation) there were vague stories in his lifetime about a secret marriage. The Russells are naturally angry, but after all nothing is imputed to the present Duke that he can resent, for if the story were true he would simply have been tricked by his cousin. . . .

9 Dec. 1878: Left Keston at 9.00, walk in to the station: at home all day till it was time for the House to meet. Rather nervous & uncomfortable, a sensation of which I shall never be cured, since 30 years' experience have not removed it. The House was fairly full, but not crowded as I have seen it. Cranbrook opened his case in a dashing splashing speech such as he loves to make, & makes well. It had the two faults of being rather too detailed, occupying 1 1/3 hours: & of being directed against Ld Northbrook & his policy in a tone of more hostile criticism than is usual when a minister makes a statement for which he asks the support of all parties. He spoke as if knowing that he was to be attacked, & resolved to take the initiative. Ld Halifax moved his amendment in a long statement, temperate & full of sound argument: but his voice is rather too feeble for that large room. – Ld Lawrence[281] came next and, talking to the table as men unpractised in speaking often do, was scarcely heard. I rose about 9.00, with the advantage of address-ing an audience prepared to welcome any speaker whom they could follow: my line of argument was not altogether easy, for I had at once to defend what had been done up to the end of 1877, for which I am responsible, however little I knew about it: and to give reasons for disapproving what was done in 1878. Towards the close I laid stress on the dangerous state of Indian finance, & the risk of causing discontent among the native population by increased taxation. I was speaking nearly an hour, very well listened to throughout. Somerset followed me, attacking the opposition rather bitterly. Carnarvon said a few words nearly in my sense. Ld Napier of Ettrick[282] harangued for an hour and a half, pompous & prosy. He wearied everybody, & we adjourned about half past eleven. – I do not think the peers have adjourned a debate since that on the Irish church in 1869.

10 Dec. 1878: Some weariness from last night, but glad that my speech is done, & not dissatisfied with anything that I have said.

Debate began again at 4 o'clock, an hour earlier than usual. Ld Grey opened it, speak-ing with intellectual force enough, but with hardly physical force to make what he said effective. It was curious to hear him state that, though a member of the Cabinet of 1839, he had disapproved the first Afghan war. His argument was clear & sound, & will be better to read than it was to hear. – Cairns followed, able as he always is, moderate in tone, with a show of logical accuracy: but he manipulated the case to suit his views with more dexterity than candour. Selborne replied upon him, very powerfully as it seemed to me, but he had chosen an unlucky hour just when men go away to dine. Some minor speakers followed, whom I did not hear. Northbrook took up the argument & handled it well, though rather long considering the hour: Salisbury had been much attacked, & was expected to make an angry reply, but whether from fatigue, or from thinking the House exhausted at past one, or from policy, he was very short, not animated, & sat down when people thought he was only beginning. Cardwell was equally brief: the Premier closed the debate, in a reply which was not one of his happiest. He dwelt on the phrase which he had used at the Guildhall 'a rectification of frontier' seeming sore at its having been described as incorrect, & quoting precedents: an odd, minute point to dwell upon at such a time. He touched in a rather desultory way on various matters, quoted me as having said that I censured the Cabinet for not having declared war on Russia – an absurd misrepresentation but it was not meant to be taken seriously. He ended by a vehement denunciation of 'peace at any price'. We divided about 2.30 [p.m.]: 201 to 65. The result was so far expected that many who would have voted with the minority did not care to come from a distance. Home at 3.00, weary, but well content.

11 Dec. 1878: . . . In the Commons yesterday, a fine speech from Gladstone, in his best style. He had mastered the blue book, which hardly anybody had, & was thus able to argue points of detail, & correct rash assertions. J. Manners was feeble even for him. The weakness of the ministry in debate will be one of its chief difficulties: Hardy being gone, there remain only Cross & Northcote who are capable of holding their own: & they are pitted against Gladstone, Hartington, Harcourt, Childers, Lowe, Goschen, & many competent speakers, not official, on the opposite side, such as Leatham[283], Dilke[284], Lawson[285], etc. A majority no doubt is an answer to all argument: but even the most thoroughgoing supporters grow uncomfortable when they feel the debate dead against them.

Note that in the Lords yesterday the opposition were under a double disadvantage, having lost their two best speakers. Argyll is in the gout at Cannes, & Granville too ill to attend.

12 Dec. 1878: . . . Stayed quietly at home in afternoon . . . well satisfied that the debate is ended, & that I have taken part in it, without compromising my opinions on the one hand as to the needlessness of this war, & without showing anything like personal animosity or faction on the other.

The little borough of Maldon, in Essex, has returned a Liberal in place of a Conservative: which would indicate some change in feeling if the constituency were not so small[286].

. . . Hear indirectly from the French ambassador that negociations are being carried on with the view of getting Alexandretta[287] for England, the intended equivalent being a guaranteed loan. But nothing appears to be settled. Hear also that – as was to be expected – the Ameer has thrown himself on Russian protection, & Schouvaloff is instructed to make some communication on the subject. It is an awkward complication, for our govt. will not willingly accept the mediation of Russia, & on the other hand the Russians can hardly altogether desert the Ameer, after having brought him into his present troubles.

Talk among other matters of Ld Dufferin, who has come back from Canada with the reputation, well earned, of a brilliant success: but with the entire loss of his private fortune, no one knows how got rid of. He has only £1,500 a year left, & his estates are mortgaged to Mulholland[288], the rich manufacturer. Except that he is a Sheridan by descent[289], the thing would be inexplicable. . . .

14 Dec. 1878: . . . With M. to enquire at Marlborough House after Princess Alice[290], who has been seriously ill for some days, with diphtheria: find that she died early in the morning. This is the first death among the Queen's children, & it is noted as strange that it should happen on the anniversary of Prince Albert's death, that same day having also been the turning point of the P. of W.'s illness.

. . . Compliment Walpole[291] on his son's book: a history of the early part of the present century: it is really well done, & considering the writer's connection with Perceval (his grandfather) the absence of prejudice is surprising. He writes rather as a Liberal than the reverse: certainly not as an old Tory.

Division last night . . . gave a majority of 101 for the govt.: less than they had in former divisions on the eastern question . . . Harcourt & Hartington both spoke well. Northcote was long, temperate, I should have thought rather heavy: but, though not able to stir up the House or rouse strong feeling of any kind, he manages it skilfully, conceding so much as to disarm moderate opponents, & evading with considerable skill what he does not choose to meet. Both Walpole & Lowe praised his tact in this respect. Walpole indeed praises everybody, but Lowe is not lavish of compliments, & I suppose therefore it was deserved.

15 Dec. 1878: Schouvaloff has seen M. more than once, and had some interesting talk. I will not attempt to record in detail conversations which reach me only at secondhand: the general purport is this. The Ameer has appealed to Russia, as he was sure to do: the Russian govt., without exactly taking up his cause, has asked ours what we mean to do, and suggested an arrangement: either that we shall withdraw from Afghanistan, leaving the Ameer his possessions, except some small rectification of frontier, in which case they will on their part remove their mission: or that we shall do what we please in and with the Afghan country, the Russians securing a countervailing advantage by occupying Merv, and so bringing their frontier into contact with ours. When these ideas were first started, Salisbury appears to have held high language, objecting to any interference by Russia: Schou. thereon reminded him that the position now was very different from what it had been during the Turkish war: then, the Russian army in Turkey might have been cut off by an English expedition: now, there was no such risk to run, and Russia in her own territory was not easy to attack. What answer was returned I don't know, but nothing is settled.

16 Dec. 1878: In London unable to see, read & wrote by lamplight. Sanderson called .. . Schou. called on M. but I did not see him. By 5.00 p.m. from Euston . . . Arrived about 11.15 at Knowsley. Found the Galloways, Margaret, & Arthur[292].
    . . . The papers are full of Princess Alice, whom they praise with much exaggeration, but as I believe with some justice: she had a good deal of talent, carefully cultivated, & tried to do her work. There was a coldness – reason unknown – between her & the Queen, who always made difficulties about her coming to England & saw as little of her as possible. But this will rather increase than lessen present regrets.
    An election for Bristol[293] has just come off, the result being that the Liberals keep the seat, which was theirs, & parties remain as they were. But they treat it as a victory, for at the last election the numbers were 8,800 to 8,500, or thereabouts: now they are 9,000 on the Liberal side, & 7,500 odd for the Conservative. The latter too was a good candidate, Sir Ivor Guest, a millionaire, who has married the D. of Marlborough's daughter.

17 Dec. 1878: . . . See Barnes, & settle as to the shooting.
    See Broomfield, & hear an account of what he has been doing.
    See Latten about library matters, & to settle accounts with him.
    See Moult, & arrange with him as to keeping a separate, or private, account, with Heywood.
    See Hale, & talk over various matters of detail: one being a new Liverpool cricket club, in which it is wished that I should take shares.
    Another a plan set on foot by Clarke Aspinall[294], for giving free breakfasts to the poor of Liverpool during the hard weather & distress – a doubtful way of helping them, but if others take it up I shall do so too.
    Walk to look at the new planting . . . but what with snow on the ground, & what with fog, which was dense, I could see nothing.
    . . . In the papers, news of a singular change of purpose on the part of ministers, though

the matter is not important. Northcote had given notice of his intention to propose a vote in aid of the sufferers by the disturbances & massacres in the Rhodope district: the amount not stated, but it was probably not meant to be large. The idea was unpopular on all sides, considering the distress that exists, & the proposal was wisely withdrawn[295]. Of course the Opposition triumph, but it is a small affair, & will soon be forgotten.

Questions were asked as to a supposed intention on our part to guarantee a new Turkish loan: which Northcote neither admits nor denies, but says nothing will be done without the consent of parliament.

18 Dec. 1878: Shooting . . .

Received from Northcote a request that I will take the chair of a committee, as he calls it, but it seems rather a small commission, to enquire into the expediency of a proposal by the Indian govt. . . . to meet the difficulties caused by the late fall in the price of silver. I answer . . . asking further details.

19 Dec. 1878: Shooting . . . we killed 318 head, nearly all hares & pheasants. . . . Snow on the ground, but not deep . . .

. . . Idle on coming home, & did nothing except read lazily for amusement: I cannot set to work readily after shooting.

20 Dec. 1878: More snow, day again dark & foggy. Desire Moult[296] to put down my name for £100 in shares of a new Liverpool cricket club, of which Sefton is president: but I much doubt whether the money will ever be raised : certainly the time is not favourable to such projects, for in all large towns distress is growing severe, & nowhere more than in the north. . . . Several banks have smashed, there is a general feeling that the worst has not yet come, & in the south the agricultural interest complains as much as the traders. In these parts the farmers live by a kind of market gardening, & I cannot learn that there is any difficulty among them.

21 Dec. 1878: Very hard frost, therm. at 8 degrees. Snow lying rather deep. We meant to shoot . . . but had to give it up.

In the papers, news that Londonderry is carried by the Liberals: 2,400 odd against 1,800 odd, a large majority. It looks as if the ministerial policy were proving unpopular, the times not being favourable to expenditure, & distress creating a disposition to find fault. It would not be easy now to make a war popular with the masses, though twelve months ago a minister who had proposed one would have been drawn through London streets in triumph.

Severe distress reported from most of the great towns, Sheffield being apparently the worst. All the papers contain articles & long reports on the subject . . . we are only at the beginning of the winter, & already soup-kitchens are open in a dozen places & special collections being raised. There is nowhere the intense destitution of the cotton famine but, if less violent, the mischief is more diffused, & so many industries are attacked that they cannot help one another as they did in 1862. – It is strange that, though times have been growing steadily worse since 1875, deposits in the savings banks continue to rise, & are now higher by a million than last year: also that there is scarcely any falling off in the excise returns. It looks as if beer & spirits were the last articles of consumption to be reduced even when food is scanty.

...The building trade, though slack, has not failed altogether, but I hear that builders are mortgaging their unfinished houses whenever they can.

Saw Hale, & arranged with him to give £100 to a Central Relief Fund, a meeting of which has just been held in Liverpool.

22 Dec. 1878: Wrote to Sanderson to look in my Cabinet for the notes of my late speech in the Lords[297], *Hansard* having sent me a proof of it which is from beginning to end one mass of incoherent rubbish – put together by an Irishman apparently, for he makes a strange jumble of 'would' and 'should'. This business of rewriting speeches for *Hansard*[298] is a real nuisance – utterly useless too, for who reads old speeches? but one does not like to be made responsible for utter nonsense.

23 Dec. 1878: Snow falling early, & day very cold. . . . Sir W. & Ly Thompson [sic][299] & Sanderson come.

24 Dec. 1878: Cold increasing, therm. was at 9° last night: snow on ground, & heavy fog outside. In Scotland railway traffic to the north is stopped, Aberdeen especially being in a state of blockade.

Gave Mary £10 as a Christmas present, & Margaret £5.

Walk with Sanderson, but I thought it better not to say much about Turkish or eastern matters, lest I should seem to be enquiring into matters which he was bound not to disclose.

. . . Made some notes for a speech at Rochdale but could not satisfy myself. It is difficult to speak of the existing distress & its causes without being either declamatory or dull.

Reading today & yesterday a strange but to me attractive book – the life of James Hinton[300]. The name of its subject was scarcely known to me, but he seems to have been an extraordinary character. Born a philosopher, caring for nothing except philosophy in the highest sense of the word, having made a religion of his own which he thought to be the christian but which, as far as I can understand it was utterly unlike any existing form of religious belief, he devoted himself to surgery for a means of living, rose to high rank in his profession, gave it up exactly when ordinary men would have thought their career begun, not from necessity, but that he might be free to philosophise – bought land in the Azores (of all places on earth), ruined himself by the speculation, & died worn out at little over 50: worn out, it would seem, by constant & intense thought. – On the face of it, a melancholy record: yet in such absolute devotion to intellectual & moral ends there must be a compensating sense of something which if not happiness is higher & better than what usually goes by that name. – I am not now often touched by a book, in the sense of having an interest excited by reading which is distinct from intellectual appreciation of the thing read: but this man's biography has affected me with a sense of inferiority, & respect for a very rare & noble type of character.

25 Dec. 1878: Cold continues, but slightly lessened. Church, & walk back with Sanderson. Made up accounts for the year, that is, of my private expenditure. Rather oppressed, whether by company, or because less exercise than usual has been possible to me. – I certainly am not suited for the life of a large country house, but this feeling is not new: it was perhaps even stronger 20 years ago than now.

. . . Finished correcting or rather rewriting my late speech for *Hansard*, which I do with infinite disgust. Made some more notes for Rochdale.

26 Dec. 1878: Up early, & drove through deep snow to the Prescot station . . . Preston by 11.00, train delayed by snow & fog. Took the chair at 11.30 . . . magistrates present about 30. Business mainly formal, but we had some discussion on the best way of carrying into effect the Highway Act of last session. We sat till 2.00, when I returned to the station. While waiting there, fell in with Carnarvon, who was married this morning, & on his way to London. He looked very cold, & less happy than a man should on such an occasion. We only talked for a minute or two, his train going on before mine. Return to Prescot, & walk back from thence, with some trouble, the night being dark & snow lying thick. The cold, however, is less, & a thaw apparently setting in.

Talk at Preston with various magistrates on the distress: the general opinion I gather to be that it is less severe in the artisan class than the newspapers make it out, except perhaps at Manchester: at least there seemed no serious alarm among them as to the future, nor any apprehension of riots. But all agree that there is a class which has suffered severely, that of the small shopkeepers & clerks: the former especially live from hand to mouth, carry on business with borrowed money, & are unable to bear the falling off of custom for a few weeks.

27 Dec. 1878: Warmer weather, & partial thaw. . . . I walked with Sanderson . . . The pipes . . . breaking through the frost . . . one of the rooms below was flooded last night . . .

. . . Letter received from F.A.S.[301] . . . yesterday, containing good wishes for the coming year, with a sort of allusion to our not now meeting as we used. I answer very simply, & in few words, returning his good wishes, but saying nothing as to our future intercourse. – I show the note to M. & consult her before answering.

28 Dec. 1878: . . . Weather milder, a partial thaw . . . Read in *Liverpool Post* the yearly report of the great savings bank there, of which I am (among many others) a trustee. Notwithstanding bad times, the deposits have increased by £36,000 in the year. They are in all over £1,700,000. The rate of increase is a good deal below the average, but it is still increase & not diminution.

Made up private accounts for the year: I have spent in all £4,374, but of this £800 has gone as pension to Sanderson, & £1,508 in other gifts & charities: so that my personal outlay is under £2,100. I need not in future keep it at so low a figure, but in the winter business prevented outlay, & during the spring, expecting a war, I determined to keep all expenses which were optional as low as possible. For the future I have settled to pay all donations, etc., through a separate account . . . so that what I allow myself for personal use shall be a fixed sum. . . . I have spent £810 on works of art, & only £268 on books, but there is a separate allowance of £200 for keeping up the library here. . . .

30 Dec. 1878: Day warm, & snow fast disappearing.

Mr. Duncan[302] left us: to the general regret.

Shooting . . . We killed 456 head, chiefly pheasants . . . My share was 93.

In afternoon there came Schouvaloff, Münster with his daughter, Sir B.[303] & Ly Brett, young Brett[304], & P. Hope[305].

31 Dec. 1878: Shooting . . . with the two ambassadors . . . We had a fine day, & killed 709 head: my share being 135. A great crowd with us, much excited & pleased.

There joined us a son of C. Münster.

The Hales dined with us.

So ends the year: more quietly & pleasantly than it began.

Notes

[1]   War with Russia, though not begun, was expected shortly.

[2]   Philip Currie, 1st Baron Currie (1834–1906), diplomatist from 1854: with Salisbury at Constantinople (1876) and Berlin (1878): permanent under-secretary 1889–1893: cr. peer, 1899. His wife was 'Violet Fane', the writer: d.s.p.

[3]   War Minister 1878–1880, entering the cabinet for the first time.

[4]   1st Earl of Cranbrook (1814–1906): Indian Secretary 1878–1880.

[5]   In summer 1876.

[6]   C.B. Adderley, 1st Baron Norton (1814–1905).

[7]   Lord Sandon (thus styled until 1882), 3rd Earl of Harrowby (1831–1900).

[8]   Family solicitor. Admiral Edward Stanley (1798–19 February 1878), eldest son of Rev. James Stanley, vicar of Ormskirk, became a captain in 1838 and a half-pay admiral in 1870.

[9]   William, 3rd Earl of Leitrim (1806–1878): succ. 1854 and d. unm. Owned 54,000 acres in Donegal and 2,500 in Leitrim, total value (1883) £11,000 p.a. An improving landlord, active in famine relief, and long chairman of the board of guardians, he was murdered together with his clerk and coachman. At his funeral the mob tried to drag the coffin from the hearse.

[10]   Derby's private secretary when in office, and factotum and family friend when out of office.

[11]   Charles Abbott, 3rd Baron Tenterden (1834–1882): entered F.O. 1854: succ. uncle as peer, 1870: asst. under-sec. 1871–1872: perm. under-sec. 1873–1882: freemason.

[12]   Chancellor of the Exchequer 1874–1880.

[13]   Sir Henry Drummond Wolff (1830–1908), only son of Jewish convert: educ. Rugby: entered F.O. 1846: priv. sec. to Lytton when col. sec.: sec. to high commr., Ionian Is., 1859–1864: in finance 1864–1870: M.P. (Cons.) 1874–1880: U.K. commr. for E. Rumelia 1878: M.P. 1880–1885: invents Primrose League 1883: commr. in Egypt 1885–1886: envoy in Persia 1887–1891, in Madrid 1892–1900.

[14]   R. Bourke, 1st Lord Connemara (1827–1902), 3rd s. of Lord Mayo: Cons. M.P. 1868–1886: cr. peer 1887: under-sec. for foreign affairs 1874–1880, 1885–1886: gov. of Madras 1886–1890: m. dau. of Lord Dalhousie, Indian viceroy (she divorced him 1890: see *Later Diaries*, 137).

[15]   C.S. = Constance Stanley, his brother's wife, dau. of the former foreign secretary Lord Clarendon.

[16]   To withdraw into neutrality.

[17]   Arthur Kinnaird, 2nd Baron Kinnaird (1814–1887), partner in London bank: succ. January 1878: philanthropist.

[18]   *Parl. Deb.*, 3, 8 April 1878, cols 789–801. Derby made a powerful anti-war speech, and denied that calling out the reserves was the sole or even the principal reason for his resignation.

[19]   William Molyneux, 4th Earl of Sefton (1835–1897): succ. 1855: lord-lieut. Lancs. and leading Liverpool Whig: socially on friendly terms with diarist.

[20]   Frederic Thesiger, 1st Baron Chelmsford (1794–5 October 1878), lord chancellor 1858–1859, 1866–29 February 1868. As a midshipman, he had served at Copenhagen, 1807. He was 3rd s. of the Collector of Customs in St. Vincent, W.I., where a volcano destroyed his father's estate, 1812. He was made a baron, 1858.

[21]   James, 2nd Earl of Verulam (1809–1895), Herts. magnate: M.P. (Cons.) Herts. 1832–1845: lord-lieut. Herts. 1846–1892: minor office 1852, 1858–1859: president of Camden Society 1873.

22   Private secretary, whose services were retained after Derby left office: Derby's executor.

23   On the day of the great Chartist demonstration.

24* The Royal Literary Fund.

25   Lord John Manners, 7th Duke of Rutland (1818–1906): M.P. with little break 1841–1888: in all Tory cabinets 1852–1892: succ. brother 1888: declined Canada April 1868 and India November 1875: postmaster-gen. 1874–1880, 1885–1886: chancellor of duchy, 1886–1892.

26   A.J. Mundella (1825–1897), Nottingham hosiery manufacturer: M.P. Sheffield 1868–1885 and Brightside 1885–1897: P.C. 1880: education minister 1880–1885: president of board of trade 1886, 1892–1894: involved in range of educational reforms.

27   J.M.W. Turner (1775–1851).

28   Sir Henry Irving (1838–1905), actor: then in *Louis XI* (1878): first actor to be knighted, 1895.

29   Alan Stewart, 10th Earl of Galloway (1835–1901): succ. father 1873: d.s.p., when succ. by bro.: m. Derby's step-daughter Lady Mary Cecil 25 January 1872: suffered from alcoholism in later life.

30   Pyotr Andreyevich, Count Schouvalov (1827–1889), Russian amb. to London 1874–1879: served in Crimea: former head of political police.

31   Georg Herbert, Count von Münster (1820–1920), German amb. in London 1873–1885: amb. in Paris 1885–1900: previously in Hanoverian service.

32   Sir Stafford Northcote, 1st Earl of Iddesleigh (1818–1887), Cons. leader in the Commons 1876–1885.

33   The budget proposed to raise income tax from 3d. to 5d., 4 April 1878.

34   Sir Willliam T. Charley (1833–1904), barrister from Antrim: M.P. (Cons.) Salford 1868–1880, when defeated: Common Serjeant of London April 1878–.

35   W.E. Gladstone (1809–1898), four times premier.

36   The diary shows virtually no sign of Derby being in poor health in the period between his resignation in March and the revival of bitter controversy in July. There is some evidence of nervous anxiety in the period between July and the end of 1878. However, in the six weeks between resignation and his visit to the Paris Exhibition on 5 May, Derby was leading a quiet but normal life of business, exercise, and estate management, and presided as usual at sessions (23–24 April). Derby even went to a play for the first time in years.

37   12 Apr. 1878.

38   Frank Hugh O'Donnell (1848–?), Home Ruler. M.P. Dungarvan June 1877–1885. Hon. Sec. Irish Home Rule Confederation of Great Britain.

39   Robert Lowe, 1st Vt Sherbrooke (1811–1892), chancellor of the exchequer 1868–1873, home sec. 1873–1874: cr. vt 1880: long an intimate of both Derbys.

40   Lord Hartington, 8th Duke of Devonshire (1833–1908): postmaster-gen. 1868–1871, chief sec. for Ireland 1871–1874: elected Commons leader unopposed, February 1875: succ. father as Duke, 1891: known as Lord Hartington 1858–1891.

41   Fairhill, near Tunbridge.

42   A.J. Beresford-Hope (1820–1887), Cons. M.P. and founder of *Saturday Review:* m. Mildred, dau. of James, 2nd M. of Salisbury: thus bro-in-law of the premier, and uncle of A.J. Balfour.

43   A small scenic estate, originally of about 1,000 acres, but gradually much extended, near Haslemere, Surrey: sold to Derby, 1875.

44   By 8th May Derby was interpreting Northcote's apparent sharp practice as a blunder rather than deceit.

45   (Sir) A.H. Layard (1817–1894), author of *Nineveh and its Remains* (1849): M.P. (Lib.) 1852–1857, 1860–1868: foreign under-sec. 1861–1866: 1st commr. of works 1868–1869: minister at Madrid 1869–1877, amb. at Constantinople 1877–1880.

46   Lionel Sackville (formerly West or Sackville-West), 2nd Baron Sackville (1827–1908):

diplomatist 1847–1888: U.K. min. in Argentina 1872–1878, in Madrid 1878–1881, in Washington 1881–1888: succ. bro. 1888: alleged intervention in U.S. elections October–November 1888 led to resignation: bro. of diarist's wife: usually called Lionel West in diaries.

47   (Francis Charles) Hastings Russell, 9th Duke of Bedford (1819–1991), succ. his cousin 1872: m. 1844 Elizabeth Sackville-West, Lady Derby's sister (she d. 1897).

48   Estate accountant at Knowsley, inheriting the post on his father's death, 1876.

49   Small estates in Kent, near Bromley and Tunbridge Wells respectively, acquired by Derby after marriage in 1870.

50   Head agent for Derby's W. Lancs. estates: seen by Derby as too easy-going.

51   Head forester.

52   Formerly Gathorne Hardy.

53   (Sir) John Pender (1818–1896), businessman: submarine telegraph magnate.

54   Sir Theodore Martin (1816–1909), Edinburgh lawyer and London parliamentary agent: humourist, translator, biographer of Prince Consort (5 vols. 1875–1880) and Lord Lyndhurst (1883): literary worthy.

55   Baron C.F. Stockmar (1787–1863): educ. Jena: physician: adviser to Leopold I of the Belgians: in 1836 came to England as adviser to Princess Victoria: for a time influential at her court.

56   R.W. Hanbury (1845–1903), Rugbeian: M.P. (Cons.) Tamworth 1872–1878, Staffs. N. 1878–1880, Preston 1885–1903: entered cabinet as agriculture minister, 1900.

57   M.A. Bass, 1st Baron Burton (1837–1909), brewer: educ. Harrow and Trinity: M.P. (Lib.) 1865–1886. Cr. baron 1886. Lib. unionist 1886, then tariff reformer.

58   Fairhill.

59   Lord Arthur Cecil, Derby's stepson-farmer.

60   Rev. E. Hornby, parson of Bury, bro. of Adm. Hornby: cf. below, 31 October 1878.

61   Thomas Statter (1816–1891), steward of Derby estates in Bury and S.E. Lancs. 1841–1891: art collector and businessman in his own right: consistently pessimistic about business prospects in later life: strict, and not popular with tenants.

62   Derby and his wife went to Paris for the Exhibition on 5 May, returning to London on 12 May. Derby felt 'the uselessness of going into foreign society, and should not do it at all but for M.'s pleasure. From growing hardness of hearing, and the rapid way in which the French talk, I cannot follow a conversation sufficiently to enjoy it' (diary, 12 May 1878).

63   Derby's feelings about Salisbury perhaps found an outlet in resigning from the Council of King's College, London ('essentially a clerical institution'), and in refusing to give active support to the projected Liverpool bishopric (diary, 26 Apr. and 4 May 1878).

64   The Paris Exhibition of 1878 drew 12 million visitors.

65   Richard, 2nd baron Lyons (1817–1887), succ. 1858: amb. in Paris 1867–1887: cr. vt 1881 and earl 1887: offered F.O. by Salisbury 1886: R.C. convert 1887. Highly regarded by Derby.

66   The Prince of Wales.

67   Lord Acton (1834–1902), cr. Baron Acton of Aldenham 1869: lord-in-waiting 1892–1895: regius prof. of modern history, Cambridge, 1895.

68   Ernest Renan (1823–1892), biblical scholar, progressive thinker, author of *La vie de Jésus* (1863).

69   Castalia, Countess Granville, née Campbell of Islay: very tall, and much younger (b. 1847) than her husband (b. 1815).

70   Mary, Mme. Mohl, wife of German orientalist: held salon in Paris: friend of Lady Derby.

71   Hippolyte-Adolphe Taine (1828–1893), dominant figure in French letters: his history of English literature (1864–) based on sociological ideas of 'race, milieu, moment'.

72   Sir William Harcourt (1827–1904), home secretary 1880–1885: Liberal leader 1896–1898.

73   Henry Fawcett (1833–1884), economist and radical: postmaster-gen. 1880–1884: M.P. 1865–1884: blind: never in cabinet.

74   Decazes, duc (1819–1886), foreign min. 26 November 1873–23 November 1877: m. a

Singer (not a chanteuse, but a U.S. sewing-machine heiress). Disliked by Derby for supposed corruption.

75   Gladstone spoke 'under an hour' in reply to 'a deputation of 130 from Manchester & the towns, and some 20 from Wales' (*Gladstone Diaries*).

76   William Henry Waddington (1826–1894), educ. Rugby and Trinity, where rowed for Cambridge in Boat Race: savant and archaeologist: twice education minister in 1870s: foreign minister December 1877–: French plentipotentiary at Congress of Berlin: succeeded Dufaure as premier, early 1879–27 December 1879: amb. in London 1883–1894: m. an American, née Mary King. Protestant.

77   Hastings Russell, 9th Duke of Bedford (1819–1891), succ. 1872.

78   Charles René Gavard (1826–1893), 1st sec. at French embassy in London 1871–December 1877. Author of *Un diplomate à Londres: Lettres et notes, 1871–1877* (Paris, 1895).

79   Lord Lyons's factotum.

80   Stratford Canning, Viscount Stratford de Redcliffe (1786–1880). Amb. at Constantinople 1842–1848. Cr. viscount 1852.

81   Society doctor, of Kensington.

82   Sir Roundell Palmer, 1st Earl of Selborne (1812–1895), lord chancellor 1872–1874, 1880–1885: cr. baron 1872, earl 1882.

83   Edward Levy-Lawson or Lawson, 1st Baron Burnham (1833–1916), editor of the *Daily Telegraph* from 1855 to 1903: cr. peer, 1903.

84   Arthur Penrhyn Stanley (1815–1881), educ. Rugby under Arnold, and Balliol: pub. *Life of Arnold*, 1844: sec. of Oxford University commission, 1850–1852: leading Broad Churchman: Dean of Westminster 1864–1881.

85   Probably (Sir) William Smith (1813–1893), lexicographer: kt 1892: ed. of *Quarterly Review*, 1867–1893.

86   (Sir) H.M. Stanley (1841–1904), explorer and writer ('Dr. Livingstone, I presume?').

87   Lord John Russell (1792–1878), 3rd s. of 6th D. of Bedford: premier 1946–1852, 1865–1866: cr. Earl, 1861.

88   Sir James Philip Lacaita (1813–1895), Neapolitan lawyer: assisted Gladstone against Bourbons, 1850: came to London, 1852, where taught 1853–1856: naturalised 1855: sec. to Gladstone's mission to Ionian Is. 1858: deputy in Italy 1861–1865, senator 1876.

89   *Pall Mall Gazette*, a Tory paper edited by Frederick Greenwood, but hostile to Derby: transformed into a Liberal organ under John Morley and W.T. Stead, April 1880.

90   Charles Newdigate Newdegate (1816–1887): educ. Eton and King's: M.P. (Cons.) Warwickshire N. 1843–1885: P.C. 1885: pub. letters on trade, 1849–1851.

91   Henry Howard Molyneux Herbert, 4th Earl of Carnarvon (1831–1890), Tory intellectual and Disraeli's colonial secretary, 1874–1878: freemason.

92   This refers to Constance, wife of his brother Frederick Stanley (see also 11, 16 and 17 July 1878 below). No indication is given in the diary of the nature of her offensive remarks. The coolness between the brothers dated, not from Col. Stanley's taking Cabinet office on his brother's resignation, but from the time Constance Stanley's talk reached Derby. On 30 May 1878, on the occasion of the funeral of an aunt, Derby pointedly declined an invitation to stay with his brother, and put up at an adjacent inn for the night.

93   Cotton Districts Convalescent Fund.

94   John Wilson Patten (Wilson till 1823), Lord Winmarleigh (1802–1892), Nestor of the Lancashire Tories: M.P. (Cons.) N. Lancs. 1830–1831, 1832–1874: educ. Eton and Magdalen: P.C. 1867: Constable of Lancaster Castle 1879–1892: cr. baron March 1874: chancellor of the duchy, 1867–1868: chief sec. for Ireland, September–December 1868.

95   Probably Georges-Douglas-Trevor-Bernard d'Harcourt (1808–1883), French ambassador in London May 1875 to January 1879.

96   President of France, 1873–1879: lived 1808–1893.

[97] (Sir) G. Scharf (1820–1895), sec. to Manchester Exhibition 1857, sec. to Nat. Portrait Gallery 1857–1882 and its director 1882–1895, retired 1895: K.C.B. 1895.

[98] Hugh McCalmont, 1st Earl Cairns (1819–1885), educ. Belfast and T.C.D.: M.P. for Belfast, 1852–1866: Q.C. 1856: attorney-gen. 1866: cr. Baron Cairns 1867: lord chancellor 1868: leader of conservatives in Lords, 1869–1870: lord chancellor 1874–1880: cr. Earl Cairns, 1880.

[99] Edward Cardwell (1813–1886): junior office 1845–1846, minister 1852–1855, 1859–1866: Gladstone's reforming war minister 1868–1874: cr. viscount 1874.

[100] G.G. Leveson-Gower, 2nd Earl Granville (1815–1891), succ. 1846: colonial sec. 1868–1870, foreign sec. 1870–1874, 1880–1885, colonial sec. 1886: Liberal leader in the Lords.

[101] Charles Carington, 1st Earl Carrington (1843–1928), succ. 1868: Governor of New South Wales 1885–1890: cr. Marquess of Lincolnshire, 1912.

[102] Sir R.A. Cross (1823–1914), Disraeli's reforming home secretary: in the 1880s, but not in the 1870s, often thought drunk in the House.

[103] Sir James Paget, 1st bart (1814–1899), surgeon, vice-chancellor of London University 1883–1895; or possibly Sir A.B. Paget (1823–1896), diplomatist, amb. to Italy 1876–1883.

[104] Sir John Lubbock, 4th bart (1834–1913), banker: campaigner for Bank Holidays and Early Closing: authority on ants: M.P. London University 1880–1900: cr. Lord Avebury, 1900: Kentish country neighbour, much visited by Derby.

[105] Sir W. Thomson, Baron Kelvin (1824–1907), kt 1866, baron 1892: ardent Unionist, b. in Ulster.

[106] W.T. Stead (1849–1912), editor: ed. *Northern Echo* (Darlington) 1871–1880: asst ed. *Pall Mall Gazette* 1880–1883, ed. 1883–1890: drowned on *Titanic*.

[107] Lady Dartrey.

[108] Sir M.E. Hicks Beach, 1st Lord St. Aldwyn (1837–1916), M.P. (Cons.) 1864–1906: chief sec. for Ireland 1874–1878, 1886–1887: col. sec. 1878–1880.

[109] G.J. Goschen, 1st vt (1831–1907), pres. of poor law board 1868–1871, 1st lord of the admiralty 1871–1874: out of office 1874–1886: in Unionist cabinets 1886–1892, 1895–1900: cr. vt 1900.

[110] Samuel Plimsoll (1824–1898), agitator: the 'Sailor's Friend': hon. sec. of Great Exhibition, 1851: coal merchant in London, 1853: Radical M.P. Derby 1868–1880: his violent protest in H. of C. 1875 led to Merchant Shipping Act 1876 and Plimsoll Line.

[111] Russell Gurney (1804–1878), recorder of London: barrister: Q.C. (1845): M.P. (Cons.) Southampton 1865–1878: served on public bodies (Married Women's Property Commission, Eyre Commission [1865], Washington treaty [1871]).

[112] Philip Wykeham Martin (1829–1878) of Leeds Castle, Kent: educ. Eton and Balliol: M.P. (Lib.) Rochester 1856–1878.

[113] Spencer Perceval (1762–1812), premier 1809–1812, assassinated in House of Commons 1812.

[114] David Plunket, 1st Baron Rathmore (1838–1919): M.P. (Cons.) Dublin Univ. 1870–1895: 1st Commr. of Works 1885–1886, 1886–1892: cr. Baron 1895.

[115] See above, 3 April 1878.

[116] Sir Spencer Walpole (1839–1907), historian: biographer of Russell and Perceval: governor of Isle of Man 1882–1893: sec. to P.O. 1893–1899: pub. *History of England from 1815 to 1856* (incomplete).

[117] Alexander Johnstone Wilson, *The Resources of modern countries . . . reprinted, with . . . additions, from Fraser's Magazine*, 2 vols., London, 1878.

[118] '. . . Since the Russians keep Kars & Batoum in Armenia which in effect give them command of the country; Bulgaria up to the Balkans: & the southern half of Bulgaria, which it is proposed to make into a separate state, will know no rest until it has obtained for itself the same complete freedom as is possessed by the northern province.'

[119] Perhaps Charles Henry Hopwood (1829–1904), recorder of Liverpool 1886–1904: Q.C. 1874: M.P. (Lib.) Stockport 1874–1885, Middleton 1892–1895: opposed severe sentences.

[120] William Jacobson (1803–1884), Bishop of Chester 1865–1884: sometime regius professor of divinity.

[121] The diarist's brother.

[122] Rev. Oswald H.N. Penrhyn, Rector of Huyton, 1876: officiated at Emma, Countess of Derby's funeral, 28 April 1876: distant kinsman.

[123] A.k.a. Scanderoon in Victorian times (now Iskenderun in S.E. Turkey), a port on which Disraeli had cast covetous eyes in spring 1878.

[124] The widow of Henry Thomas Stanley (1803–1875), black sheep of the family; she more than filled her husband's place. *Née* Anne Woolhouse.

[125] Owner and occupant of Holwood, Pitt's villa near Bromley. In 1872 Derby, then resident at Holwood, 'heard with regret that Mr. Alexander, the owner of Holwood, intends to live there, and that we must give it up in June 1873. Perhaps this is as well for we should never have left the place of our own accord . . .' (diary, 13 April 1872). Derby eventually bought the reversion, Alexander continuing to live there for his lifetime: 'Heard to my satisfaction that Mr. Alexander accepts the offer of £60,000 for the reversion of Holwood . . . I have done a wise thing in buying' (diary, 20 October 1877).

[126] Sir Arthur Gordon, 1st Baron Stanmore (1829–1912), colonial governor: s. of 4th E. of Aberdeen, premier: colonial governor esp. in Fiji 1875–1880, N. Zealand 1880–1883, and Ceylon 1883–1890: cr. baron, 1893: noted for sympathy with native races.

[127] A.J.E. Liardet was defeated Tory candidate at Greenwich in 1874.

[128] George McCorquodale (1817–1895), master printer: printer to L.N.W.R.: sheriff of Lancs. 1882, of Anglesey 1889: contested Wigan 1880, Newton division 1885.

[129] Thompson, as sub-agent for the Fylde, had little contact with Derby.

[130] James Fraser (1818–1885), bishop of Manchester 1870–1885.

[131] George V, K. of Hanover (1819–1878), succ. 1851, deposed by Prussia September 1866: lived in Paris until his death: a good musician.

[132] Lionel Sackville (former West or Sackville-West), 2nd Lord Sackville (1827–1908), succ. brother 1888: minister in Argentina 1872–1878, in Madrid 1878–1881, in Washington 1881–1888.

[133] Nassau Senior (1790–1864), prof. of political economy at Oxford 1825–1830, 1847–1852: wrote report of Poor Law Commission, 1834: biographer, interviewer, and leading economist.

[134] 6th Duke of Richmond (1818–1903), leader of Tories in House of Lords 1870–1876: Lord president of council 1874–1880: first Scottish Sec. 1885–1886: pres. of board of trade 1867–1868, June–August 1885: styled E. of March 1819–1860, succ. 1860.

[135] Henry George, 3rd Earl Grey (1802–1894): succ. 1845: col. sec. 1846–1852: not holding office thereafter.

[136] House of Edward Bootle-Wilbraham, Baron Skelmersdale (1837–1898): succ. his grandfather, 1853, in the barony: minor office 1866–1868, 1874–1880, 1885–1886, 1886–1892, 1895–1898: P.C. 1874: cr. Earl of Lathom (after his house), May 1880: m. Clarendon's dau.: leading Freemason: left £127,000 net.

[137] Emma Caroline, Countess of Derby (d. 1876), dau. of 1st Baron Skelmersdale. She m. Lord Derby (1799–1869), thrice premier, in 1825.

[138] The *Telegraph* had recently been a strong supporter of Disraeli.

[139] Though Derby had resigned over Cyprus, he was entirely in the dark as to government policy over its occupation between the time of his resignation and July. For an interim period of three months, therefore, he was unable to tell how far he had any grounds for breaking with the government, or whether, indeed, his resignation might not be made to look foolish and unnecessary. When Indian troops went to Malta in early May, Derby saw this as a sign that 'the design of an occupation is suspended'; on 5 June 1878 'the Cyprus and Scanderoon business is still a

mystery'. Derby's diary shows no suspicion, however, that the Cyprus issue, at least as ventilated in the spring, was more a means for his removal than anything else.

[140] A defensive treaty with Turkey, concluded on 4 June, was announced by Richmond on 8 July. On 8 July a proclamation by the Sultan ceded Cyprus to Britain, Baring at once annexing the island. On 16 August details of the defensive convention in Asia Minor were announced.

[141] The prosecution against Charles Marvin was dismissed. The *Globe* published the Anglo-Russian convention, 14 June 1878.

[142] Philip Currie, 1st baron Currie (1834–1906).

[143] Lords Arthur, Lionel, & Sackville Cecil, Derby's stepsons by Lady Derby.

[144] Lady Emma Charlotte Stanley (1835–1928) who m. 1860 Col. The Hon. Sir W.P.M. Chetwynd Talbot (1817–1898).

[145] Arthur Philip, 6th E. Stanhope (1838–1905), M.P. 1868, 1870–1875: junior whip 1874–1876, first church estates commissioner 1878–1905, and commoner wife.

[146] Possibly Sir George Howland Beaumont, 9th Bt (1828–1882) and commoner spouse.

[147] *Née* Lady Alice Villiers, 2nd dau. of Lord Clarendon: became Countess of Lathom, 1880.

[148] Friedrich Ferdinand Graf von Beust (1809–1886), Saxon and Austrian statesman: minister-president of Saxony (1858), chancellor of Austria (1866), subsequently Austrian amb. in London until 1878 and in Paris 1878–1882: a Protestant.

[149] Batoum or Batum, Turkish port on S.E. coast of Black Sea: repulsed Russian attack in war of 1877–1878, but ultimately gained for Russia by verbal sleight of hand at Congress of Berlin, July 1878, despite vociferous protests from U.K. public opinion.

[150] Derby was educ. at Rugby and Trinity.

[151] Correctly reported.

[152] Georges-Douglas-Trevor-Bernard d'Harcourt (1808–1883), French amb. in London May 1875–January 1879: brought up in England: sat in Chamber of Peers 1840–1848: lived in England 1848–1870.

[153] Rev. Charles Kingsley (1819–1875), man of letters: professor of modern history at Cambridge 1860–1869.

[154] Gen. Jonathan Peel (1799–1879), sec. for war under Derby 1858–1859 and 1866–1867 (resigned): M.P. Huntingdon 1831–1868: bro. of premier, father-in-law of Morier, devoted to turf.

[155] Derby's brother-in-law, Col. Sir W.P.M. Chetwynd Talbot, who was on the Carlton Club political committee and thus much involved in election preparations.

[156] Lady Mary Cecil (1850–1903), m. Alan, 10th E. of Galloway (1835–1901), leaving no issue.

[157] Lord Sackville Cecil (1848–1898): d. unm.: successful businessman.

[158] Cf. M. Swartz, *The Politics of British Foreign Policy in the Era of Disraeli and Gladstone* (1985), pp. 97–99. The main organiser of the reception was none other than Lord Henry Lennox.

[159] Cf. n. 15 above.

[160] *Parl. Deb.*, *3*, ccxli, cols. 1878–1804.

[161] Lancaster, 9 March 1848: Armstrong (Lib.) 636; Stanley (Protectionist) 620. Stanley in any case wanted a seat much further away from his father's influence.

[162] Archibald Primrose, 5th E. of Rosebery (1847–1929), premier 1894–1895.

[163] Edward Adolphus Seymour, 12th D. of Somerset (1804–1885), Whig: minor office 1835–1841, 1850–1851: in cabinet 1851–1852: 1st lord of admiralty 1859–1866: styled Lord Seymour until 1855, when succ.: offered first refusal of Colonial Office, *vice* Carnarvon, in 1878: sceptic.

[164] George Peabody (1795–1869), U.S. millionaire and philanthropist: came to England, 1827, and made fortune: founded Peabody dwellings for workmen: benefactor to Harvard and Yale.

[165] Lord Lorne (1845–1918): thus styled until succ. as 9th D. of Argyll 1900: m. Princess Louise, 21 March 1871.

[166] Frederick Temple Hamilton-Temple-Blackwood, 1st Marquess of Dufferin and Ava (1826–1902), gov.-gen. of Canada 1872–1878, viceroy of India 1884–1888.

[167] The diary throws no light on the use of Secret Service money.

[168] Queen's residence in the Isle of Wight.

[169] *Parl. Deb.*, *3*, vol. ccxlii, cols. 671–717.

[170] *Parl. Deb.*, *3*, vol. ccxlii, cols. 872–892.

[171] Lord and Lady Derby left London on 5 August for a holiday in the Swiss Alps, returning to England on 4 September. Derby's weight had fallen to 13 st. 1 lbs., 'less than I have been since 1866'.

[172] According to the diary, this arrangement was abandoned in the autumn.

[173] John Morley, *Diderot and the Encyclopaedists* (Chapman and Hall, London, 1878), 2 vols.

[174] *Parl. Deb.*, *3*, ccxli, cols. 1787–1804.

[175] Rev. Christopher Newman Hall (1816–1902), Cong. minister in London 1854–1892: chairman of Cong. Union of England and Wales 1866: divorced.

[176] Sir H. Rumbold (1829–1913), diplomatist: sec. to legation in China 1859–1862, minister in Chile 1872, in Switzerland 1878–1879: eventually amb. to Austria 1896–1900: succ. brother as bart 1877.

[177] The *Princess Alice*, a saloon steamer of the London Steamboat Company, collided on 3 September 1878 in daylight with a large screw steamer. About 500 to 600 of the 700 day trippers on board died. The principal promoter of the ill-fated vessel was none other than Mr. John Orrell Lever.

[178] Lord Sandon, 3rd E. of Harrowby (1831–1900), succ. his father 1882: entered cabinet 1878 (leaving in 1886): Disraeli's education minister 1874–1878: M.P. (Cons.) Liverpool 1868–1882: leading Evangelical.

[179] A. Trollope, *Australia and New Zealand* (London, 1873), 2 vols.

[180] Part of a lifelong pattern of Gladstone seeking, and Derby evading, the other's company.

[181] Sir Edward Malet, 4th bart (1837–1908), diplomatist: after varied career, amb. at Berlin 1884–1895.

[182] Augusta, Lady Dartrey (d. 1887), Derby's cousin and his friend and correspondent since he was 18: m. an Irish Whig landlord.

[183] The 1st baron Gerard (1808–1887) had two daughters. It was the elder who in November 1878 m. Gen. Sir Laurence Oliphant, not to be confused with the religious crank of similar name.

[184] The family estates were worth about £43,000 p.a.

[185] William, 2nd Baron Gerard of Bryn (1851–1902): prominent on the turf: succ. father, 1887.

[186] The worst ever colliery accident in South Wales occurred at Prince of Wales Colliery, Abercarne, near Newport, with 262 lives lost, and 520 widowed or orphaned. The explosion also put 700 men and 1,400 dependants out of work: 82 men and boys were rescued. The cause of the explosion was unknown.

[187] Lady Egerton of Tatton (1811–12 September 1878), e. dau. of 1st Marquess of Ely, m. W.T. Egerton, 1st Baron Egerton of Tatton (1806–1883), cr. peer 1859.

[188] At Preston.

[189] Greece had done badly under the Treaty of San Stefano. She was not entitled to full representation at the Congress of Berlin, where Greek claims were however considered, and a rectification of frontier proposed. This led, though not until 1881, to the cession of most of Thessaly and a small part of Epirus to Greece.

[190] Edward Lytton, 2nd Baron Lytton (1831–1891), succ. father 1873: cr. Earl 1880: viceroy of India 1876–1880.

[191] 1st Viscount Cranbrook (1814–1906), cr. 1878: India Sec. 1878–1880.

[192] Reginald Sackville, 7th Earl De La Warr (1817–1896), succ. his brother 1873: brother of Lady Derby: formerly Baron Buckhurst (1870–1873): Chaplain to the Queen 1846–1865: country parson 1841–1865: m. dau. of Lord Lamington: usually referred to by diarist as 'the Delawares'.

[193] Lord Odo Russell, 1st baron Ampthill (1829–1884): amb. at Berlin 1871: cr. peer 1881: s. of Lord George William Russell, who also amb. at Berlin 1835–1841.

[194] The West Highland estate of the millionaire industrialist Pender: visited by Derby, 1872.

[195] Perhaps Mr. E.W. Binney, Manchester solicitor and geologist (1812–1881).

[196] Joseph Arch M.P. (1826–1919), agricultural trade unionist.

[197] See also entry of 22 December 1878 below for evidence of re-writing of Hansard.

[198] *Parl. Deb.*, 3, ccxli, cols. 1804–1816. Salisbury here compared Derby to Titus Oates.

[199] In later life a hopeless alcoholic.

[200] Philip Stanhope (1847–?), youngest son of Philip, 5th Earl Stanhope, M.P. 1886–1892, 1893–1900, 1904–1906, was cr. Baron Weardale, 1906. He m., 1877, Alexandra, widow of Count Tolstoy.

[201] Archibald Forbes (1838–1900), war correspondent, chiefly for *Daily News*, in wars of 1870s. Cf. Forbes, 'The "fiasco" of Cyprus', *Nineteenth Century*, Vol. 4, October 1878, pp. 609–626.

[202] John Abernethy (1764–1831), a leading surgeon of his day.

[203] Sir T.M. Biddulph (1809–1878), Keeper of H.M. Privy Purse.

[204] Lord Francis Hervey, M.P. (Cons.) Bury St. Edmunds 1874–1880, 1885–1886, 1886–1892: Civil Service Commissioner 1892–1907, 1st C. Serv. Commissioner 1907–1909.

[205] Possibly Edwin Dyson, sometime curator of Dukinfield and formerly of Miles Platting: in 1881 vicar of St. John's in the Wilderness at Shuttleworth near Ramsbottom.

[206] W.E.H. Lecky (1838–1903), historian: declined regius chair at Oxford, 1892: frequent guest at Knowsley: wrote introduction to posthumous collection of diarist's speeches.

[207] Victor, 7th E. of Jersey (1845–1915), owner of Child's Bank, gov. of New South Wales 1890–1893, leading Freemason married to leading society hostess.

[208] Eustace Balfour (1854–1911), architect: brother of A.J. and Gerald Balfour: m. Lady Frances Campbell, 1879.

[209] The City of Glasgow Bank stopped payment 5 October 1878, with a total loss of £6,783,000.

[210] William Pilkington (b. 1827) of Roby Hall was a S. Lancs. neighbour, Roby being 5 m. E. of Liverpool. He was a J.P., D.L., and member of the Junior Carlton.

[211] Sir Francis Grant (1803–1878), portrait painter: P.R.A. 1866–1878: kt 1866.

[212] Lord Leighton, 1st Baron Leighton of Stretton (1830–1896), P.R.A. 1878–1896: cr. peer day before his death, 1896.

[213] Lionel Tollemache, 8th E. of Dysart (1794–1878): see also *Derby Diaries 1869–1878*, p. 139: personalty sworn at £1,700,000 (December 1878).

[214] In fact Dysart left £1,700,000 in personal property (diary, 13 Dec. 1878), mostly to accumulate in trust for 21 years.

[215] Lord Lytton, 1st E. of Lytton (1831–1891), viceroy of India 4 January 1876–1880.

[216] The French Ambassador, who was a guest at Knowsley.

[217] Shere Ali (1825–1879), Amir of Afghanistan 1863–1879, y.s. of Dost Mohammed, whom he succ.

[218] Sir T.D. Baker (1837–1893), military sec. to Lytton, 1878: accompanied Roberts in Kabul campaign, 1879–1880.

[219] Lord Arthur Russell (1825–1892), M.P. (Lib.) 1857–1885, brother of 9th Duke of Bedford.

[220] Sir Charles Rivers Wilson (1831–1916), Treasury civil servant 1856–1894: served in Egypt 1878–1879, ran Canadian railways 1895–1909.

[221] The ambassador, not the politician.

[222] Frederic Thesiger, 1st Baron Chelmsford (1794–1878): attorney-gen. 1845–1846, 1852, lord chancellor 1858–1859, 1866–February 1868: cr. baron 1858.

[223] Richard Bethell, 1st Baron Westbury (1800–1873), lord chancellor 1861–1865: father of investment trusts: not over-scrupulous.

[224] Sir James Ughtred Kay-Shuttleworth, 2nd bart (1844–1939), 1st baron Shuttleworth (cr. 1902): M.P. (Lib.) Clitheroe 1885–1902: owned about 4,200 acres.

[225] Sir C. Wood, 1st vt Halifax (1800–1885): cr. peer 1866: lord privy seal 1870–1874.

[226] T.G. Baring, 1st E. of Northbrook (1826–1904), s. of 1st Baron: viceroy of India 1872–1876, 1st lord of the admiralty 1880–1885.

[227] The local doctor at Knowsley.

[228] Sir R. Burton (1821–1890), explorer: translator of *The Arabian Nights:* consul at Trieste 1872–1890.

[229] Col. The Hon. Sir W.P.M. Talbot (1817–1898), serjeant-at-arms, House of Lords, 1858–1899: kt 1897.

[230] The politician, not the ambassador.

[231] William, 7th D. of Devonshire (1808–1891), succ. 1858: father of Lord Hartington.

[232] J.A. Roebuck (1801–1879), radical turned Tory: founder member of the Reform Club 1836–1864: chairman of Administrative Reform Association, 1856: P.C. 1878: a.k.a. 'Tear 'Em'.

[233] John Orrell Lever (1824–1897), M.P. Galway 1859–1865, 1880–1885. Speculator and director of shipping companies.

[234] Sir S. Northcote, *Conservative Finance and Liberal Fallacies: Speeches delivered in . . .* (1879).

[235] W.H. Smith (1825–1891), 1st lord of the admiralty 1877–1880. Smith made an official visit to Cyprus, 30 October 1878.

[236] Lady Margaret Cecil, the diarist's step-daughter, who never married.

[237] Steward at Knowsley.

[238] Head keeper at Knowsley.

[239] Head forester at Knowsley.

[240] Knowsley librarian, also responsible for minor local charities and almsgiving: a man of erudition.

[241] Henry Dunckley (1923–1896), Manchester journalist: ed. of *Manchester Examiner,* 1855–1889: also Baptist minister: a.k.a. 'Verax'.

[242] (Sir) T.V. Lister (1832–1902), assistant under-sec. at F.O. 1873–1894: nephew of Clarendon and Sir G.C. Lewis.

[243] W.E. Gladstone, 'Electoral Facts (No. I)', *Nineteenth Century,* Vol. 4, November 1878, pp. 955–968.

[244] Who had cut U.S. nets for fishing on Sunday.

[245] Joseph Chamberlain, 'The Caucus', *Fortnightly Review,* Vol. 30 o.s., November 1878, pp. 721–741.

[246] William George Clark (1821–1878), Derby's tutor at Trinity College, Cambridge: Shakespearean scholar.

[247] Sir John Robert Townshend, 3rd vt Sydney (1805–1890), succ. his father 1831: lord-lieut. of Kent, 1856–1890: lord chamberlain 1859–1866, 1868–1874, lord steward 1880–1885, 1886: cr. Earl Sydney of Scadbury, February 1874. His estates consisted of about 3,000 acres worth £6,615 p.a. rental.

[248] Sir Henry Ponsonby (1825–1895): maj-gen. 1868: priv. sec. to the Queen, 1870–: P.C. 1880, G.C.B. 1887.

[249] 'The peasants of our Indian empire', *Westminster Review,* No. 110 o.s., July 1878, pp. 135–150.

[250] Charles Hardinge, 2nd vt Hardinge of Lahore 1822–1894: M.P. (Cons.) 1851–1856: succ. 1856: priv. sec. to his father when viceroy: junior min. 1858–1859.

[251] Lord Ronald Charles Sutherland-Gower (1845–1911 or 1916), 4th s. of 2nd D. of Sutherland, M.P. Sutherland 1867–1874: writer and sculptor, creating the Shakespeare monument at Stratford: friend of Disraeli and Queen Victoria: bohemian, sometimes seen as 'the wickedest man in London'.

[252] Charles Darwin (1809–1882), Kentish country gentleman and naturalist, much visited by the Derbys.

[253] Derby's Manchester banker.

[254] Julius, Count Andrassy (1823–1890), Austrian foreign minister November 1871–1879.

[255] Capt. H.E. Stanley (1840–1867) died from a fall from his horse. He was the 3rd s. of Henry Stanley, the black sheep of the family.

[256] G.W. Norman, Kentish country neighbour, of Bromley: owned 2,849 acres, £4,704 rental.

[257] Sir J.F. Lennard of Wickham, West Wickham: b. 1816, succ. 1861: 4,870 acres, £7,636 rental.

[258] Col. John Ireland Blackburne (b. 1817), succ. 1874, of Hale Hall, Widnes: owned 3,148 acres, £8,490 value. 'A weak silly sort of person . . . a worthy and intensely respectable country squire, has not two ideas on politics' (diary, 22 October 1875).

[259] Sir Richard K. Brooke, 7th bart (1814–1888) of Norton Priory, Runcorn: high sheriff of Cheshire, 1870.

[260] Either Rowland E. Egerton-Warburton (1804–1891) of Arley Hall, Cheshire, Tractarian, author of *Hunting Songs* (1846), whose wife (*née* Mary Brooke of Norton) was a childhood friend of Mrs. Gladstone: or (since he was totally blind from glaucoma from 1874–1875) perhaps his son and heir, Piers Egerton-Warburton, M.P. for Mid-Cheshire 1876–1885, water-colourist and Col. of Cheshire Yeomanry, who d. 1913.

[261] George Sclater-Booth, 1st Baron Basing (1826–1894), cr. baron 1887: president, local government board 1874–1880: M.P. (Cons.) Hants. N. 1857–1887.

[262] Col. George Villiers (1847–1892), military secretary to Lytton, later serving at St. Petersburg, Berlin, and Paris.

[263] Auberon Herbert (1838–1906), s. of 3rd E. of Carnarvon: president of Oxford Union: Northcote's priv. sec.: M.P. (Lib.) Nottingham 1870–1874: vegetarian: supported Arch, Bradlaugh, and republicanism.

[264] 5th Marquess of Londonderry (1821–1884), prominent Mason, 2nd s. of 3rd Marquess: styled Earl Vane from 1854 (when his father died) to 1872 (when he succ. his half-brother Frederick): lord-lieut. co. Durham 1880–1884.

[265] Sir James Caird (1816–1892), agricultural expert: author of *The Landed Interest and the Supply of Food* (London, 1878), pp. xv and 160.

[266] Lytton took office on 4 January 1876 but perhaps discussed plans before that date.

[267] *Recte* Balkans.

[268] Carnarvon remarried, 26 December 1878, his cousin Elizabeth Howard.

[269] Arthur, 6th Earl Stanhope (1838–1905): styled Viscount Mahon 1855–1875: M.P. (Cons.) 1868, 1870–1875: whip 1874–1875: 1st Church Estates Commissioner 1878–1905: Lord-Lieut. of Kent 1890–1905: son of the historian, brother of Edward Stanhope the Conservative Cabinet minister.

[270] Henry Thomas Pelham, 3rd E. of Chichester (1804–1886), educ. Westminster and Trinity: eccles. commissioner 1841–death: chief commissioner for ecclesiastical estates 1850–1878: lord-lieut. Sussex 1860–1886.

[271] 8th D. of Argyll (1823–1900), succ. 1847: sec. for India 1868–1874.

[272] H.C.E. Childers (1927–1896), M.P. (Lib.) Pontefract 1860–1885: Gladstonian minister: 1st v-c of Melbourne University.

[273] Meeting of shadow cabinet to discuss Indian blue book and the recall of parliament (see Ramm, II, i, 90): 'Meeting at Ld Granville's. No great result but feeling on the whole good' (Matthew [ed.], *Gladstone Diaries)*.

[274] Leonard Courtney, 'The migration of centres of industrial energy', *Fortnightly Review*, Vol. 30 o.s., December 1878, pp. 801–820.

[275] Henry George, 3rd Earl Grey (1802–1894).

[276] Lord Ravensworth (1821–1903), 2nd Earl of: succ. his father as baron, March 1878: M.P. S. Northumberland 1852–1878.

[277] Edward O'Brien, 14th Baron Inchiquin (1839–1900), succ. father 1872: lord-lieut. co. Clare 1879–1900: rep. peer (I) 1873–1900: owned about 20,000 acres, £11,681 rental, all in co. Clare: left £2,614 net.

[278] *Parl. Deb.*, 3, vol. ccxliii, cols. 5–81 (5 December 1878): debate on the Address in the Lords.

[279] Hastings Russell, 9th Duke of Bedford (1819–1891), succ. his cousin 1872.

[280] William Russell, 8th Duke of Bedford (1809–1872), succ. father 1861: recluse in later life: d. unm.

[281] John Lawrence, Baron Lawrence (1811–1879), viceroy of India 1863–September 1868: chairman of London School Board 1870–1875.

[282] Sir F. Napier, 9th baron Napier of Ettrick (1819–1898), diplomatist: governor of Madras 1866, acting viceroy 1872.

[283] W.H. Leatham (1815–1889), M.P. (Lib.) Wakefield 1865–1868, Yorks. West Riding S. 1880–1885: banker (1836–1851) and poet.

[284] Sir Charles Dilke (1843–1911), 2nd bart, M.P. (Lib.) 1868–1886, 1892–1911: foreign under-sec. 1880–1882.

[285] Sir Wilfrid Lawson (1829–1906), 2nd bt, M.P. (Lib.) 1859–1906 with short interludes: temperance reformer, home ruler, and humorist: succ. to title and estates, 1867.

[286] Maldon election, 12 December 1878: Courtauld (Lib.) 671; Abdy (Cons.) 530. Result at 1874 general election: Sandford (Cons.) 622; Bennett (Lib.) 519.

[287] Minor port in S.E. Turkey.

[288] John Mulholland, 1st Baron Dunleath (1819–1895), eldest s. of Andrew Mulholland, Belfast industrialist: M.P. (Cons.) Downpatrick 1874–1885, cr. baron 1892.

[289] His mother (d. 1867) was the eldest of the three accomplished Sheridan sisters, daughters of Thomas Sheridan, known as 'the three beauties', and a grand-daughter of R.B. Sheridan, dramatist. His father d. of a morphine overdose.

[290] Princess Alice (1843–1878), Queen Victoria's 3rd child, m. 1862 Frederick of Hesse, becoming Grand Duchess of Hesse-Darmstadt.

[291] Spencer Walpole (1806–1896), cabinet minister: home sec. 1852, 1858–1859, 1866–1867.

[292] Lord Arthur Cecil, Derby's stepson (1851–1913): farmer in Scotland who made a *mésalliance*.

[293] Bristol election, 16 December 1878: Lewis Fry (Lib.) 9,342; Sir Ivor Guest (Cons.) 7,795.

[294] Clarke Aspinall, coroner of Liverpool, d. 1891.

[295] Northcote announced that the government's plan to make a grant to Turkish refugees would be dropped, 16 December 1878.

[296] Estate accountant.

[297] *Parl Deb.*, 3, vol. ccxliii, cols. 273–288.

[298] Cf. entry of 23 September 1878 above.

[299] William Thomson, Baron Kelvin (1824–1907), physicist and inventor: professor at Glasgow 1846–1899.

[300] Jane Ellice Hopkins, *Life and Letters of James Hinton* (1878).

[301] The diarist's brother Col. F. Stanley, then Sec. for War.

[302] G. Duncan (b. 1845), brother and heir presumptive of 3rd E. Camperdown: m. a New England lady (she d. 1910). His sister Julia was lady of the bedchamber to Queen Victoria 1874–1885, having married George Ralph 4th Lord Abercromby in 1858, and probably a source of Court gossip for Derby. Duncan, a Kentish neighbour, was active in business.

[303] W.B. Brett, 1st vt Esher (1815–1899), judge 1868–1897: cr. baron 1885, vt 1897.

[304] Reginald Brett, 2nd vt Esher (1852–1930), succ. father 1899: Hartington's priv. sec. 1880–1883.

[305] Philip Beresford Beresford-Hope (1851–?), e.s. of A.J. Beresford-Hope, politician, by Mildred. dau. of James, 2nd Marquess of Salisbury. He m. 1883 an American, who d. 1900.

1879

January–June

Notes on private & estate finance

I have on private account invested in 1st class railway debentures or debenture stocks
(not shares)   £200,000
Giving interest at a little over 4%   £8,000
I have in reserve   £6,500
And with Coutts or in hand   £2,200
Total nominal value is therefore   £208,700

But the securities are all at about 5% premium; therefore the real value is over £216,000.
    I have drawn from the Knowsley office in the last 9 years exactly £210,000.
    I have arranged that all charities, etc., shall be paid by a separate account with
Heywood, so that they may be independent of my private allowance.
    I shall draw this year £30,000, making total drawn £240,000. And when this is done
my savings will rather more than cover all that I have drawn.

★ ★ ★ ★ ★

Estate & personal debts

The estate owes to my brother   £170,000
Interest on which is   £7,350
There is due to C. Stanley   £24,000
Interest on which is   £1,080
Total estate debt   £194,000

In addition I owe to Ly D.[erby] which is to be repaid in the present year £10,000
    I have promised to my sister for her children £2,000 a year for 10 years: two instalments are paid

Knowsley rents are due:
In Jan., Feb., March   £20,000
In April & May   £95,000
June to Oct. inclusive   £57,000
Nov. & Dec.   £8,000
Total   £180,000

This calculation was made a few years ago; there has been an increase since, but in the main it is still correct.

In May, when the rents are in, I ought to have a surplus free for investment, varying from £40,000 upwards.

In July 1883, if alive, & unless I prefer to invest in land, I shall have invested from savings £400,000.

Knowsley estate receipts up to July 1877 were for the last 12 months	£184,858
Of the above:	
Liverpool, Bootle, & Kirkdale gave	£39,128
E. Lancashire estates	£72,443
Home estates	£49,977
Outlying estates	£23,296

* * * * *

There are due to me from railway companies various sums:

From the Cheshire Lines (to be paid at once)	about £75,000
From the L. & Yorkshire (no date fixed)	over £50,000

From the same for Bury station, amount not yet settled, but I take it provisionally at £45,000

From the L. & N.W. Railway Co. payable soon (say)	£15,000

Total (as near as I can estimate) about £185,000

The trustees have on hand or in the funds	£18,000
Making in all something over	£200,000

Of this I owe for Holwood, on [Mr.] Alexander's death	£60,000
And C. Stanley should be paid off	£24,000
Thus there is already appropriated	£84,000
Leaving free for investment, but not yet in hand	£119,000

I have paid off in the last year £12,000 due to the trustees of my late uncle H.S. This is the only debt discharged, my uncle C. Stanley positively objecting to be paid off.

I have bought but little land, Hollydale near Keston (50 acres) being the chief purchase: nothing else beyond a field or two enclosed in mine. What I have sold, though considerable in value, is nothing appreciable in point of acreage. But my savings have been large: investments were in Jan. 1878 £140,000: they are now £200,000, making an increase of £60,000 in the year.

2 Feb.: Agree to buy 85 acres in the Fylde for £4,250 (Sir U. Shuttleworth) Agree to buy 175 acres near Holwood, £22,750 (Sir W. Dyke)

20 Mar. : Agree to buy 245 acres near Haslemere (Rev. Parsons) which increases the Witley estate to about 1,650 acres

28 Apr.: Received from Moult . . . the summary of receipts . . . for the year ending 1 July 1878:

   . . . Total receipts for last year are   £182,682

The first time, I think, in 20 years that there has been a falling off, but it is not considerable: in fact with the two arrears paid, which I am told they will be, there is no falling off, but a slight increase.

15 June: Have settled to buy 215 acres more in the Fylde. To the 175 acres near Holwood, I have added 35 more, which are paid for. To meet these various payments, I have drawn from Heywood only £15,000. I have paid Ly D.'s debt of £10,000.

1 Jan. 1879: Knowsley. We have staying in the house C. Schouvaloff, C. Münster, his son & daughter: the Galloways: P. Hope: Lionel & Margaret [Cecil]: Sanderson: Sir B. & Ly Brett & their son.

Messrs. Lee & Nightingale sent over a reporter by arrangement, & I gave him the substance of a speech which I am to make at Rochdale tomorrow. It is longer than I meant, & will be nearly an hour in the delivery.

Shooting . . . we killed 470 head . . . Hale came out to see us, & he, Sanderson, & I walked home . . . together.

Sent Sanderson his quarterly cheque for £200.

. . . Rather nervous & uncomfortable about my speech tomorrow: a feeling which I find does not diminish with years: & there is something which adds to it in the sensation of going to a strange place, & addressing an audience which one has never seen before.

. . . Talk with Münster among other matters of the supposed leanings of Bismarck to protection, which he does not admit, but contends that the cost of the German military system is so great that without a general system of indirect taxation it cannot be borne: it is therefore necessary to impose import duties &, if incidentally some of these are protective, that is an accident which cannot be helped. The explanation is ingenious, but I doubt its accuracy. It does not seem, however, that the intended duties are meant to be heavy.

As usual, Münster shakes his head ominously, & predicts fresh diplomatic trouble in May, when Roumelia is to be evacuated & the people will undoubtedly make a strong effort to unite with the emancipated Bulgarians. – What are we do to in that case?

2 Jan. 1879: . . . Leave at 12.30 for Rochdale . . .arrive about 3.15: am met on the platform by Mr. J. Ashworth, president of the Workmen's Club: he drives me to see the club, & partly round the town: which is better than most in these districts: the streets wide, well paved & lighted, the ground undulating, a good pleasure ground of 28 acres in the centre, a really fine town hall, in good taste: &, though there is a large proportion of the usual red brick two-storey houses, which without being absolutely squalid are mean & miserable in their appearance, these are intermixed with others built of the grey stone of the country which look neat & substantial. We dined at 4.30 at Mr. Ashworth's house, a villa just outside the town: the party 12 persons, Ashworths 3, Hugh Mason[1], the Mayor, the vicar Mr. Molesworth[2], Mr. Hutchinson, & 4 others.

At 6.00 we went to the town hall, which was full, & a very satisfactory building to speak in. Mr. Ashworth took the chair, some speeches were made, I was called upon in about an hour after we sat down, & spoke 50 minutes, very well listened to, & with fair though not complete satisfaction to myself. The audience was evidently satisfied, & the few references made by one to peace were cheered in a way that showed what the local feeling was. All ended before 9.00, & I drove with Mr. Hutchinson to his house about 2 miles out of town.

3 Jan. 1879: I was very hospitably received . . . last night: supper, & billiards afterwards. Made acquaintance with my host's family. Mrs. H. is an heiress, has a mill of her own, which she professes to manage for her sons: a good specimen of the Lancashire manufacturer's wife, plainspoken, with a fine provincial accent, & decided opinions as to the evil ways of the lower classes. She & her husband between them have collected a good many pictures, some really good, others daubs: the house handsome, large, with good conservatory, but scarcely any pleasure ground. Mr. H. has about 1,000 acres, he says, but it is black rough land, not attractive nor probably of much value.

Visited the mill (woollen): noticed that a very small stream drove a turbine of 33 h.p. supplying most of the power wanted: drove thence to the mills of the Bright family about 2 miles off: they employ 1,500 hands, partly in carpet making, partly in cotton spinning: saw several members of the family, two sons & a cousin: called on John Bright, whose house is close by: some talk on the prospects of free trade, etc., but nothing of special significance: several persons being present, & of various opinions: saw at the works a telephone, the best I have seen, communicating with their warehouse in Manchester 13 miles away. I spoke through it, was heard & answered with as much ease as if the other interlocutor were in the next room.

. . . On the whole, this visit to Rochdale has passed off in a satisfactory way. It has pleased the people to whom it was paid: &, whether or no what I have said is a success in the sense of being popular, it embodies various ideas which I wished to bring out, & which possibly may be of use. From the conversation of the Rochdale people I have learnt less than I expected: in fact, the condition of different trades differs so much that all generalisations are apt to be inaccurate.

4 Jan. 1879: . . . See Brailsford, & talk with him about his pension: he looks very ill, & is probably unfit for work during the rest of his life. It is chiefly his own fault, but great allowance must be made for the hardship of a keeper's life.

See Barnes, talk with him as to the shooting, killing off hares, etc., & more particularly destroying the rabbits which have got into the young plantations.

Write to Mr. Torr[3], declining to help the new bishopric: send £50 to the Literary Fund, & £25 to the St. James's parochial charities.

. . . News of another (Cornish) bank having failed: which increases the general distrust.

Much writing in the papers about the bursting of a big gun on board one of the new ironclads (*Thunderer*): it killed 8 men, & wounded 33. . . . The *Pall Mall* characteristically draws the inference that, as we cannot be sure of our ships, we ought to have a great many more of them.

5 Jan. 1879: Day cold & snow on the ground. Church in morning.

In the *Pall Mall* of yesterday is a shrewd sensible letter from an old officer, pointing out that the changes made in the constitution of the army have resulted in an effect entirely contrary to what was anticipated & desired by their promoters. It was thought & said that when purchase was abolished the army would become a profession into which poor men would put their sons, & that a class of hardworking officers would thus be obtained, who would look on their work as the occupation of their lives. – Instead of this, the necessity of facilitating promotion has led to the adoption of a scheme of compulsory retirement, according to which most captains will have to leave the army with a pension of £200 a year at the age of 38 or 40, comparatively few going on into the higher grades. But such retirement does not suit men who have their living to earn, while it exactly suits heirs to estates, large or small, who have a competence to fall back upon at their father's death, & only desire employment in the meanwhile. Hence probably the service is likely to be more specially aristocratic, or rather plutocratic, than before. An odd result: but not the only instance where a reform good in itself has been of most service to the very class against which it was directed. The leading opponents of the Corn Laws sincerely believed that their abolition would break down the landed aristocracy: which on the contrary is far stronger than it was before.

6 Jan. 1879: . . . See Broomfield, as to damage done to young plantations . . . See Moult, & go with him over the list of benefactions to see if any should be omitted. I have told Hale to give notice to those concerned that I will not any longer contribute to the various county registration societies.

Walk with M. for an hour: day cold, snow still on ground, & east wind bringing fog. Did not go out again.

In afternoon, took a hot-air bath, staying in it half an hour. The feeling was agreeable, & there is no subsequent discomfort.

Saw Hale, & arranged with him to give £20 for this & the same for next year to a Mrs. Hiscock, widow of a keeper. He had not been long enough in my service for a life pension, but I had allowed her £30 for 3 years, which are now exhausted.

Lionel [Cecil] left us this evening: he has been of great use to M. & me in attending on our guests, & especially in shooting affairs. Mrs. W.E. West[4], 2 girls, & 2 boys, arrived from Wales.

7 Jan. 1879: Order from *Hansard* 100 copies of the Afghan speech[5] for distribution: a thing I have seldom done, but it is so absurdly distorted in the papers that I wish my friends, or some of them, to know what I really said.

. . . Short walk: day cold & disagreeable, with violent east wind. Rent day dinner, for the Knowsley tenants, where M. & I appear as usual, & I make the usual speech. All very cordial.

We expected Col. W.E. West to join his wife & children: but he has made an excuse not to come. He has taken to strange ways of late, adopting a vegetarian diet not on sanitary but ascetic grounds, & altogether his family are not quite easy about him. But he was the same at Oxford, & it is only an old disease that has taken a new form. There would be nothing in it beyond a little harmless eccentricity, only that it is impossible to forget his poor brother De La Warr[6]: who, however, would probably have been alive now if he had had what W.E. has, a steady & regular everyday employment to keep him straight. His last freak is insisting that he is too highly paid, & wanting to return a part of his salary on that ground: which, as Ld Penrhyn[7] himself fixed it last year, & has upwards of £100,000 a year, seems a needless piece of delicacy.

Mrs. West tells curious stories of the Gladstone family: thinks Mrs. G. one of the simplest minded & kindest hearted of human beings, but eccentric beyond ordinary measure: the children of the family complain that she will ask many more people than their house can hold, so that they have to turn out in order to make room: on one occasion Mrs. G. was short of money to pay her railway fare, & appealed to Mrs. West to help her. Next day the daughters apologised, explaining that it was impossible to leave money in their mother's hands because, whatever might be the purpose for which it was designed, she was sure to give it away in charity leaving her bills unpaid. A queer household.

8 Jan. 1879: Walk early with M. – weather very cold & disagreeable, strong east wind & snow drifted.

Tenants' dinner again, which we attended, going in at the end: my health was drunk,

& also that of M., for both of which I returned thanks. – I hear from Hale that there is no complaining, & no backwardness in making payments. In fact, with low rents, with Liverpool close at hand, & supplying market garden produce, in which foreign countries cannot compete, the farmers in this country are untouched by the general depression of industry.

. . . I receive daily notices of the Rochdale speech, from which I gather that it has produced a good deal of effect, especially that part of it (for the sake of which I made the whole) containing a warning against the influence of war interests. W.R. Greg[8] & old Warde Norman have written in specially warm terms: & I have a letter from Dean Blakesley[9] in which he says that in my present position I can exercise more influence over affairs than I could in any office. Greg's approval is natural, for I think most of my habitual ideas in politics have been suggested by his books, even where my conclusions are not identical with his: which of late is often the case, for he has grown much of an alarmist.

9 Jan. 1879: . . . Trade returns for the year published: very bad: of British produce there is exported 192 m. against 198 m. in 1877, which itself was a considerable falling off: imports are 366 m., which is too great a disproportion, though not greater than last year. – I am interested, however, in seeing that ten years ago, when there was a temporary falling off in trade, though slighter than at the present time, exactly the same things were said as to over-population, decline of English population, & so forth, as are being said now. This I verify by reference to the pamphlets & treatises of that date, some of which might seem to have been written within the last month or two, so exactly do they anticipate the present state of feeling.

Ld Beaconsfield is in the gout at Hughenden: not in danger, nor seriously ill, but I note the fact here, because it is characteristic of him that when his illness was first reported he authorised an absolute contradiction, the report going on to say that he was in his usual health: (he could never bear the notion of being supposed to be laid up, or unfit for work): this being of course known to be untrue, the contradiction made everybody believe the matter to be a great deal more serious than it was: whereas, if he had been content to let the exact fact be known, there would have been no fidget on the subject. The *Standard* persisted in its story, in the face of official contradiction, & proved to be right in the main.

Moult comes . . . & leaves a mem. of the rents paid in . . . He tells me that the proportion paid in gold is lessening: this year it is under £1,800 [out of £11,239]: most of the larger farmers use the bank, & give notes or cheques. He thinks, however, that the old habit of hoarding has not altogether disappeared.

Walk early with M. Cold & snow on ground continue, with sharp east wind.

10 Jan. 1879: Cold & snow continue, with strong east wind last night. Nothing much to do: sort & tear up old letters, throw away old pamphlets . . .

I have not noted . . . the purport of sundry conversations which I had with Schouvaloff & Münster while they were here. I learnt from Münster that Schou. is not well pleased with his position in England: that he had a promise, or something like one, from the Emperor that he should succeed to Gortschakoff's place, & it was intended that the latter should resign at the end of last year: but for some reason not known this arrangement has been altered, & Schou. has written to beg that he may be allowed to retire, not choosing to serve under Gortschakoff again. That vain old man has never ceased to court the favour of the military, or Sclavonic party, in Russia, & says openly that he had to defend

Russian interests at Berlin against his colleague as well as against foreigners. Schou. told
M. that he had lost favour with the Emperor by his successful protest against the entry
of Russian troops into Constantinople. The Emperor yielded to his argument that such a
step would probably lead to war, but has never forgotten or quite forgiven his ambassador's interference. So Schou. says, & the story is intrinsically probable. – Münster
writes that there is in Russia a revival of the military or Sclavonic sentiment, & that he is
much afraid of fresh trouble impending. (Note, however, that he has held this language
at all times during the last two years, & evidently holds it by order.) Both he & Schou.
frequently refer to the danger to be feared in May, when the Russians evacuate Roumelia,
& when there will almost certainly be a rising among the Roumelians who want to unite
with the new Bulgaria. What is to be done then? Will it be proposed, or allowed, that
English troops should be employed to keep the Roumelians in subjection to Turkey? If
not, what other troops are available, & under what conditions shall they be employed?
This is the question which perplexes diplomatists, & to which no solution appears to have
been found.

11 Jan. 1879: . . . The Lit. Fund Committee propose to select as chairman for their dinner
in May the young Prince Imperial! I express my objection to the choice on the grounds
. . . (3) that his selection is quite sure to be made use of by the anti-republican party in
France, backed by a large section of English 'society', as a demonstration in favour of
Imperialism, which is exactly what we wish to avoid.

12 Jan. 1879: Cold still continues: 18° of frost last night.
    Church: write letters, etc., as usual. Little or no business to do. Walk in afternoon with
M. Snow falling.

13 Jan. 1879: Left Knowsley soon after 10.00: . . . roads slippery & dangerous with partial
thaw: day very fine: at station met Sefton & with him to Manchester for a special meeting of the Hospital trustees[10]. The business was formal . . . All was over by 1.00. . . . There
I met the Mayor, & had some conversation with him on the distress: he took me to the
offices of the present relief committee, which is well organised, & has more than enough
to do. Help is given by tickets for meat, bread, vegetables, coal, etc., care being taken, as
is said, to prevent the tickets being sold, as they otherwise would be, for drink. The Mayor
seemed fairly confident of being able to get through the winter without worse trouble,
though admitting that the distress is more severe than has been known since 1862–63, &
that the end is uncertain. He said there are now 8,000 families in receipt of relief in
Manchester alone, not counting Salford or the outlying districts: 40,000 persons. He
spoke also of the danger lest those who are being relieved should lose the habit of work:
cases have not been rare in which low wages are refused, the men saying they had rather
draw their 8s. a week & do nothing than earn 10s. or 11s. Met Sefton again at the station,
& with him as far as Huyton, where got out & walked home.

14 Jan. 1879: Kirkdale at 11.00, got there with some difficulty, at least with some anxiety, the roads being like ice, though a thaw has set in. Sat till 5.30. Magistrates present,
about 30 at the beginning. . . . hardly any assaults: which is due to hard times, & consequent enforced sobriety. The refreshment room & all its appliances even dirtier than
before: I was glad to hear others complain.

Home about 6.30. Took a hot-air bath, which is pleasant, but I suspect weakening if taken often. Some fatigue in evening.

Read an interesting paper by Prof. Rogers[11], the radical professor & financier, on British finance in the future: the purport of which is that, if the English nation ever takes to temperance, a new departure in financial policy must be the result. He supports a graduated income tax . . . He also proposes to tax unprofitable property, such as pictures: the estates of corporations: & land in the shape of probate duty. Not on the whole a pleasant prospect for capitalists. But I do not believe that the Whigs in general would take up these ideas. Prof. Rogers who is a thoughtful economist speaks of the rise in value of gold as undoubted, & apparently deals with it as likely to continue. Is this an accepted fact? Twenty years ago, when California & Australia were first opened, all the world except a few held it certain that gold would fall at least 50%. It did fall to some extent, but far less than was anticipated, & appears to be now rising again. Prof. Rogers lays great stress on the predominance of the richer classes in parliament, saying that they do not care about even an increased income tax, for it does not seriously affect them, & hence they are indifferent to public economy. He quotes a saying new to me, that the prosperity of English finance depends on the majority of the English people being sots, & the majority of foreigners being fools – meaning that if their industrial energies were not hampered by bad govt. they would make for themselves much of what they now take from us.

The cry for protection – now called reciprocity – is growing louder, & it is evident that in manufacturing districts the Tories (I do not call them Conservatives) intend to trade upon it. In most constituencies it will not work, for everybody knows that bread & meat cannot be taxed again. The French have given notice of terminating the commercial treaty, which is unlucky at the present moment: & Bismarck's avowed intention of raising a revenue by moderate protectionist duties strengthens the hands of the anti-free-trade party here. But the same cry was raised in 1869, & died away of itself when prosperity returned.

15 Jan. 1879: Kirkdale at 10.00, only 6 or 7 magistrates present, but they are enough for the work. Sat till 2.30, when adjourned, having finished all the business. Home, & short walk with M. Slight, but not excessive weariness.

We have had good juries at these sessions, & there has been no failure of justice. One prisoner was rightly acquitted: all the rest were either convicted or pleaded guilty. The longest sentence was one of 7 years, on a returned convict, for robbery: the shortest was a month . . . The offences were all against property, except 2.

Warm weather, frost & snow all gone.

Wrote to Northcote, accepting the chair of his proposed commission on Indian silver, but on condition that Goschen also accepts.

. . . Received a long . . . letter from . . . Birmingham, in favour of what is called 'reciprocity': evidently written in order to draw me into a controversy, & to be published. . . . It appears clearly that the Conservative party in Birmingham (headed by a certain Capt. Burnaby[12], a leader among the Jingos) is going to agitate against free trade, & make that their election cry. I answer briefly, declining to argue the question.

16 Jan. 1879: Kirkdale again at 11.00, for a bastardy appeal . . . It lasted 5 hours. . . . Home about 5.00. Hard frost again, & roads dangerous, though not as bad as they were. Rather weary with three days' work, though it has not been either very long or very hard:

but, though habit has made me familiar with the ordinary questions which arise in practice, & so far lightened the burden, I find the difficulty of hearing increases &, when one has to strain one's attention to catch every word that is spoken, the fatigue of the effort becomes considerable.

Knowsley receipts from Moult for the year ending 1 July 1878. . . . The general summary is:

. . . Received £185,380. Last year the figures were £184,858: so that even in these hard times there is an increase shown, though a small one. Divided, the returns are:

East Lancashire estates	£73,463	
Liverpool estates	£40,183	
Home estates	£44,678	(and £3,536 due)
Outlying estates	£22,453	(and £1,063 due)
Total	£180,780	

Bury, as usual, shows the largest & steadiest growth.

17 Jan. 1879: Letter from the doctor attending Mrs. H. S[tanley] requesting to be allowed to call in assistance . . . Things do look as if her life would not last long. She will die unregretted by any human being: but the granddaughter remains, & what is to be done with her I cannot even conjecture.

With Broomfield through various plantations near & beyond Knowsley village. . . . Well satisfied in general . . . Settled to make a pinetum in what was a paddock . . .

18 Jan. 1879: We had meant to shoot . . . & Sefton was to join, but a fresh fall of snow stopped us . . .

. . . Col. Champneys[13] writes from Hendon that his brother, who has the living of Badsworth, is dead. The living is said to be worth £700 a year, & in my gift. I write a suitable answer & consult M. & Hale as to the successor. I think young Hopwood[14] ought to have it, but shall not decide today.

19 Jan. 1879: Day fine overhead, but cold, & snow on the ground. Wrote nearly 20 notes & letters of one sort or another.

. . . Wrote to F. Hopwood to offer the living of Badsworth to his son . . .

. . . Received a letter from Fawcett sending me his book on free trade & protection . . . In my reply I pointed out that there is the less danger of a really strong protectionist reaction, as the agricultural classes well know that to tax food again would not be possible, & that is the only kind of protection which they care about.

. . . Promised £25 to Mrs. Tait's memorial, rather against my will: but Tait[15] was headmaster of Rugby while I was there, & I do not like to seem to have forgotten old days. Besides, he has shown sense in his office, & made enemies by resisting the fanatical party.

20 Jan. 1879: Troubled with cold, & frost very hard, with high wind: but I went to Manchester, not liking to miss the meeting. Met Sefton at Edgehill. Winmarleigh, Egerton, Ashworth[16], Mason, Hutchinson, Bailey, O. Heywood, etc., present – 15 in all. We sat till 1.30, & agreed to accept the terms offered by the Corporation & other sellers at Southport, & to enlarge the hospital there. Also to increase the sum to be spent on the Devonshire hospital at Buxton.

Talk with Winmarleigh, who is helping Taylor[17] to find a new High Sheriff for the year: he complains of difficulty: from the size of the county, the cost is very heavy, over £2,000, & the heads of old families do not think it worth while. On the other hand there are always candidates for the office, but of the wrong sort: rich men without social position, who will spend any sum to get it.

Talk of the Hesketh[18] family – the imbecile baronet, it seems, is dead: and his brother has succeeded, re-uniting the estates. But I heard some time ago that he is following in his father's ways.

See Hale, & settle to send relief to the bargemen on the canal in Newborough & Burscough. They are in much want, being out of employ by no fault of theirs, since the frost set in.

21 Jan. 1879: . . . Weather continues very hard, thick ice on the ponds, & a coat of frozen snow on the ground. Did not leave the house.

In the afternoon the Mayor and ex-Mayor of Liverpool (Messrs. Royden[19] & Forwood[20]) called together, by appointment, about this new scheme of a college intended for the upper & middle classes of Liverpool. It is evidently intended to be a rival of Owen's College, Manchester: there is some soreness because Liverpool men send their sons there, as being cheaper & nearer than Cambridge: & it is wished to be able to give the same kind of education nearer home. . . . The promoters do not intend to make a beginning until they can secure £40,000: they require for efficiency at least £75,000, but would start with less, trusting to time to make good the deficiency. I promised them help to the extent of £2,000 when they have raised £40,000, another £1,000 if they reach £60,000, and perhaps another if they get up to £80,000. In short, I will take on myself 5%, or 1/20, of the cost. They seemed well satisfied. They have a good many promises of £1,000 each, but none larger.

I took them to the drawing room to have tea with Ly D. They talked of Manchester, where it is believed that a mistake has been made in granting relief too freely, & without precautions against abuse: cases had occurred where relief tickets had been presented, & delicacies such as tinned meats, potted lobsters, etc., asked for: the casual wards of the workhouses are empty, vagrants & tramps getting outdoor relief with the rest: all possible enough, but one cannot trust a Manchester man when he talks about Liverpool, nor *vice versa*. They seemed confident of getting through the winter without difficulty: but said – which was also what I heard in Manchester – that the worst suffering was in a rather higher class, that of the small shopkeepers & clerks. The shops especially suffer, for they have been encouraged by the high wages of the last few years to extend their business recklessly: & now their customers, the workingmen, cannot pay.

22 Jan. 1879: Frost harder than before, 16° in the night. Troubled with cold, & stayed at home.

See Hale, who gives me the comparatively satisfactory news that the Cheshire Lines Co. have agreed to pay down £20,000 on account out of the £74,000 they owe me. As the balance carries interest, & I do not want to use it just yet, the arrangement suits me well enough.

23 Jan. 1879: Frost continues, 15° in the night, but no wind. Still troubled with cold in the head, but went out thrice . . . Walk with M. both in morning & afternoon: but slippery roads, & cold overhead, make exercise disagreeable.

. . . The North Norfolk election is carried by the Conservatives[21], at which their journals are exultant: though it is only keeping what they had before, & Norfolk is the most doggedly Tory county in England. Their rejoicing shows the extent of their previous alarm: I cannot imagine how a Liberal victory can ever have been expected in that district.

24 Jan. 1879: . . . The newspapers, especially the *Telegraph*, have for some time past been full of vague hints of a new surprise intended for parliament: & the shape which such reports most frequently take is that of a new University education scheme for Ireland, which shall give to the Catholic hierarchy all they want, & secure the Catholic vote in return. There is much in a policy of this kind that would attract the Premier, one of whose favourite theories it is that Catholics ought to be Tories: & it would be congenial to the high-church sympathies of several of his colleagues. But the Irish Conservatives would oppose to a man: & their certain defection is probably more than a compensation for the gain of doubtful & not over-respectable allies. Another objection is the presence of Cairns in the Cabinet. Cairns has shown himself flexible enough in all conscience, & has earned his earldom thereby: but, if he has a conviction in the world, it is on the side of Irish Protestantism: & I can scarcely imagine that he would sanction any measure which conceded as much as the Catholics would accept.

Another & more probable report is that the D[uke] of Connaught[22] is to be made Lord Lieut[enant] – a doubtful arrangement as to constitutional precedent & convenience, but it would please the Queen, & also a certain section of the Irish people.

25 Jan. 1879: Walk with M. after luncheon round the lake. Plan a new clump between the Stand & the water, about halfway down the hill.

Much talk with M. as to the lads' Scotch farm. They have spent in this year over £10,000, mostly upon it &, as their whole capital was never quite £80,000, & they have drawn upon it a good deal of late years, she is naturally uneasy as to the future. It is useless to talk to Arthur, who is like a child in such matters, & is fond of boasting that no advice ever makes him change his opinion: but Lionel has sense, and may be induced to cut down his outlay. Neither of them has inherited their father's carelessness about money: but, except in this matter of farming, they have not been reckless.

Letter from Lawrence, Mrs. H.S. is not very ill, but as usual has run up bills without end, & is screaming to have them paid. I discuss the question with Lawrence, . . . & await his reply.

26 Jan. 1879: In the night, 20° of frost: the greatest cold we have had yet, & I remember no frost that has lasted so long. Stayed at home most of the day: walk with M. in afternoon.

27 Jan. 1879: Shooting . . . The bag was about 110 head, nearly all pheasants. . . . Frost continues as before but, there being no wind, the cold was not greatly felt. Pleased to see how the spaces of open unreclaimed moss are gradually getting clothed with self-sown birch . . .

... More talk with M. as to the boys: she very uneasy expecting them to be ruined, for which I do not think there is as yet any sufficient cause: but her anxiety is a good deal due to nerves & health. To make her mind easy, I promised that if, at the expiration of their lease, 13 years hence, they are losers, I will make up their incomes to £1,000 each for their lives. Arthur's property is secured in trust for his wife, so that there is no fear for him: & Lionel has sense enough not to run through his means, though he may have been over-sanguine as to returns from his farm. My pledge is therefore not very burdensome, the more so as in any case I could not let my wife's children want. I believe that she has been frightened by Arthur's foolish talk: he professes indifference whether he is ruined or not, saying that he could always find employment as a land agent: which is partly conceit, & partly said merely to tease his mother.

28 Jan. 1879: Frost continues unabated: 17° last night.
    ... Made out a calculation of personal expenses for the year, for which I allot £5,000, independent of charities, but I do not think it will all be spent.
    The papers for some days past have been full of the Zulu war on which we seem to be launched: &, as far as their articles throw light on the circumstances, the quarrel seems unprovoked & unnecessary. It seems that the Zulu kingdom has for many years past been a kind of standing army in which the whole population up to a certain age is enlisted: we are now the only neighbours of the Zulus on the south & west, having annexed the Transvaal: & Sir B. Frere[23] accordingly concludes that the military preparations of the Zulu sovereign are a threat directed against England, & sends him a peremptory order to discontinue them. But surely we have been the aggressive party of the two, & a chief who has just seen his neighbours eaten up may naturally think his own turn likely to come next, & arm in self-defence. One would think that the case was one to be dealt with by peaceable assurances & friendly intercourse, not by intimidation. Is it likely that any king, civilised or savage, will accept without resistance or resentment a peremptory order to disarm, addressed to him by the head of a state on which he has never in any way acknowledged himself dependent? Things look as if Sir B. Frere had been following in Lytton's track – possibly by order, & with the same result of bringing about a little war. It is, however, possible that the newspapers may not have got the whole story, or not have got it accurately, & for the national credit one hopes so. Meanwhile, the effect of an expensive & inglorious war in S. Africa is so far good in that it will tie the hands of our ministers in Europe, & make a quarrel there less probable & less popular.
    Arthur C.[ecil] left us for Scotland.

29 Jan. 1879: Went early into Liverpool to attend the 18th meeting of the Lancashire Rifle Association: of which I have been a member since its first foundation. We met in the Town Hall. I opened the proceedings with a short speech. The council had sat before, I taking the chair, to settle the report.
    Cold continues, though less severe.

30 Jan. 1879: ... Letter from Lawrence, by which I find that Mrs. H.S. has £400 [p.a.] from the trustees, £100 from me, & in addition I paid £315 of debt for her last year. There is now a fresh demand for £125, & I answer that the matter must wait till we meet in London. It is absurd that £500 a year should not be enough for one old woman & a girl, living together in lodgings.

Letter from Statter, about distress in Bury. I authorise him to send £100 to the local relief fund.

See Barnes, & arrange a matter which has been in discussion as to New Year's gifts to the keepers. They are to have £1 each & something extra if Barnes reports that they have had specially hard work.

. . . Gave £50 in aid of the distress in Bootle, added to £20 given before.

. . . Declined an application from Bootle that I will increase the pay of the parson: to whom I have already handed over the church, which was my property, at least so that the pew rents came to me. Declined also a request for a new organ at Bickerstaffe: there being many things more urgent.

. . . Land belonging to Sir U.K. Shuttleworth in the Fylde is offered me which, being priced too high, I had refused before: the terms are now lower, & I will consider it.

1 Feb. 1879: See Broomfield, & give him many directions for the spring & early summer. See Latter, & give some last orders. Busy for an hour or more, destroying letters & papers which have accumulated in the last six weeks. Saw Hale, & talk with him over estate affairs. Various applications are considered & refused. – I agree to give 10s. a week for 12 weeks to a man who lives near the village, disabled by illness from work. – Also to give £20 to schools in Kirkham.

After discussion, I settle with Hale for the purchase of Sir U. Shuttleworth's land, 85 acres, lying alongside of mine in the Fylde. The price asked is £50 per acre, & Hale thinks it moderate. He began by asking a much higher price, but came down, finding that he could not get it. I am not in general inclined to extend the family possessions at a distance from home, but in the present case the addition is obviously an advantage to the estate.

. . . Speech delivered by Ld Hartington at Edinburgh, as rector of the University: it would not have been easy, among able & experienced public men, to find one who *prima facie* would seem less fitted for work of that kind, for he has never been a reader. What knowledge he has is gained by experience of men & things. Still he has acquitted himself well, his lecture is good sense, & to the purpose: though it is open to the comment of being from beginning to end a panegyric of Whig principles, & rather more openly political than the custom of the place allows on such occasions.

2 Feb. 1879: Frost continues, with a fresh fall of snow, which vexes me, for it will be destruction to the young plantations . . .

Received from Chadwick a satisfactory report as to Sir W. Dyke's land near Holwood. He has secured it, 175 acres in all, at the rate of £130 an acre, which is £5,000 less than asked, or than I expected. He now wants to buy about 24 acres more, from the same owner, with a view to exchange with Lubbock.

See Hale for the last time . . . I give £20 in aid of distress at Ormskirk . . .

Write to Northcote to know whether the commission on Indian silver is to come off, as I have heard nothing of it lately. The intention of the Indian govt. to substitute gold for silver as the measure of value has become public, & is criticised in various newspapers, especially in the *Spectator*: which has an able article pointing out (1) that the yearly supply of gold from the various mines of the world is diminishing, being now about £19,000,000 yearly, as against £26,000,000 in the early days of California & Australia: (2) that the adoption by Germany & the U.S. of a gold coinage has drawn heavily on this lessened supply, which is probably not now equal to the demand: (3) that the effect of the above conditions has been to lessen the purchasing power of gold, which had previously fallen during many years: (4) that the remarkable lowering of prices in the last 5 years is in great part due to the rise in value of gold: (5) that this rise has produced commercial depression, as the fall 30 years ago produced a temporary expansion of trade: (6) that from the above data it follows that a vast demand of gold from India will aggravate existing difficulties, & disturb the markets of the world. The writer goes on to contend that, if a gold coinage is created for India, it is sure to disappear from circulation, gold being more convenient for hoarding purposes than silver, & the habit of hoarding universal in the east. To the last conclusion it might be added that gold will be hoarded anyhow, whether made legal tender or not, since its value as metal can always be realised, that probably the increased use of it in this way has something to do with the scarcity which already exists: & that the proposed measures of the Indian govt. will make little difference. The article is full of interest & I have kept it for reference.

The papers have been full of the trial of the Glasgow bank directors . . . They have been convicted of issuing fraudulent balance sheets, & sentenced, two to 18 months, the rest to 8 months' imprisonment. The sentence is thought unduly light: but Ld Moncrieff[24], who tried the case, laid much stress on the absence of personal dishonesty: they had cheated for the benefit of the bank, & not for their own. It is perhaps more to the purpose to say that they are old men, holding high positions, & that the social ruin & disgrace of the sentence is in itself punishment enough.

3 Feb. 1879: Left Knowsley at 11.00, & to London, leaving M. at the Bletchley station, where the D[uke] of B[edford] received her. Weather has changed at last, & thaw is general. – St. J.[ames's] Square at 6.00, where busy on letters & papers. Sanderson dined with me.

4 Feb. 1879: Busy all day, as one is on first coming to London, without much work done to show for it. Went through various boxes containing old letters & papers, & destroyed a great many, though there remains a great deal to do in this line.

. . . Received from Northcote a letter in which he tells me that Goschen refuses to serve on the silver commission: will I accept Lowe or Fawcett instead? He adds very frankly that the Indian govt. & the Indian council are on one side in the matter of the proposed change of currency, the Treasury officials strongly on the other: & that the position of the Cabinet is awkward in having to decide between the two. It is for this reason that a commission is desired: the evident intention being that it shall take the responsibility of smashing Lytton's scheme. Northcote is quite right to make no disguise about the matter, but the policy seems weak for a govt. which has nothing to fear in the H. of C.

Called in Curzon St. & luncheon there, but with little pleasure. Short walk. Notes & letters most of the afternoon. Sanderson dined with me. According to Ly Dartrey, who is just returned from Ireland, & takes much interest in local affairs, the priests are more exorbitant than ever in their demands as to educational matters. In the parish where Dartrey House is, the bishop refused to allow the peasantry to send their children to a National school, though attended solely by Catholics, & directed by Catholic teachers, because the priest was not made sole manager. According to this statement, even lay help from Catholics is refused, if not absolutely subordinated to the priest's orders.

5 Feb. 1879: Letter from Hale, in which he prepares me for an outcry from the clergy of

Bootle. They had a promise among them of £1,000 from my father, which I made good: & now they want as much more, on the ground that two parsons have acted separately on the expectations thus held out. I note what he says . . .

Answer a Mr. Clare of Manchester, who wants to get up what he calls a conference on the Prisons Act of 1877. In other words to organise an attack upon it. I tell him I entirely approve of the policy of the Act, & have heard nothing that leads me to think that there can be any reasonable cause of complaint as to its working. If there is in Lancashire a general movement in favour of a conference upon it, I will not refuse to take part, but neither will I support the proposal.

Northcote called as he had announced his intention of doing, & we had some talk on the Indian proposal. He repeated in substance what he had said in his letter. I told him that, if I were to advise on the question of policy, I should recommend doing without an enquiry: acting on the responsibility of the Cabinet, & rejecting the hastily considered scheme which Lytton has been induced to sanction. What had they to fear? Opinion here was probably all one way, & I gathered from what he said that the Cabinet had made up their minds. If, however, they thought a commission necessary, I would not refuse to serve, provided someone known to the public as an economist, such as Lowe or Fawcett, will serve also. It is clear from what Northcote said that the result is prejudged but, so long as it is prejudged in the right direction, I do not object. . . .

6 Feb. 1879: Heard from Northcote that the Cabinet have decided not to hold any enquiry by a commission on Lytton's proposal, but to deal with it directly: so there is an end of that matter. I think the decision is right.

Saw Drage, who thinks me not very well: I weighed on Tuesday over 14 stone, which is never a good sign with me. Walk for exercise round Hyde Park & Kensington Gardens: bought a book in Bond St. . . .

Hear of the recall of Ld A. Loftus[25], Dufferin replacing him at Petersburg: a good riddance, & a good appointment. Without being absolutely incapable or stupid, the pompous conceit & swagger of the late ambassador made him a disagreeable person to have to do with: &, though good tempered, he continued to be disliked by all the ministers with whom he came in contact. I assume that he has been bought off with an Indian governorship: which, if it be so, is hard on the Hindoos.

[d']Harcourt, the F. Amb., called, & we talked over affairs. I asked him, as I have often asked Frenchmen, what were the measures likely to be taken by a really radical govt., supposing one to be formed in France? He answered me at length, & in substance as follows . . . He thought the most alarming feature of the situation was the retirement of Gambetta[26] into a position where he could neither act nor speak. He construed that as meaning that Gambetta saw the impossibility of keeping his own party in order, & had prudently got out of the way. He thought well of Waddington[27], but did not believe that he could remain long where he was: he would be pushed out by more violent men. – As to the east, he expected great trouble from two causes: one the mental condition of the Sultan[28], who is in constant terror, suspects his ministers, & removes them without assignable cause: the state of things at Constantinople is one of anarchy, & it was impossible to see from what quarter improvement could come: the other was the certainty of outbreaks in Roumelia when the Russian troops retired. He believed that our govt. either had, or would have, an engagement with Austria as to what should be done in the event of disturbance (Q., subsidy? or joint occupation?).

Oddly enough, [d']Harcourt had just been preceded by his namesake, Vernon Harcourt: who talked of the prospects of the session, but had nothing very new. He thought the Cabinet were anxious to get out of the Afghan trouble as cheaply as they could, & would be glad to retire taking only a small slice of Afghan territory: but that the Viceroy & his advisers would be too strong for them, & would force a larger annexation: that Lytton was known to think that we ought to hold Herat & Balkh: that he had been the real author of the war, which was not desired at home: this I think possible & even probable. He wished the Irish Univ. question could be settled, or left alone, as its discussion would place the Liberals in a position of excessive difficulty: either they must lose the Irish vote by resisting what was proposed, or split up. – I could see clearly that V.H. would be ready to buy up the priests at their own price, but he has nothing of the anticlerical feeling so common on that side. He expected a deficit, & thought finance would be the weak point of the govt. He spoke of trouble in Roumelia much as his French namesake had done: observing that, if the Berlin treaty failed in that quarter, there was an end of it, for the division of Bulgaria had been the one diplomatic triumph of last year. . . .

10 Feb. 1879: . . . Called on Granville, hearing that he had called on me: it turned out that he had nothing special to say, but we reviewed the situation generally. I pressed him to lay stress on the Zulu war, & to elicit the reasons for its being made, as with our present knowledge it appeared unprovoked & unnecessary. He had heard nothing of any plan for a Catholic University.

Heard later that there is a good deal of anxiety felt in D. St. to get the D. of Connaught to accept the viceroyalty: but that he objects entirely, saying with some reason that if he once settles at Dublin it will not be easy for him to get away: that he does not wish to be banished into Ireland: that his desire is for a military life – in short, that he will not go unless absolutely commanded by the Queen, and then with the greatest reluctance. It is thought that the Premier is the more anxious to please Irish feeling in this way because he foresees that he shall not be able to do anything for Catholics in the way of education. . . .

11 Feb. 1879: Left with Hale for Witley by the 9.30 train. Arrived at Haslemere about 11.00. . . . We . . . walked up the hill . . . & through the whole length of the estate, coming out at the point nearest Witley station. In all nearly 5 hours' walking, which I was glad to find I could do without the least weariness. . . . I never saw the country look so well: shape of hills, colouring, everything was perfect. Witley is by far the most agreeable of all my estates to look at or go over, & I am more inclined to extend myself in that quarter than anywhere else. Home by about 6.00 . . . Hale dined with us – M. thinks him much aged, & I do not disagree, but he has abundance of bodily activity left.

News of a failure[29] in the Zulu war: about 600 Europeans & 30 officers killed, 2 guns lost, also the regimental colours & an enormous quantity of ammunition & rifles. In fact the English camp fell into the hands of the enemy, & the supplies necessary to carry on the campaign are lost. . . . The ultimate effect of this check will be to damage the govt.: who (not very reasonably) are always credited with success, & blamed for failure, even where from distance & the nature of the affair it is impossible that they could have secured the one, or averted the other. When a national disaster has occurred, patriotism is appealed to, & criticism of the causes seems out of place until the mischief has been repaired.

12 Feb. 1879: Mr. Gorst, whom I hardly know, except as a sort of electioneering agent of the Conservative party, sends me a letter to introduce one Hitchman[30], a political writer, author of a very absurd life of Lord Beaconsfield. I make an excuse not to see him, & send no answer to the letter, thinking the proceeding, under all circumstances, rather cool.

Letters & notes as usual. I find I have on an average nearly 2 hours' work with these, for the most part wholly uninteresting, communications; of which absurd advice & unreasonable requests form a large proportion.

. . . At 3.00, meeting of the Lit. Fund committee . . .

Home. See Froude[31], who talks freely of S. African matters: he thinks the war has been made to satisfy the people of Natal, who are in constant fear of Zulu invasion. I gathered from remarks made by him that he is beginning to see his ideas of a permanent connection between distant colonies & the mother country are unworkable. – Granville called, & talked at length over the speech he is to make tomorrow. He had got the substance of the ministerial statement, nothing sensational, all solid & sensible. Party at Ly Granville's went 10.30 stayed till 11.30.

13 Feb. 1879: Short walk, but day wet, stayed mostly at home: destroyed old letters, etc.

At the party last night, I gathered that there is a general feeling that the war had been begun with inadequate forces, & that to this the disaster is attributable. A colonist of the name of Phillips, who has been useful to young West, & who called on M. today, explained the advantage which natives have in this sort of war, being unencumbered with luggage, & moving far more rapidly than Europeans. He also gave me a new view – as follows: 'The war was determined upon by Sir B. Frere, as part of the great federation scheme. To this scheme there were two obstacles – one the existence of the Molteno ministry at the Cape, which is got rid of – the other the determination of the Cape colonists not to unite with Natal so long as the risk of a Zulu invasion continues. They say that they will not take on themselves without necessity the risk & cost of fighting the Zulus, from whom they are now divided by the breadth of a separate & independent colony. But, if the Zulu power is once broken, that objection falls to the ground of itself. Now federation is the favourite idea just at present in D.[owning] St. A war was necessary to work it out, & a war has been made.' I neither accept nor reject this solution, but think it worth noting.

Went to the opening, or rather re-opening, of parlt. with M. The House was fairly full, not crowded, the galleries much the same: it did not seem as if much general interest were felt in the announcements about to be made. – Ld Beaconsfield's speech was studiously brief, and his evident object was to present as few points of attack as possible[32]. He was scarcely half an hour on his legs, & either from real failure of memory for the moment, or affectation of indifference, he had omitted all mention of Afghan affairs, & begun upon home legislation, when he was reminded of the slip. There was nothing ostentatious or swaggering in his language, he seemed only to wish to get through his work with the least possible trouble. Of the bills to be brought in he read a bare catalogue, almost without comment. – Granville followed, speaking an hour, now & then pointed, but without much animation, & not in his best style. Carnarvon & Kimberley said a few words: all was over soon after.

14 Feb. 1879: Sent £5.5.0 to the Newspaper Press Fund for the year.

Mr. Hitchman, who called on Wednesday, writes that he wishes to produce a biography of my father: will I give him papers? I decline, but in carefully civil terms, saying (as indeed is the fact) that I think any such use of my father's correspondence would be premature[33]. . . .

15 Feb. 1879: Peabody fund meeting at 1.00, sat till 2.30: present, Sir C. Lampson[34], Mr. Welsh, & self. We settled the yearly report. (Note that the fund has received in all £700,000: £500,000 being the original gift, £200,000 accumulated interest & rents received: of this sum we have spent £550,000 as nearly as possible, & have in safe investments the remaining £150,000.) . . . It appears that the plan of clearing land by compulsory powers, where occupied by unhealthy buildings, with a view to rebuilding, does not answer in London: the spaces so thrown open cannot be let or sold, though offered by the authorities much below cost price. The condition imposed, that they shall be used only for workingmen's dwellings, operates against their sale, since no one likes to buy land which he cannot dispose of as he thinks best. This is the difficulty which thoughtful men saw from the first. It is easy to destroy houses unfit for human habitation, & to clear the sites: but supposing it does not pay to put up dwellings for the poor, which shall be at the same time good & not too dear for their use, what then? And, as a rule, it does not pay. Business men are not apt to be content with a return of 4 to 5 per cent on an investment which they cannot get out of, & more has seldom been made. It may answer to municipalities to build on these terms, but the experiment of a corporation undertaking to find lodgings for the people is open to a good deal of abuse.

Mr. Knowles[35], of the *Nineteenth Century*, called, very anxious that I should write something on the Zulu war. I declined, on the ground that anything I might have to say on that subject would be better said in the Lds, where we are sure to have a debate some day. But we talked over the question, & I gave him, but without mentioning names, the view taken by Judge Phillips, which was new to him, & striking. Keston with M. by the usual train . . .

16 Feb. 1879: Day passes quietly & without event.

I have not noted the death of Gen. Peel which, though he had in great measure retired from the world, will be felt by many as a loss. Good sense, knowledge of men, & a peculiar dry humour which gave significance to whatever he said, made him an agreeable companion & a useful friend. His politics were those of an old Tory, but he was, so to speak, a politician only by accident, & I do not think he had an enemy.

17 Feb. 1879: Left Keston at the usual hour: snow falling, & thick black fog on the south side the river, but not much in London.

Occupied an hour in sending off to various friends copies of my Rochdale speech, which is reprinted.

. . . Did not go to hear the Chancellor's new bankruptcy bill, which I should not have understood: preferring to read the new South African blue book.

. . . In H. of C. Northcote appears to have denied all knowledge of any intention to make the D. of Connaught a permanent viceroy. As the affair does not come off, he has a right to say that it is not intended: but all London knows that the attempt has only failed because of the determined opposition of the Duke himself, who is afraid that, by leaving the army, he shall lose his chance of being one day C.-in-C.

Münster brings a strange story, which I can hardly credit, to the effect that the Queen

& Premier determined to restore the office of Lord High Admiral, & put the D. of Edinburgh in that place: that the Cabinet gave a reluctant assent: but that Smith on behalf of the Admiralty held out, & in face of his opposition the scheme was abandoned. It is like Disraeli to entertain such an idea, & the Queen of course would press it: but, unless age & absence from the Commons have impaired his judgment, he can hardly have been serious in putting it forward. All the Liberals, & half the Conservatives, would condemn it. The Duke is, I believe, to be put in command of the reserves: an appointment for which he may perhaps be fit, or where at least he cannot do much harm. . . .

18 Feb. 1879: . . . Dined The Club, meeting Houghton[36], A. Russell, A.P. Stanley, Paget, Doyle[37], Maine[38], Reeve[39], Tyndall[40]: a good party & pleasant. I see with a kind of surprise that, having been elected comparatively young into The Club, I have risen to be nearly the senior member: only Prof. Owen[41], the D. of Cleveland[42], Argyll, & Gladstone being above me: & of these the first two are not likely to attend any more from age & health. There was a time when we were in danger of growing too parliamentary, too much like a copy of Grillions: but of late our elections have been, wisely, in a different line.

19 Feb. 1879: . . . Talk with Ld Lawrence, who is a good deal alarmed at the project imputed to Lytton, of compelling the native princes to disband or greatly reduce their armies. He does not deny that the thing would be good if done, but fears that it cannot be brought about at once without causing serious trouble, & that it will be undertaken hastily & rashly. He quite agreed with me as to the precarious condition of Indian finance, saying that he will neither himself put money into Indian securities nor allow any friend to do so if he could help it. He saw no end to the mischief that this war will have done in Afghanistan: thinks the chiefs will be all hostile to us, & ready to welcome the Russians: that there will be constant pressure upon us from the military party in India to seize the whole country, & that for this policy there will be a plausible excuse in the state of anarchy which will follow our withdrawal.

D. of Northumberland[43] calls on M. this afternoon, & confides to her (unasked) that he is weary of his position, doubts whether he is doing any good by staying in the Cabinet, & has to make many sacrifices of what he personally thinks right. But he did not say on what points.

Debate in the H. of C. on the Burials question. A. Balfour[44] [Cons. M.P. for Hertford] has brought in a bill conceding nearly all that the nonconformists ask: it was discussed today: & talked out. B. Hope opposed it sincerely, & J. Talbot[45] ostensibly, on behalf of the govt., but it is clear that Balfour, who is closely connected with Salisbury, would not have moved in so delicate a matter without knowing that his action would rather help than hurt the Cabinet. In truth neither side is quite honest in this matter: the Liberals, professing anxiety to settle it, are really not at all desirous of putting out of the way the only grievance upon which they can thoroughly unite with the nonconformist interest: while the more moderate Conservatives, for exactly the same reason, would be glad to make the concession demanded, & have done with it, if they could manage that without offending their clerical supporters. A strange game of cross-purposes!

Parliamentary proceedings so far have been languid & uninteresting: the political interest of the Zulu war is much lessened by the evidence of the blue book showing that the initiative has been taken by Sir B. Frere on his own responsibility, & against the rather feeble remonstrances of the Col. Office. It may be a question whether the Cabinet ought not to have recalled Sir B. Frere: but that is another affair: & it is scarcely possible that he should have had secret orders in an opposite sense from that of his public instructions. . . .

21 Feb. 1879: Snow, on the ground, 4 inches deep: & more falling. Paid £12.10.0 for new shares in the Coffee Tavern Co.

Long debate in H. of C. last night on the rules of the House & the conduct of business: which ended in nothing [having] been done, & looks ill for the prospects of the session: time being wasted, it seems intentionally. Northcote kept his temper as he always does, & showed a real wish to conciliate: but it is evident that the party of obstruction is strong: & it is reinforced by another party which, without desiring obstruction, does not like to see the initiative of legislation exclusively in the hands of the Cabinet. I do not see the way out of all this difficulty & confusion. At another time the opposition might join in helping to carry useful & harmless measures: but just now, with an election in prospect, it is not parliamentary nature that they should go out of their way to enable their opponents to gain credit for useful legislative work: more especially as the neglect of internal affairs is evidently going to be one of the chief grounds of accusation against the govt., & not one wholly unfounded.

. . . Took a hot-air bath to combat a growing cold.

22 Feb. 1879: Sent £10 to the Artists' Benevolent Fund, making £430 spent so far on the separate account to which benefactions are charged. Walk home with Lowe: he very moderate & fair in talk, says he thinks Northcote right about his new rules, but doubts their being passed. Gives N. credit for his great courtesy & wish to conciliate, but thinks he has not 'backbone' enough for his place. Talked of the oddity of the situation – in December we were discussing a war made without the knowledge of the govt., by a zealous subordinate. Said he was surprised to find the growing revolutionary feeling about land: men reckoned to be moderate thought it quite a reasonable proposal that the State should limit the extent of farms, & give the occupier fixity of tenure, which seemed to him sheer robbery. He named Shaw-Lefevre[46] as holding these ideas. Said Hartington had all the appearance of being sick of his place, & probably was so: with Gladstone on one side, & Chamberlain on the other, it was not an easy one. Did not see any future at all for the Liberal party: the state of politics puzzled him altogether. His way of conversing left on my mind the impression that he does not mean to take an active part again: but he did not say so.

Called in the afternoon on Sir C. Lampson, at his request . . . discussed with him a plan for borrowing from the Treasury a large sum at 3% for the purpose of extending the building operations of the Peabody trust: his plea for taking this course is that the Artisans Dwellings Act[47] has proved a failure in London: sites have been or are being cleared to the extent of 40 acres, but partly owing to the cost, partly to the stringent rules enforced by the Metropolitan authorities, nobody will come forward to build: the Westminster plot of 3 acres is adjudged to us without a single rival bidder having come forward: land is therefore to be had in London at exceptionally low prices, suited for our purposes: all we want is more capital, & he believes that govt. will be ready to lend at a low rate, in order to avoid the necessity of admitting that their legislation on this matter, for which they have taken a good deal of credit, has broken down. We shall thus, he thinks secure both land & money cheaper than we shall ever do again, or could do except under these peculiar circumstances. We discussed the question fully. I told him I did not like borrowing as a rule, but in the present case the advantage to be gained was clear, & I would not object, provided that we really could get the money at 3% (he declared on this that he would not wish to borrow at a higher rate) and also that a limit was fixed, both as to amount & time of repayment. I thought we ought not to exceed £200,000 (he had spoken of £300,000): & that it should be repayable in 10 years. We left the matter there for future discussion. – Keston in afternoon.

23 Feb. 1879: Quiet day at Keston: walk early, alone, later with M. . . . snow falling in afternoon.

Death of the D. of Newcastle[48] announced, at the age of 45: he had succeeded in being wholly unknown to the public, since his early youth, when he was known, not to his advantage, as having run through large sums in gambling & on the turf. His losses in this way were repaired by a rich marriage, but whether his habits were reformed I never heard. His mother was rather mad, and hated her husband: his father quarrelled with everybody he came near: so that he had some excuse for eccentricity. He is succeeded by a son, still under age.

Dinner given last night to Dufferin, at the Reform Club . . . those who took part in it were in a difficult position: but both Granville, who was in the chair, & Dufferin spoke with admirable skill & tact. There is no doubt but that the substitution at Petersburgh of Dufferin for Loftus is a gain to the country: but I hear through Schouvaloff that Ld D. is absolutely ignorant as to what has passed about the east, both in India & Europe, & has no definite ideas as to what his instructions are to be It is singular under these circumstances that he should have accepted the embassy, since he cannot well have a blind & implicit confidence in the Cabinet: but he is ruined, active, & ambitious. It is a misfortune to him to be employed in a post where his remarkable gift of speech will be useless: but he is probably as good in diplomacy as in oratory.

Some details as to the Zulu disaster: one man alone appears to have escaped from the camp that was attacked: having been wounded & unable to fight, he was in the wagons, & got away . . .

24 Feb. 1879: Hard frost & bright day: walk in to Bromley . . . St. J. Square at 10.45 as usual.

Sanderson calls, & talk about affairs in general terms: he says Layard's[49] illness is real, not political: though here it is usually assumed that he has been quietly removed as a concession to Russia. The diplomatists have a report that Drummond Wolff is to succeed him, a choice which would not be popular for, though undoubtedly clever, Wolff is more universally distrusted than any man in parliament. What he has done to earn his character as unreliable & untruthful I don't know: & it is fair to note that I have never heard of any definite charge against him: but the fact remains that he is in some way discredited, & for this reason Disraeli passed him over in 1874.

. . . Ld Beaconsfield has been laid up with cold & gout &, as usual, the clubs are beginning to speculate on his successor. The diplomatists think that Cairns will be the man – for two reasons: because it would not be easy to find a new foreign secretary, & because Salisbury is considered by the public as extreme in opinion, & rash in character. But there is no special reason for supposing that the Premier will resign, or die. He has no home to fall back upon, few personal friends, & is too old to take again to literature: so that I should expect to find that he would prefer to die in harness, like Palmerston[50]. Ld Melbourne's[51] case may probably occur to his recollection: who lived 7 or 8 years after quitting office, always distressed at the thought that he was neglected & forgotten, & wishing to return to power, [or a] subordinate position (after having held the highest) when mentally & bodily unfit for work. . . .

26 Feb. 1879: Walk early for exercise. Met F.A.S.[52] in the street: we shook hands, but nothing passed in the way of conversation.

. . . The young Prince Imperial[53] . . . is on his way to the Cape to serve as a volunteer with our army. The object of course is to qualify as a future sovereign: it being thought indispensable among his partisans in France that he should have seen a campaign. There is no harm in the matter: but it has furnished occasion for an odd article in the *M. Post*, which reads like a communiqué from the court, expressing the deep interest felt in him by the Queen, & the anxious desire of 'society' that he should in time fill a higher station. It is odd to note how the fashionable dislike to even the most moderate & conservative of republics is apt to break out.

27 Feb. 1879: More snow falling & thawing: streets very disagreeable. Short walk: called at a new bookseller's . . .

Early luncheon at home . . . H. of Lds for committee at 2.00. Home at 5.00, there being nothing in the Lords. Dined D. of Bedford's, meeting old Ly Westminster[54] & the Tavistocks[55]. Pleasant.

28 Feb. 1879: . . . . . . In the evening, went with M. & Margaret to Ly Waldegrave's[56] party. The night was rainy, & we waited the best part of an hour for our carriage: not much amused on the whole, but it is good to show oneself in society now & then. Some talk with Lawson about Roumelia: he admits the difficulty of keeping order when the Russians go out – thinks there may be a mixed occupation by the troops of various countries – Austrians, French, & English. Or that the matter may end in a compromise – but as to that he was vague. Saw Forster[57], who said the question of reciprocity would give a great deal of trouble both in parliament & out of it. – Talk with Erskine Perry[58], who thinks if possible worse than I do of the prospects of Indian finance: as to which there has been this evening a debate, & an effective speech from Fawcett. Talk with Sir C. Foster[59], who says the H. of C. is sadly changed for the worse since I knew it ten years ago – not under any control from its leaders, & time wasted recklessly. He is for the *clôture* as the only effective remedy – & I am not sure that he is not right.

1 Mar. 1879: . . . Eastwick[60] calls to talk over Indian affairs: takes the most gloomy view of the situation: speaks of Lytton as incredibly reckless, & surrounded by flatterers: who let him hear no opinion adverse to his own: quite the worst Gov. Gen. in Eastwick's opinion that we have ever had, & he has known India 40 years. Sir B. Frere he also thinks dangerous, from his acting on his own ideas without reference to instructions, & his total want of prudence. Eastwick is a Liberal, but not a violent partisan, & he says that most of the Indian council think as he does.

Keston with M. in afternoon – Sanderson goes to Fairhill.

2 Mar. 1879: Fine bright day: the first really pleasant weather we have had this year. Walk with M. . . . Walk again later with her in Hollydale & Keston grounds. Read aloud several articles in reviews, etc. No business: quiet day.

. . . I do not think I have noted the ruin of two peers & large landowners which is causing a good deal of talk in society. One of them is Ld Lonsdale[61], a drunken disreputable
being, who in two or three years has managed to run through (it is said) near half a
million of money. Being very young still, he has thus condemned himself to what may be
a long life of poverty, unless he contrives to shorten it by drink. The estates, I take for
granted, are secured, & only his life interest in them is gone. The other is a man I have
known all my life as an acquaintance, though diversity of tastes prevented our having
much to say to one another. Ld Hardwicke[62] came in for nearly £17,000 a year, saved by
great care during the life of his father, who succeeded to a deeply encumbered estate. He
has not had it, I think, more than half a dozen years: & now all that he can lay his hands
on is gone. He has lived in the Marlborough House set, raced, gambled, & thrown away
money in every possible fashion. He is liked by many for his good humour & high spirits, laughed at by others for his swagger & self-conceit: but on the whole I think his smash
is regretted. The papers have it that he will be appointed to an Australian governorship,
& the Premier has a strong personal sympathy for him, but I do not think the arrangement possible: it would be reckoned too gross a job.

3 Mar. 1879: Walk from Keston . . . to the station, a bright fine day: St. J. Square about
10.45 as usual.
   Hale writes that old Howard, who managed the coal yard, is dead: a good & steady old
servant. I have written to ask about his family & their situation. – Hale also tells me that
the Cheshire Lines have paid in £20,000 on account . . .
   Read Elton's book of African travel[63]: the author died on a journey, & nearly every
European whom he mentions appears to have been struck down again & again with fever:
yet in the face of facts there are never wanting people who declare that Eastern Africa can
be occupied & civilised by Europeans. – Elton was brave, energetic, & prudent in his anti-
slavery work, of which he had a good deal: together with Dr. Kirk he succeeded in
suppressing the slave trade for a time, but I observe his editor says it has broken out as
before. Before leaving F.O. I saw his last journal – an 8vo Letts beautifully written, with
maps & plans & drawings of scenes passed through: it is not everybody who could do
work of this kind in an African camp, surrounded by confusion & discomfort of all kinds,
& suffering from climate. . . .

4 Mar. 1879: Walk: round Hyde Park, which much improved by planting . . .
   Paid £5.5.0 to the National Training School of Cookery, S. Kensington: to which I
have subscribed for 5 years, & hear well of it.
   . . . Dined The Club: meeting Houghton, Tyndall, P. Hewett[64], Reeve, Smith, Walpole:
a small party. Pleasant enough, but I carried away nothing worthy of being specially
noted. We elected Newton[65], of the B. Museum, & Sir Joseph Hooker[66].
   . . . In H. of C. debate on extension of the county franchise[67]. It was unreal & not very
effective, all parties knowing that the question cannot be dealt with in the present parliament. The Liberal party, Lowe & Goschen excepted, is pledged to the change: the
Conservatives dislike it, but think it inevitable, & are therefore in the difficult position of
choosing neither to support nor resist on principle, but only plead for delay. On the other
hand, it is not to be assumed that all those who vote with Trevelyan[68] want him to succeed.
Many are glad to see their neighbours resist what they themselves get popularity by
supporting: & this for two reasons: they keep the 'cry' which will be useful at elections: &

they postpone a reform which they probably distrust. The confusion is increased by the fact that nobody really knows who would gain by letting in the rural peasantry as voters: many people think that in the first instance the power of the squires would be increased, whatever might happen afterwards. Lowe stood out strongly against all further widening of the franchise: & Courtney as strongly for the representation of minorities: but these were the only two speeches, made on either side, which did not show their origin in simple partisanship.

5 Mar. 1879: . . . There dined with us: Seftons, Cardwells, Tavistocks, Elliots[69], Talbots, Grant Duffs[70], Münster & daughter, Schouvaloff, Tenterden, Meade[71], Galloways, in all 22.

Some talk with Schou. as to the situation: he thinks it unsatisfactory, & seems equally displeased with the attitude of his own govt. & of ours. He is going over to Russia, as he says, to arrange for his own recall, being weary of his post, & thinking he can do no good in it. The opportunity was not favourable for much conversation, even if I could with delicacy have asked questions: but I gathered three things: that Russia is pressing for the withdrawal of our fleet from its present station: that either Merve [sic], or some point close to Merve, will be occupied by the Russian army, in return for an advance into Afghanistan: & that the question of Roumelia is being considered by the powers. It is on this last point that difficulty is chiefly feared. All the Roumelians wish to be annexed to Bulgaria: the Bulgarians wish it too: both populations are armed: &, when the Russian troops withdraw, they will declare their union, unless means are found to prevent it. But what are those means to be? Not the continuance of Russian occupation, for to that all Europe would object: nor the entry of Turkish troops, for that the Russians have declared they will not endure: a mixed international occupation seems the only resource: but in the way of that there are many difficulties: who is to supply the occupying force? who is to pay for it? will the Turks themselves consent? how long is the occupation to last? &, as it cannot last for ever, what is to happen when it is ultimately withdrawn? If I understand Schou. rightly, which perhaps I did not, the English Cabinet would be content with an understanding that, after a certain lapse of time, the two states should be merged in one: but that understanding, if it exists, must be secret, & therefore useless for the purpose of keeping the Bulgarians quiet. The difficulty is expected to begin in May.

6 Mar. 1879: . . . I did not note yesterday that I had met Ld Beaconsfield in the street, & exchanged a few words with him. Nothing passed beyond civility, but as we have not met since April of last year and, as at his age he may die any day, I was glad to see him in this way, & renew amicable relations. Nothing has passed between us personally unpleasant &, though I know that he intrigued against me while we served together, & sent secret instructions of his own opposed to those which he had officially sanctioned, yet conduct of this sort is so much part of his nature that he does not offend me as it would in anyone else. He can no more help Oriental ways of dealing than he can help his nose & hair. And we acted long together, & in early days I learnt many things from him. But, though glad that this meeting should have taken place, I have no wish to see the old man again, or to renew personal intercourse.

I have this day two curious evidences of distress (at least impoverishment) among the richer classes in Scotland: one a circular offering yachts, sailing & steam, at about half what they cost, there being no demand for them: the other a similar circular relating to the letting of Highland moors & deer forests. The loss seems to fall chiefly on the upper & middle classes for, notwithstanding all that we hear about distress in English towns, the revenue returns are good, & the consumption of liquor appears hardly to fall off.

The B. of Trade has published an interesting paper by Giffen[72], their official statistician, proving, I think satisfactorily, that the enormous falling off in British exports is almost entirely a question of prices, not of quantities. We produce as much as we did in 1873, only we get less for it by nearly £60,000,000. This is not altogether as it should be, but it puts an end to the talk about the decay of industry, & the like.

7 Mar. 1879: . . . Sent £50 to a fund in aid of the family of Prof. Clifford[73], just dead at Madeira. He was only 33 or 34, but promised to be one of the first men of science of his time. He was rather too aggressive in religious, or rather anti-theological controversy, & had become in this way best known to the public, by what was really a very subordinate & secondary part of his character: but, according to those who knew him best, he needed only longer life to have extended the range of mathematical knowledge.

. . . In afternoon Gerald Talbot[74] called, he who was my private secretary in 1858–1859. He has since been Director of the India Store Dept., with £1,400 a year, which he now gives up on grounds of health. He came to speak to me about his claim to retiring pension: the office gives him £800 a year, he thinks he is entitled to £920. (He has his Ceylon allowance besides.) On hearing all detail, I advised him not to press it . . . He acquiesced readily . . . – He told me curious things of the Civil Service co-operative society, of which he is a director: how bitter is the feeling of the tradesmen against it: if a servant defrauds them, they find it is no use prosecuting; the jury, chiefly of the small tradesman class, are sure to find for the defendant. At the Haymarket stores, the parish authorities openly said that they would make it impossible for ladies to go there, & with that view they proposed to put a public urinal directly in front of the door: but the directors appealed & stopped the scheme. He expects violent attacks on the stores in parliament, as there have already been in the press.

Schouvaloff called, on his way back to Russia: we had a very long convn., upwards of an hour: he wished as he said to ask my opinion on two points: one, whether, as his govt. suggested, they ought to make an appeal to the powers in general for the withdrawal of the English fleet from Turkish waters? As to this I told him I was quite ready to give my opinion, that any such appeal would be a mistake. It would lead to no result, the powers would not move, it would be therefore only a diplomatic failure for Russia, & would lessen the chances of a friendly arrangement here. To this he appeared to assent. The next question was, whether the Russian govt. would do well in taking the initiative of proposing a joint occupation of Roumelia? & what were the chances of its being accepted by England? We discussed this at some length: I told him sincerely that I thought the proposal ought to be made: it could do no harm in case of failure, the making it would prevent any other Power from taking up the idea in a hostile sense &, if our Cabinet refused, as seemed likely, they would be bound to make some counter-proposal of their own. I did not, however, see how they could accept. We had few troops to spare: the expense would at the present moment be unpopular: & still more unpopular would be the notion that an English force was employed to keep a Turkish province from revolting. The thing would be too dangerous to attempt, especially just before a general election. He talked freely of the state of Roumelia, said the people were all armed, the militia organised, its officers were Bulgarians: if the Porte allowed them to remain, they would be his enemies in command of the military force: if he removed them, the rank & file would refuse to obey, & probably would murder any who might be sent as their successors. His chief fear seemed to be that, on the withdrawal of the Russian forces, disturbance would break out, which would lead to the Turkish troops moving in: the effect in Russia would be to excite a violent explosion of feeling, & probably, at whatever risk, their army would return. He seemed, or professed to be, convinced that the existing Roumelian arrangement could not last, & hinted, as he did once before in convn., that the English Cabinet thought so too.

M. & Margaret went to the play. Sanderson dined with me.

8 Mar. 1879: Statter called early, to report as to the Bury station arbitration case, which is still pending. The land taken is 7 acres, he modestly values it at £96,000, which he knows to be above the mark: he admits that he would take £70,000 & does not expect that. The other side offer, or rather put the value at, £14,000: which they well know is too little: probably the real value may vary between £60,000 and £30,000: if we realise £40,000 I shall not complain, & £50,000 will fully satisfy my expectations. – I ask as to state of business in Manchester. Statter answers: 'No better, & till the workmen come to their senses it is not to be wished that it should be.' He thinks there is a great deal of rottenness still – unsound houses propped up by the banks, & which ought to come down before matters can really mend.

Sir C. Lampson called: says we were premature in thinking we had secured the lot of 3 acres in Westminster: there is some delay or difficulty: but we shall probably get it in the end. He seems to have grown cool on his borrowing scheme: does not care to borrow at a higher rate than 3%, & I am sure the Treasury will not lend at that rate, but I advise him to see Northcote & make sure. He talks of the necessity of bringing some younger member into the trust, of providing for its working when he grows too old to attend to details: hints at his son as a fit person. He dwells (quite truly) on the importance of keeping it clear of jobs: two or three trustees with ends of their own to serve might easily quarter their dependants upon it, & waste money without end. The trust now really consists of Lampson himself, with some help from me: of the other trustees Northcote is too busy to attend: Mr. Morgan is an invalid, & seldom comes: The American minister cannot know much about the matter: & Sir C. Reed[75], besides having his hands full elsewhere, seems to me a windbag.

Pender called, to talk over the question of a telegraph to Africa, which he wants to lay, but cannot get the Treasury to give him the terms he asks. He is much disgusted: talks loudly of the incapacity of the Cabinet: says their majority will be upset at the next election, less on account of anything they have done than because people are suffering, & will compare the distress of 1880 with the abundance of 1873. He says money was never more plentiful, but there is no confidence, people will not risk it. He is seriously alarmed (as are also Lampson & Statter) at the probable effect of working men's combinations in driving trade abroad.

10 Mar. 1879: . . . The tale of the day is the partial burning of Granville's house, which happened while they were away, yesterday afternoon. The two upper floors are gone, the roof of the lower rooms a good deal damaged by water: most of the valuables saved, but Ly Granville has lost all her clothes. Both he & she praised for the good humour & absence of fuss with which they have taken the annoyance. It is noticed by those who are disposed to be superstitious that the house was built by the last Duke of Newcastle but one, whose constant ill luck in all things was a matter of common observation: & the ill fortune still clings to his successors. Granville had the disagreeable surprise of seeing a crowd collected in the park &, on asking a policeman what they were looking at, he was told that his house was burning. . . .

13 Mar. 1879: . . . At the Lit. Fund meeting yesterday, a Mr. Gruneisen[76], well known in connection with the Conservative Land Society, & . . . German or Dutch by origin, spoke to me about the Transvaal. He has since written. . . . From having many friends in Holland he hears much of South African affairs: that we do not understand the Boers: their dogged Dutch pertinacity, their aversion to the English, & their determination not to submit to us: that the annexation was a mistake, & that the sooner we let the Transvaal go the better, as the whites, being disaffected, will combine with the natives against us, & make the position untenable, except at a greater cost of men & money than it is worth.

I am much of the same mind as Mr. Gruneisen about the merits of the original annexation scheme, which I disliked from the first, & opposed in Cabinet[77]: but to give back territory once annexed is not easy. The only practical question is whether the possession of the land might not be reduced to a simple protectorate, which would lessen the difficulty. We have already had warnings that the Boers, though they will not join with the Zulus, will do nothing to help us: & the adjoining govt. of the Orange Free State has shown its feeling by a refusal to allow recruiting for our service. In fact, Frere has made enemies both of blacks & whites, & we were probably never more detested in South Africa, except among the class which makes its fortune out of the war expenditure.

14 Mar. 1879: . . . Dined with Pender, a party of men only, made up to meet the Premier of Victoria, Mr. Graham Berry[78], who with Prof. Pearson[79] is in England to ask the Col. Office to alter the Victorian constitution in a more democratic sense: the party consisted of 20: Shaftesbury[80], Granville, Gladstone, Bright, Lowe, Childers, Messrs. Berry & Pearson, two other Australian gentlemen, etc., etc. . . .

– I sat next Granville, & was well entertained. Gladstone seemed ill at ease, was very silent, & went away early[81]. He has grown to look even more ghastly than formerly, his whole appearance being that of a man worn out & exhausted by overstrain of mind.

– I find that his intended candidature for Midlothian is thought a mistake. If he loses, he injures his party far more by exclusion from the House than he can benefit them by winning a seat. By those who speculate on the motives of public men, he is thought to be influenced in his choice of a Scotch seat by ecclesiastical considerations. He is willing to sever the connection between Church & State but, being an earnest High Churchman in his personal feelings, does not like to owe his seat to the support of the Dissenters who alone will stand by him in that matter. Scotland is neutral ground as regards the English church, & he can take any line he pleases about it, as a Scotch member, without giving offence.

15 Mar. 1879: . . . Talk of an attack in one of the new scandal papers on Eustace Cecil[82], for being mixed up in a company which deals in stocks, while holding a confidential office in the War Dept. I doubt, considering what City companies & their promoters are, whether it is ever wise for a politician to be mixed up in them: but E.C.'s connection with this company was open & avowed, & it is idle to contend that his official position gave him any access to secrets which he could use for his private purposes. The article gave M. some annoyance, else I should not have thought it worth noting.

In H. of C. last night, Northcote said that there is no intention of recalling Ld Chelmsford from his command at the Cape: a question which has been much discussed in the press. Thereupon Mr. Jenkins[83] of Dundee – a very irrepressible gentleman – rose to denounce the govt., moving the adjournment for that purpose. A general row followed in which everybody lost their temper, & which lasted more than an hour. It is the remark in everybody's mouth that the present House is quite demoralised, & unfit for business. Every M.P. is thinking of his constituents & the coming elections, nothing gets done, & Northcote has shown no capacity as a leader, except in the one respect of temper & courtesy. These qualities he certainly displays, but his speeches are weak & vague. Still such as he is he must go on, for there is no one to take his place. Cross is the only possible substitute, & not a good one. . . .

17 Mar. 1879: . . . War estimates in H. of C. – ending in another Irish row got up by the obstructionists, which wasted a great part of the evening. Northcote seems to have been goaded into a little impatience at last, very excusable considering the provocation, but which served the purpose of the Irish, as giving them a peg on which to hang more speeches. In the course of the wrangle Mr. Biggar[84] seems to have observed that, if England were at war with Russia, the sympathies of a majority of the Irish people would be with the Russians. Much too true to be pleasant!

Dined Travellers, the house being upside down for a party, which began at 10.30 & lasted till 12.30. Abut 700 were asked, & less than 300 came. Mr. Berry & his Australian friends were among them. The rooms looked well & were not overcrowded.

18 Mar. 1879: Letter from Hale, sending an answer about insurances. They are now, for the London house, £21,000: for Knowsley, £11,500: stables & farm, £3,000 more. I desire him to increase them to £25,000 for London, £16,000 for Knowsley, stables & farm as before: in all £44,000.

. . . Walk with M. to Chelsea, where left her with old Mr. Carlyle. . . .

A saying is ascribed to Ld Beaconsfield, so characteristic that I think it must be genuine: 'The Zulus – they talk about the Zulus – yes – they have beaten one of our best generals, & converted one of our most learned bishops – and yet we call them savages.' . . .

20 Mar. 1879: . . . Sat only a short time in the House: walk up with Carnarvon, & long talk with him on South African affairs, in reference to the debate of next Tuesday. Dined at home & quiet evening.

Great complaints in the southern & midland counties as to the difficulty of getting or keeping tenants, who are throwing up their farms in all directions. Carnarvon says he has 3,000 acres on hand, which he is thinking of laying down in grass: Bath[85] has also suffered: & I have heard several others tell the same story. In every case it is the large capitalist farmer who has suffered most: probably because he has more to pay for labour, & therefore suffers more by its dearness. In Lancashire I have not heard a single complaint: but there the tenant works with his own hands & those of his family, only hiring men when absolutely necessary. The D. of Bedford, whose farms are well managed, & not highly rented, has received numerous requests for reductions, which he answers by telling the applicants that he cannot do what they ask, but is willing to put his land into the market, so that they may see what they can do with a new owner. I have not heard that he has in any case been asked to make his offer good.

21 Mar. 1879 (Friday): Sir C. Lampson called, with the news that he has seen Northcote & Cross, & can get money for Peabody purposes from the Treasury at 3%. He thinks it will be well to borrow £200,000. We agree to call a meeting next week.

Walk for exercise: bought a few books & prints . . .

Sent £13 to the Meteorological Socy., which I have just joined: & £5 to the Newsvendors Instn. Refused to take shares in a new cottage-building society, having done enough in that line.

Pestered with begging applications, I don't know how long it is since I had so many.

Dined Sir B. Brett's, meeting Ld & Ly Lyttelton[86], Sir C. Dilke, & others. Some satis-factory talk on various subjects with Sir C.D. & I think he is a man to be cultivated. Münster was also there: talk with him about the Roumelian trouble: he thinks our govt. will occupy the territory in question, to prevent disorder: I express my doubt, for what can be less popular than to hold a Turkish province with English troops, that it may not revolt against the Sultan? The thing seems madness, yet Münster is generally accurate.

Went on to Ly Beauchamp's[87] party, to meet the K. & Q. of the Belgians[88]. Met Cairns there, & some convn. with him as to S. Africa & Sir B. Frere, against whom he expressed himself in the strongest terms, saying that I should see in the blue-book just out the censure that was passed upon him, that it was severe, but not more so than he deserved, etc., etc. – Salisbury was there, & went up to M. to shake hands, which she did not refuse (quite rightly) but it was an awkward moment for both.

22 Mar. 1879: Found the despatches which Cairns referred to last night: they were just delivered, & certainly the reprimand to Frere is sharp enough: but it ends oddly with an assurance of continued confidence, which is not very intelligible, as under the circs. it can hardly be sincere. There is also a despatch from Ld Chelmsford, in which still more oddly he tenders Frere's resignation for him: asking himself to be relieved, & adding that Sir B. thinks the officer who comes out to replace him, Ld Chelmsford, should hold the high-est civil post also. These papers seemed to me so materially to affect the position of the question that I went to call on Granville: saw him & discussed the whole matter. He was disposed to think they made no difference: that the censure was neutralised by the assur-ance of confidence, & by Frere's being kept in his post: adding, what I could not but agree in, that it was awkward to make a change of front at the last moment. He, however, said that on seeing the blue book he had telegraphed to bring back Hartington from the coun-try, & to call a meeting of the party at Devonshire House. . . .

24 Mar. 1879: Cold snowy morning. Did not walk in as usual. London by 10.40. Heard from Granville that it is intended to amend the resolution agreed upon last week. . . . H. of Lds committee at 2.30, sat till 4.30. We examined Calcraft[89] of the B. of Trade, & then discussed our report. – In the Lords, the D. of Cambridge[90] explained Ld Chelmsford's singular despatch, denying that he (Ld C.) had ever complained of being worn out or asked to be relieved, & explaining his request as merely the expression of a wish, natural under the circs., that an effective second-in-command should be sent out to take his place in case of accident. I do not doubt the Duke's accuracy, & he has no motive for misrep-resentation, but it is extraordinary that Ld C. should refer in an official communication to an alleged complaint made by him in June last, of which complaint there exists no trace, & which is apparently contradicted by letters of his written about the same date. The mystery will probably never be cleared, but it will be forgotten like others. Meanwhile the position of the Cabinet is seriously affected by what has passed. They are not responsible for the making of the S. African war which was clearly contrary to their wishes & intentions: but they are blamed by the 'jingos' for having thrown over Frere – which they have done most effectually – & by the partisans of peace for not having seen in time where he was leading them, & stopped him by positive orders. The military disaster produces grumbling: & it is felt on both sides that these two local wars – both unnecessarily undertaken – are a serious evil. The party of peace & economy object to them as a needless waste of money: the partisans of a spirited policy dislike them as making a serious quarrel with Russia impossible – a circumstance of which the Russians will of course avail themselves. The Premier is well understood to take the latter view, & to be anxious to get out of Afghanistan on almost any conditions. But Lytton & the Indian army do not see matters from that point of view: & they are masters of the situation. Nor is it easy to retire from a country once occupied since a British retreat involves the massacre or, at best, the plunder & banishment of all who have taken our side. Add to the above considerations the hard winter, the depression of trade, the heavy deficit on the last two years' expenditure, and the almost bankrupt condition of Indian finance: & it is evident that disagreeable times are coming for the ministry. They lost their opportunity in not dissolving after the treaty of Berlin, when popular feeling was in their favour, & a new parliament might have been secured as conservative as the last.

Party in evening: about 800 were asked: there came about [91]: the cold disagreeable night keeping many away, & the H. of C. debates detaining others. The rooms were all open, & looked very well. A musical performance with bells in the small room attracted many, & prevented too great a crowd in the others.

25 Mar. 1879: . . . H. of Lds. at 5.00, where debate on the question whether Sir B. Frere should be recalled or not. It was opened by Lansdowne[92], rather feebly as I thought: he kept the gloves on: & his attack was on the whole ineffective. Cranbrook followed, fluent & ready enough, but less rhetorical than usual &, as rhetoric is his strong point, less powerful. Ld Blachford[93] talked good sense in a manner which hardly did justice to his matter. –Carnarvon, I believe, delivered a panegyric on Frere: but him I did not hear. When I came back from dinner, Kimberley[94] was speaking: he discussed the whole question of South African policy, clear & able in his criticism, & more to the purpose than any previous speaker: Salisbury followed him, also able, but confining himself to the single point of Sir B. Frere's position. D. of Somerset came next, & introduced a comic element into the discussion: without descending to buffoonery he put things in a quaint way which kept up a continual laugh: the Premier answered him, not in his happiest vein: physically vigorous, but feeble as to argument. Granville closed the debate in a few telling sentences more to the purpose than most of it had been: but on the whole I did not think the Lords did themselves justice. The division of course gave a large majority to govt. I had half intended to speak, & prepared myself for the purpose: but was restrained by doubt as to whether the whole question was thoroughly known to me, & a little also by the consideration that a strong attack on Frere – which I should have made if I had spoken at all – might have provoked a reaction in his favour. It was evident that the peers on all sides were inclined to deal with him gently, I suppose on the ground of the difficulty in which he is placed, though he has brought it on himself: and I cannot see any excuse or palliation for his conduct. He knew that if he asked for leave to make his war he would be refused: he therefore prepared to make it without leave: & began it with inadequate forces rather than run the risk by delaying of being stopped by positive orders. A graver offence against the public interest it is impossible to imagine.

26 Mar. 1879: Day cold & snowy, winter come again.

. . . There dined with us the Carnarvons, Penders, Morier[95], A. Russell, & Miss Grosvenor[96]. Pleasant evening. Margaret [Cecil] was ill (as she now frequently is) & could not appear.

Morier denounced the Col. Office in very unmeasured terms being apparently of opinion that something might have been done to open Delagoa Bay by negociation with the Portuguese, & that if the Boers had got this access to the sea they would have been heartily with us. Carnarvon & he talked about the Transvaal: C. contending that if it had not been annexed, or if it were now to be given back, the best thing we could do would be to give up South Africa, retaining only the harbour of Cape Town & territory enough round it to make it safe. I could not quite follow his reasoning, but it seemed to be this – that all the Boer population would go together, that they are a majority of the whites even in the Cape colony, & that they must either be all dependent or all free. Froude is to write an article on S. Afr. politics: he says in a letter I have seen (I dare say quite truly) that the debate in the Lords shows that neither side knew what they were talking about. Some conversation with Pender as to Indian finances, which he now agrees with me in thinking almost desperate: £20,000,000 have been borrowed in 3 years, the Afghan drain continues, & taxes cannot be increased without risk of revolt.

27 Mar. 1879: . . . Walk sharply for exercise round Regent's Park: I have not had a walk for three days, owing to the detestable weather.

. . . News of the death of a son[97] of the Crown Princess of Germany – a grandchild of the Queen . . . The death was sudden, with little warning or apparent cause, & many people believe that the P. Consort's descendants have all more or less inherited his weakness of constitution.

The newspapers have got hold of a negociation now going on for a mixed occupation of Roumelia, & Northcote being questioned does not deny the story, though saying that nothing was settled: so that Münster was right. At best it is a temporary expedient to stave off trouble, for the occupation cannot last for ever, & what is to follow when the troops are withdrawn? By the treaty of last year, the Turks have a right to occupy the country in case of disturbance &, as the object of the mixed occupation is to prevent Turkish troops from going in, the Turcophiles will say with truth that already the spirit of the treaty is being departed from. Indeed they are saying it already, through the *Pall Mall*.

28 Mar. 1879: . . . Layard, who is on his way back to Constantinople, called also, & I had a good deal of talk with him. He thinks ill of the state of Turkey: men & money are both wanting: the latter is the greater difficulty: for the Turks would now accept official supervision by foreigners, only they have not the means of paying them. It is a *cercle vicieux*: we tell the Turkish authorities 'Make reforms, & you will be able to get money': they answer 'We cannot make our reforms till we have money'. And so nothing is done. He seemed to think a loan might be raised on the security of the customs duties, if they were put under European superintendence, & if the prior claim of the bondholders could be got rid of: but there was the chief difficulty. He praised the Sultan as honest & well meaning: but added that he is quite mad on one point – his personal safety – & believes anybody who tells him that one of his ministers is conspiring against him: this weakness is known, & intriguers, native & foreign, play upon it. Hence perpetual changes of hands, with the necessary consequence, that no policy is persevered in. – He thought the mixed occupation of Roumelia might be necessary, & the best way out of a perplexing situation: but he evidently did not like it, saying with truth that it put the Porte in a far worse situation than was intended at Berlin.

Peabody trust meeting at 3.00: Lampson, Morgan, & the U.S. minister present: it was agreed that Lampson & I should negociate with Sir S. Northcote for a loan at 3_% of £200 to £300,000. But we are to settle nothing without reporting to the other trustees.

Went with Sir C. Lampson to visit some houses handed over to us by a lady, in Westminster. The block is large & solid, but the houses are dirty, & not at all like model lodgings. They may be improved, however, by cleaning & a little repair.

H. of Lds, where a speech by De La Warr, on his employers & workmen bill: we adjourned the debate, as the Cabinet have a bill on the same subject, now in the H. of C. Ld Huntly raised the question of agricultural distress, speaking sensibly & well: he wanted a commission of enquiry, which would have been useless, & which the Premier refused, also in a good speech, without bounce or claptrap of any kind. There seems to be no doubt that the farmers are having a very bad time, owing to increased wages, & bad harvests, together with American competition. But it is odd that the distress should be so local, severe in some counties, hardly felt in others: in Lancashire we know nothing of it. The reason of our escape I take to be partly that our farms are more like market gardens, supplying the towns with vegetables, etc., which cannot be brought from a distance: partly that the small farmers work with their own hands & those of their children, so that the cost of labour matters nothing to them. Dined Ld Cardwell's, meeting the Bedfords, Ld Sydney, D. of Northumberland, Harcourts, etc. Pleasant enough.

29 Mar. 1879 (Saturday): . . . The debate on South Africa in the Commons, which began on Thursday, still continues: Sir C. Dilke opened it, speaking better I am told than he has ever done before: Hicks Beach followed, & being put on his defence showed more power than is usual with him: the other speeches that night were unimportant. Yesterday Lowe began a vigorous attack, but being taken ill was obliged to sit down: Sir R. Peel[98] delivered an extraordinary harangue, in bad taste, attacking Ld Chelmsford violently, & too abusive: the effect was also weakened by its being well known that a personal disappointment is at the bottom of his opposition: still he said things which were true, & said them with vigour & force. F. [Stanley] was selected to close the debate: he spoke sensibly, but heavily, & emptied the House: he evidently did not like his case. The general effect has been damaging to Frere & to the Cabinet which decided not to recall him: *The Times*, of late reckoned a ministerial organ, condemns him strongly: & the general opinion, formed on his own despatches, is evidently against him. The tide has begun to turn: the local wars, the approaching bankruptcy of India, the protectionist movement against our trade, now extending over nearly all the world, the heavy deficit in the revenue, the depression of industry, together with the strong conviction that the diplomatic victory gained at Berlin is only illusory, have cooled the enthusiasm of supporters & sharpened the criticism of opponents. But the public mind continues in a conservative mood: there is no revival of democratic zeal, only a wish for better administration. . . .

31 Mar. 1879: . . . Luncheon at Traveller's. Mr. Bartley[99] called by appointment at 3.00; he came to explain the condition of the National Penny Bank, of which he is the founder, & which so far has been a real success. He wants me to take more shares, which I am not wholly averse to do, though they will pay nothing, for the scheme is a really good one, & has worked well.

. . . Got hold of a privately printed diary of Ld Carlisle[100], or rather of a book composed of extracts from his diaries: the contents are neither instructive nor very amusing, but I read them with a sort of interest, from the constant recurrence of familiar names & allusions to events which I remember. He seems to have possessed an immense faculty of liking everybody & everything: which indeed was his character in life. I do not know why this enviable condition of existence should as a rule be incompatible with marked intellectual superiority: but it certainly seems to be so. 'Weak, kindly, & a busybody' is the impression which this diary leaves. Its author was exactly in his place as an Irish Viceroy: the benevolent bustle, & flow of sonorous platitudes, with which he would open a new institution, or preside at an agricultural dinner, suited the office & the people. He seems to have loved preaching more than is usual with public men: for the diary is full of notes recording his attendance at such & such a church: & generally with some panegyric of the performance.

1 Apr. 1879: . . . The debate in H. of C. ended last night by giving to govt. a majority of 60: large enough, but still less than any they have had in the battles of the last two years: & the language of the press on all sides indicates disapproval of the restless policy of Frere. It is singular that they should suffer in reputation by acts which they have neither prompted nor sanctioned: but it is not wholly unjust: for the spirit in which Frere has acted in S. Africa is precisely that which has actuated the Cabinet in eastern matters: & they are indirectly answerable for the tendencies which they have fostered. Perhaps the most marked incident of the debate was the defection of Sir H. Holland[101]: who having served the Col. Office was exceptionally well acquainted with the question, & who though an independent is a steady & decided Conservative. The speeches of last night do not seem to have been above, or perhaps up to, the average: Gladstone took no part, whether from personal sympathy with Frere, or from a bad cold. Dilke has improved his position: & Sir R. Peel has shown, as from time to time he does, real oratorical power, though disfigured by personality & bad taste . . . The negociations with Yakoob Khan[102] must be in the Viceroy's hands: & if he decides that they shall not end peacefully he is the master. The impending bankruptcy of India is not a matter of any moment to him, nor indeed is it a thing that the Premier would care about, if only it can be deferred till after the next elections. Meanwhile fresh trouble seems impending on the side of Burmah: the young king, said to be passionate, drunken, & a hater of western civilisation, has murdered his whole family, fearing rivals for the throne: & summoned all his subjects to take arms. War appears probable: & in this case the fault will not be on our side.

2 Apr. 1879: Sir C. Lampson called, with estimates of land to be bought, & of the sum to be raised. He now wants £300,000 which I think a heavy debt . . . but he says we can pay it off in six years, as with the new houses to be built our income will be £50,000. He may be right, but it is a sanguine & speculative kind of finance.

. . . Mr. Sheffield called, fresh from Paris. He reports the state of France as good politically: the republic appears to be established: but he thinks there is a great danger ahead:

the army is now very powerful, the people know it, & among a large class of Frenchmen a fresh war with Germany is talked of as the first serious work to be taken in hand. But, as France will not fight without an ally, it will be her policy to keep the eastern question open, & bring about a general war if possible. What French politicians would like best would be to fight together with England & Austria against Germany & Russia. But, whatever may be the details of the arrangement, France must be expected to act rather as a disturbing than a peacemaking influence in Europe. Mr. Sheffield thinks Waddington may last six months, hardly longer: that he is there only till Gambetta sees an opportunity: that he has not been a success in the Chamber, & is too pacific for the present French taste. But Gambetta doubts whether the President would act with him, & does not like the idea – in the interests of the republic – of two presidential resignations in one year.

In the afternoon Ld A. Loftus called, fatter & more pompous than ever. He dislikes the idea of a mixed occupation of Roumelia: calls it a Russian dodge: fears quarrels among the occupying powers: in short he is against the whole scheme: but he did not seem to know whether it is decided or not. He drew a very dark picture of the internal state of Russia, saying that corruption is everywhere, the Nihilists are gaining ground, the finances are ruined, etc., but the military party would not allow of these things to stand in the way of a war, if they saw their advantage in making one. The Emperor has grown very nervous & irritable, it is thought he will not live long. Not much is known of the tendencies of the son: except that he is strongly averse to Germany & German influences, in which his wife confirms him. Gortschakoff[103] will not resign, he is 82, unfit for work, but he objects to go, & the Emperor does not know how to remove him. An odd difficulty for an autocrat. . . .

3 Apr. 1879: Drage called: serious talk with him as to symptoms which he had discovered, which indicate a possible return of the complaint I had in 1843. In that case 'bonsoir la compagnie'. But they are not yet serious, & may be warded off by care.

With Sir C. Lampson to call on Cross, who was in his room at the H. of C. (a new arrangement since my time): it was agreed that we should propose our plan in writing. He seemed favourable, as well he may be, for unless we help him his act of 1875 will be a dead letter. Fairhill in afternoon, with M. & Sackville [Cecil]: Margaret [Cecil] had gone before.

4 Apr. 1879: . . .

. . . The papers are full of the budget, which is for the public an agreeable surprise. He puts on no new taxes (two trifling rearrangements of the duty on cocoa & that of tobacco being merely for purposes of adjustment, & not for revenue): leaves the income tax at 5d. as it was, & all the rest unaltered. He estimates next year's income at £83,055,000, expenditure at £81,153,000, giving him a surplus of nearly £2,000,000, which he expects will be enough to meet the cost of the Zulu war – that item being by the nature of the cost impossible to estimate. – In the year just ended he has received £83,116,000 nearly: & spent £85,407,000. In the last two years there has been created a debt, unfunded, of £4,750,000 of which but for the Zulu war he would have paid off £2,000,000 this year: but that payment he has put off till better times. For this delay in making good the deficiency he will be severely attacked, & on the whole I think it would have been better if he had put another penny on the income tax: but the general depression of industry, & the fact that we have two wars at this moment on hand & may have a third, are a strong defence, perhaps a sufficient one. He has at any rate done well in not laying on any new indirect tax, & in not suspending the operation of his sinking fund. . . .

. . . News of a fresh mishap in the Zulu country: a party of about 100 soldiers surprised in a fog, & 60 of them killed. There is no evidence to show who (if anybody) is in fault, but the accident will make the war even more unpopular than it is. If one did not know the rapid changes of opinion, or rather of feeling, in this country, it would be surprising to see how entirely the popular mind has shifted. No more big talk or bluster in the newspapers: the general wish is to get out of the Afghan & African troubles as quickly & cheaply as may be: Roumelia is little noticed, & then chiefly with the expression of a hope that we may be spared the cost & trouble of an occupation. Economy is again beginning to be in favour: the increase of debt is criticised: in short the nation is coming to its senses.

10 Apr. 1879: . . . The papers are full of a fresh trouble that has come upon us, though it need not be a serious one, unless we choose to make it so. The Khedive, having succeeded lately in getting rid of Nubar[104], has tried a fresh stroke: he has dismissed Rivers Wilson & his French colleague – which he had carefully reserved the right to do – & has thus broken loose from European control, and reasserted his personal absolute power, which from the first he never meant to part with. He ingeniously holds out to the bondholders the prospect of payment in full, instead of the compromise which the Anglo-French advisers were prepared to propose: & he is putting it about in Egypt that the foreign interference is solely on behalf of the creditors, & that he resists their attempts to ruin the peasantry by oppressive taxation. In truth he is not far from being master of the financial situation, for a hint given to his tax collectors will reduce the yield of his taxes by one half, & enable him to regain his popularity, while the inconvenience falls on his European advisers & his foreign creditors. I say this on the assumption that European control is to be re-established: but in truth it is not easy to see how this is to be done. We have expressly recognised the Khedive's right to dismiss his ministers: Northcote has said as much in the H. of C.: but not the less will his doing so be regarded as a slap in the face to England: & the French, who are in the same boat with us, are apt to be less patient under such provocation than we are. They, moreover, are in the habit of protecting their bondholders even by armed demonstrations if necessary: a practice which we never took to, & have often formally disclaimed. Hence, however we may desire to act with them, it is not certain that we shall be able to pull together. Either we must do more for the creditors than is accordant with our practice: or they must do less: & with an astute Oriental at work to set us against one another, the risk of difference is not small. It is suggested that we ought to bring the influence of the Sultan to bear: but the precedent is bad, for our policy has always been to make Egypt as far as we could independent of the Sultan: & it is quite possible the Sultan will refuse to interfere. Why should he help us, he will say, as we have not helped him? Bourke is gone over to Paris to see Waddington: though how he can expect to succeed better than Lyons is not clear to me: the Cabinet, I understand, was taken by surprise at the Egyptian move, & sat for nearly three hours on Tuesday without coming to any definite conclusion. The matter is only vexatious, not dangerous, but it comes on the back of many other troubles.

11 Apr. 1879: . . . An odd letter from a person unknown to me . . . referring to a saying that has been current abut the present Premier, wants to know if it is true that I am the author of it . . . . . . The saying referred to is harmless enough, but why it should be given to me I don't know. It is to the effect that someone remarking on the oddity of the fact that France is governed by an English gentleman (Waddington) was answered: 'I wish England were.'

12 Apr. 1879: . . . Morley, the carpenter employed here, came with some inlaid tables for which he asks £15. I bought them &, knowing that he was buying a piece of land for a house, which he means to build for himself, & that he is a steady workman, I questioned him as to his means, & found that he wanted £42 in all for the purchase. This he had settled to pay off by instalments: but I gave him a cheque for the whole, leaving him £27 in my debt. The man's surprise & pleasure were curious to see.

. . . The newspapers are full of the Egyptian complication, which is awkward for several reasons. The Khedive has dismissed his English adviser which not a month ago we, through the mouth of Northcote, recognised his full right to do. Can we coerce or punish him for so acting? Certainly not: but yet his action in this respect is a slight to us, is felt as such &, what is more important, indicates an intention of falling back into the old habits of personal & wasteful administration: still if we stand alone it might be better to do nothing beyond remonstrating: but we do not stand alone. The French are acting with us: we cannot take any steps behind their backs without a breach of faith: nor separate our action publicly from theirs without producing a coldness in our mutual relations. The French govt. has always gone on the system of protecting its bondholders: we do not: & thus our joint intervention is made difficult at the outset by a fundamental difference of ideas. It is now said that the Sultan is to be appealed to, & that he is ready to depose the Khedive if we ask him. But shall we ask him? & who is to be the successor? Never was a govt. involved in more perplexities at once than ours. Egypt: Roumelia: S. Africa: Afghanistan: possibly Burmah: & all this with trade depressed at home & India insolvent.

13 Apr. 1879: Snow thick on the ground, but it melted away gradually. Day cold & unpleasant.

Wrote, after full consideration, to the 'Lancashire Union of Conservative & Constitutional Associations' withdrawing my name. – I joined this body 7 years ago, with some reluctance, & it is now entirely in the 'jingo' interest.

Wrote also to Carnarvon complimenting him on a translation of the Agamemnon of Aeschylus which he has just achieved. It is well done, but only serves to convince me more fully of the inherent impossibility of the thing attempted. I have added a few criticisms, but rather in order to show that I have read the book than with any idea of their being of use.

. . . Read to M. some 40 pages of Froude's new book on Caesar[105]: a strange production: but I suspend my judgment upon it till I have read all. . . .

15 Apr. 1879: . . . News in papers of an attempt on the life of the Czar: but he was not hurt, & probably the incident will increase his popularity among the Russians.

No news from the Cape: people are growing anxious about the fate of Col. Pearson[106], who is shut up at a place called Ekowe, & his supplies thought to be running short.

The Afghan war remains also in the same condition: no active operations, but no peace: the tribes are hostile, & the whole country is like a disturbed hornet's nest.

The king of Burmah, who lately massacred all his relatives, or at least all within his reach, is daily expected to break out in some act of hostility to England. He is given to drink, & probably not quite sane: his strongest feeling is supposed to be one of dislike to western civilisation: and for enmity towards the British power he has cause enough in the history of the last half century. If this business grows into a war, the fault will not be on our side: which is more than we can say in other cases. The Greek, Roumelian, & Egyptian questions all remain unsettled: for years we have not been involved in such a complication of difficulties at the same time. The country is growing thoroughly weary of the whole affair: 'jingoism' is apparently dead: but I see no signs of any other than a conservative feeling in the speeches or writings of the day: what men want is peace, revival of trade, & security against ceaseless troubles: not organic change.

17 Apr. 1879: Long early ride . . . the country is pretty & pleasant, but I never saw so backward a spring: nothing is green except the grass.

. . . News has come from the Cape, but not conclusive. Col. Pearson is still besieged at Ekowe, with provisions running short: Ld Chelmsford had started with 6,000 men to relieve him, but of these only half are Europeans. The distance is short: only 35 miles, but there are no roads. It is a singular proof of how far & fast news travels in these days, that the defeat & slaughter at Isandhlwana is understood to have become known to the king of Burmah, & to be one motive for the hostile attitude he has assumed.

18 Apr. 1879: . . . Drove with M. to Tunbridge Wells, on a sudden thought . . . I did not observe much new building since our last visit. [We] . . . visited the house called 'Grecian Villa', by the 'Grove', where my father & mother lived in 1853. It is now for sale, a pretty retired place, near the springs, but not (I suppose) in the most fashionable quarter – I dare say I have noted before in this journal that T. Wells is of all places that of which I have the oldest & earliest recollection: having been taken there at the age of 3, & remembering the house where we stayed, the Sussex hotel, perfectly. It was my father's favourite resort in his short holidays out of London, before he was master of Knowsley, & when travelling was slower than now. But it has lost the character of quiet & ease which used to belong to it, & is a fashionable watering place.

19 Apr. 1879: . . . My withdrawal from the Lancashire Union of Conservative Assocns. has created more sensation than I expected, being noticed in leading articles of most of the London papers. It appears to be generally taken as a final secession, not only from the Conservative organisation, but from the Conservative cause, which is a wider inference than the act itself justifies. . . .

21 Apr. 1879: Leave Fairhill early . . . reach Croxteth at 5.30: very hospitably received: walk with Sefton. Day cold, gloomy, & disagreeable: the spring even more backward than in Kent: nothing green except the grass.

. . . Meet Wyatt[107]: he says there is no distress among farmers here: all are holding their own, & paying as usual: but they are a good deal alarmed as to the future: an enormous importation of live & dead meat from the U.S. being expected. He thinks in these parts milk is the safest article to produce, as that cannot be brought from a distance.

Talk of [Lord] Gerard: who is professing to be in difficulties: wants to let his London house, has turned off his cook, sold his horses, & generally pleads poverty. The reduced price of coal is the reason, or excuse, but I suspect his children have more to do with it.

22 Apr. 1879: Many letters, which I got up early to answer.

Kirkdale at 11.00, sit an hour on county business. Major Greig[108] sends us in a bill of £1,280 for the late riots, which involved bringing down troops & quartering them in various places. We referred the matter to the finance committee. We petitioned against two bills of Sclater Booth's, one for local boards, the other on county valuation: which, being drawn with the intention of pleasing both parties, have failed to satisfy either. They are sure not to pass. – Police reports show a decrease of petty offences: due to lower wages, & their consequence less beer. We had 65 prisoners for trial: 38 counsel present! & about 25 to 30 magistrates. We sat till near 6.00. Several defended cases: one of an ex-sergeant, with a singularly high character & a pension, who stole out of the docks a plank worth 8d. & an old brush worth nothing. As he will lose his pension by the conviction, we let him off any other penalty. Sentenced about 25 prisoners, the longest term being 12 months. Back to Croxteth, & more letters.

Observed much new building all the way from W. Derby to Kirkdale, which is strange in such bad times as these are said to be. Newsham Park especially is being surrounded with new villas, ugly enough, but indicating wealth.

Ld Winchilsea[109] writes, asking a subscription of £5 to a collection of his poems, which he is publishing. They are worthless, but I have no wish to refuse, for it is really a gentlemanlike way of begging.

News of the relief of Ekowe by Ld Chelmsford, which is so far a success, but there has been hard fighting & a good deal of loss, & after all we are not much further advanced than at first, for the place is to be abandoned: only a disaster has been avoided.

23 Apr. 1879: Up early again to dispose of letters . . . Kirkdale by 9.45 . . . Sat till past 7.00, a long & wearisome day . . . The day was cold, wet, foggy, & smoky: with the smell of Widnes very perceptible. So wretched a spring no one has seen for many years.

Croxteth again in time for dinner . . . Fairly pleasant, & Sefton is a most hospitable host.

. . . A letter of mine written on Sunday to a Manchester gentleman, answering his question as to my withdrawal from the Lancashire Conservative Assocn., has been published, as I expected it would be . . . [I have told him] . . . that I cannot support in Lancashire what I have opposed in the Lords: & that I therefore wished for the present to stand aloof from all party organisations.

24 Apr. 1879: Left Croxteth, walked over early to Knowsley. Day fine, & warm, but rather dark & dull.

Went to the office: saw Moult, looking very ill, as he has often done of late . . .

. . . Receive from Moult the yearly return of receipts & outlay for the year ending July 1878: . . . it is unsatisfactory in one respect, showing that, notwithstanding remonstrances & objections, Hale persists in keeping up an expenditure which is beyond the wants of the estate, or the usual custom of landowners. He has served too long, & in some respects too well, to be removed: yet while I retain him only a small proportion of my nominal income is in any sense mine.

Long walk about the park, but not well pleased with the look of things . . . there are but few signs of spring . . . in general all is brown & wintry. A more ungenial season has seldom been known . . . Walk later with Hale, & dined at his house. Much discussion on various estate affairs, but all on points of detail.

25 Apr. 1879: Left Knowsley at 8.20: St. J. Square about 2.45: found there many notes & letters & abundantly employed: left again for Fairhill by 4.50 train, arriving at the house about 6.20. . . . All well & nothing altered.

Here is a summary of the expenditure of last year (to July 1878):

1. Compulsory deductions. Annuities £13,005. Taxes £6,175. Quitrents £5,844. Total under these heads £25,024.
2. Household, £25,000 exactly. (There are some savings on this, but in a separate account.)
3. Estate. Buildings £39,851. Improvements £17,756. Many other items, recorded elsewhere: the total is £73,538.
4. Miscellaneous. Benefactions £7,389. Fairhill & Keston £7,000. Incidental £6,128 (Minor entries). Total £20,775.
5. Ld D. drawn for use & investment – £44,000.
6. Lands bought £15,744. This last item has I think been repaid by the trust, being only in the nature of an advance.

Including the £4,000 drawn by me for use, but excluding the lands bought, & the £40,000 drawn for investment, there has been spent £148,337.

Under the first heading there is no excess above what I know of – & it is not in my own control.

'Household' is at the fixed rate. 'Miscellaneous' is on the whole not excessive.

But the estate has cost £73,500, which is at least £20,000 more than it ought to be, though I cannot detect where the waste is.

Summary condensed

Laid by:		Spent:	
Investment	£40,000	Compulsory deductions	£25,024
Land	£15,744	Household	£25,000
Total	£55,744	Miscellaneous	£20,775
		Estate	£73,538
		Self for use	£ 4,000
		Total	£148,337

26 Apr. 1879: Day fine & pleasant.

. . . Well satisfied with the effect of an opening which I have made through the screen of trees south of this house, which lets in a view of parklike fields & distant woods, unseen before.

This afternoon the Tonbridge fire brigade came out with their engine, for the drill which it seems they hold fortnightly: 2 officers . . . and 14 men. They laid hose from the pond by the stables, & sent jets of water flying higher than the housetop. They said their engine can throw a ton of water per minute: & that they are ready for a start in 6 to 7 minutes after the signal is given. . . . They say they now know what to do in case of fire here. They are a volunteer body, formed 3 years ago: the neighbours all subscribing. We entertained the 2 officers with cake & champagne: the men had their refreshment separate. . . .

27 Apr. 1879: . . . Answer a letter from Mr. Passmore Edwards[110], editor & proprietor of the *Echo* newspaper, who wishes me to act as arbitrator in the strike of the Durham miners, which has now lasted some weeks, & involves 50 or 60,000 persons. I answer him in much the same way as I answered Mr. Samuelson[111] of Liverpool, who made a similar request in reference to the strike there: I said that, if invited by both sides, I should not feel that I had a right to refuse, but that I thought the parties concerned would do better if they selected someone who had more acquaintance with mining business. I could promise impartiality & care, but technical knowledge in addition would be desirable, & that I did not possess.

From Chadwick's[112] conversation yesterday I learnt several things. He said that the effect of the co-operative movement in London had been very great on the tradesmen: so great as visibly to affect the rent of houses in the Strand: many were giving up their shops, & those who took them would only do so at a lower rate. I asked about land, how far its value for selling purposes had been affected by the existing depression? He said, where the value was residential, there had been no decrease: land of that sort was as much in favour as ever, both with those who bought for their own use & with investors: but where the value was agricultural only the falling off had been considerable, & was likely to be greater. He did not see how English farmers were to hold their own against the competition of cheaper land & better climates. He anticipated a heavy fall in rents: &, on some soils, that cultivation would cease altogether as unprofitable.

29 Apr. 1879: Left Fairhill, reached St. J. Square about 10 a.m. At my door, I met Mr. Melly[113], whom I could not shut out, he having seen me: he talked calmly enough, showed a note which he had received from Gladstone, whom he said he wanted to bring forward for the county, & himself to stand for the borough. He is undoubtedly not quite sane, but there was nothing in his manner to show it.

. . . Debate last night on the financial policy of the govt. which passed into a general discussion of their proceedings. It had the disadvantage of being opened by Rylands[114], who is a violent & rather wrongheaded person, without much weight on his own side: the Whig opposition supported him, but coldly, & thinking the move injudicious. Goschen seems to have spoken with effect, & Gladstone delivered a fine speech in his best style[115]: but I do not think the debate excited much interest as a whole: the speeches on the ministerial side were tame & dull. Majority 73.

30 Apr. 1879: . . . Talk with Granville & Kimberley about the debate in the Lords last night: they said that Bateman's[116] speech was scarcely intelligible: it was impossible to make out what he wanted: and he speaking nearly 2 hours, he drove away his audience, & prevented a real discussion which might otherwise have been got up. The Premier appears by the report to have given him no hopes, & to have negatived any idea of a return to protection, speaking clearly & sensibly.

Dined at 6.00, in the Middle Temple Hall: a large party: Gladstone, Granville, Lowe, Jessel[117], Phillimore[118], Moncrieff, B. Hope, Froude, Houghton, etc., among the guests.

I sat between the Treasurer & Sir R. Phillimore, & was well entertained. The students gave me a very warm reception, as they did also to Gladstone. We removed after dinner into a separate room (like the combination room of a Cambridge college) where toasts were given. I answered for the Lds., Gladstone for the Commons, Jessel for the judges, he making a capital speech, the best of the evening. Mr. J. Morley[119] represented literature: I was introduced to him later, which I am glad of. – Home early, soon after 10.00, well pleased with the evening: & to my surprise, instead of having made the cold in the head worse, I have nearly got rid of it.

1 May 1879: Letter from Statter: with monthly report. . . . He reports no improvement, & seems to expect none. . . .

2 May 1879: . . . Sanderson called, & explained to me the exact state of things in Roumelia: according to him nothing is actually settled, not even whether the Turkish troops are to move in to their posts on the Balkan. . . .

3 May 1879: Drage calls, sees M. about other matters, & tells her that the symptoms which he had detected in me are lessened, but not gone. There is no new rule to follow, only caution.

. . . Academy Dinner at Burlington House. Went there at 5.15, to have time to look well at the pictures, which I did . . . We sat down from 200 to 250 at the dinner: most of the notables of London present as usual: P. of Wales & royalties, ambassadors, ministers & ex-ministers. Sir F. Leighton as president did his work excellently well: he is if not a natural orator a ready, fluent, & exact speaker: & his merits were the more felt as poor Grant, having a defect in his speech, used to fail quite painfully in that part of his business. The oratory was average: Ld B. made a hit or two, but in general was in his didactic vein, which is not his happiest. The Prince spoke with good taste, but rather as if the whole affair bored him. Froude had to answer for literature, & delivered a harangue chiefly about American reprints & copyright, which was not much to the purpose & was rather impatiently heard. We got away about 10.30, & I took the 11.15 train to Bromley, reaching Keston about 12.30.

4 May 1879: . . . Ld Hertford[120] told me at the dinner yesterday, I sitting next him, that he had 14 farms thrown on his hands at once & that most of his neighbours were in like case. I advised him to accept definitively the surrender of the leases by one or two, & see if the rest would persevere when they found themselves taken at their word. There is no doubt some real distress among the farmers: but I cannot but think that many are taking advantage [of] it merely to see if they can get rents reduced.

5 May 1879: Leave Keston at 9.00, walk in to Bromley station: St. J. Square by 10.45. . . . Sanderson called, not very well either in health or spirits. . . .

. . . H. of Lords at 5.00: presented a petition: Lord Thurlow[121] brought on the question of opening museums on Sundays: he spoke well & clearly, but where I sat I could not hear all he said. Lds Aberdeen & Kintore[122] opposed: Ripon[123] & the D. of Somerset supported the resolution. I said a few words, but rather because I had promised to do so than from any other reason. The Abp. of Canterbury[124] ended the debate. The Premier made a sort of hesitating declaration, natural in his position, which was in substance that popular feeling was not strongly enough declared to justify a change.

Before this discussion began, Granville put a question as to the execution of the treaty of Berlin, which Salisbury answered at length, enumerating the various articles which have been or are being acted upon. He passed over the question which is really material: whether the Balkans are to be occupied by Turkish garrisons? All we know as yet points to an opposite conclusion: the Roumelians declare that they will not admit them without fighting, they are organised & drilled, & the new governor is supposed to share their sympathies. The minister in his statement dwelt rather significantly on the impossibility of reforms being made in Turkey without money, & the equal impossibility of raising it. If the thing were not so utterly impracticable, one would be led to think that he was paving the way for some financial arrangement such as a guaranteed loan – but that is now out of the question. Even friends of Turkey would not support it, & the attempt would be too full of risk before a general election.

6 May 1879: Gave M. £10 to repay a present which she has made.

Drove with her to Mr. Power the oculist, where I heard what he had to say. He has no doubt but that cataract is slowly increasing, there being a change for the worse since Nov. He says that, where the patient is under 65, 90 per cent of the operations are successful[125]. He advised quiet & as much country air as possible meanwhile. Though he told me nothing which in substance I did not already know, I went away saddened & anxious.

. . . H. of Lds at 5.00: where we had the very old question of the deceased wife's sister again: Houghton moving for an alteration of the law: he was fairly successful in his speech, but novelty on such a subject is impossible: the Bp. of London[126] answered him, in a reply very carefully reasoned, dwelling as was natural mostly on the ecclesiastical aspect of the question, but delivered in so low a voice as to be ineffective: Cranbrook said a few words. We divided 81 to 101: a large minority, considering that nearly all the bishops had come down to oppose. The only new feature of the debate was that the P. of Wales & D. of Edinburgh both voted in the minority, the former presenting a petition & (rather irregularly) expressing his hope that the motion would be carried, before the debate began. Home at 8.00, & quiet evening.

7 May 1879: Drive with M. to Chelsea to call on Carlyle[127]: left her at the door, & walked home. She finds the old man much enfeebled, in body & mind, & expressing his wish to die.

Lawrence calls with papers for signature: he told me where the estate now for sale at Frensham is, just across the Hindhead common. The extent is 940 acres, with a small house. I have asked for the printed particulars when they come out, but doubt as to buying. I am already in treaty with Herries for 200 acres, which I can only pay for by sacrificing the year's savings. And there is land close to Keston which I cannot refuse if it should fall in. Still the opportunity of extending my Witley estate is an inducement, & it may not recur. About Fullock's estate, which touches mine, nothing is known except that the owner is dead. Lawrence tells me that the insurance company with which he is connected would advance the whole sum required, if I wished it, leaving me free to pay off by instalments. My position is as follows. I owe for Holwood £60,000, for other lands bought £46,000, & C. Stanley has a charge on the estate of £24,000, which ought to be paid off on his death. Thus I ought to have available £130,000 to be clear. There is due to my trustees, & available for all the above purposes, £146,000 certain (including what they have in hand) & an uncertain sum of at least £60,000 more. Thus I have at least

£70,000 available for purchases of land, without touching on my private savings. But the date of these various payments from railway companies is very uncertain.

. . . Talk with Cairns & O'Hagan[128] about Isaac Butt[129] who is just dead. They agreed in considering him the most effective Irish orator of his time. He had a brilliant career before him: but from earliest days he was in debt: He was constantly involved with women: & latterly he had taken to drink. Poverty & absence of self-respect led him into some questionable transactions with Indian princes, to whom he was more than suspected of selling his parliamentary influence: from that time he became impossible as an official personage: & his necessities increased until he had come to the habit of borrowing small sums from any chance acquaintance. With all his faults, however, he will be a loss to the Home Rulers, being by far the ablest man of that party.

8 May 1879: . . . Went to the Westminster Hotel at 12.00 to attend a meeting of the Cotton Districts Convalescent Hospital fund: we sat $1\frac{1}{2}$ hour. Present, Winmarleigh, Egerton, Shuttleworth, Maclure, Ashworth, Heywood, etc. We settled some matters of detail but rejected a plan for the new building at Southport as being too costly & showy.

Ashworth says things in Manchester are looking better, the men consent to take lower wages, & with the great cheapness of food that prevails they are as well off as before. He was right in predicting a bad winter, so perhaps he may be so [now].

Walk home with Winmarleigh: he (at nearly 80) full of the work he is about at his new home in the Fylde, making a park, planting, etc., for the benefit of a grandson who is still a boy. Is it a kind of instinct, or mere habit, that enables men to ignore the fact of old age, & to go on taking interest in the affairs of the world as though they were not soon to leave it? Certainly Ld Winmarleigh is as keenly concerned in his own affairs, & in those of his friends, as he could have been at 40. . . .

9 May 1879: News in papers of a new election for Canterbury, vacant by the retirement of the Conservative member: the seat was again carried by a Conservative, but the contest was close, 1,159 to 1,103: in 1874 the majority was 500.

Pender called early, & gave M. & me his impressions of Cyprus, which were interesting, as he has evidently examined what he saw with no bias either way. His general conclusions are: that the present harbours are bad, but a very large & good one can be made at comparatively little cost: that land is cheap, some of the best agricultural land having been offered to him at a long lease on a rent of 2s. per acre: that it is probably good, but requires large irrigation, which existed in former times, but the works are now gone to ruin: that the cheapness of native labour, & the climate, would make it impossible for English workingmen to go out there with advantage, but that if capital is only forthcoming labour will not be wanting: that a sum of not less than £2,000,000 of state expenditure is necessary in the first instance, if the resources of the island are to be developed at all: that the people expected a large outlay, & few or no taxes: instead of which nothing has been spent, & the taxation, though more justly collected, is higher than under the Turks: that there is in consequence a good deal of discontent & grumbling: that if we starve the island it will be of no value to us, but liberally dealt with it may become a profitable possession. – I think these were his views briefly summarised, & I note them without comment of my own.

. . . Miss Morier[130] came to luncheon: the likeness to her grandfather, old Gen. Peel, is remarkable. . . .

10 May 1879: . . . Read a book[131] by Dr. Hood on gout, thinking I might find in it some useful hints as to the best way of keeping off the hereditary enemy: but I find none, beyond the not very novel suggestion that abstinence & exercise are the most effectual preventives – a lesson which I need not have paid half-a-guinea to learn. The most interesting part of the work is a chapter on longevity, in which he cites the Registrar-general as proving that out of 1,000 persons 500 die before the age of 17: 440 more before the age of 60: leaving only 6 per cent who reach that age. Of the 1,000 only 2 reach 80. Q. are these figures accurate? & can they be obtained in fuller detail? . . .

12 May 1879: Fine warm morning, the first we have had.

Walk in to Bromley station: London 10.45 as usual.

. . . Many letters & notes, which keep me occupied till luncheon.

Mr. Reade[132], late consul at Rustchuk, called to pay his respects: he talked of the Bulgarians, said their chief fault was an excessive envy; if any one of their number rose to a great position all the others would combine against him: that would be a political difficulty to them in the future: all depended on the future prince: if he was able & popular, they might maintain a real independence: there was already some jealousy of Russia, & it might increase. They were determined to unite with Roumelia some day, & the Bulgarian population of Roumelia was of the same mind, but not the other races. There was a bitter feeling between Greek & Bulgarian, chiefly on ecclesiastical grounds. He added that all the cruelties of the late war had been due to irregulars on both sides: as far as he could judge, both Russian & Turkish regular troops had behaved well.

. . . Promise £10.10.0 to the fund in aid of Mr. Smith of Coalville, the philanthropic agitator, about children in brickfields: it does not seem that the appeal on his behalf has excited much interest. For this in my heart I am not sorry, having subscribed more for appearance' sake than any other reason, & it not being good that philanthropic agitation should become a profitable employment.

Passed the afternoon lazily, only writing a few letters, till it was time for the H. of Lds. There, debate & division on a bill for restricting race meetings in the environs of London, which have become a nuisance to respectable persons living near. Richmond on behalf of the Cabinet opposed the bill vehemently, which was odd, as Cross in H. of C. had supported it. Ld Enfield[133] brought it in, making a speech which seemed to me very little to the purpose, but which I suppose was meant to conciliate the racing world. Ld St. Leonards[134] moved to throw it out: what I could hear of its argument was to the purpose, but he spoke ill as to voice, etc., & produced no effect. The debate was kept up by Granville, whom Ld Rosebery followed, & answered in an odd sneering tone, as if hostile, but it may be only his manner. The P. of Wales & D. of Cambridge were both there, the former talking loudly against the bill, but he was induced not to vote. We divided for the second reading, 84 to 57: it was not at all a party question, the opponents being the members & friends of the Jockey Club, & fashionable society in general. Home by 7.00, & quiet evening.

13 May 1879: Hale sends me a bad report of Moult, which I receive with great regret, for he is assiduous & accurate. His heart is in his work, as his father's was. I answer, suggesting that I should find someone in London to take his place for a time.

Drage calls (see 2 Apr.): reports that the symptoms observed 6 weeks ago have very nearly disappeared: but the gouty tendency is there, though it may be kept down. He sums up his advice in two rules: plenty of exercise & sweating, & very little wine. He sees no reason why with ordinary care my life should not last out the full term, general health being good. . . .

14 May 1879: Sir C. Lampson[135] calls: he has heard nothing more from Cross or Northcote, & is disposed to press them again which I advise him to do. He says money is extraordinarily abundant from the reluctance of men to speculate: the Treasury could borrow temporarily at 2 or at most 2½ per cent.

. . . Fawcett (not the M.P. but the consular judge) called, & gave me his impressions of what is passing at Constantinople. The Sultan he says is well intentioned, but weak in mind & body, & may be driven to do anything by his terror of conspiracy & assassination. The oligarchy of the Pashas is if possible worse than before, quite as corrupt as before the war, & more difficult to deal with. There is no gold in the country, & but little silver: the paper currency has fallen to a nominal value, & the bakers are subsidised to supply bread cheaply, & so prevent riots. Altogether he describes the country as falling to pieces. . . .

15 May 1879: . . . Sir C. Lampson calls: announces that the Treasury are willing to lend us £300,000 at 3½%, which is to be repaid within 15 years (we shall probably be able to repay it in 10): he is now going to enquire about the lots on sale. They are going much below their value, & we shall be able to extend our operations far beyond what would have been otherwise possible, though at the cost of tying our hands for a good many years to come.

Wet day: went to the Westminster hotel to attend a meeting of Lancashire magistrates on bills that affect the county: we discussed chiefly the Valuation Bill, now in committee of H. of C., & suggested amendments. There were present Messrs. Jackson, Ashton, Holt, Bletchley, Hulton, etc. We sat an hour.

Answered a letter from the Principal of Owen's College on the subject of a northern university, which is much discussed. I profess (quite sincerely) my wish to do anything that may be in the interest of O.C. but express doubts as to its being desirable to multiply universities, & a wish to know why the examinations & degrees of the London Univ. are not thought enough.

Did not go to the Lords, there being nothing of interest: but I ought to have gone, having nothing else to do. A strange laziness has come upon me of late, partly in the absence of any very definite employment, partly connected with health. . . .

16 May 1879: . . . Hale writes that Moult has been safely removed to Ben Rhydding in Wales. His case is one of melancholia: he is decidedly not in his right mind, & made some resistance to the journey, but chiefly as it seems from fear of being 'locked up' as he put it. There is no reason why with rest & care he should not recover. It is singular that only two days before his removal he wrote me a letter showing no sign of mental disturbance either in handwriting or contents.

More news from the Cape, unsatisfactory enough. The force on the spot is large, full 20,000 men: but the difficulty of transport appears enormous, there being no roads: & the season for operations is short. In any event the cost must be greater than Northcote has allowed for . . . The Boers will not rise in actual insurrection, but they are disaffected & do not conceal it. . . . For some reason not clear to me, the Zulu armies can outmarch ours . . . even now there is terror in Natal lest they should slip between two of the invading columns, & ravage the colony.

. . . H of Lds. at 5.00, where a good attendance, & many in the galleries. Argyll rose at 5.15, & spoke exactly two hours: his speech, exaggerated in parts, was fine & effective as a whole: he contended, & to my mind with complete success, that the provisions of the treaty of Berlin to which the greatest importance was attached have been virtually annulled, & that the Russian victory has been complete. Roumelia is to all intents separated from Turkey: the line of the Balkans is not to be occupied: the Asiatic protectorate is not to be acted upon: the war debt to Russia makes the Porte dependent on the Czar: & Russian influence is greater at Constantinople than ours. To all this there is really very little answer, & the 'Jingos' are beginning to see how they have been duped. Ld Beaconsfield answered with a good deal of force & fire, in his most declamatory style, happy at the beginning of his speech, where he was replying to what Argyll had said: but he then went on to give a sort of narrative of events, which he had evidently prepared, which was not much to the purpose & rather heavy. Many went away while he was speaking, & when he sat down the audience was reduced to some 40 peers. Kimberley, Salisbury, & Granville all took part in the debate, but the interest of it was ended with the two first speeches.

17 May 1879: . . . In the papers appears a singular despatch from Sir B. Frere: he forwards a memorial from the Boers, asking for independence &, without absolutely committing himself to support their demands, he writes in a strain which makes it evident that he thinks they had better be complied with. Can this be in pursuance of orders from home? & can the object be to throw on the Transvaal annexation – Carnarvon's work – the blame of the subsequent Zulu war? This would be quite in the Prime Minister's line: but, whatever the motive, it seems clear that the Transvaal will be better as an allied state than as a dependency &, if it can be set free as part of a general policy of pacification, that would be the best end of the affair. If I was not too busy at the time to note in this journal what passed, it will show that I always doubted the wisdom of the policy of annexation, & assented to it reluctantly. It was a mistake, & one for which Carnarvon as colonial secretary is primarily responsible: but I believe that the real author was Sir T. Shepstone[136]. There is in South Africa a strong party whose ruling idea is to found an African empire which shall be a second India, extending up to, or possibly swallowing up, the Portuguese possessions.

18 May 1879: Walk in afternoon, alone, met Fawcett, Dilke, & Ld E. Fitzmaurice[137], from High Elms: they wanted to find the way to Hayes, & I took them there. Much pleasant parliamentary talk, reminding me of former days in the H. of C. – Fawcett discussed India a good deal, said it was not easy to understand how Indian securities kept up as they did, considering the almost bankrupt condition of the finances: he thought the explanation was that among English investors, even bankers & capitalists, there prevails an idea that England has 'morally' guaranteed the Indian debt: that in one way or another they will not be allowed to lose their money. It is a delusion, but has its effect. He could not see how things were to go on there: & I find this to be a general impression. He talked of the dangers of democratic finance – the state is asked to help & interfere in a hundred things which are not its business. He dwelt especially on the danger of local loans, which the H. of C. is always willing to sanction, each member thinking his constituency may some day want one: if bad times come, there will be fresh demands to have the interest reduced, or possibly to wipe off the debt altogether. – In all this Dilke & Fitzmaurice agreed. He spoke of land, said there was much of it which had been put into cultivation in the days of protection, which never ought to have been broken up, & which will not now pay to cultivate, not if the farmer had it rentfree. He spoke especially of the poor pasture & downland of the south. He was in favour of a peasant proprietary, but did not like what is proposed for Ireland, that the tenantry should be enabled to buy by having the greater part of the purchase money advanced by the state. We were creating a new class of encumbered proprietors (I think I said this, & he agreed). Either Dilke or Fitzmaurice made what I thought a shrewd remark about Argyll's speech of Friday: if it was the fact that the Cabinet had abandoned all their ideas, & taken up his, why was he, or did he affect to be, so indignant? He ought to have been satisfied with the result, & left the question of their morality & consistency to them, whom alone it concerned.

19 May 1879: Fine warm morning . . . Hale sends a bad report of Moult, whose future fitness for work he doubts. See Sanderson, & agree with him that the best thing to do is . . . . to send down an accountant to keep the current business in order. I do it accordingly . . .

. . . Write to Carnarvon proposing to see him about African affairs. Call upon him later, & discuss the situation. He does not disguise his reluctance to consent to the retrocession of the Transvaal, thinks it may be a necessity, but does not understand how Frere comes to have changed his opinion so suddenly & completely. He evidently dislikes the affair, & does not understand it. He advises that nothing should be said or done till we have the despatches in full, which is reasonable, as the telegraphic copy may be abridged or incorrect, and he also thinks it probable that Frere may have written to him. He will not oppose the giving up of the territory if satisfied that there is nothing else to do, but dwelt a good deal on its not being our business to help the Cabinet out of a difficulty. I said that I differed: if by our support we could help them to get rid of a dangerous responsibility, & put them in the way of doing a sensible thing, it was as much our business as that of anybody. But he did not quite see it.

Münster called later, & told me various things: (1) that there is an uncomfortable feeling between us & the French: they think we have thrown them over both as regards Greece & Egypt: encouraged them to commit themselves, & then refused to back them. (2) That notwithstanding the bankrupt condition of the country, the Russian govt. is adding largely to the numbers of the army: adding 400,000 men, he said, to the war complement: which makes Germany uneasy, as no sufficient reason is given. (3) That a Russian expedition is going in considerable force either to Merv, or to a point near it: the Russians arguing that now that we have occupied a large part of Afghanistan they are under no obligation to sit still. (This tallies with what I have heard more than once from Schouvaloff.) (4) That the virtual abandonment of the line of the Balkans has caused great disgust among the 'Jingo' party here but, having no one to fall back upon, & nothing that they can do, they keep in their resentment as well as they can. (5) That we are on the point of securing peace with the Ameer – he explained the terms, but I need not set them down.

There dined with us: Dow. Ly Lothian, Dow. Ly Shrewsbury, the Galloways, & Froude. Pleasant: Froude talked much of Carlyle & his early life, the roughness of it: his wife married him out of admiration for his genius, expecting a life chiefly passed in intellectual pursuits: disappointment at finding that her chief business was to cook the dinner, & keep the house in order. Froude talks also of Transvaal: thinks it would be well parted with, & would give back to the Dutch Natal also: which is a more questionable proposition.

20 May 1879: Mr. Parsons, brother to the man whose land near Haslemere I lately bought, makes me a sort of offer (but cautiously worded) of other land lying between my new purchase & Witley. I answer him in equally guarded style . . . It never rains but it pours. Here are three offers of estates touching Witley, all come at once. And yet the public goes on talking, in the face of evidence, about the difficulty of buying land. The difficulty in my experience is much rather to sell it.

H. of Lds. at 5.00: debate on an Irish bill brought in by Ld Belmore[138], for declaring the Ulster tenant right existent in certain cases not hitherto included in the law relating to it: everybody agreed that there was a grievance, but the bill went farther than its framers intended; & all parties condemned it. I was moved to say a few words, & advised him to withdraw it, & bring in another, for which in our House there is ample time. He would not do that but allowed it to be negatived on the second reading without dividing. Lord Lifford[139], a dull speaker & with strong prejudices, but not I think inaccurate, gave some curious evidence as to the kind of decisions sometimes pronounced in the land courts. He quoted one chairman of sessions as having said in court that he should take an entirely different valuation according as the owner of the land was a rich or poor man: for it was the duty of large landowners to let their estates at moderate rents, whereas a poor man might be justified in making the best bargain he could. Probably this principle is often acted upon though seldom avowed. . . .

21 May 1879: Sanderson comes early . . . to settle about a temporary substitute for Moult.

Drive with M. to Marshall & Snelgrove . . . Thence drive for air & pleasure round Regent's Park: where got out, & walk alone.

. . . Bagge[140] of Lynn calls upon me – hearty & bouncing as in old days. He is high sheriff for the year, & evidently pleased at the honour though he affects to grumble at the expense. He says the new dock has saved Lynn from ruin: at one time there were 400 houses empty in the town (so he said, but ?) now there is not one, & new houses are building out along the Gaywood road.

London U. Senate for a committee to revise the bye-laws: . . . much helped by Jessel, whose shrewdness in picking holes is especially useful in this sort of work.

22 May 1879: . . . The day being fine &, having nothing special to do, I decided on going down to Witley to see what I could of the land offered . . . Reached Haslemere 12.50, walk thence by part of the Frensham estate up to Hindhead, thence through my own lands . . . going round Fullock's estate. The latter is very picturesque, well wooded, & will be an acquisition if I can get it. The Frensham land is wild & has some wood on it, but is rather bleak & poor. I had an excellent walk & took the 4.10 train back from Witley, reaching home just before 6.00: 7 hours out or a little less.

In the H. of C. this evening a great debate on Indian finance was expected, Fawcett having a resolution which declared the danger of the situation, & announced the absolute necessity of retrenchment: it however collapsed, for Stanhope making his annual statement so fully admitted the almost desperate situation of matters that he in effect accepted Fawcett's motion: which accordingly Fawcett[141] withdrew. But to acknowledge a difficulty is one thing, to meet it is another: & there seems little hope of reductions sufficient to avert the necessity either of partial bankruptcy, or of help from this country. Lytton is not, & from his nature cannot become, an economist: the army is too strong a social interest to allow itself to be largely reduced: & no cutting down will be effective that does not include the army.

23 May 1879: . . . Much talk about the D. of Bedford having given back half a year's rent to his agricultural tenants. The act is not popular among his brother landowners, who fear they may have to do the same: & this, I think, has increased his pleasure in doing it. The discouragement among them is great & increasing: scarcely any are free from encumbrances: they are not frugal as a class: and most are compelled by their position to live in a certain fashion which they cannot easily alter. Hence a reduction of rents, small in proportion to their gross incomes, sweeps away nearly all that they have at their free disposal. The effect will be to break down a large number of the smaller squires, compelling them to sell: the largest estates will remain unaffected, or even tend to increase in consequence of the quantity of land in the market: buyers will be able to suit themselves, & on their side there will be no complaints: but owners of settled & heavily mortgaged properties will be disposed to ask for legislative relief such as the Irish Encumbered Estates Act, enabling them to sell freely. . . .

24 May 1879: . . . Went to a meeting of the Museum trustees
    . . . Walk back with Carnarvon, who excited about politics, & thinks the govt. cannot stand: which indeed he has thought ever since he left it. He says quite truly that the English public will not be well pleased when they see the bill for the Zulu war, which cannot be costing less than half a million a month. And for this reason he contends that they will dissolve in the autumn, by which time the fighting ought to be over, while the amount of the indebtedness will not yet be known.
    Peabody meeting at 3.30. Present, Lampson, Morgan, U.S. minister, & myself: we passed a resolution formally sanctioning the borrowing of £300,000 from the Treasury at 3½ per cent, not more than £100,000 being raised in each year. We decided also to negociate for the purchase from the Metrop. Board of about 10 acres of land: the price they ask is 5s. per sq. ft., or about £11,000 per acre, which considering the situation is far less than the ordinary market value of the land. Some of the plots, if sold free from all restrictions as to their use, would be worth 15s. per ft., so Mr. Vigors tells us. – Mr. Morgan scrupled a little as I had done at the extent of our borrowing, but is reconciled to it as I am by the goodness of the bargain, the obvious duty that lies upon us of extending our operations, & the certainty of being able to clear ourselves in 10 or 12 years.
    We also agreed to elect Mr. G. Lampson (Sir C.'s son) a trustee. Keston by 5.15 train. Met Hale there, but had only time for a few words, as he was on his way back into Lancashire.
    Pender has a convn. with M. which is reported to me but, being at secondhand, I note only its general features. He thinks business is not reviving: fresh failures at Middlesbrough & elsewhere have destroyed the confidence which was returning: the feeling among members of the House is one of alarm: & it is even stronger among the landowners & their representatives. Rents must fall heavily, even if tenants can be had: the smaller owners are mostly encumbered: habits of life have become more expensive, & cannot be altered at short notice, & many estates will change hands. The friends of the ministry are not sanguine as to the result of a dissolution: there is general uneasiness & depression: & the practical collapse of the Berlin treaty, just beginning to be understood, has disheartened many supporters.

To this I add two remarks: the revenue returns are bad, showing that diminished employment has lessened consumption: & the military authorities, & those interested in army matters, complain loudly of what they call the breakdown of our system. The petty war in S. Africa has drained off all our available forces: the recruits sent out are boys: & their inferiority, man for man, to the Zulus is matter of general comment. Nothing can show more strongly the general aversion to soldiering than the fact that, in a time of slack employment & general distress, it has not been easy to find recruits. The life is rough, ill paid & leads to nothing.

26 May 1879: . . . Saw Sanderson & some talk with him. No improvement in the City that he can hear of, nor prospect of employment for his brother, who I believe is living upon him still, & has done so for the last three years.

   Attended a levee, the only one this year, & I shall not go to a second: but one is a necessary duty for a peer engaged in public life. . . .

27 May 1879: Fine day, but cold. . . . See Hale . . . Settle with him (1) not to bid for any part of the Frensham estate; it is too far from Witley, likely to be dear & in the worst order . . . (2) to engage Mr. Ward, who can be usefully employed even if Moult should recover: (3) to help a cricket club in Bootle with a donation.

   . . . Hale tells me that he has continual applications for land to be let for building purposes: one firm at Burscough is applying for 8 acres in order to set up a factory: & in Lpool. the demand is lively. It is singular that the two ends of the county should differ so widely, for Statter reports nothing except stagnation.

   News in the papers that Sir G. Wolseley[142] is to take command on the South African frontier, superseding both Sir B. Frere & Ld Chelmsford: who nevertheless remain where they are, Frere retaining the government of the Cape. This is a wise move on the part of the Cabinet, and admits of no criticism except that it might just as well have been made three months ago. Hicks Beach has again taken the opportunity of disclaiming intentions of annexation. It is scarcely to be supposed that, after being thrown over and superseded, Frere will remain in the comparatively unimportant position of governor of the Cape: Natal & Transvaal being taken away from his jurisdiction. But he is poor, & has been trained in the Indian school, where resignation is an idea hardly entertained, since to the Anglo-Indian official his salary is his only means of living. Having accomplished a decided success in this announcement, Northcote, Beach, & F. proceeded to impair it by getting into a wrangle about whether, or when, the instructions given to Wolseley shall be published. It may be quite right to keep them back for a time: but no two gave the same reason for so doing: which is odd.

28 May 1879: More wrangling in the H. of C. wherein Gladstone seems to have spoken very civilly of Frere (I suppose religious sympathies are the bond between them, both being devout persons): & Elcho[143] outdid himself in military ardour, wanting to annex all South Africa, if I understand his speech rightly, or if he understands it himself. But on the whole the supersession of Frere is well taken, & ministers have a right to claim credit for it. – The House adjourned for Whitsuntide, &, unless there is a sudden reaction from the idleness of the last few weeks, the session will be one of the most barren ever known. The revenue returns are also more curious than agreeable reading, for customs & excise together show a loss of £750,000 & something more in comparison with the same date last year. . . .

29 May 1879: Letter from Statter, not wholly satisfactory: the award is given in the arbitration for the 7 acres near Bury station: he expected £70,000 which I knew was exaggerated but thought £40,000 a probable amount: the sum actually awarded is £28,000, with 2 years' interest, or £30,000 in round numbers. Except in the heart of a Lancashire town, one cannot call £4,000 per acre too little, but it is less than we had expected. . . .

30 May 1879: Left at 11.15 for Manchester, having undertaken to open a flowershow at the Botanical Gardens there. Arrived 12.45: where I was met by Ald. Booth[144], formerly Mayor . . . we had luncheon at Mr. Booth's house: I then went to the gardens & in a short speech declared them open: the show was said to be very good . . . At the suggestion of Sir J. Heron[145], the town clerk, I went with him to look at the Town Hall, which I had not seen since it was finished: there we found the Mayor, who asked me to join him in opening a new coffee tavern, which he had promised to do. We joined him accordingly, & I made another little speech, of course without preparation, but on such a subject it was safe to speak unprepared. Thence back to the Hulme town hall, where a dinner of the Botanical Socy., about 120 present. I took the chair: Dr. Watts[146], Hugh Mason, & many others locally known were present. I made the speeches short, & got away by the 9 p.m. train, reaching Knowsley by 11.00: rather weary, but not ill satisfied with the day's work.

Much interesting talk with Sir J. Heron about the municipal arrangements of Manchester. Large profits made for the public out of gas: not much out of water, it being a primary object to sell water as cheap as may be: the debt is large, but not so when compared to local revenues: it is held largely in the city itself: the debentures, or bonds, are as low as £50: this is the only respect in which improvement would seem possible: why should not every man who has a £5 note to spare put it into these securities? I suggested this to Sir J.H. but he seemed afraid of the increased complication of accounts that would follow.

He tells me that real property in the borough has fallen in value to the extent, on an average, of 25 or even 30 per cent: but the values were originally very high. In some cases £100 per square yard has been given, of course for frontage only.

31 May 1879: . . . An advertisement sent down to me mentions the proposed sale in one lot of an estate composed of waste lands in Cornwall, 36,000 acres, worth, according to the statement, £5 or £6 per acre. Probably no property of equal magnitude has changed hands in our time. I was half inclined to enquire about it, as such a purchase might in the long run be made very profitable by cutting up & reselling to small purchasers. The Cornwall people are taking much to the growing of early vegetables, etc., for London, since the general failure of their mines drove them to look for new employment. Among the marked effects of the present distress among farmers, I note a disposition to recur to the often discussed idea of peasant ownerships in England, such as exist in France & Germany. The plea for them is briefly this: that men work with more spirit & energy when they work for themselves: that, if they make but little money, they will at least be able to live off their produce: that spade husbandry will get more out of the soil than the less minutely careful operations of farming on a large scale: that a class of peasant owners will be at once very independent & very conservative: that they will be an eminently healthy class, unlike those who get their living in great cities: in short that they will be industrious, frugal, moral, & healthy. The above assertions would probably not be disputed: but it is answered: 'How are these men to buy their land? They have not the capital &, if they borrow, you have at once an encumbered class, not independent, since they will be at the mercy of their bankers, & miserably poor, since interest will eat up all their profits. Again, they will have to buy land at a rate which returns them 2 or $2\frac{1}{2}$% borrowing at 4%: which is a losing operation. They would be better off, man for man, if they put their savings into the funds & continued to work for wages. Nor is it certain that freedom to work or be idle as they pleased would be a gain. It is not always an advantage to be one's own employer.' The Continental precedent, it will be further contended, does not apply. For, in the first place, the French peasant seldom bought his land: he acquired it at a nominal rate during the Revolution: in Germany he received it from the State on the abolition of feudal tenures. Here, the first step in the process will be to buy: & that will seldom be possible. Nor is it safe to argue as to the cultivation of English moors & downs from the experience of French vineyards. Climate & sunshine make a difference which it is useless to ignore. – So the question is argued, but behind the argument on each side there is a strong unexpressed feeling, one side desiring to maintain, the other hoping to upset, the existing squirearchy . . .

1 June 1879: . . . Dr. Gorst calls, & talks to me with some reserve about Moult's case: he opens himself more freely to M. He does not expect mental recovery: poor Moult is undoubtedly insane: his case one of melancholia: no suicidal tendencies are observed: it seems that his family, & Gorst also, have long been uneasy about him: though in matters of business he was clear & methodical as ever. As is common in such matters, I observe that everybody about the place knew of his being out of sorts & queer before Ly D. or I did.

2 June 1879: See Hale early . . . Long talk with him about Moult. – Agree to engage Mr. Ward, at his own terms of £350 a year, & a lodging found for him.

. . . Drive with M. later & call on Mrs. Moult to ask after her son, & express sympathy.

Day remarkably bright & fine: a large temperance party in the park, but we saw little of them.

. . . There dined with us Hale (Mrs. Hale being in France) . . . & young Hornby, a son of the squire-parson of St. Michael's whom Hale is employing as a sort of secretary or assistant in the office. I suspect ulterior views on the part of the parents, & that it is desired to qualify the youth, who announced a taste for land-agency, for the reversion of Hale's place. But that will not rest either with them or with Hale to settle. . . .

3 June 1879: Drove into Liverpool early with M. for a meeting of the Molyneux trustees . . . We examined the accounts: income is over £1,600 a year: of which £1,400 is given away. We made one considerable change in the rules: agreeing to meet half-yearly, & deciding that no new applicant should be admitted to a pension without the case coming before us. Formerly the Rector of L.pool & the Visitor [Rev. Fairclough] settled all between them.

. . . The wind being westerly, sky clear, & a general cessation of work in St. Helens & among the colliers, the air was perfectly pure, free from smoke, & we saw Knowsley as I have hardly ever seen it during the last 10 years, but as it must have been before the great towns grew up round it.

4 June 1879: Another day like yesterday. Sky smokeless, bright sun & pure air. . . . Out nearly the whole day.

. . . In the papers death of Baron Rothschild[147] announced: a notable figure in London society: all the papers praise him, & justly, for he was kindly & liberal in the use of his wealth: very far superior to any of his sons. Historically he will be known as the first Jew who sat in parliament. Never was a change made which so entirely falsified the expectations of both sides. Jew members have been on the whole more Conservative than Liberal, their number has been small, & they have exercised no appreciable influence on English politics. The Baron's will is likely to excite curiosity, as the most fabulous ideas prevail about the wealth of the firm – probably much exaggerated!

5 June 1879: This was in the main an idle day. M. went into L.pool to see a school of cookery which she had promised to visit . . . Saw a young man named Mills, a son of my father's favourite servant, whom he had with him for many years: this youth is a broker: he had a vague notion that I could & should do something for him, but did not in the least know what. I gave him civil words, but could give nothing else.

Saw . . . poor Moult's brother-in-law . . . & talk as to his position. There is nothing more to be done, but I was anxious to hear what the family wished, & to show sympathy: for his father, old Moult, was the most devoted of all possible servants, & the son took after him.

6 June 1879: See Hale early. Agree with him to comply with a request of the volunteer officers to be allowed to have a field day of 5,000 men in the park some time next month: they to make all the arrangements, & keep order.

. . . Three members of the Lancashire farmers' club – Messrs. Neild, Whalley, & [?] – called as a deputation asking me to attend a meeting of the club next week, which I agreed to do – they sat with me an hour, which however was not wasted, for with much willingness to be convinced, & no apparent desire to ask for anything unfair, they started the wildest ideas, which seemed to have been put into their heads by somebody else, & taken up without their understanding what was implied in them. We talked the matter out, & I think I succeeded in making an impression on two of the party – the third, Mr. Neild, was a mere bag of phrases, which he kept repeating like a parrot, whenever they seemed to come in suitably. He was a great talker too, & wearied out his colleagues.

There came to stay the day & sleep here Pender & Sir C. Dilke, the latter of whom has been making a speech in L.pool on the claims of Greece. I took him out for a walk, Pender driving with M. We had much talk, though rather of a general than political character. He has a villa at Toulon, with 25 acres, & talked amusingly of his position as a landowner in France. He said among other things that most of the labour employed in his district came from Italy. The Piedmontese worked harder & cheaper than the Toulon people, & came over in considerable numbers. He did not like the proceedings of the republic – the system of the empire, he thought, was too much continued – public works carried on in all directions to employ labour, & to please the constituencies, money being borrowed for the purpose, without thought of the future. – He confirmed what I have heard from several quarters, that there is great dissatisfaction in France at the attitude of England. We have never been quite forgiven for not helping the French, at least by diplomatic means, towards the end of the German war – & now we are supposed to have thrown them over about Egypt, which has aggravated the original grievance.

Of English affairs D. talked freely. He is not sanguine as to the prospects of the Liberal party – thinks they will lessen the Conservative majority at the elections, but not destroy it. Their trouble is to find candidates for the counties – & they are a good deal divided among themselves. – He praised Ld Rosebery highly, but said he required so much time to prepare & polish a speech that he could not often be induced to speak. He spoke warmly of Ld Lansdowne. I asked if it was true that Hartington did not care for his post as a leader, & was willing to throw it up? He thought that was a mistake: it was not Hartington's nature to show himself warmly interested in anything, but when there was some question of his being superseded he had shown no disposition to give way. Of Gladstone he spoke little, but enough to show that, while greatly respecting him, he did not think his leadership safe or judicious. He commented shrewdly on Fawcett's speeches: observing that for the first quarter of an hour they were excellent, full of matter & well put: but the rest was only repetition in a different form of what he had already said. Pender, who heard the comment, agreed in its justice.

To me he said nothing about disestablishment one way or another – but from remarks made to M. I gather that he & many of the younger Liberals, while pledged to it in principle, are not zealous in the cause – not that they love the church, but that reasoning from what has happened elsewhere they think it doubtful whether disestablishment would not stimulate ecclesiastical zeal to such an extent as to make the clergy more powerful than before. This, he told me, is the view taken by Gambetta as to the French priests – that it would not be safe to withdraw the contributions which they receive from the State, as the deficiency would be made up by the devout among their congregations, while if unpaid they must necessarily be uncontrolled.

Some remark was made by me as to the position of English Liberals on the land question, as affecting their chances in the counties, since large owners do not care to be reformed out of their estates. I did not press it: but D. took occasion in talking with M. to refer to the subject & assure her that the Liberal party had no intention of raising the land question – that they knew the danger of it – & that I need have no uneasiness as to anything violent being done in that direction. I accept this assurance as sincere, & obviously it is not in the interest of Whigs to stir in a matter where their action would alienate all the large proprietors. Still it is given with an object: & no one M.P., even if in the position of a leader, can answer for the entire body of the parliamentary Liberals.

7 June 1879: Breakfast at 8.00 with Sir C. Dilke & took leave of him. . . . To Preston. There H.[ornby] left us, & at the station we met Mr. Thompson, my agent for the Fylde. Drive with him & Hale to Chipping, where first went over a farm bought 2 or 3 years ago & farmed by a quaint old man of the name of Seed. He would not believe in my identity, & when persuaded of it did nothing but stare at me. Thence to the land[148] now offered for sale, about a mile off: it is detached from mine, but not distant[149]. It . . . wants draining, & grows large crops of rushes. . . . Hale & Thompson both seemed to think the purchase worth making: saying that the rent might well stand at £220, or a pound per acre, that the farmer could pay that, & the return would then be 3%. I reserved my decision, but feel well disposed towards the purchase. It is in these northern parts of the county that our family has retained most influence: and if driven out by increasing smoke & crowding from Knowsley it is here that our natural retreat would be. A few years would be sufficient to consolidate what I now have scattered by buying up the intervening freeholds, & a little planting would add the only feature wanting – for the hills are fine, & the air healthy.

On the way I questioned Hale as to the capacity in which young Hornby is living with him. It appears that he is taken in as a pupil to learn the business of land agency, so that I have no sort of responsibility for him, which I am glad of. He is well brought up, & Hale is much taken with him, but I do not think he has much capacity for business, as far as it is possible to judge of a youth only just come from Cambridge. . . . Took the 4.30 train back to Prescot, where it was stopped for me, & walk in thence. . . . Strong smell of St. H.[elens] in the park & house.

8 June 1879: . . . Sent £20 to the L.Pool Workshops for the Blind, & £20 as required to the National Penny Bank in London.

Agreed, after consulting with M., that I could not reasonably refuse the office of umpire in the Durham arbitration case, however troublesome & thankless it may be. Wrote accordingly to accept.

. . . Examined also . . . a quaint drawing of the Derby house in L.pool, & another of the house belonging to the family in Chester. Both are small & poor: so much so that it is impossible to suppose they were used as residences: probably they served in the absence of inns to lodge any member of the family who might be passing through, or visiting the town on business for a day or two. The number of houses kept up in this way by old families, & their smallness, are equally a puzzle to me: I can only explain them in the way suggested. . . .

10 June 1879: Talk with Hale, & agree that he shall send up £15,000 to Coutts . . .

I shall now have, withdrawn from the estate, & either invested or in hand, £225,000: which is exactly the sum I have received from Moult since 1870. My private expenses have been met during these ten years partly by previous savings, partly by interest of money invested. As in the same time I have cleared off half a million of debt, bought Fairhill, Witley, Keston, & the reversion of Holwood, besides many freeholds in Lancashire, my successors will have no reason to complain.

11 June 1879: Heavy & incessant rain all day, with east wind & some smell. I drove with Hale to Bootle . . . We saw the new streets planned, & partly laid out, & the increase of building, which is remarkable considering the hard times. There are full 500 acres untouched, much of which lies near the docks. The main roads laid out for villas are well shaded with trees, & these and the gardens give a better appearance to the place than one could have expected.

Note that Hale again brought young H.[ornby] with him - & that F. Hopwood tells M. that it is understood he is appointed an assistant. I have little doubt but that this is what the family want, & what Hale contemplates: but he has not chosen to say so, & calls him only a pupil. Hale is a gentleman in mind & manners, & I get on well with him: but his excessive caution as to giving offence, combined with a strong determination to manage things his own way, makes him a little tricky & underhand in his arrangements. I am always obliged to ask myself, when he proposes anything, whether I know the whole, or what is kept back to be produced later. . . .

12 June 1879: Woke not very well, with some headache, I cannot imagine why, for a more regular or temperate life than mine it is not possible to lead. The feeling passed off, but left a certain languor & apathy behind.

Saw Hale, & told him that I had decided to buy the Fylde farm. My purchases of this year are now 300 acres north of Preston, 205 acres adjoining Holwood, & 245 near Haslemere: in all 750 acres, & there is the negociation going on for 200 acres near Fairhill. But railway sales will cover all & more.

Long walk with Broomfield, in park & meadows. All looks well, except . . . where smoke & vapours are evidently doing mischief. Near home the look of care & neatness about the place is a marked contrast to what it was a dozen years ago.

Finished putting together some notes for an address to the L.pool Farmers' Club on Saturday.

Mrs. W.E. West . . . came to dine & sleep. She reports her husband well, & apparently he is not possessed with melancholy fits as he used to be at Oxford: the work of agency[150] suits him: his only eccentricity is that he has taken up and adheres strictly to the vegetarian system, saying with much satisfaction that he can live on 7d a day. . . .

13 June 1879: Mr. Lee[151] came early to take down my address to the Farmers' Club. Mrs. West & her daughter left. Gave the girl £2 as a present. Long early ride. Walk in afternoon to look at a new clump above the lake . . .

14 June 1879: . . . Drove in to the Town Hall, L.pool, where meeting of the Farmers' Club is held. Received by Livingston[152], the deputy mayor. Both he & Steble[153] attend the meeting. About 100 to 120 present: Mr. Neild, Mr. Whalley, & Mr. Scotson, all take part. My address occupies about 50 minutes – perhaps less. Not much dissent, & indeed the speeches were but little to any purpose – rather vague complaints as of something wrong than definite suggestions.

. . . Col. Steble, whom I meet at the Town Hall, tells me that the St. Helens people have got hold of a new patent which, if generally applied, will make it profitable to consume the vapours. . . . I received yesterday . . . a funny note from Col. Blackburne[154], original in grammar & language, but imparting that Sclater Booth will drop the most material provisions of his bill for the prevention of nuisances, having some faint hope that, if he does so, he may be allowed to carry the rest. He probably has no choice, for the deadlock in the H. of C. is worse than ever. The obstructionist tactics of the Irish have so far succeeded that the session will probably be the most barren on record. The favourite device, practised with much success, is to ask a question or make a speech on some petty subject, in terms so offensive that the minister answering can hardly avoid noticing them. Then some other Irish M.P. gets up to justify his colleague, speaks more violently still, compels a reply, and a scene is got up which wastes two or three hours.

15 June 1879: Woke in the night with a sense of misery & depression as if some grave misfortune had happened: it was some time before I could satisfy my mind that all was illusion, & that there was no cause for anxiety or low spirits: the effect on my nerves has not yet passed away: I cannot conceive the reason, never having been so troubled before[155]: probably it is digestion only, or the effect of damp climate. But I am not sorry that we move tomorrow. . . .

16 June 1879: . . . Left Knowsley at 10.20: reached St. J. Square about 4.20 . . .

17 June 1879: My speech of Saturday last has led to articles in all the papers, civil enough, & for the most part containing more of agreement than of dissent. The only criticisms upon it have been in the nature of objecting that I had not mentioned this, that, or the other circumstance which it did not fall within my plan to deal with.

Received from that singular being Capt. B. Pim[156] a letter in very friendly terms, assuring me that what the public wants is the reversal of the free trade system of the last 30 years, and wishing that I should put myself at the head of the movement. As the letter is private, it must be sincerely meant. There is no doubt a real revival of the old protectionist spirit among a large class: not resting on economical grounds, but on a kind of patriotism, according to which it is the duty of every Englishman to employ some other Englishman rather than a foreigner. With such a sentiment there is no reasoning, & it has gained strength from the example of America & the colonies. But it will come to no result, for the request of the farmer to have corn taxed will be refused by the protectionists of the towns: & he in turn will not see the advantage of giving to other people's industry a benefit which is not to be extended to his own. . . .

18 June 1879: . . . London U. Senate at 4.00: sit till about 5.00. Business mostly formal. Walk with Granville. He anxious to know, & asks with apologies, what my attitude at the next election is likely to be. I tell him, as indeed I think I did once before, that I shall not make any secret of my want of confidence in the present Cabinet – that I shall give no support to the Conservative candidates in any part of Lancashire – that I shall announce this resolution to all whom it may concern – but that I shall not take any active part against them, simply holding aloof.

Had myself weighed, 14 st. 1½ lbs., which is more than I like, but the increase is not due to want of exercise, or excess in food.

. . . M. goes with Margaret to a party given by the Duchess of Northumberland: meets there Ld Beaconsfield, who very affectionate, & presses us to dine with him. – I have no personal feeling against Disraeli &, as nothing unpleasant has passed between us, there is no reason why we should not meet: but Q. whether all this revival of friendship is genuine? It may be, for he has always been fond of M. but a dissolution in autumn is much talked of, & it might serve his purpose to put about the notion that we were politically reconciled.

19 June 1879: . . . Sir C. Lampson called . . . He talked about the farmers, said he farms 1,000 acres in Sussex: that labour has risen from 12s. a week 30 years ago to 18s. now: that he did not complain of, but the labour was worth less than formerly: it was carelessly done, the men knowing that, if they were turned off at one place, they would be taken on at another. He thought the British farmer could hold his own in growing meat: that more land should be laid down in grass: which would save labour, though rents might be rather lower.

. . . After full talk over the matter with M. we agree that it is best to decline Ld B.'s invitation, but to do it in the most conciliatory & friendly way, so as neither to commit ourselves nor to give offence.

20 June 1879: See Drage, who says liver is not quite right, & orders medicine. It is never a good sign with me when my weight increases. But, taking all together, few men at 53 have had less in the way of health to complain of.

. . . Late last night came news that the young Napoleon – Prince Imperial as they called him – has been killed by Zulus. It seems he went out reconnoitring with a party of only 8 men, who had dismounted, seeing no enemy, to rest their horses . . . It is an event of political importance, for it leaves the Bonapartists without a candidate for the throne, if they should ever have a chance again. Prince Napoleon[157] (Plon-plon) is the next in succession, & his abilities are remarkable: but for some reason he has contrived to become unpopular with all sections of Frenchmen. Priests hate him as a freethinker: conservatives as a revolutionist: the army has been imbued with an opinion of his want of courage: a charge for which I believe there is no foundation but which, once put about, it is almost impossible to refute: and the republicans, with whom he has strong intellectual sympathy, cannot forget that, however he may have criticised & opposed the policy of the late Emperor, he profited by his position as a member of the reigning family, receiving some £30,000 a year from the civil list. So it comes about that, with many admirers, he has no party at his back. He has sons, but they are too young to be available for many years, even if he were willing to vacate his position in their favour. . . .

21 June 1879: . . . After luncheon, by rail with M. to Bickley, whence drove to Chiselhurst to write our names in sign of condolence at Camden Place: which it seems is the right thing to do: & we found many on the same errand. The Empress[158] is to be doubly pitied: for in the loss of her son she sees the end of the dynasty, & her sole object & interest in life is henceforth gone. But I should pity her more if it were possible to forget that for the sake of this boy she, more than any other person, forced on the war of 1870: causing calamities to Europe of which her own suffering is a very slight expiation. . . .

23 June 1879: . . . Margaret tells us – Sackville [Cecil] present – that young Brett, the judge's son[159], all but proposed to her in the spring, but she managed to convey to him the idea that his offer would not be welcome in time to prevent its actually being made. She has kept the story to herself till now, & it only came out on our speculating as to the reason of her not being asked to a party given by the Bretts to which M. & I are going.

H. of Lords at 5.00, where expected a debate on Irish affairs: but Ld Oranmore[160], who had given the notice, missed his opportunity by chancing to go out of the House: & our chief business was a dull discussion on the drainage of the Thames valley. Salisbury answered a question to the effect that the European powers acting in concert have called on the Khedive to resign: a decision which was perhaps inevitable, but will lead to a good deal of controversy. The Duke of Cambridge, before business began, volunteered an explanation as to the terms on which the young French prince went out to South Africa, by which it seems that he was a simple looker-on, not even a volunteer, nor attached to any general. It is characteristic of the time & of the men that the Duke & Ld Chelmsford have both come forward to show that they were not in fault, before anyone attacked them. Not dignified perhaps in high functionaries, but it shows how completely we are ruled by opinion, & that is well. There is a good deal of uneasiness in the public mind as to the circumstances of the young man's death.

24 June 1879: Cold raw day, with frequent showers & some thunder. The season continues the worst that I remember. . . . Stayed at home after luncheon, rain continuing: read & wrote. H. of Lds at 5.00, but no business of interest. Walk home with Carnarvon.

. . . Poor Moult is no better in condition of mind, though improved in health: he is to be removed to the asylum at Cheadle, his state being now unmistakably one of insanity.

His family write about the prospect of a cure, but that seems scarcely probable. I am afraid from what Gorst told me at Knowsley there is no doubt but that he is himself the author of the mischief.

25 June 1879: Sanderson calls, tells me his brother has a sort of offer to be secretary in Cyprus, with £1,200 a year: a better post than Galatz[161], but in a worse climate, & his health is poor. I am glad, however, that the proposal should have been made, whether accepted or not, as it shows that Sanderson's services in the office are appreciated.

. . . Sir C. Lampson calls, explains that the negociation with the B. of Works for London is in difficulties, the Board naturally disliking the idea of selling their land for a third of what it cost them: though they have not got, & are not likely to get, any better offer. We talk the matter over, & I agree to write to Sir J. Hogg[162] a semi-official letter, stating, what is really the fact, that the trustees will gain nothing by the arrangement, that at best there will be a bare avoidance of loss, that they have gone into the business solely in the interest of the public, & that if their help is not wanted they will withdraw without regret. . . . In truth I shall not be sorry if the whole matter ends, never having much liked the notion of a debt for £300,000, though it is justifiable under the circumstances, & can be worked off in 12 or 14 years.

Letter from Hale . . . Hale is selling 8,000 yds in Bootle to the canal co. – he asks 10s. a yard, which is at the rate of £2,500 per acre.

. . . Called in Curzon St. Talk of the Irish University Bill, which after much hesitation the Cabinet has decided to oppose. But at the last moment news came of an unexpected announcement – Northcote has given notice of a bill to be brought in on the same subject in the Lords tomorrow, by the Chancellor. The surprise was universal. Everybody asked: 'Is this a new intention? If so, why is it taken at the last moment? If not, why were not the House warned before, so that they should not waste their time on a bill which was condemned beforehand?' I believe that there has been nothing worse in the matter than hesitation: but, taken together with all that has gone before, it will be regarded as a fresh instance of the policy of tricks & mystification of which we have heard so much. In any case to bring in a new ministerial measure on the 26th of June, when those already before parliament have but little chance of passing, is an unbusinesslike proceeding.

A strong agitation has sprung up in Mayo & Galway against the payment of rent – opposed by the priests, but supported by Parnell & some others in a respectable position. This is a comment on the predictions of those who, like Gladstone & Fortescue, really believed that the bill of 1870 would put an end to agrarian agitation.

26 June 1879 (Thursday): Walk for exercise (not at all for pleasure) in steady rain. . . . Troubled with a loose tooth which causes irritation & some aching.

Deputation called from Southport asking me to take the first part in an inauguration – so it is fashion to call such affairs – of a new promenade, etc. They suggested August, which could not be arranged, but in the end agreed to the 18th of September.

H. of Lds at 5.00, expecting a statement from the Chancellor, after what Cross had said: but we were made April fools: for he only rose to give a notice for Monday, & even then only to 'call attention to the subject' not to bring in a bill. It seems that Cross had been hasty, & spoken without authority. The peers had come down in greater numbers than usual, & were half amused, half disgusted. The move of yesterday has not pleased the conservatives, who ask what is the use of trying to deal with a question which it is well known cannot be settled so as at once to satisfy the Irish Catholics & the bulk of the party, while more will be lost than gained by stirring it: & they also want to know why, if the thing was to be done at all, it was announced only at the last moment. The answer commonly given, & probably the true one, is that the Cabinet were waiting to see how far the official leaders of opposition would commit themselves to the Irish demands before taking a line of their own. But any tampering with ultramontane support is dangerous where English votes are concerned: more may be lost here than will be gained in Ireland. . . .

27 June 1879: . . . In afternoon to the Lords, where a brisk little debate on the state of Armenia, in which Carnarvon for some reason appears specially interested. He had no trouble in showing that reforms of various kinds have been demanded by us, & promised more or less vaguely by the Turks, none of which seem likely to get themselves realised. Hammond[163] said something about the treaties, but quite inaudibly: Salisbury in reply took a bold but imprudent line, denying all responsibility for the Turks, beyond the duty of giving them good advice. This might have been well enough if only the old treaties had been in question, but he altogether ignored & threw over the Anglo-Turkish convention of last year: of which fact he was reminded both by Ld Morley[164] & Granville. Ld Beaconsfield was absent, having the gout. But it is singular that, though there was a fair attendance on the Conservative side, & Salisbury was rather sharply attacked, not one either of his colleagues or supporters said anything in his defence.

Much teased all this day with pain & swelled face.

28 June 1879: Hear from Coutts that the £5,000 is invested: leaving £3,603 balance, & making £215,000 in railway securities, worth £225,000.

. . . Stayed at home in the afternoon, having pain in the face, unable to talk easily or to eat without discomfort. Keston by 5.00 p.m. train.

Baron Rothschild's will is proved, £2,700,000, which is far below what was generally expected: but most likely a substantial part of his property is invested abroad. He was commonly thought to be worth £10,000,000 or £12,000,000 . . .

The event of the week is the deposition of the Khedive of Egypt, nominally by the Sultan, really by agreement of all the powers. The reasons for this step will be explained in papers about to be laid. Substantially, I can believe it to have been wise & even necessary: for the government of the Khedive was one of oppression to his own subjects, & he had alternately duped & defied the powers. In short he was incorrigible, & is well got rid of. But many difficult questions will be raised by his removal – not the least so being that of the Egyptian debt. In equity, if the lenders get back half their capital, they will have as much as they can reasonably claim, for the loans were raised on excessive terms, & with a full knowledge on the part of the lenders of the risk incurred. But the French speculators, who are the chief holders of the debt, are not likely to see the matter in this light: & we may be dragged at their heels into measures inconsistent with our general policy as to lenders to foreign states.

29 June 1879: . . . Wrote to Sanderson, to offer him the use of Fairhill during August for his mother, sisters, & self: while we shall be in the Alps.

. . . Death of Lord Lawrence announced in the papers yesterday, at the age of 69, but he had long been in failing health. He was on the whole the greatest Anglo-Indian since Warren Hastings, & probably it is owing to his determination & judgement in the crisis of 1857 that India remains a British possession. There was a peculiar simplicity in his character, more easily felt than described. You seemed when in contact with him to be conscious that you were dealing with a nature incapable of meanness or intrigue. His face once seen was not to be forgotten: it was that of a man born & trained to exercise supreme power: rugged and massive, yet not harsh. I believe that few persons have been more affectionately regarded by those dependent upon them, or more respected by the natives. By the fashionable society both of Calcutta & of London he was rather under-valued: his services & capacity could not be denied, but his ways were not their ways, & sympathy was impossible. We have many good public servants left both at home & in the east: but none of the type of Lord Lawrence. There is a talk of burying him in Westminster Abbey: I hope it will be done, but the influence of court & Cabinet will not be exercised in that direction: for the modern imperialist notions were hateful to his practical and economical turn of mind, & he made no secret of his aversion.

30 June 1879: . . . Saw . . . Sanderson, who accepts the offer of Fairhill for August on behalf of his family. He tells me that the interference of the Porte in the Khedive's affairs was not at all desired by our government: but the Sultan having the legal right to do what he did, & exercising it in doing precisely the thing which we wanted, objection on our part became impossible: he has thus ingeniously managed to establish a precedent for inter-vention in Egyptian affairs, which we did not desire, but cannot help.

. . . Wrote to Herbert Spencer, the philosopher, to thank him for his last book[165], a copy of which he has sent me: & I took occasion to say something as to the effect which his writings have produced on my mind, which was very sincere, though I worded it dryly lest I should seem to be complimentary after the manner of politicians.

Went to . . . the dentist at 1.00: & there had the tooth drawn which has given me trou-ble of late, taking the usual anaesthetic, laughing gas. It produced sleep after six: not the slightest discomfort afterwards. I was exactly 11 minutes in the house, & home again within half an hour of setting out. Business as usual on coming home. Left by 3.23 train, & reached Keston again by 4.30. Walk with M. . . . Quiet evening.

Notes

[1]   Hugh Mason (d. 1886), president of Manchester Chamber of Commerce 1871–1873, Mayor of Ashton 1858–1860, M.P. Ashton 1880–1885 (defeated), D.L. Lancs.: extreme radical.

[2]   Rev. William Nassau Molesworth (1816–1890), incumbent of St. Clement's, Rochdale, 1844–1889: priest 1840: author of *A History of the Reform Bill of 1832* and much else: s. of Rev. J.E.N. Molesworth (1790–1877), vicar of Rochdale 1840–1877.

[3]   John Torr (1813–1880), Liverpool merchant (retired 1869), M.P. Liverpool 1873–January 1880 (died). Chairman of Liverpool College.

[4]   Mrs. W.E. West (d. 23 February 1883) m. 1860 Col. W.E. Sackville-West (1830–1905). Their eldest son Lionel Edward (b. 1867) became the 3rd Baron Sackville, succeeding his uncle in 1908.

[5]   *Parl. Deb.*, 3, vol. ccxliii, cols. 273 (9 December 1879). Derby argued that the Viceroy and his advisers had precipitated a war which, by a little more patience and forbearance, might have been avoided.

[6]   After a distinguished army career, Charles Richard West, 6th Earl De La Warr, drowned himself in the Cam in 1873.

[7] Edward Gordon Douglas-Pennant (Douglas to 1841), 1st Baron Penrhyn (1800–1886), cr. baron 1866.

[8] W.R. Greg (1809–1881), writer, thinker, and millowner: comptroller of the Stationery Office 1864–1877.

[9] J.W. Blakesley (1808–1885), dean of Lincoln: educ. Trinity, Cambridge, where tutor 1839–1845: vicar of Ware 1845–1872: dean of Lincoln from 1872. Wrote much for *Times:* editor of Herodotus.

[10] The Cotton Districts Convalescent Fund built hospitals in healthy locations like Buxton and Southport.

[11] J.E. Thorold Rogers (1823–1890), M.P. 1880–1886: professor 1859–1890.

[12] F.G. Burnaby (1842–1885), cavalry officer, balloonist, and explorer: contested Birmingham 1880: killed in action in Sudan, 1885.

[13] Not traced, unless conceivably Col. W.T.N. Champ (1808–1892), premier of Tasmania 1856–1857.

[14] Perhaps Edward Robert Gregge-Hopwood of Hopwood Hall, Middleton, Lancs. (1846–?), who succ. his father Edward John in 1891. He was 'family' in that in 1875 he m. the grand-dau. of the 12th E. of Derby. His 2 sons died in the Great War.

[15] Dr. A.C. Tait (1811–1882), Archbishop of Canterbury 1869–1882: headmaster of Rugby 1842–1849.

[16] Of the Cotton Districts Convalescent Fund.

[17] Col. T.E. Taylor (1811–1883), Tory whip: Chancellor of the Duchy of Lancaster October–December 1868, 1874–1880.

[18] It is not clear how far this corresponds to the facts. Sir T.H. Fermor-Hesketh, 6th Bt (1847–d. unm. 28 May 1876) had indeed been succeeded by his brother, Sir T.G. Fermor-Hesketh, 7th Bt (1849–1924), who married the dau. of a Nevada senator. The latter's son, Thomas, 1st Baron Hesketh (1881–1944) married a Californian, and became a peer in 1935. The family rental is given as £31,000 p.a.

[19] Probably (Sir) Thomas Bland Royden, 1st bt, Liverpool shipping magnate, who d. 1917: father of Maud Royden, preacher.

[20] Sir A.B. Forwood (1836–1898), Liverpool mayor 1877–1878, merchant prince, and Tory leader: M.P. Ormskirk 1885–death: 1st sec. of Admiralty 1886–1892.

[21] In N. Norfolk the government majority increased from 110 in the April 1876 by-election to 490 in the January 1879 by-election, the Liberal candidate being the same in both cases.

[22] Arthur, 1st D. of Connaught (1850–1942), Field-Marshal, Gov.-Gen. of Canada 1911–1916.

[23] Sir Bartle Frere, 1st bart (1815–1884), gov. of Bombay 1862–1867, gov. of Cape 1877–1880.

[24] Henry James, 2nd Baron Moncreiff (1840–1909), s. of 1st baron: educ. Trinity, Cambridge: advocate-depute 1865–1866, 1868, 1880: Scottish judge 1888–1905: Lib. Unionist 1886.

[25] Lord Augustus Loftus (1817–1904), s. of 2nd Marquess of Ely: diplomatist 1837–1879: amb. to Russia 1871–1879: gov. of N.S. Wales 1879–1885: sought transfer to Rome, February 1876.

[26] Léon Gambetta (1838–1882), s. of a Genoese grocer: blind in one eye from youth: embodied national resistance in 1870–1871: premier November 1881–January 1882 for 66 days: d. from revolver accident aged 44.

[27] W.H. Waddington (1826–1894), French premier 1879: French ambassador in London 1883–1894. Educ. Rugby and Trinity, Cambridge, with Derby: rowed in boat race for Cambridge: married an American: a leading archaeologist: Protestant.

[28] 'Abd Al-Hamid II (1842–1918), Sultan: succ. his bro. Murad V, 31 August 1876.

[29] Destruction of British force by Zulus at Isandhlwana, 22 January 1879, with loss of 30 officers, 500 men, and 1,000 rifles.

[30] Francis Hitchman, Tory publicist: ed. Disraeli, *The Runnymede Letters* (1885, 1st ed., 1836). Also *The Public Life of ... the Earl of Beaconsfield* (London, 1879), 2 vols; second and revised ed., 1881.

[31] J.A. Froude (1818–1894), historian and biographer of Carlyle, whose literary executor he was: regius prof. of modern history at Oxford, 1892–1894: frequently a guest of Derby.

[32] *Parl. Deb.*, *3*, vol. ccxliii, cols. 1041–1048. Beaconsfield confined himself to defending Frere as the man best fitted for the post of High Commissioner, and to denying that government policy in South Africa was one of annexation. As to legislation, he promised a Criminal Code and County Boards.

[33] Derby still lacks an authoritative biography.

[34] Sir C.M. Lampson, 1st bt (1806–1885), b. in Vermont, U.S.A.: came to U.K. as merchant, 1830: vice-chairman of company for laying Atlantic telegraph 1856–1866: cr. bt 1866.

[35] Sir J.T. Knowles (1831–1908), editor and architect: laid out Leicester Square, founded Metaphysical Society (1869–1881), and editor of the *Nineteenth Century* from 1877: inventor of the signed article.

[36] Richard Monckton Milnes, 1st Lord Houghton (1809–1885), M.P. Pontefract 1837–1863: Hon Fellow Trinity, author, and Keats scholar: cr. baron 1863: m. dau. of 2nd Lord Crewe (she d. 1874) and was succ. by his only s., later 1st Marquess of Crewe.

[37] Sir Francis Doyle (1810–1888), professor of poetry at Oxford: commissioner of customs 1869–1883.

[38] Sir Henry Maine (1822–1888), jurist: master of Trinity Hall, 1877–1888.

[39] Henry Reeve (1813–1895), man of letters: on *Times* 1840–1855, ed. *Greville Memoirs* 1865–, ed. *Edinburgh Review*, 1855–1895.

[40] John Tyndall (1820–1893), man of science: Ph.D. Marburg 1850, F.R.S. 1852: wrote on glaciers.

[41] (Sir) Richard Owen (1804–1892), naturalist: kt 1884.

[42] Henry George Powlett, previously Vane, 4th Duke of Cleveland (1803–1891).

[43] 8th Duke of Northumberland (1810–1899), succ. 1867: styled Lord Lovaine 1830–1865 and Earl Percy 1865–1867: M.P. Northumberland N. 1852–1865: minor office 1858–1859: lord privy seal (in cabinet) 1878–1880: m. Louisa (who d. December 1890), dau. of Irvingite banker Henry Drummond, 1845: leading freemason.

[44] Salisbury's nephew: premier 1902–1905.

[45] John Gilbert Talbot (1835–1910), M.P. (Cons.) Kent W. 1868–1878, Oxford University 1878–1910: parl. sec. to board of trade 1878–1880.

[46] G.J. Shaw-Lefevre, 1st Baron Eversley (1831–1928), educ. Trinity, Cambridge: minor office 1868–1874: 1st commissioner of works 1880–1884, postmaster-general (in cabinet 1885: in cabinet 1892–1895): cr. baron 1906.

[47] Cross's Artisans Dwellings Act of 1875, slightly amended by further legislation in 1879. In 1881 a report found that, of the 87 towns to which the Act applied, 77 had taken no action to carry it out. Paul Smith, *Disraelian Conservatism and Social Reform* (1967), p. 290.

[48] Henry, 5th D. of Newcastle (1811–1864): Henry, 6th D. of Newcastle (1834–1879), his s. and h.: Henry, 7th D. of Newcastle (1864–1928), elder son of the 6th Duke, who was succ. by his brother the 8th Duke (b. 1866). The 'rich marriage' of the 6th Duke was to a daughter of Henry Hope of Deepdeene, the Surrey banker.

[49] (Sir) A.H. Layard (1817–1894), amb. at Constantinople 1877–1880.

[50] Henry John, 3rd vt Palmerston (1784–1865), twice premier.

[51] William Lamb, Lord Melbourne (1779–1848), twice premier.

[52] Derby's brother.

[53] Prince Imperial (1856–1879), s. of Napoleon III and Eugénie.

[54] Elizabeth Mary, dau. of 1st D. of Sutherland, who m. 1819 Richard, 2nd Marquess of Westminster (who d. 1869).

[55] George Russell, Lord Tavistock, later 10th D. of Bedford (1852–1893), M.P. Beds. 1875–1885, m. Lady Adeline, dau. of Earl Somers.

[56] Frances, Lady Waldegrave (1821–1879), *née* Braham: had 4 husbands, the last being Chichester Fortescue, Lord Carlingford.

57 W.E. Forster (1818–1886), M.P. (Lib.) Bradford 1861–1886: chief sec. for Ireland, 1880–1882, resigning: proposed as H. of C. leader 1874 but stood down in favour of Hartington.

58 Sir T.E. Perry (1806–1882), Indian judge: member of council of India, 1859–1882.

59 Sir C. Foster (1841–1904), inspector of mines 1872–1901: kt 1903.

60 E.B. Eastwick (1814–1883), orientalist: M.P. (Penryn) 1868–1874.

61 Henry Lowther, 3rd E. of Lonsdale (1818–1876): St. George Henry Lowther, 4th E. of Lonsdale (1855–1882), s. of 3rd E.: Hugh Cecil Lowther, 5th E. of Lonsdale (1857–), bro. of 4th E. Estates: 68,000 acres, £71,333 rental p.a.

62 5th E. of Hardwicke (1836–1897), succ. 1873: previously Lord Royston: the original Champagne Charlie?

63 James Frederick Elton, *Travels and Researches among the Lakes and Mountains of Eastern and Central Africa. From the Journals of . . . J.F.E. . . . Edited and completed by H.B. Cotterill*, London, 1879.

64 Sir P. Hewett, 1st bart (1812–1891), surgeon to Queen Victoria and Prince of Wales.

65 Sir Charles Newton (1816–1894), keeper of Greek and Roman antiquities at the British Museum 1861–1885.

66 Sir Joseph Hooker (1817–1911), botanist: succ. father as director at Kew, 1865: president of Royal Society, 1873–1878.

67 *Parl. Deb.*, 3, vol. ccxliv, cols. 137–255. Trevelyan's motion for Reform was defeated 291–226.

68 Sir G.O. Trevelyan, 2nd bart (1838–1929), chief sec. for Ireland 1882–1884.

69 Sir Thomas Frederick Elliot (1808–1880), assistant under-sec. for colonies 1847–1868.

70 Sir M.E. Grant Duff (1829–1906), M.P. (Lib.) 1857–1881: under-sec. for India 1868–1874, for cols. 1880: gov. of Madras 1881–1886.

71 Priv. sec. to Granville in 1860s: asst. under-sec. in C.O. 1871–1892, perm. under-sec. 1892–1896: s. of E. of Clanwilliam.

72 Sir R. Giffen (1837–1910), economist: head of board of trade statistical department 1876–1897.

73 W.K. Clifford (1845–1879), mathematician: professor of applied mathematics, U.C.L., 1871: F.R.S. 1874: attacked by consumption 1876: works published 1879–1885.

74 Lt.-Col. Gerald Francis Talbot (1848–1904): served in Prussian army, 1870: J.P., Kent and Essex: m. a New Yorker: or perhaps Gerald Chetwynd-Talbot (1819–1885), director-general of military store department of India Office, and a distant relation.

75 Sir C. Reed (1819–1881), typefounder and antiquary: chairman of London school board 187–1881: kt 1874: M.P. St. Ives 1880–1881.

76 The Transvaal was annexed 1877–1879.

77 Carnarvon's 1875 confederation plan was 'sharply criticised' in cabinet (Derby diaries, 28 April 1875). Disraeli and Derby expressed uneasiness about South African policy, but outside cabinet. It appears that the actual annexation of the Transvaal in April 1877 took place without cabinet debate, Carnarvon telling Disraeli: 'I do not like to delay my movements for the meeting and discussion of the matter in Cabinet' (Monypenny and Buckle, *Life of Disraeli*, vi, 415).

78 Sir Graham Berry (1822–1904), thrice premier of Victoria: much feared by the monied classes: important in making Victoria protectionist.

79 Charles Henry Pearson (1830–1894), colonial minister and historian: professor of modern history at K.C.L. 1855–1865: educ. min. in Victoria 1886–1890.

80 Sir Anthony Ashley Cooper, 7th E. of Shaftesbury (1801–1885), philanthropist: styled Lord Ashley, 1811–1851: M.P. 1826–1851: succ. 1851: evangelical and social reformer.

81 Gladstone 'fought against a cold and went to dine at Mr. Pender's. Conversation with Ld Granville – Mr. Bright – Mr. Berry' (*Gladstone Diaries*, ed. Matthew, 14 March 1879).

82 Lord Eustace Cecil (1834–1921), M.P. 1865–1885: surveyor-general of ordnance, 1874–1880.

83 Edward Jenkins (1838–1910), M.P. (Lib.) Dundee 1874–1880: s. of a Montreal Presbyterian minister: educ. Montreal and Lincoln's Inn: agent-gen. for Canada 1874–1875: later a Cons. candidate, 1885 and 1896.

[84] J.G. Biggar (1828–1890), M.P. Cavan 1874–1890: bigamist.

[85] John Alexander Thynne, 4th Marquess of Bath (1831–1896), succ. his father 1837: lord-lieut. Wilts. 1889–1896: trustee of N. Port. Gallery and B.M.: High Churchman.

[86] Charles George Lyttelton, 8th Viscount Cobham and 5th Baron Lyttelton (1842–1922), succ. his father as 5th baron 1876: succ. as Viscount, 1889. M. Mary, 2nd dau. of Lord Chesham.

[87] Frederick, 6th E. Beauchamp (1830–1891), lord steward 1874–1880, m. a dau. of E. Stanhope.

[88] Leopold II (1835–1909), K. of the Belgians, m. (1853), Marie Henriette (d. 1902), dau. of Archduke Joseph of Austria.

[89] Henry George Calcraft (1936–1896), civil servant and society gossip: priv. sec. to presidents of the board of trade, 1859–1874: Mr. Pinto in Disraeli's *Lothair* (1870).

[90] George, 2nd D. of Cambridge (1819–1904), field-marshal and c.-in-c. of the army: succ. as Duke 1850: succ. Hardinge as c.-in-c. 1856: enforced resignation, 1895.

[91] No figure stated in original.

[92] Henry Petty-Fitzmaurice, 5th Marquess of Lansdowne (1845–1927), succ. 1866: governed Canada and India, then Unionist statesman.

[93] (Sir) Frederic Rogers, Baron Blachford (1811–1889), public servant: perm. under-sec. C.O. 1860–1871: cr. baron 1871: leading Tractarian.

[94] John Wodehouse, 1st E. of Kimberley (1826–1902), member of all Gladstone's cabinets: lord privy seal 1868–1870, colonial sec. 1870–1874, 1880–1882: sec. for India 1882–1885, February–August 1886: foreign sec. 1894–1895.

[95] Sir Robert Morier (1826–1893), diplomatist: minister to German courts 1853–1876, to Lisbon 1876–1881, to Madrid 1881–1884, amb. to Russia 1884–1893: P.C. 1885.

[96] Perhaps Victoria Charlotte, elder daughter of Robert Grosvenor, 1st Baron Ebury (1801–1893).

[97] Prince Waldemar, 4th s. of the Crown Princess, d. 27 March 1879, aged 10.

[98] Sir Robert Peel, 3rd bt (1822–1895), s. of premier: diplomatist in youth: then M.P. and Irish sec. 1861–1865: failed to obtain further preferment: only Tory to vote for home rule, 1886.

[99] G.C.T. Bartley (1842–1910), M.P. (Cons.) Islington N. 1885–1906 (defeated): sometime principal agent Conservative Central Office: in Civil Service (Science and Art Department) 1859–1880: wrote much on thrift: founded National Penny Bank Limited, 1875: K.C.B. 1902.

[100] George William Frederick Howard, 7th E. of Carlisle (1802–1864), lord-lieutenant of Ireland 1855–1858, 1859–1864: as Lord Morpeth, Whig M.P. 1826–1848: d. unm.

[101] Sir Henry Holland (1825–1914), 2nd baronet, and 1st viscount Knutsford: s. of the Queen's physician, whom he succ. 1873: asst. under-sec. for colonies 1870–1874, M.P. (Cons.) Midhurst 1874–1885: baron 1888, sec. of state for colonies 1888–1892, vt 1895.

[102] Yakoob Khan, Amir of Afghanistan for most of 1879: eldest son of Shere Ali, whom he succ. February 1879: signed Treaty of Gandamak, 26 May 1879, accepting large measure of U.K. control: massacre of U.K. mission at Kabul, 3 September, led to his abdication.

[103] Prince A.M. Gorchakov (1798–1883), Russian foreign minister 1856–1882, chancellor 1866–1882.

[104] Nubar Pasha (1825–1899), Egyptian statesman: born Smyrna, s. of an Armenian merchant: educ. in France by Jesuits: held high positions in Egypt over 50 years: thrice premier: retired 1895.

[105] J.A. Froude, *Caesar – a sketch* (1879).

[106] Thibaw (ruled 1878–1885).

[107] Lieut.-Col. Halifax Wyatt of Grove House, West Derby, for over twenty years Lord Sefton's agent on the Croxteth estates. M.A. Oxon.: served in Crimean War: assistant commissioner under Board of Agriculture.

[108] John James Greig (1806?–1882), head constable of Liverpool 1852–1881, C.B. 1867.

[109] 11th E. of Winchilsea (1815–1887), succ. 1858: M.P. (Cons.) Northants. N. 1837–1841: styled Vt Maidstone 1826–1858: well known racehorse owner and poetaster.

[110] John Passmore Edwards (1823–1911), editor and philanthropist: founded 70 free libraries, hospitals, etc.

[111] Ald. Edward Samuelson J.P. (1823–). A tobacco broker, born in Hamburg: on town council 1864, Mayor of Liverpool 1872, when he entertained Derby and the Shah: prominent on Libraries and Museums Committee, and a prime mover in establishing the Autumn Picture Exhibition.

[112] Land agent in Kent.

[113] George Melly (1830–1894), Liverpool businessman, author, and politician: M.P. Stoke 1868–1875.

[114] Peter Rylands (1820–1887), banker and industrialist: M.P. (Lib.) Warrington 1868–1874, Burnley 1876–1887.

[115] *Parl Deb.*, 3, vol. ccxlv, cols. 1206–1210. Gladstone cast a longing glance in favour of a general taxation of charities, as proposed by him in 1863.

[116] William Bateman, 2nd Baron Bateman (1826–1901), eldest s. of 1st baron: lord-lieut. of Hereford 1852–1901: succ. 1845: lord-in-waiting 1858–1859.

[117] Sir George Jessel (1824–1883), first Jewish judge: educ. U.C.L., bar 1847, Q.C. 1865, sol.-gen. 1871, M.P. Dover 1868–1875, when Master of the Rolls. High Court Judge 1875–1881. F.R.S. 1881.

[118] Sir R.J. Phillimore (1810–1885), judge.

[119] John Morley, Viscount Morley of Blackburn (1838–1923), statesman and man of letters.

[120] Francis Seymour, 5th Marquess of Hertford (1812–1884), succ. his cousin 1870: held court offices, general in the army, lord chamberlain 1874–1879.

[121] 5th Baron Thurlow (1838–1916), P.C., F.R.S., succ. his brother 1874: m. 1864, dau. of Lord Elgin (4s. 2d.): diplomatic service 1858–1870, lord-in-waiting 1880–1885, paymaster-gen. February–April 1886: H.M. high commissioner to general assembly of Kirk May–July 1886.

[122] 8th E. of Kintore (1828–18 July 1880), who succ. his father 1844: m. his cousin (4s. 3d.): succ. by his eldest son Algernon: 9th E. of Kintore (1852–), succ. 1880, gov. of S. Australia 1889–1895, lord-in-waiting 1895–1905: m. dau. of D. of Manchester.

[123] George Robinson, 1st Marquess of Ripon (1827–1909), succ. as 3rd E. De Grey and 2nd E. of Ripon 1859: lord president 1868–1873, viceroy 1880–1884.

[124] Dr. A.C. Tait (1811–1882).

[125] Lady Derby (b. 1824) was then around 55.

[126] Dr. John Jackson (1811–1885), bishop of London 1868–1885, *vice* Tait: a Disraeli appointment: author of *The Sinfulness of Small Sins*: cr. diocese of St. Albans, and had 1 s. and 10 daus.

[127] Thomas Carlyle (1795–1881), prophet.

[128] Thomas O'Hagan, 1st baron O'Hagan (1812–1885), lord chancellor of Ireland 1868–1874, 1880–1881: cr. baron 1870: 1st v-c of Royal University, 1880.

[129] Isaac Butt (1813–1879), founder and leader of Irish home rule party: of Tory antecedents and generally poor character.

[130] Sir R. Morier had m., 1861, Alice Peel, dau. of Gen. Peel, Cons. War Minister (1858–1859 and 1866–1867) and Lady Alice Peel.

[131] Peter Hood, M.D., *A Treatise on Gout, Rheumatism, and the allied affections, etc.* (1879).

[132] Bulgarian port on lower Danube.

[133] George Byng, 8th E. of Strafford (1830–1898), raised to Lords, February 1874, as Baron Strafford: styled Viscount Enfield 1860–1886: succ. father 1886: sec. to poor law board, 1865–1866: under-sec. for foreign affairs 1871–1874: under-sec. for India, 1880–1883: 1st Civil Service Commissioner 1880–1888.

[134] E.B. Sugden, baron St. Leonards (1781–1875), lord chancellor for 10 months under Derby in 1852: cr. baron, 1852: probably declined offer of same post from Derby, 1858: s. of a hairdresser.

[135] Of the Peabody Trust, in which he took the leading part.

[136] Sir Theophilus Shepstone (1817–1893), involved in South African native affairs 1839–1876: annexed Transvaal 1877 and administered it till 1879: administrator of Zululand, 1884.

[137] Lord Edmond Fitzmaurice, baron Fitzmaurice (1846–1935), s. of 4th, and younger bro. of 5th, Marquess of Lansdowne: his father d. 1866, his mother Baroness Nairne *suo jure* d. 1895: chairman Wilts. C.C. and quarter sessions: M.P. Calne 1868–1885, N. Wilts. 1898–1905: under-sec. for foreign affairs 1882–1885, 1905–1908: chancellor of Duchy of Lancaster 1908–1909: m. 1889 a New England lady (annulled, 1894).

[138] Sir Somerset Richard Lowry-Corry, 4th Earl Belmore (1835–1913): succ. his father, 1845: m. dau. of Capt. J.N. Gladstone, R.N., niece of the premier: had 3 s. and 10 daus.: under-sec. of state home department 1866–1867, governor of New South Wales 1867–1872. Estates of 19,000 acres in Tyrone and Fermanagh worth £11,000 p.a.

[139] James Hewitt, 4th Vt Lifford (1811–1887), eldest s. of 3rd Vt, whom he succ. 1855: m. dau. of E. of Gosford: rep. peer (Ireland): succ. as 5th Vt by his eldest son.

[140] Sir William Bagge, Bt, of Stradsett Hall, Norfolk (1810–1880), M.P. (Protectionist) Norfolk 1837–1857, 1865–1880.

[141] Henry Fawcett (1833–1884), blind 1858: Cambridge professor 1863–1884: M.P. 1865–1884: postmaster-general, 1880–1884.

[142] Sir Garnet Wolseley, Vt Wolseley (1833–1913), field-marshal: won Ashanti war, 1873: administrator of Cyprus, 1878: conquered Egypt, 1882: c.-in-c. 1895–1899.

[143] Lord Elcho, M.P. (1818–1914), later 10th E. of Wemyss (succ. 1883): as Lord Elcho, M.P. (Cons.) 1841–1846, 1847–1883: his 2nd wife d. 1945.

[144] Ald. William Booth, J.P. (1812–1886), Mayor in 1871 and 1872. He had a fine private library of 10,000 vols.

[145] Sir John Heron (1809–1889), town clerk of Manchester December 1838–1889: obtained Act for the Thirlmere reservoir, 1879: kt., 1869.

[146] Dr. John Watts (1818–1887), social reformer: Ph.D. Giessen 1844: advocate of municipal socialism in Manchester area: wrote many pamphlets on such topics.

[147] Lionel Nathan de Rothschild (1808–1879), banker: educ. Göttingen: assumed dignity of Austrian baron, 1838: M.P. (Lib.) City of London 1847–1868, sitting from 1858: see above, entry of 28 June 1879.

[148] Bailey Hey.

[149] 215 or 221 acres 'in a rather picturesque country, just under Parlick Pike'.

[150] Agent for Lord Penrhyn, in N. Wales.

[151] Shorthand writer from Liverpool.

[152] Joseph Gibbons Livingston, or 'Old Joe', for more than 40 years the chief wirepuller of Liverpool popular Toryism, the main link with the public house interest, and a frequent deputy mayor: a rough diamond.

[153] Lt.-Col. R.F. Steble (1825–1899), mayor of Liverpool 1874–1875–1876, and for 14 years on Liverpool City Council: a Liverpool solicitor: sometime Col., 1st Lancs. Rifle Volunteers: M.P. (Lib.) Scarborough 1884–1885, Mayor of Scarborough 1891, 1892. Educ. Rossall.

[154] M.P. and landowner, of Hale Hall, Widnes: worth about £8,000 p.a.

[155] An odd comment, for Derby often suffered from unexplained varieties of depression, as did his brother and (probably) his father.

[156] Capt. B.C.T. Pim (1826–1886), M.P. (Cons.) Gravesend 1874–1880 (retired): naval career, then barrister and writer: defeated Totnes 1865 and Gravesend 1868.

[157] Prince Napoléon (1822–1891), s. of Jérôme, King of Westphalia (1784–1860), Napoleon's youngest brother.

[158] Eugénie Montijo (1926–1920), wife of Napoleon III.

[159] Reginald Brett, 2nd Vt Esher (1852–1930), succ. 1899: M.P. (Lib.) Penrhyn 1880–1885.

[160] 2nd Baron Oranmore (1819–1900), only s. of 1st baron: educ. Harrow and Trinity: no degree: High Sheriff co. Mayo, 1841: representative peer, Ireland, 1869–1900.

[161] Further signs of Derby's wish to benefit Sanderson's poor relations may be suspected in

the case of Rev. Edward Manners Sanderson, presented by Derby in 1890 to be Vicar of Huyton (£329 p.a. net and house).

[162] Sir James M.M. Hogg (1823–1890), 1st baron Magheramorne, chairman of the metropolitan board of works 1870–1889.

[163] Lord Hammond (1802–1890), cr. baron 1874: permanent under-secretary at F.O. 1854–1873.

[164] Albert Edmund Parker, 3rd E. of Morley (1843–1905), succ. father 1864. Minor office 1880–1885: under-sec. for war, February–April 1886: chairman of committees, House of Lords 1889–1905.

[165] Perhaps Herbert Spencer, *The Principles of Sociology*, 3 vols., 1876–1896.

July–December

1 July 1879: Keston. The half-year begins with a violent storm of wind & rain, the worst we have had in these parts. The prospect as to harvest begins to look really bad: another failure will utterly crush thousands of farmers, who even now are only scrambling on in debt & difficulty. The quarter's revenue returns are out, & look ill for the future: customs & excise between them showing a falling off of £625,000 in three months. On the other side I ought to note that T. Hankey[1] told me the other day that the income tax returns for the City of London, which he has seen, show an actual increase in the amount of income returned on those of 12 months ago: showing that, if some persons lose heavily, others gain.

. . . In the Lords yesterday Granville said a few cordial words about Ld Lawrence, & Ld Beaconsfield was compelled to reply in the same strain, but did it with an evident coldness. . . .

2 July 1879: . . . Write answers to many requests: one an invitation to attend the yearly meeting of the Trades Unions at Edinburgh, which I declined civilly on the plea of other engagements . . .

Much discussion in the newspapers about the Chancellor's University bill: the general verdict is what I anticipated yesterday, that there is no harm in the bill, that in principle it is right enough, but that as it cannot possibly satisfy the Catholics, & as nobody else wants any new legislation, it is not likely to pass, nor of much use if it does. There may, however, be something behind which we don't know of – some secret bargain as to alterations to be made in the Commons – & the suspicion of some such transaction makes Conservatives unwilling to entertain it.

3 July 1879: Leave Keston at 7.50 . . . to Waterloo: there meet Hale, & with him to Haslemere, where we arrive a little before 11.00.

. . . Walk through Haslemere town, or rather village: a queer little place, like no other that I know: consisting chiefly of one immensely broad street, probably laid out so to serve as a market: small old-fashioned houses on each side: no new building that I could see: with two or three rows of lime trees planted to form a boulevard, for which there is ample room, it would be pretty enough in its way: but there is a curious look of decay about it.

Noticed on part of my new-bought farm, Church Hill, an enormous beech tree, the largest, I think, that I ever saw, & I wonder that nothing was said about it at the sale: but it is not in very good condition. – Walk over this farm, & by the common to the Witley estate: walked along the northern part of it, observing details & giving orders: reached Witley station at 3.30: took the 4.10 train back to Waterloo . . . met M. & with her, though very wet & dirty, to Keston by the 6.05 train. The day was very bad: heavy rain at intervals, with squalls of wind, & only short intervals of fine weather. Found 13 or 14 letters on my return: there are sure to be more than usual if I am away for a day.

4 July 1879: . . . – Short walk at night, but rain continues. Never were the prospects of farmers so gloomy.

Another unseemly & discreditable row in the H. of C. The Irish have found their tactics of obstruction successful, & are determined to persevere. To bring parliament into discredit, if not their direct object, is at least a result not unwelcome to them – for they regard it as the parliament of a foreign & hostile country: and I suspect they represent in this respect a more general Irish feeling than we in England are apt to admit. Northcote is blamed for not dealing more decidedly with the obstructers, but I doubt whether the censure is just. They want to be martyrs: and a little persecution would only help their game. It is not easy to see the end: the least mischief which they can do – and that least is not inconsiderable – is that they will compel the House to revise its rules, limiting freedom of debate, & lessening thereby the resisting power of minorities. They have secret allies moreover, in that party, now more distinctly declared than it has been in my time, who question the right of the H. of C. to the practical supremacy which it has asserted, & are not sorry to see it cheapened: though such persons, except by accident or casual indiscretion, are not likely to let their ideas reach the public.

5 July 1879: My wedding day, and I had hoped to pass it quietly at Keston. But the funeral of Lord Lawrence is fixed for this morning, and after talking the matter over with M. we agreed that I ought to attend (1) as having been a very old acquaintance, & a guest in India, of the dead man (2) as having been officially connected with the India Office (3) because there is evidently in Downing Street, and probably at court also, an inclination to make as little of the occasion [as possible], on account of the opposition offered by Ld L. to the Afghan war. To which reasons I add my own wish to do what honour is possible to one of the most honest & unselfish of public servants whom I have known. I went accordingly by the usual train, & was at the Jerusalem chamber, the appointed place of meeting, at 11.40. The service began at 12.00, & lasted till 1.00. It was all musical, for which there is perhaps more reason in the Abbey than elsewhere, for the space is too great for any human voice to be effective. Of the government only Northcote, Cranbrook, & Stanhope[2] attended: the last two in their official capacity. Gladstone, Granville, Cardwell, Lowe, & others of the opposition were there: many Indians also. There was a great crowd in the Abbey, but fewer persons of note than might have been expected. Cardwell reminded me that the last time we had met there was at the funeral of Ld Macaulay, 18 years ago. Returned by 2.13 train . . . Walk with M., and later a ride by myself for exercise. . . .

6 July 1879: . . . News yesterday of the very sudden death of Ly Waldegrave[3]: who has been a leading figure in London society for at least 30 years. She gained by four successive marriages wealth, rank, & political position: & before her death had made herself perhaps the most conspicuous female figure in London. Social distinction was her object in life, & she secured it: being liberal, hospitable, good-natured both by policy & temper, & not delicate in pushing her way. She was only 57 or 58 at her death: which will be especially a loss to the Liberal party, for whom she kept open house. She will probably be longest remembered in connection with Strawberry Hill, Horace Walpole's celebrated villa, which she inherited in a ruinous condition, restored, enlarged, & restocked with works of art.

Hear from Sir James Hogg that the Metropolitan Board accept the offer of the Peabody trustees to buy their vacant land – by which they sacrifice half-a-million. It is a good bargain for us, & our operations will be extended beyond what would otherwise have been possible. But the ratepayers will not be pleased when they see what is the practical working of the Act of 1875. Good lodgings for working men, such as modern ideas require, cannot be built in London except at a loss.

7 July 1879: . . . Froude writes to M. a remarkable letter, saying that Canada is willing to enter into a parliamentary union with England, & pressing for that step to be taken as the only alternative to ultimate separation. The Canadians, he says, cannot stand alone: they must join either England or the U.S.: & as matters now stand they prefer England. He is very anxious that advantage should be taken of the opportunity. – This suggestion raises various questions. Is he right, in the first place, in thinking that any such wish exists as he supposes? The Canadians before they could join us would have to abandon protection, to remodel their tariff, to accept a share of imperial burdens, from which as yet they are free: and to consent to submit all their more important local affairs to the decision of a parliament sitting 3,000 miles away, in which they would be a very small minority. Is it likely that they would make these sacrifices? Why should they? They have imperial protection already, without paying for it: & local freedom to the fullest extent. – If they really wished to join us in this way, the question of accepting or rejecting the offer would be a very serious one. But there will be time enough to speculate on the gain or loss to England when the proposal takes a more serious form. As matters are, I suspect that it exists chiefly in Froude's imagination.

I omitted to note the discussion in H. of C. last week on agricultural distress. Chaplin[4], who moved for a commission of enquiry, got what he wanted, though it is not easy to see what there is to enquire about. Several speakers avowed protectionist ideas. Their language roused Bright to his old fury against landowners, & he denounced the 'land monopoly' in his most passionate style. But that cry is not much responded to, & he rather interested than influenced the House. Hartington took the opportunity to say that our laws of entail & settlement required revision: which may mean a great deal, or very little. The land question will unite all shades of Liberals who are not large landowners: but the Whigs will hardly join in any very destructive measure.

8 July 1879: Walk in to the station: St. J. Square by 10.45. Find many letters . . . Write a minute on Froude's Canadian scheme, suggesting points on which explanation is desired: this for M.'s use, as she is to see him.

. . . Travellers', where waste an hour looking at new books (of which there are, however, very few): then H. of Lds, where the Irish University Bill was read a second time without opposition. Kimberley opened the debate in a critical speech, acute & temperate, the best I have heard him make: Cranbrook answered: O'Hagan came next, arguing strongly for the endowment of a Catholic University[5], as nothing would suit the Irish except a purely Catholic education. Then followed Lds Leitrim, Donoughmore, & Inchiquin, clearly put up by the government: & Ld Spencer, whom having to go home I left speaking. Walk up with Carnarvon: his impression is the same as mine, that there is no harm in the Irish scheme & that, if it leads to endowment, the endowment can be limited to assistance given in a form not open to objection.

. . . Much talk in the clubs of an attempt by one Grissel to bribe a private-bill committee of which H. Lennox[6] is chairman, & the report is that he & the person accused of this attempt at corruption are closely connected in business. It is unlucky in any case, for H.L. has no reputation to spare, & after the Lisbon tramways exposure is rather tolerated than welcomed in society.

Much talk also of a quarrel in the H. of C. between Hartington & Chamberlain last night, in one of the innumerable discussions on the Army bill. Hartington disavowed the Radicals, & begged that he might not be considered as their leader: Chamberlain in turn repudiated him. There seems to have been some temper lost on both sides. The Conservatives are pleased: the Whigs also, for they have for a long while been afraid that the Ultras were gaining the lead, & uneasy in consequence.

9 July 1879: . . . Lit. Fund meeting at 3.00: 14 present, including the secretary & myself. . . . We gave away £400, in six gifts. There remained above £1,000, of which it was proposed to invest half: but this proposal Trollope objected to, talking in a noisy blustery way for which there was no reason or provocation: but I find this is his habitual style, & he is disliked by his colleagues in the trust accordingly, though for his name as a writer it is not desirable that he should leave us. He talks as if any dissent from his opinions was a personal affront[7]. We adjourned the question, to avoid needless quarrelling.

Walk up with Dr. Smith[8]. He tells me the publishing trade is dead: new books are not brought out, from the impossibility of getting a sale: result, he supposes, of bad times, books being one of the first luxuries that rich people are willing to economise in when obliged to pull in. He talks of much larger sale of new books in America than here: in England, 2,000 copies are thought a good number: in the States a publisher will often start with 10,000. He explains this by the absence of book clubs and circulating libraries in the States . . . Keston by 5.15 train with M.: walk in Hollydale.

10 July 1879: . . . In papers, the chief news is a hot electioneering speech made by Salisbury in the City, in the course of which he again vindicates the foreign policy of the Cabinet, in a strain which seems to imply distrust of its being acceptable. He also attacks Ld Hartington, which is a mistake, since Ld H. having more than half quarrelled with his party, or at least with a large section of it, in defence of the government, it would have been more politic to encourage than to satirise him.

11 July 1879: . . . M. goes to see Mr. Darwin, now aged 76: but she finds him still full of interest in all that is going on, & meditating a tour.

. . . Letter from Gavard[9], about things in general. Write to accept the offered office of a vice-president of the Social Science Congress in Manchester from October next, but I do not suppose I shall have much to do with it.

Walk with M. . . . about the park. Day bright & sunny, the first we have had. See Broomfield again, & settle with him that the thinning of Hollydale shall be done by men sent from Knowsley, labour here being expensive.

In the H. of C. another row last night. The Speaker having employed an official of the House to take minutes of what passed in committee – as he said, for his own information only – the Irish chose to take this act as offensive to themselves, talked of having spies set upon them, of intimidation, etc., ending by giving notice of a motion for tonight censuring the Speaker. The object is merely to create delay, & in that they will succeed. The difficulty created by them is increasing, & they are quite aware of their success. They make no secret now of their intention to impede the course of all business till, as the lesser evil of the two, the English shall consent to let them sit in a parliament of their own.

12 July 1879: London by the usual train . . . Walk thence to the B. Museum. On my way,

buy one of the new penny weeklies, of which there is a sudden outbreak, & which are selling in thousands at street corners: find it full of the grossest indecency, all the articles
without exception being on subjects which admit of obscene treatment. A new, & not a
beautiful, sign of the time.

At the Museum . . . Discussion as to taking over part of the India Museum, which by
way of economy is to be broken up – a mistaken piece of economy, I think. Call in Curzon
St. but do not stay to luncheon, as I had meant, there being visitors. Travellers': thence
at 3.00 to meeting of Peabody trustees. Present, the U.S. minister, Sir C. Lampson, & his
son who attends for the first time as a trustee – Sir C. Reed has lost a son (drowned):
Northcote is too busy to come: & Mr. Morgan was either ill or occupied. We agreed to
conclude the negociation with the Metropolitan Board: securing over 8 acres of land at
about £90,000: this we can pay for without help, having still unexpended of our fund
£163,000: but to cover these spaces with building it will be necessary to borrow from the
Treasury, & they agree to lend us £300,000 at 3½% . . . If our building operations
proceed gradually, I hope that it will not be necessary to use to the full extent the borrowing powers which we have obtained. Agreed to meet once more before the autumn recess.
Keston by 4.30 train . . . Too wet for a walk.

13 July 1879: . . . In H. of C. the Speaker's conduct in taking notes of the debates through
a clerk was attacked by the Irish, but vindicated by an immense majority – 421 to (I
think) 29. There is no doubt that he was within his right, but the policy of the proceeding is not so obvious. – The victory, however, was divided, for though the attacking party
were beaten as they knew they must be, they have succeeded in stopping business during
two evenings.

14 July 1879: . . . Letter from Carnarvon, who has accepted the chair of the commission
of enquiry on agriculture &, having done it, wants to know my opinion. I tell him I think
he was right in not letting any past or present political differences with the government
prevent his acceptance of the offer – but that I have doubts as to the usefulness of a roving
commission of enquiry of this kind, & that it will be necessary for him to keep members
& witnesses closely to the two questions which they have really to deal with – are there
any grievances affecting agriculture which are of a kind that the law can deal with? &, if
there are, what remedy is suggested? I end by saying that, as the enquiry is to take place,
I am glad he is chairman.

The Irish newspapers are already setting up a scream of exultation at the success
which has attended their obstructive tactics. They point out quite truly that they can
without violating any rule of parliament make the transaction of business impossible: &
that they cannot be checked except by restrictions which will equally apply to the English
members. The time will come, they say, when the English will see that the only way out
of the difficulty is to restore the illegally suppressed Irish parliament. Here we have the
object plainly declared, & there is no doubt that it will be steadily followed.

15 July 1879: . . . The substance of Ly Waldegrave's will is announced: she leaves all she
has, except a moderate provision for her own family, to her husband[10] for his life, the
reversion to the Lord Waldegrave of the day. This is fair & right, as the lands came from
that family, & belong to it: she was not the cause of their being alienated in the first
instance, & has replaced the head of the name in the position he ought to hold.

The usual parliamentary 'massacre of the innocents' is announced: it includes nearly every bill that the government has brought in, with the exception of the Army Bill. No session so utterly wasted has been known in my recollection: the weakness of the Cabinet in the H. of C., the apathy of the public, & the obstructive policy of the Irish must divide the discredit. . . .

18 July 1879: . . . In the Commons last night, a debate & division on flogging in the army, raised by Hartington, which ended in a majority of over 100 for government. The result must have been expected, & probably the object of the move was to reunite the Liberals, & give them a common ground of attack. The victory is divided – for it places the Conservatives in the position of having to defend an institution which, whether necessary or not, is intensely unpopular: & this in face of an election: while the Liberal party as a whole is committed to the opposite & popular view, which it never was before.

Many people believe that the cause of this – certainly rather sudden – change of front by the Liberals is that they were afraid lest Ld Beaconsfield should be beforehand with them, & abolish flogging at once, leaving the Opposition the odium of having been willing to support it. There has been on both sides a good deal of manoeuvring for popularity, which is natural & inevitable before an election. But one good result is obtained – there is an end of the foolish pretension constantly put forward by our military authorities, that 'parliament has nothing to do with the discipline of the army'. Parliament has asserted its right in that respect, & in fact the punishment in question, though nominally retained, is so closely limited in its application that it has all but ceased to exist. The Queen will be furious – not so much at the thing done as at the interference with what she regards as her especial prerogative. . . .

20 July 1879: . . . Talk with L.W.[est] of what he has heard in Paris. He gave no authority – which I observe diplomatists are always very unwilling to do – but predicted that within a year Gambetta would have taken the place of Waddington, & then a war policy would be adopted, & war would follow, probably with Germany, within a short time. I asked why? and what could be the object? He said that the republicans think the republic cannot be consolidated without a war: the army is still indifferent, if not hostile: & nothing will secure the country against a military *coup d'état* except a great republican victory. 'But suppose a defeat instead?' 'Gambetta never thinks of failure: his nature is sanguine & reckless: he thinks this policy necessary, & will not count the cost, or calculate the risk.' 'But is the French army even now a match for the German?' 'The French think it so: a great deal has been done in the last two or three years.' 'Would France fight Germany without an ally?' 'Probably, if she cannot find one.' V. my convn. with Sheffield, 2nd April: which agrees with the above except on the last point.

21 July 1879: My birthday – 53. Three-quarters of life are gone, according to the ordinary estimate, but I do not feel what so many persons have described, that existence is less interesting than when one was younger. Personal & egotistical interests certainly count for less – there is nothing in the way of new gratification to look forward to – but with larger knowledge & fuller experience the position of a looker-on at the great events of the world becomes more & more agreeable. I can say with truth that I have fewer annoyances, & not fewer pleasures, at 53 than I had at 23. But then my pleasures have been intellectual rather than of the senses: and I have had good health (for which I may partly thank my own care of it) and a singularly happy home. . . .

22 July 1879: Went up to London, together with M.: . . . day as before cold & rather wet. At 11.00 went to 12 Great George St. to attend the Durham miners' arbitration case: the hour was that named, but the representatives of the men had mistaken it, & did not appear till 12.00. . . . The arbitrators, 2 on each side, sat with me at the head of the table: Messrs. Dale & Armstrong for the masters, Messrs. Lloyd Jones & Crawford for the men. The representatives of the two parties sat at the sides. It was agreed that no report should be sent to the papers. The owners read their case, which was well drawn: a general discussion followed, questions being asked & explanations given: then the men followed with their reply, which showed less literary skill, being weak in argument, & declamatory. They dwelt much on the doctrine that wages ought not under any circumstances to be allowed to fall below a certain limit: but I could not get them to explain who was to make good the difference, if the trade would not yield enough to make it worth while to go on on these terms. There was very great contradiction as to the facts, even as to facts which would seem capable of proof. The masters have asked for a reduction of 20% in the wages of the hewers, & something less in the case of other workmen: a previous arbitration settled a reduction of 8% (& a fraction over) as the provisional rate, leaving the further question to be disposed of by the present reference. It is admitted that the trade is in a bad way, & that both profits & wages have fallen greatly since 1873–74. We are to have a second day of argument: as yet I have heard no very conclusive proof on either side. – About 30 persons were in the room, a large & convenient one. Sat till near 3.00. Luncheon at the club, & return by 4.12 train. Find Mary Galloway at Keston.

23 July 1879: This being M.'s birthday, I gave her £50, Mary & Margaret £5 each. Day cold, dark, & disagreeable. Out of the 200 days & more of this year so far as it has gone, not more than 3 or 4 have been even warm: a state of things which I never remember before. Many parts of the country are flooded, & altogether the harvest prospects are worse than they have been for a generation. Pauperism has increased since January, but less than might have been expected: the very low prices of food & all other necessaries doing something to lessen the general poverty. There is no discontent, I suppose because people in all classes feel that their difficulties are not due to any political cause, nor removable by parliamentary action.

. . . The Dean of Lincoln[11] tells me that several farmers near Lincoln have put an end to themselves, being ruined, & seeing no way out of their difficulties.

News in the papers that the Zulu war is virtually over, a great battle having been fought, ending of course in a Zulu defeat with heavy loss. It is felt to be satisfactory that Lord Chelmsford, who has been exposed, perhaps unjustly, to a storm of abuse, should have effected his object before being superseded: for, though formally Sir G. Wolseley is in command, he has not gone into the field, & the honour of the success is entirely with his predecessor.

24 July 1879: London by 9.10 train. . . . By 10.30 I am sitting in G.[reat] George St. on the arbitration case: a printed reply was read containing the masters' criticism on the men's case, & the men followed with a rejoinder on the masters' case. When the reading was finished, a long verbal discussion took place: in parts vague & inconsecutive, which from the nature of the subject was not easy to avoid: & the difficulty was increased by both masters & men severally being represented by three or four persons, who did not always agree among themselves. However, I think I got out from them the substance of what they respectively wanted to put forward. We sat till 2.00 p.m., the same audience present as on Tuesday: I said I would take the papers home to consider, & give my award next Monday. – The argument has been managed on both sides with temper, & on that of the masters with remarkable moderation: the men were less reticent, but I saw & heard nothing that looked like settled hostility or bitter feeling between classes. . . .

25 July 1879: . . . Send Ld Winchilsea £5, which he applies for in a circular, in return for three small volumes of what he is pleased to call poems, privately printed. It is only a form of begging &, little as I respect the man, I regret to see the representative of an old name reduced to these straits. Ld W. started in life with some cleverness & some ambition, & might perhaps have effected a moderate success in public life: but he was early spoilt by bad fashionable company, & by the flattery of persons in society who thought him a poet & a statesman. He went on the turf, lost, & spent money in various ways, ruined himself, gave up politics, but continued to write '*vers de société*' of which the best are mediocre, & the worst very bad indeed. His only son, a disreputable kind of person, enlisted in the army as a private, & is lately dead. I do not know who is in succession to the peerage & estates. Altogether his life is a muddle & a failure, & probably he knows it. . . .

26 July 1879: Ride in afternoon . . . The main roads are alive with pleasure-vans, in which crowds of excursionists come down for a day in the country. They pack as close as possible, blow horns, stop at a roadside inn, & there lounge about the dusty road, looking hot & uncomfortable, till they have had beer enough to make them noisy. The enjoyment to a looker-on would seem small, but one must presume that they like it. Bicycles also abound on the roads, & are increasing in numbers: a wholesome harmless kind of amusement. I think I passed not less than 20 to 25 in one half-hour this afternoon. . . .

28 July 1879: London early. Walk in to the station: day hot & roads dusty. The arbitrators come at 11.30 as agreed, & sit with me till about 1.00. I then announce my award: a reduction of 10%, instead of 20% which the masters asked, and 15 which they would have taken without arbitration. The men on their part would have conceded 7: so that the difference was reduced within narrow limits. There is a provisional reduction of 8½% now in force, pending the present award. The matter was argued with temper & good sense on both sides, nothing offensive being said. I think the feeling of both parties was that it might have been worse – neither got quite all they wanted, but neither went off with a mortifying defeat.

. . . Hale has bought for me 5 cottages in Bootle, costing £900, which he has long wanted, I don't exactly know why.

29 July 1879: Fairhill. Very fine hot day, & the place in its best looks. The abundance of wood in all directions, the distant views, the varied outlines of the hills, & the rich cultivation, makes this neighbourhood singularly attractive in summer. For the winter, I am bound to own, it is too wet & sticky underfoot to be thoroughly pleasant. But we do not use it in winter. . . .

31 July 1879: . . . Look in at the club: where I find all the world full of a story about F. Wellesley[12]: how he has carried off from another man, one Delacour, a woman of the demi-monde, & gone abroad with her[13]. The scandal is twofold, for Wellesley is a married man, & this escapade cannot help becoming public – indeed it is in all the 'society' journals already: & Mr. Delacour being a rough of the upper class wanted to fight Wellesley, & has threatened a personal assault. Some add that he has followed him from place to place, trying to provoke a quarrel, but I do not know if this is true. It is doubly unlucky for Wellesley, as he has many enemies: the whole diplomatic profession felt aggrieved when he was put in over their heads at Vienna, & they are naturally making the most of his troubles. He has talent & activity, but is weak: has lost much money at play, & lives on bad terms with his wife, whom he was made to marry by her parents. . . .

2 Aug. 1879: Drage calls early, reports me better than for a long while past.

. . . See the courier, give him £50, & talk about the journey. He is the same man we had with us last year – Duruz.

. . . At Statter's suggestion, I promise the Bury Agricultural Socy. £100 to help them out of their difficulties.

Sanderson called to take leave: he says Wellesley will certainly resign: a foolish end of an undeserved promotion: but I regret it for Ld & Ly Cowley. He (F.W.) is clever, but silly: gambles & gets into debt rather because other people do than because he likes it: married a woman for whom he did not care, without a shilling: & has now gone off with another woman for whom he probably cares as little.

Sent Sanderson, after he had gone, £20 for flies at Fairhill.

. . . Called on A.D. but she was ill & in bed.

G. Duncan[14] came to luncheon: told us that the engineers' strike is virtually over, that the masters have gained a complete victory: the men do not admit defeat, but have in effect withdrawn from the struggle, & advantage has been taken of it to get rid of many of the least efficient. He said, if I understood him right, that the objection to piecework is confined to London: the men from the north prefer it to any other system. . . .

3 Aug. 1879: . . . Up at 6.00. Left home 7.25. Charing Cross 7.40: reach Dover 9.45. Passage rather rough . . . We had a deck cabin, & both escaped illness, though most on board suffered. At Calais, where arrive about 12.00, we meet the Vice-consul, who comes on board to us, & sees us off from the station. . . . Luncheon at Calais, set off at 12.30, reach Hotel Bristol at Paris 6.30, without fatigue, though day very dusty & hot. . . . Read to M. in the evening. Read a novel by Zola on the way.

4 Aug. 1879: . . . Called at the embassy, saw Lord Lyons, & talk with him as to the situation. His view differs widely from that of Sheffield & L. West. He holds that Gambetta could turn out Waddington if he pleased, but that it is not at all certain that he desires to come into political office, for the present. He looks to succeeding M. Grévy[15] some day in the presidency, and is half inclined to think any other post below him. He has more influence now than he would probably retain as a minister, and likes his present post of Speaker. In short, Lord Lyons said, he is rather like the Count of Chambord[16], who whenever pressed to come forward finds some good reason against taking action. Nor does he consider it as in any way certain that, if Gambetta came into power, he would take up a policy of war. He might, but he has never given the public reason to think so.

He says (I mean Ld L.) that there is now a complete separation between the government & what is called 'society'. Those who constitute society in Paris keep obstinately aloof from politics, know nothing of what is going on, & as Ld L. put it 'are like exiles, though living on the spot: they believe whatever they wish'.

I asked as to the prospects of the Bonapartists. Ld L. thought they had not lost much by the death of the Prince [Imperial]: the party had become very weak: the best heads in it were tired of useless intrigue, & glad like Rouher[17] to have an excuse for throwing up the whole affair: for the time Imperialism[18] seemed hopeless: no doubt in the future it might have a chance, but then Plon-plon's son would do as well as the late prince – better in some respects, since he would carry back men's thoughts to the first empire, & not revive the recollection of Sedan. Meanwhile all who want employment, officers of the army especially, are rallying to the republic, the prince's death giving them a fair excuse.

Ld L. spoke of the state of France as wonderfully prosperous, which he ascribed less to political causes than to the two French social characteristics – frugal habits & small families. He thinks there is no present prospect of trouble on the continent, as far as one can see: but he quoted Hammond's celebrated declaration to Granville in July 1870.

5 Aug. 1879: We dined early, & took the train for Basle & Zurich, which leaves the station at 8.05. We had a coupé with beds . . . & the night passed with less discomfort than was expected. Breakfast at Basle: thence on through rich, wooded, & very pretty country, to Zurich, where arrived about 10.00 a.m. very dirty & rather wearied. . . . We put up at the Hotel Bauer, close to the lake, where all is as pleasant as possible . . . Drive in afternoon about the environs, which are pretty enough, but Zurich is more smoky than Swiss towns in general, & not very picturesque . . .

6 Aug. 1879: Walk . . . by the lake, which is pretty & pleasing: the great number of villages & villas gives a look of overflowing prosperity to the neighbourhood, which I have hardly seen elsewhere.

Thanks of parliament voted for the Afghan war: which is a proceeding open to question, the operations having been on a small scale, & attended with no serious fighting.

7 Aug. 1879: By rail to Coire [Chur], 4 hours: pleasant enough: thence posted to Thusis, a very pretty drive: Thusis itself . . . in a beautiful situation, & our inn . . . looking into the gorge from which it takes its name, the most agreeable to stop at that I have yet come across. . . .

14 Aug. 1879: Hear of the death of Townley Parker[19], aged 86, the oldest magistrate in Lancashire. He was already an old man when I was his guest in 1862. In earlier days he was active, to the last he remained hospitable, & he retained a large amount of local popularity, which was unaffected by political changes. He began life as an eager radical, then turned sharp round, not effecting his conversion as many men do by gradual modifications of opinion, but with a degree of zeal which made him at once a fervent ultra-Tory. It was not by intellectual qualities that he gained & kept his position in the county: but by honesty, kindliness, & active interest in local affairs.

Wrote to the L.pool Conservative Workingmen, in answer to an appeal by the secretary, regretting that I cannot defer my resignation until next year, as requested by them, since it is impossible to say whether a dissolution may not occur in the interval, & it is better for all parties that there should be no mistake as to our relative positions.

16 Aug. 1879: Settled our bill at St. Moritz, which we are not sorry to leave, for the hotel though large is crowded, our rooms are indifferent, & altogether there is an absence of quiet & comfort about the place. We walked leisurely across to Pontresina (3 to 4 miles) ... Settled at the Hotel Saratz, where we find all that we could wish: good quarters, a fine view ... no disturbance.

17 Aug. 1879: The session is over, & its end seems to be observed without regret by all parties. Scarcely anything has been done, time has been wasted to an extent never known before, & the Irish obstructionists have gained a complete victory over the rest of the House. They have wisely altered their tactics. At first they strained the rules of debate, & made no disguise of their intention to stop business by speeches which hardly professed to be made for any other purpose. This procedure created disgust, & if continued would have been met by censure or enforced silence. They have accordingly given it up & substituted a policy more effective because less invidious. No irrelevant or extravagantly long speeches are delivered: but every bill, small or great, is debated, & every detail connected with it argued out. This is so clearly the right of parliament, & may so easily be represented as its duty, that objection cannot well be taken to it: yet, if adopted as a general rule of action, it puts the House under an impossibility of getting through half its work. As the practice has succeeded, it is taken up by other members who at first held aloof: and every Home-Rule candidate pledges himself to it. The immediate mischief & inconvenience are considerable: but much worse, to my mind, is the indication of continued hostility to England on the part of the Irish people. All has been done for them that could reasonably be asked, & more in respect of the land than is consistent with English ideas of justice to landlords: yet the land question, as it is the fashion to call it, seems as little settled as before, the demand for fixity of tenure is pressed as vehemently as ever, & of late it seems as if even that were not considered enough. A Mr. Finnegan[20], lately returned for Ennis, has declared at his election that he would take it as an instalment – reduction or abolition of rents being apparently the claim which he agrees to postpone. The priests and the demagogues are by no means in harmony with one another: but they agree in dislike of England.

The priests are especially discontented with the working of the Irish Church Act. They expected that it would break down the Protestant interest: whereas in fact the injury has been small, the Protestants have shown themselves both able & willing to support their ministers, & their position is stronger since they can no longer be represented as supported by invidious privileges. – The Irish difficulty, and the all but bankruptcy of India, are our two great sources of anxiety in the near future.

The Times observes that the leading members of the Cabinet have not increased their reputation by the work of the last few months: & this is certainly true: but I think Northcote is unjustly criticised for his alleged feebleness as leader of the House. He has shown great temper, patience, & in general discretion: the obstructionists have been too strong for him, but I am not clear that any one else in his place would have fared better.

The question, dissolution or no dissolution, remains in suspense: Ld Beaconsfield at his age can hardly wish to face a new parliament: the Queen probably will not let him retire, even if he wishes it, which is doubtful: &, though the Afghan war is over, & that with the Zulus probably ended, there has been nothing in either so glorious as to give the Cabinet a ground of appeal to popular confidence. Disordered finances & depressed trade are not in their favour: & in neither of these is there a prospect of improvement.

20 Aug. 1879: Death of Ld Bloomfield[21] announced in the papers, at the age of 77. He was a true diplomatist of the old type, a courtier, & an intriguer as far as his very limited faculties allowed. His father got an Irish peerage by doing the P.[rince] Regent's dirty work in some confidential capacity (I forget now what): & the son secured an English peerage by holding on to his post at Vienna, for which he was quite unfit, until bribed to retire by a seat in the H. of Lords. However, it is all one now, he is dead, & there is an end of the family.

Old Whitbread's[22] will is just proved: he leaves £350,000 besides the second largest estate (as I believe it is) in Bedfordshire.

21 Aug. 1879: Finished reading Stanley's narrative of his journey across Africa[23]: a remarkable & plucky expedition, and there can be no doubt about the main facts. But whether from the style, which is that of the American reporter, or from the known character of the man, I lay down the book with great doubts as to whether it is to be taken as a record of actual events, or [as] a romance of travel, founded on some real basis. I suppose it is owing to this generally prevalent doubt of his accuracy, felt & implied even where its expression was most carefully avoided, that he has always shown extreme susceptibility, & readiness to take offence on the most unsuitable occasions. A singular contrast to his book is to be found in the simple narrative of Cameron's travels in the same part of the world, almost equally adventurous, & related with less literary skill[24]: yet one feels sure that he is accurate in his statements, & almost sure that the other is not.

22 Aug. 1879: . . . Write to St. Helens bicycle club, who want me to be a patron, to know their numbers, etc., as I will not join an institution that has not some prospect of lasting.

23 Aug. 1879: Pay Duruz £50 for the journey – £200 in all for the 21 days we have been out.

. . . Mr. Oscar Browning[25] calls about an entertainment which is to be given some day next week, but we shall be gone . . . He talks about the Apostles' yearly dinner, which I have not attended for many years. I half promise to be at the next.

. . . Two notable speeches have been delivered in the last week: one by Gladstone at Chester, the other by Sir C. Dilke. Both attack the government severely: but it is noticeable that Gladstone dwells chiefly on the use of the prerogative, the unconstitutional character of many of the proceedings of the last two years, & above all on the expenditure incurred, while Dilke lays stress chiefly on the failure of their foreign policy, & on the results of the treaty of Berlin, which he quite truly represents as a surrender rather than a victory.

24 Aug. 1879: Quite unexpectedly, for I did not know he was in Switzerland, E. Malet[26] called: he is making his way back slowly to his post from England. He says Turkish affairs are going on as badly as possible: no reforms are being made, even in matters which would not cost money: outrages on peaceable inhabitants are left unpunished, remonstrances disregarded, Layard can do nothing. The Sultan is well intentioned, but suspicious to excess, so much so that the bare idea of a plot against him – an idea which he is always ready to entertain – puts him almost out of his mind. He is excessively vacillating, & it is never certain, however resolved he may appear to carry any scheme into effect, that counter-orders will not be given at the last moment. There is great soreness, Malet says, against England: we are credited with causing the cession to Austria of the two lost provinces, the three conspirators having contrived to throw the responsibility of the transaction on us. The Turks like us hardly better than they like the Russians, & they fear us less.

He talked also about the Wellesley affair: which is an even greater mess than I had supposed. Wellesley could not return to Vienna without the risk of being publicly insulted or cut – not because he has gone off with an actress who was in another man's keeping – but because the party aggrieved wanted to fight, & Wellesley refused. English ideas would justify him, but in foreign armies the point of honour as it used to be enforced here is still maintained: an Austrian officer cannot refuse a challenge without disgrace. I hear that Ld Beaconsfield is reported to have said: 'Wellesley was my friend – the friend of a prime minister – and the companion of sovereigns – and he has thrown away all his prospects for a caprice!'

25 Aug. 1879: Leave Pontresina . . . not to my regret, though our rooms are comfortable, & we have passed a week well enough. But I am hardly young or light enough for mountain excursions, even if I liked, which I do not, to leave M. alone for the whole day: and any one who does not go mountaineering, & is not an invalid, finds a certain want of employment in a place like this. Nor do I think the Engadine valley equal, in picturesque interest, to the other mountain centres with which I am acquainted. The distant ranges are fine, but the vegetation is monotonous . . . But the air & the quiet life has done M. good & it is something to have seen a place of resort which just now is exceptionally popular. – Princess Teano[27] came to see us off.

27 Aug. 1879: . . . To Porlezza, on lake Lugano . . . On the way we passed through several Italian villages: I was struck with their squalid & filthy appearance. They are quite as bad as Irish cabins in the old days . . . Many beggars, some disgusting in their appearance.

28 Aug. 1879: Went boating on the lake [Lugano] for 2 or 3 hours in afternoon. Land a little before dark at a villa close to the town, & go over the gardens, which are pretty, & fairly kept, but in England we should hardly make a show of them. Either there are few rich men hereabouts, or they don't care to lay out capital in 'making a place'. And perhaps they are right, for if they did the tourists would assuredly take possession of it. But it is odd to see how whatever is luxurious in these parts is for strangers. The hotels are palaces, the steamboats floating hotels: but a well-to-do Italian seems to live in a villa not superior to those about Chiselhurst, & with much less ground attached: nor are there many even of those. . . .

1 Sept. 1879: News . . . that poor Moult is dead. Nothing else could be wished for, since recovery was hopeless: but I regret the loss of a good & most zealous servant. Wrote to express sympathy.

Long letter from the mayor of Southport, about preparations for the show on the 18th. Applications without end, but I tear most of them up.

I have an odd feeling when on the lake of Geneva, as [if] I were returned home from foreign parts: I suppose from being familiar with the place since early days. And this hotel (Beau Rivage) is the best I have seen abroad: splendidly fitted, garden before & behind, & view over the lake. I know no place to which I should return so willingly.

Leave about 3.45. Train from Lausanne, Pontarlier, Dijon: travel all night.

Prince Alexander of Holland[28] calls on M. He is now heir to the Dutch throne: he was very weak in health, & thought deficient in intellect, but I believe that was a mistake. He called to talk to M. about his mother, knowing the friendship there had been between them. It appears that the Villiers family are very anxious to get back Ld Clarendon's letters to the Queen, which are freely written and abundantly indiscreet as his manner was: but the Queen by her will directed them to be kept, & her children do not choose to let them go.

2 Sept. 1879: Paris about 6.00: Hotel Bristol by 7.00: breakfast, lie down to rest, & dress: rather weary from last night . . .

Called on Adams[29] at the embassy: talk of F.O. matters: he confirms a report I had heard from Sanderson that Tenterden is to be married again: the lady is a Mrs. Rowcliffe, widow of a lawyer, said to have considerable independent means.

Talk of Gambetta: Adams says it is quite true he dislikes Waddington as being wholly independent of him, & will replace him if he can by a follower of his own: but it is not true that he desires himself to be in office: he is well aware that in France a politician is quickly *usé*, & he does not wish to wear out his reputation in a subordinate office. His object is to succeed to Grévy, not to serve under him, & meanwhile to exercise as much influence as he can without entering the Cabinet. He thinks it premature to speak of Gambetta as having resolved on a policy of war: but he would not be content to keep things quiet as Grévy is: he is determined to replace France in her former position in Europe, & to do something memorable. So at least his friends & those who know him best think.

3 Sept. 1879: Left the hotel a little after 7.00. Rail to Calais . . .

At Dover, met Granville & travelled up with him: no serious talk., except that I beg him to suggest to Hartington the expediency of explaining at some early opportunity what he really means, or wishes, about the land. What he has said in parliament is true in itself, & unobjectionable, but it is very vague, & wild interpretations are being put upon it by extreme politicians: which, as I told Granville, will have a thoroughly bad effect in frightening the Whig gentry. No question of our day requires more careful or cautious handling. I suspect Granville personally to be rather radical in his ideas as to large landed estates. He has none himself, & has mixed a good deal with continentals, who are generally against our English system. . . .

4 Sept. 1879: Have myself weighed, 14 stone exactly.

See Sanderson, & talk with him. He tells me that Rumbold[30] is going to B. Ayres, which will certainly not suit him: Vivian[31] takes his place at Berne: & Malet replaces Vivian at Cairo. The last choice is decidedly good: the removal of Vivian is, I suppose, a political necessity. He knew nothing of the intended retirement of Layard, which is much talked of, but apparently without reason.

Not much has happened of public interest since I left England: the chief event of the recess is the new Irish agitation got up by Parnell, O'Sullivan[32], & a few more of the same sort. Its objects are not precisely stated, but they seem to be twofold: Home Rule or, in other words, the repeal of the Union, & the management of Irish affairs by an Irish legis-lature: and the complete emancipation of the land, by fixity of tenure and (apparently) a limitation of rents to some scale fixed by public authority. Nothing can exceed the violence of the language used: Parnell himself openly advised the tenantry the other day to refuse to pay any rent which did not appear to them reasonable: &, whenever he or others spoke of putting a moral pressure on landlords, the response from the crowd was 'Shoot them', 'Give them lead', or other cries to the same purpose. It is clear that the popular Irish feeling is as strongly anti-English as in the days of the Fenian conspiracy.

. . . The harvest prospects are worse than when I left: one estimate reckons the aver-age, or rather the full value, of all British crops taken together at 260 millions, & assumes that the return for 1879 will fall short by one-fifth, or 52 millions: other calculations are more moderate, but in any case there is a heavy deficiency, falling on a class already impoverished by former losses.

5 Sept. 1879: See Duruz, our courier, & give him £20 as his fee, the same as last year. It is odd that the expenses of this year have been almost exactly identical with those of 1878 – £345 against £346 for 31 days in the one case, & 32 days in the other.

See Drage, who gives an unsatisfactory report as to the return of morbid symptoms: albumen in the water. This had all but completely disappeared a month ago. For some reason, I cannot tell what, travelling does not as a rule agree with me.

See Major Roberts[33], & ask him for a return of the expenses on game in the last 4 or 5 years, divided under heads, with a view to making some reduction. . . .

6 Sept. 1879: . . . Promise £10 to a new society called the National Thrift Society, of which Stanhope is president: but I doubt its success: economy is the least popular of virtues.

Read, or tried to read, a republication of some of George Sand's[34] tracts & addresses to the people . . . they are all meant as manifestos of socialist doctrine; but except the style I can find nothing remarkable in them.

In afternoon comes news of a revival of the Afghan war: the English embassy at Kabul has been attacked by mutinous Afghan troops, over whom the Ameer declares he has no control: there is an escort, & when the telegram left they were still holding out: an immediate advance on Kabul is ordered, & we are in for an indefinite increase of expenditure: possibly an occupation of the capital may be necessary. This is exactly the danger foreseen when the war began: to overrun the country was never thought difficult by any reasonable person: the difficulty is not to leave it in a state of anarchy which will make subsequent relations with the authorities impossible to establish on a lasting basis. . . .

8 Sept. 1879: . . . A bicycle race has lately come off, in London I think, lasting 6 days, & 18 hours in each day. The distance covered by the winner was more than 1,400 miles! If the custom of bicycling becomes general, it will immensely extend the powers of loco-motion among those not rich enough to keep horses. No horse could do 50 miles a day without overwork: but 100 miles a day is not severe exercise on a bicycle. The practice deserves to be encouraged, & in these parts it is spreading fast.

9 Sept. 1879: Fine in morning, rain in afternoon.

. . . Nothing definite from India, except that we know certainly of the massacre of Major Cavagnari[35] & his escort: but no details. It is not likely that the Ameer was a party to the murder, indeed he appears to have warned the members of the mission of possible danger from the fanatical hatred of the people. It is remarkable that this danger of assassination was always put forward by former Afghan rulers as a reason why a mission should not reside in Kabul. Dost Mahommed[36] used to say: 'Your agent will be murdered some day if you send one, I cannot prevent it, but you will hold me responsible.' Afghans as a rule hate all foreigners, they hate them more if not Mahometans, they set no value on life, & in our case two invasions of their country, both unprovoked, go far to explain & excuse the feeling of hostility. – The result of this business is that we must march on Kabul, and occupy it: for how long, & on what conditions, no one can yet decide: but the necessity is evident. The best proof that the attack was not premeditated is the time of year at which it has taken place: two months later the insurgents would have been secure against the possibility of attack for several months: now, there is no obstacle except the inevitable delay that must occur in getting troops together, & the want of transport, which may be serious. How the expense is to be borne is another question, for India is nearly bankrupt already.

10 Sept. 1879: . . . Went round Knole park, & met Ld Sackville[37] driving alone in his carriage: he looked mad as usual, but was quite friendly. He has just quarrelled with & turned off his agent, who has managed the estate for many years, on some imaginary imputation of dishonesty: perhaps it is a consequence of this quarrel that he is just now on good terms with his family: for half-cracked people seldom have more than one feud on their hands at a time.

. . . G. Duncan came . . . He tells me of the growing corruption in business matters: it is a new thing, he says, that within the last few years foremen, agents, & generally all persons employed in transacting business for employers, expect a gratuity: his firm had resisted the practice as long as they could, but without success: & he now satisfies his conscience by only waiting till the bribe is asked for, not offering it. – The practice, he says, prevails largely in the government offices, especially the Admiralty & War Office: the heads know it, but detection is impossible, since nothing passes in writing, or before witnesses: a hint is given to contractors as to the amount expected by the official who has to pass their contracts, & the sum is handed over in banknotes. It is well known, he says, that Mr. Reed[38] got £10,000 for one ship, from the builders who got the job to do. . . .

15 Sept. 1879: . . . Mr. Cazalet[39] called after luncheon, & stayed a long while talking: as he was walking home, I accompanied him as far as his gate on the Shipbourne road. He is a middle-aged man, quiet & thoughtful in manner, talks well, though in a hesitating way, is evidently full of ideas, though as to home ideas he seemed a good deal in the dark: there was something in his way of conversation odd & rambling, jumping from one subject to another & back again, so that it was not easy to follow him.

He spoke of Ld Beaconsfield: said we did not know the extent to which he had been helped by the sympathy of the Jews everywhere, not in England only, but over the Continent: they considered his position a triumph for their race, & to a man they supported him, no matter what his policy might be. – He thought nothing was to be done with Asia Minor, but Syria ought to be separated from it, & taken effectively, not merely in form, under a British protectorate: the Euphrates valley line should be constructed, & the Jews everywhere invited to return to Palestine. He seemed to think that Ld B. would undertake these things. He spoke with a good deal of confidence &, whatever his ideas may be worth, had evidently thought a good deal about the east. He is standing for Mid-Kent as a Liberal, but did not expect, he said, to see a majority in the next parliament, only that the existing majority would be cut down. He talked about Ireland, did not see why the Irish should not have a local parliament, but withdrew this opinion after a little discussion. I note the fact only as indicating how confused English opinion is, even among cultivated men, as to the real objects of the Irish agitation. . . .

17 Sept. 1879: Left Fairhill by early train: London at 10.15. Luncheon, or early dinner, at Travellers': see Sanderson, but he has no news: write a good many notes . . . Decline Capt. Cheyne's[40] request that I should be chairman of his committee for Arctic exploration, as that would make me responsible for his scheme, which I do not choose to be, though thinking it an experiment that may very fairly be tried.

Leave St. J. Sq. at 2.30, Euston at 3.00: reach Southport . . . at 10.00: not having said how I was coming, I thought I should get quietly to the hotel: but I found the mayor & ex-mayor waiting for me with a carriage, & a crowd of some 500 or more assembled round the station. They cheered me in the most cordial way, & there was some trouble in getting through the crowd. Supper, & bed at 11.30.

18 Sept. 1879: At 10.30 the mayor came, & the business of the day was talked over. At 11.00, we went to the Town Hall. Cross & Skelmersdale met me, & so did Ld Houghton whose presence was a surprise. He said he attended as a director of the L. & Y.[orkshire] Co. but nobody knew him as connected with railway matters, & his real object is a mystery to me. I am afraid he – who though one of the most good-natured is also one of the vainest of men – cannot have been altogether satisfied, for he was quite unknown to the crowd, & the demonstrations, which were very warm, were all for the local notabilities. We drove slowly in procession through the town, the streets crowded, flags flying, etc. At the point where the new promenade begins I had to dig the first sod & wheel it in a barrow, making a little speech afterwards: at the site of the new market I laid the first stone, making another little speech: then came a luncheon – luckily not a formal affair – at the Town Hall – then a visit to the public gardens, or park, a pretty little spot of 15 acres, formerly a waste of sandheaps, now bright with flowers of all sorts & colours. Then the glaciarium where on real ice artificially produced a game of curling was going on: next the large public swimming baths, where feats were exhibited, & a clever show made by a party of imaginary excursionists upsetting their boat through awkwardness – to the delight of the crowd, & the lesson may be a useful one in a place where there is much boating. One man lay at the bottom as if drowned, another fished him out, & was nearly dragged under by his struggles – in short, the circumstances of an accident & rescue were imitated as naturally as possible. After that a visit to the winter-garden, & a concert: then home to dress: then at 6.00 the dinner. About 300 sat down. Speeches fair, & not too many of them: I was too long, as I had expected, full half an hour (twenty minutes is quite enough at a dinner) but they listened without impatience, so all went well. Houghton spoke also with no great effect. Skelmersdale escaped by going away early. Cross was called upon, & I could not help noticing that he laid great stress on his old & early connection with me. I dare say he meant what he said, for we have always acted together well enough, but the election of next year seemed to have something to do with it. The party broke up about 10.00. Back to my hotel where some tea, & went to bed & slept without a headache . . .

During the day the mayor, Skelmersdale, Cross, & I occupied one carriage, I spoke to Cross seriously, as I had meant to do, about the Irish & their attitude, the danger of which to parliamentary institutions is not (I think) enough appreciated. To my satisfaction I found that he entirely agreed: saying that it was nonsense to talk of obstruction being the work of a few men – they had the nation behind them. This was what I had been trying to enforce, & no more was required. But he did not see the remedy, nor do I. He discussed also the question of London water supply, which he has some hopes of settling in the next session: as he says, the companies are alarmed & would rather make terms with him than take the chances of the future. I agreed with him that the supply ought to be in one hand for all London, & that a public trust [sic][41].

19 Sept. 1879: Leave hotel at 8.25, my indefatigable friend the mayor (Boothroyd[42] by name) meets me at the station . . . London not till 3.40. Reach Fairhill 6.30. . . . Find Hale at Fairhill, just arrived from Keston.

Well pleased with my Southport visit. The reception could not possibly have been warmer. The fatigue was not excessive. My speech, if it has told nothing new, has done no harm, & I believe it to be a fair statement of the actual state of matters as regards industry & finance. And I have reminded the public of my existence, which it was about time to do, for I had not spoken, I think, since June.

The Premier has been making a long, and in some respects very clever, speech in Buckinghamshire but, to the undisguised disgust of the newspaper writers, he has said nothing about Afghanistan. I do not see how it could be expected that he should, the dinner not being political, but *The Times* and *Telegraph* are equally annoyed. He has dwelt at great length on a principle which he has discovered but which nobody quite under-stands – that all land must pay three profits, whether to the same person or to several. He might just as well have said four, or six, while he was about it. What I understood him to mean is true enough – that the farmer who owns his land is not really better off than the tenant, since the interest on its value stands in place of rent, and in fact is a heavier charge than rent would be. He would gain on the whole by selling his land, & putting the value in consols, living upon it as a rent paying tenant. But he [Disraeli] seems to me to have complicated a plain calculation by a fanciful hypothesis.

Hartington has also been speaking but not to much purpose. It is a pity, I think, that modern custom requires these continual utterances from prominent public men, when either there is nothing to be said on the state of affairs, or when what can be said would be better kept back. They are compelled to talk for talking's sake, & that gives an air of unreality to what they say. No rational person wishes to live all the year round, & every year, in the mental atmosphere of a contested election. Yet this is what we are coming to.

20 Sept. 1879: Walk with Hale . . . He has got the Cheshire Lines to promise payment in October of what they owe me – £56,000 I think it is. . . . Talk of old Moult, & the system of his getting fees for leases, which is all wrong, & I believe illegal: Hale thinks in some years he must have made £1,000 by it. Arrange to have that altered for the future. – Talk of Church Hill farm at Haslemere: part to be planted, the rest let if possi-ble: if a tenant cannot be found we must see: in that case I think I had rather plant the whole, as stocking a farm costs nearly as much as planting, & it never pays. – Settle various small local subscriptions . . .

Lowe came to luncheon & stayed with M. some hours. We had a political talk. He thinks the H. of C. is losing its position in the country – does not see what will improve it – thinks the system of obstruction, decorously modified to save appearances, will spread from the Irish members to the English & Scotch: he notes, as one result of it, that a bill if passed at all must be passed just as it is brought in: no matter how useful an amendment might be, no friend to a bill will suggest one, lest it should serve as an excuse for delay. . . . The only great measure which had realised the ideas of those who passed it was free trade. He thought the govt. would be turned out at the elections, & seemed disappointed because I doubted: but to M. he said that personally he did not wish the Liberals to come in, since the question of county franchise will prevent his acting with them, & he was better pleased that they should all be in opposition together. He talked of the land laws: their extreme complication, the loss they caused to landowners, for the sole gain of lawyers: wished to see land put on the same footing as personal property: but would not do away with settlements altogether, & did not suppose that the results of a change would be what most people suppose, the breaking up of large estates. – He denounced the financial recklessness of the Cabinet both in England & India in very strong terms. He talked of Afghanistan: said Nemesis always overtook offenders, but seldom so quickly. He thought Afghanistan was made by nature to be a boundary between Russia & India: & that by holding it we only increased our own difficulties, & lessened those of the Russians. Speaking of the H. of C. he said that, if the Lords cared to use their advantages, they might do much useful work in the way of revision & correction: he did not know why they did not try. I said the peers were too well off and too lazy to care for work which they were not forced to: and this is true: but there is really more behind. Much activity on our part, however usefully & harmlessly directed, would rouse democratic jealousy to an inconvenient degree. – He talked of the two working-class members, Burt[43] & Macdonald[44]: of Burt he spoke well, as most people do: Macdonald he fell foul of, declaring him to be corrupt, a man who could be bought to do anything. I note that – whether this particular charge be true or not – I have heard the same said several times of late by M.P.s of one another: which is new, & not pleasant. I never heard an imputation of that kind in my time, except as regards some of the Irish, who were supposed to sell their patronage: & I don't know that even that was never proved. . . .

21 Sept. 1879 (Sunday): . . . Write up this book since Thursday morning. . . . Talk with M. who puzzled & uneasy at Margaret's odd ways: last night she would eat no dinner, today she would not sit down to breakfast because she said there was a wasp in the room: she is certainly eccentric in small matters, but I think health is the cause. T.H.S.[anderson] had a narrow escape in her refusing him, little as he might think so himself. Talk of Lionel C.[ecil] who brings a more hopeful report of the farm: the life there seems a thoroughly happy one: & I don't see that he is altered by it, except that he has grown almost ludicrously fat: [Lord] Arthur [Cecil] it seems is the same. I suppose it is the result of an active, but not very laborious, life in healthy air, joined to a total absence of anxiety or serious thought on any subject.

Forgot to note yesterday that in talking of the Irish difficulty Lowe said his solution would be to form an Irish committee composed of the Irish members, to whom all Irish bills should be referred in the first place: which would be in fact an Irish parliament, but sitting in London, & subject to the veto of the whole body of which it would form part. The objections & difficulties are obvious but, if matters cannot be left alone, perhaps this is as little objectionable a remedy as any.

22 Sept. 1879: Ld & Ly De La Warr[45] came to luncheon . . . We showed them what little there is to see about the place. It seems that the farmers in these parts who depend on hops are likely to be ruined: the crop not being worth picking: I hear of 150 acres of growing hops being offered by the grower to any one who would take them away, paying only for the labour of picking . . . Ld D. says his tenants have not as yet complained, & evidently believes that there is a good deal of unreality in the cry of distress that is raised. Many tenants cry out not because they are hurt, but because they have got a good thing, & think they see a chance of getting it cheaper. A leading tenant of the D. of Bedford lately threw up his farm, asking for a reduction of rent which the Duke thought unreasonable: as soon as it was settled that he should be taken at his word, which apparently he did not expect, he sent in a request that his son might succeed him in the holding which he had declared he could not afford to keep. . . .

23 Sept. 1879: . . . Receive, and refuse, a request from a widow of a cattle-dealer in Wales: her husband has just died leaving £4,000 of debt, & she hopes that I & a few other capitalists will pay it for her. She does not allege any claim or profess ever to have seen me. Another sample of the odd applications which every post brings.

Wet morning . . . ride in afternoon. Heavy rain, & I come in wet through.

24 Sept. 1879: Send £60 to the Birkbeck Institution.

Ride in afternoon . . . again caught in heavy rain.

One effect of the excessive wet has been that I never yet saw the grass & trees of this place in such luxuriance. The rich green of the meadows is like Ireland.

25 Sept. 1879: Münster came to luncheon with his daughter: they stayed till 4.30. Much talk as to home & foreign affairs. He says it is understood (but so many things are understood that never happened) that a dissolution had been decided on, & was about to be announced, when the news from Kabul came. He thinks the Afghan business serious: that we shall get to Kabul easily, but that it will not be easy to get away: that in one form or another we shall be obliged to annex the entire country: that the Russians will then advance on their side, until the frontiers of the two empires are coterminous.

He talked of the next elections, said the general idea in London was that the govt. would lose about 30 votes – making 60 on a division. But with the unknown elements of household suffrage, who can do more than guess?

He spoke only in general terms of the arrangements supposed to be in progress between Austria & Germany, but said that Bismarck's object was to establish a thoroughly good understanding with Austria, hinting that such an alliance would serve as a check upon any Franco-Russian combination against Germany. But he did not believe that any such combination either existed now or was contemplated.

He thought Andrassy's retirement not likely to last. Believed that it was really nothing more than a strike for promotion: he wants to be Chancellor of the Empire as Gortschakoff is: that is, I suppose, invested with a real supremacy over the other ministers, instead of being merely *primus inter pares*. He noted that Andrassy had put forward to hold his place an unknown man, having but little influence, whom he can remove again if it should be convenient to him to return to his post.

27 Sept. 1879: In afternoon drove to Penshurst with M. at the invitation of Lord De L'Isle[46], and were by him shown over the house, including the private rooms. He found the whole in bad order, modernised in the most defective taste, except where it had been altogether neglected: in fact, in Amsinck's[47] book on Tunbridge Wells, published 70 years ago, the house is spoken of as falling into decay. He has been 25 years at work upon it, & with no very large means; by constant care he has made it a nearly perfect specimen of the old English house of 4 to 500 years ago, the necessary modern additions being made to harmonise with the rest. Only three or four rooms remain to be dealt with. He is a widower [a mistake: his wife is alive, but separated]: a daughter was with him when he received us. We stayed an hour and a half, & returned much pleased. All is in harmony: the country round, the park, the woods, the garden, and the little village close outside. The owner appears to consider the keeping of it in order as the chief business of his life, & I don't think he is wrong. The estate is not large but I believe he married an heiress. Whilst there, we saw the chief drawback on such possessions: successive parties of tourists, in batches of about 20 each, walked through the house, at least through the greater part of it, which is thereby made useless for private occupation.

The Penshurst estate seems to have passed through the hands of two heiresses, the later of whom married a Shelley, who took the name of Sidney. He & his descendants appear to have selected matrimony as their road to distinction: since the next generation after the heiress secured a title by marrying one of the daughters of William IV by Mrs. Jordan[48], and the present owner has added to his possessions those of the Yorkshire family of Foulis.

28 Sept. 1879: Margaret unwell, & does not appear at dinner. At night, M. explains her anxiety lest a matter in which Margaret is concerned, quite harmless in itself, but capable of misrepresentation, should cause scandal. I do not like to set it down more plainly. Her anxiety seems to me overstrained, but it is not altogether without grounds[49].

I lately received . . . a plan proposed by a Norfolk parson in substitution for the existing poor law. He would compel every one (except I suppose on proof of inability) to pay a small sum, £10, I think it is, to the State at an early age, by way of insurance, in return for which the person so contributing should receive a weekly payment after the age of 60 enough to maintain him in old age. I did not understand, or do not remember, by what penalties this precaution was to be enforced. It is obviously impracticable, in the actual state of opinion, & probably unworkable in itself: but I note it as showing the tendency of opinion to condemn the poor law as pauperising, & to endeavour to substitute a more satisfactory system. As matters now stand, the labourer who is asked to put money into a savings bank, if he has learnt to reason at all, refuses. Why, he says, should he refuse himself such pleasure as he can get, in order to save the ratepayers' pockets? They are bound to keep him in old age, & if he is known to have money in hand he will not be entitled to relief. The argument is sound, & there is no answer to it. – The pamphlet embodying the plan mentioned above was sent for my opinion, by the Dow. Ly Lothian[50] to M.

29 Sept. 1879: Sanderson came to dine & sleep. Asked him to Knowsley.

News in the papers that the Ameer has escaped from his insurgent subjects, and taken refuge in the British camp: a step which proves that he has not been an accomplice in the murder, but which does not lessen our difficulties. He will represent himself (justly) as the victim to concessions made in our interest, & require us to put him back on the throne. If we do this, we must keep him there: Shah Soojah[51] over again! And who can feel sure that a second Dost Mahommed may not turn up?

The anti-rent agitation in Ireland continues, and is bearing fruit. Tenants refuse to pay, & threaten those who do: & they have discovered the ingenious device of agreeing not to take any farm vacated by the eviction of the previous holder: a rule which will no doubt be enforced by shooting the first man who breaks it. Even fixity of tenure with fixed rents is not now thought enough: the demand as far as it can be understood seems to be that the rent is to be fixed from year to year by some public authority, who shall decide what the tenant can spare. But in truth the object is to get rid of the landlord altogether: the Irish peasantry have never ceased to hold that the land belongs to them, and has been taken away by violence & confiscation: which as a historical fact is in most cases true. Hence they have (at least in the south) retained the notion that, when justice is done, they shall get it back again – & they think they see their chance now.

30 Sept. 1879: Long early ride & lose my way in the Weald lanes. The variety of roads fit for riding in this neighbourhood is quite inexhaustible.

Lionel C.[ecil] goes over to Witley with Sackville [Cecil], the latter having a fancy for an outlying bit of land of mine, 5 acres: I tell them that if his mind holds he may have it for nothing. It is the first time I have had an opportunity of doing him any service, & with his curiously suspicious temper I have never liked to volunteer any, as his first impulse would be to ask what my object could be: but in this case there seems no risk of misconstruction.

Margaret has got her head full of an intended visit to her uncle at Madrid, in company with Miss Franks[52]: she can think & talk of nothing else: & M. has wisely consented, as she is evidently in an odd nervous state, & change will do her good. But a winter session if we have one may upset all these plans. A nice question has been raised whether the sanction of parliament is necessary for a march on Kabul: if it is to be considered as a war, parliament under the India Act must be consulted: but it is possible to contend that, the Ameer being on our side, there is no war, but only a friendly expedition to help him against his own insurgent subjects.

1 Oct. 1879: . . . M. has seen Ld Cowley, who is in deep distress: it seems F.[rederick] W.[ellesley] is drowned in debt, so that the smash must have come soon or late. Ld C. himself is unable to help him, his rents being ill paid, & family not very well off. F. was engaged some years ago to an American girl, whom his relations liked, & thought the match excellent: she has £20,000 a year, but he broke it off at the last moment, no one knowing why. The D. of Cambridge tells Ld C.[owley] that the feeling against his son is strong in the army, & that he has had difficulty in agreeing to let him go back to his regiment. The wife is to be amicably separated: the Queen allows her £100 a year, I don't know on what ground, but F.W. knows some awkward secrets, & she can hardly afford to let him be driven to the wall. . . .

2 Oct. 1879: Send £5 to a free library set up at Bethnal Green.

In the papers yesterday appears the financial *resumé* of the last six months. It is not pleasant reading. On customs, the falling off from last year is £438,000, on excise £593,000, or more than a million on the two. According to *The Times*, whose calculation I have not verified, Northcote will have to deal next spring with a deficit of between £6 and £7 millions, incurred in the last three years. As far as one can judge, this practical proof of the costliness of a warlike policy has told on opinion. The language held by supporters of the ministry is not that of boasting and praise, as was the case a year ago, but rather of apology. The popular talk is that Disraeli takes a gloomy view of the situation, and especially dislikes Hicks Beach, on whom he throws the blame of the South African trouble. Such reports are worth little, but in the present case they have an intrinsic probability, for Hicks Beach is (though not wanting in power of speech) singularly unconciliatory, & almost offensive in his brusque way of opposing what he dislikes. . . .

3 Oct. 1879: . . . Read to her a long speech of V. Harcourt at Southport, where he has been opening a new club: it is thoroughly partisan, & of course exaggerated in its language, but vigorous & telling, as an exposure of recent foreign policy. *The Times* replies to it, but rather oddly: arguing that the ministry may not have done all that they ought but that the opposition would have done less, & of the two those who at least tried to be in the right have the better claim. – I note that Harcourt is careful to confine himself to retrospective criticism: saying as little as possible about the future, & alluding to the land laws only in a vague way.

I have not before noted that a few days ago I received from Col. Steble a note expressing his perplexity & dissatisfaction at the existing state of political affairs: & asking my advice as to his line. I tell him it is not my intention to give any support to the ministerial candidates at the coming election: that I do not intend to take an active part against them, or to connect myself with any Liberal organisation: but simply to watch events, making it clear that I am in no way connected with the men now in power. I add that I have never been a hot partisan: that I want peace economy & useful administrative measures: any govt. that holds out a prospect of these will have my good wishes.

4 Oct. 1879: Very fine bright day. Long early ride, & take the opportunity to look at a farm that is for sale about 3½ miles away, called Northstead Manor: acreage 664, of which 140 are wood, an old house which has been good . . . high, healthy, & rather picturesque.

In *The Times*, letter from the Lord Mayor saying that the intended memorial to Sir Rowland Hill[53] has failed, only £100 being collected: & that he gives it up. I write to him . . . In conclusion I offer £50 if the Lord Mayor will try again. It is discreditable that nothing should be done to honour the memory of a really useful reform.

. . . Letter from Ly Dartrey about Irish troubles, in reply to one from me. What she says is in substance that we are wrong in thinking that the Irish have any definite grievance, or that it is possible to satisfy them. They do not want to be satisfied.

5 Oct. 1879: . . . I leave the south with some regret, but yet not wholly sorry to begin the more bustling & active life of Knowsley. I should enjoy that life more if the climate did not always, within a few weeks, disagree with M. either as regards her health or spirits.

6 Oct. 1879: Meet D. of Richmond in the street, & short talk about the distress: he says in Sussex it is very bad: he will not make general reductions of rent, objecting to that in

principle, but he will give the farmers time to pay, & has put off his rent days in consequence. In the north of Scotland he finds matters even worse. On the whole he did not
seem cheerful, though he asked me whether I did not regret having ceased to be an Irish
landlord?

See Drage, & serious talk as to health. He speaks of marked improvement since my
return from abroad, the albumen has diminished to a very small quantity, & the general
condition is excellent: which indeed I could have told him. But the mischief is liable to
recur, unless care be taken: & each time it does recur the risk is greater. He lays down
three rules: (1) unnecessary drinking, even of water, to be avoided, as throwing work on
the kidneys, which ought to have rest as far as possible: (2) alcohol to be kept within
narrow limits (he is satisfied in this respect with my present regimen): he does not think
I can give it up altogether, which I told him I was willing to do if necessary: (3) chills to
be avoided with peculiar, almost with extreme, care. They may be fatal. I note in all this
the advantages of modern analysis. A century ago, no disease would have been detected
until it made itself felt in the general health, & the cure would have been long & difficult.
Now, the slightest variation for better or for worse can be traced.

Leave Euston at 5.00, & reach Edgehill by 10.00. Thick white fog, but reach Knowsley
by 10.45. Find Margaret & Lionel [Cecil]. Supper, & to bed.

7 Oct. 1879: Up early: notes & letters. Send £5 to a local library at Ulverston. Walk out
in the park, which looks well as far as fog & vapour from Widnes make it possible to see.
Day disagreeable, & some smell.

There came in the afternoon Count Münster with his daughter, & Sir W. & Ly
Harcourt.

Talk with Count Münster: he says Schouvaloff is quite out of favour at court, &
unpopular in the country: that he is thought too English & pacific: the man most in credit
is the War Minister . . . very dangerous, Münster says, & reckless. The Russian army is to
be increased by 300,000 men above the number at which it stood during the Turkish war
– no one knows exactly why. Great irritation in Russia against Germany, but Münster was
reticent as to the cause. M.[ünster] lays great stress on the cordiality existing between
Austria & Germany, which he is evidently instructed to make the most of: & he praises
Bismarck for his foresight in not imposing hard terms of peace on Austria in 1866 so that
the war then ended should not leave behind an impossibility of reconciliation & joint
action hereafter. He thinks the Russians do not really care about extension in Asia, but
that all their activity in that part of the world is for our annoyance: that they may have a
weapon in their hands to use in the event of a quarrel about Constantinople. He half
hinted that what would be best for all parties would be an alliance between Austria,
Germany, & England: so as to counteract the union of France, Italy, & Russia. This would
suit German purposes very well, but why are we to separate from France without necessity or provocation? The plan seems as though hatched at court, where an Anglo-German
dynastic and anti-republican alliance is naturally a popular arrangement.

8 Oct. 1879: Nervous & uncomfortable at the prospect of a speech. Drive into Liverpool
at 3.00, arrive at St. George's Hall a little before 4.00, where I find a dinner of 600 in the
great room, & at least 500 more in the galleries. . . . This dinner is given by the Liverpool
people on the occasion of the opening of the new Picton reading room, & in honour of
old Mr. Picton[54], the historian of Liverpool. I was asked as long ago as last May to take

the chair, but did not foresee that it was to be on so large a scale. The Mayor sat on my left, Mr. Picton on my right: the attendance was entirely unpolitical. I spoke not much to my own satisfaction, the room being too big for any voice, but all went off well. We sat till 8.30, when I got away, & sat with my guests in the drawing-room after dinner. The whole business is fully reported in the local papers.

News of a scandalous scene between Lawson of the *D. Telegraph* & Labouchere, the editor of *Truth*. The latter has employed himself of late in libelling the whole Lawson family, especially an uncle of E. Lawson lately dead, & who is said to have left £900,000. Thereupon an encounter in the street, & a horsewhipping, followed. – American manners imported into London life. There is no compassion felt for Labouchere, who has taken up the trade of libellous journalism without the excuse of poverty, but an editor of a leading journal does himself no good by such retaliation.

Receive from Mrs. Moult, through her son-in-law, Mr. Evans, a request that she may be allowed to stay on in her house: which I granted as a matter of course. She has lived there, she says, more than 50 years.

9 Oct. 1879: Woke in the night rather ill & uncomfortable as the result of yesterday's dinner, or rather of the want of one, for I had not eaten since 5.00 p.m., and but little then. . . . However, it passed off before breakfast.

Shooting with Münster, Harcourt, & Lionel: we killed 145 head. Day fair, but wind in the east, bringing fog and smoke.

Long talk after coming home with V. Harcourt in my room. – There dined with us the Mayor of Liverpool, Mrs. Royden, & Bolton. – One of the facts told me by Harcourt is curious. He has lately met Gen. Ponsonby, the Queen's secretary, who told him that he, Ponsonby, was charged with a message to the leaders of opposition, to warn them against pledging themselves to anything which would make it impossible for the Queen to receive them as ministers. One thing which she would absolutely require was the maintenance of the present foreign policy: another the retention of the Scotch ecclesiastical establishment, which it seems there is some talk in Scotland of sweeping away. This is likely enough to cause trouble in the future, for no Cabinet will submit to have the conditions of their policy dictated in the way adopted by George the 3rd. Ponsonby said further that there would be some personal exclusions: that it would be almost impossible to induce her to consent to Gladstone's holding office in any capacity: & there were one or two others (probably Argyll was intended). In short, she has been worked upon by the Premier to assert her prerogative, and will try to take a direct share in the government.

I happened to remark to Harcourt that, whereas the conservative party often found it difficult to fill the offices, their supply of available candidates being small, the trouble of the Liberals arose from an exactly opposite cause: they had more effective speakers & useful party leaders than they knew how to find places for. He said it might have been so, but was not so now: Gladstone he thought was not a candidate, though if anything would make him so it would be the notion of an attempt to exclude him by the prerogative. Lowe would not wish to serve again, & was not fit for it, having lost his power of speech in the House (Harcourt spoke of this several times as a fact generally admitted, so I suppose it is more or less true): Carlingford was too much knocked down by grief for the loss of his wife: the D. of Argyll had not health, & was weary of business. He could only find 4 peers – Granville, Cardwell, Kimberley, & Northbrook – & 4 commoners – Childers, Goschen, Hartington, & Forster – whose claims were irresistible. He laid much stress on the decided superiority of the moderate section of the party: how they had got & kept the lead of the whole – & how the ultras would really be content with much less than they seemed to ask for: which may be so, but it was obviously said with a purpose. – He seemed to be confident of the defeat of the ministry at the coming elections, saying that the last six months had made a great difference in the state of opinion. He was against making any concession to the Irish, thinking that it could not be done without recognising them as a separate nationality. He dwelt in our conversation a good deal on the land laws, not concealing that his wish is to do away with settlements altogether: recognising only the absolute owner, with full power to sell: but he did not expect any proposal of that kind to be accepted by parliament, nor did he say that it would be taken up by the party. . . .

11 Oct. 1879: Our guests left us, the Münsters after breakfast, Harcourts later. I have had in the last three days a great deal of conversation with V.[ernon] H.[arcourt]. His ability is unquestionable, & his late speeches are among the most effective that he has made. He is ambitious, but whether he is prepared to give up the law altogether & take a simply political place I cannot make out. It may be that he expects to succeed Ld Selborne, who however is healthy enough for another term of office. He calls himself an old Whig, & affects dislike of the radicals: but there is an obvious reason for his holding such language here, & I do not lay much stress upon it. The only point on which his ideas are radical is unluckily almost the only one on which mine incline in an opposite direction. He is for making a clean sweep of the land laws, & doing away with limited ownership altogether. He argued the matter at length, laying a good deal of weight on an argument which no doubt has something in it: that the power which an heir has of selling his reversion, or borrowing on the strength of it, in cases where an estate is entailed upon him, does almost as much to ruin families as the entail itself does to save them from ruin. – He did not seem to think that limiting settlement to lives actually in existence would do much one way or the other.

He talked of the D.[uke] of Sutherland[55], who seems to have embarrassed his property by speculations of various kinds, & to be in some trouble: he (the Duke) blames Pender for leading him into the trouble, & they are not now friends. – Of Ld Carlisle, who is insane, & his family affairs, he tells me that the last earl, the Lord Lieut. of Ireland, left his estates encumbered with a debt of £400,000, but tied them up so that his successor can spend nothing till the debt is paid: which is in gradual process of being effected. Of Ld Fitzwilliam[56], who was pressed to settle his estates in the usual way, & declined, saying: 'My father trusted me, and I will trust my son.' (This must have been the late lord[57].)

Ride in the park: no walk later which I ought to have taken.

See Hale, who reports no distress in the Fylde.

12 Oct. 1879 (Sunday): Church early: walk with M. in the afternoon to the Hales. Saw Mrs. H. & heard of her stay at Boulogne: Hale is evidently uneasy, & I dare say with reason. . . .

16 Oct. 1879: . . . Long discussion with Mr. Ward, whom I find shrewd & sensible, about the village insurance society, founded in 1856 by my father, and which, though at first warmly taken up, has not been on the whole a success: nor has it been managed on sound principles, being neither business nor charity, but something between the two. There are now only 26 subscribers, & my purpose is to allow no more to come in, so that the existing obligations may run off, but to assist future applicants in paying their premiums to which ever of the great public insurance offices they may prefer.

Went with Mr. Ward over the list of benefactions, & struck off a few which have remained on the list almost without my knowledge, merely because they were there, & I had never taken the trouble to revise them. . . .

18 Oct. 1879: . . . M. goes into Liverpool to see Bickersteth: he tells her in confidence that Mrs. Hale's situation is critical: considerable internal mischief has been done, chiefly by incautious use of stimulants. We had long suspected this, but did not know it with certainty.

19 Oct. 1879: Walk early with Ld Lyons about the grounds: later with Sanderson in the park. Cold much lessened . . .

A speech has been delivered at Manchester by Salisbury, to which much attention had been called, & great expectations were formed of new disclosures: not very reasonably under all circumstances, but so it was. There were no disclosures to make, & the speech, though able & vigorous, contained nothing new: its chief merit was that of being temperate in language, & offering as little handle for attack as was possible. The only noticeable feature of it was an allusion to the Austro-German alliance as a fortunate event for Europe, on which Ld S. dwelt very strongly: not however professing to know that it has been concluded. If true, the event is important, & its effects are not wholly to our advantage. It is a check on Russia in the south-east but, inasmuch as Austria in the new alliance must be absolutely dependent on Germany, the result is to increase Bismarck's power, & strengthen him against France. Can it be that our Court & Premier are meditating an anti-republican dynastic alliance, which is to check the French influence in Europe? It is an idea which would naturally find favour with them.

Sheffield tells me that when the P. of Wales showed so much civility to Gambetta, which was generally approved, but caused a little surprise to those who knew the prince's ideas, he was urged to do it by his Bonapartist & Legitimist friends. Their notion was that Gambetta as an ultra should be encouraged to the utmost against the moderate republicans, and assisted to obtain power on the calculation that his success would inevitably lead to disturbance, & bring about a counter-revolution. The prince, he says, listened eagerly to these ideas (which have just the kind of shallow cunning which would please him) & acted accordingly: the calculations of his friends have however been disappointed, & they regret the move. The prince, Sheffield says, is open-mouthed against the republic, which interferes with the popularity which he might otherwise gain by his liking for French society. Sheffield referred several times to Gambetta's influence over the Italian republicans, & how they would follow him if he made a move: but he does not think (nor does Ld Lyons) that Gambetta himself has any idea of endeavouring to press the republic on foreign states. In fact, a republic in Italy now (whatever might be the case 20 years hence) would be a clerical rather than a liberal victory. It would be the revenge of the priests on the family which has dethroned the pope.

20 Oct. 1879: . . . News in the evening papers that Merv is taken by the Russians, which if true will make a sensation here, but it is only a report, & seems improbable. There is, however, little doubt that they will advance their frontier to meet ours, being relieved from all pledges to the contrary by our invasion of Afghanistan. Our position is peculiar. We are in Kabul, the Ameer has abdicated, there is neither sovereign nor government, & the country is in that state of anarchy which was from the first predicted as the probable result of the war. The population is inevitably hostile, & we can neither retire without discredit nor remain without the cost of a strong garrison, which India can ill bear. The scheme which it is supposed the Cabinet will adopt is that of calling on the heads of clans to elect a new Ameer, promising him support in return for friendship. But will the clans agree? and, if they do, can their nominee be trusted to keep any engagement into which he may enter? . . .

22 Oct. 1879: Ld Lyons & Sheffield went away. There is no pleasanter society than that of Ld Lyons. – I regret to see that he has grown very infirm & unwieldy, more than suits with his age. Total want of exercise, & a good appetite freely indulged are the explanation. Sheffield, whom he takes about with him as his secretary, is also lively, & helps to keep up conversation among a mixed party.

Letters asking me to attend meetings at Wigan & Darwen, which I decline. – One from Mr. Waugh[58], the Lancashire author, with a book: I answer complimenting.

Ly D. & most of our guests went in to Liverpool to see the docks, warehouses, etc. I had a walk with Grant Duff, the conversation almost wholly political. His information on foreign affairs is more exact & minute than that of any Englishman I have come across: he talks of continental statesmen, their relations to one another, the parties they act with, their chances of power, etc., with as much interest & detailed knowledge as most of us would show about the affairs of our own country. Characteristically he deplored the national indifference on such matters: & started various ideas as to what should be done to remedy it. He would have a council to advise F.O. like that of India, composed of retired ambassadors & ministers: & wished to have entrance into the diplomatic service by limited competition, subject to a property qualification. We talked of the eastern question: he regretted that the opportunity was not taken to remove the Sultan from Constantinople, putting the D. of S.[?] in his place. He thought the real difficulties of the question had not been got over, but merely postponed: that the Turks could not reform their administration in Asia, & were not likely to try: that Russian intrigues would be renewed, & that massacres like those of Bulgaria in 1876 would probably recur, this time among the Armenians.

On the whole, thinking over this conversation, I was more impressed with Grant Duff's knowledge than with his judgment: he seems to me something of a pedant, though well informed & laborious: but I do not say that he is mistaken in the conclusion which I have noted above. . . .

23 Oct. 1879: I note this anniversary – ten years – but in 1869 it was a Saturday. What changes, public & private!

. . . Sensible talk on Mr. Wyatt's[59] part as to the necessity of supplying evidence to the new commission on agriculture. If this is not done, if all is left to chance, the witnesses who will be ready & eager to come forward are those of the agitating sort, who form a very small minority but, being talkers, & representing a class which is usually silent & apathetic, will give a false impression as to the state of feeling. – I note the hint as being worth acting upon.

24 Oct. 1879: Day almost wholly wet: rode early, but the ground is so full of water that it was like a marsh in many places. Did not go out again.

Ld Hartington & Mr. Grant Duff went to Manchester for their meeting: Ld Lymington[60] went with them ...

Ld Hartington came back at 10.30, having had a very warm welcome from about 5,000 people, & having spoken an hour and a quarter. He was not at all satisfied with his own performance, & said so in the most unaffected manner.

I read the speech after, & understood why he had thought it a failure: it is a sound solid argument, reads well, but the points which set a crowd cheering are comparatively few, & I dare say it was heavy to listen to in parts. Yet taken as a whole it is effective, & certainly would not suggest failure to anyone who read it in the papers. Ld H. was perfectly frank in expressing his dislike to speechmaking, of which nevertheless he has a good deal now, & will have more hereafter. He talks of politics sensibly, but without animation, & leaves on one's mind the impression of thinking the whole concern a nuisance: which perhaps is the case: but it may be only the result of a naturally lethargic habit. In some respects this apparent apathy may be useful: it would be impossible to suspect Ld H. of intriguing for office, or of using factious means of trying to push himself: it is evident from the mere manner of the man that any such proceedings would give him more trouble than he is inclined to take. He talks in a slow drawling way, as if the exertion of opening his mouth were disagreeable: but what he says is sound hard sense, conveyed in few words. He has some humour, & enjoys a joke: I cannot imagine him excited or angry.

25 Oct. 1879: With Latter[61] [the librarian] setting out books for binding, & ordering new ones out of a catalogue.

Ld Hartington went again into Manchester, this time for a meeting at the Pomona gardens, where Salisbury was received last week: on that occasion great pains had been taken to secure an enormous attendance, which was done, for the crowd was greater than the building & gardens could hold: the Liberals determined to outdo the Conservative demonstration &, if the report brought back by Ld H. is correct, they have succeeded: but in fact little is proved by these gatherings on either side. In a population such as that of South Lancashire, it is easy by a little expenditure, & good party organisation, to bring together a larger crowd than can find room in any place of meeting available, & the organs of each party will then multiply the real number two or threefold. The excitement & enthusiasm are said to have been great. Ld H. spoke shortly, leaving most of the work to be done by Bright, whose harangue was in his old style, a fine piece of oratory, effective & suitable for the time: but, as usual, all on the old subjects, free trade & peace, without a new idea of any kind, & he laid very unnecessary stress on the wish of some Conservatives to restore protection. It is worth notice that both speakers abstained from giving any hint as to what their programme would be in case of taking office.

The D. of Argyll & two daughters came about 5.30.

Hale came to dine with us.

26 Oct. 1879: Walk early in the park with Ld Hartington, wishing to have with him a more continuous conversation than had yet been possible, as to Irish affairs and the land question. I cannot say that the result was satisfactory. His remarks were sensible, but on both questions, & especially that of land, he made it plain to me that he had not arrived at any definite conclusion: indeed he said so plainly enough, admitting that he had no idea what would be proposed by the Liberal party. He was in favour of the plan proposed by Laurence in a recent pamphlet, of making universal & compulsory the system adopted in most settlements as now drawn, by which power is given to sell the land itself, the price only being reserved for the family & out of the power of the seller to spend. To this I had no difficulty in agreeing: nor did I see any great objection to abolishing the law of primo-geniture, & letting the land be divided in cases where there is no will. I argued that this would make no difference, since every estate of any importance is bequeathed by will or settlement: Ld H. did not agree, saying that custom would be apt to follow the law, but at present a man who left away any land from his eldest son felt as if he were robbing him of what ought to be his by law, whereas if division were the legal rule his feeling would be the opposite: I do not assent but I note his argument. But on the main point, whether he is prepared to do away with all settlements, or only to limit them to lives now in being, he was vague, & I could see no sign of his having considered the matter at all. In another man similarly circumstanced I might suspect intentional reserve, but not in Ld H. He told me in course of talk that his family estates were free from all settlement.

As to the Irish business he was still more vague. The only definite decision which I could extract was that he would support a plan for buying by help of the State the lands of willing sellers, to be resold to the tenants. He seemed to think that Irish obstruction would die out of itself, in a new parliament: thought Parnell nearly mad, & not unlikely to go quite so. India, which we also touched upon, he admitted that he knew nothing about. On the whole, his ideas appeared to me to be in a curiously unfixed state: I said as much afterwards to the D. of Argyll, who said it was quite true, that he had not studied these matters nearly enough, that he was a good deal in the hands of Adam[62], the Liberal whip, who told him the party expected this, that or the other to be said, & he was apt to take Adam's word for it, & commit himself to propositions which he had not thought out in detail. Ld H. left us at 3.00 p.m. Walk later with Sanderson . . .

27 Oct. 1879: Dull cold day, with east wind & smoke: wrote up this book, which was in arrear: wrote various letters: one to [Edward] Lear[63], who is trying to raise money to build a new house, his old one having been rendered uninhabitable by a neighbour building in front of it – so he says. As he is 68, & a bachelor, I ask what hinders his taking a house on lease, instead of going to the cost & trouble of building.

Ride early . . . walk with Sanderson later. The Duke would not go out, being a little gouty. The Duchess of Bedford went with M. to see Speke.

. . . Comparing notes with Sanderson, M., & others who have talked to Ld Hartington during his stay here, I find their impressions agree to a singular degree: nearly everyone says the same. His manner is frank, unaffected, and inspires confidence: in that respect nothing more is to be wished for: what he says is always sensible, always to the purpose: not striking, but not commonplace: hard sense appears to be the predominant quality in his mind: his conversation is slow, he talks as if the effort were disagreeable, but occasionally becomes animated: I cannot make out how far he has considered the various questions with which he will have to deal, whether his talk is purposely vague, from caution & reserve, or whether he has not made up his mind: I doubt his being quite strong enough for a first minister, but he would, I think, he able to head the H. of C. & his speeches are undoubtedly effective.

Much talk in evening with the Duke [of Argyll]: he seemed less afraid of American competition for English farmers than most people are: he had talked to many owners of farms & persons interested in agriculture, in Canada, & did not believe that farming was a paying occupation there any more than here: but he said there was this difference between the English & American farmer, that the latter, being the owner & anxious to keep up the value of property which he may wish to sell, tries to make the best of the situation: while the English farmer, being a tenant, & wanting rents reduced, has an equally strong interest in making the worst of it. The Duke is strongly in favour of maintaining our land system as it is: believing that without entails no estate will remain for more than 3 or 4 generations in the same family: his own uncle, he said, would have sold every acre had he been legally able to do: he thought the feeling at the bottom of the outcry against settlement was not [a] wish to have land more easily bought, or better cultivated, but democratic jealousy of a landed aristocracy. He said he had been very near resigning when the Irish Land Act was discussed in Cabinet, & had got it a good deal mitigated from the first draft.

28 Oct. 1879: . . . Drive to Kirkdale; Sanderson went with me, having business in Liverpool: found about 30 magistrates present, and 35 counsel. Cases in calendar 116: nearly the heaviest sessions in my recollection. . . . The court was crowded, & I found increased difficulty in hearing the witnesses. Air foul & close – very weary before the end of the day. We sat till 6.30. . . . The jury sensible & intelligent, no wrong verdicts. But I have great & increasing doubts whether or not to go on with this kind of business. It is really work for a police magistrate, & below my position: the only reason for continuing to perform it is that it keeps me before the public here as engaged in local business, which otherwise I shall not be: & it is good that a local magnate should be known to take his share of personal trouble.

29 Oct. 1879: . . . Quaint speech of an Irish prisoner; asked whether he pleaded guilty or not guilty: 'My lord, how can I tell whether I am guilty or not till I hear the evidence against me?'

30 Oct. 1879: Kirkdale at 10.00 . . . Home all but late for dinner. Ld & Ly Jersey[64] left us. Mr. & Mrs. Lowe came. Also Count Schouvaloff.

31 Oct. 1879: D. of Argyll & his daughter left us. We have not had much conversation on passing events, but a good deal about public affairs in general. He seems to be extremely conservative on most subjects, especially in regard to land: he does not believe that any family can long maintain its position without a system of entail, & strongly condemns all legislative interference between landlord & tenant. He is still full of the eastern subject, & intends to deliver himself again upon it before long. He is evidently not now at one with Gladstone, of whom he speaks with kindly & friendly feeling, but criticising his speeches freely. He told me that on the Irish Land Act of 1870 he had been on the point of resigning, disliking the clauses which give compensation for disturbance. He had, he said, obtained great modifications in them, it being at first proposed that tenants evicted for non-payment of rent should be compensated equally with others. – The only subject on which he was absolutely reticent was Canada: as to which he only spoke despondingly as to the character of public men in the colony, & very decidedly against Froude's view of the possibility of a legislative union with England.

Drage reports again as to the symptoms observed in me (v. 3 Apr.). They are no better during the last month, but no worse. Increased care will be necessary during the winter.

. . . Talk with Ld Northbrook[65], on various occasions, about Indian finance. I find him impressed with its difficulties, but less so than I am: I pressed the point of the increase of the population of Bengal, till that province is becoming a kind of Ireland on a larger scale. The people live on the scantiest food, have no savings, will not migrate, & are multiplying beyond the resources of the soil. The three great checks on population, war, famine, & pestilence, do not touch them, or touch them very lightly: for they are not affected by war on the distant frontiers: famine when it occurs is mitigated by lavish state expenditure: & pestilence, which usually follows on famine, is proportionally diminished. All quite right; but what is to be the end? Will not the doctrine of Malthus assert itself true at last? Ld N. did not seem to like the subject, & argued that it would be too painful to our feelings if all exertion were in this way baffled by an irresistible law: it was a conclusion he would not admit until forced to it. As to the immediate difficulty, he thought it might be got over if the price of silver rose again, but Afghanistan appeared to him an insoluble problem. We could not hold the country without ruinous expense, nor divide it, nor retire from it without discredit.

1 Nov. 1879: . . . Ld Northbrook asked me to subscribe to an Indian association for giving help to natives who want to educate their children in England. I give £10, which is the limit fixed.

. . . Talk with my sister before her departure about her future settlement. Neither she nor T.[66] can make up their minds as to whether they will give up their farm now, or wait till the expiration of their lease, 5 years hence: meanwhile they are looking out for a site on which to build a villa, if unable to buy one that shall be suitable: I strongly advise going beyond the limit of suburban villas, as they have a house in London: & specially recommend either the neighbourhood of T.[unbridge] Wells or that of Haslemere. Note that in all these plans there enters the calculation as to provision for E.[67] when left a widow: Talbot is only 61, but his health has often been bad, & his family is not long-lived.

2 Nov. 1879: Schouvaloff left us last night rather suddenly: summoned away by a letter from London: he expressed himself over & over again to all who would hear him as aggrieved by Salisbury's Manchester speech[68], which certainly contains a strong denunciation of Russian policy: we are used to these things here, & think but little of strong language, but diplomatists are more sensitive, & take an electioneering harangue as seriously as if the language held in it were that of a despatch. Ld Northbrook & I both tried to appease him, but he is deeply hurt, & I suppose he feels it as a personal injury, since he has from the first been in favour of a policy of conciliation, which has made him unpopular in Russia, & could only be justified in the eyes of Russians by success in bringing about a good understanding. He professes to deny absolutely the existence of an Austro-German alliance, but such denials are worth little. If the alliance exists it may very probably be in some secret form, either not known to him, or not officially disclosed, so that it can be repudiated in all quarters whenever its avowal is not convenient. He thinks he shall be recalled (which he says he has been asking [for] ever since the Berlin treaty) and only a secretary of embassy left in his place, which is not exactly a diplomatic rupture, but is understood as a mark of displeasure. He says the Central Asiatic expedition must now go on: the recent failure must be retrieved, that is a matter of military necessity (we should argue in precisely the same way): & English remonstrances are not now likely to be listened to. But they will not go to Merv: the point they will make for is south of Merv. I said something as to the probable result being that the two empires will touch, which is an inconvenience to both: he answered that as an Englishman I was right in saying so, but that to Russia the advantage was greater than the inconvenience. Hitherto we had no vulnerable point: we could destroy Russian commerce at sea, & reprisals were impossible: but with an Asiatic land frontier the case was altered, & the Russian army might be employed in case of war to make demonstrations on the side of India. He talked throughout with great plainness & frankness using no diplomatic circumlocutions.

Walk early with Lowe: with Sanderson later.

3 Nov. 1879: . . . The Liverpool papers are full of the municipal elections there, which are supposed to be especially significant, as they turn on party politics. The Liberals have won 8 seats out of 16 in all, of which 12 were contested. They have therefore all but reversed the majority against them. In other boroughs the result has been less marked, but generally the same.

Much excitement in London at the news that the fleet is again to be sent into Turkish waters: the report is that the Sultan is to be coerced into making reforms in Asia, & on his refusal to be dethroned, & his brother put in his place[69]. It is of course added that Russia is supporting him in his resistance.

In the course of yesterday & Saturday [1 November] I have had a great deal of conversation with Lowe: he has never been more agreeable, & I do not think that on the subjects which we discussed there have been many differences between us: but I am struck with his pessimism, which is evidently genuine, & not put on for effect. He thinks that the greatness of England has reached & passed its highest point, & that a slow decline is before us: that the greater facility of communication, bringing all the world together, is all in the interest of new countries, which have greater resources, & more attraction for working men: that the colonies give us no strength, & in any case cannot be long retained: while India, which we cannot part with, is a source of danger & weakness. At home he did not seem to fear violence or discontent so much as reckless expenditure, intended to please the working electors by spending money freely, especially in the way of local loans, which he objects to as strongly as Fawcett.

4 Nov. 1879: Long early walk with Broomfield, pointing out changes to be made, but they are in small matters. We are now (1) extending & replanting the belt below the Mizzy Dam: (2) clearing out & in part replanting the plantation between that lake & the Riding Hill: (3) extending, enclosing, & replanting one of the clumps between the great Dam & the park-keeper's house: thinning & in part replanting the upper part of the Clayholes: (4) thinning young plantations in various parts of the park: (5) putting in cage trees, about 150, in sundry places. To this I have added the extending & re-enclosing of two small clumps near the Pony Coppy lodge – & the putting on the Moss of single trees, principally chestnuts, which ought to grow well there, & require no protection from deer. On the whole I am well pleased with the state of matters. I have not included in the above list the extending of a plantation in the Meadows, & the putting in of many single trees there, as this was finished some time ago. Round the lake, & everywhere except on the Stand Hill, where old dead trees still abound, the growth of the woods, & the better order in which they are kept, have produced a marked effect, & altogether I do not suppose that Knowsley has ever looked so well as at the present time.

Walk in afternoon with De La Warr: Arthur[70*] & the fisherman Hayward employ themselves in catching two swans to be sent to Keston. . . . Arthur leaves us at night. He is much improved by years: his high spirits & good nature remain, & the conceit which was rather too obvious is greatly diminished or disguised. He is really a desirable addition to any party that we may have in the house.

Second letter from Lear: I do not well understand why building is necessary to him, but on the whole remembering how long he has been patronised by this family, & considering his age, I decide to help him. I say I will let him have £500, not as a loan (for loans are a mistake) but to be paid for in drawings or pictures – drawings being what of the two I should prefer. – Ld Northbrook, with whom he stayed in India, says that Lear has no expensive tastes, but an immense family of brothers & sisters, who live upon him & keep him poor. Certainly, though his pictures sell well, he has never been out of money difficulties since I have known him.

Receive from Mr. Malcolm MacColl[71], a writer on the eastern question, a strong ritualist, & admirer of the eastern Christians, a new book written by him on the subject of Turkey. His letter is courteously worded, & he is evidently divided between sympathy with an opponent of war with Russia & dislike of any one who does not sympathise with his protégés. I answer him civilly, but coldly: declining criticism of his production on the ground that our points of view are entirely different.

5 Nov. 1879: Letter from Sanderson, saying that he has seen Corry, who asked a good deal about my position, & tells S. that the Cabinet are seriously considering the question of Ireland, that they believe the distress to be greatly exaggerated, & that no extraordinary measures of relief are required. That Ld B. is in good health, & not oppressed by his work. He adds that there are other details which he will give verbally.

The story of the fleet being sent into Turkish waters appears to be true, & also that some pressure will be put on the Turks to induce them to make reforms: but the threat of dethronement is obviously a *canard*. The state of Turkish Asia is, however, growing worse & worse, & there being an absolute want of money one does not see how it is ever to mend. The Russian expedition into central Asia has become a necessity since their late failure, & this together with the state of Turkey points to the necessity of some understanding between us & Russia. Such an understanding ought not to be difficult to come to, but the Manchester speech [of Salisbury] stands in the way of it. . . .

7 Nov. 1879: Wrote to Coutts to discontinue my yearly subscription to the Carlton Club.

Letter from Laurence, asking an advance of £100 for Mrs. Dunn, the widow of C. Stanley, who wants to start one of her sons in business at Cork. They have each £200 a year of their own, & promise to be respectable. I agree to the advance, repayable in 4 years.

8 Nov. 1879: . . . Receive from Ly Dartrey another letter, sensible enough, about the Irish distress: she says that the principal cause of trouble among the smaller farmers is that they are all in debt. Up to the passing of the Land Act of 1870 they had no security to offer, consequently could get no credit: since that date they are able to borrow on the strength of the compensation – money to which they are entitled on leaving their farms.

The local banks have invited them to use their privilege largely, and they have done it: the great majority owe more than they can pay: & since the failure of the Glasgow bank there has been a tendency to call in debts, increased by the prevalence of bad times. The trades-men as well as the farmers are pressed by creditors, & they in turn press on customers: the only point in which all parties agree is that the landlords' claim should be postponed till everybody else is satisfied.

9 Nov. 1879: Dull cold day, rather disagreeable. Walk with Sanderson, & look in at his house in Wimpole St. which is newly done up. Call on Ly Harcourt in the afternoon. Dine – all four of us – at the German embassy, meeting there Schouvaloff, Brincken[72], & two others of the embassy staff.

Schou. in high spirits, & not disposed to conceal his pleasure at going home: which is natural, for his bed has not been a soft one during the last three years.

He told me one or two things which are curious, if one can be sure of their truth. (1) It is open, he says, to Russia to join the Austro-German alliance[73] whenever she pleases: the sole object of that alliance being a guarantee against French attack: but hitherto Gortschakoff has steadily declined to give any pledges in that sense. (2) He thinks the situation dangerous as regards Afghanistan. The Russian expedition must go on: the fron-tiers will be brought very near: the natural solution of the difficulty would be by an agree-ment of some kind, but after the Manchester speech there is no prospect of Russia consenting to anything of the kind. (I must here note that any such agreement would be wholly one-sided, since we should observe it scrupulously, & the Russians would not. But I merely record Schou's expressions.)

(3) He declares that there is no foundation, or next to none, for the universal belief that we are putting pressure on the Porte to make reforms. The movement of the fleet has not taken place: no fresh assurances have been given: in short, according to him, we have been merely deluded. – Can this be so?

10 Nov. 1879: Vernon Harcourt calls, says that there is no chance of early dissolution: the Attorney-Genl. having given up his private practice to devote himself to preparing the code for parliament. He is probably right: yet I don't think the Premier or Salisbury would feel much scruple about giving their law-officers trouble for nothing. He is full of electioneering calculations: says the Liberal agents have gone carefully through the list, they assume the Home Rulers to be 75, reckon them as neutral, & after that deduction consider that they ought to have a majority of 30. This seems sanguine, & I well know how partisans can delude themselves: the estimate, however, is one which would not have been made six months ago, & so far indicates a change in opinion.

Sir H. Elliott[74] called, on his way back to Vienna: he talked in his usual pleasant style, & professed much gratitude for what I had done in standing up for him two years ago. I could not ask as to the actual situation, but he dwelt on the complicated machinery of Austrian administration, & the difficulty of working it: did not well see either how it was to go on, or what was to replace it: thought the taking of Bosnia was a necessity: the Italians would otherwise certainly have made a push for it, & for Dalmatia at the same time: the occupation, he added, had pleased the Turkish inhabitants better than the Christians: the latter are tenants, & assumed as a matter of course that, when the coun-try was taken over by a Christian power, the Turkish landowners would be driven out, & they should have the lands for nothing: in this hope they are disappointed, & disgusted accordingly. – He did not believe in the much talked of customs union between Germany & Austria: thought the obstacles insuperable. He said there was no doubt an end of the agreement, or understanding, between the three emperors: but the new compact was not formed against Russia, but rather against France. He likes Vienna, but does not much care about the society: there is no conversation: the old exclusiveness is kept up to that degree that, though the ministers in their official capacity must come to court, their wives are not admitted, unless belonging to the old aristocracy: & if one of these marries a man not within the circle she loses her position. Consequently there is little rational talk, & the social surroundings are dull.

11 Nov. 1879: Write to Carnarvon, telling him that I have left the Carlton – that I did not intend to do it so soon, but that absolute neutrality, in view of an election, is impossible for me in Lancashire, & having felt myself obliged to withdraw from the local Conservative organisations, I could not consistently remain in connection with the central electioneering body. I don't think he will follow the example, nor does it greatly matter but, as we have been more or less in the same boat, I thought it as well to keep up communication with him.

. . . Wrote to A.D. giving a brief report of the impression produced by the Premier's speech at the Mansion House last night. – I do not remember to have seen so much interest excited by an occasion of the kind: the public had persuaded itself that some startling disclosure was to be made: & there was general curiosity to see whether Ld B. would soften down Salisbury's utterances at Manchester, or back them up by holding similar language. Never was delusion more complete. He spoke briefly, said nothing new, & dwelt more on the state of trade than on the condition of Europe. If his object had been to disappoint the general curiosity, he could not have accomplished it more effectually. Among quiet people the sensation is one of relief, for nobody knew what was coming.

12 Nov. 1879: Drage calls, reports very satisfactorily as to general health . . .

Receive another interminable letter from Mr. Miller[75] which I answer briefly, to the effect that a colonial customs-union is to my mind utterly impracticable: I stop there, not giving reasons: but they are obvious. . . . Yet there is certainly in many quarters a strong desire to bring the empire into closer union, & it is possible, & even probable, that ideas like those which Mr. Miller is trying to spread may be put forward at the elections. . . .

16 Nov. 1879: Letter from Lear, in which he offers me 7 pictures, now lying in Wardour St. & for which he has asked £765, for £500, instead of supplying drawings to the same amount: he not having these ready, or having promised them to other buyers. I write back that I like the proposal, & will look at the pictures.

. . . Two speeches have been delivered, one by the D. of Argyll, the other by Forster, on the general question of foreign policy: the Duke, as might be expected, violent & somewhat intemperate in language, &, as I think, weakening his case by showing that in his view the interest of the eastern Christians ought to have been the one main object of English policy. Effective in language, & sound in many parts of his argument, the speech as a whole reads to me too passionate & declamatory to answer its purpose. – Forster, with his hard northern shrewdness, goes straight to the point, showing that by the convention binding us to defend Asia Minor we have for the first time got a frontier coterminous with that of Russia, which gives the Russians the full advantage of their enormous army, as against ours. This is sense, & is in effect what Schouvaloff said to me at Knowsley.

18 Nov. 1879: Letter from Mr. T. Horsfall[76], about covered playgrounds & gymnasia for large towns, which he wants to have provided & paid for out of the rates. I tell him in reply that the difficulty is not to get parliamentary power to make a rate for this purpose (indeed I conceive that the power already exists) but to induce local authorities to use it. Mr. Horsfall, who has written to me before, is an enthusiast for work of this kind, arguing with some truth that the squalid unhealthy lives of the lower class in great English towns will re-act on the whole population, lowering the energy & physical power of the race. Railroads increase the mischief, for now few rich men live in any town except London: they only come in to do business, & naturally care less for wants which are not daily under their eyes.

Another letter from Lear, sending me a list of subjects for watercolours, but I will not answer it till I have seen his oil paintings tomorrow.

Ride early in the green drives of High Elms: which are well enough, but nowhere in this pleasant & pretty country is there ground as good for riding purposes as in the park at Knowsley.

19 Nov. 1879: London by the 10.00 a.m. train. . . . Call at a shop in Wardour St. to see the pictures which Lear wants to sell: they are 7, & out of them I select 4 . . . The others seemed to me inferior. The price I suppose will be about £300.

. . . Granville confirms Harcourt's estimates as to the elections, saying that Forster gives the Liberals a larger majority – not less than 40 – and he hears that the government themselves expect only a majority of 13, Home Rule being regarded as neutral. With these numbers they can go on, but they cannot do as they have been doing in the present parliament. . . .

20 Nov. 1879: Snow falling heavily all morning: did not leave the house.

. . . Gave M. £21 for the Mendicity Socy.

. . . The event of the last few days is that two of the leading agitators in the Irish-anti-rent movement have been arrested: one, Davitt[77], an ex-convict sentenced in 1870 for some act done in the Fenian conspiracy: the other, a barrister, one Killen[78] or Killeen. It was time that something should be done, for the language now held by the agitators is – not merely that indulgence should be shown to tenants unable to pay – but that rent is in its nature an unjust exaction, and the tenantry should refuse to pay it. In several counties, especially Mayo, a system of intimidation has been organised, which gives farmers an excuse for saying that they dare not pay, though willing, for fear of their neighbours. The question of property in Ireland is curiously complicated with the question of nationality: & socialist talk which would not be accepted on its own merits is justified to the Irish mind where the parties against whom it is directed are English – that is, foreigners, & enemies.

21 Nov. 1879: Snow lying deep on the ground, & roads difficult. . . .

22 Nov. 1879: More snow falling: walk about an hour on the swept road, up & down: posts delayed, & roads difficult. . . .

23 Nov. 1879 (Sunday): Hard frost, fine clear day, snow on the ground. Winter seems to have set in all over England. . . .

24 Nov. 1879: Another day of bad weather, & indoor life. Thick fog: smell of smoke as strong as it could be in London: the wind bringing it over. Snow on ground, & more falling.

25 Nov. 1879: Frost continues, snow on the ground, roads no better, & fresh snow falling from time to time.

    . . . The papers are full of the death of Delane[79], aged only 62: but from 1841 to 1877 he had been editor of *The Times*, & at last his health broke down under the incessant strain. Probably he was the most celebrated and powerful journalist yet seen in England. *The Times* of late years had had rivals, & its influence has declined: but from 1850 to 1870 it held a position which no newspaper ever attained to before in this country, & which, as newspapers multiply, it is probable none will hold again. In the Crimean war it directed opinion: I remember seeing a telegraphic notice stuck up in Liverpool: 'Sir J. Simpson is appointed to the command. *The Times* approves the appointment.' Delane on principle never wrote articles himself: thinking that he should have more control over his writers by keeping to the work of supervision. In society he played his part judiciously: flattered on all sides, & receiving more homage than the Queen or the Premier, he was very little, if at all, elated by it: his manners were simple, & his conversation agreeable. *The Times* has never recovered [from] his withdrawal from it: both in the writing & editing department the falling off is very marked.

    Gladstone has set out for his journey to Midlothian: his progress northward has been more than royal: crowds at every station where his train stopped, addresses presented, speeches in reply – all this preliminary to a week of incessant oratory at or near Edinburgh.

26 Nov. 1879: Snow still on the ground, more falling, roads hardly passable. Stay at Keston, & mostly indoors: rather lost for want of occupation, which does not happen to me five times in a year.

    . . . Read an eloquent, but interminable, speech from Gladstone, which took nearly two hours to deliver at Edinburgh, & occupies six columns in *The Times*. Except a vigorous & quite justifiable exposure of the system of creating faggot votes, which is being practised on a large scale in Midlothian, there is nothing new in it: the whole is a repetition of what he has said very often before, the old story of the eastern question, the Berlin treaty, etc. It may be that in addressing provincial audiences this frequent re-iteration is inevitable – that nothing is really taken in by the masses till they have heard it very often – &, as Gladstone evidently enjoys his share of the business, nobody can object – but it seems work of a low kind for an intellect such as his. – My criticism is not caused by dislike of the things said, for in most of his argument I agree rather than otherwise. – It is clear that one effect of the agitation which he is carrying on will be to make his position relative to Granville & Hartington more difficult than ever. Can he retire, having made himself a far more prominent figure than either of them, & being looked upon as the real leader of at least one half of the party? Can he, on the other hand, serve under them, or act at all in parliament without virtually setting them aside? And if he returns to the leadership, what will be the effect on that large section – Whig and moderate – which fears & distrusts him as extreme in views & rash in action? The difficulty is equally serious, in whatever direction a solution is looked for.

27 Nov. 1879: Snow & frost continue, but with fine weather overhead.

Walk for exercise round Holwood, but the roads are almost impracticable.

28 Nov. 1879: Snow & frost continue. Walk for exercise, & try to ride in the afternoon, but obliged to return soon.

Wrote to Mr. Ward to send me £500 more for the charity account. I ought not to want this till January, but have rather outrun the constable.

Lionel Cecil, who is travelling with Margaret in Spain, has been appointed to the honorary post of attaché to West[80], so that he may be able to see the ceremonies with advantage: this is done at the request of West, by Salisbury, & is almost a matter of course ... Some eager friend has suggested to M. that she should write a letter of thanks, by way of bringing about a better understanding with Hatfield: we talk this over, & decide against it, as a revival of intimacy in that quarter is for many reasons not desired.

Death (in the papers) of Lord Durham[81], whom I remember a year or two my junior at Cambridge. He had a good deal of his father's ability & shrewdness, & also I believe of his violent temper: but this I never witnessed, & his health, which was always weak, is excuse enough. Considering his wealth, position, & steady adherence to the political party which has been uppermost, it is singular that he should have been so little known or heard of in the world. He leaves an enormous family – 9 sons & 4 daughters.

29 Nov. 1879: Still frost, & some snow, walking disagreeable & riding impossible.

Extraordinary letter from a Mrs. Evans – whom I never saw & know nothing of – asking me to intercede on her behalf with the judge of the county court in which she has a case to be tried! ...

30 Nov. 1879: Hard frost, roads difficult with frozen snow.

The event of the week has been Gladstone's Midlothian campaign: he has spoken a good-sized octavo volume, on a moderate computation, within five days: addressing enormous & enthusiastic audiences, & altogether making a deep impression not only on the local public, but throughout the country. The substance of what he said has been less remarkable than the language: a good deal is not & could not be new, & perhaps the supposed necessity of travelling again & again over familiar ground has rather impaired the general effect: but on the whole his arguments & conclusions have been those of a decided, but not violent, Liberal. He condemned altogether the laws of settlement & entail, but in general terms: employing a far-fetched & fantastic argument: to the effect that they are against the laws of nature, & the institution of the family, because they make the rising generation dependent not on their fathers but their grandfathers. He at the same time threw cold water on the theory of peasant proprietors, though laying rather imprudent stress on the right of the legislature, if it so pleases, to divide estates, compensating the owners. As an assertion of abstract right it is impossible to differ from him: but if these words are taken up in Ireland they will encourage Parnell's agitation. – Perhaps the most noticeable expression used by him in any of his speeches was in reference to the Irish church and land acts of 1869-1870: which he admitted frankly had been brought about by the Fenian agitation, & the

Clerkenwell attempt. There is no doubt that the fact is so, but the admission is an encouragement to the Fenianism of the future.

1 Dec. 1879: . . . Very cold, & more snow. . . . Sent £25 for parish charities, in London. Sent £200 to Sanderson, with an intimation that his allowance will continue till the end of 1884 at its present rate. – A very idle day: weather made exercise impossible.

In the papers, death of Roebuck[82]: not premature, for he had outlived his strength, & in part I think his faculties also. He had been 50 years in public life: beginning life as a radical, & a zealous one, though measured by the present standard of opinion never extreme in his ideas: he was a ready, bitter, & most pugnacious partisan: too irritable & too vain to act in concert with any other man or set of men, for co-operation with him would have been possible only on the terms of absolute submission to his will. But as a free lance he was effective, & at times played a prominent part. His health failed about 1852: he became paralytic, & could neither walk steadily nor speak so as to be heard or understood: most men would have taken such an attack as a warning to retire, but he persevered, gradually regained utterance and strength, & in 1855 acted as chairman of the committee which enquired into the misconduct of Crimean arrangements. Of late years he had become conservative, partly from jealousy of Gladstone, whose popularity he could not endure: partly also from the natural effect of age, and having seen most of the measures for which he fought in early life carried. He took the side of the South in the American Civil War, and latterly was one of the hottest of the Jingos. He was fond, like Robespierre, of figuring in the character of the 'Incorruptible': & it may have been only from pique that the Liberals denied his claim to the epithet: except [for] his connection with one Orrell Lever[83], a rather disreputable sort of speculator, I know of no foundation for their imputations of venality. But it is certain that of late such imputations were common. – He was probably never more flattered than by the speech which George Smythe put into his mouth when he had praised the late Sir R. Peel in a ludicrously condescending tone. Smythe[84] said his panegyric might be summed up thus: 'If I were not the Diogenes of Sheffield, I would be the Alexander of Tamworth.'

By his vanity he was easily led, though not long by any one person or set of persons: for the mere suspicion that he was thought to be influenced by any would have been enough to make him an enemy of the person so indicated. He never accepted or sought for office: for which indeed he would have been absolutely unfit, from his contradictory humours. He has changed a good deal, though not more than most men do in half-a-century in active politics: but I think there has always been a kindly feeling for him among the masses, who like a good fighter, and are not as acute as the more educated in finding ridiculous traits in their favourites. Witness the many eccentricities of Brougham in old days, & of Gladstone lately, which lessened the influence of both of them in society & parliament, but hardly at all among the people.

2 Dec. 1879: Sudden & rather extreme cold: thermometer last night at 8°F or 9°F: and in the midland counties it was at 5°F.

London by the usual train. Travelling difficult. The house, No. 23, not having been lived in for some time, was so chilly that we sat with coats & shawls on.

. . . Saw Drage; he reports the unsatisfactory symptom (albumen) as having all but entirely disappeared: but caution is necessary lest it should return. There is, he says, a hereditary predisposition. The two great enemies to be feared are alcohol, & sudden chills. The latter especially may be fatal.

Travelled at times with pain in the face & teeth from cold.

3 Dec. 1879: Troubled overnight with pain in the face, & long in getting to sleep, which does not happen to me twice in the year. Slept at last, & the pain did not return on waking.

Letter from Hale, who says that Liverpool Corporation are inclined to buy from me the land facing their new public offices, 2,200 yards, for which he expects a sum between £40,000 and £50,000: at the rate of £80,000 per acre. This does not look like distress, or alarm about the future: only they are spending other people's money, not their own.

Statter sends the monthly report . . . He hears much, he says, of a revival in trade, but does not see it as yet.

Mr. Millyard . . . wants £180 to enable him to study for practice as a solicitor. He has no claim on me of any kind, but I agree to give him (he calls it lending) £60, or one-third of the sum, if he & his friends can make up the rest.

Received a deputation from Huddersfield, consisting of the Mayor & three leading manufacturers, asking me to . . . deliver a speech at the yearly meeting of the Chamber of Commerce chiefly for the advantage of a new school, or college, of technical instruction which is being set up. I agreed . . .

4 Dec. 1879: Severe cold continues. Woke in the night with headache – result I suppose of less than usual exercise.

Coutts's have bought for me – G.W.R. 4 p.c. deb. stock – £5,000, L. & S.W. 4 p.c. deb. stock £5,000. The cost of the two, with brokerage, £11,000 within a pound or two. This high rate proves two things: one that there is plenty of money, the other that there is difficulty in finding profitable employment for it. . . .

5 Dec. 1879: Heavy fall of snow, which lasted all day. I did not leave the house. Refused to dine with Hale, not liking to take out servants & horses without necessity. . . .

6 Dec. 1879: Snow has ceased to fall, but lies pretty deep and hard frozen on the top: travelling very difficult. . . .

7 Dec. 1879: Day nearly blank. Weather unchanged. Church in morning, not having been seen there, or indeed anywhere, for a long while by the village folks.

Walk with Hale in the afternoon, but snow made all locomotion difficult.

Death of the Duke of Portland[85] announced in his 80th year. He was chiefly remarkable for the extreme seclusion in which he lived, never of late years leaving London, never being seen outside his house, and not by more than half a dozen persons in it. He had even surrounded his garden with an enormous wall of glass & iron, so that he could walk in it unobserved from the surrounding houses. This morbid aversion to be seen was originally due to some disease of the skin from which he suffered, & which he fancied made him an object of disgust: though I believe there was nothing in it very noticeable or repulsive. But the singular part of the story is that he spent his very large income both in buying new estates and making costly improvements on those which he had inherited, quite irrespective of the fact that he never had seen, & never would see, the works of ornament & art on which he was spending hundreds of thousands. I do not think he ever attended the H. of Lords: certainly I have never seen him there in the last ten years. He is succeeded by a cousin: but it is understood that a large part of his estates will be to other branches of the family. Their rental is popularly estimated at £200,000 a year.

8 Dec. 1879: Hard frost continues, but less severe in these parts. At Cambridge the thermometer has been down at 0°F. Fine overhead, but frozen snow makes walking difficult.

Hale has an offer for Crag Hall [Wild Boar Clough, Cheshire] which has long lain vacant: £200 a year for 5 years, afterwards £400. I approve the terms . . .

14 Dec. 1879 (Sunday)[86]: The last four days are blank, for I have neither had anything to set down, nor inclination to write. On Wednesday I was unwell, but went out for a walk. On Thursday, feeling feverish, chilly, & ill in general, I sent for Gorst[87], who prescribed, & went to bed in the afternoon. Friday I passed chiefly in my room, but partly in bed. Saturday I was able to dress & go about, & the feverish symptoms disappeared. Today I am fairly well, though weak & without appetite. I do not know exactly what has been the matter, nor I suspect does Gorst: he talks of a chill affecting the liver & this may very likely be the explanation. Exercise & perspiration are to me especially necessary, & for the last three weeks the one has been difficult, the other except by artificial means nearly impossible. Frost has been incessant, on some days very severe: the roads, where not covered with snow, are glazed with ice, so that walking is a labour.

. . . Fighting continues in Afghanistan: & it is becoming evident that, as everybody foresaw who knew the Afghan character, our army at Kabul commands only so much territory as is actually within reach: no moral effect has been produced on the more distant tribes. No step has yet been taken towards a political organisation of the country: & *The Times*, which so far has supported the government in its policy, now begins to throw out hints & warnings about the danger of having no policy, the advantage of knowing where to stop, and the like.

The Irish land agitation is less noisy than before, but there is a good deal of intimidation of tenants who consent to pay rents: & naturally the tenants themselves are not unwilling to be intimidated. Distress in some districts is real: but tenant-right sells at as high a price as ever, & the movement is less a result of popular suffering than an attempt to extort money from the Treasury or the landlord class. Great efforts are being made to create a corresponding movement among the Irish in America: hitherto with little success: the Americans answer: 'If they can't live at home, why don't they emigrate & join us here?' It is reported that the government prosecutions are to be dropped, or some of them: certainly they have had the effect of making speakers at Irish meetings more cautious, & are so far justified, & it may well be that the Cabinet think the result of a trial doubtful, & prefer to rest content with the success they have gained. . . .

16 Dec. 1879: Frost slowly breaking up: a cold thaw: east wind & St. Helens more than usually disagreeable.

. . . Talk of the D. of Portland: who it seems contrary to general expectation has left all he had to leave, or nearly so, to his successor in the dukedom: it is said in London to be not less than £150,000 a year, exclusive of the London estates, which go to the Howard de Walden family[88].

Talk with Mrs. Hornby about her brother Sir Geoffrey[89]: his desire to be relieved of his command: he is very weary of it, wishes for rest; what he would now like would be a dockyard, but of that there seems no chance at present. Nothing, she says, would induce him to return to the Admiralty, he disliked so much the kind of work to be done, or rather, I suppose, the having to act with other men & consult their views: for he is a man of a peremptory & despotic turn of mind.

Talk of the D.[uke] of Westminster's son, Ld Grosvenor[90]: he is in a strange way of health, either as to body or mind: lies in bed nearly all day, & cannot be roused. He has been sent to Canada with the hope of curing him. This hopeful youth will have £500,000 a year, if there is no revolution meanwhile.

The newspapers are full of the situation at Kabul: which is not pleasant: Gen. Roberts has been obliged to shut himself up in cantonments, as the result of three days' fighting in which he has recognised that the enemy is too strong for him: he has sent to Jellalabad & Gandamak for reinforcements, & waits for their coming. A gun has been lost, & the officers engaged have suffered severely in proportion to the men, which is a bad sign, for it shows that the men want leading, & are inclined to hang back. The danger to the troops is probably none, even if the country were to rise as one man: for 5,000 Europeans, behind walls, & well supplied, can take care of themselves: nor is there any risk of the almost insane blunders of Gen. Elphinstone[91] being repeated: but it is clear that, so far from holding Afghanistan, Afghanistan holds us, & not a step has been taken in the direction of creating a government to which we can hand over the country. In fact any chief who became Ameer under our protection would by that fact alone be so hateful to the people that he could not maintain himself on the throne.

17 Dec. 1879: East wind, fog, partial thaw, & slight frost over it.

. . . Mr. Hornby tells me of old Townley Parker's will. He has died much richer than anybody expected, leaving £25,000 a year in all, £17,000 of which goes to his eldest son, about £8,000 to another son. The successor, Tom Parker[92], is respectable & reformed: when I knew him in 1862 he was a rough, sporting, drinking sort of squire, though I never heard that he had gone into any special follies. His wife very well spoken of. – Talk of E. Hornby of Bury[93], his troubles & disappointments: both his sons disreputably married, & the younger – who has taken to wife the widow of a country innkeeper with three children – does & apparently will do nothing for his own living. This is the one for whom a place under government was asked, but the request dropped on the father hearing that an examination had to be passed.

18 Dec. 1879: . . . Singular application from Col. Maude[94], whom I appointed to Warsaw three years ago. He wants an advance of £1,000, to enable him to pay off a debt incurred some time ago. According to his story, soon after taking up his post, he gave a dinner to a large number of Russians, at the end of which he was not quite sober. Some of his guests seeing him in that situation drew him on to play, & he lost £1,600. By borrowing at high interest he made up the sum, but the debt is a weight round his neck, & he professes fear of losing his appointment should he be unable to pay, & his creditors complain to F.O. This last fear I think is unfounded, for they certainly would not be foolish enough to take steps which would cause the loss of his place, which is their only security for being paid at all. – I refer the letter to Sanderson, & shall talk with him about it.

19 Dec. 1879: Hard frost continues: it is just 4 weeks since it began in the south with snow, & since then it has not ceased for a day.

Reading the diaries of Ly Sale[95] & Lt. Eyre[96], kept during the Kabul war of 1841, which are curious by the light of present events. Some passages might have been written in the last six weeks. It was officially declared, then as now, that Kabul was quiet, & there seems to have been the same determination to see nothing that made against the hypothesis. In 1841 as in 1879 it seems to have been impossible to the English mind to realise that a warlike & turbulent people, jealous of their independence, & reckless of life, would resent invasion: & our officers went on believing themselves to be rather popular than otherwise in the hostile capital which they had occupied, till undeceived by the explosion of insurrection all round them. The generals of the first Napoleon made the same mistake in Spain, so perhaps it is not a case of specially English self-deception. Possibly it is never easy for individuals, conscious of having none but friendly intentions towards the people they are quartered among, to realise that their mere presence is felt as an outrage. – The chief anxiety now felt for the army at Kabul is lest supplies should fail: Gen. Roberts[97] has about 7,000 combatants, & a not much smaller number of camp-followers, in all about 12,000 mouths to feed: according to Ld Lytton he has 5 months' provisions with him, but this calculation is not accepted at home as likely to be accurate. Fuel is scarce, & the suffering from cold will in any case be considerable . – In the old war the Afghan chiefs who followed up & destroyed the remains of the retreating British army passed the word among their men to waste no ammunition on the sepoys, since the cold would effectively dispose of them: but to attack the British only.

20 Dec. 1879: Frost continues, but rather milder. . . . Day disagreeable, with raw cold wind, & roads glazed with ice. We have now had over 4 weeks of incessant frost, & the winter is only beginning.

. . . In the office, where talk with Hale & Mr. Ward about a general revision of the accounts, striking off old & irrecoverable arrears, so that they shall not encumber the books. I proposed this years ago, but poor old Moult could not be induced to deviate from his accustomed routine. . . .

21 Dec. 1879: Walk with Sanderson early & late: day cold, windy, & disagreeable, but the frost is less severe. . . .

22 Dec. 1879: Walk with Sanderson early & late. Frost breaking, & weather milder.

. . . Talk with Sanderson, who tells me that Salisbury's changes in the routine of the office have been one after another quietly dropped, & that matters are nearly as they were before his taking the management. The plan of ignoring the departments, & working through a private secretary, has not been found to answer, & Tenterden, who at first was left out in the cold, has now got back again to his old position. But Sanderson thinks that, though able & industrious, he has never been quite able to fill Hammond's place, & that the discipline of the office, which depends mainly on the permanent under-secretary, is less strict than in old days.

23 Dec. 1879: . . . The long-expected and hard-fought contest for Sheffield has come off at last: ending in the success of the Liberal candidate, Mr. Waddy the lawyer[98], who polled 14,000 odd votes against 13,500 odd given to his opponent[99]. The fight was an unusually sharp one, owing to the fact that Roebuck, the late member, had become more than half a Conservative in his later days, & carried many friends with him. The town is much concerned in the making of iron plates for armourclads, & I believe also weapons of war, so that the Jingo feeling which exists everywhere among a certain class was strengthened by local interest. Added to this there was & is a real anti-Russian feeling among a section of the artisans. The Catholic vote was also supposed to be secured to the government: of the leading Jews, who are an important body, most go with Ld Beaconsfield from sympathies of race: the publicans are all Conservative: so naturally are the clergy: & it was generally expected that these combined forces would overbear the natural radicalism of the place. The fact that the register of voters was 12 months old, & that the subsequent changes are known to be strongly in the Liberal interest, increases the significance of the event. It had been taken as a sort of test-division, & the newspapers have been full of it for weeks past. It is in fact a gain of two on a division to the opposition, for Roebuck had quite gone over, & had received his reward in a privy councillor's title.

It is a curious coincidence, if nothing more, that not a week before this election came off the Attorney-General should have granted leave to have the legality of Tichborne's sentence argued: it being alleged that the Chief Justice, who tried him, had no right to pass more than one sentence of 7 years. (He actually sentenced the 'Claimant' to 14 years, on the ground that two distinct acts of perjury had been committed: & it was doubted at the time whether this was not a straining of the law, the offence being virtually one & the same.) Five years ago, an application to have the question argued before the judges with a view to partial remission was refused: within the last few days it has been again made, & granted: a circumstance which at any other time would neither attract nor deserve notice: but as matters stand it is difficult not to suspect a political motive. The delusion as to the injured innocence of the 'Claimant' is stronger in Sheffield than anywhere else (except, I believe, in Nottingham & Northampton): hundreds of voters believe in him: and these voters are loud in the expression of their gratitude to the Cabinet. – If the thing has been done with any electioneering purpose, it is a bad business: worse than any money job or purchase of an individual with a place: but it is of course possible that Sir J. Holker[100] may have acted without special instructions, though the coincidence of time is singular.

24 Dec. 1879: Weather milder, but frost still continues. Walk with Sanderson. Some rain. . . .

25 Dec. 1879: Sir W. Thomson came in afternoon.
Frost continues, rather sharper than before.

26 Dec. 1879: Walk early with Sanderson & Sir W. Thomson. Later with Sanderson alone. Day very cold & windy: disagreeable enough. Whether from this cause, or health, I felt & feel very lethargic & incapable of exertion.

No luncheon except a biscuit & a vapour bath in afternoon, to supply the want of perspiration.

Sir W. Thomson talks much, & in an interesting manner, of the possibilities of improved means of producing mechanical power. He says our present steam engines do not give more than one-fifth of the power which theoretically ought to be obtainable from the quantity of fuel they consume, & in this way there may be a vast economy of fuel: but it is possible they may be superseded, at least for certain purposes, by waterpower.

. . . Talk today of the D. [uke] of Hamilton[101] intending to sell his island of Arran: his own folly, and the roguery of his agent, one Padwick[102], having led him into embarrassments. If true, & the report seems to be well founded, it is a pity, for few families have a more historic name & position, & the island has been for centuries in their hands. Half in joke, half earnest, Galloway & Duncan proposed that I should buy it: &, though I treated the notion with ridicule, there are some inducements. It would be in a sense the recovery of what we lost when the Isle of Man went away from us: we are related to the Hamiltons &, if my grandfather was rightly advised, we might even have claimed some of their Scotch titles: we may be driven out from this place by the increase of building & smoke: & there is no other estate offering residential advantages (as the agents would call them) to which it is possible to retire. Arran is 165 sq. miles . . . which gives 105,000 acres: the whole interior is heath & mountain: the probable cost £300,000 or thereabouts. I could make the purchase well enough, only at the cost of all my savings: & the question is whether this is worth doing. But possibly the whole story of the sale may be a fiction.

27 Dec. 1879: Receive from Lear a list of subjects for drawings: out of which I choose 19, costing at various prices in all £230.
   . . . Send a little help to an intending emigrant. . . .

28 Dec. 1879: Frost gone at last, a mild pleasant day. Whether from the cold or any other cause, I have hardly been well in health & spirits since coming here more than three weeks ago. M. also is depressed (as always happens to her) by the damp climate, so that we both feel as if we should be better anywhere else. . . .

29 Dec. 1879: . . . Newspapers are full of a railway accident in Scotland . . . The iron bridge over the Tay . . . broke last night with a train upon it, & all the passengers were lost . . .
   . . . Death also announced of Hepworth Dixon[103]: a busy, pushing, active-minded, clever, & vulgar man of letters who by a succession of books on popular subjects had contrived to make his name widely known. His style was detestable in point of taste, but vigorous in its way: his biographies & histories are worthless from utter inaccuracy, but they as well as his travels can be read by those who are not fastidious, for they are never dull, whatever other faults they may have. He was only 57 at his death: another instance of the general unhealthiness of an author's life. He edited the *Athenaeum* for many years: & I observe that the London journals have nearly all given him an article.

30 Dec. 1879: With Sefton, Galloway, Ld Calthorpe[104], Arthur [Cecil], E. Hornby[105], & C. Stanley to shoot . . . The morning was fine, but when we reached the ground hail & sleet began to fall: which, combined with a bitter wind, spoilt our pleasure a good deal. Pheasants too were scarce, a large number having been stolen in the spring: & hares being few (which I don't regret) the day gave a smaller return than usual. We brought in 397 head: returning an hour earlier than in former years . . . I was chilled & not wholly comfortable, but have not suffered.

31 Dec. 1879: Preston for sessions. Day very wet. Left home at 9.00, reached Preston by 11.00, via Ormskirk, hang about the courthouse till 11.30, when take the chair. We sit till nearly 3.00, much business having to be done, though none important. . . . The magistrates present were only 28: those living at a distance will not take the trouble to attend, & then they complain that the business falls into the hands of a small clique in or near Preston: which is true in the main, but their own fault. Shepherd Birley[106] has disappeared from the court, having had a paralytic stroke from which he is slowly recovering: our finances used to be left in his charge, & a better chancellor of the exchequer could not be. Mr. Jacson[107] is taking his place, but is slower & longer about the business.

The usual rates were levied: the property on which they are leviable is £9,800,000 odd: so that a penny rate brings in a little over £40,000.

Left with Rathbone[108] in the 3.15 train . . . home by 6.00. Much talk with Mr. R. I think him generally right in his conclusions: he is well informed, & evidently inclined to fairness in his judgments: from his talk I suspect him to be wanting in clearness & directness of mind: he does not say things in a way which makes it easy to follow or retain them. He spoke of general politics &, details apart, his view seemed to be very much like mine: that the Conservatives came in in 1874, less on their own merits than because the country was tired of heroic legislation, & a little uneasy as to what might come next: that the Liberals, divided among themselves, & not seeing clearly what was to be the next step, were not eager to turn them out: & that if they had kept out of these foreign troubles, & given parliament plenty to do with useful domestic legislation, they would have been safe for an indefinite time. Now, he thought, it was different: most of the Liberals had made up their minds that, with Beaconsfield & Salisbury where they are, there could be no security for peace or against reckless proceedings, & they would do their utmost to get rid of them, whatever might follow. But, he added, if these two men were away, there would not be the same feelings against their colleagues.

Notes

[1] Thomson Hankey (1805–1893), Kentish neighbour and W. India merchant: Governor of the Bank of England 1851–1853: M.P. (Lib.) Peterborough 1853–1868, 1874–1880.

[2] Edward Stanhope (1840–1893), under-secretary for India 1878–1880.

[3] Late wife of Lord Carlingford.

[4] Henry Chaplin, 1st Vt Chaplin (1840–1933), M.P. 1868–1906: cr. peer, 1916: leading sportsman, protectionist, and representative of agriculture.

[5] Lennox, himself no angel, had called attention to a breach of privilege by Charles Grissell, who had told those opposing the Tower high level bridge that he could procure its rejection by the committee which Lennox chaired for £2,000.

[6] Lord Henry Gordon-Lennox (1821–1886), third son of 5th Duke of Richmond: M.P. (Cons.) Chichester February 1846–1885: minor office 1852, 1858–1859, sec. to admiralty 1866–1868, chief commissioner of works 1874–1876 (resigned following financial scandal). Married 1883: intimate of Disraeli.

[7] Cf. 'A View of Anthony Trollope' in *The Later Derby Diaries*, ed. Vincent, pp. 144–151.

[8] Sir William Smith (1813–1893), editor of *Quarterly Review*, 1867–1893: kt, 1892.

[9] Charles-René Gavard (1826–1893), 1st secretary at the French embassy in London 1871–December 1877.

[10] To her husband, i.e. Lord Carlingford.

[11] Rev. J.W. Blakesley (1808–1885), dean of Lincoln: historian.

[12] Col. Frederick Arthur Wellesley (1844–1931), s. of Lord Cowley (1804–1884): U.K. military attaché in St. Petersburg, where his 1st marriage to the dau. of the U.K. ambassador, Loftus, in 1873, ended in divorce (1882). Wellesley was secret emissary between Disraeli and the Tsar, behind Derby's back, August 1876: he had declined Derby's offer of a post as consul-general in Warsaw, July 1876, and was renewed for a second term of five years in Russia by Derby, August 1876. Salisbury, on taking office, promoted him to Vienna. Derby thought 'his only fault' lay in being 'an incurable spendthrift'.

[13] For Wellesley's fling with the actress Kate Vaughan, see *Derby Diaries, 1869–1878*, pp. 28–29, and *The Letters of Disraeli to Lady Bradford . . .*, ed. Zetland, pp. 234–235. Wellesley eventually married Miss Vaughan, previously an attachment of John De la Cour.

[14] George Duncan (1845–), bro. and heir presumptive of 3rd Earl Camperdown: Kentish neighbour, with business interests: his sister Julia, lady of the bedchamber to Queen Victoria 1874–1885, m. 1858 George Ralph, 4th Lord Abercromby: m. an American wife who d. 1910.

[15] Grévy, François Paul Jules (1813–1891), President of the Republic 30 January 1879–2 December 1887 (resigned after honours scandal): President of the Assembly, then of the Chamber of Deputies, 1871–1879.

[16] Comte de Chambord (1820–1883), as 'Henry V' legitimist claimant to the French throne: grandson of Charles X: lived mostly in exile: almost returned to throne in 1873, but made impossible conditions: died without issue.

[17] Eugène Rouher (1814–1884), Bonapartist minister, considered more honest and able than most.

[18] In the sense of Bonapartism.

[19] Robert Townley-Parker (1793–1879), only s. of Thomas T. Parker, d. 1794: educ. Eton and Ch. Ch.: sheriff of Lancs. 1817, M.P. Preston 1837–1841 and 1852–1857: constable of Lancaster castle 1874: d. Cuerden Hall, near Preston, 11 August 1879: see also n. 529.

[20] James Lysaght Finigan, M.P. (Lib. 'and advanced Nationalist') for Ennis July 1879–November 1882 (resigned).

[21] John Arthur Douglas Bloomfield, 2nd Baron Bloomfield (1802–1879), career diplomatist 1818–1871: ambassador to Austria 1860–1871.

[22] Samuel Charles Whitbread, F.R.S. (1796–1879), younger s. of Samuel Whitbread, M.P. 1764–1815: M.P. Middx. 1820–1830: one of 3 founders of The British Meteorological Society, 1850: personalty sworn under £350,000.

[23] H.M. Stanley, *Through The Dark Continent . . .*, 2 vols. (1878).

[24] V.L. Cameron, *Across Africa*, 2 vols. (1877).

[25] Oscar Browning (1837–1923), historian, Fellow of King's, and later President of the British Academy of Arts in Rome.

[26] Sir E. Malet, 4th bt (1837–1908), diplomatist: U.K. agent and consul-general in Egypt 1879–1883.

[27] The Princess of Teano was a Lancashire kinswoman, Ada Bootle-Wilbraham, who had m. (1867) the 15th Duca di Sermoneta. Ada was the 2nd dau. (but eldest surviving) of Edward Bootle-Wilbraham (1807–1882), 2nd s. of 1st Baron Skelmersdale (1771–1853). Ada's sister Emily m. (1869) Ludovic 26th E. of Crawford. Ada's aunt Emma m. the 14th E. of Derby, thrice premier, hence her kinship to the diarist. Sermoneta, a classic Italian liberal, figures in both the Crawford and Derby diaries.

[28] William *Alexander* Hendrik Karel, Prince of Orange-Nassau (1851–1884), Prince of Orange (i.e. Crown Prince of the Netherlands) since 1879. In consequence of the death of his elder brother William, Queen Sophie's youngest son Alexander had become heir to the throne. Intelligent and well educated at the University of Leyden, he never enjoyed good health and died unmarried. According to a recent publication of diaries written by Alexander's groom of the chamber, the Prince was at Hotel Beaurivage (Ouchy/Lausanne) on 1 September 1879, where he must have met Lady Derby before leaving late in the afternoon for Ceix. Cf. W. Keikes ed., *Steeds weer op reis met*

Alexander Prins van Oranje 1871–1881, Reisherinneringen van kamerdienaar Johannes Theodorus van Balen, Amsterdam, 1996, p. 199.

29   (Sir) Francis Adams (1826–1889), acting minister at Paris 1874–1881, minister at Berne 1881–1888.

30   Sir Horace Rumbold (1829–1913), minister in Chile 1872–1878, in Switzerland 1878–1879: in diplomatic service 1849–1900, ending as amb. to Austria 1896–1900: succ. bro. as bart 1877.

31   Hussey Crespigny Vivian, 3rd Baron Vivian (1834–1893), eldest s. of 2nd Baron: F.O. clerk 1851–1874, in Alexandria 1873, Bucharest 1874, Egypt 1876, Berne 1879, Denmark 1881, Brussels 1884: amb. in Rome 1892–death: succ. as peer, 1886.

32   Perhaps William Henry O'Sullivan, M.P. (1829–1887), Fenian and Parnellite: imprisoned in 1867 under suspicion of Fenianism: M.P. co. Limerick 1874–1885: chairman of his local board of guardians: a co. Limerick merchant.

33   Steward of Knowsley.

34   George Sand (1804–1876), prolific writer and controversial figure: lover of De Musset and Chopin.

35   Sir Pierre Louis Napoleon Cavagnari (1841–1879), born in France of a Napoleonic officer and his Irish wife: educ. Christ's Hospital: naturalised 1857: employed on Afghan frontier 1868–1878: appointed British resident in Kabul 1879: murdered by rebel Afghans.

36   Dost Muhammad (1783–1863), Amir of Afghanistan 1826–1838 and 1843–1863: became U.K. ally by treaty of 1855.

37   Mortimer Sackville-West, 1st Baron Sackville (1820–1888), bro. of 6th E. De La Warr (suicide 1873) and of 7th Earl (d. 1888). In 1876 he was cr. Baron Sackville of Knole, as 2nd surviving s., and heir to Knole estates. Lord-in-waiting (extra) 1876–1888: brother of Mary Derby.

38   See Note 357 above.

39   E. Cazalet, Kentish country neighbour, with City background: stood as Lib. for Mid-Kent 1880, but defeated.

40   In 1879 Commander John P. Cheyne, R.N., had proposed using balloons for Polar exploration (Richard Vaughan, *The Arctic: A history*, p. 194).

41   Word omitted in original.

42   Alderman Samuel Boothroyd, J.P. (1814–1886), Mayor of Southport 1868, 1869, 1878, 1879, and chairman of magistrates: b. Huddersfield, s. of a Congregationalist minister: member of Southport council 1867–death: resident in Southport for 52 years, and instrumental in obtaining its first Improvement Act of 1846: for many years chairman of Board of Commissioners set up in 1847.

43   Thomas Burt (1837–1922), M.P. (Lib.) Morpeth 1837–1922: miners' leader and first workingman M.P.

44   Alexander Macdonald (?–1881), M.P. (Lib.) Stafford 1874–31 October 1881 (died): sec. of Miners' Assoc. for Scotland, and President of the Miners' National Association.

45   Reginald Windsor Sackville (from 1871), Baron De La Warr (1817–1896), succ. his brother 1873: m. Constance, d. of 1st Lord Lamington.

46   Philip Sidney, 2nd Baron De L'Isle and Dudley (1828–1898), succ. 1851: m. Mary, only child of Sir Robert Foulis, Bart: 4s. 1 d.: D.L. and lieut. Royal Horse Guards.

47   Paul Amsinck, *Tunbridge Wells and its Neighbourhood, illustrated by a Series of Etchings, and Historical Descriptions* (London, 1810).

48   Dorothy Jordan (1762–1816), actress, for long mistress of the Duke of Clarence (William IV).

49   This may have concerned her artful footman Fred Capon: see *Later Diaries*, p. 18.

50   Constance, Dowager Marchioness of Lothian (1836–1901), dau. of 18th E. of Shrewsbury, and widow of William Schomberg Robert Kerr, 8th Marquess of Lothian (1832–1870).

51   Shudja-Al-Mulk, ruler of Kabul August 1839–1842 (murdered): installed by British armies.

52   Devoted companion of Lady Margaret Cecil.

[53] Sir Rowland Hill (1795–1879), inventor of penny post: dismissed from post office 1842: chairman of Brighton railway 1843–1846: sec. to the post office 1854–1864.

[54] Sir J.A. Picton (1805–1889), Liverpool author, architect, and public figure: founded Liverpool public library: wrote *Memorials of Liverpool*, 1873: kt 1881.

[55] George Granville William Leveson-Gower, K.G., 3rd Duke of Sutherland (1828–1892), m. 1861, Anne, only child of John Hay Mackenzie.

[56] The insane Lord Carlisle would be the 8th E. (1808–1889), country rector 1832–1877, who succ. his bro. the 7th E. in 1864. The 'last earl' mentioned above was George William Frederick, 7th E. (1802–1864), lord-lieut. of Ireland 1855–1858 and 1859–1864. Both 7th and 8th Earls d. unm. and were succeeded by their nephew the 9th Earl (1843–1911).

[57] Charles William, 5th E. Fitzwilliam (1786–1857).

[58] Edwin Waugh (1817–1890), dialect poet: 'the Lancashire Burns': granted civil list pension, 1881.

[59] Lord Sefton's agent.

[60] Newton Wallop, vt Lymington (1856–1917), succ. his father as 6th E. of Portsmouth 1891: M.P. (Lib.) Barnstaple 1880–1885, N. Devon (LU) 1886–1891, under-sec. for war 1905–1908. Asquith was employed as his tutor before he went up to Balliol. He m. a Pease heiress and eventually rejoined the Liberals.

[61] Librarian at Knowsley.

[62] William Patrick Adam (1823–1881), chief whip 1874–1880: educ. Rugby and Trinity: bar, 1849: sec. to Lord Elphinstone in India, 1853–1858: Scottish M.P., 1859–1880: gov. of Madras, 1880–1881.

[63] Edward Lear (1812–1888), artist, known to Derby since childhood.

[64] Sir Victor Child-Villiers, 7th E. of Jersey (1845–1915), succ. father 1859: m. dau. of Lord Leigh: paymaster-gen. 1889–1890, gov. of N.S. Wales 1890–1893, chairman Light Railway Commission 1896–1905.

[65] Thomas George Baring, 1st E. of Northbrook (1826–1904), viceroy of India 1872–1876, First Lord of the Admiralty 1880–1885: his 2nd s. lost at sea in *Captain*, 1870.

[66] Talbot, the diarist's brother-in-law.

[67] Emma, the diarist's sister

[68] Salisbury had made two recent speeches at Manchester. On 17 October at a Tory dinner he had defended the government's foreign policy and spoken of the Austro-German alliance as 'glad tidings of great joy'. On 18 October at a Tory demonstration at Pomona Gardens he had spoken cautiously of Indian policy as defensive not aggressive.

[69] Cf below, 5 Nov. 1879.

[70] Lord Arthur Cecil, the diarist's stepson.

[71] Rev. Malcolm MacColl (1831–1907), Canon of Ripon from 1884: High Churchman, controversialist, Gladstonian.

[72] Franz Egon Freiherr van den Brincken (1835–1906), German first secretary in London 2 April 1874–16 March 1881. Envoy at Weimar 1881–1882: Athens 1882–1887: Copenhagen 1887–1895: The Hague 1895–1899.

[73] Note that he denied its existence a few days ago: a proof how loosely he talks, for he can have had no interest in deceiving me. (Diary.)

[74] Sir Henry George Elliott (1817–1907), appointed ambassador to Vienna, *vice* Buchanan, 31 December 1877: left for Vienna 31 January 1878: remained in post until 1884.

[75] A Canadian correspondent (uninvited).

[76] Thomas Berry Horsfall (1805–22 December 1878), Mayor of Liverpool 1847–1848: a merchant, and 1st president of Liverpool Chamber of Commerce, 1849: M.P. (Cons.) Derby 1852–1853, Liverpool 1853–1868 (retired).

[77] Michael Davitt (1846–1906), ex-Fenian, ex-prisoner: founding figure in the Land League: leading anti-Parnellite in 1891.

[78] J.B. Killen, barrister and anti-rent lecturer, was arrested, 19 November, on a charge of delivering seditious speeches at Gurteen, co. Sligo, on 2 November.

[79] J.T. Delane (1817–1879), editor of *The Times* 1841–1877.

[80] Lionel Sackville-West, 2nd Baron Sackville (1827–1908), was U.K. minister in Madrid 1878–1881.

[81] George Lambton, 2nd Earl of Durham (1828–1879): styled Viscount Lambton 1833–1840: a Liberal, Lord-Lieut. co. Durham 1854–1879: youngest & only surviving son of 1st Earl, by 2nd wife: succ. 1840. Married, 1854, a daughter of the Duke of Abercorn (her mother was a daughter of the 6th Duke of Bedford), his estates in the north-east were about 30,000 acres worth about £71,000 p.a., he yet left no trace on public affairs.

[82] See Note 212 above.

[83] See Note 213 above.

[84] George Smythe (1818–1857), young man of promise: member of Young England: under-sec. for foreign affairs, 1846: retained friendship of Disraeli, who depicted him as Coningsby.

[85] William John Cavendish-Bentinck, 5th Duke of Portland (1800–1879), was succ. by Sir William Cavendish-Bentinck, 6th Duke of Portland (1857–1943), Master of the Horse 1886–1892, 1895–1905, chairman of the first R.C. on Horsebreeding.

[86] There are no entries for 10, 11, 12 and 13 December.

[87] Dr. Gorst, the Knowsley general practitioner.

[88] The widow (1808–1899) of the 6th Baron Howard de Walden (1799–1868) became one of the 4 coheirs of her brother William John, 5th Duke of Portland, on his dying unm., 6 December 1879.

[89] Admiral Sir Geoffrey Hornby (1825–1895), lord of admiralty 1875–1877, c.-in-c. in Mediterranean 1877–1880: took fleet through Dardanelles to Constantinople, 1878: K.C.B. 1878: admiral 1879: president of Royal Naval College 1881–1882: c.-in-c. Portsmouth 1882–1885. His father was linked by a double marriage to the 12th and 13th Earls of Derby.

[90] Victor Alexander, Earl Grosvenor (1853–22 January 1884), s. of 1st Duke of Westminster: died without inheriting, his son becoming 2nd Duke.

[91] Gen. W.G.K. Elphinstone (1782–1842), in command at Kabul, 1841: died just before the final catastrophe: fought at Waterloo.

[92] Thomas T. Townley-Parker (1822–1906) of Cuerden Hall, Preston: estates 8,000, value £13,127 p.a.: succ. 1879: see also N. 465: left no lineal successors: chairman of Chorley Improvement Commissioners, and of Chorley Rural Sanitary Authority 1852–1891: chairman of Leyland Hundred Highway Board: like his father, the renowned cock fighter, he was the oldest J.P. in Lancashire: a devotee of the turf and an ardent dog fancier: his brother was for over 30 years rector of Burnley.

[93] See Note 53 above.

[94] Col. Francis Cornwallis Maude, V.C. (1828–1900), consul-general at Warsaw 21 September 1876–1886: author of *Five Years in Madagascar* (1895).

[95] Florentia, Lady Sale, *A Journal of the Disasters in Afghanistan, 1841–1842,* London, 1843.

[96] Sir Vincent Eyre, *The Military Operations at Kabul . . .* (London, 1843); revised and corrected ed., 1879.

[97] F.S. Roberts (1832–1914), 1st E. Roberts: c.-in-c. India 1885–1893, field-marshal 1895, c.-in-c. 1900–1905: successfully conquered Afghans 1879–1882.

[98] Samuel Danks Waddy (1830–1902), s. of principal of Wesley Coll., Sheffield, and President of the Wesleyan Conference: educ. Wesley Coll. and London Univ.: barrister 1858, bencher 1876, Q.C. 1874. M.P. (Lib.) Barnstaple 1874–December 1879, Sheffield December 1879–April 1880 (defeated), Edinburgh November 1882–1885, Lindsey N. 1886–1894, when appointed Recorder of Sheffield. Defeated at Grantham 1895: appointed County Court judge, 1896.

[99] Sheffield by-election 21 December 1879: Waddy (LIB) 14,062; Stuart-Wortley (CON) 13,584.

[100] Sir John Holker (1828–1882), lord justice of appeal: Q.C. 1866, kt 1874, solicitor-general 1874–November 1875, attorney-general November 1875–April 1880, lord justice of appeal 14 January 1882: d. 24 May 1882.

[101] William Douglas-Hamilton, 12th Duke of Hamilton (1845–1895), eldest s. of 11th Duke.

[102] Possibly Henry Padwick (1805–23 September 1879), solicitor, racehorse owner, well known money lender, stockmarket speculator, and deputy keeper of Holyrood Palace.

[103] William Hepworth Dixon (1821–1879), writer and historian: author of *British Cyprus* (1879).

[104] Frederick Gough-Calthorpe, 5th Baron Calthorpe (1826–1893), s. of 4th Baron: educ. Eton and Trinity, Cambridge: M.P. (Lib.) Worcs. E. 1859–1868: d. unm. and was succ. by his brother. Will, £297,000. Rental, over £122,000 p.a.

[105] See Note 53 above.

[106] Rev. John Shepherd Birley, (1805–1883), of Moss Lee, Sharples, near Bolton, and 'premier of Lancashire', being chairman of 9 or 10 county committees (out of 17), and having sat on 14. Eldest s. of Wm. Birley, merchant, of Kirkham: educ. privately and at Brasenose: friend in youth of Cardwell, Lowe, and Gladstone: parson at Bolton, 1833–1843, but retired on health grounds: J.P. 1839: a founder of Poor Protection Society at Bolton: interested in lunacy administration: very hospitable.

[107] Charles Roger Jacson (1817–1893), of Barton Hall, leading figure in Lancashire life and Preston public business. On his death flags flew at half mast in Preston and all public business was adjourned. He was the son of George Jacson of Barton Hall, Mayor of Preston in 1840, and partner in Horrocks and Jacson. His grandfather and great-grandfather were rectors of Bebbington. C.R. Jacson was educ. privately at Chester, and at Rugby under Arnold. He was always a strong Conservative and active Churchman and philanthropist. Becoming a J.P. in 1849, he devoted his life to local matters, refusing to stand for parliament, but becoming chairman of the Preston Board of Guardians and of the County Finance Committee.

[108] William Rathbone (1819–1902), M.P. (Lib.) Liverpool 1868–1880.

1880

January–June

1 Jan. 1880: . . . I begin this year under favourable circumstances in most respects. I have had no misfortune, trouble, or source of anxiety: Ly D. is well, though this climate does not altogether suit her constitution: my affairs are prosperous, the bad times having produced but little effect in these parts: I have kept myself fairly before the public, & am free, if I should think fit, to join in any political combination that may offer: though a growing desire of ease, & perhaps less willingness than of old to give way to others in public matters, make it unlikely that I shall do so. It is only in the matter of bodily health that I have anything to complain of: in that respect no mischief is threatened which moderate care & prudence will not ward off. . . .

3 Jan. 1880: . . . Ld Calthorpe[2] went away after the shooting. I am rather favourably impressed with him as a guest: he knows many things, & people, talks well, shoots well, enjoys his dinner, & generally contributes to make a party go off satisfactorily. But he is almost avowedly a man of pleasure, making society & amusement his object, & that is not a habit of mind with which I have much sympathy. . . .

4 Jan. 1880: . . . Rather gouty all day: I notice that with the appearance of local discomfort in hands & feet all disagreeable sensations elsewhere vanish: there is no irritability: & both in point of spirits & mental activity my condition is above the average of what I am used to. M. also is unwell: & I believe that the damp of this climate in winter affects us all unfavourably. . . .

6 Jan. 1880: . . . Tenants' dinner at 2.00, but we were not sent for till 3.30: when found a great crowd assembled, more than there was room for. Many of the cottagers having brought friends with them, which I do not forbid. Reception very cordial. I made the usual speeches from the usual place. . . .

7 Jan. 1880: Reporters came & took down my Huddersfield address of tomorrow night. I do not much like it, but a failure matters little. See Hale[3] . . . He well satisfied with the receipts, says there are no complaints & but few arrears. He is uneasy & anxious about Mrs. Hale[4], & I fear with cause. Day disagreeable, east wind, fog, & smell: very gloomy, though not cold.

. . . Second tenants' dinner; this time they were from Bickerstaffe, Rainford, & Halewood: larger tenants, & the style of things rather different. Less noise & shouting, & I made them more of a speech on agricultural prospects: great cordiality. We were called in at 3.00, & got away by 3.30.

8 Jan. 1880: Woke to find myself almost disabled from walking by stiffness in the knee & thigh on the right side – I suppose rheumatic or gouty.

Reading & writing all morning: revised my speech finally: at 1.20 left for Huddersfield. Reached the station at 3.54 exactly: found a large crowd collected, though less than at Southport last year: hearty cheers, etc. Mr. Crosland[5] met me with his carriage, & took me to his house, a fine grey stone villa about 2½ miles out of the town, magnificently furnished, & in good taste: 50 acres of grounds, but buildings & chimneys spoil the view outside. . . . No fine building that I saw, but the material being stone there is not the squalid look of the Lancashire towns. We dined a party of about 20, all men, except Mrs. Crosland: Prof. Roscoe[6], of Owen's College: Mr. W. Stanhope, M.P.[7]: & Sir J. Ramsden[8], the leading persons present. The meeting was held at 7.00, & lasted till 10.15. About 1,500 present, as many as the room would hold.

There was much noise & confusion at first, but only in consequence of a scramble for places. Mine was the only long speech[9], it lasted over an hour, I kept to the substance of what I had written, but varied the style to make it more conversational. I have never had a pleasanter audience: attentive, interested, taking every point, & ready to cheer or laugh on the smallest provocation. – We returned to supper at Mr. Crosland's: well pleased with the success of the evening. The purport of what I said was to combat exaggerated ideas of the present depression in trade & industry, showing that the wealth of the nation has steadily increased, & that there is no adequate ground for the assumption that our foreign trade is declining. But I attacked the system of 'bloated armaments' & militarism gener-ally, in strong terms, though keeping clear of anything that could be construed into a reference to party politics. . . .

10 Jan. 1880: See Hale, looking very miserable on account of his wife's illness, as indeed he has a right to be. She is not now in actual danger, but her health is bad, & it seems impossible to induce her to act with ordinary prudence. Bickersteth gives medicine & advice, but it is a mere chance whether she will take one or the other. – Knowing that Hale's anxiety is increased by questions of expense, I give him £200 out of the lease-fee-fund, which I had partly intended to do before.

. . . News in the local papers that Torr M.P. is paralytic & disabled from business in future. He was the chief promoter of the new bishopric scheme[10]: an active fussy politi-cian, of no ability, but by keeping himself always before the world, & courting the cleri-cal interest, which he did assiduously, he secured the Tory vote in Liverpool. The reward dangled before his eyes was a baronetcy: but I do not think it was ever intended he should have one. At any rate he has lost his chance now.

11 Jan. 1880 (Sunday): Cold dark dull day: stayed at home all morning. Worked on a speech about savings banks[11] for next Friday . . . Mrs. Hale worse, & thought to be in danger this morning: but she rallied later. Go twice to her house with M.

Examine Mr. Ward's[12] accounts for the year ending 30 June 1879. The receipts (not including balance from the year before) are £181,517. The rents are divided as follows:

Home estates	£41,692)	
Liverpool	£33,666)	With shillings, etc.,
E. Lancs.	£72,745)	added £170,597
Outlying	£22,491)	

Miscellaneous receipts are £10,879.

Note that, the accounts being made up earlier than usual, there is a large sum in arrears, recoverable, & paid since last July for the most part.

There was paid back to Ly D. £10,000, & to me £29,000. Expenses were as follows:

(1)	compulsory deductions	£25,531
(2)	estate & incidentals	£68,474
(3)	household	£25,000
(4)	benefactions	£9,644
(5)	Keston & Fairhill	£10,250

Thus the expenses are under £140,000, the sum paid off or laid by is £39,000. In all a little under £180,000. This return is not satisfactory as regards income, but the chief reason is explained above.

12 Jan. 1880: Sent £50 to the Irish Relief Fund: I observe that in the papers it is commonly spoken of as a failure: the sum collected having been small: the fact is that nobody knows with any approach to certainty how much distress really exists, it having been wildly exaggerated for anti-rent agitation purposes: in some districts out west it is undoubtedly severe, the soil & climate being such that only in good seasons can the people get a living out of the land at all: in such cases the proper remedy would be emigration: but that is opposed to the utmost by priests & nationalists for different reasons: the priests lose income & power both by the diminution of their congregations: the nationalists dislike to see Ireland further drained of men: no great confidence, I think, is felt in the Castle authorities who will distribute the fund: which lessens its popularity: while the attitude of the agitators has chilled English sympathy. . . .

15 Jan. 1880: . . . M. returns in afternoon from Wales, better in health for two days on the sea coast. She has found her brother's[13] house & way of living satisfactory except that from time to time a fit of despondency comes upon him, in which he says that he is not earning his salary: that he is only robbing Ld Penrhyn by taking it: that he must throw it up – & more to the same effect. At other times he takes it into his head that by accepting an agent's place he has lost his social position, & that his children will not be received in society. He is a vegetarian in diet, but not a strict one, eating fish & drinking wine, which the sect in general do not. He cannot bear indoor life, even for a few hours: & came back ill from a meeting of the local board of guardians. His eccentricities are many, but they do not increase, & on the whole I think there is less risk of their taking a dangerous turn than there was when he lived at Oxford.

16 Jan. 1880: . . . Into Liverpool at 7.00 to address a meeting of the promoters & supporters of savings banks: which have flourished beyond expectation. The principal or central bank holds over £1,800,000 of money belonging to depositors, & more accounts are opened every year. Even in the worst times it increases. The subject was a very trite one, but I did what was possible to give it novelty by [discussing] the bearing of savings banks on the national debt, etc. I spoke half an hour . . . & was home again before 10.00.

News in the town of Torr's death, not more than a week after his first seizure: but he was 68, & in bad health. He was in early life an active & acute man of business, not reckoned too scrupulous in his dealings: but he outlived any little obloquy on that score, and as a M.P. was fairly respected. He threw himself into ecclesiastical work, gaining thereby the warm support of the clergy: & was usefully busy in the local affairs of the town. In parliament he never spoke, but steadily supported the govt.: he was not, however, a 'Jingo' by disposition, & I hear him credited with having repressed the pugnacity of some of his fellow-townsmen. According to the story told me, the cause of his illness & death was excitement arising out of the bishopric fund affair: he had been promised a large sum in aid of it by some society in London, which failed to keep its word, & he thought his honour compromised, as having induced others who acted with him to trust to this promise. His death just now is a local calamity: since a bye-election preceding a general election decides nothing, & only creates needless trouble & quarrelling. . . .

18 Jan. 1880 (Sunday): . . . Sefton[14] calls on M. – full of the pending election – & anxious that I should see Mr. Holt[15], the leader of the Liberals, which accordingly I agree to do.

19 Jan. 1880: Hard frost, & bright clear day.

Manchester by 11.04 train: to the Town Hall, where take the chair of the Horticultural Society's annual meeting . . . about 50 persons in the room . . . The report was taken as read . . . I said a few words, Dr. Watts[16] followed in a more elaborate speech . . . We had last year a deficit of more than £300, on an income of about £4,000. We have also a debt of £4,000, or rather more, & I offered to the meeting to put down £100 towards lessening it, if £900 more were raised within the year for the same purpose. – This was well received. Dr. Watts seems to be practically the working man of the concern. Talk with the Mayor, who asked me into his room, but heard nothing. Return by 2.00 p.m. train.

Mr. Holt, the local leader of the Liberal party, called by appointment: we had a good deal of conversation, turning chiefly on Irish affairs. The position of parties in Liverpool is peculiar: the Liberals, plus the Irish, are nearly one half the constituency &, aided by the discontent of many Conservatives, they may win: though to my thinking the chances are against them: but the secession of the Irish contingent would place them in a hopeless minority: & the problem is, how to satisfy the Irish without disgusting the English [Liberals] by an apparent adhesion to Home Rule. I say 'apparent' because the purely English vote is enough to ensure the rejection of any Home Rule scheme: &, as far as the result is concerned, it does not matter much if half a dozen members for English constituencies where the Irish vote is strong pledge themselves to support the Irish demand: the moral effect of such tactics would be bad, both in a party & a national point of view.

I thought Mr. Holt agreeable, intelligent, & well-mannered. He spoke with earnestness & apparent sincerity of his own position as leader: said he was not fit for it, had little knowledge of general politics, had taken it only because there was no one else, etc., all which he seemed to mean. We parted mutually pleased.

20 Jan. 1880: Very hard frost: therm. at 12° in the night.

Kirkdale at 11.00. About 20 magistrates present, fewer than usual. . . . Counsel present were 38, the largest number I remember. Cases, 79. . . . We had a sensible jury, no perverse or stupid verdicts.

Read on the way to Kirkdale & back a little book just published by the D. of

Somerset[17] called *Monarchy & Democracy*. It is desultory, clever in parts, but has the faults of being a mere grumble throughout – a simple expression of political scepticism. 'Everything is going to the bad, & there is no remedy': that is not, to my mind, a dignified attitude for a great peer to assume: nor do I believe his fears to be reasonable. He is rather happy in contrasting the expectations formed of the U.S. a hundred years ago with present realities: pointing out that the nation which was to set mankind an example of virtuous simplicity, & in which there were to be no rich & no poor, has developed more expensive habits, & produced larger private fortunes, than any other. . . . He also amuses himself ingeniously at the expense of J.S. Mill who, as the Duke puts it, considers that every man has a natural right to produce books, but that no one has a natural right to produce children. – But, on the whole, the book is not suggestive, nor useful, except as a warning that in politics scarcely anything turns out as its promoters expect – a true conclusion, but not a very novel one.

21 Jan. 1880: Kirkdale at 10.00, sat till 5.30.

Ld & Ly Ramsay[18] came (he is standing for Liverpool): they both made a favourable impression upon us: she handsome & pleasing: he unaffected, intelligent, & apparently clear-headed. Much political talk, & he showed me his intended address, which is good. The Irish question was discussed of course: I found him prepared to take up the Irish view of local grievances, which I did not discourage, but on the contrary told him to believe in them as much as he honestly could. Only he must be guarded in his utterances as to self-government & make it clear that he did not mean to consent to the creation or restoration of an Irish parliament, in any form. He asked many questions, showing, as was to be expected, little knowledge of politics, but much willingness to learn, & quickness of apprehension. He appears sanguine of getting the support of the Irish, saying what is no doubt true that, if the Liberals can do nothing without them, they on their side are insignificant if they alienate Liberal support by exaggerated demands. But it does not follow that they will see this, & they may prefer to sacrifice an immediate advantage for the sake of proving that nothing except compliance with their demands in full will secure their help.

22 Jan. 1880: . . . Looking over some savings banks returns which have been lately sent me, before destroying them, I find that our Liverpool bank holds £1,800,000, that of Manchester £1,300,000, that of Glasgow £3,000,000, or nearly as much as both the English banks put together. It would be interesting to know the reason [for] this difference. The three towns being nearly equal in size, the comparison is a fair one. And the population of Irish is nearly alike in all three. . . .

23 Jan. 1880: Write to Ld Hartington, in answer to a note from him which is meant to bespeak my good offices for Ld Ramsay. I praise Ld R. highly, mention his inevitable dependence on the Irish vote, say that in his speech (of yesterday) he had gone a little further than I can follow about Irish land, but on the whole it is prudent & able.

. . . Talking over the arrangements of the Kirkdale sessions with Gibbon[19], Mr. Wilson[20], & others, I find they agree with me in thinking that the increase in the number of cases has made it desirable to hold 8 sessions in the year instead of 4, & I shall make a motion to that effect in April. I shall probably also take the opportunity of retiring from the chairmanship, which I have held since July 1856. It is inconvenient to me to be bound to 4 appearances in the year, 8 would be impossible, & indeed the reluctance of magistrates to attend, & the increase of business, both point to the appointment of a stipendiary. I do not dislike judicial business in itself, but my time can be more usefully employed, both for the public & my own credit, than in doing what is really the work of a police magistrate. My only regret is that I shall lose almost the only opportunity I have of taking part in local business. The dislike to unpaid local work is growing among the younger men, & it is a bad sign: but on the other hand legal business is best done by a trained lawyer, & a stipendiary has already been appointed for the other two divisions of the county.

24 Jan. 1880: . . . Read a life of Buckle[21], the author: not well done, nor very interesting: perhaps the biography of a student who lived wholly among his books can hardly be so: but it shows in the subject of it a curious difference between his public & private character. The least emotional of writers – the philosopher who more than all others put the intellectual part of man's nature above the rest – seems to have been in his personal relations one of the kindest & most good-natured of men, & even morbidly sensitive to domestic grief.

25 Jan. 1880: Frost continues, with east wind & dull dark weather. Walk early with Ld Ramsay in the park. In afternoon, he & Ly R. went with M. to the service at the West Derby seamen's asylum.

Much talk with him & my first good impression is confirmed. He tells me that the Home Rulers have decided to abstain from voting, which if they stick to their resolution, & if all the Irish go with them, renders his candidature hopeless: but it is possible that they are only trying to screw further concessions from him.

Write to Ld Granville, in answer to a note from him. He sounds me as to dining with him before the opening, but that I decline, not choosing to commit myself to a course of policy which I do not know, or to forfeit an independent position by forming a new political connection: though, as far as the Conservatives are concerned, I have broken off finally from former ties.

26 Jan. 1880: . . . Mr. Bushell[22] told me the history of Torr's difficulties about the new bishopric fund, which by the anxiety & vexation they caused were the immediate cause of his death. It seems that he had obtained a large number of promises of gifts to be spread over 5 years: it became clear, however, that the bishop could not be appointed till the money was obtained, & a strong wish was expressed among the church party that this should be done at once, in order that the appointment might come off before the general election, & be in the hands of the present Premier: Torr accordingly set to work to press the donors to pay up at once: this some could not, & others would not do, & the request was thought unfair by many. Then came negociations with some church society in London, which promised £20,000 advance, but could not make good its promises at the last moment. . . .

28 Jan. 1880: Very hard frost continues, but bright & clear as before.

See Hale, a long talk with him. – Discuss the request of the Bootle authorities for a park: they ask for 20 acres, at a nominal rent, near the gas-works. I agree that they must have a park, so the matter is settled in principle: but the exact extent of it, & the question of rent, remain for discussion with them. They are coming as a deputation . . .

. . . In afternoon, wrote to the clerk of the peace, saying that from the increased number of cases at sessions I thought it absolutely necessary that we should sit 8 times in the year, instead of 4, &, as 8 attendances are impossible for me, living as much as I do in London, I must give up the office of chairman, so far as the criminal business is concerned. I also suggest the appointment of a paid professional chairman, but with the remark that this is a matter to be decided by the magistrates collectively, & not by me. I added a private note, requesting that the above letter should be made public.

The decision as above is not a sudden one, but I do not know that I should have announced it at this particular moment but for the fact that a good deal of attention is beginning to be attracted to the question of sessions. The judges of the superior courts are overworked, & much circuit work might with advantage be transferred from assizes to sessions. But this could not, at least it will not, be done, unless the judges to whom it is transferred are professionally trained men. One change is necessary to make the other possible.

29 Jan. 1880: See Broomfield. Direct (1) making a green drive beyond Mizzy Dam to join the upper & lower Prescot approaches – a thing which M. has long wanted . . . Also putting in Spanish chestnuts wherever there is a spare place. They thrive on the rocky soil. – I note with regret that Broomfield is losing a good deal of his health & activity. He has been here, & we have worked together, nearly 20 years. . . .

31 Jan. 1880: . . . The canvass at Liverpool goes on with unabated vehemence, & great bitterness of feeling. The Irish have reconsidered their decision &, as an excuse for doing what they lately said they would not do, they have obtained from Ld R. a slight alteration in the terms of the pledge which he gave them. I do not myself see that the difference is more than verbal, or that, having swallowed the condition of voting for what is practically an enquiry into Home Rule, the words used are important: but they treat the change as a serious concession on his side, & the Conservatives . . . follow suit. He has secured the Irish, but possibly lost some English votes, for even strong Liberals dislike the Irish alliance. He (Ld R.) wrote to tell me what he had done, but as it was done objection or criticism were useless. And it is true that he had only a choice between two difficulties.

1 Feb. 1880: London. Walk for exercise round Regent's park. Frost & thick fog, disagreeable enough: it is said that they have been more than ever abundant this winter, & many illnesses have resulted. Three of the Cabinet are laid up – the Premier, Salisbury, & Northcote.

Write to Mr. M.[artin] Tupper[23], that I will send him at once a cheque for £50 . . . and that I advise him to apply to the Lit. Fund. He relates in explanation of his request a whole catalogue of misfortunes – a son in the army who spent his money & died – one who failed in business – a brother who also failed, & whose sleeping partner he has been – investments in Spanish funds – & insurance companies that are bankrupt. In short his management of his own affairs has been what one might expect from a poet – if he has no other claim to the character.

Letter from Carnarvon, but rather to sound as to my views than express any. I answer shortly (as we shall soon meet) that I do not mean to speak on the address: that I shall retain a wholly independent position for the present: that I think badly of the state of matters, Ireland being the chief difficulty . . .

Granville calls. He is evidently uneasy about Home Rule: a question which we discussed, but not fully or earnestly. He told me that he had some idea of defending the foreign policy of the Gladstone Cabinet, which is repeatedly attacked by ministerial speakers. I doubted as to the wisdom of this: why should he stand on the defensive without necessity? *Qui s'excuse s'accuse.* And would it not look like a confession of weakness?

V. Harcourt called on Ly D. & I saw him. He seemed less confident of success than he was a few months ago, but gave no reason. He confirmed the report that Cairns has in hand a land bill[24] of some sort, probably not intended to pass, but meant to show how far ministers will be prepared to go in a new parliament. He said shrewdly that a bill of that kind brought in by Conservatives was sure to be amended in a Liberal sense, whereas one brought in by Liberals would be altered in a Conservative sense.

Talking of Ireland, I said that much of the soreness of the Irish M.P.s, I thought, arose from the feeling that in parliament they were not treated socially as equals. This V.H. confirmed, saying that most of those who took the lead were not gentlemen, nor persons with whom it was possible to associate – Biggar[25], Callan, Sullivan, etc. – In fact these men brought in contact with English society feel themselves in a foreign country, & in one where they are not welcome. Hence their animosity.

Keston in afternoon, through thick fog.

2 Feb. 1880: Keston. Day very fine & bright, frosty. . . . Walk . . . with great pleasure in this climate & the clearness of the air, very different from Lancashire.

. . . Read to M. an article by Sir H. Rawlinson on Afghan affairs[26]. He advises holding Kandahar permanently as a British possession: & ceding Herat to Persia under conditions – the latter being an entire reversal of our earlier policy in this respect, which was to prevent its being in Persian hands, Persia being considered as the ally & tool of Russia. But he says, with some truth, what else can be done, if a united & friendly Afghan state cannot be created? Herat is not big enough to be independent, & what power except Persia can hold it, unless we extend ourselves beyond what is desirable? He thinks the Russians will secure Merv, & that that cannot be helped. He would prefer seeing Kabul under a native chief, but with an English resident & garrison there.

Shrewd remark of old Mr. Norman about Irish land. He said: 'You may get rid of the landlord if you please, but the tenant will have to pay rent all the same. As soon as the land is in his own hands he will mortgage it – land always is mortgaged, both in this country & in America – & he will pay in the shape of interest & mortgages as much rent as the land will bear!' . . .

5 Feb. 1880: M. not being well enough to go to the Lords, I take Mary G. [alloway] instead. The House not very full, but fairly so. The mover was Ld Onslow[27], who spoke well, fluently, & with more self-possession than is usual in a beginner: he was judged a success. Lord Rosse[28], who seconded, spoke about Irish affairs exclusively, & was too long. Three-quarters of an hour on Irish drainage & crops are more than ordinary patience will endure on a first night. Granville made a speech of his usual sort, neat, pointed, effective, without oratory, which he never affects, but omitting nothing that made for his argument, & saying hard things in a smooth tone. The Premier followed but, whether age or gout were in fault, he was only a shadow of his former self: hesitating, feeble, with here & there a flash of the old humour, but on the whole his reply fell flat. He ended with a denunciation of Home Rule, intended to influence the Liverpool [bye-] election. Argyll[29] got up to speak on

Afghan affairs and denounced Ld Lytton as the author of the mischief, & as acting independently of the Cabinet at home. I presume he had some grounds for his charge, for it is one of an unusual kind, & not to be made on light grounds against a Gov.-Gen.

Ld Cranbrook[30] replied, but in a thin House; he worked himself as usual into an oratorical passion, & was fairly effective. We broke up about 9.30. Walk home, supper, & bed.

6 Feb. 1880: . . . News late at night of the Liverpool election being won by the Conservative candidate, Whitley: the numbers polled being greater than ever before – nearly 50,000 in all. Majority, 2,200. In this case, the Conservatives have succeeded, so far as that they have kept what they had: the Liberals may claim to have lost nothing, & that the majority against them is relatively to the numbers smaller than it ever was before – that is, for the last 30 years.

7 Feb. 1880: . . . Eastwick[31] talked yesterday about Indian affairs, suggesting some points new to me. He says the Afghan campaigns are very unpopular with the native army: Mussulmen do not like fighting against Islam, & Hindoos have a horror of serving outside the limits of India. Besides this, the climate is severe, & the winter cold kills off many. He notes the danger of leaving the whole interior of India unguarded, & that if any disturbance, or attempt at revolt, were to occur in the native states, or in our own territories, we have no means of meeting it. He says the best regiments have been sent to the frontier, they have suffered severely from climate, & the loss incurred in strength is not to be measured by the mere numerical decrease. He thinks also that the Indian authorities are not sufficiently aware of the discontent caused by heavy taxation: which in his judgment is great & increasing. He says that Lytton lives entirely with a few persons who applaud all he does – that anything in the nature of criticism or objection he receives with courtesy, but does not invite or allow a repetition of it. (This is exactly like the Queen: so easily does a royal position produce royal habits!) Eastwick is retired from affairs, & speaks with no party bias, though he has all his life been strongly opposed to the annexation policy.

Salisbury did not appear at the opening, & from what Drage tells M. I gather that he has been suffering from a severe internal complaint. Drage does not think well of his constitution, & he has persuaded himself that it is possible to live without exercise by help of drugs – which is a mistake. If he were to break down, the Cabinet would be as weak in point of ability as it is strong in supporters. The Premier cannot last long, & even in the Lords no one would be left except Cairns & Cranbrook. In the Commons, as matters now stand, they have no one who can be relied on for an effective speech except Cross & Northcote – Stanhope[32] is capable, but it is doubted whether his bodily strength would be equal to the work of taking a leading part. . . .

10 Feb. 1880: . . . The Irish debate has ended after 4 nights only: I call it the Irish debate, though it was on the address generally, but the Irish took possession of it, & the whole discussion turned on the alleged impending famine. The speeches were not violent, nor was there anything that could be laid hold of as obstruction, but the intention is evident of spending as much time as possible. It is as though the Irish members said: 'You will force us to discuss Irish affairs at Westminster – very well in that case we will take care that you shall be able to discuss nothing else.' They threaten, as is reported, to have the whole debate over again on the report.

11 Feb. 1880: Drage calls, he reports very well of me, & speaking of M., on whose account indeed I saw him, he says that she must have rest, it is for her the one condition of health, & as she can, or at least does, hardly ever get it while awake, it is essential that she should sleep long & well.

. . . Lit. Fund committee at 3.00: 11 or 12 present . . . We voted £200 to Mrs. Clifford, the widow of the eminent scientific man who died last year. We voted £30 to an old applicant, a Mr. Allen. The grant of £200 is the largest which the fund has ever made. We invested £500 after a discussion, no one dissenting except Trollope, who has laid down an odd rule that a charitable institution ought never to lay by anything.

London Univ. Senate at 4.00: the only important business was a singular letter from the Treasury, on the subject of estimates for 1880–1881, warning us that we must look forward to a time when the parliamentary grant shall be withdrawn. This, if it is to be taken seriously, is the announcement of an entirely new policy, whether due to high church tendencies, or to an ultra-rigid economy in all that does not concern army & navy. But even the present parlt., & still more the next, is very unlikely to consent to what in existing circs. would be the ruin of the University. We thought it best on the whole to take no notice of this threat – for a threat it really is. . . .

12 Feb. 1880: Sent £21 to the Manchester Hospital for Incurables . . . Sent £5.5.0 to the Female Orphan Asylum, Surrey. . . . At 1.00, to Westminster Palace Hotel, to consult with a deputation on noxious vapours who have requested me to introduce them to Sclater-Booth . . . No two were of one mind as to what they should ask for . . . With some trouble we settled the list of speakers, & agreed to keep as clear of details as we conveniently could. Home for luncheon. At 2.30 met the deputation again, & stated their case, speaking about 15 minutes. There were present Sefton, Legh of Lyme, Greenall, Rathbone, Sir C. Mills, Mr. H. Philips, the Mayor of Manchester, Ld Percy, Wilbraham Egerton, etc., about 35 in all. We were brief & the whole business did not last an hour.

H. of Lds. at 5.00, where a sensible, business-like discussion on Irish distress: raised by Ld Emly[33], who was supported by Lds Middleton, Dunsany, Dunraven, Monck, & Kimberley. All agreed in approving the govt. scheme of relief as a whole, but they object to one part of it, the power given to the baronies to set up relief works, as requiring to be carefully guarded, & open to much jobbing & abuse. Richmond was the only speaker on the other side, & he clearly knew nothing about the matter, but had got it up in haste for the occasion. However, he dashed intrepidly on, ignoring contradictions & corrections, & seemed to have satisfied himself.

The Chancellor's bill for regulating the conditions under which workmen injured by fellow workmen shall be entitled to claim compensation passed the 2nd reading without debate, & is referred to a select committee. I have intimated that I am willing to serve on this committee if wanted. The subject excites workingmen more than almost any other: they have got it into their heads that the law is purposely framed so as to shut out their claims: a delusion, but just one of the kind that they would get hold of & stick to – & the great difficulty of the subject introducing inevitable complexity into the law which relates to it favours their mistake. Home about 9.00, & quiet evening.

13 Feb. 1880: . . . Hear that Sackville [Cecil] has accepted the traffic managership of the Metrop. District line, £1,500 a year: & on the strength of it he buys the land near Dover with his own money. . . .

15 Feb. 1880: . . . Had an interesting talk with Stephen[34] on the state of India. Found that he agrees with me entirely in what I can only call the Malthusian view: the theory that in Bengal & most of Hindostan, where the soil is already fully peopled, & where the inhabitants as a rule prefer death at home to emigration, the very benefits of our administration will turn to the injury of the people. War, famine, & pestilence being averted, the first wholly, the two last in great measure, there is no natural check to the increase of population; as every Hindu thinks early marriage a duty, the ultimate result will be a struggle for food such as the world has not often seen. Stephen did not quite accept this conclusion, but talked of some new industry, such as manufactures, being set up. . . .

17 Feb. 1880: . . . There is a great scandal in the Catholic world, caused by the well known Monsignor Capel[35], whose special mission was the conversion of the English aristocracy, having been compelled to leave England in haste, in consequence of some mess in which a woman – or more than one – was concerned. There are various stories, & I do not care to set down gossip which may be untrue: but that he has been in some way indulging amorous propensities & is in consequence suspended seems to be undisputed. It is a blow for the Catholic interest, inasmuch as it tends to strengthen the popular belief that sentimental devotion & irregular indulgence in love are apt to be connected, or at least that both have an attraction for the same class of persons.

I have a singular letter from a Mr. Heneage[36], who was, & still nominally is, a member of the diplomatic service: he went off his head while in Russia, retired, & has been travelling in Australia: while there he applied to Ld A. Loftus for help in some difficulty, which Loftus refused, assigning as a reason for declining to see him that he, Heneage, had while at Petersburgh accused Ly Augustus of attempting to poison him. The absurdity of making this a ground of quarrel is obvious . . . the very nature of the statement shows that it can only have been the delusion of a man temporarily insane. . . . I have simply declined interference.

18 Feb. 1880: Sent £10.10.0 to a Sailors' Aid Society: & £4.4.0 to the Newspaper Press Fund. Called on C. Münster & Ly Cowley. Went in evening to Ly Cork's party, alone, M. being tired & unwell. Talk with Mrs. Reeve, Tom Hughes, Argyll, Ly Sefton, etc., & introduced to Mundella[37]. Some interesting convn. with him as to the relations of employers & workmen: he says they have greatly improved in the last 20 years, there is less violence, more willingness to listen to reason, arbitration is generally accepted as a method of settlement. I asked as to the alleged objections of the men to piecework, & the existence of rules intended to check inequality of wages. He said there was great misconception on that subject: that 90% of all the work done in the country was piecework: that vexatious & restrictive rules, formerly common , were now being rapidly swept away: that prejudice was created by the fact that the worst of these existed in the building trade, which more than any other lay open to public observation. The reason, he thought, was that this trade is by its nature protected against foreign competition: you can import food, furniture, or clothes, but not houses, thus the men had no check upon them, everything their own way, & they naturally assumed that any abuses found in it prevailed also in other trades: which, he said, was not the case.

19 Feb. 1880: Receive from the tenants about Bury & Manchester a memorial asking for reduction of rents for this year: I refer it to Statter, asking him (1) whether he advises a general reduction for all alike, or that separate cases shall be gone into & treated each on its own merits? (2) What is the total rental of tenants who apply for relief? (3) What amount of reduction he thinks fair, if it is to be general?

... Ld Cowley[38] calls on M. & stays to luncheon: but we had no serious convn. Both he & Ly C. keep up their spirits well: but the position is hard. After a long life of success & happiness, they have one son (F. Wellesley) disgraced & ruined: (he owes £14,000): a daughter married to an equally ruined spendthrift, Hardwicke: & another son now permanently out of his mind. The Greeks were right: 'Call no man happy till his life's end.'

Travellers' at 4.00 for Sanderson's election: he got in with one black ball but, more than 18 voting, that did him no harm. Another candidate put up with him, Mr. Reginald Yorke[39], failed utterly: the drawer when opened being half full of black balls. . . . Wrote to Sanderson at once to tell him the good news.

20 Feb. 1880: . . . Received from Ld Rayleigh[40] an application for funds to fit up his laboratory at Cambridge. He gives £500 himself, & the D. of Devonshire another £500. I promise £100.

. . . At 5.00, go to H. of Lds. with M. – The attendance was fair, not very large: the galleries fuller than the house itself. Argyll spoke more than 2 hours, his argument effective, though in point of eloquence I have heard him better: Cranbrook replied, poorly & weakly in reasoning, but with animation & fluency: as he did not begin till past 7.00, his audience thinned, & he ended with few hearers. Ld Northbrook delivered a speech excellent in substance, & which would have made an admirable minute: but he seemed to read it from a paper, & that with difficulty, so that for parliamentary purposes it was ineffective. Then followed Ld Denman[41] – mad: Ld Strathnairn[42], inaudible, & old: Ld Napier of Magdala[43], who was short, & spoke entirely from the military point of view. Ripon was followed by Cairns, whom Granville answered, & was in turn answered by the Premier: none of these later speeches was remarkable, in fact the interest of the debate was concentrated in Argyll & Cranbrook. We adjourned at 12.00 exactly. I went home with De La Warr[44], & was in bed by 1.00 a.m. – a late hour for me.

21 Feb. 1880: Heard last night with real regret of the deaths of Sir F. & Ly Elliot[45], at Cairo, of some infectious disease. She died first, & he followed in a few hours, apparently, for the news of both deaths came together. Elliot was about 70 years of age and, being the son of a father who was old when he was born, the two generations reached back to an extraordinary length of time. Hugh Elliot, the father, was ambassador at the court of Frederick of Prussia: his life has been written by Ly Minto. The son passed most of his life in the Col.[onial] Office, of which he was undersecretary when he retired, 10 or 11 years ago. I have never met a man more agreeable in society. Never dull, nor the cause of dullness in others, equally ready to talk & to listen, possessed of natural good humour & good spirits, well read, with a large experience of life & some taste for science, he could suit himself to any company, & was sure of a welcome in all. In politics he was neutral, inclining to a mild Liberalism: in religion, sceptical without intolerance, & with so much respect for the convictions of other people that, but for a tour in the Pyrenees which we made 15 years ago, I should not have suspected his real opinions. He was twice married, the first time, as I have always heard, unhappily: the second time very much otherwise. He was a devoted husband to Ly E.: &, except selfishly, I cannot regret his death, for as a childless widower he would have been lonely & unhappy. . . .

23 Feb. 1880: H. of Lds., where listened to the Chancellor's land bills: his explanation was very clear, & the bills seem moderate, but I do not feel as if I could judge clearly of their merits.

Look in at the H. of C. where the Irish had as usual got all their own way: Northcote's foolish concession to the Ultras of his party on Friday has brought its own punishment. He yielded to the pressure put upon him by the Carlton, & agreed to treat as a breach of privilege a foolish & offensive placard put out by Plimsoll, in which Sir C. Russell & Mr. Onslow were denounced by name for opposing a bill of Plimsoll's. Nothing could be in worse taste, but Plimsoll had been induced to apologise, the apology had been accepted, & the matter might have ended without harm to anybody. However, the high Tories determined to treat it as a breach of privilege, which technically any comment on the proceedings of parliament is: & they passed a resolution condemning it. The Irish saw their advantage, & have raked up all the abusive attacks on them in English newspapers – of which there are plenty – complaining of these also as breaches of privilege. They were not more in the wrong than the complainants of last week, but by this time Northcote had become aware of the absurdity of the proceeding, and resisted, & so the matter has ended. He has also given notice of resolutions against obstruction, which seems very feeble: but we must wait to hear them discussed. Parliament has now sat a fortnight & more: & with few exceptions its whole time has been taken up either with Irish affairs or with debates raised by Irish members. . . .

24 Feb. 1880: Dine at The Club: very small party, only Maine, Reeve, & Dr. Smith: but pleasant. Talk of the Dickens letters: of Charles Dickens: his quarrel with his wife: he had given her some cause for jealousy, and she set the servants to watch him & see where he went. He discovered & did not forgive it. Then he wanted the whole story of his separation to be printed in the magazines to which he contributed: & quarrelled with some of his oldest friends because they refused. Smith, who knew him well, spoke of his extreme vanity, & altogether seemed to have a less favourable impression of his character than most of his acquaintance.

25 Feb. 1880: . . . Granville tells me that the Opposition believe Northcote's resolutions (which are to be moved tomorrow) to be a trap set for the Irish by the govt.: it is hoped that they (the Irish) will oppose them violently, and give a plea for early dissolution on the ground that nothing can be done in the present parliament. But the Irish are warned, & will act & talk moderately: while the opposition front bench will give a general support. The fact is that Northcote's proposals are so feeble & futile that it seems clear he is bringing them forward only under pressure of some kind, & that he does not believe in them himself. Whether the pressure comes from the Carlton (as I believe) or from his colleagues, it is equally effective. – The remark is often made, that he gets no help, or next to none, from his colleagues: all the burden of debate falls on him: but in truth, except Cross, they have no ready speaker among them. Oddly enough, the Speaker has not been consulted on these new resolutions: & is half disposed to take it ill. . . .

27 Feb. 1880: Witley by 9.30 train, reaching Haslemere 10.50, where met Hale. Walk with him over Church Hill . . . then over most of the Witley estate, ending with a visit to Fullock's land, which is or soon will be for sale. We walked with few & short halts till 4.00, when I took the train back to London, & Hale went to his quarters at Liphook. We had a fine day, & I was more impressed than I have been yet with the singular picturesqueness of the country on all sides.

28 Feb. 1880: Meeting of Standing Cee. at B. Museum: D. of Somerset in the chair . . . Walk up with Lowe, who pleasant in talk as usual. He does not think the resolutions against obstruction will be effective, but does not see any harm in them. He remarks on the oddity of their not having been previously discussed either with the Speaker or with Hartington: which in such matters is the invariable rule, that the two front benches may act together. The omission may have been a mere accident, but the opposition all believe that the whole thing has been planned with a view to draw the Liberals into opposing a plan which is on the face of it feeble & futile, in order that there may be fastened upon them a charge of sympathising with obstructionists. If there really has been such a trap laid, it has failed, for the criticism of the opposition speakers has been almost unduly moderate, & the resolution will probably pass this afternoon.

Talk with Rawlinson, very brief, but significant, as he has from the first been the great author of the Russophobic policy. He says it would be madness for us to go to Herat – does not much like the notion of the Persians having it, but sees no other alternative – does not think it of much consequence, but would hold Kandahar.

Sanderson, whom I saw earlier, tells me there is nothing settled, & that the negociations with Persia were 'more off than on'.

Sent £5.5.0 to the National Training School for cookery.

29 Feb. 1880 (Sunday): . . . **Note** that M. yesterday saw White Cooper for her eyes: he gives the most encouraging report we have yet had, not thinking that there is anything seriously amiss with them, but that their failure is due to weak nerves & general debility.

1 Mar. 1880: . . . H. of Lds. at 5.00, where D. of Richmond moved the bill for dealing with Irish distress: he spoke shortly, & there was little debate, as the only points on which any difference exists had been discussed the other night. – Lansdowne made a neat sensible little speech, rather despondent in tone, & naturally taking the landlords' point of view. He argued that most of the distress arose from the population having settled into places where it cannot find a living from want of employment, bad climate, & the poverty of the soil (he referred, I suppose, especially to the southern & western coast): if the land were wholly theirs, without rent to pay, their position would be the same: a bad season reduces them to destitution, & must do so unless they change their way of living by a part of them emigrating: but that is exactly what they will not do: they cling to their wretched homes, & even multiply in them. – There is truth in Ld L.'s view, though of course it is not the whole truth: but he owns he sees no remedy. . . .

2 Mar. 1880: With Hale to Northstead[46], & walked over the whole farm, examining it carefully . . . We went into the house, & made acquaintance with the tenant . . . also with his mother, an old lady of 85. She was full of a recollection of my great-grandfather when he hunted with the Surrey staghounds, having stopped at the house & accepted their hospitality: & they had an old print of him on horseback with his dogs.

3 Mar. 1880: Many notes & letters, costing time to write, though unimportant. Sent £5 to a Liverpool family in distress. Sharp walk for exercise round Regent's park, early. In afternoon, call on Ly Stanhope.

Paid bills, drew £50 for use, made up accounts, etc. No public work of any kind. Quiet evening.

. . . Public affairs are singularly quiet . . . The Irish have decided apparently to keep silent for the moment: they let the Army Estimates pass in one night . . . Cross has brought in his Bill for uniting the London Water Companies into a single Water Trust . . . As far as can yet be judged, the plan is well thought of . . . Much speculation as to how the six vacant seats are to be dealt with[47].

4 Mar. 1880: . . . H. of Lds. On the stairs met the Premier, shook hands, & exchanged a few words. I have not seen him to speak to since last year. He was very feeble physically, going up the stairs by the help of the railing, & with an evidently painful effort. But his mind seems clear enough.

Debate on the Chancellor's land bill, sensible enough, but not animated, as nearly everybody is in favour of the principle, & the differences expressed relate only to details. Bath spoke strongly against the whole measure, but was not supported. Ld Carington declared in favour of abolishing settlements altogether. Ld Wentworth[48] spoke for the first time, but was quite inaudible. No nonsense was talked, but none of the speeches was remarkable. . . .

7 Mar. 1880 (Sunday): . . . The papers are busy with Cross's water bill for London: which is condemned on all sides as too favourable to the companies, whose shares have been raised enormously by the mere announcement of the scheme. Whether he could have done better I do not know, & he certainly is not a man to perpetuate a wilful job: but many of his friends think that office & administrative success have made him in popular phrase 'too big for his boots' and that a check will not be out of place. He has certainly of late assumed a dictatorial tone towards the House, which is new, and not graceful: but taken as a whole his tenure of office has been creditable enough. That this bill will drop seems certain, in whatever way that may come about: but any mischief that it may cause will not thereby be cured: for it has already led to wild speculation in shares &, if it drops, the buyers at high prices will have reason to complain that they have been duped by the action of the government. It will be a joke against them that they have burnt their fingers with cold water – a new performance.

8 Mar. 1880: Saw Mr. Saunders[49] of the Central News office, a shrewd well mannered man: he explains a plan for collecting news for all the papers, which he develops: he says among other things that, taking the aggregate of papers which have more than local sale, *The Times* sells only one-twentieth of the whole: 30 years ago, its sale exceeded that of all the other London papers put together. – I found that Mr. S. was author of a book on America, which I had received from the author, & acknowledged with a compliment: for which he was still grateful.

. . . Walk for exercise: at the Travellers', at 4.30 or thereabouts, heard the news that a dissolution is announced: which has been long expected on all sides, but now that it has come it seems like a surprise. Business in the Lds. was of course put off: & I hear that the scene in the Commons was absurd enough: 40 or 50 members jumping from their seats at the same moment to rush to the telegraph office, which they besieged. . . .

9 Mar. 1880: See Moss about the proposed purchase of 4 new carriage horses, for which £900 would be required. I demur to the cost, & in the end we settle to buy one pair only, at a cost of £400.

. . . Pender calls: excited like all the world about the dissolution: thinks ministers will lose considerably, but still probably keep a small majority: talks of eastern affairs: matters in Turkey going from bad to worse: shows me a telegram: the Sultan & his advisers are determined to resist all foreign influence, & the ambassadors can get nothing done.

Sanderson calls: talk vaguely of politics: the chief fact that has struck him is the restless eagerness of the Italian govt. to take a part in whatever is passing. They are acting with the French, & evidently mean action of some kind, but to what object it will be directed does not yet appear. . . .

10 Mar. 1880: Mr. Holt of Liverpool calls early, & tells me of the intention of the Liberals to contest the S.W. division of the county, Rathbone being one candidate. I say that he has my sympathies, that I believe they could not have a better candidate, but that not knowing the state of the register I can express no opinion as to the expediency of a contest.

Granville calls, talks generally of election prospects, thinks it a certainty that the govt. will lose 8 or 10 seats in Scotland, & at least 15 in Ireland – but these last to the advantage of the Home Rulers only. As to England, all is uncertain. He thinks it may be a tie, leaving out the Irish: an inconvenient state of things, as it will give them a casting vote.

11 Mar. 1880: Saw Granville, who wants to raise a debate on the Premier's new manifesto, & asks me if I will speak? I answer that I will not make any attack on the Premier personally, that I will leave the business of criticising his address to some one else, but that, if I see an opportunity of saying something as to the foreign policy of the future, I am willing to do so.

Note that M. has been to see old Carlyle at Chelsea, & he sends me a sort of message to the effect that I ought to speak out as to the state of public affairs.

. . . Write to Maclure about shares in the Manchester Cons. Club: one to Statter asking him to see if my name is still connected with any party organisation: one to Hale in same sense.

Mr. Holt called again [to say] that Rathbone will stand along with a brother of Ld Sefton. I repeat what I said yesterday, that my sympathies were with the Liberal candidates, & at their earnest request I wrote this to Sefton: though why they were so anxious that I should write is more than I can tell. . . .

12 Mar. 1880: Northcote's budget out last night,. It is unsatisfactory, but that was expected. He admits a deficit of £3½ millions, & that the revenue has fallen below his estimate by £2 millions. He puts on no new tax except an addition to the probate duty, estimated to yield £600,000: and of the accumulated debt of £8 millions he pays off six by creating a terminable annuity to expire in 1885. This involves a yearly charge of £1,400,000: to meet which he sacrifices his own sinking fund, created 4 years ago: a part of his scheme which will no doubt be sharply criticised. But he may plead that in 5 years the fund will revive, & be greatly increased by the falling in of annuities, so that the mischief is only for a time.

Mr. H. Thompson called, to say that Rathbone consents to stand unwillingly, as his chances in the county are bad, & he sacrifices a safe seat. He evidently hinted at the choice of someone else – I think of himself as he has stood before – but I said that I could not interfere in the choice of the Liberal party . . . though I did not put it so crudely.

Sefton called, & talked for some time about local politics. He is ready to run his brother along with Rathbone, if I will support. After much discussion in which I found him shrewd & sensible, I agreed to write him a letter for publication, making no reference to the election, which indeed as between two peers would not be decent, but saying that I cannot support the government, that neutrality, however I might wish it, would be in my case an evasion of public duty, & that I have therefore no choice but to oppose them. I know this is right, & had long made up my mind that it must be done: but the doing it is abundantly disagreeable. . . .

13 Mar. 1880: . . . Nothing is talked of except dissolution, placards are out on the walls, the papers are full of election addresses, & the work of the session is being wound up as quickly as possible. Gladstone's address is as might be supposed a slashing attack on the ministry, rather too indiscriminate, but it is only a summary of what he has been saying for months past. That of Ld Beaconsfield (I call it an election address, though it is in the form of a letter to the D. of Marlborough[50]) is a singular document, quite in character. He denounces the Liberals as having been willing to give up the colonies, & now wishing to disintegrate the empire by Home Rule for Ireland: he declares that England must exercise an ascendancy in the councils of Europe: & that it is only by her doing so that terrible wars can be averted. In short, the paper, which is ill written for him, & in a bombastic style, is an appeal to popular prejudice, without reference to facts or possibilities, absurd if addressed to educated men, but not ill adapted to be read aloud in public houses. – Hartington has replied in a well reasoned manifesto, which seems to have been arranged by the Whig leaders, & which has exactly the opposite defect. It is convincing in argument, clear in style, but rather too long to be telling with the masses.

Northcote's address is sensible and moderate, but differs curiously from that of the Premier. The latter holds out the prospect of European war only to be averted by English interference: Northcote on the contrary hopes that the time for anxiety is over, & that we shall be free to devote our energies to internal improvements. A more complete contrast cannot be, & the explanation is obvious, that each predicts what he wishes to see. Northcote left to himself would be a moderate Liberal or moderate Conservative (the difference is not great): but he never seems to think of opposing schemes and policies with which it is impossible to believe that he can have any sympathy. . . .

15 Mar. 1880: London by usual train . . . Saw Sanderson, but no special news, except that Salisbury is going to the south of France for six weeks, not being cured of his complaint, & still very weak.

. . . Call at Vernon Heath's, & buy 4 large new photographs, for Fairhill. He tells me that for his work, which is on a large scale, & requires much light, only 2 days in 1879 were available: which does not seem easy to believe.

Call on A.D.[51] who as usual vehement about the state of Ireland, saying the poorer classes under the guidance of their priests are socialists to a man, though with no definite formula or plan of action: that with the present franchise 70 Home Rulers will be returned[52] . . .: that concessions are of no use, etc. But is this not rather like saying that we hold Ireland by force only? and what hope is there of a better state of things, since little remains that an English parliament can do? The Irish difficulty is the real rock ahead, the others can be avoided but in the hostility of Irish feeling I see no change. And the agitators gain their point in one respect: they keep English capital out, which otherwise flowing there would create plenty & content: & they keep English settlers out, so that no further intermixture of population is probable.

. . . Do not go to the Lords, which I avoid because after my letter to Sefton my place is on the opposition benches, & I think it better to defer that move until a new parliament.

The letter in question, as far as I can judge, has been well received: the time had clearly come when a longer suspension of the expression of my opinions would have been resented as unfair to those who in part depend upon me. As I have said to various persons, if I had been a private person, Mr. Smith or Mr. Brown, I should have remained absolutely neutral: but when I know that many voters are saying, especially in Lancashire, 'What does Ld D. think? what does he advise?' it is impossible to put them off with the answer that Ld D. has no opinion to offer, & no advice to give. Yet I am glad that I waited till now. . . . The truth is that to my opinions as to those of most men who think there is a conservative as well as a liberal side: but I am not afraid of finding the Liberal leaders, or the party as a whole, too violent. Their difficulty will be the other way – that they fail to rouse enthusiasm.

16 Mar. 1880: . . . My office papers, or a part of them, come home – the drafts of letters alone occupy many vols. Amused with looking through them, & find references in some that I cannot now understand – so quickly does a rapid succession of events wear away memory.

. . . See a Mr. Humphreys of the Register Office about a memorial to Dr. Farr[53]: who is 72, broken in health, & has never received any recognition of his remarkable services in sanitary & statistical matters, beyond the pension to which he is entitled. I do not know why the govt. have slighted him, but they have certainly done so. He was too ill & weak to be made registrar, but at least he might have been knighted, or received some mark of distinction. He is badly off, & it is thought that we may at the same time pay him a compliment, & help to make him easy about his family. . . .

17 Mar. 1880: . . . At 4.00, go to the Gen. Register Office, Somerset House, where in the library I met some 12 or 14 gentlemen to consider the expediency of a memorial to Dr. Farr. Heywood, Newmarch, Dr. Carpenter, Wakley of the *Lancet*, were among them: most I did not know. We agreed on details of what is to be done, & I promised £50.

Dined with Ld & Ly Bath: party small, being broken up by the elections: met the Russian ambassador, Ly M.[arian] Alford, Ld & Ly Airlie, Ld Kenmare, Ld Camperdown: with ourselves 10. Pleasant enough. P. Lobanoff, the new Russian, is a curious contrast to his predecessor: a short quiet man, looking sensible, but with no great intelligence or vivacity: his passion is collecting books & works of art, of which he is said to have brought over a good many: he has not yet gone much into the world.

It is announced that Ld Salisbury goes abroad for six weeks: which looks like shaken health. I hear that both Northcote & F. [Stanley] are much worn out, and would be personally glad to retire.

There are now in the field 1,021 candidates for the 652 seats, being about the same number as in 1874. I believe no one on either side has the least idea how the English vote will go. That Liberals will gain in Scotland, & Home Rulers in Ireland, is certain: but late events have caused a confusion of parties which disturbs all calculation. Socially, the candidates seem of the same class as before. I do not see that workingmen's candidates are coming to the front. The publicans are all Conservative: the Catholics are divided, the English part of them inclining to support the govt., while the Irish are furious at Ld B.'s manifesto, & will vote in opposition without asking pledges. In Lancashire, I hear that the Catholic vote will be given to the Conservatives: but in Nottingham, where a meeting of Catholics has lately been called on the subject of Irish distress, the bishop presiding, the language was as violent as if it had been held in Ireland, England being accused of having caused every Irish misfortune.

18 Mar. 1880: Ly Granville's at night, where met a small party. – Some talk there of the Queen's life of her husband: I call it hers for, though Theodore Martin is the ostensible author, he has only been employed to put together materials furnished by her[54]. It is an extraordinary production, especially the narrative, by the Queen, from her diary, of the details of her mother's and husband's deaths. The writing is good, better than from her usual style one should have expected, and would figure well in a novel: but nobody understands how she can have brought herself to make public her most intimate thoughts & feelings which the natural instinct of delicacy would induce any one to keep private. It is not easy to believe in the reality of a sentiment thus carefully noted at the time, & proclaimed to all England afterwards. Yet that in a sense it was real I do not doubt. A royal personage, I suppose, ceases to care about privacy, which is so seldom attainable by such persons: & in the affection of the Queen for her husband there was no doubt always a feeling of superiority: he was her trusted headservant: and in telling the world how she trusted and regretted him she is still a sovereign doing honour to a subject.

Granville told me that, so far as the party agents were able to judge, they expected the govt. to have a majority varying from 15 to 25.

19 Mar. 1880: . . . Hear of the young Ld Shrewsbury[55], not yet of age, being in a scrape with the notorious Mrs. Langtry, whose photograph is in every shop window. According to the tale, the P. of Wales, who is also one of her admirers, found them in a compromising situation. The lady declares her intention of getting divorced & marrying him! A singular fate follows that family. The grandfather[56], himself nearly mad, married a mad wife, & did his utmost to ruin all belonging to him: the father[57], who died a couple of years ago, though eccentric in many respects, & conceited almost beyond the limits of sanity, yet showed sense in matters of property, & retrieved the position by clearing off most of the encumbrances: the present youth, said to be good-looking & good-mannered, failed to pass the easy examination for the army, & promises to be a merely fashionable gentleman. The three daughters, his aunts, all beautiful, attractive, & odd, are childless – Nature's way of checking the spread of insanity, which they inherit from the mother.

Much talk of Italian preparations for war: they are spending largely (which they can ill afford) on their navy, & will soon have the most powerful ironclads in the world. There is . . . a strange discontent with the position which their country holds . . . They have three wants: an extension to the north-east: possibly including Trieste: influence on the eastern side of the Adriatic, perhaps territory there: and the possession of Tunis. . . .

21 Mar. 1880: . . . Read again Mallock's book *Is Life worth Living?* being an argument that without religion . . . life as we know it would not be worth having. The author is a nephew of Froude . . .

. . . Wrote to Hale about the S.W. Lancs. election, as I had done before, telling him to let it be clearly known what my opinions are, though without pressing anybody: I wrote this letter in a rather official style, & sent a copy to Sefton for the agents on that side, not for publication, but that they might see I was doing what I had promised. . . .

23 Mar. 1880: The letters being delayed, Hale's answer to mine of Sunday did not come till the afternoon: which caused some uneasiness, as we know that there are influences at work against us, & the Liberal agents accuse Hale as the cause. In this they are unjust, for he is a man of scrupulous honour, & would do nothing against my wishes, but I can well believe that he dislikes what is going on, & is slow to take any step, while others about the place are less scrupulous. After much talk, M. & I decided to go down to Knowsley on Thursday, leaving Fairhill till later. – Hale's letter arrived at last, & is satisfactory. The Seftons distrust Mrs. Hale, believing her to be entirely in the Witherslack interest, but they give no reasons. The contest is expected to be close, & there is evidently much local excitement. . . .

26 Mar. 1880: . . . Talk with Hale as to the election: find him rather sore at various attacks made upon him by some of the Liberal agents. We agree that he shall address to the tenants a circular carefully worded, enclosing copy of my letter of Monday to him, a little altered. In the course of the day Baring[58] came out of Liverpool to see him, & I think the explanation that ensued set matters straight. Baring is active in favour of Rathbone & Molyneux, & what was said to him will reach the other agents. – I am bound to say that I had an idea myself that Hale had not been conveying my views quite correctly to the tenants, though I did not suspect him of intentional disguise or perversion of them: but merely of a strong disposition to read them in the sense most favourable to his own views. His conversation, however, has removed even that impression.

. . . Dine at Croxteth meeting the two candidates, Rathbone & Molyneux, Mr. Bilson[59] the agent, Baring, & others.

27 Mar. 1880: Settled finally Hale's letter to the tenants.

. . . Ld Ramsay called from Liverpool. He expects no contest. He says the Catholics are divided in their sympathies, the Irish strongly Liberal, the English mostly inclining the other way.

28 Mar. 1880 (Easter Day): Show myself to the village in the accustomed manner. Walk home by the Moss. Walk later with M.

Dine again at Croxteth, meeting Molyneux, but not Rathbone. . . .

30 Mar. 1880: . . . The newspapers contain nothing except reports of election speeches & meetings. There are 1,134 candidates in the field altogether. Of the English seats, 489, only 85 are uncontested, leaving 404 separate fights to go on at the same time. Naturally, not one-hundredth part of the oratory of the day is reported except in local journals: but, as far as one can judge, there is a singular absence of anything that can be called radicalism. I see no trace of the bitterness of class-feeling which certainly existed 30 years ago, & which one would expect to find in a country where the contrasts of wealth & poverty are so strongly marked. The Liberal programme is mild enough, & most of the Conservatives seem to shrink from decided expressions of hostility to change. The church too is hardly attacked & plays no prominent part in controversy: which also is new.

31 Mar. 1880: . . . Tell Sefton that I am ready to subscribe to the county contest to the amount of £3,000. He talks of giving £2,000, which with my £3,000 ought to be half the whole cost.

1 Apr. 1880: Left at 9.00 for Preston: at the Exchange station got the news: & found that the government have lost 16 seats, or 31 votes on a division: which, as the returns are from boroughs scattered all over the country, is an almost decisive indication of the general result. Liberal gains are 25, Conservative gains 9, making the balance 16. At Preston, I got out to walk through the town as usual to the courthouse, which is at the other end of it: half way I was recognised, & immediately followed by a crowd, nearly all friendly & cheering loudly, but I could have dispensed with such an event. We sat less than 1½ hours, the business being chiefly formal: we borrowed, or rather sanctioned the borrowing of, £80,000, for an extension of one of the lunatic asylums, but the work was necessary &, as the debt is made repayable within a term of years, there is no harm done. Magistrates present were only about 25 . . . Taking a cab back to the station, I was again followed by a rather large crowd, who spread about the station, & did not leave till my train went off.
 . . . M. went with Ly Sefton to Ormskirk, as a kind of political demonstration, & they were very warmly received. Both parties held meetings there during the day . . .

2 Apr. 1880: . . . Sir R. Peel[60] has of his own accord retired from Tamworth. . . . Sheffield has got rid of Mr. Waddy[61], who relied too much on the Irish vote, & suffered in consequence. In the smaller boroughs contests have been very close . . . I see it observed in one of the newspapers that ten seats have been transferred by less than 400 votes.
 . . . The returns of yesterday, received this morning, show 31 seats lost by the government, which counting 62 on a division destroys their majority. They may gain in the English counties though that does not seem likely: but they will lose in Scotland & Ireland, so that it is scarcely possible they should go on. The Liberals, who did not expect so considerable a change, are surprised at their own success. The most unsatisfactory part of the business is that, balanced as parties will probably be, the Home Rulers will be strong enough to turn the scale, unless indeed the Liberal successes continue at the same rate. In which case, the majority on their side will be sufficient to enable them to disregard them to disregard Irish faction. – M. went with Ly Sefton to Southport, & there had a very warm reception. Neither Sefton nor I joined the party, it being not thought right that peers should show themselves at election times, where canvassing is going on.

3 Apr. 1880: . . . The elections continue as before to show Liberal gains, which have now reached the number of 50 seats, making 100 votes on a division. This is a clear Liberal majority, & not only makes a change of hands inevitable, but makes it probable that the incoming govt. may be able to hold its own. – Two things are clearly proved: one that the London press does not now, as it used to do, represent the general opinion of the country: since the London press has been in the main very favourable to the present Cabinet: the other, which is perhaps only another form of the same statement, that party leaders

& election agents cannot with any certainty foretell what is to happen, with the large constituencies we have now, & with the ballot. . . . But it is odd that the Jingo cry should have been apparently so popular & powerful, & yet have exercised so little influence. Endless explanations will be given: the simplest is probably the truest: that the public gets tired of the same people and the same policy after a certain time: in 1874 they had had enough of economy & reform, & wanted something different: now they have enjoyed the blessings of a spirited foreign policy, and will be glad of quieter times. Another cause may be added: moderate Liberals were not afraid, in 1874, of any real reaction: they thought there would be a slackening in the rate of progress, & nothing more. In short they were prepared to tolerate a Conservative ministry, but were not prepared for a revival of old Toryism. With a certain class, the Premier's excessive deference to the Queen & his well known disposition to exalt prerogative have done him harm. Others have been influenced by the comparative failure of Conservative finance, which is quite as much Northcote's misfortune as his fault, since he is not responsible for the depression of trade. And every ministry makes enemies as it goes on, disappoints many expectations, & comes into collision with interests which resent attack.

. . . So far as the elections have yet gone, it does not seem as if the social composition of parliament were much changed. Macdonald, Burt, Broadhurst, & Bradlaugh are the only members returned who are decidedly outside the class which is conventionally called 'gentlemen': two of these sat before, & Bradlaugh has only replaced the notorious Kenealy[62] who is displaced. Nor have extreme or violent speeches been made, nor any wild pledges been asked or given. The new House will be decidedly Liberal, but I do not see that it will be democratic. (**Note:** I ought to have excepted Ireland, which indeed was not in my mind.)

Ride early: walk with M. in the park later, & examined a new process of fish hatching . . . M. went with a party from Croxteth to attend a meeting in Liverpool: I stayed at home: an odd reversal of parts, but it is not etiquette for a peer to be present at electioneering gatherings. Ld & Ly Ramsay came to stay with us. . . .

5 Apr. 1880 (Monday): Ld & Ly Ramsay left us early. Long ride in the park. Walk later with M. . . .

The Liberal gains are variously stated at 57, 58, & 59, several more having been announced on Saturday . . . It is announced in a sort of semi-official way that he [Gladstone] has made up his mind not to take office, but to support Granville & Hartington. This is undoubtedly the wisest course in all respects: for he could not without loss of dignity hold any place but the first in a Cabinet: indeed his serving in any other capacity would be looked upon as an absurdity, & place both parties to the arrangement in a false position: while, if he became Premier, the Radicals would be exultant, & the Whigs would probably drop off. But, with his restless temper, it is a question how long he will have patience to watch his friends doing what he will assuredly think he could do better. And, if he turns against the government, they will have an unpleasant time.

Much speculation as to the chances of the Premier throwing up the cards as he did in 1868, & Gladstone in 1874. It would be the most dignified course, & the result anyhow must be the same. But some people think that hatred of Gladstone will make him fight on to the last. . . .

7 Apr. 1880: In the papers, news of fresh Liberal successes, making the seats gained by them 68, as well as I can make out: but the Irish elections cause confusion, as it is not easy to say to what party Home Rulers belong. The *Pall Mall Gazette* is pressing hard to have Gladstone sent for instead of Granville: obviously on the speculation that his accession to power would disgust the moderates on his own side. The *Pall Mall* also hopes that Ld B. will not resign without a debate & vote, so that the policy of the Cabinet may be vindicated. *The Times* on the other hand treats the question as settled and points out that an immediate resignation will save some three weeks of useful time. This last view is the most likely to be popular, & the adoption of it would certainly be better in the interests of the Premier's dignity.

– Lowe is returned for the London U.[niversity] & has made a speech giving up his opposition to the extension of the county franchise, not as having changed his personal conviction, but yielding to the general feeling of his party: a rather noticeable change for so stiff & strong-willed a politician.

Left Knowsley 10.20, reached St. J. Square about 4.20, just six hours from door to door: day mostly fine. On arriving, heard of the Liberal defeat in S.W. Lancashire which does not surprise me, having always expected it, but M. is disappointed. . . . In the evening went to a party at Ly A. Russell's, where among others were Renan, M. Arnold, Prof. H. Smith[63], & Morley, of the *Fortnightly*. With this last I had some interesting talk as to the situation. He foresees considerable trouble for the new Cabinet – first in consequence of the number of candidates for places, next in consequence of the probable claims of the extreme, or radical party. These he says are some 25 in number, all inclined to make their voices heard, and will press for action in various ways for which the country is not prepared. They may be patient for a year, or even two years, but that will be the utmost limit. Then will come demands impossible to be granted, & not to be refused without offence. Redistribution of seats is in itself a difficulty enough to baffle any ministry – yet with a change in the county franchise it must come. – I noted the absence of church questions – he said the non-conformists generally had acted under a strict rule, in keeping back their personal opinions on those subjects lest they should divide the party. And generally speaking 'advanced thinkers' of all sorts had done the same. – He thought it not at all certain that Gladstone would waive his claim to office; if he did so he would cause great disappointment among the party in general, and his own position would be difficult. Talked of the absolute necessity of getting rid of some of the older men, who nevertheless were not at all likely to waive their claims. – I was interested in Mr. Morley's talk, & pleased with his manner. He is a man I should like to cultivate, & there is now no obstacle: formerly there was, for a man of his politics is naturally shy of entering into free discussion with a professed Conservative.

8 Apr. 1880: The Liberals now claim to have won 81 or 83 seats, but it is not clear whether they are not counting some in Ireland which belong to the Home Rulers. This would not have mattered much at the start of the election, for the H.R. party would have formed part of the opposition [with the Liberals]: but it is different now, for Parnell & his friends have no idea of supporting any minister, & in fact will always vote in opposition. There are really three parties, and I see that even Conservatives profess satisfaction that their rivals should have a majority sufficient to make them independent of the Irish vote.

Call in Curzon St. Hear only that Goschen declines office, on the ground of his opinions about the county franchise. This is a loss in regard of administrative ability, but the younger competitors will not regret it.

9 Apr. 1880: Liberal successes continue, and the chief danger of the new Cabinet is lest they should be too strong: which may easily happen. Where there is virtually no opposition, ministers grow careless, they fall into blunders, commit jobs, and in any case disappoint their followers, who cannot understand why they should stop short of carrying into effect all the most extreme views of the party. Yet, if they try to gratify these same supporters, they rouse against them the feeling of that large class of moderate non-political men, who are not apt to interfere while matters go smoothly, but become alarmed when they think the horses are running away, & the driver has lost control of them. Something of this sort happened in 1873, & explained the catastrophe. Every variety of explanation is given of the change of feeling in the constituencies since 1874, none quite satisfactory, for, if the policy of the late Cabinet (as one must call it now) was really as unpopular as the elections would indicate, how comes it that no sign was made to that effect, & that the best judges were deceived by the apparent apathy of the people? This is a question which has never been answered. On the whole I see no reason to change what I wrote a week ago, but perhaps another cause should have been noted – the curious preference of many voters to be on the winning side, even when the vote is secret: a tendency which is not easy to account for, but it certainly exists.

It is now taken for granted that the precedents of 1868 & 1874 will be followed, & that the Premier will resign as soon as the Queen comes back from Baden, and when the elections are complete. I hope in his own interest that he will & hardly doubt it. Already the dissensions between Whig and Radical are appearing & the question is anxiously raised, who is to be Premier? Gladstone is understood to waive his claim, but it will not be easy to satisfy his friends that he does so freely: & there are those who hold that, after taking so prominent a part in turning out the government, he is bound not to shrink from the responsibility of office. He cannot, they agree, plead age & infirmity, for his oratorical campaign of the winter involved exertions far greater than those of office. He is the real head of the party: & the position of irresponsible protector of a Cabinet is not one to which we are accustomed, nor one which can be long maintained. On the other hand, there is no doubt but that his accession to power will alarm many of the less thorough going Liberals, and that it will be opposed by the Queen with all the violence of personal aversion. The next ten days must decide the question. . . .

11 Apr. 1880: Hear from Drage that some uncomfortable symptoms have reappeared, though not to a considerable extent: but strict care in living will be necessary for some weeks.

. . . In the papers, a report (which I do not believe) that Layard[64] is to resign, & his place to be filled by Drummond Wolff[65]. I suspect the latter ingenious gentleman is himself the author of the story. – Another more probable rumour is to the effect that Salisbury is to be made a Duke. – Ld Holmesdale[66] is called up to the Lords, which makes no permanent addition to the peerage. The D. of Portland's stepmother is also made a peeress[67], for no very obvious reason.

Death of Ld Hampton[68] announced. He was past 80, but to the last seemed fresh & healthy. Few men have been more lucky in their public career. Up to 1852 he was known only as a good county member, and chairman of quarter sessions: the absolute dearth of qualified candidates for office caused my father to give him the Colonial Office, where, if he did not greatly succeed, he did not utterly fail: the position thus acquired he managed to keep, & afterwards held the Admiralty & War Office. As a speaker he was fluent, correct, but ineffective: I never heard him to my recollection do well in a debate. But courtesy, fairness to opponents, & the reputation of a good man of business carried him through: &, though he was confessedly placed higher in the official hierarchy than he had a right to be, I do not think he was either unpopular or ridiculous. It was a mistake on the Premier's part to have created a sinecure office[69] for him, when nearer 80 than 70: & perhaps a mistake on his part to have accepted it. The transaction savoured of jobbery, & did neither of them good. But, taking his life as a whole, he was a good sample of the country gentleman accidentally elevated to be a minister, &, though a certain pomposity & self-importance belonged to him by nature, it could not be said that his head was turned by his elevation. He had a good estate & fine old house in Worcestershire, where I was once his guest, I think, in 1853 or 54. He leaves two sons, but no grandsons, so that his peerage will probably die. . . .

12 Apr. 1880: The newspapers are still full of speculations: *The Times* makes up Ld Granville's Cabinet for him: giving me the Colonial Office. *D. News* argues earnestly that Gladstone must either be Premier, or hold a seat in the Cabinet without office. It is said that Lyons means to retire from Paris, on the ground of health (but this has been contradicted): Layard & Elliot on political grounds: Lytton the same: so that the incoming ministry will have four great posts to fill.

13 Apr. 1880: Talk with M. about writing to Ld Granville without waiting for an overture from him, to say that I will support the government cordially, but not take office. She agrees that it should be done.
    . . . By 10.50 train to London. . . .

14 Apr. 1880: Plagued with an influx of letters from strangers such as I have not often known: I sent off by the two posts over 20 answers, & there were many besides which did not deserve or require an answer.
    . . . In reply to a sensible letter from Sydney, on the question of free trade or protection in N.S. Wales & Victoria . . . I reply by suggesting that what Australians should work for is a customs-union of all the colonies of Australia, so that intercolonial tariffs & customhouses may be done away.
    Write to Ld Granville, who by a note addressed to me gives me an opening, saying that, though there is some awkwardness in refusing what has not been offered, I think it better to explain at once my position. I shall give a cordial support to the new govt., but cannot take office, as I think that, when a man is compelled by convictions or circumstances to change his party connection, he is bound to show that he is not a gainer by the change. I add that I have the less difficulty in coming to this decision, as he can be in no difficulty from the want of men. I did not add, as I might have done, that his difficulty will consist in the overabundance of candidates for every possible office. . . .

16 Apr. 1880: Letter from Granville, brief, but almost affectionately grateful for mine. He says, however, that he shall probably not be sent for: & indeed I see a strong feeling growing up that Gladstone must have the offer of the first place, whether he chooses to accept it or not. All parties wish it for various reasons: the radicals, sincerely & simply, for they consider G. as their leader: the Conservatives because they think his nomination will frighten the Whigs, & divide the party: the Whigs (not all but a majority) because, danger for danger, they think it is better that G. should feel the responsibility & be put under the restraints of office than that he should exercise a nearly absolute power over the parliamentary majority, & so over the Cabinet, without having any account to give, or any colleagues to consult. In this latter case his position would be like that of Gambetta in France: there is no exact parallel for it that I know of in England. The Queen will be frantic, having on every occasion that was open to her expressed in vehement language her determination never, never, never to employ Mr. Gladstone again. But Ld Beaconsfield can now have no motive for advising her otherwise than prudently (for rancour is not one of his faults) & he will probably smooth the difficulty.

My position will be unaffected, whoever is minister: &, while the scramble lasts, I shall have the good word of all the office-hunters who are glad to have one rival the less – probably of the chiefs also, who have three candidates for every place. And, as I really like rest & the country better than Downing St., I think it rather ingenious to be thanked & applauded for doing what suits my own taste best. . . .

17 Apr. 1880: See in the papers that Sanderson is a C.B. Write to congratulate him, warmly.

Death of Kenealy, the Irish lawyer & agitator, at the age of 61. He was, I suspect, more than half mad: & his passion for notoriety ruined his career. He set on foot, & headed, the agitation in favour of the impostor who called himself Tichborne: which for a time raged among the masses, & certainly is the most curious popular delusion of our time. Success turned his head: he insulted the judges, got himself disbarred, was sent to parliament by a large majority, & edited & wrote a scurrilous paper, *The Englishman*, which I believe still exists. In the H. of C., as might be expected, he did nothing: & on standing again he was nowhere. He died ostensibly of a slight hurt: really, I suspect, of rage & mortification at his failure. He had some literary capacity but, as a speaker, owed more to vehemence & pertinacity than to either eloquence or argument.

. . . Galloway[70] has let his big country house for 5 years, which is a relief to his finances. He has more than £30,000 rental, & hardly £4,000 out of it to spend. Is this a common condition of old Scotch estates? . . .

19 Apr. 1880: Troubled today with an odd nervous feeling, as if misfortune were impending, or as if I had some cause for great anxiety: the fact being that I have not the slightest trouble, small or great, nor anything on my mind. I was subject to this sort of foolish complaint in early life, but thought I had outgrown it. Perhaps the very absence of active or absorbing occupation tends to increase it. The sensation came rather suddenly, & passed off again in a few hours: so that I think it is due only to disturbed digestion. But possibly the incessant worry of 1876–77–78 has left behind it more effects than I am fully conscious of.

The newspapers continue full of speculations, & nothing is known, but Ld B.'s resignation without waiting for a parliamentary vote is generally assumed. Northcote, Cross, & J. Manners get the G.C.B. which the two first have fairly earned: & as to J.M. . . . his honours will not be grudged. . . . Borthwick[71] of the *M. Post* a knight (he expected a baronetcy) . . . The Queen is come back from Baden. There is to be a Cabinet on Wednesday at which I suppose the resignations will be formally decided. The public, rightly or wrongly, takes for granted that Gladstone must be in the new arrangements, either as chief or without an office, but with a seat in Cabinet. It is generally felt that he cannot take a subordinate post, which would put all parties in a false position.

20 Apr. 1880: Wrote to Ward to pay £3,000 to Mr. Eccles[72] of Huyton on account of the late election. Considering the sums expended, which cannot be less than £2,000,000, & more probably reach £3,000,000, I have not been heavily taxed.

. . . By 3.50 train to London. At No. 23 see Sanderson, who talks over the situation. He tells me that the Premier was really anxious to provide for H. Lennox[73] before going out, & meant him to have the place held by Ld Hampton: but Northcote & others remonstrated, & the thing was stopped. There could not be a better illustration of Disraeli's good qualities & his defects. He was quite ready to incur a certain amount of unpopularity in order to serve an old friend, & this though he can now have no personal object to gain: on the other hand it probably never occurred to him that he was putting a man of damaged character into an important office. I am glad for the sake of his reputation that the advice of friends prevailed. . . .

21 Apr. 1880 (Wednesday): . . .London U. Senate at 4.00 p.m. . . . Short talk with Granville, who was in the chair. He tells me that he expects Hartington to be sent for in the first instance, but that he (Ld H.) will endeavour to transfer the duty of forming a Cabinet to Gladstone, who, Granville thinks, will not persist in his refusal.

A Cabinet was held today at which the question of resignation was discussed – & there seems to be no doubt of the result. But I am told that Hicks Beach & one or two more were violent against the idea of retiring without a debate & division – the Premier taking the opposite line, as he did in 1868. One does not clearly see what there is to be gained by waiting for the inevitable vote of no-confidence, but the *Pall Mall Gazette*, & the Jingo party in general, incline to that course.

22 Apr. 1880: . . . In the papers [Ld] Skelmersdale is to be an earl[74]: so is Ld Sondes[75]: and Montague Corry, Ld B.'s private secretary, is rewarded with a peerage[76]. This last selection will not be popular in the H. of Lords, nor with the public so far as they care about the matter, for the new peer has no land, only vague expectations from relations, & has never held any post except that of private secretary. It is the first time that merely personal service has been so rewarded. Nor will the demeanour of the person so honoured make matters better, for he has always been laughed at for his swaggering ways and somewhat comic imitation of Ld B.'s occasional pomposity. But it is just to add that he has been personally devoted to his chief, & has rendered him more than ordinary official service.

23 Apr. 1880 (Friday): News at last that Ld Hartington is sent for: but it is generally assumed that he will refuse, & indicate Gladstone as the only possible Premier – & on all sides it seems to be felt that this is the best arrangement. That G. should have supreme power is not now in question – the elections have given it him – the question is whether he shall exercise it with or without responsibility.

. . . It is unlucky that the Queen has made her personal dislike of Gladstone so public. It is referred to without disguise in the papers, as a notorious fact. The result is that she, who might have appeared at least to maintain a neutral attitude, is now exposed to the humiliation of having forced upon her by the public a man for whom she is known to entertain no feelings except those of distrust & aversion. She has also more or less quarrelled with Granville, nobody knows why: & the sending for Hartington in his place is meant as a slap in the face to him. But, as the three men concerned are acting with mutual confidence & cordiality, no harm will be done.

The Whig party as a whole will no doubt accept Gladstone as inevitable & try to like the arrangement, but it is to them a disappointment. They have got a more complete victory than they wanted, & are a little frightened at their own success . . . The D. of Bedford[77] is a typical example; his disgust at the second seat in Bedfordshire being won by an independent Liberal[78], after he [Bedford] had declined to sanction the starting of another candidate, is not disguised. Even now, there are many signs of a split visible: but for the present year it cannot come to much. . . .

24 Apr. 1880 (Saturday): The ministerial crisis is ended, more quickly than any one expected. Scarcely any one doubted but that Gladstone must be Premier: but it was thought probable that there would be an interval of fruitless negociation, wasting time. The public, however, was mistaken, for the Queen appears to have given way at once, & Gladstone accepted office. He takes the Exchequer as well as the First Lord's office: which he did once before, in 1873: but it is not a good arrangement from the point of view of the party. Places are already too few to satisfy all, & the inevitable discontent will be increased when two of the most important are held by one person, however eminent. Granville is by universal consent indicated as Foreign Secretary, & in point of ability no man can be fitter: but he has grown very deaf and very lazy, which are drawbacks. No other post is known to be filled.

. . . About 3.00, received a letter from Gladstone, offering 'a place of weight' in the new Cabinet. With it came one from Granville also. I had no difficulty in refusing which I did almost in the terms used in writing to Granville ten days ago . . . I am inclined from the wording of the Premier's letter to think that he did not expect an acceptance, but considered the offer as a courtesy which was due to me under the circumstances. I had not the slightest doubt as to persevering in my refusal, by which I sacrifice nothing for, elected as Gladstone has been by the whole body of the constituencies, he is dictator, & his colleagues will be merely tools. By refusing I keep my independence, I make it impossible for anyone to say that I have acted from interested motives, & I lose no advantage which I value or wish for. The only risk I run is that of dropping out of public notice, but that can be guarded against by a moderate expenditure of trouble. Whether I shall ever hold office again is a question which may very well be left to the future. As newspapers multiply, & the system of stump oratory becomes established, a post in Downing St. grows less & less desirable from the point of view of personal satisfaction. – Sent off my answer by a messenger: & almost immediately after doing so received a telegram from Sanderson saying that he has accepted the private secretaryship[79]: telegraphed back to approve & congratulate, & wrote in the same sense.

25 Apr. 1880 (Sunday): Dull dark day, fog in the air as if from London, though it is strange that the smoke should travel so far.

. . . Wrote to Skelmersdale to wish him joy of his new title of Earl of Lathom, which he has long wanted, and related as we are I think it better to keep up a friendly intercourse. Besides, he has always been civil & even cordial, notwithstanding recent political differences.

26 Apr. 1880: See Drage, who very well satisfied with me, but gives earnest warning as to chills, which it seems are especially fatal where there is any weakness in the kidneys. Ld Durham died lately from this cause.

Leave for Euston at 4.30 . . . Knowsley 10.40. Supper, letters, & bed. . . .

27 Apr. 1880: Send £21 to a memorial fund in honour of Mr. Clerk Maxwell[80], a distinguished man of science at Cambridge, of whom I know nothing, except that he was famous, & is dead. There is to be a bust of him, and his works are to be published. I subscribe with pleasure, for it is well to make friends among the scientific party, & after all they are the men who do the real work. . . .

29 Apr. 1880: . . . The Cabinet is complete . . . Gladstone, 1st Lord [Premier] & Chanc. of Exch. – the taking this second place I have thought from the first a mistake.

Granville has F.O. – the best choice that could be made.

Kimberley has the Colonies, for which he may thank me, for I believe that was the post reserved for me if I had accepted. He is fit.

Childers at the War Office will be unpopular, but efficient.

Northbrook at the Admiralty – good.

Hartington's selection for the India Office is a surprise – it is a laborious post of which he knows nothing, but he has sense, & will learn.

Harcourt has fairly earned the Home Office but, unless Downing St. changes his nature, he will not be popular in it. Magistrates & mayors don't expect to be treated as if they were black beetles.

Selborne could not be passed over for the [Lord] Chancellorship. He is moderate about land, which is a good thing: & respected on all sides.

Bright takes a sinecure – the Duchy of Lancaster: so does the D. of Argyll, who has had enough of departmental work. He is Privy Seal. Ld Spencer has the Presidency of the Council: an easy post, but which he has scarcely earned.

[W.E.] Forster goes to the difficult & disagreeable post of Irish secretary. I do not envy him. He is honest, sympathetic, radical enough for the people, but justly intolerant of folly & lies: and he will hear little else.

The 'advanced' party are conciliated by the admission of Chamberlain to the Cabinet as Pres. of the B. of Trade. I believe the choice is a good one: Dilke would have been generally preferred, but it is understood that the Queen has set a mark against him, as having opposed various things on which her heart was set – grants to royal children & the like. Dodson has a seat in Cabinet with the Local Govt. Board – a new arrangement, perhaps a good one. Dodson himself is respectable, but nothing more. The peers are six, commoners eight: counting Hartington among the peerage (and he may be there any day) the numbers are equal.

Ripon goes to India, for which he has no special fitness: but I suppose it is the only place where his popery will not stand in his way.

29 Apr. 1880: . . . The papers are still busily discussing minor government appointments. These are on the whole good: the two oldest are Fawcett to be Postmaster-General: the first time, I should think, that a blind man has held office in this country: and Grant Duff to be under-secretary for the colonies, a department which he has probably studied less than almost any other. But he is too pedantic & crotchety for foreign affairs, & I suppose has committed himself too strongly on Indian subjects. Ld Cowper[81] is Lord Lieut. of Ireland: a respectable, but rather weak selection: I suppose it is understood that he is only to do the entertaining, & that the business is to be left to Forster. It is well that we have escaped a royal viceroy: the court is understood to wish that the Duke of Connaught[82] should be sent: which would create endless confusion.

Sir H. James[83] was inevitable as Attorney Gen. & is equal to the place. Herschell[84] is solicitor [-general], a good sound lawyer, & sensible speaker: his selection is a bitter pill to Watkin Williams[85], who had expected the post, & had done much for the party. But legal claims will be the hardest of all to satisfy, for in no former parliament have so many lawyers sat.

It is odd – reverting to the late ministry – that the three men who were most active in attacking me personally, Drummond Wolff, Sir R. Peel, & the late Attorney-General [Holker][86] are all three disappointed, Ld Beaconsfield having left office without doing anything for them. In the last case the disappointment is severe, for Sir J. Holker had a customary right to the Chief Baron's place: but Sir F. Kelly[87], though long past 80, & utterly inefficient, either does not feel his own incapacity, or is determined at all costs to hold on till by the expiration of 15 years' service on the bench he has earned a pension. So he has ignored all hints to retire (which I am told have been many & pressing) & Holker's prospects are of the vaguest kind, unless he takes a *puisné* [junior] judgeship, which I suppose the Liberals would give him.

1 May 1880 (Saturday): Leave for London, to dine at the Academy. Meet by appointment two Vienna journalists . . . I had no occasion for reserve, & told them what I thought as to the inconveniences of an Anglo-Austrian-German alliance which, briefly stated, are that it would make Bismarck master of Europe, & put an end to our cordial understanding with France: neither, to my mind, desirable results. I don't know whether they mean to publish what I have said to them, but it cannot harm me if they do.

Hear with some regret that the *Pall Mall Gazette*, the great organ of the Jingo party, is to change hands, & become a supporter of Gladstone – the editor, Greenwood[88], retiring from it. Though the views which it has expressed during the last 3 years are utterly opposed to mine, I am sorry that they are not to be expressed any more. The writing was always vigorous, & the leading articles showed real thought, though of a perverse kind. There is plenty of cleverness in the ordinary journalism of the day, but not much originality.

. . . The other speeches were indifferent. Gladstone could not speak badly if he tried, but the substance of what he said was commonplace: no particular point in it. . . . I sat [next to] Ld Coleridge[89]: he told me an almost incredible story of the Chief Baron, how within the last year or two he [Kelly] had been talking of the failure of the Chancellor's [Cairns's] health, of the difficulties of supplying his place, the weakness of the rising men: & plainly said that he thought Ld Beaconsfield would be forced to apply to him to take the place when it became vacant! The poor old man is notoriously incapable of doing the ordinary work of his present office, his memory not serving him from one hour to another. So at least the lawyers say.

Casual talk with Ld Halifax[90], who tells me that Lytton, in his late statement of Indian finance, has under-estimated the expenditure by six millions! As this statement was sent home just in time for the elections, & in fact had some influence, by representing matters as much better than anybody supposed them to be, it is difficult to think that he was not wilfully shutting his eyes to the facts. But Ld H. may have heard an exaggerated report.
. . .

4 May 1880: . . . See Mr. Hughes, late agent for the Knole estates, whom Ld Sackville[91] in a fit of insane suspicion or dislike has turned off for no assigned reason. He wants employment, & I should be glad to help him, but scarcely see how. . . .

5 May 1880: . . . Call in Curzon St. Hear that there is a good deal of grumbling & discontent at the distribution of offices, which I suppose always happens when a ministry is formed. Ld Cork[92] expected some place that he has not got: Sefton is disappointed: but the hardest case is thought to be that of Ld Carlingford, who with his wife kept open house for the party, & spent a fortune in entertainments. He gets nothing except an offer of the embassy at Constantinople, which he has refused[93]. The form which grumbling assumes is that of saying that nobody has a chance of promotion who has not paid personal court to Mr. or Mrs. Gladstone. Ld Ripon's nomination as Gov.-Gen. is sharply criticised, he not being thought strong enough for the place. This was & is my own opinion, & I hear it is that of all the world. But on the whole the distribution of posts has been good. Forster for Ireland is especially approved. . . .

7 May 1880: See Drage, who well satisfied with me, but is full of warning against chills.
Levee, which I attend . . . see Ripon there, who looks & speaks as if oppressed with the heavy work he has on hand. See Northcote, & congratulate him . . . Gladstone was standing against the wall, silent and with a very gloomy expression, as if success had brought him more weariness than pleasure. . . .

8 May 1880: . . . News . . . that Sir W. Harcourt is defeated at Oxford on vacating his seat after taking office[94]: an awkward blow for the Cabinet in the midst of their triumph, but they are strong enough to bear it. – Harcourt with all his cleverness is generally unpopular, from what strangers consider to be his sarcastic & overbearing manner: and he won at the general election by a small majority: but the reason of so sudden a change among the electors is unexplained. It is probable that the Conservatives [at Oxford] lost votes last month thinking themselves secure . . . It is more likely that a certain section of Whigs, or moderates, at Oxford are alarmed by the result of the elections, think the movement has gone too far, dislike the notion of having Gladstone at the head of affairs, & have gone round, or abstained from voting, in consequence of their fears. If so, the result is worth notice: since what has happened at Oxford may happen elsewhere. It is worth noting in this connection that Harcourt was stronger than anyone in favour of the exclusion of Gladstone, & of keeping power in the hands of the Whigs pure & simple. He swallowed his objections when he saw they were useless: but Gladstone knew of them &, if Ld Halifax is correct, Harcourt's elevation to the Home Office was not effected without difficulty. It is paradoxical, but possible, that he may now have been sacrificed to the prevalence among his friends of apprehensions & dislikes in which he himself fully shared, but which circumstances induced him to swallow.

9 May 1880 (Sunday): . . . In papers, a speech from Fawcett, accusing the late government of having been aware that the statement sent to them from India as to the condition of the revenue was inaccurate. According to him, they had a telegram to correct it which they received before the elections, but which they kept back: thus allowing the public to be misled into thinking the cost of the war £4,000,000 less than it was. This is so grave a charge that it seems equally hard to accept it as true, or to suppose that so careful a speaker as Fawcett usually is would have risked it without evidence. . . .

11 May 1880: . . . The papers are busy with a letter addressed by Gladstone to the Austrian Ambassador, for publication, in which he unsays many of the hard things which he has uttered against Austria in the course of his Midlothian canvas. Some explanation was no doubt necessary & desirable: but most people will think that, as he was unduly violent in accusation, so he is now needlessly humble in recantation. The explanation of both tendencies is the same – a vehement impulsiveness of disposition, not checked by sufficient reflection as to the effect which his words will produce. He finds he has done injustice, & hastens to make the amplest amends: but he forgets what a man less enthusiastic & more selfish would have borne in mind, that the very ease with which he abandons all defence of the language used by him is sure to be treated as a matter of reproach. It will be said: 'This kind of talk has served his purpose in opposition, & now he admits its unreality.' Nothing, I believe, could be further from the truth: but nothing is more certain to be said.

12 May 1880: To London. . . . Lit. Fund meeting at 3.00. Froude, Trollope, B. Hope [etc.], about a dozen in all present.

We voted to Mrs. Butt, widow of Isaac Butt, a grant of £80: not without some doubt, for her literary claim is slight, & her husband squandered recklessly the large income which during many years he made: but pity prevailed, though a proposal to grant her £100 was negatived. . . . In all £250 [was voted]. . . .

16 May 1880 (Whitsun Day): . . . Read again Sir C. Dilke's book on America, Australia, & India, which he rather affectedly calls *Greater Britain*: it deserves its popularity, being full of new matter & the style good. I see with amusement that protection to native industry, though treated as an economical error, is mentioned with much respect: while it was the theory of an aristocratic class, as in England, no words of censure could be strong enough: but, being taken up by democratic communities & vindicated on democratic grounds, it at once assumes a more respectable character. So also, though the American treatment of the negro as an inferior is repudiated as unjust, being assumed to be the result of feelings created by slavery, far more tenderness is shown to the equally strong aversion to Chinese labour of both Americans & Australians: though the sentiment of race superiority is exactly the same in one case as in the other. But on the whole the book is not unfair, & it is certainly interesting. The most noticeable speculation in it is whether the English race in the New World will altogether change its physical type, & reproduce that of the (so-called) red Indian, who is not red at all, but whom the New Englander already resembles far more closely than he does the typical Englishman. A more curious question can hardly be raised, but only Americans can throw much light upon it, & in their presence it is hardly safe to mention the subject.

17 May 1880: . . . News in papers that the Peace Preservation Act[95] for Ireland is not to be renewed: a bad hearing for Irish landlords, but it is believed that the late Cabinet had come to the same decision. If it had been decided to renew it, the whole short session would have been taken up with the screams of the Irish: & this objection probably had more weight than in justice it ought to have.

18 May 1880: Weather continues as before – bright, but cold & excessively dry.

News that the seat at Sandwich, vacated by the promotion of Knatchbull-Hugessen, is lost to the government, being carried by a local Conservative, Mr. Crompton-Roberts. It is odd that since their great victory they have lost Oxford, Sandwich, the Wigtown burghs, & another seat which I forget[96]. . . . The Opposition will lay the blame on Gladstone's Austrian letter, which no doubt is unpopular – the manner being disliked even where the matter is approved – but there has scarcely been time for that cause to operate.

19 May 1880: . . . Dined at Granville's parliamentary dinner, a very large party. Heard the speech read: it is long, moderate in tone, & does not promise more legislation than is reasonably possible in the time. (1) Burials, (2) Ballot Act renewed, (3) Ground game, (4) Liability of employers for injuries to workmen, (5) Extension of franchise in Irish towns. These are the subjects announced to be dealt with: the only alarming one is the last, & as to that it may be argued with some truth that nothing can make the Irish urban constituencies more revolutionary in temper than they are already. . . .

20 May 1880: . . . In Kensington gardens meet R. Montagu[97], so disguised in a grizzly beard & moustache that I did not know him at first. He talked just as he might have done 30 years ago: no man ever changed less with the progress of years: his mind the same odd mixture of cleverness & childishness as when he & I were both at Cambridge. He remains, I suppose, a Catholic, but is thoroughly disgusted with Irish priests & Irish agitators, & has said so in public. He thinks the feeling between classes growing worse & worse . . . He assures me that in 1872 or 73 Disraeli & Col. Taylor pressed him to come forward as a Catholic Home Ruler in the Conservative interest, offering him high place when they came in, or a permanent post, whichever he might prefer. He has the letters now. A singular contrast with the late Premier's attitude towards the Home Rulers in the last few months – ! Montagu is a loose talker, but he can hardly have invented this story.

. . . The D. of Marlborough rose to protest earnestly against the non-renewal of the Irish Peace Preservation Act, which expires on the 1st of June & is not to be continued. He evidently meant what he said, & I believe many of the peers on both sides agreed with him, & thought it a risk to do away with useful precautions at a time of public danger: but Ld Spencer, who followed, had an effective retort from the party point of view, for if the late Cabinet had meant to renew the Act (which they have never avowed) they left themselves no time to do it. The truth is, electioneering considerations have overridden all others, as in this country they always will. Ld Beaconsfield spoke briefly & with little effect. Physically, he showed no signs of weakness or failure: but his criticism had nothing in it that was meant to be serious: in short, his only object in speaking seemed to be to show that he held to his position as leader. Granville followed, & gave some explanations as to foreign affairs: but, though sensible, his speech was tame. In fact our debate was a mere form, & it does not seem to have been otherwise in the Commons.

Carnarvon has returned to the Conservative party, frightened by the majority & by the composition of the Cabinet. He has done right in his own interest, for the whole turn of his mind makes it impossible for him to adopt Liberal ideas as they exist in England. He is a strong churchman, proud of his ancestors having been loyal cavaliers, with a peculiar veneration for the memory of Charles I, & a good deal of sympathy with the Jacobites. He is clever & laborious: but rather flighty, like his brother Auberon[98], though their enthusiasm takes a different direction. . . . All his friends are on the Conservative side. In fact his quarrel was less with them than with Ld Beaconsfield personally. . . .

22 May 1880: Walk to B. Museum, for meeting of standing committee at 12.00. Walk back with Walpole. Much talk on public affairs. It is always satisfactory to talk with him, or rather to hear his ideas: few men are so really impartial, so incapable of doing injustice: which perhaps has been a cause of his partial failure. He tells me there is a 'cave' forming on the Conservative side: Northcote is thought too moderate & conciliatory & the hotter partisans are discontented. Chaplin, one of the hottest, is a genuine protectionist, so Walpole thinks. Just now the ultras on that side are hot to prevent Bradlaugh from taking his seat, on account of his avowed atheism. . . . Walpole is strong against the objectors, contending that there can be no right in the House to prevent a man from taking an oath which the House itself has imposed, he being willing to do so . . . to do so would be temporarily disenfranchising the constituency. I see no answer to his argument, & pressed him to speak on Monday . . . He tells me the debates are much fallen off since I knew them. They resemble a public meeting more than a parliamentary sitting: claptrap is preferred to argument, & personal wrangles distract attention from anything else. We talked of the elections; he agreed with me that there has been less of class bitterness & democratic hostility to the rich than might be expected, indeed less than in former years. But he thinks that a great social change is in progress, instancing especially the altered relations between landlords & tenants.

He told me that Ld Beaconsfield's speech to his party on Wednesday had been marked by more personal feeling than he had ever seen Ld B. display – and this touched his audience – otherwise it was not effective – and he implied that he thought Ld B.'s powers were falling off. But Ld B. has always been unequal – one day admirably good, another day heavy & long-winded. He does not know why he should have contradicted the report of the speech that appeared in the papers – which he has done even angrily in *The Times* – as to Walpole, who heard it, the summary seemed a fair one. . . .

24 May 1880: . . . Ld Granville calls . . . – He asks me an awkward question about Odo Russell – how far he (O.R.) is to be trusted when he reports the opinions of the govt. to which he is accredited? I answer: 'Odo would not, I think, mis-state a fact: but he is essentially a courtier, and extremely anxious to please the person he is speaking to: so much so that I should not trust him to report faithfully an unfavourable opinion, or to express an opinion of his own which he knew would not agree with yours.' Ld G. thanked me, saying that his impression as to O.R. had been the same as mine.

25 May 1880: Read the Bradlaugh debate of yesterday evening in H. of C. with little pleasure, for the speeches seem mostly poor . . . It is noticed that none are hotter against him than Catholics & Jews, both themselves admitted to sit within the memory of living men. It is noticed also as curious that the two leading champions of religion & morality are Drummond Wolff & Randolph Churchill. The former of these two was left out by Disraeli in forming the Cabinet of 1874 expressly on the grounds of his general bad reputation (for of his cleverness there is no question): the latter narrowly escaped expulsion from a London club, some 4 or 5 years ago, on account of a scrape in which he was involved with others: I have forgotten the details. Northcote, who must know better, was dragged at the heels of his party: & obliged to give a hesitating adhesion to their view . . .

26 May 1880: . . .London U. at 4.00, where a large meeting of the Senate: Granville in the chair. . . .

. . . Walk from Burlington House with Granville: take the opportunity of recommending to him the claims of Sir E. Thornton[99] who has been 13 years at Washington, an expensive & disagreeable post: & who has a moral claim to an embassy if one falls vacant. He tells me that the Italians are anxious to be authorised by Europe to enforce the execution of the Berlin treaty in Albania – Did I think the proposal feasible? I said certainly not – their appearance on the scene would excite extreme jealousy in Austria: they were too near to be disinterested, & they would not make the offer except with the idea of getting something for themselves out of it. Still less would it be liked in England if, as G. hinted, a vote had to be taken to pay for an Italian occupation out of English funds. – He then asked what answer I should give, if it rested with me, to a question about to be put, as to the existence or otherwise of any secret treaty with Russia. He was rather in favour of refusing to give any answer whatever. He then told me the facts, which are that Russia, in return for the cession of Batoum, has given some sort of pledge not to meddle with Turkish Asia – a pledge of no value, since it is only in the sense of what Russia is already bound to by public treaty, but it is a signed engagement. I told him, I thought the jealousy of parliament in the matter of secret treaties was legitimate, & that a refusal to answer would cause dissatisfaction. The answer I would give would be to the effect that no engagement or obligation existed on the part of England to do or abstain from doing anything, except what was already known to the public . – I thought the matter so important that after going home I wrote the form of answer which I should use – which I now rather regret doing as it may seem fussy. . . .

28 May 1880: . . . Called on Ly Cowley, & heard details of [Ld] Malmesbury's approaching marriage. He is 73, & has been infirm for years – indeed he resigned on the ground of health.

29 May 1880: . . . Mr., or Capt., Mills called by appointment to talk over South African affairs: he was requested by Sir B. Frere, or some of the family, to see me. He explained various details which were new to me: & in regard of the Zulu war acknowledged plainly that the object was policy & not defence – that the destruction of the Zulu power was necessary before the colonies can be induced to confederate, as the Cape parliament would not take on itself the liability for an impending Zulu war. He added, however, as if it were an afterthought, that we should soon have been attacked ourselves if we had not taken the first step. From what he said I gather that the Transvaal is the difficulty in the way of confederation. Troops must be kept there, the English & Dutch being on bad terms, & the natives restless. He remarked as the peculiarity of S. Africa that the black men are increasing more rapidly than the whites – making government more difficult. He spoke well of the Fingoes as docile & capable of some civilisation. I thought him a frank sensible gentleman, likely to give an honest report of things as they seemed to him.
. . . It is not yet a fortnight since the session opened, & ministers are decidedly less popular than they were with their own party. . . . Three blunders have been made – one the assumption by the Premier of a second office besides his own, thus hurting the vanity of his followers, & lessening their share of patronage. The second, the undue & unnecessary humility of the Austrian apology – right in substance, wrong in form. The last, & by far the most serious, is the non-recall of Frere, which has been received with unconcealed disappointment, & even disgust, by the bulk of the Liberal party. Whether right or wrong from an administrative point of view, it is a mistake in the party sense, since it makes the

violent language used by nearly all the present Cabinet against Frere seem to have been uttered for electioneering purposes only. The error is rather one of tact than of wrongdoing: but here, as in the Austrian case, the contrast between office & opposition is too marked. Impulsiveness & mobility look like insincerity, though in reality it is the excess rather than the want of candour that is in fault. . . .

31 May 1880: . . . H. of Lords at 5.00, where a debate . . . on the system of state-aided schools, opened by Ld Norton[100]: he was as usual well informed & sensible but ineffective from want of method: it was not easy to see what was his drift, and what he wanted to prove: his speech, however, though rather dull, was of the most inoffensive kind. To everybody's surprise, Richmond took it as a personal attack, & answered him with marked rudeness & loss of temper: seeming as if he took pains to show his contempt for the criticism which he was attempting to answer. Lowe (Ld Sherbrooke) followed, listened to with curiosity & interest: he was inferior to what he used to be in the Commons, saying the same thing over & over again, & at one moment he all but broke down, forgetting what he wanted to say & pausing in a painful manner. He has done this, I am told, several times of late. Ld Aberdare & Ld Spencer I did not hear, having to come home.

1 June 1880: Saw Sir C. Trevelyan[101] & Stansfeld, at their request, about a scheme for a new provident dispensary system, which Sir C.T. has taken up very warmly, & explained at length. He is not the most successful supporter of such schemes that could be found: want of tact and a conscientious desire to leave no part of his argument undealt with make him tedious, and at meetings where I have heard him speak he has generally ended by being hooted down. But he is very laborious, a good economist, & what he has to say is generally in substance worth hearing. I listened, & promised to read the papers they had brought: which was all the answer they expected.

H. of Lords, where Cairns got his land bills read a second time: but the govt. does not care to take them up, & they will drop.

Monthly returns from Statter, who is again in a despondent mood – indeed he has never been out of one – sees no sign of improvement, & does not believe in it. . . . It is odd that, while this depression prevails in Manchester, the growth of new building should be as rapid as ever at & near Liverpool. The cause of the difference is not explained.

2 June 1880: Pender[102] calls early: tells me of the state of feeling in the Commons: there is great dissatisfaction, he says, felt with Gladstone, who is thought to act entirely on his own judgment, & to consult nobody. The appointment of Lord Ripon[103], & still more that of Lord Kenmare[104], has caused deep resentment. The latter would seem harmless enough, but it appears that the Scotch have got it into their heads that it gives a Popish peer direct personal access to the Queen, which of course he cannot fail to use in support of his religion. Anyway, they are deeply offended. The nonconformists think Gladstone has been too favourable to Bradlaugh, though it is not easy to see what he has done that was not absolutely required by justice: but the chief grievance is the non-recall of Frere, which is considered not quite unreasonably to be a recantation of the language held by the Premier himself & his chief supporters, before & during the elections. . . .

3 June 1880: House of Lords at 5.00, where a large attendance: 40 to 50 ladies in the gallery, & nearly all the bishops. The debate was dull on the whole. The Bp. of Lincoln[105], who opened it, spoke with a certain force but his prophecies of ruin to the church establishment were such as the occasion did not justify, & seemed rather conventional than as though he really meant them. The Abp. of Canterbury[106] answered him, sensible, but not lively: Cranbrook evidently thought the question settled, & indeed it was not easy to defend the interests of the church where the primate had surrendered them. He did not declaim at all, in his usual fiery style, & scarcely spoke half an hour. Ld Brabourne[107] (Knatchbull-Hugessen) let off a fluent torrent of commonplace, rather of the sanctimonious description. Some others followed: I spoke from 8.20 to near 9.00, in a thin House, but chose that time partly as being tired of waiting, partly because the debate seemed likely to drop. At 10.00, the Chancellor summed up the arguments, & we divided a little before 11.00: 126 for, 101 against, the second reading. I do not believe the Opposition wanted to win, nor that the govt. would have greatly cared about a defeat, for an outcry against the H. of Lords might have been useful in bringing together the scattered fragments of the Liberal party – which has already begun to quarrel. The non-recall of Frere is to many Liberals a bitter mortification & not unreasonably so.

4 June 1880: . . . Mr. Morley tells me of great discontent among Liberals, in which he appears to share: the immediate cause is Frere's business, which he feels so strongly upon that he & many others want to raise the question again in parliament, & obtain a reversal of the decision not to recall him. We had some talk, & at the end of it he asked leave to call upon me, which I willingly agreed to.

Léon Say[108] talked freely of French affairs, taking a view of the situation which was rather despondent than sanguine. He thought the danger from the ultra-republican party considerable: they were numerous, & utterly intolerant . . . . . . The above is rather a summary than a reproduction of our talk, which was in French: but I am sure that in substance it is accurate.

5 June 1880 (Saturday): Keston by an early train . . .

My speech of Thursday [on burials] appears by the papers to have given satisfaction, one side being satisfied, & the other not offended. In fact the view taken by me, that the nonconformists have no claim as of right to the concession they ask for, but that it is harmless in itself, & may be granted without injury to anybody, is I believe the exact truth, but it does not suit either side to represent the matter so in argument. Thus I had an opportunity of saying what many thought, but did not care to express. I had written out enough of the substance of my speech to secure a good report in the papers: which can scarcely be got in any other way.

. . . Read another article[109] on the same subject [the general election defeat] by Kebbel, the Conservative essayist, which is more to the purpose, though still inconclusive. His reasons are that the dissolution was not expected on the ministerial side, their candidates were taken unprepared: that they were over-secure, believing in the popularity of their policy & did not exert themselves: that in many cases sitting members had neglected their constituencies, which were being assiduously canvassed in the opposite interest (but surely this would be true of both sides equally?), that there was a want of money on the Conservative side (this I believe to be true): that the working class mostly read none but radical newspapers (this also I believe, but it was equally the case in 1874): lastly, that the modern system of living, railways, & the centralising of business in

London, have lessened the importance of local magnates: which is no doubt a fact, but not more so in 1880 than 6 years ago. . . .

7 June 1880: Day windy & rather wet: drove in to the station instead of walking . . . Peabody trust meeting at 4.30, sat till 5.15. Sir C. Lampson, his son, & Mr. Lowell, the new U.S. minister, the others present. . . . We came to two decisions: one to employ Cubitt as the builder of our new houses, instead of going to competition, by which we should get worse work a very little cheaper.

I was pleased with Mr. Lowell[110], whom I had not met before: he is a gentleman of the European type, having nothing of the Yankee about him, either in manner or in voice. We had but little conversation, but I hope to improve the acquaintance.

H. of Lords at 5.30, where found Stanley of A. [lderley][111] denouncing the govt., as his manner is, in a confidential whisper: so low that Argyll, who was to answer, had to leave his place & sit in front of the Woolsack in order to hear him. . . . Marlborough[112] raised a sort of debate on Ireland, in which the two chief speakers were Dunsany[113] & Oranmore[114], neither of them lively speakers, & both great alarmists as to Irish matters, but I thought them substantially right, & told Granville so when leaving the House. They contended that agrarian intimidation is as rife as ever, & that increased protection against violence is necessary, if mob law is not to be supreme. – Home, quiet evening. . . .

11 June 1880: In the papers, news of a supplementary budget which Gladstone has brought in, & about which there was a good deal of apprehension in some quarters, it being thought that he would not be able to refrain from a general remodelling of taxation. Radicals hoped, & moderate men feared, some large change injuriously affecting property. But what he has done is harmless enough: the malt tax is turned into a tax on beer, the wine duties are reduced as part of the negociation with France for a new commercial treaty, spirit dealers' licences are increased, and a penny is added to the income tax. There is nothing in all this to object to, indeed I think it probable that Northcote would have increased the income tax if the prospect of a general election had not deterred him. . . .

12 June 1880: . . . From the papers, & from some letters received, I gather that the new budget is a success. The farmers of the eastern counties have got the thing for which they were always crying out, & probably will never discover, or not for a long while, that they are paying the same tax under a new name. The change in wine duties is right, though not very important. The extra penny of income tax for the year was expected, & will not be much grudged. So easily is public attention diverted, & so rapid is the succession of events that this well managed affair will cause Frere's business to be forgotten. The Burials Bill also seems unlikely to give trouble. The game bill is disliked, rather for the principle which it establishes than for its actual results: and Bradlaugh's case threatens to waste much time, though it cannot admit of more than one ending. What was less anticipated, I hear of a good deal of resistance to the Bill extending the powers of savings banks to receive deposits. The bankers talk of state competition & probably are right in supposing that it will lessen their profits.

13 June 1880: . . . Read a long letter, addressed nominally to M. but really meant for me, from Morier. It is in his old style. He wants Constantinople: says so frankly, & that he thinks he shall be able to make a name there. So far all is right: and I do not much dissent from a rather vehement protest which he makes against the bringing in of any outsider, as being unfair to the service. But he has got hold of an idea, right or wrong, that Ld Napier[115] is to be preferred to him: & thereupon proceeds to give Ld N. such a character as not many men outside Newgate have ever deserved. He speaks of him as tricky, dishonest, a liar, & half a dozen more such epithets. This is Morier's way, and it has done him harm in the office, giving him a reputation for intrigue not wholly deserved.

14 June 1880: Received an application from Jennings, formerly head gardener here, to the effect that he is past 70, ill, & disabled from work: of course he has not a shilling put by, & is asking old acquaintance to maintain him. I send £5 for his immediate wants & make enquiry with a view to helping him further. But it is only in England that a man, respectable in conduct and having held well paid posts for many years, would not have thought of making any provision for his old age. . . .

15 June 1880: Left for London, alone, & rather unwillingly: but, the Lords being in committee on the Burials Bill, I thought it not well to be away. Left Knowsley 10.20 . . . & in the House by 5.30. The debate or rather series of debates was not very interesting but sensible. The speakers knew their subject &, except a rather silly speech from Ld Forbes[116], they all argued to the purpose.

Salisbury moved an amendment exempting from the operation of the bill all land given for burial purposes to the Church of England within the last 50 years. This was merely a pretext for destroying the bill, since the clause, if passed, would have made the whole unworkable: though he consented to modify it so far as to require that the representatives of the donors should signify their desire that the amendment should be put into force. Two other amendments were carried, a good many Liberals voting for them – their effect being, in general terms, that the churchyards shall remain as at present wherever nonconformist burials are already provided for by their having a cemetery or burial place of their own within reach. There is nothing to my mind very unreasonable in this proviso, but the nonconformists will not accept it, for what they really value is the social advantage of seeing their ministers put more nearly on an equality with those of the establishment: this, much more than the practical inconveniences of the law as it stands, has been the motive for agitation. The House sat till past 10.00, but I left before 9.00, all the clauses I cared about being then settled. I did not speak. The discussion is badly reported. Dined Travellers . . .

The papers are full of a disreputable scene in the Commons: one O'Donnell[117], who is among the wildest of the Irish, & professes strong clerical sympathies, asked a question imputing to the new French ambassador certain disgraceful acts in the late civil troubles. He was answered, but persisted in his attack, denying the truth of the answer given, & moved the adjournment. Thereupon Gladstone, taking advantage of a form which has not been in use for 200 years, moved 'That Mr. O'D. be not heard': Northcote doubted the wisdom of the proceeding: Harcourt attacked him as sympathising with the obstructors: violent feeling was shown on all sides, & the House became a bear-garden. Nothing more unlucky could have happened. For Gladstone's action was quite as irregular as that which he tried to check: & he has brought into use a new weapon of obstruction which the Irish will know better than anyone else how to use. . . . Except *The Times* & *Standard*, no paper now attempts to give more than a brief summary of the debate: & even these ignore any debate that goes on beyond a certain hour. Parliament never was more power-ful than now: but it is not respected, at least among the upper classes, in proportion to its power.

16 June 1880: . . . The question of my right to sell any part of the Bury estates . . . is estab-lished by the discovery of a document whose existence was not known. Lawrence suggests on the strength of this discovery that a competent antiquarian should be sent down to Knowsley to examine the muniment room & put it in order.

I may now count on receiving within the year at least £76,000 from the L. & Y. Co. which was not payable while the dispute as to title lasted.

Hear that the D. of Bedford[118] has bought a place in the Isle of Wight, called Norris Castle, close to Osborne. It is only 150 acres, & he gives £65,000, but the situation was singularly good, & he is fond of yachting.

17 June 1880: Day very wet . . . with strong, warm east wind which destroys the leaves by depositing smoke & acids upon them. . . . I cannot doubt but that to the east of the park every tree of more than a moderate size & age is being destroyed . . . I often wonder – will another generation be willing to live here? If the towns continue to extend as they have done, anything like country life at Knowsley will be out of the question. But at the worst my successors will be compensated for their loss in pleasure, so far as money can make up for it: the letting value of building land in this district would be enormous.

18 June 1880: Up early, & left home at 8.00. Preston at 10.00, where met my brother: & with him to Blackpool: on the platform we met the mayor & most of the town council. Visited the Free Library which was to be opened, & then with the mayor & town clerk in a carriage drawn by four horses paraded the streets at the head of a long procession. My brother was in the next carriage & about 20 others followed. Most of the population seemed to be in the streets to look on: they cheered & shouted in a very hearty way, but with less enthusiasm than the Southport people did last year: perhaps only because there were fewer of them. After two hours of this performance we went to a place called the winter garden, where in a large room nearly full the mayor, my brother, & I made our speeches. None were long: an address of thanks was presented to me by the Town Clerk, & read aloud. We visited the sights, which are few: a fernery, skating-rink, concert room, etc. Then at 3.00 luncheon, or dinner (of course the provincials called it a banquet) in a sort of wooden house, or pavilion, on the pier: the mayor in the chair, toasts & speeches, tedious enough. The business lasted three hours. We were escorted back to the station . . . home, arriving about 9.30. Very weary, but glad the business is done. Wearisome as such ceremonies are, & an utter waste of time, they are necessary, if local popularity is to be maintained. – The day was luckily fine . . .

The H. of Lords, on the invitation of Ld Norton, has passed a resolution on the subject of education about which opinion will be a good deal divided. The object of it is to confine the primary schools, supported by rates, to elementary teaching: it being contended that the teachers have grown too ambitious, & deal with subjects which are useless to the class of scholars which they teach, & which cannot possibly be learnt to any purpose in the time allowed. In this last objection there is undoubtedly some force, & the objectors ought to have rested more upon it, instead of talking invidiously as to the uselessness of teaching ploughboys Latin & so forth – which may be quite true, but which unnecessarily stirs up democratic jealousy. The resolution was opposed by ministers, & they were right: for the Lords have really no power in the matter & they went out of their way to express an unpopular opinion which they cannot enforce. Oddly enough Richmond, who was almost offensive in his answer to Norton three weeks ago, when Norton said exactly the same thing as he has now repeated, found out that after all they were agreed, & supported him warmly. The thing is on the whole a mistake, but not a very important one[119].

19 June 1880: . . . Wrote to Hale . . . agreeing that Mr. Moore[120], a lawyer & antiquarian, who is to be employed . . . in putting the muniment room in order, shall come down at once & lodge in the house while we are away.

. . . In the papers, news that Sir W. Lawson has carried his resolution on local option for the first time by 229 to 203: not a large House, but many must have stayed away on purpose. Gladstone rather oddly voted against it himself, but said he would put no pressure on his friends, & his Cabinet in consequence supported Lawson. The result is that he is pledged to try next year to amend the licensing laws on the basis of local option – not an easy matter for, of whose who by their votes affirmed the principle, no two are agreed as to what they wish done.– It is perhaps inevitable that a long period of stagnation should lead to haste when parliament wakes up again, but to those who wish well to the ministry it is a matter of regret that the danger of 1873 should be courted again. – 'Harassed interests' will soon be the cry as it was then, & perhaps with more reason. The clergy are sore at the Burials Bill – bankers resent, & are trying to oppose, the quite legitimate extension of the savings bank system: the publicans will now draw together as one man to resist attacks on their business: landowners as a rule dislike the bill brought in by Harcourt which transfers ground game to the tenant, giving no power to either him or the landlord to contract themselves out of the bill: and Forster has rather hastily pledged himself to a measure limiting the power of the Irish landowner to evict without compensation in cases where the rent is not paid. This last proceeding is the strangest of all, inasmuch as Irish landlords had the strongest possible assurances given them in 1870 that their rights, though limited by the act of that year, were now settled on a legal basis, & would not be again disturbed.

It is not unlikely to be dropped, but the mere threat will have done harm, encouraging the agitators by hopes of more support than they will get. The Bradlaugh difficulty again will lead to angry debates & give much trouble. It is the fashion to say that it has been mismanaged but, as far as I can see, nobody had a solution ready &, the case being new, it was perhaps hardly to be expected that they should have. Altogether, government have got on hand more work than they can possibly get through in the time remaining this year: &, by aiming at more than they can accomplish, they will produce an appearance of failure. On the other hand, the budget seems certain to pass, & is accepted as a success. And, whatever happens to the hares & rabbits bill, it has answered its purpose of pleasing the farmers. . . .

21 June 1880: . . . Letter from Harcourt, the Home Sec., asking me to serve as chairman of a commission on the City charities – nearly the same request that Cross made to me two years ago. I have not refused, nor yet accepted, but asked questions as to the nature & extent of the enquiry, & arranged to see Harcourt before giving a final answer. The work will be unpopular, whoever does it, & probably laborious: if any result is to follow.

I do not care for one or other, but it is silly to work hard & be abused & after all get nothing done.

22 June 1880: . . . Sanderson called, & talked rather gloomily about ministerial prospects. He said Harcourt had already succeeded in making himself intensely unpopular, he did not know why or how, but so the fact was: & several of the bills now before parliament are much disliked. – Harcourt then talked about business at home & abroad, rather in the same strain as Sanderson had before him: he thought Afghanistan was as bad as it could be, there was no decent candidate to put forward, Yakoub[121] was imbecile as well as treacherous, Abdurrahman[122] he said would not do, he was going to explain why, but did not. However, he said they were quite determined to get out of the country, whether a good govt. could be established there or not. He said Lytton had been coming home full of anger, & ready to vindicate his policy, but the financial exposure, which he (L.) did not in the least expect, had altered his tone, & he was now deeply depressed. As to business in parliament, he thought very badly of it. The policy of obstruction was being pursued, even the budget was not likely to pass without great delay: there was no hope of getting much in the way of commercial advantages out of the French: they might probably enough have to drop nearly all their bills in order to get the financial work finished. He thought the ground game bill would not be sharply resisted by the squires, as many of them, though they did not like it, saw the impolicy of going against the farmers. But it was a chance whether it reached the H. of Lds at all, & he does not seem to care if it has to be put off till next year. . . .

23 June 1880: Lawson *(D.T.[elegraph])* called & talked about things in general. He seemed of opn that matters were not satisfactory, & that very little would be done in parliament. He confirmed what I had heard of the unpopularity of the Irish bill, & that it had never been before the Cabinet at all, being settled by Forster & Gladstone. He thought the ground game bill also would be dropped for the year. Supposed the Bradlaugh business had been mismanaged, but did not well see what ought to have been done in it.

Harcourt called a little later. I agreed to take the chair of his proposed commission & wrote to the D. of Bedford, who made his acceptance dependent on mine. He talked of the Bradlaugh business, which is in greater confusion than ever, the House having by a majority of 45 voted against allowing him to affirm, & by a later resolution declaring that he shall not take the oath either. This in the teeth of the government, who contended for his admission. In Harcourt's opinion, the fault lay with the Speaker, who ought to have overruled at once, as disorderly, any attempt to prevent Bradlaugh from taking the oath in the usual way. There is now no choice except to bring in a general bill substituting affirmations for oaths at the pleasure of the person swearing or affirming.

. . . Morier dined with us: his talk, as usual with him, alternately pleasant from the clearness of his ideas & his vigour in expressing them: & disagreeable from the uncontrollable egotism & conceit of the man, stimulated by friendly sympathy. He is vehemently angry with both the Foreign & Colonial offices – with the latter especially, which he accuses of having caused the non-ratification of the treaty which had cost him great labour & pains, & which he regarded as a signal success. It fell through at the last moment, the final sanction of England being delayed until a change of ministry in Portugal brought in the party which had opposed it from the first. But, on enquiry, I find that Morier had taken on himself to make terms for the Col. Office without the latter having been consulted: & Morier I think is unreasonable when he makes it a grievance that they wished to have a voice in their own departmental affairs. He all but quarrelled with Ld Kimberley, whose reception of him he describes as insulting – & it is true that Ld K.'s manner is often unconciliatory. But he evidently came prepared to take offence &, where that is the case, provocation is seldom wanting. I smoothed him down as well as I could: but the truth is he had satisfied himself that his treaty was a great diplomatic victory, & that he had earned by it the embassy at Constantinople: which on coming home he finds almost certain to be otherwise disposed of. . . .

25 June 1880 (Friday): Statter called unexpectedly: . . . He is more gloomy than ever in his predictions. Something is due to lowered vitality: he talks with far less than his old overbearing energy, & actually allowed me to put in a word now & then. . . . Walk: call on A.D.: . . .

H. of Lds at 5.00 for the deceased wife's sister's [Bill]: Houghton[123] opened the debate, speaking fairly well: Beauchamp[124] followed: Coleridge made an artful speech, ignoring the ecclesiastical part of the question, which as all know is with him the really important part, & jumping over the difficulties of his argument in the old style. Granville answered him: the Bp of Oxford[125] hit the real blot, pointing out the necessity of drawing up a new table of prohibited degrees: the Bp of Lincoln preached a sort of sermon, till he was put down by general impatience. We divided 101 to 90 – a larger minority than has been yet known in the Lords.

. . . Having a carriage at the House, & the night being wet, I took Granville home, & on the way took the opportunity of warning him of the extreme unpopularity of Forster's Irish bill. This bill takes away for a year & more the landlord's remedy of evicting a tenant for non-payment of rent, if in the opinion of a county court judge the tenant is really unable to pay. Practically, it will operate over the 16 Irish counties to which it applies as a relief to the tenant from the necessity of paying his rent in any case: for it will seldom or never be possible to prove that he has the means: his word will be taken: & the local judges must be more than human if they are not influenced by the universal clamour & terrorism to which they will be exposed. The unfairness of it is shown by this – that it is not proposed to relieve the tenant from the pressure of other creditors, so that his whole available means may be taken as a debt by the local tradesman or moneylender: it is only the landlord whose claim is suspended. By the Irish, who consider the land as their own, & rent as an exaction to which they submit only because they cannot help themselves, this temporary relief will be regarded as merely the preparatory step to abolishing rents altogether. How the Cabinet came to sanction such a measure I cannot imagine: probably the truth is as commonly believed, that they were never consulted as a body till the scheme was launched.

The Bradlaugh trouble has passed into a new phase. Mr. Bradlaugh on Wednesday claimed his seat, & was informed that the House forbade his taking the oath: he persisted, defied the authority of the Speaker, & was taken into custody, which was exactly what he wanted: Gladstone, having resisted the resolution which was carried on Tuesday night, excluding Bradlaugh, left the initiative of these proceedings with Northcote & the opposition, while admitting that they had now become inevitable: the victors were considerably embarrassed by their own success &, though no submission was made by the prisoner, they voted his release on Thursday: possibly the least foolish thing that could be done as matters stood, but obviously weak & inconsistent. Bradlaugh is at this moment the most conspicuous figure in England, & he is not a man to lose any chance of notoriety. The House has taken up a position from which it must recede, & it cannot recede without loss of dignity. It is announced that on Tuesday next Gladstone will state what the Cabinet mean to do. A bill would be the proper course: but, from what Granville said, I gather that they dislike that plan, as involving too great expenditure of time & loss of all their other bills by delay. They hope, he says, that the House may be induced to rescind its late resolution. In that case, all goes smoothly: but if they are mistaken?

26 June 1880: . . . Parliamentary affairs are in a curiously complicated condition. The H. of C. has before it more business than can be dealt with in the time allowed: obstruction is rampant: & it is increased by the fact that Northcote has either virtually retired from leading the opposition, or is deposed: for the more factious part of the party seem to care only for impeding legislation, in order to discredit the govt.: & they overbear the rest. We are at the end of June, two months are the utmost that can be counted on: and there remain on hand (1) Budget, (2) Burials, (3) Savings Bank, (4) Hares and rabbits, (5) Irish relief, (6) Irish compensation to evicted tenants – which is a separate bill, (7) Bradlaugh case: of which all except (5) are likely to lead to controversy, & some will be very hotly disputed. Walpole, who is as little of a partisan as is well possible to any one engaged in public life, tells me that Gladstone does not manage the House skilfully. But, if matters were otherwise, time would fail for all that has been attempted. . . .

28 June 1880: London by usual train . . . fine warm day. Sanderson called, said, as Harcourt did on Tuesday, that Afghan affairs are going badly: but did not give details, & I did not ask them: he heard there had been a good deal of difference in the Cabinet about the Irish land bill: no wonder!

. . . Mr. R. Philips[126] of Bury & Mr. Hugh Mason[127] call to ask help for the registration expenses of south-east Lancashire. They say that the contest in that division of the county cost the Liberals £10,000: in the south-west it was £8,000. They agreed that with the new large constituencies expenses are heavier than they ever were before: & this quite legally: the cost of printing is enormous, & the conveyance of voters from a distance is not effected for nothing.

. . . Gladstone gives notice of his resolution for admitting Bradlaugh to affirm, subject to the legal penalties if any: which leaves the question to be decided by a court of law. The solution is weak & not wholly satisfactory, but probably the best that could be reached without infinite trouble & delay. It is in effect a rescission of the vote of last week: but with such verbal differences as may seem to save the credit of members.

The feeling against the Irish bill, notwithstanding a very able defence of it by Forster, is apparently as strong as ever: & I doubt its passing the Lords unaltered.

29 June 1880: . . . Saw Major Roberts[128] on the question of paying our servants monthly instead of quarterly, which is a growing custom, & a good one, as it saves them from having to borrow, or leave debts unpaid.

Layard called, & we had a good deal of talk. He is naturally ill pleased with the present state of things. He says the present Sultan is undoubtedly at times mad, luckily his madness does not take the form of cruelty, but he suspects everybody, thinks he is going to be murdered, & that whoever advises him does so with a treacherous design. With all this, according to Layard, he is very clever: & has succeeded in concentrating power in his own hands to a greater degree than any of his predecessors. His ministers are mere tools. He gave an instance where one of them was caught in telling him some story notoriously untrue, which the minister being pressed could not deny to be so, but said he had the Sultan's positive commands to hold this language. Layard does not understand where all the revenue that is collected goes to: thinks it must be £14,000,000 at least, & nobody is paid, not even the troops or the high officials: he knows a case of a Turk at Constantinople, lately in high place, selling his ring to get bread for his family. He believes the Sultan is making a hoard in view of impending war. He says the Russians are playing their old game of professing friendship to the Porte, & offering to screen the Turkish officials against pressure from Europe. Does not like the state of matters in Albania: twice, he says, already the Cabinets have had to give way to Albanian resistance & the same thing may happen a third time. He spoke of the three years he has passed at Constantinople as the most disagreeable of his life: which I can well believe.

. . . **Note** that I took an opportunity of telling [Lord] Cork[129], as the ministerial whip, my objections to the Irish bill: he thought it had not a chance of passing, & said so rather exultantly.

30 June 1880: Mr. G. Smith[130] of Coalville called by appointment: I saw him for the first time: a professional philanthropist if ever there was one: full of plans for the benefit of gypsy children – the class whose interest he has taken up: but not disguising his wish for employment under the act which he is trying to get passed. I gave him some advice as to the way of proceeding, & satisfied him that he has no chance of getting a bill through this year.

. . . The Premier called on M. this afternoon[131], & talked freely of the situation: thought the Irish bill had been much misunderstood as it put the Irish landlord in no worse a position than the English (surely a strange saying!): the debate would clear up that matter: but he complained that there were twenty questions on hand, each of them enough to upset a government, yet which must be dealt with.

Notes

[1] That of Lancashire.

[2] 5th Baron Calthorpe (1826–1893): educ. Eton and Trinity: M.P. (Lib.) Worcs. E. 1859–1868: succ. father 1868: d. unm.

[3] Head agent at Knowsley.

[4] An intermittent sufferer from alcoholism.

[5] (Sir) Joseph Crosland (1826–1904) of Royds Wood, Huddersfield, a leading light in all aspects of Huddersfield life: a firm Cons., a Churchman in later life, M.P. Huddersfield 1893–1895: kt 1889: member of joint committee to further the creation of Huddersfield Technical College: mechanically gifted.

[6] Professor Sir H.E. Roscoe (1833–1915), professor of chemistry, Owens College, 1857–1885: M.P. (Lib.) Manchester S. 1885–1895.

[7] Walter T.W.S. Stanhope (1827–1911), M.P. (Cons.) West Riding South 1872–1880: 1st class in maths.

[8] Sir J.W. Ramsden (1831–1914): M.P. (Lib.) for various seats 1853–1885: educ. Eton and Trinity: m. dau. of D. of Somerset.

9   Speech on Industrial Condition of England, given at Huddersfield, 8 January 1880: printed in *Speeches and Addresses of Edward Henry XVth Earl of Derby K.G.*, ed. Sanderson and Roscoe (1894), ii, 29–41.

10   The proposed bishopric for Liverpool.

11   Speech on Savings Banks, delivered at Liverpool, 16 January 1880: printed in *Speeches and Addresses of Edward Henry XVth Earl of Derby K.G.*, selected and edited by Sir T.H. Sanderson and E.S. Roscoe (London, 1894), ii, 42–49.

12   Estate accountant at Knowsley.

13   Col. William Edward Sackville-West (1830–1905), Lady Derby's youngest brother.

14   William Molyneux, 4th E. of Sefton (1835–1897): succ. 1855: leader of Whig party in S. Lancs.: lord-lieut. of Lancs. 1858–1897.

15   Robert Durning Holt, leader of Liberal party in Liverpool: first Lord Mayor of city (1893).

16   Dr. John Watts (1818–1887), social reformer: Ph.D. Giessen 1844: leading advocate of municipal socialism in Manchester area: vigorous pamphleteer.

17   Edward Adolphus Seymour, 12th D. of Somerset (1804–1885), leading whig; 1st lord of admiralty 1859–1866.

18   John William Ramsay, 13th E. of Dalhousie (1847–1887), styled Lord Ramsay 1874–July 1880: succ. father July 1880: M.P. (Lib.) Liverpool April–July 1880: Sec. for Scotland March–August 1886: m. 1877, dau. of E. of Tankerville. He died in a French hotel one day after her.

19   Edward Gibbon of Rose-hill, Gateacre, deputy-lieut. for Lancs., a small landowner and active magistrate.

20   Possibly Col. Thomas Wilson, V.D. (1806–1889) of Hillside, chairman of Toxteth Local Board: served in Ceylon: col. 1873–death: gen. on ret. list 1877.

21   H.T. Buckle (1821–1862), author of *History of Civilisation in England* (1857 and 1861).

22   Probably Christopher Bushell (1811–1887), wine merchant at Liverpool, philanthropist, and earnest Churchman: established Liverpool Council of Education, for helping elementary school children to take their studies further: sometime chairman of Liverpool School Board, President of Liverpool Chamber of Commerce, vice-president Liverpool University College, 1880.

23   Martin Tupper (1810–1889), author of *Proverbial Philosophy* (1838–1842). His father had worked for the diarist's father.

24   This came to nothing: as Disraeli wrote (29 January 1880),: 'The Ld. Chancellor, attacked by asthma for the first time, was so frightened that he rushed to Bournemouth, where he found the fog blacker than here' (M. and B., vi, 506).

25   J.G. Biggar (1828–1890), bigamist; Philip Callan (1837–1902), intriguer and Unionist client: T.D. Sullivan (1827–1914), editor and M.P. 1880–1900.

26   H.C. Rawlinson, 'The situation in Afghanistan', *Nineteenth Century*, Vol. 7, February 1880, pp. 197–215.

27   William Onslow, 4th E. of Onslow (1853–1911): succ. his great-uncle, 1870: held junior offices under Salisbury: a senior freemason: agriculture minister 1903–1905: chairman of committees, House of Lords, 1905–1911.

28   Laurence Parsons, 6th E. of Rosse (1840–1908), styled Lord Oxmantown 1841–1867: succ. his father 1867: Rep. Peer (I.) 1868–1908: Chancellor of Dublin University 1885–1908: F.R.S. 1867: pres. of Royal Irish Academy 1896–1901.

29   Secretary for India 1868–1874.

30   Secretary for India 1878–1880.

31   E.B. Eastwick (1814–1883), orientalist: M.P. Penryn 1868–1874: sec. of legation to Persian court 1860–1863.

32   Edward Stanhope (1814–1893), 2nd s. of 5th E. Stanhope (who d. 1875): Fellow of All Souls, with First in maths.: board of trade November 1875–April 1878: under-sec. for India 1878–1880: cabinet minister 1885–1886, 1886–1892.

33 William Monsell, 1st Baron Emly (1812–1894), M.P. (Lib.) Limerick 1847–1874.
34 Sir James Fitzjames Stephen (1829–1894), jurist and publicist.
35 Thomas John Capel (1836–1911), R.C. prelate prominent in London society from 1868: ran schools in Kensington: the original of Catesby in Disraeli's *Lothair* (1870): went to U.S.A., 1883, and died there.
36 Charles Heneage (1841–1901), diplomatist, 2nd s. of G.F. Heneage, M.P. Lincoln 1832–1835, 1852–1862, and bro. of 1st Lord Heneage, formerly Edward Heneage M.P., cr. a peer 1896.
37 A.J. Mundella (1825–1897), Sheffield M.P. (Lib.) 1868–1897, educational reformer, and Nottingham hosiery manufacturer.
38 Henry Wellesley, 1st E. and 2nd Baron Cowley (1804–1884), amb. at Paris 1852–1867.
39 Either John Reginald Yorke M.P. Gloucs. E. 1872–1885, or possibly Reginald Somers Yorke (1854–), both remote descendants of the 5th s. of the 1st E. of Hardwicke.
40 John William Strutt, 3rd Baron Rayleigh (1842–1919): senior wrangler 1865, F.R.S. 1873, sec. of Royal Society 1885–1896, O.M. 1902, Nobel prize 1904, chancellor of Cambridge 1908.
41 Thomas Denman, 2nd Baron Denman of Dovedale (1805–1894), a Liberal who usually opposed his party.
42 Sir H. Rose, 1st baron Strathnairn (1801–1885): served in Syria, Crimea, and Indian Mutiny: c.-in-c. India 1860–1865, c.-in-c. Ireland 1865–1870: cr. baron 1866, general 1867, field-marshal 1867.
43 R.C. Napier, 1st Baron Napier of Magdala (1810–1890), conqueror of Abyssinia in 1868: c.-in-c. India 1870–1876: cr. peer 1868.
44 Reginald Sackville, 7th E. De La Warr (1817–1896), previously a peer as Baron Buckhurst (1870–1873): succ. as earl on his brother's suicide, 1873: bro. of Lady Derby: an unproblematical character.
45 Sir Thomas Frederick Elliot (1808–1880), assistant under-sec. for colonies 1847–1868: made walking tour of Pyrenees with Lord Stanley, 20 September–20 October 1865.
46 A small estate, recently acquired, a few miles from Bromley.
47 An abortive plan for redistributing corrupt borough seats among the counties.
48 Ralph Gordon Noel (Milbanke from 1861), 13th Baron Wentworth (1839–1906), succ. his brother 1862: was succ. in the title by his dau. despite marrying twice.
49 William Saunders (1823–1895), radical journalist, co-founder of *Western Morning News* (Plymouth) 1860, founder of *Eastern Morning News* (Hull) 1864: proprietor to 1894: started Central Press, the first news agency (from 1890 Central News Agency) in 1863. Chief manager to 1884. Principal proprietor to death. M.P. Hull E. 1885–1886 (defeated), Walworth 1892–death. Land nationaliser.
50 John Winston Spencer-Churchill, 7th D. of Marlborough (1822–1883), lord-lieutenant of Ireland 1876–1880 and father of Lord Randolph.
51 Lady Dartrey.
52 The state of parties in Ireland after the 1880 election defies exact description. The Irish 1880 elections were mainly between different home rule factions, not on British issues at all.
53 William Farr (1807–1883), statistician: compiler of abstracts in Registrar-General's Office, 1838–1879: retired, 1879.
54 Theodore Martin, *The Life of His Royal Highness The Prince Consort* (2nd ed. London, 1876, in 5 vols.).
55 Sir Charles H.J. Chetwynd-Talbot, 20th E. of Shrewsbury (1860–1921), succ. his father 1877: he m. June 1882, to a lady just divorced, and produced an heir in September 1882. For many years he was in a very large way of business as a hansom cab proprietor: he left £617,000 gross, all his free property being left to a female not his wife.
56 Henry John Chetwynd-Talbot, 18th E. of Shrewsbury (1803–1868): succ. to earldoms of Shrewsbury and Waterford on death of his kinsman the 17th Earl in 1852: formerly 3rd Earl Talbot (succ. 1849). He m. a Waterford.

57   Charles John Chetwynd-Talbot, 19th E. of Shrewsbury (1830–1877): as eldest s., succ. 1868:
M.P. for Stafford, Staffs. S., and Stamford: captain of gentlemen-at-arms.
58   Liverpool politician.
59   Alfred Bilson, Liverpool solicitor, and honorary legal adviser to the Liberal party in the city: M.P.
Barnstaple 1892–1895, Halifax 1897–1900, Staffs. N.W. 1906–1907 (died): Gladstonian and
Presbyterian.
60   Sir Robert Peel (1822–1895), 3rd baronet, son of premier: Irish sec. 1861–1865: topped the poll
at Tamworth in 1874, but in 1878 a Tamworth by-election for the second seat was won handsomely by
the Liberals. In 1880 the Liberals easily won both seats.
61   Samuel Danks Waddy, Q.C. (1830–1902), M.P. (Lib.) Barnstaple 1874–December 1879,
Sheffield December 1879–April 1880 (defeated). Sheffield and Greenwich were the only two Tory
gains outside London in populous seats in 1880. Waddy was a prominent Wesleyan.
62   E.V.H. Kenealy (1819–1880), counsel for Tichborne claimant, 1873: independent M.P. Stoke
1875–1880 on Tichborne's behalf.
63   Professor Henry J.S. Smith (1826–1883), leading mathematician: educ. Rugby and Balliol:
Savilian professor of geometry, 1860.
64   Sir A.H. Layard (1817–1894), ambassador at Constantinople 1877–1880.
65   Wolff was not appointed.
66   William Amherst, Baron Amherst of Montreal (1836–1910), of Sevenoaks, Kent: styled Viscount
Holmesdale 1857–1886: M.P. W. Kent 1859–1868, Mid-Kent 1868–1880: summoned in his father's
title, April 1880, as Baron Amherst of Montreal: succ. father as 3rd E. Amherst, 1886: fought in
Crimea, where severely wounded.
67   As Lady Bolsover.
68   Sir John Pakington, 1st Baron Hampton (1799–1880), but born plain John Russell: cabinet
minister in Tory ministries 1852–1868: lost seat and cr. peer 1874: devotee of archery.
69   Civil Service Commissioner.
70   Galloway had married Derby's stepdaughter, Lady Mary Cecil. Bateman gives the gross annual
value of his estates as £32,197 for 79,184 acres.
71   Algernon Borthwick, 1st Baron Glenesk (1830–1908), proprietor of *Morning Post* 1876: Cons.
M.P. 1885–1895: suggested Primrose League, 1883: cr. baron, 1895.
72   A prominent Liberal family rooted in shipping, insurance and cotton.
73   Lord Henry Charles George Gordon-Lennox (1821–1886), M.P. 1846–1885 and friend of
Disraeli: held minor office under Derby: first commissioner of public works 1874–1876 but resigned
after financial scandals.
74   As Earl of Lathom, after his house.
75   George Milles, 5th Baron Sondes (1824–1894), cr. Earl Sondes, May 1880: credited by Disraeli
with having kept Kent Tory in 1880.
76   As Lord Rowton.
77   Hastings Russell, 9th Duke of Bedford (1819–1891), who succ. his cousin 1872.
78   Won by James Howard, an agricultural engineer and manufacturer in Bedford.
79   To Granville.
80   James Clerk-Maxwell (1831–1879), first professor of experimental physics at Cambridge.
81   Francis Cowper, 7th Earl Cowper (1834–1905), lord-lieut. of Ireland 1880–April 1882
(resigned).
82   Arthur, Duke of Connaught (1850–1942), 3rd s. of Queen Victoria: governor-general of Canada
1911–1916.
83   Henry James, 1st Baron James of Hereford (1828–1911), attorney-gen. 1873–1874, 1880–1885.
84   Farrer Herschell, 1st Baron Herschell (1837–1899), M.P. (Lib.) 1874–1885: solicitor-gen.,
1880–1885: lord chancellor 1886, 1892–1895.
85   Watkin Williams Q.C. (1828–), M.P. (Lib.) Denbigh 1868–1880: elected for Carnarvonshire
1880, but appointed a judge later that year.

[86] Sir John Holker (1828–1882), M.P. (Cons.) Preston 1872–1882: attorney-gen. 1875–1880: lord justice, 1882.

[87] Sir Fitzroy Kelly (1796–1880), lord chief baron 1866–1880.

[88] Frederick Greenwood (1830–1909), founder of *Pall Mall Gazette* 1865, and its editor 1865–1880 until a new owner made it a radical paper: left for newly founded Tory *St. James's Gazette*, 1880–1885.

[89] Sir J.D. Coleridge, 1st Baron Coleridge (1820–1894), cr. peer 1873: chief justice of Queen's Bench, 1880–1894.

[90] Sir C. Wood, 1st Viscount Halifax (1800–1885), sec. for India 1859–1866: cr. viscount, 1866.

[91] Mortimer Sackville-West, 1st Baron Sackville of Knole (cr. 1876), 1820–1888: bro. of Lady Derby, and of 6th E. De la Warr (suicide, 1873).

[92] Richard Boyle, 9th E. of Cork (1829–1904): held court office 1866, 1868–1874, 1880–1885, 1886, 1894–1895.

[93] See Vincent and Cooke (eds.), *Lord Carlingford's Journal* (1971, p. 16). Gladstone offered Carlingford the Irish lord-lieutenancy, without cabinet office, which Carlingford declined: Granville then offered him the Constantinople embassy, which he accepted, only to find the offer withdrawn.

[94] On petition this by-election was declared void and, its second member soon after becoming a judge, Oxford City was without an M.P. 1881–1885.

[95] The 1875 Coercion Act expired in 1880.

[96] Gladstone lost 7 British seats altogether in the period between the 1880 election and the end of the year. The reaction continued into 1881, when there was a net loss of 5 British seats.

[97] Lord Robert Montague (1825–1902), 2nd s. of 6th D. of Manchester: M.P. (Cons.) Hunts. 1859–1874, (Cons. H.R.) Westmeath 1874–1880: vice-pres. of council & education minister March 1867–December 1868: introduced education bill into Lords, 1868: an R.C., 1870–1882.

[98] Auberon Herbert (1838–1906), s. of 3rd E. of Carnarvon: president of Oxford Union, Northcote's private secretary, M.P. (Lib.) Nottingham 1870–1874, supporter of Arch, Bradlaugh, and republicanism: a vegetarian.

[99] Sir Edward Thornton (1817–1906), minister at Washington 1867–1881, ambassador at St. Petersburg 1881–1884: had declined Derby's offer of Madrid, 1877.

[100] C.B. Adderley, 1st Baron Norton (1814–1905), M.P. (Cons.) Staffs. N. 1841–1878: cr. baron, 1878: president of Board of Trade 1874–1878.

[101] Sir G.O. Trevelyan (1838–1928), man of letters, historian, nephew and biographer of Macaulay: M.P. (Lib.) Hawick Burghs 1868–1886.

[102] (Sir) John Pender (1818–1896), telegraph magnate: M.P. (Lib.) Totnes 1862–1866, Wick 1872–1885: (Lib. Un.) Wick 1892–1896.

[103] As governor-general of India, 1880–December 1884.

[104] Valentine Browne, 4th E. of Kenmare (1825–1905), succ. his father 1871: M.P. (Lib.) Kerry 1852–1871: various court posts 1856–1858, 1859–1865, 1868–1872: lord chamberlain 1880–1885, February–July 1886.

[105] Christopher Wordsworth, Bishop of Lincoln from 1868 to 1885.

[106] A.C. Tait, Archbishop from 1869 to 1882.

[107] Edward Knatchbull-Hugessen, 1st Baron Brabourne (1829–1893): as Lib. M.P., held junior office: cr. peer, 1880, became conservative, wrote fairy stories.

[108] Léon Say (1826–1896), French finance minister of 1870s: achieved early payment of war indemnity: ambassador to U.K. April–May 1880..

[109] T.E. Kebbel, 'A Conservative View of the Elections', *National Review* (May, 1880).

[110] J.R. Lowell (1819–1891), New England writer: U.S. minister in London 1880–1885.

[111] Henry Stanley, 3rd Baron Stanley of Alderley (1827–1903), eldest s. of 2nd Baron: diplomatist in east, 1851–1858: a Moslem, an ardent upholder of Welsh Anglicanism, an improving landlord, and a bigamist.

[112] Lord-lieutenant 1876–1880.

[113] Edward Plunkett, 16th Baron Dunsany (1808–1889): in navy from 1826: admiral, 1877: rep. peer (I.) 1864–1889: left £137,880.

[114] Geoffrey Browne, 2nd Baron Oranmore (1819–1900).

[115] Sir F. Napier, 9th Baron Napier (1819–1898), diplomatist: minister at Washington 1857–1858, The Hague 1858–1860, St. Petersburg 1860–1864, Berlin 1864–1866: governor of Madras 1866–1872, serving as acting viceroy on Mayo's death: cr. Baron Ettrick in U.K. peerage, 1872: member of London School Board, 1873–1876.

[116] Horace Forbes, 20th Baron Forbes (1829–1914), succ. his father 1868: Scottish rep. peer 1874–1906.

[117] F.H.O. O'Donnell (1848–1916), Irish obstructionist: hon. sec. Irish Home Rule Confederation of Great Britain: M.P. (H.R.) Dungarvan 1877–1885.

[118] Hastings Russell, 10th Duke of Bedford (1819–1891).

[119] *Parl. Deb.*, 3, vol. ccliii, cols. 264–284. Resolved 'to prevent our drifting into secondary education in elementary schools', 98–50.

[120] Perhaps Stuart A. Moore (1842–1907), legal antiquary, or more probably Arthur W. Moore (1853–1909), Manx antiquary and public figure, educ. like Derby at Rugby and Trinity.

[121] Yakoub or Yakub Khan, Amir of Afghanistan from February 1879: eldest son of Sher Ali, whom he succeeded: by Treaty of Gandamak, May 1879, accepted a measure of U.K. control: after massacre of Cavagnari (3 September) Yakub fled to Roberts, and abdicated.

[122] Abdurrahman, nephew of Sher Ali: consolidated the Afghan state between 1880 and 1901, with some U.K. support.

[123] Richard Monckton Milnes, 1st Lord Houghton (1809–1885), cr. peer 1863.

[124] Frederick, 6th E. Beauchamp (1830–1891), succ. 1866: lord steward 1874–1880.

[125] J.F. Mackarness (1820–1889), Bishop of Oxford 1870–1889.

[126] R.N. Philips (1815–1890), M.P. (Lib.) Bury 1857–1859, 1865–1885.

[127] Hugh Mason (d. 1886), M.P. (Lib.) Ashton-under-Lyne 1880–1885: D.L. Lancs.

[128] Comptroller at Knowsley.

[129] Lord chamberlain 1880–1885.

[130] George Smith (1831–1895), philanthropist: his agitation successful: in 1885 received a grant from royal bounty.

[131] Confirmed by *Gladstone Diaries*, without any comment.

July–December

1 July 1880: Lawson called, talked over foreign affairs: as to which he had nothing new: then of the troubles of the government, which seemed to give him pleasure: he said the last story was that Gladstone & Hartington did not work smoothly together, the Premier insisting on taking Indian affairs into his own hands. He also mentioned a report that Harcourt would take the Speaker's place. The Speaker is sick of his work, which grows more disagreeable every year: & I believe there is no doubt of his wish to retire: Harcourt, with all his ability, has managed to make himself intensely disliked on both sides (this I have heard from various people) & probably this fact has given rise to the idea of shelving him. But he is quite unfit to be Speaker: his strength lies in debate & popular oratory: & I cannot conceive that he should accept (even if it were offered) a place where he would be silenced & without influence. – Lawson had heard, as I also had, that the Irish are arming & drilling largely: they have bought quantities of disused military rifles, sold cheap by the War Dept.: not to shoot crows with.

. . . H. of Lds for the case of the Mar peerage[1], which has excited extraordinary interest in the minds of the Scotch peers: the lawyers, however, are against them &, though Galloway moved the resolution on which we voted, I could not support him against the united authorities of Cairns, Selborne, & Ld Blackburn[2]. The division was 80 to 52. Dined at the D. of Cleveland's[3]: sat next to my old friend Ly Cork, whom I find much changed: grown grave, anxious, & rather querulous about public affairs. She said, repeating what I suppose is the common talk of the Whigs, that 'Hartington lets things slide' – the phrase she used – 'not holding himself largely responsible for matters outside his own department'. She talked of Granville as nearly worn out, in bad health, hardly equal to his work, & mortified at being passed over for the first place. Except as to his health, I take the liberty of doubting this. She wanted me to come forward, & act as a check, which I do not see how I could have done so far: &, like most women, she underrates the strength of the democracy. She seemed almost hopeless as to the state of Ireland, & I don't wonder.

2 July 1880: . . . In H. of C. the Bradlaugh business got itself settled last night: the House admitting him to affirm (subject to the legality of the proceeding being discussed in a court of law) by a majority of 54. This is the readiest way out of the difficulty: & therefore perhaps under all circs. the best: though it is neither the most logical, nor the most dignified: for it implies a rescinding of the resolution passed last week, & it does not finally settle the issue, which a bill would have done. But it cuts the knot, & saves time. The Conservative opposition was much divided: the rational part of it, represented by men like Northcote, being ready to support a bill making affirmation optional: the more violent avowing that in their view an atheist ought to be excluded as such. The Irish Catholics, O'Donnell & Sullivan, took the latter view: Parnell going against them. . . .

3 July 1880: . . . Sanderson called: he said the settlement of the Greek business would probably be resisted by the Porte, or at least not assented to: but possibly they would take no active step to retain the territory in dispute. He thinks the Italians likely to give trouble. They want a settlement on the Red Sea (for what reason is impossible to guess): &

we oppose it as inconvenient to us. But English convenience is not necessarily a measure of right: though we are apt to think so. We talked of Layard: I thought he might be given Rome when any fresh move was made: but S. thinks that his rough ways, & his indisposition to put himself out of the way for tourists, would be against him there. . . .

4 July 1880: . . . The chief event of the week has been the expulsion of the Jesuits from their establishments in France . . . The political effect of the move is that the republic is no longer considered as a mere form of government, adopted from necessity in 1870, & retained because there is nothing to take its place, but as the embodiment of secularist & democratic resistance to priests & aristocrats. It will be more vehemently opposed & more warmly supported. – I observe that moderate Liberals here dislike the state of things, & prophesy evil. . . .

7 July 1880: . . . In the afternoon Mr. Herbert Spencer, the well known writer, called: his object was to enquire as to the possibility of founding a chair of sociology in the new Liverpool College. He explained in a clear & interesting way how his late enquiries had led him to the conviction that the laws which govern the organisation of human society admit of being reduced to scientific form equally with those of political economy, and he thought they might be taught in the same way. I spoke of the difficulty of finding a man fit to be professor: & suggested that a beginning should be made by the delivery of a course of lectures on the subject, which would cost comparatively little, would show how much interest was felt in the study which he recommended, & might in time lead to more. I also advised him to speak to the D. of Devonshire, as head of the new university: which he seemed disposed to do. He was with me about 20 minutes: I treated him with the respect which I really feel for one of the few men who has done original work: & promised to help his views if I could. I had never seen him before except hastily & in company. He is not marked out for a philosopher by outward appearance, like Mill: the head is good, but not remarkable: the expression of the face shrewd rather than deeply thoughtful: if I had not known who and what he was, I should have taken him for a man of business in the City, a merchant, or possibly a lawyer. His manner is quiet & quite unaffected: without any of the dictatorial style of Buckle. He conversed fluently, & I should think would make a good lecturer. . . .

9 July 1880: Late last night Lawson called, asking to see me: what he wanted specially to know was whether it was true that Ld Lansdowne had resigned his appointment on account of the Irish bill. I could only tell him that I had heard the report, & thought it likely to be true: but it seems that a question on the subject was put & answered in H. of C. leaving no doubt as to the fact.

Ld Camperdown[4] came to see me today, as he had done yesterday: much perplexed & distressed about the bill, saying that he could not support it, wished some way could be found out of the difficulty, etc. So do I, but it is not easy to see one: the Cabinet has gone too far to make withdrawal possible: Gladstone & Forster are deeply & personally pledged, & they are not men to give way easily. The amendment has been proposed, modifying the operation of the bill (though to what extent it does so I am not clear) which has had the effect of disgusting the Home Rulers, without materially conciliating opposition from other quarters. On the whole the mess is an awkward one: Forster has been in haste to satisfy the Irish so far as it could be done without outraging English ideas: &

he has jumped at the first plausible proposal that offered, not (I think) seeing that the objects of those who suggested it to him were entirely different from his, & that the reasons for legislation which they put forward were mere pretexts.

10 July 1880: Lawrence came . . . He mentioned incidentally that his firm has been employed by the family for exactly 100 years: since 1780.

Harcourt called with a list of names for the commission[5]: D. of Bedford, Lds Sherbrooke & Coleridge, with D.[erby]: Cotton & Waterlow as representing the City, Firth[6] & James, both M.P.s, as hostile to the claims of the companies: Cross, who has overcome some scruples which he had as to serving: Burt, the 'working man representative', said to be honest & intelligent: Mr. Pell[7], a rather shrewd Conservative member: & one of the Rothschild family. In all 12: 4 peers: 4 M.P.s unpledged on either side: & 4 who may be considered as counsel for the two parties respectively.

Some talk with H.[arcourt] as to the political situation, of which it is clear that he thinks badly: he says the difficulty of making any arrangements with the Opposition is all the greater because they have no leader: Northcote is not factious enough for them, & obstruction is their game. Gladstone is fixed in his determination to carry his measures, however late the House has to sit, but H. seemed doubtful as to the chances. He thought it possible the Irish bill might be lost on the third reading: Irish Home Rulers & Conservatives combining against it. Even Bright, he said, is now compelled to admit that there is no satisfying the Irish. He thought, as the bill had failed to please them, & certainly pleased nobody else, it might be dropped or thrown out without much agitation in consequence: & I gathered from his way of talking that he would not be sorry if this were to happen: but in decency he could not say so. He thought Turkish matters were going well on the whole: but the Afghan trouble remained: it was not easy even to withdraw from the country without our troops being insulted & attacked on the way back. Kandahar had been promised to one chief to be held under our protection: but whoever was in power at Kabul would not be content without it, nor would the chiefs bear to have the country divided. Yet there was our pledge formally given: how to get out of it?

Walk to the B. Museum . . . we agreed to give £4,000 for a statue found at Rome . . . a boy taking a thorn out of his foot. Little as I know of such things, I could appreciate the wonderfully life-like attitude & expression of face.

Home. Keston by 4.12 train. . . . Letter from Lear about drawings he has made for me, which I tell him he can keep till his exhibition in London is broken up. . . .

12 July 1880: . . . Hale, who has been attending at the laying of the first stone of the Town Hall, Bootle, sends me figures showing the increase of the place. In 1850 the popn. was under 3,000. In 1860 it was 6,000: in 1870, 16,000: in 1880, it is estimated at 28,000. The rental has risen from £3,300 in 1848, to £15,028, & the growth is more rapid than ever. . . .

13 July 1880: Up early . . . the place in good looks, foliage rich & abundant.

News in the papers that Gladstone has again amended, or altered, his land bill, so as to conciliate the Irish members: the precise sense of the change made I cannot gather form the telegraphic report: but it is apparently a retraction of the concession that he made last week to English opposition &, if so, it will increase his difficulties with English public opinion, which is at present decidedly hostile.

Leave at 10.00 for the sessions, which are held in St. George's Hall, the first time I ever sat there. Sat till past 6.00: the new courthouse makes work much easier, for the air is comparatively pure, the jury are within easy reach, & the witnesses where I can hear them. Came away but little wearied.

Dined lightly alone, & wrote letters most of the evening.

14 July 1880: Liverpool again: sat in court from 10.00 to past 6.00: cases all of the usual sort, & not interesting. . . .

15 July 1880: Sessions again, 10.00 till 6.30: two appeals . . . The rest of the day was passed in trying assault cases, chiefly Irish, from Widnes . . . Dined with the Hales, & some talk with him as to affairs. In the two courts, we disposed of between 70 & 80 cases . . . the longest sentence passed by me was one of 18 months, the average about 6 months. . . .

16 July 1880: London by early train: St. J. Square at 2.30: letters, notes, & papers till 5.00, when to H. of Lords: there saw Pender, & much talk with him: he greatly dissatisfied at the state of business, says that the moderate Liberals are disgusted, Gladstone is pressing on matters too fast, that he will break up his party, etc. He believes that the Irish bill would not pass the Commons, but for the conviction that is felt that it will be thrown out in the Lords. – As to this Bill, I note that it has been changed every night, & the debates upon it have been heated: Gladstone & Forster have defended it, Hartington was reluctantly induced to make one speech in its favour on the second reading, but is known to dislike it: the D. of Argyll makes no secret of his aversion to it, & by the Whigs in general it is regarded with extreme alarm – not so much for what it actually does, as for what it threatens in the future: in short, it has divided moderates from radicals, & for that purpose is a good test question. It is thought that the Cabinet are well aware that they cannot carry it through the Lords, but wish to throw on the latter whatever unpopularity may attend its rejection. It is, I am afraid, a class question: most well-to-do people being against, most of the poorer sort in favour. – There is already visible a great deal of bitterness among the Ultras: in various quarters I hear threats of another dissolution if the House does not show itself more in (democratic) earnest. This of course is nonsense: but it indicates the general tone of feeling in that section. They have been spoilt by great & unexpected success: they have taken the talk of the hustings literally, & are disgusted to find that the very men whom they have elected, mostly rich & successful themselves, have no desire for real social change – that is, the great bulk of them, for no doubt there are some real democrats in the lot. . . .

18 July 1880 (Sunday): . . . Nothing much on my mind except the Irish bill: as to which I am in doubt whether to vote for the second reading or against, or not vote at all. I dislike the bill, think it dangerous & unjust, but the prudence of throwing it out is questionable, especially if the most objectionable parts can be amended in committee.

19 July 1880: . . . **Note** from A.D.'s conversation I gather that the Whigs are beginning to doubt the prudence of throwing out the Irish bill on second reading: & incline to suggest amendments which will take the sting out of it, without bringing the peers into direct collision with the other House. . . .

Dined with Morier at the Pall Mall restaurant: a party of men only: he had brought together all the notabilities of his acquaintance . . .

Sir G. Wolseley talked of Gen. Grant, the American, whom he had known: described him as having been obliged to leave the army on account of intemperate habits, & earning a small salary in private employment when the civil war broke out. Then he volunteered &, his determined character becoming known, was chosen to command a volunteer regiment which had shown itself insubordinate. He succeeded, and his position was made. Sir G. said that his famous campaigns, in which he ended the great war, had nothing about them remarkable in a military point of view: his principle was simply that of fighting whenever a chance was offered, knowing that he could afford to lose two soldiers better than the confederates could afford to lose one. But his earlier performances on the Mississippi were really memorable, showing great military skill. Sir Garnet said that the one great military reputation made by the war was that of Gen. Lee: whom he thought quite different from all other men whom he had known, and for whom he expressed an extraordinary veneration. He did not think any of the other confederate generals came near him – some were good subordinates, could obey his orders, but he alone was capable of directing the war. . . .

21 July 1880: My 54th birthday.

. . . London is busy with a singular story. Old Ld Malmesbury, aged 73, has within the last three months committed the folly of engaging himself to marry a young widow, more 'fast' than respectable, who had been separated from her husband before his death in South Africa. His family naturally were disgusted, & coolness has followed. The marriage was on the point of coming off when it was discovered that the lady had already a husband living, one of the Kingscote family, whom she had married immediately after the death of the first husband & before her engagement to Malmesbury. Why she should have amused herself with practising a deception which must necessarily be detected no one seems to know, but as matters stand she has extracted many valuable presents from the old man, & left him in a ridiculous position. I believe the story, chiefly because it is too improbable to have been invented, & feel some regret for Ld M. whom I knew well at one time, having served under him when he had the F.O. in 1852. But he was always under female influence of some kind: &, as a minister, was induced by such influence to perpetrate not a few jobs[8].

22 July 1880: . . . The impression grows stronger every day that the Irish bill will not pass the Lords, & that the Cabinet are more than half inclined to let it go. The Whig peers in general detest it, & their feeling is not weakened by the suspicion that it is meant to lead to some stringent measure of a permanent kind. The well-to-do classes in general think it dangerous, but by the radical section it is received as the beginning of a new order of things, less for what it does, which is little enough, than for the principle which it is thought to sanction. On the whole, I think its nominal authors now wish they had let it alone: they did not suspect the turmoil which it would create, or the dissensions to which it would lead.

23 July 1880: My brother's second son, now training for the navy, was sent over to see M., who brought him to me: he seems intelligent & spirited. Keston by 11.45 train, where the cool fresh air & quiet are very welcome after London.

The following mem. received from Ward I copy out for reference.
Rental & receipts from rent from Knowsley estates:

	Rental	Receipts
1875	£183,515	£179,033
1876	189,544	183,012
1877	193,942	184,833
1878	196,995	180,780
1879	200,486	170,597
1880	198,541	177,089 (and more to come in)

I do not quite understand the enormous discrepancy between rental & receipts in the last three years: nor yet how the rental is taken as a fixed sum due, when it includes payments for coal, clay, iron, & the like, which vary with the quantities taken out. But on these heads I will consult Ward when again at Knowsley.

24 July 1880: Fine warm day, our hay is being made . . .
Long ride by Northstead, where I see the steam plough at work, Mr. Hughes having apparently begun his operations. I have engaged him as bailiff, & shall lay out the farm anew, so as to give it a residential letting value. – Mr. Hughes was till lately agent to Ld Sackville at Knole, but has been dismissed for no intelligible reason in one of those fits of insane suspicion to which Ld S. is liable. He had not long before dismissed his house-keeper on the ground that she was watching her opportunity to poison Ly Sackville: & another servant, who he said was employed as a spy upon him. Happily he does not seem to go beyond freaks of this kind, so that his mental state is not known to the public: nor does he seem to get worse. . . .

25 July 1880: Letter from W.P. Talbot[9], containing an odd request: he wants me to advance the rest of the £20,000 which I have promised to my sister for her children, of which there is still £12,000 unpaid, in order that with it he may buy an estate near Harrow, Wembley park, which is to be sold (he says) much below its value: borrowing money to make up the rest of the purchase money. He has not consulted E.[10] & begs that if I refuse I will keep the whole matter from her knowledge. – The odd part of the request is that he absolutely ignores the fact of my having given this money to his wife for her own use & treats it as if at his disposal. I answer civilly, but say that I must know what she thinks: adding that I do not advise the purchase, as it is a speculative one in any case, the return uncertain, and if he wants the place to live at, which he hints is one of his objects, it is a great deal too large & expensive for him. This he no doubt knows, but does not like to admit to himself, attaching as he does an extreme importance to social display. She, however, has plenty of sense: and I am not afraid of her joining in this crotchet.

26 July 1880: . . . Began to read Carlyle's *Latter-Day Pamphlets*, which I have scarcely looked at again since they were new, 30 years ago. I could make little of them – perhaps from want of imaginative power, or some other mental defect – but I cannot see that the history of the last 30 years justifies the pessimism of the writer. He predicts moral and material ruin, and seems to believe in a general degradation of national character. As to the last, no one can judge: but it is certain that the period intervening between 1850 and

1880 has been on the whole about the most prosperous in the history of the nation. Nor do I see any proof that we are more dishonest, more selfish, or more untruthful than in earlier days.

27 July 1880: . . . The Irish disturbance bill passed its 3rd reading last night, by a majority of only 66: the ministerial majority, in its normal condition & with the addition of the Home Rulers, being 170. This large defection will not improve its chances in the Lords.

28 July 1880 (Wednesday): London for the day. Sundry letters . . . to Statter, to give a man £5 who has lost a cow . . . At 2.00, Sanderson [brings] news of a disaster in India: it seems that a brigade under Gen. Burrows has been destroyed near Kandahar[11], but numbers & details are not known.

Call in Curzon St., where find an Irish party: hear some rather ridiculous talk about the Irish bill, how not 50 peers will vote for it – not 40 – not 35. All the worse, I say, if it were true, but it is not. Dartrey's agent, one Galway, says the harvest is good, even extraordinary, & this will go far to lessen the angry feeling that is sure to prevail, and diminish the chance of disturbances.

Went, at Lear's earnest request, to a house where he is staying in Norfolk Square, to see the new drawings which he has finished for me, & some others: I bought two more, cost me £26, & paid for them by cheque before night.

London U. Senate at 4.15 . . . our business not important. Walk back with Granville, who owned that he was very nervous about the debate on Monday, not knowing the subject well, being aware that the House is against him, & feeling the importance of not making any mistake: besides which, as he says truly, he has no time to prepare, being full of other business. He seemed in conversation to admit that the bill must inevitably be lost: this probably affects him but little, but to a Whig of the Whigs, as he is, it must be painful to see so many of his personal friends & old colleagues against him. . . .

29 July 1880: . . . The papers are full of the Indian disaster, which appears not quite so bad as was supposed at first, since the brigade attacked & defeated has not been wholly destroyed: but our force at Kandahar will be besieged in the citadel, & the difficulty of leaving Afghanistan honourably is increased tenfold.

. . . Dined with Granville, meeting Argyll, Gladstone, Bright, Sheffield, L. Gower, Sir G. Dasent, Monck, Mr. Waddington, & the Austrian chargé . . . Pleasant enough. Left at 11.00, & by 11.15 train back to Keston.

Mr. Waddington talked freely of the state of France. In regard of material conditions, he said, nothing could be better: the increase of revenue had astonished, and even puzzled, their financiers: building was going on more rapidly than in the most prosperous days of the empire: the nation, in short, had never been so rich. . . . But he feared for the future. The next assembly would probably be more radical . . . He spoke of our English politics: expressed surprise at the extreme bitterness of feeling (so he described it) which he found in society – said the language held about the government by its opponents was like that of the monarchical parties in France where the republic was concerned. He had never heard anything like it before. – I told him that neither he nor I remembered the years 1830–1835.

Gladstone talked of Gen. Grant, whom he strongly blamed for his assumption of royal dignity while on his tour, saying that it was of the very essence of republicanism that the official, whether small or great, ceased to derive any dignity from his office when he ceased to hold it, & became like any other citizen. – Bright did not seem quite to agree, but turned the discourse by praising Grant's politeness & conversational facility, which rather puzzled the rest of us, since we had been used to think him deficient in those qualities.

Conversation turned on taxation, & the inequalities of income-tax. Gladstone said it was impossible to tax property instead of income, the complications were too great. Bright dissented, observing rather roughly that the only difficulty was that the classes owning property had too much power. Gladstone replied by pointing out the enormous power which under the American system the officials charged with collecting taxes possess, & the corruption: which was not disputed.

Gladstone dwelt a good deal on the advantages of his new beer tax, observing that it was elastic, could be revised or lowered more easily than the malt tax which it has replaced: & also expressed his belief that a substitute for malt would be found in many substances not now used: Indian corn would take the place of barley, & potatoes be made largely available. . . .

1 Aug. 1880 (Sunday): . . . Read a book[12] lately published on Italy by Laveleye the Belgian economist. It is slight & sketchy, but interesting from the conclusions reached. M. Laveleye describes the Italian peasantry & poorer classes as crushed by taxation: living on scanty food, drinking water: & in Lombardy, the richest country perhaps in the world, suffering from disease caused by want of nourishment. In Sicily the attempts to create a peasant proprietary seem to have failed so far. Over 6,000 separate estates, containing 450,000 acres, have been sold by the State, but they have been bought by 2,000 proprietors – the richer class of buyers outbidding the peasants, or purchasing from them. A significant fact, especially taken in conjunction with what has happened in Australia, where the perpetual effort of the various legislatures to break up large holdings has been as perpetually defeated. Laveleye speaks of taxation, general & local, as absorbing from 30% to 50% of private incomes: a scarcely credible proportion. Naturally there is a strong growth of socialist feeling, the result of discontent & suffering quite as much as of theory. He evidently thinks nothing can avert a revolution except economy. The country is drained by the interest of loans, payable in most cases to foreign creditors, so that the Italians are really paying a heavy tribute to the foreigner, as the result & price of their political freedom. The more favourable side of his picture is the great intellectual activity which he found everywhere.

2 Aug. 1880 (Bank Holiday): Walk in to station . . . fine warm day: the roads already full of holidaymakers.

News in the papers of Gladstone's illness – a feverish attack, which by the prominence given to it seems to be thought serious.

Statter sends his usual monthly report. There is some sign of improvement at last.

. . . Went down to the Lords at 5.00, where found a very full house, galleries full, & steps of the throne crowded. Ld Granville opened his case, speaking as if nervous, & as if he did not much like his case, which probably was the fact. He was clear, earnest, & fairly effective. Ld Grey[13] who followed him, at first inaudible, & physically rather feeble throughout: but he made some good points. Ld Emly defended the bill, but thought many parts of Ireland were included in it where there was no need. Ld Dunraven[14] spoke against it, sharply & forcibly in a thin House: Ld Lansdowne the same, in a remarkably telling speech, the best he has ever made, to my mind: about 9.30 (I think it was) I rose, & very soon had full benches. I spoke an hour, fairly well for me, taking the rather difficult line of at once expressing disapproval of great part of the bill, & yet advising the Lords not to throw it out on the second reading, but amend it in committee – arguing on the fact that we are a body of landowners & therefore not impartial: that it was an Irish bill, to be decided by English & Scotch votes: that it was a bill proposed to meet an emergency, as to which therefore we had no opportunity for second thoughts: that we should have more serious land questions to deal with shortly, & therefore had better not injure our position with the country, & lessen our influence in dealing with them, by hasty action. Then I criticised the bill, contending that it might be accepted as a necessary expedient for dealing temporarily with distressed districts, but that it should be limited in area, in time, & in regard of the class to which it should apply: that we were able to amend it in all these respects, & ought to do so, instead of throwing it out. I was very well listened to throughout. Salisbury followed me, & began with a personal attack, but was less vigorous than his opening promised: he spoke briefly, & sat down rather suddenly. We adjourned before 12.00.

Walked home with Sanderson.

3 Aug. 1880: . . . Went down to the Lords a little after 4.00, the sitting beginning earlier than usual. Cairns spoke for nearly 2 hours: too long, & with the lawyer's fault of dwelling too much on small details, giving them an importance beyond their real value: but it was a fine argument, clear, logical, & temperate, & he had many strong points to make, especially as showing that ministers have given various incompatible reasons for bringing in the bill. The truth is it was done by Gladstone & Forster, in a hasty impulse, to please the Irish: & the reasons for doing it have been supplied afterwards. Selborne followed, at an unlucky hour, for the peers went away to dine. I did like the rest, & did not hear him. Cranbrook was below his average – weak in argument, & noisy, as far as I heard him, but I heard only part. Ld Beaconsfield came next, & to me at least his performance was painful: it was so clear that his faculties are no longer what they were. He spoke in a hesitating, tedious, & slipshod fashion, repeating himself again & again, & putting one word for another. Towards the end he woke up a little, & declaimed in his old style but without much force or point. Only his voice remained as clear & strong as ever. Granville replied briefly, & we divided at 1.30, 51 against (I think) 282. The largest division for more than 10 years, & the smallest minority that ever supported a Cabinet on a question of general policy. Home, & to bed at 2.00, very weary.

I do not think that ministers greatly care about their defeat, which they were quite prepared for. In the first place, many of them disliked the bill: some are not sorry to see a check put on the impetuous impulses of the Premier: and as a matter of fact they will gain rather than lose in Ireland by the failure. For the bill, if passed, would not have effected one-tenth part of what the Irish expected from it: & the disappointment would have been visited upon its authors: whereas now the Irish will lay all the blame on the Lords, & give the Cabinet credit for having been willing to help them. Some agitation we shall have, but not, I think, to a dangerous extent.

4 Aug. 1880: . . . News that Gladstone is practically out of danger. The interest felt in his condition is intense, & nothing else has been talked of since Monday. It is thought that, though doing well, he cannot appear in parliament again this year: that the session will be shortened in consequence: & that he must give up the exchequer, the double work of the two offices being more than any man can bear. . . .

6 Aug. 1880 (Friday): . . . Gladstone's illness[15] has been the one subject of interest during this week, causing minor matters of politics to be forgotten. For two or three days he seems to have been in considerable danger. His illness began this day week, but was not generally known till Monday. He is now thought to be doing well, but will probably require a good deal of rest. The cause is overwork & constant excitement. There are many speculations as to whether he will continue to be able to lead the H. of C. & especially as to whether he can keep the exchequer: but he will not easily bring himself to part with it.

7 Aug. 1880: . . . Old Mr. Norman, the friend of Grote, called . . . He talked much & well, chiefly on economical subjects, as to which he is, as was Grote a strict economist of the older school. He told me two things which I did not know: one that in Belgium, which is constantly cited as an instance of the success of peasant properties, by far the greater part of the soil is cultivated by tenants, paying high rents, & that estates of upwards of £100,000 a year still continue to exist, notwithstanding the law of equal division: the other that excluding the vine . . . the French culture yields very much less per acre than ours: he says this is attested by quite recent calculations but did not give his authority. He noted it also as remarkable that land in England on an average sells more cheaply than in any part of western Europe, where the fertility of the soil is equal: he drew no inference, but said he had often verified the fact. Mr. N. is 87 . . .

8 Aug. 1880 (Sunday): Sanderson comes in afternoon. He does not tell me, nor do I think it fit to ask, anything as to what is passing in F.O. His brother is thinking of settling in Australia as a bank manager. His brother's wife, who has long given trouble in the family, is at last declared mad, & shut up: which is a relief to all concerned. He talks much of reorganisation in the office, & increase of pay to the juniors, which is a thing very just, if the money can be found.

News yesterday of the Liverpool election: Plimsoll beaten by Ld Claud Hamilton[16], a majority of 1,900. No one was surprised, or had a right to be: for, the majority being conservative, was sure to assert itself at a single election: the Irish Home Rulers stood aloof: & indeed their support would probably have been more damaging than their abstinence: nor was Plimsoll himself a wisely chosen candidate. He is an enthusiast, thought by many people to be not wholly sane &, like most enthusiasts, by no means scrupulous in what he does or says with an object in view: he is naturally suspected & disliked by the shipowning interest, & their hostility more than counteracts any support which he may have got from the sailors. In fact he is not a man qualified by judgment or capacity to represent such a place as Liverpool. Rathbone had previously refused to stand: whether fearing the cost, or disliking the Irish voters whom he would have been required to conciliate, I don't know. . . .

12 Aug. 1880: Pay £50 to the Farr testimonial, which has not succeeded as well as was hoped, there being only about £1,000 collected as yet. The Dr.'s services have been eminently useful, but they have not been of a kind to appeal to the popular imagination

– & as a rule the upper classes do not greatly care for sanitary reform – possibly because a good deal of quackery is apt to be mixed up with it. . . .

Much uneasiness felt as to the prospects of Irish disturbance. Arms are being largely bought by the peasantry (it is said that for 7s. a good Enfield rifle may be had in Dublin), American Irish are seen going about in Galway & Mayo without ostensible reason: supposed to be Fenians: there is a general expectation of trouble: & a very odd attempt has been made to plunder a vessel lying in Cork harbour of a stock of arms which it was imagined were there. From 60 to 70 men were concerned: they seized the vessel, & managed so well that no alarm was given, while they ransacked her: but, as usual with Fenian plots, there was a screw loose somewhere. Nothing in the way of arms was to be found, except some old smoothbore muskets, useless for fighting purposes. Thus the attempt turned out a failure: but the secrecy & skill with which it was organised show that some better heads were concerned than those of the ordinary Irish peasantry.

13 Aug. 1880: . . . It is thought the session will last till the 10th of next month, which greatly pleases the radical section. They like the notion of increased legislative activity (and they are right, for there is a great deal to do) & they like it not the worse because it vexes the country gentlemen, & those who enjoy sport. Equality is asserted if the M.P. who has not got a moor can prevent the M.P. who has one from enjoying it. There is a good deal of soreness about the Hares & Rabbits Bill: which will pass, not being seriously opposed: but Harcourt has accepted various amendments which tend to conciliate the squires, & the whole anti-game-law party are annoyed. Bright, who has constantly in these debates adopted an exasperating tone, rather in his earlier than later manner, said plainly the other day that the bill did not satisfy him: an odd speech from a colleague. The Burials Bill has got through its second reading: but the real difficulties will arise in committee. The Lords' amendments are sure to be knocked out: & the question is, shall we maintain them or not? If we do, the bill is lost for the year. . . .

15 Aug. 1880: . . . Talk among other matters with M. about the boys[17] & their farm, which is turning out a more & more unlucky speculation. She thinks they have now independent of it only £20,000 each, having started with upwards of £30,000 each. The rest is sunk, & even now they are not able to make the two ends meet. Farming is certainly not an economical kind of business. There must be large outlay: weather & other accidents make the return necessarily uncertain: the habit of paying out large sums creates indifference to small economies: & success depends on minute supervision of details & acting as a hard task-master – work which a gentleman never goes into willingly. I do not think that in this case either she or I are responsible for the results. The lads certainly would not have taken to any other employment: their minds were set on being farmers & nothing else: &, having independent fortunes & being of age, they were their own masters.

16 Aug. 1880: . . . In the papers, death of Ld Stratford de Redcliffe, at the age of 90 years or more. Having lost his only son, who was an invalid, his title dies with him. He will be chiefly remembered in history as having done all that was possible to keep alive the Turkish empire, over which for several years he was thought to have exercised more power than the Sultan. Of his remarkable ability there can be no doubt: & it may be a question whether his success was more hindered or promoted by a temperament extraordinarily imperious & irritable. My old chief, Malmesbury, used to say of him: 'Many men are thin-skinned, but Stratford Canning has no skin at all.' The common belief is that a quiet & somewhat careless temper, the disposition which inclines a man to take things easily, conduces more than any other to long life: but the two longest lived politicians that I have known have been evidence to the contrary: Ld Stratford being one, & Ld St. Leonards the other: than whom probably few persons have ever lived more easy to offend, or more difficult to get on with.

Ld Stratford was in the H. of Commons, but did nothing there: & in the Lords he rarely spoke. He tried his hand at literary work, but with no result beyond a dismal mediocrity. His power was all shown in diplomatic business: & in that profession he was recognised as the leading personage of our day: I mean, of course, among Englishmen. He gave practical proof of his belief in the Turks, & to his own misfortune, if it be true, as I believe it is, that nearly all his fortune was invested in Ottoman loans, & that in his last days he had little except his diplomatic pension to live on.

17 Aug. 1880: . . . See Lawrence . . . went with him carefully over my will, which I have not touched since 1878, & which requires to be drawn anew. Here are the chief provisions:

Ly D. & Sanderson to be executors.

My brother to be residuary legatee.

In money, I have about £300,000 to leave, which I divide as follows. – In trust to pay off encumbrances on the family estates, accumulating till the whole is paid, £100,000.

For purchase of Holwood, £60,000: Holwood to belong to Ly D. for life, & then to go to the family, as a settled estate.

To Ly D. herself, absolutely, £40,000. The above disposes of £200,000.

To the five children, £25,000. To Sanderson £10,000. To my sister, as much of the £20,000 promised her as is not paid off: the present sum is £12,000: private legacies £5,000: legacies to servants on a scale according to service, perhaps amounting to £10,000 in all: £20,000 to public institutions (1) The Literary Fund, (2) Brompton Hospital, (3) Geographical Society, (4) Manchester Grammar School: the above £1,000 each. – London University, University College, Trin. Coll. Cambridge, Rugby School, Nat. Port. Gallery, Walker Art Gallery Liverpool, Royal Society, & Royal Institution, £2,000 each.

All property at Knowsley to my brother.

All at Keston or Fairhill to Ly D.

All at No. 23 to be divided in a manner laid down.

My private papers to my executors to deal with as they think fit.

My father's & other papers inherited by me to my successor.

The above are the chief provisions.

18 Aug. 1880: . . . Found on returning that Ld Sherbrooke [once Robert Lowe] had ridden over to us from Caterham. Much talk with him, & pleasant. We discussed the colonies, he thinks better than I do of their financial future, holding that except N. Zealand they will probably continue solvent, whereas I hold that they will nearly all outrun their means & pass through a crisis of partial insolvency. M. tells me that to her he predicted the present Queen would be the last English monarch: which shows that he is in the same mind as before about the results of democracy. He expressed satisfaction that he had not been asked to take a place in the present ministry, as he should have accepted it, & should have felt obliged to resign immediately afterwards on the Irish bill: which would have looked foolish. . . .

20 Aug. 1880: . . . Letters from Hale . . .

The other letter is to tell me that the L. & N.W. Co. are at last ready to complete their Bootle purchase, paying £23,000 with interest for 2½ years: and that the Canal Co. are ready to pay £6,250 for land taken by them.

Not much has passed in parliament of late. In the Lords, Ld Strathnairn has delivered himself of a long threatened attack on Ld Chelmsford's African campaign: which, however, turned out to be rather an attack on the present military system: Ld Chelmsford, in a speech which was well put together & sensible, explained the cause of the Isandhlwana disaster, which, as he puts it, is this – that he had left in camp a force quite sufficient to defend the position, naturally a strong one: but that, contrary to his orders, the officer in command chose to go out & fight the Zulus in the open, where they beat him, the disparity of numbers being too great.

In the Commons, we have had the Indian budget, which is not pleasant reading. The Afghan war has cost £18,000,000 in all: of which £11,000,000 is paid, leaving £7,000,000 still to the bad. It is announced that the British exchequer is to give some help, but not how much.

21 Aug. 1880: Young Talbot, W.P. Talbot's eldest son, has failed to pass the army examination. He may succeed on a second trial but, if not, it is hard to see what can be done with him. There are openings in all professions for those who will really work hard: but young men of family, brought up at public schools, where hard work is thought ridiculous, & games are the most serious part of the teaching, will not submit to a life of real restraint & privation. This boy will have about £10,000 to live upon – just enough to keep him idle. . . .

24 Aug. 1880: . . . H. of Lds at 5.00 p.m. where the Employers' Liability Bill read a second time. The Chancellor spoke 1½ hours in bringing it in: his speech sensible, & I dare say in not too great detail, considering the nature of the subject, but a little heavy. Cranbrook spoke against the bill a little bitterly I thought, which was unwise as the second reading was not to be opposed: Ld Brabourne harangued against it in a tedious commonplace style, the D. of Somerset said a few words. The attendance was small, no division being expected: not above 40.

Dined with Granville, on a sudden invitation, meeting (with Ly G.), Northbrook, Hartington, & Lowe. Hartington came up from the Commons, where the Irish are having it all their own way again. Pleasant talk but I remember nothing worth setting down.

. . . News of a sortie from Kandahar, which seems not to have been a success: 200 men being killed or wounded, & a more than usual proportion of officers. The result is not clear: but after our late defeat in the open field, by a native force – a thing which has very seldom happened to us in India – opinion is sensitive, & people are over-ready to talk about failure.

I do not think I made at the time any note as to this defeat, which seems to have been caused by over-confidence, we attacking, or resisting attack from, a force 4 or 5 times our own in numbers. We trusted to better arms & discipline, but the Afghan chief Ayoub[18] seems to understand something of war, & probably had European advisers. Even now, a month after the event, we know very little in detail: but the upshot of all is that we are shut up in Kandahar, & partially besieged there, but a relieving force is being sent from Kabul and from Khalat. It is hard that, when we only want to get out of the Afghan country creditably, we should be as it were kicked from behind: compelling us to fight in defence of our military honour, though there is no longer any object to gain by fighting, since we have settled to leave the Afghans alone. – Ld Northbrook says that his successor Ld Lytton had become thoroughly convinced before leaving India of the failure of the Afghan policy, or, perhaps it would be more accurate to say, of the uselessness of our trying to stay on longer in a country where we have not a single friend or ally whom we can trust. – I believe this Afghan war to have been one of the two causes which chiefly led to the fall of the late govt. It was seen to be a failure – whereas the success or otherwise of the Berlin negociations was matter of argument, not admitting of such proof either way as could be made clear to the masses. – The other cause I think was the reserve (to give it a mild term) practised in dealing with parliament: the denial of facts afterwards proved – in a word the policy of systematic deception & concealment which was not only practised, but openly justified, as a necessary part of 'high policy'. It seems difficult to realise in this month of August the fact that not six months ago the 'Jingo' party was thought to be in a majority, not only thought so by itself, but by its opponents also. One week of polling landed us in a new world. . . .

26 Aug. 1880 (Thursday): Debate on the Employers' Liability Bill in committee. The attendance was very much larger than on Tuesday, about 120 peers being present. One clause of the bill, or rather a part of a clause, was lost on a division, & by another division the Opposition limited the duration of the Act to two years, treating it as an experiment, like the ballot. In this there is no great harm, for if it works well it will be continued as a matter of course: if not, an amending Act would have been desirable in any case. But it is not pleasant to see that the Conservative party can at any time force a collision with the Commons, & they are not likely to use their power more sparingly when Salisbury & Cranbrook succeed Ld B. in the leadership. Took a cab when all was over, & just caught the 9.25 train to Bromley, reaching Keston about 10.30. . . .

28 Aug. 1880 (Saturday): The Irish trouble in H. of C. which Hartington foretold on Tuesday culminated on Thursday night, the system of obstruction being renewed. The House sat up all night, & till noon yesterday – 21 hours at a stretch. The hours thus spent were of course wasted, the debate, if it can be called such, being desultory & dull, & the conduct of members (not all of them Irish) anything but Irish. They ate & drank in the House, lay down to sleep on the benches, & generally behaved as if their object was to turn parliament into ridicule. It is a bad sign, & all the worse because nobody seems to care.

29 Aug. 1880: Sent Sanderson his £200 for the last quarter of the year, having reason to think it may be wanted.

Gladstone has gone off for a ten days' cruise round the English coast[19], which is done by medical order, & wisely: for at sea, with only a few friends, he cannot do business, or make speeches, which he certainly would anywhere else.

Diplomatic affairs are in a sort of crisis, no one knowing what is to happen about the Greek frontier, whether the Turks will give way or not: but no one seems to care. The

English public cannot interest itself in two things at once: & just now people are thinking about Ireland. Even the Afghan trouble, which may easily become serious, attracts little notice. The Irish difficulty is as threatening as ever: & the less easy to deal with because it takes no definite form. General discontent with English institutions appears to be the predominant feeling in Ireland: & there is just as much dissatisfaction about the land as before the Act of 1870 was passed: if not more. The position of matters is most unsatisfactory. On the one hand, we cannot understand or realise, on this side the water, what the Irish grievance is: for beyond vague talk of oppression & rackrents it is never formulated, & to the English eye the Irish tenant appears to occupy an enviable position: protected & screened by law in a way unknown here. On the other hand, it is abundantly clear from the language held, & the prevailing feeling, that to leave Irish land grievances to be settled by the Irish themselves would be simply to sanction the confiscation of landed property: the landlords would be deprived of all power over their estates, & probably of half their rents at least. Gladstone is perhaps partially trusted by the Irish, or at least thought to be friendly: but for that very reason he is distrusted on Irish subjects by at least half his own followers in England.

30 Aug. 1880: This day we break up from Keston, to our great regret: there being no place where we feel so much at home, or so free from the troubles & worries of society. If Holwood should fall in during the next few years, I think it likely that we shall give up Fairhill, & settle wholly here, except as far as Knowsley & London require our presence.

Talk last night with L. West, whom I find eager for exchange to Washington. He thinks Thornton would like the exchange also, but of that he has no certain proof. I will speak to Sanderson about it.

. . . To the Lords: where I had half an intention of speaking on the 2nd Reading of the Ground Game Bill, but gave it up, partly because there seemed no wish for a serious debate, the 2nd reading not being opposed: partly because what I wished to say could be better said in committee.

Kimberley brought in the bill in a speech studiously moderate & sensible, pointing out to those who disliked it that the only other possible alternatives would be more disagreeable to them, & that a bill of some sort was inevitable. Redesdale[20] opposed, in a weak angry speech. Ld Beaconsfield followed, & showed that his failure of the other evening was only accidental, or perhaps owing to the hour being late. He talked some nonsense, but he knew it to be nonsense, & as an address to his supporters, & with a view to conciliate their prejudices, nothing could be more adroit than his general argument. It was to the effect that serious collisions with the other House are probable – that the Lords may have to put out their strength in resisting really dangerous proposals: & that therefore they had better not throw away their strength by resistance on a matter of minor importance. – I do not know how this advice was taken by the sporting peers, but no dissent was expressed, & we did not divide.

Dined Travellers'.

31 Aug. 1880: H. of Lords at 5.00, where the Game Bill in committee. There was a large attendance, over 160 voting. The debate lasted till past 9.00, & was more amusing than such discussions usually are – many peers speaking who are little accustomed to hear themselves, & who rambled away from the immediate subject to autobiographical narratives of their relations with their tenants. I was up three times, once on an amendment which really involved the whole principle of the bill: a proposal to allow landlords to contract themselves out of it. I dwelt on a point which had not been much touched: the facility with which, notwithstanding the bill, landowners might reserve the game by means of understandings & agreements. I advised the Lords to leave well alone, & be glad that the tenants were content with so harmless a measure, since if it fell through it would certainly be followed by one considerably more stringent. I spoke about ten minutes, very well listened to. Two amendments were carried against the government, one limiting the number of people whom the tenant may employ to shoot for him, the other providing a close time for hares &, absurdly enough, for rabbits also. But this last will certainly not be adhered to.

Dined Travellers', as last night, & slept in town.

1 Sept. 1880: Settle that Mrs. Brailsford shall have her husband's pension for 2 years from this date.

2 Sept. 1880: Read in the papers that the Lords yesterday threw out an Irish Registration Bill, which had been long in passing through the other House, by old Ld Redesdale's advice: a silly proceeding, for the bill was harmless, & the question was merely one of dignity. Redesdale has long complained, with some justice, that bills are sent up to us too late for effective consideration: &, if this bill had been an important one, there would have been some reason for his proceeding: but to reject now, by the votes of a very few peers, what we should have passed at any other time of year without debate is silly & spiteful. Redesdale, however, is gouty & irritable by nature, & in him a natural tendency to arbitrary proceedings is increased by the despotic power which he exercises in regard of private bills. The House has got used to his ways, laughs at him, & tolerates what it would resent in most men. It is justice to say that he is attentive & careful, though wilful, in his management of business. – I should blame myself for absence last night, but that Cork assured me there was no reason to stay.

. . . Read to Ly D. an article by Froude[21] on the state of Ireland: clever, well written, containing much truth in its analysis of the causes which have led to the present situation, but utterly without help as to the future. Indeed Froude hardly conceals his belief that the best thing which could have happened in the past would have been that the penal laws should have been effectively put in force, so as to convert or drive out of the country the Catholic population.

He ignores, I think, the fact that, though laws of extreme severity may be passed by governments or parliaments, sitting at a distance, & impressed by motives of state policy, such laws require to be executed by officials or private persons resident among the persons against whom they are directed – & the personal contact of man with man produces a state of feeling which necessarily mitigates the law in its practical administration. In fact, the Irish penal laws never were enforced, nor could be. – But Froude represents a very general feeling in the kind of hopelessness as to the future of Ireland which pervades his article. What is to be done with people who seem to hate us more & more the more we do for them?

3 Sept. 1880: . . . London by 10.50 train . . . luncheon at The Club: news . . . of an Afghan victory[22] gained by Gen. Roberts, which saves military honour, & enables us to leave the country without discredit.

The Burials Bill was restored to the state in which it was brought into our House, or nearly so: there was but one division, 61 (I think) to 26: the bishops, who attended in numbers, were divided among themselves. . . .

4 Sept. 1880: . . . The session has ended, for all practical purposes, by the reappearance of Gladstone, who delivered himself of a long & spirited speech on foreign affairs, characteristically going off into an enthusiastic eulogy of the Montenegrin people, which was quite unnecessary for his argument: but are they not good Christians, of the eastern sort, and do they not hate the Turks?

Two apologies, one in each House, varied the proceedings. One was made in person by a Mr. Callan, who divides with Mr. Biggar the reputation of being the most ill-conditioned of even the Irish gang, & who yesterday was formally put to silence for disorderly conduct: he having persisted in speaking when very drunk, & talked vituperative nonsense. The other, more important, was offered to the H. of Lds by Granville, who explained away some angry & threatening words used by Forster the day before in connection with the action of the H. of Lds. He seemed to menace the House with some great change to be brought about in its constitution, if it again put itself in opposition to the Commons. Naturally, the peers were sore; & 'society' professed to be scandalised. The incident is not important as it only shows that the incessant baiting from both sides which he has undergone, added to fatigue & hot weather, have been too much for the temper of the Irish secretary – which is not surprising nor inexcusable. But the unlucky disturbance bill has predisposed men on both sides to see revolution, or something like it, in whatever Forster says or does.

The govt. has been fortunate, as their predecessors were unlucky, in the revival of material prosperity exactly coinciding in time with the political change of hands. Trade is improving: the harvest on the whole is good: & all signs point to the return of industrial progress, after a comparative stagnation of five years. Absurd as the thing may be, I do not doubt but that the popularity of the Cabinet will be increased by this appearance of having good luck on their side.

5 Sept. 1880 (Sunday): Walk with Sanderson & with M. – Weather rather less hot, but still too much so for pleasure.

I gather that the state of matters as regards Turkey is as follows: the French & Italians are both anxious to keep out of any serious conflict, though probably at the same time not willing that an important change should be made without their at least seeming to have some voice in it. The Germans, for their own interest, will back up Austria, but otherwise are pretty indifferent to the result. The British govt. has no purpose of its own to serve & Gladstone's reopening the controversy was only justifiable on the ground that matters left alone would have gone from bad to worse: (if this be so: I hear no evidence to enable me to decide either way): but after all that had passed at the elections I suppose he could not have helped taking some action: the Russians & Austrians are in real earnest, & the only parties who are so. The Russian design is to unite Bulgaria with Roumelia when the time comes & they are advancing it by filling both countries as far as they can with Russian officials. The Austrians, I suppose, care little for a big Bulgaria, but are uneasy as to their own newly acquired possessions, & wish to keep the direction & control of the Sclave movement in their own hands. The Porte is playing its own game of delays suggesting impossible proposals, objecting to whatever is proposed by other Powers, trusting to time & to the chance of division arming its enemies. – We are detested (so Sanderson says) at Constantinople, & have no influence there. The Sultan is partly mad, morbidly susceptible to threats of conspiracy & assassination: in fact he lives in constant terror for his life & suspects everybody who comes near him in turn. With all this he is clever, extremely plausible in his talk: he used to entertain Layard by the hour with schemes of reform neatly drawn out & sounding well: but which Layard now believes he never had the slightest idea of executing, using them only to give proof of his goodwill, & perhaps with some pleasure in mystifying his tormentors. In the way of improved administration absolutely nothing has been done, nor seems likely to be.

8 Sept. 1880: Queen's speech proroguing parliament. Nothing special in it. there is a lull in party politics just now, all parties being tired with the session: & on the part of opposition it is felt to be useless to agitate against a govt. possessing so enormous a majority – no serious result can follow, as things are. The session has on the whole been a success to ministers: they have carried most of their bills, losing none of importance except the temporary measure for relief of Irish tenants, which most of the Cabinet disapproved from the first. Forster is to some extent damaged by that failure, & by his own utterances: but he has been in a position of extreme difficulty, for which allowance must be made. Hartington has done well throughout, Harcourt is said to be unpopular with the House, but cannot be called a failure. It is odd to see how little notice is taken of foreign affairs, though they have not often been in a more confused condition than now.

9 Sept. 1880: . . . In papers, news that the French have annexed Tahiti, which 25 years ago would have caused an uproar: but the world is grown wiser. In fact the change is not great: for the formerly existing protectorate could scarcely be distinguished for any practical purpose from actual possession.

B. of Trade returns show a marked return of prosperity: both as regards exports & imports: the latter are £275 million for 8 months, or at the rate of more than £400 million for the year: a larger figure, I think, than has been reached yet. The exports also have increased 20%. It is a singular piece of good fortune for Gladstone, that his return to office should exactly coincide with the revival of material prosperity. The same thing has happened twice [before]: the Conservatives taking office in 1866, just after the great financial & mercantile crash: & again in 1874, when the extraordinary advance of the two or three preceding years had begun to be checked.

10 Sept. 1880: Gave Job & John, the two gardeners here, a present each: they are respectively 78 & 77 years old, & have worked about the place since they were boys. Their interest in it is as great as if it belonged to them, which in a sense it does, for in their own department they do nearly what they please. . . . These two old men are perfectly content, & never seem to have thought of comparing their condition with that of others who are better off.

In the carriage with M. before 12.00, & drove through Sevenoaks town over to Sundridge, to call by appointment on Mr. & Mrs. Spottiswoode[23] at Combe Bank. . . . The broad level terraces of the garden are striking . . . otherwise the place is small, 500 to 600 acres: & the house is singular in its unsightliness . . .

We visited Mr. S.'s workroom, where is a complete electrical apparatus of various kinds: with this he showed some curious experiments. I took occasion to ask whether, since the new arrangements for applying electrical force had been perfected, there was any chance that it would compete with steam as a motive power? He said no, that steam would always be cheaper, but that where the thing wanted was not the creation but the transmission of power it would be very serviceable. With a certain percentage of loss, perhaps as much as one half, power might be transmitted to any distance . . . so that (to take an instance which I suggested) a waterwheel at Niagara having 100 h.p. would supply 50 h.p. at New York.

11 Sept. 1880: Sent £20 to the St. Pancras Free Library, declining at the same time a request that I should take the chair at a meeting in its support.

Busy with M. making out lists of persons to be invited to Knowsley.

12 Sept. 1880: Absolutely clear & free of all business . . . Day very fine, but cold, the summer being apparently ended. Walk alone for exercise early, & later with M. We talk among other matters of the possibility of my returning to office. I say that I neither wish it, nor should under all circumstances refuse it: it might be obviously the right thing to do: but I do not wish it, especially just now, for various reasons: (1) I can never feel sure what Gladstone will do next &, though willing to give him an independent support, I should not like to pledge myself 'jurare in verba magistri'. (2) I am not very sympathetic with him in personal character & feeling: he is an enthusiastic high churchman, I am a sceptic with a strong dislike to enthusiasts of all colours: he is an eager democrat, my sympathies are not with democracy, though I see its strength, & am not minded to fight with a certainty of defeat. If we were to act together, it is not likely that we should long work in harmony. (3) His position is so much that of a dictator just now, that no colleague of his could hold out against his wishes with a chance of success – & all that is popular in any department is ascribed to the chief, the departmental heads only getting credit for the inevitable blunders committed – not exactly the position that a man of independent temper would choose. (4) After a change of political connection, it is undesirable to seem to be a gainer by it, as I wrote to Granville & to Gladstone himself in the spring. (5) And most to the purpose, I have served 8 years in Downing St. and am happier where I am.

13 Sept. 1880: Ride early, but driven in by a storm, very wet.

Visit from Cazalet[24], who talked on various subjects in a fairly entertaining way, but he always leaves on my mind an impression of oddity for which I cannot quite account. He spoke of the state of Russia . . . He spoke of a bricklayers' association (apparently a trades union concern) with which he had dined lately, taking the chair: there were 400 of them: he began by giving the usual toast of the Queen: which was very ill received, most of those present refusing to drink it. He thought we did not know the strength of the radical feeling in that class. On my cross-questioning him a little, he seemed to say that he saw no evidence of socialist feeling, only radical dislike of a court & all that belongs to it.

We talked of Ireland, he thought (& it is evident that he has good information as to what is passing) that the object of the govt. would be to introduce the Ulster custom in some form over all the country. But do they as yet know themselves what they mean to do?

We talked of land near here: he thought nearly all the estates round us either were or soon would be in the market: he has taken nearly all his estate into his own hands, finding trouble with the farmers. . . .

16 Sept. 1880: An idle day, though not by my fault. Sanderson called early, & we had some talk: he seems to imply that the state of things in the east is not satisfactory, the Porte not having yet made up its mind to concede the piece of Albanian territory demanded by the Powers, & seeming inclined to let matters go to extremities, relying on the disunion of Europe. To this the answer is to be a naval demonstration: but a demonstration is only useful if it produces the moral effect for which it is intended: & in this case its success is doubted. I gather that it is with great trouble that the various governments concerned have been induced to go even so far as to sanction the demonstration at all: & that the Sultan is perfectly aware of their hesitation. . . .

19 Sept. 1880: Weather clear, bright, & cold, with occasional heavy showers.

. . . Death of the old Chief Baron, Kelly, aged 83, whom I knew well when we both sat in the Commons, & kept up acquaintance with till near the end. He was a remarkable character. At the bar he fought his way, with few friends, & against a good deal of prejudice (the cause of which, if there was a cause, I never knew), but certainly in his own profession he was not liked. At one time he had an immense practice, & made a large fortune, which however he got rid of: spending freely, & being unlucky in speculations. With success he grew careless, & neglected his business so much that it fell off, though his reputation lasted among the solicitors long after he had ceased to be efficient as a counsel. He was not raised to the bench till 1867, when he was 70 years of age, & had almost dropped out of the profession. As a judge, however, he regained the position which he had lost, his great knowledge of law & clearness of head supplying the want of industry. During the last 5 or 6 years he grew unfit for work, & latterly his infirmity became a scandal, but either he did not know it himself, or he was too poor to retire without a pension, which he had not served long enough to earn. He was a little, short, strongbuilt man, capable in his best days of enduring much fatigue, with perfect command of temper, & great readiness of speech. This last quality perhaps served him ill, for in the House he was intolerably prolix, taking an hour to say what might have been perfectly well said in ten minutes. If he was ever successful there, it was not in my time: I never heard him effective as a speaker, & have often heard him coughed down. But he was kept up by his reputation as a great lawyer. He leaves no son, & I should think little or no fortune.

20 Sept. 1880: . . . With Ward in the office, & got from him the balance sheet of the year 1879–1880. It is satisfactory enough. the receipts are £206,024 from rents: but this sum includes a large amount of arrears from the year before. The normal sum due, or rather which I may expect to receive, I put at £190,000. There are repayments of debt, & sums received from the trustees, which make up the gross receipts to £228,044.

The various estates have contributed as follows:

East Lancashire	£70,801
Liverpool, Kirkdale, & Bootle	£54,043
Home estates	£55,484
Fylde & outlying lands	£25,693

On the other hand the heads of expenditure are as follows:

(1) Compulsory deductions	29,675

(2) Estate	66,167	
(3) Household	27,000	including Keston & Fairhill
(4) Miscellaneous	**21,487**	
Total	£144,332	(shillings added)

I have drawn for investment or personal use, since 1 July 1879, £75,000. Practically the whole of this has been invested, & my personal outlay has been more than covered by the interest.

Looking back to the last 10 years, I observe that the growth of rental has been far in excess of what I expected – it was in 1870 but little above £160,000, excluding Ireland: & is now nominally £200,000, being an increase at the rate of nearly £4,000 in each year. On the other hand, I had flattered myself that the expenses might be kept down to £120,000, whereas they exceed £140,000. But on the whole there is an excess of income not less than £60,000, besides that much of what is laid out on the estate is really in the nature of investment. . . .

25 Sept. 1880: Notice from Lawrence . . . that the L. & Yorkshire Co. are about to pay me £50,000 on account, out of the £76,000 which they owe.

Sent through Latter some help to a Mrs. Hall, wife of a man who was at school with me, & has been in poverty ever since, & I believe not by his own fault.

Sent £20 to a coffee or cocoa room at Huyton quarry. Ride early for exercise.

At 3.00 a garden party, to which about 260 persons were asked: I do not know how many came, probably under 200: they were received in the front drawing room, passed through the gallery, & into the garden by the colonnade staircase: there were two bands, a tent, preparations for lawn tennis, & the Creek [?] took parties to the boathouse. Refreshments were in the large dining room. They seemed to enjoy themselves, & stayed till 6.00. Then at Ld Winmarleigh's request I took him out for a walk. He had been out walking early, had stood about during the whole three hours that the reception lasted, & he is nearly 80.

26 Sept. 1880: Walk in the park for exercise. Walk later with Ld Winmarleigh. Sefton comes over from Croxteth. Hear that Ld Lyons, who was coming to us next week, is obliged to return at once to his post: which looks like diplomatic trouble. Write to A.D.

Much talk with Ld Winmarleigh on Irish affairs, as to which I find his ideas perplexed to the last degree. He is a good deal alarmed, thinks an outbreak must come, thinks we ought to concede every reasonable demand, and even go beyond what is reasonable, in order to show our moderation – etc., etc., but in the same breath says that small holdings are fatal to the chance of improvement, that they ought to be discouraged, that it would be a good thing to subsidise emigration, on a great scale, that the one thing most wanted is the introduction of English capital – all true enough, but exactly the reverse of the ideas which the agitators are trying to work out. His mind seemed to be in utter confusion: yet he has been Irish secretary, has been 50 years in parliament, & is fairly clear-headed in ordinary life – though it is the fact that his unusual good-nature, combined with a certain timidity, make it difficult for him to take a decided line. He wants to agree with everybody, & will accept any argument as valid, as long as it is not pushed to its logical conclusion. But in the present case his perplexity is not greater than that of society in general.

27 Sept. 1880: Saw Ld Winmarleigh off, walking with him as far as the Prescot lodge. Talk of politics, he praised Hartington highly, in contrast to Gladstone, of whom he says a deep distrust exists on his own side.

It is a characteristic trait of him that, as he told us, he had intended his title to be Wyresdale, in which district his chief estates are: the patent was made out, & everything settled, when a neighbour, a Mr. Ormerod, protested, or rather appealed to him, on no other ground than that he also was a landowner in Wyresdale, and had called his place Wyresdale park. Patten's good nature could not resist the appeal, though utterly unreasonable, & at considerable inconvenience he changed to Winmarleigh.

Rev. E. Hornby[25] of Bury came.

In the papers, news that Lord Mountmorres[26], of Galway, has been shot, evidently by some person in the interest of the land agitators. He was a small owner of land, resident, an active magistrate, & it is said unpopular with his tenants. This act, following on several minor outrages, & on a series of violent speeches delivered at provincial meetings by Parnell, O'Connor, Redpath (an American) & others, will excite a strong feeling on this side the water – the more so as the demands of the Land League are becoming more & more wild. They now amount to a confiscation of the landlords' interest altogether – according to Parnell, he is to draw rent at a fixed rate for 35 years, after which it is to cease altogether. . . .

1 Oct. 1880: Cabinet held yesterday, to consider the crisis in eastern affairs. The naval demonstration before Dulcigno, which was to overawe the Albanian inhabitants & induce them to give up the town peaceably to Montenegro, has failed owing to the unexpected decision of the Sultan. He has instructed his commander in the district, Riza Pasha, to resist the entrance of the Montenegrin forces: and, as the Porte has 10,000 regular troops, the transfer becomes impossible, unless the fleets of Europe send a contingent to help Montenegro. But, as any such step involves war with Turkey, the admirals naturally decline to take it without express orders from their governments. Hence a crisis in diplomacy, & a Cabinet summoned.

It is to be noted that the Turks have put themselves entirely in the wrong, for they had formally agreed to the surrender of the territory in question, & are thus refusing to execute what they have promised.

It is said, but I don't know on what authority, that Musurus[27] has done a great deal of mischief by continually assuring his government that the English Cabinet meant nothing, & would not go to war with them under any circumstances. I can well believe that he has held language of this kind, for it used to be impossible in 1876–1878 to get him to convey any message of an unpleasant or menacing character. Whether from fear of losing his place, or mere Levantine servility, he was sure to soften it down so as to be utterly unmeaning.

2 Oct. 1880: I accept the presidency of a co–operative congress in June next, after some reflection: but I think the object harmless in any case, & probably useful, & it serves to divert support from more revolutionary schemes.

Garden party in afternoon which was partly spoilt by weather but some of our guests went as far as the boathouse & gardens. Most however stayed in the house, where between the library & picture gallery they were well enough amused. We had refreshments in the large dining room, & a temporary wooden staircase from the end window there to the lawn below.

De La Warr's eldest son, a boy of 11, came yesterday, & is staying in the house.

Talk with Malet[28] as to Egypt. He thinks the country is less oppressed & impoverished than it has of late been the fashion to suppose. The creditors have accepted 4% as fair interest on their money, which is not beyond the power of the people to pay: the present Khedive is so far amenable to advice, & likely to do well. He thinks there is room for an almost unlimited increase in wealth, prosperity, & population, but it must be gradual, the result of time & of better administration. Cave[29], he says, took far too favourable a view of the revenue & resources of the country; he thought it could yield in taxes £10,000,000, whereas £7,000,000 is nearer the reality . . .

He talked of the ex-Khedive, said there is no doubt but that in his time the old eastern practice of doing away with persons who were thought dangerous to the state by private assassination was still continued. The finance minister, who was supposed to have been banished to Upper Egypt, & to have died there, was really murdered in a palace near Cairo, to which the Khedive in person took him in his own carriage. When there he was seized & made away with, the Khedive disappearing so as not to be an actual witness of the murder, & returning to Cairo. (I had heard another report, that the minister was caused to set off for his place of exile, & poisoned on the way.)

Malet says that, by tacit consent of all other powers, a dual protectorate of Egypt has been recognised as vested in England & France: & that the Egyptians do not dislike this arrangement, as it saves them from pressure from any other quarter. But what is not agreeable to them is the high salary paid to Europeans employed – £3,000 to £4,000 a year, whereas the Khedive's ministers have only £1,500. . . .

6 Oct. 1880: . . . We have in the papers today the Turkish answer to the demands of the powers. It is vague & illusory but in substance a refusal thinly disguised. What is to be done now? The naval demonstration before Dulcigno, always a questionable proceeding, has failed, & cannot be renewed: the ships are gone into safer quarters, & any fresh menace must be directed against the Turkish government itself. But if the Sultan will not give way? Up to the present moment he has shown himself obstinate, & he probably reckons on the Powers not being able to agree as to the next step. The Cabinet is scattered again, but probably it would be useless for ministers to meet until the opinions of other powers are known.

7 Oct. 1880: . . . Ld Houghton & Ly G. Russell[30] came to stay.

Ly G. talks of Skelmersdale [Earl of Lathom]: his increasing interest in public affairs: his occasional failures in health: he suffers much from rheumatism at times: two of his sisters also in very bad health.

We have today the full text of the Turkish reply to the summons of the powers, & a remarkable document it is. No vagueness such as appeared in the telegraphic summary, but a simple downright rejection of the demands made by Europe, scarcely disguised under the forms of diplomatic courtesy. The substance & style of this document at least make the situation simpler. Whether the powers were wise or unwise in their original claim, they have now no choice except to press it, if they can agree on the means. But, if the Sultan remains in his present temper, coercion will become inevitable – and then what next? Will the whole Turkish Empire fall to pieces in our hands?

8 Oct. 1880: Another disagreeable day, east wind & smoke, with some rain.

Houghton left us about 1.00 to return to his Yorkshire home. He made himself very agreeable, being full of anecdote, & seeming to know, or to have known, every remarkable person in Europe. Mr. & Mrs. Cazalet came to stay . . . also Ld Camperdown.

Houghton talked a good deal of Ld Beaconsfield, & told some curious stories of him. One was to the effect that in his younger days he had said to Milnes[31]: 'I may play many parts in politics, & seem to change in many things: but there are two points on which you will always find me the same – I shall be a true Jew and a true Republican.' The second was that, talking to Disraeli about the time of his famous attacks on Peel, Milnes said to him: 'Your speech was a fine one – but somehow it seemed to me not to show much of the personal animosity which you affect.' Disraeli answered: 'Personal animosity! There is none in the case, there is nobody whom I respect more than Sir Robert, & perhaps some day I shall have the chance of doing what he is doing now.' Houghton said these words had made a strong impression upon him, & that he remembered them accurately. A third speech of Ld B. is less characteristic, but curious & I think true[32]. Soon after the Prince Consort's death, he said of him: 'That man, if he had lived, would have realised all the projects of George III. He had the will to do it, & he had the ability.'

9 Oct. 1880: . . . Talk in the intervals of shooting with Münster[33] about what is passing in Europe: he describes the situation: says Germany will take no active part in coercive measures against Turkey: nor he thinks will Austria or France: if anything of that kind is attempted, only Italy & Russia will join with England. The Russian govt. has of course its own objects to serve & does not disguise them: it wishes to push on the powers to insist on their demands, the Sultan to resist them, & so bring about a general disturbance, in the course of which the Turkish Empire would probably go to pieces. The Italians have no object to serve, but the mere desire to be recognised as a great power would induce them to join in almost any demonstration for any purpose.

10 Oct. 1880 (Sunday): Münster left early this morning for London: having before his departure informed us as a fact that the Russian squadron had started to occupy Smyrna, & that ours was about to follow. This startling piece of news turned out to be a mere *canard*. Luckily he had treated it as confidential, so that we did not spread the story. . . .

12 Oct. 1880: News that the eastern crisis is over for the time, the Sultan having given way as to the cession of Dulcigno. This settles matters for the time, and is a success for the Cabinet: but the more difficult Greek question remains behind. . . .

15 Oct. 1880: . . . Irish agitation continues unabated: the air is full of rumours of prosecutions, but it is notorious that Forster & Gladstone dislike the notion of taking any step of that kind, & that their feeling is shared by many of their supporters. In plain words, they are not sorry that the landowners should be exposed to terror, as a method of inducing them to acquiesce more readily in any plan of settlement favourable to the tenants. Meanwhile in Cork (I think it is) a sort of counter-agitation has been got up by the labourers, who say with reason that they will be no gainers but rather the contrary by a movement which simply transfers the soil from one class of owners to another. . . .

18 Oct. 1880: Sharp white frost.

Balances from Ward . . . I have now put by in the course of this year £70,000, which is more by £30,000 than what I reckon as the sum which ought to be saved. . . .

20 Oct. 1880: Sharp frost, the first real frost of the year. Also east wind & stench, from which I note that till now we have been entirely or almost entirely free.

. . . Talbot left suddenly summoned by a telegram from the Carlton. It seems that he was chairman of a committee which sent down £3,000 to Oxford: the money was used for purposes of bribery, and a commission is now enquiring into the whole matter. I do not suppose that T. [albot] is in danger of being called to account, for he knew & could know nothing as to the application of the funds, & the sum was not larger than might be legitimately wanted, but he is evidently uncomfortable, & it is a disagreeable business to be mixed up in. He went off literally at half an hour's notice. . . .

24 Oct. 1880: The political world has been quite unusually quiet: no speeches either in attack or defence. The chief interest at home is concentrated on Irish affairs, which are going from bad to worse: fresh outrages every day: the speeches of the Land League growing more & more violent & defiant: a system of terrorism established over a large part of the country, directed not merely against landlords, or to prevent evictions, but against tenants who set the bad example of paying their rents. The game of the agitators is so to depress the value of landed property, & to make the position of the landowner so insecure, that he will be ready to give up his land on very inadequate terms. The priests look on, affecting to deprecate violence, & in some instances really alarmed by a movement which has got beyond their control: but not on the whole dissatisfied, as the class attacked is foreign & protestant. Debts are occasionally repudiated as well as rents: but with less eagerness, for the leaders in the agitation feel that they cannot afford to quarrel with the local tradesmen. Home Rule is little spoken of, & appears to have drooped into the background: but in fact the anti-landlord movement is nationalist rather than socialist in character. The object is to weaken the English connection, of which landowners . . . are the steadiest supporters. At last it has been decided to prosecute the leading agitators: & not a day too soon, for on this side the Channel a strong feeling was growing up that leniency had been carried too far, and that in fact it amounted to a tacit connivance. Critics were beginning to hint that Gladstone & Forster were not in their hearts sorry that the landowners should be intimidated, since a little fear would make them readier to come into the ministerial plans: and language of this kind was being held by friends as well as by opponents. That the prosecutions will succeed is held unlikely, under the present jury system: but it is thought that the failure itself will be useful, as showing the need of obtaining further powers from parliament. If such powers had been asked without previous action, the answer would have been ready: 'Why have you not used the powers which you have already?' Possibly, but this is a mere surmise of my own; the Cabinet may not be sorry that a trial which cannot well end before Christmas should serve as an excuse for not holding an autumn session: which would be inconvenient in many ways.

In foreign affairs, the only important incident is that the King of Greece has delivered himself of an exceedingly warlike manifesto, threatening to march into Turkey on his own account if the Powers will not give him possession of what they have promised. Nobody, however, is much alarmed, for it is thought that the speech is only meant to gratify Greek feeling, and that the King will have the sense to take care that he is not allowed to do what he threatens – like a duellist who manages to let the police know of his intentions. The English government, having got the Dulcigno business settled, can afford to wait, and most people believe that they have had a warning to be cautious in future, in their very narrow escape from a failure which would have been ridiculous. . . .

27 Oct. 1880: . . . The season of political speeches has begun: several have been delivered: the only one of importance being by Salisbury. It is more temperate than usual with him, marked by no especial acrimony, but singular in this respect, that he argues at length against any attempt to execute the treaty of Berlin, he having himself signed that treaty, and all his party appealing to it as a great diplomatic success. He contends that the powers had no right to give away Turkish territory to Greece: & in this it is impossible to say that he is wrong: but, when united Europe agrees in recommending a certain cession to be made by Turkey, it is a strange plea that nothing more was meant than that the Porte should be only advised to do what notoriously it will not do except under pressure. In fact – wisely or unwisely – the treaty implied coercion in the last resort, & was so understood on all hands. And now one of the authors of this coercion policy turns round & objects to its being carried into effect. . . .

31 Oct. 1880 (Sunday): . . . Irish trouble and agitation continue as before. Parnell, whose prudence in using no language for which he can be held legally responsible has been hitherto as remarkable as his intense virulence against England, has let the cat out of the bag. He has told a meeting that the land agitation is only intended to lead up to independence – which is a mistake, since it alienates the English democracy – and he has further said that if the opportunity offered (for insurrection, though he did not actually use the word) the American people would be as ready to help them at need as they had been to assist them with subscriptions. – This is treason, & I cannot understand so cunning a speaker talking so, except on the supposition that he wishes to be sentenced to imprisonment – feeling sure of an early release when the crisis is over, & wishing to be out of the way when the time comes for fighting or giving up the game.

1 Nov. 1880: See Ward, who talks of being able to spare another £10,000 from current expenses: which if true will be £80,000 saved in all, more than ever yet in one year.

Ride in the park which looks as well as anything can look in November, the day being bright & sunny.

Miss Franks, Margaret, Arthur, & Ly D. all left about 11.00, two of them for London, the other two for Woburn. I stay on for sessions. – Though left alone, which is not cheerful, I am glad that M. is gone, for the Lancashire climate, & perhaps also the labour of receiving so many guests, has brought her into a condition of gloom & depression which is painful to witness, though I have seen it in her once or twice before. And I watch any tendency in that direction with the more anxiety from knowing the family predisposition. Probably change of air & scene will set all right for the time.

2 Nov. 1880: Drive into Liverpool, & meet the magistrates in St. George's Hall. Of them about 40 attended at the opening . . . The calendar was heavy, 84 cases. I counted 45 lawyers in court, which looks as if they had not much else to do. Sat till 5.30, none of the cases remarkable in any way, & most of them short. Home to a dinner by myself, wrote notes & letters.

3 Nov. 1880: In St. George's Hall by 10.00, & sat till near 6.00.

Again dined alone, which I do not regret when weary with a long day's work.

4 Nov. 1880: Liverpool at 10.00, & sat hearing appeals till 1.00 . . . Then jury cases came on again . . . Went off in haste, at 6.16, to dress at the Adelphi, having to dine with the Mayor: about 140 sat down . . .

5 Nov. 1880: Liverpool again at 10.00, & sat till 4.30, when finished all the cases. . . .

6 Nov. 1880: Leave Knowsley at 8.30, reach St. J. Square a little before 3.00, there meet M. & with her to Keston by 5.15 train. Much enjoyment there of quiet, rest, & pure air. M. well & cheerful; the change in 4 days is extraordinary.

My poor old friend, Ld Malmesbury, aged 73, & too infirm to walk steadily across a room, has committed the folly which he threatened in the spring and, having been thrown over by one woman, who concealed the fact that she was actually married when he proposed to her, has now married her sister. He will probably not have long to repent his mistake.

Much talk at the sessions with H. Bright, . . . whom I like . . . We discussed . . . a biography of Mrs. Grote [by Lady Eastlake]. Bright quoted a saying of Sydney Smith, new to me, 'that till he became acquainted with Mrs. Grote he never had known the meaning of the word grotesque': and another, 'that he liked the Grotes: Mr. Grote because his manners were so ladylike, and Mrs. Grote because she was such a thorough gentleman'. Perhaps the point of these sayings would be lost on any one who did not know the pair: he formal, courteous, & refined to that degree that you felt a vulgar expression would be like a blow to him: she, large, masculine, & eccentric, though amiable & highly cultivated.

Politics remain as they were. Nothing is talked of except Ireland. The prosecutions are set on foot, but I find a general belief that they are not serious: that success is not expected, & that the only object of them is to stop the mouths of the landlords, & of those who sympathise with the landlords on this side, by showing that all that was possible has been done. Those among the agitators who have been left out are deeply disgusted, having lost their best chance of notoriety: apropos to which a story is quoted, probably not true, but characteristic, to the effect that Tom Steele, a sort of Boswell to O'Connell, having given a good deal of trouble to the prosecutors in the O'Connell trial, was addressed by the law officer conducting the case: 'Mr. Steele, if you are not quiet, I'll tell you what I'll do – I'll leave your name out of the indictment!' . . .

9 Nov. 1880: My brother-in-law, W.P. Talbot, was yesterday examined before the Oxford election commissioners as to his part in sending down the money used for bribery. He admitted having signed a cheque for £3,000, which went to Oxford, but says he did so only as a member of the committee which managed such matters, in concert with others, that he had no knowledge of the purpose to which it was afterwards applied, & supposed that it would be used only for legal expenses. He seems to have told his story fairly enough, & I think he will hear no more of the matter. But, in his position as a servant of the House of Lords, it was a mistake to get himself mixed up in electioneering intrigues, however legally defensible. . . .

10 Nov. 1880: . . . One of our grants was to a Mr. Rutherford, author of a clever little book called *Sketches from Shady Places*, written from intimate personal knowledge of the vagabond & predatory classes, & showing some real literary power. One should have thought such a man could at least have got his living: but he, like all the other applicants, is in actual want of food. They generally state the amount of income which they are in the habit of earning: today none put it higher than £300, while several returned £200 as their average. . . .

11 Nov. 1880: The subject of the moment is Gladstone's Mansion House speech, & it seems to have been generally well received. Shorter than such speeches usually are, very moderate in tone, & addressed to the nation rather than to a party, it reads well, and will have conciliated doubtful friends & candid opponents by offering no point for attack. In fact its merit consists quite as much in what it does not say as in what it does. Gladstone has been suspected of an undue degree of sympathy with the Irish malcontents, & of a disposition to minimise their acts of violence: on Tuesday night he spoke firmly as to the necessity of putting down outrages, & as to the intention of the Cabinet to call for fresh powers if those they have are not sufficient: while his allusion to possible amendments of the land law was not such as to alarm owners, or encourage the friends of the Land League. The feeling of his audience was (I am told) quite unmistakable, and shown most clearly by the enthusiastic cheers which followed a very commonplace remark of Ld Selborne's on the necessity of maintaining law as well as liberty. He (I believe) meant nothing by it except a generality: but the hearers applied it to the case of Ireland, & applauded in a way that astonished no one more than the Chancellor himself.

Nothing but Ireland was thought of: references to the eastern difficulty, I am told, fell flat. . . .

14 Nov. 1880: . . . Read a striking article on the future of India in the *Economist*: the writer's argument is that we are confronted with a difficulty that will probably be insuperable – the gradual & rapid growth of population which we ourselves have caused by our improved administration. We have put an end to the three great checks on increase – war, pestilence, & famine . . . What can follow except gradually increasing distress, ending in starvation? If these views are correct, & to me they seem so, they will bring again into prominence the theory of Malthus, which of late years there has been a tendency to ignore: our great commercial wealth, & our habit of emigration, having made the question practically of little importance to England. There is nothing absolutely new in the *Economist* paper, but it is founded on figures supplied by Dr. Hunter[34], who is employed as a statistician by the Calcutta authorities, & is therefore not likely to be unduly despondent in his outlook.

15 Nov. 1880: Day fairly fine in morning: later, very wet.
Ward writes that he can spare for investment £10,000 more, which I accordingly ask him to send up. . . . I have now put by in one year £80,000 out of income, which I never did before, nor probably shall again.

Send Mrs. Freeman, the wife of our former gardener, £10.

Write to A.D., to Sanderson, & others.

Read to M. as before.

The Irish trouble has passed into a new phase: one Capt. Boycott, a land agent in Mayo, having made himself unpopular, an attempt is being made to drive him out of the country: not by violence, but by a general agreement to refuse to work for him, or to sell him provisions, such agreement being enforced by intimidation, so that his fields are unworked, and he lives guarded by constables in a kind of siege. The Ulster Protestants, whose hereditary dislike of the Celtic peasantry has been revived by recent agitation, determined to raise the blockade, & it was at first proposed to send 500 armed men from the north to guard Capt. Boycott & get in his crops. This proceeding was objected to by the authorities, as being certain to lead to a fight – which no doubt it would – & in the end it was decided that only 50 should go: but to prevent mischief they are guarded by a small army of several hundred regulars, with two guns: this force, or the greater part of it, is encamped round Capt. Boycott's house, & his potatoes are thus being got in at a cost of some £10,000 to the state. It is not disguised that this device for driving out of the country agents & landlords is the work of the Land League: & it is likely to be tried else-where, though as yet the organisation is hardly complete enough anywhere except in Mayo to make it possible. Forster & the Cabinet are evidently determined to do no more in the way of reprisal than is absolutely inevitable: partly no doubt from the unpopular-ity of coercive measures with the Liberals, partly also (I suppose) from an idea, not wholly ill-founded, that, the more disagreeable the position of the Irish landlords is made, the more willing they will be to come into such terms as government may propose.

Two plans are commonly discussed for settling the land difficulty: the first being to give the tenant a fixed perpetual right in his holding: with power to sell, and rent decided by some external authority: which is simple, easily done, & costs nothing: the objection being that it is a robbery of the landowners' reversionary right. The other is to buy out the landlord with government money & sell to the tenants, they paying back principal & interest by instalments spread over a term of years. This scheme would be willingly accepted by Irish landowners in general, though some might object. Its defect is that it involves an enormous outlay in the first instance, not all of which will be recoverable: that it creates a body of peasant proprietors, heavily encumbered from the outset: and that, the state being the universal landlord, more money than ever will be drawn out from Ireland, thus aggravating the chief grievance now complained of. – Both these proposals are open to the objection that the small farmer, left free, will subdivide his holding & thus create again the pauper population that existed in 1841: but this objection, though a grave one, is common to all schemes whose object is to free the tenant from landlord control.
. . .

21 Nov. 1880: . . . News in the papers of the sudden death of Cockburn, C.J.[35], aged 77 or 78, but still by far the most brilliant speaker either on the bench or at the bar. He was remarkably pleasant in conversation: spared much time for society, notwithstanding his heavy official duties: enjoyed music, yachting, and in younger years was noted for his appreciation of female company. This trait in his character operated to prevent his receiv-ing the peerage which was offered him more than once: but, having a natural son, to whom he was much attached, living with him, he could not bear the idea of holding a title which would not descend to this youth, and which would make public the fact of his ille-gitimacy, since young Cockburn would not have been entitled to the style of 'Honourable'. By those who envied his success, Cockburn was said to be but little of a lawyer, & this may have been true: but long experience supplied the want, if it ever existed, & certainly no complaints were heard on that score. Whatever he may have done as to law, he studied with extreme care the art of oratory: two of his greatest speeches were that on the Pacifico case in 1850, and that on the Hopwood trial at Liverpool in 1855: and I have been told that on both these occasions he not only prepared his peroration in writing, but recited it several times over to a friend to test the effect. I think my informant was the present Sir F. Holland[36] but am not sure. I know that, whoever he was, he professed to have heard the recitation. The Chief Justice's judgments on important cases were works of art, framed with unusual care, & in the expectation (probably not to be disappointed) that they would preserve his fame to posterity, at least in his own profession. We have greater lawyers left in Cairns & Selborne: but, as a legal orator, he has not left his equal. – Indeed the prospects of oratory in or out of the legal profession are not brilliant. Bright, Gladstone, Ld Beaconsfield, are all ending their careers: where is their match among the juniors? In the House of Commons there is absolutely no one – in the Lords, though Argyll, Salisbury, & the Bp of Peterborough[37] are all effective & powerful debaters, the first of the three is the only one who attempts oratory of the higher kind, and besides them I know no one who is even a competitor in that line. . . .

24 Nov. 1880: Buy Lord Beaconsfield's new novel, *Endymion*. I am told that for the copyright of this book there was given £10,000, & that 8,000 copies were subscribed for before it appeared.

See my sister at luncheon. Talbot is better, & they think his complaint curable. Bad report of Skelmersdale's [Lathom's] health, & worse of his sister.

Keston by 6.05 train. Read to M. in evening out of the new novel.

25 Nov. 1880: . . . Read Ld B.'s new novel to M. – I suspend judgment upon it till we have finished.

26 Nov. 1880: . . . Continued to read Ld Beaconsfield's novel.

27 Nov. 1880 (Saturday): Day fine. Call with M. on Mr. & Mrs. Darwin, at Downe, & stayed nearly an hour. . . .

29 Nov. 1880: Received from Ward a well drawn summary of my outlay under the head benefactions. This for last year comes to £7,103, not including the £2,000 which I draw yearly for personal distribution, nor the £2,000 paid to my sister. I thank him for it – he has enabled me to understand my own affairs much better than I did in Moult's time. Wrote to him to invest £50 in a new coffee-tavern, which is really a gift.

Ld Donoughmore sends me a pamphlet, being the case of the Irish landlords, which I acknowledge with thanks, though several copies have reached me before. One I sent to Froude, who is writing on the Irish question – the other to Sanderson for Ld Granville.

30 Nov. 1880: Many letters: one from . . . a parson, very earnest if not very original: he is much exercised in mind about the quantity of liquor consumed in Liverpool, and cries out for a bill: I tell him there will almost certainly be one next year: but I do not add that Harcourt is about the last man in public life who will quarrel with the publicans if he can help it.

. . . Sanderson came to luncheon, looking as we thought, ill & weary: but in fairly good spirits. We talked of current affairs, but with some reserve, as I wished to avoid the appearance of curiosity. He thinks, and I gather that the Cabinet do, the prospect unpleasant – the Irish expecting a land bill such as the H. of Lords will not swallow, even if the government will – there being a good deal of discontent at the alleged supineness of the authorities in regard of Irish disturbance – and the bitterness of party feeling making help or forbearance from the opposition improbable. Distrust & fear of what Gladstone may do next is scarcely concealed even by his colleagues, & openly avowed by the Whigs.

Note Sanderson's own troubles, his mother ill, brother still without employment, & sister-in-law lately in an asylum through drink.

1 Dec. 1880: . . . Ld Coleridge is Chief Justice in the place of Cockburn: a promotion to which he was probably entitled, & which was a necessity if, as is understood, the other Chief Justiceship & the Chief Baron's place are to be reduced to the rank of ordinary judgeships. Ld Coleridge is eloquent, with a singular sweetness of voice & fluency of well chosen speech: in argument he is (or was when I used to hear him) less strong than in appeals to feeling: he had a curious knack of jumping over the weak points in his own case, which sometimes served him, but created distrust when often repeated. Of his purely legal qualifications I have heard no trustworthy opinion. In secular politics he is a rather extreme Liberal: in church matters a strong and even intolerant high churchman – an unpleasant & incongruous mixture, but well suited to the Premier's taste. Brett, who knows & does not love him, says that he often talks in a strain of ridicule about church matters – but I should require further evidence before accepting that statement. His conversation is varied & agreeable: his manner rather too deferential, its extreme humility putting you on your guard at least as much as it conciliates. It is the Oxford or ecclesiastical manner, somewhat overdone. – Much doubt among lawyers whether it is wise to lessen the prizes of the profession, & not a few laymen agree with them: the end it is feared will be that the strongest men at the bar will not care to take judgeships, and that the bench will not be intellectually equal to the men who argue before it. A leading counsel can make from £10,000 to £15,000 a year without greater effort than that which a judge has to make for £5,000: nor is the dignity of a judicial position so highly rated as it used to be some 20 or 30 years ago. I do not know why, but the fact is certainly so. . . .

3 Dec. 1880: Finished Ld Beaconsfield's novel. It is like all he has written, clever, amusing, fantastic: rather a fairy tale than a picture of real life, so far as the story is concerned, but with its extravagances are mixed so many shrewd traits of character and ingenious phrases that the absurdity of the tale is forgotten. The writer's characteristic habits of thought reappear: the delight with which he dwells on details of external splendour, fine houses, parks, jewels, equipages, etc., is almost childish, were it not so obviously natural & irrepressible.

Another marked trait is the extraordinary & exaggerated prominence which he gives to merely social influences in political matters: a lady who gives receptions is in his view hardly a less important personage than the parliamentary leader of a party. – The book has the merit of being thoroughly good tempered: there are reminiscences of various eminent personages, but nothing that can be called a portrait, unless George Smythe[38] be an exception. Nor is any description of character bitter or unpleasing like those of Croker[39] & Ld Hertford[40] in *Coningsby*. – Altogether, if not a first rate work in a purely literary point of view, it is a remarkable production for a man of 75, after six years of a kind of labour which does not stimulate the imaginative faculty.

Col. & Mrs. Long came over from Bromley Hill & sat with us an hour. He talks much of my uncle H.S.[41], his strange way of disappearing for weeks, how he (Long) as a young man was sent to look for him, & found him in a small public house. There was no woman in the case: it was only oddity.

4 Dec. 1880: . . . In the papers . . . a wild letter from Gordon ('Chinese' Gordon) proposing that the state should buy up all the west & south-west of Ireland, to sell it again to the tenants, between whom & their landlords he believes there can never be peace.

A more rational proposal is signed 'W.M.J.', which initials are understood to be those of Lord Justice James. His idea is to give to all small holders, under £50 rental, fixity of tenure at rents settled by the state: the landlords, if dissatisfied, to be bought at 25 years' purchase, in which case the tenants are to become owners paying for their farms by instalments. In the case of holders of more than £50 rental, they & the landowners to be free to contract themselves out of the law. – In the above scheme there is no great injustice to the owner, since he is offered compensation should he decline to hold Irish land under the new conditions: but the writer evidently does not realise the eagerness with which the great majority of Irish landlords would come forward to get rid of their lands, nor the consequent magnitude of the charge imposed on the exchequer. . . .

6 Dec. 1880: Letter from Sanderson, giving me notice that Talbot's proceedings in connection with the Oxford election have been a good deal commented on among ministers, & hinting that from what he hears he thinks it would be as well that T. should discontinue his connection with the election committee at the Carlton, & make known to those to whom he is responsible (I suppose the [Lord] Chancellor) that he has done so.

The Irish trouble has passed into a new phase. Parnell, in a speech delivered at Waterford, within the last few days, has openly declared – not indeed for the first time, but in language more explicit than ever before, that the land question is with him not an end, but a means, the object being the restoration of Irish independence. He professes to wish to use none but constitutional means at present, but indicates in few words the policy of systematic obstruction. 'England,' he says, 'has given us our present constitution for her purposes, and we will use it for ours.' He discourages emigration to America, on the plea that there is in Ireland plenty of land left unsettled: and advises putting pressure on the owners & tenants of large grazing farms to compel them to give these up.

Whether it was politic in Parnell to speak so plainly may be a question: but he has undoubtedly made matters easier for English politicians. It is no longer possible to contend that the agitation is merely for reformed land laws: the real purpose is frankly announced. We have the old repeal agitation of O'Connell's time revived, & with more system & reality in it than it had 35 years ago. Parnell's influence is probably as great as that of O'Connell, & this although he is a Protestant: but, if it were conceivable that the movement should succeed, the priests would soon have a leader of their own in his place.

Unluckily a mistake has been made on the other side. The Irish Chief Justice last week refused, quite reasonably, an impudent application for the postponement of Parnell's trial, on the ground that he, Parnell, & his friends, would be wanted in the H. of Commons: but, as luck would have it, he took the opportunity to denounce the Parnellite agitation & the author of it, in language which would have been quite in place had he been passing sentence after conviction, but which unmistakably assumed the guilt of the parties whom he was going to try.

One is reminded of a similar performance by (I think) Whiteside, of which a friend said 'that there had been nothing like it in the way of a charge, since the charge of Balaclava'. – The nationalists see their advantage and, if a conviction is secured, they will denounce the judge as partial, & affirm that the issue was prejudged – not wholly without some plausible ground.

Much (and very idle) talk of differences in Cabinet, which are vehemently denied by Liberal papers, so vehemently as to lead one to suspect that there is some truth in the story. But nothing can be really known.

7 Dec. 1880: Receive another letter from Sanderson, and after consideration write to my sister. I abstain in my letter from any expression of opinion or proffer of advice, but simply repeat what has reached me, not naming T.H.S. but speaking of him as a person closely connected with the ministry, & who has probably received a hint to write.

8 Dec. 1880: Leave Keston with regret but, as the object of giving M. a complete rest is secured, there is no reason for longer stay – & I think I grow lethargic & dull in the comparative absence of society & employment. London by 1.45. At 4.00 to meeting of the City Commission . . . caution is necessary, for we have no compulsory powers of enquiry, though if wanted they could probably be obtained from parliament.

Some talk on general affairs with Sir N. de Rothschild, who seems to have a good deal of the family shrewdness, & information in plenty as to what is passing. . . .

9 Dec. 1880: . . . Dine with Froude & his daughter, meeting a friend of his, an Irish landowner, Mr. Mahoney[42], who remembered having seen me at Killarney in 1859. Much pleasant talk. He is one of the few improving landlords in the south-west, and has published a pamphlet deprecating the confiscation of money spent by him on his farms, under pretence of settling the tenants' rent in perpetuity. But I find on enquiry that he thinks many rents are fixed at too high a rate in his part of the country, by the small owners, & would not be averse to see a court established which should limit the amount of rents. I could not, however, get him to say by what process a fair rent was to be fixed: he seemed to think that according to Irish practice there would be no great difficulty in the matter. He said that where he lives there is a good deal of jealousy between the Fenian chiefs and the new promoters of the Land League: the former looking down on the latter as on men who have sacrificed the great national idea for a mere pecuniary object. The quarrel had gone so far that the respective parties had come to blows.

Note that Lord Claud Hamilton, whom I met in the morning, & Ld Kenmare, whom I saw at the Travellers', both agree in saying that, so far from the outrages committed being exaggerated, they continually pass without notice, because the sufferers themselves do not choose to let them be known: so thoroughly are they intimidated that they refuse to complain, & if pressed even deny the fact, knowing that to give information would presently cost them their lives.

I hear also that in Dublin there is difficulty in getting men to serve on juries – the most respectable tradesmen prefer paying a fine, lest they should be required to sit in some political case, & compelled by evidence to find a verdict of guilty: which would certainly ruin their business, & lucky for them if it did no worse. . . .

13 Dec. 1880: . . . News from London . . . that Forster has come over again, this time to press for additional powers of enforcing the law: & indeed it is quite time: for over a large part of Ireland the Land League is now supreme. There is not even agitation, or the necessity for it, since obedience is paid to the local leaders of the movement, who enforce their orders by what is called 'boycotting' . . . The Land League does not confine itself to cases of agrarian disturbance or quarrels about land, but interferes wherever there is an alleged case of oppression, replacing labourers who have been dismissed, compelling employers to alter their rules, & in many instances proscribing respectable & quiet individuals for no offence except that of having refused or neglected to contribute to the League funds. It is said that in the Western markets no peasant can buy or sell without producing his ticket of membership obtained from the League. Add to this that arms are being bought in extraordinary quantities, & these mostly of a kind (rifles & revolvers) which cannot be wanted for any purpose except that of insurrection. There is a strong disposition in England to blame Forster for not having more effectually repressed this movement in its earlier stages: but I greatly doubt whether he is in fault: the feeling of the Irish masses is decidedly with the agitators, witnesses will give no evidence, juries will not convict, even those who have suffered personally dare not make the fact public, lest matters should be worse for them.

14 Dec. 1880: Shooting . . . we brought in 673 head.

Grant Duff came to stay.

In the newspapers appears the decision come to at yesterday's Cabinet: obviously the result of a compromise. It is settled that there is to be no immediate meeting of parliament, the date of 6 Jan. is adhered to: and there will be no action beyond the limits of ordinary law in the interval. But it is given out that the suspension of Habeas Corpus will be moved at once on parliament coming together. So each side has something to go away with: neither will be content, but each will say that it might have been worse. Forster is attacked by both Liberals & Conservatives: the latter being disappointed that he does not resign, the former not forgiving his supposed desire for a more coercive policy. As far as I can see, he has done his duty fairly: but the task of keeping order in Ireland as things are now is an all but impossible one – the terror is universal, & the English papers are full of complaints of the impossibility of living in the south or west for anyone who is not prepared to accept the orders of the League.

Mr. Bence Jones[43], a well known & improving landlord, has been 'boycotted' for refusing to accept rent at Griffith's valuation: Ld Kenmare, who is rebuilding his house, has had a strike of all his workmen engaged on it because one Englishman has been employed: in fact the condition of the country is one of complete anarchy: no debt can be collected, & no claim enforced. Baron Dowse[44] received a threatening letter while on the bench: the same has happened to another judge: solicitors advise their clients (v. *The Times* of this day) that it would be useless & dangerous to apply for compensation where injuries have been sustained. I do not think that at any moment during the Fenian troubles society was so disorganised.

15 Dec. 1880: Wet morning, with east wind & stench from St. Helens: but it cleared off later. C. Münster, [Lord] Calthorpe, [etc.] shot . . . They brought in 409 head.

I did not go out with them, but walked with Grant Duff in the afternoon.

Talk with Ward: the leases of this year . . . give £7,500, nearly all new rent: an unprecedented increase, even on this estate.

Desired £500 more to be put to my charity account.

Desired Ward to put £200 to Hale's account, to be drawn when he pleases, to meet the heavy charges he has been put to by his own & his wife's illness.

Gave Margaret £10 for the Knowsley village library.

G. Duff talked freely of the Basuto war, as to which he drew a distinction: saying that the intended disarmament of the tribe could not be called an act of injustice, since they were to be fairly paid for the arms they gave up, & had no use for them of a legitimate kind: they did not want them for hunting, or for protection against wild beasts, or for defence against external enemies, seeing they have none: the object of their acquisition was to intimidate the whites, by holding over them the threat of a possible rising. The disarmament was therefore justifiable morally but not on grounds of policy: it had been rashly undertaken, without military strength to enforce it, & after the disapproval of the home authorities had been made known, which naturally encouraged resistance.

I found him much disheartened by the obstinate persistence of both the Canadian & Australian colonies in a policy of protection: as to which he did not see his way to any change: indeed he seemed inclined to admit that it was only owing to an exceptional combination of circumstances that in this country free trade became a popular cry – the chief articles taxed being food, the middle class interested in getting the tax off, & the persons supposed to be benefited by its existence being a rich & numerically limited class of landowners.

16 Dec. 1880: . . . Talk with Münster about France: his tone rather surprised me. It was contemptuous & angry, as if some recent provocation had been given, but I know of none. He said the French had no man of any capacity to guide them – that the Assembly was utterly devoid of talent . . . that their condition was one of utter decadence. I objected their extraordinary prosperity in the last two or three years, but he seemed to think that that circumstance only made matters worse: they had taken to industry & thought of nothing but increasing their wealth. – Is there a little envy at the bottom of this kind of talk? or is it an expression, simply, of the genuine contempt which a military aristocracy is apt to feel for an industrial democracy? or is there a latent feeling that the immense material prosperity of the Republic is a danger to German institutions? . . . Münster answered decidedly that things would not long be smooth in France: he did not say why, nor did I ask.

We talked of the Jews in Germany, against whom there is just now an outcry: he did not justify, but explained it, saying that the feeling was not due to religious intolerance (which I believe)but to dislike of a class of men who had no patriotism, did not really care for any German interest, did not even make a show of serving the state in any way, but confined themselves to amassing fortunes, in which they were very successful. He did not add what others have told me, that part of the outbreak of apparent fanaticism is due to the arrogance with which the richer Jews display their wealth, & part to the extraordinary hold which they have got over the German press: so that scarcely any opinion adverse to them can get itself circulated.

17 Dec. 1880: Shooting . . . we brought in 709 head . . . More than 100 lookers-on walked with us.

Lawrence writes that he has secured the cottage & garden at Witley for £200 (v. 12 Dec.) and another for £600. A third is to be had for £675, if I sanction the purchase, which I do.

It is in the papers that the Cabinet yesterday sat 4½ hours, and hints are given that the land bill is settled, at least in principle. We are further made to understand that it is very moderate, not likely to give offence, or to fail in the Lords. But who knows the truth? Meanwhile the Irish anarchy increases, & law has ceased to exist. Here is one case among many. A Mr. Healy[45], a Parnellite, was put on his trial for intimidation, he having threatened a farmer with sundry unpleasant consequences if he failed to obey some orders of the League. When the trial came on, the man who had been threatened retracted his evidence, declared there had been no intimidation, & that only friendly advice had been offered. As he was the main witness, the case broke down. The prosecutor did not dare to tell the truth in his own interest. Still more significant is the public statement of Baron Dowse, that at the assizes (I think in Galway) 291 cases stood for trial: but only 13 were proceeded with: in the remaining 278 the prosecution was dropped, the parties not daring to come forward. At last English feeling has been thoroughly roused, & I am afraid my friends of the government will have an unpleasant time when parliament meets: for beyond doubt matters would not have gone so far if active measures of repression had been taken in time. Judging by the event, it is clear that parliament ought to have been called together in November & additional powers obtained: but there has been a certain tenderness for the offenders felt in Downing Street, an extreme dislike to admit the seriousness of the case, & possibly also an idea that a moderate degree of terror would be useful in putting pressure on landowners. But, to do the Cabinet justice, I do not think they ever foresaw the length to which violence & sedition would be carried.

18 Dec. 1880: . . . Some talk with Baring before he left about Liverpool trade & the dock board. He says business never was more flourishing: the trade of the river greater than in any former year: so much so that the board have been able to reduce the dues by £110,000, & yet make ample provision for their wants. Strange that Manchester should still continue depressed while the sister city is doing so well. . . .

21 Dec. 1880: Shooting with the two Cecils, Hope, & Pilkington on the Colliery beat. Hard frost, & the road so slippery . . . we left the carriage . . . & walked 3 miles to where the men were: a great crowd of lads with us all day. We killed 399 head: nearly all hares or pheasants. . . .

24 Dec. 1880: . . . I note that there is general dissatisfaction with the acts of the government, or rather with its absence of action – all turning on the supposed sympathy of some members of the Cabinet with the Irish agitation. Of this there is not a particle of proof, except their reluctance to adopt coercive measures, which is sufficiently explained by their own former language, & by the fear of offending their political allies. It is at the same time remarkable with how much tenderness a large part of the press speaks of Irish outrages, especially among the minor journals. I suspect the very large proportion of Irish connected with journalism may have something to do with this result. How far the general public agrees in thinking that there has been slackness on the part of the Irish executive it is impossible to guess: but among the upper classes the feeling is almost universal. And Gladstone has unluckily contributed to increase it, by an ungracious reply to Capt. Boycott's demand for compensation. The demand itself he did quite rightly in refusing: but he might without danger of holding out false hopes have expressed some sympathy for the losses of a man who has in effect been hunted out of Ireland for no other offence than that of being obnoxious to the revolutionary party.

It is remarked as strange that in all this business the very name of the Lord Lieut. Ld Cowper is scarcely ever mentioned: he is nominally head of the executive, but it seems to be taken for granted that the work is to be done by Forster, & that no serious question is to be referred to the Viceroy.

25 Dec. 1880: . . . Made up accounts for the year. I have spent in presents to Ly D., £979: in other presents, £647: in works of art, £1,261: in books, £584. Casual expenses, & dress, make up the total to £3,962. Charities are in a separate account.

News that the Transvaal Boers have risen in earnest, & either killed or made prisoners of 250 English soldiers, who were marching up the country to reinforce the garrison. So we are committed to a new South African war. The worst is that their open resistance makes it impossible now to restore their independence, or to turn our annexation into a mere protectorate: a policy which might have been adopted had peace continued.

Lord Ripon has fallen ill &, though recovering, it is thought not likely that he will be able to bear the next hot weather. Health lost in India is not easily regained, especially when there can be no complete rest, nor any freedom from responsibility. *The Times* has gone so far as to name Dufferin as his successor: a good choice: & better than the original appointment which was generally thought at the time a mistake. Ripon though an honest man is weak, & his being a convert to Catholicism has not increased his popularity in the country – though I suspect it had something to do with his being selected: for Gladstone, though he has abused the papal hierarchy in unmeasured terms, has an odd sympathy with Catholics. It is a question whether, considering that Indian difficulties are now mostly financial, Goschen would not be even better than Dufferin.

26 Dec. 1880: . . . Some interesting talk with Sir W. Thomson. He is working on the magneto-electric machine, thinking it may be made practically useful in various ways, both for producing light & transmitting power. I told him what Spottiswoode had said of it – he thought power could be transmitted with a much smaller loss than 50%. But for creating force nothing would be cheaper or more effective than steam. . . . He remarked on the singular fact that, notwithstanding the enormous development of steam traffic at sea, there were more sailing ships afloat, & with larger tonnage, than before steam was introduced. Nor did he think they would disappear.

He talked also of the gradual cooling of the sun & the solar system as being a theory now universally accepted. Nothing, he said, could prevent the gradual destruction of life on the earth by cold, except the previous occurrence of some catastrophe, such as a collision with some other planet, which there was no reason to suppose impossible. I said I had supposed sudden catastrophes to be disbelieved in by modern enquirers – that the accepted doctrine was that all changes were gradual. He said no, that theory had been held, & was so still by some persons, but it was no longer in favour. . . . I could not but think from this . . . that even in what is supposed to be the certainty of exact science there is more of doubt than is admitted, & that fashion & popularity have some influence on theories which profess to be founded on pure reasoning. . . .

29 Dec. 1880: Intended to shoot . . . but steady rain & fog made us give it up.

Destroyed old letters: sent a cheque to the Cancer Hospital. Sent, for next year, £50 to the Lit. Fund, & £10.10.0 to the Brompton Hospital, of both of which I am president. Also £20 to help in founding a scholarship at Cambridge as a memorial . . . Of the man so commemorated I know little, except that he was thought to be eminent in his own line: but I like the system of memorial scholarships: they are the best kind of monuments, at least for scholars.

Read Aylward's book[46] on the Transvaal, in view of present events: & some Irish pamphlets.

Much sensation . . . caused by the death of George Eliot . . . She is described (I never saw her) as plain . . . but with attractive manners . . . As a novelist she has certainly no equal in our day: though perhaps never as generally popular as Dickens & Thackeray, her works are rated by critics higher than those of either, & will probably last longer.

30 Dec. 1880: Left home soon after 9.00 . . . to Preston. Found not less than 25 or 30 Liverpool magistrates on the platform. . . . Took the chair at 11.30, in the largest gathering of magistrates that I have yet seen – over 80, I should suppose. We had besides the usual routine three matters of real business to dispose of. One was to approve a report on juvenile offenders, to be sent to the Home Office: which we did with little difference of opinion: the second the passing of a bill for various purposes, the most important of which is the consolidation of the county debt so that we shall know precisely what we owe (which we never have done yet) & at what rate we are paying it off. This bill was approved after some talk, & is to be brought in by the county members (I have written that we passed the bill, but it would be more correct that we sanctioned it being brought forward in the name of the county: being purely local, it is not likely to be opposed). Our third affair was more serious, being the settlement of a dispute between Salford hundred and the rest of the county. It seems they – the Salford people – have paid for building their own courthouse, which we did not know of, & in an act of last year they are made responsible for paying their share of the new Liverpool sessions house. This they complained of, quite reasonably, as unfair . . . In the end a compromise was come to . . . We sat till near 4.00, the longest sitting I remember. Reached Knowsley by 6.30.

Bad news from South Africa: the Boers are in arms all over the Transvaal, & have obtained some successes. They are not formidable as soldiers, nor well armed: but their country is not easy of access, they have the sympathy of their fellow Dutchmen over the whole Cape colony, & these are the majority of the white race in Africa. What is more, it is impossible not to feel that they have much justice on their side.

Our only plea for annexing the country was that we believed the majority of the people wished it, & that we should thereby avoid a native war: but the war has come nevertheless, & the popular feeling appears to be exactly the contrary of what we were led to suppose. We are therefore in the unpleasant position of having to put down a rising which we admit to be not unprovoked, & to subdue a people whom we had much rather leave free, if they can be made to abstain from provoking troubles with the tribes round them. But there is no help for it, as matters stand, unless some terms of agreement can be found.

The Irish trials have begun, but they attract little notice. A conviction is not expected, and I hear doubt expressed as to whether it is really desired, or whether the prosecution was not undertaken solely to satisfy opinion in England. The C. Justice has declined to sit, lest his impartiality should be questioned: an awkward apology to have to make for his indiscreet speech of a few weeks ago, but it was right to make it, & the best way out of the scrape he had got into[47]. . . .

Notes

[1] For the Mar case, see G.E.C., *The Complete Peerage*, Vol. VIII, Appendix G.

[2] Colin Blackburn, Baron Blackburn (1813–1896), judge from 1859: High Court judge, 1875: cr. peer, 1876: retired, 1886.

[3] Harry Vane (from 1864, Powlett) 4th Duke of Cleveland (1803–1891), succ. his bro. 1864: a Lib. M.P. 1841–1864: had no successor.

[4] Robert Haldane, 3rd E. of Camperdown (1841–1918), Lib., then Lib. Unionist: succ. 1867.

[5] City Companies Commission.

[6] J.F.B. Firth (1842–1889), M.P. (Lib.) Chelsea 1880–1885, Dundee 1888–1889: president, Municipal Reform League: supported Home Rule and electoral reform.

[7] Albert Pell (1820–1907), M.P. (Cons.) Leics. S. 1868–1885: authority on poor law and on agriculture.

[8] For the full story, and its sequel, see *Later Derby Diaries*, Ch. iv.

[9] Hon. W.P.M. Chetwynd-Talbot, serjeant-at-arms in the House of Lords 1858–1899: diarist's brother-in-law.

[10] The diarist's younger sister Emma (1835–1928). She m. Col. Talbot in 1860.

[11] At Maiwand. Losses were 934 killed, 175 missing (similar to Isandhlwana).

[12] Laveleye, Emile Louis Victor de, Baron, *L'Italie actuelle: Lettres à un ami* (Bruxelles, 1880).

[13] Henry George Grey, 3rd E. Grey (1802–1894), succ. 1845.

[14] Windham T. Wyndham-Quin, 4th E. of Dunraven (1841–1926), succ. his father 1871: under-sec. for colonies 1885–1887: war correspondent for *Daily Telegraph*: Irish land reformer, devolutionist, and sportsman.

[15] Gladstone fell ill with fever, 30 July, and two days later 'I thought of the end . . . coming nearer to it by a little than I had done before'. By 8 August he reported good daily progress, appetite returning, and on the 9th went to stay with the Dean of Windsor. However, he did little except convalesce for the rest of the month.

[16] Lord Claud Hamilton P.C. (1813–1884), 2nd s. of 1st Duke of Abercorn: M.P. Tyrone 1835–1837, 1839–1874: held court posts in Derby ministries: defeated in Tyrone 1874, 1880.

[17] Lord Arthur and Lord Lionel Cecil.

[18] A claimant to the Afghan throne, briefly, in 1880.

[19] Gladstone left Gravesend, 26 August, returning there on 4 September. His cruise with Donald Currie on his ship *Grantully Castle* took him down the Channel, calling at Plymouth, Dartmouth, Falmouth, Dublin, Skye (where he climbed in the Cuillins), Leith and Yarmouth.

[20] J.T. Freeman-Mitford, 2nd Baron Redesdale (1805–1886), cr. earl 1877: chairman of committees and deputy speaker in House of Lords 1851–1886.

[21] J.A. Froude, 'Ireland', *Nineteenth Century* (September 1880).

[22] Roberts left Kabul on the 8th with 10,000 men, reached Kandahar on 31 August with scarcely a casualty, and on 1 September completely defeated Ayoub Khan, capturing his camp and all his guns, while himself losing less than 200 killed and wounded.

[23] William Spottiswoode (1825–1883), physicist: student of electricity: president of Royal Society 1878–1883.

[24] E. Cazalet, a Kentish neighbour, had stood unsuccessfully for Mid-Kent as a Liberal in 1880.

[25] Canon E. Hornby of Bury (1816–1888), Rector of Bury 1850–1888, s. of Rev. Geoffrey Hornby (1780–1850), Rector of Bury 1818–1850.

[26] William Browne, 5th Viscount Mountmorres (1832–1880), succ. his father, 1872: murdered by 6 revolver bullets near Ballinrobe, co. Galway, 25 September 1880: treated barbarously even after death.

[27] Musurus Pasha (1807–1891), Ottoman minister 1851–1856 and ambassador 1856–1885.

[28] Sir E.B. Malet (1837–1908), British agent and consul-general in Egypt 1879–1883, where he reorganised its finances.

29   (Sir) Stephen Cave (1820–1880), M.P. (Cons.) 1859–1880: paymaster-gen. and vice-pres. of board of trade 1866–1868: paymaster-gen. and judge advocate-general, 1874–, resigning latter post December 1875 to go on special mission to Cairo: intended as successor to Adderley, 1875, but held out for cabinet seat, which Disraeli would not give (Derby diary, 3 November 1875).

30   Lady Georgiana Russell, eldest child of Lord John Russell: m. the 3rd s. of Gen. Peel.

31   Later Lord Houghton.

32   Cf. Dudley W.R. Bahlman (ed.), *The Diary of Sir Edward Walter Hamilton*, 1880–1885 (1972), Vol. i, p. 187, for Disraeli's claim that he led the atack on Peel as a means of advancing his own position.

33   George Herbert, Count von Münster (1820–1902), German ambassador in London 1873–1885.

34   Either Sir W.G. Hunter (1827–1902), surgeon-general, or Sir W.W. Hunter (1840–1900), author of statistical survey of India.

35   Sir Alexander Cockburn (1802–1880), lord chief justice of England: attorney-gen. 1851–1856.

36   Perhaps Sir H. Holland, 1st Vt. Knutsford (1825–1914), called to bar 1849: assistant under-sec. for colonies, 1870–1874: M.P. (Cons.) 1874–1885: P.C., 1885: colonial sec., 1888–1892: baron, 1888, and vt., 1895.

37   Dr. W.C. Magee (1821–1891), bishop of Peterborough 1868–1891.

38   Original of Waldershare.

39   Original of Rigby.

40   Original of Lord Monmouth.

41   Henry Stanley (1803–1875), brother of 14th E. of Derby. Col Long was a distant kinsman of the Stanleys.

42   Perhaps linked to Pierce C. de L. Mahony (1850–1930) of Kilmorna, co. Kerry: educ. Rugby, Magdalen, and Cirencester: assistant land commissioner 1881–1884: Parnellite M.P. 1886–1892.

43   William Bence Jones (1812–1882), Irish agriculturist.

44   Richard Dowse (1824–1890), Irish judge: Lib. M.P. Londonderry 1868, 1870: sol.-gen. and att.-gen. for Ireland: baron of Irish Court of Exchequer, 1872.

45   T.M. Healy (1855–1931), gov.-gen. of Irish Free State 1922–1928: M.P. 1880–1886, 1887–1918.

46   Alfred Aylward, *The Transvaal of Today: War, witchcraft, sport, and spoils in South Africa* (Blackwood, Edinburgh, 1878; new ed., 1881).

47   Cf. above, 6 December 1880.

1881

January–June

Finances: . . . As matters now are, I ought to have £50,000 surplus every year after all expenses paid. But the estate outlay remains a great deal higher than I like, or than it ought to be. In other respects I have every reason to be satisfied.

1 Jan. 1881: . . . The tenantry are content, they have suffered less than most: & on this side of the county I have no farms vacant. Statter has three, but expects to let them soon. The rents have been well paid, & in Liverpool & Bootle land is being taken up for building more rapidly than ever before. On the Manchester side there is stagnation, as there has been for the last 4 years. But on the whole I have no reason to complain. My rental touches £200,000: the actual receipts exceed £190,000: I have invested £300,000, and can lay by at the rate of £50,000 a year if I care to do so. I have bought some land at Witley, a field at Fairhill, & a few small freeholds in Lancashire: but on the whole I have not much increased the family estates. On the other hand, I have since Jan. 1880 invested £80,000, the largest sum yet put by in one year by me.

In my personal relations I have nothing to find fault with. Health has been good: only on two days in 1880 have I been unable to appear at meals: & I have entirely escaped the troublesome & violent colds from which I used to suffer. On the other hand, increasing weight has produced, or perhaps only coincided with, somewhat diminished activity: & I have felt myself less disposed for exertion in the way of public speaking than formerly. A certain indolence, mental & bodily, is the chief danger against which I have to guard. I have been engaged in no serious dispute, & lost no friend by death or otherwise. Ly D. is less strong than I could wish, & suffers at times from her eyes: but there is nothing in her health to cause alarm.

As to public affairs, the prospect is gloomy enough. We have in India the enormous cost of the Afghan war to pay, with a revenue which is not elastic: in South Africa one war to carry on against the Boers, which everybody regrets, & another waged by the colonists in which we shall probably have to interfere: in Ireland a state of things which is hardly short of civil war, & may end in an open outbreak – law being meanwhile practically in abeyance: at home great bitterness of party feeling & demands for radical changes not likely to be obtained: abroad the eastern complication still unsettled, & likely to remain so. On the other side is to be set an improving revenue, & an apparent return of industrial prosperity. The Cabinet is strong, & so far unaffected by divisions within itself: at least if they exist they have not come to the surface. Gladstone is almost worshipped by the Radicals, distrusted, but followed by the Whigs, & hated by the Conservatives: in each case with some reason. Hartington has everybody's good word. Granville is respected & liked, but people talk of him as growing old & deaf & the hard work of office may at any time break him down. The extraordinary display of changed public feeling at the elections has destroyed the official prospects of Conservatives for some time to come. Ld Beaconsfield is too old to return to power: Salisbury is ill thought of as being violent, unscrupulous, & untruthful: Northcote is respected on all sides, but thought to want decision for a party leader: a judgment in which I agree. In the new parliament, the landed interest is weaker than it has ever been since 1832, but there are only three workingmen, & no mere agitators except from Ireland, where the Home Rulers take exactly the place in general opinion which was taken by O'Connell's 'tail' as it used to be called. It is commonly asserted that the parliament is more radical than the Cabinet, and the country than the parliament: & I am inclined to think the fact may be so. . . .

3 Jan. 1881 (Monday): In *The Times* of Saturday is an apparently inspired article to the effect that the Irish land bill is not intended to be on a new principle from that of 1870, but only to supply defects in it. Is this really meant? or is it only written with a view to reconcile dissentients by making a really violent change appear a mere development of what has been done already?

. . . Letter . . . from Sanderson, evidently written under an uneasy impression as to what the session may bring: & in truth there is reason for it, for never were more causes of discontent & alarm: trouble on all sides, & apparently a certain dissatisfaction at home. The necessity for a coercion bill is admitted, but the bill will give rise to fierce battles, & the system of obstruction invented by the Irish will have to be broken down in some way. Nor is it impossible that when the land bill appears, disappointing as it must the expectations of the Irish, an actual rising will follow. It is beginning to be seen in England that the movement headed by the Land League is really one for national independence. And it is evident that some of our ultra politicians would be prepared to give up Ireland rather than hold it by force. Indeed one or two have said so.

. . . To . . . Liverpool . . . to attend a dinner given by the Mayor in honour of Gen. Roberts . . . About 180 sat down . . . Gen. Roberts spoke with unusual modesty, not saying a word of himself or of his own services but pleading for more respect to be shown to the army – that is, to the private soldier – who he thought should be picked out for civil employment wherever possible . . . I spoke late in the evening, for 5 or 6 minutes only, but very well received, & said what I meant. Cross followed me, not altogether successful.

4 Jan. 1881: Ride early in the park. Rent day dinner at 3.00 . . . I spoke as usual. Everybody very friendly & cordial. Settled that Lionel C. shall take the chair tomorrow when the Bickerstaffe & other more distant residents come.

5 Jan. 1881: Left Knowsley at 10.20 . . . No. 23 at 4.30 or thereabouts.

. . . Ward has drawn in these two rent days £12,700 odd, which is a considerable increase on former years, the system of sending out circular notices having produced its effect in greater punctuality.

Dined with Granville, the customary official dinner: sat next the D. of Devonshire, & well enough entertained. Talk with Lord O'Hagan, both before & after dinner: he says the feeling in Ireland is far worse, & the movement more widespread, than in '48 or '65: he thinks it very serious, & does not see what is to be the end. I said: 'The plain truth is, I suppose, that we hold Ireland against the wish of a majority of the people. You could not safely refer the question of the English connection to a popular vote.' He answered: 'I am afraid that is the exact truth.' Talk with Kimberley, who seemed to take much the same view, but naturally was more occupied with his own Transvaal troubles.

The speech was read after dinner: it is long, well written, & the part that relates to Ireland will give pleasure to all except the 'advanced' Liberals, who are sure to think that too much is said about restoring order, & too little about amended land laws. On the latter question the language is studiously & skilfully moderate. The object is declared to be to amend & supplement the Act of 1870, not to supersede it – which at once excludes the 'three F.s' & absolute fixity of tenure. – I said to Cork after the reading: 'This means that you break with the Ultras': he answered: 'It certainly does, & I am very glad of it.' On the other hand Ld O'Hagan looked grave & gloomy, & feared that what was proposed would never go down in Ireland.

6 Jan. 1881: . . . At 4.45 went down with M. to the Lords. The house was full, especially the galleries & place by the throne: but not so full as I have seen it on some former openings. The mover, Ld Carington, & the seconder, Ld Yarborough[1], did their work neatly: both were as short as possible, not exceeding 10 minutes apiece, which is a new custom, but I think, good as their speeches are, by the nature of the case rather formalities than real arguments. Ld Yarborough is only just of age, & looks like a boy of 14. They were followed by Ld Beaconsfield, whose speech was not absolutely feeble, but not one of his best: the plan of it good, but in places expression seemed to fail him, & he repeated himself more than appears in the report. He chiefly accused the Cabinet of having reversed hastily & ostentatiously all that had been done by their predecessors. This Ld Granville answered rather neatly, by observing that during the last session they had been continually taunted by the opposition with adopting the measures of their predecessors. Both charges could not be true. But Ld G. also was feeble, or rather seemed to speak as if his heart was not in the business. The D. of Marlborough followed, & began to explain his views as to the state of Ireland, which he had a right to do, & I thought them sensible enough: but he is a heavy speaker, and the peers went away, some to dine, others to listen to the debate in the Commons, which was a good deal livelier than ours. Northcote attacked the government for not having taken earlier measures to keep down disturbance in Ireland, & having a good case (for they have been very dilatory), & knowing that he had the sympathy of the House, he spoke with more force & animation than I ever heard him display, making some fair hits & getting vehemently cheered. Gladstone replied, with all his accustomed skill, but less than his accustomed fire: he has been working incessantly since his illness, without a day of rest, & his friends say he is getting weary & depressed. But there was no sign of irritability, either morbid or normal. – I left him speaking, dined hastily at the Travellers', & came home, not ill pleased with the day.

7 Jan. 1881: Sanderson called early . . . Sharp walk for exercise in cold wind.

Trade returns for 1880 in the papers . . . show a steady increase in wealth, which I believe never wholly ceases, whether times are good or bad.

. . . In the Commons an Irish debate came on . . . Parnell spoke with great moderation & good sense: much to his credit in one sense, but the contrary in another, since his calmness where he has nothing to gain by violence shows plainly that he is rather playing a part in his popular harangues than a genuine enthusiast. . . . The Irish will resist a coercion bill to the utmost, as is only natural, and, being 40 or 50 in number & for the most part indifferent to English opinion, they may delay its passing for weeks, unless some such decided step as refusing to adjourn & sitting through the whole night is taken. Note that many Conservatives, who have not the smallest sympathy with obstruction as such, will yet object to strong measures taken to repress it, thinking that it is not good to give to a majority the power of closing debate when they please, & so overriding the minority: & also being of opinion that we are rather in danger of having too much legislation than too little.

8 Jan. 1881 (Saturday): . . . Walk with Ld Sherbrooke to the B. Museum. He gloomy in his predictions, saying the parliamentary machine had become unworkable, that the change between 1860 & 1880 was extraordinary, we had now in parliament a set of men who cared nothing for the old traditions of the place, or for the unwritten laws of parliament: the whole arrangement he said was artificial, it rested on conventions, & if those were not respected the whole concern would break down. I could not but agree to a certain extent: but reminded him on the other hand that no sign had appeared either of reckless faction, or of democratic envy of the rich, or of class-feeling among the working section of the electors: which in a country like ours is much to be able to say. He acquiesced, only doubting whether things would continue as quiet as they are.

. . . The Premier called on Ly D. this afternoon[2], & talked with her freely on current events. I do not attempt to note his conversation as it reaches me only secondhand: but I gather that he expressed himself strongly against the Irish schemes of fixity of tenure, & settlement of rents generally by a court, saying that both one & the other were a robbery of the landlord: which confirms what we heard last month, that he is more moderate in his proposals than even the moderate section of the Cabinet.

9 Jan. 1881: . . . The session is now fairly opened, & it is curious to see how entirely the expectation of a stormy opening has been disappointed. But the cause lies in the action of the government, which has disarmed their chief opponents. They have brought in a coercion bill &, though the Conservatives grumble, & say with some truth that it should have been done two months sooner, they are not disposed to find serious fault.

They have also given it to be understood that their land bill will not be a revolutionary scheme – to the disappointment of their radical friends, who nevertheless retain some hope that Gladstone may be better than his word – but to the relief at once of Whig supporters & Conservatives, whose dislike of the Cabinet is for the moment merged in their hope that the Land League may be effectually put down.

To other causes of trouble is now added the possibility of a fresh dispute with the U.S. It is alleged in Congress that the award on the fishery question was obtained by the use of figures which had been altered so as to make them favour unduly the Canadian claim: that the error was pointed out at the time to our government: but that the F.O. refused to reopen the award, alleging it to be binding in any case, & that the time for correcting errors was past. It is admitted, I think, that the error was originally an accident: but in the American view it was pointed out in time to have been set right, if we had been willing. . . . Is it a mere accidental coincidence that this question should be raised just when South Africa is in open insurrection, & Ireland in a state not far removed from it?

10 Jan. 1881: Walk down to the Lords, where Lytton delivered his maiden speech[3] – ostensibly in defence of his own policy, but really an attack on the policy of giving up Kandahar. He spoke well: his style excellent, voice clear, manner easy, & a little theatrical: the substance of his argument ingenious, & he certainly made the best of a bad case. He spoke rather more than an hour, very well listened to. The speech is said to have been not only learnt by heart, but so often rehearsed that his family knew it by heart also: & the delivery made this theory probable. But with all drawbacks, it was a good speech, & Lytton is a gain to the House, which has fewer able speakers than it had a few years ago. Argyll answered, with great force & severity, but which Lytton had brought on himself by being the aggressor. The effect of the reply was increased by its being necessarily unprepared, arising out of what had been said just before. The rest of the debate was poor. . . .

11 Jan. 1881: . . . H. of Lds at 5.00, where no business except a motion for papers by Ld Dunsany[4], which he supported in an incoherent speech. Walked home with Granville: he talked of the land bill, in guarded terms, but such as led me to believe that the Cabinet has made up its mind against granting fixity of tenure, but that they will try in some way to prevent the raising of rents to an exorbitant amount. I do not see how this is to be done effectually, if the tenant is willing to pay an increased rent rather than be turned out, & if the landlord has the power of turning him out. Nor is it obvious what is to prevent a landowner, having a vacant farm, which he must not let at more than a certain rent, taking a sum down from the successful competitor for it. But if the Cabinet resist unjust proposals, it is not the interest or the duty of their friends to point out that the proposals which they substitute for them are impracticable or inefficient. That is their affair. Granville confirmed what I have heard from various quarters, that there is a strong radical pressure being put on the govt. to change their course, & bring in a bill which shall in effect sweep away the landlord. He told me that full 100 English members go with the Home Rule party. –

He talked also of the state of things in the east, which gives him alarm: Greece & Turkey bent on fighting, & no feasible scheme of arbitration having been devised.

12 Jan. 1881: . . . Lawson of the *Telegraph* called, to talk over the Irish question: he confirms what I had heard from various quarters as to the bitter feeling growing up between Whigs & Radicals & the pressure which is being put on the govt. by the latter. He condemns the 'three Fs' but adds that a good many landlords will accept them, or almost any other concession that will enable them to get their rents paid. He praises a speech[5] made last night by Hartington as the best he has ever delivered – and indeed it is a very good one. He does not see the end of the Irish trouble, & believes that nobody else does: in which I agree with him.

Lit. Fund meeting . . . We gave away £220 in 5 donations. None of the applicants had any real literary claim, but were simply respectable persons in distress who happened to have written books.

Dined with the Bedfords: Tom Hughes & his wife: . . . Mrs. Hughes told me of 'George Eliot' – her extreme ugliness, of which she was so well aware that she would never be photographed . . .

13 Jan. 1881: . . . All yesterday afternoon was wasted in the H. of C. by the Irish, who did not care to conceal the fact that they were trying to stave off the Coercion Bill as long as possible. Not a chance has any Scotch or English subject had of being attended to, nor will for some time to come. I find that a good many Scotch & English members do not much regret this state of things, at least not as much as from their public professions one would think: they hold that a very radical parliament, such as this is, may as well have time to settle down before undertaking legislation on a large scale. Naturally the feeling I speak of is strongest on the Conservative side, but it extends to both: e.g. the public house interest is delighted with the prospect of a year's respite: the magistrates are not sorry that a county govt. bill cannot be brought in this year: English landowners are not eager (to put it mildly) for a bill altering the land laws: & so on through all the interests which are or may be affected by reforms. . . .

14 Jan. 1881: . . . Another Irish night in the Commons. The question of expediting proceedings will be forced on parliament: but it is awkward to have to begin with a coercion bill as the measure which is to be pushed through in haste – & the Irish see their advantage, & are sure to use it.

Went to the Lords, but there was no business, & thence to the Commons, whom I found in an exhausted condition, the house nearly empty, & the few present not listening. Mr. Synan[6], the speaker, was shouting at the top of his voice, & repeating the same idea over & over again during the few minutes that I heard him. The reporters took no notes &, except one minister left there for decency, the front bench on both sides was empty. I soon grew weary, & came away.

. . . Two curious attempts at mischief, both probably Fenian, & both childishly foolish in the way they were set about, within the last few days. The first was on the London Custom House: to which an incendiary by some means got access, & set it on fire by means of papers heaped up against a wooden cupboard: but the fire was detected & put out with little damage. The other was a dynamite explosion, intended to destroy the armoury at Salford: in which 5,000 stand of arms are stored: but this armoury being close to a barracks the project of plundering it was hopeless. As it chanced, the explosion did not hurt the building & only injured two passers-by. But it is scarcely possible to doubt what was intended. The trade in arms at Birmingham is extraordinarily active: from 6,000 to 8,000 revolvers are ordered for Ireland, the papers say: not for or by the authorities. . . .

16 Jan. 1881 (Sunday): . . . The H. of C. debate ended on Saturday morning with a division in which 51 Irish & 8 English figured as the minority against more than 400. But the Irish have carried their point: a week is wasted already, & Walpole yesterday told me that the two still remaining amendments will occupy a week more. Till they are dealt with the Coercion Bill cannot be even approached. It is now apparent to everybody that the clôture in some shape has become a necessity: since 50 members, bent on obstruction, can under our present rules throw all business into confusion. But there is an awkwardness in abridging the liberty of debate, however abused, when the object is to bring in a coercive measure.

Gladstone intended to speak on Friday, but was prevented by a cold: I believe really prevented, & that there was no trick in the matter[7]: but a good many of the public are sure to think otherwise, & the silence of Bright & Chamberlain, who have not got colds, makes the suspicion plausible. I have myself no doubt that Gladstone was not sorry to have a fair excuse for getting out of an unpleasant & unpopular necessity: & that the speech would have been a disagreeable one to him to make – but I do not imagine that he invented an illness to get rid of it. Among followers of the government, the relations of the two sections are becoming more & more strained: Hartington is spoken of by the Radicals with respect indeed, but with regret for the line which he has taken: & the *Pall*

Mall Gazette, the chief organ of the 'advanced' party, has assumed an attitude of candid criticism which is the first step towards open opposition. . . .

20 Jan. 1881: St. George's Hall again for sessions, sat till 7.00: a long day, but to my satisfaction I came away quite fresh & untired. Better hearing, which lessens fatigue, & better ventilation, make a great difference when the work is at all heavy.

. . . I have not lost much by absence from London, for the Lords have had nothing to do. In the Commons there has been some sharp debating, & a strong exhibition of feeling against the Irish attempts to obstruct business by interminable talk. Gladstone was provoked to turn upon them more angrily than he has done yet, which produced strong expressions of satisfaction from the opposite side of the House. This, & his supposed moderation on the land question (about which I am not quite so sure as some people) has revived his popularity among the upper classes & the Whigs. The Radicals are no doubt disappointed, but do not yet express their feelings in that sense. . . .

22 Jan. 1881 (Saturday): Cold still continues. If Harrison is accurate, it was down to - 1 below zero on Sunday morning: last night it was 10°F, or 22° of frost. The papers are full of stories of men & horses frozen to death: one adventurous person walked across the Mersey on ice: the Thames above London is frozen. We have had nothing like this since 1860–1861, & then it did not last nearly so long.

Left . . . by 11.00 a.m. train to Euston . . . I read complaints from villages . . . that coals, bread, meat, etc., are running short from the roads being impassable. London is worse than the country, the streets filled up with large frozen blocks of snow, originally swept off the roofs or out of the roadway, there frozen almost as hard as ice . . . There is a track in the middle of the street, but rough & narrow. Nothing seems to have been done to clear away the nuisance . . .

24 Jan. 1881: . . . To the H. of C. where listened to Forster moving for leave to bring in his coercion bill. He spoke better than ever I heard him, making out a very strong case for the necessity of repressing outrages & acts of intimidation – massing his facts skilfully, & avoiding excess of detail. There was a good deal of noisy ill-mannered interruption from the Irish members at first, but the strong plain language in which Forster denounced their friends, & the unmistakable feeling of the House, fairly cowed them: & the last half of his argument was listened to without expressions of dissent. He did not spare hard words when he spoke of the local leaders of the Land League agitation. A passage at the end was characteristic. He would not have taken the Irish office, he said, if he had known that this was the kind of work he should have to do: &, if he had expected it when he entered parliament, he should have kept clear of parliamentary life. This was weak, but it was so evident that the speaker meant what he said that it excited more sympathy than ridicule. Forster has by this speech undoubtedly regained lost ground and the very length of his previous delay is so far a gain that the whole body of English Liberals is now prepared to accept as necessary the repressive measures about which in November they would certainly have been divided in opinion. In fact this is the only real justification for not having acted sooner: & on the whole I think it is a good defence. . . .

25 Jan. 1881: Frost continues, & indeed grows more severe. The streets are now partly cleared of snow, but traffic is still difficult: everywhere, wagons & carts are seen with horses unable to draw them, stuck fast in the snow, or rather in the powdery mess which was snow a week ago. . . .

27 Jan. 1881: Thaw fairly set in . . . but the streets are ankle-deep in mud, & walking is almost impossible.

. . . Walked back with Northcote from the Peabody [trustees] meeting, & talk over the clôture which Gladstone wishes to introduce in some shape: but Northcote feels sure that the larger part of the Conservative party will not accept it, at least until milder remedies have been tried & failed: he sees the awkwardness of the situation, but feels strong objection on his own account to allowing a majority, even a $\frac{3}{4}$ majority, to close any debate when they please. This is a reasonable scruple, & it is sure to be strongly felt by the Conservatives who, though they dislike obstruction in its more flagrant shape, are not disposed to give facilities for rapid legislation, holding that it is a mistake to suppose the suspending of a member for obstructive or disorderly conduct was ineffectual: even the Irish feel a certain shame at the public reprimand, &, if the punishment of notorious offenders in this line be steadily adhered to, he thinks nothing more will be necessary. At any rate he considers that this milder method, which does not punish the innocent for the acts of the guilty, ought to be tried first.

28 Jan. 1881: . . . Sefton dined with us: very full of Hardwicke's bankruptcy[8], which is formally announced, & excludes him from sitting & voting as a peer till it is annulled. Whether from real indifference, or a wish to assume it, he (Ld H.) appears in society as usual, keeps a very handsome carriage, plays, and plays high, in short conducts himself as if nothing had happened: which would be a respectable way of taking his misfortunes if they had not been of his own creating. He owes £240,000: how spent, no one knows. It is odd that this poor creature was a special favourite with Ld Beaconsfield: whom I suppose he reminded of the fast young men of his own youth – the D'Orsay & Gore House set.

– In the Lords, a short debate on Kandahar, which had no interest since it is well known and has been officially announced that the abandonment of the place is decided upon, the H. of C. & the public approving. Military & Indian opinion is in general strongly opposed to the retreat. The argument on the two sides may be summed up in two sentences. One party contends that, though the military position is a good one, the expense of keeping it & the consequent financial mischief are greater than its military importance justifies: the other side replies: 'Very possibly: but you will have to retake it some day if you give it up now, & that will cost more than holding on to it now.'

News this afternoon of a reverse sustained by Sir G. Colley[9], who attacked the Boer insurgents in a strong position, & failed to take it. It is not known why he did not wait for reinforcements, but probably he knows that some of the detached British garrisons could not hold out unless speedily relieved, & he may have thought the risk of failure worth running. The loss is about 200 men: it does not appear that anyone failed to do his duty: the place was too strong for the attacking force to carry.

29 Jan. 1881: . . . In the Commons last night, a fine speech from Gladstone incessantly & rudely interrupted by the Irish, whom in consequence he attacked with entire justice, but perhaps with more vehemence than he would have used if they had shown him the ordinary courtesy of gentlemen. The feeling against them has grown very strong, both in parliament & in the country: increased I think by what seemed like a determination on the part of the Liberal press to excuse & support them as long & as far as possible. – The awkward part of the matter is that, while their hostility to England, & their general intemperance of language & conduct, are notorious, there is no reason to believe that they are otherwise than fair representatives of the constituencies that return them. The feeling about Ireland generally is one of great disappointment not to say despondency: 'We have tried for 50 years to give them what they want, & the end of it is that after we have removed their grievances, and shown our goodwill in a hundred ways, they hate us worse than they did in the days of the penal laws.' This is what many people are saying: it is a paradox, but it is true. . . .

31 Jan. 1881 (Monday): Dined at Grillions: a pleasant party: Lds Fortescue, Stanhope, Norton, & D.[10], Sir P. Egerton, Sir J. Paget, & Northcote, Gladstone, Walpole, [Lord] J.[ohn] Manners & one more, for we were 11 in all. The Premier seemed in excellent spirits, talked freely & pleasantly, & not the least awkwardness appeared to be felt by any of the party. The longer I live, the more I value these dinners as a means of preventing political opposition from becoming personal & bitter. Men meet there as friends who seldom meet elsewhere, and jokes & champagne drive out the recollection of sharp words spoken in debate. It certainly was so tonight. I put down my brother's name as a candidate for the club, & got Northcote to second him.

The Premier left us early[11], expecting, as he & others said, an all night sitting of the House: the Irish being determined to prevent leave being obtained to bring in the bill. That in so doing they are delaying the land bill also is to them a matter of indifference. – By an awkward accident, the coercion bill has been printed & circulated prematurely: the authorities charged with the distribution having taken for granted that the debate would end on Friday night. This mischance gives the obstructives a double advantage: they have an irregularity to comment on & complain of: & they have the details of the bill before them as a subject of criticism: supplying a fresh topic, though in strictness they have no right to deal with it. (**Note**: They made very little use of either opportunity, preferring to deliver speeches which showed unmistakably that the only object of the speakers was to waste time.)

1 Feb. 1881: . . . To the Commons, to see how they looked after a sitting of more than 24 hours continuous. They seemed jaded, & many were asleep, as was natural, though they arrange to relieve one another, sitting alternately, as men keep watches at sea. The debate was as dull as might be expected where the object was avowedly to waste time. There seems a general feeling that matters have come to a crisis, & that something must be done. Indeed I learnt that the leaders on both sides are about to confer, in order that an end may be put to a state of matters which is becoming a scandal.

2 Feb. 1881: Soon after 10.00 Pender called, with news that a *coup d'état* on a small scale has come off: the Speaker having by his own authority closed the debate at 9.00 this morning. He made the House a speech[12], in which he declared that its dignity & credit were threatened: that the usual rules had proved powerless to ensure order: that a new & exceptional course was necessary: & that he should therefore put the question at once. He did so, & the division took place. The House in general cheered vehemently: the Irish party, at that moment only 19, withdrew together, some crying loudly 'Liberty' &

'Privilege'. Gladstone announced that he should propose the clôture in form of a resolution, to be announced at 12.00 today, & brought in tomorrow.

At 11.00 came Lord Dalhousie, who had agreed to walk with me: we walked on the embankment, & returned to Westminster at 12.15, to watch what went on: the House was crowded & in a state of excitement such as I have seldom seen. –Parnell was furiously cheered when he came in. The Irish members put to the Speaker a series of questions, not quite disrespectful, but nearly so: & threatened a vote of disapproval of his ruling of this morning. They then moved the adjournment which I left them discussing at 2.00 p.m.

The sitting of Monday, Tuesday & Wednesday occupied 41 hours: a scene never witnessed in parliament till now. The Speaker's *coup d'état*, as it is generally called, is the sole subject of conversation: the general feeling is that he has acted with courage & good sense, & that his decision, though in excess of his powers (or of such powers as he has been hitherto thought to possess, for their extent is undefined) has brought about the only possible solution of the difficulty. There is not the same agreement as to the new proposed rules of debate: which, apart from objections of substance, are open to the obvious criticism that they will require as much time to get them through the house as they will save by their operation. But on these rules there has not been time for opinion to form itself.

Nothing was gained today by the refusal to adjourn: the Irish, with some English help, kept up debate till 6.00. – Little as I like the man or the cause I could not but be impressed by the remarkable ability of Sullivan[13], who led the Irish party in the discussion which I heard. Five-sixths of the House were against him, & at every minute he was interrupted: but he was not in the least put out, & contrived to maintain an attitude of half-ironical deference to the Speaker & to the majority, while saying all that was most disagreeable to them to hear.

The all-night sitting was marked by no one speech of any eloquence or power, & it was disgraced by many ebullitions of bad temper & bad taste. Lyon Playfair[14], the deputy speaker, is thought to have shown weakness in enforcing, or rather in not enforcing, order: but he had to deal with men some of whom were asleep, & would not support him: some drunk, & nearly all who were awake either angry, or disposed to turn the whole affair into ridicule.

Dined with the Gladstones, meeting D. & D.ess of Edinburgh, D. of Cambridge, Ld & Ly A. Russell, Bp. of Ely, Ly De Vesci, Mr. Bryce, etc. A party afterwards. Pleasant enough. As we were going away Gladstone, who had been in a placid & happy mood through the evening, took me aside[15] to complain of Northcote, who he thought had misled him by promises of support which he was not able to make good. I said what I really believe, that Northcote was not at all the man to mislead anybody, but I thought it likely enough that he might not have been able to induce his followers to agree to what he personally thought reasonable.

3 Feb. 1881: Walk early with Lord Dalhousie[16], who interests me. He is full of interest in public affairs, while almost entirely ignorant of them: sharp & rather clever, a good speaker, as was shown at Liverpool, but simple-minded as a child: it seems to cost him an effort to understand that the opinions he hears are largely coloured by the passions & prepossessions of the individuals who express them. He reminds me of R. Montagu in his youth, but I think will turn out to have more sense.

To H. of C. but the peers' gallery being full I could not get in. I was in the lobby when Dillon[17] & Parnell were suspended from the sitting, amidst a scene of agitation & excitement such as I never saw before, & which could hardly have been exceeded if a revolution were in progress. It was clear that the Irish members had made up their minds to defy the House, & in fact after I left they were suspended in a body, 28 of them, for refusing to vote in a division on the plea that the procedure adopted by the Speaker was illegal. – Gladstone then proceeded to move his new rules, vesting an almost dictatorial power in the Speaker and, the Irish opposition being withdrawn, they were carried with some amendments.

Up to the present date the tactics of the Irish have been skilful, but I do not understand their present proceedings. They might without blame have occupied the better part of a week in discussing the new regulations, which they have allowed to go by default: & unless they wish to excite Ireland to armed insurrection (which seems too hopeless a game to be played in earnest) one does not see what they gain by the scene of last night. It may have been a mere outbreak of rage & despair, but if it was done in policy I do not see the sense of it.

A meeting of Conservatives was held yesterday morning, at which they agreed to support the govt. with some reservations: & they appear to have kept their word. Gladstone's speech is praised as fine, & he did well in showing no sense of the great provocation he had received. But I hear it said that his voice is weaker than of old, & that signs of diminished bodily strength are apparent to those who watch him. I suppose that within the House, if he were to break down, Hartington would be strong enough to carry on business: but he would not carry the same weight with the popular party out-of-doors, nor unite the two sections as Gladstone has done hitherto.

Before the suspension of the Irish members, & when (I suppose) it was known that the crisis was coming, the police cleared the outer lobby, or hall outside the House, allowing none to stay there but peers & members: which I never knew done before. Disturbance was expected, for there were 100 police within call: but they were not wanted. . . .

4 Feb. 1881: . . . What I hear in conversation confirms the impression that the last Irish move, by which they virtually threw up the game, was a mere blunder, the result of haste & passion. They seem to have been greatly excited by the arrest of one Davitt, formerly a Fenian, sentenced to 15 years' penal servitude & who had a ticket of leave. He has been the most active member of the Land League – some say the life & soul of the whole movement – & possibly they are afraid that to save himself he may give information. Else the arrest hardly seems reason enough for such intense excitement. No doubt the two nights' sitting & perpetual speechmaking may have shaken their nerve a little. Everybody asks: 'Are they played out? What will be the next step?' But I suspect that as yet they themselves could not answer that question. . . .

6 Feb. 1881: Fine pleasant day. Walk with Sanderson round Kensington gardens. Talk of many things, of his prospects among them, which do not seem very favourable, at least in F.O., & if he moves to any other office he will lose the advantage of his special knowledge.

Some excitement caused by news of a second Ashantee war, the king having made a demand for the surrender of one of his chiefs who has escaped to British territory. We refuse to give him up, & the king threatens invasion.

Called on Ly Stanhope & Ly Harcourt. From the latter I hear that there is a good deal of anxiety felt at the Home Office lest some foolish or desperate attempt should be made by the Irish. It is not expected that they will try armed resistance, but confine themselves to acts of mischief, such as can be accomplished by few men, & without detection. Explosions, setting on fire public buildings, & possibly shooting at persons whom they consider their enemies, are the most probable forms which their resentment will take. Both the Home Sec. & the Premier are attended by police in plain clothes when they go out.

. . . There are various opinions as to the Speaker's act of Wednesday morning. Those who find fault argue that his own action on the day following proved it to be unnecessary: since the naming & suspending of disorderly members, with the universal approval of the House, was sufficient to ensure order & brevity in the debate which followed. He need not therefore, they contend, have gone out of his way to make a doubtful precedent. The majority think him justified by the emergency, & the discredit into which the House was falling. All parties agree that his personal demeanour was precisely what it should be – dignified & judicial. He has gained greatly in personal estimation. . . .

8 Feb. 1881: M. went to Windsor to see her old friend the Dean.

Walk for exercise with Ld Dalhousie, & much talk.

Went in aftn. to the Lords, where met Ld Beaconsfield: we shook hands. I thought him grown very old: his face void of expression & as if lifeless: but I hear he spoke very well to his friends in his own house, at a meeting held there a few days ago: probably he requires the stimulus of something to be done, to rouse him out of the half lethargic state in which he seems to be.

. . . Ld Rosebery talked of Albert Grant[18] & H. Lennox[19], & related tales of their financial iniquities which were new to me, & certainly to the public. If he is correct, they are closely associated, & one as bad as the other.

Talk of Sefton, who is very much abused for alleged brutality to his old friend Hardwicke. It is said that he told H. to leave the Turf club, of which they are both members, on the ground that by the rules he is disqualified as a bankrupt. I believe he does not deny having given H. a warning to that effect, but says that he did so to save him the annoyance of a public exposure. In fact it was an act of intended good nature, done in a brusque & offhand way: which is characteristic of the man. But H. is much admired & pitied by a certain set, & his friends have chosen to treat the incident as if it were a piece of party spite.

I hear on all sides of the effect produced in Ireland & among the Irish by the arrest of Davitt. It seems that he (D.) was the real head & organiser of the Land League: & the Irish peasantry believed that the govt. were afraid to touch him. His capture without resistance has for the moment entirely demoralised them. Rents are being paid up which were withheld for a year & more: & for the first time the Land Leaguers see that they are not the strongest – that force is against them.

9 Feb. 1881: Lit. Fund meeting . . . Walk back with J. Manners, & some talk about Ireland & the H. of C. I gather that the Conservatives are alarmed at the extent of the powers which the House has entrusted to the Speaker, thinking that they may be used against the rights of minorities. But I also see, or think I see, that the necessity for a cocrcion bill has brought the two parties nearer together, & that there is less bitterness of party feeling than last year.

Dined with V. Harcourt . . .

Harcourt expressed himself to Ly D. thoroughly sick of his office, the worry & responsibility of which are more than he can bear with patience. So he says, & I daresay he is
not wholly insincere. He is for a strong land bill, says no other will be of the slightest use:
& if it is thrown out, or altered by the Lords, the Cabinet will at once resign. I answer:
'What use? You cannot be replaced, & must come in again after a little waste of time.' But
he persisted. I thought his language indicated fear that the land bill will not be such as he
would like to see it.

10 Feb. 1881: Public affairs in H. of C. go on very quietly. The Land League has
prudently sent its funds, which are considerable, to be invested in France: & the less
notable agitators are coming over to England, where they will be out of reach of the coercion act. The change already produced by the attitude of govt. & of the public is marked:
rents are being paid which have been refused for more than 12 months, and the hold of
the League on the people is visibly relaxing. It is always so in Ireland: there is something
oriental in the character of the people: they submit meekly to ill usage, & grow insolent
with the consciousness of being free. Probably the same would be true of any population
similarly treated. Forster, to judge by some talk I had with him the other day, is beginning to realise this state of things: and it is a revelation to him.

The Transvaal news does not mend . . . details now received make it clear that Sir G.
Colley has had a narrow escape from serious disaster, & that his position is still awkward.
He has lost most of his officers, & from a fourth to a third of his force.

11 Feb. 1881: . . . The papers have been full of the death of Thomas Carlyle, undoubtedly our most celebrated man of letters, who ended a long illness at Chelsea a few days
ago. He was 85. . . . To the last, the public never quite knew what to make of him: but his
reputation continued to grow, & latterly he was looked up to with extraordinary reverence by a group of literary notabilities, Froude & Lecky the most prominent among
them. I do not feel qualified to pass judgment upon him: nor to decide how much of his
indisputable eccentricity was genuine, how much the result of deliberate effort to be original. It was common to compare him to one of the ancient prophets, & certainly he
looked the character. His great power, as it always seemed to me, lay in sarcastic &
humorous illustration of the doctrine he was preaching, rather than in force of argument,
or novelty in the doctrine itself. . . . His dogmatic or oracular way of announcing his ideas
was apt to repel those who did not accept them: in fact he could not help either attract-
ing or repelling: he left no hearer indifferent. On some the repulsion was strong: insomuch that they would say the great effect he produced was due to his accent & his
vehemence, rather than to higher qualities: but this was certainly not just. Froude on the
other hand believes that there has been no such English teacher since the days of the
Puritans: if then. He never argued any question, nor listened to argument. A French
newspaper describes him as 'prophet-buffoon' – not a wholly inappropriate description.
His politics were of a nondescript sort: his perpetual declamation against an idle class,
and against pleasure seeking in general, pleased the radicals, & especially the socialists:
while his contempt of popular govt., & assertion of the need of a despot to keep order,
gratified men of a different school. Thus he had admirers in all camps. But in truth he
can scarcely be said to have had a political system: nor did he greatly value systems of any
kind. Towards religion his attitude was peculiar: utterly rejecting the popular creed, &

making no secret of such rejection, yet using the language of religious men in a sense of his own. I remember Gladstone saying of him many years ago: 'There is no man who has so large a stock of *unfunded* religion.' The truth I suppose to be that his habit of mind was one of reverence and desire to find a law to obey: that mere negation, even when he was compelled by intellectual conviction to accept it as just, gave him no satisfaction: that his moral nature was formed by Calvinist doctrines, and that when they became untenable by him their place was taken by a kind of stoical philosophy, not formulated, but not the less real. 'Nobody knows the future: nobody knows what will or will not make for his happiness, nor does it much matter: do your duty because it is your duty, and leave the rest to fate.' This, I take it, was and is the practical outcome of his teaching. Of all thinkers, he seemed most to hate the Benthamite or materialist school: I suppose because their fundamental doctrine 'Happiness the chief good and object of man' was in direct opposition to his.

12 Feb. 1881: Wrote to Sanderson, in consequence of a letter which has appeared in *The Times* asserting that the Russian govt. proposed to ours in 1876 a partition of Afghanistan. The *Telegraph* has got the same story, in fuller detail, showing clearly that it is being put about by some person professing to know the facts – probably Lytton. I observe as an indication of the general feeling that Lytton, having been proposed as a member of the Travellers' Club, has been rejected by more blackballs than any candidate is known to have received. This is the more noticeable because he is pleasant in manners & conversation: at least such was his character in England, though at Calcutta he never achieved popularity. . . .

15 Feb. 1881: . . . In the Lords Lytton volunteered an explanation[20] of his proceedings on the Afghan frontier in 1876. As he had given no public notice, the attendance was small. Argyll, whom he had informed of his intentions, told him plainly, though in decorous language, that he did not believe the statement which he (L.) had made, & intended to prove its inaccuracy. A few words from Ld B. & Granville ended the conversation.

De La Warr dined with us.

16 Feb. 1881: . . . Called on Granville, to talk over the mystery of the supposed Russian offers for the partition of Afghanistan in 1876: a story which has been put into the papers evidently by Lytton, & the only explanation of it which I can suggest is that it arose out of a conversation which L. himself held with Schouvaloff before going out to India. Of this convn. no record exists either in the Foreign or India offices, which have been searched: I have asked Sanderson to look through my private papers when he returns to London, to see if it can be traced there. But I remember that an interview between the outgoing Gov. Gen. & the Russian ambassador did take place: & it is not unlikely that Lytton, in his imaginative way, may have magnified some remark thrown out in casual talk into an offer or overture, on the part of the Russian govt.

Looking back to my notes of past Cabinets, I am able to say (only it cannot be said in public) that the question of relations with Afghanistan was never brought before the Cabinet in the spring of 1876.

– I found Granville with 39 unopened boxes great & small waiting for him: an accumulation which would have disturbed my nerves more than it seemed to do his. . . .

17 Feb. 1881: . . . Sir F. Roberts[21], dining the other day in the City, took the opportunity when his health was drunk of making a speech in which he strongly, & even vehemently, condemned the system of short service introduced into the army during the last few years. He said that it gave the army boys instead of men, that they knocked up, fell ill, could not bear fatigue, & that, unless the system were modified, they would not have troops fit to make such campaigns as that which he had gone through. As the new arrangement is extremely popular at the War Office, whatever it may be in the army, Sir F.'s speech is thought a remarkable display of independence but, as he probably has the Duke of Cambridge on his side, there may be more show than reality of risk to his prospects.

The intention of establishing short terms of service was to create a powerful reserve, composed of men who had passed through the ranks, & were liable to be called upon in emergency: but the experience of 1878 has shown that except in the gravest necessity it is almost impossible to employ this reserve practically: the men called out have to throw up their employments, their places are filled while they are serving, & they come back to find that they have neither work nor wages. This at least is the case with so many that the calling out of the reserve is felt as a cruel hardship on those liable to serve in it. It is available if there were civil war, or danger of invasion: but hardly otherwise. And it does not seem that the comparative shortness of the term has induced young men of a better class than the ordinary recruit to enlist: which was long the hope of army reformers. So that it is likely the whole subject will have to be reconsidered.

18 Feb. 1881: . . . Sent to the Arundel Socy. a cheque for £15.15.0 which gives some extra privileges as to receiving prints & publications – I hardly know what, nor care, but it is the right business to 'patronise art'.

In afternoon to the Lords, where a lively wrangle (I can call it by no more dignified name) between the two front benches. Argyll renewed his attack on Lytton, for which there appeared no obvious or adequate reason, accusing him of having planned the Afghan war as long ago as in 1876. He gave what he considered proofs of this but, though believing the charge to be true, I cannot say that they were conclusive. It seemed to me that the military preparations, which undoubtedly were made, were no more than might have been reasonably explained by the circumstances of the time, & the danger of a disturbed frontier. Lytton answered with some force & skill, but shuffled a good deal, & did not rely on what I should have thought was the simple & straightforward line of defence. He had, however, so far the best of it, that the attack, having been unprovoked, could not be justified except by clear evidence, & the evidence was not clear. Granville, Cranbrook, Cairns, & Ld Beaconsfield all spoke shortly, and the scene was more animated than usual: but dinner dispersed the peers, & ended the affair. Nobody had a victory, & on the whole neither good nor harm was done.

19 Feb. 1881: . . . The week has not brought an end of the Irish Coercion bill debates, which have lasted practically for six weeks, since no other subject has been discussed. And, as the present bill is to be followed by an Arms bill, one does not see where it is to end. The Irish members have recovered from the shock caused by the new rules, & by the outburst of public feeling against them: and are exerting their ingenuity to evade these rules: not wholly without success. I do not care to note details, but it is observable that the Speaker has been compelled to reinforce his first set of rules by others of greater stringency: & that the

Conservatives, who at first backed up the Speaker, now hesitate to support him. I do not say they are wrong: for undoubtedly much has been taken away from the freedom of debate: but the House is now in such a situation that there is only a choice of evils.

This evening conversation turned on the Irish question. I found every one of our party, from the Duke downwards, agreed that the Irish masses are entirely hostile to English rule: that the Home Rulers really do represent the nation: or, in other words, that under the name & form of popular government we are holding Ireland against the will of the Irish. It is long since I have been of this way of thinking, but until lately it was not common in English society. The difficulty is grave: for, in such conditions, the more the representative system is developed, the more clearly you bring out the fact that what the people want is what you cannot give them: and how long will parliamentary institutions be possible, when one-seventh of the members use their rights as such with the sole & avowed object of making government impossible? . . .

21 Feb. 1881: . . . Somebody, I forget who, has summed up the Irish question thus: 'The Irish don't know what they want, & will never be satisfied till they get it.' I am afraid, however, that a good many of them do know what they want, & that it is what we cannot give them.

22 Feb. 1881: . . . H. of Lords at 5.00, where Ld Dunraven moved a resolution in favour of Sunday opening of museums, etc. He spoke well, though rather too long. A lively little debate followed, Rosebery answering the Abp. of Canterbury, & making some fun at his expense, Cairns speaking out plainly in favour of the 'divine authority' of Sunday observance: which was honest, & contrasted with the Abp.'s careful avoidance of any such expression of opinion. Ld Thurlow got up just before 8.00, & persisted in speaking when the peers wanted to go away & dine. Many did go, & we divided 34 to 41: a narrow majority[22], considering that the clerical party were very active in bringing up votes. . . .

24 Feb. 1881: Walk early with Ld Dalhousie.

Sanderson came to tell me of an accident that happened to the Premier last night: he fell down, cut or severely bruised his head, & is ordered to keep entirely quiet for 3 or 4 days. . . .

25 Feb. 1881: Much talk of the accident to Gladstone, which might have been serious, or even fatal, to a man 71 years of age, but it is said he will soon get over it.

. . . The Irish in H. of C. have calmed down: &, though they continue to waste as much time as the new rules allow, no violent scenes have occurred. Parnell has been to Paris, ostensibly to get support from French politicians & the French press (popular talk says there is a woman in the case): and is going back to stay some time, or else proceed to the States. It is thought here that he has lost his hold on the agitation: from the first he was disliked by many as a Protestant: and his intercourse while in France with Rochefort, V. Hugo, & others of that sort has alarmed the clerical party. Since the arrest of Davitt, outrages have ceased, & the local branches of the Land League are breaking up everywhere. In fact the evident anger of the English people has done the work of the Coercion bill: & the bill will be passed just when it is not wanted. I am not sure that it ever would have been necessary, if more energy had been shown in the autumn & early winter: but Forster did not know the Irish, & he could not have acted without splitting up his party.

The remark I hear on all sides is: 'How lucky that the Liberals are in: if they had been out of office, half of them would have been backing up the Irish.' And I am afraid that is the truth.

A court drawing-room today, to which M. went, & reports the Queen as extremely civil to her, which shows a change since 1878.

26 Feb. 1881: Walk to the Museum, where a committee meeting: we sat little over an hour, D. of Somerset in the chair. Ld Beaconsfield was there for the first time that I have seen him of late years. He seemed half asleep, & not aware of what was passing: but this was appearance only, for he roused himself, & took part in the business, which was not important. Sherbrooke, B. Hope, Spottiswoode & others present. . . .

28 Feb. 1881: London . . . Call on A.D. [Lady Dartrey] & hear the latest Irish news. It seems that the feeling among the peasantry is better than it was: six weeks ago they believed in a coming revolution, and took no pains to conceal their hopes: the young people about Dartrey all carry either guns or pistols, and used to fire them off along the road, especially (A.D. says) when any of the gentry were passing. She has heard them say when firing: 'There goes another landlord.' But matters never went beyond this harmless kind of practical joking. She noticed especially that young men whom she knew would turn away to avoid meeting her – not choosing to exchange civilities, nor yet openly to refuse them. Now all this is over, rents are being paid again, & the normal conditions of society are being restored. She ascribes the change entirely to the arrest of Davitt, & the silencing the Irish members: which for the first time showed that England was in earnest.

. . . The papers are full of a severe defeat[23] suffered in the Transvaal, in which Sir G. Colley has been killed, & several hundred men: first reports say 500 . . . It seems Sir George had seized a hill which commanded the position of the Boers, & would have compelled them to abandon the defences they have been laboriously throwing up: seeing this they determined to retake it at any cost & did so by sheer hard fighting. It is impossible for men to have shown more courage, & we seem to have made the usual mistake of underrating them.

1 Mar. 1881: . . . H. of Lords, where we heard from the govt. that the disaster in Africa has been exaggerated: the total loss being about 300, instead of 500 to 600, as was at first supposed.

Sir F. Roberts goes out to take the command.

2 Mar. 1881: By arrangement a reporter from the Central News office called here & I dictated to him the substance of the speech I am to make tomorrow. It occupied an hour & a little over.

Walk for exercise. In afternoon called on A.D. & heard more of Irish affairs.

I was all this day oppressed with a disagreeable nervous sensation, anticipating the speech to be made tomorrow. I am never free from this feeling when about to speak, & except in 1859 I have seldom felt it more strongly.

3 Mar. 1881: . . . At 4.30 with M. & Margaret [Cecil] to the Lords: the house full, galleries, throne & bar crowded. Lytton opened his case at 5.15, speaking nearly 2 hours, very good in regard of voice, manner, & style: but as to matter exceedingly rambling &

discursive. In fact, the greater part of his argument was a defence of his policy in 1878 & earlier: which it was natural he should make, but, as it related to a state of things now past & gone, the immediate question at issue was not greatly touched by it. He will be an able debater with practice: today the general impression left was 'Clever, but not much to the purpose'. Enfield answered him, speaking to a thinner audience: sensible & argumentative, not aiming at more: then came some less notable peers, Chelmsford one of them, who condemned the retention of Kandahar on military grounds, going against his party: which ought to be remembered in his favour. I got up about 9.30, and was speaking just an hour. All uneasiness left me when once started, and I satisfied myself pretty well: using the prepared text as a framework, & interpolating into it replies to what had been said in debate. I was very well heard, & on the whole am content. Salisbury followed me as usual: less bitter than he sometimes is, & arguing the question fairly: towards the end his voice & bodily strength seemed to fail. Ld Northbrook replied to him, able & vigorous in reasoning, but with a dry, jerky delivery which destroyed the effect. He could not make the Lords hear, & many went away. Naturally the reporters have mangled his utterances beyond all possibility of being understood. We adjourned about 12.00.

I walked home with Granville, who talked vaguely, but gloomily, hinted that they might break up, did not know how long Gladstone's health would last, etc. He, Gladstone, has again appeared in his place, but is said to feel the shock of his fall a good deal.

4 Mar. 1881: To the Lords again at 5.00: Cranbrook opened the debate, speaking $1\frac{1}{2}$ hours: very unequal in different parts of his speech, mixing up good and bad points as lawyers, or law-trained men, are apt to do: all that he really had to say might have been said in half an hour, . . . the only two really valid objections to the surrender were made by him. (1) To whom do you mean to hand over Kandahar? Who is in a position to hold it? (2) How can you give effective protection to natives who have sided with the British cause & made enemies thereby? He also laid stress on Ld Ripon's opinion not having been produced, implying that it was hostile to the govt. policy: but this turned out a mistake. Towards the end he grew declamatory, & made a great noise, in his old H. of Commons style, which had some effect, but less than there.

– Argyll followed, & had apparently been warned against violence, so carefully that he became dull, which is not his custom: he dwelt too long on details, quoted the opinions of Indian officials at length, & prefaced them with comments on the persons quoted – which Ld B. afterwards laughed at, fairly enough. He was unlucky too, in speaking all through the dinner hour. Dining at home, I found on returning Ld Dunraven talking quaint Yankee sense in that fine nasal tone which he has acquired out West: Lansdowne & Rosebery were to have followed: but Ld Beaconsfield begged to be allowed to speak early, age & fatigue being his plea: the request could not be refused, & it caused the debate to end at midnight.

Ld B. had seemed more dead than alive before speaking, & after his speech (& the division) he wandered about the House, & sat down on the Treasury bench, either in absence or (as I fear) seeing very little. But while on his legs he was vigorous & effective: temperate too in language, as a man neither personally attacking nor attacked. On the whole, I have not of late often heard him better. Granville's summing up was neat, but in no way remarkable. We divided (I think) 79 to 165 . . . But nothing will come of it, probably there will not even be a countervote in the Commons.

5 Mar. 1881: Walk early with Ld Dalhousie. Fine warm day.

Sent £20 to a fund for helping Ly Mountmorres, widow of the Irish peer who was murdered last autumn.

Yesterday Sir Wilfrid Lawson called by appointment: his object being to get up an agitation against the Transvaal war. He thought the govt. would not be sorry to be pressed to make terms. We talked with entire agreement on the subject itself for I have from the first considered the Transvaal business a mistake, into which the Colonial Office was led by its authorities at the Cape: but I could not agree in the wisdom of an agitation which should condemn the present Cabinet as too warlike – Bright & Gladstone being among its members. The thing would seem absurd, & would fail for want of support. Nor did the English public like the notion of negociating until they had redeemed their damaged military reputation by a success. – I could see that Sir W.L. more than half distrusts the Cabinet: and certainly its position is peculiar. The Basuto war & the Boer war are both disapproved in Downing St., yet neither can be stopped: the Irish secretary laments pathetically & quite sincerely the hard fate that compels him to bring in coercion bills, but he has no choice, & as a fact they are nearly the most severe ever passed: the Premier would like to make a great reduction of taxes: but he will probably find that Afghan & African expenses make that impossible: and, to increase the absurdity of the situation, freedom of debate in parliament is for the first time restricted, under the most democratic ministry we have ever yet known. In fact by sheer pressure of necessity, & not by choice, the actions of the govt. have been exactly such as a conservative govt. would have taken in hand: with this difference, that they pass unopposed, whereas if Gladstone had been in opposition they would have been resisted at every stage.

6 Mar. 1881: . . . There has been more trouble with the Irish this week: but they have injured their own cause by violence. On Tuesday last (I think it was) Dillon attacking the Arms bill said that if he were a tenant he should think himself justified in shooting any man who attempted to evict him – & that there would be but few evictions if every Irish peasant had a rifle. He further said: 'We have not the means of waging civil war, I wish we had' – the most distinct avowal of revolutionary intentions that I suppose ever was made in parliament. His colleagues saw the mistake & with infinite civility disavowed him: but it was too late: after that reason given, by one of the leaders of the League, why arms should be wanted, nobody could well dispute the need of an Arms Bill. Parnell spoke also, but his speech, some hearers told me, was that of a beaten man. In fact, matters have come to a point where the movement must either explode in violence, or collapse. . . .

7 Mar. 1881: . . . Busy with suggested amendments to the Alkali Bill, which comes on tomorrow, but no two of them agree, & I believe in the end nothing will be done. One set of people press for impossible strictness, & if they do not get all they want would rather have no bill at all: another set urge, quite justly, the importance of conciliating the manufacturers, & are willing so to soften down the provisions that they would cease to be of any value. . . .

11 Mar. 1881: . . . Much grumbling and uneasiness as to the state of parliamentary business, which is more in arrear than ever: notwithstanding all that has been done, obstruction is rampant, & it becomes increasingly difficult to see how it is to be checked without suppressing freedom of debate. It is impossible officially to distinguish between an honest English M.P. who is only conducting what he supposes to be an argument in a tedious manner, & a Home Ruler who gets up & declaims for the purpose of wasting time. The obstructionist movement has been more successful than its very authors could have expected, since it has profoundly disorganised the whole machinery of parliament. A less sensitive man than the Premier might be expected to feel intensely the annoyance of the situation: but I observe that Gladstone, though in trifles the most nervously irritable of men, is calm in serious difficulties. They seem to steady him.

12 Mar. 1881: . . . By 4.30 train to Keston. Walk on arriving, but I was, & still partly am, oppressed by a new sensation of discomfort: weight & sinking of the stomach, & a sort of nervous anxiety as though a misfortune were expected, or as if I had just heard alarming news. It is purely physical, for there is nothing in outward circumstances to cause it, they being all favourable: nor have I troubles or disputes of any kind. I suppose it is one of the innumerable disguises which gout assumes, but I should prefer honest bodily pain, if the choice were allowed.

I hear that F.[24] has got the gout slightly but decidedly: also that he has been of late in a morbid despondent state, thinking himself ruined, etc., which is probably only the same complaint. . . .

14 Mar. 1881: On the station walls saw newspaper placards announcing that the Emperor of Russia was murdered yesterday, two explosive bombs being thrown at him while driving in Petersburg: the first killed horses, men, etc., and shattered the carriage: the second blew off his legs as he got out. He died in 2 or 3 hours. . . . The secret of the conspiracy will probably never be discovered.

As far as it is possible to judge at a few hours' notice, the event seems an unmixed evil. Alexander was peaceable, had experience of governing, and inclined to reforms: his successor is young, not thought to have much capacity, believed to be fond of war, & certainly dislikes the Germans. He may change under pressure of responsibility but, if not, he is very likely to intrigue with the French in order to break down the German empire: which means another great European war. Further, the result of a successful attempt to assassinate is always a misfortune: it encourages hotheaded fanatics all over the world to try their chance in the same line &, where it does not create terror in the authorities, it breeds resentment & anger: in either case strengthening reaction. For the party of constitutional progress, if such a party exists in Russia, no outlook can be worse. It would not surprise me if similar attempts were made in Berlin, Vienna, possibly Rome & Madrid.

. . . Went across to the Commons, where considerable excitement, Gladstone wanting Supply to be treated as urgent, which would curtail discussion on the estimates, & Northcote having objected in a letter published this morning. As urgency cannot be declared except by a two-thirds vote, the Conservative party has a veto upon it, practically, & this veto they seem disposed to use. The fact is, they have got the coercion bills through, which they were afraid would be dropped: and they are not in the same haste to give facilities for the Land Bill, which in no case can now be brought in till after Easter. But the case is doubtful: many people think that Gladstone has been hasty, & it is a serious matter for parliament to divest itself (practically) of control over the estimates. Moreover, the proposed contribution of £5,000,000 in part payment of the Afghan war is a serious question of principle, & ought not to be assented to in haste.

15 Mar. 1881: . . . Govt. last night were defeated in the attempt to declare urgency: but only under the new rule requiring a two-thirds vote, so that they are not in a minority. Estimates were passed rapidly, the Irish not obstructing. The opinion is general that it was a mistake to ask for extraordinary powers, when they could be dispensed with: but there was only a choice of difficulties.

The House has got the Bradlaugh business on its hands again, or soon will have: the seat having been declared vacant, as far as the law courts have power so to declare it, but subject to an appeal. If the appeal goes with the original judgment, a bill must be brought in allowing all persons the right to affirm: which will be opposed, & a tedious business. I thought last year that it would have been better to cut the knot in that way, before any trial at law: & I think now that in that way what would have been saved.

16 Mar. 1881: Slept ill, nervous & uncomfortable about journey & speech . . . Maclure called, bringing . . . two Manchester gentlemen, to consult me about getting up a great meeting in aid of the Manchester Infirmary, which is largely outrunning its income. . . . It came out clearly that in Manchester, as elsewhere, all the business of giving is left to a small fraction of the richer class, the rest standing aloof.

Thence, to a meeting of the Cotton Districts Convalescent Fund . . . about the cost of building at Southport, which has exceeded the estimates . . . Home, an early & hasty dinner: left at 3.30 for Euston . . . Manchester at 8.45, where found Mr. S. Platt[25] & his carriage on the platform. Drove with him 6 or 7 miles to Oldham (Werneth park) where met Lyulph Stanley[26*]. Him I should scarcely have known again, for though only 42 he is quite grey, & looks nearer 60. He is just what he was as a young man: rather clever, fluent, confident, affecting popular or rather democratic sympathies: a man whom a mixture of conceit & superficial good intentions might make dangerous if he were in a more important position. He has not accomplished any considerable success in the House. On the other hand he has married the daughter of a very rich manufacturer, & brought some money into the family, which much wanted it. Supper, & bed about half past eleven, having settled proceedings for tomorrow.

17 Mar. 1881: After breakfast L. Stanley & I went to the nearest of the four works owned by the Platt family: the greatest machine-making establishment that exists in the world. Platt himself & one of the managers took us over. The business is in form a limited company, but only the family & some of the workmen hold shares. There are employed 8,000 men & lads, making a total dependent population of about 30,000. Wages average 31s. a week: none of the men doing mechanical work get over 40s.: foremen, draughtsmen, & others having headwork in addition get salaries up to £200 a year. I presume there are some higher, but note the figures as they were given to me.

At 12.30 went to the Town Hall where the mayor, Mr. Platt, Hibbert, L. Stanley, I, & some others had to speak, but we were all brief. Then a procession, which seemed to me a failure: then a formal inspection of the schools, a tedious business: home about 4.00, rest before dinner, dine at 5.00: a little before 7.00 to the theatre, which was crowded, about 2,500 in it as they said: more speeches, mine lasting 40 minutes, some very tedious. But the audience swallowed all & seemed to like it. Home at 10.30 to 11.00: & so with a little supper to bed.

Werneth park, my host's place, is a large detached villa, enclosed with 4 or 5 others in a joint park: close by is the house of James Platt, uncle of this man, who received me in

1856, & died from an accident the year after. . . . John Platt[27], M.P. for Oldham, now dead, was brother of James: this man is his son, & lives in the house of the widow. Another son has the estate in Wales, and there are several more. The business has been built up by three generations, the grandfather having in the first instance come over from Yorkshire & settled at Oldham, where according to his grandson he began with 4 men only, working with them himself. I note these things in case any chance should bring me back to Oldham.

18 Mar. 1881: Sleep sound & woke relieved to feel that this business was done: for I have been foolishly nervous about it – I suppose owing to health.

. . . Reached Euston at 5.00 – Found news of the death of Ly M. Hope[28], at Nice: it had been expected for some days: she was only 58, but had long been in broken health. The blow will be heavily felt by B. Hope, a man naturally affectionate, domestic, & helpless in small matters.

. . . I was told that in the Platt works nearly all is done by the piece – weekly wages are the exception – the men prefer the system and would object to fixed-time payments. I think Mr. P. said there had been some resistance by the trade unions at first, but it was long since done away. He did not fear union rules or strikes: pointing out that from the increased use of automatic machines, which can be tended by unskilled men, very few men now were in a position to dictate to their employers, as they could with only a few exceptions be easily replaced.

Mr. P. has been a good deal in America, & I noticed that he did not agree in the opinion which is common here as to the superiority of American mechanics. . . . For thoroughness of work, the English were far superior . . .

19 Mar. 1881: . . . Pender called . . . He brought from Dr. G. Clerk[29], Gladstone's physician, a bad report of the Premier's health, which indeed I hear confirmed from various quarters. Increasing irritability and a growing sense of fatigue are the symptoms spoken of.

20 Mar. 1881 (Sunday): . . . Parliamentary business in the Lords there has been none this week: the Commons occupied with estimates. Childers has a plan for reorganising the army, about the tenth time that process has been gone through in my memory: 'Plus ça change, et plus c'est la même chose.' The officers seem on the whole to like it, as far as I can judge: civilians remain indifferent, and suppose it will all come right. Trevelyan made a speech in moving the navy estimates, which is spoken of as exceptionally good. The Irish have puzzled friends & enemies by abstaining absolutely from obstruction: some say, because they wish the Land Bill to come on as soon as possible, in order to pass it: others, because they have settled with the Opposition to throw it out, or so to reduce the majority in its favour that it will be thrown out by the Lords and, having this piece of effective revenge in prospect, they are content to remain quiet for the moment.

Loud complaints from Ireland that the Coercion bill is being feebly and unequally worked: the real leaders of the movement being allowed to defy the law at public meetings, while only small unimportant persons are arrested. I suppose there is some truth in this, for nothing can be more violent or apparently seditious than the language which Dillon M.P. has been holding.

21 Mar. 1881: . . . It is announced that the Premier's Land Bill is to be brought out before the Easter holidays, & read a second time after them: a result which has apparently been brought about by pressure, for an opposite intention was expressed (though not officially or publicly) a few days ago.

Death of Ld St. Germans[30], about the age of 50, in papers: he was a poor creature, weak in brains and health, & intensely superstitious. He is succeeded by Eliot[31] of the F.O., one of the best clerks there, & a loss to the department: an able official, but also in weak health, & deaf: so the office has lost a good clerk, & the Lords have not gained a peer who will be active in their business.

22 Mar. 1881: . . . Letter to M. from Talbot, who seems alarmed at the trouble into which he has been brought by the Oxford election business: it was not easy to induce him to write offering an explanation: this he has now done, & I hope it is not too late. She promises to intercede with Harcourt, & I draft a letter for her to write accordingly.

. . . Saw Rathbone, who brings a message asking me to be the first president of the new Liverpool College. I agree, on the understanding that the office is mainly honorary, & that if I find duties belonging to it which I cannot conveniently discharge I may without blame retire.

Dine at The Club, meeting by an odd chance only the two editors, Reeve & Smith. Much pleasant & friendly talk chiefly on literary matters. It was mentioned that Carlyle has left £40,000, the produce of his literary work: but his success came late in life, after he had been severely tried, & in some measure soured, by poverty & obscurity. . . .

24 Mar. 1881: Left London with A. & L. Cecil by a special train from Charing Cross to attend the funeral of Ly M. Hope at Kilndown church near Bedgebury. We drove from T. Wells to the church, carriages being provided, & all done in order: the service, however, was as badly arranged & tedious as possible, lasting over 2 hours, & in the midst of it a controversial sermon in the worst possible taste . . . Long ceremonies on such occasions are a mistake.

Most of the Cecil & Balfour families were there. Cranbrook came as an old friend & neighbour. Salisbury & I met casually at the station door at T. Wells: he offered his hand, & I did not refuse it (which would have been foolish at any time, & brutal on an occasion of this kind): but it is not likely or desirable that any personal relations should be renewed between us. Both he & Eustace Cecil[32] looked very much worn & aged. . . .

26 Mar. 1881: Debate on Kandahar in the Commons ended last night, with a division of 336 to 216 – 120 majority. The talk last evening was that Ministers expected to win by 80. The speaking was generally good: Hartington's summing up is especially praised: Stanhope & Dilke were also able. Those who heard the debate say that it was not on the whole exciting, though the speeches were sensible & to the point: but it was known beforehand how the vote would go and, as the act of abandoning Kandahar is final, there is no question of the decision being reversed in the future. I notice – perhaps as an effect of the discussion in the Lords – that little was said as to the permanent retention of the place, most stress being laid on the allegation that the withdrawal is precipitate, impolitic at the moment, & so forth.

Ld Sherbrooke, with whom I walked home from the Lords, has got hold of a report, which he seems to believe, that Gladstone intends to take off the income tax altogether, replacing it by a heavy legacy & succession duty. He has the story from Ld Halifax. . . .

28 Mar. 1881: . . . Parliamentary business goes on smoothly: the Irish for some reason of their own have ceased to obstruct: either they really have hopes that the Irish bill will be such as to content their supporters (but that can hardly be): or they think it better tactics to throw no obstacle in the way of its being brought in, but to reserve their opposition till it is discussed: or, as many people think, they have an understanding with the Conservatives to throw it out &, secure of success in the future, they can afford to behave peaceably as yet. This last speculation is to my mind over-refined, but it is in people's mouths.

The South African business is finally settled, & in the only rational way: by the substitution of a protectorate for direct administration by the Col. Office, which leaves to us the only thing we really want, the control of foreign relations. There will be, & indeed is, some grumbling at the notion of making peace after a defeat: but the defeat was on too small a scale to affect prestige, and it would be more like a red Indian than a rational being to say: 'The terms you offer are satisfactory, but we can't accept them until we have killed a few more of you.' On the whole, if the Greco-Turkish quarrel gets itself arranged without a war, the prospect abroad will be decidedly improved.

29 Mar. 1881: . . . Hear with regret, but not with surprise, that the De La Warrs[33] are what is popularly called 'ruined' – that is they have been living up to if not above their means, & the lowering of rents due to agricultural distress, & having some farms unlet on their hands, has hastened a crisis which probably must have come anyhow. They talk of letting Buckhurst, as well as their London house, & going to live in cheaper quarters.

Much talk about the Lawson-Labouchere[34] trial, which has filled the papers for some days, & ended last night by the jury being unable to agree: so that we may not impossibly have it all over again, unless the parties come to terms. . . . Among both lawyers & laymen [there is] a strong opinion (which I fully share) that Ld Coleridge has shown a very marked partiality for the defendant – whether from dislike of Lawson & the *Telegraph*, since it turned against Gladstone, or from the fear of being libelled by Labouchere in his scurrilous paper. Brett among others expressed to me (meeting him in the street) a strong opinion as to Coleridge's language & conduct: 'If he had been retained for the defence he could not have shown a stronger bias.'

Much talk also about Ld Beaconsfield's illness – a complication of asthma & gout apparently, which has gone on for several days, but yesterday & today became serious. At 75 years there is always danger in such cases. . . .

30 Mar. 1881: . . . Ld Beaconsfield's illness increased, & he is considered to be in great danger.

31 Mar. 1881: H. of Lds. at 5.00, where a speech from Cairns on Transvaal matters, which lasted over 2 hours. It was one of his best, very able in parts, though with his common fault of being too minute & diffuse. The peroration theatrical, but fine. Apart from artistic merit, it had little in it of good: being throughout an appeal to prejudice in an electioneering strain, making no allowance for difficulties, though these were inherited from the late govt., & apparently not admitting the idea of any solution except brute force. It was addressed in fact to the clubs & to the jingo mob. Outside 'society' I do not believe its effect will be felt. Kimberley followed: but no division was intended, & the House thinned towards 8.00.

Called early to enquire at Ld Beaconsfield's door: the street was crowded: the poor old man would be happy if he knew (perhaps he does) the popular interest excited by his illness. I saw Barrington, who is in constant attendance there: the report is neither better nor worse: perhaps some improvement but still much danger.

1 Apr. 1881: . . . Drive with M. [to] a doctor, or quack, who treats her by rubbings and gentle muscular exercises, which she thinks do her nerves & consequently her eyes good. May it be so: I doubt: but Drage says the man is harmless, & the experiment gives her hope of improvement.

Call to enquire in Curzon St. Report favourable: but there is still much danger.

2 Apr. 1881: Pender calls to talk about his claim to a baronetcy. Knowing that it has been reported that he was ruined, he volunteered to tell me that he has property to the value of about £400,000, & Mrs. Pender over £200,000 in addition. Out of this, if he gets the honour he wants, he will lay out £100,000 in land to go with it. . . .

4 Apr. 1881: . . . Went across in the evening to Travellers' to learn what the budget was. It will disappoint radicals, & satisfy moderate men, being simple & unpretending. The penny of income tax put on last year is taken off again, duties on foreign spirits slightly increased, a small change made in the probate duty, which I do not well understand, but as it only adds £300,000 to the revenue it cannot be important. Other changes are trifling. He announces, but will explain hereafter, a plan for paying off £60,000,000 of debt by means of terminable annuities – a thoroughly right & sound proposal, but the details remain to be seen. The estimated expenditure for 1881-1882 is £84,705,000: the revenue as estimated £300,000 higher.

Gladstone laid a good deal of stress on the necessity of dealing with succession duties, legacy duty, etc., on a large scale, but added that it was a work that could not be undertaken except with ample time, which was not now to be had. He farther hinted that the present budget was probably his last: which no doubt was his reason for going out of the common course, & condemning a whole class of taxes which he is not in a position to reform or replace. . . .

6 Apr. 1881: . . . Walk with Dalhousie: in course of conversation he tells me that his gross rental is about £70,000, & the encumbrances £450,000. He wants to sell, which in principle I approve, but tell him not to be in haste, as this is a bad time. . . .

7 Apr. 1881: Sent £10.10.0 as a life subscription to the Kent Ophthalmic Hospital. Gave £10 to the W.E. West children, to be divided among them.

. . . Received from the O'Donoghue[35] an application for a loan of £400, or £200, to save him from immediate bankruptcy: he offers security of some kind, & on this I apply to Lawrence for his judgment. It is an odd request, for I hardly know the man, & believe that his distress is mainly owing to his own extravagance: still he is a gentleman, though a very Irish one, & the sum will not hurt me to lose.

Declined a similar request from one Haydon, a son of the unfortunate painter who shot himself about 1845 or 46. . . . He puts forward absolutely no claim, & the father was notorious for the frequency & importunity of his begging applications.

. . . In the Commons, Gladstone brought in his Land Bill in a speech of two hours which is much admired: but the bill itself is very complicated, and some time will be necessary to understand its provisions. It attempts to fix rents, but does not give an absolute fixity of tenure. Large provision is made for helping tenants to buy their farms, which is the least objectionable part of the whole. – But I cannot attempt criticism.

8 Apr. 1881: Saw Lawrence, who advises me that (as I had supposed) the security offered by the O'Donoghue for his proposed loan is entirely worthless: on which I determine to grant half his request, sending him a cheque for £100, saying that I require neither security nor interest, but excusing myself from giving help on a larger scale by the number of similar claims. He has absolutely no right to expect help from me, & what I have given is rather because I do not think it becomes me to refuse such requests than on account of any sympathy I feel for the man. He has played with disaffection all his life, & has his just reward in the refusal of his tenantry to pay their rents. – Ld Granard[36], I hear with sincere satisfaction, is in the same position: it is not many years since he made a speech in Ireland, glorifying the insurgents of Vinegar Hill, the scene of the revolt of 1798. Irish patriots of this kind are rightly served when they find their own countrymen turn against them. . . .

9 Apr. 1881: . . . Call early at Coutts, & give orders to invest £5,000 . . . I ask for Metrop. railway debentures, if they can be got. All securities remain very high, money being much more abundant than the means of employing it: & I was glad to hear from the broker that, though new companies (mostly bubbles) have been abundant of late, they have not been successful. . . .

11 Apr. 1881: Reports of Ld Beaconsfield rather worse . . .

An article in *The Times* points out the difficulties which either Ld Cairns or Ld Salisbury would feel in acting under the other, and the probable unpopularity of both with certain sections of the party: & half suggests that the D. of Richmond might be nominal leader over both.

Call in Curzon St.: talk of Land Bill: the Irish landowners are much alarmed: they object to the unlimited & arbitrary power which it is proposed to give to the commission to reduce rents without any check or any law to guide them. They say that the officials, being Catholics, & appointed from the dominant party, are sure to decide every doubtful point in favour of the peasantry, and they want some kind of rule laid down for the guidance of the court. A.D. does not believe that the tenants will wish or care to buy their farms. They had rather have a landlord who will lay out money, be indulgent to them in hard times, & who will under the new conditions have practically no power. I suspect this is likely enough to be the truth. . . .

13 Apr. 1881: See Kitley[37]. Hear the story of Garland's estate being sold: he is a wine merchant, was doing a good business, took his son into partnership: the young man gambled away the money of the firm, & absconded. The father is ruined, & likely to die, broken down by his misfortune. The estate is only 71 acres with a good though small house.

14 Apr. 1881: Wrote to F. Hopwood about his son, whom he wants to get a place for as a gaol governor[38].

Wrote to Childers, by request of the officers of the 1st L.R. Volunteers, to call attention to the services of Lt. Col. Bousfield[39] in connection with the regiment. I do not do this very willingly, for he was a noisy jingo when in parliament, & a vulgar fellow at all times: but it is a bare act of justice, he has worked hard & successfully with much expenditure of money as well as time, & no advantage to himself personally so far. . . .

15 Apr. 1881 (Good Friday): Long early walk along the top of the hills . . . a fine, rather hot day . . . The woods & lanes are full of flowers: the grass green: but, except the larch & horse chestnut, no trees have put out a leaf yet.

Walk later about the place, in a lounging way, with a book: & again with M. In all, more than 4 hours on my legs.

Letter from Sanderson, containing a curious report of the almost ostentatious indifference shown by the upper & official classes in Petersburg to the Emperor's death: he assigns no reason, but I suppose the granting of land to the serfs at the expense of the owners has never been forgiven . . .

. . . Improved report of Ld Beaconsfield, who now seems really to be mending: which nobody expected. . . .

17 Apr. 1881 (Easter Day): This day passed very idly. Not feeling disposed for a long walk, I only rambled about the grounds & plantations with a book: in afternoon walk with M.

. . . Diplomatic changes, long expected, are announced: Dufferin to Constantinople (his own wish, since he cannot get India): Layard to Rome, which is exactly what he wanted & what he is very fit for: Paget to Petersburg. This last is a disappointment to the person concerned, for the expense is heavy, & Paget has nothing but debts. But he has been hitherto quite exceptionally lucky &, as each successive promotion only made him grumble more loudly, I do not think there will be much sympathy felt for his present grievance. Morier will be disgusted, having expected an embassy, though I never knew on what ground: & Thornton also, who really has a claim from service, having been at Washington since 1867.

The Greek question is probably, though not absolutely, settled: which is a piece of a good fortune to our government, which would certainly have been blamed if a war had broken out. The Greek people are deeply disgusted: they have bragged so loud & so long as to have ended by imposing on themselves, & believing that they are a match for the Turkish army. There are many people who say that the Greek king is in danger from popular resentment: that he may be turned out as Otho was. The Greek finances are disordered by the great expense they have gone to: & the disbanding of a mass of excited & discontented young soldiers is likely to be a risky business. Still, when all is said & done, the Greeks have gained a valuable province without fighting: giving them probably more territory than they expected 3 years ago. . . .

19 Apr. 1881: Knowsley. . . . Raised Ward's salary from £350 to £400: which indeed I had half promised to do last year, for his work is heavy, & it is well done.

. . . Left at 10.00 for St. George's Hall [Liverpool] & sat there till nearly 7.00. The cases were 45: an unusually light calendar . . .

. . . Heard in court of the death of Lord Beaconsfield at 5.00 this morning. Though the event was expected – indeed for the last week it has seemed almost certain – yet it brought a shock, and I was & am glad to have received the news under circumstances where the necessity of giving constant attention to the work before me excluded other thoughts.

20 Apr. 1881: . . . St. George's Hall at 10.00. Sat till 5.45. . . . On the whole I was content with the jury. No fatigue, though the sitting lasted nearly 8 hours. Home by 7.00, read & wrote, alone all the evening.

The papers are full of Ld Beaconsfield, as might be expected. No death since that of the P. Consort has created so much sensation: perhaps even that created less interest of a personal kind, though being unexpected it set people more on speculating. The impression on my mind is melancholy, rather than painful: bringing back old times & the memory of events long gone by, in which my father also was concerned. For Ld B. himself longer life was scarcely to be desired: his part was played, his name is inscribed in the history of England, he had held supreme power, & for some years had enjoyed a vast reputation. He has died while his mind was still clear, & while his fame was fresh. Neither might have been the case five or six years hence, and no man would have felt more painfully the appearance of neglect: as Ld Melbourne did in his last years. It is better as it is: still the blank which his disappearance creates will long be felt, & not least by those who knew him personally long ago. We should probably never again have talked confidentially to one another: but recent differences are effaced by death, and only the recollection of early intimacy remains.

21 Apr. 1881: Again up early, & many notes before breakfast. St. George's Hall at 10.00 exactly, where sat hearing appeals till 4.30 or 4.40. Home: saw Ward: some talk with him: he confirms my impression that Statter's failing health & low spirits since the death of his wife make him take an unduly despondent view of the present & future situation. . . .

24 Apr. 1881 (Sunday): Received an invitation to attend Ld Beaconsfield's funeral on Tuesday, which I decide to accept, & write accordingly to Lord Rowton.

. . . Wrote to Sanderson . . . Note that T.H.S.[40] sends a bad report of Granville who is now habitually out of health, & I think will not long remain fit for the heavy work of the F.O.

I take an opportunity to suggest the necessity of accepting amendments to the Irish Land Bill, which is not likely to pass the Lords in its present shape. . . .

26 Apr. 1881: Slept ill, which I seldom do: nervous & uncomfortable, rather than melancholy. My personal relations with Ld Beaconsfield had ceased, & indeed of late years they had not been those of close personal confidence & intimacy: ever since 1874 I knew that much was being done & planned which was concealed from me, & was on my guard accordingly. But the business of today recalls many old recollections, & brings back past life in a way that is unusual, and to me disagreeable.

Went at 1.00 to the Paddington station, where a special train: men of all parties, ministers, ex-ministers, politicians, diplomatists, & private friends. Sat in same carriage with Lowell[41], Rances, the new Greek minister, Col. Taylor[42], etc. Talk with the Greek, who rather amusingly did not know me, & when I told my name said it could not be Ld D., I looked too young. He very warlike in his talk, thought his government wrong for accepting terms of peace: they ought to have fought & been beaten, when Europe would have been compelled to interfere. Taylor very cordial, & less despondent about Ireland than most landowners[43]. Walk up with Stanhope from the station nearly 2 miles. In the funeral procession I selected my brother to walk next: good for the public, & serves to check gossip as to our relations. Hughenden was much as I saw it last in 1870: except that the evergreens have grown so as to darken the house: & that the garden has almost disappeared. The day was fine, & ceremony well managed. After it was over the will was read. We returned by special: I with Stanhope, Harcourt, Hartington, & others, I forget who. Some talk with Harcourt about the Irish bill, which if unaltered will scarcely pass the Lords. . . .

28 Apr. 1881: Left . . . with Mr. Horseley[44] R.A. about 10.30: reached London at 4.00: thence on to Fairhill, arriving at 6.30.

Mr. H. talks of Ruskin, whom he denounces as the worst kind of amateur critic: utterly ignorant, & unaware of his own ignorance. Says that no artist talking or writing to another ever quotes him as an authority: that Turner himself did not understand his admirer's criticisms, & used to say so: that there was a vein of madness in him . . .

Talks of artists 40 or 50 years ago: it was accepted then as a rule that (except portraits, and of those there were but a few) no one bought pictures but noblemen and rich men of fashion. He remembers the sensation when —— (I forget the name) first gave a large order from Manchester. The custom grew, & now large manufacturers are the best customers.

29 Apr. 1881: . . . Talk of the fund she [i.e. Lady Derby] is making for [Lord] L.[ionel] Cecil, in case, as is likely, he loses all his money in the farm. It is £10,000 in the hands of trustees, she undertaking to pay £500 a year towards it, & I promising to make good what may be wanting at her death. She now suggests that I should put in £500 a year also, so as to make up the fund in less than ten years.

Troubled with the breaking-out of smallpox in our London stables . . . we have no choice except to hire others, for the season, so as to avoid the risk of infection.

Wrote to Ward to send up another sum of £10,000, making in all £30,000 this year.

I see with some surprise how the interest in Carlyle & all that belongs to him is kept up. The autobiography has provoked a burst of rage from the admirers of the old philosopher, who dislike its harsh sneering tone . . . They take their revenge in abusing Froude for having published the book: which (as he says & I believe) he had no option about doing, & indeed had trouble in preventing Carlyle from publishing it in his own lifetime. Meanwhile it is said that subscriptions for a statue are entirely stopped, the worshippers being disenchanted. – I cannot myself see the cause of all this noise. The autobiography contains a good many harsh & hasty judgments: but in what book by its author are not such marks of haste & harshness found? The explanation of the stir is, I think, the unexpectedness & incongruity of this literary reappearance of the man whom we thought of as just dead.

30 Apr. 1881: . . . Much talk of the picture of Ld Beaconsfield by Millais: which is sold to W.H. Smith for £2,100: but I heard it sharply criticised, & agree in the censure. The head is too square: the forehead is made upright, whereas in Ld B., though large & broad, it sloped back: the upper lip is made to fall in, giving an appearance of death or extreme debility, which may have been correct when Millais saw him, but was not so a few weeks ago. . . .

. . . Much discussion in the papers as to who is to lead the Conservative party in the Lords. The claimants are three – Richmond, Salisbury, & Cairns.

Richmond has the double advantage of having led before, & of exciting no jealousy: on the other hand his ability is small, his manner though frank is brusque, & he is not very popular on either side, the less so as his wife's dislike to London and to society makes entertaining difficult for him.

Salisbury is quite capable in point of ability, but is judged to be rash & reckless, a good partisan but a dangerous leader. He would not conciliate disaffected Whigs & would present the ideas of his party in the most repulsive form to those whom a prudent and temperate Conservatism might attract. His tongue has made many enemies: & in recent transactions he has got a reputation of the worst kind for an English statesman – that of untruthfulness. I am myself inclined to think that the lies he has told have been the result quite as much of forgetfulness combined with hasty assertion as of deliberate purpose: but this explanation will never be accepted by the public, & it does not cover all cases: such as that of the secret agreement with Russia publicly & formally denied. Anyway his reputation makes him just now impossible as a leader, if the party is to return to power.

Cairns is the third candidate, & has many advantages. His character is pure: no charge of deceit rests on him: he is a more powerful debater than Salisbury: more effective & less personally bitter: moderate in opinions, & ready to waive personal preferences where he is spokesman for others. But some of the country lords dislike lawyers: the high church-men dislike a strong & earnest Protestant: &, after some former experience of the lead, he gave it up. Moreover it is nearly certain that Salisbury would not act under him, & the party would be split.

On the whole, I think Richmond will return to the position which he held while Disraeli led in the Commons: & that this arrangement will be the best for all parties. Northcote is accepted without dispute as leader in the other House: & this is scarcely a matter of choice: there is no one else who could possibly take the place. The only fault found with him is too great caution & moderation: which is a compliment in the guise of a complaint.

1 May 1881: . . . Note that I saw Carnarvon last night, returned from Madeira, well in health, but smaller to look at than before: he has lost his hair, & with a glass in his eye his appearance had in it something comic, which I can hardly describe[45]. . . .

5 May 1881: . . . Granville moved a vote of thanks to the army employed in Afghanistan. He did it badly, at times confused & hesitating, once he stopped altogether. I thought he was ill, but Sanderson tells me that he was so pressed with business that he had barely time to read the papers, or arrange what he should say. Cranbrook followed, a little better, but having no one to attack made him tame. The D.[uke] of Cambridge spoke in a rambling strain, not much to the purpose. Lytton, as ex-governor-general, added a few words[46].

Home, quiet dinner, & evening.

6 May 1881: Saw Drage, who is well satisfied both with M. & me.

At 1.30 to Downing St. for a meeting of the electing trustees of the B. Museum . . . Gladstone in whose house we met was ill & in bed[47], with his now usual complaint of diarrhoea, which any worry or excitement is said to bring on: & he has had a good deal

lately in connection with the question of a monument to Ld Beaconsfield. We elected the
P. of W., Dean Liddell, & Houghton.

Walk in afternoon round Regent's park. Did not go to the Lords, there being no business on the paper: but I see that I have missed a good speech by Dalhousie, on the subject
of naval cadets.

Sanderson & Mary Galloway came to dinner. Talk with S. about the prospects of
West[48]: Washington being vacant by Thornton's late & well deserved promotion to
Petersburg. I thought it right to mention his claim, as he is thoroughly weary of Madrid,
and wishes for the change: but in truth I doubt whether he will suit the Americans, or
they him.

7 May 1881: Grillion breakfast, attended by 16 or 17 of the club: less than usual. We . .
. elected one member, Sir H. Holland[49]. A. Balfour was also balloted for, but did not
succeed.

Nothing special to note, except that Ld Coleridge[50] . . . talked with extreme bitterness
of Froude: from some expressions used, I suspect the *odium theologicum* is at the bottom
of the dislike. Froude is a sceptic, and specially averse to Catholics: Coleridge belongs to
that section of the Establishment which is more than half Catholic . . .

Went to Coutts, & settled for the investment of £20,000, or rather for the purchase of
stock to that amount, which will cost £23,000.

By an early train to Keston with M. arriving at 4.00. In the rail car met Mr. & Mrs.
Knowles[51]: talk with him as to Irish land. He says everybody tells him the same story as
to the unreasonableness of the Irish demands, & the impossibility of really satisfying those
who make them. I explain to him the Irish peasants' view of the case – that the lands were
stolen from them in the first instance, & are still theirs by right: that in consequence they
consider whatever rent they pay as in the nature of compensation offered to a person who
is found unconsciously holding stolen property, & is called upon to disgorge: that they
consider in strictness that they owe the landlord nothing. Hence an utter incapacity on
each side to understand the other.

In the Commons, the Land Bill has been sluggishly discussed, with no vehemence on
either side, & in very thin Houses: probably because it is well understood that the second
reading must pass, & that the real battle will be in committee. Bright was provoked last
night to tell the Irish members that the wretched condition of the Irish peasantry was due
quite as much to want of enterprise in the people as to bad laws: whereupon there was a
scream of Celtic indignation – he had insulted the Irish people, his ill will to Ireland was
well known, etc. It is as if Bright's strong sense, & love of plain speech, had compelled
him at last to break through the conventional parliamentary habit of ascribing whatever
is wrong in Ireland to English oppression. . . . Dillon has been arrested at last – much too
late, but better late than never – but the Land League is still vigorous, & outrages are
frequent.

Every person I meet interested in politics is uneasy as to the prospect. It is doubted
whether the Land Bill can pass the Lords without a good deal of alteration: and the
session seems likely to be stormy. There is also a good deal of uneasiness as to Gladstone's
health, which is certainly not good, & a bulletin has been issued.

8 May 1881 (Sunday): . . . A.D. writes that they are now collecting, not without difficulty, the rents due in May 1880: & even as to these there is great reluctance to pay,

though the year has been unusually good, & there is no distress. But a vague expectation has been created of relief by the legislature, which makes the tenants unwilling to meet even claims, which until now they never would have dreamed of disputing.

9 May 1881: London early: walk in to the station: very dry & dusty, but not unpleasant.
. . . Write to subscribe to a testimonial to Mr. Spedding, the editor of Bacon's works, lately dead: a man who has done good service in the literary way, the more so because he devoted most of his working life to a single object of study.

H. of Lords at 5.00 exactly: where an address was moved to the Crown for a public monument to Ld Beaconsfield: Granville did his part of the work in excellent taste: his speech was a difficult one to make, & he was evidently nervous, but it was a success: Salisbury seconded, & was less fortunate: he was awkward & embarrassed, which under the circumstances was not unnatural: & towards the close he dwelt on Ld B.'s anxiety that England should be great & respected, in a tone which suggested the wish to revive recollections of the policy of 1878-1880. But he stopped just in time to avoid saying anything inappropriate to the occasion. He was very brief, which was as well. Malmesbury followed, no one knew why, & talked wretched twaddle, not even made endurable by sincerity: for he was no friend to Ld B., at whom he used to sneer (rather vulgarly) on the ground of his Jew origin and inferior social position.

In H. of C. Gladstone made the same motion: & his speech (which I tried to hear, but could not, the gallery being full) was skilful for his purpose. It reads as if rather laboured, & as if the speaker was trying to convince himself as much as his audience. – It is pretty well known that the proposal for a vote of public money for a monument originated with the Queen, & was accepted rather reluctantly by the Cabinet: she has been at pains to mark her interest in the family, not only visiting Hughenden after the funeral, but having the boy who is heir to his uncle on a private visit at Windsor. The talk is that she wishes to make him a peer: but, as he has absolutely no fortune, this would be a doubtful kindness.

10 May 1881: . . . Sanderson called . . . He complains of the French in the matter of Tunis, saying that they have been utterly unscrupulous as to truth, etc. But it is more the business of the Italians than of ours.
. . . At 5.00 to the Lords, where a good debate on Transvaal politics: Carnarvon defended the annexation in a rather high-flying style, speaking well enough: Kimberley answered as I thought with much sense & point: Argyll followed in the same sense: three good speeches, after which some nonsense from Ld Brabourne, & a few inaudible words from Stanley of A.[lderley] – In reference to the latter Lowe quoted a [Latin] epitaph, probably of his own making, on some bore. . . . It was certainly true as regards S.[tanley] for the peers scattered as soon as he began.

Some talk with Granville, at his request, about the vacancy to be filled up at Washington. I told him I was not an impartial judge, but I really thought that West had as good a claim as any: especially as I knew that Stuart[52] did not wish to go. In short I said what I could in my brother-in-law's interest, though I have my doubts whether he will not soon be more tired of America than he is of Spain. Thence he proceeded to talk about affairs in general: as to which I can see that he is anxious & not sanguine. He thought Argyll was not now hostile, but would easily drift into opposition – said he carried no weight in Cabinet, from his hasty impulsive ways: but in debate they had lost a useful speaker. Some talk about the Irish bill followed, but vague.

Dined The Club . . . old Prof. Owen in the chair. He is grown old & feeble, but talked well on his own subjects, dwelling a good deal on the necessity of preserving specimens & remains of the existing larger animals of the world, as they are so rapidly being destroyed. He mentioned two or three kinds of whale which have been nearly extermi-nated. There was some good conversation from him . . .

11 May 1881 (Wednesday): . . . Call at Coutts, & try & settle for the investment of £20,000, which I tried on Friday, but found it impossible to get the securities I wanted at any price. . . .

12 May 1881: Letter from Coutts. They have bought for me Metrop. District 4% deben-tures £10,000, & S.E.R. debentures, £10,000: total cost, £22,876. I have now £340,000 invested, worth at present rates £380,000.

Pender called yesterday, & talked with me a long while – partly about his baronetcy (of which he is sanguine so far as Gladstone's approval is concerned),but it is believed, he says, that the Queen in her dislike of the Premier will grant no titles of any kind at his request. This may or may not be true, but it pretty accurately represents the state of the royal mind. The tone of the court is unmistakable: it is the fashion of people about the Queen to question Gladstone's sanity, & to say that he meditates giving up the colonies & India!

P. has heard, & believes, that he will not sit in the Commons after this session, but take his seat in the Lords.

P. very full of a scheme for a freshwater Suez canal, papers about which he left with me though I did not ask for them.

At 1.00 p.m. to Cotton Districts Conv. Fund meeting, Sefton, Winmarleigh, Egerton, Birley, Curtis, Maclure, Dr. Watts – I think these were all. We settled to reduce our plans for building, Egerton alone objecting. Walk back with Winmarleigh, who is recovered from a dangerous bronchial attack, & looks & feels as young as ever – at nearly 80. He says he thought himself hopeless of recovery, & with great difficulty induced his medical man to allow him a little port wine, for which he had a craving. He began to mend at once on its being allowed. He talked about the land bill, more in its favour than I should have expected, saying that on the small estates owned by native Irish the oppression of the tenantry had been great. He thought it ought to pass with some amendment.

Troubled with lumbago, which made walking impossible. H. of Lords at 5.00, where two bills of the [Lord] Chancellor's, one about pawnbrokers, the other about charitable trusts: both were attacked rather bitterly by Salisbury, but he did not offer to oppose them except verbally. Dined at home & quiet evening.

13 May 1881: . . . The lumbago . . . is relieved, but not gone.

Gave M. £15 for a Swedish quack, whom she consults, & who she believes has done her good.

. . . See the sec. to the Middlesex Hospital, for the dinner of this evening, & give . . . £52.10.0.

Note that I gave £10 yesterday to the Early Closing Assocn. . . .

. . . Sheffield called, & we talked over the Tunis business, which is not creditable to France, for what is being done amounts to a virtual annexation of the country, a quarrel having been picked on the plea that it was necessary to punish certain plundering tribes on the border. The Bey has accepted the French terms, as to which he had in fact no option. The affair is unlucky in many ways. It discredits the new republic: it embitters the mutual relations of Italy & France: & it threatens Europe with a revival of the old French pretensions to military supremacy, which kept the world in constant fear of war. It is Gambetta's doing, & is done in view of the approaching elections.

I note it as curious that when I spoke to Sheffield of the ill-feeling likely to be created among the Italians (who intended to annex Tunis for themselves at the first opportunity) he agreed in the main, but said it would not be so strong as might be thought, since the republicans were a powerful and growing party in Italy: & none of them would quarrel with a neighbouring republic if they could possibly help it. We cannot complain, for it is certain that at the time of the Berlin treaty Salisbury told Waddington[53] that France was free to take Tunis: & even suggested it as a set-off against Cyprus: though he afterwards denied, or rather explained away his words.

The Germans are well pleased, & with reason: for the satisfaction given to French vanity tends to heal the wounds of 1870-1871, & so to make a war of revenge less probable.

At 7.00 to Willis's rooms for the Middlesex Hospital dinner . . . About 200 sat down. The whole affair lasted till near 11.00. Over £3,000 was collected.

14 May 1881: Stayed at home, having still some lumbago: worked on my address to the co-operative congress, & made some progress with it. I like the subject, but there is much to read up in regard to it, & care is necessary neither to chill the enthusiasm of adherents, to whom co-operation is a new gospel, nor to indulge in predictions which to the outside world may seem Utopian. . . .

15 May 1881 (Sunday): . . . Read a book of African travel[54], by one Thomson, a young Scotch naturalist: plucky, & a good writer: he dispels a good many illusions as to the African interior, pointing out that the country, which has been represented as a garden, is really poor, scantily peopled, & excessively unhealthy. The ivory trade is falling off, from the rapid destruction of elephants: & there is no other valuable article of export. In short, he makes out that, however interesting Central Africa may be to explorers or naturalists, there is very little of material advantage to be derived from it. The French & Belgian colonising expeditions appear to have failed utterly.

The more the Tunis affair is looked into the worse it looks from the point of view of political morality: the aggression was absolutely unprovoked, & the excuse put forward for it (trouble given by some marauding frontier tribes) can scarcely be treated as deceptive, since it could take in nobody, but it involved a good deal of unnecessary lying. There is no doubt but that Bismarck has been the instigator: he has a real object to gain, for whatever occupies French troops, & satisfies French ambition without disturbing European peace, renders a war of revenge less probable, & so far secures Germany. The chief danger, I think, is from the side of the Italians: they are not strong enough to go to war with France, & they know it: but they in their turn will find consolation by laying hands on a piece of convenient territory belonging to any weaker power – if they can find one. The arrangement made with the Bey is in fact the establishment of a protectorate – though the word is not used – which after a convenient interval can be turned into absolute annexation without difficulty or resistance.

16 May 1881: . . . Send £10 to Working Men's College . . .

H. of Lds, where a tedious interminable speech from Galloway on the subject of the new regimental arrangements, which I believe he understands thoroughly, & there is some force in his objections: but he spoke more than two hours, & not in a way to make the question intelligible to an outsider. He emptied the House, and I came away before he had done.

Long talk with D.[uke[of Bedford, who dislikes the Irish bill so much that he proposes to withdraw the Duchess from her place in the Household, in order that he may be free to vote as he pleases upon it. – I encouraged this idea, but decidedly objected to throw out the bill on second reading, as being dangerous to the H. of Lords, & to public order also, since Irish agitation would instantly be renewed, & it would not be easy for ministers to act vigorously against it, when the agitators were in fact fighting on their side against the Lords. I thought it premature & irregular to raise a discussion in our House before the bill came up to us (as had been suggested) & in this the Duke agreed. He thought the radicals were having their own way, & that the Whigs would secede. But where can they go? There are no Whig constituencies, & they cannot well join the Conservatives. This he admitted. I hear that [Lord] Tavistock[55] is strong against the Ultra party on his own side, & seriously thinks of giving up parliament.

17 May 1881: . . . Read Gladstone's speech on the land bill, which he delivered early last night, feeling unwell as he said, & wishing not to keep back his explanation any longer. The speech is said to have been a fine one but, after going over it twice, I can make out nothing more than I knew before as to the main points in dispute. His chief argument appears to have been that the Irish would take nothing less, & that if this bill was not passed a worse one would follow.

Much talk & interest about Gladstone's health. He is in bed[56] today with a renewed attack of his old complaint of diarrhoea or dysentery &, though his speech of last night is praised as a fine effort of oratory, it is noted also that he showed signs of bodily weakness at the beginning & of exhaustion at the close. The precedent of Pitt & Fox, who died within a year of one another, is much in people's mouths.

. . . Received . . . a singular application from Beauchamp[57]. It is for help to provide for Ld Beaconsfield's old servants, about whom he had left a memorandum in his will but the executors have no funds. I agreed to give £50, though it is the first time I was ever asked to pay for pensioning off the household of a friend.

18 May 1881: Saw Northcote, at his request, about a proposed memorial to Ld Beaconsfield, which he (N.) wishes to be so put forward that men of all sections can subscribe, but some of his supporters think otherwise. We discussed at length what it should be: he had thought of a Free Library, which I partly approved, but pointed out the objection of cost: it would be useless to start such a concern with less than £30,000, for land, building, & support: would they get £30,000? I thought not. Then we fell back on the idea of a statue, in which the matter will probably end. N. supposed that £10,000 would be raised: which is more than enough.

Some talk on the Irish bill followed: N. spoke temperately & frankly, as is his custom: did not think it safe that the bill should be thrown out in either House, especially not in the Lords: wished it could be amended: asked what the Whig M.P.s would do? I laid stress on the importance of knowing clearly what it meant, & insisting on the wording being clear: as it now stands, nobody can interpret it, & Gladstone's explanation has not made it plainer. N. promised to tell me what he meant to propose: & it was understood, though not expressed, that I would use what influence I may have with Whigs to secure their help if I agreed in his modifications.

Drive with M. in afternoon to Boehm's[58] studio, where Froude met us: the object being to see a cast of Carlyle taken after death. It was striking, but unpleasant. He had in progress a very fine head of Gladstone, & one of Bright. There was also a cast of Ld B., remarkable chiefly as it made the head look smaller than it did in life. Suggestion by M. that we should have our busts taken, & I know of no reason against it, except the trouble.

19 May 1881: Send £10.10.0 to an 'Industrial Home' for boys.

Pender calls, & consults me . . . on his Suez scheme . . .

He tells me a wild story of a friend of his, an engineer, crossing the Channel in company with three Italians, one disguised in a beard, which he pulled off on reaching land. The engineer heard their talk, which they supposed he did not understand: they seemed to be nihilists, were going to see what could be done in Ireland, & spoke of various people who were to be taken off – Gladstone & the King of Italy among them. He (Pender) repeated the story to Harcourt, treating it lightly, but was surprised to find that the Home Sec. looked grave over it, & wanted the engineer's address. He (Pender) believes that foreign revolutionary agents are busy in Ireland, hoping to raise a civil war, which may spread to England. I tell him for consolation that any plot which has an Irishman mixed up in it is pretty sure to fall through.

20 May 1881: . . . The Irish land bill was last night read a second time, by 352 to 176: after a speech from Northcote, which temperate & sensible in substance, clearly showed that he thought the division on second reading a mistake. And this it undoubtedly was: but, as has happened before, he was, or thought himself, unable to resist the pressure of his own supporters. Parnell told the House that the bill would do no good, & that agitation would go on as before: a significant utterance.

It is remarkable that no one has yet been found to express even a hope that this measure will be final – often as that was said about the Act of 1870 – so that the owners of land who suffer by it have not even the consolation of feeling sure that they know the worst. The real fight is to begin next week in committee: but whether the bill passes unaltered or not, no very satisfactory result can be expected. Its failure involves a political crisis, & possibly a civil war: its success is another step towards weakening the English influence, & making Ireland what the Irish want it to be, a purely Celtic & Catholic country. It is commonly remarked that Gladstone in his speech of the other night dwelt little on the justice of the bill, but treated it exclusively as a matter of political necessity.

21 May 1881: . . . At the meeting, Argyll expressed a wish to see me, & a time was fixed. He is very full of the evidence taken by the Bessborough Commission, which he says is utterly one-sided, the commissioners having framed their questions to elicit the answers they wanted, & cross-examined sharply those who answered in a different sense. From my own reading of the report & evidence, I fancy he is right. He talks of bringing the matter before the Lords, as a kind of preparation for the real debate, which cannot be till July.

[Lord] O'Hagan also talked freely of the state of Ireland, which he thinks is growing worse instead of better. He thinks the peasantry have grievances: but now rents are being refused, on ostensibly patriotic grounds, by tenants who are well off, & have no pretext of being overcharged: they simply refuse to pay anything. 'The people,' said Ld O'H., 'are losing sight of the difference between *meum* and *tuum*.' He does not see what the end is to be: and, if the land bill comes to grief in the Lords, he thinks there will be an outbreak, or something like one. But what is the state of the country now but one of undeclared, but existing, war?

22 May 1881 (Sunday): . . . There is triumph in the Opposition at the result of the Preston election, caused by the death of Mr. Hermon[59], one of the members. Yates Thompson[60] contested the borough on the Liberal side, an able man, once a candidate for the county, & owner of the *Pall Mall Gazette*, edited by [John] Morley. The Conservative candidate was a Mr. Ecroyd[61], locally known, but else of no special note, who hoisted protectionist colours. He won by a larger majority than had been obtained in Preston for many years. The explanation I believe to be that the Irish on principle voted with the opposition for the time being – in other words, they voted Liberal in 1880 to turn out Ld Beaconsfield, & Conservative in 1881 to turn out Gladstone. There is no seat lost or won, the balance of parties remains the same. But, coming after Knaresborough, the increased majority at a place like Preston is enough to set party men talking about reaction.

23 May 1881: . . . H. of Lords at 5.00, stayed till 6.30 when all was over. Lansdowne moved for a committee to enquire into the Irish jury laws, temperate & terse, in which he brought together a mass of evidence as to the habitual failure of justice in Ireland, from juries being either afraid to do their duty, or sympathising with the offenders. He was very well listened to, & carried the House with him. His committee was granted, & I have agreed to serve upon it.

. . . Talk with the D. of Bedford about the Land Bill in H. of C. & suggest to him that he should advise Tavistock as to the amendments which he (Lord T.) should support. To my surprise after what he had said the other day he hung back, thinking that interference on his part would be unwise. He added gravely that T. is strongly in favour of the bill as it stands. This I know to be the contrary of the fact: & suspect some undercurrent of intrigue on the Duke's part. An intimate friend of his tells me that he does not really care about the Bill either way, but only wishes for an excuse to get the Duchess out of her place at court, which he never liked her accepting. In any case, I note the difference of his language in so short a time as a trait of character.

24 May 1881: . . . [Lord] Tenterden calls, explains to me at some length his wish to succeed to the place [chairman of committees] which [Lord] Redesdale is understood to be about to vacate: saying that he wishes to take his seat in the Lords: that the work of the office is too much for him, is hurting his health, & so forth: (which I believe is the truth): that, his circumstances having changed, he no longer wishes for a mission or an embassy (Ly Tenterden having a good house in London, naturally does not care to live at Washington or Petersburg): that the office of chairman of committees would suit him in all respects, & that he thinks he could do the work of it in a satisfactory manner: he has spoken to Lds Granville, Salisbury, & Lathom[62], who all gave encouraging answers: he now came to consult me. I encouraged him too, really thinking the choice will be a good one for the public, as he has habits of business, is hardworking, lives in London all the year round, & so will always be ready when wanted[63]. And the vacancy which his retirement will cause at F.O. gives T.H.S.[anderson] a chance of early promotion.

H. of Lords: where charitable trusts bill in committee: two divisions were carried against the government, & the bill a good deal mutilated, but this matters less, as it is in any case not likely to pass the Commons, where the block of business is absolute.

25 May 1881: . . . D. of Argyll called by appointment to talk over the Irish bill: his objections to which he explained. He does not seem to find fault with a land court for the settlement of rent, thinking that in the actual circs. of Ireland it will be quite as much a support to the landlords as a restraint upon them: and he would be glad to see the purchase clauses extended & made the leading feature of the bill. But he objects strongly to granting the right of free sale, & also as to the uncertainty which remains as to the standard which should be adopted for fixing a fair rent. He agreed with me that it would be a mistake to try to throw the bill out, even if that could be done: & he had no wish to introduce amendments which would compel the govt. to drop it. But he thought it might be amended in various ways, and made clearer than it is. He disliked the divided ownership which it creates, & would encourage owners to sell altogether. He thought the question of buying out owners who objected to hold under the new conditions might be at least entertained: though, if many took advantage of the option given, the question of cost would become serious. He did not see much use in excepting from the operation of the bill holdings over £100 yearly, they being very few, & mostly on lease: but considered that there was a good deal to be said in favour of not meddling with rents which had not been raised for 10, 15, or 20 years. His language altogether was moderate, & not at all that of a man going into strong opposition: he used one remarkable expression –that he disliked the bill itself much less than the arguments by which it was defended. He thought Gladstone was failing: his intolerance of opposition or dissent, always his weak point, had grown excessive. He (G.) had taken the Exchequer with a view to work out a great financial scheme for the budget of this year: but the difficulties in his way had been too many, & it was given up. . . .

27 May 1881: Sir R. Temple[64] calls . . . Like many people who have no personal knowledge of Irish feeling, & have not thought on the subject, he saw no reason why Home Rule should not be granted.

H. of Lds at 5.00, stayed till 6.30: discussion first on a new valuation of Irish land: Lansdowne made a sensible practical speech.

There dined with us, Duchess of Cleveland & daughter, Ld & Ly Somers, Ld & Ly Airlie, Ld & Ly Sherbrooke, Ld & Ly Reay, Ld & Ly Enfield: Mr. Lowell, Ld Houghton, Count Setchery, Count de Franqueville, Mr. Leveson-Gower, De La Warr & Ly D. Pleasant enough: with selves, 22. . . .

29 May 1881 (Sunday): . . . There is not, I think, at the present moment much political excitement, but a strong feeling of hopelessness or, if that word is too strong, of disgust at the unpromising appearance of matters in Ireland. The disorder in that country is steadily increasing: throughout the south the movement is directed first against payment of rent generally (no matter whether high, low, or moderate): next against the enforcement of any debt or obligation by legal means. The most ordinary police duty is performed with the help of a force 150 or 200 strong: and even so it is not always that the object can be secured. In fact the state is one of civil war: only it is a kind of guerrilla war, in which no attempt is made to drive out the authorities, the insurgents being content if they can prevent them from exercising any power. We have had nothing like it since 1848: & even then the insurrection was less organised than now. The plea of distress is not even put forward by the tenants who refuse payment: they are waiting to see if parliament will strike off their arrears, as they have been led to hope it will: when disappointed in this respect, as they must be, the explosion is likely to come. The Irish executive has been feeble in its action, but the necessity of using force to repel force seems now to be understood, & a good many arrests have been lately made.

In parliament, the progress of business is excessively slow: open & barefaced obstruction has been put an end to: but needless questions, foolish personal wrangles, & generally a disposition to waste public time, have made this session, so far as it has gone, the most discreditable in my recollection. . . .

31 May 1881: . . . Sent Ld Beauchamp £50 as promised, in aid of the subscription he is making up for Ld Beaconsfield's old servants. Promise £50 to the other Beaconsfield memorial.

. . . Newdegate[65] called, to my surprise, for we have not talked on public affairs for years: his object in coming seemed to be to prepare me for the coming triumph of protectionist ideas, which he seems to think are regaining influence in the country: & indeed it must be allowed that the example of America & the colonies has deeply discouraged free-traders, & made many people wish that we had some advantages to offer by way of treaty to foreign govts., which seem more & more inclined to shut out our trade. Newdegate said, with more shrewdness than he usually shows, that if England had been divided into small peasant properties a much harder fight would have been made for the Corn Laws: but that large owners were afraid of raising dangerous questions, or giving a pretext for agitation. He dwelt a good deal on the fact that democracies, where the working man is the master, generally favour protection – & I suspect in that he is right.

Pender called to talk over his Suez scheme, & said that there was much talk in the House about Gladstone's excitable manner: that he seemed to be in a state of constant irritation caused by overwork & anxiety: the general belief was that he could not stand another session. He said also that an insurrection in Ireland was expected & predicted by the Irish members generally.

Morier came to luncheon: & for once fairly disgusted M. with his bragging & unreasonable pretensions. He talks of the offer of Madrid – which is promotion – as a result of the discreditable intrigues against him, & as intended to prevent his having the credit of securing the treaty, for which he has worked so hard. He was, however, easily persuaded that it would be folly to refuse Madrid, which he talked of doing, but I do not think he seriously meant it. . . .

1 June 1881: . . . More rioting in Ireland: in one place, Clonmel I think, the cavalry had to charge the mob, & a company of infantry, who were pelted with stones but not allowed to fire, cheered them vehemently as they passed. The tension is too great to last.

2 June 1881: Another very hot day.

Donoughmore[66] called at his own request to talk over the Irish bill: I found him moderate in tone, not at all disposed to throw it out in the Lords, or to mutilate it so that it should be rejected in the Commons, but only wishing to amend it in detail. The four points on which he dwelt most were: (1) Landlord as well as tenant to have power to initiate proceedings in the court: (2) Fair rent to be more clearly defined: (3) Estates on which rents have not been raised for a certain time to be exempted from the operation of the Act: (4) The State to buy up properties which the owners do not care to hold under the new conditions created by the Act. Of these, the first is not material: the third is doubtful: the second is partly promised by the govt. & I suppose we shall accomplish it to some degree: the fourth is a manifestly just provision but, if many owners take to selling, it will involve so enormous an outlay of public money – not all of which will be got back – that the Cabinet may reasonably hesitate. On the whole, D.'s conversation gave me better hopes of things going smoothly in the Lords than I had before.

More reports of Irish trouble: throughout the south there is now a general refusal to pay rents: evictions follow as the necessary consequence: they are resisted, & fighting ensues. At a place called Scariff, the police & soldiers were obliged to fire: one hundred shots are said to have been fired, & six men are reported killed. The Irish press, & that part of the English press which sympathises with the Irish, cries out for the suspension of evictions: in other words, for leave to tenants to withhold rents if they had rather not pay.

The Catholic hierarchy professedly stands neutral, but nearly all the priests are in their personal capacity with the Land League: & one, Archbishop Croke[67], is making speeches to the peasantry which go very near to incitement to outrage. . . .

6 June 1881: Sleep disturbed, & up very early, not very comfortable in mind. Wrote letters, etc. Breakfast at 8.30 . . . reached Leeds by rail at 10.20. . . . At the Leeds station, received by the Mayor & a considerable crowd. With the Mayor to the building where the co-operative meeting was to be held, which by an odd chance was opened by myself about 20 years ago. The hall was large, quite full, & very hot: but excellent for hearing. I never had a more cordial reception anywhere. My address which, though in print, was spoken rather than read, lasted 70 minutes: some passages I cut out fearing to be too long. The effect was considerable, & from the heat of the room I felt the sweat running down my face & hair and dropping on the desk before me. Hughes followed . . . A Mr. Lloyd Jones[68] spoke well, though a little too florid for my taste: Holyoake[69], the lecturer, talked good sense in a thin sharp voice . . . Then followed luncheon with the Mayor, a long sumptuous feast, though our entertainer being a Quaker & teetotaller would give no wine: an improvement I think in hot weather & early in the day. Thence went to the Liberal club, where an address was presented to me, but in private: then on to Temple Newsam, 3 miles off, where I was a guest on my former visit to Leeds. My host of that time was unmarried: he afterwards took a wife, a daughter of Ld Halifax, who survives him, and owns the estate absolutely, his own family being extinct. The house & park are very fine, but spoilt by smoke, which has destroyed many of the trees, & injured all.

Walk & talk with Ld Halifax, who is full of the Irish bill but, though usually clear-headed & lucid in explanation, he seemed quite unable to explain the nature of the amendments which he wished to see made in it.

7 June 1881: Found a bazaar going on in the park, at which the ladies of the house kept stalls: it was formally opened by Houghton in a neat little speech, about 11.30: then visitors from Leeds (who came in thousands) were let in, as indeed they were all over the house also. I bought rubbish, as is expected in such cases, to the value of about £12 or £13.

Walking about the place with various companions nearly all day: one while with Houghton, another time with his son, later with Mr. S. Buxton[70] & others.

. . . All were weary with the bazaar business, & went to bed soon after 11.00.

8 June 1881: Left Leeds at 11.00: reached Knowsley 2.30. Found only M. & Margaret. Weather very fine, but cold for the time of year.

See Hale: some talk with him . . . he confirms my impression that building is going on in Bootle & Liverpool faster than he can meet the demand for land. . . .

10 June 1881: . . . News – which turned out to be true – of an Irish attempt to blow up the Town Hall, at 4.00 or 5.00 this morning, by placing a heavy charge of some explosive material against the wall. A policeman saw the bundle in which it was wrapped, lying there, and rolled it into the middle of the street. No great harm was done by the explosion beyond breaking windows. Two men concerned in the attempt were caught by the police: both Irish returned from America.

Left at 6.30 to dine with Mr. & Mrs. Holt at their house in Sefton park: a large pleasant villa, with garden looking out on the park. Sir A. & Ly Hobhouse, Mr. & Mrs. Hornby, Mr. & Mrs. Brocklebank[71], Lord Kilcoursie[72], Col. Bird[73], etc. The last an Indian official, with whom I had some pleasant talk. Mrs. Holt an intelligent woman: the family are Unitarian, a sect among whom, whatever be the reason, there are very few stupid people.

11 June 1881: . . . Letter from Ld E. Fitzmaurice[74], on the Irish land bill, asking to see me, & suggesting amendments, very nearly in the sense of those proposed by Donoughmore: except that he only speaks of the claim to compensation on the part of the landlords as arising in the event of the changes asked for being refused. I answer to the general effect that: (1) I agree that landlord as well as tenant should have access to the court: (2) I agree entirely as to the necessity of obtaining a clearer definition of what is held to be the tenant's interest, & on what principle it is to be estimated: & this I consider as the question on which trouble is most likely to arise: (3) I agree in the justice of exempting from the operation of the bill holdings above £100 in value, if there are enough of them to make it worth while: (4) as to the exemption of estates managed on the English system, which he asks for, I do not object in principle, but doubt whether they can be defined with sufficient clearness.

. . . To Liverpool in afternoon, to the Reform Club in Dale Street, where a sort of afternoon party, or tea, was being held, attended by women as well as men. M. & Margaret both came with me. Mr. & Mrs. Holt seemed to take the leading part. We stayed about an hour.

Talk among many others with the Mayor of Bootle: he very proud of the increase of the town, saying it had 6,000 inhabitants in 1861, 17,000 in 1871, 26,000 in 1881, and that ten years hence it will contain 40,000. I think this likely enough . . .

12 June 1881: . . . Public affairs seem to remain where they were: it is more & more evident that the Irish land bill is the only bill of importance that can pass in the present year: and it daily becomes clearer that the legislative machine has got out of order, & cannot be made to work. Part of this unpleasant result is due to the oddities of the Prime Minister, who as his friends say talks out his own bills: he will not consent to leave the slightest objection unanswered, and encourages the superfluity of debate which it is his business to repress. He is also said to show plainly the marks of failing health in an excessive irritability & impatience of opposition – always his failing, but now grown to a disease. Irish rows break out perpetually, & are so common as to be accepted as matters of course.

13 June 1881: Saw Ward, & settled with him as to payment of the £10,000 to Liverpool College. Also as to increasing the charity account by £500.

. . . Mrs. Hale is seen by M. who has also an interview with [Dr.] Gorst. It is the old story: stimulants perpetually applied, until the habit has become incurable. Hale is informed, but will not believe the story. . . .

14 June 1881: Give Latter £30 to buy a choice advertised copy of Ruskin. Very well pleased with the library altogether. . . .

15 June 1881: Received an extraordinary number of letters, 15 or 16 I think by one post: luckily none of importance: most to ask something. A son of Ld Dundonald begs for employment. (**Note**: This was an impostor. I heard of him afterwards in gaol for a robbery.) A beggar whom I relieved at Keston has had the impudence to refer to me as able to vouch for his character, whereas I can vouch for nothing but his rags. A Manchester parson writes to complain of a subscription being stopped, which I referred to Statter: luckily it is under the parson's own hand that he had only asked for it for 2 years, for which term it had been paid. Answered him accordingly, but sweetened the correction by letting him have it for one year more. . . .

16 June 1881: . . . Often as I have noted the ease of travelling between London & Knowsley, I never did so more than today. Luncheon was half an hour earlier than usual, dinner half an hour later: otherwise the day's arrangements were not more disturbed than if we had taken a long drive in the afternoon.

17 June 1881: . . . Heard that Gladstone has made, or promised, some concessions to the landowners in his Irish bill: especially that he undertakes to remodel the 7th clause, round which most of the controversy will gather.

An amendment excluding 'English-managed estates' from the operation of the bill was lost by only 25. In principle it is just, but I do not see how such estates could be defined in legal form.

Talk at some length with Lansdowne on the bill: to which as a whole he is less adverse than I expected: saying that Irish rents are as a rule low (which is true) and that he does not believe the new court will reduce them except in a few exceptional cases. We agreed that the one thing important is a more exact definition of what is called the tenant's interest: if it is to be expressly recognised at all. It is understood that some concession to the landowners has been promised in the sitting of today, but we do not well know what.

18 June 1881: . . . Ld E. Fitzmaurice called to talk over the Irish bill: we went over various clauses: it is what somebody called it in the House, a series of conundrums: and there is strong suspicion that its obscurity is not accidental, but intended to prevent English M.P.s from seeing what its operation will be. Ld E. says that it is impossible to get from the Irish law officers any consistent explanation: they say one thing one day and another the next, & as there is scarcely any report of what passes in committee they cannot be called to account. There are about 35 Whigs who in the last division either went against Gladstone or stayed away. He thinks a late concession made by Gladstone important: in the 7th clause, on which the principle of the bill depends, all express mention of the tenant's interest has been struck out, & it is simply left to the court to fix a fair rent: a large & arbitrary power: but of two evils it seems better to leave it so than to recognise a joint interest in the land.

As a sample of the confusion which exists about the bill, nobody can make out whether, at the end of the 15 years' lease to be granted by the court, the landlord will have a power of re-entry or not. Gladstone apparently says yes: the law officers say no. This is one of the points that will have to be cleared up.

My convn. with Ld E. lasted about an hour.

Left for Keston about 2.30: arrived at 4.00: walk & lounge there in peace, the weather being perfectly fine & the place in its best looks. . . .

20 June 1881: . . . Gladstone has announced some large concessions on the Land Bill. Landlords as well as tenants are to have access to the court, which is obviously just: the foolish plan of fining a landlord who attempts to raise his rent is abandoned: and the 7th clause is so far altered that all reference to the tenant's alleged interest in the land is struck out. If the principle of allowing rents to be fixed by a court at all is to be adopted (and, though a bad principle, its adoption is inevitable) there is now as little fault to be found with the method of its application as can well be: though some points remain unsettled still. There seems no doubt that these changes have been made in consequence of the display of Whig, or moderate Liberal, feeling. The cave that had begun to be formed threatened danger to the party. The Premier is not often so willing to yield: but in this case it is probable that he has been driven by his colleagues farther than he wished to go, and in giving way he is really falling back only on his own original opinion.

21 June 1881: . . . H. of Lds committee, sat from 12.00 to 2.30, Lansdowne in the chair: when we adjourned for want of witnesses. Great difficulty is found in getting the evidence of judges, stipendiary magistrates, & persons employed in the administration of justice: partly because they are wanted at home, & partly because with the usual moral cowardice of the Irish they will not give evidence if they can help it, knowing that what they say must necessarily be unpopular among their neighbours.

22 June 1881: . . . The Irish census is out, & shows what will not please the nationalists of Ireland, a reduction from 5,400,000 to 5,150,000 (in round numbers) in the popula- tion: being a loss of 250,000: more, I think, that anyone expected. It is curious that the most prosperous counties have sent out the largest number of emigrants: there is no decrease among the starving cottiers of Mayo & Galway, or next to none, while Carlow & Monaghan show a diminution of 10%. – The census returns for England & Scotland are not yet known: but they are believed to show a popn. of more than 35 millions, or an increase of nearly 4 millions in the last 10 years. So that the Irish, who were in 1845 nearly a third of the whole, are now scarcely more than one-seventh, & the Catholic Irish (4 millions in round numbers) considerably less than one-eighth.

Dined with Sir J. Lubbock . . . Went afterwards out of civility to a party at Ly Harcourt's. . . .

24 June 1881: . . . H. of Lds committee at 12.00, sat till past 3.00: examined 4 witnesses: they agreed as to the breaking down of the jury system in Ireland in regard of agrarian cases – and, some added, in regard of all cases in which the crown is prosecutor. But the remedy is not so clear. It seems agreed that a mere raising of the qualification for jurors is useless: if slight it produces no effect, the feeling throughout the lower & middle classes being the same: if carried far, it limits the number of persons liable to serve so as to throw a heavy burden on each: and to take unpaid trouble on behalf of the public is a thing which does not enter the Irish mind as possible. Moreover a high qualification would in most parts exclude the Catholics altogether, and a cry of unfairness would at once be raised. To allow the verdict of a jury to be given by a majority, as has often been proposed, would in some cases be useful, but in others it would merely do harm: for the majority would acquit the prisoner against evidence, & he could not be tried again: whereas now [when] there is a disagreement, no verdict is entered, & the man does not wholly escape. Something may be done to lessen the right of the accused to challenge the jurors: which, as it is practically exercised, means that the counsel defending strikes off every man of education & intelligence, leaving only those who can be intimidated, or whose sympathies are against the law: but on the whole it is clear that a jury system cannot be worked where popular feeling & law are on opposite sides, & the only remedy I see (a very partial one) is to extend the power of the magistrates to punish summarily: the sentences so imposed would be light, and the penalty would be certain: which is the main point. . . .

26 June 1881 (Sunday): . . . Read today & yesterday a singular book[75], a collection of letters written from Africa by 'Chinese Gordon'[76]: the officer who commanded a Chinese army, & afterwards took service with the Khedive. He seems by his writing to be a Puritan of the old sort: a real fatalist, not valuing life & absorbed in extra-mundane ideas. I suppose, if Oliver Cromwell were to revive, he & Gordon would understand one another better than either of the pair would understand the ordinary Englishman of the day. Apart from his creed, Gordon has the reputation of a daring & brilliant officer, with an extraordinary power of dealing with savages, but it is said that his disposition is such that he cannot act with or under anybody: he must be in command, & absolutely independent. . . .

28 June 1881: Dr. Drage called: I saw him chiefly in order to talk about M. & the expediency of her going abroad, but he thinks her well in health, & that there is no need.

Morier writes asking me to subscribe & give my name to a fund for raising a monument to Lord Stratford de Redcliffe. I agree.

H. of Lds committee: we examined, besides two other witnesses, Mr. Justice Barry[77]: a shrewd clever lawyer, one of the judges of the Irish Queen's Bench. He had condemned the administration of justice and the misconduct of juries in the south of Ireland, in the strongest possible terms: but contrived to explain what he had said – or in plain terms to shuffle out of it, with a determination not to commit himself to any unpopular expression of opinion that was amusing to hear. They are all alike in that respect: no moral courage: mortal fear of what will be written about them if they go against any prevailing prejudice.

Dined at The Club, the last dinner of the season: we were a large party, the Duc d'Aumale, Gladstone, Abp. of Canterbury, D. of Cleveland, Rosebery, Houghton, Sir G. Wolseley[78], Sir F. Doyle[79], Prof. Owen, Reeve, Lecky, P. Hewett, Newton[80]. In all 14: a good party, the best of the year: but the result was dull. Gladstone was worn out & very silent[81]: the Abp., though sociable enough, is not brilliant in talk: Owen, our chairman, is old & very shy: & the presence of great dignitaries rather silenced others, Houghton always excepted. I was myself weary, though with little cause. The dinner & wine very bad. Altogether it was a failure.

29 June 1881: . . . At luncheon we had young E. Stanley[82], the lad who will one day be in my place: I looked at him with curiosity & a sort of interest: he is rather oddlooking, but lively & has good manners. He is reading for the artillery.

Left at 2.30, Euston at 3.00, Preston at 9.25: put up at the Bull, my own property (half of it at least is): comfortable enough: supper & bed. Read again Schweinfurth's travels in Central Africa[83]. . . .

30 June 1881: . . . Sessions . . . sit till past 3.00: the longest attendance we have yet had, over 60 magistrates present: Sir J. Heron[84], from Manchester, attended, whom I never saw before. Several motions were before us, the object of which was to secure a larger representation for the Salford hundred, which is apt to think that it has not a sufficient voice in disposing of the funds to which it contributes largely. . . . A discussion, rather sharp at times, arose out of the question of voting a new courthouse at Liverpool: the sum required is larger than expected at first (when was it otherwise) and the Salford people resent this, as contrary to an understanding come to with them. Salford was in a minority, & the matter is settled: but the feeling between different ends of the county is not friendly.

Notes

[1]   Charles, 4th E. of Yarborough (1859–1936), styled Lord Worsley 1862–1875; at Eton 1873–1878; at Trinity 1878–1881; M.F.H. 1880–death; minor office 1890–1892; senior freemason; lord-lieut. Lincs. 1921–death.

[2]   '. . . Lady Derby (a long conversation) . . .', Gladstone, *Diaries*, 16 January 1881.

[3]   *Parl. Deb.*, *3*, vol. cclviii, cols. 856–862 (15 February 1881), denying allegations of an aggressive policy in 1876.

[4]   Edward Plunkett, 16th Lord Dunsany (1808–1889), naval officer: Admiral 1877; succ. 1852; rep. peer (Ireland) 1864–1889. A Cons.

[5]   *Parl. Deb.*, *3*, vol. cclx, cols. 1842–1851 (vote of thanks for military operations in Afghanistan), 5 May 1881.

[6]   E.J. Synan (d. 1887), M.P. co. Limerick 1865–1885. A Lib. Home Ruler; barrister and graduate.

[7]   The cold was certainly genuine, the premier being laid up for much of the time from Tuesday to Sunday: e.g. '16 Jan. Saw Dr. Clark. Strictly inhibited from going to Church . . .' (Gladstone, *Diaries*).

[8]   Charles Yorke, 5th E. of Hardwicke (1836–1897), formerly Lord Royston; succ. 1873; a.k.a. 'Champagne Charlie'; M.P. Cambs. 1865–1873: court office 1866–1868, 1874–1880; m. dau. of 1st E. Cowley.

⁹ Sir G.P. Colley (1835–1881), Sandhurst professor, secretary to viceroy of India, and chief of staff in Zulu War: governor of Natal, 1880: defeated by Boers at Laing's Nek, January 1881, and at Majuba Hill, 26 February 1881.

¹⁰ Derby.

¹¹ Gladstone's diaries make no comment on his meeting with Derby, 31 January 1881.

¹² *Parl. Deb., 3*, vol. cclvii, cols. 2032–2033 (1–2 February 1881).

¹³ Probably Timothy D. Sullivan: possibly A.M. Sullivan.

¹⁴ Sir Lyon Playfair, 1st Baron Playfair of St. Andrews (1818–1898), M.P. (Lib.) Edinburgh and St. Andrews Universities 1868–1885; postmaster-gen. 1873; peer 1892; chemist.

¹⁵ Gladstone was 'simply delighted' with the Duchess of Edinburgh – but despite his pleasant evening '. . . lay awake till four' (*Diaries*, 2 February 1881).

¹⁶ Lord Dalhousie (1847–1887); styled Lord Ramsay 1874–1880; succ. his father, a Cons. retired admiral, and succ. by his son, also Cons.: but himself, after naval career and Balliol, M.P. (Lib.) Liverpool Mar.–July 1880, when, on inheriting, appointed Lord in Waiting 1880–1885: Sec. for Scotland Mar.–Aug. 1886: for private difficulties, see *Later Diaries*: m. 1877, d. of Earl of Tankerville, outliving his wife by one day.

¹⁷ John Dillon (1851–1927), leading Home Ruler.

¹⁸ Albert Grant (1830–1899), né Gottheimer; a.k.a. Baron Grant; M.P. 1865–1868, 1874–1880; bought and embellished Leicester Square for public use; fraudulent company promoter.

¹⁹ Lord Henry Lennox (1821–1886), M.P. (Cons.) 1846–1885; held minor office, arranged 'Peace with Honour' junketings, was Disraeli's boyfriend.

²⁰ *Parl. Deb., 3*, vol. cclviii, cols. 856–862, 15 February 1881 (Lord Lytton).

²¹ Sir Frederick Roberts (1832–1914), cr bart. and c.-in-c. of Madras army 1880; conqueror of Afghanistan 1880.

²² i.e. majority against Sunday opening.

²³ Majuba (26 February 1881).

²⁴ His brother.

²⁵ Samuel Radcliffe Platt (1845–1902), Oldham's most prominent citizen, and head of the largest firm of textile machinery makers the world has ever known: s. of Mr. John Platt (d. 1872): educ. Cheltenham Coll. and Berlin, where he lived 6 years, and as a workman in the family firm, where he showed great mechanical skill: a Lib. Unionist, an Anglican, Mayor of Oldham, but not politically ambitious: keen cricketer, musician, and educationalist: a lifelong yachtsman, died on his steam yacht off Anglesey: gave food and coal wholesale to the poor of Oldham each Christmas.

²⁶ [Edward] Lyulph Stanley, 4th Baron Stanley of Alderley (1839–1925), educationalist; M.P. (Lib.) Oldham 1880–1885; succ. Moslem brother as Lord Stanley, 1903, and kinsman as Lord Sheffield in the Irish peerage, 1909: member, London School Board 1876–1885, 1888–1904, & its vice-chairman 1897–1904; a Cambridge First.

²⁷ John T. Platt (1817–1872), MP Oldham 1865–death: thrice Mayor of Oldham: chairman of Hibbert, Platt and Sons Ltd. 1868–death; of Hemeth Park, Oldham. He was bro. of James Platt (1823–1857), M.P. (Lib.) Oldham April–August 1857 (accidentally shot on the moors). They were sons of Henry Platt.

²⁸ Wife of A.J.B. Beresford-Hope (1820–1887). She was Lady Mildred, *née* Cecil, dau. of James, 2nd Marquess of Salisbury, by his 1st wife *née* Gascoyne.

²⁹ Sir Andrew Clark (1826–1893) was Gladstone's physician; cr. bart 1883.

³⁰ William Eliot (1829–1881), d. unm.: 5th Baron Eliot & 4th Earl of St. Germans: diplomatist 1849–1865: M.P. (Lib.) Devonport 1866–1868.

³¹ Henry Eliot (1835–1911), 5th Earl of St. Germans & 6th Baron Eliot: s. of 3rd Earl: entered navy, then junior clerk in F.O. 1855–1872; assistant clerk in F.O. 1872–1881: succ. to title 1881; m., 1881, dau. of 1st Lord Taunton.

³² Lord Eustace Cecil (1834–1921), M.P. (Cons.) Essex 1865–1885; surveyor-gen. of ordnance 1874–1880; 2nd s. of James, 2nd Marquess of Salisbury, and thus full bro. of the premier.

33 Reginald Sackville, 7th E. De La Warr (1817–1896), previously Baron Buckhurst (1870–1873); succ. his bro. 1873; m. Lord Lamington's empty-headed dau.

34 Barely mentioned in A.L. Thorold, *Labouchere*, 453.

35 Daniel O'Donoghue (d. 1889), M.P. (Lib.) Tipperary 1857–1865, Tralee 1865–1885: lived by sponging.

36 George Forbes, 7th E. of Granard, in the Irish peerage (1833–1889), succ. 1837. Educ. Eton; diplomatist 1852–1854; lord-lieut. co. Leitrim 1856–1872; a Lib. until 1886. An R.C. from 1869.

37 Derby's land agent in Kent.

38 Perhaps Rev. Frank George Hopwood of Winwick Rectory, Warrington, where he had been Rector since 1855. Formerly he was incumbent of Knowsley 1840–1855. Winwick was a rich living whose patron was Lord Derby.

39 Lt.-col. Nathaniel G.P. Bousfield, J.P. (b. 1829) of Windermere, M.P. (Cons.) Bath 1874–1880 (retired); leading light in Liverpool Rifle Volunteers.

40 Sanderson, Granville's private secretary.

41 J.R. Lowell (1819–1891), U.S. minister in London 1880–1885.

42 Col. T.E. Taylor (1811–1883) of Ardgillan Castle, Co. Dublin: sometime chief whip and chancellor of the duchy of Lancaster.

43 Probably because Col. Taylor's 10,000 acres of Irish land were largely in the counties of Meath and Dublin, a part of the country which had experienced little upheaval.

44 Possibly John Callcott Horsley R.A. (1817–1903), painter, of Kensington: elected Treasurer of the R.A. 1882.

45 Carnarvon left Madeira 9 April 1881 after a residence of 5 months, spent with his wife and children. He had had a long spell of unspecified ill health beginning in the second half of 1879 (Hardinge, *Carnarvon*, ii, 57–62).

46 *Parl. Deb., 3*, vol. cclx, cols. 1803–1814 (5 May 1881).

47 Gladstone, troubled by having to speak of Beaconsfield's life, noted: '. . . Bed all day. In the evg. I began to get quiet. Clark came twice' (*Diaries*, 6 May 1881).

48 Mary Derby's brother.

49 Sir H.T. Holland, 1st Vt Knutsford (1825–1914), colonial minister 1888–1892; cr. baron 1888, and vt. 1895.

50 Lord Coleridge (1820–1894), M.P. (Lib.) 1865–1873; judge 1873, peer 1874, chief justice 1880–1894.

51 Sir J.T. Knowles (1831–1908), editor and architect; laid out Leicester Square, founded Metaphysical Society (1869–1881), editor of *Nineteenth Century* from 1877; inventor of signed article.

52 Hon. Sir William Stuart, K.C.M.G., M.A. Cantab. (Trin.), diplomatist; at Paris Embassy 1845–1858, including priv. sec. to Lord Normanby when amb. 1846–1852; sec. of legation and/or chargé at Rio, Naples, Washington (1861–1864), Constantinople, St. Petersburg, 1858–1868; minister at Buenos Ayres 1868–1872, Athens, 1871–1877, Netherlands 31 October 1877–1888. Retired 1888..

53 W.H. Waddington (1826–1894), French premier; educ. Rugby and Trinity: placed second in the Classical Tripos, First Class, 1849; achieved distinction as an archaeologist: entered politics 1871; one of French plenipotentiaries at Congress of Berlin; premier early 1879–20 December 1879; amb. in London 1883–1893; devoted his life to preparing a definitive catalogue of all Greek coins, a project sadly never completed.

54 Joseph Thomson (1858–1894), *To The Central African Lakes and Back* (1881).

55 George Russell, 10th Duke of Bedford (1852–1893), succ. his father 1891; M.P. Beds. 1875–1885; styled Lord Tavistock 1872–1891.

56 'Better, not well', Gladstone, *Diaries*, 17 May 1881.

57 Frederick Lygon, 6th Earl Beauchamp (1830–1891), succ. 1866; educ. Eton and Christ Church; President of Union, Fellow of All Souls; M.P. (Cons.) Tewkesbury 1857–1863, Worcs. W.

1863–1866; minor office 1859, 1874–1880; lord-lieut. Worcs. 1876–death: paymaster-gen. 1885–1886, 1886–1887.

58   Sir J.E. Boehm (1834–1890), leading sculptor; R.A. 1880; sculptor-in-ordinary to Queen Victoria.

59   Edward Hermon, M.P. (Cons.) Preston December 1868–6 May 1881 (died).

60   Henry Yates Thompson (1838–1928), book collector and traveller.

61   W.F. Ecroyd (1827–1915), worsted manufacturer of Burnley; M.P. (Cons.) Preston 1881–1885.

62   Formerly Lord Skelmersdale (until May 1880).

63   Lord Tenterden had recently married money.

64   Sir Richard Temple (1826–1902), Indian official; lieut.-gov. of Bengal 1874–1877; gov. of Bombay 1877–1880: M.P. (Cons.) 1885–1895.

65   C.N. Newdegate (1816–1887), M.P. (Cons.) Warwickshire N. 1843–1885.

66   John Hely-Hutchinson, 5th E. of Donoughmore (1848–1900), succ. his father 1866: served in the European Commission for the Organisation of Eastern Roumelia 1878–1879.

67   T.W. Croke (1824–1902), R.C. Archbishop of Cashel 1875–1902.

68   Lloyd Jones (1811–1886), Owenite and biographer of Robert Owen.

69   G.J. Holyoake (1817–1906), co-operator, secularist, radical publicist.

70   Sydney Charles Buxton, 1st E. Buxton (1853–1934), Liberal politician; M.P. (Lib.) 1883–1885, 1886–1914; held ministerial posts 1892–1895, 1905–1910, 1910–1914; gov.-gen. of S. Africa 1913–1920. Created vt 1914, earl 1920.

71   Sir Thomas Brocklebank, 1st Bart. (1814–1906), né Fisher; Liverpool shipping magnate; cr. bart. July 1885.

72   Frederick Lambart, 8th E. of Cavan (1815–1887), succ. his grandfather 1837. A Conservative. Styled Vt Kilcoursie.

73   Col. Stanley G. Bird of Ashdown House, Tunbridge Wells (1837–1905), ex-President of Builders' Institute; commanded 1st Middlesex Rifles; served in the Volunteers longer than anyone else (1859–1899).

74   Brother of Lord Lansdowne, and thus with family estates in Kerry.

75   *Colonel Gordon in Central Africa, 1874–1879 . . .*, ed. G. Birkbeck Hill, London, 1881.

76   Gen. Charles George Gordon (1833–1885).

77   Possibly Charles Robert Barry (1825–1897), Irish legal career 1848–1865; M.P. 1865–1868; law officer 1865–1872; lord justice of appeal (Ireland) from 1883.

78   Sir Garnet Wolseley, 1st Vt Wolseley (1833–1913), field-marshal; conquered Egypt 1882.

79   Sir Francis Doyle (1810–1888), 2nd bart., poet, professor of poetry at Oxford 1867–1877, friend of Gladstone in youth.

80   Sir Charles Newton (1816–1894), Keeper of Greek and Roman Antiquities at the British Museum 1861–1885.

81   Gladstone's diary entry for this occasion is of no interest.

82   Edward Stanley (1865–1948), 17th E. of Derby, nephew of diarist, 'Uncrowned King' of Lancashire.

83   George Schweinfurth, *The Heart of Africa. Three years' travels and adventures in the unexplored regions of Central Africa from 1868 to 1871 . . .*, 2 v., London, 1873.

84   Sir Joseph Heron (1809–1889), town clerk of Manchester December 1839–1889.

July–December

1 July 1881: Heard of the death of my old nurse, Madame Montaudon . . . whose face & appearance are still clearly visible to me, though it is 48 years at least since I saw her.

. . . Wrote to Reeve about setting up a cellar of our own for The Club, the wine with which we are supplied being very bad.

Went over to No. 7, Lord Egerton's, for the yearly meeting about the [St. James's] Square gardens: we ought to be 7 ratepayers, but only Ld Egerton[1] & Ld Tollemache[2] attend: and the former of these I found in a pitiable state of health & nerves: he seemed as if he might die at any moment. Trouble with two clubs, which decline to pay, as we won't give them a key. Expenses are about £100, income £120 if we could get it. Went into the garden with Ld T. & the clerk, & condemned some half-dead trees. From increasing smoke, it is less & less easy to get them to grow.

Lds committee. Examined three witnesses. All agree that in the south-west of Ireland there is no chance of getting a conviction in any agrarian case, or indeed in any case where the crown prosecutes, from a jury.

Back to the Lords at 5.00, where heard a fine speech from Argyll, attacking the report of the Bessborough Commission as not warranted by the evidence, & complaining of the conduct of the enquiry as indicating a foregone conclusion. He made out a strong case, & I am inclined to believe that he is right in the fact: but the move seems to me a doubtful one just now, as its effect can only be to incline the Lords to reject the Land Bill, which they are ready enough to do: & what will follow is not clear if that happens. But it was impossible not to sympathise with Argyll whether his speech was prudent or not: Lord Bessborough got up to defend the commission, a simple honest-looking gentleman, no speaker, & his very helplessness served him, for his defence consisted in little more than a protestation of honest intentions, which all of us were ready to believe. Whatever sharp practice there has been in the matter is not of his planning. Waterford followed at length, going over the same ground as the Duke, but in a very inferior style. Still he cited a few cases of apparent unfairness which strengthened the charges against the commission. Ministers did not like the business, & kept out of it as far as possible, deprecating argument which might prejudge the land bill. Salisbury could not resist a speech which by its violence augurs ill for the line he is likely to take when the bill comes up. But I did not hear him, having gone to dinner with Ld Camperdown. Met there by Ly Abercromby[3], who acted mistress of the house, the Galloways, Morier, Jowett, Sir C. Aitchison[4] (a rising light of the Indian civil service, now commissioner in Burmah), Miss Octavia Hill[5], & others. Pleasant enough. Day very hot, but not disagreeable.

2 July 1881: See Paley the architect[6], who calls at Hale's request, & settle with him for the repair & renovation of the burying place of my ancestors at Ormskirk. The cost will be about £1,000. I take no interest, & feel no pleasure, in this kind of work, but it is a family obligation.

. . . Receive a deputation of the anti-slavery society . . . they want a question asked, or motion made, about the slave trade in the Soudan, & the establishment of a consul at Khartoum: I ask for some further details before an answer: but am well disposed to do what they ask. Not that I care about negroes, but central Africa is a favourite subject in the northern towns, where exaggerated ideas prevail as to the amount of trade to be developed there: and it is certain that no trade can be created until slave hunts are done away. Besides, Khartoum is a centre for exploration, & we ought to have an accredited agent there.

. . . Day very hot so that I scarcely went out. Keston in afternoon. Received while at dinner a telegram from Pender, with the news that President Garfield has been shot. . . .

5 July 1881: Very hot night & morning. At noon the streets were comparatively empty, as in tropical countries. I see it reported that the temperature has been over 90° in the shade. At a review held yesterday at Aldershot, two men died of heat, and two more are dying, besides many disabled & ill.

. . . Lords committee 12.00 to 3.00 . . . Three witnesses: one a Mr. Monahan, son of the chief justice, poor & confused: the next a very shrewd lawyer, Gibson Q.C., brother of the Gibson who is now fighting the Land Bill in H. of C. – his evidence excellent, especially as to the unwritten law of the class from which juries are taken, they will never convict for assaults unless there has been something considered as foul play: nor in land cases. In fact they have a law of their own, which they execute as far as they can.

6 July 1881: . . . The Belgian economist, M. de Laveleye, called by appointment. His object was to talk of the abuse which has grown up of enticing away English girls to Brussels for purposes of prostitution. The subject did not much interest me, but he was full of it, & I listened.

He then passed on to bimetallism, for which he is very eager, & which he wished to explain to me his reasons for supporting. He talked well & clearly, & had the advantage of me in conducting an economical argument in French. His main argument is as follows. Gold is growing dearer: the production of it is not equal to the consumption, and to the increased demand for it by the growing population of the world: consequently the process of 30 years ago is being reversed, debts public & private are growing heavier, prices are falling, and – which he laid great stress on – it is everywhere the worker, the producer, who suffers, while the capitalist gains without labour. This statement is interesting, for it shows the real purpose of the bimetallists – to enable debtors to pay off their creditors in cheaper coin – though no doubt M. de L. would answer, as in fact he did, that he did not want to make it cheaper, only to prevent it growing dearer. I did not given an opinion of my own, beyond asking questions & suggesting doubts in order to draw out his ideas more clearly.

7 July 1881: Saw Mr. Chadwick again, & agreed with him to make another attempt to secure the land lying between Keston & Farnborough [Kent] which belongs to a Mr. Wilson of Leeds, I believe the same whom I met a month ago at Fryston. He will ask a high price, but the land is necessary, if Holwood & Keston are ever to be made into a single estate. Having this purchase in view, I am confirmed in my intention of not buying more land between Holwood & Fairhill.

. . . To a meeting of the executive committee of the Beaconsfield memorial: present Northcote, J. Manners, Smith [W.H.], Salisbury, Wilton[7], Lansdowne, Rosebery, Barrington, etc. We met to choose the sculptor of the proposed statue, & agreed on an Italian, Reggi[8]. The other candidates were Count Gleichen[9], & Mr. Bell[10], whose Byron statue is not generally approved.

8 July 1881: Very little walking, more from laziness than want of time. . . . At 12.00 to committee [on Irish juries] . . . We examined 4 witnesses, who differed in every particular . . . H. of Lords again at 5.00, where only a dull Scotch debate. Walk away with Houghton. Quiet dinner & evening.

9 July 1881: Sanderson calls early. Trouble at the German embassy where one Lynar, secretary in some grade, has been arrested for an unnatural offence. Diplomatic privilege released him, but the charge is true, & he will have to leave the country.

B. Museum, where a dull sitting of 1_ hour: walk home with Lord Sherbrooke, who is much pleased with having detected some jobs in the stationery office, being chairman of a committee on that subject: & enjoys the idea that he is preparing a report so plainspoken that nobody will vote for it.

He talked a little also about the Irish bill, but that he thinks is a hopeless affair, & is not much concerned to deal with it.

Peabody meeting at 3.00 . . . The only matter of interest discussed was whether we should go on with the 3½% loan from the Treasury, which we thought it a great matter to have secured 2 years ago. Money is now at so low a rate of interest that both Lampson & Morgan think we can borrow at 3% or even at 2½%. We had some discussion on the subject: they contending that interest was going to be low for many years to come: I (rather with a view to elicit their opinion than to express mine) arguing that a great war, or an outbreak of speculative enterprise, might bring things back to their former condition. They admit that war or other forms of waste may lessen the excess of capital for a time, but maintain that any loss so caused is very quickly made good by the savings of the people. Perhaps they are right.

Walk home with Northcote, talking of the Irish bill.

Keston by 5.15 train. Fine evening, & quiet.

Drage informs me that some unfavourable symptoms affecting the kidneys, which had almost disappeared, have returned: & I shall in consequence adopt a stricter rule of diet, with more exercise when possible.

10 July 1881 (Sunday): . . . Write to Mr. Holt, who has asked me by letter to deliver a speech on the new form of protection called reciprocity: which as he says is gaining ground in the country. I believe he is right: and that protectionist doctrines, except where the food of the people is concerned, are rather popular than the reverse. The fact is that free trade as a system belongs rather to the middle-class system of thought than to that of the working class: the former says to the state: 'Let me alone that I may make my own way': the leaders of the artisans are much more inclined to say: 'Protect us & organise our labour, for we are not strong enough by ourselves to stand against the capitalist.' Every nation where the working classes really govern – France, America, Australia, Canada – is strongly protectionist: and I see no reason for supposing that a change will come. In England many people believed that free trade would in some mysterious way break up the aristocracy, & help the poor in their struggle against the rich: they did not know how, but they expected some such result. Finding themselves deceived, they are apt to think that the whole thing has been a delusion, and take up the cry that the idle capitalist is the only gainer by cheaper production: that higher money wages are the labourer's true interest: & these require state encouragement to trade.

. . . News of the Volunteer review, which seems to have been a success in all respects:

no deaths from heat (which were feared), no drunkenness, & the means of conveyance were sufficient, contrary to universal expectation. Over 50,000 volunteers were on the ground, the largest number that has yet been brought together.

11 July 1881: . . . In papers, death of Ld Hatherley[11], an amicable & respectable man, of an old Whig-Radical family (his father the chief adviser of Queen Caroline): a sound lawyer by the report of the profession, & who became Chancellor without anybody calling the appointment a job: in the H. of Lords he was a bad confused speaker, so that his explanations of law bills were almost unintelligible: luckily he spoke seldom. He was a strong churchman & personally inclined to devotion: a great frequenter of services & sermons: which gave him the good will of the clergy, notwithstanding his Whiggery. He was respected also by the Bar for his honesty, & liked for his honesty & patience. I have heard that he never wrote his judgments, which may in part account for his rambling & perplexing style as a speaker.

12 July 1881: Write notes & letters. . . . Sent £5 to a literary beggar, which I half regret, believing the fellow to be a rascal: but it is done.
St. George's Hall at 11.00 . . . Cases seem all of the usual kind. Very bad report from the chief constable as to increase of petty offences, chiefly drunkenness. Workingmen in Liverpool are earning higher wages, as prosperity returns – hence the increased consumption of liquor. . . . The charges were all of theft or embezzlement. I sentenced 21 prisoners in all, the average term of sentence being a little over 8 months. The longest was 18 months. Most were old hands: habitual offenders. Home by 6.30 . . .
. . . Receive from Ward a summary of rents received in the year ending 30 June 1881. The total is £206,820, against £206,024 in 1879–1880. Better than I expected, and an increase of £40,000 since 1870, deducting the Irish rents then received. It is odd that in Bury, about which Statter is always grumbling, there is shown a growth of £5,000: £75,000, against £70,000 last year.

13 July 1881: Up early, & busy with notes & letters. . . . Left home a little after 9.00. . . . Early in the day the cases were short & easy . . . The jury was good, & no failure of justice occurred. There was one acquittal, quite justified by the evidence. Nearly all the prisoners were old offenders. Home by 6.30 & short walk in the park.

14 July 1881: Up early again, & busy with letters till 9.00, when left for Liverpool. Sat from 10.00 to 5.20: the day as I was told extremely hot, but sitting in a large airy building I hardly felt it, except that I was drowsy after luncheon, which never happened to me in court before. I kept on taking notes mechanically, but not very sure whether they were sense or not. I did not actually fall asleep.
There were 2 bad cases of wounding, 3 men concerned in the one, 2 in the other: all were Irish: the strange feature of both was the utter absence of provocation: in both the persons attacked were inoffensive strangers, & the weapons used were loaded sticks. There was not even the semblance of a quarrel. . . . They got 8 months for one offender, 6 months each for the other 4.
. . . An old soldier, a desperate ruffian, but intelligent, got 12 months for stabbing a policeman, whom he had repeatedly threatened to murder. I was pressed to send this case over to the assizes, but saw no reason for doing so.

15 July 1881: . . . Leave at 11.15. Reach London at 5.30. Call at No. 23. Leave again, & reach Keston soon after 8.00.

The day is said to be the hottest on record in England. Heat in the shade variously estimated in different places at 95°, 93°, & by one observer 97° (this was the official reading at Greenwich). But on the line there was not much dust, & it was never very oppressive.

16 July 1881: Another very hot day, though less than yesterday. Walking in the sun was impossible, at least disagreeable. sat in & lounged about near the house: read & wrote.

. . . Nothing has passed in the Lords since I left London, except some discussion on the Transvaal, leading to no result. In the Commons, the Irish land bill has made steady way, notwithstanding an outbreak of attempted obstruction by the Irish members, whose special aversion is the clause encouraging emigration. They provoked Gladstone into a fine rhetorical denunciation[12], which is said to have produced a great impression on the House, but it served their turn well enough, giving them a fresh peg on which to hang speeches for which otherwise there would have been no excuse.

17 July 1881: Great heat continues, making exercise impossible. In the room where I write, carefully cooled & shaded, the glass stands at or near 80°. The grass is burnt to the colour of a gravel road. The roads, usually noisy with excursionists at this time of year, are silent. No one stirs that can help it.

18 July 1881: Heat continues, undiminished if not increased. Very little done . . . Rode late in afternoon.

19 July 1881: London by 9.12 train, driving to the station: reached No. 23 before 10.00. . . . Got myself weighed, 15 stone exactly: walk down at 12.00 to committee: the streets nearly empty from heat & glare: sat 3 hours . . . By 3.23 train to Bromley, whence home again at 4.30.

Ride in the evening, but temperature remains at 80° till late.

In papers, death of Dean Stanley[13], who had been ill for some days, but till yesterday not so as to alarm his friends. He was only 65 years of age, & looked younger: though I do not believe he ever got over the death of his wife in 1876. Except among the clergy, who cordially disliked him as an enemy of hierarchical pretensions, he was popular with everybody: in his own rank of life his conversation made him a welcome guest: the poor knew his sympathy for them: and all who appreciate good literary work enjoyed his books. If a church establishment could be kept going in our day, he was the man to have done the work: for he believed it possible to include within the establishment most of the dissenting sects: a theory held also by Arnold before him: but which is open to the objection that it pleases nobody: neither the dissenters, who do not now wish to be included, nor the clergy, whose notions of their own spiritual authority grow higher & higher. – The Dean was I think most thoroughly at home in his position as official guardian of Westminster Abbey: the history of which in its minutest details he had by heart: & no man ever devoted himself more earnestly to any work than he did to the care & improvement of the old building. . . .

21 July 1881: My 55th birthday: now an event which does not create any interest in my mind: nor do I care in the least to conjecture how many more may follow. Yet few people have had less in the way of trouble or vexation: whether as regards health, domestic affairs, or relations with the outside world. . . .

22 July 1881: . . . See Ld E. Fitzmaurice, & discuss a possible amendment in the Land Bill, exempting holdings of £100 & upwards. This I approve of, & he agrees to give notice of it. . . .

24 July 1881 (Sunday): Much talk & discussion as to accepting Pender's invitation to cruise in the Mediterranean. I rather encourage acceptance, though personally not caring for the voyage – my travelling days are ended, as far as interest & keen enjoyment of travel are concerned: but I believe that some change is needed to keep M. from falling into a state of habitual low spirits – the complaint of all her family – and this is an opportunity of seeing much, & making a complete change, without inconvenience or fatigue. No immediate decision is necessary.

In afternoon, walk by Downe & call on Mr. Darwin: with him I had some interesting conversation, though less than I could have wished, for he was so anxious to hear about Ireland & affairs of the day that it was not easy to get him to talk on his own topics. The chief thing he told me was that some foreign experimentalists are trying the effect of inoculation in various diseases: that is the virus which causes the disease being known is applied to the animal in a mitigated form, causing only slight illness, & by this process security from infection is obtained in the same way as vaccination prevents the catching of smallpox. There are hopes, he said, that dogs may be insured in this manner against hydrophobia. Some Italian physicians believe, he said, that they have detected the cause of malarious fever in a certain very minute organism which they had collected from the air, & which administered to a dog produced the ordinary symptoms of poisoning by malaria.

Mr. D. insisted on showing me a better way home than by the road, & gave me his company for some distance. I was glad to see him as well in health & looks as before, though he said he had given up riding in consequence of a severe fall.

25 July 1881: . . . The Irish land bill is at last out of committee in the H. of C. & it is understood that the second reading will not be opposed in the Lords.

At 3.30 went to the late Dean's funeral in Westminster Abbey . . . The only thing strange that I noticed was that both the Cardinals, Newman & Manning, had been invited, & were apparently expected to attend, for their names were called out: but they were not there.

Dined Grillions . . . This will be my last Grillions dinner for the year.

26 July 1881: . . . In the papers – H. of C. debate on the Transvaal question last night, ending in a majority of above 100 for ministers. . . . The subject seems to have lost its interest, though it ought not to have done so, for matters are not settled, & possibly may not be for a long while yet.

. . . Working both today & yesterday on notes for a speech on the Irish bill, which will displease both sides, if made as I intend, for it will tell the naked truth as to Irish disaffection. We go on in England talking about the anti-Union agitation as if it were the work of a few interested mob-orators: whereas, so far as I can judge, it is simply the expression of a unanimous feeling on the part of the Irish masses. . . .

30 July 1881: . . . The Irish land bill is now out of the H. of C. and will be read a second time at once in the Lords. . . .

1 Aug. 1881: . . . House of Lords about 4.30: where found Ld Carlingford on his legs, & explaining the ministerial scheme. He did his work weakly with very little argument, & as if unaware of the magnitude of the interests concerned: but possibly this was calculated, & meant to disarm opposition. If so, it was not successful: for the feeling of his audience was strongly shown: dead silence in general, & ironical cheering (very rare in our House) whenever a remark was made that seemed to provoke it. He spoke about 1_ hour, cheered only by colleagues. Salisbury followed, & criticised the bill sharply & effectively: I have heard him speak with more force, but he showed judgment in avoiding any extreme bitterness. O'Hagan followed in defence of the bill: then others whom I did not hear: including Lansdowne, whose speech as it reads in the papers seems to have been effective, & is generally praised. Lytton closed the case for the opposition: eloquent & clever, but his argument was pushed to exaggeration & had an unreal tone. Ld Spencer's reply was mild & sensible, but so dull that I did not wait to hear the end.

I dined with Sanderson at the Travellers'.

2 Aug. 1881: See Drage, chiefly to talk about M., whose nerves are much strained & her spirits depressed, without any obvious cause for anxiety. This has happened to her before but, knowing the family tendency to morbid melancholy, I never see it without uneasiness. He does not think there is anything constitutionally wrong, but is not satisfied. She has this morning seen a new German oculist who of course has some new remedy: whether likely to be more effective than the rest remains to be seen. His opinion agrees with that of others, that there is no serious mischief in the eye itself: a beginning of cataract, but which may probably not increase: but that the nerves which communicate with the eye are affected, & the treatment to restore them must be general, not local.

Ld Lansdowne called by appointment to discuss various proposed amendments in the Land Bill, & also his draft report on Irish jury laws, which we went over carefully. After turning the matter over in my mind a good deal, I decided not to deliver the speech which I had prepared, though it would have been effective: but on considering it carefully I could not but see that its tendency would have been more against the ministerial scheme than in its favour: &, though ready to oppose the govt. if necessary, I see no reason for doing so where a protest only is possible, & no result can follow. If circs. render it inevitable that one should accept what one disapproves, it is neither useful nor dignified to make more fuss about the matter than one need. So at least on a balance of the arguments it appears to me: but my mind is not quite at ease, though I can truly say that what I have done (or rather left undone) was not to save myself trouble, for the speech is written out in full. Part of it, however, will be available in committee. . . .

3 Aug. 1881: Chevening. Party in the house are the Danish minister and his wife, a native of St. Thomas in the W. Indies – pretty & amusing: Sir F. & Ly Pollock[14]: & Mr. Knowles, editor of the *Nineteenth Century*. We passed nearly the whole day out-of-doors: first I walked with M. about the grounds: then took Mr. Knowles to the top of the hill near Knockholt: in afternoon we all drove to Brasted Chart, Stanhope & I walking back: later again I took Mr. Knowles another walk in the park. The day was fine, conversation pleasant, & my only drawback was the fatigue & depressed spirits of M., who wisely went to bed soon after dinner.

Stanhope talks of his ecclesiastical commissionership, & tells me that the feeling is general among his colleagues as to the expediency of disposing of some at least of the land they hold, & putting the proceeds into the funds. But the law must be altered in order to make this possible. The bishops, who at first preferred land, are now changing their minds, and three, he said, have given up their estates, taking instead the sum which these estates are calculated to yield.

Knowles talks among many other things of the growth of the new protectionist movement: seeming to think that it will succeed, & that the artisans will agree even to a moderate tax on corn & other articles of food, as a measure of retaliation for the exclusion of English manufacturers abroad. I cannot believe this, but he is a man who hears many opinions on all sides . . . .

I had much interesting conversation with Mr. K. Though not, I think, a man of any great original ability, his business as an editor has brought him into contact with a large number of thinkers, & made him acquainted with the ideas of the time. He is, or professes to be, a real believer in 'progress': adopting to the fullest extent the idea that man is perpetually raising himself to a higher civilisation, & not much liking to admit that there may be a limit to the process, or even that it may be interrupted altogether. He discussed these matters eagerly, with an earnestness that showed that they were to him much more than simple intellectual problems: indeed he contended that a man ought not to allow himself to be sceptical on such questions, lest he should weaken his own capacity for action. We ended our controversy in a friendly way: he holding me to be a sceptic (which indeed is my nature), I thinking him an enthusiast. One of his notions was that men would soon grow ashamed of possessing, or at least of bequeathing, more than a moderate share of wealth: & that the rich man of the future would feel it a duty, after making some moderate provision for his children, to give or leave the surplus to the state. He praised sumptuary laws, preventing extravagant expenditure, & thought them likely to be re-enacted by the democracy. But, when I pointed out that compulsory limitation of outlay was the surest way (assuming it to be practicable & not wholly ineffective) of preventing the dispersion of wealth, he changed his tone. He said that Gladstone, whom he often sees, had talked of the growth of a plutocracy as one of the chief, if not the chief, dangers of the future. He himself (Mr. K.) thought that a legal limitation of inherited fortunes within a certain amount would be a good thing, & would not willingly admit that it was sure to be evaded. – I note these scraps of talk because I suppose them to represent the notions that are floating through the minds of many men: especially of literary men: though they seem to me neither very wise nor likely to be translated into action. They are socialist, though of a mild type.

Brasted Chart very pretty: Stanhope has 200 acres there: . . . Mr. Tipping, once an M.P., has most of the land about Brasted: Brasted village very neat & pleasant. . . . At Chevening nothing changed except a new billiard room. The house comfortable & agreeable. I saw the young Mahon[15]: a baby: the fourth generation of Stanhopes I have known[16].

4 Aug. 1881: Left Chevening by the 10.30 train from Sevenoaks: . . . very hot . . . did not go out again till near 4.00, when walked down to the Lords. The House very full, about 300 peers present: we went at once into committee on the Land Bill, & remained at it till

12.45. The discussion was necessarily dull, turning on verbal amendments & involving few points of principle: I spoke 5 times, I think, but only in a conversational way, no regular speech. I voted thrice with the government, & once against them: not of set purpose, but following my own judgment simply. Every division went against the government, as was inevitable. –I dined at the House: very badly of course: &, the evening being hot & sultry, I have seldom felt more weary than on setting out to walk home. . . .

5 Aug. 1881: Very hot morning . . .

. . . Talk with M., who is beginning to be alarmed at her own state, which is one of almost constant low spirits, without any cause except health. I press upon her going away somewhere – either abroad or on a tour at home: but, though she approves the idea, the effort seems to be more than she can make. I have never been more uneasy about her state: for, though the symptoms are not new, indeed they have existed to some extent for 7 or 8 years, they seem to increase steadily, & no remedy is effective for more than a short time. It is impossible not to think of the late Ly Amherst[17], whose last years were passed in profound melancholy, with occasional delusions. And Col. West[18] is little better: and the last Ld De La Warr[19] destroyed himself in what was evidently a fit of insanity. I do not fear the worst: but I do fear a state of chronic unhappiness. She has never suffered so much from this cause as in the last week.

House of Lords at 4.00 & stayed till 8.00: spoke once in committee & voted once: then dined Travellers' &, being very weary, & not caring much about the clauses which remained for discussion, I did not return. There was the less need, as divisions are at least 2 to 1, & a few votes more or less make absolutely no difference. Still it was a piece of laziness on my part, only excusable from not being quite well. . . .

7 Aug. 1881 (Sunday): . . . Odo Russell[20] has had an audience, or more than one, with the Queen, & says she is full of complaints of Gladstone's treatment of her: saying that he does not consult her, tells her nothing, seems to forget her very existence, or to consider that she has no business to interfere in affairs. She also found fault with Hartington as not showing her proper respect.

. . . There is some curiosity, & even excitement as to what the Lords will do – that is practically, the opposition – when their amendments to the Land Bill are returned, rejected by the Commons. Will they persevere, & risk the throwing out of the bill? & the consequent agitation? If they do, they raise at once the awkward question of the constitution of the H. of Lords: if they give way, they make their own previous action ridiculous.

It is worth notice that at the Mansion House dinner, last night, Bright spoke in a very hesitating & guarded manner as to the prospect of the Land Bill restoring peace. Ld O'Hagan said the same thing to me the other night: I asked him whether he hoped the agitation would cease. He said: 'Yes: but it is hoping against hope.' In fact the Land League announces that its operations will continue as before, & the agitators profess to hold that the bill will make no difference. Their aim is the extinction of the landlord's right, not its simple limitation: & this only as a preliminary to the restoration of the Irish parliament: that is, of Irish independence. . . .

9 Aug. 1881: London by usual train . . . Lds committee at 1.00, and sat till 3.45. We finished the report, considering it para. by para. Nearly all present. We had only one division: the concluding sentences of the report intimate our belief that, if the present state of lawlessness continues, no mere reform in the system of constituting juries will be sufficient, but trial by jury must be suspended altogether in a certain class of offences. Carlingford & Spencer did not in substance disagree to this, indeed they brought a report framed in the same general sense, but vaguely worded, so that (as I told them in the discussion which followed) it could be explained away at Irish public meetings as meaning nothing. It seemed better to us to say plainly what we meant, & the original report was adopted by 7 to 4.

In this committee, as in the Irish debates of the year, Lansdowne has shown ability & judgment above what he was credited with, though his good sense was always recognised. He is certainly the best of the rising men on either side in the H. of Lds. The Conservatives as far as I can see have none: for Donoughmore, though a good fellow, will not go far: and, though Waterford[21] has come out with more force than his friends expected, he has kept (very prudently) to his special subject of Irish land tenure.

. . . There is talk of Forster retiring from the Irish office, & being succeeded by Shaw Lefevre. If true there are only two possible explanations: one that he is sick of the place . . . the other that he is sacrificed to the resolution of the Cabinet to propitiate the disloyal party at all costs, an idea which Gladstone is quite capable of acting upon, rather than admit the failure of his plans, but which will scarcely be avoided.

10 Aug. 1881: . . . Continued to write on the Irish subject: but with no great interest, for I ask myself what is the use?

The D. of Argyll's amendment on the Land Bill, the only one in favour of which I voted, is partly conceded by Gladstone: the others seem likely to be rejected: &, though some of them are reasonable in themselves, they are not worth fighting for. The bill as a whole was perhaps inevitable, in the revolutionary state of Ireland: but it goes farther than any act of recent legislation in its interference with proprietary right & though, as a matter of prudence & for political reasons, I should have voted for the second reading had a division been taken, I am heartily glad to have no responsibility for it.

The whole transaction increases (if possible) the distrust I have long felt for Gladstone, who is equally uncongenial to me as a high churchman and *dévot* and as an ardent democrat. He alone keeps Whigs & Radicals together, it is said: but the Radicals have the best of the bargain. They laugh at his churchmanship, but excuse it on the ground of his general dislike to the richer classes: a dislike in general very cordially reciprocated. There is a strong belief that his holding on to the office of C.[hancellor] of the Exchequer is due to a wish to make some great increase in the burdens on real estate, especially on land. . . .

12 Aug. 1881: . . . H. of Lords at 5.00: a full attendance: about 220 peers voted in the various divisions, & many ladies & M.P.s filled up the room . . . The first sight showed that fighting was intended. A Conservative meeting had been held in the morning, at which it was decided not to give way to the Commons: &, as the ministerial project is not much better liked by Whigs than Conservatives, & many Whig peers were away, the result was certain beforehand. We divided 4 times, the divisions about 2 to 1 in each case, or rather more: the speaking was not good, indeed the nature of the debate hardly allowed it: to be rhetorical and impressive on details is impossible. I voted once with Argyll against ministers, thinking him absolutely right, & them absolutely wrong: the other three votes I gave for government. I dined at the House, & came away about 12, the voting being all over.

We are now in a difficult position: to give way after two votes is less easy than after one: the first dissent might have been accepted as a simple protest, but persistence in it leaves no choice except dangerous conflict with the Commons, or undignified withdrawal. The latter is not in Salisbury's line: the former is: & his eagerness is not likely to be controlled by the prudence of Cairns, of whom moreover he feels a good deal of personal jealousy. The Commons, headed by Gladstone, will certainly not give way: in fact they hardly can, their followers in the country would not let them: nor is Gladstone a man of yielding disposition.

The talk is that, in the event of no understanding being come to, the bill will be allowed to drop, and revived in the autumn, a November session being held for the purpose. If that session too should end in failure, resignation or dissolution must follow. The danger of the situation lies in the largeness of the majority in our House: to make peers is useless when you are in a minority of 100: there is no alternative except to yield, or to set about altering the constitution of the Upper House – a difficult business!

13 Aug. 1881: . . . Received a letter from the Mayor of Manchester, asking whether I am willing to part with 10 acres of land at Cheetham Hill for the purpose of a park . . . I answer civilly . . . and refer the application to Statter. I have no objection to sell, but doubt whether the corporation are prepared to pay the value, which cannot be less than £1,500 per acre, & may be a great deal more. . . .

14 Aug. 1881 (Sunday): . . . Ld Camperdown came to luncheon, & stayed to dinner. A good deal of talk with him. We walked together in Holwood & on the commons. He talks of his grandfather, who has a large estate in Warwickshire, of stiff clay land: 2,000 acres of which he has now in hand, Ld C. managing for him. At first there was outlay without repayment, but the land is now paying not only expenses but a fair rent also. Talk of politics: he bitter against Gladstone, whom he accuses of an inordinate love of flattery, of listening to no opinion that does not tally with his own, of extreme violence towards opponents, etc. I suppose this is the general language in private of Whigs. He praised Ld Hartington, but distrusted Harcourt: which also is not an uncommon state of mind.

. . . An odd letter from one Maccoll, a parson, who has been constantly writing on the subject of the Turkish war, being a devoted believer in the eastern Christian races: he excited a good deal of ridicule in 1876 by declaring that he had seen a man impaled, which other people believed to have been only a scarecrow. He now writes after 5 years to appeal to me (whom he has abused through thick & thin) whether his story is not true. I decline to settle the dispute, replying however civilly, since he apologises for having (as he says) done me injustice.

15 Aug. 1881: Mrs. Long[22], Sir J. Lubbock, & Grant Duff all called together. Talk with the last about Madras, of which he professes to like the prospect, but I do not think he would have accepted if he had not thought his chances of promotion at home were small. He is able, cultivated, industrious: but there is something in his style dry & pedantic, which does not suit the H. of C. nor indeed any audience. And among the rising men he is outstripped by Dilke & Chamberlain.

16 Aug. 1881: . . . H. of Lords at 5.00: where a full attendance, though not so full as last week: it had come to be generally understood that some sort of compromise had been, or would be, arrived at, & the prevalent feeling was one of simple curiosity, not of anxiety. Salisbury spoke at some length, & in a tone of creditable moderation, a complete contrast to his language when the Commons' amendments were discussed. He announced that accepting the concessions made last night in the Commons, of which he naturally made the most, he should not press the other points in dispute. Lansdowne followed suit, & in less than an hour all was over, or would have been but that Lord Monck, in general a sensible man, insisted on delivering a set oration on the whole subject, which came too late to be either useful or amusing. Why he did it I cannot imagine.

I believe the cause of the Lords giving way to be mainly the pressure brought to bear on the Conservative leaders by Irish peers who, though disliking the bill, dislike still more the notion of leaving the question unsettled till next year.

The most disappointed party are the Radicals, or ultras, who hoped for a collision between the two Houses, & a consequent change in the constitution of the Lords.

I walked home with [Lord] Dartrey, whose plain good sense may be trusted in such matters: & asked him what he thought the effect of the bill would be? He thought on large estates, & those held by well-to-do proprietors, especially English absentee landlords, there would be little or no change: the people knew well enough when their rents were moderate, & would not go into court unless they had a fair chance of success: especially as they would have to pay costs in case of failure. He did not expect his tenants to give any trouble. On the smaller properties, with needy owners, he thought there really were cases of over-renting, where reductions would be expected & made. What he feared was a continuance of the agitation, in which the priests are now he says everywhere active, & a general refusal next winter to pay rents. He thought the Land League ought to be proceeded against in an effective manner, now that the pretext or justification for its existence had been taken away. His priest had given the tenants advice to pay nothing except on compulsion: & to send all their claims for reduction at once into the court, in order to choke it with business. But he did not think the advice would be followed.

Dined Travellers', where met Sir H. Elliot[23] . . . He remarked . . . on the oddity of the English people: how their attention is always concentrated on a single subject at a time: at the present moment the Foreign Office might do what it pleased, no one would care. Ireland was the only thing thought of. Next year it would be something new. . . .

19 Aug. 1881: . . . Gave M. another £100, as a beginning of repayment of what she has spent on her cousin D'Arcy[24]: which as well as I can make out is about £700. He has been governor of the Falkland islands, and held other colonial appointments: but being unluckily not to say disreputably married could never get the promotion which otherwise he might have expected. He spent more than his salary, got into debt, and has been slowly extricated by his friends – M. doing the most, the Duchess of Bedford assisting a little at first, but she soon got tired.

. . . No special event in the week: I do not know whether the death of Ld Gainsborough[25] at 62 is worth noting: he was one of the earliest of persons known in society to turn Papist &, as usual with converts, carried his zeal for his new faith to absurdity: a weak harmless man, of whom the only trait I remember is that, being put to serve on a private bill committee, he was too shy or too simple to excuse himself on the ground of being almost entirely deaf: and only after several days sitting he announced that he had not heard a word of the evidence. The losing side thereon pressed to have the whole case tried over again by a fresh committee: I forget whether they succeeded.

20 Aug. 1881: . . . Much talk with M. about her brother, L. West, who is about to start for Washington. He is perplexed about his family – three girls and two sons. The sons are in South Africa, at least the eldest is there, the other if not gone is going to join him: they are therefore disposed of: but the daughters remain, the eldest 15: and, while it is inconvenient to leave them behind, their illegitimacy makes it awkward to take them to Washington. M. has done what she can in favour of their being recognised: I have approved her action, though not disposed to be personally mixed up in the matter: but for some unknown reason, probably more from temper than from conviction, the D. of Bedford has declared vehemently against any notice being taken of them, & almost quarrelled with the rest of the family on the subject.– The girls are said to be good looking and well mannered: but who will marry the bastard child of a Spanish dancer, brought up abroad, & in the Catholic religion?[26] It is an unlucky affair. The mother, besides entangling L.W. in a connection which has prevented his marriage & hindered his advancement, managed during her life to spend the whole of his private fortune. There, however, she was obliged to stop: for he would not be drawn into debt beyond a small amount which he has now cleared off.

21 Aug. 1881: . . . Wrote to Mr. Knowles, declining to send him an article on Ireland: though mine is written all but a page or two. My reason for disappointing him is that, with every desire to speak favourably & hopefully of the ministerial scheme, I cannot do so: the more closely I look into the matter, the stronger are my reasons for believing that it will not check disaffection, & that at the bottom of the whole movement is the desire for Irish independence. But there is nothing to be gained by saying so at the present moment &, as the only sincere opinion I could give would tend to discredit the government, & give pleasure to the opposition, I think silence best. But the M.S. is not destroyed, & may possibly be put in print.

22 Aug. 1881: . . . Read in *The Times* that the Land Act is received without a single expression of thanks or satisfaction, and preparations are being made for attacking the landowners under it by the help of Land League funds on a large scale. This is legal, & perhaps legitimate: but, if they fail before the court as in most instances they will, the ground will be laid for a new agitation at once. Next year the question of Home Rule will come to the front: or, if not next year, then within two or three years at latest. . . .

26 Aug. 1881: . . . In the papers, reports of the Edinburgh volunteer review, at which 40,000 men turned out. It was spoilt as a show by the worst possible weather, but is spoken of as a success in the way of a military display of strength. But, out of 40,000 men obliged to pass the day & evening in clothes wet through, how many will have their health destroyed?

Dismal complaints from all quarters as to the harvest, which promised to be fairly good, but the storms of the last three days have injured it everywhere, & in some places it is nearly destroyed. The political result will be bad: for there is no remedy so wild or hopeless that ruined farmers will not grasp at. And many will be ruined: for persistent misfortune during five years has left them no reserve of capital to fall back upon.

27 Aug. 1881: I note that The O'Donoghue, who extracted £100 from me this year, is bankrupt at last. Query – whether for the first time? . . .

28 Aug. 1881: . . . Parliament prorogued yesterday: but in fact for the last ten days none but officials & a few M.P.s who have nothing else to do have attended. The session has been one of the longest & most barren on record. 'It is the session,' somebody said, 'of one measure and one man.' Gladstone has kept the Irish bill in his own hands, & his colleagues have had little chance of showing what they could do as debaters. . . .

30 Aug. 1881: Sent off . . . to Mr. Knowles at his request the M.S. of the article I had prepared . . . but determined not to publish. He is free to use any ideas he can find in it. The main drift is to warn the English public against the mistake of supposing the Irish difficulty settled, when in fact we are at the beginning rather than the end of it.

. . . News of six new peers created: two, Lord Reay[27] & Lord Tweeddale[28], are already Scotch peers: both these are good selections: one, Lord Howth[29], is an Irish peer: of him I know nothing: Sir Harcourt Johnstone[30] and Sir D. Marjoribanks[31] are both old M.P.s, both respectable, neither notable for either talent or success: one hardly sees why they were chosen, but there is nothing to be said against either: the latter, Sir H. Tufton[32], represents in a certain way the extinct family of the Earls of Thanet, his father being a bastard son of the last lord. What his claim may be I cannot imagine, but he is a large landed proprietor, & so far suitable.

Wrote to Ld Reay to congratulate. Ld R. is a cultivated thoughtful man, & seems anxious for distinction: he would be a useful addition to our House, if there were anything to do there.

See Morley the carpenter, to whom I advanced money to pay for land on which to build his house. He has built it, & values the whole at nearly £300: on which he has borrowed £150 at 5%. I think about relieving him of part of this charge, for he is a hard-working energetic man. . . .

1 Sept. 1881: . . . Settled to lend Morley £30 . . . The £30 advanced I can repay myself by taking it out in work, at which he is very handy.

. . . Long sharp walk for exercise . . . in all I think between 10 & 11 miles.

. . . Receive from Ly Dartrey a melancholy description of Irish troubles: she is apt to colour a little, but well informed, & in the main I believe her story to be true. The popular demand, she says, has changed. It used to be for low rents only: now the tenants are told to pay no rent at all. Trade is nearly destroyed: the railways pay diminished dividends, the large Dublin shops are paying nothing: servants are discharged in all directions, & begging for places. The smaller landlords are leaving the country: & many would sell out & out to the tenantry, but the latter are not willing to buy, thinking they shall get their farms without payment by waiting a little. . . .

3 Sept. 1881: . . . In the papers, news that James Lowther[33] is returned for N. Lincolnshire, against Col. Tomline[34]: which is the loss of a seat, or two votes, to the government. The constituency was always Conservative, & its being carried by the Liberals in 1880 was a matter of surprise. The only importance of this contest lies in the fact that the Conservative candidate has distinctly raised the cry of protection & has been returned upon it: the first time for many years that such a thing has happened.

Northcote has been obliged to make a speech to a party meeting at Sheffield, in which he has spoken ambiguously on the question of what is called 'reciprocity', using words which may be interpreted in various ways. He could perhaps scarcely help it under the circumstances of the Lincolnshire election, & knowing how strong is the feeling of many of his followers: & so far his fault may be only that of speaking at all when nothing was to be gained by it: but, as he is well known to be a convinced free trader, the effect is unsatisfactory. The tail of the party is wagging the head.

4 Sept. 1881: News in papers of the loss of another seat to government – N. Durham[35]: carried by Sir G. Elliot against Mr. Laing by a small majority, thus reversing the decision of last year. The change is mainly due to the Irish voters, said to be 900 strong, who last year were apparently divided, but now seem to have polled as one man against the party in power: following in this Parnell's advice & the tactics of the Land League: the object of which is to make all government impossible, so that Repeal may become a necessity. Two things are clear: one that the Irish trouble is not settled, but only beginning: the other that protection, which never was really dead in the counties, is now reviving as a cry, and Conservative county members will be obliged to swallow it, or lose their seats.

5 Sept. 1881: . . . Wrote to Ward to take shares for me in the new Mersey railway to the value of £1,000: I do not well know how far the undertaking is likely to pay, but it may reasonably be expected of me that I should help it, interested as I am in Liverpool.

Wrote to Ward also to pay £50 to the Tonbridge Free Library Building Fund – a thing I cannot well refuse. . . .

6 Sept. 1881: Up early, & leave Fairhill by 8.15 . . . In papers, news of a serious riot at Limerick, several persons shot: the police & soldiers having been attacked with no apparent provocation.

Left London at 3.00, & reached Southport by 9.30, where received by the Mayor . . . & driven in the Mayor's carriage to the Prince of Wales hotel: very large & comfortable. There supper & bed.

7 Sept. 1881: A little before 11.00 the Mayor fetched me to the Town Hall, where met Lathom, Maj. Gerard, my brother, & a large party of local notabilities. We drove in procession through the streets to the new promenade, which Lathom opened in a short speech: another speech was made by a Mr. Smith, to whom the chief improvements in the town are ascribed: he was once a workman – a navvy, they say: he spoke roughly & bluntly, yet with sense of humour. Then followed more processioning: till we arrived at the new market hall, the same of which I laid the first stone two or three years ago: this building I was to declare open, & did so, making a speech as required by custom . . . The market was a very pretty sight, decorated with flowers & fruit, & the sellers in fantastic costumes. I walked round it with Ly Lathom, having pressed upon me offerings of fruit & flowers which it was not easy to dispose of. Then followed a visit to the aquarium: then at 3.00 o'clock a dinner which lasted till 6.30 or perhaps later, for I left it going on. Lathom & my brother spoke, but very briefly. I took the opportunity to discourse on the industrial condition of the country: &, though I could tell the public nothing new, I was very well listened to, & have been pretty accurately reported. My argument was to the effect that taking the last ten years together we have gained much ground instead of losing any: & that the depression of the last two or three years is essentially temporary, due mainly to bad seasons. This view I supported by figures. I do not think my audience in general agreed with me, but they seemed interested & attentive. In the streets & everywhere I was very warmly received.

Left by 7.00 p.m. train, reached Knowsley about 9.00 . . . Found a heap of letters & wrote till late.

Desired Ward to invest another £100 in the London Labourers' Society.

8 Sept. 1881: Knowsley. Waited early on the princesses, who with their governess went over to Croxteth. Drove there with Lionel, arriving about 10.00 a.m. Met the P. of Wales, Princess, & suite. Drove in procession by Newsham Park – where the Mayor met us – into Liverpool and to the pier head. An immense crowd, cheering enthusiastically, all the way. Ly Downe & Hartington in my carriage.

At the pier we embarked on board a steamer, & went down the river to the new docks, which were opened in form by the royalties: we steamed round them, landing to inspect the machinery, & in a vast shed found luncheon for about 400 persons. All very well arranged, no crowd nor confusion, everybody in their place. No speeches except by the Chairman of the Dock Board (Hornby) & the Prince. They were both short & to the purpose: Hornby especially was praised for saying just what ought to be said & no more. After luncheon through the worst & dirtiest parts of Liverpool, Scotland Road, etc., the crowd dense & dirty, but delighted & shouting at the top of their voices. To the Town Hall, where an address read by the Recorder, & reply: then looked out from the front of the building to see the Volunteers march past: a fine show. Returned through streets more thickly packed, if possible, than before: reached Knowsley at 6.00: saw Hale there & signed some papers: then to Croxteth for dinner. Sat next the Princess of W. A large party. The royalties left at 11.00 for Edgehill: and we went home.

I have never seen a public ceremony go off so well: the weather was perfect: fine, clear, & cool: not one mishap or accident, great or small: every arrangement worked out as it had been intended. Liverpool probably never held so many visitors before: full half a million were in the streets (I hear since that the police say a million): & it was specially noticeable, because odd, that the enthusiasm was greatest in the poor & squalid streets, where one would think the inhabitants had little reason to be satisfied with the world as it is, & English institutions generally: but, if there was a difference, they were noisier & warmer in their demonstrations than the rest. My reception was excellent everywhere, the warmest, I think, I ever had.

9 Sept. 1881: . . . Parted with Lionel, thanking him warmly for his trouble, for he has taken a great deal: gave him £20.

Left by 11.00 a.m. train . . . London at 4.00 . . . Fairhill about 6.30, rather weary, but well pleased that these two days of ceremonies & bustle are over without mishap of any sort, & indeed with success: for both at Southport & at Liverpool, but the latter especially, reception was unusually cordial: I don't know when I have been so incessantly cheered. And this in Liverpool I did not expect, party feeling running high, & the place being very Conservative: or rather Orange, for dislike to the Irish is the predominant feeling among the working class.

10 Sept. 1881: In afternoon, drove with M. to look at Oaklands, the Garland estate, again: as chance would have it, we stumbled on the family, whom we had supposed absent: gaining, however, by their presence a sight of the house, which is excellent, solid, & in good taste. Mr. G. a little vulgar, but natural in the expression of his regrets, & it was impossible not to be sorry for him – ruined by his son when old, & compelled as he said to leave a place which he had lived at for 23 years. There was no disguise, beyond what civility required, as to the object of my visit: & the family evidently wish that I should buy. The land is 71 acres: improved & dressed: worth at £80 per acre £5,600 in round numbers: he now asks £9,300 for the whole but would probably take less. The house, I dare say, may be worth £3,000: altogether I think better of the transaction than I did in April (v. 13 Apr.): the more so as land in these parts is bound to rise in value. . . .

11 Sept. 1881: Day dull & mostly wet . . .

Many notices in the papers of my Southport speech, which seems to have been a success in the sense of having expressed the feeling of many people, just at the moment when they wanted expression given to it. I have agreed to correct the proofs with a view to its being reprinted. There is an active & noisy protectionist agitation going on, though not I think supported by more than a section of the Conservative party. But this section is the loudest . . .

Received from Ward . . . the balance sheet of the year ending 30 June 1881. It is a satisfactory document.

Rents received in the year are	£208,220		
They were last year	£206,024		

Total year's receipts were	£218,821	but this includes some arrears
(excluding a sum repaid by the trustees)		

Classified, the rents are as follows:

Home estates	£49,765	Last year	£55,484
Outlying	£10,991	" "	£7,376
Liverpool	£53,688	" "	£54,043
E. Lancs.	£76,144	" "	£70,801
Fylde	£17,631	" "	£18,317

I may reckon with some confidence on a return averaging: Home estates, £50 k: Liverpool, £60 k: E. Lancs. £80 k: all the rest £30 k. In all £220,000 certain to be reached in a few years, & if the increase stops there I have no reason to be dissatisfied.

12 Sept. 1881: Drive in afternoon to call on the Cazalets at Fairlawn, & found T. Hankey sitting with them: half amused with the contrast between their splendid decorations & the simplicity of our Fairhill home. Cazalet gave £150,000 for Fairlawn, & has spent at least as much more upon the place & estate.

. . . Interesting article in the *Fortnightly* on the future of gold, by Laveleye. He reckons the total known produce of gold in the world at £1,400,000,000 of which perhaps £1,000,000,000 may be in existence now: the average yearly production at about £20,000,000: which in his judgment is not enough to supply the increasing wants of the world. . . . Both in Australia & America the production seems to be falling off. – It is curious . . . to look back to the time, not so long ago, when the gradual future depreciation of gold, & consequent increase in all prices, was treated as an axiom, not to be argued about or discussed, but accepted as a basis of reasoning. Another proof how little we can really look forward in dealing with national affairs.

13 Sept. 1881: Day warm, & very free perspiration, which was what I desired. In after-noon Ld Sherbrooke came to dine & sleep. We thought him much altered & grown old, his memory often failing, & he saying the same thing several times over: yet he talked pleasantly.

Read to M. an article by Goldwin Smith on Canada, which is sour as his comments on events are apt to be, yet shrewd & worth notice. He argues that Canada is not & cannot be one country, being composed of 4 parts very slightly joined together . . . that the natural connection of each of these is with the U.S. lying to the south of it . . . that sooner or later a complete commercial union between the two is inevitable: & that we had better admit the fact. . . .

15 Sept. 1881: . . . In morning W.P. Talbot came with two of his sons, to shoot, dine, & sleep here: he did not do much in the shooting way, birds being plenty, as he said, but wild. And the woody country with thick frequent hedges is bad for sport. His eldest son, who as a child used to be so great a favourite with my father, is now 19: a tall youth, neither handsome nor ill-looking, quiet & gentlemanlike in manner, with an air of much good nature: he is in the militia, having failed to pass the necessary examination for the army. I talked to him a little, but could not make out that he had any strong tastes or likings. His father & mother complain that he has an invincible dislike to take trouble: I should think him quiet, unlikely to get into scrapes, & if he manages to get a commission in the line, which he is trying for, he will make a fair average regimental officer. The parents are both disappointed, & do not conceal it, though matters might have been worse, but they at one time thought he would have distinguished himself.

T. talks a good deal of the young Ld Shrewsbury, who seems to be a fool: he is not yet of age, & is living with a Mrs. Mundy, who has got complete control of him. Her husband luckily has not sued for a divorce, else she would make the boy marry her. T.[albot] says the estate is clear of debt, & worth over £50,000 a year: but he is not always accurate where his family is concerned. I console him by pointing out that Ld Waterford made just as bad a start in life, but has outlived it, & is respected & well thought of. The last Ld Shrewsbury too was an unpleasant mixture of vanity & madness; yet he did nothing to discredit the name, & relieved the property of a heavy debt. . . .

17 Sept. 1881: . . . Much talk with M. about the Talbot children – the sons –& generally as to the chances of young men. We agreed that there is something in the training of public schools as they are now, which seems to disable lads from great or continued exer-tion. Good manners are usually acquired there, & athletic exercises, & a certain amount of teaching, not in general of a very useful sort: but it would be a moral impossibility that an English public schoolboy should work for his living, & in the hope of future distinc-tion, as for instance the late Lord Campbell[36] worked. The youth would feel he was doing something exceptional, & would not be sure whether anything exceptional was 'good form'. The fact I suppose, is that the training of these schools is arranged to suit the sons of rich men, who have no need to work hard, & could not be induced to do so. For them it is suitable enough, & as an introduction to society: but not for those who have to make their way. These last are beaten in competitions, & probably in after life also, by lads otherwise brought up, with inferior manners, & probably not better brains, but who have not given up half their energies to cricket & boating. Hence the perpetual complaint: 'What can we find for young men to do?' There is plenty to do, if they would do it, but it is dull disagreeable work, of a kind they dislike: & they had rather vegetate on a very small income than change their habits.

18 Sept. 1881 (Sunday): . . . Examined again my balance sheet from Knowsley (v. 11 Sept.) and this time with less pleasure than before for, if the gettings are great, so is the outlay:

In 1880–1881 (30 June to 1 July) I have:

(1) Paid in compulsory deductions, taxes, quitrents, annuities, & the like £28,501. This not being under my control does not trouble me, & it will be lessened by at least £5,000 in a few years, though increased taxes may eat up the gain.

(2) Paid for household, parks, stables, game, etc., etc., £27,000, which is at the old rate for Knowsley [i.e. £25,000] with £1,000 each for Keston & Fairhill. This I do not grudge or find fault with.

(3) Benefactions figure for £24,174, which includes £10,000 to the Liverpool College, £2,000 to Manchester for the University, and £2,000 to my sister: all extras, & two will not recur. So here also I am satisfied in reason, especially as both the Manchester & Liverpool endowments are of a permanent kind, & will help to keep the family name alive.

(4) Kent & Surrey estates have cost £9,000, Northstead £7,000, which is a monstrous charge, but I suppose that it must soon come to an end, & that these estates will be self-supporting.

(5) Estate expenses, with incidentals, come to £76,854, which ought not to be, & must not continue, but I do not know how to hinder it. It is here that the great leakage has always been, & so it continues, & so it will while Hale goes on acting: yet I should be sorry to lose him, not only from personal friendship, but because he understands the estate, & the people, & keeps all quiet, though he certainly does not spare my pocket.

In all there is spent £172,000, which is monstrous, though not much of it has gone in waste. I have put by £60,000 in the year calculated as above, which is not the worst part of the business. But the outlay ought to have been at least £30,000 less.

19 Sept. 1881: Ride, & took leave of Fairhill with regret . . .

20 Sept. 1881: Saw Mr. Knowles, & agreed to publish the article which I sent him lately (v. 30 Aug.) with a few additions & corrections. It reads better in print than I expected &, though I should not be surprised if it gave offence to both parties, it is I believe a plain statement of the truth – at any rate of the truth as it appears to me. It will at any rate not be considered as too optimist, which is the criticism often made on my utterances.

Employed myself in sending to friends copies of the Southport speech, which has been reprinted.

L. West dined again with us. He now seems disposed to go out alone, leaving his daughter to follow: which I am glad of. This (illegitimate) family is likely to give trouble & it is well that the girls should go to Washington where they may very probably marry: but it is not well that much public attention should be called to them: which will be the case if they or one of them go out with the minister. The lads are luckily provided for: one is settled at the Cape, & the other will follow.

Talk of the children of W.E. West, who already show signs of the father's oddity. The eldest boy very sharp & quick, but in weak health. . . .

23 Sept. 1881: . . . The Duchess of Bedford & her daughters, being in town, came to tea, & I sat with them half an hour. It is settled that the Duchess keeps her place at court till the beginning of next session – the Duke wishes to get out of the connection with government, but hardly knows how – he refused to support Gladstone on the Land Bill but, if the Premier does not consider that a reason for resigning, he, the Duke, can hardly treat it as such. The truth is that, with his independent & rather eccentric way of looking at things, he ought to have stood wholly aloof, & he himself probably thinks so now. But it is too late, & he cannot get out of the connection without some appearance of quarrelling with his party.

24 Sept. 1881: This was another day of compulsory idleness – and perhaps want of employment concurred with health in bringing a return of the disagreeable nervous feeling from which I have suffered of late. It passed off in two or three hours, & I note it only because, being absolutely without external cause of any kind, I see it is a sort of bodily complaint which must be considered & dealt with as such. I can only describe it as the sensation which would be produced by the first information of impending misfortune. Business in which I can take an interest drives it off at once: especially if transacted in company with other people: solitary employment does not much relieve it. . . .

26 Sept. 1881: . . . **Note** also that Hale says not more than a third of the soil of my estate in Bootle is yet built upon (I thought it had been over one half) and he sees no reason why the rental of that estate should not double its value.

Ld & Ly De La Warr came to stay.

27 Sept. 1881: In papers, news of death of Ld Airlie[37], in the far west, where he had gone as I understand to buy land for one of his sons. He was exactly my age, 55, & seemed healthy. A man not shining, but of good sense, & who would have had more credit for it but for the accident of his having married a clever talking wife, who seemed to assume to herself the headship of the family, & reduce him to a cypher.

. . . I was surprised at my brother-in-law's [De La Warr's][38] activity: he is past 60, & does not look strong, but he walked better than any of us. To be sure, he is lean, long in the legs, and up to the age of 45 lived an almost ascetic life as a country parson: when he married, [he] began a new existence as a man of society & pleasure: but chiefly to please his young wife. She (Baillie Cochrane's daughter) is or was very good looking, perfectly good tempered, & not a little silly. . . .

29 Sept. 1881: . . . Sycamore grows best of all trees here[39], but sheds its leaf early. Birch does well also, but in masses it is monotonous. Horse chestnut grows fast & healthily, but is open to the same objection as the sycamore, that it is bare early in autumn. Elm has been but little planted of late, but I see no reason why it should not be. The old elms are among our best trees. Spanish chestnut is suited only to sheltered places & dry ground. There are some very fine ones in the park near the Octagon. Lime prospers, & I have planted a good deal of it, but it does not flower as in the south, & there is but little scent. Beech grows slowly, & kills even the grass under it, so as to be objectionable in general, though there are fine old specimens in the park.

Ash does not seem to do well. It grows freely to a certain height but then dies off.

Oak I have almost ceased to plant. It will not bear the smoke.

The same rule applies to most kinds of fir, which are apt to look as though they had been used to sweep a chimney with. On the whole I prefer (1) sycamore, (2) elm, (3) horse chestnut, (4) alder, (5) birch, (6) lime. Spanish chestnut, beech, & ash here & there. Scarcely any oak. Conifers only in a few places, where they make a show in winter, & are not seen too closely.

We must give up the hope of having fine old trees here in future: between smoke & sea winds they mostly begin to decay at 50 or 60 years of age. Perhaps it was always so, & that is why in the old pictures the trees are mostly represented as pollards cut closely in.
. . .

3 Oct. 1881: . . . I have not noted before that (as might have been expected) the Irish land bill has borne fruit in an English & Scotch agitation for similar measure. Fixity of tenure is not exactly & in so many words demanded: but it is implied in the right which is claimed for the tenant of selling his holding to the best bidder when he goes out – the pretext being that in no other way can the value of his improvements be ascertained. This of course is a pretext only: the object is to enable him to sell the goodwill of the farm, which belongs to the landlord. This demand is put forward by a body called the Farmers' Alliance – which is in effect an alliance against the landowner. James Howard, of Bedford, the machine maker, is at the head of it. So far it has not made much way, but one cannot feel sure as to the future. There are now four distinct parties or sections working on questions connected with the land each from their own point of view: (1) the protectionists, under their new name of fair traders, wanting to tax foreign imports of agricultural produce: (2) the party, not known by any distinctive nickname, who claim a large reduction of the local burdens on land: (3) the 'Free Land' party, who believe the whole secret of a reformed agriculture to lie in the sweeping away of settlements & entails, & placing land on precisely the same footing as money – this party being more political than economical, & desiring rather the breaking up of great estates than the improvement of the farms upon them: and (4) the tenant right party, whose idea, worked out to its full logical development, is to turn the landowner into the holder of a rent charge, & the occupier into a virtual owner. The check on this theory, as applied to English practice, lies in the fact that the landlord at present finds nearly all the capital for improvements: which naturally he would cease to do if he lost control over his estate.

4 Oct. 1881: Write to the Dean of the Faculty about the prizes which I distributed to the medical students yesterday: I have it in my mind to found & endow one, if the opportunity seems suitable.

Smell from St. Helens early very disagreeable: in fact it woke both Ly D. & me at 5.00, but it passed off before 10.00 a.m.

5 Oct. 1881: Very fine bright day, no smoke, wind in the west.

See a Miss Mason, a young lady out of Liverpool, whom Ly D. thinks of engaging as a kind of secretary: a plan I entirely approve, as it will save her much needless fatigue.

. . . Mr. and Mrs. Lecky came. Pleasant evening: much talk with L. especially as to Carlyle, whose consistency & coherence in his opinions he defended, I rather doubting than disputing. He said one thing which was true & rather striking: 'Carlyle's reputation in the future will depend much on what happens in regard of parliamentary government. He did not believe in it, & always said so: if he proves right, & the democratic movement fails by its own excess, & ends in despotism, he will have seen what nobody saw, & will have been right before anybody else. In that case he will leave a great name: if his predictions are falsified, his reputation will suffer in proportion.' This is fair, & well put. – I was less successful in obtaining an explanation of the reason why Carlyle detested John Stuart Mill: Lecky's interpretation of the fact, which he did not deny, was that Carlyle considered Mill to have ignored, or at least undervalued, the distinction between right & wrong: if his (Mill's) philosophy were true, & utility the only test, nothing could be good or bad in itself, & all the higher instincts of man revolted against this doctrine. . . . I asked again how Carlyle came to take Goethe for his idol – they having as far as I could see absolutely nothing in common? He said that Goethe's books were the first that Carlyle had read after breaking loose from Puritanism, & when he wanted a religion of some kind: & they had given him an ideal, something to live for – a service which he never forgot. But if he had come across these same books later, the result might not have been the same.

6 Oct. 1881: News from Chadwick that he has secured the Garland estate, Oaklands, for £8,000, which I did not in the least expect, nor should I have cared to pay heavily for it: but it is worth that sum, & more, as an investment.

News also from Statter that the total sum due from the L.[ancs.] & Y.[orks.] R. Co. is £59,800: due in November next . . . it is a satisfactory accession of means, being much more than I had anticipated.

. . . Walk with Lecky in afternoon.

Letter from Knowles: great praise of the article on Ireland: I believe it has been much read. **Query**: Shall I leave well alone, or write another on Home Rule?

Two speeches have been made lately in Yorkshire by Sir S. Northcote: both sensible & in good taste, but not effective as party manifestos. The truth is that Northcote is too good a man intellectually & morally to do that kind of work well: he cannot set himself to exaggerate, overcolour, & misrepresent: & without some admixture of these arts a party speech is seldom successful. The only part of his two manifestos which excited warm applause was when he gave something like a hesitating approval of the principle of reciprocity: when there was great cheering: & he was glad to escape from a dangerous subject by vague phrases which might mean anything or nothing. . . .

8 Oct. 1881: Garden party from 3.00 to 6.00, to which about 300 of our neighbours were asked. . . . We had the usual collection of ex-mayors & mayoresses. The weather luckily remained fine, & many of the party drove about the grounds & went boating on the lake.

I was attacked by several people about the Irish article: one man fastened upon me with a plan of emigration, so that I had trouble in getting away from him: another (whom I did not know) said in a solemn tone: 'You have not gone to the bottom of the subject. The root of the evil is – Popery.' Holt said that everybody in Liverpool had been reading it.

The newspapers are full of two speeches delivered by Gladstone at Leeds, one chiefly on free trade, the other on Irish affairs. They are of course eloquent & able, but considering their length there is perhaps less in them than might have been expected.

The Irish speech is the more important, but contains chiefly praises of the Land Act, & a strong attack on Parnell – well deserved, but which the object of it will take as a compliment to his influence. There is an emphatic declaration that the principles of the Land Act are not intended to be applied to England or Scotland: which on the whole I believe, but do not forget that in this very year Mr. G. was loudly denouncing fixity of tenure for Ireland, while he had practically embodied it in his bill.

There is a notice of the increased wealth of the Irish peasantry, as shown by the savings banks – which does not quite prove what the speaker intended, since it shows (1) that the Irish peasant cannot have been much oppressed, if he could lay by so largely, (2) that the undoubtedly existing disaffection has not been caused by distress. There is a strong and good declaration of the intention of government to keep order: though rather oddly worded, the phrase being that 'the resources of civilisation are not yet exhausted', which may mean a stronger coercion bill, or some equivalent measure, or on the other hand some fresh attempt at conciliation. Probably the sentence was left purposely ambiguous, so that England might read it in one sense, Ireland in another.

There is also a marked reference to Granville as Gladstone's probable successor: which may mean a good deal.

On the whole the speech is not one of the most remarkable delivered by the Premier: but it has the great merit of alarming nobody, & of containing no phrase which is specially open to comment. . . .

10 Oct. 1881: . . . Two fresh speeches by Gladstone, very long, & rather more of a partisan character than those delivered on Friday: but he has avoided saying anything significant as regards the future, or which can be laid hold of.

Lecky shows me some numbers of the *Weekly News* and *United Irishman* – intensely bitter against England but well written, as the seditious press of Ireland usually is. Matters are not mending there: the last development of the popular movement is that fox-hunting is to be stopped: the reason apparently being that it is a sport popular with landlords, & that doing it away will be annoyance to them. There is at the same time an attempt to promote the use exclusively of Irish or American manufactures, English goods being excluded: but a policy of that kind requires more care & discipline to work it than the leaders of the Irish mob have at their command. Outrages & shootings continue as before, & we grow so accustomed to them that they pass as matters of course, & are scarcely commented upon in the English papers.

11 Oct. 1881: . . . From Gladstone's late speeches the inference is drawn that he intends to propose an English tenant right bill drawn on the lines of the Irish Act: I do not myself believe it, but note the fact that this expectation exists among some of his followers, as significant at least of their wish. But to any scheme of that kind there is (apart from all question of its justice) the almost insuperable obstacle that in England improvements are made by the landlord mostly, & that the tenant would lose more by having nothing done for him than he could gain by security against disturbance. . . .

12 Oct. 1881: Intended to go shooting, but heavy rain prevented.

. . . Send copies of the article to D. of Argyll, D. of Bedford, Dalhousie, Camperdown, & Houghton. Write to Knowles for more copies if they are to be had.

. . . Dr. Gorst dined with us. Bad report of Mrs. H.[ale] & entirely by her own fault. She not likely to live.

Day mostly wet. Short walk for exercise. Read & write chiefly. Rather lazy & lethargic, which I suspect is the result of a damp climate: but since coming here I have been entirely free from that disagreeable nervous sensation which I sometimes suffer from in the south.

More speechmaking: this time by Salisbury & Northcote, but it is all an attack on the government, & I can discover no new idea. Salisbury dwelt chiefly on the disturbed & practically anarchical state of Ireland – as to which I wish I did not agree with him – but to my taste, though probably not that of the public, he spoilt the effect of what was real & sound in his objections by stating them in an exaggerated form. It is increasingly clear that there is in the minds of the popular leaders a fixed intention of driving out of the country any men who will not accept the supremacy of the Land League. The priests are getting frightened, for socialism is not in their line & the mob seems to make no distinction between Protestant & Catholic: but they have no power of resistance. For the first time, as I should think, in Irish history Catholic landlords are calling in to help them the armed Orange parties who go by the name of 'Emergency Men' & who volunteer to do police work, protect threatened property, & do jobs for employers who being boycotted can find no other labourers. It is a strange condition, & cannot last.

13 Oct. 1881: Shooting on the Roby beat . . . brought in 217 [head] mostly hares.

Home at 4.00 where news of Parnell being arrested. Sanderson & Pender both telegraphed, but we have no details, except that Gladstone announced the fact at the Guildhall, where the enthusiasm was immense. It was quite time that some action of the kind was taken . . .

Letter from Froude, very civil about my article, which I had sent him, & characteristic in his mention of Irish affairs. He argues that the policy of conciliation has been a failure throughout . . . His argument, if I follow it, is really in favour of despotism: which is Carlyle's leading idea, but that of nobody else.

14 Oct. 1881: We had intended to shoot . . . but a heavy gale of wind & rain – one of the heaviest I remember – compelled us to stay at home. While I write, the walls of the old house are shaking, some plaster has fallen in the gallery, & I hear of much destruction among the old trees. Towards evening the storm abated: it was at its worst about 11.00 a.m. but it still came in gusts against which it was not easy to stand. . . . The park & grounds are strewn with broken boughs. . . . There has been no such gale since that of 1859 in which the ship 'Royal Charter" was lost.

15 Oct. 1881: . . . Biddulph & Ly E. talk much about the Duke of Teck[40] (Ly E. was attached to the Princess Mary as lady-in-waiting) who has gone over to Ireland as chairman of a company to speculate in land (I believe it is) Orrell Lever and H. Lennox[41] being the promoters. Two more disreputable speculators are not to be found, & it is something new to have royalty mixed up in such transactions. He seems to have dined with the Lord Mayor of Dublin, got drunk, & made a most absurd speech, in course of which he said that he supposed there was some reason why the royal family did not come over to Ireland, but he, Teck, did not know what it was. – The man is a blockhead, but till now has had the sense to hold his tongue, so that it could not be known publicly what he was. . . .

18 Oct. 1881: Letters, etc. Very busy early. Left at 9.20 for Manchester, reached the Town Hall at 10.50, & took the chair at a meeting in aid of the Infirmary at 11.30. Some 250 were present. I spoke about 25 minutes, not to my own satisfaction, but saying what was necessary to be said. The Bishop of Manchester, Jacob Bright[42], Agnew, & others followed. We sat till 1.30, when I was again taken to the Infirmary, in order that I might go thoroughly over it, the chairman of the board saying there had been some dissatisfaction because yesterday I visited some wards & not others. Found in one ward a patient who said he had worked for me, left £2 with him. Luncheon in the boardroom, where one or two speeches, & great cordiality. Interested in seeing the new process of disinfection by means of spray, or vapour, from carbolic acid, which prevents impurities floating in the air from getting into wounds & poisoning them: a simple device &, they say, quite efficient.

About £14,000 was promised towards making up deficiencies in the Infirmary funds: I gave £20 a year for 5 years. One rough-looking fellow, whom I should have taken for an artisan, sent up his name for £1,000. On the whole the meeting was a success.

. . . News of Dillon & Sexton[43] being arrested, & a warrant is out for O'Connor[44], but he has escaped to England. Violent speeches at an Irish meeting in Liverpool last night, & rioting in Dublin.

19 Oct. 1881: Shooting. Very fine day, & pheasants swarming. Brought in 681 head: my share was 141. Some weariness not from walking but from incessant noise. Hares were few . . . Lionel shot a boy, but not badly . . .

I had barely leisure to read the papers, & answer a few urgent letters, before setting out . . . such business as I have to do is getting into arrears. But it is only for a day or two.

All the newspapers are full of Ireland, & no wonder: for the crisis has come at last. The people are furious – that is the mob, the Irish journalists, and I suspect the lower classes generally. How far upwards the anti-English feeling extends no one here can judge . . .

In England, all feeling that can make itself audible is one side: the press of London is virtually unanimous: Liberals acknowledge a necessity which they regret: & Conservatives find no fault except that the thing was not done earlier. Ministers no doubt rely on the moral effect of the blow they have struck, & with reason: but if the organisation of the Land League be really as strong as it is supposed to be, the arrest of a few leaders will not crush it. And, if there is any considerable number of leaders willing to make martyrs of themselves, one asks what next? . . .

21 Oct. 1881: . . . Write to M. Arnold, who has sent me his book containing extracts from Burke on Irish affairs: I say among other things of Burke in my letter: that he was above the work he had to do: that his speeches are wonderful when read, but that one understands why & how they were not successful, as a rule, when delivered: 'He pelted his opponents with pearls, when pebbles would have been more effective.' I end by expressing a wish that his political writings should be sifted, so that what is of lasting value might be reproduced separately. No one reads Burke now: now what do we not lose by not reading him?

The news of today is that the Land League has been declared illegal, and its meetings suppressed. This is a decided step, & a bold one, but it is necessitated by the fact that after Parnell's arrest the League issued a manifesto directing the tenants to refuse all rent: a direction clearly illegal, as inciting to illegal acts. From another point of view it may be said that the proceeding was politic: for, in the actual state of Irish feeling since the arrests were made, it is clear that conciliation was impossible, & nothing could be worse than a policy of coercion attempted & not carried through.

But the whole affair is a disappointment to Gladstone & the more sanguine Liberals, for they undoubtedly believed that their Land Act would quiet the people without the necessity of using force.

22 Oct. 1881: Into Liverpool to see L. West off to America. . . . The Americans made a point of his crossing by this line, as it lands him in the State with which he has an old hereditary connection – De La Warr. We left home before 9.00, & were at Knowsley again by 11.15. West took his departure very coolly. I told him as he left that 'the road to Paris lay through Washington' – & I think he feels the importance of doing his utmost in the post where he is now. The next few years will determine whether his diplomatic career is to be a success or a failure. He has plenty of ability, perfect manners, & an excellent temper: what I fear for him is the giving way to a feeling of mixed indolence & shyness, which sometimes leads him to neglect obvious duties, with an odd indifference to personal consequences. It is difficult to get him to write despatches even on important subjects: he says the Foreign Office don't read them, & don't want to be bored: but I think he has been persuaded that that theory, comparatively harmless at Madrid, will not do for America. His eldest daughter is to follow him in a few weeks or months.

All our guests left us . . .

Wet windy day: walked in afternoon 4 miles on the measured terrace, for exercise, in much rain.

Write to Reeve, suggesting among others the name of M. Arnold as a candidate for The Club. Barring a little coxcombry, he is a companionable sort of man, & his literary reputation stands high.

23 Oct. 1881: . . . In afternoon, Mr. Holt called: he showed me an odd letter from Gladstone, not very intelligible, but from which we gathered that he does not want to make a public appearance in Liverpool, or to speak there: that he does want to make a speech on Irish affairs which shall go forth to the public (his last being ten days old) and will take the opportunity, if I don't object, of receiving a deputation here: of course I agree: & we settled the time & manner of receiving them.

Read the new *Quarterly Review*: it comes out undiguisedly in favour of protection, under the new name of 'Fair Trade': so that there can be no reasonable doubt but that the party as a whole is committed to that movement: a bad thing for them, since many of their supporters will stand aloof, & a good thing for the government. It is curious that now that the old Tory section is predominant among Conservatives, there comes out a sort of odd socialist tendency, which has disappeared of late years on that side of politics: cheapness is represented as a gain chiefly to the idle capitalist, & he is held up to odium as unpatriotic, whom the fortunes of the country do not interest since he can always send his money abroad: the laissez-faire doctrine is energetically repudiated: & it is alleged to be the duty of the State to see, in one way or another, that the labourer has sufficient employment. . . .

26 Oct. 1881: . . . In the afternoon there came to stay with us: Ld & Ly Halifax, Sir J. Lubbock & two daughters, the Premier[45], wife, & daughter, Ly Reay, Pender, Knowles, Baring, H. Russell – I think these were all. The Seftons dined with us.

Great precautions were & are taken against any attempt on the Premier's life: police day & night, all round the house, & others along the road from Edgehill.

27 Oct. 1881: After breakfast we took our guests into the libraries, where much talk, the Premier discoursing on every possible subject with infinite volubility, & in a manner more genial & pleasant than his usual demeanour would lead one to expect. Then followed a walk, which it was arranged I should propose to Gladstone, in case he wished to discuss any public affair seriously but, Mrs. Gladstone volunteering to join us, the walk was short, & there was no discussion.

After luncheon came a deputation from Liverpool, of 12 or 14 persons, followed by a train of reporters. They presented an address to the Premier, which he acknowledged, & then proceeded to deliver a speech on the state of Ireland which occupied more than half an hour. The audience being small, he spoke in a low voice, & turned his back on the reporters, so that they had trouble to follow him. His language was more sanguine than I could have used, or could agree in: but I suppose a minister is bound to be optimistic in his views. He spoke of the Land League as a body whose object was rapine, denied that they represented any considerable section of the Irish people, affirmed that their influence was due wholly to terror, & seemed confident that they would be speedily put down. Apart from his under-stating the danger of the position, which I think he does, his language was likely to please all except extreme partisans, being firm & uncompromising as to the necessity of maintaining order. I observed that he spoke from full notes, occupying several pages of M.S., but he did not refer to them much.

When the deputation left about 4.00 p.m., M. took him a drive, & I walked in the park with Knowles & L. Gower[46].

Lionel Baring, H. Russell, & Campbell shot Simmons wood: 313 head.

There dined with us Sir T. & Ly Earle, Brocklebanks, father, son, & wife: Mr. & Mrs. Holt: Seftons again – I think these were all. We sat down over 30: the largest gathering we have had this year.

28 Oct. 1881: It was settled that I should walk alone with the Premier early, which I did, taking him by Singleton's hill and the Trap wood & so round the park to the Pony coppy gate.

Walk in afternoon with Pender.

M. took Mr. & Mrs. G. after luncheon to Croxteth, & thence round to Court Hey.

Lionel [Cecil], Ld Sefton, Campbell, H. Russell shot the Eccleston side: 681 head. L. Gower left us.

There dined with us: Mr. & Mrs. Rathbone, Mr. Lyster, Mr. A. Gladstone, Mr. Bilson: I think these were all. We sat down 28 in all.

Mr. G. talked freely of politics during his walk, but with no special significance. He praised very highly the young men of the party who would form the Cabinet of the future: especially Dilke & Trevelyan. He was not uneasy, he said, as to the feeling of the English people: they were quiet & contented: I interposed that there seemed in England no feeling against the rich, such as one saw on the Continent. No, he said, there was none: the fault of the English lay in the opposite direction, in the excessive deference paid to wealth. He said little of Ireland, spoke bitterly of Parnell, but to my surprise passed a high compliment on Healy, whom most people think the worse of the two. (But Healy has praised the Land Act.) He did not think there were more than 10 or 12 really disaffected Irishmen in the House. He believed the Irish people as a body to be loyal. (I did not dispute, but could not agree.) But he said he foresaw trouble in the future – there would be great noise & talk in parliament, & but little done: he was not sorry to be nearly out of it all. As to foreign affairs he was anxious. He thought the war of revenge between France & Prussia must come: he would not be comforted when I observed that the same threats had been used after Waterloo. He was deeply disappointed as to Italy, which he had expected to be the most conservative power in Europe, owing to the boundaries of Italy being for the most part fixed by nature: but, on the contrary, they were a disturbing element, anxious for military glory, & for the possession of territories beyond sea, which could be of no use to them. He talked of the treaty with France now pending, but in a tone of greater indifference than he showed on any other subject – observing that he had great doubts as to the policy of commercial treaties, but if we failed to make one with France the political effect would be bad – it might make a coolness between them. He confirmed something that I said as to the unceasing exertions of Bismarck in various ways to make mischief between England & France – saying that he (B.) had caused it to be signified to him (Gladstone) while in opposition, at the time of the Constantinople Conference, that he ought to press for the seizure of Egypt. At the same time Bismarck was telling the French that we meant to seize the country, & stirring them up to resist the attempt. (This is exactly what he did in regard to all the proceedings of the Conference, which he was determined from the first should fail.)

Gladstone's curious interest in the eastern Christian broke out in his treatment of a document which he had received, being a complaint from certain Bosnians of ill usage by Austria. As it came from unknown persons, & stated no facts, except in the vaguest terms, I should not have thought it of much importance – nor do I see how our government could interfere in the matter – but he recurred to it again & again, with an earnestness which to me seemed disproportionate to the cause. He talked a great deal (but not to me) about the Hungarian bishop, Strossmayer, about whom I am told he was enthusiastic, but I don't know on what grounds.

We had some conversation about land & tenant-right, but on that his ideas were as he said himself unfixed. He seemed to favour the notion of establishing in England something like the Ulster custom, allowing the tenant to sell his interest. He did not seem much moved by the plea that in that case the tenant would be selling, not merely the value of his improvements, but the right to appoint his successor, which is not his but the landlord's. He was more impressed by the argument that in case of such sale the incoming tenant would be entitled to demand that his rent should not be unduly raised – and that a land court would be necessary to decide what rents should be. He had evidently no plan, but it was equally evident that the bent of his mind was to give everything to the tenant that could be given without too manifest injustice. On one point he was clear. He did not believe in a peasant proprietary for England, & said so distinctly. He thought that, whether desirable or not in itself, it was impossible in the actual economical state of the country. The smallholder would always be bought out[47].

29 Oct. 1881: All our company left us, except Sir J. Lubbock & his two daughters, Ly Reay, the Campbells & Mary Hope.

Occupied till midday in seeing them off. Ride in afternoon.

During the whole of Gladstone's stay, some 12 or 15 policemen surrounded the house, watching it day & night. He received one threatening letter while here, & according to Mrs. G. no day passes that does not bring one or more. The Home Office are uneasy, & insist on precautions: not I suppose fearing a conspiracy against his life, so much as the possible act of some half crazy fanatic, excited by the reading of Fenian newspapers.

. . . Much talk & comparing of notes as to the Premier. The general impression seems to be, & certainly it is that left on my mind, that he is more agreeable, more light & easy in conversation, than would be expected from his manner in public: no subject comes amiss to him, he is ready to discourse on any, great or small, & that with the same copiousness & abundance of detail which characterises his speaking. He has no humour, rarely jokes, & his jokes are poor when he makes them. There is something odd in the intense earnestness with which he takes up every topic: I heard him yesterday deliver a sort of lecture on the various ways of mending roads, suggested by some remark about the Liverpool streets. He described several different processes minutely, & as if he had been getting up the subject for an examination. So again somebody talked about a cathedral for Liverpool, & he went off at score on the respective merits of three or four sites. Since the days of old Lord Brougham, I have heard nothing like his eager & restless volatility: he never ceased to talk, & to talk well. Nobody would have thought that he had cares on his mind, or work to do. His face is very haggard, his eye wild: a lady who saw much of him said: 'He has the eye of a madman.' And it is certain that in his way of thinking & conversing there is much that suggests eccentricity. M. was much struck with his singular power of becoming enthusiastic in his admiration of what he likes or appreciates: talking before her & Ly Reay of a woman (one Miss Pattison[48]), who had taken up the life of a hospital nurse, he said it made him proud of human nature that such characters could be found – or words to that effect. He spoke much of Cobden, of whom a biography has just appeared: thought his intellect over-rated, his views more narrow and mistaken than his admirers would readily allow, but praised in vehement terms what he called the nobleness of his moral nature. On this Pender tells me that, when asked on some occasion to pay a public compliment to the leaders of the anti-corn law movement, he [Gladstone] had done so warmly as regards Cobden, moderately in respect of Bright: but, though the name of Charles Villiers was repeatedly pressed upon him as that of the real pioneer of the movement, he would take no notice of him whatever: which Pender & his friends ascribed to the fact of Villiers being a shrewd cynical man of the world, a character specially odious to G. – He talked of Carlyle, to whom he would not allow the character of a thinker, but considered him a great poet who preferred to write in the form of prose. – He gave some reminiscences of the past. Thought the history of England might have been different if Sir R. Peel had come in as he ought in 1839: at that time he was not specially pledged to protection, & might have adopted free trade without incurring the reproach of inconsistency, or quarrelling with his party. He did not think Sir Robert had ever seriously considered the matter, till forced to do so by the exigencies of office – nor had he, Gladstone. His opinions were therefore rather developed than changed. . . .

30 Oct. 1881: Walk early with Sir J. Lubbock. He talks of clôture – under what safeguards it is possible – thinks it necessary in some form. Difficulty about a new Speaker: Brand[49] wishes to resign. Whitbread[50] has not health: is Dodson[51] fit? Talks of Gladstone, praised his conversation, but said it left no clear impression on his mind (this criticism I could not quite agree in). Noticed the intensely theological or ecclesiastical turn of his thoughts. – Walk later for exercise on the terrace. Very sleepy & drowsy, I do not know why, before dinner.

31 Oct. 1881: Ly Reay, the Lubbock family, & Mary Galloway left us.
    . . . Ordered payment of £50 to the Lancaster Grammar School.

Saw Broomfield . . . he says there are between 300 & 400 trees down, but few of any consequence. I believe we have lost less than most large parks: partly because we have less to lose.

1 Nov. 1881: M. left for London . . .
Left at 10.00 for St. George's Hall. Sessions lasted till 5.20.
Calendar very heavy, 99 cases: one of attempted suicide, four of indecent assault, all the rest thefts . . . or assaults.
Gave one man, a returned convict, 5 years' penal servitude.
Two others had 12 months for theft.
One had 12 months for embezzlement from Bootle corporation.
Two were acquitted, rightly.
Average of sentences under 8 months, excluding the one of P.S.

2 Nov. 1881: Left home at 9.00, in court by 10.00. Sat till 6.00 p.m. exactly.
No sentence of P.S. Three of 12 mos. each. Average about 6 mos.
There were three acquittals, all reasonable. No verdict against evidence.
Went to Adelphi Hotel, there dressed, & to dinner with the Mayor, where about 120 guests. Speeches as usual, but no reporters. We met at 7.00, & sat till 10.30. I sat between the Mayor & Sir A. Walker[52]. My speech was not good, but well received.
Note that the Conservatives in Liverpool are half triumphant, half ashamed. The Irish have voted in a body for them at the late municipal elections, & thereby given them a large majority – voting power having in the last few years been pretty equally divided. In the particular case no great harm is done, but it is an unpleasant sign of what Irish influence may do. The Mayor tells me that the Irish in Liverpool are 180,000 out of 600,000, or nearly one-third of the whole.

3 Nov. 1881: Liverpool at 10.00 for appeals. All were public house cases.
Three were allowed, six dismissed.
. . . Home 6.30: rather harassed by the necessity of answering a multitude of unimportant letters, after a long day's work. When I returned to Knowsley, I had passed 19 hours in public – the dinner in the Town Hall included – out of the last 36. Yet the fatigue is less than it used to be 20 years ago: either because a wholly sedentary day has grown more familiar, or because the court in which I now sit is better aired than that at Kirkdale. But the strain on hearing & attention is considerable, especially as these sittings come too seldom to create a habit.

4 Nov. 1881: In court again at 10.00, & sat till 6.00 exactly . . . One man had tried to hang himself, nobody knew why: he was let go without punishment: for I hold that to punish attempted suicide is an absurdity.
One woman got 4 months for biting off the nose of another woman: an amusement commoner among men than women. She was Irish. Home a little before 7.00. Saw Hale, & settled some estate affairs.

5 Nov. 1881: This was the last day of sessions: the longest sessions I remember, & probably about the longest in England. We sat from 10.00 till 8.15, 10½ hours: making 41 hours' sitting in all.

. . . Drove home by moonlight: bonfires up & down in the fields: Guy Fawkes seems more popular here than in the south. Perhaps antagonism to the Irish explains the interest felt in this rather antiquated ceremony.

6 Nov. 1881: . . . I have agreed, though not without hesitation, to buy Cazalet's land adjoining Fairhill. His price (£100 per acre) is not reasonable but it is in the nature of a fancy price & I believe that he did not care to sell, & would not take less. I have now 1,200 acres in a ring fence, having begun in 1873 with 540 acres.

The chief event of last week is the death of Macdonald[53], the so-called workingman's representative. He had accomplished the feat of being more universally disliked & distrusted than any member of the House (Irish excepted): & this though at his coming in there was a wish to show special civility to the first of a new class. His only colleague of the same class, Burt, gained & kept the respect of parliament: which shows that there was no class feeling mixed with the general censure of Macdonald. He was accused of excessive arrogance: of habitual bad manners, such as unnecessary dirtiness, & spitting about the House in the American manner: and also very generally of corruption: but as to this last charge the stories were so vague, though widely spread, that they ought not to go for much.

7 Nov. 1881: Left Knowsley by the 9.15 train from Edgehill, after a six weeks' stay. It is worth notice – whatever may be the reason – that the annoyance of stinking vapours from St. Helens has been lessened this year to an extraordinary degree. In a note which I kept daily, I find that out of the first five weeks, or 35 days, of our stay the smell was absolutely imperceptible on 29 days: that it was noticed as disagreeable in the morning on 4 days, but went off by 10.00 a.m. or even earlier: & that it was felt as unpleasant during the whole or a large part of the day on 2 days only. In the last week, being busy, & all day at Liverpool, I have kept no count. The cause is not in the wind, for that has been frequently in the east: I can only suppose that the new act of parliament, & the stir made about it, has caused the manufacturers to exert themselves more than before in preventing the nuisance.

. . . I find a strong report going about that Gladstone is about to resign, but believe it to be only an echo of his own words at Leeds, & of the language which he now habitually uses as to his public life being at an end, & so forth: which is, I dare say, sincere enough, but in the mouth of a minister does not mean much. Another story is that of my approaching entrance into the Cabinet – result of the Knowsley visit.

The Bedford business is ended by the Duke withdrawing the Duchess's resignation, which he tendered on finding that he could not support the Land Bill: it seems that he has been reassured as to the future &, if the Cabinet choose to ignore his dissent of last session, he could not well make that a ground of separation.

8 Nov. 1881: . . . Sanderson dined with us. We did not talk about foreign affairs, in which indeed I now take little interest. He is in trouble about his eldest brother, who, having a wife nearly mad from drink, & never having recovered from the shock of failure five years ago, is apparently living on what T.H.S.[anderson] can spare from his own wants.

Much talk, & newspaper writing, about the Irish land court, which has begun its work in Ulster by several apparently sweeping reductions of rent: these may be exceptional cases, & there is an appeal from the sub-commissioners, by whom they have been made, to the court: it is therefore premature to cry out against them as unjust: but reasonable alarm has been created by an extraordinary speech of a sub-commissioner, Prof. Baldwin, to the effect that 'in determining the rent they have set up no standard of what the farming ought to be' – that 'they consider only the capabilities of the land in the hands of the present tenants' & have nothing to do with the question whether the value in other hands might not be greater. – This doctrine is so extraordinary, & so unlike the language held when the creation of the land court was before parliament, that it has excited a good deal of sensation. It in effect declares that a tenant who is a bad farmer is entitled to hold at a lower rent than if he were a good farmer: which is a singular way of encouraging agricultural improvements: & also that the landlord is to be fined for the tenant's shortcomings: which is not justice.

I am afraid it will be found that the apparent concessions made to socialist ideas in the land bill will have influenced opinion very injuriously to the government in England, & produced a conservative reaction of which there are even now some signs.

9 Nov. 1881: . . . Saw nobody, I think, except Sanderson. I find him uneasy, & he admits that the office is so, as to Egyptian affairs: the cause of trouble being the insubordination of the army, which may at any moment make the Khedive a prisoner, & take all power into its own hands. In that event the only two obvious alternatives would be, either a Turkish occupation to which the objections are many: or an Anglo-French occupation, which might be indefinitely protracted: for the French certainly would not leave sooner than they must, & while they stayed we should be obliged to stay also.

10 Nov. 1881: . . . Statter called . . . [he] hears much talk about a revival of trade, but as yet does not himself see it.

. . . The Lord Mayor's dinner of yesterday went off flatly. Gladstone has delivered so many speeches of late that it was known there was nothing new to be told: popular curiosity was satisfied, not to say satiated: he had fired off all his ammunition & had nothing left to make a noise with. His speech was below the usual mark of his oratory: & Granville, though prudent & polite, was not eloquent. . . .

12 Nov. 1881: . . . Some talk with B.[eresford] Hope[54]: he very squalid & dirty in appearance, as if not caring to look after himself: tried to be cheerful, & made bad jokes, accompanying them with his strange laugh: the attempt at good spirits seemed more melancholy than silence would have been.

Walk back with Sherbrooke: he very ill pleased with the state of public affairs, at which I am not surprised: thinks parliament has been duped as to the land court, which is engaging in a competition of robbery with the Land League: whereas, but for assurances that rents in general would be little affected, parliament would not have agreed to the establishment of the Court. (But, as I told him, it is premature to judge the court by a few decisions of sub-commissioners, from which there is an appeal.) He noted also the tendency of present legislation to undo the work of the last 50 years: from 1830 to 1880, we acted generally on the principle of leaving individual energy as little fettered as possible by legal restrictions: now, all goes the other way: inspection & control are more & more introduced into all trades: rents are fixed in Ireland, & may be so in England: the inclination is to employ wherever possible the power of the State to check that of the capitalist. We agreed that, if the usury laws had not been repealed in the last generation, it would probably have been found impossible to repeal them now: prejudice would have been too strong. . . .

13 Nov. 1881: . . . I have read, at intervals during the last fortnight, Morley's life of Cobden, so much praised by Gladstone at Knowsley. It bears out on the whole his judgment as to the subject of the biography. Cobden appears to have been a man as free from personal motives as any one engaged in public life well can be. Except a bitter & unreasonable dislike of the landed gentry, which suggests social jealousy, there is nothing to find fault with in his character: & this dislike was not peculiar to him, but shared with the manufacturing class generally, as they were then. But intellectually he seems to me to have been essentially a narrow-minded man – a man of few ideas – quite incapable of understanding, or entering into the various ideals of life which different nations make to themselves. In one word, he really believed mankind to be governed in their actions by enlightened self-interest: whereas experience shows that motive to be almost powerless as against passion, prejudice, superstition, or national vanity. No Frenchman believes a fresh war with Germany to be for the material benefit of France: yet probably a majority of the French people would vote for such a war if they saw a chance of success. This was the kind of feeling which Cobden never could understand: he thought it peculiar to England, & due to the influence of the aristocracy: whereas in this, as in many other matters, the aristocracy have only seemed to lead a movement which they were really following.

14 Nov. 1881: . . . Called on Northcote, at his request, to attend a meeting of the Beaconsfield memorial committee: he & Barrington, with myself, were the whole party. The sum raised is a little under £65,000: the statue, which we went to see at the sculptor's, is nearly modelled, & promises to be fine: the immediate object of our meeting was to settle certain questions as to extra expenses incurred. Barrington left us on the way, & Northcote & I walked together down to Pall Mall: talking of many things, Ireland among others. He ridiculed the 'fair trade' or protection movement, which indeed seems to be dying out. He agreed with me that, if anything like the indiscriminate reduction on which the Irish land court appears to be bent had been suspected beforehand, parliament would not have assented to the establishment of the court: the assurance having been repeatedly given that rents in general would be left substantially unaltered. There will be a good deal heard on this subject when parliament meets: unless the decisions hitherto given are exceptional, or unless they are reversed on appeal. . . .

15 Nov. 1881: . . . Lawrence called, & told me that Mr. Knowles, my neighbour at Witley, agrees to take £15,000 for his land, 191 acres . . . This purchase was unexpected, for he had delayed so long . . .
  I have bought in this year

(1) The Hazels   - 162 acres
(2) Oaklands   - 71 acres
(3) Cazalet's land   - 128 acres
(4) Knowles's land   - 191 acres
(5) Some land near Haslemere, but only a strip, say 10 acres.

I think this is all, except a field or two, & a few cottages, in various parts of the

Lancashire estates. In all about 550 acres. And on the other hand there are a few acres sold to railway companies. But the increase of the estate cannot be less than 500 acres.

I have about £96,000 to pay for land, including Holwood: but the railway payments will make up £60,000, now due partly to me, partly to the trustees: & there is more to come, so that all required is to give up investing for one year. – I have now made up the Witley estate so as to include all that I want: Fairhill requires two or three small additions, but they will not be obtainable at present, even if I wished to buy: Holwood is still incomplete, while Ninham's wood & the piece opposite the workhouse are not mine, as also Mrs. Smith's fields bordering on High Elms lane. But these also are not to be had without waiting, nor will the cost be heavy when they come in. . . .

16 Nov. 1881: . . . Letter from Ld Spencer offering me a seat on a committee of the Privy Council, which is intended to hear appeals from the decisions of the University Commissioners of Oxford & Cambridge.

17 Nov. 1881: News in the papers that the Old Admiralty & War Office are to be pulled down: which ought to have been done long ago: & that they are to be rebuilt on the site adjoining the Horse Guards, where the Admiralty & Pay Office now are.

. . . Call on Ld Spencer to talk over his offer of yesterday: agreed to accept conditionally, if the sittings do not begin till near the end of January, but I cannot settle in London before that date.

18 Nov. 1881: The papers are busy with a celebration at Rochdale of Bright's 70th birthday, which seems to have been a popular triumph. The occasion is utilised for reviewing & analysing Bright's career. *The Times* sums up all in a shrewd comment, the purport of which is that Bright has succeeded in his immediate objects, but not in the social & political results which he expected from them. He has carried free trade, & largely helped to carry the popularisation of the franchise: but both the landed aristocracy & the church, which he expected to destroy, are to all appearance stronger than 40 years ago. And if changes come affecting both, they will not be in the direction expected by the anti-corn law leaders. The power lost by the clergy will not be gained by dissenting preachers, or by Agnostics or Deists: the authority of the landed gentry will be shared with the working class, not with the manufacturers, whose existence as a distinct class is scarcely felt.

M. had yesterday a long conversation with the Dean of Windsor[55], much of which she repeated to me, but talk at second-hand can seldom be written down with accuracy. The chief topic dwelt upon was the continuance of unpleasant relations between the Queen & the Premier: he complains bitterly that, whereas she used to be the most constitutional of sovereigns, she has now grown an 'imperious despot'. He (Gladstone) ascribes this change to the influence of Ld Beaconsfield: but I imagine it would have come in any case, though Ld B. may have encouraged it. She now interferes in everything, great & small: quarrelled with G. because the Under Sec.ship of the Colonial Dept. was given away without her being consulted, though in the case of undersecretaries this has always been done: offered the Deanery of Westminster to one Canon Pearson[56] without consulting the Premier: but he was induced to decline & so prevent an unpleasant conflict of authority: and writes incessantly to express her wishes, or rather commands. The Dean thinks this perpetual warring does much to induce G. to think of resigning. He says he cannot bear it in addition to all his other work.

Saw Mr. Warr, & went with him over the City Companies' reports. All the large companies except the Mercers have given information, many of them freely, & in much detail. Their income is larger than we expected to find it. Warr thinks it will be about £500,000 per ann. of property, & £200,000 more held in cash. Yearly total £700,000. . . .

19 Nov. 1881: . . . Saw a day or two ago, in the papers, news of the death of W.R. Greg[57], the well known essayist, who has more than once been a visitor at Knowsley, and whom I knew personally, though my most real acquaintance with him was through his writings. These were of two kinds, political or rather economical, for on politics he wrote as an economist chiefly: and theological. In economics his ideas were always shrewd & rational, inclining to the despondent rather than the sanguine view of things. He began life as a decided, though moderate, Liberal, but never was a democrat: latterly his dislike of democratic passions and caprices made him to all practical purposes a Conservative. As a writer on theology, he took a place quite peculiar to himself: starting from the Unitarian sect, he became a theist, & about 30 years ago wrote a book called *The Creed of Christianity* which made a deep impression on the educated public. Free thought was then less common than now, & an argument directed against miracles & revelation seemed a novelty: while the singular fairness & tolerance of adverse opinion shown in the conduct of the argument secured attention from readers whom a more pugnacious controversialist would have repelled. I consider that volume as the starting point of the anti-theological movement which has made so much progress of late. I read it again and again, & it fastened itself in my mind – though I was then already familiar with Strauss. In later days Greg changed his ground a little, & from having been a convinced theist became an agnostic: or rather it might be more true to say that the sceptical tendency of his nature grew stronger, & the devotional weaker.

20 Nov. 1881: News of the Stafford election which is carried by a Conservative. The votes 1,480 odd to 1,180 odd – majority about 300. There are not many Irish in Stafford, so that the cause must be looked for elsewhere. The Conservative candidate, a Mr. Salt[58], is a local gentleman well known & respected in the town, & was unseated by a small majority at the general election. The Liberal was a man named Howell[59], a working-class candidate, of rather extreme opinions, & a stranger. Probably he failed to get the support of middle class voters, who under the ballot can change their minds as often as they please without fear of seeming inconsistent. But, allowing for these causes, it would certainly seem as if the enthusiasm of last year had led to a natural reaction. And I cannot but suspect but that Gladstone's Land Act for Ireland has alarmed holders of property everywhere – as it very well may. Personally, I think this check to the government is far from being an evil: they are strong enough for all useful purposes: and would still be so if twenty bye-elections went against them: while it is a good thing that the extreme section should see that they cannot have everything their own way.

21 Nov. 1881: . . . Mr. Warr called again at my request, & we had further talk as to the City Companies. The more the question of reforming them is looked into, the harder it seems to turn them to any practically useful purpose. Many of the trades with which they were originally connected are extinct: & in most cases the connection appears to have been merely nominal for centuries. I do not see my way at all. Meanwhile we have obtained data for action: & the public will know for the first time what the Companies are, how they came by it, & how they spend it.

22 Nov. 1881: . . . Marriage of the D. of Albany[60] announced: which means more grants, & the inevitable grumble from a section of the Liberal party. They do not receive much sympathy, for the outlay after all is small: but a more awkward question is raised: what is to become of the descendants? Half a dozen dukes, with no land, little money, & a position which makes all professions impossible for them except the army or navy, will form a curious & rather inconvenient element in English society. Nothing except the singular barrenness of the royal family has prevented this difficulty from being felt long ago.

23 Nov. 1881: . . . Saw Münster . . . [he] did not apprehend a warlike policy on the part of Gambetta: thought he had too much sense. Did not believe that the French had any wish for a renewal of the war: they were occupied in peaceable pursuits & especially in money making. But he thought a financial crisis was impending in France, & that it would be followed by great discontent. He said . . . the corruption among official men, & in the public service generally throughout France, had never been so bad as now, not even during the Empire. He said it was a common remark among diplomatists that for years there had not been so complete a lull in international politics as at the present moment. He explained this state of things by the theory that every country had its own internal troubles . . .

Ld Camperdown dined with us. Some talk about farming. He had noticed, as I also have, that the farmers who have suffered least in the late hard times are not, as might have been thought likely, the capitalists who farm high & do everything in the best style, but the comparatively small & poor tenants who put little into the soil & get little out of it at any time. The only explanation I can find is that men of this class live plainly, whereas the modern farmer is luxurious in comparison with his predecessors . . .

27 Nov. 1881: . . . Read to M. out of a new & last volume of Greg's essays[61]. They are in his old vein. One striking thought I noted . . . He observes that in youth, when we have all life before us, we think of it as scarcely worth having, unless an immortal existence is to follow: in old age, when life is nearly exhausted, we grow comparatively indifferent to the prospect of re-existence, while clinging to what remains of interest here. He ascribes the change to a gradual loss of vital powers, making the idea of rest, of cessation from labour & trouble, more welcome than that of renewed activity. And he regards it as a happy instinct, intended to make death easy when it comes in the ordinary course of nature. I believe he is right, & that the feeling is common, though I never before saw it noticed in print. . . .

29 Nov. 1881: . . . It is announced that parliament is to meet on 7 Feb. Probably it is wise not to anticipate the ordinary time, for no advantage came of the early meeting this year, & any unnecessary shortening of the holidays is always unpopular: but a different decision was expected, in view of the state of Ireland which shows no improvement. It is possible, however, that this very reason has operated in an opposite direction. Ministers habitually cling to the hope that things may mend before they are called to account: for if they had to defend their Irish policy now on the ground of results their task would not be easy. Outrages are not diminished in number: the refusal to pay rents still continues in many places: & there is not the slightest sign of an improved condition of feeling. Even men of democratic opinions talk freely of the necessity of strong measures, & proposals for strengthening the police, suspending trial by jury, & similar measures, are constantly discussed. It is impossible to doubt that a strong reaction of opinion has begun, not so much in favour of the conservative opposition, as against the apparent weakness & apathy of the Cabinet. They have been unwise too, I think, in meeting seldom, which creates an appearance of indifference & inaction.

30 Nov. 1881: Sanderson dined with us. No particular news: but it seems that some alarm is being caused by the incorporation of a company for the government of a vast tract of country in Borneo, ceded by the Sultan to certain Englishmen. There are Dutch & Spanish claims on the territory in question, neither of them of much account, but which may possibly give trouble in the future. The policy of the Col. Office in granting this charter is criticised: I think not reasonably, since it merely legalises the acts of private persons, without even pledging the nation to their defence if attacked. And it is wise to give free vent to the colonising & conquering tendencies of the English race, where it can be done with little risk of international complications. – I was in favour of taking over Sarawak in 1858, & I think it might well be done now. . . .

2 Dec. 1881: . . . Much talk in the south about reductions of rents. Ld Salisbury has given back to his tenants half a year's rent, & many others are remitting a quarter. It is strange that we have suffered so little (or rather, not at all) in Lancashire. Near the great towns our escape is intelligible, but why the farmers of the Fylde should be doing well when those of Yorkshire are complaining is less clear.

. . . In the *St. James's Gazette*, which though not exactly Conservative, yet carried on an independent & very effective opposition to the Gladstone ministry, there is today a singular article, deprecating the adoption of the system of *clôture*, as a remedy against obstruction, not merely on the merits (which is a question fairly arguable) but on the ground that the government would probably fail to carry it, & be left in a minority. One naturally asks: why should the writer object to a result which he must necessarily feel to be desirable? and he answers the question –because no other government could be formed just now, or, if formed, could deal with the Irish troubles. This is, I take it, the exact truth: the radical party are giving even now a not very willing support to the inevitable measures of repression &, if their own leaders were not in power, they would express something very like sympathy for the disaffected party.

3 Dec. 1881: . . . Two new baronets announced, both oddly selected. One is an Irish lawyer, Sullivan[62], of whom I never heard before, and whose services have certainly not been remarkable or exceptional: the other Sir R. Phillimore[63], who in the H. of C. was a failure & reckoned a bore, & I do not hear that his reputation as a judge stands high. But he is an extreme High Churchman, & when in parliament was a devoted, not to say servile, follower of Gladstone, who is never insensible to merit of that kind.

4 Dec. 1881: . . . Met Reeve in the street, who talked rather warmly about the apparent indifference of the government to the state of anarchy & turbulence in Ireland: which was never worse. But it is not easy to see what they could do.

The papers are full of a singular robbery committed (if it can be called a robbery, for

I believe legally the offence is not theft) on the body of the late Ld Crawford[64], which was sent home from Italy embalmed, placed in a family mausoleum, & is now gone, none knows where. The object of course is blackmail, & the same trick has been played in America . . . It seems uncertain when the body was abstracted, & there is no trace of the offender.

5 Dec. 1881: *The Times* begins to cry out against the seeming indifference to Irish outrages, which indeed rather increase than diminish. It cannot be agreeable to Gladstone & his colleagues to find that their message of peace has acted as an incitement to increased violence: but the extreme party among English liberals is evidently disposed to treat these outbreaks as excusable in themselves, & in the result beneficial since they tend to get rid of landlords. And the *Pall Mall Gazette*, the organ of philosophical radicalism, deplores the arrest of the Land League orators as the primary cause of mischief. There is much in what is passing in Ireland to suggest a parallel with the early days of the French revolution, when mobs went about the country, intimidating & robbing the proprietors – very feebly resisted by the government of the day, which thought them only a little too zealous in a good cause. The comparison has been worked out in detail, & supported by quotations from Taine's history, by a writer in the *Nineteenth Century* for this month. . . .

9 Dec. 1881: . . . Miss West, natural daughter of L.[ionel] West, came on her way to join her father at Washington: she is good-looking, very well mannered, & but for the unlucky accident of her birth would be a suitable person in all respects to take charge of the mission: as things are, she is rather an encumbrance than a help, & it was long doubtful whether he would take her: the proceeding is not free from risk, & probably there will be unpleasant notices in the papers. But a young girl, especially if handsome, is not likely to be an object of dislike: it is only unlucky that in her position publicity of any kind is a disadvantage. – She speaks broken English, but in all other respects is quite what one might wish the daughter of an English gentleman to be.

The Hales dined with us.

10 Dec. 1881: . . . Examined the new muniment room, just completed, & which is perfect in its way. Talk with Mr. Moore, who is setting in order the old family papers: he confirms my impression that there are very few of any historical or even domestic interest. The destruction of Lathom in the civil wars, & the subsequent break-up of the family when the elder branch died out in the male line, account for the disappearance of all old correspondence[65]. . . .

13 Dec. 1881: . . . Mr. Adams[66], the diplomatist, came to stay.

In papers . . . the burning of a theatre at Vienna, with loss of 800 to 900 lives as supposed, has created a good deal of sensation: as also the loss of one Powell, an M.P.[67], in a balloon, which was carried out to sea some days ago, & has not been heard of since.

Irish murders & outrages continue unabated, & have almost ceased to attract notice.

14 Dec. 1881: We intended to shoot . . . but heavy rain with south-east wind & fog made that impossible. In afternoon, the day mending a little, most of the party went out: I walked with Froude. He fell down . . . the road being a sheet of ice, but no harm was done.

Saw Ward, signed leases: & verified with him the amount of my private drawings from the estate, which is exactly £360,000 in the 12 years that I have held it, or at the rate of £30,000 a year. But I had at least £120,000 to pay off of legacies, succession duty, & debt to the bank: so that in fact I have laid by at the rate of £40,000 a year, or £480,000 in all.

. . . The Hales dined with us – Mrs. H. rather exposed herself, being obviously not sober when she arrived.

Mr. Moore, the lawyer employed on my family papers, also dined: a clever man, rather too free & easy in his manners to suit fastidious tastes, but a gentleman.

15 Dec. 1881: Went to shoot . . . and did so for an hour but, fog setting in heavily, we were obliged to give it up, & walk home. We left home at 10.00, & got back at 1.30.

Froude left us today. I had several interesting conversations with him. He is now more than ever Carlylian, his business of editing Carlyle's papers naturally filling his mind with ideas of that sort: &, so far is the unconscious imitation carried, that when discoursing on his master's favourite subjects he falls into the peculiar Scotch intonation of the old 'prophet', which from an Englishman has an odd effect. I imagine Froude to be essentially & by nature a hero-worshipper, & that if he had not fallen under Carlyle's influence he might like his brother have yielded to that of Newman. – He told me quite seriously that he considered Carlyle to be one of the two or three men of our century, out of all Europe, who would be remembered a thousand, or perhaps two thousand, years hence: that his reputation would depend mainly on the truth or fallacy of his fixed opinion, repeatedly put forward in his books, that modern society was drifting rapidly to destruction: he thought Carlyle was as much in earnest in his depreciation of parliamentary government as in anything he had ever written, and that the event would prove him right: that all existing institutions were breaking up, a period of anarchy must follow, & we & all other nations could only be saved by a master. This, or something to this effect, was what Carlyle believed: he, Froude, believed it too, & if they were wrong Carlyle's authority would suffer in proportion as he had always preached this doctrine.

16 Dec. 1881: [We shot.] . . . The day was very bad, rain almost without ceasing, but luckily not heavy enough to send us home: we brought in 554 head, which is a good deal above the average. There were about 100 hares. – As usual, a crowd gathered, attracted by the shooting. Some of the party had waterproofs to shoot in. I had none, & on coming back felt rather chilled: but no harm came of it.

Well pleased with the party generally: L. Gower, Cowper, & Ld Lymington[68], being old & intimate friends, entertained one another: & Mr. Munro, though not quite of the same mental habits, conciliated all by pleasant manner & great amiability. . . . On Wednesday his son arrived, fresh from South Africa, where he has been serving as a volunteer in the Basuto War. He was formerly secretary to Sir G. Colley. . . .

18 Dec. 1881: Day very wild, strong wind, hail & rain. Went out for a short time only. Feeling lazy and incapable of exertion both in mind & body. . . . Cleared all [post] except one, as to which I could not satisfy myself, whether to decline briefly & civilly, or to enter into explanations. The applicants wish to get up a movement against the continual extension of the functions of the state in all departments of life. I agree with them in opinion and in feeling, but doubt whether there is any use in protesting against so marked a tendency of the time, strengthened as it is by various powerful influences. There is not much moral courage among politicians, & few will stand up in parliament or at public meetings to point out that a popular & philanthropic scheme is foolish, unjust, or in any way unworkable. The public whose interests he is defending does not care: the philanthropists whom he opposes throw mud at him (and no class of men can be more abusive): & all he gets for his trouble is the reputation of a cynic, indifferent to human suffering: which in our gentle & rather sentimental age is a grave reproach. Further, all extension of the functions of government creates patronage, which no parliament or Cabinet dislikes. And the poorer class, those who have voting power but not capital, are naturally inclined to use their votes, in order to get through their votes a better bargain in dealing with the rich than they could make for themselves.

This was what I meant to say in answer to my querists: but I doubt whether the letter will be sent. . . .

21 Dec. 1881: Day very fine & pleasant, except a cold wind: some rain later, but not enough to interfere with shooting . . . 398 head brought in.

. . . Young E. Stanley left us this morning: I gave him £20. He made a favourable impression, being well mannered, natural, and intelligent. I do not see any sign of more than ordinary ability in him, but it is early to judge. He seems to work fairly well for his examinations. He is rather small, but has not done growing. On the whole I am well pleased. How long will it be, 25 or 30 years, before he is master here? And what at that date will be the status of a great English peer?

Very lazy on coming home from shooting: sat in my chair & read for amusement: but there was no work to neglect. . . .

24 Dec. 1881: . . . Talk with Sir W. Thomson on electricity & other possible motive powers: he believes, as some engineers have already said in public, that the steam engine is destined to be superseded by the gas engine, which is not yet sufficiently perfected to work on a large scale, but which in principle is more economical of fuel.

. . . Gave one Hedley Jones £10 to help him to emigrate though strongly believing the fellow to be a rascal. He wrote on both sides, took money from all parties, & was prosecuted on a charge of false pretences, but acquitted. But he is clever, & one of the sort that it is worth paying to get quietly out of the country.

25 Dec. 1881: . . . Rather weary & depressed. No walk, the day being mostly wet, & not very much to do. M. is harassed by never being left alone from morning till night, & my spirits are not habitually up to the mark of a Christmas family party. Yet they are all welcome, & I am glad they are here, though not sorry to escape from them, to the quiet of my own room. . . .

28 Dec. 1881: . . . Ward came with leases to sign, making total new rents for the year just ending £5,902: a remarkable increase, even if times had been good. Assuredly I have no reason to complain, whoever else may. He tells me that the total number of tenants paying rent is as nearly as possible 5,000: of whom 3,000 are holders of leases in towns, about 1,000 agricultural tenants, and another 1,000 cottagers. . . .

29 Dec. 1881: Left early for Preston . . . To the courthouse: we sat from 11.30 to 1.30, the business chiefly routine, though a good deal of money was voted for various local purposes. But there was no serious discussion, & no difference except on points of detail. From 35 to 40 magistrates attended, not a large proportion out of 800, but there would not be room for them if all came, nor anything for them to do. . . . Home at 5.30.

Of public news there is very little. A report of Ld Selborne's illness is contradicted, but he is thought not likely to be able to go on, & there is much speculation as to his successor. Coleridge would naturally be preferred by Gladstone, as a strong High Churchman & Radical: a combination which the Premier especially loves: but he being a peer already has little to gain, & may not care to change a permanent £8,000 a year for a precarious £10,000,. notwithstanding the retiring pension.

Irish affairs show no improvement: but Forster has just adopted a new plan of more stringent police supervision from which he hopes for some results. Hunting is stopped by mobs in several counties: in one place a mob killed a herd of tame deer before the eyes of the owner: & in several places the people have turned out to destroy all the game they could find under the pretext of sending it to the prisoners detained in Kilmainham. The movement against paying rents is spreading, & so far has been successful. The failure of their attempt at conciliation is a blow to the government, who have been hitherto unduly, not to say absurdly, sanguine. I do not think Gladstone would now repeat the speech he delivered in my dining room two months ago.

30 Dec. 1881: . . . Read with pleasure the yearly report of the Liverpool Savings Bank, of which I am a patron: it shows deposits to the amount of £1,939,200, & surplus property £14,000 more. The increase in deposits is £82,374 since last year. Depositors are 72,214. This is satisfactory enough, for Liverpool can scarcely contain more than 120,000 families, & from those must be deducted the rich, who have other investments, & the very poor who cannot be expected to save. It is a better return than I should have anticipated from what is probably the most drunken town in England.

31 Dec. 1881: . . . Sent Sanderson £200 . . .: Lit. Fund £50: Brompton Hospital £10.10.0 & gave Latter £13 to draw upon for the small gifts I make through him. I have left for London charities up to July only £400, which I shall probably exceed.

I end this year happily & peacefully, in good health, without anxiety or trouble of any kind, satisfied with my position, & having nothing to wish for except that no change may come for the worse.

Notes

[1]   W.T. Egerton, 1st Baron Egerton of Tatton (1806–1883), cr. peer 1859. His estate was worth about £32,000 p.a.

[2]   John Tollemache, 1st Baron Tollemache (1805–1890), cr. peer 1876.

[3]   Lady Abercromby, née Lady Julia Duncan, V.A., Lady of the Bedchamber to Queen Victoria 1874–1885; only dau. of Adam 2nd E. of Camperdown (1812–1867) and sister of 3rd E.; m. George, 4th Baron Abercromby (1838–1917) who succ. his father as 4th baron 1852; a source of Court gossip for the diarist.

[4]   Sir C.V. Aitchison (1832–1896), chief commissioner of British Burma 1878–1881.

[5]   Octavia Hill (1838–1912), housing reformer, philanthropist, co-founder of National Trust.

[6] Paley was also the architect of his brother's house, Witherslack, N. Lancs.

[7] Thomas Egerton né Grosvenor, 2nd E. of Wilton (1799–7 March 1882), 2nd s. of Robert, 1st Marquess of Westminster (d. 1845). He m., 1821, Lady Mary Stanley (d. 1858), dau. of 12th E. of Derby. He succ. his grandfather Sir Thomas Egerton, 1st E. of Wilton (d. 1814). His estates, mainly in Lancs., were thought in 1882 to be worth £65,000 p.a.

[8] *Recte* Raggi. Mario Raggi (1821–1907), an Italian, came to London in 1850 and became a leading sculptor, portraying both Gladstone and Disraeli.

[9] Count Gleichen (1833–1891), admiral, prince, and sculptor: properly Prince Victor of Hohenlohe-Langenburg; his mother was half-sister to Queen Victoria: in British navy 1848–1866; governor and constable of Windsor Castle 1867; admiral 1887, but chiefly a leading sculptor.

[10] John Bell (1811–1895), sculptor: produced Wellington Monument (Guildhall) and Guards' Memorial (Waterloo Place).

[11] William Page Wood, 1st Baron Hatherley (1801–1881), cr. peer 1868; lord chancellor 1868–1872; Sunday School teacher.

[12] *Parl Deb., 3*, vol. cclxiii, cols. 941–943 (14 July 1881). A handful of Irish had spent 3 days trying to force ministers to drop the emigration clause, thereby delaying the progress of the land bill as a whole: hence Gladstone's stiff rebuke.

[13] Arthur Penrhyn Stanley (1815–1881), Dean of Westminster 1864–1881; biographer of Arnold, leading Broad Churchman.

[14] Sir Frederick Pollock, 3rd Bart. (1845–1937), jurist; succ. to title 1888; professor of jurisprudence at Oxford 1883–1903; editor-in-chief of *Law Reports* 1895–1935.

[15] James, 7th Earl Stanhope (1880–1967)), 1st Lord of Admiralty 1938–1939.

[16] Philip, 4th Earl (1781–1855), antiquary: Philip, 5th Earl (1805–1875), historian: Arthur, 6th Earl (1838–1905), 1st Church Estates Commissioner: and the baby.

[17] Mary (1792–1864), née Sackville, dau. and co-heiress of 3rd Duke of Dorset; widow of 6th E. of Plymouth; she m. secondly the 1st E. Amherst (1773–1857) as his second wife; with her bro. the 4th D. of Dorset she was from 1815 co-heiress of the Knole estate.

[18] Lady Derby's brother.

[19] Lady Derby's eldest brother.

[20] Lord Odo Russell (1829–1884), diplomatist: s. of Lord George William Russell, who was s. of 6th D. of Bedford. Odo was bro. of 9th D. of Bedford; U.K. rep. at Rome 1858–1870; asst. undersec. at F.O. 1870–1871. In 1884–1885 Derby wrote: 'Except Lyons, we have no better diplomatist . . .' (*Later Diaries*, 101). Odo was amb. at Berlin 1871–1884, where his father had been before him, 1835–1841. Odo was cr. peer 1881 as Lord Ampthill.

[21] John Beresford, 5th Marquess of Waterford (1844–1895), eldest s. of 4th Marquess; succ. his father 1866; lord-lieut. co. Waterford 1874–death; M.P. 1865–1866; army 1862–1869; master of the buckhounds 1885–1886; chairman of Irish Landlords' Committee; took his life by shooting himself after painful injury.

[22] Lt.-Col. Samuel Long (d. 31 August 1881) was a distant relative of the diarist by his first marriage. On 18 April 1825 he had married Louisa Emily Stanley (d. 11 December 1825), 2nd dau. of Charles James Fox Stanley, the 3rd s. of Edward Smith, 13th E. of Derby (1775–1851). Both Longs (assuming he must have remarried) were respected friends and Kentish neighbours until 1881.

[23] Sir Henry George Elliot (1817–1907), ambassador at Constantinople 1867–1877; appointed ambassador to Vienna 31 December 1877; left for Vienna 23 January 1878, where in post till 1884.

[24] Colonel George Abbas Kooli D'Arcy, Governor of the Falklands 1870–1876 (retired). Army career 1837–1858. Assistant private secretary to five successive governors of Bombay; governor of the Gambia 1859–1867, commanding its army in battle against a fanatical sect of Mahomedan negroes. D. Plymouth 22 October 1885 aged 67.

[25] Charles Noel, 8th Earl of Gainsborough (1818–1881): he and his wife became R.C.,1851: succ. 1866.

26   Lionel Edward, 3rd Baron Sackville (1867–1928), whom Derby did not expect to survive boyhood, married in 1890 his cousin Josephine Victoria Sackville-West (d. 1936), mother of V. Sackville-West, who thus succeeded to one of the greatest English houses.

27   Donald James Mackay, 11th Baron Reay (1839–1921), governor of Bombay 1885–1890 and 1st president of British Academy (1902–1907); b. The Hague and educ. Leiden; settled in England 1875; cr. U.K. baron 1881; under-sec. for India 1894–1895.

28   George Hay, 8th Marquess of Tweeddale (1787–1876), A.D.C. to Wellington in Peninsular War; gov. of Madras 1842–1848; cr. field-marshal 1875; his dau. m. Peel's son Sir Robert; succ. his father 1851; leading freemason; succ. by his eldest surviving s.

29   William St. Lawrence, 4th E. of Howth (in the Irish peerage) (1827–1909), was granted a U.K. barony, as Baron Howth of Howth. Since he was unmarried, it was probable in 1881 that all his honours would die with him, as in fact occurred. But since his mother was from the great house of Clanricarde, and his Irish titles were very ancient, it is likely that some sort of gesture towards the Irish landlords was intended. Howth became a Unionist in 1886, having been a Liberal M.P. 1868–1874.

30   Sir Harcourt Johnstone, 3rd Bart., 1st Baron Derwent (1829–1916), M.P. (Lib.) Scarborough March 1869–1880. Cr. peer October 1881.

31   Sir Dudley Marjoribanks, 1st Baron Tweedmouth (1820–1893), partner in Coutts Bank, director of East India Co., and M.P. (Lib.) Berwick 1853–1859, 1859–1868, 1874–1881. Cr. bart. 1866, peer 1881. Left personalty of £650,000 net.

32   Sir Henry James Tufton (1844–1926), succ. father as 2nd bart. 1871; cr. Baron Hothfield 1881, but a Unionist by 1890: his father, born in France in 1813 at Verdun, was Sir R. Tufton, 1st Bart. (1813–1871), the illegit. s. of the last E. of Thanet, and inherited about 40,000 acres.

33   James Lowther (1840–1903), M.P. (Cons.) York 1865–1880 (defeated), Lincs. N. September 1881–November 1885; Isle of Thanet 1888–death. Minor office 1868, under-sec. for colonies 1874–February 1878; chief sec. for Ireland 1878–1880.

34   Col. George Tomline (d. 1889), M.P. (Cons.) Sudbury 1840–1841, Shrewsbury (LC) 1841–1847, 1852–1868, Grimsby 1868–1874.

35   Durham N. by-election, 2 September 1881: Cons. 5548, Lib. 4896. (1880 general election, Lib. 6233/5901, Cons. 5092). The Cons. candidate was the same on both occasions.

36   John Campbell, 1st baron Campbell (1779–1861), lord chancellor June 1959–1861; of humble origin, as Fife minister's son; left grammar school for university at 11; chief justice 1850–1859.

37   David Ogilvy, 5th E. of Airlie (1826–25 September 1881), who succ. 1849; rep. peer (S.) 1850–1881 and Lord High Commissioner to the Kirk 1872–1873; m. Henrietta (b. 1830), 2nd dau. of Edward, 2nd Lord Stanley of Alderley, and a Whig hostess.

38   Reginald Sackville (né West), 7th E. De La Warr (1817–1896), Rector of Withyam, Sussex, 1841–1865, and Chaplain to the Queen 1846–1865; became Sackville–West 1843, and Sackville 1871; on his mother's death, 1870, became Baron Buckhurst; in 1873 he succ. his bro. as E. De La Warr, though the Knole estate passed to his younger brother. A Conservative.

39   At Knowsley.

40   H.H. Francis Paul Charles Louis Alexander, Duke of Teck, G.C.B., G.C.V.O. (1837–1900), who m. H.R.H. Princess Mary Adelaide (d. 1897), younger dau. of H.R.H. Adolphus Frederick, 1st Duke of Cambridge, son of George III; they were parents of Queen Mary.

41   Lord Henry Lennox (1821–1886), Disraeli's boyfriend, held minor office, was a Tory M.P., and a promoter of dubious companies. J.O. Lever (1824–1897) was M.P. Galway 1859–1865 (defeated) and 1880–1885 (retired); a shipping speculator and seeker after subsidy.

42   Jacob Bright (1821–1899), bro. of John Bright; M.P. (Lib.) Manchester 1867–1874, 1876–1885, and for S.W. Manchester 1886–1895.

43   Thomas Sexton (1848–1932), at this time Home Rule M.P. for Sligo Co. (1880–1885).

[44]   Probably T.P. O'Connor (1848–1929), journalist; M.P. (Home Rule) Galway 1880–1885; M.P. Liverpool (Scotland division) 1885–1929; first president, Board of Film Censors, 1917.

[45]   For this visit, see Gladstone, *Diaries*, 26–29 October 1881, esp. 26 October, n. 4: 'As we drove, we talked of Ld. Derby's being Lib. P.M. Papa expects it more than I do.'

[46]   Cf. Gladstone's diary, 27 October: '. . . Much pleased with this spacious house . . .' and G. to Spencer, 27 October: 'I have been holding forth today in Derby's dining room to a very hearty Liverpool deputation . . . with a view of stamping in the proper public impression.'

[47]   '. . . Longer walk with Ld D mg . . .' (diary, 28 October, but no other comment by G.).

[48]   Perhaps Margaret Lonsdale, *Sister Dora. A biography*, Kegan Paul, London, 1880. Dorothy Wyndlow Pattison (1832–1878), the sister of Mark Pattison, was Sister Dora, a nurse in Walsall.

[49]   Sir Henry Brand, 1st Vt. Hampden (1814–1892), speaker 1872–1884; cr. peer 1884.

[50]   Samuel Whitbread (1830–1915), M.P. (Lib.) Bedford 1852–1895 (retired); educ. Rugby and Cambridge; m. dau. of E. of Chichester; a Lord of the Admiralty 1859–1863.

[51]   J.G. Dodson, 1st Baron Monk-Bretton (1825–1897), M.P. (Lib.) 1857–1884; deputy speaker 1865–1874; cabinet minister 1884; cr. peer 1884; Lib. Unionist from 1886.

[52]   Sir Andrew B. Walker (1824–1893), wealthy brewer, benefactor of Liverpool, founder of Walker Art Gallery.

[53]   Alexander Macdonald (d. 31 October 1881). Miners' leader; M.P. (Lib.) Stafford 1874–death.

[54]   Lately bereaved.

[55]   Gerald V. Wellesley (1809–1882), dean of Windsor, 1854–1882; 3rd s. of 1st Baron Cowley.

[56]   Hugh Pearson (1817–1882), canon of Windsor 1876–1882; friend of Dean Stanley.

[57]   William Rathbone Greg (1809–1881), comptroller of the Stationery Office 1864–1877; writer on divers topics, social, religious, and economic.

[58]   Thomas Salt (1830–1904), banker, of Stafford; M.P. (Cons.) Stafford 1859–1865, June 1869–1880 (defeated), November 1881–1885 (defeated), 1886–1892 (retired); cr. bart. 1899; parl. sec. to local government board January 1876–April 1880.

[59]   George Howell (1833–1910), bricklayer; trades union leader; sec. of the Reform League 1864–1869; sec. of the T.U.C. 1871–1875; M.P. N.E. Bethnal Green 1885–1895.

[60]   H.R.H. Prince Leopold (1853–28 March 1884), the 4th s. of Queen Victoria, was made Duke of Albany May 1881. On 27 April 1882 he was to wed Princess Hélène (b. 1861), dau. of the late George Victor, reigning Prince of Waldeck and Pyrmont. On the death of Alfred, Duke of Edinburgh, in 1900, their son became reigning Prince of Saxe-Coburg-Gotha.

[61]   William Rathbone Greg, *Miscellaneous Essays*, Trübner, London, 1881.

[62]   Sir Edward Sullivan, 1st bart. (1822–1885), lord chancellor of Ireland 1883–1885: Irish M.P. (Lib.) 1865–1870, judge, and law officer.

[63]   Sir R.J. Phillimore, 1st bart. (1810–1885), judge, High Churchman, intimate of Gladstone; judge from 1867; cr. bart. 1883.

[64]   Alexander Lindsay, 25th E. of Crawford (1812–13 December 1880), who succ. his father 1869. He died in Florence and was buried in Scotland, whence his body was stolen 3 December 1881, and where it was eventually rediscovered 18 July 1882. The episode remains a mystery.

[65]   Moore was Stuart A. Moore (1842–1907), legal antiquary. He produced *A Calendar of the Muniments of the Right Hon. The Earl of Derby. Compiled by Stuart A. Moore F.S.A.* London, priv. pr. 1894. The muniments, though calendared several times before 1844, were seriously confused. There was (and is) a distinct lack of older muniments. Most of what was listed by Moore is now in the Lancashire (and Liverpool) Record Offices.

[66]   (Sir) Francis Adams (1826–1889), acting minister at Paris 1874–1881; minister at Berne 1881–1888; educ. Rugby: small Lancs. landowner.

[67]   Walter Powell, M.P. (Cons.) Malmesbury December 1868–10 December 1881, when lost in a balloon: educ. Rugby.

[68]   All these were Whigs. It is notable how easily and quickly Derby gave up seeing Tory parliamentarians.

1882

January–June

1 Jan. 1882: . . . The rental stands higher than it ever did, new leases bringing in £5,900 in 1881, and in 1880 over £7,000. It cannot now stop short of reaching £220,000.

. . . The last year has passed quietly & prosperously: I have continued well, have suffered no misfortune or trouble, engaged in no quarrel, and generally have nothing to regret. My public appearances have been sufficient to keep me from being forgotten, and to give some sense of public usefulness. Lady D.'s health though not restored is improved: & her spirits do not grow more depressed. In regard of outward circumstances I have nothing to wish for. My health is better at 55 than it was at 35: I do not recollect having felt really unwell more than one day last year & that was from eating or drinking something that disagreed. But I am conscious of an increased disinclination to bodily exertion, which must be guarded against.

I have added to the family estates: at Knowsley, The Hazels, 160 acres: at Witley, 190 acres: at Fairhill, over 200 acres: in the Fylde and home estates, nothing important: in all I suppose the addition has been 600 acres. Nothing has been sold except small patches to railway companies, not enough to diminish appreciably the area of the property.

The family papers are being arranged, catalogued, & put in order for the first time under the care of Mr. Moore. When this is finished, I shall have to consider the expediency of putting any of them into print, with a view to greater security.

In regard of public affairs, the outlook is not altogether pleasant. We are quiet abroad, & there seems no present reason why we should not remain so: the South African trouble is for the moment at an end, though not unlikely to break out again: Indian finance continues bad, but the country is at peace, & peace ought to bring prosperity. At home our troubles are more serious. Ireland is deeply discontented: the no-rent movement has spread all over the south & west: the whole machinery of coercion is being put in motion – arrests, seizures of newspapers & arms, dispersion of public meetings – quite rightly & necessarily, yet so far with little effect. The Land Act has not yet conciliated the people, while it has injured & exasperated the owners of the soil. We are as far as ever from a settlement: & the mind of the nation appears to be more & more fixed on Home Rule, the one thing which we cannot grant without breaking up the Empire. Some loss of credit to the government has ensued – not perhaps justly but inevitably – but their immense majority can bear some diminution, and no organised attack by the opposition has a chance of success. The feeling against Gladstone in the upper & part of the middle class is intensely bitter, and he is distrusted by many (I suspect) even of his own colleagues. No reasonable person believes him to be consciously unscrupulous, but his mind is so framed that whatever is in the interest of his party or of his policy is apt to seem to him justifiable. How far he is really a genuine democrat is not clear: his dislike & jealousy of riches & rank as a social force are curiously interwoven with respect for the authority of the church. But it is thought that he would go all lengths in the line of increasing democratic power, were he not held back by the fear of breaking up his party. He talks much & often of his wish to retire: whether really meaning it, or in order to lessen envy, is not clear. If he retires it is as certain as anything can be in politics that his successor must be either Granville or Hartington: the former if his health will bear it, which seems doubtful.

In England & Scotland there is political quiet: no question seems to occupy the public mind. Trade is reviving, the revenue promises well, & only the farmers are grumbling, nor even they in all districts. The Irish precedent has affected them to some extent, & fixity of tenure is being claimed for them by some of their advocates, but this demand is not taken up by politicians except a few of the extreme sort. . . .

3 Jan. 1882: Victor Stanley[1] left us: he seems a promising lad. Gave him £5.

. . . A reporter came from Lee & Nightingale[2] to take my speech.

There came to stay, Sir B. & Ly Brett[3], C. Münster[4], his son & daughter: Mr. Lowell[5]: Ld & Ly Crawford[6]: Mr. Thornton, son of Sir E. Thornton[7].

Rather nervous all day at thought of speech tomorrow.

4 Jan. 1882: Letter from Ld Halifax to Ly D. alarmed lest Gladstone should propose anything violent in regard of English land, which he thinks him disposed to do, but on what ground I cannot say. He wants me to refer to the subject, which indeed I had intended.

Took out Sir B. Brett & Mr. Lowell to walk in the park early: in afternoon shut myself up with notes for speech, & went over it several times.

At 6.00 set out for Liverpool, & met Sefton[8] at the Reform Club: where from 150 to 200 dined. Sefton was in the chair, & said what he had to say well & briefly. I was very warmly received, & spoke about 50 minutes, keeping in the main to the substance of my written text, but enlarging upon it a little. Dalhousie[9] followed me, & was not happy, as I thought, not having much to say & saying it rather diffusely. .. I got home about midnight, glad to have finished the affair, & fairly satisfied with my own performance . . .

5 Jan. 1882: Ld & Ly Crawford left us. He seems ill, & worried by the extraordinary outrage practised on his family, of which the papers have been full: I mean the abstraction of his father's embalmed body from the mausoleum where it lay. No clue has been obtained as yet: the most probable explanation is that blackmail was the object & that, finding it was not to be had, the body has been destroyed. Another story is that it is an act of revenge, the work of a poor man who conceives himself to have a claim to the family title & estates, & has gone crazy, or nearly so, at being unable to make it good. Ld C. left us sooner than he meant, having been called away by a story that his grandfather's body had been carried off in the same way as his father's – a report which he did not much believe but was anxious to verify.

It seems that his father, absorbed in literature & study, has left upwards of 80,000 volumes in his library, but has much impaired the estate, so that the present owner has only about £3,000 a year to live on as yet: but it will increase as charges drop off.

. . . Death announced of Bernal Osborne[10], the wit, sometimes the buffoon, of the II. of Commons for 20 years & more. He was a Jew by descent, married an Irish heiress, & once or twice held minor offices, but his forte did not lie in official work. He was a bold rough speaker, sometimes coarse in his wit, but usually telling: his influence was increased by a rather ostentatious display of independence, which enhanced the value of his support when given. He was popular in private life among men, not I imagine among women: a diner-out & fond of company. Though he & Ld Beaconsfield belonged to opposite parties, there was a good deal of sympathy between them, arising out of common origin, & some similarity of mental qualities – though of course Osborne made no pretension to be a great man in politics or a leader. The present House would be less dull than it is if a few men like him sat in it: but they are not of the sort that the democracy will take to. A satirist & a joker of jokes is not usually thought to be 'earnest' enough for working men with a social ideal, or safe enough for voters of the shopkeeping class.

Another death is announced – that of 'Jim' Macdonald[11], well known in society, and who served with credit in the Crimean War. I saw nothing of him, except casually, in later days: but at the old racing parties here (1840-1850) he was a constant visitor, along with the Chesterfields, Bradfords, Anson, & that fast & fashionable set. Very lively times they were, but when my sister came out[12] it was thought that the style of things was not quite such as a young girl should become familiar with, & the parties ceased, or were made up of men only.

6 Jan. 1882: . . . Much talk with Sir Balliol Brett as to the present state of the legal profession. He says that there is a difficulty in finding good men for judges: promotion has been rapid of late, the best of the seniors have been picked out already, & those youngest men who are in the largest practice object to take a judgeship until they have made money enough for their families. He believes the gains of the bar were never greater, though perhaps no one counsel is doing as much as Bethell[13] or Cairns. A Mr. Davy[14] of the Chancery bar is making over £20,000 a year: Mr. C. Russell[15] perhaps as much: several over £10,000: & none of them will give up $\frac{1}{3}$ or $\frac{1}{2}$ of their income for the dignity of the bench. For himself, he said frankly that what he should like would be one of the new legal life peerages. He hinted that the prospect of the chancellorship might once have tempted him, but he had no thought of it now. He did not in the least know who would succeed to the vacant place if Ld Selborne (who has been much out of health of late) were to knock up. Coleridge would not willingly resign a permanent for a temporary post: James[16], he said, dislikes responsibility, & would not take that or any judicial office, liking his present place better: Harcourt is supposed to wish for it, but no one except himself thinks him competent: his practice has been all at the parliamentary bar, & he has no law. Still the judicial duties are few, & the temptation to him of reviving an old family peerage might be strong. Jessel[17], the Master of the Rolls, Sir Balliol thought about the ablest lawyer who could be named: but his Jewish faith would be against him in the Lords, & his manners are uncouth, not to say brutal. This, I think, was the substance of our talk.

7 Jan. 1882: The Bretts left us, to the general regret . . . Mr. & Mrs. Pilkington of Roby Hall dined with us . . . Ld & Ly Dalhousie came to stay: also Mr. [Eustace] Balfour[18] & Ly Frances Balfour[19], a daughter of the Duke of Argyll & very like him.

. . . Took a vapour bath before dinner: a practice which I think useful when the short days & wet weather make much walking, & free perspiration, difficult.

My speech of Wednesday has been much criticised in the papers, favourably on the whole, though it is amusing to see the perplexity of party writers at finding in a speech delivered on a party occasion no attack on the opposition, nor praise of the Cabinet, but simply suggestions as to what ought to be done. – I note that the Liberal journals are disposed to contend that the closing of debates ought to be voted by a bare majority, so that no opposition to any measure should be carried on longer than those criticised like it to last: in my mind a despotic rather than a liberal proposal. But it is only one sign among many of the disposition increasingly shown by 'advanced' radicals to enforce their ideas by coercive means: of which the often proposed anti-liquor legislation is another instance. I suppose this is everywhere the true temper of democracy: since men who are at once uneducated & in earnest are by habit of mind intolerant of difference. And, in the present instance, it is likely enough that a minority not able to resist by votes the passing of measures which it dislikes may deliberately resort to the tactics of impeding all legis-lation, so as at least to delay them for a few years. But the mischief of this is not great: the life of a nation is long: & in the present almost apathetic temper of the public the putting off of county elective boards, or municipal reform in London, would excite no anger.

Exports of last year are £233 million, a large increase. Imports £395 million, a falling off from 1880, when they were £411 m. But the figures show a marked beginning of improvement. . . .

9 Jan. 1882: Walk with Dalhousie to The Hazels, where Broomfield[20] was in attendance, & went carefully over the ground, marking out extensions of clumps, etc.

Walk in afternoon on the terrace, 3 miles.

Ward came to me with leases to sign. Examining his book, I find the new leases signed in the last three years to give: in 1879, £2,900: in 1880, £7,600: in 1881, £5,900: total, with small figures added, nearly £16,500.

. . . Ward took the opportunity of asking for an increase of his own salary to £500: as to which I gave no immediate answer, preferring to consider it at leisure. He has done well, & put the accounts into order: but he has been already raised once. –Spoke to him about getting an accurate return of the total area of the estates, which at present we have not, that made by Moult some time ago being rough & conjectural. I believe them to include a little over 70,000 acres in all, but there is no certainty.

Saw in the papers a notice of sale in Yorkshire, unusual from its magnitude: Swinton park in Yorkshire, with over 22,000 acres, yielding £12,000 a year . . . I shall watch this transaction with curiosity: for purchases on so large a scale are rare.

Cabinets have begun: the newspapers are full of guesses & gossip. It is believed that Gladstone has decided on *clôture* pure & simple: he will have his hands full if it is so.

One very awkward question which will not keep long is whether Parnell (to whom the freedom of the city of Dublin has been voted) shall be kept in gaol or released. The diffi-culties either way are serious. If liberated, he comes out without having made any submission, & practically victorious: for the party which he leads is as active & as mischievous as ever: in fact, the government will have acknowledged themselves defeated so far as he is concerned: if he is kept in, the Irish, & possibly a good many of the English radicals, too, will scream indignantly at the notion of detaining a leading Irish M.P. while Parliament is in session, & while Irish ideas are being discussed. The position of the Cabinet in regard to Ireland is not pleasant: conciliation, their first policy, has failed utterly: and as yet coercion has not been more successful. The fault is, I think, not theirs, for it is difficult to see what they could do beyond what they have done: but they have increased their own difficulty by obstinately persisting in an optimistic view of the situation: an obvious mistake in tactics, for their interest lay the other way: they should have magnified the risk rather than lessened it, so as to gain the more credit if they dealt with it successfully, & less discredit if they failed.

10 Jan. 1882: Ride early: rent day dinner at 2.00: we came in towards the end of it at 3.00, & I made the usual speech to the Knowsley villagers & small tenants. They had had full as much beer as was good for them, & though cordial in their reception were disorderly & noisy: One drunken fellow insisting on shouting 'Order' till he was put out. I have not of late years seen any sign of excess, & suspect there must have been some mismanagement.

. . . Sent £5 apiece to the Westminster Hospital, Cancer Hospital, & Early Closing Assocn.

. . . The newspapers are full of an eccentric manifesto by the old Emperor of Germany: in which he asserts his right to the personal direction of affairs, objecting to the popular reading of the constitution according to which ministerial responsibility makes the minister & not the sovereign, be considered as the author of the measures proposed. . . . It is curiously like what Albert would have written, had he dared to speak out. In fact, the leading idea is identical with his: that the sovereign ought to be the real head of his or her Cabinet.

11 Jan. 1882: The Balfours left us on their way to Canada: where they stay with Ld Lorne[21], in the absence of the princess. They are both agreeable & lively in society: he by profession an architect, though not much employed as yet: she a daughter of the D. of Argyll, with something of her father's brains, but without his conceit.

. . . Second rent-day dinner, attended by the larger tenants . . . They were sober & orderly . . . I made them a speech on matters connected with land: very well received.

. . . We have been continuously occupied in receiving society, M. & I, since the second week in Dec. &, though all has gone off pleasantly, we are neither of us sorry to rest.

In the papers, no considerable event. Sir J. Holker[22], the late Attorney General, is appointed to one of the judicial vacancies, as a 'Lord Justice': a sensible act on the part of the Chancellor, since he thereby secures a strong lawyer for the bench, & takes away one of the opposition speakers from the H. of Commons. My brother has delivered a speech at Blackpool, not as able or effective as some of his earlier utterances: but singularly fair & temperate in style & substance so much so as to make it clear that he is not inclined to commit himself to indiscriminate opposition: which in the interest of the family I am glad of.

12 Jan. 1882: Ride early: walk in afternoon, arranging a speech for Saturday . . .

Mrs. Burton[23] having represented herself as in difficulty for want of £100, I offer to lend her the amount: not to be repaid.

Wrote to A.D.[24]

Heard more of the Swinton park estate: it belongs to a Mr. Danby, a descendant of a very old family, but who has passed all his life in Australia, & has no wish to return home. He is specially anxious to keep it unbroken . . . the idea of purchase runs in my head, for the country round is picturesque, the place itself is very fine . . . an estate of 22,000 acres is not often in the market . . . 'Why wish for any other place in the north when you have got Knowsley?' a friend might ask . . . But Knowsley is even now scarcely in the country,

& it is quite on the cards that if the prosperity of Lancashire continues, & Liverpool increases as it is doing now, it may be no more a country place than Holland House in London or Heaton near Manchester . . .

13 Jan. 1882: . . . Gladstone has been delivering a speech of an hour or more to his Hawarden tenants at a dinner: chiefly on the question of land, but vague & leaving matters nearly where they were[25]. . . .

16 Jan. 1882: . . . Sefton tells me that it is proposed to print & circulate 30,000 copies of the speech I made at Liverpool on the 4th.

Two seats are vacant, & may be contested. One is Preston, where Sir J. Holker has retired to be made a Lord Justice, but it is certain that the Conservatives, reinforced by the Irish, are there in a majority, & probably there will be no fight. Raikes[26] is the Conservative candidate. Ayrton[27] is talked of as the Liberal if any one stands.

The other constituency is the N. Riding of Yorkshire, vacant by the death of Lord Helmsley[28]: the Liberal party in that division have put up a tenant farmer, a Mr. Rowlandson[29], locally popular, but who stands in opposition to the landlords: as a natural result, some of the latter hold aloof, & will support the rival candidate, a brother of Ld Downe[30]. It is no good sign, if our party divisions become class divisions also: which in the matter of land they seem tending to be.

Death of Sir R. Malins[31] announced: he had lately retired: I knew him well in H. of C. He was an honest, well intentioned man, but heavy & tactless as a speaker. As a judge he meant well, but his indignation against what seemed to him injustice often led his judgment astray: he would strain the law, & create a dangerous precedent, to avoid pronouncing a decision which bore hardly on the party concerned. In other words, he set himself above the law. But, though blamed on this ground, & often ridiculed, he was respected & not disliked.

Report of Manchester savings bank, of which I am a trustee: it has over £1,800,000 of assets, an increase of £125,000 from last year. The depositors are over 60,000, or about one for every two families in the district served.

17 Jan. 1882: Into Liverpool early for sessions. Another dull sunless day, but dry & not cold.

Sat till 5.30, when adjourned. The calendar lighter than usual, only 53 cases . . . the longest sentence passed was one of 2 years . . . the average of 21 cases 9 months each.

Cross appeared on the bench, which he has not done since he was Home Secretary. We had some friendly talk about things in general. He expected a sharp fight over the question of parliamentary procedure. We talked about local boards & county government, & I found he took the same view that I do, that the elected county boards would have very little to do: since the outlay on police & that on lunatic asylums are practically controlled by the Home Office, schools are managed by school boards, highways by special boards, & poor relief by the guardians. It is possible that the care of highways may be transferred to the new tribunal, but schools & poor law administration scarcely will be. – If this is his view (& he seemed sincere in it) why has so much difficulty been made about a simple matter? He thought (as also I do) that the question of municipal government for London would give far more trouble, from the great complexity of the interests involved.

18 Jan. 1882: Sessions again: sat from 10.00 till 6.25. Nothing unusual or in the least interesting in the cases tried. The longest sentence was 12 months.

... Commins[32], the Home Rule M.P., is vulgar & violent at meetings, but with a wig & gown on he has always behaved well when I have heard him.

19 Jan. 1882: Sessions again: appeals from 10.00 till 4.00 ... Business went off quickly towards the end of the sessions, most of the counsel being engaged to attend the assizes just begun at Manchester. Fees are higher there – & when that is the case the cases at sessions are rapidly disposed of: prosecutions abandoned where there is a conflict of evidence, & prisoners induced to plead guilty where they have no reasonable chance of escape.

Cross said on Tuesday that the importance of sessions to the bar had greatly diminished: he himself had in early years often carried away as much as £100 from one sessions, whereas nothing of the kind can be done now. This he ascribes in part to the increased powers of summary jurisdiction given to magistrates: in part to the greater simplicity of the law as regards settlement, rating, etc. We had as usual over 30 lawyers in attendance, of whom not more than 5 or 6 made anything, & they but little.

I spoke to Cross about appointing a stipendiary to do the quarter sessions work for all the county – a plan I have long favoured – but he says in the north it would not be popular & obviously is against it.

20 Jan. 1882: A quiet day, except for the accumulation of letters – over 20 – that had to be worked off ... Ride early, but not with much pleasure, the ground being too heavy for a gallop: though little rain has fallen of late, the weather has been absolutely sunless, so that it does not dry. It is noted all over England that the barometer has stood higher than for 40 years: nearly up to 31°.

Walk in afternoon on the measured terrace, a habit which grows upon me. Where walking is taken merely for exercise's sake, there is a certain pleasure in not needing to think where one goes, & in doing exactly the distance intended.

English politics remain much as they were. Childers has made an excellent speech on army matters, explaining his changes, half the credit or responsibility of which he gives to my brother: whether truly, or to disarm opposition, I do not know, but either way it is good policy. Lytton has delivered another speech, which curiously contrasts with that of Childers: it is clever, even eloquent: but otherwise such as might have come from Randolph Churchill: a mere piece of party invective, not worthy of an ex-viceroy. – Irish affairs seem to go on as before. It is settled that Parnell & his friends are not to be released for the opening of parliament. – The land court is beginning to hear appeals, but no definite principle or precedent has yet been laid down. The question of parliamentary procedure is much discussed in the newspapers, & evidently it is that on which the first fight of the session will come off.

21 Jan. 1882: Ride early, walk later with M.

Read to her a curious, & to my mind quite just, criticism in the *Economist* on the decreasing popularity of the H. of Commons which I believe to be a fact, & which the writer treats of as a fact generally recognised. The causes ascribed are two: first, the growth of journalism in all its branches, one result of which is that debates seldom contain any argument or statement of importance that has not already been dealt with by the press, & hence less interest attaches to them than of old, when they were the chief source of political information. This is inevitable, & on the whole it is a gain: the second cause is the entrance into the House of a class of men for whom the old traditions of parliament have no meaning or interest: who are not bound by its unwritten laws, & for whom therefore definite rules must be laid down – a necessary but imperfect substitute for customary obligations of courtesy. So far the writer, with whom I agree: but he might have added something more: that exactly in proportion as the House has become more representative, as its members embody the feeling of the average middle class or the average democracy, so less interest is taken in them. The constituent feels that he could say what his member has been saying, & say it quite as well. Why should be look up to the politician who is socially his equal, & politically his servant? I do not believe that the aristocracy will recover its lost power, or that the democracy can be anything but the governing class: but the body which professes specially to represent it seems likely to exercise less power than formerly. And the marked tendency among the masses is to choose a dictator – to take some one leading man, Gladstone, Gambetta, whoever he may be, & insist on his being followed blindly by all who are elected as his supporters.

22 Jan. 1882: Walk in afternoon with Hale . . . In general, the result of 20 years' work in setting things straight is showing, & Knowsley is more agreeable to the eye than ever it was in my time, notwithstanding increase of smoke.

In a volume of extracts[33] from Ld Beaconsfield's writings & speeches, got up by Ld Rowton, I found a curious blunder: a long & well known passage from one of Macaulay's essays, quoted in *Henrietta Temple*, & now reproduced as though it had been Disraeli's own. I thought it worth while to write a note to Lord Barrington to point this out.

Accepted from Dr. Watts an invitation to join the Manchester Reform Club as an honorary member.

Letter from Mr. Jesse Collings[34] of Birmingham in which he explains & vindicates his plan of enabling local authorities to buy up estates to be divided among workingmen. This he justifies on the ground that it is essential to bring back the working class to the soil, & check overcrowding in towns. He dwells a good deal on the growth among the poor of a feeling of jealousy at the spectacle of great inequalities of fortune – and I dare say he is right, though the existence of such a feeling is better not acknowledged in public. He would not allow buyers of land under his conditions to mortgage, but he does allow them to sell. I answer his letter in one of which copy is kept, to the effect that I take no objection of principle to his plan, but see two main difficulties: one that land cannot be bought to yield more than 2½%, & if a town or county is to invest in land, borrowing for the purpose at 3½%, the loss will be considerable: the other, that land bought by working men will always go back to the capitalist, unless sale as well as mortgage is forbidden: &, if it is so forbidden, the system is one of perpetual entail not on a family but on a class.

23 Jan. 1882: See Ward . . . I settled to increase his salary as requested to £500, which is only fair, as he has done much more than poor old Moult ever did, & the rents to be collected have increased from £180,000 to £208,000. He is active, able, & understands business: but I am sorry to see that there is a growing jealousy of him on Hale's part which may give trouble.

Walk early with M. Walk later, sharply, on the terrace, 4 miles. Vapour bath afterwards.

I have been plagued all this day with a sort of nervous lowness of spirits, absolutely without reason, from which I suffer at times & which is disagreeable, though I think it rather sharpens than dulls the wits. I believe it to be gouty, & best walked & sweated out.

24 Jan. 1882: Bright sunny day, the first we have had: the weather quite extraordinarily warm, insomuch that primroses have been sent here from Fairhill.

. . . Odd incident in yesterday's *Times*. In the middle of the report of a speech by Sir W. Harcourt . . . is interpolated a line, wholly irrelevant, & ending with a word too grossly indecent to be put in print. It looks like a practical joke of some one employed in the printing at the expense of the editor. I do not remember anything of the sort having happened before. The newspaper was as far as possible suppressed, but the early editions had gone out before the mistake was detected.

25 Jan. 1882: Thick heavy weather again, & east wind. Though there is no cold, I have seldom known even the Lancashire climate so persistently gloomy. It is impossible not to feel the influence of it in some degree, & the prospect of a speech for tomorrow does not make things pleasanter.

. . . See Hale, & talk with him about one Powell, the tenant of Finch farm, who is in arrears 4 years' rent. He ought to pay £170, but has managed to get behind with his rent to the amount of £700. He was under notice to quit, but I have respited him for a year, not for his own sake, but to avoid bother & trouble . . .

. . . Received the annual list of Grillions Club, of which I have now been a member for 25 years. We are 208 members in all, of whom about 80 are living. Our oldest member is Ld Harrowby[35], who was elected nearly 62 years ago. I chose, as is always done, six candidates for the year: my six were: F.A.S. [the diarist's brother], Dalhousie, Dilke, Penzance[36], M. Arnold, & Trevelyan.

26 Jan. 1882: The North Riding of Yorkshire, after a sharp contest, has been won by the Conservative candidate: the numbers, 8,100 odd against 7,700 odd. The winner is a brother of Lord Downe: the loser a tenant farmer & small owner of land. Unusual interest has attached to this election, not only because the constituency is large, but because several Whig peers – Lord Grey, Lord Zetland, & the Duke of Cleveland, have openly seceded – not indeed from their party, but from the cause of the candidate chosen by it. Mr. Rowlandson, though as far as I can see a man personally of moderate opinions, was understood to represent the 'Farmers' Alliance' which is in fact an anti-landlord alliance, & hence the fight became one of class rather than of party simply.

I do not regret the result: on the contrary, I think it good: first because a tenant revolt is not a thing for landowners to encourage: & next because the government is strong enough, & an increase of numerical power would rather increase its difficulties than diminish them, causing more to be expected, & exciting the ultra party mischievously. There is in reality no victory on either side, for the opposition have only kept what they had before.

I agree to give Mr. Prescott £100 for his Upholland school, subject to certain conditions. I decline a request to help the Liverpool Council of Education farther, thinking I have done enough for the town in that line.

. . . Left at 1.30 . . . Reached Bury at 3.30. With the rector [Hornby] to his house, where talk with him & Mrs. H. till it was time to dress. At 5.30 went to the dinner of the 8th L.R.V. in uniform, & unexpectedly found it pleasant. Sat next Col. Mellor, the host,

& Col. Gillespie, in whom I found a student and critic of history, rather to my surprise. We talked agreeably enough: leaving at 8.00 for the distribution of prizes, which lasted till 10.00. Then home with Hornby, & supper, with cigarettes, an indulgence rare with me, & from which I expected a headache but it did not come.

27 Jan. 1882: Having business in Manchester at 2.00, & none earlier, I walked in from Bury, 8 miles or more: the road excellent for walking, but very dull & smoky country all round, except just about Prestwich.

. . . Meeting of the County Rifle Assocn.: I took the chair, made a short speech, & explained the position of the society, which is not satisfactory . . . though there was a little conversational discussion, nothing disagreeable was said. . . .

28 Jan. 1882: Talk, which began casually, with Margaret about her future: she discusses it quietly & rationally, saying that she thinks a single life will suit her best, that it is her wish & purpose to lead one, that she is quite aware that personal feeling for someone who really pleased her might lead to a change of intention, but that she does not expect, & certainly does not wish, that this should happen. I did not dissent or dissuade, partly because it is useless, partly also because I really believe that, with her independence & singularity of character, she is not likely to find any man whose tastes would agree with hers. Therefore it is not at all clear to me that marriage in her case would be a desirable experiment. . . .

30 Jan. 1882: . . . So ends a stay at Knowsley of eight weeks & a day, during which we have been almost perpetually occupied with receiving company, local business, speeches, etc. I have seldom had less of a really idle time. . . .

1 Feb. 1882: . . . Among other speeches, a long one from Sir C. Dilke delivered to his constituents, which I note only because there was a persistent attempt by the Irish party to create a riot, which so far succeeded that the rioters took possession of the room, & had to be cleared out by a strong body of police[37]. One of the fruits of Irish disaffection is that we are unable to hold a political meeting in London, or indeed in any great town, without the probability of organised disturbance.

2 Feb. 1882: Heavy fog through all the morning: read & wrote by lamplight.

. . . Note that Hale wants me to buy the tithes of Burscough, which are or are likely to be for sale: I say I will consider, & am really not unwilling: they can then be merged in the rent, & I shall have added £1,000 a year to the value of the estate.

In papers, report of a meeting held yesterday in the City to protest against the persecution of the Jews by Russia: old Ld Shaftesbury & Cardinal Manning the leading speakers. Politicians for the most part kept away, I think wisely: the government as not wishing to give to the movement an appearance of being inspired by them: the opposition, lest they should seem to be taking a factious advantage. This is right enough on both sides. But it is remarked with some reason that the Liberal journalists & speakers who now dwell on the necessity of caution, the danger of doing more harm than good by officious interference, & so forth, are precisely those for whom no exaggeration was too reckless, & no language too violent, when the massacres of Bulgarians by Turks were in question. Even the Premier himself is believed to think that the Jews are not wholly innocent victims: & that an eastern Christian is too pious a person to commit murder without reason. – The truth I believe to be that there is quite as much of socialism as of fanaticism in the anti-Jewish movement. The Jew is prudent, saving, & accustomed to manage money: the peasant is lazy, ignorant, improvident: the one lends, the other borrows: until the working class throughout eastern Europe finds itself in the power of a race which it hates & looks down upon. The same feeling, produced by the same cause, prevails in India, though there the moneylender is a Hindoo: and it is growing in Ireland, where the peasantry having since 1870, for the first time, something to borrow upon are using their advantages freely, and three-fourths of them will in a few years be hopelessly in debt. At least this is what those who know them best predict: & probably they are right.

3 Feb. 1882: News in papers of the Preston election: The Conservative, Raikes, returned by 6,000 odd to 4,000 odd: a result not to be regretted, for the so-called Liberal candidate, one Simpson[38], was a mere charlatan. He has been long known in Liverpool, where he keeps a refreshment shop, & was in no sense a fit representative of the party, which did not invite or sanction his appearance. He bid for the Irish vote, swallowing all the pledges asked for by that section of the electors. Yet it is remarkable that he polled nearly as many as the thoroughly unobjectionable Liberal gentleman Yates Thompson[39]: which looks as if personal fitness were not much thought of in large constituencies.

See a Mr. White who wants employment: also a Mr. & Mrs. Thomas who came with a note of introduction from Sir S. Northcote. He is an Exeter tradesman: she a natural daughter of Peabody the American: they are in difficulties, & she wants help out of the Peabody Fund.

A Mr. Escott[40] called, a friend of Carnarvon's, & author of a book called *England*: he is independent, & a gentleman, but does something in the way of writing for the *Standard*: his manners & intelligence pleased me, & I told him to call again if he wished for information.

Called on Ly Harcourt, some pleasant talk. Found her uneasy as to the prospects of the government, thinking a dissolution probable, & saying that is the opinion of many people. I do not see why: but such prophecies tend to fulfil themselves.

Wrote to a Mr. Thorn, who wants to reprint my speeches[41]. I say if he does I will look over them, but I dissuade him, as such collections never pay: and it would be strange if they did. Who reads old speeches?

. . . Dalhousie dines with us.

4 Feb. 1882: See Lawrence . . . Agree to send £100 to the cousin in New Zealand[42], though he has not been heard of since last year.

Lawrence brings me some deeds to sign, & shows how they have been shortened since Cairns' Act came in force. A few lines take the place of several sheets. This is because certain provisos, which formerly required special insertion in each deed, are now taken for granted unless the contrary be stated. Yet the public has scarcely taken notice of this change, though it makes transfers of land much cheaper.

Letter from Bagge . . . he mentions incidentally that land in Norfolk is supposed to be now worth 40% less to sell or let than it was a few years ago.

Meeting in afternoon of the Peabody trustees: Northcote, the two Lampsons, & myself present. . . . Our funds now amount to over £780,000, expended chiefly in land & buildings . . . Walk back with Northcote: some talk as to the coming session, but nothing of much interest.

Keston by 4.30 train. Very thick fog . . . Quiet evening.

5 Feb. 1882: Keston. Walk early with M. in Holwood.

. . . Write to Hale in answer to his suggestion that I should buy more land in the Fylde, asking where the money is to come from? as I cannot well understand what it is that he expects to receive from the railway companies, & I do not mean to apply my private savings in that way.

Read to M. a good deal: among other things an article by O.K. (Madame Novikoff[43]) against the policy of Austria in Servia, by which it appears that the Russian & Austrian parties in that country are fighting fiercely, & that Austria has got the upper hand. Ecclesiastical questions are as usual in these countries either the cause or the pretext. This statement explains in part a fiery speech delivered by Gen. Skobeleff at a public dinner not long ago, in which he spoke of the Slavs as still an oppressed race, & of the historical mission of Russia. It read like a declaration of war against some foreign state, & it is now clear that Austria was intended. – Meanwhile the Austrians have an insurrection in Bosnia to deal with: not on a grand scale, but the country is difficult & the people warlike.

Westminster is to be contested: Sir C. Russell[44], the sitting member, having retired from ill health. He was distinguished as a soldier, had the V.C. and is popular in society: but in politics was only known as a noisy 'Jingo' & in the House he had no weight. A son of the D. of Northumberland[45] is the chosen Conservative candidate: the Liberal is not yet chosen: Morley of the *Pall Mall Gazette* has been spoken of & would be quite fit from the intellectual point of view, but his opinions on Irish matters are extreme – in private he does not disguise that he thinks Home Rule inevitable – & he would probably divide the party. (**Note**: He has since declined to stand, on the ground of private business.)

6 Feb. 1882: London by early train . . . reach No. 23 by 10.40.

. . . Letter from West at Washington, in which he speaks of the alarm & jealousy which foreign immigration is causing in the U.S. . . . Wrote to West in answer.

E. Talbot [diarist's sister] came to luncheon. Her son, in the militia, does not expect to qualify by examination for a commission in the line, for which the competition is excessive. Badly paid as the army is, & small as are the prospects of advancement in it, it seems more than any other profession to attract the sons of the gentry: whether from inherited feeling, such as that which on the continent makes every noble an officer, holding no other employment fit for him: or because the work is supposed to be light: or because it holds out chances of adventure. What this lad is to do if he fails to qualify I cannot imagine. He will have £400 a year to live on, & no occupation.

Heard with regret of the serious illness of Ly Lothian[46]: who has destroyed her health by devoting herself to the work of a guardian in one of the London parishes: a singular line of business for a most refined & sensitive nature: but she has sacrificed time & strength to it, & is not expected to live.

Nat. Port. Gallery at 3.00. Long sitting. Present, Hardinge, Baillie Cochrane, Gladstone, E. Fitzmaurice, Millais, & Scharf.

In evening, dined with Granville, a party of 40 or more: the speech was read, & the general opinion seemed to be that it was of a very unaggressive kind. Local government & a new government for London are the chief measures promised. Nothing is said about parliamentary procedure, as that would not be etiquette for the Queen to interfere in. Party at Mrs. Gladstone's afterwards.

7 Feb. 1882: A little headache from hot rooms, etc., last night: but it passed off early. Much fog, so that I read & wrote by lamplight.

. . . After luncheon received a deputation [including] H. Brand, the Speaker's son . . . to ask me to support a new insurance company.

. . . At 5.00 to the House of Lords, which was moderately full: the mover & seconder, Lds Wenlock[47] & Fingall[48], did their work fairly well, & had the merit of brevity: Salisbury spoke for $\frac{3}{4}$ of an hour, in the customary critical tone of an opposition leader: but was in general neither animated nor effective, though he made one or two happy hits. Granville followed, & was even more below himself: wordy & dull. He was very little cheered, & towards the end of his speech lost the ear of the House. Waterford[49] spoke at length on the wrongs of the Irish landlords, the only subject which seemed to interest the peers, but, as they know that nothing can be done, the interest was not very warm. On the whole, I have not known so dull & tame an opening since I sat in the Lords. . . .

8 Feb. 1882: . . . Called on Ly Dartrey, who is just returned from Ireland: both she & Dartrey look older & harassed by the constant anxiety from which they have suffered. She describes the state of things as worse than ever but I think (though agreeing in the main) that she over-colours a little. She says that the tenants on their estates do not refuse to pay rents, but make excuses for delay, promising to pay a little later, etc. There is no distress, but the notion has gone abroad that parliament will be driven to deal with the question of arrears, wiping them off wholly or in part: & with this idea in their hands they hold back, thinking that they may perhaps escape payment altogether. They all believe that the government is on their side against the landlords &, if what Ly D. says of the sub-commissioners is accurate, they have reason to think so. . . .

10 Feb. 1882: Drew £100 in gold & notes for use.

. . . Much excitement is created in the political world by some words used last night by Gladstone in debate. They are too long to quote, but the purport is that, while nothing is to be allowed which takes away from the authority of parliament, it is desirable to give larger powers of self-government to Ireland[50]. The meaning probably was only that, when the times become quieter, county boards may be set up in Ireland as well as in England – or something of that kind (but the expressions used were so ambiguous as to enable the Home Rulers to claim that their demand has been at least in part conceded to be just). The speech admits of being explained away, but it is unlucky & imprudent in the present state of opinion. It will discourage the loyal party & strengthen the hands of their opponents. The new rules for restricting debate, just issued, & to be discussed next week, are complicated, & seem unpopular. Altogether the outlook for the government is not agreeable: though they have too great a following to be displaced, even if any one wished to displace them at this moment.

. . . Forster made a plain, strong, manly speech in defence of his coercion policy[51]: which produced, I am told, a good effect: the contrast of tone between him & the Premier was very marked.

News in the last day or two of the death of Lord Lonsdale[52], at the age of 26. He was never sober, & died of drink. He was taken ill at the house of a disreputable female acquaintance in Bryanston Square, whence to avoid scandal the body was removed at night to his own. Ly Lonsdale is abroad, having not long ago been brought to bed of a daughter whose paternity is doubtful, but with which certainly Ld L. had nothing to do. These are the things that make it difficult to defend aristocracy.

11 Feb. 1882: . . . Much excitement among politicians who are pleased to assert that the new rules for the business of parliament will be pressed on the House with the full force of government, that they will be rejected, that the Premier will treat the rejection as a question of confidence, & that a dissolution will follow. This report I find [it] hard to believe. Gladstone can never again have an election so favourable for him as that of 1880: the Irish policy has not been a success up to the present date: the Bradlaugh business is disliked: on the whole he has lost rather than gained, & the old Whig landowners, disgusted by the Irish legislation, & fearing its introduction into England, will certainly not exert themselves in his favour, even if they do not leave him as they did in Yorkshire. A dissolution now would strengthen the hands of the opposition, & weaken his. There is absolutely no reason for it: if the thing is done, it will be a *coup de tête* like that of 1874, & probably end as disastrously. There is always the alternative that G. may resign, & leave Granville & Hartington to get out of the mess. But his most sensible plan would be to accept the decision of the House, which on a question of parliamentary procedure he very well may do.

Westminster has been left to the Conservatives without a contest. The balance of parties remains as before. The sensation created by the Premier's speech, hinting at some possible modification of Home Rule as being what parliament could accept, has done him harm: creating that vague uneasiness as to what he may do next which is a dangerous sentiment for a minister to inspire. It is not clear whether the concession so made was a verbal imprudence, dropped in the haste & heat of debate: or whether it is a bid for at least a section of the Irish party. I cannot decide: & perhaps the person most concerned does not know himself. . . .

14 Feb. 1882: . . . Left at 12.00 for Tunbridge Wells with M., Arthur & Margaret to see the experiments on electric light being carried on by Mr. Siemens, the eminent engineer. His villa is about 2 miles from the station, pretty, & surrounded by grounds of nearly 200 acres. We saw the transmission of power through the electric wire from a small steam engine, to work a pump, drive a circular saw, etc., and, what was more curious, we saw fruits & vegetables being forced by electrical light & heat, which is turned on when the sun goes down, & thus gives the plants no rest, day or night. The flavour is said not to be spoilt: but I should doubt whether the expense would not be too great to make it worth while to use the process on a large scale. The place very pretty – views fine. Mrs. Siemens Scotch: he German, with a strong accent of his country. We were met there by Count Münster, who with one of his attachés returned with us to London.

Mr. Siemens said that for naval engines gas would supersede steam, and an equal power be produced with ½ the consumption of fuel.

Dined The Club. Pleasant, and we sat on till 11.00.

15 Feb. 1882: . . . Rather low & depressed in spirits, but cured myself by a sharp walk of nearly 2 hours.

. . . At 4.00 p.m. meeting of the City Companies Commission. We sat 1½ hours: all the members present. It was agreed to take oral evidence, which will last some time. The property of the companies, as stated in the returns made to us, may be taken roughly at a figure of £14,000,000, the greater part represented by building land and ground rents. Another fact of some interest has come out. It is clear that the connection between the companies & the trades whose names they bear has been little more than nominal for 300 years, so that there seems no possibility of going back to any former application of their funds, which in fact have been accumulated since the companies became substantially what they are now. I cannot as yet in the least see what our recommendations are to be: most likely we shall not agree on any, but split up into sections, each having a plan of its own.

Dined with Sir W. & Ly Harcourt: meeting Mr. & Mrs. Gladstone, Ld & Ly Spencer, the Russian ambassador, Mr. L. Oliphant, etc. a party afterwards. The Premier talked of the Channel Tunnel, against which there is a violent opposition now being directed, on military & patriotic grounds. Tennyson, the poet, is one of the most vehement, & Sir G. Wolseley has joined the cry – rather, I suspect, in order to please the Queen, who has always disliked the scheme, than from real conviction.

Oliphant talked freely of his plan of repatriating the Jews, seeming to think that there would be a large emigration from Russia & Eastern Europe to Palestine. It is odd in him that, though a wild fanatic in reality, not a trace of his feeling in this respect appears in conversation. He spoke of the Jews as though interested in them from feelings of general philanthropy.

Harcourt, as usual, confided to Ly D. his intense desire to be free from the cares of office: which on the whole nobody more enjoys, though being indolent by disposition I dare say the work is sometimes harder than he likes.

16 Feb. 1882: Walk down to the H. of Lds with Bath, & question him as to the working of the Land Act on his Irish estates. He tells me he sees as yet no reason to complain: he has on the whole suffered less by depression in Ireland than in England: he considers his Irish estates to be highly rented, & has offered a general reduction of 12%, which his tenants seem to be hesitating whether they shall accept or not. He thinks the outcry against the Land Courts exaggerated. In England he finds great differences: grazing land in Somerset has been unaffected, there is no loss there: in Wiltshire, close by, where light land has been broken up for corn, which had better have been left in pasture, the farmers are ruined, & rents will fall heavily. On the whole, Bath talked on this subject more fairly & rationally than I ever heard him talk before. . . .

17 Feb. 1882: . . . H. of Lords in afternoon, where debate on the Irish land courts, Donoughmore moving for a committee, which he carried by a large majority. . . .

18 Feb. 1882: To a sub-committee of the B. Museum at 12.00, where met Ld Sherbrooke, Walpole, & Hope: we agreed on a report on the subject of providing space for newspapers elsewhere than in the Museum. The bulk of them is enormous, they accumulate at an increasing rate, & it seems to be held that the state must keep them all somewhere, as evidence to be referred to in trials at law. But it is a question whether they should not have a building & a department to themselves. They are scarcely in our line.

. . . The political excitement of the moment is Gladstone's unlucky speech, understood by many people as in favour of some form of Home Rule. I do not believe he really meant it in that sense, but it is a misfortune, & generally a fault, in a minister if he speaks on such a question in a way to be misunderstood. His words have encouraged the Irish party both in parliament & in Ireland, & alarmed the loyalists in proportion. He explained it in an elaborate defence on Thursday, but to my judgment 'the interpreter was the harder to be understood of the two'. In fact his curious ignorance of mankind was never more clearly shown. He seemed to think it possible that a parliament could meet in Dublin, armed with powers to deal with local affairs, without disputing the supremacy of the imperial parliament at Westminster, or trying to go beyond the narrow & humble function assigned to it. If he really believes this, he is the only politician in England who does so: if not, his language is an unscrupulous bid for Irish support. I prefer the former alternative.

A speech by one Sexton, an Irish M.P., formerly a clerk & then a journalist, has attracted much notice. It was able, bitter, & uncompromising in its tone of hostility to England. There is a vacancy in the Irish representation, and the man selected to fill it is one Egan, the treasurer of the League, now in Paris, who went there partly lest he should be arrested, & partly to keep the League funds out of the reach of English officials. He will certainly be returned, & will take his seat as a pledged enemy to England. There are 500 suspects in gaol: they cannot be kept there for ever, & every man of them who is released will be a popular hero. The prospect, I think, was never bleaker. The English radicals are beginning to cry out for the sweeping away by parliament of the arrears of rent due to Irish landowners, saying with some truth that, as long as the tenants are liable to them, & unable to pay, they are not free to go into court & have their rents fixed: consequently, that the Act fixed for their relief is inoperative. But, even in the present condition of things, the H. of Commons would not listen (and still less the H. of Lords) to a proposal to cancel debts by retrospective amendment. That is a little too strong, even for men like Bright & Chamberlain. It could only be done if coupled with some large grant from parliament towards the payment of these debts, when the landlords might be induced to accept a composition, taking (say) two-thirds down & agreeing to sacrifice the rest. . . .

20 Feb. 1882: To H. of Lords, where we had a short but significant notice from Granville that the government would take no part in the proposed committee sanctioned by the vote of last Friday.

. . . Thence to the Commons, where found great excitement, Gladstone having just announced a resolution to be proposed condemning the appointment of the Lords committee, not by name, but with a direct reference to it. This step is in point of form unprecedented, & may lead to grave complications. I have seldom seen politics look more stormy.

Dined Grillions: present, Coleridge, Sherbrooke, Fortescue, Walpole, Gibson, Mills. Pleasant enough.

21 Feb. 1882: Promised £50 to a Mr. Aspden, who has lost money, or says so, by writing a (very indifferent) *History of the House of Stanley*[53].

Lawson called: very hot against Gladstone's last proceedings, which he cannot understand, & thinks there is more temper in them than policy. He says he has never heard more wild radical talk among the working classes, & believes many of them want a change of government, & to turn out the present ministers, not out of hostility, but because they think agitation would be easier & more likely to succeed, with Conservatives in power. Not an unskilful calculation for their purpose. . . .

22 Feb. 1882: Lansdowne called, we discussed the situation: I told him it was useless to make a public appeal to the Conservatives, as he had proposed, unless he had first secured an understanding with them. I advised him to see Cairns, who is more likely to be moderate than Salisbury, & who may be willing to put off the committee, on the ground that, as the government take no part in it, it can only be a one-sided and unsatisfactory enquiry. Gladstone's notice of Monday undoubtedly complicates the matter, as it is never easy to give way gracefully after threats have been used. But even an awkward retreat is better than perseverance in a blunder: & in the present case it looks as if Gladstone were trying to divert attention from the *clôture*, & from the unsatisfactory state of business generally, by picking a quarrel with the Lords.

To the two existing complications, a third has been added: Bradlaugh last night took an opportunity of slipping into the House after a division, reading the oath from a paper which he held in his hand at the table, & kissing a bible which he brought with him. He was ordered to retire, & did so: but it is a question whether he has or has not taken the oath according to law, though in an irregular way, & another question what the House is to do with him by way of marking its sense of his disrespect. He may be expelled: but he would probably be re-elected: & he would rather enjoy the notoriety than otherwise. I do not think I have ever known public affairs in such confusion, nor so little prospect of useful legislation.

Münster (who hears everything that has happened, & some things that have not) has got hold of a story that the Queen sent lately a message to Salisbury to say that she could not long endure her present ministry: that she was thwarted in everything (that, considering her political tendencies, is likely enough): and that at the earliest opportunity she would get rid of them: he must be ready to form a government! A hopeful prospect, with 150 majority against him.

23 Feb. 1882: Report in the papers of the death of Schouvaloff, but it turns out to be only a cousin, much to the relief of M. to whom the news came as a shock.

. . . Saw Lansdowne, who is trying to stop this Irish committee being formed: he could not see Cairns, who is out of town: but did see Salisbury. He did not get much encouragement, but intends if he has a chance to try & get it postponed by an appeal in the House tomorrow. Saw Camperdown, who came on the same errand. Dined at home & quiet evening.

24 Feb. 1882: Day foggy & dull, so that I read & wrote by candlelight. It is the general saying that fogs were never so abundant as during this winter.

Called on Granville & agreed as to what should be said in the House. . . . At 5.30 it was proposed to nominate the committee on the Land Court: Lansdowne got up, & in an excellent speech, sensible & conciliatory, urged the postponement of the committee: Donoughmore refused it in a rather pert reply, as if feeling his own importance as the spokesman of the Irish landlords: I followed in the same sense as Lansdowne, Salisbury followed me, & Granville replied. It was evident that nothing in the nature of compromise was intended or desired by the opposition. The House was not full, but a good many M.P.s, Gladstone among them, stood on the steps of the throne.

Neither party has acted wisely in this matter. If Granville last week had objected to the committee in terms as strong as those used by Gladstone in the Commons, it is quite possible that he would have secured at least its postponement: for the Lords in general had, & have, no wish to bring about a collision between the two Houses: but he did not do so, and now they are irritated, not unnaturally, by Gladstone's extraordinary notice. One result of the Premier's proceeding is that he will bring on a general debate on Irish subjects, which will probably last a week: & this at a moment when he is professing his anxiety to put a stop to the actual waste of parliamentary time. On the other hand, an appeal made to the majority of the Lords by the executive, on grounds of public safety, is seldom disregarded: & the feeling is strong even among the opposition, that it would have been better to make terms, either limiting the scope of the enquiry or stipulating that it shall take place a little later. The only gainers are the Irish, I mean the disaffected Irish, who are delighted with the prospect of more delay, confusion, & wrangling. Their language this week has been more outrageous than ever: one member accused Forster of passing his time in a gambling house when he ought to be attending to business: at another time it ws suggested that young Herbert Gladstone should take the place of Marwood, the hangman, because on one occasion, as a tourist, he had been present at an eviction carried on by the help of the police[54]. These are samples: but the habitual ill manners, rowdyism, & intentional disrespect to the House are not to be described. There has been nothing like it before, unless possibly in the parliament of 1832-1834. One trouble is for the moment got rid of. Bradlaugh is expelled the House, on a sudden resolution & without being heard in his own defence: a questionable precedent, but he so obviously wished to bring about the result that no great sympathy is felt for him even by those who think the proceeding unwise. If he fails to be re-elected, that question is settled for the time: if he is returned again, the wrangle begins anew: but in any case there is a respite.

Much talk about an early dissolution: which I should treat as absurd, but for the Premier's impulsive nature, & the precedent of 1874. It would be a mistake: the fear of jingoism & a war policy influenced many voters in 1880 who would now be on the Conservative side: parliament has been mismanaged & business muddled: the Irish Land Act has frightened holders of property, & as yet it does not seem to have done anything in the way of restoring peace & order. The secrecy of voting, moreover, makes it possible & even easy for electors to give effect to their changes of feeling without publicly compromising themselves or formally leaving their party.

Dined Sir B. Brett's: meeting Münster, Harcourts, Ld & Ly Hothfield[55], Ly F. Cavendish, Ld Coleridge, etc. Party afterwards, & pleasant evening.

25 Feb. 1882: I did not notice yesterday the last development of Irish patriotism. Meath being vacant, the electors have chosen Davitt, the founder of the Land League, now in Portland prison, to represent them: he is ineligible by law, & the return will be declared void: when Egan[56], the treasurer of the League, will be chosen in his place. Thus a double insult will have been offered to English authority: & another Irish debate will be made possible, on the annulling of the first election.

B. Museum at 12.00: the standing committee sat till 1.30: D. of Somerset in the chair. Walked back with Ld Sherbrooke: talk of the state of matters in parliament: the inevitable deadlock: where is the remedy? I hazarded the opinion that . . . composed [as it is] of men who nearly all want to speak, and are wanted to speak by their constituents, the H. of C. is too large for its work. There is not room for 650 members all wishing to take their part in debate. Even as lately as 30 years ago, when I first knew the place, the whole work was done by about 200 or 220 members – the other two-thirds attended occasionally, &

voted, but scarcely ever spoke. . . . The longest session on record has occupied about 1,400 hours: so that if every M.P. thinks fit to speak one hour in the course of the year (and less will hardly satisfy the people who sent him there) half the available time, or nearly half, will be absorbed to gratify provincial vanity. No plan of curtailing debate will thoroughly remedy this evil . . .

26 Feb. 1882 (Sunday): Day mostly wet & windy. . . . Received from Col. Maude[57], consul-general at Warsaw, an application for a loan of £300, which after a day's consideration I have declined. He has absolutely no personal claim upon me, for I have only seen him once or twice in my life: he is a good officer, but plays heavily, & I know from others that ten times the sum he asks would not set his affairs straight. So I have refused, & think myself justified, but I do it with a little regret.

The O'Donoghue, lately bankrupt, begs for £10, which I send him. He also has no claim, but the sum is too small to be worth refusing. . . .

27 Feb. 1882: . . . Heard later that Gladstone, who had called together a meeting of his party in the afternoon, at which he was very cordially received, spoke with great force & skill in moving his resolution: having previously said that he would not press it if he could have an assurance that the committee would limit its enquiry, so as to exclude the judicial decisions of the Act. This assurance, however, could not be given: & indeed I suspect that the Premier would have been greatly disappointed if it had been: wanting only to show moderation by the offer. The debate that followed was not very animated: it stands adjourned till Wednesday. – There was a division previously to decide whether the question should now be discussed: but it was forced on, I am told, by the Irish, & so is no test.

28 Feb. 1882: Pender called early: he had attended the Premier's meeting of yesterday, & was much impressed with its unanimity & success. He thinks the effect of that, & of the speech made last night, which he praises as one of Gladstone's very finest, has been to make ministers stronger than they have been this year: the grumblers are silenced, the doubters satisfied, & confidence is restored. He says also that he never saw Gladstone so nervous & anxious as he appeared at the meeting, till reassured by his reception.

Went at 11.30 to St. James's palace by invitation, to attend a meeting called by the P. of Wales to discuss the question of founding a national college of music. The Prince & the D. of Edinburgh both read addresses, evidently written by the same person, fairly good, & not too long. The Abp. of Canterbury followed: then Ld Rosebery, as representing the Lords Lieutenant of Counties: his speech was amusing: I don't know if there was any malice in the emphasis with which he dwelt on the patronage of music by early English kings, especially Henry the 8th and Charles the 1st. It was impossible not to draw the inference that good musicians might be bad rulers: but he glided over that. Gladstone harangued with as much eagerness as if a vote of confidence were in question: characteristically he talked most of church music, and spoke of it as a thing monstrous & disgraceful, hardly now to be credited, that in his youth he had known the services of the church performed without a note of music from beginning to end. The Lord Mayor & Northcote each said only a few words. The Princes talked very big of making this a national movement drawing subscriptions from every parish, & even from the colonies & the U.S. I doubt they will be disappointed, for the number of people who care enough about music to pay largely for a college of music is, I suspect, but limited.

. . . Dined with The Club: meeting Coleridge, Gladstone, Walpole, Reeve, Smith, Maine, A. Russell, Tyndall, P. Hewett, Hooker. Pleasant. After dinner, & as he was going away, Gladstone took me aside, & began to talk earnestly about Ireland. He did not explain why he said it, but the substance of what he said was that now was the critical time: if the Irish party came back after the next election 60 or 70 strong their demand for an Irish parliament would be irresistible. They would be strong enough to make their own terms.

1 Mar. 1882: Long visit from Statter, who in a flood of words vindicates himself from the charge of spending too much money on the Bury estates. The fact is with a nominal rental of £10,000 more than when I succeeded to them they yield me now a smaller net return. Whether there is jobbery, or only waste, I cannot judge, but rather suspect the former, as Statter is anxious for popularity with the tenants in order to support his son's claim to the reversion of his place.

2 Mar. 1882: Bradlaugh is again returned for Northampton by a narrow majority[58], & we shall have the old trouble over again.

News in the evening of a man having shot at the Queen: with no result. He is thought to be mad, & probably the object was only to create alarm, & secure notoriety.

3 Mar. 1882: . . . Promised £200 to the new college of music, half this year, half the next. It will most likely be a failure, for the princes talk of wanting £10,000 a year, which means a capital of £300,000, & if they get £50,000 it will be much. The middle classes care little about music, & the provinces are not fond of sending money up to London. . . .

4 Mar. 1882: . . . A French workman out of employ was tried for shooting a doctor whom he had never seen, & against whom he had no cause of complaint. But he considered that he & all his class were 'exploités' by the 'bourgeois' . . . This Frenchman does not seem to have been mad, but possessed with a spirit of vindictive hostility against all who were better off than himself . . . Something of the same feeling appears to mix with national animosity in the Irish anti-landlord movement: though there it is stimulated by direct pecuniary interest. The cause I take to be in the main twofold: (1) with education, & some increase of leisure, there has come an increased appreciation of the comforts of life, & a clearer perception by the masses that by them most of these comforts are unattainable: (2) the religious belief in a future state which is to compensate for the inequalities of life, even where not theoretically destroyed, is losing its hold on men's imaginations: so that poverty & suffering appear in the light of injustice, & on the other hand the sufferer who, to relieve or revenge himself, commits crime is not restrained by fear of consequences after death. I suspect that we shall see a good deal more of the results of this state of feeling in a few years, though in England they will be less violent than elsewhere.

5 Mar. 1882: Gave M. £16 to pay her Swedish doctor for the month. He is really to outward appearance doing her good, both as to health & spirits: the depression which was so common last year has almost entirely disappeared.

Talk of lending Hollydale to Ld & Ly Halifax, which M. wishes, & I shall be glad of, but fear the house is smaller than they will care to live in. They are, like many other landowners, a good deal pinched by non-payment of rents, and have no house in London having let their own.

The Parnell party have taken a new departure. They now propose to raise a fund to pay their members regularly, so as to secure their attendance in parliament, & I suppose also to keep them in subjection to the authorities of the League. They talk & write confidently of returning 70 members, in lieu of their present number of 35, at the next dissolution: & are anxious to bring it about as soon as possible. It is too early to say either that they will or that they will not succeed . . .

6 Mar. 1882: . . . Home: dined Grillions, where met a good party, Cairns in the chair: . . . Cairns told some Irish stories in his peculiar vein of dry humour. He talked to me seriously afterwards about Irish affairs: said in his judgment the only thing possible to be done now was to make the Irish farmers proprietors by large assistance from the State to them to buy their farms. He did not see any other basis on which the land question could be settled. . . .

8 Mar. 1882: . . . Several notices of Ld Wilton[59] appear in the papers. His character was one of the most singular that I have known. A man of pleasure from his youth (he succeeded to the earldom as a boy) he laid himself out for a life of energetic amusement. He rode hard until within the last few years, & was said to be one of the best gentlemen riders in England: shot well, though dangerously to his neighbours: loved yachting, & managed his own yacht on occasion: was an excellent musician, & composed music which is said to be good. He never drank, nor smoked: but in eating was an epicure, & would talk about it more than is the custom of modern society. He ran after women incessantly, causing much trouble & vexation to his first wife. Even when near 60, he could not keep from connections which created scandal. With all this, he was pious after a fashion of his own: attended church regularly, composed hymns, & would have been genuinely shocked if any one connected with him had shown signs of heterodoxy. He was very hospitable, living in & for society to the last. Added to his other pursuits, he had taken up amateur surgery in his youth: & I believe really knew something about it. His manners were peculiar: very courteous & refined, but artificial in the highest degree: he spoke always in the languid & drawling tone which I suppose was once fashionable, & which Ld Strathnairn also uses. My father, who was nearly his contemporary, used to be curiously divided between liking for an old friend & companion & impatience of his follies. He had energy enough to have done something in active life but preferred the kind of social distinction which he got at Melton, Cowes, & in the racing world. His income was large, & I am not aware that he lived beyond it. Naturally his sons have come to no good: the eldest[60] is a fop, harmless but insignificant: the second[61], a great musician like his father, took to drink & women, sold his reversion to the estates, which Lord Wilton bought back again, & is living somewhere in obscurity, from which he will not emerge. The estate is a fine one, being near Manchester, & if the town continues to grow will be all building land. . . .

10 Mar. 1882: . . . W.E. West[62] came to luncheon: he has been staying in the house, but dining with friends elsewhere: he left in the afternoon for Wales. His is domestic trouble in another form. He has work, as an agent, well paid, & which [he] likes: but it involves the necessity of living nearly all the year round in a country town (Bangor): & the absence of fitting company, & want of occupation, has developed in the daughters a growing tendency to eccentricity (to which there is a family tendency) already unpleasant, &

alarming for the future. West's own habitual melancholy & oddity has probably had a larger share in this result than he knows: but it is not the less disagreeable on that account.

. . . H. of Lords, where no business: call on Ly Harcourt, who let out in plain words the secret, that the attack on the Lords was arranged by the Cabinet as a means of bringing together the party, disunited and disorganised by the *clôture* proposals. (These are now again put off for a week or ten days.) The move was probably a good one in a party sense: but it is early for a strong government, which has never been seriously attacked, to be driven to these expedients. Home, dined quietly: rather depressed in spirits & irritable, without cause, except that I have no work of any interest to do.

11 Mar. 1882: The press is beginning to remark, not without reason, on the absolute waste of the session so far. Nothing has yet been done, & nothing seems likely to be done soon. The Irish members have managed to secure most of the time passed in debate: & their language has been if possible more unseemly than that of last year. Last night, Biggar referred to the visit paid by Forster in the famine time when at great cost of labour, money, & risk from disease he distributed the relief funds sent by English Quakers: Biggar's comment on this was that some people took pleasure in the sight of human suffering, & probably that was the motive. He was called to order, but the Irish applauded. The insults poured on Forster every night exceed in virulence anything I remember in parliament: neither he nor any one else takes them seriously, but they lower the credit of the House, besides wasting time. A more serious trouble is that the Coercion Act expires next autumn. It cannot be renewed without infinite agitation nor safely dispensed, unless Irish feeling alters more than seems in any way probable. There are over 500 untried prisoners in gaol now, the whole number detained having been nearly 800. Yet outrages have not ceased, hardly slackened: and rents are still withheld. . . . As regards the stoppage of business, & the prospect of a session in which scarcely any legislative work will be done, I do not see that the public at large cares in the least. The reforms proposed are useful, but they do not touch the popular imagination, & scarcely anybody not a politician by habit & employment thinks that county boards, or a new local government for London, will really do much either in the way of good or harm.

12 Mar. 1882 (Sunday): Dull foggy day . . . dined early at Travellers', & left for Euston at 4.30. On the platform met Londonderry[63], Colville[64], & others on the same errand as myself. Met also F.A.S.[65], with whom I travelled down to Manchester. There Colville joined us, & we drove together to Heaton. At Heaton I found the new owner, Grey[66]: his brother, G. Egerton[67] (who at one time nearly killed himself with liquor, but is now apparently in good health again) . . . We had supper & went early to bed.

13 Mar. 1882: . . . There was a large crowd gathered both outside & within the church: & evidence of real sorrow among the people. Birch, the parson, who read part of the service, was crying like a child. The old earl was evidently popular among his neighbours. – His eldest son, Grey, has grown absurdly like the father in appearance, voice, & manner: & looks 60 instead of being under 50.

Some talk of the will: it seems the new Lord Wilton will have from £60 to £70,000 a year: with the London house, & of course Heaton. The widow has £6,000 a year for life: the daughters, moderate fortunes, I think £10,000 each, & one is residuary legatee to the personal estate.

Talk with R. Grosvenor[68] about business in parliament: he takes a desponding view of the situation: says the Conservatives are united with the Irish for purposes of obstruction: that Northcote cannot control them . . . He admits that no regulations for closing debate can be really effective, though they may lessen the nuisance: he thinks the Parnellites will be stronger in the next parliament, probably 60 or 70: and that no scheme of Home Rule which leaves to the imperial parliament a real supremacy will satisfy them. He says most of the government, as far as he knows, believe that the end must be a civil war: there seems no other way out of the difficulty: Gladstone himself was beginning to despair. He thought a bill might be carried establishing county boards, but not one for the government of London: the opposition being too strong. He agreed with me that the public is really indifferent to delay, & not in haste to see any of the new plans adopted. There was no strong feeling as to the existence of any grievance: people were quite content to wait. they cared just now only about Ireland & Bradlaugh.

14 Mar. 1882: . . . To the Lds in afternoon: where Cairns' land bills went through committee without alteration, or a word spoken: a proceeding rather surprising when one considers that these bills affected the personal interests of every peer, present or absent, & dealt with the subject on which they are most sensitive – their estates. But I am not sure that the instinct of the peers was not right: they felt that the questions concerned were in the main legal questions, they knew that both Cairns & Selborne were agreed upon them: they knew also that both chancellors are strongly conservative in their ideas upon the land question: & they concluded rightly enough that the best arrangement was being made on their behalf that could be made, & that their interference would do more harm than good. So that probably they were wise: but the proceeding looked odd. I at least have no right to find fault, since I joined in the general silence.

. . . Kimberley talked after dinner of South African affairs: thought they would continue for a long while to give trouble: at the bottom of all the difficulty was the inevitable conflict between white and black races for the possession of the soil: he thought it must end, as in Australia & N. Zealand, by the victory of the whites. I doubted, for the negro of South Africa is a tougher & more improvable being, up to a certain point, than the Australian native or the Maori. And opinion will not tolerate his being got rid of by the summary process practised in other colonies on natives.

15 Mar. 1882: Walk with Dalhousie, who tells me two curious facts. One that Chamberlain has declared publicly that there can never be another Irish coercion bill: parliament will not have it: this was at a dinner where he seems to have talked very freely. And he intimated in plain terms that the present Act could not or should not be renewed at the end of the session. If he sticks to his words, & the state of Ireland does not greatly alter, there must be a secession from the Cabinet, for it is impossible in actual circumstances to fall back on the ordinary law. The other story also came from Chamberlain: to the effect that Bright had objected strongly to the principle of the Irish Land Act from its first introduction: preferring his own plan of buying the landowners out with public money. But Gladstone objected absolutely to that, as involving a vast amount of public expenditure. It is quite extraordinary what a knack my young friend seems to have of extracting secrets from his informants: perhaps because in his frank sailorlike way he has no scruple in asking downright questions which more experienced politicians would think indiscreet.

In afternoon, I attended the City Companies Commission . . . Two facts come out clearly in this enquiry: (1) that the wealth of the companies is greater than any one had supposed, certainly exceeding 14 millions, & possibly amounting to 17 or 18: (2) that their ceasing to be really trade associations is not, as most people thought, a modern abuse, but dates from the 16th century at latest, since which time they have had no functions to perform, but have been really middle class clubs as at present.

16 Mar. 1882: . . . In parliament, the Irish continue to occupy, & almost to monopolise attention. They took up the greater part of yesterday's sitting with a criticism of the Land Act, not very consistently, after having most of them joined in the vote condemning the House of Lords for wishing to enquire into it. The last demand made by them is the modest one that landlords shall be compelled to give up their arrears of unpaid rent, so that the tenant may start free of claims which they cannot pay. But this proposal is too strong even for their friends in England. It is true enough, as they contend, that a tenant who may at any moment be evicted for unpaid arrears is not free to go into the Land Court if his landlord & creditor objects: but that was known & foreseen when the Act was passed, & was accepted by many persons as a useful check on its working.

17 Mar. 1882: In parliament: the Irish again! They kept up a childish & angry wrangle about Forster's late speech at Tullamore, & the alleged conduct of certain policemen, with the object of preventing the navy estimates from coming on: and in fact they succeeded so far that Trevelyan did not get his chance till near midnight . . .
. . . Walk home with [Lord] Dartrey, who gives a rather better description of the state of Irish feeling. He says that his tenants in the north are beginning to pay: they have hitherto held back under some vague impression that parliament would cancel the arrears: a certain number have applied to the Land Court, but he does not expect any considerable reduction. On the D. of Abercorn's estates he says reductions have been either refused or when granted they have been so small as to leave matters practically where they were.

18 Mar. 1882: Pender called early to ask me to a party at Sydenham on Monday, which I accepted willingly, as it is to see the new electrical inventions. We talked of parliament: he joins in the general disgust at the waste of time and hopelessness of useful legislation, but says (and I agree with him) that one cause of this state of things is that the public are really indifferent: there is no eagerness for county boards or for an improved government of London: &, if nothing is done in the present session, none except politicians will complain. This I suspect is about the truth. . . .

20 Mar. 1882: . . . At 7.00 p.m. to Victoria station: where joined Pender's party: Gladstones, Granvilles, Goschens, Forsters, Wolseleys, Ld Sherbrooke, A. Russells, etc. We travelled in Pullman's [sic] cars, lighted by electricity: nothing can be more luxurious or comfortable. At Sydenham we found a great crowd &, as seeing the various lights involved walking all round the building in a sort of procession, it became rather wearisome: the noise making it impossible to hear explanations, & the mob, though civil & cheering loudly, pushed us about a good deal. Ly Granville was my partner in the walk, which lasted about $\frac{3}{4}$ of an hour. Then came dinner: good & not too long: then some explanations of the mode of working the lights, which could not be well heard. One huge light up aloft is said to have the illuminating power of 150,000 candles, & is driven by a

30 h.p. engine. The applications of the light to domestic purposes were, however, the most interesting part of the display. We were shown a small glass lamp inside which is a vacuum, & the light burns in it: on the glass being broken, as was done with one, the light goes out instantly from the admission of air. The inventor says that he would not be afraid to break one in a barrel of loose gunpowder. On the whole the sight was well worth seeing. Back at Victoria by 10.30, & walk home.

. . . Forster talks about Ireland: complains bitterly of the general want of moral courage: & tells a story of an Irish landowner at some place that he went to who, though entirely friendly to the government, & eager for protection, refused to be seen in pubic with him, Forster, lest he should become unpopular: & apparently made no secret of his reason. I agreed, but defended the Irish gentry on the ground that they have been for two or three generations discouraged in any attempt to take an active part in local affairs, lest their doing so should give offence to the priests & the peasantry.

21 Mar. 1882: . . . In H. of C. debate on county franchise, which everybody agreed must be reduced to the level of that in the boroughs, but nobody seemed to be in a hurry about it. 'Concede the principle, & postpone it indefinitely' seemed to be the feeling of members generally.

22 Mar. 1882: . . . Dined with Ld & Ly Reay: meeting Gladstone, Mrs. Goschen, Ld Coleridge & daughter, Mr. & Mrs. Howard[69], Mr. & Mrs. Trevelyan, Sir T. & Ly Brassey[70], Mr. Morley: I think these were all. Lord Coleridge very amusing: told stories without end. Trevelyan reported a saying of the Speaker, that in all his parliamentary experience he had never known party run as high as it does now. (I suppose he was referring to the assistance given by the Conservatives, or rather by a part of them, to Irish obstruction.) Some talk with [John] Morley on Irish affairs: he almost despairs: sees no way out of the trouble: laughs at Gladstone's optimism, believes as I do that the Irish all want Home Rule: and that the English will not concede it: in short, his view is almost as despondent as mine, which where Ireland is concerned is saying a good deal.

23 Mar. 1882: . . . At 5.30 to the Lords, where found [Lord] Redesdale[71] arguing for his bill, which is to exclude atheists by enforcing a declaration of belief in some deity: an absurd proposal on the face of it, and which nobody supported except Lord Oranmore[72]. Shaftesbury was put up to argue against it, as a man who could not be accused of favouring atheism: he spoke as might be expected, with much artificial solemnity, & with a large intermixture of canting phrases: but in the main sensible enough, pointing out the obvious objections of policy to any new test, & the inadequacy of this test for its professed purpose, since a man might take it who believed in supernatural powers of any kind, though holding (like Epicurus) that they do not interfere in human affairs. The Bp. of London[73] took the same line, & as sensible & temperate. Ld Dunraven went over ground already traversed, & was rather too long. Granville summed up in a speech which showed his extreme fear of giving offence on such a subject: but, oddly enough, & with no apparent reason, made a violent attack on Salisbury for some expressions lately used by him in a letter, personal to the Prime Minister: he was right, I think, in substance, but the occasion did not seem a fit one. Salisbury saw his advantage, & answered in good temper: adding to other criticisms on the bill an odd one: that it did not include any article of belief except that in a deity. Ld Aberdare[74] said to me: 'I suppose he wants to put in the whole Athanasian creed.'

I had forgotten the speech of the D. of Argyll, which was a very odd one. He denounced the abetters of Mr. Bradlaugh, in a tone of fervent Scotch pietism, but at the end declared that the only way to avoid future troubles of the same kind was to substitute affirmations for oaths universally: a conclusion more reasonable than his premises seemed to lead up to. On the whole the debate was good, if one could forget the extreme absurdity of the proposal which led to it. Redesdale withdrew without dividing.

Home. Dined alone with M., whom I regret to find again despondent about her eyes, which till lately she believed to be improving under Kehlgren's treatment.

24 Mar. 1882: Made notes for a speech at Bury, not to my own satisfaction, but about hospitals what is there new to be said? Feeling bored & uncomfortable at the prospect of a useless journey & tedious day tomorrow. . . . Left Euston at 4.00 . . . read on the journey Windham's diary, which I had not looked at since it first came out. A strange life. . . . The oddity of the character is increased when one knows that [there] occur in the M.S. journal passages of an entirely unreportable character, describing minutely his amours, which were many, & the physical peculiarities of the ladies concerned. This was told me by a friend (Reeve, I think) who had seen the original.

25 Mar. 1882: I reached Manchester last night at 8.45: found Statter's carriage . . . Supper, & bed at 11.00. Admired Statter's water colours, china, etc., in regard of which he has shown more taste than I should have credited him with.

Breakfast early, & at 9.30 drove to the office in Bury: where met Mr. Philips[75], the Mayor, [etc.] . . . Settled some details as to the opening. It began by a procession in which . . . half Bury walked or drove: flags without end, carriages, & huge vans. The show was not much, & it was spoilt by frequent heavy rain: but that nobody seemed to mind. There was a kind of wooden platform put up in front of the hospital . . . on which the principal performers mounted. I spoke first, then Philips, then Wrigley, a son of the old papermaker. Then the hospital was gone over: the we returned to the office: the function ended with a public luncheon at 2.00, which I left, after making my speech, at 4.00. . . . By 5.00 p.m. train to London, where supper, & slept, M. being gone to Keston.

The reception at Bury was very cordial indeed at the luncheon: fairly so by the crowd, though less than at Liverpool. Having been so little in the town, & with a not very conciliatory agent, I am rather surprised not to be actually unpopular.

Statter admits some improvement in business, but is still not sanguine. He notes as curious that the working class have suffered little, if at all, in the last five bad years: they have always been employed, & at fair wages, though as he says the employers have been working at a loss. This I find hard to believe. Yet it is true that, while cottage building goes on steadily, many villas of the larger sort are unlet. The loss, if there is loss, has fallen on the rich. Statter says there are plenty of men doing well in a small way, but no large fortunes being made.

Note that nearly 300 of the old life leases still remain.

Note also that I signed a receipt for £31,000 odd from the L. & Y. Rlwy. Co., thus settling that business, which has dragged on for 7 or 8 years.

26 Mar. 1882: . . . Gave M. a present. Heard with regret that she intends to discontinue her visits to the Swedish doctor, thinking he does her eyes no good.

. . . Troubled while walking with a slight but unpleasant feeling of oppression on the chest, which is new to me: it seemed to make breathing difficult while it lasted: but I dare say it is only stomach.

27 Mar. 1882: Walk in to the station . . . Some return of the oppression of yesterday. Just in time for the P. Council meeting at 11.00 . . .

. . . Received a visit from Sir H. Parkes[76], of Sydney, who is head of the N.S. Wales ministry, passing his holiday in England. He was ready to talk freely of colonial affairs, & sensibly: though rather long-winded, & measuring his words with an odd preciseness. The chief thing that he told me was that he believed confederation to be nearer than we supposed: it was true that people did not think or talk much about it, but any chance event might stir up an interest in the question. He was sanguine as to the prospects of Australia: Australians were now 3 millions, & would soon be 7 or 8. He thought their prospects better than those of America, the immigration being more purely English. He said the danger of too great an Irish admixture was strongly felt. He explained the state of the land question: which, as he related it, appeared to be a struggle on the part of the legislature to prevent capitalists settling on the soil, & to reserve it for labour: which they had failed in doing.

28 Mar. 1882: M. troubled with a story of her brother, Ld Sackville, having just turned off without cause a keeper who with his father has been over 40 years about the place: no reason assigned. Gave her £10 to send to the family in their distress.

. . . Walk: called on A.D. who is leaving for Ireland . . .

. . . Dined The Club: meeting A. Russell, Walpole, Reeve, Smith, Froude: P. Hewett & Sir G. Wolseley: a pleasant party, & good talk. Much was said about South Africa, & I could see that Wolseley agrees with Ld Kimberley that troubles must be expected there for a long while. The black races, so far from dying out or decreasing, are multiplying: and will hold their own: the white settlers want the land, & will have it, being the stronger: but not easily or without a struggle. The Zulus Sir Garnet thinks quite untameable. the Basutos milder in disposition, & with more intelligence. Even if they died out, there are fresh hordes always ready to pour down from the north & fill their places. . . .

29 Mar. 1882: . . . Agreed with reluctance to open a bazaar on behalf of the Stanley Hospital at Liverpool on Whitmonday: a silly waste of time, but such things are not to be avoided if one lives in a populous district.

. . . City Companies Commission at 4.00, and sat till near 7.00. We examined a Mr. James Beal[77], who is a shining light among municipal reformers, and whose proposal was to abolish the companies simply & absolutely . . . This scheme . . . he defended with much fluency & vehemence . . .

. . . Dined with Ld & Ly Tweedmouth: a large stately party, 27 or 28 sat down: I was placed opposite Gladstone, & well entertained with his talk[78]. Carlingford sat near him, & left an impression of feeble obsequiousness which jarred on my taste. The house very fine, with marble pillars, inlaid floors, & a kind of magnificence which one does not often see in London interiors.

Party at Ly Granville's later: to which I went alone, M. being tired.

Much talk about a wrangle last night in the Commons, when the Irish exceeded their usual insolence, & provoked Forster to speak out. He told them that the outratges must be put down, that it was the business of government & parliament to do it, & that if the present methods would not suffice others must be tried. The House cheered vehemently, as I am told: & the English public will think Forster right to use plain words. But Carlingford shook his head & regretted the speech: Mrs. Gladstone, reflecting her husband, said it was a pity it had been made: & the ministerial press holds the same language, though guardedly. The fact is, they – the majority of the Cabinet – will not recognise facts, & persist in believing that the Irish people are well affected. Forster made in the same speech an honest admission that he & they had underestimated the gravity of the situation: which they certainly did. But, with all Gladstone's extraordinary powers, & though nobody could better afford to own that he had been in the wrong, that is a thing which whether from temper or system he will not do. . . .

30 Mar. 1882: . . . In the Commons, close of the long debate on *clôture* by a bare majority: which was carried . . . by 318 to 279. The majority is larger than ministers expected: they would have been glad to be sure of 25: but it is small compared with their ordinary strength. The Irish were divided: the moderate section supporting the government, which they can do without risk as they are sure not to be returned . . .

31 Mar. 1882: Dined with the Sherbrookes, they being anxious to make up a party to meet Sir H. Parkes. It was a good one: Gladstone, Lowell, Kimberley, Mr. & Mrs. Childers, Ld Monck[79], Sir C. Trevelyan, Dodson, & one or two more. Sir H. Parkes did not much impress us. His manner & talk were like those of a sensible London tradesman who has a seat in his parish vestry . . .

. . . Childers talked a little about the young men who go as officers into the army: said they were distinctly a poorer class than formerly, but not socially inferior, rather the other way: sons of poor gentry, clergy, & the like. The class whom recent regulations tend to exclude is, he says, the class of rich tradesmen's sons, with much money, & little education, whose parents want them to be officers as a means of getting social promotion.

The division of yesterday . . . has been a relief to the feelings of ministerial supporters, who had worked themselves into a fear, not exactly of defeat, but of a majority so small that the practical victory would have rested with the opposition . . . . . . From another point of view the debate & its results are less satisfactory. The session up to Easter has been absolutely wasted for purposes of legislation: nothing done, nor likely to be: the discussion of parliamentary rules will occupy most of the disposable time till Whitsuntide: and what chance is there then for a county board bill, or a municipal scheme for London, getting passed? We must assume that whatever is decently possible in the way of obstruction will be done, the Irish and Conservatives being agreed so far: the Irish do not disguise their wish to make parliamentary government impossible, until they can have a parliament of their own: the Conservatives believe that opinion will come round to them again, & by means of delay they hope in the meanwhile to avert legislation of a kind which they dislike, but cannot openly resist. In this object they have succeeded so far.

1 Apr. 1882: . . . Talk with Northbrook about Ireland: I observed to him that it was lucky the Liberals were not in opposition, as they would have made a point of resisting coercion in any & every shape: he agreed emphatically, saying that it would have been utterly impossible for a Conservative government to use repressive measures as the present government has done . . . he hinted strongly that the Prime Minister would probably have been among the opponents. The Irish know this: hence their anxiety to bring about a change. . . .

5 Apr. 1882: . . . Debate on Ireland again in H. of C. which really seems incapable of discussing any other subject: it was remarkable only for the tone of despondency, & almost of despair, in which Gladstone spoke. His eyes are opened at last. It is admitted now that the Land Act has not pacified the people, & that new methods must be tried. What will they be? The Conservatives wish to create a peasant proprietary by advances from the Treasury, but to do this on a small scale is useless, & on a great scale ruinously costly. Nor is it likely that the loans so made would ever be repaid. But we shall hear more of the project. It is about the only expedient left untried.

Meanwhile, the Ultra Liberals, represented by [John Morley] of the *Pall Mall Gazette*, are opening an attack on Forster: trying to force his resignation. The precise grounds I do not clearly understand, but the allegation against him is that he has become unpopular with the Irish: as if any one could be popular in a country which is virtually in a state of insurrection, without failing in his duty towards England. The explanation I suppose is that they know he will propose a renewal of the Coercion Act in some shape, & this they are determined to resist. Another possibility is that he has made up his mind to resign, if he cannot get certain things done: & his colleagues, or those of them who have no mind to do them, are forestalling him by making his retirement appear involuntary.

6 Apr. 1882: . . . Rather weary & depressed in spirits, I think from digestion being disturbed: though I have been living quietly enough. The truth is that, though often tired of work when I have it to do, it is necessary to me, & when it is not to be had (as now) I suffer from the want of it.

Herbert Spencer sends me his last new book: to be acknowledged suitably.

7 Apr. 1882: . . . [Lord] Tavistock[80] came for the day from London, but brought no special news. He talks very freely of his family, which is not a happy one. His relations with his own wife[81] are those of virtual separation: & he allows comments upon her which would be better unmade by his sisters, cousins, etc., in his presence. The Duke[82] is an object of respect, but of terror [too], to his children: he has brought them up carefully, done well for them in substantial matters, but he spoils all by an odd habit of teasing – ordering this & forbidding that – merely to show his power. The consequence is they all dislike him & keep out of his way as much as possible. He does the same to his two brothers[83], whom he lectures & almost insults one day, giving them presents sometimes of £5,000 in a lump the next: and without any assignable reason either for the quarrel or for the benefit, except his own caprice. M.[84], who knows him well from early days, ascribes this curious trait of character to the state of dependence in which he was long kept by his cousin, the late Duke[85]: & which she believes has created in him the desire to retaliate on those who are similarly in his power. Of the daughters[86], one refuses to go into the world, devoting herself to study & drawing: she is already eccentric in character, & will probably grow more so. The other is lively, likely to marry, & become a member of fashionable society. The Duchess[87] is, I think, the happiest of the family: she likes balls, parties, &

dinners: enjoys her fine dress, fine houses, & command of means: leaves affairs to the Duke, & goes placidly through life, enjoying no great happiness, but troubled with few anxieties. Tavistock himself has good sense, shrewdness, & knowledge of the world: he is not likely to discredit himself or his family, but neither will he do anything to raise it. He is very indolent: has no serious pursuits & no active amusements: likes lounging & gossip better than suits a young man: and is something of a *gourmand*. In politics he is ostensibly Whig, really Conservative: not with any Tory leanings to church or crown, but with a strong & natural aversion to encroachments on the rights of property. I forget how he voted on the Land Act, but he certainly did not hide his dislike. He may very possibly leave the H. of Commons, for the work of which he does not care, and where he has never yet spoken. The younger son, Herbrand[88], is in the army: I know little of him, but believe that in general temperament he resembles his brother. There is a common belief that Tavistock can have no children: founded, I suppose, on his peculiar conjugal relations, which are no secret[89]. . . .

14 Apr. 1882: . . . Salisbury, Northcote, & others have been making a Conservative demonstration in Liverpool, their speeches fill several columns in today's & yesterday's papers: they contain nothing new, only the old ideas in new words, which indeed is all that can be expected on such subjects as the state of Ireland. The one thing in them worth noting is that Ld S. strongly recommends the buying out of Irish landlords, & so creating a peasant proprietary. The scheme is popular in Ireland, as it naturally may be, since it can only be worked by a large application of English money: landowners will be glad to obtain a fixed income free from the annoyance of an Irish tenantry: tenants will accept an arrangement by which they may hope to get their farms as freeholds without paying more than half the price: but if the thing is meant seriously, & not as a mere bid for the Irish vote, two objections occur: (1) where is the money to come from? (2) what is the chance of the advances made by the State being repaid? If the whole Irish soil is to be bought by the tenantry, England advancing the capital, it is hard to say what sum would not be required: £200,000,000 is a modest estimate. And how much of this would ever be seen again? . . .

15 Apr. 1882: Finished the reading to M. of Froude's life of Carlyle . . . It is an interesting, not an agreeable book. . . . [Against his defects] it is only just to set his dogged honesty and independence of character, sustained by the conviction that he had a 'message', a 'mission', something which he was bound to say to the country as best he could, & which he would not suppress or soften, however unpopular it might be. What this message was is a point on which no two of his followers agree: & possibly a certain admixture of mystery is essential to a new religion. But it is odd to find a great teacher deriving his ideas from a German novel (Goethe's *Wilhelm Meister*): & odder still to find an intolerant impatience of religious unbelief in a man who rejected the Christian religion in all its forms. An intense faith in deity & immortality, founded on no external evidence, but solely on feeling, or intuition, is the apparent foundation of Carlyle's creed. The morality superimposed on this foundation is simply that of all ages – work – tell truth – deny yourself – act justly, etc., etc., and these very elementary precepts are repeated by him so often, in private letters as well as published, as to be wearisome. Two of his favourite tenets seem to be, one that we lived in an age of decadence, not of progress, & that our decadence is due to our not having a religious belief really & firmly held. The other, that happiness, either personal or collective, is not, ought not to be, & cannot be, the object of life. – On the whole, while I heartily admire Carlyle's genius, & endure his eccentricities & mannerisms for the sake of the ideas of which they are the medium, I feel that I understand him rather less than more as I study him longer – & I do not regret not having cultivated his acquaintance in earlier years.

16 Apr. 1882: . . . Wrote to Froude on his Carlyle book: praising, & adding a hint that it would be well to explain more clearly what the doctrine was, to the teaching of which Carlyle attached such extreme importance.

17 Apr. 1882: Left Fairhill early, not with reluctance. A party of 9 or 10 in a small house, and with nothing special to do, suits me less than either London, or the same society at Knowsley, where there is room for each to go his own way.
 . . . Euston at 4.00: reached Knowsley at 9.30. Reading Lecky's new history[90] on the way down. . . .

18 Apr. 1882: Up early: letters till 10.00, when left for Liverpool.
 Sat in court . . . from 10.00 till 5.00 . . .
 Cases in calendar 74: one attempt at suicide, 2 charges of keeping a disorderly house: 10 assaults (none indecent): all the rest thefts or other offences against property.
 The only thing noticeable in the calendar was the unusual number of old offenders: several had been convicted 8 or 10 times before.
 . . . Home at 6.00: letters again till 7.00.
 Then read the papers, & dined alone.

19 Apr. 1882: Up early, busy with letters & notes: at 9.00 leave for Liverpool.
 Sit [in court] from 10.00 till 5.00 . . . No incident: the day dull enough.
 Home at 6.00, & short walk.
 Letters again: read, write, dined, & early to bed.
 Sent £5 to the Bethnal Green Free Library.
 The H. of Commons has met again, but done nothing, nor does there appear to be any impatience among the public at this waste of time: it is not now thought that any measure of importance can pass: Ireland is the only subject which people care to discuss.

20 Apr. 1882: Up early . . . Liverpool again at 10.00, & sit till 5.30 . . . Home at 6.30.
 Answer from Col. Maude to my letter. He is as full as ever of his plan for sending back the Jews to Palestine.
 . . . The Irish anti-rent agitation has spread to Skye, where there are riots, police sent for, & a prospect of further disturbance. Strikes in Wales have also caused some rioting, & in Cornwall there has been an outbreak of the native population against Irish labourers. All indicates an excited state of mind among the working class on labour questions, though as regards politics properly so-called there is complete freedom from agitation.

21 Apr. 1882: Saw Ward, who is well satisfied with the way the rents are coming in, but less so with the expenditure, which is very heavy, & a good deal of it he evidently thinks unnecessary. I am inclined to agree, but while Hale remains at his post any considerable reduction is hopeless.

. . . Dined at Croxteth, which in good manners I could not refuse, after frequent invitations: else I would as soon have stayed at home.

22 Apr. 1882: . . . Euston at 4.00 . . . reached Fairhill about 6.30. . . .

23 Apr. 1882: . . . Again proposed to M., & pressed upon her, a foreign tour some time in the summer: but to no purpose. She has been disappointed in regard of the success expected from the Swedish doctor's treatment, & now thinks the weakness of her eyes incurable & increasing: for which belief I hope & think there is no adequate cause: but to reason against it is useless: & it is in part the cause, in part the consequence, of the habitual low spirits, amounting to despondency, which have returned upon her. In these moods, which now prevail with few exceptions, nothing seems to give pleasure, & the only interest excited by passing events is of a fanciful kind. A disagreeable piece of news is dwelt upon as if with a sort of satisfaction, referred to again & again, & not allowed to drop out of sight: while anything of an opposite character is as far as possible ignored. It is a family affliction, & probably cannot be cured, but may be mitigated by care & watchfulness. – I believe it to be constitutional, & that the failure of eyesight only supplies a reason & justification for feelings that would equally exist if that exciting cause were withdrawn. (This description was not exaggerated when written, but matters have mended since: it is only at intervals that these gloomy fits occur - Aug. 1882.)

Heard, two days ago, of the death of Darwin: the greatest scientific discoverer of our age: who has revolutionised opinion to a greater extent, & with farther reaching consequences, than we are as yet aware of. He was 73, & had been all his life in feeble health, requiring him to live in a quiet & retired way: he seldom left his house at Downe, & avoided all personal publicity, while known through his books to the whole civilised world. It is impossible to conceive a character more free from envy, jealousy, or vanity in any form. Indeed his apparent ignorance of his own world-wide fame would in a man of less simple & natural manners have seemed like affectation. He has had his reward: for surely no one ever yet produced such an overthrow of existing beliefs, who provoked so little personal hostility. I am asked by his sons to be one of the pall bearers at his funeral in Westminster Abbey, on Wednesday, & have of course accepted . . . The subject of the moment is state purchase of Irish lands, to be resold to the tenants, & by them paid for in instalments. This was originally Bright's scheme: it is now taken up by the opposition, whether wishing to outbid their opponents, or possibly as an indirect method of securing to landowners a fair equivalent for their estates: now unsaleable in open market.

In the abstract it is not objected to by any party: but the obstacles to working out a scheme of the nature indicated are very serious.

(1) Will the Irish tenant care to buy? He has got fixity of tenure, which is what he most wants, & he has vague hopes of some political convulsion, in which, helped by American sympathisers, he may get his land for nothing. Moreover he knows that the State would require & enforce payment more effectively than the private owner.

(2) If he does buy on a large scale, where is the money to come from? Two hundred millions is a moderate estimate of what would be required if all Ireland is to be bought up. Probably the figure would stand much higher.

(3) Assuming the bargain made, what are the chances of the rent, or interest, due to

the State being paid with any regularity, or through a series of bad years? Every Irish M.P. would be called upon to vote for remission of arrears, & probably for reducing the sum originally fixed. How long would the English & Scotch members be able to resist their appeals? The Irish vote would be promised to the party that bid most largely: & how long would our political virtue hold out?

(4) Assuming the payment to be regularly made, would the State become more popular in the character of universal creditor than when, as at present, trying to hold the balance fairly between landlord & tenant?

(5) If more capital is one of the first of Irish wants, will not things be made worse rather than better by the proposed scheme in that respect? The capital paid to the landlords will for the most part be taken out of the country, & the interest will necessarily revert (if paid) to the British Treasury – no part going back for local improvement?

These are a few of the doubts that occur: if leisure serves, & laziness does not intervene, I may perhaps put them into a more formal state for the public.

24 Apr. 1882: . . . In the papers, death of Sir Erskine Perry[91], an accomplished & agreeable man, son of Perry the publisher & editor, who was intimate with the Whig leaders at the beginning of the century: the son became a lawyer, an Indian judge, & later an M.P. In that last capacity I saw a good deal of him during the session of 1858, when he was a violent opponent of the bill establishing a council for Indian affairs. I remember his telling me, when the bill was on the point of being carried, that I had thrown away a great opportunity: next year, however, he had an offer of a seat in this same council, which he accepted, & became the strongest defender of its rights, almost quarrelling on that ground with Sir C. Wood[92], from whom he had the appointment. He remained a member of it till near his death, & did good work, being a man of sense, industry, & culture. In fact he succeeded everywhere except in the H. of C. where, though respected, he was thought a tedious speaker.

I see also recorded the death of Ly Minto[93], who has left a record of herself in several volumes of interesting family biography: and of Sir H. Cole[94], long head of the S. Kensington museum: a shrewd, active, & useful public servant, supposed to have supreme influence with the Court in matters of art, & unpopular accordingly with parliamentary men, especially with the Chancellor of the Exchequer. He was thought to be a jobber, but I never heard proof that he really was so. He spent public money freely, even lavishly: but for that the permanent head of a department cannot well be held responsible. Every department spends all that it can get: & a department which has the Court behind it can get a good deal.

25 Apr. 1882: Lionel C.[ecil] left us: not much talk about farming affairs, but I gather that he is spending his capital as fast as ever. He & his brother [Lord Arthur Cecil] are content with knowing that it all goes on the farm, & do not seem to know or care whether any part of it will come back. However, they behave perfectly well in all other respects, & at worst it will not be hard to provide for them.

In H. of C. the budget last night: contrary to expectation, it is the least important that Gladstone has ever brought in. People believed that being his last he would try to make it memorable by great financial changes. This he has not attempted: partly on the plea that his surplus (£305,000) is too small: partly on the ground, I suppose, that the Cabinet have troubles enough before them already, that the House is overburdened with business which it cannot or will not do, & that it is not advisable to engage in fresh controversy.

Moreover he could not do what it is thought he most wishes to attempt – increase the duties on real property – without finally alienating the Whigs, who are not too friendly even now. So he has contented himself with readjusting & increasing the tax on carriages, and contributing £250,000 (in what way I do not clearly understand) to the highway rates. – I have no doubt that in existing circumstances his decision is wise: but to ardent reformers it will be a disappointment. It is announced that the bills for local government in counties, & reform of the municipal government of London, are dropped: so that the session will be nearly barren.

Gladstone took occasion to complain of the too great love of expenditure, & of not enough being done for reduction of debt: in both of which complaints I sympathise, but as regards the debt I think he overstates his case, for by his own showing we have paid off 7 millions in the last financial year: which is quite enough, if we can keep it up. . . .

26 Apr. 1882: By early train to attend the funeral of Mr. Darwin . . . The pall bearers with me were, D. of Devonshire, D. of Argyll: Lowell, Huxley, Hooker, Spottiswoode, Mr. Wallace the naturalist, & Canon Farrer[95]. Sir J. Lubbock was named one, but I did not see him. Possibly he was shut out, for the arrangements were confused. The grave was close by that of Sir Isaac Newton: which was well.

Saw Walpole, & wished him joy of his son's appointment to be governor of the Isle of Man.

Note that E. Stanley[96] of Cross Hall is returned to parliament as a Conservative: without contest. He was a mild Whig (very mild) in his earlier days – probably frightened by the new developments of politics. He has good sense & cultivation, but is too indolent & indifferent to do anything in public life. Probably he has no ambition of the kind. But I am glad for the sake of the name that we have three Stanleys sitting in H. of C.

Meeting . . . of the City Commission. Only about half our number present. Walked away with Ld Sherbrooke, who more than once forgot what he was going to say, repeated what he had said a minute before, & complained of having lost his memory. He is certainly failing, but the failure may go no farther for a long while. . . .

27 Apr. 1882: . . . Government promise a bill dealing with arrears of rent, in what sense they do not say. They seem to be waiting for the opposition proposals as to purchase before they will declare themselves.

28 Apr. 1882: . . . After dinner, Lawson called to ask if I had heard the news: Ld Cowper[97] resigns Ireland, Spencer takes his place, as reported: I had no information & could give none. What he evidently wanted to know was whether I had had, or should have, an offer to join the Cabinet &, if so, what answer I had given or should give. But as to this, I had nothing to say.

29 Apr. 1882: Up early, & find the news of Ld Spencer's going to Ireland is true: which surprises me, for he is in weak health, and his present post is one of the highest & pleasantest that a man can hold. It is a real sacrifice to public duty: Ireland is the grave of political reputations, & Spencer can be under no illusions as to the nature of the work. I read the matter in this way – there is a cry for change in the Irish executive, & for the removal of Forster: which is unjust, for he has done all that a man could do, hampered & pulled in various directions as he has been: but if on the one hand some concession is to be made to the discontented, & if on the other Forster cannot be sacrificed, the appointment of a new Lord Lieut. is a good expedient – Ld Cowper's position has become ludicrous: nominally at the head of an administration, with the country in a state of smothered war, he is literally never mentioned either for praise or blame: his name is hardly known: he is vaguely believed to disapprove much of what has been done: but nobody knows, & nobody cares. Spencer, it is understood, retains his seat in the Cabinet, which if true is a new arrangement, but perhaps convenient, though he can very seldom attend.

Much speculation as to his successor in the Presidency: I hear Ld Rosebery named as probable[98].

Wet morning – busy . . . the secretary to the Hospital for Consumption called to ask me to attend the opening of the new building in June – I gave an ambiguous answer: but, as president of the hospital, I suppose refusal is impossible: though these frequently recurring ceremonies are a waste of life.

. . . Sanderson called again to explain that the papers are mistaken: Ld Spencer does not go over to Ireland, it seems, but only on a kind of special mission, retaining his post as Ld President: which saves the trouble & fuss of a reconstruction. So much the better: but it can only be a temporary arrangement.

. . . Tore up letters . . . read a book on political economy by Bonamy Price: less dry than such treatises usually are[99].

Gave my name[to] a memorial to Newmarch, the late statistician & writer on economy[100]. . . .

1 May 1882: . . . To the Lords, where a dull debate raised by Carnarvon on religious teaching at the University of Oxford. He brought up Camperdown, & two bishops, also the Chancellor, who was tedious & inaudible. Nothing came of it. De La Warr asked one of his many questions about Tunis[101]: and Salisbury asked about Ld Cowper's retirement, & the consequent changes, in a tone of acrimony, & almost insult, which was unprovoked, & jarred on the feelings of the House. He got no answer, Granville asking for notice.

. . . Several of the papers mention my name in connection with the Presidency of the Council: but, as it is not vacant, the question has not arisen. I hope it will not arise: for of the three alternatives, either that I should not be asked to join, or that I should refuse, or that I should accept, there is probably no one that would not injuriously affect my personal position. The Cabinet, though still strong, is discredited with the public by the failure so far of its policy: since rents are not paid, & Ireland is not pacified. On the other hand, it is scarcely possible to give this as a reason for refusal – one cannot say to a government which one supports: 'You are too unpopular, & I will not act with you.' A refusal would make it difficult to return to active public life. And to be passed over is never agreeable. I hope therefore that matters may remain as they are, & that there will be no reconstruction.

The Irish trouble may be said to have reached its height. Three questions are pending: (1) the release of the suspects, or of some among them: (2) State help to the tenants to pay off arrears: (3) State help to them to buy their farms. None of these questions admits of an entirely satisfactory settlement. The two last I shall notice later on: as to the release of the prisoners, opinion is divided. On the one hand, it is argued, they must be liberated some day. You cannot keep them in for ever: &, if the thing is to be done, why not now? It is added that their detention is a discredit to us in the eyes of foreign nations, & increases the sympathy that is felt, or professed, for Ireland abroad: & that they have already undergone as heavy a sentence as would have been passed on most of them, had they been regularly tried. All this is true: but with equal truth it is answered they have made no submission, they make none now: they will not even promise to abstain from agitation in future: if released they will begin again, & with the glory of being political martyrs: you have not won yet, & if they are let out they will claim, with justice, that they have beaten you. The arguments are sound on either side: probably the result will be, as it usually is, a compromise: a few of the worst will be kept in, the rest set free.

2 May 1882: . . . Read & wrote after luncheon till near 4.00, when to H. of Lords. There a statement was made by Granville, not merely that Ld Cowper had resigned, & Ld Spencer taken his place, which we knew before, but that the suspects now in gaol are for the most part to be released, & that Forster, apparently dissenting from the policy of this step, has left the government[102]. This was not expected, & caused much sensation: for the most part unfavourable. There was no cheering on either side, & faces looked grave. A similar & rather fuller announcement was made in the Commons.

Dining with Mrs. Meynell Ingram[103], we met Gladstones, Halifax's, the Duchess of Somerset, the Abp. of York, etc. Gladstone seized upon me before dinner, & began eagerly to explain the situation. I do not set down in detail what he said, not remembering it with sufficient accuracy: but the substance was that the government had carried their point as to putting down the no-rent agitation (I doubted, but said nothing), that they had failed to put down outrages, & that he at least was convinced it could not be done by any police arrangements: he had no doubt but that these outrages took place at the instigation of the Land League, & he believed that if the suspects were released, & proper legislation adopted on the question of arrears, the influence of the League would be used to restrain them. He was sanguine of success: but he said: 'I admit that all depends on success: & if we fail we are done for altogether.' In fact it is a new departure, founded on partial alliance with the Land League, & on an emphatic repudiation of the policy of coercion which has been accepted as a necessity up to this date by parliament & the public. The effect one way or the other must be grave, if not decisive: & the sections of the Liberal party will be wider apart than before. The immediate question is, what will be asked by the Irish – will it be no more than England can fairly give? and will not Parnell return as master of the situation? It is too early to judge. Forster's explanation has to be heard, & we do not know all the facts.

But I augur ill of the result. It will be felt both in England & in Ireland as a humiliation to have given way, as by Gladstone's own admission we have done: & I should not be surprised if many elections are lost in consequence.

I note it as odd that Gladstone should have denied officially that any negociation had taken place with Parnell: when to me he said distinctly that a Mr. O'Shea had acted as the go-between, & had had interviews with Parnell in Kilmainham. It is possible that O'Shea volunteered his services, & so was not in the strict sense of the word employed: but surely that is rather a fine distinction? The very time of his going over was named: he crossed on Friday night, was at the gaol on Saturday, & returned Saturday night.

3 May 1882: . . . Received a deputation headed by Broadhurst M.P. asking me to attend the trades union yearly meeting (congress they call it) at Manchester in September. I reserved my answer, but probably shall not go.

. . . The son of Mr. Beal, the agitator for municipal reform, who appeared before us the other day, writes to ask for a loan of £1,500 or £2,000 to save his father's business. I decline, but civilly.

4 May 1882: Slept little & disturbedly last night, half smothered with cold in head & throat, & feverish into the bargain: I do not know when I have passed so uncomfortable a night. It is a real influenza cold, said to be epidemic just now, & rather severe, involving in most cases a week's illness. . . .

5 May 1882: . . . In H. of C. Forster's explanation of his retirement has been given[104]: he spoke temperately, gravely, in a spirit of friendship to his late colleagues, but as if deeply convinced of the danger of relaxing the grasp in which Irish agitation is held & restrained. A debate, or rather a wrangle, followed: &, as far as I can make out, the feeling of the House seems to have been with Forster. The opposition of course take up the cause of any minister who has seceded, in order to damage those who remain: but among Liberals many think him ill-used – that he has been made the scapegoat of a policy which was common to the whole Cabinet – and, others add, that he has been got rid of by an intrigue of which the chief promoter was Chamberlain. It looks as if the Premier, who is liable to sudden impulses, had been converted by the party of conciliation, & not only wished to release the prisoners (which must have been done sooner or later) but to give to their release the utmost importance, letting them out all at once, instead of a few at a time, so as to mark & emphasise the fact of a new departure having been taken.

6 May 1882: Up to breakfast, much better in health: indeed there is now but little amiss, except great weakness, result of fever & remedies for it.

. . . Left at 4.00 for Keston, with M., where we enjoyed the fine air & quiet. Walked about the place, but neither far nor fast.

Wrote among others to L. West at Washington, & to A.D. on the Irish policy.

The new departure in Irish policy, as it is called, has occupied all tongues & pens for the last few days. And no wonder, for it is a bold and questionable step. It is announced that the coercion act will not be renewed, but that fresh powers of some kind will be taken by the executive to restrain outrages: that there is to be legislation about arrears, & probably also to extend the purchasing power of the tenants. What strikes me is that a modification of policy, perhaps necessary, has been accomplished in a specially awkward way. The suspects could not have been kept in for ever: whether they were released a little sooner or later could hardly be made a very serious issue: & the executive might fairly have been trusted to act on its own discretion in the matter: again, legislation about arrears is in no sense necessarily a concession to the Land League: in fact it may be very much to the advantage of the landlords: and the plan of enabling tenants to buy their holdings is expressly supported by Smith & Cairns. Against the announced cessation of the coercion act might have been set the promise of new powers to be obtained for the repression of crime: in short, there is nothing in what has been done, or announced as intended to be done, that may not be defended on even conservative grounds. The misfortune is that it has been done in the most tactless manner. Gladstone, while verbally denying negociations with the imprisoned Land Leaguers, has in fact admitted that something of the kind took place: & the immediate denial of Parnell & Sexton that they had accepted any conditions looks suspiciously like a determination to get out of an understanding which had been formulated in purposely vague terms. The resignation of Forster, whose reluctance to adopt a policy of coercion was extreme & well known, & who may be assumed to have supported it only from a conviction of necessity, has been a heavy blow: not the less so because it is believed to be the result of an intrigue conducted by Chamberlain, who wanted the direction of Irish affairs to be in his own hands. If this be so, and I believe it is, the plan has failed: for the vacant place is given to Ld F. Cavendish, Hartington's brother, a good sensible official, but about the last man who would have been thought of for the post.

One story is that Chamberlain might have gone as secretary, but insisted on dictating the conditions of his policy, & these were so entirely in the sense of the Land League that even Gladstone could not accept them[105]. In any case, the selection of Cavendish has disappointed the radicals (for he is a Whig of Whigs) while it has not reassured the moderate section of the party: for they consider him as a clerk put in to do what the Premier wishes.

The first effect of the whole business has been undoubtedly to weaken & damage the Cabinet: which is more shaken than it ever has been before: but all really turns on two points: (1) the result in checking outrages, & quieting outrages, during the next 2 or 3 months: (2) the character of the legislation promised. Till we know more, any final judgment is premature.

7 May 1882 (Sunday): I had scarcely written the above when news came of the murder of Ld F. Cavendish & the under-secretary, Mr. Burke[106], in the Phoenix park, close to the Viceregal Lodge, between 7.00 & 8.00 last night. It is too early to speculate on the results of an event which will profoundly affect the situation: raising the hopes of the irreconcilable party, discouraging the friends of conciliation, & possibly causing in England & Scotland a violent outbreak of anti-Irish feeling. A more disastrous incident could not have occurred, nor could it have occurred at a more inconvenient moment. The first impression left on my mind is that it will be a heavy blow to the Cabinet. 'We were told,' the English public will say, 'to rely on Irish good feeling, to conciliate instead of coercing, & here is the answer that comes from Ireland.'

Passed the day as usual: G. Duncan called.

8 May 1882: London by usual train . . .

H. of Lords at 4.00, a considerable attendance, many peers in mourning: it had been agreed to do no business, but adjourn at once, after a few words said in honour of the memory of the late Irish secretary. Granville moved the adjournment accordingly, Salisbury seconded, Cowper, Marlborough, & Carlingford each said a few words. None was eloquent, all in good taste. I heard that a similar scene passed in the Commons, Gladstone being deeply affected. Indeed he had reason to be so, for not only was F. Cavendish a connection of his by marriage, but the families were intimate, they had been in the closest possible official relations during the last two years, & it was the earnest request of the Premier that alone induced Ld F. to accept the Irish post. More than this, Gladstone must have felt that the murder was, in fact, the Fenian answer to his message of peace, & in that sense the immediate result of it.

There is no reasonable doubt that the murder was committed by Fenian desperadoes, & that the motive was fear lest conciliatory offers on the part of government should produce a better feeling between the two countries. The object was to keep alive the old feeling of dislike on both sides, & it cannot be said that the means were ill chosen with that end [in view]. The skill & daring shown in the commission of the crime are remarkable: firearms, which would have given the alarm, were not used, & the murderers actually drove off unsuspected, having killed two men in daylight in a publicly frequented park. They were probably Americans: natives would have blundered the business. I am inclined to think that my first impression as to the injury done to the government was mistaken: but reserve my opinion on that point a day or two longer. Dined quietly at home, & early to bed.

9 May 1882: Still troubled with much cold in the head, though not now generally unwell.
. . . It is announced that Trevelyan is to be the new Irish secretary: probably a good choice: he is clever, industrious, ambitious: his only defects a somewhat too obvious good opinion of himself, which hindered his early success in parliament, has much decreased with increasing age & literary fame. He is radical in his general opinions, but too clear-headed, I think, to be mystified by 'Irish ideas'. . . .

10 May 1882: . . . All that passes confirms me more & more in the opinion that the Cabinet will gain, in a political point of view, from the event of Saturday night. Party opposition is for the moment at an end: the threatened attack, consequent on the 'new departure' of last week, will be no more heard of: Gladstone escapes from the false position into which he had put himself by his quasi-alliance with Parnell: he has used the opportunity to get out of another difficulty by compromising the question of *clôture* on which he might very possibly have been beaten: (his excuse for withdrawal being that Irish affairs require the whole attention of the House): he will carry his new police measures whatever they may be, the Irish not daring in the present state of feeling to obstruct: the question of arrears remains his only trouble, & as to that there is quite as strong a wish on the Conservative as on the Liberal side to get it settled. He holds better cards than he has held since the beginning of the session. But personally he is said to be suffering much from the shock: being a man of nervous temperament, & feeling responsible for having sent Ld F.C. to his death.

11 May 1882: . . . Herbert Spencer called by appointment, wishing to see me about a new society called the Anti-Aggression League, having for its object to prevent unnecessary wars . . . I expressed general sympathy . . . though having little faith in his proposed remedies: but the object is good. He came to luncheon . . . & talked very agreeably.
    Funeral of Ld F. Cavendish today: & all the papers are full of the subject. It is said that Parnell has applied for police protection: whether really feeling himself in danger from the Fenian party (who no doubt are distinct from the Land League) or, as is more likely, wishing to divert odium from himself & his friends, by seeming to be in the same danger as landlords & loyalists. . . .

12 May 1882: . . . H. of Lords . . . Drove home with Dalhousie, who has seen a good deal of the Irish & finds them furious at the new coercion bill, proposed last night in the Commons: well they may be, for it is about the severest ever passed. Another complaint he reports which is new to me: the moderate Home Rulers and Liberals are especially angry that as they say advice given by them is left unnoticed, though they are friendly to the English connection, whereas any word that falls from a prominent Land Leaguer is caught up at once. The truth I suppose to be that, as in revolutionary times always happens, the moderate party has ceased to have any influence: not being feared, they are not important. Shaw[107] complained with peculiar bitterness of the demoralisation produced by English policy: 'You have taught us that reason, argument, appeals to justice, are useless: but that you are always ready to yield to threats. It will take Ireland a century to recover from the effect of the last two years.'

There is truth in this: at the same time it must be remembered that Shaw is a disappointed candidate for the Irish secretaryship.

Talking to Kimberley about the question of state assistance to enable Irish tenants to pay up their arrears, I said: 'You are going to make a general distribution of public money, by which both Irish tenants & Irish landlords will profit: one class only you exclude from the benefit of the subsidy: & that class is made up of landlords who have been moderate enough to waive demands which could not be met, & tenants who have been honest enough to pay as much as they could.' Kimberley answered: 'I cannot deny it: what you say is perfectly true, but I don't see how we can help ourselves.' Nor do I: but the transaction is an Irish one throughout.

13 May 1882: . . . Knowles[108] called in afternoon, hinting at an article on Home Rule. I find that he is convinced of its necessity in some shape: chiefly on the ground that the Irish M.P.s will make all business impossible till they get what they want. I do not think highly of Mr. Knowles's personal judgment, but he runs about & sees everybody, & probably what he says is being said by many others of the younger Liberals. He says the Irish will use every device to delay the passing of the new coercion bill: & indeed nothing else can be expected: so that we shall probably sit late, & pass very little else.

Another foolish attempt, supposed[ly] Fenian, to create a scare by exploding powder under the walls of the Mansion house: as in former cases, it was detected before mischief was done. It is not easy to understand what object is served by tricks of this sort, too trifling to cause terror, though they may irritate. . . .

14 May 1882 (Sunday): . . . Read Renan's book, a translation of & comment on Ecclesiastes[109]: interesting, & all the more so because Renan by the nature of his mind is exactly fitted to understand & sympathise with the sceptical, désillusionné Jew who assumed to write in the character of King Solomon. He has made some passages intelligible which are nonsense in our version, but at the cost of their poetry. . . .

15 May 1882: . . . After luncheon Granville called, & with a little circumlocution proposed to me, on the part of the Prime Minister, that I should join the Cabinet. His offer was either the post of Lord President or that of Indian secretary: in the event of my accepting the latter [*vice* Hartington] Hartington would take the Exchequer. He did not think any further changes would be made in the Cabinet. I told him, with compliments, that I received the proposal with gratitude: that I knew of nothing in the state of politics to make acceptance impossible: but that I must consider the matter at leisure. He should have an answer on Wednesday. I added that if I accepted either place it should be the India Office, as that gives some real work to do, which the Presidency of the Council does not[110].

H. of Lords at 4.30: walk down with D. of Cleveland[111], who full of stories about the Irish in the mining districts about Raby. He believes they mainly sympathise with the murderers, & some of them make no secret of it.

At the Lords, talk with O'Hagan: who says the new cardinal Maccabe[112] [sic] is in fear of his life, thinking himself marked out as the next victim: I don't know why: but O'Hagan says the old feeling of respect for the priests is greatly diminished, the American or Fenian influence being used against them.

16 May 1882: In the Commons, a very angry scene arising out of the negociations with Parnell[113]. Balfour talked of the 'infamy' of the conduct of the government, a word which I should have thought the Speaker would not have allowed. Gladstone answered, in anger as was natural, & did not say too much. It is a confused business: I cannot see that anything substantially wrong has been done, but it was unwise to do or say anything that bore the appearance of negociation with Parnell: & still more so to deny the existence of an understanding with him, when to ordinary minds it seemed clear that what had passed amounted to one. There was no deception in all this, for the facts were frankly admitted: only an odd habit of refining & drawing distinction, such as has damaged the Premier before now.

Labouchere had a motion to abolish the H. of Lords: whether seriously meant or not I don't know: but the House was counted[114].

17 May 1882: Saw Trevelyan, & walked with him in the street. He talks cheerfully & sensibly of the situation: says he must expect to be knocked about a good deal (his own words) but that at his age, 43, that is of less consequence than to Forster, who was past 60. He has found the Castle officials in alarm, thinking there was to be a general clearance of them, which among other things the Irish are crying out for: but he says he has reassured them. He is determined to take no offence, & be conciliatory to everybody: a good resolution, not easy to keep where Sextons, Biggars, & such like are in question. He thinks Forster was much injured by the presence of his adopted son, Arnold-Forster[115], who lived with him & used to write in the papers, or in reviews (I don't know which) on Irish subjects. He asked me whether I thought the Whigs were alienated? I said yes, for the moment, but it would not last. I thought the parliamentary difficulties were mostly overcome: what remained to be done was not likely to be opposed, except by the Irish.

. . . Dined Sir J. Lubbock . . . Talk with Buxton[116] as to Home Rule: I find him strongly convinced that no federal system of government will answer, that an English & Irish parliament would inevitably come into collision: but he seriously doubts whether it would not be better to let Ireland go altogether than retain it by force. He admitted, however, that national sentiment would make a surrender of that kind impossible, & that practically there was no remedy except to keep things as they are.

18 May 1882: . . . I yesterday wrote to Granville, declining office at present, but in such a manner as to show confidence in the government, & ascribing my refusal to private reasons exclusively. There are some circumstances connected with this offer & refusal which I think it better not to note down: though I have no reason to be ashamed of them. But they are entirely personal, & do not concern me alone.

19 May 1882: . . . Dined with Granville, a large party . . . sitting next Ly Harcourt, & having much talk with Dilke, I was well entertained.

Dilke says that Tenterden, who used to be very hard-working, has grown lazy, is often away, & throws all on Pauncefote[117]: the fact is he is now happily married, well off, & tired of the office. Lister[118] does nothing at all: which is not new. Pauncefote bears the whole burden, & Dilke speaks of him in terms of high praise. He also praises young Villiers[119], Ld Clarendon's son.

Talk of the Irish office. Dilke expressed something like displeasure at its having been offered him without a seat in Cabinet: which considering that he is young in politics I thought pretentious: but I see that he values himself highly, & indeed he has had enough of success & flattery to make a little elation natural. Then we fell on Gambetta & French politics: he thought Gambetta had intended to fall, but expected to be picked up again, & was disappointed at there being no return of opinion in his favour . . .

. . . We had some more conversation on various matters connected with foreign policy: I could not help noticing that Dilke assumed the tone of a partner in the business rather than of a subordinate: & I suspect that Granville, who is no longer as young as he was, accepts the situation, & lets him take a larger share in the management than is usually allotted to an under-secretary.

20 May 1882: . . . The vacancy caused by Ld F. Cavendish's death is filled by a Mr. Holden[120], a manufacturer, in the same interest. The seat was sharply contested by one of Ld Cranbrook's sons[121], but the majority is large. The Liberal papers are crowing rather more loudly than is wise for, after all, parties only remain where they were: they make it clear that they thought a beating probable.

There is great bitterness against Forster: which is not reasonable, for he has held his own in the most difficult of all positions, & his policy was that of the Cabinet: while, as to pleasing the Irish, the thing was impossible in the mood they are in. But the party are sore at his resignation, though it was the consequence of an intrigue directed against him by Chamberlain & others: the ostensible ground of difference was probably only the plea for doing what both sides already desired. There is a struggle going on between Whigs & Radicals, of which a recent quarrel in the Reform Club is one symptom. The Whigs, or moderates, there blackball every candidate of the ultra party, & an attempt was lately made, headed by Granville & Hartington, to put the elections into the hands of a committee: on this proposal a vote was lately taken, & it has been rejected. The radicals are angry, claiming their share in the club, & from a political point of view they are right: but the Whigs allege that their candidates are not gentlemen in the conventional sense of the word (which is probably quite true) & do not choose to associate with them. The matter is important only as an indicator of what is going on outside on a wider scale. . .
.

22 May 1882: . . . H. of Lords at 4.30, where two ecclesiastical bills occupied a long time: most of the bishops were there. Then came De La Warr, with a bill about railway brakes, which the railway interest opposed, & he was obliged to withdraw it: but he made a good fight. Stratheden had intended to deliver one of his incomprehensible harangues, but put it off: & Waterford, who had given notice of a question about the so-called 'treaty of Kilmainham', withdrew it. I moved the second reading of a Boilers Explosion Bill intended to give the B. of Trade power to enquire into accidents arising from explosions: this is the bill which H. Mason asked me to support. I spoke about five minutes: there was no opposition.

. . . Death of the Duke of Grafton[122] announced: he was only 63: a kindly, simple man, popular, & deserving to be so: in politics, an old Whig. His chief occupation was hunting.

Sir J. Holker, appointed a Lord Justice only a few months ago, has resigned his office: he was thought dying, but appears to have partially recovered: but his active life is over. He was a sound lawyer: a solid heavy speaker: a strong partisan while in political life: but would probably have made a fair judge if his health had lasted.

Lord Westbury[123], grandson of the Chancellor, is to marry a sister of the present Ld Dysart, with a fortune of £200,000: another illustration of Disraeli's favourite theory, that in England to give a man a title is to put into his hands the means of acquiring fortune. Ld W. has taken no part in the business of the Lords.

23 May 1882: . . . I hear from various quarters facts significant of the state of Ireland, & all unsatisfactory. It has been necessary to take precautions to prevent the grave of Mr. Burke, the lately murdered under-secretary, from being violated: it was believed that the mob would have opened it to drag about & insult the body. Ld Spencer has written to say that the feeling in Dublin about the murders is one of undisguised exultation among the lower classes: & this Ld O'Hagan confirmed. The daughters of a Mrs. Smythe, lately murdered by a shot not intended for her, were hooted & hissed on their way to the railway station: it seems that though the shot was really meant for another person the mob supposed that she must have done something to deserve shooting & so vented their anger on the family. At a concert in Dublin, attended by the Lord Mayor, 'national' songs were sung, & applauded with extraordinary vehemence by the audience. The 'Fenian Council' in New York (I think it is) has issued a manifesto applauding the late assassinations. Davitt, released on ticket of leave, has been delivering a speech in Manchester as defiant in tone, & hostile to British rule, as if he had never been in gaol. Maccabe, the new Cardinal, has asked to be put under special police protection: but this may only be a device to make it appear that he is threatened by the Fenians. Whether rents are being paid or not seems doubtful: accounts vary in every district, & I cannot get at the truth. Taking it altogether, I should judge that as regards obedience to law, abstinence from acts of violence, & honesty in recognising obligations, the people are worse now than last year: & one does not see how they are to recover from their present demoralisation.

24 May 1882: Left Keston by the usual train . . . Called on A.D. . . . Death of Sir J. Holker announced . . . he was only 54.

Derby Day: notwithstanding which the H. of Commons sat, the first time they say for 35 years. When I first came into parliament, the motion to adjourn over the Derby was always opposed, the radicals thinking it unseemly that national business should stop on account of a horse race. But whether from the influence of Ld Palmerston, or because politics in general became more easy-going after the Crimean war, the adjournment came to be a matter of course, & was not usually opposed.

. . . In H. of C. the Prevention of Crime Bill was discussed: Dillon taking the lead in opposition, & delivering a speech which Gladstone called 'heart-breaking'. The phrase is curious, as indicating what the Premier's hopes must have been: for what Dillon said was only what everybody would have expected, except that he expressed it in rather plainer terms than has been usual in parliament. His strongest utterance was a declaration that so long as evictions continued he, Dillon, would not denounce outrages. He evidently looks on the latter as a natural & necessary consequence of the former. The object was probably to show that the Irish party do not acknowledge any compact (if such exists) with Parnell as binding on them. The effect on the House was to secure support for ministers: since it is felt that the avowed encouragement of crime must be checked.

Gladstone called on M. again this afternoon[124]. . . .

26 May 1882: Left by 9.00 a.m. train, & reached Knowsley about 3.00.

. . . Parnell last night made a speech in the House, in a tone new to him, apologising for Dillon, but in a style which showed that there was no great agreement between them[125]: it is clear that he for his part is willing to act up to the understanding which the opposition have named 'the treaty of Kilmainham'. He is of course not less hostile to the Union, or to the British connection, than he was: but probably he wishes for an interval, during which the buying out of landlords may be effected, & the Home Rule party strengthened. He sees that the Land League have got all they can expect to get for the present, & that the irritation of the English would be an obstacle to any immediate concession of importance on the question of legislative independence.

27 May 1882: . . . Dined with Mr. & Mrs. Holt, meeting Gen. Fairchild . . . Holt says: 'You may just as well take away all representation from the Irish, if you will not let them manage their own affairs: what is the use of their having votes in parliament if they can always be outvoted?'

I can see that the feeling of the English public, & especially of the Liberals, is quite unsettled on the question of Home Rule: the desire to satisfy the Irish by giving them what they want conflicting with the conviction that nothing short of independence will really satisfy the discontented. . . .

29 May 1882 (Whit Monday): . . . At 12.00 left with M. & Margaret for Liverpool: where luncheon at the Town Hall with the Mayor . . . & Mayoress: about 30 to 35 guests invited: rather a long affair, though well done, & happily no speeches. Thence to Stanley park, where we drove in procession: M. & I with the Mayor & Mayoress in their carriage, our carriage with Margaret & some others. I opened the bazaar on behalf of the Stanley hospital, which was the reason of my coming: speaking about ten minutes. We then went through the bazaar, buying as was expected: and got home by 5.00 p.m. The day was very fine, a great crowd, but no excessive heat or dust, & all went off well.

Serious trouble in Egypt . . . the struggle is between Arabi Pasha at the head of the army & the Khedive: the military party professes to represent national ideas, & opposition to European interference. England & France have sent ironclads to Alexandria, partly to protect their own people, partly as a hint. The Khedive has put himself into our hands. The Porte professes to wish him well, but is suspected of favouring the disturbance in order to assert its own supreme authority, being called in as a mediator: & possibly Turkish troops may have to be employed to keep the peace: which would gratify Turkish pride, & certainly be a curious comment on Gladstone's utterances of 1876 and 1879. . . .

31 May 1882: In the papers, unsatisfactory news: the Land Leaguers have made an assault on the Poor Law Guardians (quite legally & acting within their right): they have displaced landowners & respectable persons from the post of guardians, Lord Emly[126] being one of those so removed, & elected suspects or violent partisans in their place. They are thus masters of the distribution of poor law relief, & may use it as they please to fine the landowners, & compensate evicted tenants by giving them an allowance out of the rates. The danger of this move is the greater because it is strictly justifiable: they are only doing what the law entitles them to do in making their choice. Apart from financial mischief, it is a safe display of anti-English feeling.

Trouble in Egypt continues undiminished, & if possible increased: Arabi Pasha & the mutinous army are masters of the situation: the Khedive entirely in their hands. We must interfere, & probably have done so: but the talk is that the French are hanging back, unwilling, as their nature is, to join in any expedition or negociation in which they do not take the leading part.

1 June 1882: Drove into Liverpool to lay the first stone of the new sessions house: where a fair attendance of magistrates . . . A crowd assembled. I had most of the talking to do, & spoke about ten minutes . . . We then went back to the Adelphi, & ended with a stately luncheon, some 40 present, with toasts, etc. I got home at 3.30.

. . . Saw Ward, & signed more leases. The new rents for which I have signed leases this year amount to £2,200 nearly: in 1880-1881 they came to £13,000 & more. The increase cannot go on at this rate: & I hardly wish that it should. Being of a moderate disposition, I consider all over £200,000 a year as superfluity. But if I were accused of receiving what Mill called 'unearned increment' I might fairly plead that the increase of the Knowsley rental, great as it undoubtedly is, does not do much more than give a fair interest on the capital sunk in the estates. In the last 20 years, more than a million sterling has been laid out upon them.

2 June 1882: . . . The Egyptian affair remains as it was: the Channel fleet is sent down to Gibraltar, I suppose as a demonstration: the Porte has been appealed to: & a conference of European powers is proposed. The objection to employing English or French troops, or both, is obvious: there is the risk, or rather the certainty, of creating jealousy: & some doubt as to their coming away again, where the French are concerned. Hence, if Turkish troops can be got to act on our terms, that solution is thought the best: but the Porte may object to figure merely as a policeman under the orders of the powers, & claim authority on its own account: which will be a new complication. The French Cabinet seems unwilling to do more than it can help: for which it has been angrily (& foolishly) attacked by Gambetta.

Bright has been making an extraordinary & characteristic speech at Birmingham, on the opening of a local free library: he talked in praise of books . . . & selected out of the literature of the world for special praise Bancroft's history of the U.S.[127] – one of the most unreadable of all so-called historians – & the American poets, Whittier & Longfellow. It would not be easy to find a stronger proof of the power of political bias to warp the judgment on non-political matters. I have no doubt but that Bright was quite in earnest, & that the books he names are to him more interesting than any others: because they relate to America, & represent American thought, & he believes in American society & the American constitution as the one great achievement of the human race. Extraordinary narrowness is the secret of his strength & his weakness both.

3 June 1882: Left Knowsley at 10.15 . . . reached St. J. Square a little after 4.00 . . .: found a fog . . . for at 5.00 p.m. I could scarcely see to read. On the way down I read a book by Wallace, the naturalist, intended to prove that the State should be the only landowner, &

that, as living landowners & their heirs now alive die out, their estates should revert to the community[128]. Except the book of the American socialist, George, entitled *Progress and Poverty*, which is in the same sense, I have seen no such distinctly revolutionary doctrine put forward by any man claiming to be a thinker. Mr. Wallace argues that an owner is not injured by having a distant reversion taken away from his successors, provided that the rights of all living persons, or of children whom he may have, are respected: which is ingenious but not conclusive. He reasons cleverly against all perpetual rights of property, in this way: that, as fresh capital is created far more rapidly than it is destroyed, its continual accumulation must end by rendering it worthless, since investments cannot be found for it: & this result is in fact only prevented from taking place by the fact that it is perpetually perishing: that no investment in fact is secure for ever, or in general for more than a generation or two. Hence he argues there is no reason why landed estates should possess a character of perpetuity which no other security, not even the funds, can have. – I do not accept the inference, but it is undoubtedly true that the constant increase of debts, national, local, & private (like railway debentures) is a danger: the time may come when the burden of them will be intolerable – & will there then be no danger of their being shaken off violently? . . .

In the papers, death of Garibaldi, which a few years ago would have been an event: now it is a piece of news.

Dined with Gladstone in Downing Street, which indeed is what I went up for: P. of Wales there, & a large party[129]. Sat next Tweeddale, who said there was a great change among tenants in his district: they used to think the rent must be paid, whoever else went without his money: now they grudge it more than any other payment. D. of Cleveland very lachrymose about the Irish revolt, & the danger of Irish notions about property spreading. Party at F.O., stayed there an hour, well enough pleased: met Burton[130], just returned from Africa: Musurus[131] & the other diplomatists: & half London society.

4 June 1882 (Sunday): . . . Knowsley 4.30.

. . . Called with M. on Mrs. Hale, who not quite sober.

Parliament has begun to sit again: besides the two Irish bills, it is hoped to carry one against corrupt practices, & another making the ballot permanent: parliamentary procedure will not be touched, nor county boards, nor London municipalities. In a word, the session will have been barren: yet no one greatly cares: the democratic excitement of 1880 is calmed down, & a feeling of practically conservative indifference has succeeded: increased no doubt by the fact that of the measures proposed none is objected to on principle by the opposition: so that the stimulus of excited party feeling is wanting.

Oddly enough, among many conversations on public subjects last night, I did not once hear the name of Garibaldi mentioned: so completely does he belong to the politics of the past. His character & career will puzzle posterity. In intellect he was a child: his letters & manifestos were merely absurd: it seemed impossible that they should have proceeded from a man who had played a great public part. Nor did he show any talents for generalship, nor (according to soldiers) any military qualities except unusual personal courage. He was perfectly brave & perfectly honest: but these qualities alone do not explain the enthusiasm which he created, or the devoted attachment felt for him by thousands with whom he had little or no personal intercourse. His invasion of Naples seemed a desperate venture: but he had really no enemy before him: the Neapolitan officers having been largely bribed, & the men indifferent to the cause in which they fought. In short, he was rather a figurehead than a living force in politics: yet, if fame be an object worth working for, he has got it: for his name will be remembered as long as Italy is a nation & perhaps longer. . . .

6 June 1882: . . . I have never seen so much injury done to the trees as this year . . . The possibility of being smoked out of Knowsley, at least in the next generation, has never presented itself to me so strongly.

. . . In the Lords yesterday, a sharp discussion on the so-called treaty of Kilmainham, in which nothing was remarkable except that Cowper strongly condemned the release of the prisoners – or rather, the time & manner of doing it – which he said was regarded as a victory by the disaffected party throughout Ireland.

In the Commons, the Irish bill is going slowly through: but there have been no especially violent scenes.

7 June 1882: . . . More Irish wrangles in the Commons: one Irish M.P. talks of Forster's 'infernal speeches' & is reproved accordingly. There does not seem to be systematic obstruction, but debate is spun out by every clause being discussed in detail. The prospects of the session are less hopeful than ever.

8 June 1882: . . . Heard to my regret that Mrs. – has grown worse in her habits, & now seldom consumes less than a bottle of spirits daily. The fact is known to all the village, but apparently not to the person most concerned: or, if so, he shows skill & sense in seeming to know nothing.

Talk with Hale as to the capacities of Thompson, my sub-agent in the Fylde, of whom I am glad to see he thinks very highly. He is probably the fittest successor that Hale could have, when his time comes to retire.

. . . Irish affairs still in the House of Commons: not much progress made. The end will be that Englishmen will grow so utterly weary of Ireland & its affairs as to be willing to agree to almost any arrangement for getting rid of them. At least I fear so, & this is what the Irish themselves are working for.

9 June 1882: . . . Another Irish landowner murdered: a Mr. Bourke[132], a Catholic, in Galway. He was guarded by a soldier, who was shot at the same time. The cause, that he had tried to enforce payment of rents due to him.

Great wrangling again in the Commons over the Prevention of Crime Bill, as the new coercion bill is called. But there seems to have been no violence of language. The predominant English feeling about Irish affairs appears to have become one of weariness, & almost of despair. I am not sure that this is not a state of mind favourable to Home Rule. If that experiment is ever tried it will be under the influence of some such feeling as this: 'We can do nothing with these people: we cannot settle their affairs, & they will not even let us do our own business: matters cannot well be worse: so let them go.' I do not say that we shall argue so, but that if we ever come to the conclusion supposed it will be on those grounds.

10 June 1882: . . . In the papers, three more Irish attempts to murder, though no life actually taken. In each case the mode of attack was the same, though the localities are far apart: pointing to a general plan.

. . . Mrs. – calls again, in a strange condition, visible to all who came near her.

Hale called, bringing a plan of some land to be sold in the Fylde, adjoining mine, along the bank of the Hodder, near the Yorkshire border. It is in a wild picturesque country, though rather bleak: 6 farms: 476 acres: 60 acres of wood: rental £364: luckily there is no house. I think seriously of offering for this estate: it is in one of the pleasantest parts of the county, near land which I have already, probably not dear for the acreage & rental, & the trustees have plenty of funds in hand. The time, moreover, is favourable for buying, as there are many estates in the market, & capital is less abundant than it was a few years ago: at least capital available for purposes of optional expenditure. . . .

12 June 1882: Left Knowsley at 10.20 . . . reached No. 23 a few minutes after 4.00. M. & I alone together.

Drage came to see me . . . I have now been a week troubled with a heavy cold & cough, which I cannot shake off: but, unlike that which I had in May, it is only a local annoyance: I do not feel ill. – I see, however, that both Gorst & Drage think great care necessary to prevent aggravation of the kidney symptoms. I will take care, for it is stupid to die prematurely by one's own negligence: but the imagination does not easily realise the existence of disease where there is a total absence of pain or discomfort, or even weakness. I accept the medical opinion, but I do it by an effort of reason. . . .

15 June 1882: . . . H. of Lords at 4.00, but very little to do. Salisbury made a bitter & violent speech, without public notice given, attacking ministers for what they are doing, or not doing, in Egypt: the state of things there is certainly disagreeable enough: general panic, 250 Europeans killed, all who can escaping, & the result of the Turkish mission is not yet visible. But I do not see how Granville is responsible for it.

Irish affairs no better. Payment of rent is obstinately refused, & necessarily has to be enforced by evictions: of which there have been a thousand in the last week. The new coercion bill is doggedly resisted, clause by clause, & when it will pass no one can foretell. This day, I am told, 65 questions were asked in the Commons: half of them probably with no other object than to waste time. In regard of the conduct of business, though there has been no frequent scandal like that of last year, matters are steadily growing worse. I do not believe that any plan of *clôture* can be more than an imperfect & partial remedy.

16 June 1882: . . . Walk with Dalhousie. He related a conversation he had had with Gladstone, in which, with the courage of a young man & a sailor, he seems to have questioned the premier on various delicate subjects. He says that Gladstone disavowed the Coercion Bill of last year, ascribing it entirely to Forster, & saying that it was against his wish: which seems strange. He had been among a party of the wild Irish M.P.s who assure him that, though they want an Irish parliament, they do not want separation: but they excused their language in public by saying that no one in England realises the intense hatred of the Irish masses to the English government. This piece of frankness astonished D. but does not astonish me.

Heard from Coutts late in the day that they have bought for me £10,000 more of the same stock as before, making in all £390,000 invested, & leaving about £1,400 in hand.

This completes my investments for the year.

In 1878 I had invested £195,000

1879	£220,000
1880	£300,000
1881	£350,000
And now	£390,000

Mrs. West dined with us: & her two boys.

17 June 1882: Had my self weighed, 15 st. 1 lb. – practically unaltered.

Drage calls, advises leaving off wine for a fortnight, as the kidneys are not yet right again. I agree.

. . . The Irish have got a new grievance. Whether pressed by creditors, as in many cases is likely, or wishing to anticipate the arrears Bill, landlords are now acting vigorously in the enforcement of payments due to them: & all the more so because of the Land Act of last year. They are willing to sacrifice arrears, if by any means they can get back the land into their own hands. Evictions are going on rapidly: at the rate of 1,000 a week, it was said (but I think that figure must be exaggerated): in any case there are enough of them to keep up the prevailing feeling of discontent: & prevent the country settling down. The Irish M.P.s accordingly begin to cry out that these must be stopped, or at least suspended till the Arrears question has been dealt with. It is not likely that they will succeed: & it is worth notice that the Arrears Bill will be a very partial settlement: for in the first place it excludes all tenants whose holdings are above £30 a year, & these are no better inclined to pay up than the smaller holders: in the next place, which is perhaps more important, it requires payment of a year's rent before the benefit of the Act can be claimed: &, in the poorer districts of the West, the number of those who have not got the year's rent in hand is very large. They have had it, most likely, but not expecting to be required to pay they have made away with it. – On the whole I cannot look forward hopefully to the coming autumn. – The public in general takes very quietly the stoppage of legislative business, as I have more than once noted: but this feeling is not universal. The teetotallers or temperance party, especially, are growing restless at their favourite hobby, the so-called Permissive Bill, being indefinitely postponed.

18 June 1882: . . . News in London of 400 rifles, & a quantity of revolvers, seized by the police: intended for Fenian use.

Darwin's will is in the papers: he leaves £146,000, which is more than any one thought, and more than any, I should suppose, of his brother philosophers.

19 June 1882: London by usual train . . . Sent £5 to a student: & as much to an athletic society in Crewe . . . Sent Sanderson £400 for the half year from July to December . . .

Read & considered a report by Thompson on the Fylde estate . . . I thereon authorised Hale to offer for it . . . going if necessary as high as £14,000. . . . What I have offered is too much, but it is investment up to £11 or £12,000: the rest fancy expenditure. When all is said & done, I know of no investment that in the long run is safer than land. It is less likely to be squandered than a sum in the funds. Only perhaps some people may think that I, or rather the family which I represent, have got enough already.

Call on A.D., who full of the Arrears Bill, which it seems the Irish landlords object to vehemently, though in many cases it will give them sums which they would otherwise certainly lose. But they say (and there is truth in the objection) that it will demoralise the peasantry: that the mere prospect of it excites to fury the solvent & respectable tenants, who have paid, & who now wish they had kept their money in their pockets. These vow that they will not again do an act so foolish, since government favours those who pay nothing: & they are likely to keep their word. It is thought also that the sum which the State will have to contribute is greatly under-rated: to distinguish between cases of real and fictitious distress will be impossible &, if all applications are granted without enquiry into the means of the tenants, the total will run up to several millions. – Much exaspera-tion has been caused by a rather sweeping speech of Trevelyan's, in which he speaks of evictions as 'cruel & unpatriotic' – forgetting, or not caring to note, that they are most frequently caused by deliberate refusals to pay (I think he has since denied using these words, but they were so reported), and that landowners themselves are pressed by cred-itors, from whom no one proposes to relieve them.

Talk also of the extraordinary precautions which Ld Spencer has adopted against assassination: the Phoenix surrounded with police, all business done there & not at the Castle, the garden searched by constables before any one is allowed to walk in it, & more of the same sort. It is right enough, as matters stand: but even the Czar is not more closely guarded, or more a prisoner in his own house.

The Hamilton pictures have sold well: £43,000 paid in all for them, & some are reserved: two, a Rubens and a Hobbema, went for more than £4,000 each. Well enough this in the interest of art: but I am sorry that these prices appear in the papers. The effect on the poorer part of the community cannot be good. To a man earning £50 a year, it must seem monstrous that the year's wages of 80 labourers should go for what he would call a mere fancy. Every such display of wealth strengthens socialism. In the last century, & even in my own boyish days, the stories of what Roman nobles would give for a piece of furniture, a vase, or a statue, seemed monstrous & incredible: they astonish nobody now: & in democratic America they cause even less surprise than here. . . .

21 June 1882: . . . Dined with Ld & Ly Jersey . . . In the course of the evening Ld Northbrook told M. that 'England was humiliated by what was passing in Egypt: things had never in his memory been so bad in that respect: &, what was worse, he did not see the way out of it.' A strong utterance from a member of the Cabinet.

22 June 1882: . . . Drew £500 more in notes, making reserve £10,000 in all &, as I have £390,000 invested, the sum of £400,000 is complete. Here I may stop, & consider at leisure whether to invest more, or buy land with the yearly surplus.

. . . Pender called, & talked a long while about the disorganisation of the H. of C., the waste of time, increased by Gladstone's habit of replying at length to everybody, the dissatisfaction about Egypt, etc. He says he never remembers parliamentary politics in so confused a state. As to Egyptian affairs, he did not seem especially alarmed: & I think he is right. That trouble will pass off: not so the Irish. . . .

23 June 1882: . . . H. of Lords in afternoon, where Salisbury asked a question about Egypt, & then made a violent attack on the proposed conference at Constantinople, argu-ing that the Sultan was quite right in resisting it, that it is an insult to him, & so forth. This is a mistake for, whether he is right or wrong in the abstract, it is clearly no part of the business of an English politician to encourage a foreign sovereign to refuse the demands which our government is making upon him. This was felt, & the judgment of the House was unfavourable.

24 June 1882: . . . The Cabinet is a good deal divided on Egypt: Kimberley, Northbrook, & Chamberlain are believed to be for active interference: Gladstone & Granville against it: nothing is said about Bright. Sanderson, talking to M., quoted Granville as saying that this was the worst (or the most troublesome) crisis of any that he remembered at the office.

25 June 1882 (Sunday): Keston . . . day dull & inclined to rain. Feeling languid, & indisposed to exertion, which I ascribe to sudden leaving off of wine: in the 8 days since Drage advised this, I have used absolutely none on 5 days, & very little on the other 3. I shall go on with the experiment. I passed most of this day in the grounds, but lounging with a book, or else with M. No strong exercise.

Sent . . . to a Liverpool hospital £20: and £20 to the Charity Organisation Society in answer to an application. Read to M. out of a singular American novel called *Democracy*[133] which has lately appeared, & is much talked about both there & here. The object is to expose the corruption & jobbing of Washington politics, & by all accounts the picture is not overdrawn. But it is a new thing for Americans to hear satire directed against their institutions, even by a countryman of their own: formerly they would not have endured it. I suppose that, their position as a powerful & important state being now universally recognised, they have grown less touchy.

26 June 1882: London by usual train . . . day warm & fine.

. . . To the Commons, where found questions going on, 50 or 60 at least: Dilke had the most to answer: he did it well, but in a summary offhand tone which ministers used not to adopt when I knew the place: & the whole scene, though not actually disorderly, was rough: perhaps sitting in the Lords has made me more sensitive on such points: but I was struck with the want of courtesy shown: rude laughter & interruptions when there seemed no cause. An Irishman, absolutely without provocation, asked Dilke for an answer, 'though he supposed it would be as inaccurate as the hon. member's answers usually were': & the House seemed to treat this deliberate insult as a good joke. Altogether the tone & character of the place seemed changed.

. . . There is, I am afraid, a good deal of suppressed discontent on the part of Liberals, as well as of noisy discontent on the part of the opposition, at the state of things in Egypt. It is thought that our govt. ought to have acted at once, & done something (it is not said what) to keep Arabi from exercising power. But it is not easy to see what right of interference we have. Self-defence justifies action if the Suez canal were threatened: & perhaps the rights of the bondholders deserve support, though that is more doubtful: but, so long as neither of these is in danger, it is an awkward matter to interpose between the Khedive and a too powerful minister. The difficulty is increased by the fact that Arabi is probably backed, underhand, by the Sultan, who wishes to use him as a means of exercising direct power [over] Egypt. The alarm at Cairo & Alexandria does not lessen: they are pouring out of the country in fear of a general massacre.

27 June 1882: . . . I hear from various quarters that Granville is suppos[ed] to be growing physically unequal to his work. He is certainly older in looks, and very deaf: & at times seems irritable, which was not his custom: but the strain upon him of late must have been very heavy. A divided Cabinet, Europe not agreed, & great difficulty in deciding how far our rights extend make a combination of difficulties formidable to any minister. I do not add to the list of difficulties that of an impatient & somewhat unscrupulous opposition, for criticism which is hasty & obviously one-sided helps rather than hurts: & the thought of what Salisbury might be in power reconciles many men to Gladstone.

28 June 1882: . . . Sent £5 to the Ulverston Cottage Hospital but declined to subscribe.
    . . . Talk with R. Bourke[134] last night, who fully confirms what I say as to the roughness & discourtesy of the present parliament: in which Harcourt also concurs.
    Talk with Northbrook, to whom I said, referring to some conversation that had passed between Lecky & myself: 'Here is a man who if possible takes a more despondent view of Irish affairs than I do.' Ld N. answered: 'It is impossible to take a more gloomy view than the reality justifies.' . . .

29 June 1882: . . . Dined with the D. of Bedford, meeting . . . the Master of Balliol, Jowett. Some pleasant talk, but noticed what is said to be a habit of the Duke's: that he will not discuss anything, but passes incessantly from one subject to another: which becomes in the end unsatisfactory. He is a modest man personally, but has a strange idea of the power of his family: he said quite in earnest to M.: 'I could turn out Gladstone tomorrow, but I don't see what other government could be formed.' I suppose he meant that the half-revolted Whigs would follow his lead, which perhaps they would: but surely they would not be enough to turn the scale?
    News of more Irish murders: the most important that of a Mr. Blake, agent to Lord Clanricarde, who was shot in his car while driving with his wife: the shots being fired from behind a loopholed wall showing careful premeditation.
    The Irish bill drags on: it has been now 18 or 19 days in committee, & the amendments on the notice paper are more than at the beginning. The English are getting angry, & we shall probably have another all-night sitting.

30 June 1882: . . . Preparations making in H. of C. for an all-night sitting: probably a necessary step to overcome obstruction, but always a disagreeable one: undignified, & generally leading to some exhibitions of bad manners.

Notes

1   Victor Stanley (1867–1934), s. of Frederick, 16th E. of Derby (1841–1908): naval career, rising to Admiral.
2   Liverpool news agency.
3   William Baliol Brett, 1st Lord Esher (1815–1899), judge 1868–1897: cr. baron 1885 and vt 1897.
4   The German Ambassador.
5   The U.S. Minister.
6   Ludovic Lindsay, 26th E. of Crawford and Balcarres (1847–1913): succ. father 1880.
7   Sir E. Thornton (1817–1906), diplomatist: minister at Washington 1867–1881: amb. at St. Petersburg 1881–1884.

[8] Liverpool Whig leader.

[9] Lord Dalhousie (1847–1887), 13th E. of Dalhousie: styled Lord Ramsay 1874–July 1880, when succ. his father: as Lord Ramsay, was M.P. (Lib.) Liverpool March–July 1880: lord-in-waiting 1880–1885.

[10] Ralph Bernal Osborne (1808–1882), wit, Jew, and M.P. (Lib.): friend of Disraeli.

[11] 'Jim' Macdonald (1810–1882), 2nd s. of 3rd Baron Macdonald, and deputy ranger of Hyde Park; priv. sec. to c.-in-c. army 1856–1882: colonel 1881, general 1882: fought in Crimean battles.

[12] The diarist's sister Emma was born in 1835. If she came out at 21, that would be in 1856.

[13] Richard Bethell, 1st Baron Westbury (1800–1873), lord chancellor 1861–1865: father of investment trusts.

[14] Horace Davey, Baron Davey (1833–1907), judge: educ. Rugby and Oxford (double First): Q.C. 1875, sol.-gen. February–July 1886, kt 1886: lord justice of appeal 1893, baron 1894: Lib. M.P. 1880–1885, 1888–1892.

[15] Charles Russell, 1st Baron Russell of Killowen (1832–1900), lord chief justice of England, 1894, on death of Coleridge: Q.C. 1872, M.P. 1880–1894: counsel for Parnell, 1888–1889: judge, 1894–1900.

[16] Henry James, Baron James of Hereford (1828–1911), attorney-gen. 1873–1874, 1880–1885: long subsequent career in politics: Hartington's adviser: baron, 1895.

[17] Sir George Jessel (1824–1883), first Jewish judge: Q.C. 1865, sol.-gen. 1871, M.P. 1868–1875, then judge of high court 1875–1881.

[18] Eustace Balfour (1854–1911), brother of A.J. Balfour.

[19] Lady Frances Balfour, *née* Campbell (1858–1931), dau. of 8th D. of Argyll: m., 1879, Eustace Balfour.

[20] Head forester.

[21] Lord Lorne (1845–1914), gov.-gen. of Canada 1878–1883: m. Princess Louise, 1871: became 9th D. of Argyll 1900.

[22] Sir J. Holker (1828–24 May 1882), attorney-gen. November 1875–1880: lord justice of appeal, 14 January 1882: kt, 1874.

[23] Lady Isabel Burton (1831–1896), wife of the explorer and translator Sir Richard Burton (1821–1890).

[24] Lady Dartrey.

[25] At a rent audit-dinner of his tenantry, Gladstone said his first task would be reform of parliamentary procedure: That dealt with, he hoped to turn to the reform of local government and local taxation.

[26] H.C. Raikes (1838–1891), Conservative activist: from a church family: important in party organisation 1867–1875: deputy speaker 1874–1880: M.P. Chester 1868–1880 (defeated), Preston February–November 1882, Cambridge University November 1882–death: postmaster-gen. 1886–1891.

[27] A.S. Ayrton (1816–1886), lawyer and radical M.P.: M.P. Tower Hamlets 1857–1874: minor offices 1868–1874.

[28] Vt Helmsley (1852–1881), thus styled 1868–1881: d. at Madeira December 1881: educ. Eton 1866–1870: M.P. (Cons.) N. Riding 1874–1881.

[29] Samuel Rowlandson, of Newton Monell, contested no other elections. His platform consisted mainly of reform of the land laws, free trade, and electoral reform.

[30] Hon. Guy Dawnay M.P. (1848–1889), M.P. (Cons.) N. Riding 1882–1885: defeated, N. Riding (Cleveland) 1885: s. of Lord Downe: his platform included a 5/- duty on imported corn, and elected county boards.

[31] Sir R. Malins (1805–1882), M.P. (Cons.) Wallingford 1852–1865 (defeated): Q.C. 1849, judge 1875–1881, kt February 1867.

[32] Andrew Commins (1832–1916), lawyer and Home Ruler: M.P. 1880–1892, 1893–1900.

[33] Probably the anonymous *Wit and Wisdom of Benjamin Disraeli, Earl of Beaconsfield. Collected from his writings and speeches* (Longmans, London, 1881).

[34] Jesse Collings (1831–1920), M.P. (Lib.) 1880–1918, land reformer, and Chamberlain's *alter ego*.

[35] Dudley Ryder, 2nd E. of Harrowby (1798–1882), M.P. 1819–1847, minister 1855–1857.

[36] J.P. Wilde, Baron Penzance (1816–1899), judge 1863–1872: cr. peer, 1869.

[37] See Gwynn and Tuckwell, *Life of Dilke*, i, 437. One rioter howled Bright's slogan: 'Force is no remedy'!

[38] W. Simpson, the defeated Liberal at Preston in February 1882, had fought one other election, when he came bottom of the poll at Liverpool in 1874, standing as a Liberal-Conservative. He does not figure in Orchard, *Liverpool's Legion of Honour.*

[39] Henry Yates Thompson (1838–1928), traveller and collector of illuminated manuscripts.

[40] Thomas Hay Sweet Escott, prolific author and leading journalist: perhaps s. of Bickham Sweet Escott (1802–1853), M.P. (Lib.) Winchester, 1841–1847: defeated W. Somerset 1832, 1835, 1847.

[41] No speeches by Derby appear in the British Library catalogue as having been published by Thorn.

[42] Burke gives no indicator of a New Zealand cousin.

[43] Olga Kiryeeva, later Novikova, pro-Russian publicist active in U.K.: co-operated with W.T. Stead and J.A. Froude during Eastern Question as 'the M.P. for Russia'.

[44] Sir Charles Russell V.C., Bart. (1826–April 1883), M.P. (Cons.) Berks. 1865–1868, Westminster 1874–January 1882.

[45] Lord Algernon Percy (1851–1933), M.P. Westminster 1882–1885, St. George's Hanover Square 1885–1887: 2nd s. of 6th Duke of Northumberland.

[46] Lady Lothian (1836–1901), wife and widow of 8th Marq. of Lothian (1832–1870: childless). She was dau. of 18th E. of Shrewsbury.

[47] Sir Beilby Lawley, 3rd Baron Wenlock (1849–1912), succ. his father November 1880: active in volunteers and held minor court offices.

[48] Arthur J.F. Plunkett, P.C., 11th E. of Fingall (1859–1929), who succ. his father April 1881: styled Lord Killeen 1869–1881.

[49] John H. De La P. Beresford, 5th Marq. of Waterford (1844–1895), who succ. his father 1866: chairman of the Irish Landlords Ctee.: died by shooting himself.

[50] '. . . We attach the greatest value to the extension . . . of local self–government in that country [Ireland]' (Gladstone, 9 February 1882, *Parl. Deb., 3*, vol. cclxvi, col. 260). But, he added, the onus was on the Irish to show how the division of jurisdictions was to be achieved: 'Who is to say what purposes are Imperial?'

[51] Forster's resignation speech, 9 February 1882, *Parl. Deb., 3*, vol. cclxvi, cols. 286–325, was a remorseless catalogue of Irish criminality.

[52] S.G.H. Lowther, 4th E. of Lonsdale (1857–8 February 1882), who succ. father August 1876: elder bro. of 5th E.: m. dau. of Sidney Herbert: held 68,000 acres worth £71,000.

[53] Thomas Aspden, *Historical Sketches of the House of Stanley and Biography of Edward Geoffrey, 14th Earl of Derby* . . . (Preston, 1877, 2nd ed.).

[54] Cf. J. Vincent and A.B. Cooke, 'Herbert Gladstone, Forster, and Ireland, 1881–1882', in 2 parts, in *Irish Hist. Studies*, vol. xvii, no. 68 (September 1971), pp. 521–548.

[55] Sir R. Tufton (1844–1926), cr. Baron Hothfield 1881.

[56] Patrick Egan (1841–1919), leading Fenian: treasurer of I.R.B. till expelled in 1877: treasurer of Land League: U.S. minister to Chile.

[57] Col. Francis Cornwallis Maude, V.C., C.B. (1828–1900), consul-gen. at Warsaw 1876–1886 and eldest s. of Francis Maude, capt. R.N. (1798–1886), who was 6th s. of Cornwallis, 1st Vt Hawarden (1729–1803).

[58] Bradlaugh was re-elected by 3,796 to 3,688, with a reduced majority, was again excluded and then again re-elected in February 1884.

[59]   Thomas Egerton *né* Grosvenor), 2nd E. of Wilton (1799–March 1882), 2nd s. of Robert, 1st Marq. of Westminster.

[60]   Arthur Grey Egerton, 3rd E. of Wilton (1833–1885), M.P. for Weymouth, then Bath: left no children.

[61]   Seymour J.G. Egerton, 4th E. of Wilton (1839–1898), who succ. his bro. 1885: the youngest son of the 2nd E.: succ. by his son, the 5th E.

[62]   Lady Derby's youngest brother.

[63]   George Vane-Tempest, 5th Marq. of Londonderry (1821–1884), who succ. as Earl Vane 1854, and as 5th Marq. on death of his half-brother 1872.

[64]   Charles John Colville, 1st Vt Colville of Culross (1818–1903), who succ. to Scottish title 1849: made U.K. baron, 1885, and vt, 1902: held court office 1852–1858, 1866–1868, 1873–1903: succ. by his eldest son.

[65]   Brother.

[66]   As n. 928 above.

[67]   As n. 929 above.

[68]   Richard Grosvenor, 1st Baron Stalbridge (1837–1912), 2nd s. of Richard, 2nd M. of Westminster: M.P. Flintshire 1861–1886: chief whip 1880–1885: cr. peer, March 1886: chairman of the L.N.W.R. 1891–1911.

[69]   Possibly Henry Charles Howard (1850–1914) of Greystoke Castle, M.P. Penrith 1885–1886, and bro. of Carnarvon's 2nd wife.

[70]   Thomas Brassey, 1st E. Brassey (1836–1918), educ. Rugby and Oxford: M.P. (Lib.) 1868–1886: civil lord of admiralty 1880–1884: baron, 1886. His wife Anna (1839–1887) was an authoress.

[71]   John Freeman-Mitford, E. of Redesdale (1805–1886), chairman of ctees. in House of Lords 1851–1886: cr. Earl 1877: succ. as Baron 1830: d. unm.: left £195,000. Left his estates to a distant cousin who was cr. Baron Redesdale, 1902.

[72]   Geoffrey Guthrie, 2nd Baron Oranmore (1819–1900), who succ. 1860.

[73]   Dr. John Jackson (1811–1885), bishop of London 1868–1885: Disraeli's choice: author of *The Sinfulness of Little Sins*.

[74]   Henry Austin Bruce, 1st Baron Aberdare (1815–1895), M.P. Merthyr 1852–1868: home sec. 1868–1873: cr. peer 1873: leading figure in Welsh education.

[75]   R.N. Philips (1815–1890), M.P. (Lib.) Bury 1857–1859, 1865–1885 (retired): educ. Rugby and Manchester: Manchester merchant and manufacturer.

[76]   Sir Henry Parkes (1815–1896), Australian premier: thrice premier of New South Wales, including 1878–1882: advocate of federation.

[77]   James Beal (1829–1891), London municipal reformer.

[78]   Gladstone's diaries mention the dinner at Tweedmouth's, naming eleven guests including Carlingford - but Lord Derby is not named as present.

[79]   Charles S. Monck, 4th Vt Monck (1819–1894), succ. father 1849: cr. U.K. baron, 1866: gov. of Canada 1861–1868.

[80]   George W.F.S. Russell, 10th D. of Bedford (1852–1893), M.P. (Lib.) Beds. 1875–1885: succ. his father 1891: styled Lord Tavistock to 1891.

[81]   His wife Lady Adeline Somers-Cocks, dau. of 3rd E. Somers.

[82]   (Francis Charles) Hastings Russell, 9th D. of Bedford (1819–1891).

[83]   Lord Arthur and Lord Odo Russell were brothers of Hastings Russell, 9th Duke.

[84]   Lady Derby.

[85]   William, 8th D. of Bedford (1809–1872), who died unm., and was succ. by his cousin the 9th Duke.

[86]   The elder dau., Lady Ela, never married: the younger, Lady Ermyntrude, was to marry the diplomatist Malet in 1885 (see below).

[87]   Lady Derby's sister, Lady Elizabeth Sackville West (d. 1897), m. Hastings Russell, later 9th D. of Bedford, in 1844.

[88] Herbrand Russell, 11th D. of Bedford (1858–1940), succ. his bro. in 1893.

[89] Tavistock's marriage was childless.

[90] Presumably part of W.E.H. Lecky, *A History of England in the Eighteenth Century* (London, 1878–1890, 8 vol.).

[91] Sir Erskine Perry (1806–1882), Indian judge: member of council of India, 1859–1882.

[92] Sir C. Wood, 1st Vt Halifax (1800–1885), Whig minister: sec. for India 1859–1866: cr. peer 1866: lord privy seal, 1870–1874.

[93] Emma, Lady Minto (d. April 1882), who m., 1844, William, 3rd E. of Minto (1814–1891).

[94] Sir H. Cole (1808–1882), civil servant: sec. of Science and Art Department, 1858–1873.

[95] Canon F.W. Farrar (1831–1903), author of *Eric, or Little by Little* (1858): head of Marlborough, 1871–1876: canon of Westminster 1876–1895 and dean of Canterbury, 1895–1903.

[96] E.J. Stanley M.P. (Cons.) Somerset W. Apr. 1882–1885 and Somerset (Bridgwater Division) 1885–1906.

[97] Francis Thomas De Grey, 7th E. Cowper (1834–1905), lord-lieut. of Ireland 1880–April 1882: left Dublin two days before Phoenix Park murders: succ. father, 1856.

[98] Archibald Philip Primrose, 5th E. of Rosebery (1847–1929), who succ. grandfather, 1868: premier 1894–1895 and party leader 1894–October 1896.

[99] Possibly Bonamy Price, *Chapters on Practical Political Economy* . . . (London, 1882, 2nd ed.).

[100] William Newmarch (1820–1882), banker and economist.

[101] Lord De La Warr did indeed fire off a series of well informed questions about the French takeover of Tunis, of which country he seemed to claim personal experience. He was knowledgeable about the 10,000 U.K. subjects resident in Tunis, the highly favourable terms enjoyed by U.K. merchants under the Treaty of 1875 between the U.K. and Tunis, and French policy as stated in the Paris press. In this he was a voice crying in the wilderness.

[102] Granville first stated that Cowper's resignation 'some weeks ago' was 'not founded on any difference as to the policy of Her Majesty's Government'; and then announced Forster's resignation and Spencer's Appointment: 'My Lords, we have no fresh policy.' This meant 'it is not our intention to ask Parliament to renew the Coercion Act as it stands', only parts of it. The 3 M.P.s were to be released, the cases of other non-criminal detainees to be examined, and the Bright Clauses and arrears clauses to be subject to legislation (*Parl. Deb., 3*, vol. cclxviii, cols. 1920–1924).

[103] The Hon. Mrs. Meynell Ingram (b. 1840) of Burton-on-Trent: owned estates worth £45,000 p.a. She m. in 1863 and succ. in 1871.

[104] Forster's explanation of his resignation, despite a flowery concluding tribute to Gladstone, provoked the premier into an immediate rebuttal, and marked the opening of an enduring public rift (*Parl. Deb., 3*, 4 May 1882, vol. cclxix, cols. 106).

[105] Chamberlain had decided to accept the Irish Secretaryship if offered but it was not offered him, either before or after Cavendish's murder. The post was offered instead, without cabinet membership, to Dilke, who declined, and then to Trevelyan, who accepted, again outside the cabinet. Spencer's combination of cabinet rank and the senior Irish office meant that Chamberlain could not accept Irish office without losing his cabinet membership.

[106] Thomas H. Burke, Under Secretary at Dublin, an R.C., whose mother had been niece to Cardinal Wiseman: formerly priv. sec. to Carlingford and Peel.

[107] William Shaw (1823–1895), Irish merchant and banker: M.P. (Lib.) 1868–1885: chairman of Irish party, 1879–1880: bankrupt, 1886.

[108] (Sir) J.T. Knowles (1831–1908), ed. of *Nineteenth Century*.

[109] *L'Ecclésiaste, traduit . . . par E. Renan*, 1882.

[110] Granville's proposal was that France and the U.K. each send 3 warships to Alexandria, to continue a policy of joint action.

[111] Harry Powlett, 4th (and last) D. of Cleveland (1803–1891).

[112] Edward McCabe (1816–1885), R.C. priest: archbishop of Dublin, 1879: cr. cardinal, 1882.

[113] A long attack by the Tories on Gladstone, led by Balfour, which deeply nettled the premier: Balfour used the words 'infamous' and 'degraded' of his former host.

[114] Not traced in *Parl. Deb.*

[115] H.O. Arnold-Forster (1855–1909), priv. sec. to his stepfather, W.E. Forster, 1880: M.P. 1892–1909.

[116] S.C. Buxton, 1st E. Buxton (1853–1934), Lib. M.P. and minister: gov.-gen. of S. Africa 1914–1920: cr. vt 1914, earl 1920.

[117] Sir Julian Pauncefote, 1st Baron Pauncefote (1828–1902), permanent under-sec. at F.O. 1882–1889: minister, then first ambassador to U.S., 1889–1902: legal under-sec. at F.O., 1876–1882.

[118] (Sir) T.V. Lister (1832–1902), assistant under-sec. at F.O. 1873–1894: nephew of Clarendon and Sir G. Cornewall Lewis.

[119] Sir Francis Hyde Villiers (1852–1925), sometime assistant under-sec. at F.O.: minister at Brussels, 1911–1919.

[120] Sir Isaac Holden (1807–1897), M.P. (Lib.) Knaresborough 1865–1868, W. Riding N. 18 May 1882–1885, Keighley 1885–1895.

[121] Hon. Alfred E. Gathorne-Hardy (1845–1918), 3rd s. of 1st E. of Cranbrook: M.P. (Cons.) Canterbury 1878–1880 (re-elected but unseated on petition) and E. Grinstead 1886–1895: First in History at Balliol and biographer of his father.

[122] William FitzRoy, 6th D. of Grafton (1819–1882), M.P. (Lib.) 1847–1863: d. of typhoid.

[123] Richard Bethell, 3rd Baron Westbury (1852–1930), who succ. father 1875: a Cons., and committed suicide.

[124] For this abortive effort to get Derby to enter the cabinet, see especially W.E. Gladstone, *IV: Autobiographical Memoranda 1868–1894*, p. 60: 'Lady Derby most frankly spoke of her husband's indecision . . .'

[125] Gladstone described Dillon's speech as 'the worst Irish speech I ever heard' and 'this outrageous speech', worrying that 'Parnell has thus far run quite true, but it seems doubtful whether he can hold' (*Diaries*, 24 May 1882).

[126] William Monsell, 1st Baron Emly (1812–1894), M.P. (Lib.) Limerick 1847–1874: cr. peer, 1874.

[127] George Bancroft, *History of the American Revolution*, 3 vols., 1852–1854.

[128] Alfred Russel Wallace (1823–1913), naturalist, *Land Nationalisation, its Necessity and Aims: being a comparison of the system of landlord and tenant with that of occupying ownership*, etc. (London, 1882).

[129] Gladstone's diaries (3 June) record 'Wrote to Lady Derby –'.

[130] Sir Richard Burton (1821–1890), explorer and translator.

[131] Musurus Pasha (1807–1891), Ottoman minister 1851–1856 and ambassador 1856–1885.

[132] Mr. Walter Bourke of Rahassan, co. Galway, shot dead near Gort together with his escort, Corporal Wallace of the Dragoon Guards. A reward of £2,000 was offered by government for his murderers.

[133] Henry Adams, *Democracy* (1880).

[134] R. Bourke, 1st Baron Connemara (1827–1902), M.P. (Cons.) Lynn 1868–1886: 3rd s. of Lord Mayo: under-sec. for foreign affairs, 1875–1880, 1885–1886: gov. of Madras 1886–1890: cr. baron 1887: divorced 1890.

July–December

1 July 1882: . . . Walk down to Westminster to see the H. of Commons, which has been sitting up all night: but it seems that both the government & the Irish had adopted a system of relays, by which all got their rest, some early, some late: so that there was less appearance of disorder than might have been expected. The scenes of violence in the night were many: and 16 of the Irish were suspended, for wilful obstruction, early in the morning. Later in the afternoon, 9 more were suspended, making up the whole Parnellite party. The justice of some of these suspensions is doubtful: several men were included who had been taking no part in the wrangle actually going on, & whose offences, if committed at all, must have been committed some days before. This is doubly unlucky, both as it gives them a legitimate grievance, & as it will be made to appear that the object was less to inflict a deserved penalty than to silence members who might become troublesome. But the House was determined to end the discussion somehow, recognising that it had degenerated into a purposeless waste of time: & the shortest road to that end seemed the best. O'Donnell, Healy, Biggar, Sexton, and two or three more were purposely offensive both to the committee & to the chair. The sitting lasted till near 8.00 p.m.

. . . At 6.15 I went across to Willis's rooms to attend the dinner of the Cobden Club, of which I am chairman (mean of the dinner, not the club): the gathering was large, nearly 300 . . . Lesseps[1] & Cyrus Field[2] were my neighbours . . . Lesseps talked of his Panama canal, the success of which he seems not to doubt: of the Channel Tunnel, as to which he ridiculed (quite justly) the prevailing fear that it might be used for purposes of invasion: and of what I had always considered the visionary scheme of flooding the Sahara, which he seems to believe in at least as a thing easy to do, if worth while. I kept clear of Egyptian topics, having heard that Lesseps is excited about the canal, & inclined to violent language. Mr. Field talked about America, rather in a braggy style: enquired who were the richest men in England, & what their fortunes were estimated at: then observed that we had none that could compare with Vanderbilt, the reputed possessor of £40,000,000 . . . the thought of beating us in the number & amount of enormous incomes seemed to give him great pleasure.

2 July 1882 (Sunday): . . . Read to M. an excellent article in the *Contemporary* on Home Rule by a Mr. Dicey: in which the writer shows conclusively the difficulties & disadvantages of a federal system as applied to England & Ireland[3]. It has nearly decided me not to write on the subject, as I could only repeat, & perhaps weaken, the arguments used.

3 July 1882: . . . Wrote to Mr. Boehm the sculptor to make a bust of me for preservation at Knowsley. If it succeeds, I will have one of M. also to correspond.

4 July 1882: . . . Called on A.D. who as usual full of Irish grievances & will talk of nothing else. In her view, and her husband's, Gladstone is the author of all the mischief: the Land League might have been put down easily at the beginning: it was encouraged for party purposes – & so on. I cannot think this true on the whole though willing to believe that more severity in repression at the beginning would have lessened the mischief.

Walk down to the Lords, where Argyll moved the second reading of a bill to do away with compulsory parliamentary oaths, allowing any one to affirm who conscientiously objects to an oath. He spoke an hour, well, but less well than I have heard him on more exciting topics: Carnarvon followed, & made a sad exhibition: solemnly indignant at the wickedness of the proposal, & canting to a painful degree. He is certainly, from whatever cause, losing in weight & intellectual power. He was not much cheered, even by his own side. The Abp. of Canterbury spoke in a trimming style, but ended by opposing the bill on the ground that it was intended to let in Bradlaugh, & that there was no use in raising the question without necessity. We divided 62 to 138, I think. I am bound to say that many peers thought with the Abp. that it would be time enough to discuss the subject when it came up as one on which action was required, & that to raise it now could serve no useful purpose. As a matter of political tactics, I am inclined to agree with them: we should have made a better division if the bill, or one like it, had come up from the Commons, instead of originating with us at a moment when all the world is thinking about other matters. . . .

5 July 1882: My wedding day in 1870. Gave M. £100 as usual. . . .

6 July 1882: . . . Saw Drage, who is well satisfied with me.
   . . . H. of Lords, but Granville would tell us no more of what is passing than what we know already – probably he knows no more himself – and the other business was not important.
   Called on old Ly Lyndhurst, now aged 75, at her request: she complained a good deal of age & infirmity, wished herself dead, & really seemed suffering: but a little conversation revived her, & all her troubles were forgotten. She said she was anxious that the life of Ld Lyndhurst should be written by someone who would do it justice, that the slanders of Ld Campbell's memoir[4] might not remain unanswered: of these she spoke with natural anger: she had asked Sir T. Martin to take the work in hand, & he had accepted. She said he [i.e. Lyndhurst] always destroyed letters when done with, even those of most importance: he disliked writing himself: therefore, as I gathered, the materials will be scanty[5]. She wanted me to give Sir T.M. some recollections of Ld L. which I promised to do if able, but added that I did not think I had any worth sending.
   . . . Some excitement about Egypt, as the military party under Arabi are throwing up batteries at Alexandria against the fleet. Our admiral has ordered them to desist, in which he is justified, as the operation is distinctly intended as a threat: & so far nothing has happened, but it is possible at any moment that a collision may occur.

7 July 1882: . . . Mr. Escott, the new editor of the *Fortnightly Review*, called, & hinted at the possibility of articles from me, an idea which I did not encourage. He told the details of Mr. Morley quitting the editorship, but they are not worth noting: a quarrel with the publishers. He does not wish the review to be extreme in politics, saying (I think with truth) that his habit of mind is not that of a partisan. We talked of the growth of a kind of vague socialist feeling, not revolutionary in conscious purpose, but leading people to call out for State interference whenever anything was wrong, without reference to the question whether the remedy lay within the proper functions of government. He talked of church matters also, guardedly, but so as to show that his ideas are positivist in the wide sense of the word. He told me (to my surprise) that Salisbury is very unpopular in the rank & file of the party, who much prefer Northcote. He quoted Gladstone as having boasted lately that he had put down a social revolution in Ireland – whereas most people think that the social revolution is very much alive, & on the whole gaining rather than losing. – I invited him to call again when so disposed. . . .

Mrs. Butler, the philanthropist, called upon me in the afternoon, with a heap of petitions in favour of the better protection of young girls, which she wants me to present. I agreed. She is a strange woman. One would be curious to know how far the motive in such cases is really the wish to do good, & how far it is love of excitement, fuss, & running about, attending meetings, making speeches, etc. . . .

8 July 1882: . . . Went to Boehm the sculptor at 11.00, & sat for him till 12.20. . . . I was interested, & Mr. Boehm himself was good company. . . . He seems to have an immense quantity of work on hand, several rooms full of statues or busts in various stages. . . .

9 July 1882 (Sunday): . . . Politicians are interested & excited by the prospect of a crisis: in which I think they will be disappointed. The circumstances are odd. In the original draft of their coercion bill ministers had inserted a clause giving power to search houses by night (I think it was): this the Irish objected to, & the Cabinet gave way, & agreed to amend the clause. But when it came on for discussion on Friday evening the House, annoyed by the deference shown to the party of anarchy, declined to accept the amendment, & adhered to the original bill. Gladstone, no doubt overworked & excited, & who had shown great irritation in the debate, broke out violently, & hinted in plain words at resignation or dissolution. So the matter stands, but all the world feels that to resign or dissolve on so small a matter is practically impossible, & believes that the threat was a mere outbreak of temper. For, in the first place, the vote was one not taking away power which ministers asked for, but giving them power which they did not want – a vote, as somebody called it, not of want of confidence, but of too much confidence – & in the next place, the proposal adopted was not that of any one else, but their own in the first instance, which the House preferred to their second thoughts. – The numbers were small: 194 to 207. The defeat was caused by many of the old Whigs either voting against them or staying away: partly also by the refusal of the Home Rulers to vote in their own cause. They retired to the gallery, not choosing to interfere to save the government from defeat, & probably wishing to make the bill stronger rather than weaker, that it may be more unpopular.

10 July 1882: . . . At 4.30, House of Lords, where the Crime Prevention Bill was read a second time: Carlingford brought it in, feeble & tedious as he always is, so that even Ld Oranmore, who followed, did not do worse. I left the place, knowing that there would be no debate, as it is agreed on both sides that it shall be passed without amendments, so as not to make a second discussion in the Commons necessary. In the Commons, where I went to hear Gladstone, he made the slightest possible allusion to his threat of resignation the other day, being probably ashamed of having uttered it: & indeed it was a mere outbreak of temper, excusable after so much provocation. He proposed an adjournment instead of prorogation, & an autumn session, beginning in October: which the House in general seemed to dislike, all except the decided Liberal, or Radical, party. He talked of amending the Irish Land Act in five particulars: emigration, purchase by tenants, & something to be done about leases being the chief. The latter has an ominous sound, as it suggests breaking leases freely entered into: which is a new development of Irish ideas. The House listened, as I thought, with no great pleasure to the announcement of another Irish session. He also spoke of the necessity of dealing with procedure, which was cheered by the Liberals: but on the other hand some questions as to the impending collision at Alexandria produced loud Conservative cheers, & dead silence on the Liberal benches.

11 July 1882: Drage called: he has made a fresh examination & finds marked improvement. He says that the liability to disease in the kidneys will require constant care not to excite it, but with care there is no reason why it should shorten life. The morbid symptoms may disappear entirely, though they will always be liable to recur.

. . . News in the papers of Alexandria, or rather the forts commanding its harbour, being bombarded by the English squadron: after attempts to negociate which probably were not very sincere . . . We have lost 5 killed, 27 wounded: the forts are apparently destroyed. It is too early to judge either whether this act of war was justified, or what its political effect will be. In the country generally it will be popular: but among a section of the Liberal party very much otherwise. How Bright & Gladstone made up their minds to it I cannot guess: probably they began by agreeing to demonstrations which they thought would serve the purpose, & found themselves committed to action before they knew it. – As a military operation the thing seems to have been a complete success: but hardly a glorious one, the resistance being so feeble: it was a *battue* rather than a battle. Its chief importance is as a test of the new weapons & armour, both of which seem to have answered.

12 July 1882: In H. of C. a violent attack by Sir W. Lawson on the Egyptian business, supported by other members. Gladstone replied.

13 July 1882: Received from Ward the summary of rents received in the 12 months ending 30 June . . . the total being £213,196 against £208,220 last year at the corresponding date.

The yield of the various estates is as follows:

Bury & E. Lancs.	£73,792
Liverpool & Bootle	£60,905
Home estates	£54,281
Fylde & outlying	£24.210

The chief feature of this return is the great increase in the Liverpool rents. Ten years ago they were not above £35,000: and, as Stanley Street does not yet bring in a full return, they will grow still more. I have fixed in my own mind on £220,000 as the ultimate average of the whole rent receipts, but probably they will in fact greatly exceed this.

. . . Sanderson called: thinks there is no fear of a rupture with France, which is the present danger. Fresh news from Egypt: the city of Alexandria on fire, & deserted: probably having been burnt by the retreating troops . . . Arabi falling back apparently on Cairo. The question discussed in the clubs is – shall we occupy Egypt or not? . . . Saw Knowles the editor who much excited, hopes we shall hold Cairo, hopes the French will not be allowed to join us – in short wants to hold the country. He is not a specially wise man but probably represents pretty fairly the average British public.

. . . Fawcett[6] talked about the American socialist book, *Progress and Poverty*[7*], as the best statement of that side of the case which he had seen, & thought it was having effect in England. He also lamented deeply the effect of the Egyptian bombardment, thinking it would alienate a large section of the Liberal party from the government: & I suspect he is right. They would not secede, he said, but they would take no part in elections: as was the case with the dissenters in 1874. . . .

15 July 1882: News this morning that Bright has resigned: which was expected. The only ground of surprise is that he did not resign earlier: but probably he thought the affair would end without blood.

To Boehm for a last sitting . . . I expressed to him a wish that he would undertake a companion bust of Ly D.: which he agreed to, but it cannot be begun at once. . . .

16 July 1882 (Sunday): . . . Note also that I called on A.D.[8] and there learnt that the Irish landlords are undecided about the Arrears Bill, but on the whole inclined to throw it out. They profess not to care about recovering the arrears of rent (though one would think that £2 or £3,000,000 was not an offer to be despised) but fear the effect on the peasantry. They say with truth that the tenant who has paid his rent is now an object of ridicule as well as resentment: he is told by all his acquaintance that he might have kept his money in his pocket, & government would have paid it for him: naturally he determines never to be guilty of the folly of honest dealing again. This is true, & is the great objection to the bill: but is not the mischief done already? And will it not be foolish on the part of the Opposition to provide the government with a ready-made excuse for the possible failure of their policy? If the bill is passed, & Ireland is not pacified, the responsibility rests with the Cabinet, who have been left free to work out their plans in their own way: if it is rejected, & Ireland continues disturbed, the plea will always be available: 'You have spoilt our arrangements, & if they don't work the fault is yours, not ours.' Why are the Conservatives to give such an advantage to their opponents? . . .

18 July 1882: Nothing very new from Egypt: order has been restored in Alexandria, though most of the town is burnt: Arabi is supposed to have fallen back about 15 miles: what he will do next, or what we shall do next, nobody knows. The first feeling of irritation & surprise caused among the French by our unexpected action has died out, & they appear willing to act with us. The war party here are all for a single-handed occupation of the country, partly because it looks like a defiance to all the world, partly because they hope it may end in annexation. The danger of quarrels in the event of a joint occupation by France & England is admitted: & our Cabinet, as I gather, wish to avoid it by the employment of Turkish troops: which has the additional advantage of being in accordance with international law.

Bright's speech of yesterday was meant to be conciliatory to his colleagues: but the reason which he gave for retiring was that he considered the moral law applicable to nations as well as to individuals – the inference being obvious, that in his view they held an opposite doctrine. Gladstone disclaimed the theory ascribed to him, but the imputation coming from Bright will have some effect. . . .

19 July 1882: . . . At 4.00 p.m. City Companies Commission . . . Asking for a share of the plunder was Lucraft[9] [on behalf of] the London School Board. Lucraft talked some sense, saying that, as teaching was now given, all the cleverest sons of artisans wanted to be clerks, overstocking that trade, & making good workmen scarce. He wanted more technical teaching.

. . . Found M. returned from Haslemere, well pleased with the country, & on Hindhead she found that she could see better, which shows that nerves have much to do with her affliction of the eyes. . . .

20 July 1882: . . . H. of Lords, where Salisbury raised the question of the Oxford statute regulating examinations which he asked us to disallow. He spoke about 20 minutes, temperately enough . . . We divided 70 to 57, thus confirming the statute, & defeating the motion for its disallowance. The division was not altogether, though mainly, on party lines: Redesdale, Bath, & other Conservatives voting in the majority. Except on the supposition that Salisbury was only acting in discharge of his obligations as head of the University, & did not really care for success, I cannot account for his making so poor a fight. The debate was all on one side. Even Carnarvon took no part. . . .

21 July 1882: My 56th birthday: there will not be many more. Notes & little presents from Mary & Margaret: which I answered. . . .

22 July 1882 (Saturday): . . . Saw a letter, or rather two letters, from young Victor Stanley, serving in the *Monarch*, remarkably well written, with a total absence of bounce or swagger. They might have come from a man of 25 or 30, instead of a boy of 15. I was well pleased with them & wrote to congratulate my brother on his safety.

In the papers, notice of a vote of credit for the Egyptian expedition. It is understood, or believed, that it will be a small one, & that France & Italy will be somehow associated in our action.

In the afternoon I drove over to Chevening to pass Sunday there: M. had declined on account of her eyes. It was just an hour's drive . . . Stanhope was away attending a meeting and did not arrive till night. The party were: D. & Duchess of Cleveland[10], Ly Donoughmore[11], Sir W. Harcourt, Ly M. Primrose[12], E. Stanhope[13], P. Stanhope & his Russian wife[14], Elliot M.P.[15] (a son of Lord Minto) & Mr. Newton[16] of the B. Museum.

23 July 1882: Walk early with Harcourt in the grounds: walk later with the whole party, or nearly the whole, up the London approach, with its fine view over the Weald: later, with Stanhope, P. Stanhope, & Harcourt, to call on the Spottiswoodes[17] at Combe Bank . . .

I had at intervals a good deal of talk with Harcourt & learnt much as to the situation. It seems that there is difficulty in filling up the vacancy caused by Bright's withdrawal from the Cabinet. The Radicals claim the place, alleging that if it is given to a Whig they will be worse off than before: and the claim is reasonable: but the natural candidate would be Dilke, who waived his pretensions in favour of Chamberlain 2 years ago: he is not disposed to waive them again: & the Queen, who seldom forgets any grievance that is personal to herself, has not overlooked his opposition to former grants to the royal children. If she is over-ruled, there must be a sharp struggle first: if not, the whole left wing of the party is alienated: & it is possible that Chamberlain might find his position impossible, & resign too.

Harcourt thinks that Gladstone is only waiting to settle the question of procedure before he resigns. He did not say why he thought so. When that happens, he anticipates infinite trouble, as Gladstone alone, he says, keeps discordant sections together. He doubts whether the left will follow Hartington: even if they do, the difficulty is only postponed, for Hartington must in the course of nature go to the Lords before long[18]: and who then can lead? He himself, Harcourt, would not undertake it for any consideration: the strain on health & strength would be too great: nobody knows, he says, what a bear garden the House has become: the Irish example has infected English & Scotch members, & there is no consideration of public convenience: everybody uses obstruction as a legitimate weapon when an opportunity offers. (Putting all this talk together, I am inclined to think that Harcourt would like to succeed Ld Selborne as Chancellor: not a very good arrangement, but possible: if he remains in the Commons, he must follow the lead of somebody much his junior: which is not likely to suit his taste.) He praised Dilke, Trevelyan, & Courtney[19] as three rising men who might show themselves equal to the highest places. Forster, he considered as having put himself out of the running: Fawcett, as incapacitated by blindness, since all his papers must be seen by a secretary. Contrary to what Gladstone said at Knowsley, he thought the Liberal party weak in rising talent. He saw none who were fit for much, except the three named above (Q. as to Shaw-Lefevre?). He criticised the opposition in the same spirit: thought Northcote immeasurably superior to his colleagues, though they do not hold that opinion: Hicks Beach was next best: Cross he had thought highly of while in office, but he had now gone down in the estimation of the House, speaking ill – so ill that Harcourt believed him more than once to have been drinking when he got up (this I do not believe, though H. spoke without any appearance of jealousy or dislike).

We talked of county government, on which H. took the same view that I do: that there is no harm in [elective]county boards, but that they will have very little to do: the schools, & the poor law administration, would of course be kept out of their hands. He was sanguine of passing a bill for the better government of London, which he explained: to me his plan seemed complicated, but he says he has consulted those who take most interest in the subject.

He was strong against further concessions to the Irish, saying that English & Scotch members were losing all patience with them, & that a third Irish session would not be endured. He thought Gladstone was disposed to refer all Irish affairs to an Irish committee of the H. of Commons, which he, Harcourt, could not agree to: it would be Home Rule in another shape. The Irish would propose something that the rest of the House could not possibly agree to: then make a grievance of being overruled.

He talked of Gladstone, said the common opinion of his character was entirely mistaken: he was thought obstinate to excess, a man who refused to listen to any opinion differing from his own. Harcourt's experience of him was exactly the opposite: he (H.) thought him too yielding, too much inclined to be led by others when his own mind was not made up. – I have heard from others that Mr. G. never reads a newspaper, disliking the irritation produced by criticism. I suppose, however, he is told by somebody what is in the papers, else he must be strangely ignorant of much that a minister ought to know.

24 July 1882: Left Chevening early, after a pleasant visit. Drove with Mr. Newton to Sevenoaks: some interesting talk about Carlyle, agnosticism, the state of opinion on religion and science, etc. . . . London soon after 11.00 . . .

. . . House of Lords at 4.30, where heard Granville's statement about the Egyptian business: it was clear & plain, & seemed to carry evidence with it of its accuracy: there was no apparent attempt to colour anything. But the delivery showed signs of age: he lost himself several times, began sentences which he did not finish, & showed confusion, though rather in words than substance. Salisbury followed, speaking well, without bitterness, & with more evident sense of responsibility than is common with him. I did not think his criticisms much to the purpose: the question whether it was necessary to quarrel with Arabi & fight him(which is the really doubtful part of the case) was not a question which he cared to ask, nor would it have pleased his friends. Ld Northbrook replied, & I heard no more of the debate, going over to the Commons, where Gladstone was expected to speak: but the Irish would not have it, & got up a wrangle about the order of business, intended only to waste time, in the course of which one of them (O'Donnell, I think) insulted the Speaker. This led to a fresh dispute, the House disgusted but helpless: I have never seen it more disorderly. The scene was amusing to witness, but yet sad, when one thought that five-and-twenty rowdies could so discredit & enfeeble the House of Commons. I left while the turmoil was still going on: dined at home: and by 9.30 train to Keston with M. . . .

25 July 1882: Keston. Read the details of Gladstone's plan for an expedition, & the cost of it. He asks for £2,300,000, & raises all by income tax, 3d for the half year or 1½d for the whole year, not resorting to loans for any part of the outlay. This is right & wise, & the more bellicose party will be sobered down by having to pay for their pleasure: as was no doubt the intention. . . .

26 July 1882: Left Keston before 8.00 . . . to Haslemere, where met Hale at 11.10 . . . Walk over the whole estate, & never better pleased . . . The hills covered with heather & scrub give an appearance of wildness hardly conceivable so near London (40 miles). . . . By 4.20 train back to London. Thence Keston in time for dinner, a little weary, but not much, & well satisfied with the day.

27 July 1882: M. goes up early to see Mrs. W. E. West, as to whose state she is very uneasy, & indeed with reason.
    . . . Sent through Ward £50 to the Victoria University: an old promise.
    To the Lords at 5.00 p.m. where Carlingford moved the second reading of the Arrears Bill. He did it, to my thinking, very poorly, jumping over the difficulties instead of arguing them out: the only merit of his speech being that it was conciliatory all round. Salisbury followed in a sharp telling speech, commenting on the defects of the bill, which in truth is easy to do. His argument only failed in this, that, if it were as bad as he represented it, he ought to have tried to throw it out on the second reading. But he undoubtedly hit many blots: & there were many to hit. Lansdowne & Cowper, & Dunraven later, defended it not the less successfully because they showed a full consciousness of the objections to the policy which it embodies. I had half intended to speak, & made notes, but waiting till 8.00 o'clock found the House thin, & the debate apparently languishing. Debates seldom last through the dinner hour where there is not a division to follow. This – the want of an audience – and some feeling of exhaustion – induced me to put off what I had to say till Monday: which I do not regret, though a speech deferred is always disagreeable.
    . . . Mrs. W. E. West better, & out of immediate danger: but her state of health is bad: either heart, or lungs, or both, diseased.

28 July 1882: . . . Lawrence tells me that Scotch, & even English, estates are beginning to be in request among American capitalists: a new development, & useful to landowners if the taste grows. There is no reason why it should not: an English country house is the only luxury which transatlantic wealth cannot command at home: Scotch moors are already pretty often leased by Americans: & the passage is now only an affair of 7 days. These gentry if they come will keep up the residential value of land, whatever may become of the agricultural value.

. . . Keston by 4.30 train: fine warm evening: walk about the place.

. . . News during the day that Arabi has offered terms of peace, & is ready to give up the game if guaranteed his rank & pay, & not to be molested in Syria to which he will retire: but we know no further details.

29 July 1882: Fine hot day: excursionists in swarms along the roads, noisy enough: but they never go off the main lines of highway.

. . Walk later with M. in Hollydale, which is now in really good order.

[Tom] Hughes[20], who is my senior only by two or three years, but whom I saw the other day with hair & beard completely white, has been made happy with a county court. He might have accomplished a personal success, having abundant energy & some intellect: but early in life he was inspired by Arnold's notion of a Christian democracy, & in that line he has worked on, defending trades unions, promoting co-operation, helping workingmen in various ways, but always a little too scrupulous – or, as some people would put it, too crotchety, to be accepted by any section as a leader. The democracy did not know what to make of his religion (for he is a strong churchman of the Maurice school): the churchmen were afraid of his allies & of his popular sympathies. He made himself impossible among the constituencies by promoting co-operative stores, & so making enemies of the tradesmen: he has too much sense to have gone in for the fanaticism of the teetotallers: & his love of fair play is too strong to allow of his ever having been a hot partisan. Altogether he has made less mark in the world than he seemed likely to do: but his honesty & kindliness are respected as they deserve, & in literature he has achieved a considerable reputation by his novel of *Tom Brown*. I am glad he is provided for: his zeal for the public interests having left him very poor.

30 July 1882 (Sunday): A Mr. Saunders of Exeter writes to me about savings banks, complaining that depositors are limited to £30 in each year, & quoting a speech of mine to show that the restriction is unreasonable. I quite agree with him but as Fawcett, who is an eager reformer, did not see his way to make the change, I suppose that the influence of the private banks was too strong on the other side.

31 July 1882: . . . H. of Lords at 4.30. Salisbury moved his amendment. Carlingford replied: other speakers followed: I got up between 6.00 & 7.00, & spoke for 20 or 25 minutes, well listened to, & I think what I said was sense: but I did not please myself in the manner of saying it. Cranbrook followed, noisy & vehement as his way is, with but little matter: his style does not in general suit the peers: it is rather that of a popular platform. The Chancellor was good in argument, but rather inaudible. The division was 98 to 169: 71 majority for the Opposition: but, this result being foreseen on both sides, excited no feeling. I paired, & went back to the club to dine: not caring to return for the second amendment, which was carried, I think, by 120 to 45.

The two Houses are now committed to opposite opinions on this bill, & it is certain that the Commons will not give way on the main points at issue. What is to come next? The alternatives are as follows: (1) Resignation of the ministry. If the Conservatives refused to try their chance, as probably they would, this would only leave matters where they are, besides wasting time. If they played the bold game, a dissolution must follow: by which they would gain something, but the Parnellites more, & the general confusion be increased. (2) Dissolution by the present government: a possible expedient, but open to the objection of strengthening the Parnellite party, & perhaps it would be thought that the occasion is hardly important enough for this last resource. (3) Prorogation, an autumn session, & the bill brought in again, so that the Lords may have an opportunity of reconsidering their decision. That course is simple, & involves less disturbance than either of the other two. The objection to it is that it may only irritate, instead of conciliating, the peers, & if it fails we are where we were, with some loss of time & temper. (4) Compromise, which is difficult, but ought not to be impossible. The man to manage it, if it can be managed, is Cairns, who has kept in the background probably reserving himself for the inevitable emergency. – The Irish landlords no doubt dislike the whole bill &, as regards the principle of it, they are right: but they will think twice before refusing a gift of three millions (it cannot be less) which they may not get another offer of. – The chief difficulty in the way of a settlement is the language of Ld Salisbury, which both in the House & to his party has been uncompromising. But he could pledge only himself: &, if he wishes to give way without seeming to do so, he can always give a hint to his friends that they may stay in the country while he comes up to vote.

1 Aug. 1882: Hot close night. See Drage early. He advises my seeing Dr. Garrod, which I agree to do.

Have myself weighed: 14 st. 12 lbs.

Send £5 to the London Working Men's Club & Institute Union.

. . . H. of Lords, where present some petitions, & listen to a desultory debate on the Arrears Bill: report & third reading. The only thing worth noticing was a hint of possible compromise, thrown out by the D. of Abercorn, caught at by Granville, but repudiated at once by Salisbury, who denied that the Duke had used words which we had just heard. The Chancellor contradicted, & the words were admitted: at least the denial was not repeated.

Left the House before 6.00, & by 6.35 train to Keston . . . Day & evening very hot.

2 Aug. 1882: Hot night & day.

Endless applications:

(1) That I will be a patron of the Preston Guild[21] – yes.
(2) That I will present an address from the magistrates – yes.
(3) That I will subscribe for a chain to the Mayor of Preston – yes.
(4) That I will give a living to a colonial parson – Answer: I have none available.
(5) That I will take charge of the fortunes of one Brailsford, now in South America, on the strength of his being first cousin to my late keeper. – Declined civilly.
(6) That I will find a place for one Dr. Taylor: an active shrewd Scotchman whom I met long ago at Minard. Gave him a civil answer.
(7) That I will patronise a meeting of bicyclists at Preston – yes.

(8) That I will find work & subsistence for the rest of his life for a labourer partly disabled in the Liverpool docks – on the plea that nobody else will employ him. – Declined, but sent him money.

(9) That I will contribute to a statue to be put up in honour of Lord F. Cavendish at Barrow. Agreed to.

There were other requests, but these were the chief. I have noted them as samples of those I usually receive: though the number today is perhaps above the average.

3 Aug. 1882: London early with M. – Went to see the drawing of her by Eddis, with which she is pleased, and I am so likewise.

Called by appointment on Dr. Garrod[22], & there heard his opinion of the complaint which Drage & Gorst have detected. He takes apparently a less serious view of it than they did, saying that the mischief at present is slight, & that with care it may be kept from increasing. He gave in the main the same directions as Drage, but with more tolerance in the matter of wine. He is to see Drage again about me, when I shall have his final judgment – I left him with a more hopeful feeling as to my prospects of life, though it is a puzzle to myself how little I really care about the matter, one way or the other. Most of the things I wished to do are done, & I have no plan on hand in the success of which I feel any very lively interest. Only it seems like blundering & mismanagement to go off the stage before one's time.

. . . Keston again by 5.15 train . . .

8 Aug. 1882: . . . M. went up to London, & returned by 5.30, very weary & low in spirits: I think uneasy about Mrs. W.E. [West's] prospects of eventual recovery: & certainly it is not for that family a cheerful outlook. The Welsh climate is too cold for her in winter[23]: but her husband[24], whose private fortune is small, & whose agency brings him in £1,800 a year, cannot afford to throw it up: &, being naturally of a melancholy disposition, the loss either of his wife or of his business (which he likes) would probably throw him into a morbid condition in which he might come to the same end as his eldest brother[25]. Their boys are clever, but have weak health: the daughters show signs of being peculiar, objecting to society, & so forth.

9 Aug. 1882: Heard with regret that Tavistock thinks of going out of parliament, & that his successor is informally nominated. He is influenced partly by natural indolence, which I fear grows upon him, for he thinks it too much trouble even to dine out, or answer his letters of business: & partly by the more creditable feeling of dislike to profess opinions which he does not really hold. He is in fact conservative in feeling, very heartily disliking the radicals, yet naturally unwilling to join the so-called Conservative party. He would support cordially a pure Whig Cabinet: but no such combination is possible. His dislike of the late Irish legislation is natural & not unreasonable: but it is a mistake on account of that, which is already done & settled, to throw away his political future. I question whether or no to write to him on the subject, which nothing but a strong aversion from meddling uncalled for in other people's affairs prevents my doing.

10 Aug. 1882: . . . To the Lords, where a full house for the time of year: but it was understood that there would be no fighting, & so the fact turned out. Carlingford explained what the Commons had done: Salisbury immediately replied, attacking & criticising the principle of the bill as though on the second reading: he spoke forcibly, & with evident conviction but, the more earnest he was, the less it was possible to see how he meant to reconcile himself to letting his amendments drop without a division. He did extricate himself from the difficulty, but in an unexpected way. He said that his own opinion was that the bill should have been rejected, and he was prepared to act accordingly: but that on consulting his friends he found them of a different opinion and, as he should be left in a small minority if he divided, he would not give the House that trouble. – This very frank avowal of difference in the party took the peers by surprise: & was especially distasteful to the front opposition bench: the general feeling was that it was imprudent & damaging to the speaker: such, however, was not my impression, for by no other explanation could he have vindicated his personal consistency, after the very strong declarations of the other day. It is a slap in the face to his colleagues, & perhaps was so intended. It seems a meeting was held in his house, at which there was considerable division of opinion: Richmond, it is said, being foremost in advising concession. Cairns, who is well known to inspire Richmond , was not there – possibly from mere accident, but if done on purpose it was ingenious. Having lighted the match, he leaves the charge to explode.

Dined Travellers' & Keston again by 11.00 p.m.

11 Aug. 1882: Last day at Keston for some time . . . Tore up letters, threw away papers, etc. . . . Received further details as to the scheme for making a deep navigable canal up to Manchester, which seems practicable & may pay, but it is so much against the interests of Liverpool & so unpopular there that I think I had better leave it alone.

12 Aug. 1882: Left Keston a little before 11.00, and riding leisurely reached Fairhill a few minutes after 2.00. The day was the hottest we have had this year . . . M. who came by rail joined me again at 3.30.

The papers continue full of the Arrears Bill, or rather of the Conservative opposition to it: they all treat Salisbury's speech as a grave indiscretion &, as the test of such matters is the effect on public opinion, I suppose it was so: to me it seemed a frank avowal of a disagreeable situation, & better than if he had pretended to believe that he had gained his objects – which is the line mostly taken by the Conservative press. But there is no doubt that his position as a leader is shaken: it is shown that he does not really lead more than a section, & that a small one. It is shown also that Richmond is more trusted of the two: which, considering the difference in capacity of the two men, must be annoying. As it is well known that Richmond acts under the inspiration of Cairns, I suspect the latter to have arranged for this defection of the party: which would be gratifying to him personally (for he does not love Salisbury), as well as advantageous for the public. The decision not to resist was finally taken at a meeting held only just before the sitting of the Lords: it is variously reported that the numbers were equal for concession & for holding out: and that only 17 peers were for the latter course. The fact I take to be that, when the question came to be finally decided, the Irish landowners did not see the advantage of rejecting a free gift of probably three millions for the very doubtful benefit of retaining claims which they cannot enforce. . . .

14 Aug. 1882: . . . The session is ending for the time, but it is announced that parliament meets again on the 24th October. The Liberals in general are pleased at this appearance of energy: and certainly it looks well: but I doubt whether business is really advanced by it. Six months' work out of the twelve is as much as can be expected from unpaid M.P.s & the attempt to drive them faster than they like to go seldom answers.

15 Aug. 1882: . . . I have been turning over in my mind the expediency of writing an article on Irish Home Rule: and have decided to give it up at least for the present, for two reasons: (a) because I see that just now all interest is concentrated on Egyptian affairs: people are tired of Irish subjects (no wonder) & do not care to read or hear more about them: (2) because, though I believe I could put the case strongly & clearly, & point out some difficulties which the public does not think of, yet the question is hackneyed, the English public is convinced already, & the Irish will not read anything that appears in an English periodical. I doubt therefore whether I could accomplish any result worth the trouble it would cost.

16 Aug. 1882: In papers, death of Stanley Jevons[26], the economist: an able thinker, who has written much & well. He died by accidental drowning, at Bexhill, Sussex. We have now scarcely any one left who has made a study of theoretical economics, except Fawcett: & he is unavailable for controversial purposes, while in his present employment. It is a pity: for socialist ideas, in a disguised form, are making way rapidly: the idea of the state controlling & regulating industry is as much in the ascendant as the opposite theory – the doctrine of laissez-faire – was 30 years ago.

[**Note**: In the last 3 or 4 years, Bagehot, Cairnes[27], and Cliffe-Leslie[28], have all died prematurely, being the chief authorities in this line.]

Another scene in the H. of Commons: Callan, the hero of it, succeeded in getting himself suspended, after wasting much of the evening. He was probably drunk, if that is any excuse.

In Dublin, the opening of an exhibition meant to be national, & in regard of which English or official help has been repudiated: together with the unveiling of a statue of O'Connell: gave occasion for an extraordinary demonstration of national feeling, in which the whole city seems to have taken part. Order was kept: & the only sign of disaffection to England seems to have been the negative one, that among all the flags, inscriptions & other displays of a national character, there were scarcely any bearing references to the Queen or to England.

17 Aug. 1882: . . . At a public dinner last night, at which the mayor of Dublin presided, the toast of the Queen was received with hissing . . .

. . . In the evening, some pain as well as weakness in eyes: which I ascribe to using them too much, & reading small print. When I remember how they gave way in 1856-7-8, I may be well content that they trouble me so little now. . . .

18 Aug. 1882: . . . Cazalet called in the afternoon: he sat with me for an hour: full of a scheme for restoring the Jews to the east, not exactly to Palestine, but to the region lying along the Tigris & Euphrates: this scheme he connects with the Euphrates valley line, for which he is enthusiastic. He says all that is required is a subsidy of £200,000 yearly by way of guarantee from the English or Indian governments: that the country would be peopled up as fast as the line was made: that the Jews would flock to it: that they would become cultivators & soldiers as they used to be, etc., etc. He said (& on a matter of fact like this I take his authority to be good) that in Russia they had no chance of decent treatment: the feeling against them was violent, & extended to all classes. It was partly socialistic, he thought, a revolt against capital, or perhaps rather a revolt of debtors against creditors. The same sentiment he thought was increasing in Germany, & the state would hardly be strong enough to hold out against it. The Crown Prince, with whom he had talked on the subject, admitted its violence & deplored it. I asked why the Jewish emigration in America had been a failure? which it has. He said the emigrants had not gone out willingly: they were sent by committees of benevolent persons: they had no wish to become Americans: they wanted to retain their nationality. On the whole this conversation left on my mind the impression that Cazalet, while eminently shrewd & successful in business, in which he has made a great fortune, is an enthusiast, or perhaps rather a man given to riding hobbies. But he is cultivated, & a good neighbour, which is much.

19 Aug. 1882: . . . Heard with an oddly mixed feeling of the sudden death in Switzerland of Alexander, the owner of Holwood: he had heart disease: but seemed as if he might have lasted for many years. . . . The news was unexpected, & I may say unwished for, for in buying the reversion I had secured the park of Holwood for my own enjoyment & that of M. & prevented its being spoilt by builders. The house I did not care for, & it will be a question what to do – whether to let it or live in it. The place is finer than this (Fairhill) but, being nearer to London, is less entirely quiet & rural in character[29].

20 Aug. 1882: The decision to restore Cetewayo to the throne of Zululand is announced, & is received with no great interest either way. It is a complete reversal of the policy of Sir B. Frere, but that policy was not endorsed by the Conservatives, & they are not bound to defend it. The arrangement for government by 13 chiefs under a British resident has in effect broken down: & by its very nature could not have been permanent: it was accepted by the colonists (I fancy) as necessarily leading up to annexation, which they would have preferred. But no party in England wishes for, or would willingly accept, the alternative of annexation: &, if so, the thing done seems as if it were not merely the best, but the only thing to do. There is no fear of Cetewayo quarrelling with us again – if indeed he ever did so, for it was rather Frere who quarrelled with him – & he will keep the Zulus in order better than any one who could be put in his place. The only serious objection is the feeling of resentment, almost of fury, that will be created throughout Natal & in S. Africa generally. The colonists consider all South Africa as ultimately theirs, they grudge any part of it to the black race, & will look on the step now taken as an act of oppression to them. Being largely Dutch, & sufficiently inclined to disaffection as it is, we may have trouble from them hereafter.

21 Aug. 1882: . . . News of some fighting in Egypt, but it does not appear to come to much: only the Suez canal, or most of it, is occupied by English troops.

In the afternoon, T. Hankey called with Sir T. May: the latter talked a good deal, sensibly, only in a very optimist strain. He thought Irish affairs were looking well, rents were better paid, outrages decreasing: it was said in London that Parnell is disgusted with his followers, & that the Land League is on the point of breaking up. (All this may be true, but two murders have just been reported, the worst we have heard of yet, & a new League is being formed to include the labourers, & make them the basis of a fresh agitation.[30]) In short, he thinks the worst is over – just as Gladstone did this time last year – & that the next session will be employed in English business. . . . He qualified his sanguine predictions by adding that all we could expect was a respite: that no doubt after a few years the Irish would break out again: but that it was something to have secured peace for the moment.

22 Aug. 1882: . . . There came to luncheon with us, C. Stanley & Mrs. Stanley: I was glad to be able to show them civility, and glad that they are well pleased with their house. He is what he always was – placid, contented, & harmless: quite satisfied to do nothing, & not desirous of finding employment, though he professes to look out for some. He lives cheerfully on very little, glad of help, but asking none, & as absolutely inoffensive as it is possible for man to be. He has been here three months, but did not know where Knole or Tunbridge Wells were: he does not seem to have stirred a mile from home, except that he was once at Penshurst.

. . . Papers are full of another Irish murder, the worst yet committed, 5 persons being killed at one time: a father, grandmother, sister, brother, & one of two sons: the other escaped wounded. The place was in one of the wildest districts of Connemara – Joyce's country: the cause not yet known. Many persons were engaged, it is thought not less than 10 or 12.

It is remarkable that, though the times cannot be called quiet, either at home or abroad, the political speeches delivered by members have been few. There has never been a more complete absence, in my recollection, of agitation, or even of subjects on which agitation is thought to be possible: church, land, expenditure, even county & municipal government, rouse no interest, nor the extension of the county franchise, since that is felt to be inevitable, & nobody knows how it will work or who will profit by it.

23 Aug. 1882: . . . Ly De La Warr came over from Buckhurst, with two children: she stayed from 12.00 to 4.00: perfectly good-humoured & rather silly: she has lost her looks & is growing unwieldy. . . . She reminds me continually of her father, Baillie Cochrane[31]: in manner & mind as well as in looks: but he, though foolish, has some literary culture: she has none. . . .

25 Aug. 1882: Sent £5 to a woman who begs of M.

Day wet, cold, & windy.

Passed a good part of the morning in revising my will, which I have not done for two years or more, & it is necessary to make changes, Holwood being paid for & in my possession, & the capital of which I have to dispose much increased. Here it is in the latest shape.

To Lady D. Holwood, Keston & Hollydale for life. A sum of £50,000 (increased from £40,000) and £1,000 a year to keep up Holwood.

To her five children, £40,000 equally divided (increased from £25,000).

To T.H. Sanderson £10,000 as before.

To sundry public uses, not altered, £20,000 as before.

To various persons, about £7,000: . . . to all servants employed, sums proportionate to their length of service. I cannot estimate the amount, but it will be under £15,000.

The above, with legacy duty, will come to about £150,000 besides the annuity of £1,000.

Another sum of £150,000 I leave in trust to clear off all encumbrances on the Knowsley estate, accumulating till the whole is discharged.

I have thus disposed of £300,000. What I shall do with the remaining £100,000 is left over for consideration.

29 Aug. 1882: Wrote over 20 letters & notes . . . Much & frequent discussion with M. as to Holwood, which will probably end in our living there: whether we shall let this place, or keep it for occasional use, I do not know.

Wet morning: . . . walk in afternoon for exercise, but with no pleasure, only health must be attended to.

Illness of the Archbishop of Canterbury . . . Though not loved by the clerical party, he will be a loss to the Establishment: his cool Scotch sense has enabled him to discourage & repress fanaticism, without giving much offence, or being suspected of not believing what he professes. For the peculiar business of keeping together the ancient & complicated concern which he directs, it would be difficult to find anyone fitter. However, he is not dead yet, & may recover.

News of Sir G. Wolseley's advance, & some fighting . . . loss on British side 120.

Answered letters, cleared off papers, packed up books: preparations for leaving. Our quiet time, on holiday, is over: & perhaps it is as well that it does not last till weariness sets in. It is also well that we are leaving before the hop picking begins: when the influx of tramps & vagrants from London makes the lanes disagreeable.

30 Aug. 1882: News in papers that the D. of Albany will not be able to visit Preston next week for the Guild: which will disappoint many in Lancashire, though it can hardly spoil the show. Illness is assigned as the reason. . . .

31 Aug. 1882: Left by 8.40: London at 10.00 . . .

Saw Drage, who is well satisfied with his interview with Garrod & talks more cheerfully than he did. He says with truth: 'Only keep as well as you are, & nothing more can be desired.' He believes the amount of internal damage to be small, though admitting that it is impossible to judge with absolute certainty.

Saw Lawrence . . . read over again the draft of my will with recent alterations. I desired him to put his own name down for a legacy of £1,000, finding, which I had doubted, that this is not contrary to professional etiquette.

. . . Wrote to Rathbone to thank him for a sensible pamphlet which he has sent me on Suez Canal. The object of it is to show that, though an interruption of traffic on the canal may be very inconvenient, it is not of the vital importance commonly supposed, since steamers built & engined as they are now can go round the Cape, taking only 4 or 5 days longer than they actually do to make the present passage.

Wrote to Sclater-Booth, asking him to reprint an excellent paper which he lately read before the British Association on county finance – in which he shows how little of the local expenditure is really controlled by the magistrates. This is the truth, & if understood it would get rid of a good deal of useless dispute.

At 3.30 left for Euston. Reached Knowsley at 9.30 exactly. I read but little in the train, my eyes being weak & inclined to ache. Nor could I sleep much, & conversation being almost impossible for noise the journey was tedious. Supper & bed between 11.00 and 12.00.

1 Sept. 1882: . . . Troubled during most of this day with aching eyes: result, I suppose, of railway travelling & reading in the carriage . . .

2 Sept. 1882: . . . Agreed to be a vice-president of the British Association for their next year's meeting at Southport.

. . . In the papers, ill news from Ireland: 240 of the Dublin police dismissed, & the rest have struck. I do not suppose that any outbreak is likely, but the effect of the strike is to weaken authority.

. . . Talking over future sales of land to railway companies, Hale estimates £50,000 as due from the Midland, & about £22,000 from other sources, within the next year or two: but of course this is all conjectural.

Agreed to give about £5 yearly in small charities – two at Haslemere, one at Bootle. . . .

3 Sept. 1882: Day fine & bright: much needed for the harvest, which the late rough weather has endangered.

. . . Sent Mr. Bailey Walker[32] for his vegetarian publications £5. I do not accept his theory either as a theory or in practice: but the increased use of vegetable food would be an immense saving to our poorer classes, and the productiveness of the soil would gain by a multiplication of gardens in lieu of pasture farms. So I am willing to give the herbivorous party assistance & encouragement in a small way, only not with my name.

. . . The troubles of the government do not lessen: all the Dublin police, about 900 in number, if the newspapers are accurate, have thrown up their posts: ostensibly the reason is connected with questions of pay & other advantages as to which their demands have been refused: but it is impossible to doubt that other causes have been at work. They may not be actually disaffected, but they probably feel the unpopularity to which they are exposed, & have been influenced more or less by nationalist agents. They are, it seems, distinct from the [Royal] Irish Constabulary, which also is in an unquiet condition.

. . . Left Huyton at 7.00, reached Preston at 9.00.

4 Sept. 1882: . . . It is said that the railways have prepared to carry 800,000 passengers here to see the Guild show . . . There was a procession to the Parish Church: a most tedious service, nearly all music: then a return in state to the Town Hall, where Latin speeches by the master & boys of the Grammar School . . . Before going to the church, what is called a guild court was held: a long ceremony consisting in the reading over in full of sundry ancient documents. Then a list of freemen, of whom I was one. (**Note**: The office of a freeman imposes no obligation, & confers no advantage.)

A balloon ascent from the park . . . ended the day's performance, except that there was a ball somewhere, which we did not attend.

5 Sept. 1882: Preston. D. of Cambridge arrived. We, with the leading people of the town, met him at the station: went thence in procession to the Town Hall, then to a tent close by to lay the first stone of a new free library, which was done with masonic forms by Ld Lathom: he then spoke a few words, & so did I. At 4.00, luncheon in the Corn Exchange, rather tedious, but I sat next Lady Crawford, & also escaped having to make a speech. A tree was planted in Avenham park, & the Duke left for Lathom. We went back to the hotel, & had a quiet evening. Great crowds in the streets all day, & I had a very warm reception.

6 Sept. 1882: Preston. D. of Cambridge again came from Lathom, & we again went in procession to the Town Hall: where the Trades filed past with a long line of wagons containing illustrations of their various occupations. This lasted till it was time to go to the Agricultural Show, which we did not see, but sat down to luncheon in a large tent: Lord Winmarleigh in the chair. The speeches were short, & remarkable in that some were very good (Sefton's especially) & none tedious. I spoke about ten minutes, with little preparation, & satisfied myself better than usual.

Lady D. distributed some prizes at a flower show in the ground adjoining . . .

The streets all today were crowded to excess. Every window was taken: I have seen nothing like it except the show at Liverpool about this time last year. My reception was quite extraordinarily warm, which is the more curious as I have never laid myself out for social popularity.

Home about 6.00, I think, rather weary.

Read to M. & wrote letters in the evening.

7 Sept. 1882: This was almost a blank day. The Catholic guilds, as they call themselves, walked in procession: but we thought it well not to go to look at them from the Town Hall, as the thing is a party demonstration, & I am rather surprised that it was allowed to form part of the ceremonies of the Guild. Cardinal Manning attended & made them a speech, as I see in the papers.

Walk with M. in the parks by the river which are very pretty & well laid out, & make Preston a more habitable place than any other large town in Lancashire: though that may not be saying much.

. . . At night, fireworks, very handsome.

We should hardly have stayed over today but for a reception given by the Mayoress tomorrow, which we are told it would not be polite to miss.

8 Sept. 1882: Meet Mr. Thompson[33], & talk with him over the state of the Fylde property, & land in these parts generally: he thinks that since the depression began it has fallen in value, but not to any great extent: about 2 years' purchase on the average.

At 11.00 to the Town Hall, for the reception of the Mayoress, where we showed ourselves, & paid the expected compliments. Margaret went on to a concert. At 3.00 we left Preston & returned to Knowsley . . .

I hear that on Wednesday, the great day of the show, the station was so completely blocked with passengers arriving that some of the last comers were sent to Blackpool instead, to keep them out of the way till time was given for the others to disperse. The crush in the streets was certainly great: but I do not think it was equal to that at Liverpool at the same time last year.

. . . I had every reason to be satisfied with the feeling shown by the Preston people towards my family & myself: & as far as I know nothing went wrong in connection with the ceremonies of the week.

9 Sept. 1882: . . . Of public news there is little: in Egypt a battle is thought to be impending, but nothing has yet happened: the public is beginning to grumble, impatient for sensational news, & [inclined] to make the most of every little mishap or accident such as in war must always be expected. It is becoming plain that the war, whether short or long, will cost much more than the Cabinet seem to have expected. And people begin to ask: 'When Arabi is put down, what next?' Are we to hold the country or, if not, who is to guarantee order?' It is singular that, while in reality England was never more free from ideas of annexation or aggression, they are ascribed to us by all parties on the Continent &, having undertaken to do the work of Europe gratis, we are unpopular & suspected.

In Ireland there is a temporary cessation of outrages: at least no new murder has been committed: & the strike among the Dublin police, which for a time seemed serious, has collapsed. Irish affairs generally are not worse: perhaps they are a little better.

The stagnation of party politics is for the moment complete: few speeches are delivered, & those of no importance.

The Abp. of Canterbury . . . is apparently mending again.

10 Sept. 1882 (Sunday): . . . In afternoon walk with young Palmer[34] . . . Palmer is acting as private secretary to Childers at the War Office: he is well mannered, cultivated, intelligent, & has something of Lord Selborne's peculiar style of address. Whether he has much capacity I cannot judge, but doubt it.

11 Sept. 1882: . . . See Broomfield, who agrees with me that the destruction of trees in the park is greater than ever before . . . As to the east side, by St. Helens, it seems useless to plant there till we see what will grow. But in my mind the injury done in the last two years suggests a larger question. How long will Knowsley be a possible residence for the family? unless improved processes do away with the chemical vapours which are the main cause of our suffering. And this again suggests other considerations – how about a Scotch estate? how as to throwing open land on this side of Huyton to builders?

. . . In the papers, death of Sir George Grey[35], aged 83. He had retired from public life since 1874. He was a useful, honest, and straightforward politician: I never heard him spoken of by any one on any side except with respect. A typical Whig in politics, his hard dry sense was apt to be disagreeable to enthusiasts & philanthropists, & indeed to holders of extreme opinions in general: perhaps for that very reason he made a good Home Secretary, his judgment being seldom at fault. As a debater, he was effective in the House: but his speeches did not read well. His fluency was excessive: his utterance too refined for reporters to follow, & in consequence they rarely did him justice. His matter was always good: strong clear sense delivered in an animated & earnest manner. He was a strong party man, who looked on a Tory as a natural enemy, to be resisted by all fair means: & on a Radical as a well meaning person to be patronised & kept in his place. If I know anything of his feelings, he must have been glad to be spared the necessity of passing judgment on Gladstone's Irish policy, which would not have suited him. He played an important part between 1846 and 1866: to the younger generation his name of later years was almost unknown: so short is the duration of an ordinary political generation.

12 Sept. 1882: Ward came . . . He brought a comparative statement of rental & receipts for the last 7 years.

	Rental was:	Receipts were:
In 1875	£183,515	£179,033
1876	£189,544	£183,012
1877	£193,942	£184,883
1878	£196,995	£180,780
1879	£200,486	£170,597

1880	£198,541	£206,024
1881	£206,629	£208,220
1882	£211,986	£213,903

The explanation of the difference is that in most years there is a considerable amount of rent due within the year, but not paid: on the other hand, the arrears of former years are often recovered, wholly or in part, & thus swell the receipts of the year in which they are paid beyond its normal amount. It appears from the above that the increase on 7 years is in rental, over £28,000: in receipts, over £34,000, giving a yearly growth of more than £4,000: which is the most rapid rate of progress yet achieved.

In addition to the above, there is an income of £15,600 from private investments, making, in all, gross receipts £229,500.

13 Sept. 1882: Lord Winmarleigh & daughters left. He, now past 80, shows no sign of age: his spirits excellent, & he keeps up his interest in passing affairs.

. . . Day again very fine, an absolutely smokeless sky.

News by telegraph of a complete victory gained in Egypt at a place called Tel-El-Kebir . . . which will probably end the war. The entrenched position held by Arabi was stormed in the night, or at earliest dawn, & carried, as it seems, partly by surprise, with very little loss. There is nothing now to hinder the British army from marching on Cairo, & holding it.

What is to follow? To Sir Garnet Wolseley, probably a peerage. To the Cabinet, the credit of a successful military operation, and the more substantial advantage of stopping the war before the cost of it has become a subject of complaint.

To the Egyptians, the crushing of Arabi is probably an advantage. There is no reason that I can see to suppose that he represented national feeling, or that if left in power he had the capacity to found any durable reform. – The English nation will be pleased: for, if peaceable by an effort of reason, we are warlike by instinct & temperament, as indeed I suppose that most nations are: & failure, or the absence of signal success, in military operations is resented by us as though necessarily proving that our ministers or generals are at fault. Continental feeling is mostly against us: but not so strongly as to be likely to lead to hostile action. The diplomatic difficulty remains, & may yet give trouble: it is, however, likely that we shall claim no exclusive rights & that our moderation will disarm foreign jealousy: unless, which is quite possible, it is ascribed to some deep & incomprehensible design. – The drawback is the bill we shall have to pay, not less certainly than £10,000,000, & very possibly more: which will spoil the budgets of the next few years.

14 Sept. 1882: Left home at 8.30, a very wet day . . . Preston 10.25: went straight to the new county hall: a handsome building outside, & still more so within. By 11.30 there was a fair gathering of magistrates: I was voted into the chair: made a short speech opening the hall, as was expected . . . At the end we had a luncheon, with speeches: my health was drunk, I answered, & gave one in return. Home . . . Knowsley about 5.30. Did not dine, having dined in the middle of the day: tea in my room, & joined the party in the drawing-room. – It may be worth noting . . . that, though I drank only two or three glasses of champagne, it produced an uncomfortable feeling which lasted all the afternoon, though the same quantity, or more, at night, would have been unfelt.

Received from Ward the balance sheet of the estates, made up to 1 July . . . The rents

& other receipts combined amount to £249,051: but of this £35,148 is from miscellaneous receipts, of which £32,000 odd is interest paid by a railway company, the accumulation of several years.

The expenditure, as usual, is less satisfactory, being as follows:

(1)	Compulsory deductions	£27,116	say, £27,000
(2)	Estate expenses	£79,709	say, £80,000
(3)	Kent & Surrey	£18,500)	
(4)	Thornley farm	£ 1,500)	say, £20,000
(5)	Household	£27,000	£27,000
(6)	Benefactions	£12.108	£12,000
Total, with some minor items		£166,097	£166,000

besides £40,000 invested, & £60,000 spent on the purchase of Holwood.

The expenditure, if I looked after it properly, ought not to exceed £140,000: but I despair of reducing it to that figure. There ought to be a clear surplus of from £60 to £75,000 over outlay.

15 Sept. 1882: Day very fine.

Newspapers all full of the victory, crowing their loudest, & with some cause: for the business seems to have been well managed, though the actual fighting was not much. A telegram says that Arabi has surrendered, & that Wolseley is on the point of entering Cairo. The war is over: what remains is to settle the country, & in this there may be a good deal of trouble.

16 Sept. 1882: From 3.00 to 6.00 we had a garden party, as it was called, though half the guests stayed in the house: a temporary staircase was rigged out from the dining room window, making access to the outside easy. Refreshments in the dining room & stucco room: & tea also at the boathouse (for those who liked it). I believe that from 200 to 250 came, but the exact number was not counted. Among them were the High Sheriff & the Mayor of Liverpool. . . .

18 Sept. 1882: . . . In afternoon, drive with M. to Mossborough farm, & thence to the house of Tom Barnes, the keeper of that beat, who was struck suddenly with paralysis two or three days ago: he is not in danger of life, but probably disabled. I saw him, promised that all should be done to make him comfortable, & gave Mrs. Barnes £5 for immediate expense.

19 Sept. 1882: Heard last night of the death of the Dean of Windsor: who married us in 1870: for which M. is much grieved, he having been an old friend, & I am sorry, having known him off & on for a good many years. He had held his post at Windsor for 28 years, & acted as private adviser to the Queen in ecclesiastical matters – some say, in many secular affairs also. She used him much to report to her what was passing in the world – what was thought of men and things – who was popular & who disliked – so that he had a good deal to do with forming her opinions. For this sort of work he was well adapted, being shrewd, & concealing much art under an appearance of rough & careless bluntness. He seemed to blurt out whatever came into his head, whereas he had in reality weighed every word, & watched keenly the effect of what he said.

Like all the Wellesleys, he professed indifference to party, & exclusive devotion to the Crown. He enjoyed his confidential position, cared little for money or rank, & refused a bishopric more than once[36]. No doubt he gratified his personal likes & dislikes in the exercise of power: otherwise I never heard that he used to his own benefit the influence which he exercised: & on the whole it is probable that it was wisely employed in the public interest.

His marriage was the chief mistake of his life: he was notoriously impotent, & incurred considerable ridicule when his wife presented him with a child – the fruit of an intrigue with one of the Grosvenor family. Complaint under the circumstances was impossible, & he took the matter philosophically. . . .. M. goes to Croxteth: she in low spirits, & her eyes very much worse. . . .

22 Sept. 1882: Left Knowsley early . . . Cumloden[37] at 8.00.

Read on the way . . . the correspondence of a respectable bourgeoise who lived at Paris in the worst days of the revolution . . . She meets Robespierre, thinks him 'doux comme un agneau' but too much of a dreamer or student to be the leader of a party . . .

23 Sept. 1882: Cumloden itself is a small place, about 100 acres, joining on to the estate, & bought by the present owner. Close to it is a rough wild deerpark of some 1,500 acres. . . . The village of Newton Stewart lies close to it, but is not seen or felt as a nuisance. . . . I cannot conceive of a pleasanter country house on a small scale. The house itself is built at various dates, odd & rambling, not especially good. It was let to the High Sheriff of Lancashire, MacCorquodale, until lately. The family place, Galloway House, is let to a Manchester man, a Mr. Broadhurst.

The whole estate of the Galloway family is about 80,000 acres, more than half of it in a solid compact lump round Loch Troch, Cumloden being on the edge: the rest being a long & rather narrow strip running down along the sea coast to Garlieston.

The rent I believe to be about £30,000 a year, of which encumbrances eat up £10 or £12,000. I mean mortgages, & there are family charges besides.

24 Sept. 1882: . . . Saw . . . what I read with a painful shock of surprise, the death of [Lord] Tenterden: which to me was quite unexpected. He was only about 48 years of age, but had led an unwholesome life, always at his desk, taking no exercise, swallowing his meals when he could get a chance, & in former days smoking incessantly. Of late he had grown weary of office work, & was looking out for other employment. He will be a great loss: as a writer he was at once singularly rapid & perfectly trustworthy, his style clear, his arrangement logical: I know of no man in the public service who was his equal in drafting a despatch or a minute. I may claim to have given him his first rise in official life, by appointing him précis writer in 1866: the rest he did for himself. – I remember that he had a fit not long ago, & was thought in danger: but he rallied, & nothing more was thought of it. His personal position was peculiar: he succeeded to a peerage absolutely without a shilling, having only his clerk's pay: his grandfather, the first peer, had made about £100,000: which his uncle, the second lord, entirely squandered[38]. By his industry he had secured an official income of £2,500: & by his marriage with a rich widow some £3,000 or £4,000 [p.a.] more, so that the fortunes of the family were retrieved. If he had succeeded to Redesdale's post, which was what he wanted, his ability would have been as well known to the public as it was to those who worked with him.

Wrote to Granville, to put in a good word for Sanderson, & to Sanderson himself. . . .

25 Sept. 1882: . . . In afternoon walk with Galloway, more than 3 hours, among the hills
. . .

In the papers, news that Sir G. Wolseley & Sir B. Seymour, the admiral in command at the bombardment, have both received peerages. The first of these is undoubtedly well earned, & if, as I understand, Sir G. has only a daughter, there is no permanent addition to the peerage. The admiral has had less to do, & I should have thought his honour had scarcely been earned: but probably it was considered that to do nothing for the navy would be invidious. In point of family he is well qualified: who more so than a Seymour? I don't know whether he has children, or how many, or what provision for them will be made.

26 Sept. 1882: . . . Set off by rail to see Galloway House . . . The house we did not go into. It is occupied by a Broadhurst family from Manchester, who have also taken a moor for highland shooting in Aberdeenshire. They have it for 5 years, paying £1,500 a year: but G. keeps up the place, which must make a large hole in the rent. It is a difficult question for G. to decide whether he shall renew their term . . . G. House is large, Cumloden small, & in point of dignity he would gain by going back: in some respects he would gain in convenience also: but he could not afford to live at both places, & Cumloden is in a far pleasanter country & more in the heart of the estates.

27 Sept. 1882: . . . Walk in afternoon with Lord G.[alloway] . . . It is evident that the owner is deeply attached to this place, & indeed I do not wonder. Though the extent is large, the estate lies compactly, & includes much exceedingly picturesque ground. It is also in a secluded out of the way district, free from the nuisance of tourists, & where the leading local landowners are very great people indeed. The only drawback is the extent of the encumbrances, which leave only a narrow margin to live on. I doubt whether G. has a clear £5,000 [p.a.] into his pocket, when all estate expenses are paid. The habits of the family during the last two or three generations have been liberal, though not reckless: charges have been piled up: and they have indulged in enormous numbers of children, 10, 12, or more: which no estate can long bear[39].

. . . Heard from Sanderson: it seems that Tenterden had been often ill of late, had become irregular in his habits of work, & was laid up for some time before his death: which thus did not come on the office as a surprise. Sanderson evidently thinks that he shall not be chosen to fill the vacancy: & I see in some of the papers that Pauncefote is to be the man. He is a fit person, inferior to Sanderson in ability, but steady, safe, & a conscientious worker. . . .

29 Sept. 1882: Left Cumloden with M. a little after 8.00 . . . reached Knowsley at 5.30.
. . . Among other recent applications I have had one noticeable for its sheer impudence. It is from the son of one Murray[40], formerly a consul-general in Odessa, whom I removed for misconduct: he thereupon took to scurrilous journalism, got into various troubles, & had to leave the country. He died some time ago, & now his son applies to me to lend him £50, on the ground of his father's sufferings, & my being the cause of them. I refused him curtly enough.

Wrote to Lawrence . . . declining finally to bid for the Meggernie estate. . . . It seems as if £125–£130,000 would be the selling price. I have hesitated, for there is something attractive in the idea of a valley 22 miles long . . . The reasons against it [are]: (1) I should seldom be able to visit a distant estate, . . . and am growing too old for Highland walks, nor have I anyone to whom I should care to leave it: (2) It is impossible to say what new legislation there may be about land, & for the present capital invested in securities is safer: (3) I have as yet only £400,000 put by, & that is hardly enough to allow of so large a deduction, consistently with what I want to do. Scotch estates are not rare in the market, & another chance will be offered later, if I care to avail myself of it.

30 Sept. 1882: . . . At 2.00, left for Liverpool with M. Meeting in St. George's Hall, for the opening of the University College session. M. Arnold the author & professor had been brought down to deliver a lecture, which he did. I introduced him in a short speech, made another on delivering the prizes, & a third about the state of the college: none long, all well received. The audience was large. Arnold's lecture was in substance a repetition of thoughts already in his essays, & not very new: but the style was good, & the delivery a success. The whole affair lasted less than two hours. –

M. Arnold came out to stay with us at Knowsley. –

Long letter from Granville, from which I gather that Pauncefote is to replace Tenterden, & Currie[41] to have the assistant secretaryship. The first of these appointments is probably right, since P. had done much of Tenterden's work in the last year (which I did not know before) & had established a claim which it would have been difficult to pass over: the preference of Currie to Sanderson is I think a mistake, though defensible on the grounds of seniority. He is capable, but less capable than Sanderson: but he is an intriguer, & I suspect the knowledge that he would resent being passed over, & make mischief in the office, has had something to do with Granville's choice. He may also have been naturally unwilling to lose the benefit of the best private secretary he is ever likely to find: which is intelligible but scarcely just. On the whole I am disappointed, having confidently [hoped] that S. would be a gainer by this change.

1 Oct. 1882 (Sunday): M. Arnold went with Lady Derby to church, which is a curious piece of conformity, he being an avowed agnostic: but he is also a government official.

. . . Showed Mr. A. the library, & walk with him round the park . . . Pleasant talk on many subjects, but nothing specially to note. He has a fair share of literary vanity, repeating with pleasure compliments paid to himself, & inviting them: but the desire of praise thus shown is simple, natural, & does not offend.

He told me he had persuaded Morley to accept the editorship of the *Pall Mall Gazette,* in the expectation that by his ability & influence he might secure for himself a high political appointment. This he said was the case in France, & why not here? I did not argue the question, but thought that the H. of Commons is not likely to approve or support a minister who passes over M.P.s to appoint men from outside. His idea, as I understood it, seemed to be that Mr. M., by securing promotion for himself, would elevate the position of journalists & literary men generally.

Note that A. Arnold, the member for Salford, is not a relative, nor an Arnold at all. His real name is Abraham & he is a Jew by birth, who for journalistic purposes thought Arnold a good name to appear under[42].

Talk of Lord Coleridge, his strange mixture of kindly feeling with intense bitterness:

his sceptical talk & love of ceremonial worship, which made Brett, his colleague, say that he never knew whether Lord C. was a catholic or an atheist. Arnold knows him well, & accounted for his peculiarities by saying that, so far as intellectual convictions are concerned, Lord C. is absolutely sceptical: but that he retains his interest in, & sympathy with, the ceremonies & rites of the church, & while at home attends daily service. – I confess that this union of devotion & incredulity is to me very unintelligible, but Arnold knows the man well, & seemed convinced of the truth of his description. . . .

3 Oct. 1882: . . . Left with M. for Winmarleigh . . . After dinner, Lord W. talked much in a desponding strain about the temper of the farmers, who he thought were on the way to make the same demands as had been made in Ireland. . . . He expressed a good deal of alarm at the state of public feeling: but I remember that for 30 years he has always been inclined to despond, predicting a social convulsion, & the plunder of the rich. . . .

6 Oct. 1882: . . . Little news in the papers. The troops are being withdrawn from Egypt. An army of occupation 10,000 strong will be left for the present. Ireland is fairly quiet, though there have been one or two more murders. Party politics though not dead are sleeping: Northcote has made a long speech at Glasgow, temperate & as fair as a party speech can be, but not effective, because he had really nothing to attack. His strongest point was that he got hold of some of Gladstone's rather wild denunciations of public expenditure, & showed that it had not been reduced, but increased: which is a good *argumentum ad hominem*, & indeed a reasonable criticism on exaggerated promises of impossible reforms.

7 Oct. 1882: . . . I took out of the Blue Book a list of the leading Lancashire landowners, with their acreage:

Derby	47,269	(should be nearly 57,000)
Sefton	18,769	(I think understated)
T. Clifton	15,802	
D. of Devonshire	12.681	
Sir T. Hesketh	8,944	
Blundell	8,672	
Ld Wilton	8,013	
Ld Lilford	7,552	
Ld Lathom	7,213	
T. Parker	7,336	
Ld Gerard	6,192	
Bridgewater trustees	6,701	
De Trafford	6,454	
Ld Stamford	5,231	
Starkie	5,895	
Petre[+]	5,754	
Ormerod[+]	5,290	

The above are all that I can find over 5,000 acres. In all 17.

Hesketh	4,127
Legh of Lyme	4,997
Brockholes	4,600
De Houghton	4,112
Dicconson[+]	4,323
Dugdale[+]	4,016
Garnett	4,703
Hornby of Dalton	3,736
Martin[+]	3,706
Milton[+]	3,223
North[+]	3,471
Winmarleigh	3,711
Rawsthorne[+]	3,445
Scarisbrick	3,133
Blackburn	3,143
Ld Ellesmere	3,379
Fenwick[+]	3,165
Fitzgerald	3,105
Forster[+]	3,684
Garnett	3,511
Ld Headfort	3,993

In all under 5,000 and above 3,000, 21: or 38 holders of land in Lancashire over 3,000 acres. As part of the county is moorland, & part urban, the acreage of various estates tells nothing as to their value.

Those marked with a cross are personally unknown to me.

8 Oct. 1882: Fine bright day: walk early for exercise, 3 miles on the measured terrace, with a book: when reading as well as walking the pace is just 3 miles an hour: when without one 3½ miles. . . .

10 Oct. 1882: . . . Talk later with Lowell on various subjects. About Hawthorne, whom he praised as I thought extravagantly, reckoning him one of the few great writers of the century: of Disraeli, to whom he would grant no merit except that of cleverness, thinking him absolutely selfish & cynical, & not appreciating highly even his novels: of Gladstone, whose speeches & writings he thought in substance commonplace, & was at a loss to understand the extraordinary influence of the man, unless it arose from his great earnestness: he observed what I have often felt, that G. becomes wearisome at times by the extreme importance which he seems to attach to everything which he is discussing, whether in public or private.

Talk about the Jews (I think begun by C. Münster): Lowell shares very strongly the popular prejudice against them, & does not conceal it. He & Münster agree in this. I ask why – what harm have they done? Answer: they have no national feeling, & do their best to destroy it: they are against all religious bodies: they do nothing to increase the wealth of the country they live in, but only try to get its money into their own hands: they monopolise the press: they play into one another's hands to the exclusion of other races: I think these were the chief allegations. Lowell said: 'I fear their influence in America: I think them very dangerous.' He added that most of the socialist leaders are or were of Jewish origin. He dwelt seriously on a notion which seems to me purely fanciful – that many of the great English families are of Jewish descent. He instanced the Russells, on no other ground apparently than that Roussel or Rousseau, the French variety of the name, means 'the red man' & was a common alias taken by Jews in France who wished to disguise their origin. He claimed the Fox family as Jews on the strength of their features: and Cecil, the first Lord Burleigh, I forget, or did not rightly understand, on what evidence: in the States, he spoke of Jay Gould, the financier, as undoubtedly a Jew: & named some others. He believed they controlled the whole European press, & united in writing down any one, statesman or author, who showed a prejudice against them. He said the persecutions to which they were exposed in the old days, & that in Russia now, were due to the same cause. People found all the money of their town or province in Jewish hands: and everybody in debt to the Jew: then they rose against their creditors, & killed them.

I tried to argue that a race who are so uniformly successful in industrial enterprise could not be a very immoral race: but this was not accepted. – I see the subject is with Lowell a favourite one, & that he really has a strong feeling upon it: & I remember that it is shared by Goldwin Smith who copies, & sometimes exaggerates, the prejudices of the new world.

[**Note**: 18 Oct.] Fawcett, who knows Lowell well, says that nothing is less agreeable to him than to be complimented on the *Bigelow Papers*: which he considers as a work of youth, & dislikes the idea that his fame will rest upon it: which nevertheless is probably what will happen, for he has done nothing since which has hit the popular fancy to an equal extent.

Of all Americans whom I have met, Lowell seems to have least of his country's peculiarities: I should not know him to be other than an Englishman: if there is anything special to note, it is a certain precision & purity with which he speaks, treating the English language, as it were, with more respect than we do. He notes as vulgarisms many phrases used by English talkers who do not think themselves vulgar: e.g. the pronunciation of the word 'figure' as though spelt 'figger' which he says none but uncultivated people do in the States.

11 Oct. 1882: A party had been made to go out shooting, but incessant rain prevented. Sorted out some books to go to the Manchester library & others to be bound.
Sent £5 to the Howard Association.
. . . Stayed indoors till luncheon, then walk with Mr. Lowell to call at Croxteth . . . Lowell talked again on the subject of the Jews, which I cannot but suspect is with him a sort of craze. He claimed sundry notable personages in history as of Jewish race, saying that he believed the first Napoleon was one, though the proofs were not absolutely conclusive. He had no doubt but that the order of Jesuits was founded by converts of Jewish descent.

His conversation on other subjects was very pleasant & easy, but I carried away nothing that could be noted.

Talk with Lord Lyons about the state of France: I asked what was the explanation of the general popular determination to have nothing to do with foreign expeditions? which, though reasonable, was utterly opposed to the traditions of the country. He said it was entirely due to fear of Germany. French statesmen thought that not a soldier should be sent out of France, & no expedition entered into, nor any engagement made, which might involve the country in a little war. The feeling as I understand him was twofold: apprehension lest the Germans should again attack them: & desire not to lose an opportunity of revenge, if an opening should occur for a coalition against Germany.

12 Oct. 1882: . . . I left home at 9.45 . . . to go with Lord Northbrook & a party round the docks: which we did . . . going along the whole line . . . In all there is about £25,000,000 spent on the river: of which about £16,000,000 is debt: the income is over a million a year, & there is a yearly sinking fund of £100,000 (far too small I should think). . . . The dock estate contains about 1,500 acres. Lyster[43] employs nearly 5,000 hands: men employed by piecework make as much as 6s. daily, or 36s. a week. No objection is made here to piecework by the unions – it was not explained to me why. There has been as much as 350,000 tons of shipping at one time in the docks . . . We noted the contrast between the bustle & business on the Liverpool side & the stagnation on the Birkenhead shore.

13 Oct. 1882: . . . Lord Northbrook arrived about 11.30 after a great meeting of the Liberal party. He . . . had passed the morning in a series of public appearances. He had made three long speeches within 24 hours, & seemed heartily glad that his work was done.

14 Oct. 1882: . . . Lord Northbrook has more than once observed that, while his reception was cordial beyond what he could have expected, he found the feeling cold, not to say hostile, on the subject of the Egyptian War. If anybody, he said, had attacked it at the meeting or at the dinner of the night before, as unjustifiable, the majority would have taken the speaker's part. He was the more surprised at this state of feeling, as in London everybody is for it. Fawcett argued with him, & added that, if the war had gone on, it would have broken up the Liberal party. People, he thought, endured it solely out of confidence in Gladstone. They could not see the necessity or the justification, but they were willing to suppose that he did, & in any case they felt sure that he would not have gone in for it without a conviction of there being no alternative.

Fawcett expressed alarm at the prospect of this & all future wars being paid for solely by an increase of income tax, or by borrowing. He thought it was absolutely essential that the working classes should be made to pay part of the cost – since that is the only check on the love of fighting. He admitted that the masses are quite indifferent to economy, which is a middle-class idea. He fears also the increasing demands that will be made on the State, both on the score of cost and that of over-governing. He believes ideas about the nationalisation of the land to be widely spread, & dangerous. (A part of his speech yesterday was devoted to refuting these ideas.) He talked of the extreme poverty of women well educated & well brought up, but who were, by thousands, literally in want of food, & ashamed to beg. He inferred that their services might be utilised in many ways, especially as clerks, etc. I think he also meant to infer that their not having votes had something to do with the neglect with which they are treated. He had had several hundred competitors for 30 vacant clerkships, of small value.

15 Oct. 1882: . . . Walk with Fawcett & Lord Lymington[44], nearly 2 hours.

Fawcett talked among other matters of the question of church disestablishment: said he thought that would come to the front as soon as Gladstone died or retired: the nonconformists forbore to press it just now, only out of respect for his feelings. He mentioned Mr. Dale of Birmingham as a probable leader in that agitation. He spoke of the Premier with respect, but with no great affection: laughing at his oddities, but saying that his hold on the people was something quite extraordinary. Stiff dissenters & radicals, to whom this Egyptian war is an abomination, swallowed it, he said, believing that, as Gladstone had made it, there must be a good reason for it, though they could not see where the reason lay.

Talk of the leadership of the House: he thinks Harcourt anxious to get into the Lords as Chancellor, on the ground, as I had supposed before, that he neither wishes to lead the Commons himself, nor to be led by a junior.

Talk of savings banks: he is proud of what he has done to increase their number: said the number of depositors was now about 1 in 11 of the population of England & Wales, & it was increasing at the rate of 400,000 yearly. – He wanted to reduce the telegraph rates from 1s. to 6d., but it would cost £170,000 a year at first, & the loss would not be made up for 4 years: Gladstone will not give him the money. – He would also like to increase the amount allowed to be deposited in one year, but the jealousy of the bankers stands in the way. He talked very sanguinely of his new scheme of insurance through the post office, which was a scheme of Gladstone's many years ago, & is at present in existence, but the power given by the law is scarcely at all taken advantage of. He repeated his objections to throwing all sudden increase of taxes on the income tax only: thought the duties on tea & beer might both be raised when heavier outlay required it. Thought economy could not be carried further: in fact, as fresh duties are constantly thrown on the State, the tendency is towards increase rather than restriction.

16 Oct. 1882: The Fawcetts left us, & Lord Lymington: making an end of all our receiving of company till December.

Fawcett's visit has been on the whole a success: his conversation is interesting, full of information, & not wanting in liveliness: some people might think he talks too much & too didactically, & he is certainly not a man to invite where any others in the company wish to hold forth: for he monopolises conversation almost as much as Macaulay did. Still he is worth hearing, & his defect, if it be one, is natural in a man who cannot see his audience, nor well judge of the impression he may be making. His voice loud & rather harsh is against him, & he has a strange accent, or brogue, which I never heard in anyone else. He requires very little looking after, considering his infirmity: & seems content to be anywhere so that he can find a listener. He most willingly discusses political & economical subjects, the characters of public men, the traditions of the House, & matters of that sort. I don't think he has much wit or humour, or much appreciation of them, & he is a little egotistical in expatiating on his way of managing so as to let his blindness interfere as little as possible with what he wants to do. Probably he has been often questioned on that point, & knows that what he says will be heard with interest. – Mrs. Fawcett[45] we thought pleasing & simple in her manners: with nothing about her to show that she speaks at public meetings, & is a strong advocate of women's rights. . . .

22 Oct. 1882: . . . Read some pamphlets lately sent me on the Chinese, or Indian, opium question: read them with an unpleasant sensation caused not exactly by the strength of the arguments against the trade, for with these I was familiar long ago: but by their fitness to touch the popular mind exactly on those points as to which it is most sensitive. The archbishops & many of the clergy have apparently joined in the agitation: &, as temperance & missionary work are things which a considerable section of the public really cares about, whereas nobody cares for the solvency of India except politicians, the difficulty may grow serious.

23 Oct. 1882: . . . Dined at the Germany Embassy, meeting the Granvilles, Sanderson, & C. Bismarck. Much talk after dinner with Granville: he says that Arabi clearly ought not to be executed as a rebel, unless there is proof of murder against him: that the chief trouble in that matter has been with the Queen who is furious (his own word) for Arabi's death, writing daily, or more than once a day, on the subject: she was very angry that English counsel were allowed to the prisoner. I observed that if the American war had ended differently George III would certainly have tried to hang Washington. He confirmed my opinion that the real cause of the war was the French first pushing us on, then suddenly drawing back, which encouraged the insurgents to resistance, even if they did not through their agents encourage them, which seems likely. Talk of French designs on Madagascar: I said I thought we ought rather to encourage than discourage French plans of colonial empire, since occupation in that way would keep them quiet in Europe, & in a military point of view their colonies would be a weakness rather than a strength. In this he agreed, but seemed troubled at the prospect of the Madagascar natives appealing to us, & our being unable to help them. And in truth the French appear to have been as shameless in seeking a pretext for quarrel as they were in the case of Tunis. – He made very light of the cost of the Egyptian expedition, assuring me that it would not come near the figure of £8,000,000 at which I had guessed it: but I doubt there may be more expenses than he knows of.

I asked if he could explain the curious outbreak of anti-English feeling in Italy. He could not, except that the seizure of Tunis by France had caused great disgust among many Italians, & they thought we might have prevented it. And, now that we had taken the Egyptian business into our own hands, they thought themselves excluded from the Mediterranean. – Talk of an absurd Persian proposal to raise their minister to the rank of ambassador, which would give him precedence over the representatives among others of Spain & the U.S. – Talk of Tenterden: Ld G. confirmed what Sanderson had said, that whether from failing health, or social distractions consequent on his marriage, he had of late become very inefficient in the office: working as well as ever at times, but only at intervals & only when he chose.

24 Oct. 1882: . . . To the Commons . . . Randolph Churchill had taken an ingenious, but foolish, objection to the mode of procedure adopted, on the ground that the House ought to have been prorogued instead of being adjourned. Gladstone answered in his most effective style, but it seemed a waste of power: he gave more importance to the attack than it deserved. Northcote followed with an awkward question (at least I should have thought it so if I had had to answer it) about the finances of the Egyptian war . . .

25 Oct. 1882: . . . Froude came to dine with us, agreeable as usual & less Carlylean than when we saw him last: a long holiday has restored his health, & he no longer thinks the country going to immediate ruin. He talks of bringing out two volumes of Mrs. Carlyle's letters, & then one more summing up the whole work & giving his own reminiscences of the pair. But he is puzzled how far to disclose, or how far to pass lightly over, the quarrels of their later married days. It seems that, when Lady Ashburton took up Carlyle & made a friend of him, the wife dropped into the background: &, being a woman of proud & jealous disposition, & knowing that she alone had made her husband's success possible, she resented the neglect with which she was treated. Hence disputes & angry words – though it appears that he never knew the full extent of his wife's alienation from him until he read her journal after death. – I did not venture to ask how far the last publication had been a success, but gather from M. that it has been less popular than it deserved to be. Froude is now in trouble as to a lecture which he is to deliver at Birmingham, which he says will mainly turn on the dangers of oratory to a state, as exemplified by the Greek republics. I gather that the moral will be pointed against Gladstone, Bright, & parliamentary government in general, so that if the application is taken it will cause an excitement.

Saw Tavistock, & casually Sir J. Mowbray[46]: the latter thought the discussion of parliamentary procedure would not last long: but T., who had heard the debate of this afternoon, doubted. The supporters of government have agreed to say as little as possible, but to leave the debate wholly to the opposition – a difficult system to work upon for more than one debate, & which always irritates opponents so much that little is gained by it in the end.

26 Oct. 1882: . . . At 4.15 to the Lords, where the vote of thanks to naval & military forces engaged in Egypt came on. The House was fairly filled, considering the time of year. Granville did his work in a rather heavy prosaic style, without animation or eloquence, but with a certain carefulness, dwelling in detail on some features of the campaign. Salisbury followed, & did what was expected well enough. The D. of Cambridge thought it necessary to speak also, & delivered a long rambling address, which seemed like a reminiscence of all the speeches he had made at public dinners about the army & navy. It was chattering rather than haranguing. But he was not very long, & had a patient audience.

. . . The procedure debate continues in H. of C. with what result I cannot gather. I hear that the Opposition are much displeased with Northcote's temperate & prudent leadership, & want a more dashing chief. But they cannot well put R. Churchill in the place, & there is no one on the whole half so competent as Northcote. The first question on which difference has arisen is whether the exceptional powers given to the Speaker shall be also vested in his deputy, the chairman of committees? An embarrassing dilemma, for, if not, obstruction will be unchecked in committee: and, if these powers are so extended, the whole argument founded on the peculiar position of the Speaker, as the one man in the House placed above party, falls to the ground. It is noticed that Gladstone on the first night went out of his way to express the readiness of the Cabinet to accept whatever decision the House may come to – which means that he will not make it a question of confidence, as by some eager supporters he has been pressed to do. . . .

30 Oct. 1882: Left Keston by the usual train: did not walk in, the day being rainy. At the station met Margaret: gave her £28, this being her 28th birthday. – Knowsley in afternoon.

31 Oct. 1882: Knowsley. Sessions 11.00 to 5.45. About 35 magistrates present at the opening: counsel nearly as many. Cases were 18.

1 Nov. 1882: Sessions, 10.00 to 6.15. Cases 27. One sentence of 7 years, one of 2 years, two of 18 mos., one of 15 mos., two of 12 months, the rest 8 to 4 mos.

2 Nov. 1882: Sessions from 10.00 to nearly 6.00.

. . . Liverpool papers are full of the municipal elections, which in Liverpool have left matters practically unchanged, and in the country generally the result is the same: there is a slight Conservative gain, but not enough to indicate a reaction in popular feeling.

3 Nov. 1882: Sessions again from 10.00 to 5.40. We passed the greater part of the day in trying two bankrupts, father & son . . . for fraud committed on their creditors . . . They had to be tried separately, I hardly know why: for the evidence was the same in both cases. One got 18 mos., the other 12 mos. Afterwards came assault & wounding cases: one peculiarly brutal assault, by a son on his mother, at Bootle: he knocked her down, . . . kicked her till she lay insensible, & in much danger of her life. . . . I gave the man only 8 mos., which I now think was too little: it ought to have been 12.

. . . I notice at these sessions an extraordinary increase in the number of boys charged with house breaking. It seems a common practice among the young roughs of Widnes, St. Helens, & parts of Liverpool. The parents do not care about their being sent to a reformatory, as it costs less, probably, to keep them there than at home, & they are out of the way. We have no choice but to flog, which I do not much believe in as a cure, but it acts as a deterrent for the moment.

. . . I have adopted the plan during these sessions of doing without luncheon except two hard biscuits: and I find it answers: there is less weariness in the afternoon. Exercise has of course been impossible: but I have not felt the want of it so far.

Letters from M. show that she is well & happy at Paris but I cannot make out what the new oculist has done for her.

4 Nov. 1882: . . . The week has been a busy one in the Commons: the Lords have not met. Briefly the result is that ministers have carried their plan of clôture by a simple majority, as against the proposed alternative of a two-thirds vote. The division was on Thursday – majority 84. Gladstone made a very fine speech in defence of his proposal, which seems to have had the success it deserved: but it is a little odd that he declared the two-thirds vote scheme to be worse than nothing, denouncing it with his most vehement rhetoric, in the face of his own offer to accept it in May or June, if the opposition have come to terms.

This is another illustration of what Fawcett said to me at Knowsley: that the Premier involves himself in apparent inconsistencies (apparent rather than real) by his habit of treating administrative details as questions of principle. When circumstances require a change in regard to some of these details, which must often happen, he is in the position of having to unsay what he said before, or (which is his more common alternative) to ignore it. . . .

6 Nov. 1882: Walk for exercise: at 2.30 to S. Kensington to the Nat. Port. Gallery: where the trustees met to consider the financial position, prepare estimates, & examine the pictures now rearranged. We were present – Hardinge, E. Fitzmaurice, E. Stanhope, Gladstone, Hope, Sir R. Wallace, & Scharf[47]. The Premier seemed quite at leisure, free from business, & I heard him in eager discussion with Scharf as to the best method of hanging pictures. He talked to me about the late & still continuing debates, & said among other things that he had seldom known a question of which the importance was so greatly exaggerated as this of the closure [*clôture*]. He had himself he owned been in doubt whether it was worth proposing: so strongly did he feel that it would not fully meet the requirements of the case. I observed that the proposed plan of grand committees seemed to me immeasurably the more important proposal of the two, though it had been so little talked about: he agreed, adding that what they were doing was merely tentative, they wished to see how it would work[48]. . . .

7 Nov. 1882: Still troubled with cold: did not go out.

Lawson[49] called early: some talk with him about public affairs . . . Talk as to divisions in the Conservative party: he thinks as I do that they will come to nothing, since there is no man who could be put into Northcote's place. Talk as to the future leadership of the House: who is capable? Hartington will be in the Lords: Forster is out of the running: Chamberlain, Dilke, Courtney, Trevelyan, all possible but all untried: Harcourt would not be accepted &, being rather indolent by nature, does not wish it. Lawson says like everybody else that Harcourt's wish is for a peerage & the Chancellorship: which I also believe, but it would be an odd proceeding.

Lawson was followed by Mr. Escott of the *Fortnightly Review*, who came to discuss things in general, especially Egypt. We discussed especially the possibility of arranging a compromise of the claims of the bondholders. . . . This was all the company I had for, my cold increasing, I stayed within, saw Drage, & did little beyond answering a few notes. . . .

8 Nov. 1882: . . . The Premier called on M. having sent word that he meant to do so, which put her into some confusion, thinking that another offer might be coming, but there was no cause. He talked freely & pleasantly on various subjects. He had just been speaking in the House, as I saw afterwards, for nearly an hour[50].

In the papers, I see with regret, the retirement of Walpole from parliament. He is 76 and has sat in the House for 36 years, so that his withdrawal is justified. He had of late taken little part in affairs. Though in no sense a strong man (for he did not aim at brilliancy, & his judgment, though sound, was not acute) he was respected on all sides, & deserved to be so: for a more blameless life in public & private has seldom been led by any one. He was almost too gentle for the ordinary work of the world: I cannot imagine him saying a harsh or cutting thing: and he was too modest, for his own convictions were generally wiser than those which he allowed to be substituted for them. He was often talked of for the Speakership: & in that place he would have succeeded better than as a party politician. He had the sense to aim only at what he could effect: & he has had his reward in general respect & esteem.

9 Nov. 1882: . . . In Gladstone's speech of yesterday on the clôture occurred a passage, not closely connected with anything that preceded or followed, but apparently introduced for its own sake, assuring the Irish that their claims to local self-government should be recognised: the words used were vague: so much so that they might mean a great deal or almost nothing: in Ireland they are read as a concession to Home Rule, & will do mischief[51].

The debates this autumn session are thought to have been unusually dull, scarcely a single speech made of any merit as an argument or in point of eloquence, except one by

Gladstone (not the last). The really important part of the question to be dealt with, the division of the House into grand committees, has not yet been touched: & probably less will be said upon it because the arguments *pro* and *con* have not become familiar by repetition. . . .

10 Nov. 1882: . . . Forgot to note yesterday a story which Reeve told me, having heard it from Lord Malmesbury: Ld M. said that Palmerston had talked to him about the Suez Canal, while it was making, & summed up his objections to it as follows: 'I am opposed to the canal mainly for a reason which cannot be assigned in parliament: if it is made, I have no doubt but that the English will use it more largely than any other nation: they will then want a share in the management, & we shall be drawn into a closer connection with Egyptian affairs than is desirable.'

Assuming that Ld M. has not coloured this prediction, to make it suit the event, it is a curious instance of foresight. . . .

13 Nov. 1882: . . . In the papers, news of an attempt to murder Lawson[52], the judge, in Dublin: which came to nothing, the intending murderer being seized before he had time to fire his revolver. . . .

15 Nov. 1882: . . . Dined out with the Penders, meeting Sir H. Vivian[53], Sir R. Cross, Fowler the engineer[54], Sir Cooper Key[55], Mr. Hill[56] of the *D. News*, etc. . . . Mr. Hill told us of the failure of Tennyson's play[57], which it seems was produced with a high moral purpose, as a protest against free-thinkers & agnostics: it is badly & clumsily arranged, for theatrical effect – in fact a poem, not an acting play. Hence its ill success. He said the Premier came to the first night, & was deeply pained by the collapse of his friend's attempt: characteristically he looked at it from the moral, not the artistic side, & thought the disapproval of the audience indicated sympathy with atheism. So Mr. Hill said: & I gathered that he had been talking to Gladstone himself. Mr. H. spoke of Ruskin: how he had been entirely out of his mind during part of his illness: fancied himself an elephant, etc. He agreed with me that, with all Ruskin's genius, there is in him a vein of insanity. . . .

16 Nov. 1882: M. having been cupped last night, as an experiment to relieve her from the feeling of oppression about the eyes, remained all day in a dark room: which she thinks has done her good.

. . . Dined Travellers', meeting Lord Kenmare[58], some Irish talk with him. – The last development of Irish troubles is not the least odd. After all the outcry raised in favour of the Arrears Bill, it is now found that the number of tenants who have applied for a grant under it is insignificant: the time for application is almost expired, & instead of £2,000,000 which was allowed for, the actual demands are as yet only £150,000. The explanation of this state of things is not easy. In many cases the tenants do not know, probably, where to go or how to proceed: some possibly have never heard of the Act for which they were supposed to be so anxious: some are kept back by agitators, who do not want to part with a grievance: and many, perhaps the larger number, cannot comply with the requirement that they shall have paid half the rent due. Anyway, it is characteristic that a legislative remedy which was accepted on all sides as effectual, & only objected to as unjust to the landlords, should be ignored or refused by the people who were most eager for it.

I asked Kenmare whether there was any emigration from his part of Ireland. Very little, he said. Why? did the priests or the local agitators oppose it? No – the priests would not have power, even if they wished, to do so: the trouble was that they could not raise money to pay their passage. Then if they were better off they would go? Yes, certainly: it is their poverty keeps them where they are. Impossible not to observe that it is only in Ireland that the surest sign of the country being well-to-do would be found in the people leaving it. But I believe that what Ld K. said is true.

17 Nov. 1882: . . . Forgot to note yesterday that Lord Kenmare told me that the Arrears Act had left a certain disinclination to pay rent in the minds of those who had paid hitherto – they of course get no benefit, and one of them said to him lately: 'I have got no good out of this Arrears Act, but I will take care that I get some out of the next.' It is not strange that this feeling should exist – I only wonder that there is not more of it. The failure of the Act – and apparently it must be held to have failed – is a serious matter. An enormous multitude of the tenants either cannot or will not pay: and the landlords, naturally angry at recent legislation, are not disposed as in ordinary times they might have been to treat them with leniency. They are glad to get rid of them – and no wonder. But what is to be the end?

18 Nov. 1882: . . . **Note** that seeing all my contemporaries obliged to use glasses in reading, which I will never endure, I have come to the resolution to spare my eyes more than has hitherto been my habit. Less reading at night, & intervals after half an hour or so of reading at any time, will be desirable.

Note also that, though deafness is not increasing, it may be as well to consult an aurist before leaving the south, for I can seldom hear what passes in general conversation, at least not without effort.

Review in the park today of troops returned from Egypt.

Odd incident. At the first, or second, performance of Tennyson's play – a very absurd one, in which the hero, or villain, is a freethinker, and is made to soliloquise in a highly immoral manner – Lord Queensberry[59], who has identified himself with the secularist party, got up to protest against the piece as a caricature of his opinions. He repeated this proceeding, after which he was induced to leave. It is possible that one reason of the piece being so decidedly condemned is its sermonising tendency, which playgoers naturally dislike: but it is said to be dull, unnatural, and unpleasing.

19 Nov. 1882: . . . Heard, with regret of a certain kind, of the death of Lord Otho Fitzgerald[60]. He was a mere man of fashion and of society, but a frequent visitor at Knowsley in old days, fond of shooting and, like many such persons, miserable if he did not make a good score. For the rest, a handsome, good-natured Irishman, and one of the last persons one should have thought to die prematurely. He was only 55.

20 Nov. 1882: . . . I note as odd that I have heard nothing from Hale since I left Knowsley, though he said that there were many matters which he wished to discuss. I suspect he is losing energy, from gradual failure of health, & perpetual worry about his wife.

News in the papers that Lord Harrowby[61] is dead, aged 85, which sends Sandon[62] to the Lords, & vacates a seat for Liverpool. The late peer was only remarkable as having just contrived to win the prizes of public life, having sat I think in two Cabinets, with no talent to speak of, & no considerable debating faculty: at least not in the last 20 years, but I did not know him in his best days. The new Lord Harrowby has average capacity, some power of speech, intense obstinacy, & strong devotion to the church: a man in all ways respectable, but dull & somewhat fanatical. . . .

22 Nov. 1882: . . . Sanderson to luncheon: talk about Bouyond the cook who has now quarrelled with the housekeeper in London as he did with the housekeeper at Knowsley, and behaved indecently to one of the maids. So it is settled that he must leave but, to avoid trouble, he gives warning of his own accord, & is not discharged. I am supposed to know nothing of the last row. I don't know that he has been actually dishonest, as cooks go, but he has used his right to perquisites very freely. . . .

23 Nov. 1882: . . . Talk at The Club the other night about Tennyson & his play: it seems that he reads no newspapers as a rule, & on this occasion his family have taken care that he shall not even see them: so that he is under the impression that he has had a dramatic success, instead of absolute failure, as the truth is. Gladstone has written him a complimentary letter, & so have one or two of the bishops, I suppose in the interest of morality & religion: which tends to keep up his delusion.

Maine talked of Paris, where he has been lately: sees a great change: less strictness in the police: less order kept: he was particularly impressed by the extraordinary number of indecent publications sold in the streets. Thinks that there is a general uneasiness, & wonder as to what is to come next.

24 Nov. 1882: . . . Debate on the Arrears Act: Gladstone seems to have been firm in refusing further concessions to the tenants. He had in reality no choice: but ambiguous language, such as he is fond of using, might have raised false hopes, & made mischief.

Salisbury has been haranguing the Edinburgh people: clever as usual, but not very effective, for the determination to find fault with everything that the government has done is too conspicuous, & it destroys the effect of criticism, in which at least a show of fairness is expected. Northcote is gone abroad for health: suffering from weak heart.

I suppose that for years past there has not been so entire an absence of political or social agitation in England. Various reforms are expected, & approved of: but there is no eagerness about them. Except the Irish, nobody has a grievance that they are in earnest about. The result is a certain air of unreality about speeches on both sides: there is nothing to quarrel over. . . .

. . . With M. to call at Addington & enquire after our neighbour the archbishop, who has relapsed.

25 Nov. 1882: Sent £50 to the London school board election committee: rather against my will, for I know little about the matter, & the contests seem rather personal than based on any principle.

. . . Debate in the Commons on the so-called Kilmainham treaty, which began & ended in a foolish personal wrangle: and another, the night before, on the Arrears Act, sensible & useful. It seems that the tenants hang back, & will not claim the benefit of the Act, hoping in a vague way that it may be altered more in their favour, & disliking, as their way is, to part with money till the last moment. There is yet time for more to come in, & possibly they will: but a friend writes that in some districts they are altogether indifferent, saying: 'The landlord will not turn me out if I bring him a year's rent, anyway: so why should I trouble myself with applying to the government, for his benefit?'

The pinch will come next year when, with rents fixed, & arrears in part settled, the tenants will have to decide whether they mean to pay or to refuse: dilatory excuses will be at an end. And in the south & west there are thousands who can no more pay than fly, & must be evicted, if they are not to live rent free. The difficulty is not over, nor near it.

26 Nov. 1882: . . . In the papers, another Irish murder, this time of a detective, who was attacked in the street by several men, & shot dead. . . .

29 Nov. 1882: Long talk with Warr about the City Companies Commission, the upshot of which is that the Companies are to be heard, a request impossible to refuse: they are confident of being able to refute many of the charges against them, if not all: & Mr. Firth is extremely dissatisfied. He is pushed on by one Beal, a noisy agitator, who has been in the habit of writing in the minor papers, & ascribes to himself the honour of causing the Commission to be appointed. Both Beal & Firth find to their disgust that neither the opinion of their brother commissioners, nor that of the public as far as it can be gathered, go to the full length of theirs. They wish to sweep away the companies entirely, & put their property in the hands of the new municipal govt. of London: which is not yet created, & from what I hear Harcourt is not willing to take in hand the enormous work of creating it. In the meanwhile the reformers are beginning to complain of delay, & wish to cut the knot at once. . . . As to the (so-called) private property of the companies, I do not yet see my way.

. . . At 6.00 I went to Granville's by appointment, & discussed again the question of joining the Cabinet. We talked of many things – Egypt, as to which he gave the strongest assurances that they will withdraw at the earliest possible period. Ireland – as to which he said the Cabinet were strongly averse to meddling with the Land Bill again, fearing to reopen that question without absolute necessity. Home Rule he entirely disclaimed, but believed in more local self-government for the Irish: on this matter we went into no details, & indeed I do not think he was very familiar with it. Our conversation [ended] by my promising to write or call on him next day. He told me that, if I accepted in principle the idea of joining them, the India Office would probably be that offered to me: and that Hartington would probably take the War Office, Childers going to the Exchequer, if not disabled by health. (He is just now invalided, & in the country.)

I thought it well to talk of Ly D.'s eyes, & the injury done to them by glare & hot rooms, as a reason why she would be unable to do what is usually expected of a minister's wife in the way of receiving, in the event of my acceptance. And I thought it right that the Premier should be told of this. I left Ld G. feeling anxious & weary, & had much talk with M. as to acceptance or refusal. She was entirely for my accepting, both on public & private grounds.

30 Nov. 1882: . . . Called again on Granville, & settled the matter by saying that I was ready to accept the India Office. My decision had been carefully considered beforehand, & at intervals during the year. On public grounds I have no doubt. I am sure that the present government is on the whole the best that can be formed: & that its expulsion from office by the Conservatives would lead to a far more violent outbreak of radical feeling than now seems possible. That being so, I am bound to do what I can to strengthen it, &

especially to prevent the two sections of Whig & Democrat from quarrelling. If it is thought by those who ought to know that I can be of use in this way, I have no right to refuse. Some concessions to the ideas of others may have to be made, but in what Cabinet can such be avoided? I am not an ultra-radical, but I have as much sympathy with the ideas of that class as I have with those of High Tories, & more than with those of High Churchmen. Personally I have to consider that younger men are growing up: that a place left vacant is soon filled: that to refuse office now would probably be to retire from it altogether: and that at 56 I am not old enough to be put on the shelf.

Though fond of reading, I have no taste for authorship: I am by nature & habit indifferent to most amusements: & I cannot occupy myself in the affairs of my own estate as I can in those of administration. Further, I have (I will acknowledge it to myself) some satisfaction in defeating the predictions, founded on their wishes, of those who thought that my action in 1878 had made official life impossible to me. It would not have been fitting to accept office in 1880: but after a five years' interval changes of connection cease to operate as a disqualification. M. entirely approves of what I have done: & indeed if she had personally disliked it I do not think I should have moved in the matter. Right or wrong, the thing is done now, & I shall dismiss from my mind all doubt as to its being wise. It was settled that I shall go to Manchester (as I am pledged to do) in the character of a free man: the change not being made till afterwards.

. . . Keston in afternoon.

1 Dec. 1882: . . . I have oddly enough forgotten to note that before I left London, yesterday afternoon, Gladstone called on me. He was very friendly & civil, but in substance he only confirmed what Lord Granville had said: which was what he came to do[63].

Considering my future colleagues, I find that five of them represent the Whig aristocracy of large landowners – Spencer, Hartington, Kimberley, Carlingford; and I include Granville, though himself a very small landowner, but all his connections are with that interest. Gladstone is also a considerable owner of the soil (6,000–7,000 acres): Harcourt is of an old aristocratic family, though landless: & by marriage is a rich man. The Lord Chancellor is very nearly a Conservative: probably would have been one, but that Gladstone is much more of a Churchman than Ld Beaconsfield was. Childers, though of a good county family, is more of a professional politician than the rest, being very poor. Northbrook is also of a Whig family, & rich, though rather in money than land. Chamberlain & Dilke belong to a distinctly different class, & probably represent a different class of ideas: but neither is poor, or dependent on office for their private comfort.

Grouping them, we have:

Large landowners:Derby, Hartington, Spencer, Carlingford, Kimberley, Gladstone, and I suppose Northbrook should be added

Connected with county families:Harcourt, Childers, Dodson &, above all, Granville

Middle class: Dilke, Chamberlain

I do not think these details unimportant: since the social position which a man holds is apt to affect his conduct more than the opinions which he supposes himself to hold.

2 Dec. 1882: Dull foggy day, with frost in morning, & no sunshine at any hour. Winter is beginning, & I think it grows more distasteful as I grow older.

. . . Sent £50 to Mr. Sedley Taylor for the Cambridge [University] election[64]: rather reluctantly, for the contest was a mistake. What is called the representation of the universities is really the representation of the country clergy: no other class or profession has an appreciable influence on the result.

Wrote to Mr. Firth [about his complaints over the City Companies Commission]. I suggest a doubt whether the new constitution of the City, or rather of London, will be completed in 1883. The fact is I hear that Harcourt is reluctant to incur the enormous labour & risk of failure: & that is not to be wondered at.

Here is a more exact classification of the Cabinet than I made yesterday:

Large landowners (present or in prospect): Hartington, Derby, Spencer

Moderate-sized landowners:Kimberley, Carlingford, Northbrook, Gladstone

Having little land, but connected with the Whig aristocracy, or with the landowning class: Granville, Harcourt, Dodson, Childers(?)

Of the middle or trading class: Dilke, Chamberlain

And, of these two last, one is a baronet, & the other they say not far from a millionaire.

It would be difficult to find a Cabinet with less admixture of anything that in France would be called democracy in its composition.

I do not know where to class the Lord Chancellor. He has very little land: but must be rich, & has all the feelings of a squire. I think he ought to be included in the third category.

Read to M. We finished Gibbon's autobiography, with great interest. Few lives have been either happier or more productive. An intellect always active, and a temperament always calm: congenial employment in the present, and conviction of fame in the future. He secured all that he wished for, & did not miss what fortune had refused. He reminds me in many things of Macaulay: both born students, finding their chief pleasure in books: both bachelors, & neither apparently desiring to change his state: both members of parliament in stormy times: both dying before the age of 60: both expecting literary immortality, & likely to have their wish. Yet there are differences too: Macaulay was an orator in the full sense of the word, Gibbon had no speaking power: Macaulay wrote poetry which had a certain success: Gibbon never made a rhyme that we know of: Macaulay frittered away most of his strength in essays which, excellent as they are, will not rank with the history: Gibbon threw his whole energy into one great work, & completed it, whereas the other has left only a fragment. It is hardly worth adding, as another trait common to the two, that both were born to moderate wealth, & both impoverished by the fault or ill luck of their fathers.

3 Dec. 1882 (Sunday): Wrote to Sanderson to consult him as to the choice of a private secretary for the India Office.

. . . Day mild & warm, but very damp, & some mist.

Received from Lawrence details of my purchases of land in the present year. They are as follows:

In the Fylde, two farms	490 acres
Holwood	346
Additions to Fairhill	159
Halewood, Newburgh, Cheshire, etc.	103
Total added to the estate	1,098 acres

Of these Holwood was bought by me out of my own funds, the rest by the Trustees on my account.

4 Dec. 1882: . . . In papers, death of Archbishop of Canterbury, which had been so long expected as to be scarcely an event. He was only 71 . . . He will be regretted by many . . .

Wigan election carried by the Conservatives[65]: which, however, is no gain, as they had the seat before, though the writ has been suspended for two years. The defeated candidate, Mr. Walter Wren[66], had the Irish against him: & probably did not improve his chances by canvassing in company with Arch, the agricultural trades unionist & agitator. He (Wren) is extreme in his opinions, & I am not sure that the result of the election is a bad thing for ministers. They do not want more radical pressure upon them: & with a majority of 100 they can spare a vote.

One story, perhaps legendary, is that Wren, on what provocation is not explained, amused himself with vindicating the character of Jack Cade, from the misrepresentations of Shakespeare. He may have been right historically, but the natural result was to supply a very effective election cry against himself.

5 Dec. 1882: London by the usual train . . . Saw Sanderson, & talk with him as to the choice of a secretary: he gives me several names, but I must enquire further.

In papers, opening of new lawcourts yesterday by the Queen . . . Selborne is to be made an earl in honour of the occasion: which seems an odd reason for promoting a peer: but perhaps it was desired to put him on a footing of equality with Cairns. . . .

6 Dec. 1882: . . . Münster called in the afternoon, & talked about affairs in general, but had no news: he seemed rather in search of information. He said it was generally believed that Hartington was to take the exchequer: also that the finance of next year would be bad, & that some increase of customs duties would be necessary to meet the expenses of Egypt, so that the entire burden should not fall on the payers of income tax. . . .

7 Dec. 1882: . . . News in the papers of the death of Trollope, which was expected: he was only 67 or 68, but had worked double tides all his life. A more prolific novelist has never existed: in bulk of publications he far surpasses Walter Scott: some are good, some indifferent, but all entertaining: and as pictures of the manners of our time they may have an interest beyond the moment. A strong family likeness runs through them all, producing to those who know them well a certain sameness. They are not works of original genius, but better than any writer now living can produce in the same kind. – Trollope personally was not agreeable as a casual acquaintance, & still less to do business with: he had a blustering manner, which was not conciliatory, & which I believe did injustice to his real character. But [it] is possible that my judgment may be prejudiced: I saw him only at the Literary Fund, in regard to which he was jealous of interference, and I fancy that my appointment to the presidency was disagreeable to him – though I don't know why.

8 Dec. 1882: . . . In *The Times* today is a leading article, announcing the intended reconstruction of the Cabinet, & the inclusion in it of Dilke & myself. There is also a hint (? whether from authority) that Gladstone will retire some time in the course of the coming session. He has talked so often of retiring (I dare say quite sincerely) that when the event really comes it will be a surprise to everybody. It will also be a signal for the radical section to separate itself from the Whigs, or to try & make terms. They are weaker in the Cabinet than they were in 1880: having got Dilke for Bright, & having lost Forster.

9 Dec. 1882: Letter from Chadwick, saying he can obtain Ninham's wood & the adjoining fields for £15 or £16,000: which offer I authorise. If these are secured, I shall have above 800 acres of land in a ringfence, most of it laid out in an ornamental manner, & all capable of being so: a historical place (Holwood) & grounds planted with extreme care: all within 14 miles of London. It will be what I have always desired: a model villa. Had I known that it could be secured, I should not have bought Fairhill: but having it, & having spent money upon it, I shall not sell. Witley has a distinct character of its own: it will probably pay as an investment, if I choose to part with it, from the rise in value in land about Haslemere: and it is equally suitable for a park with large country house, or for a lodge or box, standing among woods & wild ground. On the whole, considering the dismal appearance, & disagreeable surroundings, of most of my Lancashire property, I do not regret the outlay in Kent & Surrey: though it must exceed £250,000.

. . . In the *Pall Mall* and *St. James's* are articles treating my adhesion to the Cabinet as a certainty: so that I presume no secrecy is observed or required: but I shall not admit that anything is settled: indeed nothing is settled in a formal manner.

Liverpool election has ended in an unexpected result: the return of the Liberal candidate, one Smith[67], whom I did not know, & who certainly is not among the notabilities of the place. But he is an active philanthropist, & professes to take Lord Shaftesbury as a model. His rival, Forwood[68], was reckoned certain of success, but as I judge lost the election by too great anxiety to secure it. He began by describing himself as a 'Tory Democrat' which must have puzzled a good many of his supporters – & appears to have gone on with a half-socialist programme, according to which the State is to do everything for the poor man and to make itself responsible for abolishing distress. I have not seen his words, & possibly they were so vague as to mean anything or nothing: nor are election speeches to be taken literally: but he has no doubt frightened away a good many of his supporters for 9,000 fewer voted for him than for his predecessor on the same side. I see this infusion of socialism into our politics with regret, but not with surprise. It is a kind of wholesale bribery of the poorer voters, who are always disposed to ask what is the good of having votes, if they are to get nothing by them.

The *Daily Telegraph* always sensational takes up the cry, with many taunts at the exploded doctrines of political economy and laissez-faire. But it is easier to talk in this strain than to take corresponding action.

10 Dec. 1882 (Sunday): . . . News that in Dublin a jury has failed to convict the murderer of Lord Ardilaun's bailiff in Galway, the evidence being absolutely beyond doubt: but one or more of the 12 was, or were, intimidated, & they disagreed. The man is to be tried again, which is right. We hear less about Ireland than we used, & fancy that all there is quiet: but that I take to be an error.

11 Dec. 1882: London. Hard frost & heavy fog: I could not read nor write without a lamp.

. . . Knowsley by the 12.00 o'clock train: fog most of the way . . . Find the house at Knowsley very cold, & not able to warm it thoroughly.

12 Dec. 1882: See the reporters from Lee & Nightingale, for tomorrow.

See Hale, and long talk with him . . . Sale of land to the Midland Co. They agree to give £50,000. No date is fixed for payment, but it will be soon.

13 Dec. 1882 (Wednesday): Letter from the Premier, asking me to come up to town, which I will do on Friday.

Weather less cold, but thick & gloomy, with snow on the ground.

The papers are full of the ministerial changes, & have at last got them accurately. There is general civility shown to me, which I scarcely expected: but the reason is plain. Liberals are glad to see the Cabinet strengthened by accessions from without: & Conservatives think that my adhesion is a gain to the moderate section.

. . . Wrote to excuse myself from attending a meeting in aid of the Liverpool Infirmary on Friday, & promised £1,000, to be paid by instalments. . . .

15 Dec. 1882: Left Knowsley at 8.30, reached St. J. Square about 2.45. Snow all the way north of Rugby, south of Rugby none, but a cold thaw, mud below & fog overhead. At No. 23, on arriving, I could only write or read with the aid of a lamp.

At 4.00, the Premier called, as appointed: & entered at once on a long explanation of his difficulties with the Queen. The purport of it was that she had disliked all his arrangements, would not have Dilke for the Duchy, & he would be provided for either by an exchange with Chamberlain, or by taking Fawcett's place, if Fawcett were disabled. As to me, she did not like my going to the India Office, & he was unwilling to engage in a conflict with her if it could be avoided, as such matters always became public, & tended to endanger the institution which she represents. He wished therefore to know whether I would object to take Kimberley's place at the Colonial Office, he moving to India. He suggested as a possible alternative the Presidency of the Council, but not pressing it, & admitting that, though it gives high rank, it is an office of less practical importance. That idea I put by at once but, after some discussion of colonial affairs, I told him I would not add to his difficulties by raising objections, the two places (India & colonies) being equal in rank & dignity, & there being the same amount of work to be done in each. I doubted whether he was acting wisely from an administrative point of view, since he displaces Kimberley from a post with which he was familiar, & does not utilise whatever experience I gained in the Indian department: but that to be sure was long ago. The Premier agreed in what I said, & thanked me warmly when we parted for assenting to his proposal. He wished the ceremony of swearing in to take place tomorrow, which I could not but agree to, though it is inconvenient.

What he said of the Queen was that during the five years of his first administration he had comparatively little trouble: now & then she would raise difficulties, but not often. In 1880, he found her quite changed, with a disposition to self-assertion which was new, & what added to the inconvenience was that there was no one near her who could or would speak plainly: nor did he know that she would listen to them if they did. She had been greatly pleased, he said, at the Egyptian war: but was furious (he used that word) in her objection to all proposals to recall the troops. 'One thing,' he said, 'I must say for her: she has never failed as regards truthfulness, & her manners are always perfect.' I remarked that her letters used to be sometimes violent. He assented, & said they were as forcible as epithets could make them.

He said when we parted that the D. of Wellington had been accustomed to talk of the difficulties of carrying on the Queen's government: that if the work was difficult then it was now all but impossible.

He talked of Fawcett, said his blindness made him impracticable, as was apt to be the case with blind men. He worked out his own conclusions without help: his mind was isolated.

Saw Sanderson, & talk. Dined Travellers'.

16 Dec. 1882: Wrote letters, etc., till 11.30 when to Paddington & by special train to Windsor, leaving at 12.15. The Premier, Hartington, Kimberley, Childers, & the clerk to the council, Peel[69], were the party. A council was held, & we were all sworn in. I had not seen the Queen close since 1878: & thought her much aged: very grey: with a look of settled unhappiness on her face, which was new. She did not seem out of humour, but thoroughly miserable. She makes no secret of her dislike to this government, & is probably ill pleased at its reconstruction, & at the weakness of the opposition. – I am inclined to think that her disposition to assert her claims to personal power is not due to Lord Beaconsfield, though by flattery and assent he may have encouraged it: but much more to the influence of her children, & of her relations in Germany. She sees what is called constitutional monarchy in that country worked in a manner to make the sovereign almost absolute, & does not understand why that should not be equally possible here. After all, the position is a false one: to be addressed habitually in the language which would be used to an all-powerful despot, & at the same time excluded from all real exercise of power, is an anomaly which habit reconciles us to, but an anomaly all the same: & what wonder if ceremonial language is sometimes taken as meaning more than it does?

St. J. Square at 3.30. Ld Kimberley with me: I had asked Mr. Herbert[70] of the Col. Office to call: & we talked over matters. Lord K. left us, & I made sundry arrangements with Mr. H. for the work of the next few weeks. I find him agreeable: an excellent manner, & apparently a clear head. I decided to continue Mr. R. Antrobus as assistant private secretary, he having acted in that capacity for Lord K. & being well spoken of. This relieves me of present difficulty as to letters, etc., and leaves me time to consider the more important selection.

Left No. 23 at 4.30 and reached Knowsley at 10.30 exactly.

– I now rather regret that I had not the curiosity to ask what were the Queen's objections to my having the Indian department: probably they were connected with Afghan policy & my speech on Kandahar last year. It is odd that unconsciously she should have done me a real kindness, for the Colonial Office is that which of all I should have chosen: I left it with regret in 1858, & should certainly have asked for it in preference to India had it been vacant: but I could not have requested that Lord Kimberley resign it to me. I thought it well, however, in my conversation with the Premier to make a favour of my willingness to accept the altered arrangement.

My speech of Wednesday is commented on in all the newspapers, more than any I ever made: the Egyptian part of it offends the Jingos, which is quite right: the Irish part offends the Home Rulers, which is also as it should be: and what I have said about land does not go far enough to please the radicals – as I never supposed it would. But the general effect on Liberals I think has been good – & Conservatives of moderate opinions will not quarrel with the general tone, & will be inclined to look to me (whether justly or not) as a possible drag on hasty action in Cabinet. So on the whole I am well content.

17 Dec. 1882 (Sunday): Received papers from the [Colonial] office, & worked on them.

Many letters, sent some to be dealt with by my new secretary, whom I have never seen: but he is only assistant, and if he does not suit I need not have much to do with him. If on the other hand I like his ways he can be promoted to the higher post, supposing no one with higher claims comes in my way.

Walk early, 4 miles on the terrace: later with M. an hour.

From what I can learn, the state of colonial affairs is as follows. In Canada & Australia, nothing of importance doing, & no trouble expected. In Hong Kong, some small local troubles, not serious. In Ceylon & Singapore, nothing. In the West Indian group, finances unsatisfactory, & some reforms required, more especially in Jamaica. Of West Africa nothing was said. In Malta there is some discontent & trouble. Cyprus is fairly prosperous & quiet but a heavy expense. Fiji does well. – South Africa is the real difficulty. The Transvaal, the Zulus, & the Basutos are all three uneasy, & in that quarter, more than any other, complications may be expected. On the whole the outlook is satisfactory, but the scene may change at a day's notice. I do not wish for absolute quiet, & the worry, from whatever part of the world it comes, can hardly be equal to that of the Foreign Office.

18 Dec. 1882: Rode round the park, which was very wet & heavy. Walk on terrace after luncheon, for exercise.

– Read to M. yesterday an article by one Hyndman[71], in the *North American Review*, predicting a social revolution to be made by the working class within the next few years. He, however, admits that they never appeared more indifferent to their wrongs than now: so that we may hope for a respite.

19 Dec. 1882: Received from the office three large pouches, which are used more than boxes in transmitting C.O. papers. Disposed of all except one or two. All the questions dealt with were small but, being administrative, & directly under the control of the office, had some interest. Sent letters to Mr. Antrobus. Walk early, with Mr. Rathbone[72] in the park: his talk an odd mixture of sense & simplicity. He was very full of the details of a local government bill of his own, which he seems to have fully considered: and wanted to transfer the income tax to the local authorities, a notion which I never heard before, & do not think likely to be adopted. He wished the measure to be a large one, including poor laws, schools, etc., else he said it would not rouse enthusiasm in the country, & would not be carried. He talked very hopefully of Ireland: admired & praised the Irish character: thought the Irish were children now, but only because we had treated them as children: the great thing was to attract their sympathy: justice was not enough: they were governed by ideas, not by interests &, if once made loyal, would be more loyal than anybody. He was strong in favour of emigration as a remedy – but only if the emigrants could be sent straight up the country, not to New York, where Father Somebody told him they lost their morals & their religion. He thought a Lord-Lieut. of Ireland ought to be appointed irrespective of party for a fixed term, & that the two sides of the H. of Commons ought to agree to treat Ireland as lying outside the range of party politics. He added, simply enough, that it was odd that he had never found anyone to agree in this last proposal. I shall be surprised if he ever does. –

Saw Ward . . . He is making out the total acreage of the estates, which to my surprise he thinks will come to nearly 80,000 acres. . . .

23 Dec. 1882: I passed the day lazily as regards exercise, the morning was stormy, & later indolence & business combined to keep me indoors. Took a vapour bath before dinner & much relieved from a kind of gouty or rheumatic stiffness which I often feel now: pain-less, but making rapid motion disagreeable.

The daily work which comes from the office is as yet very light: 2 to 3 hours suffice to dispose of it, looking into everything: & there are very many matters of detail which if pressed for time one might very well leave to the under-secretaries. But this is holiday time & no fair test. . . .

24 Dec. 1882 (Sunday): . . . Received from Kimberley a collection of papers on the ques-tion whether & how much India shall contribute to the Egyptian expenses. Fawcett sends a letter, strongly protesting against any charge being imposed on Indian revenue. He has pledged himself to this view publicly, & is likely to resign if he does not get his own way. He dwells much on a resolution voted for in 1878 by the whole Opposition in the case of the late Afghan war: for, if the Cabinet can draw money and men from India for war-purposes without reference to parliament, where is the check on its action? On Fawcett's letter Granville, Selborne, Carlingford, Chamberlain, Dodson & others have made minutes. I added mine, to the effect that I would not argue the question of our right to levy the proposed contribution on India: that I believed India to be too poor to pay any considerable sum: that the demand would cause discontent there: & that, considering the risk of a radical secession in the Commons, I doubted whether it would not be wiser to take the more generous course of waiving all claim on Indian revenues. That I thought this way of acting would not be unpopular in England: more especially as the whole cost of the expedition was so much below what had been feared.

Of all the ministers who have put their opinions on record, I note that Selborne & Chamberlain (an odd pair) are most favourable to the line I have taken. Granville, I think, the least so, & admits in his minute that the Opposition went too far in their resolution of 1878.

25 Dec. 1882: Letter from Gladstone, enclosing one from Sir A. Gordon[73], in which a promise from Kimberley of the government of Ceylon is claimed, though admitted not to be necessarily binding on me. I answer without hesitation that I am willing to consider myself bound by it, as indeed I should have done in any case. Gordon is a son of the old Lord Aberdeen, rather uncouth & a fanatical High Churchman, which is not a character I love: but he has done fairly well in former colonial offices &, even if I had some other candidate for the post whom personally I preferred, I should not feel free to disavow an engagement entered into by my predecessor.

. . . Showed myself at church, for decency.

. . . Some excitement in society, caused by the publication of a memoir[74] of Bishop Wilberforce (Soapy) of which the first two volumes related chiefly to dead controversies, & interested none but ecclesiastically minded persons: but the third contains extracts from a diary which the Bishop kept, in which he seemed to have indulged himself freely in the practice of recording gossip & the opinions of his contemporaries on one another. There is frequent abuse of Disraeli, to whom he paid much court: & a furious attack on my father, conveniently put into the mouth of the late Lord Clarendon. Also a conversa-tion with Dean Wellesley, in which he is reported to have disclosed various matters, which he could only have heard from the Queen. The book is rather a scandal, & has astonished not the London world, to which the Bishop was well known: but the country clergy, who regarded him as a saint. It is fair to add that there is no proof that the Bishop meant his diary to be published: so the chief fault rests with the editor: and also that the most spiteful of these entries dates from a time when the writer was deeply mortified by his failure to obtain the Archbishopric – the object of his ambition in later life.

26 Dec. 1882: . . . Disposed of all work that came from the office. There was nothing in it but matter of detail, & I have kept no note of it. The variety of subjects to be dealt with is interesting, but I observe that we use less printing than is the custom at F.O. which increases the trouble of reading. . . .

27 Dec. 1882: Shooting . . . We brought in 614 head. The day pleasant, but ground wetter than ever I saw it yet, water lying in pools & plashes.

. . . I got through a little business after coming home, but was obliged to leave much in arrears, which I dislike.

. . . Letters, too, from Goschen, who wants a Rugby memorial to Tait. I agree to his proposal, & promise to subscribe & give my name to the committee if desired.

28 Dec. 1882: It was intended to shoot . . . but rain prevented. Worked on C.O. papers all morning. I have noted the subjects as a sample:

Trinidad: Proposal to establish a govt. line of coasting steamers: declined, but we ask some further explanations.

Perak: Question of slavery: nothing to do.

Singapore: Refused an increase of salary applied for.

Cuban refugees: Spanish govt. refuses to give them up. Nothing to do.

W. Australia: A bill for protection of cattle, etc., reserved by the governor. Wait for explanations.

W. Australia: Proposal for a telegraph to Ceylon. Refer to Treasury.

Gibraltar: Criminal jurisdiction to be amended by an O. in C.

Hong Kong & Kowloon: Question of leases & building there. We propose to approve, but first consult W.O.

Transvaal: The Boer govt. has issued a consular exequatur on its own authority, which is all wrong. Question how to deal with this. Refer to E. Ashley for his opinion, as we shall probably hear more of this matter in parliament.

Natal: Constitution amendment. This I have still got in hand.

It would not be easy to find a wider range of subjects in the same quantity of business. See Hale . . . Agree to give £200 to the Liverpool Eye & Ear Infirmary, which is rebuilding: £10 to a school in Preston, & £10 for new bells in Prescot.

. . . In the afternoon, went to work again on papers, & took up the question of a new constitution for Malta. It was proposed by Lord Kimberley to send out a commission to enquire into & report upon various grievances, & there was a doubt whether a plan for extension of the Maltese franchise, which nearly trebles the number of electors, should be referred to this commission: Herbert, & Lord K. himself in his last days of office, were inclined so to refer it, Ashley objected on the ground that it would be thought a mere excuse for shelving the subject, & that the delay before the commission reported might be indefinite: I thought his argument sound (it had partly converted Herbert) & sanctioned the Maltese reform bill.

I read papers for an hour on the subject of reforms in the Natal constitution, but I do not yet see my way. I did not go to luncheon, wishing to have the whole morning for work, & I am now clear of all except Natal.

29 Dec. 1882: The party went to shoot . . . they brought in 558 head: less than usual, but it seems that hares were few . . .

I stayed to work on C.O. papers, which came in good number. Here are a few of the subjects: Coolies, 1,700, for Fiji. W. Indies: Council of Jamaica – local promotions – etc., etc.

Malta: Question of publishing official documents in the newspapers. Also of the constitution.

Esquimalt harbour: The colonists want a ship there. Adm. declines.

W. Australia: Prisons. Pearl fisheries. Quarrel of Lord Gifford & the Chief Justice.

Cyprus: Consular rights.

W. India committee: Want a loan from the Treasury, or guaranteed, to repair the loss by fire at Kingston.

Natal: Appointment of a resident to be with Cetewayo. Corresp. with Treasury as to expenses. (All this was in substance settled by Lord K., only details remain.)

I have omitted many, but the above are a fair sample of the day's business.

Mr., Mrs. & Miss Pilkington dined with us.

30 Dec. 1882: We went out to shoot . . . but . . . We were stopped by rain & snow, which lasted till late in the day . . .

Home at 12.00, & working on C.O. papers most of the afternoon. I did not keep a note of what they were, nor shall I in future, unless there is something special to note.

Letter from Trevelyan, in which he says that he 'regards the struggle with Irish pauperism – and economical and moral demoralisation – as far more arduous than the struggle with Irish crime'. He foresees, not merely the loss of popularity, but 'the certainty of furious & unrelenting unpopularity in Ireland', with the prospect of the effect extending to England. 'The conditions of administration & Irish work in parliament, during the next few years, are such that it can only be a question of time as to when those immediately conducting it shall fall a sacrifice.' 'The cry for public works is tremendous. Landlords who want their rents, priests who want their dues, labourers who prefer to idle on higher wages than those on which they would otherwise have to work, are all united in describing the Irish government as cruel & heartless.' It is evident that Trevelyan has found out the Irish, & his prediction as to unpopularity is likely enough to get itself realised.

Sent £50 to the Literary Fund for 1883.

Gave Mary Galloway £5 for her card-playing, which helps us with our guests in the evening.

Sent £10.10.0 to the Brompton Hospital for 1883.

31 Dec. 1882: Another wet day. Stayed at home & work all morning on boxes. In afternoon, short walk, work again, letters, & wrote up this book.

. . . The most important papers this morning were – Jamaica finances, which seem in an encumbered condition: and negociations with France & Portugal about their claims on the west coast of Africa, as to which it seems Lord Granville has made some proposals to Portugal, implying the recognition of Portuguese claims to the Congo: which may lead to trouble with the French if we are not careful.

There is also a boundary question with Venezuela, which Kimberley & Lord G. have been trying to settle: I shall be agreeably surprised, knowing the South American Spaniards, if we succeed.

There is a question of colonial defences, consequent on the report of a commission of which Carnarvon was chairman, which will probably give us trouble, but it concerns the whole Cabinet rather than any one department. Wrote to Kimberley on this subject, in answer to a letter of his.

. . . So ends this year, of which the last day has not been the least laborious, but the work being mostly interesting I do not complain.

Notes

[1] F. de Lesseps (1805–1894), creator of Suez Canal.

[2] Cyrus Field (1819–1892), indefatigable promoter of the first Atlantic cable.

[3] A.V. Dicey, 'Home Rule from an English point of view', *Contemporary Review,* vol. 42 (July 1882), pp. 66–86.

[4] John Campbell, Baron Campbell, *Lives of Lord Lyndhurst and Lord Brougham . . .* [1869]: E.B. Sugden, Baron St. Leonards, *Misrepresentations in Campbell's 'Lives of Lyndhurst and Brougham' corrected* [1869].

[5] Sir Theodore Martin, *A life of Lord Lyndhurst, from letters and papers in the possession of his family* [1883] [2nd ed., 1884].

[6] Postmaster-general.

[7*] Henry George (1839–1897), *Progress and Poverty* (1879).

[8] Lady Dartrey.

[9] Benjamin Lucraft (1809–1897), London radical activist.

[10] Harry Powlett, 4th D. of Cleveland (1803–1891), succ. 1864: m. Lady Dalmeny, widowed dau. of 4th E. Stanhope.

[11] Perhaps the Dowager Lady Donoughmore, perhaps her daughter-in-law, a contemporary in society.

[12] Lady Mary Primrose, Rosebery's sister, elder dau. of Lord Dalmeny (d. 1851).

[13] Edward Stanhope (1840–1893), Tory politician: under-sec. for India 1878–1880, cabinet minister 1885–1886, 1886–1892.

[14] Philip James Stanhope, 1st Baron Weardale (1847–1923), M.P. (Lib.) Wednesbury 1886–1892, Burnley 1893–1900, Harborough 1904–1906: trustee of Nat. Portrait Gallery, president of Inter-Parliamentary Union (1906). He m., 1877, Alexandra, widow of Count Tolstoy.

[15] Hon. Arthur R.D. Elliot, 2nd s. of 3rd E. of Minto (1846–1923), M.P. (L., then LU) Roxburghshire 1880–1892, Durham City 1898–1906: ed. *Edinburgh Review*, 1895–1912.

[16] Sir Charles Newton (1816–1894), Keeper of Classical Antiquities at the British Museum.

[17] William Spottiswoode (1825–1883), physicist, student of electricity, president of the Royal Society 1878–1883: Kentish neighbour.

[18] As it turned out, Hartington's father, William 7th Duke of Devonshire, lived until December 1891, much longer than seemed likely in 1882.

[19] Leonard Henry Courtney, 1st Baron Courtney of Penwith (1832–1918), *Times* leader writer 1865–1881: professor of pol. economy, Univ. Coll. London 1872–1875: M.P. (Lib.) (1875–1884): junior minister 1880–1884 (resigned over PR): deputy speaker 1886–1892: baron 1906.

[20] Thomas Hughes (1822–1896), educ. Rugby: co-operator, Christian Socialist, and author of *Tom Brown's School Days*: judge 1882–1896.

21   A quinquennial assertion of ancient privileges, celebrated with popular mirth.

22   Sir A.B. Garrod (1819–1907), physician: professor at London hospitals 1849–1874: author of *Treatise on Gout* (1859).

23   They lived at Bangor.

24   Lady Derby's brother.

25   Lord De La Warr, who committed suicide in 1873.

26   W. Stanley Jevons (1835–1882), logician and economist: professor at Owen's College and later at Univ. Coll. London.

27   J.E. Cairnes (1823–1875), professor of political economy, Univ. Coll. London from 1866.

28   T.E.Cliffe Leslie (1827?–1882), professor of political economy, Queen's College, Belfast (1853–).

29   Holwood, Pitt's villa and estate near Bromley, had been Derby's first married home in 1870–1872, when it was reclaimed by Mr. Alexander. On 20 October 1877 Derby agreed to purchase the reversion to Holwood.

30   On 17 October 1882, at an Irish National Conference at the Ancient Concert Rooms, Dublin, the Irish National League was formed to replace the Land League.

31   Alexander Baillie-Cochrane, 1st Baron Lamington (1816–1890), sometime member of Young England: cr. peer, 1880.

32   (Rev.) Robert Bailey Walker, vegetarian publicist (1839–1885), b. Preston: schoolmaster and editor of *Co-operative News* (1871–): sec. of Vegetarian Society (f. 1847) and ed. its monthly magazine, the *Dietetic Reformer*: a founder of the Ruskin Society: ordained as an Anglican, 1884, with a Manchester parish, 1884–1885.

33   Sub-agent, Fylde estates.

34   W.W. Palmer, 2nd E. of Selborne (1859–1942), succ. father 1895: M.P. (LU) 1885–1895: under-sec. for colonies 1895–1900, 1st Lord of Admiralty 1900–1905: high commr. for S. Africa 1905–1910.

35   Sir George Grey (1799–1882), Whig minister: home sec. 1846–1852, 1855–1858, 1861–1866: abolished transportation and made sodomy no longer a capital offence.

36   In fact his place, £2,500 a year with house, & no claims upon him, was quite as good as an ordinary bishopric in regard of money: not being a public speaker, a seat in the Lords would have done him little good [Diarist's note].

37   Lord Galloway's house near Dumfries.

38   Charles Abbott, 1st Baron Tenterden (1762–1832), was lord chief justice: cr. peer 1827. His elder son John Henry Abbott, 2nd baron (1796–1870), d. unm. and was succ. by his nephew the diplomatist.

39   The 10th E. d. childless in 1901. His father the 9th E. (d. 1873) had 6 s. and 7 daus. The 8th E. (d. 1834) had 2 s. and 3 daus. and at least 11 grandchildren. The 7th E. had 8 s. and 8 daus. The 6th E. had 3 s. and 7 daus.

40   [Eustace Clare] Grenville Murray (1824–1881), diplomatist and writer: consul at Odessa 1855–1868: horsewhipped by Lord Carrington 1869: novelist, satirist, pornographer.

41   Philip Currie, 1st Baron Currie (1834–1906), diplomatist: with Salisbury at Constantinople, 1876–1877, and at Berlin, 1878: assistant under-sec. at F.O. 1882–1889, permanent under-sec. 1889–1893. Cr. peer 1889. His wife was the novelist 'Violet Fane'.

42   Arthur Arnold (1833–1902), M.P. (Lib.) Salford 1880–1885: chairman of L.C.C. 1895–1897: author, *History of the Cotton Famine*.

43   G.F. Lyster C.E. (1821–1899), from an Irish gentry family: educ. King William's College, I.O.M., 1835–1838: built Guernsey harbour 1853–1861: appointed engineer-in-chief, 1861, to Liverpool and Birkenhead Dock Estate: retired 1889 and succ. by his son.

44   Newton Wallop, 6th E. of Portsmouth (1856–1917), styled Lord Lymington to 1891: M.P. (L, then LU) (1880–1891).

45   Dame Millicent Fawcett (1847–1929), a.k.a. Mrs. Henry Fawcett, leader of women's suffrage movement: opposed home rule and suffragettes.

[46]   Sir J.R. Mowbray (1815–1899), *né* Cornish: educ. Westminster and Christ Church: barrister: Judge advocate-general, 1858–1859, 1866–1868: church estates commissioner August 1866–December 1868, 1871–1892: chairman of standing orders and selection committees from 1874: cr. bart. 1874. M.P. (Cons.) Durham City 1853–1868, Oxford Univ. 1868–1899.

[47]   Sir G. Scharf (1820–1895), director N.P. Gallery 1882–1895.

[48]   On 2 November 1882 Gladstone proposed, for a trial period of one session, the appointment of two Grand Committees, one for law and one for commerce, each of 60 to 80 M.P.s. This was approved.

[49]   Ed., *Daily Telegraph*.

[50]   Gladstone's diaries (8 November) name Lady Derby but without comment.

[51]   Gladstone argued that clôture was even more essential to Ireland than to Britain: and dangled the reflection that there was no subject 'on which I personally feel a more profound anxiety than local self-government on a liberal and effective basis' (*Parl. Deb., 3*, cols. 1085–1086, 8 November 1882).

[52]   J.A. Lawson (1817–1887), Irish economist and judge: professor of economics, 1840–1845: Irish law officer, 1858–1865: judge in Ireland 1868–1887.

[53]   Sir H. Vivian, 3rd Baron Vivian (1834–1893), diplomatist: minister to Denmark 1881–1884: succ. as peer, 1886.

[54]   (Sir) John Fowler, 1st bart. (1817–1898), president of Institution of Civil Engineers 1866–1867: played large part in creating the Forth Bridge.

[55]   Sir Astley Cooper Key (1821–1888), admiral: rear-admiral 1866: admiral 1878: first naval lord of the admiralty, 1879.

[56]   Frank N. Hill (1830–1910), ed. of *Daily News* 1859–1886.

[57]   Cf. Hallam Lord Tennyson, *Tennyson a Memoir* (1897), ii, 266–269.

[58]   Valentine Browne, 4th E. of Kenmare (1825–1905), succ. father 1871: M.P. (Lib.) Kerry 1852–1871: court office 1856–1858, 1859–1865, 1868–1874, 1880–1885, February–July 1886.

[59]   John Sholto Douglas, 8th M. of Queensberry (1844–1900), succ. 1858: divorced 1887: Wilde's accuser.

[60]   Lord Otho Fitzgerald (1827–1882), M.P. (Lib.) co. Kildare 1865–1874: court office 1866, 1868–1874: 3rd s. of 3rd D. of Leinster.

[61]   Dudley Ryder, 2nd E. of Harrowby (1798–1882), M.P. (Cons.) 1819–1847: high office 1855, 1855–1857, 1874.

[62]   Lord Sandon (thus styled 1847–1882), 3rd E. of Harrowby (1831–1900), M.P. (Cons.) 1856–1859, 1868–1882: office 1874–1878, 1878–1880 (cabinet), 1885–1886.

[63]   Cf. Gladstone diaries, 31 November 1882: 'Called to see Ld Derby & finally settled that he take the Indian Office. We took a slight survey of public affairs. It was altogether hearty and satisfactory.'

[64]   Cambridge University election, November 1882: H.C. Raikes (Cons.) 3,491; Prof. James Stuart (Lib.) 1,301.

[65]   Wigan election, 2 December 1882: Hon. A.F. Egerton (Cons.) 2,867; Walter Wren (Lib.) 2,243. 18 January 1881: Cons. 3003; Lib. 2,536.

[66]   Walter Wren (1834–1898) had won Wallingford in 1880 but was unseated on petition. He was defeated at Lambeth in 1885 and 1886. He was educ. Elizabeth Coll. Guernsey and Christ's Coll. Cambridge.

[67]   Samuel Smith (1836–1906), M.P. (Lib.) Liverpool 1882–1885, Flintshire 1886–1905.

[68]   Sir A.B. Forwood, Liverpool worthy (1836–1898): M.P. (Cons.) Ormskirk 1885–death: 1st sec. of Admiralty 1886–1892: cr. bart. 1895.

[69]   Sir Lawrence C.L. Peel (1823–1899), clerk of privy council 1875–1898: army and civil service career 1841–1875: bro. of Edmund Yates Peel, who was 2nd s. of Jonathan Peel.

[70]   Sir Robert Herbert (1831–1905), official: scholar of Eton and Balliol, Fellow of All Souls: priv. sec. to Gladstone, 1855: to Queensland as colonial secretary, 1859: 1st premier of Queensland 1860–1865: permanent under-sec. for colonies 1871–1892.

[71] H.M. Hyndman (1842–1921), active in founding (Social) Democratic Federation, 1881: long the leading figure in English Marxism.

[72] William Rathbone (1819–1902), M.P. (Lib.) 1868–1895: social reformer.

[73] Sir Arthur Hamilton-Gordon, first Baron Stanmore (1829–1912), colonial governor: gov. of Fiji 1875–1880 and New Zealand 1880–1883. Cr. baron 1893. S. of 4th E. of Aberdeen, premier.

[74] Dr. Samuel Wilberforce (1805–1873), bishop of Oxford 1845–1869 and of Winchester 1869–1873: effective in restoring the powers of Convocation.

1883

January–June

1 Jan. 1883: Knowsley. The new year begins with a fair promise of prosperity – whether to be realised, who knows? I never feel less certain of the future than when the present is favourable: & for this feeling there is some ground of reason: since it is when matters go well that we grow careless, sanguine, & inclined to run needless risks. My health is good on the whole: I have been warned of the possible danger of a serious disease, but by reasonable care & prudence it may be kept off, & may not even shorten my life to less than the normal term. In politics, I am again actively engaged &, though looking forward to some trouble & anxiety, I do not regret having accepted office. It is too early at 56 to lay oneself on the shelf: & if I wished to utilise my remaining years of health & strength I had no time to lose. My position before the public is I think better than it has ever been, and I have got office work of a kind which suits me, & which I like.

Estate & financial affairs are in a good way: rents have increased by £4,000 a year in 1882, & in three years by more than £17,000. Nor does the increase seem to be checked. They have doubled since my father succeeded to the estate, 31 years ago. My successors therefore have nothing to complain of: & I have put by £400,000 which may be disposed of as I think fit.

My only anxiety proceeds from the state of Lady Derby's eyesight, which however has not grown worse of late, and her health in general is excellent. All her children happy & usefully or at least respectably employed.

In regard of public affairs, the condition of the country is quiet & moderately prosperous: trade neither very good nor bad: a total absence of agitation, and general confidence as far as I can judge in the government. The extreme radicals are not altogether satisfied, thinking that the Cabinet has been modified in a conservative sense: and the high Conservatives, or rather Tories, have not lessened in their distrust & dislike of the Prime Minister. But the great bulk of moderate men on both sides are apparently satisfied, & do not desire to see in power a weak Conservative administration attacked by a furious radical opposition. Neither do they trust Salisbury. And the Conservatives suffer from the fact that their strength is almost entirely in the Lords, where they do not want it: in the Commons they are very feeble.

. . . On coming home we heard of the death of Gambetta[1]: an event of European importance. . . .

3 Jan. 1883: Received & disposed of a considerable mass of papers. The most important related to (1) a quarrel in which the bishop of Colombo is involved, & where he has made a curious exhibition of bad manners & bad taste: (2) a case of embezzlement in Trinidad: (3) trouble with chiefs on the Gold Coast, & a possible mission, or rather [message?] to Dahomey.

Walk early with Pender: but he was so full of his plan of a new Suez canal that he would talk of nothing else.

. . . The papers today & yesterday have been full of Gambetta: & not the English papers only, but that of all Europe. – No death could have caused an equal sensation except that of Bismarck. Gladstone's would be more felt in England, but in England only. It seems as though Gambetta, though not yet 45, was completely worn out. . . . A splendid orator, he failed as a minister, & might have proved an incompetent president. His chief function was that he reconciled the middle classes to the Republic: while he lived, they held themselves safe from a Red insurrection: though it may be a doubt whether strong revolutionary feeling really exists in France . . . On the whole, his death is probably a loss to the Republic: but not an unmixed loss.

. . . Lord Wemyss[2] is gone at 87: bringing Elcho[3] into the H. of Lords at the age of nearly 65: the oldest heir to a peerage that has succeeded for a long while, and Lord Stamford[4] is just dead, whom I remember at the Hatfield school, six months my junior: otherwise not worth notice: a racing, shooting, money-wasting sort of man, who married two women of bad character & low connections: at a considerable interval of time, & lived surrounded by toadies. Yet he was popular in a certain set, as almost any man who spends his money freely is.

The party went shooting . . . & brought in 422 head. I was not with them.

. . . Lyster[5] talks of the docks: already they are full, more room is wanted, & he is thinking of a further extension beyond Bootle along the coast . . . He does not much believe in the projected Manchester ship canal, but says if made it will do Liverpool no harm: which is pretty much my opinion also.

4 Jan. 1883: Letters & papers in abundance: walk with Pender, otherwise working upon them nearly all day.

5 Jan. 1883: Left Knowsley at 8.30, taking three large pouches of papers with me to read on the way, which I did, & finished them. Reached No. 23 by 2.30. Saw Herbert[6], & talk with him. We drove together to the office, where I stayed from 4.00 till 6.00. Well pleased with my room & the place generally. I was introduced to Messrs. Bramston[7], Wingfield[8], & Ebden[9]: the latter, the senior clerk, who remembers me in 1858, being then himself one of the juniors. He says, which I can hardly believe, that there is no one else left who was there in '58. Promotion must be very rapid: or I misunderstood him. (**Note**: I did not misunderstand him: & the fact is so: but it is probably a unique case. Every other office that I know contains men who have served in it for 35, 40, or even 45 years.) Meade[10] was away for his holiday, so that I did not see him: & Ashley[11] is abroad, tending a sick wife.

Dined Travellers', & idle in the evening.

I see that in some of the papers, especially the *Daily News*, there is a dead set being made at Kimberley's arrangements for Zululand[12], & the partial restoration of Cetewayo. The complaining parties contend that he should have been restored to his full sovereignty as it was before the war: & they have got an idea (which is mistaken) that it is intended to annex a part of the Zulu territory to Natal. I must admit that they are right so far as this – the arrangement made is not easy to work, & satisfies nobody entirely. But it may very probably have been the best which circumstances allowed. At any rate it is concluded, & I have neither the right nor the wish to alter it now.

6 Jan. 1883 (Saturday): Mr. Antrobus[13] called early: saw him, work on papers, etc.

Walk: looked in at Macleans & bought three drawings, which will cost me £85: but they are worth it.

. . . Luncheon at the club: thence to C.O., where stayed from 2.00 to 4.00. Saw Herbert, & did some work.

Left at 4.00, left the Square 4.30 . . . & Knowsley not till 11.00, delayed by a dense fog which spread everywhere north of Crewe, & near Knowsley smelt abominably from Widnes. – Supper, & bed at 12.00.

7 Jan. 1883: Woke with some headache . . . Day foggy, damp, with bad smell from Widnes: altogether disagreeable. M. nearly knocked up with a month of entertaining.

Stayed at home all morning, & worked on papers, especially one long set, on the constitution of Mauritius. Wrote to Herbert, apropos of this, suggesting a more extensive use of printing in C.O. They scarcely ever seem to put papers into print: and the loss of time in reading long bundles of M.S. is serious.

Wrote to Lawson, to correct the impression as to Zululand & the restoration of Cetewayo.

Made up accounts for the last year: I have spent in all on the private account £4,160, of which £851 has gone to Ly D., £664 in other presents, £1,436 in works of art, & £664 in books: these four items include nearly the whole outlay, for less than £600 remains. I might have allowed myself nearly £1,000 more, but did not care to do it.

I have bought in 1882 nearly 1,100 acres . . . It is odd that I cannot ascertain accurately what my total acreage is – something over 70,000 acres, but I do not know how much more.

Walk 4½ miles on the terrace, partly with M. Rather sleepy & drowsy in afternoon.

8 Jan. 1883: . . . Since I took office, the H.O. has sent down two detectives to be constantly about the place: not by my request: I suppose they have their reasons. There was a silly story sent from Washington of an intention to blow me up: but it can hardly have been thought worth attending to.

Saw Hale. Talk of . . . railway payments to be made shortly: the Midland owes me £50,000, & ought to pay soon: the Lanc. & Yorkshire will owe probably as much or more: but the date & amount in this case are both uncertain.

. . . Working in afternoon on Mauritius papers, which are heavy. Again drowsy before dinner, which I hope is not a sign of coming old age.

9 Jan. 1883: Working early on papers, & rather worried by them, though neither in number nor importance are they exceptional.

News in the papers that Andrew Clarke, the doctor, has been sent for down to Hawarden[14], & has forbidden the Premier to make his intended journey to Scotland declaring him to be suffering from overwork. It is perhaps just as well that the intended speeches should not be made: since there is no special need for them, & it is useless to give fresh openings for attack. But in a man of 73 the breaking down even for a time is serious, especially when coupled with his frequently repeated wish for retirement. Already the *Pall Mall Gazette*, the organ of the better sort of radicals, is sounding the alarm, & in vague, but very intelligible, terms is warning the radical party to prepare to assert itself as an independent body.

. . . Cold raw day with east wind. . . . Attended the first (Knowsley) tenants' dinner & made a speech as usual. All very cordial, & there are scarcely any arrears.

10 Jan. 1883: . . . Rather low in spirits, partly from the bore of a second speech to be made to the tenants today, which had to be made, & was. Mr. Burton, who has a farm in Bickerstaffe, & a shop in Liverpool, proposed my health. All were very friendly. I took the opportunity in returning thanks to point out that under the Irish system (the three Fs) landowners would have no motive to spend money on their estates, & would keep in their pockets what they now lay out in improvements. This was understood, & well taken.

11 Jan. 1883: Sanctioned the payment to Margaret of £300 for a sort of shop she has set up in the village, on the co-operative stores principle, though I doubt it is not likely to work long or well.

Morning wet, & I worked at home on papers, clearing off nearly all.

Papers still busy with the Premier's health: but there does not seem to be really much the matter beyond overwork. The extreme sensitiveness of the public on the subject is due to a feeling that the present balance of parties rests on his life: that at his death or retirement Whigs & Radicals would fly apart, & general confusion follow. The fact may or may not be so: but this is what the public supposes.

. . . Sanctioned the building of two cottages . . . & approved the plans.

. . . Agreed to give £50 towards a school in Urswick.

12 Jan. 1883: [Lord] Arthur [Cecil] & Ly A. [Cecil] left us, with their children. I find A. excellent company, & always ready to assist in whatever wants doing. The prospect of losing all his money in the farm which he has taken (except what is settled) does not in the least disturb him: nor affect his spirits, which are exuberant. He enjoys country life & all its pursuits with the keen pleasure of a boy: & in fact he will remain a boy (one of the best sort) all his life.

Papers as usual: one set about the Gold Coast mines, which Burton[15] went out to look at, & reported upon so enthusiastically: by the official reports they seem to be a delusion. The gold is there, but costs more than its value to work. Most of the mining companies are to all appearance swindles.

It is announced that the Premier will go to Cannes[16]. The papers are full of vague speculation as to what is to happen next: premature, as it seems to me, but when a man is past 73 people will discuss the chances of his death.

From various indications I gather that South Africa is likely to give trouble in parliament & out of doors. The 'Aborigines Protection Society' wish the C.O. to assume a kind of protectorate of the districts lying beyond the Transvaal: so as to stop the forays of the Boers who, acting each on his own account, are in fact conquering that country & destroying the natives. The Cape Colony does not know what to do with its Basutos, whom it has annexed, but cannot disarm: & I do not see that anybody likes the new settlement of Zululand, or believes in its permanence. Here are elements enough of disturbance.

13 Jan. 1883: . . . Drove out to Sefton park to dine with Mr. & Mrs. Holt: a party of 18: the object of it that I should meet Mr. Smith[17], the new member for Liverpool. – I did meet him, & we had a good deal of talk: he is middle aged, with no grey hairs, a long beard, and a soft compliant manner: not quite what one conventionally calls a gentleman, yet with nothing vulgar or displeasing. Talks very modestly: professes surprise at his election: which is possibly sincere: doubts his success in parliament: dislikes late hours & fatigue: means to live at Clapham, & be out of the London world. On the whole, I liked him rather than not: & am willing to think that the rather socialistic turn of his speeches was due to ignorance and not design.

14 Jan. 1883 (Sunday): Working on papers, 10.00 to 12.00: then an hour's walk on the terrace, reading an essay, or critique, on Macaulay, by one Morison.

. . . Sent on to Kimberley as requested a F.O. mem. pointing out supposed American designs on the Sandwich islands: I sent it with a note stating my opinion that the authorities at Washington aim at establishing a paramount influence there, but do not desire annexation, which with their form of government would be inconvenient: their constitution making no provision for the holding of distant dependencies[18].

Letter from Kimberley enclosing two from Gladstone to him & one written reply, on the subject of Zululand. He wishes some hints given to the press in order to avoid misrepresentation. I answered, but kept back the copy of his letter to serve as a brief. The *D. News* has a correspondent in Natal who incessantly attacks Sir H. Bulwer[19] (a Mr. Statham, editor of a Natal paper, who I believe wanted employment, & failed to get it) & has published some extraordinary fictions about the dealings with Cetewayo.

Walk with M. Call on Mrs. Hale, who not quite right – Hale present, & had the good sense to seem unaware of her state.

15 Jan. 1883: Day fine & bright, the first we have had for a week. Edgehill at 11.00, Euston 3.45 . . .

Antrobus called. Later came a messenger, bringing a large pile of boxes, which arrived just before dinner. Worked upon them from 9.30 to 11.00, & cleared off most. The only one of importance was a request for the sanction of a loan in Jamaica of £150,000 to meet the losses incurred by the fire which has destroyed Kingston[20].

16 Jan. 1883: Saw Warr[21], & talk with him about the City [Companies] Commission. He says the advocates of the companies are anxious to bring out the fact that both Beal & Firth, the leaders of the agitation against them, are discredited men in their personal character: Beal having been a bankrupt, & notoriously open to money inducements (as indeed he proved by asking me for a loan of £2,000): & Firth having narrowly escaped being disbarred for unprofessional conduct, in regard to which the Corporation were the prosecutors. It seems there will be an attempt to refer to these things before the Commission: which will not do, for it is none of our business.

Saw Lawson, & some friendly talk. He told me nothing special.

Saw Kimberley, & long conversation with him, all on one side, for he never gave me a chance to speak, & it was best so: he chiefly dwelt on the arrangements for Zululand, which he is not quite satisfied with himself, but does not see what else could be done: & I suppose this is the true line of defence.

Received a paper sent by Chamberlain, suggesting that the Local Govt. Bill should be postponed till after the county franchise has been dealt with: I put in a brief mem. expressing dissent, as the postponement proposed would be really indefinite, & nobody wants a franchise bill this year.

Received the agents of the various self-governing colonies, Sir A. Galt[22] at their head, who read an address, to which I replied. Remained at the office till 4.30, having gone there at 1.00.

Received & sent on for enquiry & explanation an awkward charge made by a gold-digger against Hudson[23], our commissioner in the Transvaal, of using his official influence to promote his private interests. I am afraid, however, the fact may be as to that, that Hudson is more mixed up in speculations than in his place he ought to be. Another South African complication: & more were not needed.

Dined with the Harcourts . . . Not much amused, perhaps by my own fault.

17 Jan. 1883: Walk 11.00 to 1.00, when to the office. There saw a Mr. Campbell[24], head of the police in Ceylon, who came to state his claims to promotion. He impressed me rather favourably, & reminded me of what I had entirely forgotten, that some proceeding of his in the Indian mutiny had been approved by me as Sec. for India.

Next came Sir G. Bowen[25], late of Mauritius, and now on his way to Hong Kong. He talked with pleasure of a dinner which the returned Mauritius colonists (Frenchmen) had given him in Paris, to the great surprise of the authorities, who did not understand so much affection to a foreign governor. . . . I thought Sir G. a weak sort of man, by his manner & talk: but one can scarcely judge on a first interview.

Sir A. Galt came with a scheme of assisted emigration which he had proposed 3 years ago, & which was then rejected. He was not charged to propose it again, & indeed he came, as it seemed to me, only to assert his right to be the first of the colonial agents to do business with me. We talked of the double difficulty of helping the Irish to emigrate: their own representatives object in the most violent way, & the English taxpayer has to pay.

Harcourt came over from the Home Office at 4.00, & sat with me till 5.30, talking pleasantly enough on the political situation generally: but, as only last night he was indulging in bitter complaints of being overworked, I thought his visit a curious comment on them – for there was really nothing to settle. He took a gloomy view of affairs, thought the Premier had made up his mind to retire at Easter, & did not see what was to follow. Thought Hartington, not Granville, ought to be the next chief, was inclined to think the Local Govt. Bill would be a failure, from the county boards having nothing to do. – I agree, but don't see the harm. Was disposed to push on the county franchise this year, which nobody expects. I thought that a mistake, & said so. – Home at 6.00, all business finished. Quiet evening.

18 Jan. 1883: Sent £20 to the Longfellow memorial fund.

. . . Office at 1.00.

Ly D. went to Woburn, to see her sister[26], who is ill & harassed: there seems to have been something like a quarrel between her & the Duke[27], on the subject of her resigning the court office which she held, & which she accepted in the first instance against his wish. Strange how hereditary qualities remain & reappear. The Duke & his brothers were tyrannised over in youth by their mother – a clever, selfish, & despotic woman, who had been a heiress & a spoilt child: he now inflicts on his own family what he suffered when himself dependent. He is an active-minded man, with few amusements, & not enough to do to occupy his time: which makes him restless & inclined to find fault.

Worked at the office till about 5.30, when home, but more boxes followed me, & I was busy till dinner, & rather hurried, with the consequence of some fatigue.

Saw a Mr. Neale Porter[28], now employed in the W. Indies, who called to ask for promotion, & I think he has a right to it. An active eager official, with a good opinion of himself, & some ground for it. He told me he had never been in any place without leaving his mark upon it: &, though this would have been better said by someone else, I believe it was true.

– Granville called, talked of the situation. I told him what Harcourt had said. He did not agree: did not believe in the Premier's retiring: praised Harcourt's ability, but said that he was never in the same mind two days together: thought his objection to the programme already agreed upon was purely personal: he did not like the trouble which the London bill would give him, & would be glad to stave it off for a year. Talk of France: he thought the state of things there very bad: the expenditure & consequent taxation were both enormous: the manifesto of P. Napoleon & his arrest[29] showed that people were not easy in their minds: he seemed to think it possible that a revolutionary proscription of persons or classes supposed to be disaffected to the Republic might follow. – He complained of the new Russian ambassador[30] as the most tedious personage he had ever come across.

I thought Lord G. well, but deaf & old: & inclined to agree with Harcourt that Hartington would be a more efficient chief. I fear there will be some soreness when the question comes to be decided.

19 Jan. 1883: Saw Drage: he reports an increase of albumen since his last examination, but not enough to cause uneasiness. Only care is required. In fact, it has not been easy to give due attention to diet or exercise in a country house, in weather which has been generally bad, & with guests to attend to. I am more my own master in London.

Walk: office at 12.30, & stayed till 6.00.

Appointed Mr. Antrobus my private secretary: he is nephew of Dr. Gream[31], his father was a resident near Buckhurst, so that his family is known to us, & he came into the office in 1877 by open competition, having done well at Oxford.

I verified what seemed hard to believe, but is true: that of all the present C.O. staff only one clerk, Mr. Ebden, was there in 1858. There have been great clearances, & rapid promotions: which accounts for the efficiency of the department.

. . . Froude dined with us: pleasant as usual.

20 Jan. 1883 (Saturday): Worked at the office from 1.00 to near 5.00: the subjects various.

1. Tariff of the Gambia settlement, to be amended.
2. Changes in Ceylon civil service: this I kept to be considered at leisure.
3. Prosecution of an embezzling official in Trinidad.
4. A grievance of some merchants on the Gold Coast, about restrictions on the coin they are allowed to import.
5. An interminable quarrel at Grenada . . .
6. A boundary question between Sierra Leone & Liberia.
7. Land grants in W. Australia.
8. A squabble about official fees in Hong Kong.

To the best of my recollection, these were the chief matters that came before me: & it would not be easy in any office to find a greater diversity.

Walk to Victoria: Keston by 5.15 train: evening wet & foggy.

. . . I do not know if I have noted Gladstone's temporary absence from England: he has been ordered a journey to the south of France, & three weeks' holiday as a remedy for sleeplessness arising from nervous exhaustion, from which he was suffering. Consequently there can be no Cabinets, & we shall meet parliament with little preparation. The matter is more important to those of us who are in the Commons than to the peers.

21 Jan. 1883 (Sunday): . . . More details from Jamaica as to the great fire, by which it seems that the Governor was in a hurry to ask for a loan of about £150,000, since the whole loss is computed only at £200,000, including what is covered by insurance. Sir A. Musgrave's[32] reputation in the office is that of being hasty & imprudent: he is certainly unpopular among the negroes, who hooted him while Kingston was burning: one report has it that the fire was the work of an incendiary, directed against the public buildings, & intended as an expression of popular discontent.

22 Jan. 1883: Walk on the commons . . . but they were mere swamps, ankle deep in mire. A messenger came down with papers, but not many, nor of great importance.

Read to M. out of the reviews.

Saw nobody except Sackville[33]. An easy, idle day, good for a change.

Qu. as to investing my yearly surplus in future in colonial securities? They are safe if not too much be put into any one: & in these times it may be as well to have some funds which cannot be affected by revolution at home.

23 Jan. 1883: London by early train . . . Worked at home, 11.00 to 12.30, then to office, where stayed till 5.30 . . .

Saw Sir R. Alcock[34], who came to talk about the new settlement in Borneo (though it is not a colony, nor under C.O.). He had nothing to ask or propose. He seems to rely on Chinese labour mainly to develop the country, which is mostly now a wilderness.

Saw Mr. Wingfield, & went with him over the new criminal code proposed for Ceylon . . . It is mainly taken from the Indian code. I wish it could be referred to any independent & competent authority, but I can find none.

Talk with Mr. Herbert as to Jamaica affairs. There is much discontent, & it is clear to me that some elective element must be introduced into the constitution: he thinks that any reform of this kind would be better inaugurated by a new governor, & suggests the expediency with that view of sending Musgrave to Queensland, which is vacant almost immediately. Note that M. has married a daughter of Cyrus Field, & is very well off: but likes the dignity of office.

Then who will do for Jamaica? Longden[35] from Ceylon? Or an outsider? Or Sir A. Clarke[36]?

A messenger came to me about 6.30 with more papers, & I had the satisfaction of clearing off all, leaving nothing undone in the office. Dinner at home, & quiet evening.

Pope Hennessy[37] called on M. this afternoon, & in presence of Dalhousie & Sir J. Lubbock expressed his conviction that Home Rule was a necessity for Ireland – there would be no peace there till the demand for a local parliament was conceded. This is the first time that I have heard the language of the nationalist party from anyone holding office, though only colonial office. Hennessy is essentially an intriguer: his skill in that line recommended him to Ld Beaconsfield, & he long tried to bring together the R.C. hierarchy & the Conservative party. This I suppose he found hopeless: but he still knows & speaks the mind of the Irish priests. –

24 Jan. 1883: Sent £105 to the Jamaica fire relief fund.

Office at 12.30: worked there till 4.30, when home.

The chief subject of importance was a despatch just received from the Transvaal, in which it appears that the Boer government, not satisfied with evading the convention which recognised their semi-independence, are violating it without disguise, & indeed justify their doing so. By patience & care we may avoid collisions for a time, but our relations with them are not of a kind to be permanent. They must either have more freedom or more restraint.

In the papers, news that Cetewayo has reached his capital: all quiet so far.

. . . Dined at the Middle Temple: the usual large party . . . I was very well received by the students. . . . Talk of Jessel; he is recognised as the first lawyer of the day, after Selborne & Cairns: but regret that his manners are so bad. But for that drawback he might be [lord] chancellor. But the experiment of putting in a Jew would require a more popular candidate. . . .

25 Jan. 1883: . . . L. Stanley[38] talked of Home Rule & an Irish parliament as things certain in a not remote future: arguing that the demand for them grew stronger with every concession made, that even Ulster would go with the rest of Ireland, that Parnell or some leader more violent than Parnell would have 70 or 80 followers in the next parliament, that in the balanced state of parties they would turn the scale, & make steady government impossible, that the movement could only be checked by a system of repression such as the English democracy would not endure – in short that the thing would be done whether we liked it or no. L. Stanley, though clever, is flighty, & given to disputation for its own sake, which lessens the value of his opinion: yet there is something in it. The defeat of the solicitor-general for Ireland at Mallow, by one O'Brien, a nationalist of the most pronounced type, is significant & disagreeable[39].

At the office, appointed one Stubbins[40] a *puisne* judge on the Gold Coast: I had given the place to a Mr. Lunn, but he took fright at the climate & refused, after having asked for it.

Saw Mr. Burnside[41], the new chief justice of Ceylon: we had some talk . . .

Saw Mr. Newton[42], the colonial secretary of Jamaica. He gave an interesting report of things there.

Received from Granville a proposal that the Cabinet should join in requesting the Premier not to hurry back to England. I agreed, on the condition that he was medically advised to take a longer holiday, for otherwise I am sure he would not listen to the suggestion.

26 Jan. 1883: . . . Walk early. Meet Lowell. He tells me of an American citizen imprisoned at the Cape. – I promise enquiry. Talk of France: he believes as I do that monarchy there is impossible, but thinks the Republic has taken no root.

Office at 12.40, left about 4.40. Much business, but all detail. Saw Sir J. Gonne[43], last chief justice in Fiji, now going to the West Indies: Scotch, with a noble accent, & the quiet shrewd manner of his country. He tells me that, under Sir A. Gordon's rules, no white man is allowed to buy native lands at all, though he may hold them on lease: a summary remedy against overreaching or fraudulent purchases, but not one that can be permanently available.

Saw Sir Lewis Pelly[44], just my age, but he has not a hair on his head: he has been unemployed 4 years, & says it is the hardest work he ever did: would like colonial if he cannot get Indian employment. I hinted at his writing some account of what he has seen, for he has been in strange places, but he said he did not care to go over again what was done with: he preferred something new to do if he could get it. I could not give him much hope, & indeed, accustomed as he has been to wild races, held in order by military force, he would be a bull in a china shop if put in charge of a constitutional colony.

My sister dined with us. Family talk. She quiet & not inclined to complain, but feels the weight of having five sons to look after, none of whom seems as yet disposed to do anything for themselves. It is odd that almost every boy of a well known family seems to choose the army as a profession, though it is difficult to get into, the pay when employed small, & the chance of distinction infinitesimal.

27 Jan. 1883: . . . Walk: office at 12.45: stay till 4.45, when leave, & join M. at Keston. Day mostly wet.

Some heavy papers about finances of the Straits Settlements which I disposed of: & of Cyprus, which I ordered to be put into print.

Saw a Mr. Brownlee, a magistrate in S. Africa, at his request. He was intelligent, but did not know much about the Basutos, or the Zulus. He spoke well of the natives, as regards their peaceable disposition if let alone.

In my conversation with Mr. Newton on Thursday, he told me that he did not believe Jamaica generally to be discontented. The whites, chiefly attorneys & agents for estates, complain, but the negroes are well satisfied. Estates as a rule pay badly, but there are exceptions. One (I think he said owned by a coloured man) brings in £15,000 a year. The most powerful class in the island he thought were the Kingston Jews. They command the press & most of the trade. Next to them the Baptists have influence. They are a political body, all blacks, & inclined to stir up jealousies of race – disliking the whites, & England.

28 Jan. 1883 (Sunday): Keston. Passed a quiet day. Read, wrote, walked, both alone & with M. Read to her out of the *Edinburgh Review*.

. . . Wrote to Granville about the conduct of business in parliament, advising that London municipal reform, county government, & corrupt practices, be the three subjects taken up: patent law, bankruptcy, & the criminal code to follow & fill up the background. I added that after Hartington's late speech I assumed no attempt would be made to touch Irish local affairs, as unless we throw him over we can do nothing that will satisfy or even please the Irish members. I added also, as I did at Manchester, that Ireland, having had the whole, or nearly so, of two sessions, it was not unreasonable that England & Scotland should come in for their turn.

A messenger came, but brought nothing of importance, except a secret despatch from Lyons, which the F.O. has had put in print. This document speaks of the existence of general uneasiness & alarm in France[45] . . . On the whole, the sketch is as gloomy as it well can be . . .

29 Jan. 1883: Heavy gale in night & morning, with rain. . . . I am entirely clear of office business, not one paper left to deal with . . .

Letter from A.D.[46] . . . she gives the worst possible report of Ireland: socialism rampant: public feeling fairly represented by the Mallow election: rents withheld, & as little disposition to pay them as ever: while those tenants who last year paid honestly are disgusted at finding that they have lost by their fair dealing. Great efforts making, she says, to get up a famine cry, which is not justified by the fact, except in a few districts. – I am afraid all this is true in the main, though my friend may colour the facts too strongly.

30 Jan. 1883: Walked in to Bromley. London by usual train. No. 23 at 10.45. Worked at home till 12.30. . . . To office at 1.00, stayed there till 5.30. Then home: more papers came for me, but cleared off all by dinner time. Dined at home & quiet evening. Business was mostly routine, not specially interesting.

Only there is some apprehension of trouble in the Malay states, I remember little else.

Saw Sir H. Barkly[47], now retired, whose guest I was 33 years ago in Demerara. He called nominally to pay his respects, really to recommend his son for promotion.

Mr. Barlee[48], late governor of Honduras . . . called to pay respects, & suggest his wish for re-employment, which I think he ought to have.

The bishop of Victoria called to take leave: he is just going to Hong Kong. He pleaded earnestly, but in a gentlemanlike way, that the salary of the colonial chaplain (£800 a year) might not be withdrawn, as is intended. I could not give him much hope.

Sir G. Bowyer[49] called to talk over Maltese affairs, which he did at length, & very tediously: he was one of the recognised bores of the H. of C. & has not improved with age. His interest in the Maltese arises from their being the most uncompromising ultra-montanes in the British empire. He dwelt on the loyalty of the people, on their dislike to the irreligious Italian government, lamented that the English did not show more defer-ence to the Maltese clergy & nobility: of the latter he seemed to have a high opinion: though from others I have heard that they are poor, ignorant, & indolent. He wished to see a civil governor, or a secretary fully acquainted with the wants of the island. Also that the elective members of the council should be a majority, or else that the official members should not vote on purely local affairs. There is some sense in what he said, & indeed he is not a fool except where his popish prejudices are concerned: though wanting in tact, & wearisome from not knowing when to stop in his expositions.

31 Jan. 1883: . . . Business of today was all detail . . . We wrote to consult Sir G. Rowe[50] as to accepting a kind of protectorate over certain tribes near Lagos.

There is a curious quarrel between the chief justice of Fiji . . . & the governor . . . The governor wrote to ask for the judge's notes, which he refused to give up, & went away taking them with him. . . . Note that he would be better moved to some other colony, as a quarrel between ch. justice & governor is a scandal anywhere & especially so in a place like Fiji.

Saw Evelyn Ashley for the first time, & talk with him. His face did not prepossess me – it is a foolish face – nor was his manner that of an able man: but he seems to know the H. of C. well, & that is the chief thing.

Sir W. Sargeant[51] called, the senior of the crown agents: he has served in Natal, St. Vincent, & the Transvaal: a pleasant sensible sort of person. He dwelt specially on the great improvement in colonial credit: the leading colonies can now borrow at 4% whereas

20 years ago the rate was 6%. He thinks the leading Australian colonies are going too fast – selling land & raising new loans at the same time. I agree.

Sir G. Kellner[52] called, an old Indian civil servant who is working on W. Indian affairs for love: talk of Jamaica: he says labour, so far from being scarce, is overflowing: Jamaican negroes go & work in S. America, Costa Rica, etc. Has a plan which he is working out for settling them on crown lands.

1 Feb. 1883: Letter from Granville, in answer to mine: he speaks of one serious difficulty ahead: the question of local self-government for Ireland. Hartington in his late speech is pledged to resist it, & Gladstone by what he said last year is pledged to give it. Which is to give way? It is a difference that may very well break up the Cabinet, or (which is nearly the same thing) determine the Premier to carry into effect his intention of retiring.

. . . Walk. Bought two old prints of London out of a shop in Oxford St. kept by a Jew, from whom I escaped with trouble, for he would have sold me his whole stock.

. . . Office at 1.00, stayed till 5.00. No interviews, & the business was only routine.

Received from Ponsonby a note written by order of the Queen, short & dry, saying that H.M. had all along disapproved of the restoration of Cetewayo, which she thought likely to lead to serious disasters. I answered briefly, that the restoration had been settled before I joined the Cabinet: it was now an accomplished fact: but I added that between Boers, Basutos, & Zulus, I fully expected a lively time in South Africa. . . .

2 Feb. 1883: Day very wet & windy: at times a heavy gale. No walk. Office at 1.00, & stayed till near 6.00. Dinner at home. Quiet day & evening, without event.

At the office saw Mr. Sendall[53], the man who was selected by Kimberley for governor of Natal, but the colonists would not have him, & K. wisely gave way. I believe the grounds of objection were that they wished for somebody better known: & that they suspected an intention of putting them again under the Cape, which they disliked. He seemed an intelligent sort of person, but not remarkable in any way.

Saw also Mr. Hutchinson[54], [Lord] Donoughmore's brother: now col. sec. at Barbadoes [sic]: he wants promotion to a similar office in Ceylon, which I could not promise. I liked his manners. He told me of the Barbadians: the island is crowded, the negroes will not emigrate except under pressure of hunger: the supply of labour is therefore more constant there than in the W. Indies generally: the white residents are some of them owners, but mostly agents & managers: one firm is supposed to hold half the soil, not in form, but virtually, by means of mortgages. Some absentees are rich: Lord Harewood[55] draws a steady £5,000 yearly from his estates, which he has never seen. Mr. H. said that the state of things reminded him of Ireland, but the parallel does not hold altogether, for there is no agitation. He said that since 1876 the white population had lived in constant fear of having their constitution taken away, as was done in Jamaica: & indeed I recollect that Carnarvon talked of doing something of the kind, but let it drop.

A Mr. Longden[56], now or lately in S. Africa, is recommended to me by Lawson of the *Telegraph*, Lord Wolseley, & W.P. Talbot. I have given a half promise of doing something for him in the way of employment.

3 Feb. 1883: Walk early round Regent's park. Day very fine. Office at 12.40, stayed till 4.40. Walk to the station: Keston at 6.30. No business of much interest, though enough to do all day. No interviews, except with men employed in the office.

It is now settled that we go on with the London government bill, & probably with the county government bill too, though I hear that there is a certain pressure being put on the Cabinet to postpone the latter, & substitute for it a bill giving tenants compensation for their improvements. The sole reason for the change suggested I believe to be that the former will be in the main supported by the opposition: whereas the latter will call out party feeling, which Harcourt in his conversation of the other day with me thought was necessary, if the session was to be a success. . . .

4 Feb. 1883 (Sunday): Day very bright & fine. Read to M. A messenger came with boxes, but nothing of importance.

. . . Walk in all about 4 hours, which is more than I have done of late. Sleepy on coming home, & slept a little, when quite rested.

5 Feb. 1883: Day cold, but fine. Long early walk. Short walk in afternoon with M. Read to her. . . . Messenger came at 5.00, bringing papers & letters: by hard work I cleared away all that was necessary before 7.00, & sent him back.

. . . Letter from Granville enclosing a rough sketch of the intended speech, & two letters from the Premier, one written in a very enigmatic style, alluding to his probable retirement at Easter, & deprecating his being required to bring in a local govt. bill or a franchise bill, in which case he should certainly resign. Why the local govt. bill should seem to him more laborious than the London bill is not clear, since the latter involves many more details. But the whole letter, which I read twice carefully, is odd & obscure. I remember that he regrets Hartington's speech against Irish self-govt.: & describes himself as pledged to a measure of the kind.

6 Feb. 1883: London by usual train: walk in to station: No. 23 at 10.45. Work at home till 1.00, when to office.

Appointed a Mr. Just[57], a junior clerk, assistant private secretary. He is a German by birth, trained at Oxford, hardworking, & intelligent.

At 2.30, Cabinet. All present except the Premier. Some talk about inviting him to stay abroad longer, which he seems to wish himself, but Granville disposed of it by hinting that he did not desire to be taken at his word, & indeed would be disposed to consider the invitation as the reverse of a compliment.

Spencer had come over from Ireland. He thinks the state of the country improved as regards crime, but he did not say that the feeling towards England is any better.

We had, what I never saw before, several policemen in plain clothes in the anteroom.

Long & rather confused talk as to the business of the session: Spencer very decided against a bill dealing with local government in Ireland at the present time: nearly all present went with him: Dilke & Chamberlain, who sat together, & backed one another up, agreed that no bill of that kind could pass, but wished it mentioned in the speech, to satisfy expectation. The end was that we agreed to put municipal reform in the front: & refer vaguely to other measures of local self-government being introduced if time allowed: which it will not. A number of minor measures were agreed to in principle. We read the speech in a rough draft, & settled it more or less. At the end of all, Harcourt proposed a commission of enquiry into the condition of the crofters of Scotland: I objected to this being decided without more discussion: Kimberley backed me: & we got it postponed.

I noticed that Granville, though clear & sensible in all he said, was very deaf, & seemed to hear little of what passed.

Chamberlain, referring to the new rules of procedure, treated them with the utmost contempt, saying that they were good for nothing except to serve as a foundation on which really useful rules may be framed hereafter. This I note as significant, & justifying much of what has been said by the opposition.

I noticed that, except Chamberlain, nobody seemed to care much about the county government bill for England: it was acknowledged that the farmers did not want it or care about it: unless it were accompanied by a large offer of relief from local taxation: which offer we are not financially in a position to make. And it seemed to me that Chamberlain preferred to put it off till the new constituencies could deal with it.

Sanderson dined with us.

7 Feb. 1883: Busy till 11.00 with letters & papers. Wet dull day.

. . . Office about 1.00, & stayed till 5.00, when walk: dined at home & quiet evening.

At the office, received a deputation from missionaries & others, interested in the New Hebrides. They wanted three things: (1) an assurance that France should not annex the islands: (2) the regulation or, as some said, the suppression of the labour traffic: (3) measures for the punishment of crimes committed in the various islands of the Pacific by Europeans, who at present escape altogether, as not being under the jurisdiction of any civilised authority. They talked for the most part reasonably enough: except one old man, who wanted the New Hebrideans not to be allowed to emigrate at all, on the ground that contact with the whites corrupts their morals. But he spoke only on his own behalf. As to the rest, they had sense on their side, & there was very little cant. As the question concerned F.O. as well as C.O. Granville came over & received them with me. Sir A. Gordon, Ashley, & Herbert were also present. Sir T. Buxton[58] introduced them: I think they went away satisfied.

Convn. previously with Sir A. Gordon, whom I had not seen to speak to since college days. He has a rather mean unprepossessing appearance, & bad manners: but his experience of colonial governments is large, & he has always done well. From his talk I found that he had strong opinions in favour of the natives against the European settler. He seemed to think that, where the latter were admitted to establish themselves & buy lands, there was no chance for the aborigines. He defended the prohibition to buy lands in Fiji on the plea that they were the property of the whole tribe: no one person could give a title to them: but he admitted that they could not always remain locked up in this way. In N. Zealand he said he had been sickened by the injustice which he was compelled to witness practised on the Maoris. He believed in missionary influence, & in that alone, as a possible civiliser: though admitting a doubt whether in any case it would be possible to protect against stronger races.

I offered Sir A. [Gordon] Ceylon, which he accepted, though ungraciously enough, saying that he thought that had been settled by Lord Kimberley: which was not the case. I believe he will make a good governor, but should not care to have much to do with him personally, for he is an uncouth being.

8 Feb. 1883: Wet dismal day: walk early to far end of the embankment: office at 12.30, stayed till 4.30, when left, all current business being disposed of. . . . Home, where found more boxes, & work on them till 7.00. Dined with the Reeves[59]: meeting Ld & Ly

Fitzgerald, Sir H. & Ly Loch[60], the Portuguese minister, Lord Morley[61], Froude, Venables[62] (who grown very old) & two young ladies. A pleasant party & evening.

Lord Fitzgerald[63] talked of Ireland, thought the party of order would win in the long run, but it would be a long struggle. He also said that in his belief one half the value of the land had been transferred to the tenants by successive acts of legislation.

Sir H. Loch full of the subject of replanting the royal forests, which he thinks might be done with profit: but this was disputed by others.

Granville sends round a telegram from the Premier about his movements, which it is impossible to understand: he (Lord G.) and I both read it as meaning that he intends to stay on, but it may mean anything.

Saw at the office Sir H. Lefroy[64], formerly in Bermuda & Tasmania: he came to ask for re-employment. He says the whole Bermudian group is very slowly sinking so that reefs formerly dangerous are no longer so. – Tasmania is becoming the playground of Australians: the cool climate & fine scenery attract them. But no business doing there.

9 Feb. 1883: . . . Cabinet at 12.00, sat till 2.30. All present, except the Premier & Lord Spencer. We did not all assemble till 12.20 &, as happened last time, business was not very orderly done, much talking & confusion at first, but things mended later.

Talk of the Premier's telegram, which nobody could make out, but it is thought that he wishes to stay abroad till Easter.

Much discussion as to whether we shall have a bill for licensing reform separate, which all the teetotal party want. They would have a licensing board appointed by the people, for that sole purpose. No one took that view of the case, & we agreed that the power of granting licences should be given in London to the new municipal authority, & in the country to the county boards: which means that the question except as regards London will stand over to a new parliament.

Some talk as to whether the police should be put under the municipal authority: all present are against, but the Premier is known to have a strong opinion the other way. Granville referred back to the time when in the conversations of Holland House Peel's new police was denounced as a disguised attempt to bring in despotism, the old constables having been parochial officers. Chamberlain let fall a remark that struck me. He said in Birmingham they had adopted the principle of working their municipal affairs on strictly political lines, because they found that in no other way was it possible to get men of note to take interest in them. We agreed to bring in a bill giving tenants compensation for unexhausted improvements: on which a verbal wrangle: Harcourt wanted 'protection' or 'security' to 'the interests of the tenant', which would have been taken as meaning compensation for disturbance. Several objected, I among them: Dodson & Kimberley with me: we carried our point. The Skye crofters were mentioned, & it was agreed to give an enquiry if asked for into their case, but not extending to all Scotland. This I assented to. The Bradlaugh business was next discussed: & it was agreed to bring in a bill enabling any one at his pleasure to affirm instead of swearing. Some wished to go farther, & to abolish oaths entirely: among them the Chancellor: but the reasonable objection was taken that by so proceeding we should increase the difficulties in our way, which are already great enough: and that no harm is done by merely allowing men to swear if they choose.

Some talk as to the question of making India pay a part of the expenses of the Egyptian campaign: I argue against it, as we shall only get £500,000 anyhow, as India can ill spare the money, & as the principle was strongly denounced by Gladstone when the Afghan war was in question. This his colleagues did not deny: but it seems that he has established to his own satisfaction a difference between the two cases, not obvious to other people, & is now determined to assert at least the principle of Indian liability to pay.

Office: & there stayed till 5.00, when home. Business followed me: but by 8.00 all was clear. Quiet evening.

10 Feb. 1883 (Saturday): It is announced that the Premier has decided to stay on at Cannes, for a time not yet fixed. Qu.: has it ever happened, since the time of Lord Chatham, that a first minister was absent from parliament at the opening of a session? I doubt it.

Bought some china . . . Walk round Regent's park for exercise, mostly in rain. Office at 12.30: not much business.

Talk with Ashley & Herbert about Malta: Ashley wants a commission sent out: I doubt, thinking that policy weak, & that we know enough to act. We agree to limit the power of the governor to overrule the elected members of council by his official majority: a practice which is the chief cause of complaint, & which the natives say truly reduces the council to an absurdity. The power must be retained for exceptional occasions, but I think its use may be prohibited as a regular practice. I liked Ashley's way of talking, which was shrewd & sensible. . . .

11 Feb. 1883 (Sunday): . . . Ireland continues to be as much a trouble as ever. Crime & outrage have diminished, as Trevelyan said the other day in an excellent speech to his constituents: but this improvement is due to the operation of coercive laws and to an improved police organisation, not to any change in the feelings of the people. As far as one can see, nationalism is as strong as ever, if not stronger: the speeches of its supporters are fully as violent: Parnell has withdrawn into the background, but Healy & Davitt are taking his place, with as much influence, & more rhetorical power. There is no sign of the Land Acts having done what they were meant to do, produced a change in the popular feeling towards England: so far the policy is a failure, & the sense that it is a failure may be one of the causes on which the Premier's half formed decision to retire is based. Meanwhile Irish land is unsaleable: I have heard of 11 years' purchase being asked & refused. All points to the probability that the Irish difficulty will be more & not less serious than it has been. Englishmen who hate the idea of Home Rule begin to talk as if resistance were useless: & to argue whether of two evils total independence would not be the less.

12 Feb. 1883: Wet windy day, so that walking was impossible. Stayed at home, wrote letters: one to Hartington on the proposed tenants' compensation bill.

. . . Messenger came from the office, bringing a few papers, but very few: I had not in all 2 hours' work, which is strange at the opening of a session, but there was no more left to do.

Read much to M., & quiet: but I am not sure that this was gain, for one is never more apt to be anxious about future possibilities than when there is nothing immediate for the mind to dwell on. And there are many causes of possible anxiety just now. The Premier ill & talking of resignation: the Cabinet likely to be divided on the Irish question: finance indifferent: Egypt still unsettled, wild ideas in the air about land & property generally: the necessity of a large extension of the franchise, & the utter uncertainty on all sides as to what may follow: all these promise a future not absolutely dark or gloomy, but full of possible troubles.

13 Feb. 1883: Left by usual train . . . busy till near 1.00, when to office. Thence I was summoned in haste: the Cabinet which was fixed for 2.30 having been put on to 1.00, in order to enable Granville to hold a conference in the afternoon.

All were present except Ld Spencer & the Premier.

We went again over the speech, but the criticism was only verbal: then proceeded to the intended Affirmation Bill, when the Chancellor again expressed his preference for a bill doing away with oaths entirely, on the ground that leaving the matter optional tended to create a distinction between those who took the oath & those who made the declaration: to which it was answered that to prefer the form of a declaration is not a profession of atheism, & that a man may think it enough to give his solemn promise without imprecating curses on himself if he breaks his word. Ld Selborne said if choice were left free as we propose he would be the first to take the declaration, so that it might not be misconstrued.

The [Lord] Chancellor had a bill limiting the power of the judges to commit for contempt of court. There was some rather vague talk as to this, of which I remember only that Harcourt talked of the judges in terms of extreme contempt, which seemed to me out of place. We appointed a committee to consider the question of unexhausted improvements, on which I agreed to sit.

We discussed the question of an Indian contribution to Egyptian war expenses: & in the end it was agreed to fix the sum at £500,000. I pointed out as delicately as I could that several members of the Cabinet had pledged themselves strongly against the principle of such payments: but they did not seem to care, & certainly it was no business of mine. Indeed the Premier, who went furthest of all in his criticisms of a similar act being done in the case of Afghanistan, is now eager to assert the principle that India ought to pay.

Talk about Bradlaugh. R. Grosvenor called in.

Question of the training of the Irish militia, which the military authorities dislike, but Spencer is eager for. We thought the opinion of the Lord Lieut. ought to prevail, & sanctioned it. Childers told a story of how an Irish militia colonel who was found fault with by the inspecting general on the ground that his men could not shoot: & who defended himself by saying that if they could there would not be a landlord left in the county. . . .

14 Feb. 1883: Short walk in rain & wind. Office 12.30. . . . Went at 3.00 to the Peabody trust . . . We settled the report for the year. We have spent on the two trusts over a million, and are lodging 14,600 persons: the result of 20 years' work.

Back to office, and stayed till 5.00. Then read at home, a new *Life of Lord Lawrence* by Bosworth Smith[65], well done, & where I am concerned very civil, but the editor has printed private letters of mine to Lord Lawrence without asking my consent . . .

Dined at Ld Granville's, the usual full-dress dinner before the opening. Sat by Ld Durham[66] & Ld Aberdeen . . . Party afterwards, the usual crowd without conversation of the London world. Amused to find the diplomatists all eager to speak to me, as being again in place: which in their eyes is the sole source of importance. They would be greatly puzzled by the notion that a great English peer may lose rather than gain importance by accepting office. Introduced to Mohrenheim, the Russian ambassador: the only man I have seen whose capacity of boring was too much for the patience of Lord Granville.

15 Feb. 1883: Walk with Dalhousie, & much talk on Ireland. He has been over there for some weeks, talking in his frank sailor fashion to people of all sorts &, being receptive of new ideas, & not given to criticism, he has taken up with those of Healy & Parnell, & is more than half inclined to doubt whether landlords have any right to exist. He says he is struck by three traits of Irish character – (1) the enormous power exercised by the priests: (2) the universal hatred felt towards England: (3) the impossibility of trusting any Irishman on a matter of fact. He distinguished three parties – the Ulster man, who are for the English connection as it stands: the middle class, with something to lose, who are nearly to a man Home Rulers, but would be satisfied with a parliament of their own: & the peasantry, who are frankly anti-English & nationalists. He said that nobody talked of Gladstone in connection with the Land Acts: the entire credit was given to Parnell. He found the conviction general among those he talked to, & not only among the uneducated classes, that of the men lately hanged for murder several were innocent: the cases against them having been got up by the police to make a show of activity. The police, he said, are detested: they are accused of harshness & rough dealing with the people, as if they were a military force occupying a conquered country.

. . . Office. On the way down I was caught in Bradlaugh's crowd, & had some trouble in getting through, though not recognised. The mob seemed in perfect good humour, & rather given to larking than inclined to listen to the speakers.

At 4.00 to the Lords, where a full house. . . . Lds Durham & Reay[67], the mover & seconder, both did well: the first speaking like a young man, in the ordinary style, & saying nothing new, but saying it well: the latter took a wider range &, though rather longer than is customary or in general desirable, he made a favourable impression on the House. It is probably the first time that any peer has spoken in the Lords whose experience had been gained in a foreign parliament: but in his way of speaking there was nothing foreign except a slight accent. – Salisbury followed, clever & amusing: but it was evident that he meant no serious attack. Granville answered, explaining & defending his Egyptian policy. Then the debate shifted to Ireland: the D. of Abercorn warning us as to the dangerous state of feeling there, Ld Waterford complaining of the sub-commissioners who administer the Land Act as partisans. (I suspect there is much truth in these charges.) Cowper said a few words, & Carlingford answered feebly, but by this time the peers were gone. Home at 8.30, & quiet evening.

16 Feb. 1883: I forgot to notice that yesterday Hicks Beach called at the office to ask some questions about Jamaica & the Pacific. He was very friendly & civil, much more than he used to be when we were colleagues.

17 Feb. 1883 (Saturday): At 10.00 to the Grillion club breakfast, where some 20 present: Ld Eversley[68] in the chair: he is 88, but shows very few signs of old age. . . . We elected Sir J. Lubbock: A. Balfour was proposed, had two black balls, & failed.

. . . Cabinet at 2.30, all present except the two who are out of England[69]. Little business, except settling answers to parliamentary questions. A great deal of gossip & desultory talk.

Harcourt announced that one of the leading men in the assassination plots – one

Carey[70], a Dublin town councillor – has been accepted as an approver, & will be able to show that a close connection has long existed between the Land League & this secret society. I noticed, or thought I noticed, that Dilke & Chamberlain both looked very grave & ill pleased at this announcement, but they said little, except to question the wisdom of Carey being allowed to escape. Harcourt expressed himself confident of being able to show that Land League funds had been used to secure the services of assassins.

Parnell has a violent motion on the paper about alleged violations of law in Ireland, which it is said is not his own, but forced upon him by O'Donnell[71], whom he detests, & who wants to take his place.

Talk of the Speaker, who has long been wanting to retire: but it is thought may now be persuaded to stay. There is absolutely no competent successor: Whitbread probably the best, & not much is known as to his fitness.

Talk of division last night, when by want of care in keeping a house the government was nearly beaten on Egypt. The majority was only about 30, & taken a little sooner it would have been on the other side.

Talk of affirmation bill, which some want to alter so as to make it only prospective, not admitting Bradlaugh: but this is foolish, as he would certainly be re-elected. We decide against it, unless it should appear that the passing of the bill depends on a compromise of this sort.

Talk of half-a-dozen minor bills, which are to be brought in, I don't know why: since there is little chance of their passing. – I left at 4.30, when the sitting was not quite ended . . . Keston at 6.30.

18 Feb. 1883 (Sunday): Another wet day. General complaints of the extraordinary season: floods over all low-lying lands, the farmers cannot plough or sow . . . read to M. . . . Sent £50 . . . to the Bootle Cricket Club . . . Walk for exercise.

Read a large bundle of papers on Mr. Moylan's case, but . . . suspended my judgment till tomorrow. He is a violent, quarrelsome Irishman of some ability who has made Grenada too hot to hold him, & provoked his brother officials into bringing charges, some of which they cannot prove . . .

19 Feb. 1883: London by usual train . . . Worked at home till 1.00. . . . Levee at 2.00, a very long one, & not being specially busy I thought it well to stay till the end: while there much talk with Kimberley: he praises Sir H. Norman[72] & Sir A. Clarke as possible candidates for governorships: thinks well of Sir J. Longden, except that he is dilatory: Musgrave he considers has been a failure in Jamaica. In the office he says both Herbert & Meade are very good – the first inclined to be an optimist, the second to take desponding views: Wingfield he thinks remarkably able, & every way trustworthy: Bramston safe & industrious, but of less capacity.

H. of Lds at 4.15, stayed till 5.30: Granville again asked me rather anxiously whether it was desirable to press the Premier to return or the reverse. I said: 'Do neither: leave it to him: it is his duty to come home as soon as he is well enough: & we cannot judge when that will be: if he is recovered, being the man he is, he will be eager to return: if he is not eager to return, that is evidence in itself that he is not fit for work.' G. agreed civilly, but was not apparently satisfied: I suspect something behind, but cannot make out what. – Office, where worked till 7.00: cleared off most of the current work, but not quite all. Dined at home, & quiet evening.

The papers are full of Carey's confession: which if true shows that a regular organisation for purposes of murder existed, perhaps still exists, in Ireland: & that some men are mixed up in it who were trusted agents of the Land League. The effect on opinion is to throw a strong light on the folly of the Kilmainham understanding, & immensely to raise Forster's reputation for judgment, he having resigned rather than agree to it. The two ministers who are responsible for it are Gladstone & Chamberlain: & perhaps it is the knowledge of this, & fear lest his defence should do the Cabinet more harm than good, that makes Granville so anxious to keep Gladstone away.

It is significant of the state of feeling, even in Dublin, that the prisoners about to be tried for murder are cheered by the mob (so I was told) wherever they are seen.

The question of granting local self-government to Ireland is settled for some time to come. . . .

21 Feb. 1883: Committee of Cabinet at 12.00: Kimberley, Northbrook, Dodson, Chamberlain, & Shaw-Lefevre was added, as having special knowledge of the subject. Kimberley talked in an odd strain: saying that the bill we were discussing, for giving compensation to tenants, could do no possible good; all that was to be hoped for was that it should do no harm: but the tenants wished something to be done, & we must satisfy them. They were suffering, he said, & would catch at any proposal that offered a remedy. The great majority did not in the least know what they wanted: those who did wanted a slice of the landlords' property. Chamberlain agreed with the rest that we must keep clear of anything like the Irish system – the three Fs – and that it was therefore impossible to grant compensation to a tenant while he remained on the farm, or to prevent his being charged a higher rent, in consequence of his own improvements. I said that logically I could see no standing ground between free contract on the one hand and fixity of tenure on the other: which was not dissented from in theory. My impression is that Chamberlain & his party do not expect, or even wish, to pass a satisfactory measure: but rather to pass one that may lay a foundation for larger claims hereafter. When we came to details, all were moderate, & pretty well agreed. We sat 2 hours.

Office, 2.00 to 4.00: when to the City Companies Commission. . . . Back to office, & stayed till 6.30. . . . After dinner was introduced to Mr. Broadley[73], the lawyer who defended Arabi. – Thence to a party at Ly Harcourt's: not home till near 12.00.

22 Feb. 1883: Office at 1.00, & stayed till 4.00, when to H. of Lds. There, a very thin attendance, & no business. Walk back to D. St. with Granville, who much perplexed by the outcry which is being raised in certain quarters against the removal of Paget[74] from the embassy at Rome (his term having expired) & the proposed appointment of Layard to replace him. He said that Paget had been intriguing in all directions to secure a re-appointment: and that Labouchere, Drummond Wolff, & some others were trying to get up a combination of both parties to censure Layard. He asked my advice.

I told him that on the question of Paget's removal I thought he ought to stand firm: P. had had more than his share of the good things of the service: had not earned them by any special service, & did nothing but grumble & intrigue for further promotion. If the fixing of a definite term for ambassadors had any meaning, it ought to be adhered to in such a case as this: & above all the S. of State having expressed his intention should not let himself be bullied out of it. When Paget found he had nothing to gain by it for himself, he would cease to get up a cry against Layard. As to that appointment, I thought it unfair that an ambassador should be ostracised for his supposed opinions: & I hold Layard to be an honest & able man: but the appointment might be delayed a few months if it was thought likely to produce a bad effect in the House.

Ld Emly called to ask promotion for a Mr. Wood – of course a Catholic.

23 Feb. 1883: At 12.00, committee of Cabinet, which met at the India Office, & sat till 2.00: we finished the general outlines of the bill.

Office, 2.00 to 4.00: where a long visit from Pope Hennessy, with whom I had never so much conversation before. He talked well, but conceit & a certain arrogance, of which he is accused by colonists where he has been governor, had replaced his former manner of extreme deference. He magnified his own services a little more than strict good taste allowed: & told me that he had been named by Kimberley for Queensland, but threw up the appointment on finding that it would be very unpopular among the planters. He wished for an Australian govt., being tired of the tropics after 15 years. (I asked K. as to the Queensland story, & found it true.) He spoke of the Chinese, sensibly, & with great respect for their national character: thought our officials were too stiff & haughty in dealing with them, refusing all social intercourse, of which he gave instances. Q. whether he may not be right? He pointed out, what is true, but often forgotten, that Chinese authorities are not likely to welcome Europeans in the interior, while the system of extraterritorial jurisdiction continues: in other words, while foreigners have practical impunity for any offence they may commit.

At 4.00, to the Lords, where a dull debate in a very thin house, raised by Ld Waveney[75], on Ulster tenant right. It was hardly a debate, for no one answered him, & Ld Leitrim[76] followed with an interminable story of grievances against Trin. Coll. Dublin, under whose authorities he holds land. – As many of the peers as could get into the H. of C. gallery were there, to hear Parnell speak.

. . . M. dined in Eaton Square: & on coming away called to ask after Mrs. W.E. West[77], who was suddenly much worse . . . & stayed till 2.00, when all was over.

24 Feb. 1883: . . . Saw Sanderson, who came from Granville to talk about W. Africa: I advised that we should not for the present attempt to negociate with France, unless events made action inevitable: but that we should wait till the French soreness about Egypt had subsided.

Cabinet at 1.00, sat till 3.30. The situation in the H. of C. was fully discussed, & it was agreed not to give a day, as requested by the opposition, for the discussion of the Kilmainham business of May last, on the plea that it has already been discussed more than once, at great length, & that there are no new facts. There is a slight awkwardness about this, for the Premier in November last volunteered to promise an enquiry by committee if desired: but his pledge was personal to himself, given without consultation, and (his colleagues say) repented of as soon as given. There is plausibility in the argument that, as the invitation was not accepted when given, he is not bound to repeat it some months later. But there was evident doubt in the minds of some present how the person most concerned would take it: and I see, what I had not suspected before, that Gladstone's judgment is quite as severely criticised by his colleagues as by any part of the outside public. 'A man of wonderful genius, but a little mad' – such seems to be the prevailing opinion in the Cabinet: and in this case they were very anxious to announce their decision before his return, so as to make it irrevocable.

We went through the Tenants' Compensation Bill in a general way & agreed to have it drafted.

The Lord Advocate was called in about the business of the Skye crofters: &, as it appeared that Scotch members on both sides wished for an enquiry, we could not refuse to grant one, but the terms were left open for discussion. There was a rather warm little discussion on the subject: Kimberley, Dodson, & I, with one or two more, insisting on knowing what was to be enquired into, & what was intended to come of it: Harcourt (who reminded me of Disraeli in that respect) laughing at the notion of our caring what came of it, saying it could not report for a year or two: all that mattered now was to get rid of the parliamentary question, & not to offend our supporters: the future might take care of itself. He swaggered a good deal, & his talk left on my mind a disagreeable impression of recklessness, which however may have been partly affected or provoked by opposition. But I can now understand why he is distrusted & disliked in the House. He has copied some of the most doubtful traits of poor old Ld Beaconsfield's character, without the unaffected good nature which caused them to be excused in him.

A committee on the Channel Tunnel was discussed, & some minor matters.

I notice that Granville says little, & always with a view to conciliate differences of opinion, which he does very skilfully. The [Lord] Chancellor seldom takes part, & then mostly with a question: 'How will you deal with so-and-so?' Harcourt talks most, & talks big: Hartington sensibly, but seldom: Kimberley less than one would expect from his volubility in private: Dodson little: Northbrook never speaks except when appealed to: Childers hardly ever. Dilke inclines to lay down the law (today he was silent, having his head tied up, & suffering from a toothache): Chamberlain has an odd, peculiar manner, of referring everything to the judgment of friends outside, rather than giving an opinion of his own: as though he considered himself in Cabinet less as an adviser than as the representative of a party or section: which indeed is the case. So far we have got on well: but I see wide divisions possible in the future.

Office at 3.30 to 4.45: then walk to station & Keston by 6.30.

25 Feb. 1883 (Sunday): Keston. . . . The last week in parliament has been taken up with an exciting debate on Ireland, produced by an amendment moved by Gorst. It brought up Forster, who on Thursday delivered a most powerful speech, denouncing Parnell in the plainest terms as having connived at assassination, or at least wilfully shut his eyes to the fact that murders were being planned by his supporters & friends. I do not suppose that such a charge has ever been made in the H. of C. before, & the effect on those who heard it is described as tremendous. This speech, having the effect of utterly alienating the Land League, & making union between them & the Radical section in England impossible, is disliked & criticised by the 'advanced' section: Chamberlain on Friday spoke of it with great disgust: but it has exactly hit popular feeling here, & the Irish in parliament are more intensely disliked than ever. Parnell replied on Friday, scarcely justifying himself, except on points of detail, & telling the House plainly that he cared only to justify himself to Irish, not to English opinion. Though he spoke half an hour, not a word fell from him of censure or regret at the outrages which were the subject of debate. His whole attitude was unconciliatory & defiant to the last degree: & in these characteristics he was even exceeded by O'Brien, who spoke earlier in the week. On the whole, I doubt if since the Union England & Ireland have ever been so wide apart.

26 Feb. 1883: . . . Talk with Herbert, Ashley, & later with Kimberley, about giving protection to the natives of Bechuanaland from marauders & adventurers who come across from the Transvaal & the Cape: but we fail to discover any hopeful way out of the trouble. All the whites, English & Dutch alike, are in favour of the filibusters, & against the native inhabitants. Kimberley is in favour of negociating with the Boers for a revision of the convention[78]. . . .

28 Feb. 1883: . . . Committee of Cabinet to draft the Tenants' Compensation Bill: Kimberley, Dodson, self, Lefevre, & Sir H. Thring[79]: Northbrook & Chamberlain did not appear. Kimberley delayed business by his excessive talking, but what he said was sensible, only too much of it.

Office, 3.30 till 6.30 . . . &, having no visitors, I was able to get through a great deal of work. Home rather weary, quiet evening, early to bed.

Debate on the Address still drags on: monopolised by the Irish, who will let nobody else speak. So far the new rules have done nothing to lessen obstruction.

J. Morley, the late editor of the *Fortnightly*, & still editor of the *Pall Mall Gazette*, is returned for Newcastle: a powerful addition to the radical section of the House. He is very poor, very ambitious, & is a democrat of the intellectual or literary sort: with an intense dislike to privileges & class distinctions: & (I imagine) sanguine notions of indefinite human progress in the future. If he can speak, he will make his mark in parliament: but he may not have that special gift, & without it the rest is of little use.

1 Mar. 1883: . . . Office about 12.30: stayed till 4.00, when to the Lords: no business there, office again till 6.00, when home, quiet evening.

It is announced that the Premier stays away till Monday: I asked Granville why? He said: 'I suppose he is keeping out of the way of the Kilmainham debate.' But I rather suspect that he is doing a little diplomacy at Paris on his own account, not to the entire satisfaction of his Foreign Secretary[80].

. . . Debate on the address ended, after 11 nights of talk. Ashley tells me that it is said in the House that obstruction will be more rampant than ever. Certainly the Irish language has never been more violent – Parnell talked of Ld Spencer's policy of extermination, & another member said that Trevelyan had imbibed the worst traditions of the Tory Castle clique – all this because government will not establish a system of public works by way of giving relief to the peasantry in the West, who are in a state of chronic distress, cannot live on their holdings, & will not leave them. The common talk, I am told, in London, is that the Irish are irreconcilable, that Home Rule, or government by mere force, are the only alternatives. This is at least premature. The Nationalists have failed at Portarlington & in Dublin county, which is good so far, but leaves us only where we were[81].

2 Mar. 1883: . . . Office for an hour, then home for luncheon: office again 2.30-5.00, when no more business.

Occupied with Mr. Wingfield for an hour on a confused & difficult question of regulating marriage laws on the Gold Coast.

Telegrams from Sir H. Robinson show that the Bechuana trouble is growing more serious. The Cabinet must soon decide whether to leave the native chiefs alone to be eaten up by invading Boers, or to protect them by armed force: there is no third alternative. I desired a mem. to be drawn out for the Cabinet, & have put the latest papers in print. There is an awkward hint given by Sir H.R. of protection having been promised to these chiefs by Sir B. Frere, but happily no evidence can be found of the fact, & if the promise was given it was not authorised from home.

3 Mar. 1883 (Saturday): Walk early, round Regent's park: office at 1.00, work there till 4.30, when to station: Keston by 5.15 train . . . At office, see Mr. Clifford Lloyd[82], the Irish police magistrate, who has been successful beyond others in keeping his district quiet and repressing crime. He is in consequence hated by the people, & Ld Spencer wishes to find him employment elsewhere than in Ireland – whether or no this is a wise concession to popular sentiment I cannot judge, but should doubt it. So he sends him over to me with a letter, & a request that I will find him a post in the colonies. I received him civilly, & liked his manner. He is an Indian official, aged 38, but looks 50: quiet in manner, with no swagger, but an air of resolution well suited to act on the minds of Irish peasants. I could give him no promise, but received him cordially, & sent him away, I think, well satisfied.

The Premier returned last night: I wrote him a note, but excused myself from calling, on the plea of not giving him trouble, when I had nothing to ask or tell.

I have not noted that two or three days ago I had a visit from Mr. Archer[83], the agent for Queensland, who came with a new & startling proposal. It was to the effect that Queensland should be allowed to annex on its own account the unappropriated half of New Guinea: the local authorities taking all cost & the whole management of the affair. The motive is twofold – one, the chief, inducement is the fear lest some other state should seize upon the unclaimed territory, & so get what is called 'the command' of Torres Straits, through which an increasing traffic passes every year: the other – rather put forward for appearance's sake than really felt – the inconvenience of having the New Guinea coast occupied by adventurers & ruffians, who live there beyond the reach of law, ill using natives & committing all crimes with impunity. – The idea is rather bold than wise, considering the enormous area of Queensland still lying waste, & much of it unexplored, & the strain on finances which are not very sound. But that is the business of the Queenslanders. I gave Mr. Archer no definite answer, which indeed he did not expect: but invited his government to develop their plan more in detail, promising that it shall have careful consideration. . . .

5 Mar. 1883: London by 10.12 train . . . Letters & papers till 12.00, when to office.
. . . Cabinet at 2.00, sat till 4.00: the Premier present. We settled, with much discussion, the course of business in H. of C. We discussed the question of re-appointing Layard, which Granville had proposed, but was uncertain about owing to the strong feeling against Layard in the party. Hartington said it would be very unpopular: Harcourt: 'You might as well employ Lytton or Frere.' All were against, on various grounds.

Then followed some conversation as to commercial treaties: not leading to much result, except a general agreement not to pledge ourselves. – Talk about the advance of Russia towards Herat, & a proposal of the Persians to sell or cede a piece of Khorassan. Kimberley thought the territory in question was not really held by Persia, but inhabited only by wandering tribes. Hartington did not like it: thought the Russians were already where they ought not to be. Harcourt asked what would happen if they took Herat? The Premier wished to find out exactly what Russia wanted before giving an opinion. Northbrook did not see how it could be helped: but thought that, if Russia took a piece of Khorassan, we ought to seize or occupy points on the Persian Gulf.

Then followed a curious discussion. The Queen, it seems, has of late developed a wonderful fancy for a guard of Indian troops: not necessarily more than 20 or 25, but to attend at state ceremonies, & represent the Indian army. Northbrook thought the Indian army would not like it. Hartington & Harcourt agreed that a special act of parliament must be passed to bring them over. I pressed the probable unpopularity of the scheme: people would talk about this being the thin end of the wedge, the object being to accustom Englishmen to the sight of Asiatic troops here, & then larger numbers would be introduced. Chamberlain supported me: & the Cabinet, which at first seemed indifferent, gradually became hostile to the proposal. Northbrook & the Premier both said that the discussion had altered their views. It was agreed to represent the difficulties, not absolutely to refuse, but to gain time.

(If she had this scheme in her head, I can well see why the Queen objected to my having the India office.)

H. of Lds 4.20 to 7.20. Debate on creating Irish peasant proprietors, raised by Lansdowne, in a good speech. Dunraven & Carlingford followed, & some others.

Dined Grillions: meeting a very Conservative party: Cairns, Salisbury, Smith, G. Hamilton, Gibson[84], Plunket . . . I was in the chair.

6 Mar. 1883: . . . Office at 2.00, stayed till 5.00 . . . At the Lords . . . a lively little debate on a bill of Stanhope's for prohibiting payment of wages in public houses. Bramwell[85] opposed, as did Salisbury: Cairns spoke for it, reasonably & well: & old Ld Shaftesbury ranted, as he is apt to do . . . talking in a stilted style, very displeasing to me. Rosebery threw cold water on the bill, but supported it: on a division it was carried.

Dined at The Club: present, Salisbury, A. Russell, Walpole, Maine, Reeve, Smith, Lecky, P. Hewett, & Hooker. Pleasant enough. We elected Sir J. Stephen, the judge, a member. I was in the chair.

The H. of C. having wasted every day of the session till now found itself exhausted, & was counted out at 8.00. The truth is that the public does not care about any of the bills now in hand, though possibly it may be irritated at the continued loss of time, if obstruction continues. I went in there yesterday & heard half a dozen members in succession get up (the subject being navy estimates) & talk about everything under the sun, the object of some of them being evidently to draw the Premier into a wrangle.

7 Mar. 1883: . . . Office at 12.00 . . . home for luncheon: office again, & stayed till 5.30, when all work done. . . . Dinner at the Devonshire Club, Hartington in the chair, about 200 sat down. I was next Ld H. – Cork on my right – Lds Kensington & R. Grosvenor, the Att. Gen. & a few others whom I knew. The rest were for the most part respectable M.P.s, lawyers, men in business, & others of the upper middle class. There were no set toasts after dinner, but Hartington made a good sensible speech: my health was drunk, & I made a speech also, with no preparation, but as reporters were excluded I cared less, & satisfied myself & the audience pretty well. I praised H. highly, spoke of the legislation proposed, & recommended union: glancing at Labouchere's late democratic manifesto, which Liberal papers in general have disclaimed, & pointing out that threats directed against property, & exaggerated ideas generally, could only do harm by frightening away moderate men. This was very well taken, & agreed to. We broke up about 11.00. I agreed to become a member of the club.

I was told that our new member for Liverpool, Mr. S. Smith, being entertained at some public dinner, made a speech of an hour & forty minutes, in which he expounded his idea of Christian Socialism: with the effect of being set down as a bore of the most pronounced type. He may learn, but I doubt it. Philanthropy & politics do not seem to go together.

8 Mar. 1883: Snow falling at times, very cold wind, & streets disagreeable. Short walk. Office: then to the Lords, where presented a vast heap of petitions in favour of the Manchester ship canal . . . Cranbrook gave notice of a motion on the Transvaal question, but fixed no day. It is evidently going to be selected by the Opposition as one of their grounds of attack: & I am not surprised, for the state of things there is disagreeable enough, though probably under any other arrangement it would have been worse. Talking it over with Kimberley, I find his view to be that, if the war against the Transvaal had gone on, it would probably have brought out a strong Dutch and anti-English feeling in the Cape colony itself: possibly have led to insurrection there. Hence the rather precipitate conclusion of the convention. He was determined, he said, not to play over again the part of Lord North. The more I see of Kimberley, the more I like him: his judgment is cool & clear, free of all cant & sentiment, & not running into the opposite extreme of cynicism, which is the weak point in Ld Sherbrooke's intellectual character. His views are in the main Whig, like mine: in short, we see things much in the same way:

'C'est un homme d'un génie extrême,
Car nous pensons toujours de même.' . . .

9 Mar. 1883: Cold bright day, snow fell in the night & ground is covered.

. . . Last night, in the Commons, estimates were discussed at least nominally: the Irish members again monopolised the debate, Mr. O'Brien telling Trevelyan that he would be held up to the execration of Ireland: Trevelyan retorted that four persons had been similarly held up to execration[86] – Forster, Burke, Justice Lawson, & Field the juryman – and it was known what had followed. He was quite justified in the reply & in the insinuation which it conveyed: but such talk is new in debate.

. . . Dined with Froude: meeting Ld Wolseley, & a Mr. & Mrs. Hussey[87], he being the agent on Ld Kenmare's estates. He talked well about Ireland, but told me nothing in substance that I did not know. He threw out a hint that landlords & tenants might for once unite in demanding some relief from the pressure of mortgages. He thought there would be a general resistance to the payment of rent this year: tenants would wait for the chance of another Arrears Act. One of them said so to him: 'I let slip the last chance' (he had paid up honestly) 'but I will take care not to miss the next.' Nevertheless, Mr. Hussey said that, out of £38,000 of rent due to Ld Kenmare, he had collected £35,000. I asked: 'Do you think we are near the end of the Irish trouble?' He answered: 'You're only at the beginning.'

Mr. Hussey said the priests were divided in opinion: but the curates, & the younger men generally, were furious nationalists . . .

Lord Wolseley talked about the liability of England to invasion, & said that the French would find no difficulty in putting 150,000 men into the field, and that, assuming they could get across the Channel, there was no force here that could prevent them from occupying London. He seemed to imply that they could move without long preparation: but on this point, which is material, I was not able to question him.

10 Mar. 1883: Walk sharply for exercise: day fine but cold: office before 1.00: Cabinet at 2.00, which was held at the Premier's private room, H. of Commons: we sat till past 4.00: all present. Talk first of business in the Commons: Harcourt thinks the state of things worse than ever: the opposition, or a section of them, are determined to waste as much time as possible, & they do it by raising discussions on every point of the estimates: it seems that Labouchere is the prime mover in mischief: he avows that his object is to discredit the government, which he calls a Whig government, & ultimately to turn them out, to make way for one thoroughly radical: he has an understanding with R. Churchill & a few others of that sort, & they induce every M.P. who has a hobby to bring it forward: Northcote & the official opposition take no part, but do not object – & indeed if they did it would be useless. Harcourt sees no chance for his London bill, which will accordingly be dropped, though we do not say so publicly: the Affirmation & Tenants' Compensation Bills go on. – Trevelyan was then called in, & a lively discussion on Ireland followed.

Ld Spencer had written to Gladstone, wishing to amend the Land Acts in two particulars: (1) its application to leases: (2) the date at which the new rents shall come into operation. Gladstone strongly supported the application: Carlingford & Chamberlain backed him up: all the rest of us were against disturbing the settlement, on various grounds: (1) that we are pledged not to make further changes at present: (2) that the mischief of unsettling the tenants' minds, & leading them to expect further concessions, would be very great: (3) that, the question once opened, nothing else could be done in this year: (4) that the bill would certainly be lost in the Lords, & there would be no pressure from outside to carry it through. This last argument was used chiefly by me, Granville confirming it. In the end the Premier, who had shown a little warmth in the earlier part of the conversation, gave way, in perfect good temper, with an easiness which I did not expect. We then went to the Transvaal, & agreed unanimously that to send an expedition to Bechuanaland was inexpedient, & that it would be best to compensate by money or land elsewhere the chiefs who are alleged to have been dispossessed on account of their friendship to us. There was some talk about Madagascar, but all agreed that nothing could be done[88]. Also about harbours of refuge, but this I did not closely follow.

The last subject was the Queen's Indian bodyguard, as to which it was ascertained that a special act would require to be passed – & Ponsonby wrote: 'The Queen has a horror of parliamentary interference in military matters', implying that she would rather drop the idea than have legislation on the subject. It was also found that the men must be discharged from the Indian army before they could serve here. These two objections we agreed to represent, not doubting that they will put an end to the whole scheme. . . .

11 Mar. 1883 (Sunday): I see in the papers that the H. of C. sat till past 10.00 last night: nearly the whole time on Irish affairs.

12 Mar. 1883: Cold, & snow falling. . . . Levee at 2.00: stayed till 2.30, when slipped away, as did all the ministers except Harcourt.

Home at 7.00, & quiet evening, after a bustling day, in which little done.

Talk with Chamberlain at the levee: he says it is understood in the House that Northcote's health will not allow him to go on as a leader: in consequence there are sundry candidates for the place: Smith would like it, but the country gentlemen will scarcely follow a bookseller, nor indeed is he fit: Cross is somewhat discredited, Chamberlain says that he is generally drunk when he speaks late in the evening – I don't believe the story but Harcourt said the same last year[89]. Plunket, Gibson, Stanhope, Hamilton, are all in the second rank still: R. Churchill has more cleverness than any, but is hardly a gentleman notwithstanding his birth. On the whole I do not see how Northcote is to be replaced.

Chamberlain talked of the utter disorganisation of the House, of the failure of the new rules, of the necessity of rules more stringent: on all of which points I am reluctantly obliged to agree with him, for it is impossible that all business should be brought to a stand. But when he says that the public is indignant, I doubt: the public seems to care very little about the matter.

Much talk with Granville about diplomatic appointments.

13 Mar. 1883: Office at 1.00. The Premier called, & went over the S. African case with me. I noted his quickness & clearness of apprehension, & also a characteristic trait: an inclination to lay hold of small points & give them more importance than most people would have thought belonged to them.

. . . At 4.00 to the Lords, where Cranbrook made his attack, quoting largely from the Blue Book: I followed &, as I had determined to do, stated the case with entire frankness, concealing nothing, & giving the plain uncoloured facts, as to Boer aggressions, & our having no remedy against them, that would be effective except the extreme measure of re-occupying & holding territory which we had deliberately abandoned. My statement was not a pleasant one to make or hear, as I was fully aware: & the dead silence, though deep attention, with which it was heard, was scarcely encouraging: but nothing else was to be expected, & I went steadily through with it, speaking about half an hour.

Cairns followed, & made the obvious comments: 'We always told you what your Pretoria convention was worth, & now you see we were right': which indeed they were, & it was a pity (though perhaps inevitable) that we did not get out of the Transvaal altogether in 1881 instead of retaining a shadow of authority which we cannot enforce.

Kimberley backed me up: Brabourne chattered: Stanhope said a few words: Salisbury took the same line as Cairns but more strongly, & evidently proposed to recommend war, which Cairns was not: Granville said a few words in reply.

– The plain English of the matter is that Carnarvon's original annexation of the Transvaal was a mistake, as I thought at the time, & as the result has shown: that one false step involved a second, & that we cannot extricate ourselves from the difficulty without damage in one shape or another. There is plenty of room for criticism but, where no party has been entirely in the right, retrospective criticism is not of much use.

14 Mar. 1883: Received from the Duc de la Tremoille[90] a magnificent volume of his family history including some letters of Charlotte. He is right to preserve his family records . . .

. . . Office soon after 2.00: sent for to attend a committee of Cabinet, which sat till 3.00: office again till 6.00, & disposed of all business.

. . . I note the attitude of the press in regard to the debate of yesterday: *The Times* approves the line we have taken, the other papers criticise the convention, which is reasonable, & express themselves more or less strongly according to their politics on the awkwardness of the situation, but I do not see that any of them think us wrong in declining to send out an expedition: which is the one real issue to be decided.

15 Mar. 1883: Office at 1.00, & stayed till 5.00 . . . Then to Windsor . . . The Queen very civil both to M. & to me, as if anxious to make up for former coldness. . . . But I believe that she dislikes & distrusts me, & shall be on my guard, though with all possible deference.

Sir H. Elliot in conversation after dinner assured me that he did not intend in any case to accept another diplomatic post when his present term is expired. He says the longer he lives abroad the more of a John Bull he grows to be, & he wishes to end his days at home.

Late at night a telegram arrived to the effect that some part of the government offices are blown up: supposed by Fenians, or other Irish plotters . . .

At the office saw Lord Sidmouth[91], who had a grievance about the precedence which ought to be, but is not, given to the Maltese nobility: an odd subject for a British peer to interest himself in, but he has followed it up for years.

. . . In H.C. yesterday, debate on Irish land bill: Parnell proposed a large extension of it, discussed last week in Cabinet: Gladstone, who had proposed concession to us, and was overruled, resisted in strong & plain terms, giving great satisfaction to the House, though not to the radical party. Of course his speech was the signal for a fresh outbreak from the Irish, who in their hearts are well pleased at the chance of a fresh agitation. The worst is that among the petitioners for further gifts out of the landlord's estate are the Ulster tenants who, loyal and conservative in all things else, are demoralised by the Land League, & as unscrupulous as the rest where their own interests are concerned. The change in the Premier's attitude is marked, & will be ascribed to Whig influence (Hartington's & mine) though not justly.

16 Mar. 1883: A busy day. Left Windsor at 9.00. Work at home till near 12.00, went to a committee of Cabinet at the India Office: stayed there till 2.00: then office till 4.30, where many papers, & rather hurried. H. of Lds 4.30-6.00, when home, and work again on office papers till past 7.00. Dined at home & quiet evening. Some weariness in afternoon, went to sleep in the Lds, which I do not often do.

A Cabinet box was circulated with letter from Harcourt, & other letters addressed to him, urging the great unpopularity of putting off the London reform bill till next year, & suggesting that it should have precedence of the Tenants' Compensation Bill. I contributed my suggestion that we should try to pass both, dropping if necessary the Corrupt Practices Bill, which is not urgent, since a general election is still remote. But we shall no doubt have this in Cabinet.

Went on my way to the India Office to look at the scene of the explosion last night: met there Prof. Abel[92], of the War Office, who kindly explained the circs. Dynamite, not gunpowder, was the explosive used . . . In some plans the Home Office is represented as occupying that site . . . The ceiling & floor of the room most exposed are nearly destroyed . . . & hundreds of windows broken . . . The immediate occasion was no doubt the rejection of Parnell's bill, & Gladstone's strong speech against it.

17 Mar. 1883: Cabinet at 2.00, sat till 5.00: office again till 6.00, when left for Keston. Cabinet began with talk about Transvaal affairs, & the late debates. Chamberlain expressed a strong opinion against giving any compensation to the chiefs who are being driven out. (Note that this language is repeated almost word for word in the *Pall Mall Gazette*, showing the close connection between Chamberlain & Morley, which I have noted before.)

Then followed general talk as to business in the H. of Commons. Then a discussion as to the creation of a separate department of agriculture, which the H. of C. has by a resolution forced upon us, though we all know that it will have nothing to do. Harcourt expressed a hope that some relief would be given in the shifting of duties to the Home Office, which was overloaded. Chamberlain said in a sneering way that it was generally thought to be a light office, & hoped none of its work would be thrown on the B. of Trade. Harcourt answered rather sharply that he never expected help from that quarter. Much confused talk followed, ending in the resolution that the Duchy of Lancaster should be charged with the duty of the agricultural department – details to be settled hereafter.

Thence we went on to another similar question, the conduct of Scotch business. Ld Rosebery is now specially charged with it, being in form Under Sec. for the Home Dept., but *de facto* minister for Scotland. He thinks he ought to have the title also, & be like the Irish secretary: and, what is more important, he is stirring up the Scotch to ask for a change in this sense. To this the Premier vehemently objected: but was willing to give the Scotch members a committee. Others disliked that idea, thinking the Scotchmen would get control of the committee, & the matter would end in a demand for another S. of State. A separate under-secretary for Scotland it was admitted would be reasonable, but that would not satisfy the discontented. In the end we agree to have papers circulated, & deferred the decision.

Talk as to the late explosion. Harcourt thinks the time was chosen because the boat race on the river had drawn off 1,500 police (so he said) to look after the crowds there. He warned us that the danger was as great in London as in Dublin, & implored Gladstone to be cautious. He said the authors of these attacks on life & property were well known: they were the agents of O'Donovan Rossa, who did not disguise the fact. The material used had been found more than once: a peculiar compound of the nature of dynamite but not made in England: known to be of American manufacture. Discussion began as to whether the U.S. govt. should be asked to take proceedings against Rossa: not with the idea that they will consent, but lest it should be said that the trial should have been made.

Kimberley said plainly that, of all the governments now existing in the world, that of the U.S. was the most unfriendly: that, whatever they might profess, they never lost a chance of annoying or injuring England: nobody dissented, & several seemed to agree. In the end it was agreed to telegraph to West[93], ask for information, & see if upon it there was sufficient ground for remonstrance.

Not a word was said as to parliamentary proceedings – whether the London bill or the tenants' bill should come first – which I thought strange – for the bill which is postponed will not pass this year. But possibly there are reasons, for the Premier & the Home Secretary are not of one mind as to some essential provisions of the bill – police, for instance, & it may be thought as well to avoid discussion for the moment.

18 Mar. 1883 (Sunday): Keston. Walk early . . . in afternoon walk with M. & Sanderson (who came to luncheon) to Holwood, & in the park.

Messenger from office with boxes as usual, nothing important.

Read a good deal to M., chiefly out of Baring Gould's book on Germany, the chapters headed 'Social Democracy'[94].

Sleepy & drowsy in afternoon, which has become too common with me in the last year or two: I hope it is not a sign of approaching old age.

The political events of the week are: (1) the debate on Parnell's motion: (2) the explosion: (3) the Mid-Cheshire election[95], consequent on the death of Lord Egerton, which is claimed by Conservatives as a great victory, though they have only kept what they had before. But it shows that the tenant farmers, though distressed, are not in revolt against their landlords: and is so far important.

19 Mar. 1883: . . . Dined Grillions, meeting Coleridge, Norton, Carlingford, & Salisbury, a small party but pleasant. The chief justice surprised me by the extreme bitterness with which he talked of Wilberforce, the late bishop: quoting a friend of the bishop's, who had known him well, as having said 'that he was the most selfish man he had ever known' and that in his latter days not a word that he said could be believed. Ld C. is habitually bitter & violent in his judgments of men: & I imagine that in this case he has a special grievance, thinking that Wilberforce betrayed the cause of High Church, or at least did not do what he might to promote it, in view of his own interests.

. . . Talk of the viceroyalty of Canada: Ld Lorne is, we believe, desirous of resigning before next winter, though he might have another year of office: it is hinted to me that Ld Lansdowne would like the place. If he would accept, no man could be fitter. He has considerable ability, pleasing manners, ready speech, high rank, & a celebrated parliamentary name. I note him for this employment, if it can be managed. Prince Leopold[96] also is said to wish for it: but he shall not be selected, if I have my way.

20 Mar. 1883: . . . Later telegrams from S. Africa show that the Bechuana chiefs are less helpless than we had supposed: their followers are reckoned at 25,000 men: but if so, & if the usual proportion of these are fighting men, how come they to be mastered by 500 or 600 Boers? In any case it is clear that they neither want a refuge at present nor, if they moved in a body, could one be found for them.

21 Mar. 1883: Long early walk for exercise: walk with M. later.

Day very cold, with east wind.

Boxes, or rather pouches, came down, but with not more than 2 or 3 hours' work in them.

Received from Harcourt a printed mem. as to the inexpediency of putting metropolitan police under an elective board, very ably done, & to my mind conclusive. I wrote to him to say that he had convinced me, & I thought would convince the Cabinet. But I doubted whether his victory might not be fatal to the bill.

The papers are full of an alleged attack on Lady Florence Dixie[97], in the grounds of her house at Windsor, by two men disguised as women, who, as she says, pushed her down, stabbed at her with knives, but were driven away by a dog she had with her. She has been writing in the papers against the Irish Land League, & ascribes the attack to revenge on that score. But the story is so strange, & she so strange a woman, that the public inclines to disbelieve, especially since no one else saw the men, since she escaped unhurt, though in their power, as she says, and as there is madness in her family. Her mother, Ly Queensberry, used to write letters of sympathy, & send contributions, to the leading Fenians. The eldest son Ld Q. professes agnosticism, & that in so aggressive a way as to have given general offence. This lady has travelled in Patagonia & S. Africa, & is a warm supporter of Cetewayo. If her story is not a hallucination, it is probable that the object was to intimidate rather than injure, as has often been done by Land Leaguers in Ireland. . . .

22 Mar. 1883: Cold dismal day, with high east wind & snow falling. Walk sharply for exercise. Three pouches came down: nothing of special interest.

. . . In papers, saw to my regret the death of Sir G. Jessel, which was not expected so soon, though he was known to be under a disease which must in the end be fatal. He was only 58 or 59: his last 8 years were passed on the bench. By common consent he was the strongest judge of our time: respected equally by the profession and the public: very swift in despatch of business, & so sure in judgment that his decisions were scarcely ever appealed from. His manners were bad: rough at all times, & intolerable when opposition roused him: his arrogance was great, though tempered by kindliness: dissent from his opinions he could not bear, but submission disarmed him: he had the good humour which Jews are seldom without, & was less unpopular in private than might have been expected from his habitual want of courtesy. But for that drawback, he might have been selected as the next Lord Chancellor. – I have often met him at the London U. & got on well with him, our ideas never having been much opposed: but I have heard him put down dissentients disagreeably enough: not with any show of anger, but rather treating them as children who talked too much, & should be silenced.

23 Mar. 1883 (Good Friday): Day again very cold & disagreeable: high east wind, though bright sun. Walk alone for exercise: later with M.

Business came from office but nothing special: three pouches.

24 Mar. 1883 (Easter Saturday): Day fine & comparatively warm. Long walk early, ride in afternoon.

No event. Only one large pouch from office.

25 Mar. 1883 (Easter Sunday): Fairhill. Day nearly blank. Walk early alone, later with M. Three large pouches from the office, all routine.

. . . Herbrand Russell[98] came.

26 Mar. 1883 (Easter Monday): The last three days have been newsless: except for a speech by John Bright, or rather two or three speeches, at Glasgow, in which he told the old story again, as to repeal of corn laws, wickedness of Conservatives, absurdity of the minority vote, & expense of war. There were fine rhetorical passages here & there, but the absolute absence of ideas was striking. The only remark he made which had any novelty in it was new by virtue of its exceeding foolishness. He thought a time was coming when we should all be of one mind in politics. That means, being interpreted, that he, Bright, has seen most of the things done which he wanted to do, and it is inconceivable to him that any one else should want more – just as it was inconceivable that any one should object to these. I have a kind of respect for Bright, & have tried to like him in former years: but his extreme narrowness of mind, his incapacity to travel beyond a certain range of ideas, has always repelled me. His unconcealed dislike of peers & landowners may have helped to create this repulsion: but I think I should have been equally affected by the spectacle of prejudice & bigotry, even if not interested in the classes who are the objects of it.

A calculation has been made by Mr. Hoyle of Bury, & is printed in *The Times* today, as to the decrease of drink among the people of the British islands. It seems the total cost of liquor was in 1876 £147,000,000, being the highest point reached: in 1880 it had fallen to £122,000,000, & is for 1882 £126,000,000. . . . The consumption of alcohol seems to have varied together with the change of political feeling: it was highest in 1876, when everybody was Conservative: lowest in 1880, when a genuine radical feeling prevailed: & has risen again now, when the fervour of two years ago has considerably abated.

. . . Read to M. out of Bagehot's *Essays*.

. . . Rather at a loss for employment, which I ought not to be.

27 Mar. 1883: . . . Not much business from office . . . Fine sunny day, but occasional falls of snow.

Fairhill is improved (I hope the last improvement) by adding some rooms on the servants' side of the building, & raising the whole to the same height. It is not & never can be a handsome house, but there is now nothing unsightly about it. The new planting about the place is not on the whole a success . . .

29 Mar. 1883: Walk with Collins about the place [Fairhill] . . . The land belonging to Mr. Hardwicke, which runs into mine, may probably be obtainable by purchase: which if it can be done will be a great advantage, making the estate compact. – I tell him to enquire as to the Herries estate, part of which adjoins mine, & is not unlikely to be for sale. In ten years I have increased Fairhill from 540 to 1,300 acres, & its growth need not stop yet.

Three pouches from the office: nothing urgent or troublesome: received my quarter's salary, £1,216.

Sent £20 to the Heligoland relief fund . . .

In the papers, death of John Brown, the Queen's confidential servant, about whom there was much silly scandal some ten or fifteen years ago, the foreign papers especially alleging that the Queen had married him privately. She certainly treated him with more confidence than is usual in the case of a servant, & created a good deal of jealousy in her family by consulting him on family matters, & sending orders to her children through him. It was thought also that he meddled in politics: but how far this was true I do not know, & I doubt if anybody knows. But ministers, actual or expectant, who wished to be well at court were always advised to shake hands with Brown, & treat him as an equal (which I never did nor would). I believe he had more influence over the Queen than any one of higher rank: partly because she considered him as owing all to her, & solely devoted to her interest. It is to the man's credit that so much favour did not turn his head: but I never heard that he displayed any offensive pretensions: Scotch sense, & the innate dignity of a Highlander, kept him from being ridiculous. Had he died ten years ago, his disappearance would have checked a good deal of stupid & vulgar gossip: that, however, had died out of itself, & his peculiar relations to the Queen were recognised, & had even ceased to be thought odd. She will feel the loss, for he was with her, or ready at her call, every day and all day: the only person with whom she could really be said to live.

. . . Read in *The Times* a long & able letter by Bartle Frere, in defence of his South

African policy. He admits, & pleads for, the policy of creating a second India in that part of the world, & civilising the negroes by means of protectorates & missions, to the latter of which he ascribes great influence. The cost to the English taxpayer he ignores altogether.

31 Mar. 1883: From the office, five large pouches: but I disposed of all, though rather hastily.

Bright warm day: spring beginning at last.

Satisfactory report to effect that the French have given up the idea of forming a penal settlement in the New Hebrides, which would have led to many complications. Two of these islands have been converted & civilised up to a certain point by English missionaries, mostly Presbyterians: but it is curious that without hard work, ill usage, or any other obvious cause the population so dealt with begins to die off, & in fact is decreasing rapidly. It seems as if the continual, though not very destructive, wars in which the natives indulge were a necessary excitement to them, & when these are stopped they lose interest in life, & die out from sheer dullness. Liquor would be a more simple explanation: but I believe this is rather carefully kept from them.

From Natal, Bulwer sends a long & very able despatch reviewing the situation as regards Cetewayo, whose restoration he evidently considers a mistake, & I am not sure that he is wrong. It is hard to blame an official who foreseeing failure wishes to put his dissent on record: but the despatch if published will supply weapons to the opposition more effective than they could make for themselves: and, if asked for, to keep it back may not be easy.

Read to M. a long critique from *The Times* of Froude's new book, the letters of Mrs. Carlyle[99]: which judging from extracts will be more damaging to Carlyle's memory than even the reminiscences or the former biography. Yet the publication was by Carlyle's own oft expressed desire: & one cannot choose between the rather fanciful theory of a posthumous act of penance – which is that adopted by his friends – and the more intelligible though less flattering explanation that he wished to interest the public in his biography, though at the expense of his character for humanity. Froude's position is odd: devotedly attached to Carlyle's memory, he has done more to blacken it than all Carlyle's enemies could have done. But either he thinks himself bound by a promise or he likes the notoriety – which?

1 Apr. 1883 (Sunday): Much business from the office, but cleared off all.

. . . Note that I have given £1,000 (£200 a year for 5 years) to a restoration of the cathedral at Manchester, which from old family connection I could not well avoid, though the money might have been more usefully employed.

Note that a letter of Ly Abercromby[100] to M. says that Brown, the Queen's favourite, died of whisky: he never got drunk, but was in the habit of soaking steadily. It is doubted whether she will regret him after the first, for of late he had grown imperious & rough in his manner to her, so that she was thought to be afraid of him.

Note that on Friday Mr. A. Arnold[101] brought on a motion about the county franchise, but was counted out early in the evening[102]: whereat the radicals are angry, & Conservatives talk about indifference to the question. Both are wrong: the subject is in everybody's mind, & is felt to be one which must be dealt with: but the discussion of it by a private member, of no weight nor influence in the House, was useless for all practical purposes, & wisely was dropped. The loss of time is *nil*, for it was a private member's night, when no government business could be done. Still the thing looks bad, & is so far unlucky.

Note that the revenue returns for the year are just out: the income exceeds £89,000,000, from ordinary sources, not loans: the largest sum ever yet raised so far in this country, & raised without complaint or suffering. Excise & Customs together are exactly as they were in 1881-1882, between £46 and £47,000,000. We shall have the budget before us on Tuesday: but, unless new taxes are put on, there is not room for any large remissions, since the extra 1½d. of income tax put on for war purposes cannot be kept on, without extreme unpopularity, & its loss will leave little margin. The state of the country seems fairly prosperous: steady but not rapid improvement, wages still low: which explains the increased temperance of the people. . . .

3 Apr. 1883: Went up for the day, leaving by 8.45 train . . . Found in the City a yellow fog . . . In the country the day was bright & fine.

. . . A mountain of accumulated papers & letters, which by hard work at home & at the office I got mostly disposed of before 2.00 p.m. when to the Cabinet. We sat from 2.00 till a little past 4.00.

The chief business was the budget: which Childers opened briefly & not in the clearest way, but the substance was that he takes off the extra income tax put on for the Egyptian war: that he proposes a reduction of railway duty, to cost £150,000 this year, & £400,000 next year: & that he reserves £170,000 as the cost of cheapening telegrams, but the precise plan to be adopted is not yet settled. These remissions leave an estimated surplus of about £200,000. Childers originally proposed to increase it by an extra £150,000, to be obtained by taxing corporate bodies: this plan led to much discussion, & in the end he agreed to drop it. As he excluded all ecclesiastical & educational endowments – an exemption which Harcourt, Chamberlain, & Kimberley objected to as unsound in principle – his proposed tax would have yielded so little as to make it not worth the noise it would create, & the delay consequent on its being opposed.

The total estimated revenue is about 86 million.

Something is to be done about the silver duty, which I did not well understand, & it is not important: & something also about game licences. On the whole the budget is one which will satisfy quiet people, & frighten nobody: which in our circumstances is a gain.

There followed a discussion on the Channel Tunnel business: which brought out the fact of wide differences of opinion in regard to it, though all agree that in the existing state of public feeling it cannot be gone on with. But the question is, how to get out of what has been said & done? Two successive governments have approved the scheme, & the French may reasonably complain if they are thrown over without apparent cause.

Next came a debate over the manner in which to deal with Mr. Rylands[103], who has a motion on the paper pressing for greater economy. This led to a general conversation. Harcourt pressed eagerly for the acceptance of the motion, saying it means very little, & will settle the question for this year. The Premier agreed in substance, but treated the matter in a very different spirit, saying that it was very grave, that we were giving a serious pledge, he was willing, but we must consider what it implied, etc.

Hartington objected strongly, on the ground that the cost of the army could not be reduced: on the contrary, it would probably have to be increased. He would rather oppose Rylands & be beaten. (General dissent.) Childers complained of the Duke of Cambridge

& his perpetual demands for increased estimates, in which he was backed by the Court. – I declared in favour of accepting Rylands' proposal, & took occasion to say that by so doing we should be pledging ourselves to the old & sound doctrine of economy, as against the new semi-socialist ideas of spending freely on all things that the public wants or likes, & paying for them out of the taxes. In the end we all agreed.

Office again: work till near 7.00: then home: dined at The Club . . . I was in the chair.

4 Apr. 1883: Busy all morning, though day very fine, & warm as summer.

. . . Received notice of election to the Devonshire Club (where I shall never go) and paid £42.

Corrected a speech for Hansard, which I had nearly to rewrite: a stupid waste of labour, yet inevitable for, though it is no evil not to be reported, it is disagreeable to be made responsible for nonsense.

. . . Great activity & excitement in the Conservative opposition caused by the prospect of Northcote's retirement from ill health. Randolph Churchill, prompted & helped by Wolff, has brought out a violent attack upon him in *The Times*, which however has recoiled on himself, producing a strong reaction in favour of the leader, thus causelessly attacked by a not very respectable follower, while suffering from overwork in the service of his party. On rising to ask a question, Northcote was received with very significant cheering by his supporters which lasted long enough to show that they do not share the feeling imputed to them. I am glad of it, for Northcote's sake, & also for the sake of the H. of Commons. Meanwhile, Cross, Smith, & others are looking out for the reversion of the leadership, which no one of them is fit to hold.

5 Apr. 1883: . . . In H. of C. the budget, which lasted 2 hours, & was well received: the statement seems to have been clear & interesting, only Childers made the mistake of attacking the finance of the late Cabinet, & drawing invidious comparisons: which is never wise for a minister, unless challenged. He gave a satisfactory report of the revenue, which far exceeds the estimate, & explained his proposed reductions. He also added a scheme for dealing with the debt on a large scale, which oddly enough he had never mentioned in Cabinet: I suppose he did not think that necessary, inasmuch as it is based on Gladstone's scheme of 1881, which dropped for want of time. But the omission is odd. He proposes to turn £70,000,000 into terminable annuities at once, & £102,000,000 more within the next 20 years: which last part of the plan I think questionable, for what security can he have that he shall be able to work it out, that his successors will accept it, or that some unforeseen event will not make it impossible? Still the intention is good, & the immediate reduction of debt by 70 millions is a substantial gain.

6 Apr. 1883: Work at home till 11.00: wrote a minute on Zululand affairs for the Premier, who had sent me a letter on that question.

Office at 12.30. Committee of Cabinet on Tenants' Bill at 2.00. Office again at 3.00: H. of Lords at 4.30. Back to office at 6.00, & there saw Mr. Jorissen, the attorney-general of the Transvaal, whom I received with Herbert. He was with us an hour: talked well, which was the more noticeable as he evidently thought in Dutch, and had to translate mentally as he went on. I made a note afterwards of what he said: his chief points were That the chiefs in the frontier wars which have been talked of fought on their account – the Boers did not make the quarrel– and both sides invited white volunteers to take part.

That peace is now re-established, the natives not being driven out, though it is admitted that they have lost a good deal of their land. That there would be no native wars if Boers & English were united: the quarrels arose from disunion between them, encouraging the black men to side with one or the other. That the Boers did not treat the natives cruelly: but they felt that the question at issue was which race should be master. He admitted that they did not believe in the capacity of the negro for improvement beyond a certain point: and he instanced the Basutos, who have been 40 years under a process of civilisation by missionaries, & are not much better than at first. He spoke of articles of the convention of 1881 which the Boers wished to see altered, but discussion on that point was put off to another meeting.

Bought in the morning a drawing and two china vases, cost £21.

Much talk in the papers, & in the world, about Childers's budget: which seems approved on all hands: the state of finance is better than expected, the operation on the debt is thought right & wise, & all except ultras are pleased that no new taxes should be put on. We paid off last year over 7 millions of debt.

7 Apr. 1883: A busy day. Letters & papers early, so many that I scarcely got a walk. Then office about 12.30, & stayed till 2.00: when to a Cabinet, held at Granville's house, he being ill with lumbago, & feeble: in fact during the whole sitting (3 hours) he scarcely spoke, & seemed in pain. All present, except Northbrook, who was at Sandringham. Harcourt asked leave to bring in a bill at once to provide more severe penalties against the keeping or use of explosives: an American having been arrested the other day with over 200 lbs. weight of nitro-glycerine in his possession, and five others being arrested on suspicion of being concerned in a conspiracy to blow up public buildings or set fire to London. Harcourt talked very big about this conspiracy: whether really alarmed, or wishing to give it (and himself) more importance, I cannot judge. I noticed that his colleagues were not much impressed &, though not refusing belief, evidently thought the matter less serious than he did. He said we were in a state of civil war. There was a plan to blow up or burn London. The waterworks were to be destroyed. Conspirators were coming over 'in shoals'. He could not be answerable for the slightest delay. Every hour lost was an additional danger. There were tons of dynamite in London now: they knew it, though they did not know where. Whoever opposed or delayed legislation was a public enemy. It was a mistake to suppose that O'Donovan Rossa was the prime mover: persons of far more importance were concerned. He would not answer for it that London might not be on fire this very night. He could not tell parliament, or even the Cabinet, one tenth of what he knew. Spencer was in despair at the incredulity with which his warnings were received. He believed the Irish masses sympathised, 999 out of every 1,000 (Carlingford protested, & the Premier looked amused). Some talk followed on this.

Harcourt denied that Ulster was loyal as supposed here, & said the worst conspirators came from thence. Gallagher[104], the supposed ringleader lately arrested, was an Ulsterman. After this preface, we were prepared for more stringent measures than he proposed: his bill, which was agreed to, being only to impose more severe penalties on the keeping or use of explosives. He wished to suspend the standing orders, & run it through at once: but this was not judged necessary.

Talk as to the Affirmation Bill: shall it be made retrospective or not? Said that a good many votes may turn on this, as M.P.s are willing to support the principle, but do not like the notion of seeming to legislate for the benefit of Bradlaugh. I did not clearly make out how we decided, if we did decide: but it is a H. of C. question.

Some desultory conversation followed as to a motion by O'Connor Power[105], advising migration to other districts as a remedy for the distress in western Ireland. Nothing important was said or settled: the only thing I remember is that the Premier took occasion to distinguish Healy from the other Irish members, & praise him highly: rather to our surprise, for he is as violent & hostile as any: but he has spoken strongly in favour of the Land Bill, & been civil to Gladstone personally.

On the way back to our offices with Childers, I asked him for some details of his plan for paying off debt. He thinks he has understated its efficacy, & that much more than the 170 millions of which he spoke will be paid off in 20 years: he said not 20 men in the H. of C. understood the system of terminable annuities – which sounds strange – and that he thought it just as well that they should not, as there would be less disposition to meddle.

Home: dressed in a hurry at 6.30 & to the town hall, Kensington, to the civil engineers' dinner: an odd & inconvenient place . . . The speeches were dull: Bright not at his best: & Cross putting one word for another, & confusing his sentences, in a way that made me understand why he is supposed to be drunk when he speaks late[106]. But I don't think it was the effect of drink, at least I saw no other sign of intoxication. – I had to return thanks for the H. of Lords, & was well received: but Cross was the favourite: the engineers are always conservative . . .

Reached Keston by 12.30.

8 Apr. 1883 (Sunday): Fine bright day . . . An idle, quiet, pleasant day. No messenger came down, & indeed there was no business. It is long since I have had a complete holiday.

9 Apr. 1883: London by 10.12 train. St. J. Square by 10.50.

. . . Office early, where so little business that I came home for luncheon. Later, Mr. Errington M.P.[107] called, the same who has been negociating at Rome, whether by order, or on his own account . . . I walked down to the Lords with Mr. E., who lamented on the way over the tendencies of the Irish clergy. He said the Pope could not keep them in order: one of the worst, Archbishop Croke, was in the last resort to be sent for to Rome to be personally reprimanded, but he did not know whether even that would be of use: there were many parish priests who openly advocated outrage & murder, etc., etc. Mr. E. seemed a mild gentlemanly man, talking almost in a whisper, & with a deprecatory manner such as ecclesiastics often have.

At the Lords, sat from 4.30 to 11.30, when home, very weary, which I should not be, for in the Commons the sitting would have been thought a short one: but habit is all. Dined there with W.P. Talbot[108]. . . . The debate was on India, raised by Lytton in a speech of an hour and a half, clever and even powerful, but open to the reply which was made, that he was raising up imaginary enemies in order to knock them down. Kimberley answered in a speech of an hour, the best I ever heard him make, showing from a long series of authorities that Ripon's projected reforms are not innovations, but only the natural development of a policy which has been acted upon during the last 50 years. Cranbrook followed, violent, bitter, & very unfair: the Chancellor replied to him, good sense, but dull: Carnarvon I did not hear: Northbrook summed up the case on the government side, very ably in substance, but a little heavy at times: he spoke 1½ hour. Salisbury replied, cleverly enough, but in a tone which seemed to show that he did not either know much or care much about the question.

The truth I take to be that there is nothing in what Ripon had been doing that is in itself revolutionary or very dangerous: but he has indulged too much in a kind of sentimental philanthropic talk, not perhaps wise in anybody, & certainly not in a Gov. General.

Late in the evening we heard that Harcourt's bill on explosives had run through the Commons unopposed: and we with equal speed passed it too: Salisbury protesting violently & not very wisely, as it seemed to me.

10 Apr. 1883: Herbert brought me the notes that he & I made together of Mr. Jorissen's conversation, confidentially printed for the Cabinet.

Sent £10 to the W. Derby fire brigade, £5.5.0 to the Law Clerks Society, & some other sums which I forget.

In papers, news that a cousin of the Premier's, one of the Gladstones settled at Liverpool, has poisoned himself: apparently mad.

11 Apr. 1883: Sir C. Lampson called on Peabody trust affairs. He said we had spent, or should spend by the end of the year, all our borrowed money as well as our own (£300,000) & the question was whether to delay . . . or borrow another £100,000. I was decidedly against more borrowing, & we agreed to call a meeting to settle the point.

Short walk: office 12.30 to 2.45. Saw Ashley, & much talk. He in good spirits, thinks the opposition on the Transvaal business will collapse, having been much in fear of it before. . . .

12 Apr. 1883: . . . Received a message from the Premier, & went over to speak to him as to the answer to a question on Transvaal affairs. I found him apparently very much at leisure, & inclined to talk over the subject generally. From what I hear, I gather that his correspondence, & all work of detail, is done for him, & that he reserves himself for great occasions: which is right enough, especially at his age. . . .

13 Apr. 1883: Walk early, chiefly on the embankment . . . Office at 12.00 . . . stayed till 4.00. Sir B. Frere called, & gave me some unasked advice as to S. African matters, which I listened to with respect, but was not much the wiser.

H. of Lds at 4.30, stayed till 7.00. The time was mostly taken up with a discussion raised by Dunraven on the position of the Irish labourers, whose expectations, he said with truth, have been raised by what parliament has done for the farmers, & who are more than ever discontented at getting no share of the good things going. Ld D. however weakened his case by using it as a cover under which to attack the Land Act: which he had a right to do, but it seemed as if he were really dwelling on a grievance quite distinct from that which he professed to bring forward. He was talking of the labourer, but thinking of the landlord. Carlingford was optimist, plausible, & feeble, as usual.

I went across to hear the Transvaal debate in the Commons: & came in for part of a vigorous, well reasoned speech from Chamberlain. He is certainly an effective debater.

14 Apr. 1883: Startling telegram from Reuter, stating that the Queensland government has annexed New Guinea, which is impossible, being beyond the rights of any colony to do, but I telegraphed out to enquire.

Cabinet at 2.00, which sat till past 5.00: wasting much time, as it seemed to me, but a great deal of the discussion turned on questions which interest the H. of C. only, so perhaps I am not a fair judge.

It was settled, after long discussion, to give a night to finish the Transvaal debate, which drags on. Note that Goschen spoke strongly against the government last night, & with evident intention to damage. He & Forster work much together. Note also that I complimented Chamberlain on his speech last night, which was a remarkably good one: and he seemed pleased.

Settled also to get the Bradlaugh bill through as soon as possible, several saying that it does us harm in the constituencies. The Premier complained vehemently of an article in the last *Quarterly*, which none of us had seen, accusing him of personal sympathy with Bradlaugh, which he said if he had seen when it first came out, he would have demanded an apology. As it has only just appeared, the reason does not seem conclusive: but the decision was evidently right.

Talk about a commission to be appointed on the question of local government, to settle areas, & so forth: but it was negatived. In all probability that whole matter will stand over until after the new reform bill.

The Irish have got a new grievance. By the new scheme for an appeal in criminal cases, every man sentenced to death may claim to be tried over again: & the demand is being made that it shall apply retrospectively to the case of the Dublin murderers, one of whom has been convicted already. Of course this cannot be done, but it gives a plausible ground of complaint, of which the most will be made in H. of C. 'Why should a man be hanged without appeal in April, when three months later he would have been entitled to appeal as a right?'

Talk of the C.D. Acts, which are to be an open question: Chamberlain violent against them, Gladstone doubtful, Harcourt strongly for. Comic confusion caused by Carlingford being suddenly appealed to: he had not been listening, thought the C.D. Acts relating to animals were concerned, & began to talk about slaughtering at the port of landing, & importation being forbidden. A general laugh followed, which I noticed left the Premier very grave.

Talk of purchase of the Ashburnham M.S.S. as to which we divided, 7 to 6 in favour of buying. Kimberley, Harcourt, Chamberlain, Northbrook, Dilke & I think Dodson against. In the end we agreed to spend about £80,000, if the collections which we want can be got separately.

Talk, private with Kimberley. He says the Speaker is bent on retiring at the end of this session: and confirms what I had heard that Harcourt wants the Lord Chancellorship.

Office again, 5.00 to 6.00: work & hurry: Keston by 6.35 train.

15 Apr. 1883 (Sunday): Walk early with M. & again later. Read to her. Quiet & pleasant day.

16 Apr. 1883: Balances from Knowsley . . . Ward estimates the sum to come in by July at £63,000: which would make a total of £102,000. . . . I shall be able this year to invest, not £40,000, but £80,000. But the matter is not certain.

. . . Saw Mr. Archer, the Queensland agent: he could give little explanation of the performance of the Queensland authorities, except that they had got it in their heads that

Germany was going to annex New Guinea, & thought it better to take the initiative. We shall know all about the matter when the mail comes in.

To the Lords, where sat an hour: then slipped away, & called on Ly Stanhope.

Dined Grillions: meeting Kimberley, Fortescue, Stanhope, Norton, Sherbrooke, M. Arnold, Northcote, Mills, Gibson, H. Cowper. Pleasant: but these Grillions parties always tempt me into drinking more wine than suits my constitution, or agrees with Drage's orders.

Letter from D. of Argyll in *The Times* of today, written from Cannes, violently attacking Chamberlain for a late speech in which he sneered at Salisbury as being one of those 'who neither toil nor spin'. The Duke goes on to wonder how Chamberlain's colleagues, especially some who are 'mammoths of their kind' (i.e. Hartington & myself) can endure such companionship. He evidently wishes the Whigs to secede: but it is shortsighted policy to turn a war of parties into a war of classes, if that can be avoided.

17 Apr. 1883: Walk for exercise round Regent's park, briskly. Luncheon at home, then office.

At 3.00, Stansfeld brought with him a deputation on the Contagious Diseases Acts, which had swelled from a small number to more than 100: Sir W. Lawson, Smith, the new member for Liverpool, Dean Butler[109], & other known names, being among them. Stansfeld read a speech, or address to me, & was followed by half a dozen speakers. I told them in reply that it was for parliament & not for me to settle the principles on which the subject should be dealt with: complimented their earnestness, & offered some criticisms on their proposals. They stayed over an hour. Ashley received them with me. Stansfeld told me privately that he knew he should be beaten in the House, but he thought a strong agitation would spring up in the country.

There dined with me – Sir H. Barkly, Sir A. Gordon, etc. Having a new cook, I was doubtful as to the dinner, but it was good, & the evening a success.

Sat by Sir A. Gordon, & impressed with the odd mixture in him of brusque disagreeable manners with knowledge and intellectual ability. He talked or rather declaimed violently in the evening against the proposed annexation of New Guinea: saying that it was devised by the Queensland planters in order that they might have 4 million of serfs for their estates: he could tolerate, though disliking, annexation direct by the Crown: but not annexation direct by a popular government. I observe that he (& I suppose his is the view of a large party in colonial matters) looks entirely to the interest of native populations, & sees with great jealousy the intrusion of the English settler upon their lands. He talked of his father, said he was printing many of his papers, but would publish nothing. Said he, the late Ld Aberdeen, was really in his own mind a man of decidedly advanced opinions: but, being modest & retiring, let himself be controlled by others – first Lord Castlereagh, then the D. of Wellington & Sir R. Peel, lastly Sir J. Graham.

Spoke to Dr. Smith about the article in the *Quarterly* of which the Premier complained so bitterly on Saturday last[110], saying I had not seen it, but if by inadvertence anything had been inserted that went beyond the fair limits of political criticism, I was sure he would be glad to explain or withdraw it, etc. To my surprise I found that the article referred to was in a number now 15 months old, & which probably not one man in all London except perhaps the writer now remembers. There was no more to be said: but why the Premier should have taken up this old story & made a new grievance out of it it is not easy to imagine.

18 Apr. 1883: Sent £10 to the Artists' Fund, & £5 to the Bethnal Green Library. Office early, where much business.

Saw again Dr. Jorissen: Herbert with me: he spoke out plainly, said what the Transvaal people wanted was to get rid of the convention & the suzerainty (whatever that may mean) & return to the state of things that existed under the old Sand River Convention[111]. I made a note for the Cabinet of this interview.

Worked on office business till near 6.00, when a short walk, & home.

19 Apr. 1883: Thick fog. Writing by lamplight. . . . No walk. Office at 12.00, stayed till 4.00. Then to H. of Lds where a useful but tedious discussion on the Medical Councils Bills in committee: we sat till 7.30. Home very weary, rather from want of air & exercise than actual fatigue. To business again at 10.00, & worked till past 11.00.

On my way to the office I looked in at Coutts, & bought there £5,000 more L. & N.W. pref. stock . . . I have now £400,000 invested, all in railway securities, worth over £450,000 at present rates. Though they are as safe as anything well can be, I think it better not to put more eggs into that basket, & shall try colonial securities, or corporate debts, next.

At the office, among other visitors, saw Sir Julius Vogel[112], formerly prime minister of New Zealand . . . He is a Jew of the Jews, his race unmistakable: rather dirty & mean in appearance, short, fat, with the look of a speculator: which he is, both publicly & in private. And, being such,, it is to his credit that he has never been accused of dishonesty, though his finance was thought rash, & probably led to a good deal of jobbing. He is a desperate gambler at cards, & a friend of Sir R. Peel. He is deaf & pretends to be more so than he is, so as to make his interlocutor say the same thing twice, & gain time. He talked freely of Australian affairs . . . He was strongly against confederation, as tending to lessen the tie to the mother country – five or six governors were better than one.

20 Apr. 1883: Woke with eyes weak & aching . . .

Sent £20 to a fund getting up to buy certain drawings for the Manchester Fine Art Gallery.

Office 12.00 to 1.15: then home: office again 2.15 to 4.00.

Saw a Mr. Powell[113], just returned from New Guinea, where he has been travelling among the tribes . . . the country is held in small separate districts, there are no great or powerful chiefs as far as he knows: the natives on the north coast are distinctly superior in civilisation to those nearer Australia: they have enclosed fields, neat fences, & irrigation. The country is not unhealthy, except on the coast where there are swamps. Inland is a grassy plateau, 2,000 ft. above the sea: cool & pleasant, with rich pasture. Mr. Powell was strong in favour of annexation, & thought the feeling was universal in Australia.

Saw also a deputation of the civil service, who want to set up a provident fund for widows & children, & ask me to take the chair at a meeting: but I did not think the plan sufficiently worked out, or the support of the service assured, & so put them off.

H. of Lds at 4.00, where a question & speech from Carnarvon, very friendly in tone, on the N. Guinea business. I answered, speaking about 10 minutes, without showing any bias either way. The Lords seemed satisfied, & nothing more was said.

Home at 6.30: quiet evening: worked an hour on C.O. papers.

21 Apr. 1883 (Saturday): . . . Office at 12.00, work till 2.00, when to Cabinet. We sat till

5.30 or rather later. Back to office & worked in some haste till 6.20, when to station, & by 6.35 train to Keston.

Corrected with Herbert our note of the interview with Dr. Jorissen, & ordered it to be circulated.

Telegrams have come in from all the Australian colonies, except Tasmania, approving annexation of N. Guinea in general terms.

At the Cabinet we had two disagreeable subjects of discussion. The first was the vote of Friday, condemning the C.D. Acts. The question arose on this – can we continue to enforce the Acts? Gladstone argued that a resolution of the Commons could not dispense with the obligation of obeying an act of parliament. Harcourt agreed, adding: 'How if it had been a resolution of the Lords?' Northbrook was originally in favour of the Acts, but thought the resolution must be accepted as decisive. Hartington observed that the whole question would be raised again on the estimates, giving great opportunities for obstruction: & in this the Premier agreed. Kimberley & I took the same line, arguing as to the impossibility of enforcing the Acts – especially if the fanatical party opposed to them encouraged resistance, which they probably will. It is not easy to enforce by severe penalties a law which the H. of C. has condemned. In the end we agreed that Harcourt, Hartington, & Northbrook should consult the Law Officers, & deferred further action.

The next topic was the vote of pensions for two lives conferred on Lords Wolseley & Alcester[114], which the House passed ungraciously & with much opposition on Thursday night, the radicals sneering & finding fault, the Conservatives giving little help. The fact is that both parties are sore. The one disliked the Egyptian war from the beginning, holding it to be inconsistent with the principles & professions of the government: the others grudged Gladstone his success, & comfort themselves by saying (not wholly without truth) that it was no such great military exploit after all, not nearly equal in difficulty to the last Afghan campaign, for which Sir F. Roberts got only a baronetcy. This comparison was again drawn in the course of the debate. Add to all this, that the idea of a pension for more than one life is on purely theoretical & abstract grounds, distasteful to the radical mind: & the opposition, unusual & ungracious as it was, is pretty well accounted for. The Premier said more than once that the result was humiliating, & to him unexpected: & it seems the opposition is to be further renewed. In the end, after much talk, it was agreed to vary the proposal, & to substitute a lump sum of £25,000 for each for the pensions originally intended. Harcourt objected to this course as weak, & Granville disliked the precedent, saying that it would never be possible, if we give way, to grant a pension for two lives again. The Premier disliked making the change, but yielded rather than incur the loss of time that would follow on resistance. It was agreed that he should communicate with the two Lords. – I suggested for each £30,000 instead of £25,000 but it was judged too much.

We then went on to the Tenants' Compensation Bill, about which we had rather a sharp discussion. Hartington objected to it in principle, & the Lord Chancellor did not like it. The question of applying the law to existing leases was especially opposed: & in the end was allowed, with other details, to stand over. I defended the bill (which I do not like, but judge to be necessary) on the ground that, if we did not pass something of the kind, the demands of the farmers would increase, & we should have to concede fixity of tenure, as in Ireland, or something like it. Ld Selborne accepted it, with expressions of dislike, on the plea that it is for the general interest that farmers should be induced to lay out money freely on their farms. Hartington rested his opposition mainly on the ground of injury or, as he said, ruin to the poorer landlords, if they were called upon to pay a large sum to an outgoing tenant when unable to find a new tenant. Chamberlain characteristically said nothing about the merits of the bill, but repeated more than once that we should be outbid by the Tories if we offered less. He sees everything from the point of view of a wire puller: which in fact is his line of business.

22 Apr. 1883 (Sunday): Keston. Sackville & G. Duncan came. Walk alone early & later with M. Read to her.

. . . Sent £5.5.0 to an asylum.

23 Apr. 1883: London by usual train . . . Saw Sanderson & Antrobus: work at home till the levee at 2.00. Stayed till near 3.00: then to office till near 5.00, when to Lords. There heard speeches from Lansdowne, Dunraven, & Carlingford, on Irish emigration. Walk back with Kimberley. Dine at home, & quiet evening.

Saw a letter from the Lord Chancellor to the Premier, strong, & almost vehement, against the proposal to annex New Guinea to Queensland: at which I am not surprised, but rather surprised that he should seem to fear lest the thing should be done without his having the opportunity of objecting. I spoke to him on the subject at the House.

Drummond Wolff, talking of the recent division on the C.D. Acts, said: 'The only liberty of contract which Liberals seem disposed to allow is liberty to contract disease.' Another critic has altered the old popular saying 'Vox populi, vox Dei' – turning the V into a P.

24 Apr. 1883: Gave a convalescent hospital £10.10.0 donation.

Work on boxes till near 11.00, when walk for exercise.

. . . A Cabinet box came round, saying that Ld Wolseley is not satisfied with £25,000 down in lieu of his pension, & asking opinions. I put in a note to effect that I adhered to my opinion of Saturday: £30,000 each. The Chancellor took the same view: Dilke & Chamberlain were for less: one (Hartington I think) wanted £40,000 for Wolseley.

H. of Lds at 4.15: short discussion on Zulu affairs, raised by Camperdown . . . Back to office at 5.45, & there till 7.00, when home, quiet dinner & evening.

Affirmation bill in H. of C. where a violent foolish speech from Cross against it: the debate in general dull. I do not think the bill is liked &, if passed by a small majority, it is sure to fail in the Lords. Bradlaugh has been lucky enough to succeed in two lawsuits &, if this foolish business makes him a martyr, he will have gained a political position which nothing that he could have done in parliament would have secured for him.

It is announced that the Tenants' Bill will have precedence of that for London: which is equivalent to giving up the latter, & will put the Radical section into worse humour than before. But it cannot be helped.

25 Apr. 1883: . . . Harcourt tells me that the police enquired into Ly F. Dixie's story, & believe it to have been a simple invention: the alleged stabs or cuts in the upper & under clothing do not tally, showing that they must have been made when the clothes were not worn on the person: & it is impossible that the injury inflicted on the dress, if she was wearing it at the time, should not have left a cut or scratch, or mark of any kind, on the wearer. So that it is probably a case of simple hallucination, or rather of hallucination complicated with imposture[115].

One of the Dublin murderers, Kelly, has been twice put on his trial without result, the jury disagreeing: two convictions had been obtained before, but it is feared there will be no more.

26 Apr. 1883: At the office saw . . . Sir A. Galt, who talked of Lord Lorne's retirement, & hinted at the Duke of Albany as a popular choice for his successor.

27 Apr. 1883: . . . Part of my work at the office was selecting colonial officials for decorations: GCMGs, KCMGs & CMGs. I went through the lists with Meade & Herbert, & settled them provisionally.

Much talk about a speech of Gladstone's last night on the Affirmation Bill, said to be one of the finest he ever made[116]. It was certainly ingenious as well as eloquent, since he managed to argue for the abolition of a theistic test on the purely religious ground that a theistic test from the point of view of Christianity or Church-of-England-ism was so vague as to be worthless. He quoted Lucretius at some length, & it is said the members below the gangway, for whom the Latin might just as well have been Hebrew, listened in awe & amazement. I doubt if there has been a piece of Latin poetry quoted before in the present parliament.

28 Apr. 1883 (Saturday): Went with Antrobus to examine the C.O. library: a fine room, but poor collection, no regular librarian, but a clerk attends to it. He thought there were 20,000 or 25,000 vols., but was not sure.

Sent £5 to a Wigan flower show.

Cabinet at 2.00, & sat till 5.40, when obliged to leave before all was done, but others had gone before. Scrambled through a few papers at the office, in more haste than I like, then to station, & by 6.35 train to Keston. Though my office work is not disagreeable (far pleasanter than that of F.O.) I look forward to the quiet & rest of these Saturday evenings & Sundays, & should do ill without them.

At the Cabinet much of our time was taken up by discussion of the grants to Lords Wolseley & Alcester: whether the pensions at first proposed, but which the House seemed to dislike, should be commuted to a lump sum: and what should be the amount. In the end we agreed to £30,000 for Ld Wolseley, & £25,000 for Ld Alcester. The Premier expressed his willingness to acquiesce in whatever the Cabinet preferred. Some doubts were raised as to the expediency of making a distinction between the two grants: Childers, Harcourt, & I, were for £30,000 apiece.

Talk about the London bill, the state of business, obstruction etc. Kimberley & I think Chamberlain wanted to announce that the bill must pass, the House not to separate till it was decided on. The Premier opposed this as impossible. I suggested bringing in the bill, that people might see what was intended, & then letting it stand over till next year. But Gladstone thought the idea dangerous, & quoted Palmerston & Peel against it.

Talk as to the Affirmation Bill. R. Grosvenor being called in says that the worst that can happen is a majority of 3 or 4 for the second reading.

Talk about the Russian coronation. Harcourt very strong against the grant of £2,000 to the D. of Edinburgh for attending it. But as the French give their representative £15,000 we do not see the force of the objection, though Dilke backs it.

Discussion on details of the Tenants' Compensation Bill. Nothing special to note.

Discussion as to representations to be made to the U.S. govt. on the subject of encouragement to assassination given by Irish in America. West, not very wisely, has taken the matter into his own hands, and sent in a remonstrance, to which Freylinghuysen[117] returns an answer barely civil. Harcourt attacks West as incapable, & expatiates on his folly. Granville says he was wrong in acting without instructions. I agree in this, but defend him otherwise. We settle a draft to be prepared, putting the question on a somewhat different footing from that of West's despatch. Dilke, appealed to about West's character as a diplomatist, describes him as 'rather wooden, but not hitherto unsafe'. . . .

30 Apr. 1883: Many letters, including another from Ld Sidmouth, on the subject of the precedence of the Maltese nobility – a subject which he seems to be rather mad upon.

Office 12.00–1.15 & again 2.15–4.15 . . . Then H. of Lords, when only a debate . . . on Irish affairs, intolerably dull. Escaping before it ended, I went back to Downing Street & worked till 6.30, when home, where quiet evening.

Talk at the Lords with Granville: he, like other people, is ill pleased with the state of affairs: too much talk & too little done: obstruction as rampant as ever, but more carefully veiled. No one subject is discussed at obviously excessive length, but every subject is discussed more or less, without reference to its importance: nothing taken for granted: a way of going on which makes parliamentary action impossible. He says the Premier now talks of retiring in the autumn. The Speaker announces that he will not go on beyond July: pleading health as his reason: the choice of a successor will be difficult: Whitbread has not strength for the place, & would refuse: he thinks Dodson on the whole the best man, though wanting in dignity of presence, & not as considerable socially as most of his predecessors.

1 May 1883: Up early, cleared off all letters & papers, leaving nothing undone. Letter from Statter, in his now invariable doleful style (with which I suspect health has something to do): he says business is stagnant . . .

. . . There was nothing in the Lords, except a question put by Cairns as to the conduct of the Irish Land commissioners, in which I am afraid he was right, & Carlingford, who answered, made a weak case.

At office, received a deputation from the African Trading Co., Sir S. Hill[118] chairman: they came to complain of the loss of certain exclusive privileges enjoyed by them in virtue of a grant from the native chiefs near S. Leone, which grant is made of no effect by the chiefs having accepted British protection, & submitted to our customs duties. I saw them . . . & promised consideration.

Dined at The Club: but our party very small: only Walpole, Lecky, & Stephen. Stephen did most of the talking, & was very agreeable.

Engaged a long while yesterday & today in examining a case of alleged embezzlement by a Mr. Bannerman, on the African coast: but it could not be proved. I note a singular laxity in such matters in the tropical colonies. A Trinidad postmaster who has failed to account for £2,000, & whose prosecution was ordered, writes home to ask that, if discharged from his present office, he may be allowed a pension, & be noted for re-employment.

Chose a Mr. Galty attorney-general for Grenada: Ld Halifax & Sir H. Rawlinson recommend him strongly. . . .

3 May 1883: Day cold, east wind, very busy, with heavy work left over from yesterday. Rather low & depressed in spirits, with no cause: for which I resolve to put myself on a regimen. Worked at home till the afternoon, when to office.

Saw there Mr. Jacob Bright, who came to see whether Chinese labour can be secured for the Congo expedition, now being sent out under the patronage of the King of the Belgians.

Mr. O'Shaughnessy, M.P.[119], called later to ask for a place in the colonies. He is said to be one of the best of the Irish M.P.s: a home ruler, but not a Parnellite: a lawyer, & one who was thought of for the permanent under-secretary's place in Dublin. I gave him a friendly, but vague answer.

Lord Lansdowne came by appointment: I made him the offer of the Canadian vacancy: enjoining absolute secrecy: dwelt on the importance of the position, the pleasantness of the climate, on Ld Lorne's regret at leaving (which I believe to be sincere), the uncertainty of all political prospects at home: the last a subject to be touched on delicately, but I tried to point out that between Conservatives on one side, & Radicals on the other, the chances of the old moderate Whig party were slight: & that he had better not refuse a great post while it could be had. He listened, seemed grateful for the offer, but did not commit himself in any way. I told him to take his own time for consideration.

4 May 1883: Saw Drage. Walked: weighed 15 st. 4½ lbs.: too much.

Office at 12.00, & stayed on till 4.00, not coming home. Much business, nearly all work of detail. I had the curiosity to note in turn each separate subject with which I had to deal. They were 33 in number, including the removal of a magistrate in Jamaica, the increase of a salary at Hong Kong, a pension to an official at Singapore, certain claims of traders at S. Leone, sanitary orders at Gibraltar, the case of a wreck on the Falklands, coolie emigration to Jamaica, a complaint against the consul at Panama, the lighting of Belize in Honduras, a new plan for mail communication with Mauritius, a legal difficulty about an arrest in the Pacific islands, a question of laying S. African papers, one concerning the trial of soldiers at Gibraltar, the Fiji estimates (which are all in confusion), a loan for Trinidad, secret service money spent in Bermuda, and a Catholic school at Hong Kong. These were the chief: the rest less important.

. . . Home by 6.00. Read Ernest Renan's biography. Note that the feeling of low spirits & worry has been entirely removed by leaving off wine for one day, though I slept less soundly in consequence. But I doubt whether this effect would continue, & Drage does not advise a regimen of water only for a permanence.

In the Commons last night, the bill substituting affirmations for oaths was lost by 3: 292 against, 289 for: which is a defeat, & so far an injury to the government: but less, probably, than a small majority would have been: for in that case it could not have been dropped without discredit, and its failure in the Lords was certain if persevered in: so that the same result would have been reached with only an increased loss of time & temper. The debate was dull & unreal: the only fine speech Gladstone's of last week: the fact is that personal dislike to Bradlaugh had more to do with the vote than any abstract liking for oaths: & naturally the opposition saw their opportunity & used it. The non-conformists were nearly all, I believe, on the side of toleration, but many of them not very hearty in it: their judgment convinced, but their feelings doubtful.

5 May 1883: Cabinet at 12.00, which sat till 2.30 . . . Academy dinner, I went at 5.30, &

had an hour to look at the pictures . . . Sat at dinner between Granville and Kimberley: the former is usually very pleasant company, but he grows extremely deaf, & in the noise of general talk it was hard to make him hear: besides, he had a speech to make. – Kimberley noticed with regret the falling off in Gladstone's energies: formerly he would let nothing pass in Cabinet that he did not discuss, now he rather collects the opinions of his colleagues, & acquiesces in them, & his manner is much more subdued. I cannot say that I have noticed any want of vivacity in the Premier, who takes his full share of the talk: but I cannot compare with last year.

In Cabinet today, we began with some discussion on the funds in the hands of the ecclesiastical commissioners, which I did not much care about, or well understand. Then Childers brought on his plan of assisted emigration to Canada: a loan of £1,000,000 without interest, taken from the Irish church fund. On this a general discussion followed: Dilke objecting strongly on the ground that similar claims will be put forward on behalf of the English labourer: Lord Granville taking nearly the same line, & adding that in the interest of Canada it is not desirable to send out a large body of men who are bitterly hostile to England: Chamberlain thought the remedy was only temporary: other small tenants would crowd into the vacant holdings: Dilke added that the assistance would kill voluntary emigration: which indeed is the only serious objection. Kimberley expressed strong disapproval of the principle of using the rates to force up the price of labour against the employer. To these Carlingford answered, not to much purpose: saying the Irish people wished it, & that was enough: the Premier would not argue the matter, but said he thought opinion was ripe for what we proposed: I argued that if, once the landlords got their holdings consolidated, they would take care not to let them be subdivided again. Harcourt talked dogmatically, said he did not expect to hear the antiquated nonsense of political economy: that arguments of that kind were only suited to the last generation: & so forth, adding more sensibly that Ireland was not like England, & that what was suggested was in the interests of the employers.

The Premier then talked of the course of business: lamented delay & loss of time: said the Tenants' Bill & the Corrupt Practices Bill must pass, that for London must be finally dropped: then raised the question of Scotch administration, which led to a long debate. The Scotch, instigated by Rosebery, are asking for a Sec. of State, or minister to be on the footing of the Irish secretary: there is no work for him to do, & in the judgment of most English persons the proposal is a mistake: but it seems that a certain amount of Scotch feeling, real or factitious, has been got up on the subject. The Premier suggested a committee, in which the Scotch should be called upon to state their case. To this objection was taken by Harcourt: (1) that the committee would be unmanageable, would insist on a Scotch Sec. of State, or something equally inconvenient: (2) that Rosebery would resign in order to be able to give his evidence freely, & to head the movement. The opposition would join with the Scotch, & promise anything: Chamberlain & Dilke both spoke strongly as to the bad effect produced if we lose Rosebery. I said it seemed very much a personal question affecting Rosebery: if we gave him promotion, & promised a bill next year, would not that be enough? Granville took the same line. The Premier disliked the notion of a bill, should not like to argue for it, thought the opposition would make out a strong case against. However, in the end he gave way, & a bill is to be brought in.

General business came next. Dilke wanted a meeting of the party called, to explain what bills must be dropped, & why. Chamberlain spoke strongly in favour of dropping nothing, but announcing that we should sit on till we had carried all, the London bill included. Harcourt said the London bill might be carried by a great effort, but unluckily the Cabinet was not united upon it. Gladstone argued strongly against the notion of compelling the House to sit on till all was done, appealing to his long experience, & assuring Chamberlain that the only effect would be to irritate. For himself, he was not equal to a struggle of that kind.

Some talk of an Indian resolution to be proposed by E. Stanhope ended the business. We shall accept that as we accepted Rylands. Hartington was the chief dissentient: he thought the committee useless, & that expense was more likely to increase than to diminish. . . .

7 May 1883: London . . . St. J. Square a little before 11.00. Office at 12.30, Cabinet at 2.00: where we sat till 3.45, going over & correcting a draft of Granville's to West, on the subject of Irish publications exciting to murder. It was a good draft, & I thought we altered it for the worse, as often happens when a dozen men join in the work of revision. Nothing else of any importance was discussed. Chamberlain was absent: passing his Bankruptcy Bill, I believe, through committee.

. . . It seems to be generally thought that the government has received a heavy blow, in the defeat of the Affirmation Bill last Thursday: &, as parliamentary success lies wholly in opinion, the existence of this belief makes it a reality: but in truth it proves nothing as to the general strength or weakness of the ministry. Bradlaugh is disliked & to some extent feared, as a noisy unscrupulous agitator, the more dangerous for having some real convictions: & he damaged his own cause by professing willingness to take the oath which he at first refused. It is an unlucky affair, but not one in which the ministry deserves blame, unless it be for not at once bringing in a bill in 1880, when it might have been carried without difficulty. Our real trouble lies in the impossibility of inducing the H. of C. to do any business: in Irish obstruction, & in the support given to it by the Conservative opposition, under a very thin disguise. I hear that on Thursday the Irish were especially clamorous after the division: shouting 'We have done it', 'No coercion', 'We have done for Spencer', etc., etc. Ashley says that one of them, in his excitement, threw up his hat into the air, so that it fell in the gallery, & stuck there. The clôture has so far been an utter failure.

Lansdowne spoke to me in the Lords, & to my great satisfaction announced his acceptance of Canada, stipulating only that, if he wished to come home after 3 or 4 years, he should not be bound to stay out the full term. I wrote at once to the Premier.

8 May 1883: A dismal wet day with fog, so that (11.00 a.m.) I am writing by a lamp. . . . To Coutts, where invested £10,000, half in Tasmanian, half in South Australian 4 per cents: cost £9,988. Office at 12.00 . . . There much business of detail, but nothing very important: the chief thing done was the ordering . . . a Jamaica district judge, to be brought before the executive council for sundry acts of misconduct.

News that the French have made a settlement at Porto Novo[120] on the West African coast, or rather revived one which formerly existed: which our traders will not like. They have also made an attempt to occupy a post on or near the Bonny river, but that did not come off, the chiefs being hostile.

H. of Lds at 4.30, where debate on Sunday opening: Dunraven spoke well, though on an exhausted subject: Ld Shaftesbury declaimed, or preached, in his stilted pompous style, a bad copy of the platform oratory of Exeter Hall: Cairns argued well, as he always does, but went on too long, & lost the ear of the House: the motion was lost, about 160 peers voting. . . .

9 May 1883: . . . Wrote to the Queen to propose Ld Lansdowne for Canada, having previously asked the Premier whether he would do it, though aware that the right lay with me: but I imagine him to be sensitive on such points, & to expect deference, which in this case costs me nothing. . . .

10 May 1883: Day very dismal, wet & foggy. – Bryce Wright called with specimens of rare stones: I bought a few. Read & wrote by lamplight, which is not usual on a morning in the middle of May, even in London. Letter from Ponsonby telling me secretly (what I knew before) that the D. of Albany is a candidate for the Canadian appointment.

. . . Refused to consider an application from the respectable people of Hong Kong, who are angry that the ecclesiastical grant has been cut off, and that they are not allowed any longer to tax the Chinese for their worship.

. . . Saw Sir A. Gordon, who came to plead for two protégés of his, whom he wants to have decorated . . .

. . . Saw Lord Clifford[121], a young man of about 30, not before known to me: the head of an old Catholic family . . . this youth seemed inoffensive and gentlemanlike. He came to talk about the Straits Settlements, of which his uncle, Sir F. Weld[122], is governor.

Saw Morier, who came ostensibly to talk about Gibraltar: but he chiefly harangued on his own successes with the Portuguese, on the impossibility of dealing with Spaniards, & on the incapacity of all the officials abroad & at home with whom he has had to do.

– Morier is a man of ability, but when I see him I come to understand how by incessant blowing of his own trumpet he has set everybody against him. His vanity & loquacity tax my patience, even when I believe that in the main he is right.

H. of Lords, where an Irish question put by Cairns, & very lamely answered by Carlingford, as to the removal of certain subcommissioners under the Land Act, who had failed to satisfy the expectations of the tenants in the matter of reductions. There was no reasonable defence possible: & Cairns & Salisbury improved the opportunity. Luckily Waterford & other speakers diverged into a general attack on Irish policy: which weakened their case, & made an answer possible. Lord Fitzgerald spoke well for the defence. Home late: after dinner M. & Margaret left for Holwood. Worked through the evening in my room.

11 May 1883: Saw Statter, who exuberant & energetic as ever, but this time in the despondent line. He is as confident now that Manchester is being ruined as ten years ago he was that the prosperity must go on increasing indefinitely. He talks much of Belgian & German competition: how English workmen are brought over at high wages, for 2 or 3 years, & turned adrift when the natives have learnt what they can teach: how the leading manufacturers are losing money every year, & only hold on in hope of better times, etc., etc. But with all this he is not less eager than formerly to lay out building land.

. . . At 1.00 I went over by appointment to the Treasury, & there met Gladstone, Granville, & Hartington, to talk over the Canadian business. Childers had come on other business, & stayed to discuss this.

We all agreed that the selection of the Prince was undesirable on various grounds: his absence of official or political experience, his liability to epileptic fits, the impossibility of dealing with him as with an ordinary governor in the event of his going wrong, & the probable unpopularity of the choice among the English constituencies, who would call it a job. I was prepared to fight for this view of the case if necessary but, finding that Granville took it, & the Premier agreed, I stated my opinion in agreement with theirs, but moderately. It was settled that I should write to Ponsonby, which I agreed to do.

Office again till 4.00: saw Herbert, Meade, & Sir A. Galt. The latter took leave: he disclaimed wishing for an audience of the Queen, but I think he wanted one. He is succeeded by Sir C. Tupper[123], an able but rather violent politician.

Ld Moncrieff[124] writes to ask colonial employment for one of his sons: I give the usual answer, but will help him if able.

Left London by 5.15, & settled at Holwood for the first time since 1873. I occupy the end room looking over the garden.

12 May 1883 (Saturday): Wet cold morning. Settled myself with much pleasure in the garden room, which I shall use as mine, except possibly in winter or very cold weather. The house [Holwood] is comfortable, much improved by Mr. & Mrs. Alexander, but pictures, books, & ornaments are wanting. Worked on papers till 12.00. Read to M. Sent £10 to the Newspaper Press Fund. Walk . . . in afternoon, though weather still wet.

. . . Three pouches came from the office.

13 May 1883: Walk early alone, in afternoon with M.: both times in Holwood, Keston, & Hollydale. Very well pleased with the appearance of things in general, but alarmed to find how much in the way of ornament is wanted. The furniture seems tolerably good, but the books, prints, & paintings on the walls are worthless: & to replace them as I could wish will be an affair of some thousands. However, it will be an interesting occupation for leisure time, and I have the money.

Considering in my own mind whether I shall leave Holwood, which ought in the end to revert to my family, to one of M.'s children after her, for life: the trouble is that none of them will be able to keep it up. There is also a certain difficulty connected with the difference of the tenure by which I hold the various properties forming the Holwood estate: Holwood proper being my own, while Keston, Hollydale, & the land bought from Sir W. Doyle, are vested in my trustees. –I can if I please redeem them: for in all probability if alive in 1886 I shall have £600,000, & in 1890 £800,000 laid by. But my life is precarious, & will probably not be long.

Four large pouches from the office. – Corrected a speech for Hansard.

The newspapers are busy with comments on the session, of which half has gone by with very little advantage to anybody. We complain, with some justice, of obstruction by the opposition: they reply with criticisms on the alleged mismanagement of government in bringing forward their measures: as to which I am not able to judge how far they are right: but I have a suspicion that Gladstone is not as well qualified to arrange a debate as he is to make a great speech: & that he has not the art of treating little things lightly. But the root of the mischief lies deeper. When I entered the House in 1849, it used to be reckoned that about one-third of the members, say 200 to 220, took some part in business, the rest hardly ever interfering except to vote: now the proportions are reversed, & probably the entirely inactive are less than a third, instead of being two-thirds. Then the House is more tolerant of loquacity, & men who have really no qualification except impudence waste hours, night after night.

The conclusion is forcing itself on many men that the House is too numerous – that 650 men, all wanting to take some part in affairs, cannot carry on the work of the country.

Perhaps if this view were taken, some of the difficulties of a redistribution of seats might be overcome, by not redistributing them?

Stricter rules must be framed & kept to: perhaps also hours altered: for it is idle to expect that M.P.s or anybody else will be inclined to discuss matters of detail in a businesslike way long after midnight. But the difficulty of day sittings is – how can ministers take part in them?

14 May 1883 (Whit Monday): Letters & papers till 11.00, then rode, but the lanes were full of excursionists, even those most remote from any station. . . . A messenger came unexpectedly, bringing among others a letter from Ponsonby, to the effect that the D. of Albany is pressing his claims to the government of Canada, & the Queen inclined to give way.

. . . Letter from Bulwer in a very despondent strain, saying that Cetewayo is discontented, intriguing, bent on recovering his lost territories, & totally unable to understand or accept the conditions under which he has been restored. It is impossible to send a less satisfactory report.

. . . At the sale of a collector of prints lately dead, an engraving from Rembrandt, of which only two other copies exist, sold for £1,500 . . . Probably such prices for works of art were never given in the world before . . .

15 May 1883: Very fine, warm, & pleasant: the first day of summer. Long early ride . . . Walk with M. in afternoon. Drowsy from heat, & slept before dinner. Not much business from the office, only two pouches, & those only routine.

Articles in various newspapers on the condition of South Africa, which indeed is not pleasant. The Zulus are fighting in the north: the Transvaal people have a war going on with the chief Mapool[125]: the Pondos are at war with a neighbouring tribe: & the Basutos, nominally under the government of the Cape, refuse to acknowledge any authority. In each case the British government is called upon to restore order: the secret hope of every colonist being that large forces will be sent out from England, at once protecting them free of expense & enriching them by the outlay of English public money. They will be disappointed so far as I am concerned.

16 May 1883: London . . . Saw there Sir A. Galt, who had taken leave, but came back to read a telegram from Sir J. Macdonald[126], in which he begged that Lord Lorne might stay another year, and the D. of Albany succeed him if that was impossible. I told Galt that as to the first I had tried to induce Ld Lorne to remain, but he would not: and it was useless to press the matter further. As to the Prince, I could say nothing: the matter was being considered. There is something going on that I do not know of in the case of Galt: something that he wants & is working secretly for (qu. a baronetcy?) behind the backs of the office. But he is a pleasant shrewd old man, & I shall be sorry when he goes.

Saw Sir Hercules Robinson, fresh from the Cape: long talk with him, Herbert being present, & taking notes. The substance of what he said was: 'If you do not mean to enforce the Transvaal convention, which you can only do by war, you had better drop it: it only gives false hopes to the natives, keeps up irritation, & makes the British government responsible for actions over which we have no control.' I agree entirely in this view.

As to the Basuto question, which we also discussed, he takes for granted that the Cape colonial authorities will give up Basutoland. They have tried to manage it & failed, at heavy cost. We have only to choose between entire abandonment of the country or holding it nominally, giving the people freedom to manage their internal affairs as they think best. The latter alternative he prefers, & on the whole I think he is right. But the Cabinet will have to be consulted, & possibly may not agree.

I agreed, at Lord Northbrook's request, to join an Indian club in London which bears his name, & which is to be opened next week.

17 May 1883: Holwood: did not move all day . . . Heard from Coutts that £10,000 more is paid in there, making £40,000 in all this year, & £440,000 since I succeeded.

Received from the office three pouches full of papers, none very important, but with letters they kept me at work till 2.00 p.m. Received from Ponsonby the Queen's sanction to Lord Lansdowne's appointment, & wrote to him accordingly. H.M. asks . . . why the Cabinet objected to the D. of Albany: a delicate question . . . Wrote to Granville & Gladstone, & suggested to both that we might hold out to the Duke hopes of the reversion of the government of Victoria, which will be vacant in a year or two.

Sent to the Premier a list of 4 colonial knights to be made, if he approves.

18 May 1883: Ly Jersey came to luncheon, & for the afternoon. Rode early, walk alone . . . walk with M. later. Three large pouches by post, & a messenger later, but he brought little except papers for signature. All the office work . . .was work of detail.

The papers are full of a condemnation by the Pope of the Irish agitation, or rather of its being taken up by the priests. The turbulent archbishop, Croke, has been sent for to Rome, & rebuked, & the decision is announced in a public letter. Whether it will produce the desired effect is uncertain, the agitators being as a rule not under clerical influence, & the younger priests ardent nationalists. But it will, at least, prevent the bishops from taking an open & active part in preaching socialism. And in any event England gains: for either the Pope's authority will be lessened among the Irish, in consequence of his opposition to national feeling: or the anti-English movement will be checked: or possibly both will happen in a certain degree.

19 May 1883: New leases signed, to value of £180.

One pouch only, & not much in it. Troubled with slight cold in the head (the worst I ever had was just at this time last year).

Letter from Lear, begging me to go & look at some drawings which he has sent over. He talks of his age & health, & that he will never return to England. I answered him.

. . . Examined the library which, as I expected, is nearly all rubbish, & useless to keep, but the books may remain till I can replace them.

20 May 1883 (Sunday): Three pouches came by post: not important. Letter from Granville who has been to Windsor & seen the Queen:

'She thought your decision quite right, & had expected it: but could not help forwarding the application. Had never heard of his wish till then. I unluckily said that I was afraid the P. of Wales was disappointed.

"What has the P. of Wales got to do with it? Why is he to be consulted?" Her chief argument against it was the impropriety of the Sovereign's son (except as a soldier) receiving orders from a Secy. of State. But she asked afterwards whether it was necessary to exclude him from all hope of being employed? I did not answer. But I think you might safely say something consolatory on these lines, without committing yourself.

She touched on Lorne for India. I said that it was the most important appointment she had to make, as much or almost more so than that of the Prime Minister.'

Sanderson came for the day. Walk with him early & late . . . Walked between 3 & 4 hours, & rather, though not unpleasantly, weary.

21 May 1883: Letter from Hale: he is negociating with the L. & Y. [Rlwy.] Co. for the sale of land at Bootle, nearly 10 acres: at the far end, & only agricultural land at present: price agreed on, £33,000.

Settle that the 1st Lancs. R. Volunteers, of whom I am hon. colonel . . . shall have their yearly inspection in the park at Knowsley, at the request of their officers.

Remarkably little business at the office . . .

22 May 1883: Lansdowne's appointment is well received by the press on all sides: though I observe as curious that it is spoken of everywhere as being made by the Prime Minister, who had nothing to do with it beyond assenting to my choice.

Not much work from the office. Day hot & fine. Call at Hachette's & buy a book. Call at Coutts, & settle to buy £10,000 N.S. Wales 4% stock, making £35,000 invested this year.

At 12.40 left for Paddington: Windsor by special train: a large party, Carlingford, Sydney, Kimberley, Harcourt, Sir H. Robinson . . . We held a council . . . We got back to London by 4.40: office at 5.00. Stayed till past 6.00, when left for Holwood.

Harcourt talked to me in the train about the London bill, which he wants to drop, & the Premier to go on with. I am compelled to agree with Harcourt that the attempt is useless, from mere want of time, unless (which I suggested as a possible expedient) we reserve it for a special session in November. Even so, the well known difference of opinion on the subject of police, as to which neither Harcourt nor Gladstone will give way, makes the subject an awkward one to deal with.

The Queen seemed to me aged & weakened: very grey, larger than before, & still lame from a recent fall: she sat in her chair without moving, except her head: but she was in good humour. . . . She makes no secret of saying that, since the death of her husband, the loss of Brown is the heaviest blow she has ever suffered – that she could say anything to him, & trusted him on all subjects.

23 May 1883: Very fine hot day. Not much business from the office.

. . . The Duchess of Bedford, with H. Russell[127], came to stay with us.

. . . This is the Derby day. The H. of C. adjourned over it &, having decided to take one holiday, took another by counting itself out at 8.00 p.m. It is clear that, whatever may be professed in public, there is not much real activity among our present M.P.s. They have lost their early ardour for legislation & have grown apathetic.

24 May 1883: Very fine & hot. Ly Russell, with her daughter[128], came over from Pembroke Lodge for the day.

Read, or tried to read, the diary of Henry Greville[129], brother of the Charles Greville whose memoirs created so much sensation. But it is written with no malice, & little point: so as not to be very interesting. Reminiscences are seldom a success unless flavoured with a little scandal.

25 May 1883: . . . Saw . . . Münster, who called about the claims of German settlers in Fiji, they being discontented with the decision of the court which has sat upon their titles, & rejected many as invalid. I called in Herbert, & we talked the whole question over: in the end I think Count M. went away satisfied that we cannot reopen the German claims without dealing in the same way with all others: which is impossible.

   . . . Dined with Dr. & Mrs. Smith, meeting Stanhopes, Ld Crewe[130], Huxley, Mr. Stubbs the historian, Mr. Cotter Morison who has lately written an essay on Macaulay, & some others. . . . I was puzzled by the appearance of Ld Crewe, but it seems Dr. Smith's eldest son is agent of his Wiltshire estates: as also on those of Ld Lansdowne. He gave us no trouble, going to sleep quietly after dinner & so continuing.

26 May 1883 (Saturday): . . . The H. of C. was again counted out early last night. Whatever may be the cause, it appears to be completely demoralised, & will do no work that it can help. And, apart from the small clique of party politicians, I do not believe the public cares. There is nothing that England really wants in earnest: nothing that has touched the popular imagination.

Cabinet at 2.00, which sat till near 6.00. Then home in the wet. At 8.00, back to Downing Street for my full dress birthday dinner, at which 47 or 48 sat down . . . Then came the F.O. party, where I stayed till 12.00, & came away rather weary.

At the Cabinet, Gladstone asked me to state the Basuto case, which I did, & we agreed that the territory should not be abandoned, but that, before taking it back from the Cape Colony, we should make conditions with the latter as to payment, & ascertain that the Basutos themselves desire protection.

Kimberley agreed, thought there was nothing else to do, but that some day we should have a Basuto war, as they are a turbulent people, & will probably fight among themselves. He feared also that the Cape would in like manner saddle us with the Transkei country.

Harcourt does not like it, Chamberlain would be glad to get rid of the Basutos altogether, but admits the parliamentary difficulty & would propose stringent conditions in the hope that they may be refused. He also predicted a Basuto war, to come off within 10 years. But in the end we were all practically agreed.

The Premier said we were at Whitsuntide no more advanced than we ought to have been at Easter. Dilke would not object to let drop the London bill if it could be taken up next year, but feared that if abandoned now it would not be taken up again for some years. He spoke as the only metropolitan member in the Cabinet. The effect on elections in London would be bad. The party would be thrown into great confusion.

Chamberlain agreed that the bill if dropped now would be lost for a long while. The effect on the party would be such that nothing more could be done this year. In that case our only chance would be to announce a franchise bill & dissolve upon it. Even so, the general election would probably end in defeat.

The position he thought thoroughly unsatisfactory. But if we determined to sit till the end of September we might possibly carry all our bills: in any case we should have shown energy.

Childers said his reports from the West Riding convinced him that the Cabinet had fallen into extreme discredit there. He would ask for the whole time of the House. Our friends were desponding: that would rouse them.

Harcourt thought that, if we failed to carry our programme, the failure would be fatal. We should die by inches. The strength of the Cabinet was already much impaired. He did not mind going out, but did not like the notion of going out in a stink like a tallow candle. He would sit on till August, then adjourn till October, & sit again.

Hartington believed we were in a bad way, & should probably go out before long. Did not think the plan of Chamberlain & Harcourt would be of any use as regards carrying the bills, but it might be a good preparation for an election.

Gladstone said it was insanity to ask for the whole time of the House. It would be jumping down a precipice to propose such a thing. He did not agree that the session would be a failure if the London bill were dropped. It would still be a fair, though not a glorious session. He had no doubt the opposition were obstructing to the utmost of their power, but there was no proof of it. Harcourt thought there was a great deal of proof. Dilke said the opposition were in the habit of announcing that they did not practice obstruction, since the government had given them nothing to obstruct. Granville asked whether the country was so anxious for an autumn sitting as to counterbalance the dislike that would be felt in the House itself. Gladstone again warns us that the House will not bear highhanded proceedings, that to meet in November for a London bill would not be popular, that to ask for the whole time of the House would not be thought reasonable. He spoke very earnestly, & settled the matter by so speaking. Dilke asked whether a meeting of the party should be held? Harcourt: 'What have you got to say to them? *Morituri vos salutant.* That is all we have to tell them. There is nothing to propose.' Granville: 'Party meetings are very effective, but you can't repeat the performance. Is it not better to wait till the difficulty grows more serious?' Derby: 'Is for the meeting. A speech from the Premier will do good.' Chamberlain: 'Even with your reduced programme, an autumn session is inevitable. It is agreed that the London bill must be finally dropped.'

Some talk follows about the Ashburnham collection purchase, which is strongly opposed, & a majority appears against it: but the trustees must be seen & heard first.

Talk lastly about Ld Ripon's Indian legislation. Kimberley dislikes the Ilbert Bill, but thinks the government is pledged & that it cannot now be dropped, but it may be modified. Says Ripon is extremely sensitive to criticism, thinks the council at home are against him, whereas they have been very careful to spare him, though against their own opinions.

Vague talk about the Congo, Whyday[131], the Privy Seal, Sunday closing, & the Wellington statue[132], but nothing was settled on any of these points.

27 May 1883 (Sunday): Holwood by 10.25: fine day, & cool after the late rain. Sent £10 to an Artists' Fund, & £10 to a Cabdrivers' Assocn. . . .

28 May 1883: Leave Holwood at 9.00, walk in to Bromley: No. 23 at 10.40: day fine, cool, & pleasant.

See Lawson, who agrees that the dropping of the London bill was a necessity: & thinks there is a great indifference to politics in the public mind just now. He does not believe the government is discredited, though it may have lost momentarily by the failure of the Affirmation Bill.

. . . Levee at 2.00: inevitable but foolish waste of time. . . .

29 May 1883: Fine warm day: very clear of letters & papers, having cleared the office yesterday. Office at 12.00: there found work enough, & busy, chiefly with South African matters.

A new complication: the Queen suggests through Granville that Lorne shall stay another year [in Canada]: luckily I was able to point out the fact that he had already in positive terms declined to do so, when I proposed it. Evidently Lorne was ordered by the Queen to throw up the government a year before the regular time, with the intention that D. of Albany should succeed: that having failed, she, or rather the family, are now pushing to get the change put off for a year, when there may be a new ministry. But it is too late.

. . . Gladstone called together his supporters in H. of C. & had a successful meeting[133]. It was held at F.O. & from my room I could hear the cheering.

30 May 1883: Paid for the dinner of Saturday, wine, illuminations, etc., £240, which I gave in one cheque to Ly D. Work at home till past 11.00 . . . Call at Coutts, & invest £3,000 more in Victoria 4%, cost £3,034. Total investments now £438,000.

Office at 12.00: where for a time little business. Ld Napier of Magdala called to talk over Gibraltar affairs, fearing lest some of his decisions should be reversed by his successor. He has been a good administrator, except in regard of money, as to which he is always inclined to profusion.

Long talk with Herbert & Ashley as to French proceedings on the West African coast. We do not want to annex, or to establish protectorates, but the French make it difficult for us to avoid doing one or the other, for they negociate treaties with native chiefs, under which they claim exclusive rights of trade: & that our merchants reasonably object to.

At 4.00, to City Companies Commission: where sat 2 hours, nearly all present. We agreed to recommend: (1) restraints on the Companies alienating their property: (2) publication of their accounts: (3) membership of a Company not in future to confer the parliamentary franchise. All these proposals were carried by a large majority: Cross & 2 others dissentient.

Office again at 6.00, & work till 7.00, but did not succeed in clearing my table, the business being heavy: in addition, I think I received 40 letters in the day.

I hear that the meeting of yesterday has revived confidence (if indeed it was ever shaken) and that the abandonment of the London bill was accepted with little grumbling, having in fact long been foreseen as inevitable.

31 May 1883: Signed new leases, about £350.

Saw Drage, who reports very well of me: better than I feel myself for work & worry are creating in me an uncomfortable state of nerves – but I dare say it will pass off. He chiefly fears for the want of exercise & consequent increase in bulk. He did not seem to attach importance to the symptoms of last year.

Sir A. Musgrave called, having left Jamaica on his way to Queensland: I had not seen him before: he did not impress me favourably, though intelligent & fluent, being evidently conceited & opinionated. He gave a flourishing account of its prosperity: the negroes doing well, industry reviving, estates being cultivated that had lain waste, labour abundant & fairly efficient. (This I believe is not far from the truth.) Several planters were

making from £5,000 to £8,000 a year out of the island. He admitted that the white population was dissatisfied, but thought they had no reason: did not see why the present regime
should not be permanent: the governor was the only impartial authority, & power should
rest with him: the whites desired a restoration of the old planter oligarchy, & the blacks did
not know what they wanted. He denounced the Kingston Jews violently: said they owned
the press, exercised great influence, & always for mischief: the West India committee at
home was also very troublesome: in short he seemed to think that a despotic governor was
necessary, & that everybody ought to be satisfied to have it so. . . .

1 June 1883: Met F.A.S.[134] in Regent's park, & much friendly talk.

Office, where saw the governor of Newfoundland, Sir H. Maxse[135] . . . He is in bad
health, & looked very feeble, though gentlemanlike, the last sort of man I should have
thought in his place in a rough fishing colony. He says there are many rich
Newfoundlanders who have houses in London, & pass the winter here.

Received a deputation on the subject of New Guinea, headed by the D. of
Manchester[136]: they had nothing new to say, nor was it possible they should have: but
representing the Colonial Institute they were reasonably afraid that the question might be
settled without their having figured in the settlement. I could give them no definite
answer, but we talked the matter over for an hour.

H. of Lds at 4.30. Found a debate on naval affairs in progress: Ld Sidmouth violent
about the abolition of flogging, which he wished to restore, & would have divided on
a clause to that effect, but that Salisbury interposed at the last moment to stop
him. . . .

2 June 1883 (Saturday): . . . The Cabinet occupied an hour in discussing postal affairs,
& the conduct of the P.M. General, Fawcett. Childers complains of him for holding
language as if independent of his colleagues, & almost hostile: when asked to do this or
that, he answers that he would, willingly, but that the Treasury refuse their consent: 'He
forced upon us the parcels post against everybody's opinion in the department, by pledging the government to it without consulting them.' The present grievance is that he has
sent in a demand for half a million now, & a million later, to meet the cost of extending
the postal business: of which he said nothing till after the budget. The Premier joined in
the complaint as to Fawcett: 'He dissociates himself from his colleagues entirely, speaks
as if he had no one to consult.' The Premier objected strongly, & with some vehemence,
to creating a departmental debt.

Except in extreme cases, the cost of the year ought to be met within the year. Harcourt
thought that borrowing a necessity if you mean to extend a concern: citing the precedent
of railway companies. Chamberlain would follow the precedent on which local public
works are undertaken – payment by borrowed money, the loan to be wiped out after a
certain number of years. Harcourt thought the P.O. was starved, that we ought to make
no profit out of it.

Gladstone, rather angrily: 'Then you must put on three million more taxes – where do
you expect to get them? I had rather walk out at once than be responsible for finance of
that kind.' D. [to avert a controversy]: 'What explanation does Fawcett give?' Childers:
'Very little.' Granville: 'He ought to be called on to explain: but he is very sensitive, & will
go out at once if censured.' Chamberlain confirms this, adding that Fawcett, though
recovered[137], seldom cares to attend the House. – In the end nothing definite was settled.

It is clear to me that, from whatever reason, Fawcett is decidedly unpopular among his colleagues in the Commons: & no doubt he is dogmatic & unconciliatory.

We then went on to African matters: a draft of mine, embodying last week's decision on the Basuto question, was approved: and the question of revising the Transvaal convention was gone into. I asked for leave to negociate with the Boers: Hartington thought the revision might be necessary, but was very unpleasant: 'I suppose some of us thought the convention meant something.'

Ld Selborne: 'I may have been a fool, but I thought so too.' Kimberley: 'The Boers are not as black as they are painted. In the case of Mipoch[138] they have right on their side.' General talk followed as to the power to cede British territory in time of peace, etc., which was premature, as we were only discussing the expediency of hearing what the Boers have to say. Objection was taken to Sir H. Robinson as not representing the views of the Cabinet (he is very bellicose) and it was decided to send out somebody as a special negociator with the Transvaal government. Lord Reay was mentioned as fit, he being more Dutch than English. Chamberlain, Dilke, Granville, Northbrook, all think him competent: Harcourt is vehement against him: 'I like the man personally, but he has not the requisite qualities: of all the blunders ever made in S. Africa, sending out Reay will be the greatest.' But nobody else took this view.

A long & rather confused discussion followed as to what shall be said on the question of Mr. Errington's alleged mission to the Pope. As to this, my colleagues did not seem agreed what to admit, or what his real position was: but I gather that they thought the denial of his having had any official character had been carried farther than strict accuracy justified. It seems that he has had neither pay nor instructions, but has been supplied with information which it was thought desirable the Pope should see, as he is misled on Irish subjects by Irish priests about him. . . .

4 June 1883: London . . . New leases, signed since 1 Jan., give increase of rent £3,200: the result of 5 months.

Statter sends monthly report: doleful & despondent: stagnation of trade never so bad, etc.

To Grillions, which is driven out of its old quarters, & took refuge in a room belonging to the Ralegh club. The room, the dinner, the wine, were all bad: & the party not amusing. . . . Lord Sherbrooke, whether from fatigue or illness, more evidently failing than I have yet seen him. He asked the same question . . . three or four times, receiving the same answer. He is, I am afraid, aware of his condition: but it is not always as bad as today.

Home tired, & not over pleased by the sight of a heap of boxes, which I have not had time to deal with.

A fresh trouble for the Cabinet, though not of the gravest kind: Rosebery has resigned, partly in consequence of his claims to a seat in the Cabinet not being admitted, partly, I believe, in consequence of something said by Harcourt which he construed as an affront. Harcourt is not conciliatory, & has a way of treating everybody, colleagues included, as inferiors, which his friends only laugh at, but which to subordinates must be disagreeable. The affair is not yet public, & very likely will be made up.

5 June 1883: M. very unhappy last night & this morning about the loss of some memorandum books which she has kept for many years: luckily they are recovered.

Office at 2.30, & stayed till 5.30, when left, having cleared off all the routine work. I ought to have walked but, being lazy, & the day hot, went home.

. . . Dined at home, & quiet evening. Much progress has been made in parliamentary business, & on the whole matters are mending.

Messrs. Warr, Firth, & James called . . . to discuss the City Companies report. Their plan is more moderate than from Mr. Firth at least I should have expected. They would take three-fifths of the income of the companies for charitable or public expenditure, leaving them the other two-fifths free at their disposal.

6 June 1883: Wrote to the Premier about Lord Reay, & saw him afterwards: talk as to Basuto question: find he agrees with me that the one object of colonists in all parts of the world is to extract money from the British exchequer: . . . saw Mr. Merriman[139] with Herbert as to the Basuto business: he fights hard as to terms, but is fairly reasonable on the whole . . . Letters & papers till near 6.00, when walk, & called on A.D. but she was ill.

Rosebery has resigned: the premier says, in a quite friendly spirit, & the official explanation is that the H. of C. wished to have an undersecretary who was not a peer: I imagine this was really little more than an excuse, that he got on badly with Harcourt, & thought he should improve his chances of promotion by cutting himself clear from a subordinate office. He wants the direction of Scotch business & the ostensible as well as the real control of it. He is very clever, very rich, & I fancy quite unscrupulous, so that he must be kept in good humour at whatever cost.

Meeting at St. James's Hall in favour of London municipal reform, Lubbock in the chair: a strong feeling was shown, & much disappointment that the bill is dropped: but I do now know how far this feeling is general. Out of 4 millions of people, it is easy to get a roomful who are enthusiastic about any public movement.

7 June 1883: . . . Talk with Granville about the Rosebery affair: he confirms my impression that the resignation is simply a strike for promotion, the state of Scotch business being an excuse. It seems that R. had strong promises, or what he construed as such, of being taken into the Cabinet after a short period of probation: he thinks the probation has lasted long enough, & claims a seat there as his due: the Premier, either having promised less than R. supposed, or having forgotten what he promised, or disliking to be pressed, is disposed to let him wait a little longer, & this R. resents as unfair usage.

I pressed strongly on G. the absurdity of the arrangement by which Spencer, while living in Ireland, is nominally retained in the Cabinet, which he never can attend: I thought that he ought to resign or, if that were thought likely to have an unfavourable effect on Irish opinion, that he should be considered as a sort of honorary member, not to be counted in the list of Lords as against Commoners: or, failing that, that another member of the H. of C. should be brought in to keep the balance even. G. listened to my argument, but did not seem convinced.

The successor to Ld R. is Hibbert[140]: a good choice: & a young Russell[141], nephew to the Duke, replaces him: said to be clever, & now a radical in opinion, but he will not be one always.

8 June 1883: Letter from F. Hopwood[142], asking for a post office appointment. I answer I will do what I can.

. . . Receive a deputation from some 20 Cape colonists, merchants & others, on the Basuto question: they were introduced by Sir D. Currie[143], & behaved sensibly, making only short speeches. I gave them an outline of what we intended to do, & sent them away satisfied.

H. of Lords, where a foolish violent speech from the D. of Rutland[144], against free trade & emigration, & urging a return to protection as the sole remedy for existing distress. It was listened to with a certain sort of amused interest, the speaker being evidently in earnest, & his opinions such as no other peer could support. Granville & Kimberley each said a few words, & Salisbury delivered a clever ambiguous speech, in which every sentence contradicted its predecessor: but it served the purpose of conciliating the Duke without committing the speaker to his views. . . .

9 June 1883 (Saturday): . . . Wrote to the Premier about negociations with the Transvaal. It is thought that he has lost much of his former influence with the House: which if true is due I think mainly to the habit he has acquired of talking about himself as on the point of retiring: people take his words more literally than he perhaps intends or wishes: and naturally conclude that there is nothing to be gained by following, or lost by opposing him.

How far he is disappointed with the results of his own policy will probably never be known, for he is not likely to tell, nor any one to ask him: but the Egyptian business cannot have been agreeable to his feelings, & the failure of his attempts to pacify Ireland is undeniable: though in that case it may fairly be contended that no other course would have answered better.

Goschen came into the Lords last night to speak to me, as he said, on a question of church property (he is one of the ecclesiastical commissioners). He said the clergy were now well disposed to take fixed money payments in lieu of land, & the commissioners were disposed to favour this arrangement, but some doubts were felt, & it was asserted that I had expressed a strong opinion as to the superiority of land over all other forms of investment. He wished to know if that was really my opinion? I said I drew a wide distinction between public and private property. If I wished to leave property to a friend or relative, it should be preferably in land, because ready money is always liable to be spent, whereas land is not sold or even mortgaged without some delay: and many people would hesitate before selling an estate who would have no scruple in selling out of the funds. But with public bodies the case was exactly reversed. It was not desirable, I thought, that they should hold land, which they lock up from private owners, & derive no residential advantage from, while they exclude buyers who would live on their estates.

On the other hand, the more of the public funds they held the better, both on account of the stock held by them never being thrown into the market, & so the value of it being kept up: & because of the facilities which stock held by public bodies gives for dealing with the Debt by way of terminable annuities. We discussed the matter, & it seemed to me that Goschen agreed in the general principles that I had laid down. He said what the clergy were now most anxious to buy was ground rents – as paying better than the funds, & less uncertain than the return from land. . . .

11 June 1883: London . . . I am quite curiously free from business – that is from business that requires to be done at once, for there is plenty in prospect.

H. of Lds, where found the fullest house of the year, the Deceased Wife's Sister Bill being on for second reading: Dalhousie opened the debate in a speech which though neatly delivered was not a good one, for he jumped over difficulties & begged the question in a manner which was peculiar: Cairns followed, effective as always, but he only went over the old familiar ground, adding nothing new, which indeed would have been difficult: Bramwell answered him, original in style & sometimes powerful in argument: he kept the peers thoroughly amused, but aimed rather too much at being funny, & was occasionally coarse: he spoke in an odd broken ungrammatical way, leaving sentences unfinished and arguments only half worked out: half of what he said would have been more persuasive than the whole: the new Archbishop[145] delivered his maiden speech, neither good nor bad: it seemed to be judged somewhat feeble & commonplace: Coleridge argued the case in his usual smooth strain, but not with much originality . . . The division was 165 to 158, a majority of 7 for the bill, which was not expected.

The P. of Wales & his brothers have caused some scandal by their exceedingly active canvass in favour of the bill, calling men to them & begging for their votes as a personal favour: which is thought unseemly: especially as personal motives are hinted at: but these may be purely imaginary.

The vote, not of much importance in any other respect, is felt as a blow by the High Church party: since the chief real objection to these marriages is founded, not on a doubtful interpretation of biblical words, but on the teaching & practice of the 'Catholic Church'. It is not certain that we have yet heard the last of the dispute, for the bill may be fought again on going into committee.

Home 8.30, quiet dinner.

12 June 1883: Office . . . saw there Sir T. Shepstone, who talked freely about South African matters, but did not help me much: he is still in favour of the policy of advance, & would keep Cetewayo in order, hold on to the Transvaal, etc.

H. of Lords . . . brought in a bill about transferring colonial prisoners from one colony to another . . . a fresh debate on the Mar peerage, in which Galloway was more violent than ever, so that the whole house laughed. He really has a craze on this particular question.

. . . M. not very well, I think from hot close weather, & exceedingly depressed in spirits, as she has been from time to time. But she knows the cause is bodily illness & that it will pass away again.

13 June 1883: Office at 12.00. Work there till 2.00. Then Cabinet 2.00 to 4.30. Office again till 6.00, when called on A.D. whom I found looking very ill & worn out.

Weighed at the Coffee Mill, 15 st. 4 lbs.: which is more than I can like, but office makes much exercise impossible.

In Cabinet, colonial affairs were chiefly discussed. The draft on Basuto affairs, to which Mr. Merriman, representing the Cape govt., had objected, was altered in one particular: I brought the subject of negociating with the Boers before my colleagues, & obtained their sanction to Lord Reay being employed, if he will accept: after which came a discussion on the proposal for annexing New Guinea.

I said it was impossible after the general expression of Australian feeling to put a stopper on the whole affair. Gladstone agreed, though saying he wished it could be stopped altogether. Northbrook & Granville both believed that there was no reality in the notion that any foreign power would establish itself in the island. Childers & Dilke agreed that, whether we like it or not, the annexation will come some day & in some shape. Childers agreed with the rest that the present demand must be refused, but thought the question immensely important, & that it might rouse a feeling in Australia for which we were not prepared. I observed that the Australians were loyal to the British connection, but only on condition they were not controlled, & that we helped them to get all they wanted. Harcourt objected to being dragged into an enterprise of this kind at the tail of any colony.

The Chancellor made a sort of speech, in which he talked of his conscience, thought the question not one of policy only. The proposed seizure of the island would be a crime, leading to the oppression & ultimate destruction of the natives, & he could not reconcile himself to it.

In the end we agreed to repudiate the annexation, but to word our refusal to sanction it in such a way as to leave the door open in the future.

Kimberley explained to us, for information, that Ripon has threatened to send in his resignation, on account of some very mild criticisms passed by the Council at home on one of his bills. He (R.) declares that he is surrounded by enemies, that everybody in India is against him – which as regards the European community is true – that the authorities at home do not support him – in short that he finds his position intolerable.

Kimberley says it is true the Council think he has gone too fast & too far – & Kimberley himself agrees: 'We are agreed, he & I, on the Afghan policy, & on nothing else.' But he is anxious to conciliate, & prevent a resignation. Hartington bears witness as to Ripon's extreme touchiness: 'He takes up schemes hotly, with little consideration, & cannot bear to have them criticised.'

Question of reduction of the army in Egypt. This was taken up, but at the end of the sitting, when several had left, & nothing was settled. It is now 5,000 to 6,000 strong: the Premier wants it reduced, Hartington strongly opposes. The former contends that it is wanted only as a symbol of British power: the latter that it ought to be stronger than the Egyptian army: which seems hard, as Egypt must pay for both. . . .

15 June 1883: Work at home till 11.00, when Lord Reay came: walked with him in the park, discussing South Africa. He presses for definite instructions, which without reference to the Cabinet I am not in a position to give: but the request is reasonable, as he must wish to know what his chances of success are likely to be. He offers to write to the Transvaal committee in Holland, whose president is an old friend: & thinks he can in this way get at the real mind of the Boers. He offers also to go over & make personal enquiries, but this I discourage, as it would attract too much notice. I left him more than ever convinced of his clearness of head & general ability.

. . . H. of Lords [where] Carnarvon opened the question of our relations with the Boers. He attacked them with great vehemence, speaking three-quarters of an hour: his speech if more moderate would have been less easy to answer: but he exaggerated their real misdoings so wildly that it was possible to dispute much of what he said without screening them unduly. He was civil enough to me personally, & to the government. I was about half an hour in reply, a pure debating speech for, as I did not know what he was going to say, I could not prepare: the style was therefore rough, but the argument I think sound.

Cranbrook took the occasion to beat the war drum violently speaking shortly, but with a degree of passion that is rare in our house: Kimberley answered him: Salisbury followed on the same side, with less warmth, though not less bitterness: Granville closed the debate. We had a thin house, not more than 50 or 60 present. All was over by 8.00 p.m.

The excitement of the opposition leaders was not shared by other peers for, of the small attendance named above, not half stayed to the end. The conclusion of the opposition, hardly disguised in their language, was that we ought not to lose the opportunity of making war on the Boers, & so wiping out the stain of our defeats in 1881. But this is not a view that will be popular in the country.

16 June 1883 (Saturday): Called on the Premier, to talk over the Reay business with him: Granville was there, & other subjects were discussed: among them one which is not urgent, though very important – whether in the bill dealing with the borough franchise next year anything should be done as to redistribution of seats, or whether that question should be relegated to the new parliament to deal with. The Premier threw out a hint that it might be enough to fill up the seats actually vacated for corruption, not attempting to touch redistribution at all. I forget how this discussion began . . .– I rather think, by some comments on a late speech delivered by Chamberlain at Birmingham, in which he has foolishly & recklessly pledged himself to universal suffrage, electoral districts, & payment of members.

It is true that he spoke in a vague way of a future possibly remote, & also that he did not profess to speak for anybody except himself: still the speech was not one that ought to have been made by a Cabinet minister, & it will do harm, by alienating the sympathy of moderate men.

Office: worked there till 4.30, when to station & to Keston.

The event of the week has been a function at Birmingham in honour of Bright, at which various meetings were held, & speeches made: one by Granville, clever, courteous, & conveying little definite meaning – another, referred to above, by Chamberlain: which is blamed as an error of taste even by those who agree in the substance of what was said, for they think that Chamberlain had no business to take the opportunity of putting himself forward as Bright's successor in the lead of the democracy, & that he seemed to be ostentatiously announcing: 'Bright is the man of the past: I am the man of the future.'

This is one of the results of Gladstone's age & of his repeatedly intimated intentions to retire: that some of his colleagues are beginning to make their plans for the future: which tends to disorganise a Cabinet. . . .

18 June 1883: London . . . M. left on a visit to Norris Castle[146] & for a day or two of yachting in the Solent.

Hale asks leave to buy 3 acres of land in Ormskirk, which I agree to . . .

Office . . . Deputation at 3.00, of about 50 persons, who came on the subject of state assistance to emigration. Sir Eardley Wilmot[147] & Lord Brabazon[148] were the leaders: several east end parsons (one of whom talked very sensibly) & some trades union leaders & agitators: one a secretary of some so-called 'Democratic Association' who proved his democracy by sprawling in a large armchair, with his legs in the air. This youth began an attack on employers generally, but the rest had the sense to hoot him down. Another of the party ranted about the impossibility of a poor man buying land: he also was ill received. The speakers were many, & short: except these two, they spoke to the purpose. I gave a vague answer: in fact I could give no other, pointing out that I was only one of a Cabinet, & that the question they raised was one for the government as a whole.

H. of Lords, where our chief business was a bill for the protection of young girls. Salisbury attacked Chamberlain's late speech, but did not raise a debate.

Into H. of C. where Northcote & the Irish had got up a quarrel with Bright, for something lately said at Birmingham, in which he accused the Irish & the Conservatives of being in league for purposes of obstruction. This was treated as a breach of privilege, & Northcote called attention to it, in courteous terms: doing what he had to do well enough, if it was worth doing at all. Cross supported Northcote, & O'Connor delivered a fierce harangue . . . Nothing came of it except a wasted evening . . . Business moves slowly, & things look as if even with our reduced programme obstruction would win: at least so far as to compel an autumn session. I was struck, & I hear other people are likewise, by the tone of general ill humour & even acrimony that seemed to prevail. – In the Lords, I see plenty of it in Salisbury & Cranbrook, but very little among the rank & file.

Dined with Sanderson at the Travellers'. I think him altered: his good spirits of old times gone: and little wonder: for he has a brother to support: with a mad wife & children: no prospect of their ever becoming independent: and, but for the £800 a year which I allow him, the household would have become insolvent before now. He is certain of an undersecretaryship if his health lasts: but it may not come for years, & meanwhile the pay is very small. He does not complain: but his former power – which I used to envy – of finding amusement in everything has left him.

19 June 1883: Walk with Sanderson. Luncheon at the club. Office 2.00 to 4.30. See there Lord Reay, & talk with him over a telegram just come in, according to which the President or Vice-President of the Transvaal State proposes to come over here to negociate. Ld R. thinks, & I incline to agree, that the Transvaal people having themselves proposed this method of treating it may be better to accept their offer than to send out a commissioner to them. I spoke later to Granville & Kimberley, who both took the same view.

Deputation of 14 or 15 West Indian planters, chiefly from Jamaica, on the labour question. They question the alleged great increase of the negro population, contending (which may be true) that the earlier censuses were imperfectly taken, owing to fear & suspicion on the part of the negroes. They do not deny that there is labour enough in quantity, but say that it is irregular, not to be relied upon, & inferior to that of coolies or Chinese.

. . . I see with regret that there are secessions from the Cobden Club, Ampthill & A. Russell being the chief. The dissentients say that it has become a purely party organisation, and some resent the introduction of Clemenceau, who is half a socialist, as an honorary member. I have declined to attend the dinner . . . not caring to support Chamberlain after his recent utterances.

20 June 1883: . . . Tried to see the Premier, but he had gone to a concert at Sydenham.

Sir P. Wodehouse[149] called, at his own request, to talk over South African matters: but he told me nothing that was of value. He indulged himself in congratulations on the prosperity of his own term of office: had considered Kafir wars as things of the past, etc. He said emphatically that in the quarrel with the Basutos all the fault had been on the side of the Europeans, or rather of the colonists, & seemed disposed to generalise on this, & to assume that it is always so.

He observed that the country reserved to natives, lying between Natal & the Cape, is the pleasantest & most fertile part of all South Africa: & inferred that trouble would continue, since the whites would never rest till they had got hold of these lands, & the present holders would never let them go till forced. Sir Philip seemed to me an honourable, straightforward, rather simple-minded sort of man: what he said sensible, but dull, & his conversation somewhat tedious.

City Commission . . . We made good progress with the report . . . Cross went the length of contending that corporate property stood on the same footing as private property, in regard to the right of parliament to interfere in it: a doctrine which I cannot accept, & which indeed was not supported to the full extent by any one else.

. . . Mr. Firth moved the dissolution of the companies, & the handing over of their property to official trustees: he had no supporter except the workingman M.P. Mr. Burt.

Found M. returned, in good spirits, & thoroughly revived, by two days at the seaside . . .

21 June 1883: Cleared off all papers & letters last night, & early this morning: so that (10.00 a.m.) I am clear of everything.

. . . Called on the Premier at 1.00, & talk to him & Granville about the offer of the Transvaal president to send an agent over here: which G. and I both prefer to our own original proposal of sending out a commissioner. The Premier doubts, but we agree that the matter shall be brought before the Cabinet on Saturday.

– He consulted me on another matter, of a peculiar & secret character. Cross (Sir R.) is an applicant for one of 4 pensions of £2,000 a year which by law are tenable by persons having served in certain high posts for 4 years, & being able to prove that they have not the necessary means for keeping up their rank as privy councillors. Cross claims this pension as a matter of right, a thing which he can claim, if he fulfils the statutory conditions, & in no way a favour: is he justified in so claiming it?

During 50 years no pension of this kind has been given by a minister to a political opponent: yet the statute certainly seems to place it on the same footing as the pensions of the permanent civil service, which are independent of party. The matter is farther complicated by the fact that young Northcote has hinted at a similar demand on the part of his father. I took away the papers, promising to consider them.

. . . Granville tells me the Queen, at the instigation of the princes, is pressing for Lorne to remain another year in Canada, and Ld Lansdowne's appointment to be postponed. This of course is impossible, the thing being now done & disposed of. The excuse alleged is that the princess wishes to remain another winter in the colony! which she notoriously hates, & has always been trying to get away from.

22 June 1883: Disposed of all business by 10.30 . . . Office early, & stayed there till late . . . Wrote a mem. for the Premier on the question of pensions. My conclusion was that political friends were undoubtedly entitled to priority of selection, but that, assuming none such to be qualified nor likely soon to be so, I did not think that members of the opposite party should be excluded. If anybody was placed in a false position, it was the member who applied under those circs., and not the minister, who had only to consider whether the application was reasonable in itself. As between Northcote & Cross, if either is to have it, I thought the claim of Cross the stronger.

He has no estate, or next to none, whereas Northcote succeeded to 6,000 acres: and he sacrificed a lucrative profession to go into public life, which Northcote did not. Moreover I doubted whether Northcote, though no doubt poor, is statutably qualified: in the case of Cross there can be no doubt that he is.

23 June 1883: . . . The Midland R. Co. is to pay me, or rather the trustees, £25,000 immediately, on account: the rest when conveyances are completed.

Cabinet at 12.00, sat till 12.30: then office till 4.00, when home, & was on the point of leaving with M. for Knowsley, when Drage called & absolutely forbade the journey, saying there was a good deal of fever (of which I was not aware) and that travelling would increase it. M. agreeing, I consented to stay in London, dined very lightly & early to bed. Temperature, Drage says, is 102 nearly: but it is odd that I felt no inconvenience.

At the Cabinet, Gladstone came late: he asked us to begin without him, but we would not. Some talk about a bill allowing new companies to pay interest out of capital, which hitherto has been forbidden. Chamberlain defends the relaxation, on three grounds: (1) The law as it stands is continually & easily evaded: (2) It practically shuts out small investors, as they cannot afford to lie out of their capital: (3) It is no part of the duty of the state to protect men against their own imprudence. Harcourt improved on this doctrine, saying that it was always good that new lines should be made, whether they pay or not. Selborne, Dodson, Kimberley, & I, oppose this view, & are against the change. In the end it was settled that the peers should do as they please.

Childers announced that he had secured part of the Ashburnham collection, which it was thought could not be got separately, for £45,000: which was agreed to. Harcourt mentioned that a man had written to him, offering to find the £20,000 difference between what Ld A. asks & what we are prepared to give – the compensation to be a baronetcy.

I stated the case of the Transvaal, & we agreed without dispute to drop the notion of sending out Ld Reay, & instead to accept the offer of the Transvaal authorities, & negociate here.

Much discussion followed as to the arrangement of H. of C. business, in which the peers took no part.

Carlingford complained bitterly, & I thought rather foolishly, of the conduct of the Lords committee on the Irish Land Act. Says they have picked out exceptional cases, received evidence which is not trustworthy, & generally made out a quite one-sided case. He admitted in subsequent conversation that some of the commissioners had been badly chosen. Hartington said bluntly they had given many very strange decisions: I expressed the same opinion more mildly: & I think it was generally agreed in, except by Harcourt, who declaimed against the Irish landlords, & would back up the commission right or wrong. . . .

25 June 1883: . . . I forgot to note on Saturday a discussion in Cabinet as to help to be given to tramways in Ireland. Childers was in favour of helping them by guaranteeing interest up to 2½%. He expressed an opinion, but only in a speculative way, in favour of buying up Irish railways as a whole. On this the Premier appealed to me, remembering the railway commission of 1866, & I stated the objections. Chamberlain was for buying: thought we were spending a good deal of money in Ireland to no purpose. Harcourt remarked on the enormous increase of expenditure that would follow. Childers cited Australian precedents. Carlingford thought it very important that money should be freely lent to the Irish but was vague as to the application. The Chancellor mentioned gross jobs that had arisen out of such loans.

The Premier said he was in favour of the state owning railways, but not of the state working them: he thought the system of guarantees dangerous, & that it had been pushed too far: if loans are to be offered for tramway purposes, the Act should be temporary, for three years only, & the amount limited: at the end of that time, the whole system ought to be reconsidered.

We had also a conversation on the Suez canal, but it was vague & inconclusive. It seems to be agreed that we shall work with Lesseps, help him to double the canal, help him to find the money, & in return insist on a reduction of charges, & on a larger share in the management. But I could not hear all that Childers, who brought the question on, said: & it seemed to me that, except Gladstone & Granville, few of us knew much about the matter.

26 June 1883: London . . . saw Drage . . . saw Lawson . . . He thinks . . . there is complete apathy in the public mind, that people do not really care about many bills being passed, though failure to pass them may produce bungling: he agreed with me that the Premier's perpetually repeated talk of retirement, though not taken seriously, weakens the concern: people think of the Cabinet as provisional, & speculate on what will come next. Did not see much harm in Chamberlain's late escapade: it was an indiscretion, but would soon be forgotten.

[The House of Lords] agreed without a division to negative the standing order which the H. of C. has passed, authorising payment of interest out of capital. Selborne, Salisbury, & Granville agreed in opposing it.

. . . Keston by 6.05 train.

27 June 1883: . . . Office: saw Meade: Herbert is in the gout: settled the New Guinea draft, which must go round the Cabinet.

. . . City Commission, where sat till 6.00. All present except the D. of Bedford, who, having sat with extreme patience through all the very tedious evidence, now stays away when our real work begins, & when a vote might turn the scale. We discussed resolutions & made good way: Cross & Ald. Cotton the chief opponents. Cross takes the line that corporate property stands on the same footing as private property, & that parliament has no more right, except in the case of extreme abuse, to alter the application of one than of the other. But in this doctrine he is not supported. Ld Coleridge is very active and useful. Sherbrooke from loss of memory is now quite inefficient: he forgets what has been done, says the same thing three times over in five minutes, etc. D. of Bedford stays away, whether purposely or from mere laziness I don't know. Rothschild began by going against the companies, but now sided with them: Sir S. Waterlow tries to mediate, advising concession on the part of the companies, & moderation on ours: James goes with the reformers: Burt & Firth would sweep away the companies altogether: I say no more than I must, as chairman, & try to keep the balance fairly.

28 June 1883: . . . Strange letter from my brother: his eldest son has been rejected as medically unfit for the army, & declared by the medical examiners to have one lung gone, & the other partly so: he was not satisfied, went to the war office, got a second board to sit on the boy, & this board reversed the judgment of the first: so that the immediate object is gained: but he does not know what to think of his son's health. There never was an idea of his having anything amiss before[150].

Walk: asked after J. Manners, & saw him: called on my brother, & heard his story. He is less uneasy than I expected, thinking the first board merely made a mistake. We talked with more cordiality than we have done since 1878.

Office: saw there the five Australian agents, who came to me with a gigantic scheme of annexation, including not only New Guinea, but the New Hebrides, Samoa, & in fact all the South Pacific within about 1,000 to 1,500 miles from the Australian coast. They were very much in earnest, said this was a turning point in the fortunes of Australia, the danger was imminent, any foreign settlement established near them would be their ruin. I asked more than once why or how? but could get no answer. I tried a little mild sarcasm, asking whether they did not want a whole planet to themselves, & talking of the western settler who complained of being crowded up because another man had established himself within a day's journey: but I found the matter too serious for joking: they could not think themselves safe in a country as big as Europe, if Italy or Germany had a harbour within three or four days' steaming of their shores. In the end I asked them to give me a memorial which I might lay before the Cabinet: & talked in the most exalted style of the future prospects of Australia, which were at least to equal those of the U.S. This they took quite as matter of course, & hardly as a compliment. I also dwelt on the facilities which confederation would give for dealing with questions of annexation: to which they agreed readily. They left me surprised, & puzzled at the wildness of their plans, and the quiet conviction which they expressed that we should do all they wanted.

H. of Lds, where short debate on the wife's sister, third reading: the bill was lost by 140 to 145 against. It seems that 20 Conservative peers had voted for the second reading, who were induced by their friends to stay away.

29 June 1883: . . . To Coutts to invest £2,000 in 4% Victoria bonds . . . I have now in all £440,000 invested: of which £40,000 in the colonies.

Saw Meade, & struck by the exceeding gloominess of his views on all colonial subjects. Herbert is in the gout.

H. of Lords at 4.30, where a tedious speech from Lord Strathnairn[151], hardly audible to any one . . . Then a bill for the protection of young girls, which has been through committee, but we had all that ought to have been discussion in committee over again on the report. Home about 9.00.

30 June 1883 (Saturday): . . . Saw Lawrence before leaving & agreed . . . to buy from Mr. Heseltine a stockbroker 17 acres of land touching mine at Witley, near the station, at the large price of £150 per acre. It is I believe quite worth the money to sell again or let for building, but it will not be a paying investment. Still I can afford it, & Witley is worth spending money on. . . .

Notes

[1]   Gambetta died at his home near Paris from the effects of a gunshot wound, 31 December 1882.

[2]   Francis, 9th E. of Wemyss (1796–1883), who succ. 1853.

[3]   Francis, 10th E. of Wemyss (1818–1914), eldest s. of 9th E.: styled Lord Elcho till 1883: leading Adullamite, 1866.

[4]   George Harry Grey, 7th E. of Stamford (1827–1883), who succ. his grandfather, 1845; twice married, he d. without issue, 2 Jan. 1883; worth £58,000 p.a.; hon. col., Lancs. Volunteers: a

Conservative: cricketer, racehorse owner, and Master of the Quorn Hounds 1856–1863; contemporary of Derby at Trinity.

[5] G.F. Lyster, C.E., engineer (1821–1899), engineer-in-chief to Liverpool and Birkenhead Dock Estate, 1861–89.

[6] Sir Robert G.W. Herbert (1831–1905), permanent under-sec. at the Col. Office, 1871–1892: educ. Eton and Balliol: first premier of Queensland 1860–65.

[7] (Sir) John Bramston: s. of T.W. Bramston, DL, MP South Essex 1835–65: educ. Winchester and Balliol 1850–1854: Fellow of All Souls, 1855: barrister, 1857: assistant under-sec. for cols., 1876–78: acting judge, Hong Kong, 1874: career in Queensland politics, 1859–1873: kt 1897.

[8] (Sir) Edward Wingfield (1834–1910): educ. Winchester and New Coll. (fellow 1850–1872), barrister 1859: colonial assistant under-sec., 1878–1897, permanent under-secretary 1897–1900: m dau. of Archdeacon of Gloucester.

[9] Richard Powney Ebden (1833–1896), educ. Huntingdon Sch. and Christ's 1852–1856: entered C.O. 1858: assistant senior clerk 1866: chief clerk 1879: priv. sec. to Lord Blachford 1864–1866.

[10] Sir Robert Henry Meade (1835–1898), assistant under-sec. in col. office 1871–1892: educ. Eton and Exeter Coll: permanent under-secretary 1892–96: cf Luke Trainor, *Robert Meade 1835–98* (priv. pr. 1976).

[11] Hon. Anthony Ashley (1836–1907), biographer of, and secretary to, Palmerston; 2nd s. of Lord Shaftesbury; minor office 1880–1882, under-sec. for colonies May 1882–1885; M.P. (Lib.) Isle of Wight 1880–1885 (defeated): educ. Harrow.

[12] See *Parl. Deb.*, 3, vol. cclxxiii, cols. 1803–1804, 1805–1807 (15 Aug. 1882), when Kimberley announced the partial restoration of Cetewayo, then in England, to Zululand, which was to be divided between 13 appointed Chiefs, and Cetewayo's portion, with a British Resident to be maintained in the country.

[13] (Sir) Reginald Laurence Antrobus (1853–1942), educ. Winchester and New Coll. 1872–1876, s. of Rev. George Antrobus of Withyam, Sussex: served in Colonial Office 1877–1909: Crown Agent for the Colonies 1909–18. Antrobus's father was for 15 years curate to Mary Derby's brother.

[14] Sir Andrew Clark was at Hawarden, 7–8 Jan. 1883.

[15] Sir Richard Burton (1821–1890), explorer and translator; consul at Trieste, 1872–1890.

[16] Gladstone left for Wolverton's villa at Cannes, 17 Jan., returning to Downing St. on 2 March.

[17] Samuel Smith (1836–1906), M.P. (Lib.) Liverpool 1882–1885, Flintshire 1886–1905; bimetallist, opponent of the opium trade, philanthropist.

[18] The U.S. had just acquired the use of Pearl Harbour.

[19] Sir Henry Ernest Bulwer (1836–1914): educ. Trinity: colonial service 1859–1892: Lt.-Gov. of Natal 1875–1880: Gov. of Natal and Commr. for Zulu Affairs 1882–1885: High Commr. in Cyprus 1885–1892: nephew of Salisbury's mother.

[20] Fire destroyed most of the business quarter of Kingston, Jamaica, 11–13 Dec. 1882.

[21] Secretary of the Commission.

[22] Sir Alexander Galt (1817–1893), Canadian finance minister 1867–1872: Canadian high commissioner in England, 1880–1883.

[23] George Hudson (1839–1900), Cape civil servant: civil commissioner at Kimberley 1878–1880, Colonial Sec. of the Transvaal Feb. 1880–Aug.1881, British Resident in Transvaal Aug. 1881–1884: on conclusion of London Convention returned to police work at Kimberley.

[24] Not traced.

[25] Sir George F. Bowen (1821–1899), academic and governor: gov. of Hong Kong 1882–1887 (retired): Fellow of Brasenose, 1844, and president of Univ. of Corfu, 1847–51.

[26] *Née* Lady Elizabeth Sackville West, eldest dau. of 5th E. De La Warr, and Lady Derby's sister. The Duchess d. 1897.

[27] Hastings Russell, 9th Duke of Bedford (1819–1891).

[28] Sir Neale Porter (d. 1905), Colonial Secretary, Leeward Is., 1883–1887, Jamaica, 1887–1895: Kt, 1894: possibly author of *The Army of India Question* (1860).

[29] Prince Napoleon was arrested and imprisoned, 16 Jan. 1883, for publishing a manifesto abusing the Republic.

[30] Baron Mohrenheim: 'The only man I have seen whose capacity of boring was too much for the patience of Lord Granville' (Derby diary, 14 Feb. 1883).

[31] Dr. George T. Gream, possibly the author of *Remarks on the diet of children: and the distinction between the digestive powers of the infant and the adult* (London, 1847). Gream, who resided at Upper Brook Street and evidently prospered, was an uncle of the Antrobus family.

[32] Sir Anthony Musgrave (1828–1888), colonial governor 1864–1888; gov. of Jamaica 1877–1888, of Queensland 1888.

[33] Lord Sackville Cecil, Derby's stepson.

[34] Sir R. Alcock (1809–1897), diplomatist in Japan and China, 1858–1871: kt 1862: pres. of Geographical Soc. 1876–78: publ. many works on Japan.

[35] Sir James R. Longden (1827–1891), colonial governor 1865–1883: gov. of Ceylon, 1876–1883.

[36] Sir Andrew Clarke (1824–1902), military engineer and imperial official: director of engineering at Admiralty, 1864–1873; gov. of Straits Settlements, 1873–1875; head of Public Works Dept. in India, 1877–1880.

[37] Sir John Pope-Hennessy (1834–1891), Irish M.P.(Cons.) 1859–65: colonial governor 1867–1889: gov. of Mauritius 1883–1889: M.P. Kilkenny 1890–1891 as anti-Parnellite home ruler: R.C., and the first R.C. Cons. M.P.

[38] Lyulph Stanley, 4th Baron Stanley of Alderley (1839–1925), M.P. (Lib.) Oldham 1880–1885.

[39] William O'Brien, editor of *United Ireland*, defeated Naish, solicitor-general, by 166 to 80.

[40] Not traceable in standard works of reference.

[41] Chief Justice Sir Bruce Burnside, formerly Att-Gen. of the Bahamas, then Queen's Advocate in Ceylon from 1879: much at odds with his fellow Scot, the Governor Sir A. Gordon: his son became a Supreme Court judge in Australia. See Dr. A.R.B. Ameresinghe, *The Supreme Court of Srilanka.*

[42] Sir Edward Newton (1832–1897), colonial secretary, Mauritius, 1859–1863: colonial secretary, 1868–1877, and Lieutenant-Governor and Colonial Secretary, Jamaica, 1877–1883.

[43] Not traced.

[44] Lt.-gen. Sir Lewis Pelly (1825–1892): educ. Rugby: M.P. (Cons.) Hackney N. 1885–death.

[45] Eugenie's startling visit to Paris, 22 Jan. 1883, had not calmed matters.

[46] Lady Dartrey, whose name is the only one in the diaries, family apart, to be regularly represented by initials (or by discreet references to her London home in Curzon St.).

[47] Sir Henry Barkly (1815–1898), M.P. (Peelite) 1845–1848: colonial governor 1848–1877, including Cape Colony 1870–1877. His son became governor of the Falklands and of Heligoland.

[48] Not traceable in standard works of reference.

[49] Sir George Bowyer (1811–1883), lawyer: Irish M.P. 1852–1868, 1874–1880.

[50] Presumably Sir Samuel Rowe (1835–1888), originally an army surgeon: successively gov. of Gambia, Sierra Leone, W. Africa, and Gold Coast and Lagos, 1876–1881.

[51] Not traceable in standard works of reference.

[52] Perhaps Sir George Welsh Kellner, assistant paymaster of Supreme Court of Judicature, who d. 1886.

[53] Sir Walter Joseph Sendall (1832–1904), educ. Christ's (1st in Classics): civil servant in Ceylon 1860–1872 (director of education 1870–1872): U.K. poor law inspector 1873–1878, assistant sec. of Local Govt. Board 1878–1885: gov. of Windward Is. 1885–1889, Barbados 1889–1892, Cyprus 1892–1898, Br. Guiana 1898–1901.

[54] Sir Walter Francis Hely-Hutchinson (1849–1913), 2nd s. of Richard, 4th E. of

Donoughmore (1823–1866): barrister, 1877: priv. sec. to Sir H. Robinson when Gov. of N.S. Wales, 1874–1877: col. sec. of Barbados 1877–1883: chief sec., then lt.-gov., of Malta 1884–1889: gov. of Windward Is. 1889–1893: Gov. of Natal and Zululand 1893–1901: Gov. of Cape 1901–1910: High Commissioner for S. Africa June–Sept. 1909.

55   Henry Thynne Lascelles, 4th E. of Harewood (1824–1892), who succ. his father 1857.

56   Not in *Dictionary of South African Biography*.

57   Hartmann Wolfgang Just, e.s. of Heinrich Just of Bristol, gent.: educ. Bristol Grammar Sch.: matric. 1873 aged 19: scholar of Corpus, Oxon., 1873–1878: B.A. 1877: not mentioned by diarist further.

58   Sir Thomas Fowell Buxton, 3rd Bt (1837–1915), educ. Trinity: succ. father of same name 1858: M.P. (Lib.) King's Lynn 1865–1868: gov. of S. Australia 1895–1898.

59   Henry Reeve (1813–1895), man of letters: edited *Edinburgh Review*, 1855–1895, and *Greville Memoirs*, 1865–.

60   Sir H.B. Loch, 1st Baron Loch of Drylaw (1827–1900), governor of Isle of Man 1863–1882: gov. of Cape 1889–1895: cr. peer, 1895.

61   Albert Edmund Parker, 3rd E. of Morley (1843–1905), who succ. his father 1864: under-sec. for war 1880–1885, 1st Commissioner for Works Feb.–Apr. 1886: chairman of committees, House of Lords, 1889–1905.

62   George Stovin Venables (1810–1888), journalist and fellow of Jesus, Cambridge: barrister, 1836–1882: contributor to *Saturday Review*, 1855, and *Times*, 1857–1888: friend of Tennyson.

63   John David FitzGerald, Lord FitzGerald of Kilmarnock (1816–1885, when title extinct), M.P. Ennis 1852–1860, judge 1860–1882.

64   Sir John Henry Lefroy (1817–1890): army career to 1870: gov. of Bermuda 1871–1877: gov. of Tasmania 1880–1882.

65   Reginald Bosworth Smith, *Life of Lord Lawrence*, 2 vols., 1883: reached 7th ed. by 1903.

66   John George Lambton, 3rd E. of Durham (1855–1928), succ. father 1879.

67   Donald James Mackay, 11th Baron Reay (1839–1921), cr. U.K. baron 1881: b. The Hague, educ. Leyden: gov. of Bombay 1885–1890: under-sec. for India 1894–1895: first president of the British Academy 1902–1907.

68   Charles Shaw-Lefevre, 1st Vt Eversley (1794–1888), Speaker 1839–1857: cr. Vt, 1857.

69   i.e. Gladstone (then at Cannes) and Spencer in Dublin. Gladstone was absent 17 Jan.–2 Mar. 1883.

70   James Carey, the Dublin builder and town councillor, appeared in court as an informer on 17 Feb. 1883, but disappointed the authorities in that his evidence led to no new arrests and did not implicate any well known names. See T.H. Corfe, *The Phoenix Park Murders* (1968), 246.

71   F.H.O. O'Donnell (1848–1916), M.P. (Home Rule) Dungarvan June 1877–1885 (retired): Vice-Pres. and Hon. Sec. of Irish Home Rule Confederation of Great Britain: a Fair Trader and Imperialist: opposed Home Rule, 1886: his brother made a district commissioner in Bengal by Churchill.

72   Sir H.W. Norman (1826–1904), Indian official: member of viceroy's council 1870–1877, resigning over Lytton's forward policy: member of Council of India 1878–1883: general 1882: gov. of Jamaica 1883–1889 and of Queensland 1889–1895: declined viceroyalty 1893.

73   A.M. Broadley (1847–1916), lawyer: practised as advocate in Tunis, 1873: represented Bey against France: *Times* correspondent in Tunis and Egypt, 1881–1882: senior counsel of Arabi, 1882: advocate at French bar, 1883, by presidential decree: prolific author.

74   Sir Augustus Paget (1823–1896), minister (1867–1876) and ambassador (1876–1883) to Italy, ambassador at Vienna, 1884–1893.

75   Sir Robert Adair, Baron Waveney of South Elmham (1811–1886), when the title became extinct: a senior Freemason: M.P. (Lib.) Cambridge: cr. peer, 1873.

76   Robert Bermingham, 4th E. of Leitrim (1847–1892), who succ. his murdered uncle, Apr. 1878: formerly a lieut. R.N.

[77] Wife of Lady Derby's brother Col. West, the land agent resident in N. Wales.

[78] Boer freebooters were attempting to expand the western frontier of the Transvaal by taking part in the quarrels of native chiefs, 1883–1885.

[79] Sir Henry Thring, 1st and only Baron Thring (1818–1907), counsel to the Home Office 1861–1869: parliamentary counsel to the government 1869–1886: cr. peer Aug. 1886: m. Cardwell's sister.

[80] Gladstone met the French President, Prime Minister, and Foreign Minister while passing through Paris.

[81] Col. King-Harman won Co. Dublin by 1,086 over a Parnellite, while at Portarlington, with only 138 voters on the register; the Parnellite lost by 13.

[82] Charles Dalton Clifford Lloyd (1844–1891), Irish R.M.: suppressed Land League in Limerick 1881–1883, Egyptian official 1883–1884 (resigned), later gov. of Mauritius 1885–1887: consul for Kurdistan 1889–91: d. Erzeroum, 1891.

[83] Thomas Archer (1823–1905), Queensland pioneer: agent-general for the colony in London Nov. 1881–May 1884 and 1888–1890. Owned a sheep station in central Queensland, but spent much of his life in London, Norway, and Scotland: father of William Archer, the influential dramatic critic.

[84] Edward Gibson, Lord Ashbourne (1837–1913), lord chancellor of Ireland 1885–1886, 1886–1892, 1895–1905.

[85] Lord Bramwell (1808–1892), judge: lord justice 1876–1881, cr. peer 1882.

[86] Forster had been the object of several murder attempts: Burke had been murdered: Lawson had been set upon by a gang of Invincibles: Field had been stabbed seven times by Brady. All had been held up to execration and in effect designated as targets by nationalist politicians.

[87] Cf. Samuel Murray Hussey, *The Reminiscences of an Irish Land Agent . . . Compiled by Home Gordon, etc.* (London, Duckworth, 1904).

[88] See P.M. Mutibwa, *The Malagasy and the Europeans: Madagascar's Foreign Relations, 1861–1895* (1974), p. 248 *et seq.* The French cabinet decided to use force against Madagascar on 6 Feb. 1883, although English and Protestant influence was dominant there.

[89] Cf. below, 7 Apr. 1883.

[90] Charlotte de la Trémoille, wife of James 7th E. of Derby: the heroine of a famous siege of Lathom in the Civil War. Her husband was beheaded, 1651.

[91] William Addington, 3rd Vt Sidmouth (1824–1913), succ. his father 1864: estates worth £8,000 p.a.

[92] (Sir) F.A. Abel (1827–1902), chemist: chief official authority on explosives: invented cordite, 1889: bart., 1893.

[93] Minister in Washington.

[94] Sabine Baring Gould, *Germany . . .* (Sampson Low, London, 1883): reached 8th ed. by 1905.

[95] Result: CONS. 4,214, LIB. 3,592; Cons. majority up from 336 (1880) to 822.

[96] Prince Leopold, Duke of Albany (1853–28 Mar. 1884), 4th s. of Queen Victoria: married, 1882, and left issue, who after the death of his brother (formerly Alfred Duke of Edinburgh) in 1900, became reigning princes of Saxe-Coburg-Gotha.

[97] Lady F. Dixie (d. 1905) was dau. of 7th Marq. of Queensberry and sister of the 8th Marq. She m. Sir Alexander Dixie, 1875.

[98] Herbrand Russell, 11th Duke of Bedford (1858–1940), who succ. his bro. the 10th Duke on his early death in 1893.

[99] J.A. Froude, *Letters and memorials of Jane Welsh Carlyle* (1883).

[100] Lady Julia Duncan, Lady of the Bedchamber to Queen Victoria 1874–1885: only dau. of Adam, 2nd E. of Camperdown (1812–1867) and sister of 3rd Earl: m. 1858 George, 4th Baron Abercromby (b. 1838, succ. 1852): a source of court gossip.

[101] Arnold, (Sir) Arthur (1833–1902), progressive publicist: organiser of Mill's memorial: chairman of L.C.C. 1895–97: author, *History of the Cotton Famine.*

[102] *Parl. Deb.*, *3*, vol. 277, cols. 1118–1152. No vote was taken, fewer than 40 members being present. At no time were more than 13 Liberal M.P.s present.

[103] Peter Rylands (1820–1887), ironmaster, banker, Mayor of Warrington 1853–1854: M.P. (Lib.) Warrington 1868–1874 (defeated), stood at S.E. Lancs. 1874 (defeated), M.P. Burnley Feb. 1876–Feb. 1887 (LU from 1886).

[104] Dr. Bernard Gallagher was charged with treason-felony over an alleged attempt to blow up Parliament and Scotland Yard, at Bow St., 19 Apr. 1883.

[105] John O'Connor Power (1846–1919), Lib. and H.R. M.P. Mayo 1874–1885 (retired).

[106] Cf. above, 12 Mar. 1883.

[107] Sir George Errington, Bt. (1839–1920), R.C., Lib., and H.R. (1874–1881): M.P. co. Longford 1874–1885 (retired): stood for Lancs. (Newton division,), 1886: cr. bt. July 1885.

[108] Col. the Hon. Sir W.P.M. Talbot (1817–1898), the diarist's brother-in-law, and serjeant-at-arms of the House of Lords 1858–1898: kt 1897.

[109] Rev. George Butler (1819–1890), principal of Liverpool College 1866–1882: canon of Winchester, 1882: never a Dean: husband of Josephine Butler the agitator.

[110] No article fits the bill exactly, but Lord Salisbury's 'Ministerial Embarrassments', *Quarterly Review*, Apr. 1881, pp. 535–567, perhaps comes nearest. There are also various polemics by L.J. Jennings.

[111] The Sand River Convention (1852) established the Transvaal as an independent state, called the South African Republic. In 1854, in a different sequence of events, the Orange River Sovereignty became the Orange Free State.

[112] Sir Julius Vogel (1835–1899), Premier of New Zealand: resigned premiership, 1876, and came to London as N.Z. agent-general: resigned as agent-general, 1884, returning to N.Z.

[113] Wilfred Powell, author of 'Visits to Eastern and Northeastern Coasts of New Guinea', *Proceedings of the Royal Geographical Society*, vol. V (new series), 1883, and *Wanderings in a Wild Country: or, three years among the cannibals of New Britain* (Sampson Low, 1883: German ed., 1884). I am indebted to Dr. Pam Sharpe for assistance with this reference. Cf. Donald Craigie Gordon, *The Australian Frontier in New Guinea, 1870–1885* (Columbia U.P., 1951).

[114] Sir G. Wolseley had defeated Arabi's forces by land at Tel-El-Kebir, while Frederick Paget, first Baron Alcester (1821–1895), a dandy known as 'the Swell of the Ocean', had the easier task of bombarding Alexandria.

[115] See above, 21 Mar. 1883.

[116] *Parl Deb.*, *3*, vol. 278, col. 1192 (for the six lines from Lucretius).

[117] Frederick T. Frelinghuysen (1817–1885), U.S. sec. of state Dec. 1881–Mar. 1885: negotiated naval base at Pearl Harbour.

[118] Sir Stephen Hill (1809–1891), colonial governor: army career 1823–1849, gov. of Gold Coast 1851–1854, gov. of Sierra Leone 1854–1859, 1860–1862 (leaving his son as acting gov.), gov. of Leeward Is. 1863–1869, gov. of Newfoundland 1869–1876 (retired): kt 1874.

[119] Richard O'Shaughnessy M.P. (1842–?), b. Limerick: educ. Clongowes Wood: called to Irish bar, 1866: M.P. Limerick City (Lib./H.R.) 1874–1883, when resigned on accepting office as Registrar of Sessions Clerks.

[120] Bonny is in the Niger Delta area, Porto Novo lay on the eastern edge of Dahomey.

[121] Lewis Clifford, 9th Baron Clifford of Chudleigh (1851–1916), who succ. his father 1880: an R.C.

[122] Sir Frederick Weld (1823–1891), colonial governor: N.Z. Premier 1864–1865, gov. of Straits Settlements 1880–1887: returned to England 1887: educ. Stonyhurst.

[123] Sir Charles Tupper, 1st bart. (1821–1915), Canadian politician: Canadian high commissioner in London 1884–1896: Premier of Canada Apr.–June 1896.

[124] James Moncrieff, 1st Baron Moncrieff (1811–1895), Scottish M.P. 1851–1869: lord advocate 1851–1858, 1859–1866, 1869–1899: lord justice clerk 1869–1888: cr. peer, 1874.

[125] Not traced: perhaps written in error by diarist for Mapoch (see n. 138 below)?

[126] Sir J.A. Macdonald (1815–1891), first Premier of Canada.

[127] Herbrand Arthur Russell, 11th Duke of Bedford (1858–1940), who succ. his brother, 1893.

[128] Lady Russell, *née* Lady Frances Elliot, and her only dau., Lady Mary Agatha Russell.

[129] *Leaves from the diary of Henry Greville* [1832–1872], ed. by Alice Byng, Viscountess Enfield, 4 vols., 1883–1905.

[130] Hungerford Crewe, 3rd Baron Crewe (1812–1894), who died unm., his title becoming extinct.

[131] A port on the coast of Dahomey.

[132] The lowering of the Wellington equestrian statue of 1846, prior to its removal, was begun on 24 Jan. 1883, and its future long remained a subject on the cabinet agenda.

[133] Party meeting on the state of business. Gladstone announced that the London bill would be dropped, and the Agricultural and Corrupt Practices bills pursued. Gladstone described the meeting as 'very good'.

[134] Diarist's brother.

[135] Cf. below, 10 Sept. 1883, for Maxse's death.

[136] William Drogo Montagu, 7th Duke of Manchester (1823–1890).

[137] Fawcett had been pronounced convalescent, 23 Dec. 1882, after a long and dangerous illness.

[138] Mapoch, an African chief to the west of the Transvaal, was defeated by the Boers, who blew up his stronghold (7 Feb.), induced him to sue for peace (Apr.), and forced his general to surrender (10 July). His tribe was then hired out to Boer farmers as farm workers, and Mapoch was sentenced to life imprisonment.

[139] John X. Merriman (1841–1926), politician: in Cape cabinet 1875–1877, 1877–1878, 1881–1884, 1890–1893, 1898–1900: Cape Premier 1908–1910.

[140] Sir J.T. Hibbert (1824–1908), politician: M.P. (Lib.) Oldham 1862–1874, 1877–1885, 1892–1895: held minor office in Gladstone's four administrations: poor law reformer.

[141] G.W.E. Russell (1853–1919), y.s. of Lord Charles Russell M.P., the 6th s. of the 6th D. of Bedford: M.P. (Lib.) Aylesbury 1880–1885, N. Beds. 1892–1895: minor office 1883–1885, 1892–1894, 1894–1895.

[142] Probably Rev. Frank George Hopwood, rector of Winwick (a Derby family living) and canon of Chester, who d. 11 Mar. 1890, leaving issue. He had m. Ellinor Mary Stanley, dau. of 13th E. of Derby, in 1835.

[143] Sir Donald Currie (1825–1909), shipowner: founder of Union-Castle Line, 1900.

[144] Charles Manners, 6th Duke of Rutland (1815–1888), styled Lord Granby till 1857: eldest son of 5th Duke: succ. by his brother Lord John Manners.

[145] Dr. Benson (1829–1896), archbishop 1882–1896.

[146] The D. of Bedford's house, recently bought, in the Isle of Wight.

[147] Sir J.E. Eardley-Wilmot (1810–1892), judge 1852–1871: M.P. (Cons.) Warwickshire S. 1874–1885.

[148] Perhaps Sir Reginald Brabazon, later 12th Earl of Meath (b. 1841, succ. father 1887), is meant.

[149] Sir Philip Edmond Wodehouse (1811–1887), colonial governor: served in Ceylon, British Honduras, British Guiana: gov. of Cape, 1861–1870: declared Basutos British subjects, 1868: opposed responsible govt.: gov. of Bombay, 1872–1877.

[150] The army was right. The youth was to die soon after of consumption.

[151] Sir Hugh Rose, 1st baron Strathnairn (1801–1885), Indian mutiny hero: c.-in-c. Ireland 1865–1870: cr. peer 1866, field-marshal 1877.

July–December

3 July 1883: Received from Lawrence what I had asked for, a statement of the acreage & cost of the Witley estates. They are 2,088 acres: or, with the addition now in progress, 2,105: the cost £118,200, to which £2,500 must now be added. . . .

4 July 1883: Judging by the newspapers, I gather that our decision not to annex New Guinea at the present time (for it is really only a question of doing the thing now or later) has satisfied the public: it will not please the Australians, but that can't be helped, & they have no right to claim that we shall seize on strange & unknown countries for their benefit.

5 July 1883: I passed this day quietly at Keston with M. We walked together in Holwood, & sat about in the garden as we did 13 years ago. Despatches in the morning, & a messenger in the afternoon, interfered a little with our holiday, but not much. We went late to see a family of hawkers who had managed to set fire to their van, with the result of destroying it, & burning one of their children badly. We gave them £3.

News in the evening papers of the sudden death of the Duke of Marlborough[1]: aged only 61, & after no previous illness: but it seems he had been something of an invalid, & had an affection of the heart. He must have died while getting into bed, & probably without suffering. He was found dead in the morning. He is one of those men who, being perfectly inoffensive, & useful according to the measure of his capacity, will be missed & regretted for a time. He had no conspicuous or shining ability, but in ordinary matters a fair share of sense. He spoke seldom, & then not with much force, but to the purpose. In all ecclesiastical matters he was biased by his strong pietistic tendencies: which were probably sincere, & rather needlessly obtruded on the world. As a landlord he was unpopular, not by his fault: being much encumbered with debt, he could not do for his tenants all that tenants in the present day expect.

His loss will be felt by those who have to do with the family, for his successor, Lord Blandford[2], though not without talent, is thoroughly disreputable: & probably more or less mad, which he has a right to be in virtue of his mother's descent[3]. – Randolph Churchill has more brains, but scarcely more character: his violence of language exceeds the usual licence of public speech, & he is not trusted by anybody. Indeed the more vehement radicals are half disposed to claim him: recognising justly that in his so-called toryism there is nothing conservative. And the same language is held about his brother, who affects democratic principles, but is thought to have taken that line chiefly out of opposition to his father.

6 July 1883: London by usual train . . . Saw Drage, who orders a tonic, as I am not feeling very well, though with no definite complaint. . . . To the Lords . . . Walked home with Kimberley, discussing South Africa: work at home till near 8.00 . . .

. . . Read the emigration returns of 1882, from which it appears that we have sent out 280,000 persons last year, not including foreigners on their way through. This is the largest outflow ever known, greater than that of 1852–1853, after the Irish famine. That without this kind of relief over-population would cause distress, discontent, possibly even revolution, is admitted on all hands: but it is more open to doubt whether the relief is permanent. The gaps fill up at once: & if the loss of a quarter of a million hands yearly is in some sense a gain (since there is not work for them to do) it is unluckily not always or often the right sort who go. The more timid & helpless stay at home: the best leave us: & the cream of our working population is being perpetually skimmed off. On the other hand, those who emigrate, by their activity & energy, are precisely those who would least willingly endure the superiority of the richer classes: so that there is a certain compensation.

7 July 1883 (Saturday): Work at home till near 12.00: then to Cabinet, which sat till 3.15. Office till past 5.00, when to Keston . . . Quiet evening.

At the Cabinet, we began with some informal talk as to sanitary precautions in Egypt, where the cholera is spreading, & public alarm is great. Nothing was settled as well as I could make out.

Then Childers followed with a narrative of his negociations with Lesseps as to the Suez canal. He wants some concession made to the French with regard to the rates which they are to be allowed to charge. Chamberlain objected, saying that the dividends of the company are enormous, & that the French will give way if we are firm. Gladstone thought our shipowners ought to be content with a moderate reduction, & that the investors who had taken the risk had a right to large profits. Granville & Dilke thought we ought to give a stiff answer, but leave the door open for negociation. Dilke said that Lesseps had come over expressly to negociate with us, & would not be satisfied to go back with a failure. Kimberley told Childers he was too much inclined to yield, & that he ought to fall back on his colleagues, & say he could concede nothing without leave from the Cabinet. In the end we left it pretty much to his (C.'s) discretion.

The Premier then raised the question of what bills are to be dropped & what proceeded with. We went through the names of 15 or 16 bills, & sacrificed nearly all: keeping alive: (1) Corrupt Practices, (2) Tenants' Compensation, (3) National Debt, (4) Sunday Closing Bills – all or some, (5) Naval Discipline bill, as I understand: Northbrook pressing strongly for it. We were disposed to sacrifice the Sunday closing bills, but Harcourt pleaded for them strongly, saying we could not afford to alienate the temperance party, which was the most important section of the Liberal party. Chamberlain took exception at this, & seemed to think it only a small section. The National Debt bill was in danger, but I pleaded very earnestly for it, backing up Childers, & the Premier joined: but there is much doubt of its passing.

We had a sharp little discussion on the question whether government departments should be liable to pay inventors who have patents – in other words, whether patents shall be valid as against the state: Chamberlain contended strongly for the principle that they should, on the ground of fairness: I supported him, but was almost alone: Kimberley, Hartington, Northbrook, took the opposite side: Childers said sensibly that he was not afraid of the claims of real inventors, but did fear sham inventors. Granville thought the whole system rotten from top to bottom. We talked for some time, but came to no clear conclusion.

I stated the case of Zululand, & got leave to protect the reserve against Cetewayo if necessary: subject only to this proviso, that we are not to take any step that may seem to indicate an intention of annexing the territory. In short we are to protect the people, but it is not to be a protectorate.

I accepted this rather vague indication of my colleagues' opinion – in fact there is scarcely an option, for having said that Cetewayo was not to have this territory six months ago we can scarcely let him take it now.

8 July 1883 (Sunday): . . . Read an article by the new D. of Marlborough in the *Fortnightly* on present politics: the conclusion from which is that he has been thoroughly alarmed, as was likely, by Labouchere's late pamphlet[4], & is anxious to show that his radicalism does not go as far as was supposed. It is quite possible that with no motive to take the Liberal side (which it was thought he did mostly to spite his father) he may return to the Conservatives.

9 July 1883: London by usual train, with M. St. J. Square about 10.50. Work at home till 2.00, then office . . . H. of Lords at 4.30. Elcho, or rather Wemyss, then took the opportunity of making a long speech on the militia, which led to a general debate on the state of the army, & in the end to a division. Cranbrook & Bury condemned the resolution, & voted with us . . . Morley made an excellent speech, clear & conclusive to my mind . . . The military party, which in our house is strong, voted against the two front benches, & beat us, 29 to 26. But nothing can come of the division, & its importance is null.

Elcho is to me a curious study: he is 65, has suffered family losses & troubles, & on the whole his political life cannot be described as a success: yet he is younger in his ways than most men of 30, and the air of self-satisfaction with which he lays down the law, & then looks round for applause, must be seen to be appreciated. In fact, though far from being stupid or a fool, he is a coxcomb: and the good humoured sense of superiority with which he addresses the Lords, or indeed any other audience, is comic to see. He has suffered, I think, in the serious competition of life by his remarkable good looks, which he has kept even to the present day: they made him a universal favourite with women in youth, & increased a natural tendency to conceit which has been his chief obstacle.

I went into the Commons, & heard part of Gladstone's statement about the course of business: which was listened to, as it seemed to me, with little interest: in fact the House looked apathetic & fagged. The hot weather has done its usual work: political passion is to all appearance dead, & not likely to revive till next year.

10 July 1883: Up early, much work before breakfast. Walk 9.30 to 11.00, a new fashion with me, but better in this hot weather. Work at home 11.00 to 1.30 . . . at 2.00, to office.

Saw Mr. Gabbett[5], an Irish Home Rule member, but a gentleman: who wants a place, being as he says ruined. I gave him fair words, but no promise.

Wrote to the Prime Minister, proposing to lengthen Ld Normanby's[6] term at Victoria for another year, for 3 reasons: (1) He is exceptionally popular: (2) He has been disappointed in not getting Canada: (3) It is advisable to put off the vacancy at Victoria for as long as possible, so as to avoid another wrangle with the court, for the D. of Albany will certainly claim the place. – The last was of course the operative reason. (The Premier agreed to this.)

Talk with Herbert about Jamaica, but did not absolutely settle anything: I have dropped the notion of employing Sir J. Longden, not thinking highly of his capacity from the despatches he sends: the choice rests between Sir H. Norman, strongly recommended by Northbrook, & Sir A. Clarke. I incline to the latter, for Norman is an Indian official, & they are inclined to expense, & to despotic ways. I think Clarke must be the man.

To the Lords at 4.30: Ld Sidmouth raised a debate on colonial defences, with hardly any notice, for his motion for papers told nothing of what he meant to discuss: he talked in a dull rambling style: I answered him briefly: then Carnarvon got up, & delivered a careful & rather able speech on the whole subject: very anxious that the Australians should spend more on armies & navies, & insisting that we should press them to do so, though it seems rather their business than ours. Two or three others followed, & all ended.

11 July 1883: . . . To the City Companies Commission: where, though 4 of our 12 members were absent, we carried through the resolutions on which our report is to be based: Ld Coleridge was away on circuit, I believe, & Sir R. Cross has withdrawn, objecting to the policy indicated.

Called on A.D. who has been & still is very ill. She was not to be seen.

. . . M. now declines all invitations on account of her eyes.

The complications of this week are many – Chaplin has carried a motion for restricting the importation of foreign cattle against the government, 28 Liberals supporting him through fear of their farmer constituents. We have reports of what seems like an outrage[7] on the part of the French admiral on the Madagascar coast: he appears to have used our consul ill, & imprisoned one or more British subjects. The Suez canal scheme is launched, & will lead to much debate in the H. of C. Cetewayo has been fighting again, & seems to have defeated Oham & Usibebu, his chief opponents in the north. The Transvaal government has dismissed Jorissen summarily, & has also passed an extraordinary resolution condemning the resumption by England of Basutoland: which is in no sense a matter concerning them: the Cape parliament is discussing the Basuto scheme, result still doubtful. We have business enough on our hands, & some of it abundantly disagreeable. Yet the stream of parliamentary talk flows on, & the session is rapidly wasting.

12 July 1883: The Suez canal scheme, as announced in H. of C., does not seem popular. We advance £8,000,000 to Lesseps at 3½% to make a second canal, obtaining in return a larger share of the control, & reductions of dues for our shipping: a fair bargain enough, as it seems to me, but our merchants & shipowners want a new canal made, which shall be entirely in English hands: & they will be content with nothing short of that. The unfairness to Lesseps, the probability of a quarrel with France, & the breach of legal engagements to which we are consenting parties, does not weigh with them. – I should not wonder if this business damaged the government seriously, & it is even possible that parliament may refuse to sanction the arrangement.

13 July 1883: . . . Cabinet at 2.30 in Gladstone's room at the House: I could take no note, & did not try it: nearly the whole discussion was on the Suez canal scheme, which evidently does not go down with the public, & the question is whether to withdraw it, postpone it, or refer it to a committee. The last course is weak in appearance, & only a method of gaining time. We settled nothing, but agreed to meet again in a few days.

. . . To dine with Sir W. Macarthur[8], a late Lord Mayor, great Australian merchant, who entertains Sir H. Robinson. The D. of Manchester was there, simple & good-natured as ever: & very much enjoying his position as one of the largest landowners in Australia. . . .

16 July 1883: . . . Wrote, or rather dictated, a letter to be signed by Antrobus in answer to one from Sir H. Ponsonby, asking whether I saw any objection to the D. of Teck[9] becoming chairman of a mining or landjobbing company in the Transvaal: I did see a strong objection, & said so. The letter was addressed to Antrobus, so that I left it, in form, for him to answer.

17 July 1883: Send £50 to a fund which is being got up by Cork & others on behalf of Miss Burke, the sister of the murdered Irish secretary.

Very clear & free of business: at 11.00 today I have hardly anything left to do.

. . . H. of Lords at 4.30, where Carlingford withdrew a bill about lunatics, which has dissatisfied everybody: the ratepayers because it threatens expense, & the reformers because it does not cost enough, at least does not do enough.

The Suez canal concessions remain unpopular: in the press, the *Standard* defends them, oddly enough, considering its connections: *The Times* writes furiously against them, & practically in favour of ousting Lesseps from his own undertaking: *D. News & Pall Mall Gazette* in favour of modifications: *Telegraph & St. James's* decidedly against the whole scheme.

Drummond Wolff is reported to have said exultingly to a friend: 'Keep it up: in six months we shall have driven the government into a war with France.' And there are many who no fear of provoking a war would deter from a party move. But in such matters I place confidence in the judgment of Northcote, who will neither do anything very unscrupulous himself nor connive at others doing it.

18 July 1883: Home: idle for half an hour, which is rare with me in the mornings: till papers came from the office. I have literally at this moment not a letter unanswered, nor a paper undealt with.

. . . A successful experiment – as far as I know the first – has been made on the Thames with a boat propelled by electricity. The speed was good (9 knots) . . . the only fault was in the exhaustion of the power in 5 or 6 hours, after which the boat had to be . . . recharged from the machine on shore.

19 July 1883: At 3.00, Cabinet, which lasted till the H. of Lords. Carlingford was at Windsor: all the rest, including Spencer, present.

A letter was read from the Att. Gen. in which he seemed to qualify the opinion which he has given, & on which we have acted, as to the absolute character of Lesseps's monopoly. The Chancellor thought there was no doubt possible as to his rights. Granville believed that Cairns took the same view. Harcourt: 'If our own law officers are shaky, how can we hold our ground?' D.[erby]: 'Our proposal rests on the assumption that Lesseps's exclusive right is certain: if we abandon that ground, where are we?' The Premier: 'No need to settle our course today, & it would be premature.' Granville: thinks opinion is changing. Harcourt: 'Does anybody really think a majority possible on our proposal?' Chamberlain: 'Agrees that opinion has changed. People who began by condemning us violently now think that the proposal contains a good basis for agreement. But they will not take it as it is.' Dilke: does not think it can be carried. Harcourt: 'We are strong enough to resist a vote of censure, but not to carry our plan.' Childers: suggests giving up the loan of 8 millions, which is unpopular with a certain set, & which the French don't care about. Would get the matter postponed, & communicate with Lesseps. Northbrook: is for delay. Hartington: would drop the plan at once. Harcourt: would not agree to remain in office an hour if we are beaten. Hartington: agrees, but does not think that withdrawal will be much better. The Premier: thinks they are making the matter more serious than they need. D.[erby]: thinks Lesseps may himself wish for the arrangement to be dropped if he is made to understand the situation. Granville: fears complications with France: how is the Madagascar business ever to be settled if we quarrel with the French on this? General talk: we agree to promise an answer to the H. of C. next week, to send R.[ivers] Wilson over to Lesseps: & to discuss the subject again. – Lords, 4.30–7.00: dine at home, quiet evening.

20 July 1883: . . . Went to see Lear's drawings in Wardour St., & saw with regret that he has sold very few. Bought two of the best, at price of £50, for Holwood.

. . . Mr. Jacob Bright came with the agent for the Manchester canal bill, to talk about its chances in the Lords.

H. of Lds 4.30–7.00: a debate raised by Ld Bury[10] on regimental arrangements, to the intense delight of the military peers, & the weariness of all others: most of them sensibly went away, including Granville, but Kimberley & I, being on duty, stayed to the end.

21 July 1883: Finding that the Cabinet intended to be held today is put off till Monday, I finished rather hastily such office work as there was to do, & left for Keston by the 11.35 train. Rain & thunder, bad for farmers, but the leaves & grass are very green . . . Much rain interfered with walking.

In H. of C. last night, an absurd motion by Mr. Jesse Collings, who wishes to create peasant proprietors by buying farms for them out of public money, they being forbidden to let or to mortgage, but compelled to cultivate or to sell. This was too much for the House, which counted itself out.

Note that the radical party has miscalculated parliamentary feeling where land is concerned. The press on that side has been constantly saying: 'The Tenants' Compensation Bill is feeble & almost useless as it stands, but the H. of C. will make it more stringent, & the Lords will not dare to alter it.' On the contrary, the action of the legislature has been rather to weaken the bill than to strengthen it: Liberals joining with Conservatives for the purpose: & this though the bill was really in the first instance a very mild one. Whatever may happen, the land has not yet lost its hold on parliament.

22 July 1883 (Sunday): Four heavy pouches from the office, but disposed of them in the course of the morning. Nothing of importance, except the question whether Sir S. Rowe[11] shall go up to Coomassie to attend the installation of the new king of Ashantee? which he is for, I am against, but will put the despatch in print, & send it round the Cabinet.

The papers on New Guinea, including my despatch, are published, & well received. Walk, but only in the grounds, storms being frequent. The promised hot summer has turned to a very wet one. Rather an idle day, but I am clear of arrears, & have really nothing pressing to do.

23 July 1883: London by usual train . . . Work at home till Cabinet at 12.00: we sat till 2.30. Then office, where stayed till near 5.00: much business . . . H. of Lords till 6.00: walk & made calls: dined Grillions: meeting Gladstone, Holland, Houghton, Fortescue, Norton, Sherbrooke, Mills[12], etc. Pleasant enough.

Occupied in the evening with an interminable story of quarrels among officials in

Cyprus, silly & discreditable. Luckily the parties concerned are all soldiers, so that I can hand them over to the War Office, & get rid of them so.

24 July 1883: Paid Lear £50, & Maclean £67 for drawings.

Sent £5.5.0 to the N. London Consumption Hospital.

At 12.00, to meeting of the Cotton D.[istricts[Convalescent Fund, where a large gathering . . . The business was not much, & was disposed of in half an hour. We have left to the fund about £100,000, yielding £4,000 a year income, after all payments made.

. . . H. of Lords: Manchester ship canal bill brought on for second reading: Winmarleigh moved it, speaking too long & in a feeble voice, though to the purpose: Redesdale opposed the bill violently, & seemed to have lost his temper, for he spoke with great bitterness, & seemed excited: I followed, & spoke for about 5 or 6 minutes: we divided 87–24 (I think). Met M. at the station, & so with her to Holwood.

25 July 1883: . . . Walk on the commons till 12.30. Home, & found a telegraphic summons to a Cabinet suddenly called. Left at 1.20 . . . found I had been summoned half an hour too soon, & discovered the Premier in his room, where the meeting was, lying on a sofa, half asleep, with a novel in his hand (he is quite right to get all the rest he can). Met at 3.30, & sat till 5.20. Almost the only business was to discuss in what way a resolution to be moved by Northcote on Monday next is to be met. We talked it over, & ended by agreeing on something like the previous question. Gladstone at our meeting produced a form of words which was unanimously condemned by us as imprudent & clumsy: he took our respectful criticisms in good humour &, after several of us had tried our hands, he produced another formula which we all agreed was perfect. Granville noticed the oddity of this to me, & others, as we went away.

Spencer brought before us a proposal for emigration from the distressed districts to be aided by state funds, which the Premier disliked, Dilke, Chamberlain, & Kimberley also objecting: on the general ground that emigration ought not to be subsidised, & on the more special ground that compliance with the Irish demands will lead to a similar movement in England, especially in London: which I am afraid is true.

Spencer however pressed his wish, Carlingford supporting him with the convincing argument that the Irish bishops were entirely favourable to the plan, & in the end we agreed to give £100,000 out of the church fund, which is less likely to create a precedent as the fund itself will soon be exhausted. Holwood again by 6.05 train.

26 July 1883: By usual train to London. Reached No. 23 at 10.45. Work on office papers & letters till 1.30, when luncheon, & to office. There busy till the Lords met. [Answered] a question as to the alleged death of Cetewayo[13] . . . It is not absolutely certain, but generally believed. . . . Walk with Granville to Marble Arch: called in Curzon St.: dined Travellers'.

Much talk about a bazaar . . . lately held for . . . some charity in Berlin, at which the princess of Wales & a dozen or so of the greatest ladies in London kept stalls, & sold all sorts of things, refreshments included, to any one who chose to pay for admission. The general feeling is that there is some loss of dignity . . . & that duchesses & countesses might be better employed than in serving out brandy and water to the shopmen of Regent street. The Queen thought the same, & made no secret of her opinion: but she was not told until the thing was done.

Gossip also about the D. & Dss. of Teck selling off their furniture, etc. They are £50,000 in debt, having chosen to keep up royal state, which cannot be done on £6,000 a year. Neither the Queen nor the Duchess of Cambridge will help them, except on condition of their living in Germany: which they do not choose to do. The sale has created a good deal of talk, though the excuse is put forward that they are going to move into a smaller house at Richmond, & therefore do not want the property they are disposing of.

27 July 1883: . . . Ascertained that last year the letters & despatches to & from the Col. Office were a little over 40,000: those to & from the Foreign Office 70,000. This I think is a very fair measure of the amount of work in each department respectively.

There called at the office Sir T. Shepstone, whom I asked to see, . . . thinking he might know something of the circs. which led to Cetewayo's death: but he did not. He utilised the opportunity to ask for a place for one of his sons.

. . . Occupied some time with dealing with a characteristic case of embezzlement at the Gambia . . . a negro official has made away with £500 . . . his guilt is not doubtful, but the intended prosecution . . . has fallen through, it being clear that a negro jury would not convict. Ireland over again!

28 July 1883 (Saturday): Only one pouch from the office, & little in it.

In afternoon, drive over to Chevening, 1½ hour from door to door: found there the Roseberys, E. Stanhope, Sir A. & Ly Hayter (she a Hope, handsome & pleasant): Shaw Lefevre: Ly Donoughmore: Lord Kildare[14]: Mr. White[15], now minister at Bucharest: & one or two more, whom I forget.

Driving down the hill, where there is so fine a view over the Weald, I was forcibly reminded of a visit – or more than one – which I paid there in 1858, fresh from passing the India Bill, & with the heavy responsibility of putting together the new machinery of the India Office. On the whole, I think life is pleasanter at 57 than at 32. There may be fewer enjoyments, but anxiety & worry are less acutely painful: & a casual failure is not felt as so grave a disaster.

Chevening is the only house except my own where I feel at home: & where visiting does not bring any sense of constraint or awkwardness. It was always pleasant, & has lost none of its attractions under the present management.

Debate last night on the Irish land courts & their working: . . . I was glad to be away, for in truth I believe there is more foundation for the charges of injustice so freely made by Irish landlords than Spencer & my other colleagues are willing to allow. When a hungry young attorney is made a sub-commissioner & has to fix the rental of a farm, he knows that a decision in favour of the landlord will set the whole neighbourhood against him, ruin his business, & perhaps endanger his safety. He has no reasons to give, & is very unlikely to be called to account. What is the chance of his being absolutely impartial?

29 July 1883 (Sunday): Chevening: a very fine day: walk early with Rosebery, & much pleased with his talk. He says he is going to Australia when the session is over, not to return till Easter: partly, I suppose, wishing to avoid political entanglements & see how the movement in favour of a separate secretaryship for Scotland will turn out. Walk later, with the whole party. In all, over 4 hours on my legs: but rather weary before dinner. I cannot walk as I used.

. . . Talk of an odd event in Lord Cairns' family: his eldest son, a rather fast youth, is engaged to marry a Miss Fortescue, an actress, who will find herself in very uncongenial surroundings. Cairns, with his usual good sense, has taken the affair well: & finding it could not be stopped has given his approval. So at least the talk ran today.

Letter from Mrs. Gladstone, begging £100 for her convalescent home: an odd kind of solicitation from a prime minister's wife, whom it is not easy to refuse: but it is an old habit of hers, & young officials, & aspirants to office, are now regularly warned of the expediency of propitiating the Premier's family by offerings to her favourite charity.

The papers are full of an earthquake in Italy, in the island of Ischia, by which 3,000 persons are said to have been killed . . .

A cholera panic is spreading over Europe, & has begun to show itself in England, caused by the outbreak of that disease in Egypt. . . . There have been recorded about 7,000 deaths, but probably the real number is much larger.

Nothing more is known as to Cetewayo, beyond the total rout of his army, & his own disappearance: he is supposed to have been killed, but nobody knows for certain.

30 July 1883: Left Chevening early, about 8.30, with Rosebery, & by Sevenoaks to London, arriving about 10.10 at No. 23. There found M. come up early from Holwood. She returned in the afternoon.

[From Ward] receive notice of the rents of 1882–1883: there has been brought in £215,933 against £213,196 in 1881–1882. An increase of more than £2,700: which is good, though in some years it has been greater.

Hale called from Fairhill: long conversation with him . . .

. . . To the Lords . . . Debate on a Sunday closing bill for Cornwall, which was well discussed, Wemyss opposing, & speaking better than I have yet heard him: Bramwell, Argyll, Salisbury, Kimberley, all argued with force & point. The only failure was Lord Mount Temple[16], who talked as if addressing a missionary meeting. The division was quite unconnected with party: the numbers were equal, 38 to 38: so the bill was lost. . . .

31 July 1883: Sent Mrs. Gladstone £20 for her home, promising a subscription but I did not say for how many years.

Soon after 5.00 we were summoned to an informal Cabinet, or consultation, in the Premier's room, on the state of H. of C. business. It seems that the Irish have broken out worse than ever, they kept the House sitting till 4.30 this morning, in opposition to a bill for improving the efficiency of the Irish police, which they object to on that ground solely.

Grosvenor, who was called in, spoke dolefully of the state of things: said the men were tired, he had difficulty in keeping them together, they would not now stand an all-night sitting, the Speaker too had caused it to be understood that his strength was failing. He did not see what was to be done: unless we were prepared to sacrifice all other business. Spencer thought the bill important. I made some remark as to the unpleasantness of allowing the Irish to have a practical veto on legislation, which seems to be the state of things to which we are coming: this set off the Premier, who said: 'Long as you have known the H. of Commons, you have not known it of late years, & you can form no conception of the impotence, the humiliation, the servitude, of its present condition.' And in this strain he went on for some time. Nobody dissented, and I am afraid it is true that parliament is discredited as it has never been before. We did not sit long, some of us being wanted in the House to answer questions. I came away, & by 6.35 train to Bromley . . .

1 Aug. 1883: The papers are full of details as to the murder[17] of Carey, which is spoken of by the Irish popular journals without even an affectation of disapproval, & in Dublin the event has been celebrated by bonfires & other marks of rejoicing. It is a victory of the rebel party, & they know it.

. . . I omitted to notice yesterday the total collapse of Northcote's resolution on the Suez business. For whatever reason, he was not cordially backed up by Salisbury, & Cairns, who is absent, is believed to incline to the opinion that Lesseps really has an exclusive right. Moreover, his resolution was so worded that it might mean anything or nothing: & the withdrawal of the agreement which had been objected to prevented any defection on the ministerial side. The majority was 99.

Monthly returns from Statter, who is despondent as usual about the prospects of business, but thinks the farmers are doing better.

2 Aug. 1883: Troubled part of yesterday, last night, & this morning with pains in the right hip, leg, & knee, which I suppose are rheumatic. They broke my rest, & are unpleasant still, but not enough to interfere with business.

3 Aug. 1883: Saw . . . Gen. Feilding, Denbigh's brother, who has been 5 years in command at Malta, & professes to be very fond of the Maltese: speaks their language, & knows some of them well, which few English do. He professedly came only to give information, but let out before leaving that he wished to be governor at the next vacancy[18]. He dwelt on the density of the population, & its poverty: 150,000 already, increasing at the rate of 1,800 a year. The gentry have no career: the only professions highly thought of are law & medicine: two lawyers make £800 a year apiece, the rest think £100 a very fair yearly earning. There are 1,500 priests but, as I understood him, taken from a lower class. He proposed two remedies: (1) emigration, aided by the State: (2) exceptional advantages for getting into the civil service at home. The latter is absurd: the former may be possible, but I also gathered from him that the elective members of council have an extreme dislike of all outlay (not a wholly bad trait) & will sanction nothing that involves increased taxation. He said the native gentry are very sore because the English will not admit them to their clubs: but admitted that their habits are so different from those of the English that no real association is possible. . . .

4 Aug. 1883 (Saturday): Very busy, & rather hurried, a heavy load of papers having come in late yesterday evening, when I thought the day's work over: but rising early I cleared off all.

Sent £10 to a railway servants' society, £5 to the Orthopaedic Hospital . . . Left London by 11.35, reached Holwood at 12.45.

Just as I was leaving came the secretary to the Peabody Fund, with proposals for the purchase of a plot adjoining our land at Islington . . . a little over £2,600. As the land is cheap, & will be useful, I agreed.

The H. of C., though with more business on hand than it can possibly get through, counted itself out at 9.00 last night. I suspect there is a certain limit, which is now reached, beyond which M.P.s will not sit: they are worn out, body & mind. . . .

5 Aug. 1883 (Sunday): Holwood. Three pouches from the office, worked on them till between 11.00 & 12.00. Read to M. Gave her £30 as a present to Mrs. Smith the housekeeper, who is leaving: she adding £20.

Sanderson came. Walk with him by Downe & High Elms. Walk with him again later in Keston & the park. H. Russell came in afternoon. . . .

7 Aug. 1883: London by the usual train . . . work at home till 1.00: luncheon at Travellers': office before 2.00: there till 4.15. . . . In the Lords, debate on the Tenants' Compensation Bill: Carlingford explained it, feeble & dull as he generally is: but his weakness mattered less, as there was no real opposition.

Wemyss followed, with an amendment, condemning the principle of the bill as a violation of the rule of free contract: he spoke cleverly, more cleverly than he used to do in the Commons, but the substance of his speech was extravagant & even silly: he discussed the Irish bill of 1881, which was not in question: rambled over a variety of subjects &, condemning the leaders on both sides equally, assumed an air of superiority that was partly comic, partly irritating. He was warmly cheered by a few men sitting round him, but not by the opposition generally.

Argyll pronounced for the bill briefly, but decidedly: Richmond supported it in a plain sensible statement of the position of affairs: Ld Bramwell objected, but not with much force or point: Carnarvon criticised, but would not oppose: Kimberley & Salisbury each said a few words. We sat till near 10.00 p.m. I dined with Northbrook at the House. Home, work on letters, but rather late.

8 Aug. 1883: Up early, cleared off all work on hand. M. [goes] to Southampton, intending to pass 3 days on board the D. of Bedford's yacht. Walk at 11.00 for exercise, but driven home by rain. Weighed, 15 st. 1 lb. Sent £5 to the Beckenham Cottage Hospital.

Office at 1.00: work there till 2.00, when Cabinet, which sat till 5.30. We meet too seldom, in my judgment, & sit too long, for after the first two hours business is apt to be discussed in a very desultory way.

Home at 6.00, dressed, & to the Mansion House, where ministers were entertained: the dinner lasting from 7.00 till past 10.00. The speeches were below the average on such occasions: even Gladstone was as nearly dull as he knows how to be: Kimberley, Hartington,& Childers all thought it safer to stick to commonplaces. . . . In truth there was not much to talk about, for the session, though not absolutely barren, has not been glorious: & the public is apathetic, not deeply interested just now in anything.

At the Cabinet, we first discussed the conduct of parliamentary business. Trevelyan & Grosvenor were called in. We decided to push on some bills – Irish emigration, bankruptcy, & National Debt bill – certain others, I forget which, being practically abandoned. Harcourt wanted special facilities given for a Durham Sunday closing bill, which we saw no reason for: on this Harcourt lost his temper, said he should vote on the question exactly as if he were a private member: he could not understand why we took pleasure in flouting & insulting the temperance party ,which was the strongest section of the Liberal party. This intention was duly disclaimed & the matter ended in an agreement that the question should be left open, government as such taking no part. Another wrangle arose on the question of taking Fridays for government bills, which Harcourt wished, & Gladstone, with Grosvenor, opposed.

A letter was read from Lord Coleridge, asking whether we wished him to execute his intention of going to America, & whether we would apply to the U.S. government for special protection for him, as he had repeatedly received threats of assassination. Harcourt, it seems, had spoken to Lowell on this. Lowell had telegraphed to Washington:

& the answer came to the effect that the authorities would give all necessary protection. But they wished it to be done on our suggestion. (I suppose lest the Irish party should find fault.)

We then got into a debate, the most animated which we have had since I joined the Cabinet, on the question of reducing the force in Egypt with a view to ultimate withdrawal.

Chamberlain was for going at once. He thought we should be charged with breach of faith. Dilke argued in the same sense, so did Harcourt vehemently, & Childers in a milder tone. I backed them up, arguing on grounds of home politics that our stay pleased only our opponents – who begin to think, or at least profess the belief, that a real annexation is intended: while our friends, who disliked the Egyptian business from the first, are alarmed & suspicious, though discipline keeps them from finding open fault.

Granville took the other side, admitting that permanent occupation was impossible, but thinking an early withdrawal premature. The Premier said little, but made it plain on which side his sympathies were. Hartington alone stood out, disliking the idea of even reducing the actual force (about 7,000 men). He said all the military authorities were against it. To this was answered: 'No doubt they are: they wish us to keep the country, & make no secret of it.' The Queen too, it was said, is violent against withdrawal. Somebody, I think Harcourt, said: 'My dear Hartington, you might just as well consult the bishops on the question of disestablishing the church as ask the military men about the War Office whether we should leave Egypt.' In the end, it was agreed to discuss the matter again, there being some difficulties of detail: but the feeling of the Cabinet was decidedly shown.

Lastly, we got into a long discussion about the D. of Wellington's statue. It is condemned by general opinion, including that of artists, & the question is what to do with it? Whether to get rid of it simply by melting down, as some proposed: or to melt & recast it: or to find a new place for it. I objected to the first proposal as impolitic: it was sure to be considered as a want of respect for the Duke's memory: which would give the Jingos a cry: I pressed this strongly, & I think influenced the decision[19].

Of the other two alternatives, the last was rejected as impossible: the committee of art appointed to enquire being unable to find any spot where the statue would not be an eyesore. In the end the proposal to recast, & place the new statue near the former site, opposite Apsley House, was adopted, & I believe on the whole it is the best solution.

Some talk passed as to a possible debate in the Commons on Lord Ripon's policy, but it was generally agreed to avoid this if possible, not out of fear for the result: but because in such a debate many things are sure to be said that will increase the irritation felt on both sides in India. . . .

10 Aug. 1883: . . . **Note** that I yesterday spoke to Granville, as I have done to some others, about our Cabinets, suggesting that they should be more frequent & shorter. He personally agreed, I think sincerely, but said that there was nothing which the Premier disliked so much as a Cabinet: that his extreme gentleness, & readiness to submit to contradiction, were not natural to him, but imposed by an effort of will, & that he made no secret of its being a painful one.

This I can believe: but certainly no head of a government can be less dictatorial in discussion: which is the opposite of what I had been led to believe.

. . . To the Lords at 4.30 and there sat till past 1.00 a.m. discussing the Tenants' Compensation bill in committee: the discussion was mostly to the purpose: & well sustained, though a few lords talked foolishly, as among so many was sure to happen. I took part two or three times, but briefly.

11 Aug. 1883: Very weary last night & this morning, for which there was no adequate cause, since the sitting was not especially long or late: but my hours are so regular that a slight departure from them is felt.

Work at home till 1.00: then left for Holwood. A messenger came down with routine business, which I disposed of.

12 Aug. 1883 (Sunday): Holwood. Walk early . . . Sanderson came in afternoon: walk with him by Downe . . . Ly Abercromby came . . . One pouch only from office . . . Ly A. talks of the Teck sale: it has brought very little in money directly, but has accomplished its object, which was to compel the Princess's family to give help by an ostentatious display of poverty. The Queen, the old Duchess of C.[ambridge] & others have contributed, and their immediate wants are relieved. . . .

14 Aug. 1883: Called in Curzon St., & found both sisters together: met there Wemyss, who seems in a state of chronic excitement over politics, & talked very wildly: I sometimes wonder if his brain is quite right, for he seems to me the sort of man who might go mad.

Office: where saw a Maltese, Mr. De Cesare, who has been out in Australia to find a suitable place for Maltese emigrants to go to. He has returned well pleased with the country, but finds that the local governments are not disposed to favour a Maltese immigration. They are controlled by the workingmen, who get enormous wages for little work, & do not like the influx of a hardworking, sober, saving body of men who would probably reduce their gains by one-half. In fact it is the case of the Chinese over again. I asked if the Maltese government would not help its surplus population to go out. He doubted whether the elected members would spend money to help them – not that they dislike emigration, but they fear any expense. I enquired whether a few could not be helped out by subscription among the richer Maltese? Mr. De Cesare laughed, said I did not know Malta: that no Maltese ever subscribed voluntarily for any object . . .

15 Aug. 1883: Mr. Goldsworthy[20] from St. Lucia called, with plans for a harbour at Castries, to cost £70,000: but he thinks it will be well worth the money, & I incline to agree. The matter is not absolutely settled, but I think I shall sanction it. The object is to enable St. Lucia to supersede St. Thomas as a port of call for ocean steamers.

At 6.00 to the pier by the houses of parliament, where met the Ld Chancellor, & with him & some others embarked for Greenwich for the [end of session] fish dinner . . . Dinner was at the Trafalgar Hotel: about 45 sat down: Russell, as the youngest official present, in the chair. He did his duty very well. Granville, Hartington, Trevelyan, & R. Grosvenor spoke, all in good humour & good taste, though I don't know that the wit was brilliant. My health was drunk, & I answered, briefly, not indeed having expected to be called up. Gladstone, Harcourt, & Chamberlain, were the most notable of the absentees. Home by water, & to bed about 12.00.

16 Aug. 1883: Saw Antrobus & gave him directions.

Wrote to Hale about a man named Brisley, employed about the Knowsley stables, who has been accused of getting drunk: the charge not being conclusively proved, I concluded to give him a warning as to his conduct, & not to dismiss him.

We left for Holwood by 11.35 train. . . . Messenger came down in afternoon, with boxes & letters.

17 Aug. 1883: Three pouches came by post: worked off all by 11.00.

Letter from Sir C. Dilke, recommending a son of the late Justice Shee[21] for judicial employment in the colonies: but, as the young man is an ardent Catholic, & Sir C. mildly states that he has been a little embittered by poverty – which probably means that he is a radical of the revolutionary sort – I am not much disposed to help him. – I remember his father, the judge, well in the H. of C. He had very little ability, at least I never heard him say anything that showed the slightest intelligence: but his voice was one of the finest ever possessed by man: I have heard him distinctly through closed doors in the lobby when speaking quietly & without effort: & he turned Catholic – whether from calculation or mere coincidence – just at the time when the Irish wanted a leader. It is fair to say that he was gentlemanlike & courteous as a politician – very unlike the Irish of the present day. As a judge, he was feeble, pompous, & prejudiced: one of the weakest appointments of the time: in fact his seat on the bench was due to politics only.

18 Aug. 1883: Left Holwood by early train, walking in to the station. Day hot, & on reaching No. 23 I had to change my clothes, which were wet through.

Granville yesterday gave me notice of a Cabinet for this morning, but it turned out a mistake of his. However, I do not regret that I came up, for there was much to do at the office. Went there at 12.30, & stayed till 4.30.

Sent money to two beggars, & £5 to certain Liverpool people who have taken up the cause of the oppressed shop assistants: there is no risk in encouraging an agitation which is directed only against the shopkeepers.

Cut out & kept a notice in *The Times* of the Meggernie[22] estate, 30,000 acres, £4,500 a year, now on sale: it attracts me strangely, though my reason tells me that if acquired it would be a white elephant: for grouse & deer do not interest me: what does interest me is the possession of a large tract of picturesque wild country, capable of improvement & ornament by planting. But when should I be able even to see it?

Saw Herbert: settled with him to draft a plan for the new, or reformed, constitution of Jamaica: which must include a partly elected council.

Saw Wingfield, & settled with him a plan for putting on a sound footing the savings bank at Gibraltar, which is in a bad way.

Much routine business. Holwood by 5.00 p.m. train: Galloways arrived later.

19 Aug. 1883: Holwood: very fine day . . . Sent Antrobus £20 for sundry expenses: & sent £25 to the relief fund for sufferers by the earthquake at Ischia, seeing that the Premier & Foreign Secretary have done the same.

Rather depressed in spirits, with no special cause, but I have been rather hard pressed with work lately, & constant running up & down by rail does not suit me, leaving an impression of haste & worry which is disagreeable.

In parliament, extraordinary efforts have been made to recover lost time: the H. of C. has sat on one morning till 5.30, & on several others till nearly 5.00: probably the first time in the history of the world that legislative business has been done at such hours. The

progress has been good, but Irish members have taken the opportunity to make themselves more offensive than even they have been till now: Healy, Biggar, Callan,
Harrington, O'Brien, the worst. No kind of insult is too gross for them to use: they seem
to have set themselves systematically to discredit the assembly they sit in, by displays
which no decent public meeting would tolerate. A specimen is the following. Gladstone,
deeply vexed by their attitude, as he had a right to be, delivered a fine & pathetic speech,
which had only the fault of treating them with far too great civility: in the course of it he
spoke of his own interest in the matters at issue as small, since in the course of nature he
could not expect to serve the public much longer. The House was touched: but the
Parnellites, headed by Biggar, set up a wild yell of rejoicing, as much as to say: 'And a
good riddance too.' . . . Another talked of the 'spitting on bayonets' of women & children.
And so on indefinitely. No Irish member protested or objected. The most violent phrases
were the most applauded. Where is it all to end?

20 Aug. 1883: Left Holwood at the usual time: the day being very hot, I did not walk. . . .
Worked at home: did not go to the office. At 3.20 left for Waterloo: reached Portsmouth
harbour 5.50: found a steamer ready, & so to Cowes: the tide being low, I was transferred
to a steam launch for the last mile or so: reached Osborne house at 7.40.

Found there the Queen, Princess Beatrice, Ponsonby, Ly Ely, Ly Abercromby, etc.
H.M., from whatever cause, was in the best possible humour, laughing & talking freely.
After dinner, she talked to me for nearly half an hour, on various subjects, in so frank &
cordial a manner that I should have believed her to have forgotten old grievances, only
that I know how thoroughly royal personages have acquired the art of disguising their
feelings.

21 Aug. 1883: Left Osborne at 8.00, reached Portsmouth harbour at 9.30: there found
the admiral, G. Hornby: friendly & pleasant talk with him: he grumbles loudly at what he
calls our system of starving the navy, thinks it is in a very bad condition, the French are
getting ahead of us, etc. But he has said the same thing as long as I can remember.

London at 11.50, a very hot & dusty journey: home, washed, etc., to Cabinet, which met
at 12.00, I got there at 12.30: the only business done while I was present was discussing the
amendments made in the Lords to the Agricultural Holdings bill: we agreed as to the necessity of resisting most of them, & also agreed to give way on one: but there was one,
supported by the D. of Richmond, which we differed upon, & settled by a division: we were
6 to 7, Gladstone, Dilke, & Chamberlain being in the minority. They accepted their defeat
quietly: Harcourt got angry, said we might just as well throw up the bill altogether, or accept
all the amendments made by the Lords at once – we had ruined the prospects of the party
– & so on. Childers & Northbrook were the other two against concession. Granville,
Kimberley, Selborne, Dodson, Carlingford, Hartington, & I were the majority.

I asked & obtained sanction to send troops into the Zulu reserve if necessary: Bulwer
sending a rather pressing request to that effect. I at the same time announced my intention of transferring Bulwer to Jamaica, if he will accept: which disarmed Chamberlain, his
chief opponent in the Cabinet.

Office, & sent Meade over to the War Office to settle about troops.

H. of Lds at 4.30, sat till 8.00: . . . the Lords threw out the Irish Registration bill, &
the Scotch Local Government bill: both measures which have been forced upon us, &
which we need not regret.

22 Aug. 1883: Very hot & close night, with partial fog in morning. Slept ill, which is rare with me.

Cabinet at 12.15, to consider the Queen's speech. We went over it paragraph by paragraph. The Premier had sent me overnight those which referred to colonial affairs. No dispute arose, the criticisms being chiefly verbal. Other matters were then talked over, but in a vague & perfunctory way, result I suppose of general fatigue. The question what shall be done with the Privy Seal was gone into at length, no decision being come to.

Office, & very much pressed with business. H. of Lds at 5.00 . . . discussed the amendments on the Agricultural Holdings bill. On one, the most important, allowing the Act to be invalid where there has been any previous agreement to the contrary, the numbers were equal, 48 to 48: &, a second division being taken on the same point in slightly altered form, the opposition carried their point by 1. But it is clear that they will not fight the other House with a majority of 1.

I spoke briefly in the debate: Kimberley more at length, & better. Carlingford had charge of the bill: he was neither eloquent nor argumentative: but it is justice to him to admit that he has courage & readiness. He is always willing to get up & make the best case he can, though often it is a very bad one.

Richmond spoke & voted with us: he could not well do otherwise, seeing that the bill is based on the report of his commission: but it was done in a plain manly way that commanded respect. He said just enough about his regret at differing from his friends, & not too much.

The Queen sent an odd telegram to the Cabinet to ask 'what course we intended to pursue' as to the Scotch & Irish bills thrown out yesterday. It was interpreted as meaning to ask whether we intended to resign on the defeat: & caused some laughter. I can hardly suppose she meant it so – but, if she did, if she really thinks we have lost the confidence of parliament, her good humour on Monday would be explained. . . .

24 Aug. 1883: . . . Letter from Harcourt alarmed as to the safety of Ld Coleridge in Canada, & begs I will take certain precautions.

. . . Letter from Granville referring to certain Irish threats to murder Ld Lansdowne, which I will attend to, but I do not think the matter is serious.

. . . Letter from the Princess Mary[23], begging a place for a protégé of hers, one Dunbar. In 1878 there was no language which she could use that was violent enough where I was concerned: she being Jingo of the Jingos: but that is conveniently forgotten when she wants something.

. . . Office about 2.00. Saw there a Mr. Fraser, an intelligent man, who has lived as a trader in Basutoland. He confirms my opinion that the hostility of the Basutos is not against England, but against the Cape administration: provoked partly by the foolish attempt at disarmament, partly by jobbing among the colonial agents, who are distrusted & disliked. He thinks they can be governed without trouble, but that they could not govern themselves, & would be sure to fall into the hands of the Free State. He speaks very highly of the industry & intelligence of the Basuto race.

Saw Sir J. Longden, fresh from Ceylon: he is about my age, but looks older: mild in manner, not quite a gentleman in the social sense, but civil: his talk seemed that of a cautious and careful administrator . . . He reports well of native feeling, & of the island generally except (an important exception) in regard of finances . . .

H. of Lords at 3.30, & sat an hour. Salisbury gave up his amendment, carried the other day, with tolerable good humour, but he spoke of the bill generally in a tone of hostility which is not, I think, that of landowners as a body, whether Conservative or Liberal. Wemyss of course spoke, & two or three others. The attendance was very small. – Office again, where much business: home at 7.00: dined Travellers'.

25 Aug. 1883 (Saturday): . . . Office at 12.00, where little business. Prorogation of parliament at 2.00: the Chancellor, Sydney, Kenmare, Monson, & I being the commissioners. Office again till 5.00, when to station, & Holwood by 5.15 train. So ends the session.

26 Aug. 1883 (Sunday): Holwood. Very well pleased to rest, though my work in the Lords has been comparatively easy, & though the rest will not be long before the Knowsley life begins.

The session just ended has been long, wearisome, but not so wholly barren as was expected & feared a month ago. The amount of legislation has been fair: we certainly made the mistake at first of expecting & aiming at too much, which I note for future guidance. The Irish & the regular opposition have obstructed a good deal, but with more art & concealment than at first, so that it is difficult to prove the charge against them. In point of violence & offensiveness, the Irish have been worse, if possible, than before: in fact they pride themselves upon it, wishing that the general disgust created by their presence should reconcile the English mind to Home Rule. No reputation has been made or lost in the last seven months: Gladstone has spoken as effectively as in his youth, but avoids great efforts & is generally short for him (under an hour): Chamberlain is said to have managed his Bankruptcy bill well, & the Att. General to have achieved a success.

In the Lords no great debate has come off: Salisbury has shown himself what he is, a clever & skilful debater, but does not command confidence: being thought rash in attack, & apt to be precipitate in retreat. The secession of Richmond the other day was a blow to his influence, the more so as it obviously did not arise from pique, or temper, or intrigue: Cairns does not love him: & it is no secret that his & Northcote's relations are strained. He has done the Liberals good service, & will do them more: for it is impossible for Whigs to join him, as they might join Richmond, & thus desertion in the opposite ranks is checked. –

– My part has been quiet and even obscure, for colonial affairs have attracted little attention, & I do not know when official life has been to me so little of a burden.

In Ireland, matters are improving. Rents are being regularly paid, & outrages have almost ceased: but those who know the country well believe that the feeling of the people is unchanged, & that the present calm is due rather to repressive measures which cannot be kept in force for ever than to real content. Parnell has gained in the year 3 followers: as between Liberals & Conservatives the numbers are practically unchanged: & on the whole the Cabinet is as strong as when first formed, though there may be less enthusiasm among its supporters. This is unusual for a ministry in its fourth year. Ld Beaconsfield used to say that every government might expect two years of success: its troubles would begin about the third session. Perhaps the disinclination shown just now to sharp party fighting may be due to a feeling that the present state of things is provisional only: that with a new franchise must come a new political world.

. . . Invested through Ward £200 more in the Nat. Lib. Land Co. which is paying 6% & seems well managed.

Bulwer has refused the offer of Jamaica, at least so I read his telegram, but it is obscure.

27 Aug. 1883: . . . At 3.00, set out to ride to Fairhill[24], which I did in 3 hours, 3.00 to 6.00: the roads hard & dusty, the weather not too hot. More than ever impressed with the fine effect of Morants court hill: which perhaps will be mine one day.

29 Aug. 1883: Two pouches from the office: nothing urgent.

Walk early about the place, looking at improvements, where any have been made, & well pleased with the general appearance, but I must own that Fairhill suffers by comparison with Holwood. There is no wild ground, & nothing at all equal to the views over the old ramparts, & Keston common. On the other hand, the [Fairhill] surroundings are more entirely rural, & the lanes more pleasant for riding.

. . . News in the papers that Gladstone is about to publish in one of the monthly reviews a translation into Italian verse of some popular English hymn. A more characteristic sample could not be found of the small eccentricities in which the Premier loves to indulge to the perplexity of his friends, & the amusement of the outside world. It is impossible that Italian verse written by an Englishman should be more than tolerable: even if it were good, what does he gain in reputation, or any way, by accomplishing a successful translation? Nor is a Protestant hymn likely to be acceptable to any Italians: to the non-Catholics it is ridiculous, to Catholics heretical. It looks as if the great minister & orator were not free from the childish vanity of liking to show that he can do things which nobody would expect him to do. But more probably it is a mere freak: he has written these verses as a kind of school exercise, & some friend (Lacaita[25]? whom he has been seeing lately?) has foolishly persuaded him to publish them.

30 Aug. 1883: Fairhill. Pouches from the office, two, & business all routine.

. . . In the papers, speech by J. Bright on the liquor question, in regard to which he condemns the Local Option bill & all the prohibitory schemes favoured by Sir W. Lawson, & would leave the business of licensing (as I understand him) in the hands of an elective local authority. This in my view is the right solution.

. . . Received a letter from Hartington, enclosing one from Ld Wolseley, by which it seems as if the War Office believed that we were going to dethrone Cetewayo again, for they suggest an increase of force, whereas we wish only to guard the frontier of the colony against attack.

31 Aug. 1883: Two pouches from the office, one full of the Cyprus scandal, but as I knew the case before it gave me little trouble. Disposed of both in time for the early post.

. . . Drove with M. for our yearly visit to T. Wells, where walked on the common, bought sundry little articles on the pantiles, & passed two hours pleasantly enough. We left 11.45 & returned 4.15.

Found a messenger specially sent from the office, who brought a long & rather confused telegram from Bulwer concerning Cetewayo's proceedings in the reserve territory. He wants instructions, naturally.

The substance of Bulwer's news is that Cetewayo is in the reserve with a large force, seems to want to establish himself there in an independent position, assumes an attitude of defiance, refuses to see Osborne[26]. Bulwer has sent to require him to disband his troops. If he refuses, it will be impossible to avoid using force, unless we are to acquiesce in his taking the reserve, which I do not see how we can.

I arranged to go up to town tomorrow, & telegraphed to the office that I would do so.

1 Sept. 1883: Two pouches from the office: disposed of all except one set of papers relating to W. Africa, which I kept for consideration. News of the Rutland election, which ended in an almost ludicrous defeat of the Liberal candidate, a Mr. Handley. He polled 194 votes against 860. As he had committed himself to the extremest anti-landlord doctrines of the Farmers' Alliance, I do not regret the failure, which shows that the existing land system is not unpopular in purely rural districts, at least in the farming class. What an extended franchise may bring forth no mortal can tell.

. . . Arranged a telegram in answer to Bulwer's, approving his proposal with some cautions & conditions. Wrote to the Premier for his sanction, & to Hartington to let him know what is doing.

. . . Note this day 28 years. . . .

4 Sept. 1883: In one of the papers of yesterday, a remarkable article dwelling on the change made in the last 7 years by the disappearance of most of the notable men of that date (1876) without leaving successors. In England, Disraeli gone, Gladstone going. In France, Thiers and Gambetta. In Germany, Bismarck. In Russia, Gortschakoff. Beust might be added. That they should die out is in the course of nature, but they do not seem to be replaced. We have no man on either side who is likely to occupy the position of the two great leaders of whom one is dead, & the other wishes to retire. Especially I do not see our future Prime Minister. Granville is growing old & very deaf: Hartington, with every disposition to like & respect him, I cannot think equal to the post: and who else is there? But it is idle to speculate, when a new parliament may bring a new world.

5 Sept. 1883: . . . Wrote to Lord Lorne in answer to a letter just received, in which he speaks of the necessity of taking police precautions when Ld Lansdowne arrives: the feeling among the Irish being very bad. 'Joe Brady'[27] is a hero with them, & they are as full of the wrongs of Ireland as if they lived there. – A club in Quebec, he says, goes by the name of Brady.

. . . By 1.05 train to London . . . reached Knowsley by about 10.30.

6 Sept. 1883: Up early: saw Latter, & settled with him about books, bindings, etc.: very pleased with the library, which is now in better order than any collection I know: morning being wet, I did not go out. . . . Saw Hale . . . Took him with me to the Liverpool agricultural show, for which I have come down: . . . met Winmarleigh, Lord Combermere[28], Cross, Blackburne[29], etc. Luncheon was at 2.00: I took the chair. Speeches followed: mine lasted 20 minutes: the rest were short. Returned to the show, & stayed there till 4.30, when home.

Three pouches from office.

Went to look at Boehm's two busts of Ly D. & me, which are in the gallery, & look remarkably well, especially hers. They are well worth the 600 guineas which they will cost me.

I have received of late sundry complaints about the management of the Bury estates, which resolve themselves mainly into charges against Statter. His honesty & care are not disputed: but his manner is rough: he is alleged to be too much occupied with other affairs, such as surveying & valuing, to pay adequate attention to the wants of tenants (in truth I suspect his activity is decreasing with age & impaired health): and it is farther thought that he puts too high a value on the land which he lets for building, though, as this is the opinion of the buyers or lessees, I do not hold it to be proved. But the feeling against him is general, and I shall have to consider how to proceed. I have consulted E. Hornby[30], the rector, in the first place: but, as he has had differences with Statter, I do not rely absolutely on his opinion, though wishing to hear it.

7 Sept. 1883: Left Knowsley at 9.00 . . . arriving at Euston 2.30 . . . Saw Antrobus, & disposed of letters & current business: luncheon at Travellers': Fairhill by 4.55 train, arriving about 6.40 p.m.

The papers are full of a possible quarrel between France & China, on the subject of Annam: which if it happens will be not only a misfortune but a danger. They will expect us to respect a blockade of the Chinese coast which they will not be able to enforce: & they will be aggrieved by the presence with the Chinese forces of English volunteers, who are sure to be attracted by the chance of fighting. But it is hard to suppose that the French nation, which has nothing to gain by such a war, will embark in such a policy of adventure. The first necessity for colonising is to have colonists: and the French population is stationary in numbers, & does not care to emigrate.

In my speech of yesterday I dwelt on the fallacy of supposing that land cannot be bought freely: in fact it is now easier to buy an estate than to sell one: I threw cold water on the theory of peasant proprietors, pointing out that, if there were any demand for estates in small lots, no legislation was necessary to meet it: I praised the late act for compensating tenants, said that if English tenants wanted fixity of tenure they would probably be able to get it, but that I did not think they would ask for it, since in that case the landlords' capital would cease to be available for improvements: & I expressed a hope that further legislation between landlord & tenant would not soon be required. My speech was generally conservative in tone, & will be liked by the landowners, but not by the ultra reforming party.

8 Sept. 1883: . . . Read to M. an article in the *Fortnightly* of this month called 'The Radical Programme'[31]: the writer graciously spares the Queen & the H. of Lords – the latter only as long as it is content to do nothing: but abolishes the church, makes education gratuitous, and discusses, without absolutely fixing on any one, a variety of plans by which large fortunes may be discouraged. It is an article eminently calculated to frighten moderate Liberals, & drive them into opposition. The only really noteworthy point about it is the explicit declaration that the liberalism of the future must be socialist: that the State must interfere with the relations of individuals in a way in which it has never interfered till now: and, as the writer somewhere puts it, that the power of capital over labour is so great that the legislature cannot look on & see it exercised without control. No doubt all this is the language of an extreme section only, and which even that extreme section if it got into power would not be in haste to translate into action. Still it is significant of the direction in which the contests and the dangers of our future lie.

9 Sept. 1883: Walk early for exercise . . . The day was fine & walking pleasant: but I cannot conceal from myself that whether from age or increased weight I have become less active, & two hours is enough for me at one time.

. . . M. tells me of symptoms of an internal complaint which she thinks she has detected in herself: the impression made on my mind was at first one of alarm: but it does not seem that there is any proof, & I believe as well as hope that she is mistaken. I urged her to have the matter fully enquired into, which she agrees to.

There is something going on in Bulgaria which I do not clearly understand: the Prince, having got into the hands of the Russian party, has been compelled to submit to retain ministers whom he had intended to dismiss: it is even said that one of them, when ordered to resign, refused, & appealed to the Russian ambassador, who reinstated him. F.O. seems alarmed, & Dufferin has been sent back to Constantinople in the midst of his holiday: not that I see what we have to do with the quarrel.

The Premier has gone off on a sea trip from Barrow in which he asked us to join: but we declined[32].

10 Sept. 1883: Hardly any letters, & no papers from office: the nearest approach to a whole holiday I have seen this year.

Ride early, in the Weald: walk later. Evening wet.

In the papers, death of Maxse, governor of Newfoundland, whom I saw only a few months ago, in good spirits, & on his way back to his post: but he had then a strange colour on his face, as if painted, which I believe is a sign of consumptive disease[33].

Another death – Hugh Birley[34], the Conservative member for Manchester, aged only 66, but he had long been in weak health. He was locally popular & respected, being liberal with his money, & cultivating the clerical interest assiduously. From all I saw of him, which was not much, I should judge him to have been an honest man, of sound sense & with cultivated tastes: not much of a politician by the natural turn of his mind, but useful in the discussion of details.

11 Sept. 1883: Walk early with Collins, marking trees & directing small improvements near the house. My plantations of 7 or 8 years ago are beginning really to make a show, so that I plan walks to be made through them.

12 Sept. 1883: Two pouches, I think, from office: nothing special.

Long early ride . . . to Penshurst. This is the prettiest ride I know of any in these parts.

Read much to M. as I have during each of the last 3 days.

My sister & her eldest son came to stay the night & part of tomorrow. . . . Bad report of my old uncle, C. Stanley, who now seldom leaves his room, & often passes his days in bed. There is no actual disease, but a general failure of strength.

13 Sept. 1883: One pouch from office: several letters applying for the vacant governorship of Newfoundland, one from Lord Canterbury[35], who has absolutely no claim, but is cousin to Sanderson: his reason for applying.

Letter from the Premier about New Guinea, which I answer. . . .

14 Sept. 1883: Two pouches from the office: nothing special.

Letter from Childers enclosing one from Australia about the New Guinea affair, or rather the annexation question of which New Guinea is the beginning. I answer it, & keep copy . . .

Singular dearth of news: the Premier, unable to endure a week's silence, has been making a speech somewhere in the Orkneys[36]: Chamberlain & Harcourt are both in the north of Scotland on their own account: Childers is at Balmoral: Granville, I believe, at Walmer. There is nothing to do, which is lucky, since there is no one to do it.

15 Sept. 1883: Three large & heavy pouches: disposed of nearly all. Many applications for Newfoundland . . . Walk early, in much heat . . . Rather an idle day, but there was no reason to the contrary.

16 Sept. 1883: One pouch only from office. Disposed of business early. Day very fine: indeed I have seldom seen this country looking so well, and greatly regret to leave it – the more so as life at Knowsley is far less of a holiday: there are twenty demands on my time to one here. . . .

17 Sept. 1883: Up early, breakfast before 8.00: London with M. Sent to the office, saw Antrobus: did business with him.

Sir S.[eymour] Fitzgerald[37] called, whom I had not seen for years. To my great surprise, he told me that he wished to give up the place which he holds, and take a governorship in the colonies. He said he thought he had made a mistake in leaving the H. of Commons: when he returned from Bombay he found that new men had come up with claims of recent service to the party: and he was shelved, with the permanent appointment which he now holds. He had a further grievance in the salary having been reduced from £2,500 to £2,000. But it is still one of the most desirable posts in the permanent civil service: &, involving no outlay, is quite as good in real value as a governorship with £5,000. The only reason I can assign for his wish to leave is that which led him to go to Bombay: debts which made it impossible for him to stay in England.

We talked in a friendly, even cordial tone: but I was glad not to be obliged to give an answer, since I could have held out no hope. Fitzgerald is a clever, eloquent, jobbing, impecunious Irishman: suspected of corruption at Bombay, though nothing definite could be proved, except that he had borrowed right & left from natives: but his reputation in that respect was so questionable that I well remember that Disraeli was thought to have made a mistake in giving him office.

Left London by 4.00 p.m. train & were at Knowsley by 9.15, with no contretemps except that the footman who came with us got unmistakably drunk on the way. He was reckoned a good servant: but it is strange how many fail in respect of sobriety.

18 Sept. 1883: Three pouches from office.

Saw Scott, and at his intercession decided to let off the footman who misbehaved yesterday, with a caution.

. . . Hear that Mrs. Hale is gone into an asylum, or retreat, where abstinence is enforced, for 6 or 12 months, by her own consent: Gorst saying it is her only chance of life. She has been worse of late than ever before.

19 Sept. 1883: Three pouches from office: disposed of all early. Nothing of consequence except a scheme by Sir A. Gordon for repairing the old irrigation works of Ceylon by means of borrowed money, to be repaid in a series of years. This I agree to in principle, but the details will want consideration. – Intended to have gone into Liverpool to look at the yearly exhibition, but put it off: not wishing to prevent the servants from attending the funeral of one of their number, Elizabeth, the old housemaid, who had been here more than 30 years. They joined in a request – which of course I agreed to – that her death should be announced in the papers as a mark of respect. – I note this as curious, since it shows how the desire of publicity pervades all classes.

A large meeting was held at the east end of London yesterday, on the subject of state aid to emigration: which however the east enders present did not seem to care about: the language held by them was that they had a right to be supported at home, that there was plenty of land for all, etc. It is increasingly plain that a strong socialist tendency is show- ing itself in the masses – not always revolutionary, nor even hostile to property in inten- tion, but involving demands that the state shall do for them many things which no state in modern times has undertaken to do, & for the doing of which the state is very ill fitted. Another queer sign of the times. Marwood the hangman being lately dead, his place is open to be applied for: & it is announced that 1,200 competitors have come forward.

. . . A fresh nuisance has sprung up, a steam hammer . . . about Huyton Quarry, which works all night, & with so much noise as to hinder sleep, when the wind is S.E.

20 Sept. 1883: One pouch only from office, & but little in it. Day wet, though still warm & close.

Went with Margaret into Liverpool to the Walker Art Gallery, to see the yearly picture exhibition, & buy some for Knowsley. We stayed an hour, & chose 5, costing £280.

Letter from Ld Spencer about a Mr. Blake & a Mr. Carran, whom he wishes provided for in the colonies. I answer promising to do what I can: and sincerely: for Ld S. deserves all help that can be given him: but I doubt the wisdom of what the Irish executive is doing: removing out of the country magistrates such as Clifford Lloyd, who have done their duty efficiently, & made themselves unpopular in consequence. . . .

21 Sept. 1883: Three pouches from office, but the business all routine.

Sir E. Thornton and Lord Gerard came to stay.

22 Sept. 1883: Four pouches from office. Kept some papers about Gibraltar to read at leisure. Walk with Sir E. Thornton . . . Sir W. & Ly Thomson came to stay . . .

In afternoon, a garden party, to which all members of the British Association now meeting at Southport who chose to come were invited. In all we had, I believe, 700 visi- tors: some of a very rough sort. I saw several in shooting jackets: some walking down the gallery (full of ladies) with their hats on: & I heard that the scene in the dining room, where refreshments were supplied, was peculiar: that they gorged & scrambled for the food till none was left. It was not on the whole a beautiful sight: but I suppose it will have been popular, & such things must be done from time to time. – Lady Sefton came to help M. & was very useful. – Lord Gerard left when all was done.

. . . The Premier, returned from his cruise, sent me a telegraphic invitation to Hawarden, but I could not accept it.

23 Sept. 1883: Three pouches from the office, all business of detail.

Gave an Oriental student, who wrote to beg, £10: after verifying his references.

Walk with Sir E. Thornton in the park early: after luncheon took him to Croxteth to call on Ly Sefton.

Talk with him as to his American experiences: he believes official corruption to be very general, purity in that respect being the exception: but no very serious mischief ensues, & the country is indifferent. The senate is better than it was: some years ago there was a ring of 12 senators who were notoriously purchasable: but this attracted attention, & it was broken up. Imputations in the newspapers of venality are so common that no native politician takes notice of them, nor is any one thought the worse of for having been so accused. . . .

25 Sept. 1883: . . . M. went into Liverpool to see Dr. Drysdale, believing herself to have some internal complaint: but he finds nothing amiss except as regards her eyes, and some general weakness. His decision is a relief to both of us.

Sir E. Thornton left us. Though a grave man, & seemingly always depressed in spirits, he is good company, & I am glad to have had him as a guest.

Read to M. – Rather an idle day.

26 Sept. 1883: High wind early, almost a gale: walk morning & afternoon.

Four pouches from the office.

Letter from Sir H. Bulwer, describing the state of things in Zululand as critical, & evidently alarmed. Cetewayo is in the reserved territory, gathering his forces, & apparently inclined to stay there whether we will or no. This it is impossible to allow, since we sent him back last year on the express condition, agreed to by him, that he was to have nothing to do with that territory: and, whether the condition was necessary or not, we cannot now modify it under compulsion. I wrote in this sense to the Premier, & have kept copy of my letter.

Read to M. both early & late. Ld Camperdown came.

27 Sept. 1883: Wet morning, & very windy. Only one pouch from the office.

Wrote to Childers, asking on behalf of Ceylon for some remission of the military contribution, as the colony is much distressed by failure of the coffee crop.

. . . Saw Hale: talk as to the Bury complaints: he advises me not to take the initiative in meeting them . . . since nothing has been said to me direct: but to wait and see whether the parties complaining really have any grievance which they care to put forward &, if so, what it is. This is just the advice which I should myself have given in another man's case, and I shall follow it.

Walk in afternoon with Camperdown, 5 to 6 miles. Much wind, but being from the west the air was pure . . .

There came to us Carnarvon's daughter, Ly W. Herbert: aged 19, with pleasant manners & intelligent: her father is in Canada with his second wife.

28 Sept. 1883: Day very fine & bright: three pouches from the office: disposed of most of the business by 11.00 . . .

Walk with Camperdown. He talks of Dalhousie: likes him as I do: but says nothing can be more reckless or silly than his dealings with his tenants. He has taken without enquiry or verification every complaint they make as well founded, has given them all they wanted without even consulting his agent, & is consequently a good deal embarrassed, his estate though large being heavily encumbered, & his reductions having largely diminished the available margin of income.

The papers are full of Shaw, the Madagascar missionary, who was imprisoned & ill used by the French admiral. He has returned to England, & told his story in Exeter Hall. If it is accurate . . . the conduct of the French has been foolishly & even absurdly high handed. But this is the temper they have shown of late everywhere: it is not easy to see why, for bombarding Madagascar towns & taking forts in Tonquin will not restore their prestige in Europe, whatever that may be worth. – I am afraid our Egyptian performances of last year have had something to do with creating this disposition in them.

Will of the D. of Marlborough proved: he leaves £146,000, which is more than anyone expected.

29 Sept. 1883: Lord Camperdown left us. I like him as a guest: he knows much, talks well, & his ideas are sensible. I scarcely understand why he has never received official promotion, unless it be that there is thought to be madness in the family[38].

Letters & papers from the office: worked till 11.00, when to Liverpool to attend the yearly meeting of Liverpool University College. A dismal wet day. Disposed of such business as we had in less than an hour: then with the treasurer, R. Gladstone, to the Palatine Club, where luncheon . . . Thence to St. George's Hall, where heard a lecture . . . on the study of biology . . . I gave away prizes to the students, & said a few words as to the position of the College: well received. Home about 5.20 . . .

30 Sept. 1883: Feilden, our Knowsley parson, brother of the M.P., having received an offer of a better living in Staffordshire, has made up his mind to leave us, after more than 25 years of residence. I talked the matter over with M. and, finding that she greatly regretted his going, I determined to offer him a personal allowance of £200 a year to stay. This offer I have sent, but probably it will not be accepted[39]. I believe that Mr. F. would have stayed on to the end of his days, but for a foolish son, who without means married a woman equally poor, & is trying to maintain a family by setting up a school somewhere in the south.

1 Oct. 1883: Letter from Chamberlain, recommending a Birmingham lawyer for colonial office: I answer civilly, & in a friendly style. (**Note**: We asked Chamberlain here, but he could not come.) No pouch from office . . .

I have allowed my office business to get into arrear, which is sheer laziness on my part, for there is not much of it, but so the fact is.

2 Oct. 1883: . . . The papers are full of an unlucky event at Paris, where King Alphonso of Spain, on his way through from Germany, has been violently hissed and hooted by the mob, not all of the lowest class . . . In the main the demonstration was intended to show dislike of a king as such . . . The French behaved with admirable temper & patience after 1871, and have been rewarded by a more rapid recovery from disaster than any one foresaw: but now that they are reaping the fruits of their self-repression they seem to have grown tired of it, and Tunis, Tonquin, Madagascar, with sundry minor incidents, show a growing restlessness which may easily become dangerous . . .

5 Oct. 1883: . . . Several days have passed without bringing news of Cetewayo, whose attitude is now extremely dubious: he is in the reserved territory, has been required to disarm, & has so far sent only doubtful answers.

A Mr. Briggs[40], M.P. for Blackburn, is one of the candidates for Newfoundland: and, though a man in no way fitted for that sort of place, has induced (I should think) not less than 20 M.P.s to write in his favour: some of them saying plainly that they had been pressed to write & did not like to refuse. A proof of what may be done by pertinacity.

. . . The Manchester election has ended in the rejection of Dr. Pankhurst[41], the extreme democratic candidate, by 18,000 against 6,000, or thereabouts. The effect is to leave the representation where it was, a Conservative succeeding a Conservative. The local Liberals are for the most part well pleased, and have reason to be: for the victory of Dr. Pankhurst would have proved that there was neither discipline nor cohesion in the party, whose leaders had opposed his candidature: & it would have made a split between the two sections certain probable, if not certain. . . .

6 Oct. 1883: This was one of the finest & brightest days I ever saw at Knowsley: not a trace of smoke in the air, hardly a cloud in the sky, & the park & woods looking as they used to look before the towns had encroached upon us. If many days were like this, I should not care to live anywhere else. . . .

7 Oct. 1883 (Sunday): Many letters & papers from office, & two pouches. Busy most of the morning. Walk an hour in the morning, & walk in afternoon with M.

Heard from Coutts that they have bought for me £5,000 N.S.W. bonds at £5,150. This makes up investments to £445,000 . . .

Sent £25 to Rev. J. Kempe for parochial charities, and £20 to the Charity Organisation Society.

. . . More letters from & about Mr. Briggs, who has induced half the Liberal party to write on his behalf. I must find out what he really is: for, though I dislike putting men fresh from parliament into colonial posts, it is not easy altogether to disregard so strong an expression of feeling.

8 Oct. 1883: Wrote to Harcourt about Mr. Briggs, & also asked as to the legislation of next session.

Sent Granville a mem. on the position of France in West Africa, in which the cession of the Gambia in equivalent for certain French settlements is recommended. I kept another copy of this paper for the Premier.

. . . About 6.00 the Premier[42] came, with Mrs. & Miss Gladstone, also Miss Hope. He was in good spirits, & talked abundantly. He dwelt on the increasing liability (as he thinks it to be) of the English people to panics & terror without cause: instancing the Channel Tunnel, & the continual talk about our being undefended. He thought there was no feeling of the kind before the date of the Crimean War, & mentioned that the D. of Wellington used in the time of Sir R. Peel's government to write alarmist letters on the subject of defences, of which no notice was ever taken.

He talked very eagerly about some calculation which he has seen as to the increase of the English-speaking race (English & American): which according to this reckoning was to number 600 millions a hundred years hence: I said something as to the extreme uncertainty of such speculations on the remote future, the impossibility of foreseeing all the conditions, & so forth: which he took well, but did not seem to agree in.

He volunteered to speak freely about Ireland & Irish politics: believes that the time of outrages is over, & that the movement will now be, as he put it, confined within the limits of legality. I tried to induce him (being alone) to give his real views as to the prospects of Home Rule: he went readily into the question but, perhaps by my own fault, I could not follow him: he talked about the prejudice & timidity of the English mind where Ireland was concerned, said that he would never agree to anything that would destroy the supremacy of the imperial parliament: but did not seem absolutely to reject the notion of a subordinate Irish parliament, but as to this he was very vague, & I think did not wish to be otherwise.

He did not think the Parnellites strong enough ever to cause real danger or do serious mischief: they would be, he said, like vermin about a man's person, troublesome & disagreeable, able to give annoyance, but not to interfere with his action. Before he gave any public answer to a demand for Home Rule, he would ask what it meant, & require to have a definite proposal before him. This was the clearest utterance that I could obtain from him, & certainly it is to the point. He referred to Forster in a very disparaging tone, having evidently not forgiven: & praised Trevelyan warmly.

9 Oct. 1883: Up early: four pouches from the office, & a good many letters. Worked off nearly all before 12.00 . . ., the Premier not caring to go out till the afternoon.

At his special request, Irving the actor came out from Liverpool & passed the morning here, returning about 6.00 p.m.[43] I took him, Mr. Gladstone, & Miss G. for a walk about the gardens & grounds.

There came later Sir J. Lubbock, & two daughters: & Miss Grosvenor. There came to dinner Sir T. Earle, the Holts, Mr. & Mrs. Brocklebank, Rathbone, Hale, Bolton, Mr. Galty. – I think these were all. Talk with the Premier about Trevelyan, whom Ld Spencer wishes to put into the Cabinet, but he (Mr. G.) does not wish it: partly alleging general objections such as the danger of giving offence to other candidates, partly dwelling on the extreme dislike which the Queen, as he says, expresses to Trevelyan personally. Talk of a Speaker: he discusses claimants for the place: likes Dodson well: but thinks there is an objection to transferring any man direct from the Cabinet to the chair: prefers Hibbert who he says is popular in the House, & he seems to think that the objection to a Cabinet minister does not equally apply to a minor official.

Talk of the Queen: he finds her wholly altered: thinks she is now more reactionary (his own word) that any politician living.

Talk of the order of measures – he is decidedly in favour of dealing with the county franchise alone next year, & adding if possible the county government bill: redistribution of seats to be dealt with in the next session, but in the same parliament. He says this is Bright's view, & he believes it to be right.

At dinner, he & Rathbone discussed the growth of American fortunes of late years: agreeing that in the States 50 years ago it was rare to find a man who owned £100,000: whereas now millionaires in the English sense are common. they both agreed that the American system of protection was the chief if not the sole cause of this change. I could not see it so, but did not dispute the point.

10 Oct. 1883: Three pouches from office: which I managed to dispose of at intervals of time.

Sent £10.10.0 to the Scottish Corporation. Gave Ly W. Herbert a bracelet, cost £25: she has made herself very useful to M. & is liked by everybody.

At 12.30, into Liverpool with Mr. & Mrs. Gladstone, to luncheon with the Holts: a most tedious business, which lasted 1.30–3.30. Some 30 or 35 guests made up the party. Returned by Croxteth, & walk home with Mr. G. He seemed to know well the suburbs of Liverpool, & was full of comparisons between their past & present sate.

Before we set out, I left him in the library with Latter &, rejoining them, I found Mr. G. explaining to the librarian the various styles of bookbinding in Paris & London, with the names of the leading binders, & the merits of each. One would think that he had made bookbinding a special study.

We did not talk much English politics, but something set him off on the subject of Servia, as to whose internal politics he discoursed at length, but I have forgotten what he said.

He talked of Northcote, said he had every quality of a leader except backbone: did not see who could take his place if he were disabled or deposed: Hicks Beach was the best of the other oppositionists, if only he could keep his temper, which he was apt to lose: Cross he thought greatly fallen off, & repeated the old story as to his seldom being quite sober late at night (qu. whether true? I doubt): thought Smith a good man of business, but quite incapable of leading, & not much liked in the House.

Talk of French affairs: he traced the financial difficulties of France mainly to the system which he describes as having been founded by Napoleon III (but I think it of older date) of bribing the constituencies by large outlays of public money. Yet he thought that, however heavy the taxation might become, France would remain solvent. He praised the wonderful frugality & skill in all kinds of work, of the people: & thought their wealth increased more rapidly than that of any other European country.

11 Oct. 1883: . . . The new rents for this year are over £8,000 already. This is in that respect the best year we have ever had.

Went early with a large party to see the works of the Mersey Tunnel, about which the Premier was anxious. We left at 10.00, got there at 11.00, went under the river nearly to the end of the boring, the way being muddy, with some dripping from above: there was not much to see, but what there was was well seen by the electric light. Spending about an hour there (**Note:** Mr. G. made a short speech to us in the tunnel, being asked, as I suppose, to do so by the directors) we drove to the Walker Art Gallery, where we passed half an hour: I bought another drawing, cost £50: then drove home through a crowd, whose cheering & shouting seemed to give Mr. G. keen pleasure – more than one would have thought a man would feel who has been so much used to it. All the way to Liverpool & back, & during the sightseeing, he continued to talk in his most animated style: I have heard nothing like it since Macaulay. The matter was nothing extraordinary, except for the vast variety of subjects over which he ranged: but the manner, words, & voice gave an interest to even ordinary remarks on ordinary topics.

Short walk in afternoon with Sir J. Lubbock.

. . . I heard the Premier after dinner discussing eagerly with Rendall the exact position of French students in science & art, & comparing their system with ours. He seemed to know all about it, & to think the foreign method superior to ours, but I could not make out in what respects.

12 Oct. 1883: Three pouches from office: . . . in one of them a wonderfully foolish despatch from Sir G. Bowen, who has misunderstood & taken offence at something in a despatch from the office. How Kimberley came to choose such an old Polonius I cannot guess.

Talk with the Premier in his room &, later, out of doors: he began by saying that he wished to discuss some pending questions with me: but after the first five minutes he seemed to forget them & wandered off into a general dissertation on politics, interesting in parts, less so in others, but curious as beginning out of nothing in particular, & leading up to no conclusion. For the first time, a suspicion crossed my mind that there is something beyond what is quite healthy in this perpetual flow of words – a beginning perhaps of old age. He dwelt on very various subjects – on the Prince Consort, Stockmar, & the mischievous influence which these two had exercised on English affairs – on the cost of the Indian army, & that which it involved to the English army also – on the necessity of economy, to which we were pledged by a resolution of the H. of C. – I asked where he thought savings could be made? He said in the judicial departments especially, the salaries of the judges were too high, & they had many well paid officials about them with little to do – in education also, which was managed on a wasteful system – and, above all, in grants-in-aid for local purposes, which he denounced as calculated to encourage needless expenditure, & educate the people in habits of profusion. He seems to think a great deal may be done in the way of reduction in these matters. He praised Childers as having been an admirable administrator, but feared ill health had weakened his power of work. He reverted often to the government of Sir R. Peel, as that in which administrative matters were better looked after than ever before or since.

– He left us at 3.00 for Hawarden: at the last moment there was a scramble & bustle about missing or forgotten luggage, & in the end he went off with a greatcoat of mine, his own being lost. I imagine his & Mrs. Gladstone's domestic arrangements to be incoherent. He talked much, I forget on what inducement, about the Newcastle family: said his friend, the Duke[44] who was minister, had an extraordinary power of self-delusion: & one of his fancies was that he was ruined: he having in fact a good & even large income, though his estate was a good deal encumbered. He thought the present Duke in danger of being led into bad company, his mother[45] having gone into disreputable society, & ended by turning Catholic. Wished us to be acquainted with him: but as he described the youth[46] as being a cripple, of little natural ability, & with a strong turn to devotion, I do not feel disposed to cultivate the acquaintance.

In Mr. G.'s conversations he referred several times to the Queen, & always in a tone of regret, not unmixed with bitterness.

He told me that he now regretted the fusion of the English & Indian armies in 1860, & thought it a mistake. I heard this with pleasure, having been one of a very small minority who objected to the amalgamation at the time.

13 Oct. 1883: All our party left us ... Letter from Carnarvon about Canadian affairs: he thinks well of the prospects of the colony, but ... is alarmed lest Lansdowne should be shot by the Fenians.

I answered at once, & asked his opinion on the great subject of a general federation of the empire, which I do not think possible, but I find that many people do, & it will certainly be discussed some day. I am clear that the present relations cannot last long: we are neither really identified with the colonies nor independent of them: the tie is so loose that a war, or any violent shock to the empire, would snap it.

14 Oct. 1883 (Sunday): ... Read to M. an article in the *Fortnightly* on the rehousing of the working classes[47]: which modestly proposes to take the land wanted at a price not exceeding ten years of the rental (i.e. to confiscate two-thirds of the value): and to pay for that by a tax on the real property of the district or town. This plan, put forward as the 'Radical programme', has excited some attention, & been very generally repudiated by the Liberal press: but it will do mischief.

Received from Ward the year's accounts: which are not in all respects pleasant reading:

Receipts:	Home estates	£52,633
	East Lancs. (Bury)	£73,971
	Liverpool & Bootle	£64,780
	Fylde & outlying	£24,851
	[With exceptional items]	£216,842

This is good, & shows increase everywhere save in the Bury district. But the outlay is enormous & extravagant!

It stands as follows:

	£		£
Compulsory deductions	29,143		30,000
Household, etc.	27,000		27,000
Benefactions	12,535		13,000
Investment	40,000		40,000
so far all is right			
Estate	88,089)	at the outside,	
Miscellaneous	21,466)	these should be	75-80,000
	£218,235		£190,000

There is at least £30,000, but more likely £40,000, that ought to be saved if I knew how to keep my agents within bounds. I ought to be able to put by at least £60,000 instead of £40,000: but with little leisure & less knowledge of the business of an agent, I do not much hope that I shall do it.

15 Oct. 1883: One pouch from office, & but few letters. – One of these is a request from an ex-nationalist editor, who has quarrelled with Parnell, to set him up in business in Australia. I did not see it.

Walk with Hale later . . . the occasion was convenient, & I took it, to tell Hale of the necessity of limiting outlay. He admitted frankly that for the last year it has been excessive, & exceptional. I admitted my share, having sanctioned large outlay on Northstead, Witley, etc. But £60,000 a year spent upon an estate which yields £220,000 ought to be an ample proportion. . . .

17 Oct. 1883: . . . Saw Ward . . . talk with him as to estate finances: and my resolution if possible to keep down the whole expenditure to £150,000, which would leave a margin of £60,000 & upwards. He promises help, & will do what he can.

. . . Read with interest an autobiography by the late A. Trollope . . . He describes himself as having been incessantly bullied & ill used in youth, & miserable until he reached the age of 25. Possibly this is the explanation of the singularly arrogant & swaggering manner which he assumed in later life, though, as I believe, a kind & good natured man when not opposed.

18 Oct. 1883: . . . Read in the *Quarterly* an article supposed to be by Salisbury[48] which is a kind of review of the political situation. It is very clever, the style excellent, and free in general from the personal bitterness which disfigures so many of Ld S.'s utterances: but gloomy in the extreme in its predictions, & open to the objection that it is really an attack not so much on the Liberal party or policy as on the whole tendencies of modern society. As an article in a review, nothing can be better of its kind: but as the manifesto of a statesman it can only serve to drive away the moderate & timid Liberals whom it ought to be his object to attract. Whatever force or effect it may have is due to the crotchets of men like Dr. Pankhurst or Labouchere, who put before the constituencies radical programmes, such as no rational man is likely to accept: with the natural result of frightening Whigs & neutrals into opposition.

19 Oct. 1883: . . . In some casual talk about Italy, Sermoneta[49] said that on some of his estates local & general taxes absorbed from 40 to 50% of the rent: the income tax alone is 13% . . .
He mentioned also that it was calculated that in Southern Italy since 1860 upwards of 11,000 banditti had been shot: the law as still existing gives the right of summary execution to every officer having the rank of captain or above. And this right extends not merely to the brigands themselves, but to the peasantry who may help or shelter them. . . .

21 Oct. 1883: Sefton talks of the estate (Dunalastair) in Perthshire which he has been looking at: says there are 70 applications for it: thinks the real value much under £150,000, but it will very likely fetch £200,000, though to an owner who let it the gross return would be scarcely £3,000 a year. So keen is the competition for Highland estates.

22 Oct. 1883 (Monday): Sent Mr. Smith[50] of Coalville £10. He is a philanthropist by profession, who declares that he has given his time & money to the public, & is in want accordingly. I do not greatly admire the man, but help him for mixed reasons. He might become an agitator, & it is as well that he should subside into a beggar.
. . . Troubled in afternoon by a telegram announcing that the Cabinet is called (quite unexpectedly) for Thursday: which for me is awkward, since I have accepted for that very day an invitation from the Mayor of Liverpool to a formal, semi-public dinner. I wrote to the Premier, putting the case before him, & asking an answer. –I cannot even guess at the reason for this sudden summons. It was understood that we did not meet till near Lord Mayor's day.
Talk with Hale as to railway payments . . . There is at least £60,000 due.

23 Oct. 1883: . . . Received a telegram from Hawarden, dispensing with my attendance at the Cabinet on Thursday.
. . . The Highland estate which Sefton is looking after has been bought . . . for £200,000: exactly the sum I had expected. – I cannot but see in his wish to buy the first signs of a desire to leave this part of the country: at which I cannot wonder: but, if Croxteth were broken up for building land, Knowsley would be untenable as a residence.

24 Oct. 1883: Letter from the Premier, in which he says that the business to be discussed in Cabinet is the withdrawal from Egypt, not, I suppose, immediate, but to be decided in principle: from the language he uses, it is obvious that he expects difficulties with the Queen. There is also the settlement of the Madagascar dispute with France, by our acceptance of the French offer of £1,000 to the missionary Shaw, & an expression [of] regret. I have written expressing my entire agreement with the proposed policy as to Egypt, & as to the second question I imagine no difference is likely.

Sent £5 to a Liverpool cricket club, & £10 to the Edgehill reform club: neither has much claim, but the sum is small. . . .

25 Oct. 1883: Woke feeling nervously uncomfortable at the prospect of a public dinner & speech this evening: which is absurd, but nerves do not depend on reason.

Sent £50 to help pay for an observatory on Ben Nevis: an old promise, & useful purpose.

. . . I have seldom seen the newspapers so utterly without news . . . They are now occupying themselves chiefly with an article written by Salisbury in the *National Review*[51], advocating the assistance of the State towards rebuilding the poorer quarters of towns. The *Pall Mall Gazette*, which of late has adopted decidedly socialist views, tries to make out that this is a new departure, & urges on the Liberals the necessity of taking up the subject, lest their rivals should be first in the field. But in fact there has been legislation on the subject on more than one occasion: & it is not abstract dislike to deal with it, but reasonable prudence, & doubt how best to proceed, that has caused so little to be done.

. . . At 6.15, left for the Town Hall: the party numbered about 70: the dinner long, according to custom . . . No reporters were present. I spoke about 12 or 15 minutes, fluently & without notes, but not very well. Home by about 11.30. . . .

27 Oct. 1883: . . . Margaret [Cecil] unwell & exhausted during the last few days – M. despondent about her – thinks her life will not be long. I see little mischief beyond fatigue, & the effect of a damp climate which rest & change of air will remove. . . .

29 Oct. 1883: A very dismal day, with steady east wind & smell of chemicals all over the house: worse than yesterday.

30 Oct. 1883: I went to Southport for the opening of the new convalescent hospital there: arriving soon after 12.00, I walked about the town, & on the sea wall, which is a fine thing of its kind . . .

At 1.30, went to luncheon with the Mayor at the Queen's hotel: about 120 sat down: Winmarleigh, Ld Egerton, Dr. Watts, H. Mason, Maclure[52], etc., among the party. Speeches followed: but short. At 3.00, I went to the hospital, which is close by: & opened the building by delivering a short speech, in one of the larger rooms, which was very full. Others spoke also: the Mayor, Ld Winmarleigh, etc. The proceedings lasted about an hour: after which we examined the hospital in detail. Home, returning a little before 8.00. The day was fine, & all went well. Note that at Knowsley St. Helens made itself more unpleasant than almost ever before – but it has spared us for six weeks.

This being Margaret's birthday, I gave her £30. She looked ill, & admits that she is so, but would go down to dance at the servants' ball, & stayed late.

I went down for half an hour to look on: they kept it up till 5.00 a.m.

. . . On the Metropolitan lines (underground) in London, two explosions nearly at the same time, caused by dynamite or some such substance, & evidently not the result of accident.

31 Oct. 1883: A busy day, having all yesterday's work in arrear. But east wind, fog, & a vile stench from St. Helens, which has continued more or less ever since Sunday, made work at home easier: since there was no inducement to leave it. . . .

1 Nov. 1883 (Thursday): . . . Leave at 3.00 p.m. for Hawarden, with M. – Margaret, who was to have come, stays behind, being unwell.

The party were: Mr. & Ly C. Milnes Gaskell: Mr. Bright: Mr. W.H. Gladstone: his brother Herbert, & Miss Gladstone: Mr. Harcourt, with selves, 11.

There was a good deal of talk in the evening, of which Bright, I think, took the principal share: he was gentle in his language generally, but blazed out once or twice, as when Ferrand[53] was alluded to, whom he called a ruffian, and a disgrace to the H. of Commons. He took an opportunity of saying (not in the best taste under the circumstances) that Harcourt was a man in whom he had no confidence whatever: & quoted something from Whittier, an American writer, whom he called 'a first-class poet'. But in general his talk was retrospective, & for him not dogmatic: and he seemed to wish to be agreeable.

The Premier talked of Lord Aberdeen as having after his retirement exercised more influence over the Lords than any peer he had known: and this, he said, owing to character, not to eloquence. Lord Lansdowne had enjoyed something of the same sort of power: Lord Russell none.

Young Harcourt told us that the H.O. were aware of the intended explosion on the underground line in London: which was only one of many: but it came off two days before the day originally fixed for it. It seems that a revival of dynamite outrages is anticipated, at least by the Home Secretary: but he has always been, or at least professed himself to be, an alarmist.

2 Nov. 1883: . . . I shall not attempt to note the various subjects discussed by the Premier. He seemed oddly interested in some internal quarrel which is going on among the Servians, & handed me letters to read upon it. – He talked of the Speakership. Young Harcourt, who is here, seems to think that his father would accept it if offered: & if so we agreed there could not be a better choice. Harcourt has all the traditional requisites: a good voice, an imposing presence, old family, social & political position, & knowledge of parliamentary law. His fault as a minister is imperiousness, but that in a Speaker is useful, & not disliked. He wants to be a peer, & the Speakership is a sure road to a peerage. The only question is – would his natural impatience allow him to endure the life? and would his health bear it?

He [Gladstone] spoke of the growing tendency to increased state interference: did not like it, thought it open to abuse: had himself been brought up in the school of laissez-faire, but thought the current of opinion too strong to be resisted: all that was possible was to guide it. He held a very strong opinion that moderation, & avoidance of extremes, would always characterise the English people: and that no attacks on property by them were probable. They, or some of them, might talk wildly: but when it came to action they would not be unreasonable.

3 Nov. 1883: We walked in the morning: Ly D., Mr. & Mrs. Gladstone, & I, to the village, parsonage, & church of Hawarden: the last is rather handsome, the parsonage dingy & dull, though large, but the garden has fine views. The smoke of Liverpool is plainly seen: & our hosts assert that the rising ground about Knowsley is visible, but we could not make it out. The rector[54] is a son of the Premier, not unlike him, but with a very priestly appearance.

After luncheon, we took leave of him [Gladstone[& went as a party to Eaton[55]: Mr. & Ly C. Gaskell, Sir R. Welby[56], Mrs. Gladstone & ourselves: the place, which I had never seen before, was in the main what I expected, but more magnificent. . . . The house exceeds in grandeur anything I ever saw or could have imagined . . . yet there is no appearance of undue gorgeousness . . . I suppose no private residence in Europe approaches it[57]. Yet I saw it with no such feeling of envy, or wish to possess, as has sometimes been excited in my mind by a fine park, or wild bit of forest land, belonging to somebody else. . . . The cost is said to have exceeded a million . . . but spread over 14 years. The library is small & ordinary: I mean the collection of books, not the room: & there are few pictures, comparatively speaking. The Duke[58] . . . is a man of simple tastes: and his successor[59] is an invalid, unfit for work, & incapable of much pleasure. . . . Reached home by 7.15.

4 Nov. 1883: . . . Note that Northcote has beaten Trevelyan for the Lord Rectorship of Edinburgh. Also that the municipal elections have given, on the whole, a considerable gain to the Conservatives – 84 seats won, 45 lost: showing probably a certain amount of reaction.

5 Nov. 1883: I leave Knowsley free from all arrears, & able to give all my attention to official business. . . . Reached Euston about 3.55. Saw Antrobus, & got to work on office business without delay. At it till dinner, or nearly so: disposed of three large & heavy boxes.

6 Nov. 1883: Up early, & at work soon after 8.00 . . . Saw Antrobus early, & disposed of sundry matters with him. Day very wet . . . Had my hair cut, was weighed (15 st. 6 lbs., to my disgust): then home: Sanderson called: talk of Russian advances in Persia & towards the Afghan frontier: I agree with him as to the uselessness of understandings or engagements with the Russians: we keep our word & they don't.

Sanderson says the prospect of war between France & China is causing alarm in the City & may bring down some houses engaged in eastern trade. The French are in an awkward position: neither Chinese nor Madagascar people seem disposed to give way, & they made too much noise about their demands to both countries to be able to drop them quietly . . . Paid Antrobus £10 for petty expenses . . .

. . . Lord Lorne called, just returned from Canada: conversation with him but nothing important. He said he did not know of a single question unsettled, or likely to cause trouble, in Canadian politics. – I thought Lord L. much altered by his five years of dignified authority. He has acquired a certain air which becomes his position as a future duke & a statesman: courteous & grave, showing civility & expecting deference: in former years I used to think him shy & embarrassed. He said (as he had done by letter) that he liked his position in the colony, but made no disguise of the fact that the Princess did not like it.

7 Nov. 1883: At work by 8.00: read papers on the Malta elections under the new constitution: they have turned out badly for the English party. It seems that in Malta the ordinary conditions of politics are reversed. Economy & reform are the watchwords of the
unpopular side: for these mean fewer places for the small lawyers, doctors, & clerks, who
chiefly influence the constituencies, & who if they had their own way would ask for larger
outlay, & none but indirect taxation. The mass of voters appear to have been quite indifferent, & not to have cared to go to the poll. The clergy, whose influence is very great,
appear to have taken no active part.

. . . Office at 2.00 (luncheon at home, Ly Cowley & Mary Galloway came): saw there
Sir H. Robinson, who talked chiefly about the Basuto business, which he is anxious to
have settled as soon as possible: saw afterwards Mr. Scanlen[60], the Premier of the Cape
colony: later came the Transvaal deputation composed of the President Kruger[61], a Gen.
Smidt, & a third, one Dutoit, who I believe has been a preacher. Neither of the first two
spoke English, & they brought an interpreter. Kruger is a solid looking man, tall & rather
thick set, with a large head: nothing in his appearance or manner to distinguish him from
an Englishman: met in the street, you would take him for a provincial lawyer or manufacturer. The General is like him in figure, but looks a rougher sort of person: he might
pass for an old India officer whose life had been spent at up-country stations. The third
is more evidently a foreigner: small, lean, wide awake, with keen eyes & bristling hair. He
understands English, & evidently followed what was said, but would not speak. They sat
with me about half an hour, & arranged the course of proceedings. Herbert was present,
& kept a minute of what passed. – Home at 5.30 – Sanderson dined with us.

8 Nov. 1883: At work by 8.00: all clear by 10.00. Application from Miss Thesiger for the
government of Malta for her brother: I answer sympathetically, but it is too early to say
anything. Indeed I believe the appointment rests with the War Office. Antrobus called
early. – Lawson called to ask news, but I had not much to give.

Sanderson came at 11.00, walk with him round Kensington gardens . . . Home by
1.00: office work till luncheon at 2.00. Office at 2.45.

. . . Left the office soon after 5.00. – A Mr. Macdonald from the *D. News* office called
to ask about the reception of the Transvaal delegates. *The Times* has published an imaginative article in which their demands are fully set forth, & it is stated that they will get
what they want. Probably they may, but as they have not put forward their case it is
premature to decide. – Work at home, & before dinner disposed of all that was to do.

9 Nov. 1883: . . . Office at 2.30. Saw Herbert, & arranged to have a mem. on Basuto
affairs circulated to the Cabinet. Saw Wingfield, & discussed with him a rather complicated question as to the leasing of lands in the Falkland Islands. Saw Mr. Warr, who came
about City Commission affairs. Saw a Dutch gentleman (name forgotten), an M.P. in his
own country, who came with a letter from his legation. He wanted to know if his acting
as an assistant to the Transvaal people in preparing their papers would be considered here
as an unfriendly act. I said certainly not, as we only wished to come to an amicable settlement.

Saw Mr. Blake[62], an Irish magistrate, who impressed me strongly by his manner & way
of talking. If he has not both sense & firmness beyond most men, appearances are deceptive. He has done excellent work in his district, & by what I think is an act of weakness
Ld Spencer wants to get him out of Ireland, where his presence in office irritates the peas-

antry. He has therefore been recommended to me for a colonial appointment: and he shall have one if I can manage it.

At 4.00, went across to No. 10 Downing Street to help in electing a trustee of the B. Museum: the Premier proposed Lord Bath[63]: nobody dissented.

Home, dressed, & at 6.15 left for the Lord Mayor's Guildhall dinner. The Premier had a very warm reception: so had Sir R. Carden: I was a good deal cheered, which in that audience I did not expect: we went in to dinner at 7.00, & sat till 10.30. . . . The electric light was tried, but did badly: two lamps went out, & others flickered. Waddington made an excellent speech in English, Lesseps a short one in French. Gladstone spoke a quarter of an hour, excellent as usual in style, but he told the meeting absolutely nothing: & it was a fair comment which I heard, that there was not an idea in his speech from beginning to end[64]. This however was intentional, & perhaps it is better so. . . . Home by 11.00, not very weary.

10 Nov. 1883 (Saturday): Drage sees M. The symptoms which he is watching in me have increased, but not materially.

Work at home till near 12.00: then to Downing Street, where met Gladstone, Hartington, the Speaker, Chamberlain, R. Grosvenor, Granville, & the Chancellor, to discuss the question of the Speakership. Many names were mentioned. The Speaker named Whitbread first, but his health is an obstacle: Goschen has every mental requisite, but is too shortsighted: Arthur Peel was recommended by him, rather to my surprise, for, though capable, he is but little known: but he also is believed to be physically unfit, having resigned office on account of health. Sir J. Lubbock was referred to, but only to be rejected: in fact he would not take it. Courtney's name came under consideration, but he has no fortune[65] &, though able, is deficient in 'h's' – a fatal fault in a Speaker. Hibbert was praised by the Premier, but scouted by the Speaker as not important enough. The two law officers were also canvassed: Herschell, who is fond of money, & making £18,000 a year, would not look at the appointment: James might accept, but would prefer the Home Office, and in his case there is the drawback of a houseful of illegitimate children, which does not suit with that office, as the Speaker must live in public. Sir H. Brand praised Dodson: thought he would do, though not exactly popular: Childers he thought still more highly of: lastly Harcourt was brought before us: the agreement seemed general that he would be the best of all, if he would accept: but his acceptance was thought very unlikely. He has in fact declared with his usual vehemence that he would have nothing to say to it: but Chamberlain remarked that he made just the same professions as to taking office.

Cabinet at 2.00: which sat till 5.00: I explained the state of matters in S. Africa, at the Premier's request: and it was agreed that the Basuto affair should go on. Some talk as to Cetewayo & Bechuanaland followed, but led to nothing.

I explained the plan for a new constitution for Jamaica, which the Cabinet has seen in print. This was sanctioned. Ld Granville introduced the subject of a commercial treaty with Spain: about which there was some desultory conversation. The Spaniards want the 1s. scale of the wine duties raised from 26s. to 30s.: in return for which it is thought they will give us M.F.N.[66] treatment. Childers reckons the cost at £600,000.

Ld Spencer wants us to bring in bills for: (1) Registration: (2) Sunday closing: (3) Police Reorganisation: (4) Union rating. But we did not give him much hope that these could be carried.

Question of payments due by Egypt for maintenance of troops was discussed, principally between Hartington & Childers. Hartington took the opportunity of saying in his bluff way that there must be a large increase of the army estimates, which was received in a silence which did not imply assent.

Talk about Lesseps, who is visiting the various English ports, & interviewing the shipowners. Question whether somebody should be sent with him semi-officially: but this idea was dropped. Northbrook read a despatch approving the conduct of Capt. Johnson in the Tamatave[67] affair. Some dispute arose as to the word, which is not very material, since it is not to be published. Northbrook referred to us a request by the D. of Edinburgh for the command in the China seas. It was agreed to refuse.

Some discussion took place on the recent meetings in Ulster, which have provoked riots, especially at Derry, where the Orange party took possession of the hall, & would not allow the Home Rulers to meet. Ld Spencer explained that in the south nationalist meetings had been stopped, because it was found that they were followed by an outbreak of crimes & outrages: Trevelyan, he said, wished to stop them in Ulster too: but there the danger was not the same. In conversation Carlingford talked violently against the Orange party & their 'lawless proceedings': ignoring, as it seemed to me, the equal lawlessness on the other side by which they were provoked. I was sorry to hear the Premier hold the same language, though more moderately. No decision was required or come to. . . .

12 Nov. 1883: . . . To the new law courts . . . for the making up of the list of sheriffs . . . The business lasted nearly an hour . . . Ld Coleridge[68] made some jokes, not extraordinary in merit, but it was strange to see how all the bar laughed with one accord.

Office at 3.00, sat there till near 6.00: saw Herbert, & much talk with him about filling up the two vacancies – Newfoundland & the C.J.ship of Mauritius.

Note that the Irish attorney general has written a letter to the Premier, which was circulated, stating the general belief that to lower the Irish franchise will entirely sweep away the Liberal party in Ireland – nearly all the seats will go to nationalists, & the rest to Conservatives. This view he does not personally endorse, indeed he disclaims it: but in such language as to make it doubtful whether the disclaimer is more than a form of courtesy.

13 Nov. 1883: Slept ill, I do not know why: a thing which does not happen to me twice in a year. Walk round Regent's park, for exercise.

Cabinet at 2.00, which sat till near 5.00: Northbrook absent.

Granville told us that the French have decided to go on with their campaign in Tonquin, so far as to take the two places which they are now threatening: after which they will make peace. They will not make a naval war on China, & will ignore the fact that Chinese troops are fighting against them, assuming them to be only local forces: a queer but convenient device, which the Chinese also will be glad to resort to. It is clear that the French very wisely mean to avoid the danger of interfering with German & English trade. Gladstone mentions a movement for separating the sees of Gloucester & Bristol. The promoters of it want to collect a capital representing £2,000 a year by subscriptions, to which the see to be divided will add £1,000, when the new bishop is to be created. A bill will be necessary, & he is in favour of it. Nobody objected.

The Speakership was again discussed: or rather discussed in Cabinet for the first time. The Premier thought we ought not to appoint any one from the Cabinet or government, at least until we had tried what could be done with outsiders. But he made an exception for the law officers, as to whose transfer to the chair there were precedents.

He would offer it first to the Sol. Gen. There were reasons against the Attorney. Some discussion followed, & strong opinions were expressed that it was useless: but the Premier persevered. Next to him were named Goschen & A. Peel: Goschen was much discussed. Everybody admitted his ability: but Harcourt thinks him unfit from want of dignity – his manner is hurried & nervous – Hartington doubts his discretion – Chamberlain does not think him a good chairman of a committee – I remarked on his want of sight – in short the general verdict was hostile. On the other hand, he is very able, much respected, rich, & might reasonably wish to be out of the way while the franchise question is dealt with. Little was said of A. Peel: it is believed his health puts him out of the question. Whitbread is impossible for the same reason.

Some talk followed as to the franchise bill. The Premier said a bill of 8 clauses would be sufficient for England. Hartington hoped we should deal with redistribution at the same time. The question of a bill for London was discussed. Kimberley very sensibly said that there seemed no chance of both that & a county government bill going through together with a franchise bill: & Gladstone added that a county bill was a necessity. It was settled to appoint a committee of Cabinet on the latter.

Fawcett was then called in. He objected to a proposal of the War Office that postmasters should be employed to help in recruiting for the army: but, as it appeared that they were only put on the same footing as everybody else, we overruled the objection. He said one sensible thing: that the want of attractiveness in military service is due to the fact that a soldier has no future: he spends in the army the six years during which he would otherwise be learning a trade, & leaves it unfit for any work except that of a labourer, & glad to take up with odd jobs. . . .

15 Nov. 1883: . . . At the office, long talk with Herbert as to the best method of negociating with the Basuto: in the end we agree to follow the advice of Sir H. Robinson.

In evening, received & read the Dutch (Transvaal) case, which is not long, & much to the point, though not very conciliatory in tone.

16 Nov. 1883: At the office, a committee attended by Granville, Kimberley, Northbrook, Chamberlain, & myself: Courtney, Ashley, Herbert, Lister, & Fitzmaurice. I put Granville into the chair as our senior. The subject was how to deal with the French encroachments in West Africa: they are sending gunboats in all directions, making treaties with native chiefs, in fact leaving no means untried to monopolise the trade of the coast. Our merchants are getting alarmed, & with some cause. They are trying to carry a railroad from Senegal to the Upper Niger: a wild project, as it seems, but which at least shows that they are in earnest.

We discussed various projects: among them a renewal of the often proposed exchange of territory, we giving up the Gambia, France the settlements lying south of Sierra Leone: but this was judged inexpedient for the time, the feeling in both countries not being favourable to such a transaction, & a general election being near in England. In the end we agreed to recommend to the Cabinet the sending of an expedition up the Niger, where our main trade is, to make treaties with the various chiefs on the river bank, not claiming for ourselves any exclusive advantage, still less pointing towards a protectorate, but pledging them not to grant exclusive rights as against us to any one else.

The question of accepting an offered territory on the Camaroons river was also discussed, but no conclusion come to.

Saw afterwards Sir H. Robinson, & talk on the Basuto business. Home at 6.00, quiet evening.

17 Nov. 1883 (Saturday): . . . Cabinet at 12.00, which sat till 2.30. All present, except Ld Spencer. We heard that Herschell has refused the Speakership, but after some hesitation: last night he was believed to have accepted.

Talk as to the French in China, without result.

Granville brought before us the plan of the proposed Niger expedition, which was agreed to with little discussion, & no difference of opinion.

Then we came to the letter of the Transvaal delegates: a long, & rather desultory, discussion followed: the general feeling seemed to be indifference as to the convention of 1881, willingness to release the Transvaal state from obligations as to debt, & if necessary to recognise its independence, but a strong desire to do something to prevent the Bechuanas from being eaten up. In the end we agreed to put certain questions to the delegates, before going farther.

Talk as to a new commercial treaty with Spain. The Cabinet appeared willing to make a sacrifice of £500 or £600,000 a year on the wine duties if M.F.N. treatment can be obtained. They were also agreed that Morier should not have the sole making of the new treaty, as he is thought rash, given to disregard instructions, & act on his own account.

The rest of the time was passed in discussing bills of minor importance which are to come on if possible next session. – Office, where worked till 5.30: then walk to station: Keston for dinner, rather weary.

18 Nov. 1883 (Sunday): Keston. Quiet day. Walk early . . . Read much to M. G. Duncan called in afternoon. Talk with him as to the impending strike in the coal trade. He thinks there is a dangerous feeling among artisans generally as to their right to higher wages: that they are inclined to ask more than the state of the market will allow to be given: & that much business has already been driven to Belgium.

. . . In evening rather troubled with stomach discomfort, flatulence, & distension, but no actual pain. The old enemy in a new shape! for it is gout.

. . . Wrote to the Premier, suggesting Sir J. Glover[69] for Newfoundland, Sir C. Lees[70] to replace him in the Leeward Islands, & Blake, the Irish magistrate, to succeed Lees in the Bahamas. Reading papers on Malta, but they come to the same result as before. The educated classes in the island seem to form a sort of local bureaucracy, & to them the very name of reform is hateful, as it means economy, which implies curtailment of their numbers, & reduction of their salaries. Luckily they seem to have no very active grievance, & chiefly want to be let alone. The extent of their attachment to England I believe to be fairly measured by the saying popular among them, to the effect that 'all foreigners are bad, but of all foreigners the English are the least bad'.

19 Nov. 1883: London by 9.17 train, with M.

. . . At 2.00, committee of Cabinet at the Local Govt. Office: present, Kimberley, Carlingford, self, Dodson, Dilke, Childers, Sir H. Thring, Fitzmaurice, & Mr. Owen. We sat 1½ hour, & all was not over when I left. We settled one point of importance, viz. that schoolboards, & education generally, are not to be included in the functions of the new local councils: Dilke & Childers were disposed to include them, Carlingford objected strongly as representing the education department: I objected also, on the general ground that schoolboards are working well, that men are willing to serve on them who would not care to be mixed up in all the other details of local administration: and that the difficulties of passing any bill such as that before us were so great that we ought not to add to them without necessity. Dilke gave way at once, admitting that he had expected no other decision, & feeling sure as he said that the Cabinet would see the thing in the same light. We then went on to the question of including poor law business in the work of the new councils: to which also I was opposed, but less positively than in the other case: nothing was concluded, & opinions differed. But I left a little before the end.

Office, where stayed till late. Settled with Herbert a draft of questions to be put to the Transvaal delegates: & read with regret a letter from Sir H. Robinson, saying that he cannot afford to go on at the Cape with his present salary, by which he says he loses £1,500 a year.

20 Nov. 1883: Cabinet at 2.00, which sat till 4.45. Heard that Goschen hesitates as to the Speakership, is inclined to accept, but distrusts his eyesight, & also believes that, having on one occasion been provoked into telling the Irishmen some plain truths, they will never forgive him. (But that matters less, for they will insult any Speaker, merely as such.)

Some discussion as to Transvaal affairs. The feeling seemed to be that we should keep a modified control over the foreign relations of the Boer government, leave them free within their own territories, reduce the debt, but endeavour to lay down such boundaries as shall save part of the Bechuana lands. Then we passed on to Cetewayo, & framed a telegram to Bulwer, rejected the idea of extending the reserve, agreeing that the restoration of Cetewayo is impossible, asking if Usibebu is strong enough to hold his own, & expressing a desire to leave the Zulus as much as possible to themselves.

Granville told us of his desire to bring about arbitration between France & China, which he seemed to think could be done.

Egypt came next under notice: it seems that the army in the Soudan under Hicks Pasha (a retired Bombay officer) is in danger, & it seems not improbable that the province may be lost to Egypt. As it has never been anything but a burden, the loss will not be great, if Egypt itself is safe: but how as to this? We agreed that no English force could be sent there, nor officers lent. I agree, but suspect that this decision, which was taken after little discussion, may be more important that it seemed at the moment.

The rest of the time was spent in talking over bills for next session, of which a great many were mentioned to be proceeded with if possible.

Harcourt & Hartington both spoke strongly of the mischief done by the resolution of last year, condemning the most important part of the C.D. Acts. The amount of disorder & indecency in garrison towns, now that the women are no longer under control of the police, is said to be enormous. The House is so divided in opinion that no legislation is possible, either to repeal the Acts or amend them, without infinite waste of time.

Office till 6.15, when home, & quiet evening.

21 Nov. 1883: At 2.30, committee of Cabinet in my room at C.O. – Granville, Kimberley, Northbrook, self, Chamberlain, Herbert, Lister, Meade, Ashley. We agreed that a sanatorium should be set up at Ambas Bay, under the Camaroon mountain, where some missionaries have already an establishment which is de facto British: and also that two 'kings' on the Camaroons river, who have asked for British protection, should have it. That is to say, these things are to be recommended to the Cabinet[71]. I note that Chamberlain inclines strongly to annexation in these parts, in the interest of British trade.

At 5.00, saw, together with Herbert & Ashley, the Rev. C. Mackenzie[72], a missionary, who has come over as the representative of Markaroane[73], the Bechuana chief. He is a shrewd & energetic Scotchman. He wants England to take over the Bechuana country. . . .

22 Nov. 1883: At Dublin, a Fenian named Poole has just been sentenced to death for the murder of one Kenny, committed 16 months ago. The murdered man was also a Fenian, & was supposed to have betrayed his friends to the police. The affair is noticeable because in the dock, after the verdict was announced, Poole made a defiant speech, saying that he had been condemned as an Irish republican, & was willing to die in that cause. He seems to have spoken with courage & some eloquence, & among the peasantry he will be a hero. I cannot see any sign that Irish popular feeling is less hostile than it was. Talking about this to Harcourt, he said: 'No, we have hanged a dozen of these men, & sent as many more to penal servitude, but they are not in the least intimidated. They are indomitable.'

. . . At 2.00, Cabinet, where all present except the Ld Lieut. The Premier held out to us hopes of Goschen accepting the Speakership[74].

We had a desultory conversation, the results of which, such as they were, I embodied in a mem.

Granville told us that the Sultan inclines to a Russian alliance. We telegraph, advising him to abstain from any entangling arrangements. Ignatieff, according to Granville, is again coming to the front: which bodes no good. And all the reports from Turkey describe the state of things there as growing worse & worse.

News, officially, of the total destruction of the Egyptian army in the Soudan under Gen. Hicks – a fresh difficulty in the way of evacuation[75]. We agreed to advise that no attempt should be made to recover the Soudan, but that ships shall be sent to secure the Red Sea towns from attack.

Report of the W. African committee read: the making of the proposed settlement in the Camaroons was agreed to without opposition, Hartington only asking grimly: 'How many places have we annexed this morning?'[76]

Some talk followed as to the possibility of putting a franchise bill & a redistribution bill before parliament in the same session. Hartington argued in favour of trying: but the Premier with more earnestness than I have ever yet seen him show in discussion, & at considerable length, explained the reasons against. Briefly, they are these. That he personally cannot undertake the labour of working through a redistribution bill. That the subject cannot be dealt with by a small measure – it must be a very large one. The proportional share of England, Ireland, & Scotland must be considered. The new register – that is after the extension of the franchise – must be consulted before you can tell what the new constituencies will be as to numbers. The mere bulk of such a scheme will break it down, if combined with franchise.

– Some of us observed that he proved too much, for his argument went to show that a redistribution bill was not likely to pass at all – I said, if you can't deal with them together, better put off redistribution indefinitely, & treat it as a wholly separate subject – perhaps to be dealt with by another parliament. – In the course of a long conversation, the Premier took occasion to say that Ireland, so far from being over-represented, had scarcely numbers enough. We stared. Carlingford of course supported his chief: but the question is simply one of figures, & we showed them that they were wrong. The true proportion is about 94 or 95, instead of 105.

Cabinet sat till 5.00. Work at office till near 7.00. Quiet evening.

23 Nov. 1883: . . . Office 2.30. Received the Australian agents, who came to talk about the French system of convicts in New Caledonia. They seem to believe that the French government intend to let their prisoners loose over the New Hebrides & New Guinea, whence they will escape to Australia & give trouble. I do not believe it, but promised enquiry & remonstrance if necessary.

Office till near 6.0, when home. Dinner to Sir H. Norman at the Northbrook Indian club, Lord Northbrook in the chair. – Much talk about the destruction of the Egyptian army in the Soudan, which it seemed to be thought would be a danger to India by rousing Mahometan fanaticism. . . .

24 Nov. 1883 (Saturday): . . . Saw . . . the Premier, who wished to see me about Transvaal affairs: but he soon passed away from these, & spoke with anxiety & apprehension about the Soudan business, which he foresees (as everybody does) will seriously interfere with the early evacuation of Egypt. He said that our position in Egypt was 'radically & essentially a false position': that it could not be maintained: that we must either leave the country soon, or else some other arrangement must be made. I said I did not suppose he meant to annex Egypt? He laughed, said no, we were pledged up to the eyes on that point, we at least could never do it, nor would the Cabinet ever consent: but then added he had no doubt it would be a very popular thing in England. His language left on my mind the impression that he thought such a result in the end not impossible: though personally he could have nothing to do with it. – I could not but think there is something comic in the situation: Gladstone, of all men in the world, compelled (as we shall be) to annex New Guinea & escaping with difficulty the necessity of seizing Egypt! . . .

26 Nov. 1883: Wet morning . . . No. 23 at 10.50 . . . Long letter on the franchise by Mr. C. Powell, the election agent at Liverpool[77].

Home, where received a Cabinet circular box with a mem. by Lord Wolseley: I agreed with the Premier & Northbrook that for the moment the intended withdrawal of troops must be suspended: future Egyptian policy to be decided, not in hurry or panic, by a future Cabinet.

The Premier consults me as to appointing Prof. Stubbs, the historian, a trustee of the Nat. Port. Gall. I assent.

. . . Much discussion in the papers on an article written for the Fortnightly Review by Chamberlain, on the housing of the poor[78]: which is angry and radical in tone, & unjust in substance, insomuch that even the radical papers do not accept its teaching as sound. Much of what he proposes is fair enough: but what is not reasonable is that the whole cost of sanitary improvement should be borne by a rate on the ground landlord, so that, if an owner has got his own estate into order, he may still be taxed to an indefinite extent to make good the deficiencies of his neighbours. This is not justice, & will do mischief in alienating men who have anything to lose. The article is evidently written as that of Salisbury was, to which it is a reply: for a definite party purpose, to make it appear that the radicals alone are able to deal with this question so as to do what is necessary, without taxing the ratepayers. In short it is a bid for leadership, as against Hartington. I do not think it will succeed.

27 Nov. 1883: . . . Received in evening the full answer of the Transvaal delegates, in print, & their draft of a new convention.

28 Nov. 1883: No interviews at the office, but long talk on Transvaal affairs with Ashley & Herbert. We settled two letters – one to Scanlen, to ascertain decidedly whether the Cape colony will take any step to secure the freedom of the trade road through Bechuanaland. (I am pretty sure they will not, they fear the Dutch & dare not offend them): but it is well to ascertain the fact, if only for our own justification. The other is to the delegates, telling them they must deal first with the question of boundary, before we can take up any of the other points which they have raised. – I wrote to the Premier, explaining the situation. . . .

29 Nov. 1883: . . . Talk with Herbert & Antrobus about the possibility of introducing young Talbot into the office, unpaid, to learn the work of a private secretary. They both approve the idea, & I think it will do, but will consider it farther. Dined at home, & quiet evening.

30 Nov. 1883: . . . Very little business. The contrast is curious between the comparative quiet of the place I hold & the constant bustle of F.O. And, in the absence of social claims on my time, I have really been more free during the last month, more master of leisure, than at any period of the year. M. too is well satisfied with London: the treatment of the Swedish doctor whom she attends improves her health & spirits, & as she thinks her sight also. . . .

1 Dec. 1883: . . . Wrote to Ponsonby about the Boer negociations, which have reached a critical stage.
     Committee of Cabinet at the Local Govt. Board: met Dilke, Dodson, Fitzmaurice, & Thring.
     Then office, where with Herbert studied the Bechuana boundary on a large map, for the Boer negociation. . . .

3 Dec. 1883: . . . Ward reports that the new leases signed in the year now exceed £10,000 of rent: the greatest increase that has ever been yet.
     . . . Telegram from the Cape reporting that the Basutos are divided: about two-thirds of them under their head chief Letsea are willing to put themselves under the Queen, but the other third, headed by Masupha, refuse[79].
     All the work today was routine, & not much of it: giving me an odd sensation of involuntary idleness.
     Ld Ripon's[80] unpopularity among the Europeans at Calcutta appears to increase, & is becoming serious. He was received on his return from Simla in silence, broken only by some hisses: the usual volunteer guard of honour refused to turn out: and at a non-political dinner his health was drunk without a speech, & received in silence: while an attack made on his policy by a later speaker at that same dinner was enthusiastically received. It is a bad state of things: though Lord W. Bentinck[81] was treated in the same fashion.

4 Dec. 1883: Walk round Regent's park for exercise, sharply, it being a cold morning. . . . Office at 2.15, stayed till 5.15, when home: the business mainly routine. Letter from Sir A. Gordon[82], which I answered. I can see that he thinks as I do, that all annexations in the Pacific, or even increased contact between white & native races, mean the ultimate extermination of the latter: &, while disliking the process, he does not see more than anybody else how it is to be averted.

Sent a letter to the Transvaal delegates, with map, showing the Bechuanaland boundary as we are prepared to allow it to be.

In *The Times* Goschen's refusal of the Speakership is announced, being indeed generally known &, as far as I can see, regretted on all sides.

5 Dec. 1883: . . . Wrote to a Rev. Mr. Hodson, to thank him for the biography[83] of his brother, the celebrated cavalry officer, killed at Delhi in 1857, whose panegyric it was my duty to pronounce in the H. of Commons. I did not know then that, remarkable as he was for daring and military skill, there were imputations on his character which but for the outbreak of the Mutiny would probably have ruined him, & from which his brother's book does not wholly clear him. His men plundered as energetically as they fought, which is saying a good deal. But in the moment of extreme danger the military authorities could not afford to be squeamish: they ignored Hodson's failings, & they were right. I remember Sir F. Currie[84] saying to me: 'Now he is dead, we can make a hero of him: if he had lived, he must have been tried by court-martial.'

. . . Talk with Herbert & Ashley about the Zulu trouble: but we could arrive at no satisfactory conclusion. We want the Zulus to settle for themselves who is to be their king: they are divided & helpless, & want us to decide the question for them. But, if we set up a king, we must keep him on the throne: in other words establish a protectorate, which is exactly what we want to avoid. Bulwer & the Natal colonists, if they could have their own way, would annex the country.

6 Dec. 1883: . . . Office . . . discussed with Herbert at some length the Australian proposals: which are all in the papers – some of them wild enough: they want New Guinea of course, which we knew before: they ask us to call on the French to put a stop to their system of transportation to New Caledonia: they hint that France ought to be induced to give up that colony itself (a hopeful proposal): and they lay down a kind of Monroe doctrine forbidding all annexation in the S. Pacific, without limitation of space, extending their claim for all that appears, as far as the S. American coast. This last suggestion is so far beyond all practical requirements, & so utterly without justification (for what rights have England or Australia over islands 4,000 [miles] distant from our nearest colony?), that I can scarcely suppose it serious, & probably it is meant rather as a piece of swagger than as pointing to real action. . . .

7 Dec. 1883: . . . Wrote to the Premier on Australian claims: ridiculing their extent & vagueness, but saying that I thought we must be prepared for a protectorate of New Guinea.

. . . It is settled that Arthur Peel, Sir Robert's youngest son, shall be proposed as the new Speaker[85]. His name & personal qualities are in his favour: he is less known to the public than perhaps is desirable in the case of an intended Speaker: but on the whole I believe it is as good a choice as could be made, assuming, as I see that the Premier does, that it is not desirable to choose a Cabinet minister.

8 Dec. 1883: . . . Many departmental affairs on hand:

(1) Gold Coast: Finances in a bad way, & want of public works much complained of: luckily there is a reserve fund put by for bad times, which was not meant to exceed £60,000, but has grown to £99,000. Of this, after much consultation with Meade, I agree that part may be taken for roads & necessary improvements: but I do this rather reluctantly, not liking to spend savings.

(2) Malta: A quarrel between the two elected councillors & the governor: turning chiefly on the question whether English or Italian is to be taught in the schools. This is a matter of some political importance, as the object of the Italian party is to draw closer the connection between Malta & Italy, with a view to ultimate annexation. I have referred the papers to Ashley, who has been passing some weeks on the island. Probably, if we stand firm, the opposition will give way.

(3) [Alleged sundry acts of fraud & corruption by the Att.-General of Grenada . . . 'but he has created so strong a prejudice against himself that I do not trust the judgment of his accusers.']

(4) Basuto: No news yet as to whether the refractory minority will give way. If they do, all is well, if not, our proposed arrangements fall to the ground, for we undertake to take them over only on condition of their unanimity.

(5) Answer from the Transvaal delegation, vague & not satisfactory as to the Bechuanaland boundary, but they do not close the door against further negociation.

(6) Zululand: Here again there is a deadlock: the natives apparently unable or unwilling to choose any chief: the whites in Natal & throughout S. Africa generally hoping that we shall interpose & declare a protectorate: the last thing I wish or mean if it can be helped.

(7) Australian conference: The rather wild resolutions in favour of general annexation are now followed up by others of a much more practical character. The conference proposes to create a federal council, with certain limited powers, able, within the range of these powers, to deal with questions affecting all the Australian colonies. This is a sound & reasonable proposal, & we can support it.

These, I think, are just now the principal subjects to be dealt with: and they are enough. . . .

9 Dec. 1883 (Sunday): . . . Called on . . . Ly Harcourt, whom I found – Harcourt came in while we were talking, and the conversation became political. To avoid interruption from visitors, he took me down into his study to finish what he had to say. He thought badly of the position of the government: was inclined to think that the reform bill would not go beyond a second reading in the Commons: possibly would not pass that stage: I asked why? He said that to give a lower franchise to Ireland, while it was necessary, would be very unpopular with a certain section: there would be a Whig cave: & he had much fear that Hartington might be disposed to resign: he, Hartington, had been dissatisfied with Chamberlain's language, & had hinted to the Premier that he did not see how he could support the bill as it stood. Harcourt thought Gladstone was to blame for calling so few Cabinets (in this I agree): the fact he said was that G., intending soon to resign, had become indifferent, & chose to shut his eyes to difficulties. Chamberlain, he added, knew the big towns well, but not the rest of England, & over-rated the strength of the radical party. He dwelt a good deal on the risk of Hartington leaving us, which certainly would be a blow, though in point of personal ability I think him over-rated. I said, by way of testing him, that if Gladstone & Hartington both went we should have to look to the Home Secretary for a leader. He shook his head & negatived the idea in a decisive manner.

Some talk about the murderer of Carey, O'Donnell[86], now under sentence: his counsel, C. Russell[87], has taken the extraordinary step of calling on the American government to intercede for him: which however will be ineffectual.

10 Dec. 1883: News of another Egyptian defeat[88], near Suakin, which is one more obstacle to our withdrawal.

. . . My sister came. . . . I suggested what I have for some time thought of, that her eldest son, who is hanging about London doing nothing, should come into the C.O. as an unpaid[89] assistant private secretary, to give him something to do, & in order that he may learn how business is done. She liked the notion, but must of course refer to her husband.

. . .I chose a new colonial secretary for the Falklands, £360 p.a., for which the happy recipient has to do nearly all the business of the islands.

11 Dec. 1883: The papers have been much occupied in the last few days with the story of Tennyson the poet laureate being made a peer . . . Generally the proceeding seems to be thought odd – it will not do the Premier any harm in opinion, but I doubt its doing him much good . . . No peerage has till now been given on purely literary grounds: Lytton, Macaulay, & Monckton Milnes had all three sat in parliament, & played there a part, one a very important part. And two out of the three had sat in Cabinets.

12 Dec. 1883: . . . Deputation of merchants trading with the west coast of Africa, who came with certain grievances affecting Lagos & the Gold Coast. Their chief points were: – the want of a resident at Coomassie, objection to the administrative union of the two colonies (in which they are possibly right): complaint of over-taxation & deficiency of public works (the two objections neutralise each other): allegations as to the indiscipline & uselessness of the Houssa police force, about which I promised enquiry: and some minor local grievances. They were very long, stayed with me two hours: but I think I sent them away fairly satisfied. They contended strongly that the long leave given to officials, & the frequent changes, were unnecessary: the climate not being really unhealthy! This I could not admit, they maintained their point, but all in good humour.

13 Dec. 1883: . . . Long interview with Herbert & Sir H. Robinson on the Basuto question, which ended in my being satisfied that we have received sufficient promises of submission to justify our taking over the country. According to Sir Hercules, about eleven-twelfths of the people are in our favour, only one chief, Masupha, standing out. I drafted a mem. on the subject which I enclosed to the Premier in a letter expressing my opinion, and hoping that it may not be necessary to wait for a Cabinet. But I do not feel sure that he will see the matter in the same light.

. . . I received at dinner three of the Transvaal Dutchmen, Kruger, Du Toit, & Esselen: the fourth, Gen. Smidt, was ill & sent an excuse: Mr. Scanlen, Capt. Mills, Herbert,

Antrobus: Camperdown, Tavistock, Sir E. Malet, Mr. Courtney, Lecky, Froude. Harcourt was expected but excused himself, being ill. The dinner was rather dull, I thought, for Kruger can speak no English: and it is not easy to make conversation through an interpreter.

14 Dec. 1883: . . . Office at the usual hour. Saw the Transvaal delegates, & had a long & unsatisfactory conversation with them on the subject of the western frontier. They absolutely refused the extension of frontier which we had proposed, & in effect claimed the whole country. We talked the matter over for more than an hour, but came no nearer to agreement. Sir H. Robinson & Herbert were with me.

Received by telegram the Premier's approval of our proposed action in Basutoland, which may therefore proceed at once. . . .

15 Dec. 1883: . . . Call on Harcourt, with whom I had an interesting but unsatisfactory conversation. He is more & more confirmed in the idea that Hartington means to resign[90]: the reasons given by him are inadequate: but Harcourt thinks that his real motives are twofold: one, the influence upon him of the fashionable racing set in which he lives, & by which he is continually taunted with being overruled by Chamberlain & Dilke: the other, fear of being compelled to take the lead of the H. of Commons, to which he does not feel equal, especially with the belief that Chamberlain is waiting to trip him up. Harcourt farther speculates on the probability that Gladstone will retire also, if Hartington does: foreseeing failure as inevitable, & wishing to escape the responsibility of it. (But I think this impossible – a Premier cannot throw up his office at a moment of difficulty, merely because he thinks defeat probable. And, though Gladstone has faults of temper & judgment, he is not in the habit of running away from his work.) He talked ingeniously about the absurd situation of a political party, itself united & ready for action, but paralysed because its leaders cannot agree.

Talk of O'Donnell: the American government has interceded on his behalf, assigning no definite reason: I saw Lowell's letter on the subject: but the Premier, at one moment inclined to yield, stood firm, & O'Donnell is to be hanged. Harcourt said, I think sincerely, that if Gladstone's decision had been the other way he should have resigned.

Office 2.30–5.30. Saw only Herbert & Antrobus: but much paper work. Home & quiet evening: but anxious in mind, for we have many political troubles. The reform bill difficulty is directly ahead: the Egyptian perplexity seems if possible more entangled since the loss of the Soudan: we cannot leave the country, yet our position is anomalous and false while we remain in it: the Australian demands are in part impossible to assent to: the Transvaal business does not promise well: & the chances of getting a London bill, and a county government bill, through parliament next year seem smaller than ever. Add to all this a Premier who wants to retire, a probable secession, and the Irish vote: not many elements of confusion are wanting.

I asked Harcourt about Chamberlain & Dilke, both of whom he knows well: he expressed a decided opinion that the former is the abler man ('Dilke might be cut out of a corner of him'): and seemed to predict for him great success in the future.

16 Dec. 1883 (Sunday): . . . Day dark, cold, & disagreeable: some snow fell.

17 Dec. 1883: Dark dull morning: can hardly see to read (10.00 a.m.) . . . A deluge of begging letters – the beginning of Christmas . . . Weighed, 15 st. 4½ lbs. Went to a water colour exhibition, but did not buy. Prices very high, nothing good under £35 or £40.

Office . . . Saw Forster, who came to talk about Bechuanas & Basutos. He has 'nigger on the brain' but was friendly enough.

Saw Sir H. Robinson, who is under the impression, I am afraid mistaken, that he has convinced Kruger, with whom he had a conversation of three hours. Saw, at his own request, Du Toit, one of the Transvaal delegates, the only one who speaks English. He was with Herbert & me for an hour, but we came no nearer to an understanding.

. . . O'Donnell was executed this morning: dying with courage, as all these Irish murderers do. He made no confession. Another martyr! but there was no choice, if anybody is ever to be hanged, for the act was deliberate, unprovoked, & done for a political object.

18 Dec. 1883: Dull foggy morning . . . Office early, saw Herbert, talk with him on Zulu & Transvaal affairs. Luncheon at the club . . . With M. to Knowsley by 4.00 p.m. train. Arrived 9.30.

20 Dec. 1883: . . . In the papers, some wild speeches by Ld R. Churchill, whose undoubted cleverness seems to be mixed with a certain degree of insanity. He is praised by the *Morning Post*, disapproved by the Standard, & ridiculed by the *St. James's Gazette*. The point on which he lays most stress is that the English army went to Egypt in the interest of the European moneylenders, whose investments in Egyptian debt were threatened by Arabi! . . .

22 Dec. 1883: Shooting . . . Brought in 565 head. Day very fine. Work having ceased, and the wind being from the west, there was a total absence of smoke. – . . . I observe . . . with pleasure that a long day's shooting does not now give me headache, or affect my nerves as it used: which I ascribe mainly to the use of a new & comparatively noiseless sort of gunpowder. . . .

24 Dec. 1883: Shooting on the Mossborough beat: Sefton, Galloway, Münster, the two Cecils, & self: we brought in an enormous bag, 1,108 head, of which 359 were hares. . . .

25 Dec. 1883: Nothing to record: three pouches came from office.

Showed myself in church: walk back with Sir W. Thomson: walk in afternoon with Lord Reay. . . .

27 Dec. 1883: . . . Saw Ward, with more leases: £11,700 the increase in this year, & by his book I see that in the last 4 years, since Jan. 1880, it is very nearly £30,000.

Saw Hale . . . Donations, to Halewood schools £10: to Rev. G. Lester, for the poor, £10: to Rev. Holmes £20: & something . . . to the St. Helens Volunteers. . . .

28 Dec. 1883: Shooting . . . 443 head. Day dull with a little rain, east wind & fog: disagreeable enough: the walking over moss land rather severe.

Some but not excessive fatigue. Five pouches from the office, a considerable mass of work, but less in reality than it seemed.

Sent a donation to the Cancer Hospital, Brompton: & paid away some other sums in charity . . .

Made up accounts for the year. I have spent £5,980 nearly in all: £6,000 being the limit I had fixed. Of this Ly D. had £951: other presents came to £692: books to £994: works of art £2,143.

As an estimate for next year, I allow:

Ly D.	£1,000
Other gifts	£500
Books	£1,000
Art	£2,000
All the rest	£1,500
In all	£6,000

In other words, one-fourth given, one-fourth to miscellaneous uses, and one-half to literary & artistic collection.

29 Dec. 1883: Sent £20 to a Mrs. Okeden, whom I never heard of before, but she is certified by Lawrence as a distant cousin. She writes a good modest letter, neither whining nor canting. . . .

30 Dec. 1883: . . . Wrote to Cross, who offers to attend quarter sessions. Wrote to Harcourt on the political situation.

31 Dec. 1883: Letter from the Premier, which he marks secret: to the effect that matters look badly as regards Hartington & the question of reform. He is to meet him in London today: 'will try my best with him, but I am not very sanguine': thinks it probable that I may be wanted in town. I answer, as of course, that I shall be ready to come up whenever required. It is odd that Harcourt, who wrote to me three or four days ago, thought the danger over[91]. . . .

Notes

[1] John Spencer-Churchill, 7th Duke of Marlborough (1822–1883), lord-lieut. of Ireland 1876–1880.

[2] George, 8th Duke of Marlborough (1844–1892), who succ. his father 1883: previously styled Lord Blandford.

[3] His mother, Lady Frances Vane, dau. of Charles, 3rd Marq. of Londonderry (d. 1854), had, beside her descent from Castlereagh, a half-brother, Frederick, the 4th Marquess, who passed many years in mental illness.

[4] Not mentioned under his name in B.M. Catalogue.

[5] Daniel FitzGerald Gabbett (1841–1898), M.P. (Lib. Home Ruler) Limerick City 1879–1885 (retired): bankrupt 1896.

[6] George Phipps, second Marq. of Normanby (1819–1890), thrice colonial governor: gov. of Victoria 1879–1884.

[7] The French Admiral caused the sudden death of the U.K. Consul, imprisoned a U.K. missionary on a charge of poisoning French soldiers, and refused to allow a U.K. naval vessel to land for supplies.

8   Sir William McArthur (1809–1887), merchant: lord mayor of London, 1880.

9   H.H. Francis, Duke of Teck (1837–1900).

10   William Keppel, Lord Bury, 7th E. of Albemarle (1832–1894), under-sec. for war 1878–1880, 1885–1886.

11   Sir Samuel Rowe (1835–1888), governor of Gold Coast

12   Perhaps Sir Charles Mills (1825–1895), soldier: first agent-general in London for Cape Colony from 1882.

13   A canard. For Cetewayo's sudden death, see below, 9 Feb. 1884.

14   Charles William FitzGerald, Baron Kildare, 4th Duke of Leinster (1819–1887): cr. U.K. baron, 1870.

15   (Sir) William Arthur White (1824–1891), minister at Bucharest 1879–1886, amb. at Constantinople Oct. 1886–1891 (dying in post): rose from consular service.

16   William Francis Cowper-Temple, 1st and only Baron Mount-Temple (1811–1888), Palmerston's stepson and inheritor of Broadlands.

17   The informer Carey was murdered on board ship, 29 July 1883, by Patrick O'Donnell, a fellow countryman without specific political ties. O'Donnell was hanged in London, 17 Dec. 1883.

18   Gen. (Sir) Percy Feilding (1827–1904), Crimean veteran, and 2nd s. of William, 7th E. of Denbigh (1796–1865). His younger half-brother also became a general.

19   Wyatt's equestrian statue of the Duke of Wellington (1846) was removed from the arch at Hyde Park Corner, 24 Jan. 1883, to Aldershot, after much acrimonious discussion.

20   Not at Oxford or Cambridge, or one of the great schools: untraced.

21   Sir William Shee M.P. (1804–1868), judge: M.P. Kilkenny co. 1852–1857: judge 1863–1868: first R.C. judge since the Revolution.

22   A Highland sporting estate in Perthshire, near Pitlochry, on the River Lyon.

23   H.R.H. Princess Mary Adelaide of Teck (d. 1897), younger dau. of H.R.H. Adolphus, 1st Duke of Cambridge.

24   Derby's other Kentish estate, in the direction of Tunbridge Wells.

25   Sir James Philip Lacaita (1813–1895), Neapolitan lawyer: assisted Gladstone in 1850s: naturalised in U.K., 1855: deputy in Italy, 1861–1865, and senator, 1876.

26   Sir Melmoth Osborn (1833–1899), Commissioner and Chief Magistrate of Zululand 1880–1893.

27   One of the leading Invincibles, Brady had murdered Burke in Phoenix Park, and was hanged on 14 May 1883.

28   Wellington Henry Stapleton-Cotton, 2nd Vt Combermere (1818–1891).

29   Col. John Ireland Blackburne (1817–93) of Hale Hall, Widnes: M.P. (Cons.) S.W. Lancs., Nov. 1875–85 (retired): educ. Eton.

30   Canon E.J.G. Hornby of Bury (1816–1888), Rector of Bury 1850–1888, s. of Rev. Geoffrey Hornby, Rector of Bury 1818–1850 (and cousin of Lord Derby, patron of the living of Bury).

31   T.H.S. Escott, 'The Radical Programme (No. II): measures', *Fortnightly Review*, Sept. 1883, pp. 443–447.

32   Gladstone sailed from Barrow on Sat., 8 Sept. 1883, returning to Gravesend on Friday, 21 Sept. 1883. The party called at Oban, Kirkwall, Norway, and Denmark, where Gladstone met the Tsar, quite by chance.

33   Cf. above, 1 June 1883.

34   Hugh Birley (1817–9 Sept. 1883), M.P. (Cons.) Manchester 1868–death: educ. Winchester.

35   Henry Charles Manners-Sutton, 4th Vt Canterbury (b. 1839), who succ. his father (thrice a colonial governor) in 1877. The family estates in Norwich were worth £8,000 p.a.

36   Gladstone and Tennyson received the Freedom of Kirkwall, 13 Sept. 1883, before a crowd of 1,500, Gladstone in reply paying a gracious tribute to the poet.

37   Sir (William Robert) Seymour (Vesey) Fitzgerald (1818–1885), M.P. (Cons.) Horsham

1852–1865: foreign under-sec. 1858–1859: gov. of Bombay 1867–1872: chief charity commissioner, 1875.

[38]   Camperdown was able, active, and ambitious, and his lack of political success is hard to explain on the information now available.

[39]   Feilden declined.

[40]   W.E. Briggs (b. 1847), M.P. (Lib.) Blackburn 1874–1885 (defeated): educ. Rugby.

[41]   R.M. Pankhurst (1836–1898), educ. Manchester Grammar and Owens Coll;. Ll.D. (London Univ.) 1863: original member, Nat. Assocn. for Prom. of Soc. Science, and a member of its council to death: working member of Nat. Soc. for Women's Suffrage from its start, Oct. 1867: m. Emmeline, 1879: wrote legal treatises. Contested Manchester (1883), Rotherhithe, and Gorton.

[42]   Also printed, with some cuts, in *The Gladstone Diaries*, H.C.G. Matthew ed., XI, pp. 654–660 (visits to Knowsley, 1881, 1883).

[43]   'Mr. Irving here 1½–6. We conversed freely on divers matters: he was treated with singular courtesy' (Gladstone, *Diaries*, 9 Oct. 1883).

[44]   Henry, 5th Duke of Newcastle (1811–1864).

[45]   Adela Hope (1843–1913), heiress of Henry Hope of Deepdene, and widow of the 6th Duke of Newcastle (1834–1879), became an R.C. in 1879 and remarried in 1880. In later life she gave herself up to good works in the East End, living in Whitechapel with two other ladies.

[46]   Henry, 7th Duke of Newcastle (1864–1928): succ. by his bro., the 8th Duke, b. 1866.

[47]   Frank Harris, 'The Radical Programme (No. III): the housing of the poor in towns', *Fortnightly Review*, Oct. 1883, pp. 587–600.

[48]   Lord Salisbury, 'Disintegration', *Quarterly Review*, Vol. 156, Oct. 1883, pp. 559–595.

[49]   Leone Caetani, duke of Sermoneta (1869–1935), distantly related to Derby through Caetani's mother, Ada Bootle-Wilbraham, princess of Teano: a great Islamic scholar, author of *Annals of Islam* (1905–1926, 10 vols.). A liberal, his distaste for fascism led to his settling in British Columbia, 1927–1935.

[50]   George Smith of Coalville (1831–1895), philanthropist, agitator, and writer.

[51]   Lord Salisbury, 'Labourers' and artisans' dwellings', *National Review*, Dec. 1883, pp. 301–316 (see also note 1290).

[52]   Sir J.W. Maclure (1835–1901), sec. of Lancs. Cotton Relief Fund from 1862: bart., 1898.

[53]   William Ferrand né Busfield (1809–1889), M.P. Knaresborough 1841–1847, Devonport 1863–1866: looked on 'labour as the source of all wealth;': a Cons.

[54]   Rev. Stephen Gladstone, Rector of Hawarden from 1872.

[55]   Cheshire home of the Duke of Westminster.

[56]   Reginald Earle Welby, 1st Baron Welby (1832–1915), Treasury official: cr. peer 1874.

[57]   The Duke employed 300 people at Eaton.

[58]   Hugh Lupus Grosvenor, 1st Duke of Westminster (1825–1899), created Duke 1874.

[59]   Then Victor Alexander, Earl Grosvenor (1853–1884): never inherited, but father of 2nd Duke.

[60]   Thomas Charles Scanlen (1834–1912), Cape politician: Assembly member 1870–1896, Premier 1881–1882, legal adviser to British South Africa Co. 1894, senior member of its executive council 1896: retired 1908.

[61]   Paul Kruger (1825–1904), President of the South African Republic 1883–1902.

[62]   Sir Henry Arthur Blake (1840–1926), colonial governor: resident magistrate 1876, special R.M. 1882: gov. of Bahamas, Newfoundland, Queensland, Jamaica, Hong Kong, and Ceylon, 1884–1907.

[63]   John Thynne, 4th Marq. of Bath (1831–1896): High Churchman and Tory dissident.

[64]   In fact Gladstone '*intended* a hint to the Princelets of the Balkan' – to be more liberal (*Diaries*).

[65]   **Note**: The Speaker said no man could perform satisfactorily the social duties of his office who was not able to spend £3,000 to £4,000 a year of his own.

66 Most Favoured Nation.

67 The main port on the east coast of Madagascar, attacked in 1883 by France, an event which led to the sudden death of the British Consul, and more seriously to the arrest of a British mission-ary, Shaw, on a charge of poisoning French soldiers. France eventually apologised and paid Shaw damages.

68 Lord Chief Justice 1880–1894.

69 Not traced.

70 Sir Charles Cameron Lees (1837–1898), colonial governor: gov. of Labuan, Bahamas (1881–1884), Leeward Is. (1884–1885), Barbados, Mauritius, and British Guiana (1893–1898).

71 This meeting figures in Gladstone's cabinet notes for 22 Nov. 1883 as: '5. Report from West African Committee of Cabinet – accepted' (*Diaries*).

72 Perhaps Rev. John Mackenzie, Tutor of the Moffat Institution, Kuruman: author of pamphlet, *Bechuanaland, The Transvaal, and England: A Statement and a Plea*: U.K. commissioner in Bechuanaland.

73 Mankorwane, native chief endeavouring to set up small fiefdom astride the Missionaries' Road to the north.

74 The Speakership was offered to Goschen, 4 Dec. 1883, who declined.

75 The Egyptian army under Hicks Pasha, 11,000 strong, sent to subdue the Soudan, was massacred to a man near El Obeid, 3 Nov. 1883.

76 Often cited to show the speed of British expansion, although the Cameroons in fact became first German and then French.

77 Not traced; not in Orchard, Liverpool's *Legion of Honour*.

78 J. Chamberlain, 'Labourers' and artisans' dwellings', *Fortnightly Review*, Dec. 1883, pp. 761–776.

79 See also below, 8 and 13 Dec. 1883.

80 Viceroy 1880–Dec. 1884.

81 Lord W. Bentinck (1774–1839), governor-general 1833–1835.

82 Gov. of Fiji 1875–1880, and of N. Zealand 1880–1883.

83 William S.R. Hodson (1821–1858), soldier: educ. Trinity: raised 'Hodson's horse' in Mutiny: captured Delhi and seized king: killed at Lucknow.

84 Sir F. Currie (1799–1875), Indian official: senior Indian official 1842–1853, chairman of East India Company 1857, vice-president of Council of India.

85 Arthur W. Peel announced his acceptance of the Speakership, 8 Dec. 1883.

86 Patrick O'Donnell, murderer of James Carey, was hanged at Newgate, 17 Dec. 1883.

87 Sir Charles Russell, 1st Baron Russell of Killowen (1832–1900), lord chief justice of England: M.P. Dundalk 1880–1885. Cr. peer 1894.

88 After a force was cut to pieces at Tokar, inland from Suakin, on 6 Nov., a further attempt to rescue the Sincat garrison failed in early Dec. 1883, only 40 out of 800 surviving.

89 Derby offered him a private allowance of £120 p.a., remarking: 'I do not believe that he will learn anything or be of any use: but it is well he should not be able to say (nor others for him) that he has not had a chance' (diary, 12 Dec. 1883).

90 For the cabinet crisis of Dec. 1883–Jan. 1884 over Hartington's opposition to a 'single-barrelled' Third Reform Bill, see Patrick Jackson, *The Last of the Whigs: A Political Biography of Lord Hartington* . . . (London, A.U.P., 1994), pp. 161–173.

91 Hartington accepted Gladstone's partial compromise on 2 Jan. 1884 (Jackson, *ibid.*, pp. 172–173). Over Christmas Hartington had written a memorandum which widened a gap which had appeared to have been closed. A meeting with Gladstone on New Year's Eve was crucial in resolving the crisis.

1884

January–June

Jan. 1884: Knowsley . . . The last year has been to me one of great prosperity and ease. My health has never failed, except that I was kept indoors for two days in May last by a heavy cold: & even on these days I was quite fit for business: the disease with which I am threatened[1] may be kept off by reasonable care in living: in point of strength & activity I am as well off as a man can expect to be who is approaching 60. Political anxieties weigh upon me less than they did: and of private anxieties I have had none. Ly D.'s health is improved by her new treatment: and her eyesight has not grown worse. I have lost no friend, & been engaged in no personal dispute. My political position is good, and I have not lost influence with the public, nor been much attacked for anything done by me officially: though the South African difficulties continue little if at all diminished. I have passed the whole recess without making a single political speech[2]: but this has been from deliberate choice, & not from indolence or want of opportunity. The Cabinet holds its own without apparent loss of popularity: but its time of trial is coming on, & many of our well wishers do not expect it to survive the year. As to that I have no opinion, & indeed do not greatly care. But for the first time I have got official work of a kind that suits me, & do not look forward to its cessation as to a release.

Estate affairs have been unusually prosperous: the rental shows an increase of nearly £30,000 in the last 4 years, though of this not the whole is yet realised: with the new leases of '82 and '83 it cannot fall short of £225,000. – I have bought in the year 370 acres in the Fylde, 66 at Halewood, & scraps elsewhere: in all about 460. I have invested in the year £55,000, & my total investments are now nominally £445,000: in real present value nearly £500,000. I have also about £14,000 uninvested, at home or with Coutts. Altogether the financial position is better than I could possibly have expected in 1870. If I should live 6 years longer, so as to complete 20 years of possession, I shall have laid by at least £800,000 in money or land, and shall have a rental (to leave to my successor) of £240,000. Probably no family in England has grown so rapidly in material resources.

. . . Day raw, cold, & dark, with east wind. Three pouches from the office. Sent £50 to the Lit. Fund, & £10 to a Miss Ford, a sort of exceedingly distant cousin.

. . . In afternoon received a telegram announcing Cabinet on Thursday. For this, after the Premier's letter of the 30th, I was prepared, but fear that it means a serious crisis.

2 Jan. 1884: . . . Scott, who has been head servant in the family for 15 or 16 years, writes to give notice of leaving, his own & his wife's health being the reasons. I regret it, for he has been a good servant: & I promise him a pension – amount not fixed.

Leave Knowsley 2.20 . . . Reach Euston at 8.10 (should have been 8.00) and sit down to dine at the club at 9.00. Many letters & papers, which occupy me till near 12.00 . . .

3 Jan. 1884: Up & at work early . . . Sent £10.10.0 to Brompton Hospital.

Saw Antrobus, & Lawson, who called for news. Talk of his son[3]: young: ambitious: just married at 21: has a seat ready for him at Truro[4]: etc. I note that Lawson had heard enough of differences in the Cabinet to be aware that Hartington is ill satisfied, but he knows it only in a vague way.

Walk, look at pictures: luncheon Travellers': meet Lord Houghton looking very ill & old[5]. Cabinet at 2.00 p.m., all present except Dilke. We sat till between 5.00 and 6.00. Thence office till near 7.00: saw Lawson again: dined Travellers': sat next D. of Cambridge: he very loquacious & confidential about the army: 'good material, but too young: impossible to get non-commissioned officers fit for their work': these were his chief complaints. I asked how the competitive system worked as to officers? He said there was nothing to complain of, most of them were very good. Talk of foreign armies: he thought the French had not improved, whereas the German military machine was far more perfect than in 1870.

The question dealt with in Cabinet was that of Egypt.

Granville opened, said the Egyptian government wanted to ask the Porte to send 10,000 men to the Soudan &, if he refused, then to abandon it. The discussion lasted long: the Premier expressed fears lest Cherif[6] if pressed to abandon Khartoum at once should resign. Northbrook would prefer an avowed protectorate for 5 or 10 years to the present anomalous state of things. D.[erby] disliked the affair altogether, but thought it was no use trying to screen ourselves behind the Egyptian government: 'We are the Egyptian government for the moment, & all Europe regards us as such.' As to the Soudan, I did not believe that the Turks would care to reconquer it, or that they could if they tried. Childers spoke of the impossibility of Egypt bearing the burden of the Soudan govt., even if it were reconquered. Kimberley would keep the Egyptian authorities alive, as a matter of form, but agreed with me that they must be under our orders absolutely. Hartington did not think the Egyptian garrisons in the Soudan could now be relieved. In the end a telegram was drafted, to the general purport that England will co-operate if necessary in the defence of Egypt proper, but will send no troops to the Soudan: that we have no objection to Turkish troops going there, but do not expect that they will be sent: that we do not object to the ports on the Red Sea being handed back to the Porte. These, I think, were the main points.

Some talk followed about S. African affairs.

4 Jan. 1884: . . . Childers talked to me of his expected surplus, which he thinks will be fair, though not very large: he will not try any ambitious experiments this year, there being so much already before the Cabinet that will lead to debate. He would like, he said, to reduce the tea duties by half, as from the lowered price of tea the percentage has become very heavy: he would like also to increase the spirit duties, which I cannot but think dangerous as regards smuggling: he thought that whenever county government is dealt with in earnest (which will not be this year) it would be necessary to make a large surrender of imperial taxation, in aid of the rates: and he wished to deal on a large scale with the question of succession and probate duties. His plan as I understood it was to substitute for both a single duty of 3% on the life interest of the person to whom property passes, whether real or personal, & without reference to the degree of relationship: he thought this would give a small increase, say half a million, over the present duties, & be a fair settlement[7].

I had also some interesting talk with Chamberlain as to the future of Ireland: he admits the almost universal hatred of England: thinks it may die out, as a similar feeling has done in Scotland: he seemed to me to admit that a federal union is practically impossible, & that federalism is only a step to separation. He did not say in so many words that he was ready to accept separation as a possible solution, but implied it by arguing that after all the danger that could arise from Ireland being free was rather imaginary than real: that the Irish could do us no harm 'a miserable little island at 4 hours' distance': but he seemed to ignore the possibilities of French or American alliance.

At the Cabinet today, all were present except Dilke. The Premier opened the discussion, explaining his plan in general terms. Occupying & lodger franchises to be uniform in town & country. Freehold franchise to continue in the country as now, but not to be transferred to the boroughs. Faggot votes created by sham rent charges to be as much as possible put an end to.

On these propositions various discussions arose. Chamberlain contended for the principle of 'one man, one vote': would sweep away plural votes altogether. Harcourt would enforce residence as a qualification: the Chancellor would fix the same polling day everywhere: which would practically abolish plural voting. Hartington would not exclude any *bona fide* owner from voting, whether resident or not.

Harcourt (with whom I agreed) did not see why property should vote in a county and not in a borough. Thought we were taking up a position which was not logical. We were not establishing uniformity either in regard of property voting or of residence.

These matters talked over, the Premier addressed us on the subject of redistribution. It could not, he thought, be dealt with this year. But he would give it out that it should be taken in hand next year: and he himself would waive his objections to remaining a minister, & introduce it. He was against electoral districts, would maintain the distinction of county & borough: thought there must be a large change: would give more members to a diffused than to a concentrated population: London for instance should not have 70 members which in point of numbers it had a right to. The south of England was over-represented: the north & Scotland had not members enough. He thought a moderate addition to the House desirable. Ireland had too many members, but it would be invidious to take any away, & the same object might be better attained by adding to England & Scotland. He wished the representation of minorities left an open question.

Hartington followed, saying that he disliked the extension of the bill to Ireland, & would have preferred that the subject should be dealt with as a whole: had doubted whether he could remain in office, but was satisfied by the Premier's assurance of a moderate scheme, & by his staying on in power to carry it. – (It was evident from his way of speaking that he had received private assurances on the points at issue, & that this talk in Cabinet was prearranged.) Spencer was glad that we did not give the Irish a fresh grievance, & would like minorities represented, but did not see how it could be done in Ireland & not in England. Chamberlain spoke violently against representation of minorities – it was a vital question – it struck at the root of Liberalism – he could not accept it in any form or under any circumstances. He retained his opinions as to manhood suffrage, which he thought would be rather conservative than otherwise (this raised a laugh) but the present settlement was not final, & he did not press it now. Some general talk followed. Carlingford felt sure the Irish would now be loyal! & added, sensibly, though apropos of nothing in particular, that an Irish parliament sitting in Dublin was not to be thought of as possible – once in existence, you could put no limits to its power. With this we ended.

5 Jan. 1884: . . . To Euston: Knowsley by 4.30. Day mild & wet.

6 Jan. 1884 (Sunday): Three pouches . . . Wrote to the Premier, enclosing a letter in which the D. of Albany applies for the government of Victoria. I express no decided opinion, but rather favour his candidature. . . .

8 Jan. 1884: Wet morning: four pouches from the office, with a good deal of work. Rent day dinner, the Knowsley tenants. All the usual ceremonies, speeches, etc.

9 Jan. 1884: Three pouches from the office . . . Very fine day . . . Second rent day dinner. I spoke about 15 minutes, about American competition, rates, fixity of tenure, etc., well heard & listened to. One negro was among the tenants, which is a new thing. I find he occupies a public house lately bought in Halewood.

. . . Sent £5 to a literary beggar.

. . . Ward tells me he now receives rent from not less than 5,000 tenants. Of these 3,000 are urban tenants, & pay on a single house: the other 2,000 are pretty equally divided between farmers & labourers, or cotters hardly removed from the position of labourers.

. . . The receipts from rents will soon be £240,000: when I reckon that £80,000 should go back on to the estate in improvements, £80,000 be invested, and £80,000 cover all charges, taxes, & expenses other than those connected with estate management.

I copy, for comparison, the rental at various dates:

1800	£31,881
1810	£40,270
1820	£48,614
1830	£58,331
1840	£72,616
1850	£95,199
1860	£126,196
1870	£165,000
1883	£216,000

showing an increase in 83 years of nearly 700%.

10 Jan. 1884: Left Knowsley . . . reached Euston at 3.50 . . . Day very fine, bright, & sunny: a singular kind of winter: we have not had one really cold day as yet.

. . . The papers are full of an American lecturer, a Mr. George[8], author of a book . . . which I remember Darwin enquiring about when I saw him last at Downe, the title of which is *Progress and Poverty* . . . Davitt, the Fenian convict, joins him, & Labouchere, who dares not profess entire sympathy with his ideas, consented to be chairman of a meeting which he has just held in St. James's Hall. . . . It is increasingly plain to me that a real wave of socialism is passing over Europe: and by socialism I mean, speaking generally, a demand that the state shall interfere to lessen inequalities of condition, to diminish the wealth of the rich, and to increase at their expense the comforts of the poor. Here, probably, it will assume a comparatively mild form: but we shall not altogether escape. . . .

11 Jan. 1884: . . . I note as curious the unanimous feeling expressed by the newspapers,

& at public meetings, against the Boers, & in favour of extending our influence in S. Africa. It is impossible to doubt or to mistake the strength of this sentiment: & it is exactly the opposite of that which prevailed 10 or 20 years ago, when colonies were generally regarded as encumbrances, & the burden of empire was thought greater than its benefit. My personal sympathy with the new movement is not warm: but I have no scruple in recognising and accepting it. If England chooses to throw away a million or two on Bechuanas, Basutos, & such like, she is rich enough to afford the amusement: and in fact the state of opinion leaves little choice. When the *Daily News* and *Pall Mall Gazette* are with the *Standard & Morning Post*, the practical unanimity of opinion which may be inferred is irresistible by any minister.

12 Jan. 1884: . . . Note as very unusual with me: I slept ill last night, & am nervous & rather irritable in consequence today. But there is nothing the matter that will not quickly pass off.

. . . Saw Herbert, & long talk with him as to current business.

Our principal affairs just now are: (1) Transvaal negociations: (2) Zulu settlement: (3) Australian demands on New Guinea: (4) new constitution for Jamaica: (5) squabbles with the new council in Malta: (6) quarrels & scandals among officials in Cyprus (but these I hope we have nearly got rid of): (7) request of D. of Albany to be sent to Victoria as governor. I think these are all that are urgent. Among them 1, 2 3, & 7 must come before the Cabinet. . . .

14 Jan. 1884: . . . The papers are full of Egypt: the advance of the Mahdi, & the evacuation of Khartoum, as to which there is a growing apprehension that it may be impossible from want of means of transport, & that a massacre may ensue. If it does, the British government will certainly be held responsible, not wholly without justice, for we are & must be just now the rulers of Egypt, though we are not willing to acknowledge the fact.

15 Jan. 1884: . . . Day foggy & dull . . . Osborne by 2.45 train . . . reach Osborne a little before 7.00.

Some talk with the Queen after dinner: she seemed in a placid mood, not fussy nor excited. She said a few words about Egypt & the Transvaal: I thought the opportunity a good one for telling her of the D. of Albany's wish to succeed Lord Normanby in Victoria: it was the first she had heard of it, & she evidently did not like his having asked me without her previous consent. Indeed she said as much, adding that having two sons abroad[9], & her eldest son having his own occupations & interests, she thought it hard that the Duke should leave her too. She also said that the position of a governor of a colony was not suited to a prince: which I thought it well to agree to, though it is not easy to see in what respects his position differs from that of a general or naval officer, who is also under the orders of non-royal persons.

She spoke of the coming session & its difficulties, & enquired what we should do if the reform bill were to fail to pass? I said I could not answer for the Cabinet but, as this parliament would by that time have sat for 4 years, I thought the natural course would be to ask H.M.'s leave to dissolve, & so obtain the opinion of the country. She seemed thoughtful, & it occurred to me that she had expected & wished for a different answer – that we should resign. But she did not pursue the subject.

Ponsonby was sent to my room, just as I was going to bed, to talk over the D. of

Albany's affair again: but he had nothing new to tell, nor had I, except this, that if the Queen wished on personal grounds to forbid his going, it was for her to say so.

16 Jan. 1884: Left Osborne . . . home by 12.30. Did not go to the office, but sent for Antrobus, & disposed of the arrears at home. They were not heavy . . .

. . . Speeches have broken out again after the calm of Christmas: Chamberlain has been making one[10], but in a style comparatively subdued and moderate. There is nothing in it to alarm anybody, and indeed nothing that is new. I do not see the advantage of all this skirmishing just before a decisive parliamentary battle – but probably it pleases the constituencies.

. . . I was told the other day at Coutts by the clerk employed for investments, who has a good deal to do with such matters, that a great change has come over the British capitalist of late years. He is cautious, does not go in for speculation, avoids limited liability companies, & will not look at a foreign loan. This improvement is due in part to the losses caused by Russian and Turkish loans, & by the repudiations of S. American states: in part to the committee set on foot by Sir H. James in 1875? 76? which showed up the rottenness of the defaulting governments.

17 Jan. 1884: Dull foggy morning: work by lamplight till 1.00.

. . . Saw Childers . . . He told me that Fawcett's parcel post has been a failure: the return from it in 8 months only half of what was estimated. He said Fawcett had forced the scheme both on the Department & the Treasury, against everybody's advice: and he feared the cheap telegrams would fail also.

. . . Gen. Gamble[11] called – a gentlemanlike & seemingly sensible man, who has administered Jamaica affairs for 8 months. He says the negroes are loyal, & in the main contented. The coloured or mixed race were those who made trouble: they & the Kingston Jews, who he said (and everybody agrees) control all the press of the island. The whites grumbled a good deal, chiefly about expense, but would support the government. The complaint everywhere in the island is the old one – no steady labour to be got. The negro will work hard at times, but in a desultory way, staying away when most wanted. Yet the General complained of the drain of labourers, by emigration of the best of them to the Panama canal: where surely the work is hard enough?

. . . Sir H. Elliott called, retired from Vienna: he talked of the doubt whether he should find enough to do as an idle man, & regretted that most of his papers had been accidentally burnt, but seemed pleased when I hinted that he had seen & done enough to supply material for interesting reminiscences. Talk about Austria – he thought the position of the empire difficult: the Hungarians were as impracticable as the Irish: no scheme of federation would be accepted by them, nothing but entire & absolute independence: there was discontent in Croatia & elsewhere. It was only the powerful influence of the Crown that kept the concern together.

The Jews were hated throughout the empire, & especially in Hungary, quite as bitterly as in Germany, which Sir H. explained by the extraordinary power they acquired wherever they settled. If there were any Jews near, the peasants were sure to be in their debt: they owned & controlled the press: they were detested, but very much feared. At the Berlin Congress, Gortschakoff (in the debates on their condition in Roumania, I suppose) described them as 'une vermine' & it required much persuasion before he could be induced to strike the phrase out in the printed protocol.

18 Jan. 1884: Another partial fog: work by lamplight till 11.00.

. . . To Coutts, & there bought £5,000 more N.S.W. 4% stock . . . I have now £50,000 in Australia, & shall probably stop there. Total investments £450,000. . . .

19 Jan. 1884 (Saturday): . . . Weighed, 15 st. 8 lbs.: which is more than before, & too much: but I cannot take a great deal of exercise, which would be the only remedy.

Office at 1.30, & stayed till 5.00 . . . then to station, & Keston by 5.17 train.

At office, long conversation with Herbert[12] & Sir H. Robinson considering the last answer of the Transvaal delegates, and we agreed on a reply, which is in substance an acceptance of their proposals. The controversy looks nearer to a settlement than it has done yet: but there may still be difficulties.

. . . Letter from the D. of Albany, who seems sanguine that he shall overcome the Queen's reluctance to his going out to Victoria: he thanks me warmly for what I have done on his behalf, which he evidently supposes to be more than it is. – I have no objection to his appointment: the governors in Australia have no power, their sole function is to keep a court, a prince will do this better than another man, other things being equal, and the selection of a royal personage will be taken by the colonists as a compliment. Moreover, the prince's position as a kind of unofficial adviser to the Queen, irresponsible & capable of making mischief, is not a satisfactory one: & it will be a good thing to get him away.

. . . The papers are full of the appointment of Gordon, of Chinese & Soudan reputation, to serve in Egypt in a somewhat undefined capacity: the object of employing him being to bring away safely the garrisons now in danger at Khartoum & elsewhere. The choice is good, for he knows the country, & has extraordinary influence over wild tribes: it is a pity that if it was to be made it was not made earlier, for he had actually left England to serve with a Belgian expedition on the Congo: & opposition critics will not fail to say that, if the thing was to be done, it might as well have been done sooner, when there would have been a better chance of rescuing the Egyptian garrisons. But this is the natural result of the position in which we are: governors of Egypt *de facto*, without any minister or department specially employed to supervise the work of government, & therefore unable to give proper attention to it. – Gordon, I should add, is not a man whom it will be possible to keep permanently in any administrative office. A fanatic of the Puritan type, satisfied that his way in all affairs is the best, and determined to have his own way, he has broken with his various employers successively – the Chinese government, the Khedive, the Cape authorities who wished him to settle Basutoland for them, and lastly Ripon, who had the odd fancy of taking him as private secretary: but they parted in a few months. . . .

21 Jan. 1884: . . . Peabody trust meeting . . . We shall soon have completed all the building possible to us at present, and must pass some years without further action, paying off debt, of which we have about £360,000. But it has been incurred for a reasonable purpose, is only temporary, & with the borrowed money earning 4%, while in interest we only pay 3%, we have gained by borrowing.

. . . Hartington sends round a paper, backed by one from Ld Wolseley, in which they ask for an increase to the army of 8,000 men, consequent on the occupation of Egypt. At least this is Ld Wolseley's suggestion: Hartington, I think, names no figure, but thinks an increase necessary. Another matter of dispute.

22 Jan. 1884: . . . Busy till 2.00, when to office, and at 3.00 to a Cabinet, which sat till nearly 7.00. Thence back to office, and work till 7.30, & again at night.

We were nearly 2 hours in Cabinet discussing the question of a loan of a million which the Egyptian government want from Rothschild. Granville introduced the subject, said Rothschild was hesitating from not knowing whether we meant to stay in Egypt or not. This led to general discussion of our position there. Harcourt talked of the Mahdi, the strength of his following in Syria, Arabia, etc. Granville said that Gordon speaks of the Mahdi with utter contempt. The Premier thought we could not alter our declarations of policy in order to satisfy Rothschild. Hartington said bluntly that we could not stay where we were, it was time to take up a more defined position. Granville remarked that everybody in England would be pleased if we were to annex Egypt bodily. Carlingford said it was not easy to justify ourselves for having let the Egyptian authorities do as they liked about the Soudan (referring to Hicks and his army). **Granville**: We could not compel them to give up the Soudan when they said they could defend it. **D.[erby]**: You must treat Egypt for the present as a protected native Indian state. Somebody in the Cabinet should have the special duty of looking after it: the work can't be done by F.O. in addition to all the rest. **Kimberley** agrees. What we have done has virtually destroyed the Egyptian government. **Granville** & **Gladstone** both protest: **Kimberley** insists: a general & rather discursive conversation follows. **Dilke**: This proposed loan is only the first. Others must follow. **Kimberley** would cut down Egyptian expenses severely. **Chamberlain** objects, would rather cut down the interest of the bondholders: argues that, if Egypt were independent like Mexico, there would have been repudiation long ago. **Gladstone** would steadily refuse to admit any special responsibility for Egyptian expenses. To admit it is virtually annexation. **Kimberley**: How can we say that, when we have forced them to increase their expenditure? **Childers**: The trouble is caused by the Alexandria indemnities which are a swindle. Hopes the whole matter may stand over. – In the end we send a vaguely worded letter to Rothschild, approving the request for a loan. **Harcourt** again (I forget on what provocation) denied the possible existence of an independent Egyptian government, & said it was useless to talk as if one existed. **Chamberlain**: You are arguing for annexation. **Harcourt**: Either that, or leave the country. Does not believe a native government possible. **Granville**: Six months may make a great difference. **Gladstone**: There is a strong Anglo-Egyptian interest, which will always press for annexation, apart from questions of party at home.

There followed a long discussion as to Gordon's position, by which it appears that he has fully accepted the policy of evacuation, though at first opposed to it, & goes to see whether his personal influence with the chiefs & the promise of respecting their independence will not enable the garrisons to be peaceably withdrawn.

Some talk later about the D. of Albany's appointment, the Wellington statue, etc.

23 Jan. 1884: Ward has sent up £10,000 to my account with Coutts, making the balance there over £95,000. Office soon after 2.00, & stayed till 5.00. Not much business.

24 Jan. 1884: . . . To Cabinet, which met at 12.15. All present except Spencer.

I mentioned the Queen's objection to the D. of Albany going to Victoria, which we all agreed must be treated as conclusive. I have never cared which way this matter was settled, the arguments *pro* and *con* the Duke's going being fairly balanced.

We occupied some time in a discussion among the H. of C. men as to bills to be brought forward, the order in which they should stand, & the referring them to grand committees.

Harcourt raised the question 'What shall we do for the temperance party?' saying they were our backbone, far more so than the non-conformists, except that they were often the same persons. He argued for a general Sunday closing bill &, when pressed to say why Sunday should be differently treated from other days, admitted that there was no reason, and said that for his own part he went beyond the principle of local option, and would close all the public houses absolutely. – I do not think he really meant this, but was provoked by contradiction. The Premier thought our promised bill for local government would do all that was necessary. Chamberlain thought, if we must do anything in that line, Sunday closing would be the easiest thing to do. Hartington said the teetotallers wanted to introduce the principle of a plebiscite, & we had never pledged ourselves to that. Much talk followed: Dilke asked sensibly whether we meant to carry a bill on the subject? If not, we should endanger other bills by wasting time. The Premier thought as we were not agreed, & there were more urgent matters, we had better let this stand over.

Childers then proceeded, with a view to the estimates, to explain the financial situation. He had evidently received a hint to make the worst of it: for he spoke of the revenue as likely to fall short by half a million of that of last year: the post office would require £600,000 additional: and the army & navy together asked for £1,600,000 increase. If this were conceded, we should have to provide by fresh taxation for nearly 2½ millions. Then the Premier followed. He spoke in a grave & almost solemn tone: he was wholly unprepared for the statement just made. He was the more surprised, because the demands were such as ought to have been foreseen: they arose out of no sudden emergency, nothing that might not have been calculated upon.

He reminded us of the resolution of last year in favour of economy, accepted by the consent of the Cabinet, & passed by the H. of Commons. That resolution pledged us to reduced expenditure. How, in the face of it, could he propose increased taxation? It was with him a question of personal honour. If a motion were made, condemning our conduct as contrary to last year's pledges, he saw no answer to it. He hinted plainly that he would rather resign than make such a demand as was suggested on the House.

– Silence followed, then general & rather confused talk. Chamberlain thought that to propose increased taxes would destroy this Cabinet. Northbrook objected to any reduction in the navy. Dilke said the French were reducing theirs. Harcourt observed that, if this increase in military expenditure were really necessary, it showed that the boasted army reforms had been a failure. Hartington denied the failure, said they had been and would be enormously costly. Reserve stores were absolutely wanted. The Portsmouth forts had not been armed. If a second operation like the bombardment of Alexandria had been necessary, it could not have been undertaken for want of material. – In the end we broke up without any formal decision being come to, but the sense of the meeting was clearly against the proposed demands. Hartington was gruff, almost surly, in his manner of speaking, but did not lose his temper. The Premier had evidently arranged with Childers how the discussion should be raised: his tone of surprise & indignation was quite dramatic: I don't know whether he meant it to be taken seriously, but he said, laughing, after the Cabinet: 'We have saved a good deal of money this morning': and expatiated on the rapacity of the War Office, or rather of the Horse Guards.

I wonder when he does his work? He had a breakfast party yesterday: Cabinet from

12.00 to 3.00: at 5.00 he called on Ly D.[erby] & sat gossiping for an hour, as if quite at leisure[13]. Yet he says that he does not work at night, as a rule.

Office till 5.30, when home. Quiet evening.

25 Jan. 1884: Wrote to the Premier suggesting Lord Morley for Victoria: other names mentioned were Camperdown, Dalhousie, & Lyttelton. But of these three the first is somewhat eccentric & difficult to work with: the second would almost certainly refuse: and the third is unknown to the public. **Note** that the D. of Albany now wants N.S. Wales, which will be vacant in 1885.

26 Jan. 1884 (Saturday): Cabinet at 12.00, which sat only till 2.00. Then office, where saw Mr. Du Toit, one of the Transvaalers, who wished to explain some points in their last letter. Keston by 5.17, arriving late, in consequence of the heavy gale, against which it was not easy to move.

. . . At the Cabinet, it was explained that Childers & Hartington had come to an agreement. Something is to be saved by spending out of the balances of this year what would usually be charged to next year, and Childers reckons his requirements at £$86\frac{1}{2}$ millions, which he can meet without fresh taxes. It was observed that, except in the item of education, & contributions to local expenditure, the cost of civil administration is no greater than it was 20 years ago. Kimberley spoke of waste in Ireland, where money is lavishly spent in the vain hope of conciliating disaffection. The Premier complained of the cost of the Irish constabulary, & wished it could be put on local funds. But Kimberley & Carlingford both pointed out, with general agreement, that local outlay involved local control, that the police was really an army of occupation (from this Gladstone dissented warmly) and that it must remain an imperial charge. We discussed some minor economies: then reverted to military matters. Hartington complained of the process of cutting down, of the want of reserve stores, etc. Harcourt & Childers asked why the marines could not be employed. There were 6,000 of them on shore in England, doing nothing. Northbrook objected to their being sent to Mediterranean garrisons: they are the reserve of the navy, not of the army. Childers said the D. of Cambridge had objected also on the quite different grounds that their presence would be made a reason for lessening the garrison. – The question was then raised of sending the Guards abroad. Hartington did not like it: the Guards are the only force you have in England which you can send anywhere. Chamberlain did not understand why, with a larger army at home than we ever had before, there was not a man to spare. **Harcourt**: 'We must not admit that Egypt has caused any increase in military expenditure.' **Hartington**: 'The effect will be worse if Egypt compels you to send the Guards abroad.' **Northbrook** thought it useless to treat the occupation as temporary: we could not be out of Egypt in less than two years. **Gladstone**: 'The question is whether our occupation of Egypt is temporary or not? If it is not, I agree with Hartington: but we shall know more in 2 months.' Granville talked in the same sense. In the end we agreed to the reduced proposals – as I understand the matter, the army estimates to be very slightly increased.

Then followed a conversation about an intended bill transferring control over liquor dealing to local elective boards – town councils in the towns, county councils when they are formed in the counties. Everybody agreed that it could not be carried, but it was thought likely to please the temperance party.

Some talk about cattle disease closed the sitting. . . .

28 Jan. 1884: . . . At 1.00 I called on the Premier, at his request, professedly to talk about the Transvaal: but the subject was scarcely referred to, beyond two or three questions, though our conversation lasted more than half an hour. It was a monologue on the part of my interlocutor, interesting to listen to, but very discursive: he seemed quite at leisure, & free from business or worry. He discussed the characters of rising men in the Lords, especially of Lord Rosebery, whom he described as 'intensely ambitious', ready to spend his great fortune in complying with public demands, an admirable speaker: but he doubted whether he would show equal capacity as an administrator. [Lord] Dalhousie he praised also, called him 'a noble fellow', 'he has the true liberalism, the spirit of self-sacrifice'. Thence, apropos of Dalhousie's encumbrances, he took occasion to diverge to the system for mortgaging estates, which he condemned in vehement terms: 'it was a blunder, a folly, he had almost said a sin'. Then he began to talk about a new dictionary of the English language which is being published, & recommended me to subscribe to it. Then he told me an amusing story of his having been recognised somewhere in the Strand, & a little crowd following him, to escape which he turned up Drury Lane, & heard the people asking what the noise was about, to which a woman answered that it was only the Salvation Army. This seemed to tickle his fancy greatly. It seemed to me that he was tired of business, & glad of a little gossip.

Office 2.00 to 5.00. Business all routine. Home & quiet evening.

29 Jan. 1884: . . . Saw Mr. Escott, editor of the *Fortnightly Review*, who wanted a place in Mauritius for his brother. . . .

31 Jan. 1884: . . . Cabinet at 2.30, sat till 5.00. But all our business was to discuss the speech, as to which there was no substantial difference, but much verbal criticism. I remember nothing special being said, except that among the H. of C. men there was a good deal of anxiety expressed as to the fate of a motion about checking importation of cattle, by way of preventing cattle disease, which it is thought Liberal members for counties will be obliged to vote for, & of course all the opposition, including the Irish. They seemed to think a defeat upon it possible.

To office, where saw [Lord] Morley, & discussed his acceptance or rejection of Victoria, which I offered him by letter. I pressed upon him the difficulty of obtaining promotion in the Lords, from the number of qualified candidates compared to the vacancies: besides those now sitting in Cabinet, there are Hartington, who must be a peer before many years: Lansdowne, now in Canada: Dufferin: Rosebery: Dalhousie: Enfield[14]: & not improbably Harcourt. Excluding the Chancellor, there is not room for more than six peers Cabinet ministers: so that the chances of a young peer on the Liberal side are small. Ld M. saw this clearly, & admitted that the opportunity was one not likely to come again if lost. But he was in difficulty about accepting on account of his mother who is old, infirm, & has no one to take care of her. He promised an answer on Saturday. . . .

1 Feb. 1884: . . . The O'Donoghue[15], who has twice before begged of me, asks again for the sum of £12: which being little I sent it: but his case is not one which deserves much sympathy: he had a fair fortune, which he ran through: & supported every demand of the Irish party irrespective of his own interest as a landlord. Now his tenants will not pay: his means are gone: & he lives, I believe, by doing odd jobs for the press.

... Work at home till 3.00, when to a meeting at the W.O. on colonial defences: – Present, Hartington, Northbrook, Childers, Kimberley, D.[erby], Sir A. Clarke[16] & Mr. Brand[17]. We sat an hour and a half, & settled that some works of fortification ought to be begun. – The Cape, Aden, Singapore, & Hong Kong were the points considered most essential.

... Sir R. Morier ... dined with us. – Morier full of his Spanish negociations, bragging a good deal, as his way is, but this time not complaining of want of support at home.

2 Feb. 1884 (Saturday): Troubled with rheumatism in the left shoulder & side, & very stiff in consequence: but it did not interfere with business.

Office at 2.00, & work there till near 5.00, when left for Keston.

Saw Lord Morley, who declined Victoria, with many expressions of gratitude, on personal grounds, not liking to leave his old mother to die with none of her family about her.

Decided to offer the place to Lord Enfield, who will certainly accept (in fact he has asked Granville for it). He is personally quite fit, and has a sort of claim on me, since it was the transfer of Kimberley to the India Office, caused by my joining the Cabinet, that compelled him to give up the under-secretaryship as it was necessary that that place should be held in the Commons.

3 Feb. 1884 (Sunday): Keston. ... Still plagued with rheumatism, & unable to sit down or stand up without pain, though otherwise well.

4 Feb. 1884: ... News in the papers of the death of Hayward[18], the essayist & diner-out: he was an admirable storyteller, having an immense fund of anecdotes, which he was always ready to pour out. There is no one of the same sort left: no one who, with equal ability, makes it a business to amuse society: I don't know why, but the art of talking seems to have gone out. Hayward was a Jew by descent: which did not prevent, or perhaps caused, his having a bitter hatred of Disraeli.

Letter from the Premier, not objecting to Enfield, but suggesting Lord Reay: I answered sticking to my choice, pointing out that Reay, though accomplished & agreeable, is half a foreigner, which colonists would not like ... The Premier gave way ...

5 Feb. 1884: ... Lawson called, talked of the future, doubted what a dissolution would bring: thought that the bad state of trade, cattle disease, & deficient harvests, would tell against government: in 4 years every ministry made enemies, people began to wish for a change, etc., etc.: in short he thought the majority would be considerably reduced, perhaps swept away ... He thought a dissolution in the course of the year inevitable.

Enfield called, & asked for two days to consider the offer of Victoria, which he feared for private reasons he should not be able to accept: he was evidently pleased with the offer, having felt a little sore at being left out in the cold.

... Met Pender, who gave me the bad news that Baker Pasha has been beaten in his attempt to relieve the Soudan garrisons, with a supposed loss of 2,000. ...

6 Feb. 1884: Work at home till 11.30, when to an early Cabinet suddenly summoned: which sat only an hour, on account of the H. of Commons. The subject was the motion about to be brought on, in favour of increased restrictions on the importation of cattle from countries where disease exists. This it is understood can & will be carried against us, which would be a vote of censure, compelling dissolution or resignation. We decided therefore to meet it by bringing in a bill, which will at any rate stave off the danger. All were substantially agreed, but the Premier was in a bad humour, the first time I have seen him so, contradicting everybody & showing impatience. When Egypt was mentioned he withdrew saying that he must go to the House. Harcourt & Chamberlain went with him, the rest stayed, & agreed that the day ought not to pass without our having considered the state of Egypt: this was settled, we leaving it to the Premier to fix the hour of meeting again. (The news of Baker's defeat is confirmed, & another Egyptian force under Tewfik seems to have been destroyed also.)

Home for luncheon: then office again. A meeting was settled to be held at the Premier's rooms at Westminster, but it was cut short by the necessity of his attendance in the House: &, the summons being delayed, I did not arrive until it was over. I however met him accidentally in the passage: he had recovered his temper, and had been making a speech. I saw Childers too, who told me that nothing had been settled except that some marines should be landed at Suakin or Seyla: everybody had agreed that it would be madness to send an expedition inland. Our anxiety is now for Gordon, who is travelling alone through a country which by this time is probably in insurrection, & certainly in a disturbed state.

Dined at the National Liberal Club by invitation, it being a house dinner: I was chairman . . . We sat till near 11.00: all went off well. My neighbour was Rogers, the professor & economist[19]: a rough sort of being, & not very much of a gentleman, but well informed & amusing.

7 Feb. 1884: Work as usual till 11.00. F.A.S.[tanley] called on M. & I saw him for a few minutes. All cordial & pleasant.

Walk with Dalhousie round Regent's park.

. . . Notice was given in both Houses of a vote of censure to be moved next week.

Details of Baker's defeat are coming in: they show that the Mahdi's Arabs fight with all the energy of religious fanaticism, & that the Egyptians will not fight at all. In fact they seem not to have had even the courage to defend themselves when attacked, but lay down to be slaughtered like sheep. They were 3,500 in number, the Arabs who attacked them probably not over 1,500: yet there was no battle, only a flight and a massacre . . . their conduct helps to explain how the peasantry of Egypt have submitted for innumerable generations, to every master in turn. Or perhaps the statement should be inverted: it is because they have been so trodden under foot that they cannot be made soldiers.

8 Feb. 1884: . . . Cabinet suddenly summoned met at 3.00, and sat till 4.20, to consider a proposal of Hartington's originating with Ld Wolseley, for the sending of an expedition to Suakin to fight & disperse the Arabs there, with a view to the moral effect to be produced, thereby making easier Gordon's mission to Khartoum. So he put it but, in a later part of the mem. which Hartington read, Ld W. lets it be seen that the real object of this expedition should be to recover the eastern Soudan. Much general & rather confused talk followed. **The Chancellor**: 'It is one thing to take steps for the personal relief of Gordon, & quite another to alter our general policy.' **Harcourt**: 'Our policy is the relief of Khartoum.' **The Premier**: 'Is there reason to suppose that the garrison of Khartoum is in danger?' **Dilke**: Is against so large an expedition as that proposed, but would hold the coast in greater force. **Kimberley**: 'The step proposed will take you further than you mean. You will have to follow the Arabs into the interior.' **D.[erby]**: Does not see how strengthening the force at Suakin can help the garrison at Khartoum.

Hartington: 'If anything goes wrong with Gordon, you will have to go to Khartoum or go out.'

Northbrook: 'Baker's defeat may alter everything. We ought to ask Gordon how we can help him.'

Much talk on this, & in the end it appears that a message in this sense was sent yesterday, but we draft & agree upon a second, enlarging the terms of the first. Hartington maintains to the last his proposal of an expedition to Suakin, but is alone.

To office, where by appointment met the Transvaal delegates, & discuss with them for an hour the question of debt & foreign relations. Sir W. Gurdon of the Treasury & Herbert were with me. Work at office till near 7.00, when home, all business cleared off.

9 Feb. 1884: Grillion breakfast, about 25 present . . . Two candidates were balloted for – A. Balfour[20] & Waddington[21], but to the general surprise neither got in. Balfour may have made enemies by his rather dictatorial style of writing & talking, but Waddington can have none, & is popular everywhere.

. . . News in afternoon that Cetewayo is dead, suddenly, of disease of the heart. A good deliverance: but I suppose the natives will say that he has been poisoned[22]. What we could have done with him had he lived I cannot imagine: he could not have remained long in the reserve without danger of disturbance: Natal would not have received him, nor probably the Cape, except as a prisoner: to deport him beyond seas would have caused clamour in England: and to send him back among his own people was to ensure his being killed. Bulwer[23] will be happier, & we also. With the Transvaal settlement, as I hope, nearly completed, and the Basutos pacified, if they are so, the worst of our South African troubles will be over. – I telegraphed at once to Bulwer to know what he would recommend under the new conditions.

My colonial or departmental difficulties are just now few. Malta & Jamaica are both dissatisfied, but not I think to any serious degree: in Canada there is no trouble of any kind: South Africa I have mentioned: Ceylon & the east are quiet: Australia is maturing the plan of confederation, & until that takes some definite shape the question of New Guinea need not be seriously dealt with.

For the moment, the franchise bill & all other legislation seems forgotten: Baker's defeat, Gordon's mission, the probable fate of the Egyptian garrisons & the conduct of the Cabinet, past & future, in relation to Egypt, occupy all attention, & fill the newspapers. I do not expect a large majority in the Commons on the vote of censure: especially if matters go badly at Khartoum. . . .

11 Feb. 1884: . . . Cabinet at 12.00: which sat till near 2.00, entirely occupied with discussion on Egyptian affairs, the aspect of which, both parliamentary & on the spot, is disagreeable enough. The feeling in favour of doing something to relieve the garrisons on the Red Sea coast is intensely strong, & evidently cannot be resisted. But the Premier does not sympathise with it, & will stand out as long as he can. The discussion in Cabinet was confused, turning chiefly on details, & I remember little of it. . . .

12 Feb. 1884: Cabinet suddenly summoned at 11.00, sat till 12.30. Egypt the only subject discussed. The necessity of bringing together a force at Suakin, and of relieving the Tokar garrison if possible, was admitted: that of Sinkat is destroyed, as we learn by a telegram of today. The Premier was very averse to taking any step in the matter, reasoning quite logically that, if it was our business at all, it should have been done long ago: and that our only justification for not acting till now was that we were not called upon to act at all. This is unanswerable, but popular feeling knows nothing of logic: & we all pressed upon him the parliamentary danger of absolute inaction when English sentiment was strongly roused. He assented at last, not willingly, but yielding to reason. It was impossible not to think of the outpouring of rhetoric which there would have been, had he been in opposition while these transactions passed, & Disraeli in office: for, however small may be our responsibility for the massacre of Egyptian garrisons, we are certainly more responsible than the government of 1876 were for the Bulgarian massacres of the Turkish irregulars. However, it was nobody's business to say this, though more than one thought it.

. . . House of Lords at 4.00, where a large muster, nearly 300 peers, & the galleries full. Salisbury spoke ½ of an hour: not badly, for he did not spoil his case by excess of violence, which is sometimes his fault: Granville answered, rather long, & in parts tedious, as when he enumerated in detail the reforms which we are making in Egypt: but I suppose the statement of them will be of use out-of-doors: his argument was sound but, as I thought, a little too much occupied with small points, & losing sight of the facts that needed most to be dwelt upon. Cairns followed, less effective than usual. He was followed by the [Lord] Chancellor: then came Lamington, Aberdeen, Dunraven, & Bury: I rose at 10.00, & spoke till near 11.00, arguing the whole case pretty closely, right enough in substance, but not always satisfying myself as to words & voice. However, I was very well listened to & I said what I meant to say. Cranbrook wound up on his side with one of the speeches that he always makes: weak in argument, but violent in language, & still more so in manner. Towards the close he yelled and ranted in a style which would have been very effective at a public meeting but only made the peers stare & wonder what it all meant. Kimberley answered shortly. We divided 181 to 87: but nobody seemed much excited, as it was known that no result would follow. Home by 12.30, well pleased to have got this business over.

13 Feb. 1884: . . . Called on F.A.S.[24] & walked with him in Regent's park. Talk of his eldest son[25], whom I wish F. now to consider & recognise as the future heir to title & estates: if the socialists leave us any estates to succeed to.

Office at 3.00, work there till past 6.00: settled draft of a new convention for the Boers. Saw Ashley & Herbert, & long talk with them.

. . . Much talk everywhere as to the Egyptian debate: it seems agreed on all hands that we shall have a majority of 50. The Irish it is said will vote for us, not out of love for the government, but in revenge on Northcote, whose Ulster campaign they have not forgiven, though no language could be milder than his. He is said to have failed to use his opportunity yesterday: his speech[26] being tame & feeble, so much so as to disgust his own party. This enhanced the effect of the Premier's reply[27]: which except that his voice had lost its old power is said to have excelled the performances of his best days. It has, however, provoked the general remark: 'What would he not have made of the attack, if he had been in opposition?' Certainly, the destruction of the Egyptian garrisons is a tempting subject to anyone disposed to get up an 'atrocity agitation' & capable of doing so with effect.

The public also observes, quite truly, that the opposition have selected a wrong point for their attack. We have not been inconsistent: the fault that may be most reasonably imputed [to] us is that we have been too consistent: that we have refused to recognise our responsibilities as rulers of Egypt in deference to the fiction of an independent Egyptian government which we have tried to keep up. For this the Premier is mainly responsible: but his opinion engages that of the Cabinet. If the vote of censure had been directed to this aspect of the case, it would have been much more difficult to resist: but to attack us on this ground would have implied the adoption of a rival policy by the Conservative leaders: & for this it seems they were not prepared. They have abstained therefore from blaming us where we may have been wrong: and they have accused us instead of not knowing our own minds: which they cannot prove, since it is not the case.

14 Feb. 1884: . . . The Queen has published a second book[28] about her life in the Highlands, about which the newspapers are trying to be civil, not very successfully. It is in plain English feeble egotistical gossip about herself and her family, with perpetual reference to Brown, her confidential servant, to whom as representative of the Highlanders generally the book is dedicated . . . It is a pity for her own sake that she has produced this publication, which will give the world a much lower impression of her good sense than is the truth. It is characteristic that she praises the Scotch Highlanders enthusiastically for their attachment to the Jacobite cause – the cause in fact of despotism against parliamentary government – though she probably did not herself see the inference that would be drawn as to her sympathies. . . .

16 Feb. 1884: . . . The vote of censure is the general subject of conversation: & it seems to be generally felt that the battle is being fought on a wrong issue, as I have noted above. There is no doubt a general feeling, on both sides, that the Cabinet ought to have taken on itself the whole responsibility of Egyptian administration at the time when we first occupied Egypt: that, had we done this, a more decided policy would have been pursued about the Soudan, & the inevitable retreat would have been effected with less injury & loss: & that our idea of setting an independent Egyptian government on its legs is a chimerical one. How far this judgment is accurate, or how far it is inspired by dislike of the idea of giving up Egypt a year or two hence, I am not well able to judge: but evidently, if acted upon, it implies annexation, or a protectorate which would differ from annexation only in name: and this policy the opposition, however they may incline to it, have not ventured to embody either in their resolution or their speeches.

Northcote is much found fault with for the timidity – which his friends call moderation – of his speech, & many of the party do not disguise their preference for Randolph Churchill as a leader. The latter is very clever, active, and pushing: but, though a duke's son, he is hardly a gentleman: his personal attacks are pushed beyond what the English public will tolerate, & even those who are amused & pleased by them have not much respect for the speaker. Still, he is young, & may mend, if his health does not break down, & if he does not go mad: both possibilities.

17 Feb. 1884: . . . Another death during the last few days has excited some notice: that of Chenery[29], the editor of *The Times*. He was only 57: a good scholar, learned especially in eastern languages, & an agreeable member of society: but a very unskilful editor. He seemed to know nothing of the art of journalism as distinguished from literature: his articles were essays, & his news was often a day late. Report says that Walter, the proprietor, employed him as being a man who would allow him, Walter, to take part in the management, which Delane never would do: but, whatever the cause, *The Times* has certainly lost for the moment the position which it has held ever since the Crimean War. The *Standard* and *D. News* are both better written: the *Telegraph* is better informed. It is really now the worst of the dailies, except as to foreign correspondence, & not the best even in that respect.

The changes & fluctuations in newspapers are remarkable. Two years ago, the best written daily papers were the *Pall Mall* & the *St. James's Gazette*, both coming out in the afternoon: now the *Pall Mall*, having lost Morley[30] as its editor, is a very inferior concern, & the *St. James's*, having caused heavy loss to its owners (the story is £10,000 or £12,000 yearly), is managed on a cheaper system, & has fallen off in proportion. The *Standard* & *Telegraph* have more & more taken the lead, & seem likely to keep it.

18 Feb. 1884: London by 10.12 train . . . Office at 1.00. Received the Transvaal delegates at 2.00, till 2.30, when I was obliged to go away to a Cabinet suddenly summoned: but they stopped on with Herbert & Sir H. Robinson, discussing & settling points of detail. I found them on return from the Cabinet at 4.00.

The object of our meeting was to consider the necessity of increasing the force in Egypt by one or two battalions: which we decided to do, without objection anywhere. Also to discuss the answers to be given to sundry parliamentary questions. One of these relates to a proclamation alleged to have been issued at Khartoum by Gordon, in which he is said to have legalised the slave trade: a thing so utterly opposed to all his tendencies that there must evidently be some mistake. Possibly all he has done is to assure the people that he has not come with orders to emancipate the slaves, which would of course set all the owners against him. But we do not know what he has said: and the Premier wisely told the House so. . . .

19 Feb. 1884: . . . Lawson called: talk chiefly about Gordon's proclamation. I was able to show L. a passage in Gordon's published letters, which explains it, & wrote to the Premier referring to this passage, as it shows Gordon's line of thought & action in questions relating to slavery.

. . . Office, where saw the Transvaal delegates from 3.00 to 4.30. They were very troublesome to deal with, raising over again difficulties which we thought had been disposed of, and showing great obstinacy on small points. But we went half through the draft convention, & another meeting ought to finish the business.

20 Feb. 1884: . . . Office 2.00 to 4.00. Saw Capt. Moloney[31], lately promoted from the Gold Coast to the Gambia, & talk with him. He tells me of the existence of a range of hills some 25 miles from the coast of the G. Coast colony, where Europeans can live in a comparatively healthy climate. Talks also sensibly of the establishment of a botanic garden at the Gambia as a means of introducing useful plants from other tropical climates.

. . . The intended vote of censure ended at 2.00 this morning in a majority for ministers of 49: about what was expected: the Irish party was divided: Parnell took 30 followers into the opposition lobby, and 17 other Home Rulers voted with the government. The speaking was better on the last night than before: Goschen & Cowen both took a line of their own, & were listened to as men who really contributed something to the general stock of knowledge. Morley who spoke (I think) on Friday delivered an essay which those who cared to listen to it thought able: but as a speech it failed. He has like Mill made a mistake in leaving literature & journalism, for both of which he was well fitted, and taking to parliamentary life.

Marriott[32], the member for Brighton, spoke strongly against government, & created a sensation by offering to resign his seat & stand a new election, to see if his constituents would support him. This sounded brave, & drew loud applause: but in fact he risks nothing, for the Liberal voters would certainly turn him out at the next election, & by retiring now he makes it difficult for the Conservatives not to support him: so that he has done a prudent thing which looks like an act of audacity – very clever.

Hartington threw out hints of staying longer in Egypt than we had thought of: I believe he is right, & it is necessary, but the Premier will hardly agree with him. The effect of the debate has been, I think, to show two things: (1) that the Irish are not in a position to throw all their weight into one scale, & so affect party politics: (2) that the opposition have just now neither a leader in the H. of C. nor a policy. – Northcote is universally, though very unjustly, abused for timidity & moderation: Randolph Churchill is not equal to the place, except as to audacity, of which he has plenty: and no one else has shown any sign of wishing to hold so difficult & thankless a position. Nor has the Conservative party announced any policy on which they could rally their supporters.

We are safe, as much from the weakness of our rivals as from our own strength. On the other hand, if the object – or one object – of the debate were to take up time, & so delay legislation, that object has been gained, and I have no doubt but that obstruction, more or less disguised, will be the system of fighting adopted.

21 Feb. 1884: . . . Cabinet at 2.45, which sat till 4.15. Talk very confused, no order, & it was impossible to be sure what was or was not decided. The subject was Egypt, & a perplexing telegram from Gordon, in which he proposes to give over the Soudan to one Zebehr Pasha, who was in former times his chief opponent, whom he wished only a few weeks ago to remove out of Egypt, & who is head of the slave hunting & slave dealing Arabs on whom Gordon made unceasing war.

Granville said when he read this telegram he was disposed to think that Gordon must have gone out of his mind – the Premier made some remarks on the mixture with his undoubted genius of something like insanity. In the end it was settled to let him know that the choice of Zebehr would be much objected to here, & that we did not wish to take on ourselves to choose a ruler of the Soudan. At least this I believe to be the decision, but there was so much confusion that I could not be sure. – Spoke to Northbrook & Kimberley, with whom I went away, as to the want of order in our proceedings: both agreed, Northbrook especially saying: 'It is very dangerous, & will bring us into trouble some day.'

. . . Wrote to Sir G. Bowen[33], a private letter, which I did with no pleasure, for in truth his vanity, fussiness, & pomposity have thoroughly disgusted me: if ever capable of good work, which I doubt, he is now past it: but he has written often to me, & complained of not getting answers.

22 Feb. 1884: . . . Saw there Sir T. Macilwraith[34], the late Premier of Queensland, who started the movement in favour of annexing N. Guinea last year. He is a heavy, rather clownish Scotchman of 50: shrewd & plainspoken, with a strong Scotch accent. He did not seem to care much for the annexation for its own sake, but was very earnest about the prevention of French convicts landing in Australia. Some he says come over every year, & the French do not care to reclaim them. He described himself as representing the party of property, the landed or squatting interest: & imputed to his opponents, the popular party, a policy of continually increasing debt. He said the doctrines of H. George[35] had had a wonderful run in Australia: where no doubt there is less difficulty in putting them in force than in an old settled country.

At 3.00 the Transvaal delegates came again, & stayed till 4.30. We settled all except one point, & that I believe will be arranged without difficulty. Their usual slowness & obstinacy was counteracted by impatience of longer delay, for they want to get back to their Volksraad, and they were in a more conciliatory mood than I have found them hitherto.

H. of Lords at 4.30, where Salisbury moved for his commission of enquiry into the dwellings of the working classes, which had been agreed to, & the debate which followed was therefore a mere waste of words. He spoke well, without exaggeration or any introduction of controversial matter: the P. of Wales said a few words, to show the deep interest which princes always take in workingmen, when workingmen have votes: Lord Shaftesbury harangued in his Exeter Hall style, at great length, & very tedious: Wemyss chattered: the Bps of London & Rochester said something as to the general condition of the poor: on the whole the discussion was rational, but dull, as it must be when everybody was agreed as to what should be done. . . .

23 Feb. 1884: . . . Dined at Marlborough House, a large party . . . Interesting talk with Lord Alcester[36] about the Alexandria affair. He admitted that nearly all his ammunition was expended, & that in case of continued resistance there would have been difficulty on that score. . . .

25 Feb. 1884: . . . Hearing from Childers[37] that Lord Reay would accept Victoria, which I had always thought out of the question, I determined to make him the offer, & wrote accordingly.

At the Cabinet, we discussed first the question of a proposed enquiry, which Sexton[38] has asked for, into the legality of Orange societies: he asserting that they have secret passwords, illegal oaths, & practices contrary to law. The Premier introduced the subject, & seemed inclined to grant the committee which is asked for. The Chancellor thought Sexton ought first to produce his evidence in support of the charge he makes. Dilke said that Ld Crichton[39], who must know, had publicly denied that any oaths are taken. Harcourt said the manifest object of Sexton's proceeding was to embroil us with the loyal party in Ireland. I suggested that the recognised leaders of the Orangemen should be called upon, in a friendly way, to give a public denial of the allegations against them after which it would be easy to refuse enquiry. Kimberley said all the alleged violations of the law were of very old date: he would not go back on proceedings of 20 years ago. He would refuse enquiry. The Premier, who seemed annoyed, said warmly that to refuse enquiry in such a case would be 'an insult, & almost an outrage': if that answer was to be given, somebody else must give it, for he would not. More talk followed: the end being that enquiry by a committee is refused, but the Lord Lieut. is to be authorised to look into the matter, & report his opinion whether there are grounds for any further proceedings. It seems that Ld Spencer had himself suggested this course.

Much conversation followed on the subject of Gordon's proclamation, & the Egyptian business generally. Hartington complained that all orders, questions, & communications from the War Office are published at Cairo. Harcourt took the opportunity of discoursing on the uselessness of the Egyptian army, & the impossibility of constituting a self-governing Egypt. The Premier dissented, but would not argue. I noticed this to Dilke while leaving, & he said: 'The Premier & Granville have been in a minority of two on that point ever since the Egyptian business began.' We ended by a discussion as to strengthening the garrisons at Malta & Gibraltar. Harcourt went strongly for it, the Premier against, Hartington argued moderately for a moderate increase. In the end it was agreed to put a battalion under orders, but not to move it as yet.

26 Feb. 1884: News early of an explosion at Victoria station, supposed to be the work of Irish Fenians: it happened in the night. Three men are injured & the front of part of the station is destroyed. I went to see the damage: but there was no great crowd.

. . . Saw Lord Reay & discoursed to him about Victoria. He was much pleased, & I could plainly see that his personal inclination was to accept: but there is Ly Reay to be consulted, & she may naturally dislike the idea of transportation. He asked for two or three days to consider it, which I could not well refuse.

28 Feb. 1884: . . . Puzzled by a strange telegram reporting that Gordon has addressed to the people of the Soudan a proclamation to the effect that British troops are to be in a few days at Khartoum. It comes from Baring, therefore there can be no mistake. But what troops can Gordon mean? or is the whole thing an invention on his part? It is unintelligible as it stands. We ask for explanations.

The convention[40], which is published at full length in *The Times*, is on the whole well received by the press. *D. News* approves thoroughly: *The Times* approves in the main: *Standard* criticises in a very mild tone: so (for a wonder) does the *St. James's Gazette*: the *Pall Mall* also is pleased, though writing in a wild strain as to new departures, & a future policy. . . .

29 Feb. 1884: At 2.10 received summons for a Cabinet at 2.30, which is rather an incoherent way of doing business, to my mind, & after all there was no need of special haste. We sat till 4.15, when with others to the Lords. There, on a question put by De La Warr, the opposition, evidently acting in concert, raised a rather angry debate, or rather conversation, attacking Gordon, though cautiously, & dwelling on the injustice done to the Sultan in not consulting him about Soudan affairs. Granville answered first, I spoke later, & the Chancellor concluded. There was a small attendance: but the intention to make mischief was obvious, & it is clear that these tactics are adopted in view of an early dissolution, which they think they can force by throwing out the reform bill in the Lords.

Much talk about the Premier's speech[41] on Friday, which is generally thought a fine one, though some, especially Harcourt, dissented: the reception given to it was cold, according to the general opinion, & some one remembered that it was the first time a reform bill had been brought in without there being any crowd outside or in the lobbies or any sign of public interest. The fact is that everybody is thinking about Egypt, & the public has never attention to spare for two subjects at once. . . .

1 Mar. 1884: . . . Dined with the Lord President[42], all the Cabinet present except Spencer and Hartington, & in addition we had Lords Sydney[43] & Kenmare[44], Col. Peel[45] &

another official whom I did not know. Pleasant on the whole. I sat between Granville, who is growing very old & deaf, & Chamberlain.

Chamberlain talks of Birmingham, says a remarkable feature of its industrial population is the absence of very great fortunes – no man in the whole place, he believes, has made £500,000: & the general diffusion of prosperity among a large number. He questioned Granville a good deal about Clemenceau, who has lately been over here, & who is supposed to be the coming man in France: but Granville did not seem to think much of him.

Harcourt talked a good deal about the late attempts to wreck railway stations, of which there have been 4, though only 1 succeeded, & that but in part: he said the police knew the men who did it, there were only 2 concerned but he would not tell us whether he thought a conviction possible.

News coming in gradually since noon of fighting near Suakin yesterday, Gen. Graham[46] with 4,000 men against the Mahdi's lieutenant Osman, with 10,000(?). It has ended in complete victory[47], & recapture of the guns lost by Baker, who was himself present at this last action, I suppose as a volunteer, & was wounded.

At the Cabinet of Friday, discussion on a bill of Parnell's, to amend the Land Act. Chamberlain wished to assent to the principle, but postpone the application. Harcourt, Trevelyan, Kimberley, & I all protested against holding out hopes, & unsettling men's minds. The Premier said ambiguously that a small bill would be of no use, & that he had rather not speak on the subject. (He hardly conceals his fear of offending the Irish, which perhaps at this moment is politic.) The rest of our meeting was occupied with Egyptian affairs. Great perplexity has been caused by Gordon's telegrams & proclamations – in one of the latter he has told the Soudanese that British troops are coming to Khartoum: an absolute invention. In a telegram he says that we must 'smash the Mahdi' – whom he has just declared Sultan of Kordofan. Baring telegraphs that he has received a fresh batch of proposals from Gordon, so confused & contradictory that he does not send them on, not knowing what they mean. He is a strange being, & I think a little mad, but all depends on him.

2 Mar. 1884 (Sunday): Keston by 10.25 train . . . Passed the day as usual, reading, writing, reading aloud to M.[48] & walking with her. Talk of the Swedish doctor Kehlgren, who she thinks has done good to her eyes, & certainly has produced a marked improvement in her state of nerves & spirits. Gave her £25 to pay his bill for the month.

3 Mar. 1884: . . . Busy with papers on Merv & on the Egyptian army, circulated among the Cabinet. Newspapers full of the battle near Suakin (at a place called El Teb) and the consequent capture of Tokar. It seems to have been well managed, & the troops showed more steadiness than they did in South Africa.

Mr. Marriott, the Liberal member for Brighton who voted against the government on the question of confidence, has been returned by a large majority: all the Conservatives backing him[49] . . .

. . . Saw Sanderson, who came to tell me of the rather sudden death of his elder brother, whom with his family he has been maintaining for the last 7 or 8 years. This brother was once making £10,000 a year in the City, but lost all, & became bankrupt. Sanderson owned to me that he had allowed him £400 a year out of the £800 that I give him. There are now only the children to keep.

4 Mar. 1884: Office at the usual time, worked there from 2.30 to 5.30 with little disturbance. Saw Mr. Mackenzie[50], whom I have appointed commissioner among the Bechuanas. About his energy, shrewdness, & knowledge of the country there can be no mistake, and his rather excessive partiality to the native interest will be at once utilised & moderated by his being placed in a position where he will be its official defender. I scarcely know whether I should have selected him, nevertheless, but for the strong desire of Sir H. Robinson that he should be appointed – and, as Sir H. is to be his official superior, it is fair that his wishes should be consulted. Ashley[51] too pressed the choice upon me, & no doubt it will be popular among the missionary & dissenting interest.

Ly W. Herbert came to stay a few days with us.

The papers are still full of the victory at El Teb, which will apparently have much effect in pacifying the Soudan. But the more we succeed in settling the country, the greater becomes the difficulty in knowing how or when to leave it. It would be quite as true to say that Egypt holds us as that we hold Egypt.

5 Mar. 1884: Office early: saw there Sir H. Robinson, who sails for the Cape tomorrow. We had a last conversation, & walked out together, when the Premier met us, & joined in the farewell compliments to Sir H. – which I was glad of.

Cabinet at 2.30. It sat till past 6.00, at Westminster, but in that little room I could make no note. We talked a little of procedure. The opposition want special facilities given for a second vote of censure: which we do not see the use of, as they can say all they have got to say on Egypt when the vote of credit is being discussed.

It was determined to resist the demands of Parnell & the Irish for an extension of the Land Act, which was done accordingly, the debate going on while we were in discussion on other subjects.

The principal subject was a series of extraordinary telegrams which Gordon has been sending to Baring from Khartoum. His present idea is to put Zebehr . . . as his successor to keep order, & govern the tribes as best he can. Now this Zebehr is the chief of the slave hunters from whom Gordon was sent years ago to deliver the Soudan, & whom in fact he defeated & destroyed, subsequently executing his son for attempted rebellion. When Gordon went last to Egypt, a few weeks ago, one of the points he pressed most strongly was the necessity of deporting this man to Cyprus, or elsewhere, out of Egypt. They had an interview later on, which did not end in a reconciliation. Why Gordon's distrust of him should have suddenly turned to confidence is unexplained. Harcourt does not hesitate to call him a 'raving lunatic': & in truth it does [seem] as if his incoherence of mind approached insanity. But then, how has he accomplished such results as he undoubtedly did both in China & the Soudan? One day he makes the Mahdi sultan of Kordofan: the next he is full of plans for 'smashing' him. One day he wishes to be supported by the authority of the Porte: the next, he tells the natives that he has come to protect them against the Turks. We cannot reconcile his contradictions: but it is awkward that on this question of employing Zebehr he has convinced Baring, who is a cool and clear-headed official. If we reject their joint application, Gordon will probably resign, possibly Baring also. If we comply, we do an act which does not in itself seem very rational, and which will in the eyes of England & Europe look like showing special favour to the leading slave trader of Africa – hatred of the slave trade & slavery being in England a sort of fanaticism. We sent a long string of questions, & deferred decision.

6 Mar. 1884: Ly Russell came to luncheon with us.

Office 2.30–4.30. Received there a small deputation, Sir W. Macarthur & his brother, Mr. W. Fowler M.P., & Mr. Chesson. They talked freely & sensibly about Natal affairs. They wanted all native affairs in S. Africa put under one authority, who should be governor of the Cape: holding that Zululand was governed, or regulated, by us, too much in accordance with the ideas of the Natal colonists: I gave no answer, nor was it expected.

H. of Lords, where Ld Bury[52], under pretence of asking a question, raised again the whole subject of Egypt. He was answered by Granville, who spoke with tact & adroitness: Ld Wentworth[53], who as far as I know has not spoken before, rose from the cross-benches and delivered a violent invective on the policy of occupying Egypt at all, as I understood him: saying that we were to answer to God for blood shed in a bad cause, & so forth. He seemed thoroughly in earnest, & as great a fanatic, as the Mahdi. But from that very cause his speech was effective in its way, though nobody agreed with him: Salisbury followed, & was answered, remarkably well, by Kimberley: after him Dunraven, Huntly, Hardwicke, & others emptied the House: I was ready to speak if wanted, as was Northbrook, but we were not wanted. . . .

7 Mar. 1884: . . . Office 2.30 . . . House of Lords . . . Thence to a Cabinet suddenly summoned, according to what is now the Premier's custom, not a convenient one when there is no pressing business & in the present case there was none. We sat till past 7.00, discussing Egypt. The immediate question was whether & how the Porte should be invited to garrison the Red Sea ports, which Egypt cannot & we will not hold: Chamberlain & Harcourt were against employing Turks at all, on parliamentary grounds: Granville was on the other side: Gladstone warmer for employing them than anyone, which caused some remarks, considering his antecedents, but he has said the same thing all along in this Egyptian business.

Talk of Chamberlain and his Merchant Shipping Bill, which it seems he will not be able to carry: the shipowners on both sides having combined with the opposition against it. He wants to press it, and if defeated to resign: but this is merely temper, or at least a hasty impulse: and his colleagues in the Commons will not agree: the shipowners will be content to refer it to a select committee, & this solution will probably be accepted. But it is a defeat, disguise it as we may.

Talk also of the vote of credit last night, which it seems was carried in a very thin House, & little interest taken in it . . . It looks as if the late outcry had grown out of the unsatisfied fighting instinct of the English public, & was appeased now that blood has been spilt.

. . . Lord Reay, after much hesitation, refuses Victoria – the third peer who has done so: £10,000 a year going begging!

8 Mar. 1884 (Saturday): This has been a very quiet and almost idle day.

Wrote to the Premier, asking whether his nephew, Ld Lyttelton, will accept Victoria. When first suggested, I thought his claim less strong than that of some others, but Morley[54], Enfield, Reay, & Dalhousie have all refused, & he is as good as any that remain. . . .

10 Mar. 1884: . . . Office at 2.30, thence to the Lords, where Lytton raised a debate on the subject of the annexation of Merv to Russia. He spoke fluently, with good voice &

manner, & knowledge of his subject: but somehow the speech was not a success, being coldly received on his own side, & not exciting interest anywhere. There were sarcasms carefully prepared, but they fell flat: the whole performance seemed unreal.

Argyll answered, speaking well as he always does, but rather discursively: he defended the Russian policy in Asia, but defended also the Crimean war, in which he said he was proud to have been concerned as a minister. His tone was meant to be judicial, but it left, at least on my mind, an impression of vagueness, & of distinctions without a difference. Cranbrook was short, & surprised the House by moderation: Kimberley talked plain sense in plain words: Carnarvon had come up from the country to deliver a prepared harangue, which was too retrospective to be much to the purpose, but the Lords had gone away to dine, and his audience was limited to 19 peers, so that he had not a fair chance: Northbrook followed him, full of knowledge, & clear in argument, but dull: Salisbury replied, in his usual style, Granville summed up, & Lord Napier said a few words. We ended a little after 9.00, but the last hour and a half the speakers addressed nearly empty benches, & all life had gone out of the debate. . . .

11 Mar. 1884: . . . Cabinet at 2.00, which sat till 4.00. The Premier absent, having as reported a cold, but I believe it is an attack of diarrhoea, from which he suffers[55].

. . . Long discussion in Cabinet on two points: (1) Shall the Turks be invited to occupy the Red Sea ports? (2) Shall Gordon's wish to employ Zebehr be acceded to?

As to the first, Granville recapitulated what had passed. Harcourt disliked bringing in the Turks: they would discourage all trade except slave trade: it would look ill, & as if we were only evading responsibility. Chamberlain did not think the House would stand it. If a division were taken on the question, we should be beaten. The Turk would be an enemy if he went to the Red Sea, & would never be satisfied without extending his power inland. D. asked what was the alternative? Were we prepared to garrison Suakin? Northbrook, being appealed to, said we could hold Suakin with marines, but it would be dangerous in the hot season. Harcourt (dramatically, & with a probably unconscious imitation of Disraeli): 'We can't hold Suakin in hot weather! And we are the people who made the Indian empire!'

Granville observed that whatever we might do we were pretty sure to be in a minority on some question affecting the Soudan. In the end it was determined to decide nothing as to the Turks, but to ascertain whether in case of need a small force could be sent from Aden or India.

As to Zebehr being employed, Harcourt, Dilke, Dodson said that his employment was impossible, the House would not endure it: Granville concurred: Chamberlain expressed himself more moderately: he would not consent to put Zebehr in a place of power, but would use & pay him as an agent for a temporary purpose. I backed up this idea, asking what the House of C. would agree to support? They don't want us to conquer the Soudan for ourselves: nor to let it go: nor to send British troops there: nor to employ the only means recommended by those who are on the spot. The Chancellor said it was a stalemate, no move seemed possible. Harcourt was for recalling Gordon at once, foreseeing endless difficulty if he remains: but nobody supported him. Kimberley wished him to stay on indefinitely, which I said I thought was the first step to permanent occupation. In the end we agreed to telegraph, objecting to Zebehr being employed, offering to give money, & to sanction Gordon's obtaining any other form of help, but saying that no British troops should be sent. (But this decision really settles nothing.) . . .

13 Mar. 1884: . . . A sudden summons to a Cabinet in the Premier's room at H. of C. We sat from 6.00 to 7.30. the Premier & Chamberlain both absent.

News of another battle[56] near the Red Sea coast, 70 killed, 100 wounded: a great slaughter of Arabs: they seem to have fought desperately, & at one moment captured some of the English guns.

Our Cabinet was caused by the receipt of a perplexing telegram or rather series of telegrams from Gordon: who again asks for Zebehr, & for a relieving expedition to be sent to Berber, which latter is a new demand: & an impossible one: for the march from Suakin takes at least 20 days, & the hot season is coming on. The truth is that Gordon does not seem to accept the policy of evacuation which he went out to assist, but is trying to stay on at Khartoum, & arrange for the government of the Soudan provinces. We framed a reply, leaving him as is necessary a large discretion, but pressing withdrawal. The worst of the affair is that the British public is more than half disposed to hold on to the Soudan, & will resent its abandonment, not having any clear idea of the cost and risk attending its recovery: a load which Egypt cannot bear. Gordon ends by suggesting a wild scheme of taking steamers and (I suppose) native troops up the river into the equatorial provinces, & holding them in the name of the King of the Belgians!

Northbrook & Kimberley, with whom I talked, think the situation grave, & not unlikely to lead to the breaking up of the Cabinet. But the belief out-of-doors that we are quarrelling among ourselves is quite unfounded. Indeed it would be better if we had quarrelled a little more, & so secured a thorough discussion of doubtful points. Our fault has been taking the whole business too easy, being more occupied with matters of less real importance nearer home.

14 Mar. 1884: Mrs. Gladstone called on M. to talk over Ld Lyttelton, to whom I have made through the Premier an offer of Victoria. He has been in doubt, but on the whole concludes not to accept, as there is no saving possible out of the salary, & he would lose a permanent place of £1,500 a year[57]: while, as to usefulness & distinction, there is not much of either in a self-governing colony, where the governor is only a very constitutional sovereign. I thought he was right, & said so, This is the fourth refusal . . .

15 Mar. 1884 (Saturday): Ld Wharncliffe[58], of whom I had seen nothing for years, called early, to recommend to me for the vacancy at Victoria his friend Lord Auckland[59], son of the bishop: of whom he speaks in warm terms of praise, and I hear well of him in other quarters.

I thanked Ld W. for his suggestion, which may come to something: I have now only two possible candidates in my mind: Sir H. Loch[60], former governor of the Isle of Man: and Sir T. Brassey[61], who might perhaps be tempted by the social position of a governor.

Cabinet at 3.00, at first in Downing Street, but we moved to the room at Westminster, in consequence of a debate going on in H. of C. The sitting was held to discuss estimates (Saturday sittings at this time of year are unusual): but Ashmead Bartlett[62], Labouchere[63], & a few others had determined to raise another Egyptian debate, in which they were readily joined by the main body of the opposition. The chief object no doubt was to waste time, & so obstruct business: but in the present awkward state of Soudanese matters there was some excuse for it. Less defensible was the plan to steal a division by surprise, for it is not common to raise debates and take votes of confidence without any notice. The motion, however, was lost by 111 to 94: a small but sufficient majority. The debate went on far into [Sunday] morning. I do not know when it ended. A Sunday morning sitting in March is new in my experience.

The Cabinet sat from 3.00 to past 5.00, greatly divided & perplexed: the immediate occasion of its meeting was a telegram from Baring remonstrating strongly against our decision not to employ Zebehr, expressing doubt whether the evacuation of Khartoum is possible as things now are, & in fact suggesting an entire change of policy. There was no irritation or temper shown (except a little by Harcourt) but a strong sense of the difficulties, & no agreement as to how they should be met. Granville, Harcourt, Dilke, Northbrook, Dodson, & Kimberley were against employing Zebehr in any circumstances or for any purposes: Hartington, Chamberlain, Carlingford, the Chancellor, I, & I think Childers took the opposite view, thinking anything better than the failure & possible destruction of Gordon, for which we should be held responsible if we refused him what he seems to consider as the only means of safety & success. It was understood that the Premier leans to this latter view, but he was unwell with a cold, & could not attend. We separated without coming to a conclusion, & agreed to meet again tomorrow (Sunday). Harcourt said two or three times that the Cabinet had better break up: that agreement among us was impossible, that he could not give way, etc., but Harcourt says more than he means. – The situation is altogether as perplexing as any I remember.

16 Mar. 1884: Stayed in London, which I have seldom done on Sunday . . .

Cabinet at 2.30, which sat till nearly 5.30: the Premier absent, but as we met in Downing St. he could be & was consulted. The discussion of yesterday was renewed. Letter from the Premier read, generally in favour of giving a large discretion to Gordon. **Harc.** thought the question of Zebehr had lost much of its importance. What Gordon & Baring seemed to wish was that we should send troops to Berber. That he believed to be impossible. It meant a march on Khartoum if it meant anything, & to that he would never consent. **D.[erby]** reminded Harcourt that he has frequently said if Gordon were in danger we should be forced by public opinion to send an expedition to rescue him. **Harc.** said that some government might have to do it, but not ours. **Chamb.** on full consideration believes that parliament will not sanction the employment of Zebehr: and, if so, it is useless to try it. **Harc.**: R. Grosvenor says if we agreed to it a resolution condemning us would be passed within a week. **Kimberley** agrees. **D.[erby]** has not altered his opinion on the question of policy but, if the House will not sanction it, there is no use in discussing the matter. We inform Gladstone accordingly: he regrets the decision of the Cabinet, but accepts it. General talk follows. It is said that, from want of water, only a small force can pass from Berber to Suakin or the other way, at least in summer: and a small force is not enough in view of the hostility of the tribes. Some one asks why a force should be sent? What do we mean? Is it to crush the Mahdi? **Kimb.**: This is the turning point. If we send an expedition we must hold the Soudan. That is what Baring & Gordon want, but that is not our policy. **Chanc.**: Would the Liberal party support us in withdrawing? **Several**. They may or may not: but they certainly will not support us in staying. **D.[erby]**: If we meant to stay there & hold it, we should have settled to do so six months ago. **Chamb.**: If we are to be censured either way, which seems quite possible, it had better be for adhering to our ideas rather than dropping them. – In the end we frame a telegram, refusing to employ Zebehr, pressing early evacuation and rejecting the idea of a Berber expedition unless (1) it is declared practicable by the military authorities, and (2) it is considered as indispensable for the safety of Gordon & his party.

17 Mar. 1884: . . . The debate in H. of C. on Saturday lasted from noon till near 6.00 a.m. on Sunday morning: the Irish keeping up an incessant wrangle all night, using violent language, & cheering triumphantly as they left the House. [They] talked of Ld Spencer's untruthfulness: & Parnell openly advised the Irish farmers to resist payment of the extra police rate levied in districts where outrages have been committed. The Irish temper has never been worse: & they know that, if obstruction is kept within the limits of outward decency, they will have the support of the whole opposition. It is [as bad a] look-out for business as ever I saw in parliament. . . .

18 Mar. 1884: . . . H. of Lords . . . Granville announced our disapproval of a proclamation by Adm. Hewett[64], in which he offers £1,000 reward for Osman Digna, dead or alive. In this time when nihilists & Fenians are so busy, it is not good to encourage assassination: nor indeed is it seemly at any time.

. . . Strange how much talk & gossip goes out as to resignation of the Premier, splits in the Cabinet, dissolution, etc., all growing out of his cold & our Sunday Cabinet, for there is nothing else to account for it. . . .

19 Mar. 1884: In the H. of C. a bill brought in by Broadhurst[65], so-called for the enfranchisement of leaseholds according to which any leaseholder for a long term might buy his landlord, at a rate to be judicially fixed, was lost, but 104 members voted for it, including some Conservatives. Among the latter I do not reckon Ld R. Churchill, who made a violent radical speech in favour of the bill.

20 Mar. 1884: . . . The Premier has gone out of town to Wimbledon, said to be much better, but still needing care[66]. Much complaint as to the state of parliamentary business: Chamberlain's merchant shipping bill appears to have no chance of passing: the London government bill is equally unlikely to get through: the franchise bill alone has a chance, & probably will get through the Commons, but of course only to fail in the Lords. The opposition is bitter & unscrupulous: the Irish party use their opportunity: and the attention fixed on Egyptian affairs has caused home policy to drop into the background, & altogether the outlook is unsatisfactory. The progress which ideas of a more or less socialistic character seem to have made has undoubtedly frightened many Liberals, & not wholly without cause.

21 Mar. 1884 (Friday): . . . Saw a letter from the Premier, in which he speaks confidently of being in the House on Monday: accompanied by one from his secretary, saying that this is quite out of the question.

Two elections have gone against the government, but neither so as to indicate any change in public feeling.

22 Mar. 1884 (Saturday): Working on arrears of yesterday, which are rather heavy: but all was clear by noon, when to a Cabinet. We sat 2 hours, the Premier absent. Thence office till near 5.00, where disposed of all current business. Keston by 5.17 train.

In Cabinet, we discussed first the course of debate on the franchise bill: R. Grosvenor called in. This being wholly a question of detail, & concerning the H. of C., I made no special note: but I remember that Fawcett was spoken of as discontented & out of humour, & not unlikely if he speaks to take a line of his own: he refused to vote on the vote of censure, but walked out, & advised others to do the same. Some talk passed as to redistribution, but it was felt & said on all sides that we must not let ourselves be drawn into discussion on that, lest opinions should differ. Reference was made to the premier's speech as to not reducing the Irish representation[67], on which I took occasion to observe that we are not pledged to that theory. Some doubted: but Kimberley supported me, & Carlingford said sensibly that Gladstone contemplated an increase of the total numbers of the House: if that proposal were disapproved, as it probably would be, then we were in no way pledged to keep the Irish vote undiminished[68]. Conversation followed on the cattle bill, & on a bill for relief from rates, as to both of which it seemed to be thought that we should be beaten. Agreed to try & pass second reading of the franchise bill before Easter.

Childers raised the question of Egyptian finances, which he prefaced with a sufficiently uncomfortable statement. The deficit, he said, had been £900,000 in 1882, £1,200,000 in 1883, and this in addition to the Alexandria indemnities, & to the expenses of getting the garrisons away. **Harcourt** & **Chamberlain** pressed for a partial repudiation, or bankruptcy. **Childers** pointed out that the law of liquidation cannot be altered without the consent of all the Powers. **Granville**: France will be backed up by Italy & Russia in her claims. **Harcourt**: Abolish the Egyptian army. It is the real danger of Egypt, besides the expense. If we had left Arabi alone, he would have got rid of the bondholders. Europe tolerates us where we are because it is supposed that we shall support them. But we cannot guarantee this payment, & had better say so. **Granville**: What have you to propose to them? You can't annex the country, nor yet withdraw from it. **Harcourt** (rather excited): You can withdraw. I would go out at once. Egypt will give us far more trouble than India. You will have European interference at every moment. You must defend it against the Powers. It is an affair of many millions a year. **D.[erby]**: Would like to go out as much as Harcourt does, but it is impossible as matters stand now. **Chamb.**: Does not see how it can be done but believes it would be popular. The whole affair is disliked by the party. **Kimb.**: It would simply upset the government, & our successors would reverse our action, so nothing would be gained. – Much general talk follows as to what shall be said in answer to queries as to Egyptian policy. Harcourt takes occasion to complain that he was not consulted when Gordon was sent out. (Neither were half the Cabinet: the thing was done in a hurry.) Chamberlain again repeated that the English public would be heartily glad to see us go out, and the French come in: but this was not agreed to. Granville complained rather sharply that Harcourt found fault with everything that had been done, never having taken any part, or shown interest in the business, till matters went wrong. The general feeling seemed to be that this Egyptian embarrassment is constantly growing more serious, & may yet upset the Cabinet. . . .

24 Mar. 1884: London . . . Lawson calls: talk on state of H. of C. He says nobody is minded there except Gladstone: Northcote, Hartington, Harcourt have no influence. . . . As to the future, he does not believe in Chamberlain as a leader: he is not popular &, though clever, exercises no authority. (I remember that Ashley lately said very nearly the same.) Dilke he thought much more likely to take the first place.

Wrote to the Premier to propose Sir H. Loch as governor of Victoria, or rather to say that I have chosen him, for the selection rests with me.

. . . Odd & confused telegrams about Gordon: the river is blocked between Berber & Khartoum, communication intercepted: the last we know is that he had gone out to attack a party of insurgents, but with what result has not been heard: his chief difficulty seems to be this, that he cannot attach to himself a party or get men to declare themselves on his side, in the uncertainty in which they are as to what is to follow when he retires: they do not care to make enemies of the Mahdi & his followers, if the Mahdi's party is to be allowed to walk into Khartoum in a few weeks or months. – The best that can be hoped for under these circumstances is neutrality.

There is an odd story of a Mr. O'Kelly being on his way to the Soudan – qu. with anti-English intentions?

In the meanwhile it seems we are to attack Osman Digna again[69]: that is, if he is foolish enough to let us do so: for he can at any time fall back into the desert, where we cannot follow, & wait till increasing heat has driven our troops away.

25 Mar. 1884: . . . At 3.00, a Cabinet held in the room at H. of Commons, in consequence of a long & perplexing telegram of yesterday evening from Baring. It is to the effect that Gordon cannot come away without bringing the garrisons: that he is expecting help from Suakin, and that if possible an expedition should be sent from thence to Berber. We are farther warned that if [it is] to be done at all it should be done soon, as the difficulties from climate will increase as the season goes on. Much talk among us as to the possibility of such an expedition. Ld Wolseley is said to think it practicable, but very difficult, & attended probably with great loss. – The trouble of it seems to me that a small force would be in danger from the tribes, while for a large one there is not water. It was pointed out that Gordon, when we last heard, had no fears for his present safety: that he has six months' provisions, and that, if an expedition is possible at all, it will be easier in the autumn when there is plenty of water. It was also noticed that an expedition sent to Berber would of itself be useless, unless connected with a further plan of marching on to Khartoum. It was remarked that Gordon & Baring have both in fact reversed the policy decided upon here: they think that in the interest of Egypt & the natives the Eastern Soudan ought to be held, & they mean to hold it. – We were unanimous, & framed a telegram, saying that troops cannot be sent to Berber: that Graham should be warned not to advance into the interior: and that full discretion should be given to Gordon to act as he thinks best.

I raised a discussion on Zululand, Kimberley supported me, but Chamberlain opposed, & we came to no agreement.

26 Mar. 1884: . . . The Premier still shut up at Wimbledon[70]: general talk as to the chances of his returning to the H. of Commons: but as far as I can make out there is nothing serious the matter. He is probably, like the rest of us, a good deal embarrassed by the turn which affairs have taken in Egypt, almost compelling us to adopt a line of policy against which he is deeply & personally pledged.

27 Mar. 1884: . . . Cabinet box comes round, with a well written paper from Harcourt, urging as Lawson does the necessity for a definite policy, but in an opposite sense. He asks whether we are to direct our agents, or be directed by them? I put in a mem. to the effect that, as a Berber expedition at this season is impossible, the question does not press in point of time: I agree in desiring a full discussion: but add that it is useless for us to pledge ourselves to send no expedition to the relief of Gordon if he be surrounded & in danger, since that is a pledge which the English public will not let us keep.

. . . At 5.30, Cabinet in the Premier's room, but he is still laid up at Wimbledon: Chamberlain also was not there. We sat till 7.30. Walked home with Childers, talking about Egyptian finance. At the Cabinet, sharp discussion about Egypt. Harcourt complained of Baring in violent terms, saying that he refuses to obey, & that his language against us is as strong as that of Randolph Churchill. He said the fact was that both Baring & Gordon do not wish to give up the Soudan, & hope to force us to adopt their policy. Kimberley & Carlingford observed that Gordon did not choose to leave Khartoum without making provision for the safety of the people there – it was with him a point of honour. Northbrook observed that when he was sent out it was with no expectation of receiving military assistance. I reminded the Cabinet that it was useless to say that we would not attempt to rescue Gordon if in danger, since the public would in all probability compel us to do it, whether we liked or not.

Harcourt reverted with some bitterness to our tel. of the 16th, which he said was altered after it had left the Cabinet, & as it stood did by implication promise relief if Gordon were in danger. He insisted on our deciding now that there should be no expedition. Selborne, with more heat than I ever saw him in before, said he would resign rather than acquiesce in any such decision. Granville pointed out that it was not a question which needed to be settled now, & we separated after something very like a wrangle. . . .

29 Mar. 1884 (Saturday): . . . About 1.00 p.m. received a sudden summons to a Cabinet at Wimbledon, where the Premier is staying: it had been settled, as I understood, last night not to hold one, & when we came to meet there seemed no particular reason.

Most of the Cabinet met at Waterloo, thence took the rail down to Coombe, then drove or walked about a mile to the villa (Coombe Warren): a large handsome house, very artistically decorated, with rooms of every possible shape, a great deal of painting & panelling, & all the modern requirements: but very little land, & a poor dull garden. There was a ring of police all round, which would have seemed a strange sight only 20 years ago. The great man seemed perfectly well in health, except a little paleness natural after being kept indoors: his voice clear, though he seemed careful not to raise it: no sign of ill health in his manner or appearance[71]: in fact I could not help suspecting, and I saw that others did the same, that his complaint is chiefly political. He cannot escape speaking about Egypt if he shows himself in the House, & he cannot speak about Egypt without holding language which will not harmonise well with what he said before.

We discussed the possibility of negociating with the tribes about Berber: the question of slavery at Suakin: the quarrels of Clifford Lloyd with his European colleagues: and a draft prepared at F.O. which is intended to sum up the correspondence that has taken place, with a view to our defence if necessary. Much talk also about Sunday closing, & the arrangements of H. of C. business. We sat nearly 3 hours. Walked back to the station: by train to Vauxhall: thence to Victoria, but no train available for Bromley: so in a cab to the Travellers', where dined, & by 9.30 train, & fly, to Keston. A disagreeable, wasted day, for there was nothing that required a Cabinet to settle.

30 Mar. 1884 (Sunday): . . . It may be noted as curious that at the Cabinet yesterday the death of the D. of Albany[72] was not once referred to – I mean when business had begun. Nor was anything said as to the defeat sustained by the government on Friday last on a question of giving relief to ratepayers at the national expense. This defeat had indeed been foreseen, and it is well understood that many who voted in the majority had no other wish than to satisfy their constituents. It does not seem to be thought important, & probably is not so.

31 Mar. 1884: Letter from Hale saying that the payment of the L. & Y.[orks.] R.[ailway] C.[ompany] for land & houses taken at Bootle is fixed at £99,771. He expects the payment to take place soon.

In the papers, telegrams from Khartoum reporting the defeat of Gordon's Egyptian force by an apparently very inferior force of Arabs, who did not wait to be attacked, but drove back the Egyptians with the loss of several guns. This is serious, not in itself, but as showing that Gordon's force cannot be trusted even for defensive purposes. But nothing can be done, even if we wished it, for to send troops up the Nile in the hot season would be simply murder. . . .

1 Apr. 1884: . . . Saw Lawson . . . He said the funds rose on a late rumour of the Premier's retirement, the notion being that he is the only obstacle to a protectorate of Egypt: but he admitted that the Cabinet would probably break up without him. Thought Hartington too indifferent & apathetic for a leader, Harcourt too unpopular, & not ambitious of the place: Dilke seemed the only man, & about his health there is a question. . . .

2 Apr. 1884: . . . Cabinet at 2.00, where sat till 5.20. . . . Office again till near 7.00.

In Cabinet, the talk was almost entirely about Egypt. We discussed the Egyptian army, which is nearly worthless, & it is a question whether it should be disbanded: but nothing got settled. We accepted a suggestion by Ld Wolseley that we should negociate with the leading tribes, to open the Berber & Suakin road. A letter was read from Gordon to his brother, of which we could not make sense: he says that the evacuation of the Soudan is a necessity, & in the next sentence adds that he is condemned, he supposes, to penal servitude for life at Khartoum. Talk followed as to the expected debate on Egypt in H. of C. Chamberlain with some vehemence denied that the country took much interest in the matter: he thought the interest expressed was factitious, created by the London press, which was in the hands of Jews chiefly, & in the interest of the bondholders. He was against giving the Opposition any special facilities for debate, but would let them obstruct as much as they pleased, thinking that would tell in our favour in the country. Childers introduced the subject of Egyptian finance. Chamberlain & Dilke pressing strongly the necessity for a bankruptcy. The Premier objected to this as a revolutionary proceeding & not yet necessary. Granville spoke of the necessity of applying to the Powers for a change in the law of liquidation: and it was agreed that this must be done. Kimberley supposed the thing must be done, but disliked the notion of reopening the whole Egyptian question before Europe. Harcourt was for a conference, because he felt sure that the Powers would not grant what we wanted, & we should have an excuse for getting out of the whole affair. 'Then,' it was answered, 'the French will take our place.' 'Let them,' said H.[arcourt], 'they will guarantee the interest, & why should they not be there?' But this was not generally agreed to. Somebody observed that we were going into a conference without knowing what we meant to propose. The Premier replied that he was ready to make certain financial concessions, such as a reduced charge for the European army. So it was settled to apply to the Powers. Childers had meant to propose that we should borrow £7,000,000 to lend to Egypt, but put it off to another day, seeing, as he told me, that the Premier was not well disposed to any such plan.

3 Apr. 1884: . . . In the Commons yesterday, the Sunday closing bill was talked out[73], by tacit consent of all parties, few people wishing it to pass, & none liking to vote either for or against it, with the certainty of offending some section of their constituents. . . .

8 Apr. 1884: News in the papers that the franchise bill is read a second time[74] by a majority of 130: 340 to 210: which is more than anybody expected, the highest figure having been 100, and from 50 to 70 what was thought most probable. It is possible that opposition may have been less strenuous owing to the conviction that the bill will be thrown out in the Lords. . . .

9 Apr. 1884: Sir W. Harcourt has brought in his London government bill[75], which appears to be better received than was expected. A scene in the Commons, caused by Healy, in which the [new] Speaker seems to have shown firmness.

A sudden Cabinet summoned yesterday afternoon but, as notice was not given till within an hour of its meeting, I was not telegraphed to, which indeed would have been useless. . . .

10 Apr. 1884: Received from office six pouches, which gave me enough to do.

. . . Letter & telegram from H.[ome] O.[ffice] asking me whether I can go over to Eastwell some day next week, when the Duchess of Edinburgh is confined, to make the usual attestation as to the child being hers. I answer agreeing, partly because some Sec. of State must go, and I have perhaps the lightest work of any, so that I ought not to grudge these little troubles: partly that I shall not be sorry to see Eastwell, of which I have heard much, it being reputed the finest park in Kent. . . .

11 Apr. 1884 (Good Friday): . . . Wrote to Ward to take for me 100 shares in the Bootle Reform Club: a waste of money, but politically necessary. Declined to be president of the club. . . .

12 Apr. 1884: . . . Received back from Sir T. Martin the Lyndhurst letters which I had sent him, with a civil note. He has made little use of them, nor could he. Lord Lyndhurst wrote like an indolent man and a man of business, so far as the two are compatible: that is, briefly, without ornament or attempt at style, saying what he had to say in the fewest words, & often in such a way as not to be intelligible, without the letter which he was answering. He had also the peculiarity of never, or seldom, dating his notes. I think it likely that his objection to have his correspondence published was due to the fact that he felt it could not enhance his immense reputation, founded on the personal impression which he made on his contemporaries. Nor was it in his nature to care for posthumous fame. Martin's life of him is a dull book[76], not by the fault of the author, but in part from the want of adequate material, in part from its controversial character. It was written as a reply to the attacks in Ld Campbell's biographical sketch[77], and the object of vindicating the person written about from unfounded charges is manifest throughout. Moreover, he has attempted too much: no man is misunderstood through the whole of a long & active public life: & it is imposing on our credibility to represent Lord Lyndhurst as a scrupulous, or consistent, or very high minded politician.

The truth I take to be that he was neither better nor worse than the average of lawyer-politicians: that, like most clever men, he may have talked radicalism in his youth: that he was never a Tory in the sense of feeling any great veneration for existing institutions, but probably had a thorough contempt for the intolerant zeal of half educated reformers, & thought them just as likely to do harm as good: that his predominant habit of mind was a good-natured & easy-going cynicism: and that, by talking freely & loosely, & indulging in paradoxes for the purpose of making his audience stare, he got the credit of even less principle than really belonged to him. That he was a great orator & a delightful companion his worst enemies never denied. He was socially damaged by the conduct of his first wife, a handsome fashionable woman, whose extravagance was great, & was certainly not paid for by her husband: but paid for it was, & the scandal of the day asserted, with his knowledge & connivance. He was Voltairian in religion, during most of his life, but is said to have become a believer in old age. I knew him in his latest years: when, though nearly blind & very infirm, his spirits were generally high, never depressed. He was kept informed of the latest news & gossip of the clubs, which he would discuss eagerly: I noted as a peculiarity that he seldom cared to talk of the past: indeed it was not easy to lead him to do so: contrary to the nature of old men in general. . . .

13 Apr. 1884 (Easter Sunday): Received from office six pouches, but more in bulk than in importance.

. . . Wrote to Sanderson to ask as to the value of the living now held by his brother, as it may be possible that he would suit the Ormskirk people, & they him.

Rather perplexed by the necessity of finding a new governor for St. Helena which is destroyed as a colony by the opening of the Suez route: revenue & trade have fallen off, & population is migrating to the Cape: the governor just dead, a Mr. Janisch, was a native of the island, & had never left it. I do not know how we shall find anybody to go to a place where there is nothing to do, no society, & very little pay.

I have a vacancy too in British Honduras, a disagreeable & obscure situation: but yet easy to fill as it generally leads to some better appointment, if the holder does not die in the meanwhile.

14 Apr. 1884 (Easter Monday): . . . News that the Premier, who was nearly well again, has knocked himself up by too much walking in a cold east wind. At least this reason is assigned for his not coming to London[78]. . . .

16 Apr. 1884: . . . In the papers, death of the Duke of Buccleuch[79], aged 78: he had reigned (for his estate was a small sovereignty) just 65 years, probably the longest tenure of a title & territory of any now in existence. He had the good fortune to be universally respected: in politics a very moderate Conservative: in estate affairs a good & careful landlord: active, but not fussy, in local concerns, & not desirous of being more before the public than his position made inevitable. I scarcely know anyone of whom it can be said that he filled an important position with so quiet & consistent dignity. His estates are supposed to give a rental of £250,000: but the number of large country houses which he had inherited – 7 or 8, I think – reduced his real income: and, as he made it a point of duty to live part of the year in each of them, his existence was as nomadic as that of a gypsy. The only foolish thing which I know of his doing was building that huge palace at Whitehall: a mistake for anyone who does not care about taking a lead in fashionable society. He had a singularly fortunate life, with few troubles, of which perhaps the chief was his wife turning papist. He concerned himself more directly & closely with the management of his estates than most large proprietors do: being in fact, like the D. of

Bedford, his own head agent. He was not a man of superior ability: if he had been, he would probably have created more antagonism, & received less general respect: for the public does not as a rule like to see unusual ability combined with great wealth & high rank . . . He represented fairly the average opinion of the conservative part of the upper class: & so bore himself that those who opposed him had little personal fault to find. Dalkeith[80] will not fill his shoes: being a kindly, well meaning, amiable, but very indolent gentleman: who will not take trouble as his father did, nor care to assume the same position in local administration. But he will act respectably, & keep up the family credit, though not increase it.

17 Apr. 1884: . . . Strange telegram in the papers (Reuter) saying that Gordon has written to offer to Zebehr the lieutenant-governorship of the Soudan: which, if true, is exactly what we refused him leave to do: & there are other details which make the story more perplexing.

Three political speeches in *The Times*: one by Harcourt at Derby, a clever effective party harangue: another by Salisbury at Manchester, clever also, but going over old ground & rather stale: a third by R. Churchill, the best he has made yet, with fewer faults of taste & judgment. He has shown real power and considerable skill in bidding for radical support while pleasing conservatives by denouncing their opponents.

18 Apr. 1884 (Friday): Two pouches from office, all disposed of by 11.00. The clerks are taking their holiday. Summons to a Cabinet on Monday.

To the singular telegram announcing that Gordon has offered the Soudan to Zebehr comes the addition that Zebehr has refused it: probably on advice from Baring. So we are out of that trouble, to all appearance. . . .

20 Apr. 1884: At 7.30 I received a telegram from Capt. Monson at Eastwell . . . so took the 9.25 train . . . I saw the child, a daughter[81], not half an hour after its birth. Then my business was ended, but there was no train to return by till 4.20. Walked in the park . . . Returned to Ashford station . . . Capt. Monson, as equerry, & his wife, seemed to be in charge, & responsible for everything.

Eastwell probably did not show to advantage, the day being cold & sunless, & the leaves not out: nor did I see the best parts of the park: they being at a distance from the house: but what I saw did not come up to the report. The park is immense: but near the house at least it is rather tame: the house itself, comfortable within, is ugly outside, the greater part of it being of yellow brick . . . There is a pleasant lake, but the pleasure grounds are nothing remarkable. The estate is too small for the place, only about 7,000 acres . . . the nominal owner, Lord Winchilsea[82], has nothing to live on except what the Duke [of Edinburgh] pays him as rent. But his only son, a great scamp[83], died of drink at the age of 26: the successor is a cousin[84], who inherited half the estates at the father's death, & will have all: said to be a sensible man into the bargain. The present owner wanted to sell to the Duke, & the Duke wanted to buy: but they could not agree on price, & now a sale is impossible. On the whole I was disappointed with the place but may be only that I had heard excessive praise of it.

21 Apr. 1884: . . . Work at home [St. J. Sq.] till near 2.00, then to Cabinet, which sat till 4.20. Thence to Lords, where a thin attendance & little business: so to office, & finished all there was to do. Home between 6.00 & 7.00: dined Grillions, only Northbrook, Norton, & Walpole present.

At the Cabinet, mention was made of a demand by the Queen for allowances to her grandchildren, the occasion being given by the death of the D. of Albany. It was not pressed, there being more urgent business.

Granville mentioned the French complaint of alleged insult to their flag on the Gold Coast, as to which they seem disposed to give trouble, but we do not yet know the facts accurately.

Then we went on to discuss Egypt. The situation is worse. Khartoum appears safe, but Shendy[85] is surrounded, & Berber seems likely to be so. The Premier observed that Gordon seemed to have given up his originally pacific ideas, & now thinks of nothing but crushing the Mahdi. This is a complete change of policy on his part. Granville thought that Gordon might be ordered to withdraw at once. He had seen objections to this proposal some weeks ago, but thought they were not now so strong. Harcourt would have him removed, & was entirely against an expedition to rescue him, now or later.

I expressed doubts whether he would consent to come away, & Kimberley did the same. It was always open to him, I said, to declare that it was impossible to get away, or to deny having received the order. Among his many extraordinary telegrams is one in which he says that if deserted he will retire to the equatorial provinces. I repeated the warning that if Gordon were really in danger we should be compelled to send an expedition to rescue him, & said it was better to undertake at once to do this in case of need rather than wait till our hand was forced. The Premier pressed again for the sending of Turkish troops to Suakin, he did not clearly explain why. Harcourt objected to this vehemently, & Chamberlain with some reserve, saying that the public would tolerate it if for the relief of Gordon (which it will not do much to help) but not otherwise. He thought, and I supported him, that the immediate question was what should be done about Berber.

Our discussion was long and, as usual in such cases, rather desultory: quite amicable, no sign of temper on the part of anyone, but much perplexity, & no agreement as to what should be done. We settled to meet again tomorrow, & meanwhile sent off a rather helpless telegram to ask what Baring advises. I thought I saw very plain indications that some of the Cabinet think our position dangerous, & expect an outbreak of popular feeling.

22 Apr. 1884: . . . Had myself weighed, 15 st. 6 lbs. . . . Office soon after 1.00. Busy there till 3.00, when to Cabinet. This sat till 4.30: then H. of Lords, where we had no business.

Granville, Kimberley, the Chancellor, Fitzmaurice, Meade, Herbert, & Pauncefote met at 6.00 in my room to talk over (1) Troubles with the French on the Gold Coast: (2) German claims in Fiji. We settled two drafts on the former question, & agreed generally as to the line to be taken on the last[86]. Home a little before 8.00 . . .

The Cabinet today was chiefly occupied with home questions. Childers opened his budget. He expects a surplus of £250,000: leaves taxes unaltered, except as to two very slight changes: proposes to set right the gold coinage, which has fallen below the proper weight from wear & tear: & will make an attempt to reduce the interest on the debt, by conversion of as much as he can deal with into 2½% at 108, or 2½% at 102. He said that, if his plan were worked out to the full extent, it would in the end give a saving of £1,200,000 a year, but not for a long while to come. I thought it a little ominous, & said so, that the last time this question was taken up by a government was just before the

Crimean War. In consequence of loss incurred by the parcels post, the cheapening of telegrams must be deferred, as also the abolition of the duty on silver plate which, as a tax
on art, everybody wishes to see done away, but the difficulty is the large drawback necessary.

Then followed a discussion on the Queen's request made to us that something should
be done for her grandchildren. She thinks the occasion favourable, while there is a strong
feeling about the D. of Albany, but Childers thought the House would not entertain the
idea, & Dilke objected to any grant not covered by former precedents. Something was
said as to an enquiry by committee into the civil list generally, which it was agreed would
be a large business, but safer in the Queen's lifetime than later. I suggested that the Queen
should be advised not to raise any question as to a provision for the Albany children till
we knew whether the dukedom dies out or continues[87]. The Premier seemed to accept
this view of the case, which at least gains time.

Then followed a short but rather sharp discussion on Gordon & Egypt: Hartington
vehement for an immediate announcement of an expedition to be sent out: he lost his
temper, at least his patience, & grew more excited than I thought he could be: Harcourt
with more calmness, but quite as much decision, took the opposite side. Nothing was
settled, as it was necessary that we should go to the Lords, but we agreed to meet tomorrow.

23 Apr. 1884: News in all the papers of a shock of earthquake yesterday morning which
was scarcely felt in London, but threw down buildings, & did much damage, in the eastern counties, especially at Colchester.

. . . In H. of C. last night we were beaten on the Cattle Diseases Bill, which the majority wish to make more stringent. There was a good deal of cross voting: it was not a question of party, but of town against country: & the defeat was expected. Went to Coutts, &
settled for the purchase of £10,000 Liverpool Corporation stock. The price is, including
expenses, £10,088.

Office at 2.00 . . . Cabinet at 3.00, which sat till past 7.00.

. . . In Cabinet, we began with a discussion on the Cattle Bill, & various compromises
were suggested, to escape either accepting the amendments made in it by the majority,
or having to drop it altogether. But we could not well agree as to what should be done in
case these attempts failed: nor was it necessary to determine the point yet. – Then came
the question of Egypt again, which occupied the rest of the sitting. Many papers were
read as to the possibilities of an expedition up the Nile, how far the river is navigable, for
what sized boats, what force could be sent, & many other such details. The policy of an
expedition was then discussed at length. Hartington pressed for a large force, with immediate announcement that it will be sent, & preparations to begin at once: the object being
not merely to save Gordon, but to extricate all the garrisons. Chamberlain objected to
doing anything for the garrisons, would let them take their chance, & face the possible
unpopularity. Granville took in substance the same view. Kimberley wished Gordon to be
desired to withdraw, by any route, & that the garrisons should make terms. I thought a
force might be moved as far as Wady Halfa, which we are bound in any case to defend,
& in this, to my surprise, Harcourt entirely agreed. Hartington thought Gordon could not
& would not leave the people of Khartoum to take care of themselves, & that his policy
of a large expedition there should be accepted. In the end we agreed that want of time &
the season make it impossible to do anything for the relief of Berber: & that Gordon

should be questioned in some detail as to his chances of getting away, the relief he wants, & his motives for staying. We believe that his object is to fight the Mahdi, & reconquer the Soudan, which is not ours, & that if asked he will frankly avow it.

– A report was mentioned that he has quarrelled with Stewart, the friend who keeps him quiet & checks some of his wild schemes.

– The Premier, in the course of discussion, returned more than once to the idea that these Arabs of Soudan are fighting for their country & their freedom, & that we have no right to meddle with them[88]. (But is not that discovery made rather late?)

Ld Wolseley put forward a wild plan, as it seemed to us, of bringing Red Indians from Canada, accustomed to canoe work, to help his expedition over the rapids of the Nile.

– Notwithstanding, or perhaps because of, the length of time during which we sat, the telegrams which embodied our decision were huddled up in haste at the last moment – I asked to have drafts of them in print, & read them over at leisure, but this was not liked, the whole Cabinet being weary. The substance of the decision, however, I approve of, & think entirely right.

24 Apr. 1884: . . . Very little business from office . . . Office 2.30 & stayed till past 6.00.

. . . Sir R. & Ly Morier dined with us, & their daughter. Sir R. much improved, now that he has got a post equal to his pretensions: less inclined to find fault with all the world, & his bragging has nearly disappeared. He expects an embassy, & will probably get one, for there is no man in our diplomatic service of equal ability, with all his faults.

The budget of last night went off well: not much was expected, for it was known that the surplus was small, & the state of trade not such as to encourage sanguine estimates: & I think there was a general feeling of relief that no new taxes were proposed. The operations connected with the debt seem generally approved: the plan of turning the half sovereign into a simple token, in order to get funds for restoring the sovereign to its full weight, is not equally popular: but it is a small detail & can if necessary be dropped without injury.

The Premier called on M. this afternoon, & sounded her as to offering me the vacant Garter[89]. She advised the offer. . . .

28 Apr. 1884: . . . Letter from Hale, stating . . . the various sales now in progress. They ought to bring £45,740 by the end of June . . . But there is additional, certain as to amount, but uncertain as to date, £114,000 to come in, chiefly from sales in Bootle, and a farther sum from the Dock Board, perhaps £10,000.

. . . Fog increased. Read & wrote by lamplight: office at 2.15: Cabinet at 3.00 . . . The Galloways dined with us . . . G. in much distress at the almost total destruction of his woods by the late gales[90]. Not only can he not sell the timber, but he does not see how it can be removed before it rots on the ground.

29 Apr. 1884: Another foggy day: work by lamplight till 11.00.

Office at 2.00: committee of Cabinet at 3.00, in Trevelyan's room at the H. of C. – Spencer, Kimberley, Childers, Trevelyan, Chamberlain, Lefevre[91], & myself. Our discussion was irregular & interrupted, owing to a debate going on in the Commons, which T. & C. were called away to attend. What we had to deal with was the question of providing funds with which to enable the Irish peasantry to buy their holdings. They do not care to do so, being satisfied, & no wonder, with their position as tenants who are irremovable:

but the landowners want to sell, so as to get rid of their encumbrances, & in many cases they wish, I have no doubt, to be quit of the country altogether. It is felt that they have been hardly dealt with, & that some reparation is due: & this circumstance perhaps justifies what is on other grounds a doubtful step. The objection to it obviously is that the State becomes the landlord, that there will be a constant pressure on parliament to reduce the rent & that a premium will be held out by insurrection for the people will argue that in getting rid of the British government they will get rid of their debts as well. Various plans were discussed: that which found most favour was a proposal that the county rate should be made liable for any deficiency in payment. None of these proposals is free from objection, but probably this is the least faulty.

To the Lords, where . . . an Irish debate on the subject which we had just been discussing among ourselves, the purchase of Irish lands. Lord Castletown[92] opened it, a new peer, formerly an M.P. He spoke remarkably well, with good temper & good sense. Kimberley answered, in a conciliatory tone, promising a bill . . . Home, & dined at The Club, meeting [Lord] Houghton, fresh from Egypt. – Houghton's social energies are remarkable. He has had a stroke, which at first affected his speech: but this disappeared with wine & talk, & he was livelier than anybody.

At the Cabinet of yesterday, we had a renewed discussion on the provision which the Queen wants made for her grandchildren. The Premier said she was very indignant at the decision to postpone any proposal of the kind. We talked the matter over, agreed that nothing could be done now, but did not object to some vague hope being held out for the future.

Question raised, but not settled, as to a vote of thanks for operations on the Red Sea.

Then the Att.-Gen.[93] was called in: he had a proposal to make as to the franchise bill, to the effect that it should not be brought into operation until 1886: we promising a redistribution bill in 1885: on this a lively discussion ensued: Gladstone approved the suggestion as tending to save time: R. Grosv.[enor][94], who was consulted, thought the party would not object. Harcourt was ready to acquiesce in the proposal if forced upon us, but not to propose it ourselves: the Chancellor saw no objection: I supported it, on the ground that it would take a powerful weapon out of the hands of opposition: Harcourt ridiculed it as absurd, said it would make a dissolution impossible: you could not appeal to the old constituencies, and the new would not exist: Chamberlain objected on the odd ground that he was sure the scheme emanated from Randolph Churchill, and that it would be disgraceful to adopt any plan of his. In the end the matter dropped, with a renewed expression of regret from Gladstone that we did not see our way to adopt it.

There followed a desultory conversation as to the buying out of Irish landlords: which ended in the appointment of a Cabinet committee.

30 Apr. 1884: . . . Saw Sanderson, who wants the governorship of St. Helena for Lord Canterbury, his cousin! It is exile, poverty, & little to do, & so I told S. but he was not convinced[95].

Saw Sir E. Baring, who gave a lamentable report of Egypt. The taxes are not paid, the fellah, who depends a good deal on corn, is ruined by low prices, & the confusion & disorder are great. 'You cannot stay where you are: you interfere either too little or too much: you have no option except to take the whole administration into your own hands or else to call in other Powers and divide your authority with them.' Of Gordon he talked freely, admiring his character, but describing him as impossible to deal with. 'He telegraphs whatever comes into his head: often in direct contradiction to what he has said a few hours before: nothing can be more wild than his ideas: I do not send them on to England until I have been able to put them a little into shape: & even so they are incoherent enough. I have never in my life had a similar experience.' . . .

1 May 1884: The Premier called at 1.00 to offer me formally the vacant Garter[96], which I accepted, having made up my mind to do so, though it is not a thing I value, but I am told that a refusal would be ungracious, and I have a kind of respect for our family tradition: I believe all my predecessors have been 'decorated' after this same fashion.

Cabinet at 2.30, which sat till 4.15. Then to the Lords, where Salisbury had a personal grievance, alleging that some words of a dispatch of his had been misconstrued by Gladstone. He seemed to make a good case, but Granville in reply quoted a passage from a speech delivered by him in 1882, which he had evidently forgotten, and which completely justified Gladstone. The scene that followed was comic: Cairns was evidently prepared to speak, but on hearing this quotation read he looked at his colleague, who also appeared considerably astonished, & they thought it better to say nothing[97].

. . . In Cabinet, the Premier signified the Queen's pleasure that there shall be no official birthday dinners this year: which we all readily agree to, but it is an odd way of showing grief, as the illuminations will go on.

The Queen also desires that Ld Torrington's[98] place shall be filled up by a 'personal friend' who shall not be removable on any change of ministry. Granville objects, as every vote in the Lords is of consequence, where we have so few. And it is believed that the 'personal friend' is Lord Rowton[99], whose influence will certainly not be used in a sense favourable to the present Cabinet. It was settled to protest.

The question of a vote of thanks for the operations in the Red Sea was considered, & the general feeling seemed decidedly against it, but no conclusion was come to. The rest of the business chiefly turned upon questions to be answered in parlt.

2 May 1884: . . . I did not note that yesterday the Premier, before the Cabinet, in conversation with me, reverted to his notion that a Turkish force might be sent to the Red Sea ports: to which strong objection was taken by Harcourt & others. He referred to this opposition, & said, as if surprised: 'I think there is among some members of the Cabinet a prejudice against the Turks': he himself having denounced them in the most violent language ever used in oral or written discussion. But he seemed to have forgotten this, & made his remark in utter unconsciousness of its oddity. . . .

5 May 1884: London . . . little business . . . Work at home till 2.00, when a Cabinet, which sat till past 4.00: office for a few minutes only: H. of Lords till 7.30, chiefly occupied with a discussion on the lunacy laws, brought on by Ld Milltown[100], in a fairly good speech. Lord Shaftesbury, as a lunacy commissioner, replied, speaking an hour: but inaudible during much of the time, & not effective when he was heard. Whatever power of speaking he possesses lies in declamation, not in argument. The Chief Justice[101] spoke shortly, but with weight, both from the force of what he said & the position of the speaker. He laid his finger on the sore place – that the keeper of a private asylum has a strong interest in his patient not being cured. As to the other question in dispute, whether any person ought to be shut up as a lunatic without a more public enquiry than our present system provides for, he balanced the objections fairly. Without publicity, you cannot be sure that abuses will not occur: but by insisting on publicity we should induce many sensitive persons to conceal the fact of their relations or friends being lunatics, & possibly bring about a return to the old state of things, when lunatics were kept for years shut up without form of law, by members of their own families. The Chancellor promised a bill: but I would not give much for the chance of its passing.

In Cabinet today, a desultory discussion as to provision to be made for the Queen's grandchildren. It is agreed that we can do nothing now: the question is, shall we promise any action in the future? Dilke pressed again for an enquiry into the whole civil list: thought the best time would be when the P. of W.'s son comes of age. Chamberlain objected to any pledge as to the future, 'however vague'. Talk as to the Queen's savings, which Dilke thought must be enormous, & the Premier very small. Then came the question of the proposed Conservative vote of censure. Gladstone observed that there had been more of these in the last 4 years than in the preceding half century: but it was agreed that we must not seem to avoid discussion. Then came the settling of answers to various parliamentary queries. Then talk about the intended conference. – The French answer is reckoned satisfactory. The language held by Waddington is that France makes no claim to a restoration of the joint control: and will disclaim any intention of occupying Egypt on her own account if we go out. But these pledges, as I understand them, are conditional on some arrangement being come to. Much conversation followed: I said that, having doubted at first as to fixing a limit of time for our stay, I now inclined to it, since if some pledge of the kind were not given we should never get away at all: the Premier agreed in this view, but in vague terms. A good deal of time was spent in discussing the appointment of one Raoul Pasha whom the Khedive supports, whom Baring thinks a bad choice, but also thinks we had better not interfere. We agreed in this opinion.

6 May 1884: . . . Talk with Herbert about affairs at Angra Pequena & the Germans[102].
. . . The papers are full of a quarrel between R. Churchill & Salisbury . . . Both are intemperate in language, & the dislike (mutual) is publicly expressed . . .

7 May 1884: . . . Cabinet at 2.30, which sat till near 5.30. Then office, where not much to do. . . . At the Cabinet, we discussed, first, Nubar's wish to visit England: which all agreed was not desirable. Then the possible appointment of Clifford Lloyd[103] to some colonial or Indian post: as to remove him simply would have a bad effect in Egypt, while yet he is making himself impossible there. Talk next about the negociations with France: Granville read a draft of his conversation with Waddington, but it does not seem that the French have made any definite suggestion. They want an international financial control to begin at once, which we say is impossible while the English occupation continues. This led naturally to discussion as to the length of our stay in Egypt. Dodson thought we should want 10 years. Harcourt would prefer 10 days. I said from 3 to 5 years. We all seemed to admit in principle the fixing of a term for our occupation, to be settled with the consent of Europe.

The Premier fired up, & made us a sort of speech. He said it was an unnatural proceeding to attempt to govern a Mahometan country. Somebody suggested: 'India'. 'India – yes, but you well know that with our parliamentary system India could not be conquered as it was. The thing was done without the knowledge of the English people: it could not be done now.' It was monstrous to suppose that we could manage the affairs of the Egyptians for them better than they could for themselves. For himself, pledged as he was up to the eyes, he should be a disgraced man if he listened to any schemes of either protectorate or annexation. This little harangue was delivered with much energy, & seemed to be an answer to suggestions made to him by some one outside, or to his own thoughts, rather than to anything that had passed in Cabinet.

He mentioned also, I recollect, that he received some 500 letters weekly on public affairs: of these 150 were on the franchise: the rest on various subjects, & hardly any on Egypt. He stated this as proof that there was no general feeling on the subject. – R. Grosvenor was then called in, & after discussion we agreed to meet the vote of censure by a direct negative.

8 May 1884: To Coutts, where bought £5,000 S. Australian & £5,000 Tasmanian 4% stock, at cost of £10,238. Total investments now £490,000.

. . . To a committee of Cabinet on bill for purchase of Irish lands. Kimberley, Childers, Carlingford, Trevelyan, Lefevre, & self. Most of our conversation turned on matters of detail, but we had a dispute as to the amount of inducement which should be held out to tenants to buy. Chamberlain admitted that, if the landlords were not willing to sell, he would be in favour of making the Act compulsory, & would like to see the principle extended to England & Scotland. This was too much for Carlingford, who, though a hot supporter of the Irish Land Acts, declared that he did not mean to injure the landlords, & was shocked at the notion of their being swept away: Lefevre & I agreed with him: in the end we settled to limit the amount of the funds to be supplied by the State for purchase of land, so that not more than a certain number of the peasantry should be debtors to the State at one time.

9 May 1884: . . . In the H. of Lords, Ld Balfour[104] brought in a bill to abolish pigeon shooting, which was lost by 78 to 48. The speeches were all poor, except one by Lord Aberdare[105]: those by Fortescue[106] & Galloway[107] especially silly. I should have been sorry if a stranger had judged our House by this debate. Neither ministers nor ex-ministers on the opposition bench took any part. The bishops all voted for the bill: all that is who were present.

. . . At the opening of the International Health Exhibition yesterday the Premier was received with cheers, which led to a counter-demonstration of hissing, of which the opposition papers today are making the most[108].

The quarrel between Salisbury and R. Churchill . . . is still occupying the newspapers . . . the tendencies which they respectively represent are divergent, & will remain so[109]. . . .

12 May 1884: London . . . very hot & dusty . . . Saw Antrobus, but there was very little business . . . Work at home till 2.00: then to office, where saw Herbert & Ashley on affairs of Zululand, which are growing perplexed . . . Cetewayo's friends have rallied, & attacked Osborn[110] in the reserve, getting beaten: however, Bulwer[111] is now clamorous for annexation: which the colonists have wanted all along: and Natal will back him. But Sir H. Robinson[112], I am glad to see, takes a different view. . . .

13 May 1884: . . . Walking home with me & Kimberley, Granville complained of the Premier's way of answering questions, which by its ambiguity leads to farther enquiries. 'Yes,' said Kimberley, 'he qualifies every statement that he makes, & then qualifies the qualification again.' But they agreed that it was his extreme anxiety to deal with every possible case, & to meet every possible objection, that led him to answer in a way which seems at first sight evasive. . . .

14 May 1884: Debate on vote of confidence ended last night with a majority of 28 for ministers: a victory, but not a complete one, for we ought to have had 50. The Irish all voted against us, which is not to be regretted. . . . From one cause or another, nearly 70 must have stayed away. The excitement was great, & feeling very bitter on both sides. Forster has turned violently against us, & Goschen takes the same line more moderately. Cowen delivered a speech which must have been rhetorically effective, though wild: on the whole I think the debate was maintained with more spirit & eloquence than any which we have had of late. But the Premier's speech on Monday[113] was not judged worthy of him or of the occasion: less from any falling off in argument & eloquence than because some new disclosure of policy had been expected &, failing to get it, the House was perhaps unreasonably disappointed.

We have suffered throughout from the disadvantage of not being able to state our case fully: it would be ungenerous, as well as impolitic, to throw any blame on Gordon: yet his inexplicable contradictions and changes of mind have created the greater part of the difficulty in which we are. The mistake was in sending him: which we did at last in a hurry, as important things are apt to be done when much time has been spent on small ones.

Cabinet at 2.00, which sat till 6.15: too long, & there were many interruptions, from members of the H. of C. having to go backwards & forwards to attend divisions. We sat in the Premier's room at Westminster. Office, where settled in haste what was urgent, & let the rest stand over. Home 7.30, very weary . . .

In Cabinet, Zulu affairs were first discussed at my request, & we agreed without division or debate that the annexation [which] Bulwer & the Natal people want shall not take place[114]. The talk of a protectorate is now abandoned: & Sir B. Frere's policy again proposed. But we will not extend our responsibilities in that part of the world, more especially when there may be demands on our military resources elsewhere.

Egypt was the subject discussed afterwards. Childers announced his scheme for relieving the money difficulties of the Egyptian government. We are to raise 8 millions by loan, which we shall do at less than 3%: we shall lend to Egypt at 4%, leaving 1% for sinking fund: the charge will be £320,000 a year on Egypt, which will be met by the bondholders giving up ½% on their holdings: this it is thought they may be willing to do, as without our help there will be bankruptcy: a few other minor economies will restore the balance. This idea was approved, but I am not sure whether it is definitively accepted.
It was agreed that Clifford Lloyd must resign, he & Nubar finding it impossible to work together, & having had many quarrels.

Sir E. Baring[115] was called in, & gave his opinion at length. He repeated what he has said in his telegrams: that we ought either to take over the whole administration or leave it more to itself. He thought 5 years the least time in which we could get away. Complained of the machine being hard to work, with the French so very hostile, & none of the other foreigners friendly. He thought Zebehr an element of danger, & that he is probably now intriguing with the insurgents. 'Everybody in Egypt,' he said, 'is against us. If we were to annex the country, interest would lead some to take our side: but, as it is, we have nobody for us.' The debt is too heavy, & must be reduced. And we must not go on pressing for expensive reforms, & at the same time urging economy. As to the garrisons, he did not believe in a fellaheen army. 'The men are cheap, but no force is so costly as a force that will not fight': but he did not seem clear as to the best substitutes. He praised Nubar as an administrator & negociator, but said he had no idea of economy. The above are the leading points in his narrative or exposition of the state of things.

Much talk followed as to: (1) Fixing a time for leaving Egypt: (2) Admitting an international control in matters of finance: (3) Future arrangements for neutralising Egypt, 'making it the Belgium of the east', as the phrase is. I could not accurately note it, & do not remember all that passed. But I remember that the Chancellor, Hartington, & I think Kimberley, dwelt strongly on the point that the conference had been announced to be financial only, & that if its basis were enlarged we were bound to inform the public of the fact. This seemed generally agreed to, though Dilke remarked that preceding Cabinets had not always been so scrupulous. . . .

17 May 1884 (Saturday): . . . Cabinet, which met at 12.00, and sat till nearly 4.00: thence in haste to the office, where settled a few pressing affairs, & with M. away for Fairhill by the 4.55 train . . .

At the Cabinet, debate, & considerable difference of opinion, on the question of Irish land purchase by the State. The plan of the committee of Cabinet is that the whole price of the land be advanced by the State: that the tenant shall repay it by an annuity of $4\frac{1}{2}$% for 42 years: that the county rate shall be charged as security for repayment: and that the operation be limited to £20 millions. – Spencer opposed this plan in a set speech. He said it would help the agitators, that it would disturb the working of the Land Act, that there was danger of a combination among the tenants not to pay, that government would find it impossible to collect the rents after a bad harvest, that the limit of £20 millions was illusory & could not be maintained, that the plan would encourage solvent landlords to leave the country – in short, he objected to the whole scheme. But he admitted that there was on both sides a strong wish for it, especially on the part of embarrassed landlords. Dilke agreed with him. Chamberlain took the opposite view, arguing that we have either gone too far or not far enough. A small proposal would be rejected. The present system gave no security against the Land League & farther agitation. Agitation would continue while any rent was paid. He was in favour of the universal conversion of occupiers into owners. The Premier said he was not enthusiastic about the plan, did not like a wholesale displacement of Irish landlords. Did not think the limit of £20 millions would stand. Did not like giving a premium to tenants who buy, by fixing their payments below their present rent. – We talked much, & were equally divided, so agreed to adjourn the question.

The strongest argument in favour was Trevelyan's – that much land must be sold by reason of the charges upon it, & that, if the State did not interfere, it would be bought up by speculators of the worst sort.

Granville opened a discussion on the conference. He said the Queen had objected so strongly to our fixing any term for withdrawal from Egypt that he had put off his interviews with Waddington. Waddington says the French will undertake not to go in if we come out, but they consider our fixing a time for withdrawal an indispensable part of any arrangement. Harcourt did not like any arrangement that was not at once avowed to parliament & to Europe. Nor did he like separate negociations with France. They were too like the old dual control. He wished to arrange for retirement in a way which would commit the nation & bind our successors. Then let us fight it out in parliament, & if we are beaten the Opposition will be responsible for working out the policy of permanent occupation. The Premier was very strong on the question of telling parliament nothing until we had got into conference. Premature disclosure would ruin everything. He dwelt on the danger of delay, & the imminence of Egyptian bankruptcy. Granville said he must tell the Powers what was doing with France: at least he must tell Italy & Germany. Kimberley, Chamberlain, & I agreed in urging that parliament should be informed at the earliest date. Dodson observed that whatever we told the Powers would be known, & we ought not to try to keep it from parliament. The Premier, in some heat, dwelt on the danger of intrigue if the thing [*sic*], & drew a distinction, which I could not well follow, between questions to be discussed in conference, & questions to be settled as a condition of going into conference. He seemed to agree that we might keep the latter secret, yet deny, with truth, that the scope of the conference had been extended. But the Cabinet were not with him on this point, & he did not press it. Indeed, though I think he meant what I have noted above, I am not quite sure of it, & I do not feel certain that we any of us quite understood his meaning. In the end it seemed agreed that we should tell parliament all as soon as we conveniently could, the precise time being left undetermined. . . .

19 May 1884: . . . Office soon after 2.00: work there till 3.30, when to a meeting (not called a Cabinet)[116] at the Treasury. The chief subject discussed was Irish land, and in the end Spencer withdrew his objections, though reluctantly, & saying he was not convinced. There was some further talk about the conference, but desultory: Harcourt seeing the impossibility of going out of Egypt at once, & intensely disgusted but not objecting. . . .

23 May 1884: . . . Talk with M. as to Galloway, whose habits of drink have grown unpleasantly upon him, so that he is seldom quite his own master in the evenings, & Drage says that he may at any time have a stroke of paralysis. We agreed that nothing can be said to him except by a medical man, & that he must be induced to consult one.

In the Lords, Granville spoke to me complainingly about the Premier, whom he thinks indiscreet in his conversations with the diplomatists. He seems to have told them that he had great doubt as to his being able to carry his Egyptian policy through the H. of Commons – which is certainly a needless piece of frankness – and this Granville says they have telegraphed all over Europe, thus lessening the influence of the British government.

A paper has been circulated among the Cabinet today, in the sense of recommending that Egypt should at the conference be placed under some international guarantee, as Belgium is, whereby all risk of its annexation either by England or any other Power might be averted. Hartington was, of those who had noted the paper, the only dissentient. I agreed in principle, believing this to be the only effective alternative to annexation, which most of the English people wish for.

24 May 1884 (Saturday): . . . Summons, at 11.00, for a Cabinet at 2.00: which was followed by another, half an hour later, calling it for 12.00: an odd way of doing business, but, being by chance at home, I received both. Several ministers were absent when we met, but all dropped in later except Harcourt: we sat till 4.30. Disposed of some pressing business at the office, and by 5.17 train to Keston, where all quiet, & the place in full glory, though rather dry.

In Cabinet, we began with a discussion on the expediency of fixing a date before which the franchise bill should not come into operation, so as to give fair opportunity for passing a redistribution bill before it does so. The object as Gladstone put it is not so much to give the bill a chance of passing in the Lords, for of that he despairs, as to show that the Cabinet will not, if by concession it can avoid the necessity, make itself responsible for a struggle between the two Houses: out of which he thought it impossible that the Lords should issue with the constitution of their House unchanged. Dilke disliked the concession, thought his friends would dislike it, believed that it would be useless for its object, but was ready to give way to the Prime Minister.

Then followed the question of female suffrage, as to which, it being agreed that it is not to be included in the bill, Courtney & Fawcett ask leave to stay away when it is divided upon. This the Cabinet think cannot be: and it is expected that Fawcett will resign. He has been dissatisfied ever since the Egyptian occupation began: he is not on good terms with the Treasury, whom he persistently ignores as Postmaster: & he is probably disappointed at not being in the Cabinet. Courtney it is thought will give way. Dilke told us to our regret that if Courtney went he must resign too, though he would not do so if Fawcett retired alone: an odd distinction, & not intelligible, but there is no argument possible when a man talks about obligations of honour.

There followed a long discussion as to the conference, & possible neutralisation of Egypt. All accept it in principle, the chief question in dispute being whether we should pledge ourselves to it now, or wait till the close of our term of occupation. – Several of us expressed alarm lest we should be accused of breaking faith with the H. of C., and a long & rather tedious reference to former answers to former questions followed: Chamberlain & Kimberley were especially uneasy. In the end it was settled that a fresh explanation should be made, lest we should seem to have pledged ourselves to more than we have. – Some talk as to the length of our stay in Egypt. Gladstone, though disliking a long term, thought 5 years would be more popular than 3, & most of us agreed, but Dilke & Chamberlain denied it vehemently, saying the sooner we were out of Egypt the better the public would be pleased.

Complaint was made that the *Pall Mall Gazette* gets information it has no right to (Brett, Hartington's secretary, is the person suspected). Talk about the French in Morocco. Waddington lays all the blame on a turbulent agent: but both Nigra[117] & the Spaniard here say there is a plan of annexation, & indeed it seems that the French government admit that there may be need of a rectification of frontier.

Hartington then raised a discussion on the necessity of preparing for an expedition to Berber, to be made by laying a light railway from Suakin. It is thought the line could be laid for £1 million, & that an expedition of 7,000 men would cost only a million more. The chief objection taken was that, if once a British force got to Khartoum, the British public would not allow it to come away again. – In the end we agreed to wait for farther details.

25 May 1884 (Sunday): Only one large pouch from the office: but in afternoon came a messenger with unpleasant telegrams from Zululand, saying that an immediate increase of force is necessary. Meade[118] had wisely sent this down at once, that I might have time to consider it: but in truth there is little to be considered, for we cannot refuse assistance which the governor and the general in command consider indispensable. . . .

26 May 1884: London . . . day hot & very dusty . . . saw Meade as to the reinforcements wanted for Zululand, wrote to W.O. & Admiralty accordingly.

... D. of Richmond[119] told me that the Manchester [Ship] Canal Bill, which has been passed after a 41 days' sitting, was carried in the committee of which he was chairman by 3 to 2, he being one of the dissentients, Barrington[120] with him: Norton[121], Lovat[122], & Dunraven[123] the majority. His ground of objection was that on which the Liverpool people insist most, the risk of injury to the river.

27 May 1884: ... Cabinet at 12.30, which sat less than two hours, the M.P.s having to go to the House.

... H. of Lords at 4.30, ... an angry wrangle was got up, in which Cairns & Salisbury both took part, professing, & perhaps feeling, alarm lest any irrevocable settlement should be come to with France before the Lords met again. Granville answered with extreme (and, as Kimberley & I thought, unnecessary) reserve, which irritated them still more. In the end, as they complained of too long an interruption of our sittings, we offered them to shorten the holidays by a week, which they could not help accepting though taken by surprise, & I imagine not at all desiring this compliance with their wishes[124].

At the Cabinet today we were chiefly occupied with devising the answers to be given in both Houses. The Premier read a mem. containing the statement he was about to make, Granville wanted to know whether there would be any objection to our stating the conditions on which we went into conference before the conference began? Carlingford, Chamberlain, Harcourt, & I, supported this proposal. Chamberlain would have the whole question fought out in parliament before going into conference. If we carried our point, all would be well: if not, our responsibility was at an end, & our successors would be responsible. The Premier doubted at first, saying the opposition would use their knowledge to spoil the conference: but in the end I understood him to assent. Granville read a report of his conversation with Waddington, & a letter from Ferry to the latter. He (G.) said he thought well of the prospects of a settlement with France. Hartington objected strongly to limit the term of our stay in Egypt at the demand of France. He did not see what right the French had to interfere. The preliminary negociation with them might be a necessity, but it was unlucky. In this expression of opinion nobody agreed. Gladstone dwelt on the importance of the French pledge not to go in when we withdrew. He said it was with extreme reluctance that he had consented to so long a term as 5 years. Hartington ended the discussion by repeating that he disliked the whole affair, & would not be sorry if it broke off.

The question of a possible expedition to rescue Gordon was next considered. Hartington, who raised it, wanted to spend £300,000 at once on a railway from Suakin. But we objected on constitutional grounds, & it was agreed to wait until we could ask parliament in due form.

28 May 1884: Saw Warr, the sec. to the City Companies Commission, & signed the report. He tells me that the Companies are fairly well satisfied, having expected, or at least feared, total dissolution, whereas they are let off with only some restrictions imposed on their dealings with their estates, & the obligation to spend a larger proportion of their revenues on public uses.

... With M. & Margaret to Holwood.

The session up to this date has been laborious – and the results are not quite adequate to the time expended. The London government bill excites little general interest, &

provokes much local opposition: so that it will probably have to be dropped. Chamberlain's bill for the protection of seamen, though its principle is approved, seems also in a bad way: he has defended it with remarkable ability but not in a manner to conciliate the shipowners, & they will oppose him by all means in their power: which is natural, but scarcely wise. I have a suspicion that he does not really care to pass it this year, preferring the advantage which the 'cry' will give him at the general election. The most important of all, the franchise bill, is safe in the Commons, & goes on with comparative smoothness: possibly because its fate in the Lords is considered certain. The budget attracts little interest, & indeed was not meant to be interesting.

The Egyptian question has in fact monopolised attention – for the English public cannot really concern itself in more than one subject at a time. And there is no doubt but that the line taken by us – though in my view the only one that is either honest or wise – is unpopular in London, & in the press. Whether it is equally so in the country is a disputed point, but I am less sanguine than Chamberlain & Dilke, who believe that the constituencies may want to get away, the sooner the better. . . .

30 May 1884: Four or five pouches from the office, with much work, but all routine, or nearly so. . . . At night, received . . . a telegram saying that there had been a dynamite explosion in the Square, & another in Scotland Yard, but No. 23 was not injured. There was nothing to be done: and we went to bed.

. . . News, which I see with some regret, of the death of Sir B. Frere, in his 70th year. Next to the brothers Lawrence, he was certainly the ablest & most distinguished of the Indian civilians of our day, & his reputation would have been greater but for the rashness which led him, 7 years ago, to undertake the government of S. Africa. In that capacity he made the Zulu war of 1879, whose folly as well as injustice revolted all parties at home: for neither Disraeli nor Hicks Beach concealed their dislike of it. Whether he really thought it necessary as an act of self-defence, or, as most who know him believed, he mistook the English temper, & expected a peerage & the governorship of India as his reward, will remain undecided. But, whatever the motive, he, & Lord Lytton, copying & exaggerating the 'jingoism' of the Cabinet at home, brought upon it that kind of discredit which awkward imitation is sure to produce. He felt his recall, & consequent exclusion from public affairs, very deeply: & it probably shortened his life.

Of his Indian career there is little to be said except in praise. His manner was eminently courteous: his judgment sound: and he adhered firmly, indeed obstinately, to decisions once taken. He understood natives, & was both liked & respected by them. He was thought lavish in the expenditure of public money, but it was on useful objects, public works & the like. He favoured the missionary interest, & was fully sensible of the value of its support: but I believe that in this there was as much at least of conviction as of calculation. Whatever mistakes he may have made, he was a remarkable man, & well deserves the posthumous honours which he will no doubt receive. He managed to secure a baronetcy, which descends to his only son.

31 May 1884: . . . The papers are full of the dynamite explosions, of which there were three – one at Scotland Yard, where a wall was blown in, & great damage done: but the plotters, who must have meant to destroy the offices of the detective police, missed their mark, & only destroyed a building used for some other purpose. The other two were intended to smash the Junior Carlton Club, but only injured some servants, & broke a great many windows. A third attempt was made on the Nelson Column in Trafalgar Square, but the dynamite did not explode. – We are growing used in London to these disagreeable surprises, & they create only a momentary sensation. . . .

2 June 1884: . . . No pouches or letters from the office: but in the afternoon late a messenger came from the Home Office with a warrant for signature, & request that I would sign it on behalf of Sir W. Harcourt, who is out of town. It was addressed to the Postmaster General, & requested him to deliver up the originals of all telegrams within certain dates, addressed to Paris or Dublin, the object being to get some information as to the late explosion. I signed the document & sent it back. . . .

5 June 1884: One pouch only from the office, chiefly on W. African affairs. . . .

6 June 1884: From office came six large & heavy pouches, giving me work enough for the day . . .

Sent through Statter £25 to the family of a parson . . . who died lately leaving a wife & 8 children without any means of support. It is a case for assistance, and I do not grudge the gift: but one is apt to ask, has any man a right to marry & bring a large family into the world, with the absolute certainty that they must be maintained at the cost of their neighbours?

Saw an interesting letter from Sir H. Robinson to Herbert, giving an account of the formation of the new Cape ministry, which is distinctly Dutch, though the ostensible leader of the Dutch party has not chosen to act as prime minister. It seems as if they would be disposed to take Bechuanaland into the colony: the best solution of our difficulties there, if it can be reached.

Maltese elections have turned out as badly as possible: all the most extreme men returned to the council: so says the telegram. They are a queer people . . .

There has not been much political oratory during the recess: only two speeches delivered by Salisbury at Plymouth, able and powerful, but singularly injudicious, even for him. In one of these he contends that the various ministerial bills are not brought forward with a view to being passed, or to remedying abuses, but solely with the object of setting class against class: a childish accusation when the nature of their subjects is considered. In the first, & more effective of the two, he dwells at great length on the necessity of not only keeping together, but increasing the empire: on the ground that, when empires cease to grow, they begin to decay. Historically, there is something to be said for this proposition: but, used as the foundation of an argument as to our present duty & position, it leads to this conclusion that we must go on conquering, or submit to be conquered ourselves. It is impossible to hold language more calculated than this to confirm all the unfavourable judgments of those who believe that the Conservative party has become, or is becoming, exclusively a military & clerical party. It is in fact saying that our national policy ought to be a war policy habitually & permanently. I do not believe that Salisbury's opinions – though I quite believe sincerely held by him – are shared by the great bulk of his followers. Certainly they are not those of the middle class, and probably not of the artisans.

Another noticeable feature in the speeches of the opposition is their undisguised eagerness to force on a dissolution: the reason being plain: that they wish the popular vote to be taken while everybody is thinking about Egypt, & while few people are thinking, or at least feeling, much about reform. But only a vote of censure can force a dissolution and even in that case it may be a question whether resignation would not be a preferable alternative.

7 June 1884: The office sends only two pouches, & little in them.

... Many letters & papers ... Among them were two numbers of a new socialist paper called **Justice**, the organ of the so-called Democratic Federation, which appears to have for its programme the nationalisation of the land, abolition of rent & debt, & general confiscation of property. They were sent to me as containing the report of a so-called disturbance at or near Ormskirk, where, as stated, a tenant of mine, a Mr. Williams, refused to pay rent, on principle, called a meeting & addressed them, & resisted the police. Though in all this I have no doubt there is gross exaggeration, there must be a substratum of truth: it cannot be all invention: I accordingly wrote to Hale, enclosing the article, & asking to know what has passed. I shall await his answer with some curiosity[125].

8 June 1884: Three pouches from the office. The only thing important in them is a letter from C. Münster to Granville, by which it appears that the Germans intend to claim possession of Angra Pequena, or at least to object to our claiming it. This is a sudden decision, for a few months ago they only asked protection for German settlers & traders there.

A disagreeable piece of news from America: the chosen candidate for the presidency is a Mr. Blaine[126], well known as a politician, a strong protectionist, and decidedly aggressive in his foreign relations. He is believed to desire the annexation of both Canada & Mexico, & the extension of a U.S. protectorate, in some form, over all South America. He is now the chosen representative of the party which to appearance is most powerful in the Union. His success would not promote friendly relations between the two countries: but there is the double chance: he may not be elected, or he may find it necessary if elected to change his policy: which American statesmen find it easy to do.

Judging by the language of the press on all sides, the intention of the Cabinet to place Egypt under some form of European control appears generally unpopular: and unless we are lucky it may lead to a breakup of the government or a dissolution: for the failure of the H. of C. to approve what we have done would involve one or the other. ...

9 June 1884: ... London by 10.00 o'clock train ... Very few traces of the late explosion left in the Square: only one house has its windows still unmended.

... Drew £100 from the bank, making up reserve to £10,000 in gold[127], & £2,000 notes: the latter to be increased to £5,000 in the autumn.

... Office, 2.00 to 3.00: then Cabinet, which was not very interesting. Granville occupied much time in reading a long despatch which he had received from the French ambassador, & pointing out the inaccuracies which it contained. After some talk, we obtained from the Premier an agreement to say in the House that no decision should be taken binding on the country without parliament having an opportunity of discussing it. He seemed at first not very willing but acquiesced: observing that he had already given a pledge to that effect: but, if he did, it must have been in so vague language that it was not understood. Harcourt, always in extremes, talks of the certainty of our being out in a few weeks: does not regret it, thinks we could not fall in a better cause, is sick of his office & will be glad to be rid of it (in this I believe he is sincere): but will not admit the possibility of our pulling through. Dilke & Chamberlain, though not despondent, think the position in the H. of C. critical: & Chamberlain adds that, if we fail, it will be rather on account of the public thinking our original interference in Egypt a mistake than because they consider that we ought to stay there permanently.

10 June 1884: Office at 2.00, & stayed till 4.00.

Saw Herbert & Meade on the question of the Jew colony in Cyprus, which has been a complete failure: the immigrants will do no work, object to the land which it was intended to assign to them: and ask to be sent home again. The society which sent them to Cyprus ought to help them away: but they seem to have no funds. The experiment goes to confirm the old theory that Jews never made good agriculturists[128].

. . . Saw Mr. Gorst M.P.[129] about the so-called Maori king, Tawhino: to whom he wishes civility to be shown, saying that the king is very attentive to Europeans who visit his country. He, Gorst, was employed in N. Zealand long ago[130]: hence his connection with the question.

Cabinet at 4.00 p.m. in the H. of C. room. It was very disorderly & irregular, not by anybody's fault, but because members were constantly called away to answer questions or attend divisions, the House sitting. Talk first of the woman-franchise question, as to which both Courtney & Fawcett are expected to resign, & if they do it will not be easy to keep Dilke from following suit. Talk – in an interval of business – as to what we should do if beaten on the Egyptian question in the Commons – dissolve or resign? Harcourt & Chamberlain were strong against dissolving, on the ground that Egyptian affairs could not be hung up for two months while the elections were pending: and also that we should embarrass our successors more by letting them try their hands at once than if they came into power after a dissolution ending in their favour. The force of this latter argument I do not see: the other has something in it. Kimberley & I contended that we had no right to throw up the game without playing it out to the end: that our followers had claims upon us: that the opposition coming into power would probably embroil us with France, perhaps annex Egypt, & do mischief which would not be easily repaired. Some others joined, but the conversation was interrupted.

Hartington brought forward a scheme for laying down a railway from Suakin inland, & we agreed to certain preparations being made. They involve as yet but little outlay, so that it will not be necessary to ask for a vote. . . .

13 June 1884: Another very hot day. Six large pouches from office.

. . . Letter from old Ld Malmesbury, now 77, who intends to publish his memoirs[131], & sends me letters of my father's, & some of my own, to know if I object to their being used. I answer in a friendly way, & ask a few days to look at the letters. . . .

14 June 1884 (Saturday): . . . Luncheon at the club: Cabinet at 2.00, which sat till 4.40: then office . . . Disposed in a hurry of a good deal of business, by 6.35 train back to Bromley, & reach Holwood 7.45.

The Cabinet was summoned at an hour's notice, according to the inconvenient practice which the present government has adopted. Harcourt was absent, having gone down to the New Forest. All the rest there, except Spencer.

In Cabinet, various matters were discussed. Dilke, Fawcett, & Courtney, having refused to vote with their colleagues on the female franchise question, offered their resignation: which the Prime Minister thought it better not to accept, considering the critical state of affairs in parliament, & the inconvenience of seeming disunited when about to be attacked.

Hartington mentioned the wish of the Queen to make the D. of Connaught[132] C.-in-C. of the Bombay Army, for a term not exceeding 18 months. This is proposed undisguisedly, as a first step towards giving him the command at home. To make the thing more unpopular, H.M. stipulates that he shall come home during the hot weather, lest his health should suffer. We all agreed with Hartington that the proposal is inadmissible.

Much talk about the case of Baker Pasha[133], whom Hartington, Northbrook, Carlingford, Granville, & I wish to reinstate nominally in his old rank, so that he may regain his lost status, & the price of his commission. The Premier leant to that side also, but nothing was settled. Dilke, Chamberlain, & Kimberley opposed – the two first very strongly, but solely on the ground that by condoning his offences we should alienate the dissenting interest. The arguments for mercy were: (1) that if we did not mean to recognise in any way Baker's services in Egypt we ought not to have accepted them: (2) the strong feeling of the army in his favour: (3) the fact that nearly half the H. of Commons (307 members) have memorialised the government in his favour: (4) the fact that he has undergone a double punishment: imprisonment by sentence of the court, & loss of his commission, & prospects in the army. Of these pleas the first is the only one to which I attach much weight, but that one I think strong. . . . To employ an officer on responsible duty is in effect to condone his previous acts: for a man who is still to be treated as a criminal ought not to be put in military command. The matter remains undecided.

Most of our time was spent in considering the French answer to our proposal – they refuse to give the English chairman of the commission a casting vote – we have insisted upon it. In the end we agreed to leave it to be settled by the conference when it meets.

We met at Granville's house, he having the gout. Waddington was in another room most of the time.

15 June 1884: One pouch from office, which gave little trouble. During these three weeks of partial holiday, I have been on the whole very free from departmental difficulties. The chief just now are:

(1) Malta: where the attempt at a conciliatory policy has failed, to judge by the new elections. But there is nothing at the present moment to be done.
(2) West Africa: continual disputes & quarrels with the French, who are pursuing an aggressive policy.
(3) Zululand: where reinforcements will be required to protect the reserve. The rest of South Africa is exceptionally quiet for the moment.
(4) Angra Pequena and the German claims: but that is more a trouble for F.O. than for us.
(5) Jamaica: the new constitution and the report of the commissioners, which must be decided upon point by point.
(6) Cyprus: the late military scandals, & their consequences: but I hope these are over, & that we shall hear no more of them.
(7) Newfoundland: where it seems to me probable that the colony will reject the arrangement, though very favourable, which we have made with the French about fisheries. This, however, is rather in the future than an actually pressing question.

(8) The Australian convict question, & in connection with it the new Monroe doctrine preached by Australian politicians, but which does not seem to have laid hold on the masses. The connected plan of confederation is dead or shelved: if opposed here, it would probably have become immensely popular in the colonies: being left alone, indeed rather favoured, by the C.O., it has lost its charm, & the mutual rivalry of N.S. Wales & Victoria has caused it to be laid outside.

16 June 1884: . . . Office at 1.30, where stayed till 3.00: then to Ld Granville's, to meet Kimberley, on the question of Angra Pequena. I took Sir R. Herbert with me. I found Ld G. rather worse with the gout: and not in good spirits: but as fit for business as ever. We talked over the whole matter, which appears awkward, for Bismarck, though not wanting colonies, is disposed, in view of coming elections, to make a show of great activity in protecting German settlers abroad. Our claim is not a strong one, but if we waive it we mortally offend the Cape colonists: if we press it we risk a quarrel with Germany. It may be possible to establish a *modus vivendi* for the time, if a permanent settlement is impossible.

At 4.30 to the Lords, where Argyll in a speech of $2\frac{1}{2}$ hours, discussed the Irish Land Act, against the working of which he certainly made out a strong case. He had a good audience, & was warmly applauded by the majority of the House. His speech was fine, & sound in argument, but it was a speech against the second reading of the Land Act, & useless now for all practical purposes. It was unpractical too, inasmuch as it wholly ignored the only justification of the Act of '81, the revolutionary condition of the country, making some measure of the kind inevitable. Carlingford answered in the feeblest of all possible replies, confused, incoherent, & pointless[134]. He overdid his defence too, refusing to admit the existence of any defects in the law, & treating the complaints of the landowners as if they were merely ridiculous. Luckily, the peers had gone to dinner, & it did not much matter what he said. Waterford[135], Fortescue, & one or two more spoke shortly: I closed the discussion, but in an empty House. Home at 8.30, rather weary.

17 June 1884: Office at 1.00. Saw there the Boer delegates on their way back to S. Africa. Nothing passed beyond civilities. . . .

19 June 1884: Sanderson called: uneasy as to Angra Pequena: thinks the German claims will be pressed: & does not see how to evade them.

It is now virtually announced that, as soon as the proposals of the government about Egypt are known, a vote of censure will be moved by the opposition. Opinion seems to have changed a good deal in the last few days as to its chances of success: the opposition is divided, not hopeful, and its leaders probably are not very anxious to take office in a time of so much difficulty. Still there is the chance that the House may refuse to vote £8 millions for Egypt, when we have not an undivided control: and a failure on that vote will be just as fatal as on the vote of censure.

20 June 1884: . . . Peabody fund meeting . . . Business chiefly formal: we shall finish our buildings in a few months, after which there must be a long interval of inaction till we have worked off the debt. We have secured a return of 3½% on the whole capital invested, which is just what we proposed to ourselves 20 years ago. . . .

21 June 1884 (Saturday): Cabinet at 12.00, which sat till 3.00: then to office, where worked till 5.00: then to the station, & reached Keston soon after 6.00. Day very fine & bright, but . . . I was too weary to enjoy it as much as usual.

In Cabinet, the first subject discussed was the purchase of the Blenheim pictures. Should we offer for them all? Or for three only – a Raphael, a Van Dyck, & a Rubens? or for the Raphael alone? The first alternative was rejected by common consent: in the end we agreed to offer £70,000 for the Raphael alone, or £100,000 for the three. I noticed that Chamberlain & Dilke were more eager than anyone else for the purchase. It was odd too that, in the midst of our discussion, the Premier should interpose by dwelling at some length on the impropriety of pronouncing the Italian painter's name as if it were French – it should be either, he said, Raffaelle as in Italy, or Raphael as in England.

We then went on to Egyptian finance, & Childers laid before us the state of matters in detail. Chamberlain objected strongly to our scheme on the ground that we ought not to tax the Egyptian peasantry, nor put fresh burdens on the English taxpayer for the sake of the creditors of Egypt. He would rather have a bankruptcy & let the creditor get what he could. But this view was not supported & in the end only one important change was made in what had been agreed: viz. instead of lending £8,000,000 ourselves to Egypt, as had been intended, we thought it better to let the Egyptians borrow on the security of an English guarantee: which is substantially the same thing, but avoids the appearance of adding to our debt, & is less likely to meet with opposition in parliament. It was also agreed to reduce the interest on all the debt alike by ½%.

Some conversation about Angra Pequena followed, in the course of which a general wish was expressed to conciliate German opposition as far as possible, in view of the coming conference. A few words were said about the preparations for a Gordon relief expedition. Hartington pressed them: & weakened his case by adding that we ought never to have given up Khartoum. The Premier agreed that we could not defer action indefinitely: but doubted whether Gordon wished to come away if the chance were given him. Dilke spoke much in the same sense: but Chamberlain, whether forgetting or preferring to ignore what has passed in former Cabinets, denied rather vehemently that we were pledged to any expedition, & thought that to send one would be an act of folly. Granville answered him: but nothing came of the conversation.

It is practically agreed, as I understand, to drop the London government bill for this year: it not having a chance of passing, as we knew from the first. Many meetings have been held in support of it, but artificially got up, & there seems no real feeling on the subject. The movement has suffered by being in the hands of inferior men – Firth, a briefless barrister, & Beal, an auctioneer (I believe) not very well thought of, nor exercising any influence on opinion. Londoners for the most part do not complain: and there is a vague apprehension that any change is sure to bring about an increase of rates, which makes for keeping things as they are.

Two elections, Mid Surrey & S. Hants, , have ended in leaving parties exactly where they were. Both were Conservative seats & have remained so[136]. . . .

23 June 1884: . . . At 4.30 to the Lords: where Granville made his statement: he read the despatches that have passed, which would have been tedious but for the great interest felt in the subject. He then related what had passed, speaking remarkably well, very concise and clear, his manner earnest without being declamatory. I never heard him better. A confused conversation followed, and a shower of questions: but naturally there was no sustained debate. On the whole the result was favourable, & I hear from those who heard Gladstone that the effect produced in the H. of Commons was the same. The rest of our business was uninteresting. Called in Curzon St., but A.D. was out of town.

. . . I hear that in the Commons Gladstone's statement was well received: in the debate which followed, R. Churchill made a wild speech, attacking the French nation violently, & by his intemperate language doing much good to his opponents. The attitude of the opposition was hesitating & perplexed.

24 June 1884: . . . Lawson called: thought the result of the statement in both houses last night satisfactory for the government: did not believe that a vote of censure would be proposed: still less that if proposed it would be carried. It is evident that, though his paper is blustering and (in the vulgar phrase) 'jingo' in its style of writing, he is prepared to help the government as far as he can.

Office: Cabinet at 3.00, in the room at H. of C. – the least regular & least useful that we have held. Some did not come till 3.30: others had to go away: Sir E. Baring was called in, & consulted on various points affecting Egypt, but nothing was or could be settled: all ended in desultory conversation. The Premier seemed exhausted[137] & hardly spoke. I made no note; indeed there was nothing to record.

I asked Harcourt if the newspaper report was true, that the London government bill would be withdrawn? He answered as if huffed, that newspaper reports were never true: but Chamberlain told me that from want of time there was no chance of its passing. He said the same as to his own Merchant Shipping bill, which I am sorry for, for it is a useful measure. But he, Chamberlain, has made the mistake of attacking the whole shipping interest as though they were concerned in defending the abuses which he wants to put down: &, instead of dividing the interest, he has it solid against him. I am not sure that he does not now see his mistake.

H. of Lords where, contrary to custom, the peers amused themselves by debating over again on the third reading the bill for protection of young girls[138] – I suppose attracted by the flavour of impropriety which hangs round the subject . . . We sat till past 7.00.

25 June 1884: Busy on a difficult set of papers relating to Ceylon finances, which have been affected by the recent failure of the Oriental Bank. Sir A. Gordon[139] has acted on his own authority in guaranteeing its notes: an irregular proceeding, for he ought to have asked for instructions, but there is truth in his reply, that he could not have explained the state of things by telegraph, & without explanation it would have been useless to ask leave: whilst there was no time for communicating by despatch. By taking a power beyond his right, Sir A. has no doubt gratified his strong despotic instincts: and the precedent is a bad one: but it is scarcely fair to censure an act, though irregular, which has probably averted a serious crisis.

Lawson called: he hears that the opposition are preparing an attack on the Egyptian business, & thinks them right in their tactics, though they are sure to be beaten.

. . . Received also a deputation of the Maltese nobility – three men & two ladies . . . who came with the very practical object of claiming for the Maltese nobles a share in the council – 4 to be elected by the rest to sit there. It was not easy to explain to them civilly the utter impossibility of any such idea. They said the nobility was extremely popular. I asked why in that case should they not come forward as candidates for the elective seats? Oh, they said, that would be useless: the **avvocati** would always be preferred by the electors. The inference was obvious: but I did not draw it. One of the ladies spoke most to the point: she said the English were unpopular among the upper classes of Malta, because they did not treat them with respect. That is about the truth, & not to be remedied by law.

Called in Curzon St. A.D. returned, but ill.

26 June 1884: Office: Cabinet at 3.00: but Gladstone, Harcourt, & Carlingford were at Windsor: our business was to settle whether we should give a day for the proposed vote of censure in the Commons: we were all of one mind that we ought, and it was settled accordingly. Reasons (1) that the Opposition have made a tactical mistake (which is admitted) in bringing on this vote, & we ought not to let them get out of it: (2) that a vote of censure ought always if possible to be met at once, a contrary course showing timidity & weakness: (3) that it will be impossible to negociate in the conference with any weight or success until foreign powers are assured that we have parliament with us. The Premier, I don't know why, had expressed himself disinclined to give a day: whether from grudging the time, or annoyed by the frequent repetition of these attacks, but he left word that he would be guided by the advice of his colleagues.

Granville & Kimberley joined in regretting the irregularity of Cabinets, & the desultory way in which business was done at them. They ascribed it to Gladstone's dislike of these discussions, which they say he has always shown, & which increases upon him. But I have never seen in him any disposition to deal with them in an arbitrary manner, or to cut short debate.

27 June 1884: Night very hot, & sleep disturbed, partly by heat, but more by anxiety: for the state of things is disagreeable. In Egypt, Berber fallen, with loss of its garrison: taxes in default, & the country generally in a bad way: in South Africa the Zulus troublesome on the border, & news of impending disturbance on the Bechuana frontier. In Australia, Bismarck's last colonisation speeches have revived the alarm about New Guinea – and, if any part of the island is annexed by Germans, the outcry will be more furious than ever: at home, the almost certain rejection of the franchise bill by the Lords threatens an outbreak of agitation directed against the weakest part of the constitution: &, though we have no fears as to the result of the threatened censure, it is possible that the majority may not be a large one. On the whole it is an unsatisfactory outlook: and I begin to feel as if wanting rest which I am not likely to get, especially with two important debates coming on in the Lords.

Cabinet at 12.00 . . . we sat till near 2.00, when the H. of C. begins its sittings. Nearly all our time was passed in discussing the conference & the impending debate. We heard that the Rothschilds are opposed to any reduction of interest on the Egyptian debt: that the French government, through Blignières[140], their agent, is inclined to take the same view: that the necessity for a new loan will be denied: that the French press generally supports these ideas, & is violent against Ferry[141] & Waddington: that they themselves, F. & W., are inclined to be despondent, etc.

We renewed our discussion of yesterday on the best way of meeting the vote of censure. Harcourt was for the previous question, believing that we should be beaten on a direct vote, or at best have only a majority of 7 or 8: Hartington saw no use in putting off the evil day: Granville, Kimberley, Childers, Dodson, & I, were for the direct negative, arguing that a mere dilatory motion (the previous question in any form) would not give us sufficient strength in the conference, especially after the inevitable vote of the Lords: Chamberlain & Dilke produced in succession several ingenious resolutions, which everybody applauded, but nobody agreed to: the Premier hesitated a good deal, said it was a question where the advantages were very evenly balanced, but in the end preferred the direct course.

I introduced the subject of New Guinea[142], as connected with Bismarck's late declarations on colonial policy, which will produce a sort of panic in Australia: Childers & Kimberley supported me strongly: the Premier wished for a memorandum. . . .

28 June 1884: . . . Day very warm . . . Office at 2.30. A Cabinet box came round discussing for the third time the question how to deal with the vote of censure, which we have twice settled: but it seems all unsettled again.

. . . Circulated to the Cabinet a mem. about New Guinea, chiefly drawn by Herbert. Keston by 5.17 train . . .

29 June 1884 (Sunday): . . . It is singular that while we believe, & have reason to believe, that the Cabinet has not lost public confidence, the London press with almost the sole exception of the *D. News* is decidedly hostile to our Egyptian policy. *The Times* openly & strongly attacks: *Telegraph* makes the best of what it evidently does not like: *Standard* & *Post* represent the opposition view: *St. James's* & *Pall Mall Gazette*, from opposite points of view, unite in condemnation. Is it the influence of bondholders, or is the Jingo spirit always stronger in London? Or are they growing weary of Gladstone? I do not know, but all are probable.

The Premier, whether out of temper or in pursuance of a deliberate policy, has held language lately which certainly not all his colleagues think judicious. He took the opportunity of the third reading of the reform bill to warn the peers in menacing language[143] of the danger of throwing it out. Now in fact this danger does not exist: for to appeal to the constituencies from the decision of the H. of Commons is a recognised right of the Lords: and there is no such feeling in the country as should make delay dangerous.

But, if his object was to goad the peers into throwing out the bill by stirring up their natural dislike to yield to threats, & thereby to prepare for an agitation against them, it is skilful, though unscrupulous: more in Chamberlain's line than his: but it is possible that Chamberlain may have suggested the warning being given, & Gladstone not have seen his real intention. Or possibly this is refining too much, & there was nothing in it beyond a fit of bad temper, due to fatigue & hot weather. In either case, the effect has been bad, & the very slight chance which the bill had of passing has pretty nearly disappeared. . . .

30 June 1884: . . . Hale writes that the Midland will pay £25,000 next week, & the L.[ancs.] & Y.[orks.] Co. £100,000 very shortly.

Lawson called . . . He said everybody he met condemned the Premier's menace as ill judged: he did not think it contrived purposely to irritate.

. . . Called in Curzon St. Found A.D. looking very ill, & for the first time I begin to doubt whether she will ever recover her health.

Home, & found to my surprise that the vote of censure in the H. of C. had collapsed. Goschen, it seems, took the lead[144], objected to its coming on, as being inopportune & contrary to public interests &, though formally opposed by Gladstone & sincerely so by the Opposition, carried his point by 190 to 148. So the fight is put off.

Notes

[1] Either a kidney or a liver condition, present since youth.

[2] Derby had last spoken outdoors at Liverpool University College on 1 October 1883 and at Southport, 31 October 1883. His next public engagement was at the National Liberal Club on 7 February 1884.

[3] Hon. Harry L.W. Lawson (b. 1862), e.s. of 1st Baron Burnham: M.P. (Gladstonian) St. Pancras W. 1885–1892, Tower Hamlets (Mile End) as Unionist, 1905–1906, January 1910, December 1910.

[4] Edward Lawson (the *Daily Telegraph* proprietor) had a sister, Emily, who in 1882 had married Edward Brydges Willyams, M.P. for Truro 1880–1885: hence perhaps these lively expectations, which never came to anything.

[5] Lord Houghton died aged 76 at Vichy, 11 August 1885.

[6] Cherif Pasha (1819–1888), Egyptian chief minister under the Khedive: opposed Egyptian withdrawal from Sudan and resigned 7 January 1884: succ. by Nubar.

[7] These plans are not elaborated in *The Life and Correspondence of . . . Childers*, by Lieut.-Col. Spencer Childers. For the finance of 1884, see *ibid.*, vol. ii, pp. 159–170.

[8] Henry George (1839–1897), U.S. publicist: author of *Progress and Poverty* (1879).

[9] The Duke of Connaught (in India) and the Duke of Edinburgh (with the Fleet).

[10] Chamberlain spoke at Newcastle, 15 January, expressing optimism about Egypt and Ireland, urging a policy of Egypt for the Egyptians, and treatment of the Franchise separately from Redistribution. Next day he set out his policy for reducing loss of life at sea.

[11] Gen. Dominic J. Gamble (1823–1887), commander of forces in W. Indies 1878–1883: director-general of military education, 1887–death.

[12] Sir Robert Herbert (1831–1905), permanent under-secretary for colonies 1871–1892: first premier of Queensland, 1860–1865: agent-general for Tasmania, 1893–1896.

[13] The premier noted both writing to and visiting Lady Derby in his diaries, but without comment.

[14] George Byng, 8th E. of Strafford (1830–1898), styled Vt Enfield 1860–1886: under-sec. for India 1880–1883.

[15] Daniel O'Donoghue (died 1889), M.P. (Lib.) Tipperary 1857–1865, Tralee 1865–1885.

[16] Sir Andrew Clarke (1824–1902), inspector-general of fortifications from 1882.

[17] Hon. H.R. Brand (1841–1906), Surveyor General of the Ordnance from January 1883: succ. as 2nd Vt Hampden, 1892.

[18] Abraham Hayward (1801–1884), man of letters: wrote *The Art of Dining* (1852).

[19] Thorold Rogers (1823–1890), economic historian.

[20] A.J. Balfour (1848–1930), the future premier.

[21] W.H. Waddington (1816–1894), French premier and ambassador in London 1883–1893: educ. Rugby and Trinity, rowing in Boat Race: eminent archaeologist.

[22] Cf above, 26 July 1883, for false reports of Cetewayo's death.

[23] Sir Henry E.C. Bulwer (1836–1914), Governor of Natal 1874–1880, c. 1881–1886: High Commissioner in Cyprus 1886–1892: raised British flag at St. Lucia Bay on 21 December 1884, thus blocking Boer access to the sea: supported responsible government for Natal and federation for South Africa. Lord Salisbury's mother was his aunt.

[24] The diarist's brother.

[25] The future 17th Earl of Derby.

[26] Northcote's resolution was defeated by 311 to 292. The Conservative failure to assert a bold policy of establishing a Protectorate over Egypt was much remarked. The narrow vote perhaps indicates willingness by Liberals to put the Franchise Bill in jeopardy.

[27] *Parl. Deb., 3*, vol. 284, col. 700.

[28] *More leaves from the journal of our life in the Highlands* (1884): also published in a Gaelic translation by a Highland poetess, and in a Hindustani version.

29   Thomas Chenery (1826–1884), editor of *The Times* 1877–1884, orientalist, and sometime professor of Arabic at Oxford.

30   John Morley (1838–1923), man of letters, to be distinguished in this diary from Albert Parker, 3rd Earl of Morley (1843–1905).

31   Capt. (Sir) Cornelius Alfred Moloney (1848–13 August 1913), s. of Capt. P. Moloney of co. Limerick: probably R.C.: educ. Sandhurst: army officer *c.* 1867–1874: career in Gold Coast from 1873, rising to colonial sec., 1879–1884: administrator of Gambia 1884–1886: later administrator and governor of Lagos (1887): gov. of Br. Honduras 1891, Windward Is. 1897, Trinidad and Tobago 1900–1904: retired 1904: kt 1890. Author of *Sketch of the Forestry of West Africa, with the Principal Products* (1887).

32   Sir W.T. 'Iscariot' Marriott (1834–1903), judge-advocate-general 1885–1892 and financial speculator: renounced orders 1861 and called to bar: Q.C. 1877: M.P. (Lib.) Brighton 1880–1884 and M.P. (Cons.) Brighton 1884–1893: chancellor of Primrose League.

33   Sir George F. Bowen (1821–1899), academic and colonial governor: Fellow of Brasenose, 1844: president of University of Corfu 1847–1851: 1st governor of Queensland, 1859, then successively governor of New Zealand, Victoria, Mauritius, and Hong Kong (1882–1887): retired, 1887.

34   Sir Thomas McIlwraith (1835–1900), premier of Queensland 1879–1883, 1888, and 1893.

35   Henry George, author of *Progress and Poverty* (1879).

36   Lord Alcester, then Admiral Seymour, commanded the bombardment of Alexandria, 1882.

37   When young Childers had played a part in Australian public life, 1851–1857, serving as 1st vice-chancellor of Melbourne University, and as agent-general for Victoria from 1857. Perhaps this led him to be the main spokesman for Australia in the second Gladstone cabinet.

38   Thomas Sexton (1848–1932), M.P. (Home Rule) Sligo 1880–1885, Sligo S. 1885–1886, Belfast W. 1886–1892, Kerry N. 1892–96 (accepted C.H.): joined *Nation* paper, 1869: lord mayor of Dublin 1888, 1889: chairman of Freeman's Journal Ltd. 1892–1912.

39   Sir John Crichton, Vt Crichton (thus styled 1842–1885), b. 1839: succ. his father as 4th E. of Erne 1885: lord of the treasury 1876–1880: M.P. Enniskillen 1868–1880 and Fermanagh 1880–1885: thrice chairman of Fermanagh County Council: 'storied bust and animated Erne'.

40   The Convention of London was signed on 27 February 1884, to replace the Pretoria Convention of 1881, and was ratified by the Volksraad in August 1884. Its most important provisions were to define the Transvaal western border, keeping the trade route north out of Boer hands, and to allow the U.K. to veto treaties by the Transvaal with other powers.

41   Gladstone introduced the Franchise Bill on 28 February 1884, concentrating on specific provisions rather than general arguments. The Bill received its second reading in the Commons, 3 March 1884, without a division.

42   Spencer had relinquished the office of Lord President to Carlingford, who had previously been doing the work informally while Lord Privy Seal. The change occurred in March 1883.

43   Sir John Townshend, 3rd Vt Sydney (1805–1890), succ. 1831, cr. Earl 1874: held court offices between 1828 and 1886, first as a Tory, then a Peelite, then a Liberal.

44   Valentine Browne, 4th E. of Kenmare (1825–1905), who succ. father 1871: M.P. (Lib.) Kerry 1852–1871: held court offices under Liberals, 1856–1886.

45   Probably Lt.-col. Edmund Yates Peel (1826–1900), 2nd son of Gen. Jonathan Peel (1799–1879), war minister and brother of the premier.

46   Gen. Sir Gerald Graham, V.C. (1831–1899), commanded expedition against Osman Digna in eastern Soudan, 1884, winning battles at El Teb (29 February 1884) and Tamai (13 March 1884).

47   Of 4,000 English and Egyptian troops involved in a four hour battle, only 38 were killed. This success made little difference to the overall position in the Soudan as a whole or even in the Suakin area.

48   Mary, Lady Derby.

49   Brighton byelection, 1 March 1884: Marriott (Cons.) 5,478, Romer (Lib.) 4,021. Cons. gain.

[50] Rev. John Mackenzie, British Resident in Bechuanaland, and Deputy Commissioner, April–August 1884, entering into treaties with leading Bechuana chiefs: succeeded by Rhodes.

[51] Evelyn Ashley (1836–1907), M.P. (Lib.) Isle of Wight 1880–1885 and under-sec. at Colonial Office 1882–1885.

[52] William Keppel, Vt Bury (1832–1894), thus styled 1851–1891: succ. father as 7th E. of Albemarle, 1891: originally Lib. M.P. to 1874, then Tory junior minister (1878–1880, 1885–1886): R.C. convert, 1879.

[53] Ralph Gordon Noel, 13th Baron Wentworth (1839–1906), who succ. his brother, 1862: took the name of Milbanke, 1861: d. without male issue, and succ. by his daughter.

[54] Albert Edmund Parker, 3rd E. of Morley (1843–1905), under-secretary for war 1880–1885: Devon peer.

[55] Gladstone was off sick with respiratory ailments 9–20 March 1884.

[56] Arabs defeated at Tamai, near Suakin, 13 March 1884, with 100 British dead.

[57] Lyttelton was land commissioner for England and Wales 1881–1889.

[58] Edward Mackenzie, 1st E. of Wharncliffe (1827–1899), eldest s. of the 2nd Baron: succ. as baron, 1855: cr. earl, 1876: d.s.p. 1899, and succ. by his nephew.

[59] William George Eden, 4th Baron Auckland (1829–1890), e.s. of the Bishop of Bath and Wells: chargé at Karlsruhe.

[60] Sir H. Loch, 1st Baron Loch of Drylaw (1827–1900), governor of the Isle of Man 1863–1882.

[61] Sir Thomas Brassey, 1st E. Brassey (b. 1836), M.P. (Lib.) Devonport 1865, Hastings 1868–1886: cr. baron 1886, earl 1911: s. of Thomas Brassey, railway contractor.

[62] (Sir) Ellis Ashmead-Bartlett (1849–1902), M.P. (Cons.) Eye 1880–1885, Sheffield Ecclesall 1885–1902: president of Oxford Union: held minor office 1885, 1886–1892.

[63] Henry Labouchere (1831–1912), radical journalist: M.P. (Lib.) Northampton 1880–1906: founded *Truth,* 1876.

[64] Sir W. Hewett (1834–1888), commanding naval operations in Red Sea, involving defence of Suakin, 1884: rear-admiral 1878, vice-admiral 1884, commanded Channel Fleet, 1886–1888.

[65] Henry Broadhurst (1840–1911), working man M.P. 1880–1906.

[66] Gladstone went to Coombe Warren, Kingston, Bertram Currie's house, on 19 March 1884, on health grounds, not finally leaving till 21 April 1884 (see Note 137).

[67] Gladstone introduced the Franchise Bill, 28 February 1884, including a reference to leaving the number of Irish members unchanged. Hartington queried this, as not having been approved by the Cabinet in January. In fact Ireland was seriously over-represented.

[68] The Seats Bill introduced by Gladstone on 1 December 1884 proposed to increase the total numbers of the House by 12, all of which were to be given to Scotland. The members for Ireland (103) were to remain unchanged.

[69] Adm. Hewett, governor of Suakin, had just offered a reward for Osman Digna 'dead or alive' but had been thrown over by the Cabinet, to which this smacked of assassination.

[70] The premier was at Coombe Warren, Kingston, Currie's house, 19–31 March 1884, and 2–7 April, more convalescent than actually ill, and able to transact business each day (see Note 137).

[71] Neither the premier nor his secretary Edward Hamilton mention Wimbledon. It is not clear whether Derby's reference to it is a slip of the memory. Gladstone ventured out for a short walk in the garden for the first time during the day.

[72] H.R.H. Prince Leopold, 1st Duke of Albany, d. at Cannes after a fall, 28 March 1884. He was the 4th and youngest son of the Queen: 'He would have made his mark,' wrote Gladstone in his diaries.

[73] *Parl. Deb.,* 3, vol. cclxxxvi, cols. 1390–1452 (2 April 1884), debate adjourned without a division.

[74] The Franchise Bill passed its second reading in the Commons by 340 to 210, 7 April 1884, after six nights of debate.

[75] *Parl. Deb., 3,* vol. cclxxxvii, cols. 40–70 (3 April 1884): Harcourt brought in a bill of 73 clauses which was generally well received.

[76] Sir Theodore Martin, *A life of Lord Lyndhurst* . . . (1883).

[77] John Campbell, Baron Campbell, *Lives of Lord Lyndhurst and Lord Brougham* . . . (1869).

[78] Gladstone was out of sorts for several days over Easter.

[79] Walter Francis Montagu-Douglas-Scott, 5th Duke of Buccleuch and 7th Duke of Queensberry (1806–1884), died aged 77 at Bowhill, Selkirkshire, 16 April 1884.

[80] Lord Dalkeith (1831–1912), M.P. (Cons.) Midlothian 1853–1868, 1874–1880: succ. father as 6th Duke of Buccleuch, 1884: held local and court offices.

[81] Beatrice Leopoldine Victoria, youngest dau. of Alfred, Duke of Edinburgh: b. 20 April 1884: m. 1909 Alfonso, Infante of Spain.

[82] George James Finch-Hatton, 11th Earl of Winchilsea (1815–1887), racehorse owner and poetaster: styled Vt Maidstone 1826–1858: M.P. (Cons.) Northants. N. 1837–1841: succ. his father, 1858.

[83] G.W.H. Finch-Hatton, Vt Maidstone (1852–1879), d.s.p.: gunner in the Royal Artillery, 1876.

[84] M.E.G. Finch-Hatton, 12th E. of Winchilsea (1851–1898), succ. his half-brother June 1887, and was succ. by his own brother: Fellow of Hertford: M.P. (Cons.) S. Lincs. 1884–1887.

[85] Shendy is on the Nile, between Khartoum and Berber.

[86] See A.J.P. Taylor, *Germany's First Bid for Colonies, 1884–1885: A Move in Bismarck's European Policy* (Macmillan, 1938), pp. 29–32. German traders who had bought tribal lands in Fiji had been dispossessed by the British authorities. The Germans claimed £150,000 compensation: in 1885 a mixed commission awarded them £10,000.

[87] Prince Leopold, Duke of Albany (1853–1884), was posthumously succeeded by his son, the 2nd Duke (b. 19 July 1884), who later succeeded his uncle Alfred, Duke of Edinburgh (Reigning Duke of Saxe Coburg and Gotha 1893–1900) as a German prince.

[88] For Gladstone's view of Mahdism as 'a people struggling to be free' see also Patrick Jackson, *The Last of the Whigs* (1994), p. 154, citing its use in the censure debate of 12–13 May 1884.

[89] The Premier noted his visit to Lady Derby without comment in his diary for (inexplicably) 25 April.

[90] No reference traced in Gladstone's diaries for this period, but 'severe gales' on 23 January 1884 were followed by 'terrific gales' on 26 January, both sweeping western counties. Gladstone was away at the time, and there is no diary mention.

[91] J.G. Shaw-Lefevre (1831–1928), 1st commissioner of works 1880–1884: postmaster-general 1884–1885, succeeding Fawcett: promoted to Cabinet February 1885: cr. baron Eversley, 1906.

[92] Bernard Fitzpatrick, 2nd Baron Fitzpatrick of Upper Ossory (b. 1848), M.P. (Cons.) Portarlington 1880–1883: succ. father, 1883.

[93] Henry James, attorney-general 1880–1885.

[94] Lord Richard Grosvenor, 1st baron Stalbridge (1837–1912), Liberal chief whip 1880–1886.

[95] One of several indications that Derby had come to be regarded as a patron of the whole Sanderson tribe.

[96] Derby had turned down Disraeli's offer of the Garter, April 1878.

[97] *Parl. Deb., 3,* vol. cclxxxvii, cols. 1013–1020 (1 May 1884).

[98] George Byng, 7th Vt Torrington (1812–27 April 1884), governor of Ceylon 1847–1850: held court offices 1833–1835, 1835–1837, 1837–1841, 1859–death: suppressed a native revolt in Ceylon with controversial vigour.

[99] Montague Lowry-Corry, Baron Rowton (1838–1903), Disraeli's private secretary.

[100] Edward Leeson, 6th E. of Milltown (1835–1890), who succ. his brother 1871, and was succ. by his brother: an Irish rep. peer (Cons.) 1881–1890, barrister, and lord-lieut. co. Wicklow.

[101] Lord Coleridge (1820–1894), chief justice of Queen's Bench 1880–1894.

[102] After much dilatory correspondence, Angra Pequena was placed under German protection by a German naval vessel, 7 August 1884.

[103] [C.D.] Clifford Lloyd (1844–1891), Irish R.M., then Egyptian official 1883–May 1884 (resigned): governor of Mauritius 1885–1887.

[104] Sir Alexander Hugh Bruce, 10th Lord Balfour of Burleigh (1849–1921), secretary for Scotland 1895–1903.

[105] Henry Austin Bruce, 1st Baron Aberdare (1815–1895), home sec. 1869–1873, educationalist, and Welsh reformer.

[106] Hugh Fortescue, 3rd E. Fortescue (1818–1905), styled Vt Ebrington 1841–1861: M.P. (Lib.) Plymouth 1841–1852, Marylebone 1854–1859: whip 1846–1847, sec. to poor law board 1847–1851.

[107] Alan Stewart, 10th E. of Galloway (1835–1901), previously Lord Garlies: succ. father 1873: m. Lady Mary Cecil, Derby's step-daughter, 1872, but d.s.p. 1901 when succ. by brother: touched by scandal and drink.

[108] 'A warm reception, strangely falsified by the newspapers,' wrote Gladstone (*Diaries*, 8 May), but *The Times* recorded a 'quite unmistakable manifestation of popular disfavour' caused by public concern about Gen. Gordon.

[109] A struggle for control of the Conservative organisation, made public by Lord R. Churchill's resignation as chairman of the National Union on 3 May, followed by acrimionious correspondence, and ending in reconciliation (9 May) apparently largely on Churchill's terms.

[110] (Sir) Melmoth Osborn (1833–1899), British resident in Zululand 1880–1893 (retired), kt. 1893: career as administrator in S. Africa 1854–1880, including sec. to Transvaal government, July 1877–1880.

[111] Governor of Natal.

[112] Sir Hercules Robinson, 1st Baron Rosmead (1824–1897), colonial governor: held various governerships 1854–1880: governor of Cape Colony and high commissioner of S. Africa 1880–1889: again governor 1895–1897: cr. peer, 1896.

[113] Sir M. Hicks Beach moved a Vote of Censure (12 May) accusing the ministry of endangering Gordon. It was defeated 303–275, majority 28, with many Liberal abstentions: 31 Home Rulers and 6 Liberals opposed the government, while Forster and Goschen abstained. See *Parl. Deb., 3*, vol. cclxxxviii, cols. 31–137, 180–306.

[114] Gladstone minuted the Cabinet decision as 'Decline annexation and only defend the Reserve . . .'. Tribal war prevailed in the part of Zululand outside the Reserve, with Boer forces heavily involved. In August 1884 a Boer Republic was proclaimed in part of Zululand.

[115] Sir Evelyn Baring, 1st E. of Cromer (1841–1917), U.K. agent and consul-general in Egypt from 1883.

[116] Gladstone recorded: 'Quasi Cabinet 3½ (Purchase) & Conclave at H. of C. (Egypt.'

[117] Constantino Nigra (1827–1907), appointed Italian ambassador to London, 1882.

[118] Sir R.H. Meade (1835–1898), assistant under-sec. in colonial office 1871–1892, then permanent under-secretary 1892–1896.

[119] Charles Henry Gordon-Lennox, 11th Duke of Richmond (1818–1903), who succ. 1860: leader of Cons. party in House of Lords, 1870–1876: Lord President of the Council, 1874–1880: cr. Duke of Gordon, 1876: first secretary for Scotland, 1885–1886: reliant upon Cairns.

[120] George William Barrington, 7th Vt Barrington (1824–1886), M.P. (Cons.) Eye 1866–1880: held court office 1874–1880, 1885–1886, August–November 1886: sometime priv. sec. to Derby when P.M.: cr. Baron Shute (U.K.), 1880, with remainder to his brother Percy, 8th Vt Barrington (1825–1901), holder of both Irish and U.K. titles.

[121] C.B. Adderley, 1st Baron Norton (1814–1905), cr. peer, 1878: pres. of the board of trade, 1874–1878.

[122] Simon Fraser, 13th Lord Lovat [Scot.] and 2nd Baron Lovat [U.K.] (1828–1887): succ. father, June 1875: m. an R.C.

[123] W.T. Wyndham-Quin, 4th E. of Dunraven (1841–1926), who succ. his father 1871: *D. Telegraph* war correspondent, devolutionist, land reformer, sportsman.

[124] *Parl. Deb.*, *3*, vol. cclxxxviii, cols. 1439–1447.

[125] 'Hale writes that the Mr.Williams who . . . was reported to have set on foot an anti-rent agitation has done nothing of the kind: but he has had some kind of quarrel with the owner of the great tithes, & refused to pay those, which served as a foundation for the story in *Justice*' (Diary, 11 June 1884).

[126] J.G. Blaine (1830–1893), leading Republican: set his cap at the Irish vote: as sec. of state (1877–1881), and after, the most significant policymaker between Seward and Hay: believer in pan-Americanism: sought to put any central American canal under direct U.S., not international, control: nominated 1st ballot as Republican candidate against Grover Cleveland, 1884.

[127] For Derby's obsessive hoarding at Knowsley in 'an iron box with a slit in it', see *Derby Diaries 1869–1878*, p. 161, n. 22.

[128] The abortive Jewish settlement in Cyprus lay a mile or so inland from the route between Kolossi and Paphos; Col. Fyler, *The Development of Cyprus* ... (London, Lund Humphries, c. 1897), p. 113.

[129] (Sir) J.E. Gorst (1835–1916), M.P. (Cons.) Cambridge 1866–1868, when anti-Reform: party agent, 1870–1877: M.P. (Cons.) Chatham 1875–1885: refused junior post, 1875: member of Fourth Party in early 1880s.

[130] Gorst had a somewhat turbulent career in New Zealand, 1860–1865.

[131] For Malmesbury's amorous propensities in old age, which probably prompted him to publish, see *Later Derby Diaries* (1981 ed.), ch. iv, pp. 90–91.

[132] ArthurWilliam Patrick Albert (1850–1942), 3rd s. of QueenVictoria: cr. Duke of Connaught and Strathearn 1874: m. Princess Louise of Prussia, 1879: commanded 1st Guards Brigade in Egypt, 1882: commanded in Bombay, 1886–1890: Gov.-Gen. of Canada 1911–1916: became Field-Marshal.

[133] Col.Valentine Baker (1827–1887), guilty of unwelcome attentions to lady in railway carriage, and dismissed from U.K. army: later in Turkish and Egyptian service.

[134] *Parl. Deb.*, *3*, vol. cclxxxix, cols. 372–380 (16 June 1884): not obviously feeble.

[135] John Henry De La Poer Beresford (1844–1895), who succ. his father 1866: master of the buckhounds 1885–1886: chairman of the Irish Landlords Committee: died by shooting himself.

[136] The Hants. S. byelection was a good result for the Tories, giving them a majority of 1,437 against 932 in 1874 (there was no contest in 1880). In Mid-Surrey they also had grounds for complacency, with a majority up from 2,533 in 1880 to 3,606 in 1884. Both byelections were on 20 June.

[137] The Premier had had a normal very busy day, but otherwise had undergone nothing remarkable (*Diaries*).

[138] *Parl. Deb.*, *3*, vol. cclxxxix, cols. 1208–1223 (24 June 1884): Criminal Law Amendment Bill, dealing with the age of consent.

[139] Sir Arthur Gordon, 1st Baron Stanmore (1829–1912), colonial governor: s. of 4th E. of Aberdeen, premier: gov. of Ceylon, 1883–1890: noted for sympathy with native peoples: cr. baron, 1893.

[140] French agent in Egypt.

[141] Jules-François-Camille Ferry (1832–1893), French premier September 1880–November 1881, February 1883–March 1885.

[142] Gladstone minuted: 'Fresh alarm about New Guinea from Bismarck's announcement. Postponement.' Discussion was renewed in the Cabinet of 5 July: 'New Guinea. Much discussion, & scruples of Chancellor, Harcourt, & W.E.G. Subject postponed.'

[143] Moving the 3rd Reading of the Franchise Bill, the Premier warned: 'A collision between the two houses on this question would open a prospect more serious than any he remembered since the first Reform Bill . . .'

[144] The motion for a censure debate was defeated by 190 to 148 (*Parl. Deb.*, *3*, vol. 289, col. 1698).

July–December

1 July 1884: Sent £20 to the Charity Organisation Society for this parish.

. . . To the Lords at 4.20: a full attendance: Carnarvon announced the postponement of his motion, in a speech which showed some natural soreness: and he had the doubtful taste to hint his suspicion that the interposition of Goschen had been preconcerted with the government: which was certainly not the case. Granville had anticipated some suggestion of the kind, & read a note from Goschen, in which he expressly denied it: notwithstanding which Salisbury repeated the charge in a tone which was, & was meant to be, offensive: likening the action of the government to that of a man who should accept a challenge to fight, but give private notice to the police. Kimberley answered briefly: & the affair dropped.

– Home, & quiet evening. The truth I believe is (at least so Goschen himself told Kimberley) that he went down to the House intending to protest against a discussion which seemed to him useless & dangerous: but not expecting that his words would have any effect beyond relieving his own mind: when he spoke he found the feeling of the House unmistakably with him, & the thing was done. In plain words, we were probably rash in accepting the challenge given by the opposition, & the House showed more sense than the leaders on either side in stopping the fight. The only point open to criticism so far as we are concerned is that the Premier ought either to have spoken more strongly as to the inconvenience of the proceeding in the first instance, or less strongly at the last moment. There is undoubtedly a discrepancy between his language on the two days which invites comment.

2 July 1884: Letter from Statter, who reports that no business has been done in the month: the first time since 1869 that this has happened.

Office at 2.30: saw there the Australian agents, who came to talk about New Guinea: and very wildly they talked. At one moment they said that Australia had a right to all the islands lying beyond New Guinea: at another that, provided order were maintained there and no convicts sent out, they did not care who had them. It seemed impossible to make them understand that any foreign government could have a voice in the matter: they took as a matter of course that if we wanted the islands & said so the rest of the world would acquiesce. I promised to bring the question of New Guinea before the Cabinet, and indeed it is rendered pressing by Bismarck's recent language & action. Herbert received them with me. We parted, moderately satisfied on both sides: they, I fancy, thinking me indifferent, & I thinking them unreasonable.

Granville came with Pauncefote to talk over Angra Pequena: we discussed other matters: he seemed not very sanguine about the conference: & complained of Dilke: who from his F.O. experience knows all the diplomatists, gossiping & letting out secrets among them. He also spoke with strong dislike of the intended agitation against the H. of Lords.
– Home, & quiet evening.

3 July 1884: Thick foggy morning, with close heat, disagreeable enough. It is noted that this is just the weather of the cholera year (1832-1833?) . . . Walk in Hyde Park & Kensington, which were almost deserted, on account of the heat.

... Sent Freeman, my late gardener, £5, as he writes in distress. (On second thoughts, I made it up to £10.)

... Talk with Kimberley about the attitude of the Lords, as to which we do not entirely agree. I hold that they are doing an unwise thing in throwing out the franchise bill, but one strictly within their constitutional right: he argues that they have no business to deal in this way with a bill which concerns the representation of the people, & that the agitation which will be directed against them is just, as they will be exceeding their powers. At least this is what I understood his view to be &, if so, we shall not be exactly in accordance.

4 July 1884: To the Treasury at 12.00, where met Childers, Carlingford, Lefevre, & Mr. Pearson the architect, to consider the new plan for replacing the front, or side, of Westminster Hall. The plan preferred is to build a two-storeyed cloister along it, which the architect declares to be a reproduction of something that was once there before the law courts were built. The cost is about £35,000: but of this half at least must be incurred in any case, as the wall cannot be left rough as it is. We could not finally settle anything, only recommend to the Cabinet.

... Lds Jersey[1] & Brownlow[2] came to speak to me, wishing to suggest some compromise & avert the impending collision between Lords & Commons. I heard what they had to say, sympathised very sincerely, & promised to talk it over with Granville, but did not conceal my fear that the time was gone by for any such arrangement. The opposition leaders wish to force on a dissolution thinking to gain by it: while a large section of the Liberal party desire rather than deprecate a quarrel with the peers. The peacemakers as usual are few & unpopular on both sides.

5 July 1884: Another very hot night & morning. Gave M. £300 as a wedding day present ... Office early: Cabinet at 2.00, which I left sitting, but nearly finished, at 5.00: and met M. at the station. Thence to Keston ... Heavy rain fell in afternoon, & cooled the air.

In Cabinet, we began by some general talk as to the coming debate. It was noted that the object of Cairns's amendment[3] might have been equally secured by an amendment in committee, after the second reading was passed.

Harcourt & Chamberlain were strong against doing anything that would make it easier for the Lords to pass the bill, considering that the opposition leaders had brought themselves into a difficulty, & that it was not our business to help them out.

Hartington asked whether we had considered what we should do after the Lords had thrown out the bill? It seemed to be considered certain that there would be an autumn session: but that had never been decided. Granville pointed out the objection that in an autumn session there must be discussions on foreign policy, which might be awkward. He rather leaned to the idea of an immediate dissolution. This the Premier would not listen to: objecting on the ground, which to me seems a fanciful one, that we should be conferring a new privilege on the Lords if we allowed them to fix the date when parliament should be dissolved. I observed that if the Lords threw out the bill a second time a dissolution would be inevitable. This he agreed to, but said in an ominous tone: 'If the Lords throw out the bill a second time it will be a very serious matter indeed.' Some talk followed as to the session & the H. of Commons. Harcourt said dogmatically that the House had determined to do no more work: that was clear.

A rather sharp discussion followed on the *Nisero* business[4], about which a feeling is growing up in the country. Granville proposed joint action with the Dutch to get the men released. Harcourt would have nothing to say to the Dutch, would send an expedition at once. Northbrook said that was impossible on account of the monsoon. Harcourt grew impatient at this, & ranted, saying that the navy used to do what it was told, & make no difficulties: now nothing could be attempted except in the finest weather & with a great force of ironclads. Northbrook observed mildly that the force could not land, owing to surf and absence of harbours & that, if they could, it would be of little use, since the Rajah would carry off his prisoners into the mountains, or kill them. Harcourt grew worse at this, & fairly lost his temper, which was not improved by somebody suggesting that he should take command of the expedition himself. In the end we agreed to Granville's proposal, but after the least harmonious discussion we have had yet. The Premier was suffering from lumbago, which made him irritable, & Harcourt's swaggering talk irritated most of us.

I raised the question of New Guinea: Kimberley, Chamberlain, Dilke, & Granville were in favour of a protectorate: Harcourt, Selborne, & the Premier violent against one – the latter wanted me to ask the Australian agents what precedents they could find for the annexation of a country not occupied by the people claiming it? We cited Australia itself & N. Zealand: but he was not satisfied, & objected to the Australian claim as 'mere piracy'. I reserved the whole question, and at present I do not see how the Cabinet is to decide the matter, our differences being so wide. . . .

7 July 1884: . . . H. of Lords at 4.30. The house was full enough, but not so full as I have seen it: the bar, steps of throne, & galleries crowded.

Kimberley moved the second reading of the franchise bill, in a speech[5] which lasted just an hour: excellent in all respects: temperate & courteous: very clear: giving details enough, & not too much. It was better done than anything I have heard him do, & nobody could have improved upon it. Cairns followed, & moved his amendment in three-quarters of an hour[6]: also very moderate in tone, & confining his argument exclusively to the one point on which he relied. There was no oratory or declamation: all was quiet, sober, & very skilful reasoning. Argyll followed him, & seemed to wander from the subject, dwelling chiefly on the functions of the Lords: but he had an object, which was to persuade Conservative peers that they ought not to treat a question of this sort as one merely of party. These three speeches were all worthy of the occasion & the place. Afterwards the debate languished: Richmond was feeble & apologetic: & none of those whom I heard (for I went home to dinner) were above mediocrity. The D. of Marlborough[7] spoke for the first time, but showed none of his brother's cleverness, being long, dull, & rambling. Morley closed the debate, but in a House comparatively thin, it being known that there would be no division that night. Home a little after 12.00.

8 July 1884: Very hot close night and, being full of thoughts about the debate & my speech, I slept ill, that is, for me, but woke fairly rested. I had but a few letters & papers from office, & cleared off all early.

. . . Working at home on notes for speech, & fairly satisfied with the substance, but nervous as to the delivery.

. . . Luncheon at home, & did not walk, nor go down to the office. Again went over notes, & passed about as disagreeable a morning and afternoon as I have often done: but comforting myself with the thought that my trouble will soon be over, and that at bottom

I care very little for success or failure. Only it is hard to find that custom does not make speechmaking less disagreeable: but it was my father's case to the end of his life. Perhaps the hot oppressive weather aggravates the sensation. Drove down to the Lords with M. Found a very full house. Carnarvon began at 4.30, & spoke exactly an hour: his speech was thoughtful, & in parts able, but rambling & discursive, as if he rather wished to say all that was in his mind about reform than to argue the question actually before us. I followed, & spoke an hour also[8], very well listened to, but I am afraid my argument was rather dry & heavy. It was not a failure, but might have been better. Brabourne came next, then Rosebery, who was excellent. He is the inevitable leader of the Lords, if he sticks to politics. Going home to dine, I heard no more till 10.00, when Wemyss was speaking, not much to the purpose: the Chancellor argued for an hour, sound, but a little long & heavy: Salisbury summed up on his side in his best style, not being angry or acrimonious, which is his common fault: and some of his hits were very happy. Granville answered him, fairly well. We divided 146 to 205: the largest division as I believe that has been known in the Lords. The majority was rather less than commonly expected. The heat very oppressive. Walk home, & in bed by 2.00 a.m.

9 July 1884: Sanderson called: he tells me what I should not have suspected, that Ld Granville often writes out his speeches, & that he is very nervous before speaking: which if so he conceals from all the world.

Lawson called: he said he thought the debate had been one of the best that have come off for a long while: the average of speaking very high: nothing foolish, no waste of time. I think this is true, & that the Lords will lose no credit, though their decision may be regretted.

Troubled with some headache & bilious sickness, so that I sent an excuse to the organisers of a dinner to Lord Normanby ..

. . . Cabinet at 2.15, which sat till 5.30. Then home, & work on office business, of which there was an unusual quantity, till dinner, of which I ate little, & went early to bed.

In Cabinet, some talk about the conference. Granville & Childers both say that the French are making delays, though it is not well seen with what reason: other representatives seem disposed to settle the affair. It is believed that France will ask to share in the £8 millions guarantee. We all agreed that this was undesirable, as it will look like a revival of the Dual Control, & would moreover weaken our claim to presidency in financial matters. The main subject discussed was the action to be taken on last night's division. The Premier inveighed against the pretensions of the Lords to dictate the time of a dissolution – said they were claiming a new privilege – the precedent was abominable – he believed in the constitution, & would not sanction or condone a breach of it: nothing would induce him to give the Lords a victory by consenting to dissolve now. He would far rather resign. Granville declined to argue the constitutional question, but thought what we had to consider was what time would suit us best for a dissolution. He was inclined to prefer the present time: matters might get worse in Egypt: the feeling about this division might be less strong three months hence: he regretted it, but saw no ground for a general attack on the Lords. Spencer took the same view. Harcourt talked very big. The one thing necessary was to compel the Lords to retract, and that in the most marked & public way. It was making too much of them to allow them to force a dissolution, either now or later. All business should be stopped: the bill sent up to them again without debate: and if they refused it prorogue again & send it up again. Nothing else should be thought of till that was done. Selborne agreed that an autumn session was necessary. Chamberlain dwelt on the advantage of dissolving on the new register rather than the old, and thought the longer the agitation was kept up the more effective it would be. He agreed, however, to take no personal part in it outside his own constituency. In the end we all agreed to the autumn session, & in consequence to a general sacrifice of the bills now before parliament: which is a pity, [though] inevitable, for members have had enough, & will do no more work.

10 July 1884: ... To the Commons, where Dilke, Hicks Beach, & R. Churchill were quarrelling, amidst great noise & disorder: the place was a bear garden.

Gladstone held a meeting at F.O. at 2.30 & addressed the members of the H. of C. warmly, but not with excessive violence. Goschen deprecated agitation, & was hooted: the temper of the party being hot. The end of all is that the session practically closes now, & we begin again at the end of October[9].

11 July 1884 (Friday): ... H. of Lords, where expected no business & indeed there was none: but a very angry wrangle between Granville on the one hand & Cairns & Salisbury on the other. I have seldom seen either of these two so moved. Salisbury was too much irritated to speak effectively, & Cairns also had lost his temper. The subject of the quarrel was an overture made by Granville on Tuesday to the leaders of opposition, with a view to coming to terms: they rejected it, & the affair came to nothing. But afterwards a misunderstanding occurred: it seems that Salisbury & Cairns regarded the overture as confidential: Granville perhaps did the same, but did not tell Gladstone so: Gladstone regarded & treated it as public, & referred to it in his speech to the party at F.O. The opposition chiefs were furious at this disclosure: no doubt thinking that they will be reproached by many of their party for rejecting the proffered compromise & keeping it concealed. Granville himself was not well pleased, thinking that they had some ground of complaint, & that the Premier had acted hastily if not unfairly in making public what had passed. The subject was taken up in the Commons also, and another very hot dispute followed: R. Churchill accusing the Premier of 'traducing' his opponents, & Gladstone complaining of Churchill's 'foul language' – though at the Speaker's suggestion he withdrew the epithet. In the end both sides cooled down: & suggestions for an arrangement were exchanged: but I fear it will come to nothing.

Called on A.D. who is now constantly an invalid, & does not seem to expect to live long.

12 July 1884: Wet morning ... Saw Sanderson, who said that Ld G. had been much annoyed by the attack made yesterday, thinking there was some ground for it: & that Gladstone had no right to disclose what had passed in private. This indeed he had said to me.

Saw Lawson, who told me that he can always judge how far public interest is excited on any subject by the increased numbers sold of his paper: anything relating to Gordon sent it up at once: but the franchise debates had not had the slightest effect. ...

14 July 1884: Left Fairhill ... Home before 11.00.

... Rents received in 1883-1884 are £217,643 against £216,237 in 1882-1883. The increase is not large, but in these times it is well there is no falling off.

. . . Office at 2.30, when suddenly summoned to a Cabinet at 3.00, to consider a proposed resolution of compromise to be moved by Wemyss[10]. (It is unlucky that he should have stepped into the gap, for he is a weak vain man, though a ready speaker, & carries no weight, but he has offered himself as a mediator, & cannot be got rid of.) We all agreed to support him, lest it should seem that on our side there was some disinclination to a compromise: but we did so with little expectation of any result. We sat only an hour: & not much passed.

Granville told us the conference was 'going on as badly as possible': & Münster, whom I met in the street, said the same thing. Blignières, the French representative, seems to wish to break it up, & the other foreigners follow his lead.

The Queen has been very busy negociating with both parties to try & settle the quarrel between the Houses, & is I believe quite sincere in wishing to make it up: she has written angry letters to the Premier & Granville saying that they ought to dissolve, & that if bad consequences follow from the agitation we are responsible: but she is equally ill pleased with the Opposition, who she thinks were bound as Conservatives to accept her orders as binding. The P. of Wales is also running about & advising the Opposition to make terms. They, the royal people, follow a sound instinct: for they know that an agitation directed against the peers must shake the hereditary principle on which their own existence depends.

In the Lords, Salisbury said a few words, pronouncing strongly & even angrily against Wemyss's motion, & complaining of its inconvenience[11]. Rosebery again brought on & again dropped his resolution about French convicts in New Caledonia . . . Granville was equally reserved, & wisely so: but Carnarvon could not resist letting off a speech, which however, if it did no good, did no harm. . . .

16 July 1884: Meeting of Conservatives at the Carlton yesterday who, with few exceptions, determined to stand firm, so that, according to present appearances, Wemyss's resolution is as good as lost.

In the papers, I read of the sudden death of Lord Cowley, who in a few days would have been 80: since his retirement in 1867 he had been but little before the public: but during the 15 years 1852-1867 he was in the centre of European affairs, as ambassador at Paris: and played his part well. He had no conspicuous ability, but commanded respect & confidence by truthfulness, honesty, & strong sense. He was I believe more trusted by the late Emperor than any other Englishman: and had the full confidence of his own chiefs of both parties. Being naturally shy, & latterly deaf, he disliked the merely social part of his diplomatic duty: & travelling Englishmen complained of his shortcomings in this respect: he had, however, nothing to live on but his pay till he came unexpectedly into the Mornington fortune[12], & the salary of an ambassador without private means is scarcely enough to keep up his position. By the general public he was almost forgotten at the time of his death: not so by diplomatists, & by the public men with whom he had to do. I have known him long, & should regret his end, but that life prolonged beyond 80 is seldom desirable.

Office, where at 3.20 received a summons to a Cabinet at 3.30: rather a confused way of doing business but, as nobody else made any remark, I did not. We talked first about the conference. The report of it was bad. The French object to any reduction of interest, say that we underestimate the revenue, & that more ought to be screwed out of the peasantry. The Premier observed that we are proposing to do for Egypt more than we have ever done for any colony, & that it was monstrous to ask parliament to do it unless the bondholders on their part made some sacrifice. He thought there would be trouble in the House. Members want to go away, & an early debate is hardly possible. Harcourt said there was only one thing to do – to go out of Egypt at once, no matter whether the French come in or not. Else we shall be let in for annexation, whether we like it or no. From thence we passed on to the question, raised by Hartington, of an expedition to Khartoum. Harcourt said he would not agree to it, now or at any time. Dilke and Chamberlain were against it at present. The Premier after much talk declared against it, admitting that the case is doubtful, & that there is risk of error, but contending (1) that we have no reason to believe Gordon is blockaded in Khartoum, (2) that he probably does not wish to come away, (3) that if we go to Khartoum there is a probability that we shall have to stay there. – Some others added that the H. of C. would not like to be called upon to vote the cost of an expedition, after having guaranteed £8,000,000 for Egypt. We sat till 6.00, but I could make few notes, the meeting being in the room at H. of C.

Office, work till 7.00, dine Travellers': work again at night.

17 July 1884: . . . At 4.30, to the Lords: a crowded House. Wemyss made his motion[13] in a speech which was neither good nor bad, a little spoilt by his usual conceited egotism, but conciliatory in tone. The other speeches were poor, till Salisbury rose. His tone was one of defiance[14], & his followers evidently sympathised. Granville replied, briefly, but with nearly equal warmth. We divided a little after 7.00: 132 to 182: 50 majority: 9 less than on the 8th. The result was pretty well known beforehand, so that no excitement followed its announcement.

18 July 1884 (Friday): . . . Cabinet at 2.00, which sat till 4.15 . . .

In Cabinet, we agreed to drop the Medical Law Amendment Bill, it being strongly opposed by quacks of all sorts who, as Chamberlain admitted to our amusement, are especially strong at Birmingham. I note that Chamberlain is more anxious than anyone to make a clean sweep: to pass no bills this year, great or small: evidently with a view to lay on the Lords the blame of their failure, & so increase the feeling against them. This is more the policy of an election agent than of a statesman, but Chamberlain, who is at least frank, admits that he does not wish the quarrel made up.

Some talk about grants to Welsh colleges, & about the monster procession of Monday: but then went on to discuss the conference, as to which the H. of C. is growing impatient, & we are not in a position to satisfy its curiosity. The French delegate declares that the bondholders will submit to no reduction of interest, & that there is no need of any. All the continental delegates seem to take the same view, so that we stand alone. Much discussion followed. Childers suggested a partial bankruptcy. Granville thought we could not advise Egypt to break pledges solemnly given to Europe. – Harcourt thought that, having called the conference, we were bound to abide by its decision: this opinion caused general dissent. Hartington thought we might take on ourselves part of the liability.

Harcourt quoted a saying of Ld Rowton, that by Christmas the franchise bill would be forgotten, we should be engaged in a European war. Granville thought, if we could not agree, the conference should be broken up, but we need say nothing as to what we meant to do next. The Prime Minister believed the failure of the conference ought to lead to evacuation so far at least as that an offer to retire should be made to Europe.

Somebody, Hartington I think, remarked that there was always the alternative of annexation: to which Gladstone answered that for another ministry there might be, but to us it was impossible. In the end after much discussion it was agreed to decline the French amendment on our proposals: but to offer the new proposal of reducing interest for a term of years only, 10, 8, 6, or 5, during which Egyptian finances might have a chance to recover.

Hartington raised the question of a mass meeting in Lancashire which he is pressed to attend. There is a question whether reform of the H. of Lords will be discussed there. The Premier said we were pledged not to encourage any movement for organic change in the Lords. Dilke observed meaningly that radicals would not favour any plan for reform of that House meaning that it should be abolished altogether. In fact the difficulty seems to be to prevent resolutions being carried at these meetings in favour of abolition. . . .

21 July 1884: . . . Office, but got there with some trouble, as the streets were occupied by a 'demonstration' on the franchise question, which passed in procession from the Embankment . . . by Piccadilly to Hyde Park. The crowd was immense, but quite orderly & peaceable as far as I could see. Kimberley came over to the office, & we watched it from the windows looking on Whitehall. . . .

22 July 1884: . . . The newspapers are full of yesterday's demonstration, which appears to have gone off remarkably well. The crowd was good humoured, there does not seem to have been disturbance anywhere, & the general public suffered less inconvenience than might have been expected. Nor do the roughs who usually crowd to such scenes appear to have broken out in disorderly fashion. Of the numbers that 'demonstrated', and of the degree of interest felt by them in the political object of the gathering, there are of course various reports. The day served them well, being cool & dry with the exception of one not very heavy shower.

Lawson called, & gave his impressions. He thought the success complete: & the people in earnest, at least so far as to know that they wanted something, though they may not have known very clearly what their grievance was. He had talked to a good many of them: had not seen one drunken man in the crowd, which he left about 8.00 p.m. Some were earnest politicians: they talked freely about the royal family: liked the P. of Wales: were warm in praise of the Princess: indifferent about the Queen: did not understand why she shuts herself up: 'she draws a large salary & she ought to do something for it' was one man's phrase. Another thought it wrong that the nation should pay the D. of Marlborough for his pictures as he had heard that the first Duke did not come by them honestly – a good sample of popular logic.

. . . Office at 2.30. Received there a deputation of between 30 & 40, many being M.P.s, with the chief called the 'Maori king' and 4 of his followers. Gorst introduced them, & they stated their grievances temperately enough. I gave a civil & sympathetic answer, but could not promise much, for in truth we have handed over all power in regard to native affairs to the local legislature: & I am afraid it is with reason that the Maoris complain that the Treaty of Waitangi has been ill kept. But all the world over it is impossible to make the average Englishman understand that natives can have rights which they are bound to respect. Probably other Europeans are no better, but if they have the same tendency they have less opportunity of displaying it.

To the Lords, where Granville tells me the conference is going on as badly as possible.

23 July 1884 (Wednesday): Hearing from Ward that he can spare the money, I desired him to send up £20,000 to Coutts, which will make the drawings of the year for investment £60,000, which is enough.

Went at 12.30 to a meeting of the Cotton Dist.[ricts] Convalescent Fund at the Westminster Palace Hotel . . . Business lasted less than an hour. On going away, Winmarleigh stopped me, & in his amiable undecided way began to talk about a compromise on the franchise question: when however we came to the point he had nothing to propose. . . .

25 July 1884: . . . Signed deed completing the purchase by the L. & Y. Co. of land in Bootle, for which they are to pay me £100,000.

. . . Cabinet at 2.00, which sat till 4.20. Whether from the late heats, or the work of the session telling towards the close of it, my colleagues were in a curiously drowsy condition: Harcourt, Northbrook, & Spencer were all fast asleep: the Premier yawned & stretched himself: and several others seemed in a comatose state. But discussion roused them, & we had plenty of it.

. . . In Cabinet, we first, & chiefly, discussed the conference. The French proposal was read, & our counter-offer. Waddington is believed to be friendly. Italy supports us. Russia is not disposed to give trouble. Bismarck presses for raising the sanitary question, of protection against the plague, in conference: no one knows why, unless it is to stir up a new dispute. The difficulty with France seems to be that Ferry has pledged himself to the chamber, not to consent to any reduction of interest. The Prime Minister dwelt a little impatiently on the necessity of getting things so far settled as to allow of a parliamentary statement being made. Granville said mildly that it did not rest with us: we could not hasten the decision of the other powers. Harcourt pointed out the absurdity of the position. We have thrown over all our bills in order to close the session at once, & now we find that we can't do it, & that the House must be kept sitting with nothing to do. Everybody agreed, but neither he nor anyone else had a remedy to suggest.

Hartington then asked whether we are to take a supplementary vote, before closing the session, or to wait till October? He dwelt on the difficulty of getting stores at short notice. Some discussion followed, & in the end we agreed that it would be legitimate to wait till October. Then we came back to the eternal question: what shall we do about Gordon? Hartington & the Chancellor were strong in favour of a rescue expedition, Harcourt & Gladstone as strongly against it: the latter showing some heat. Spencer expressed himself so doubtfully that I could not make out what he wished. Chamberlain & Dilke spoke very cautiously, but seemed to say that a small force might be pushed up to meet him – from 1,000 to 2,000 men. Kimberley objected to send any force to Khartoum, on the ground that if we did so Gordon would certainly keep it there, & we should end by having to keep Khartoum. Hartington said finally: 'If we do not make preparations now, we can do nothing for Gordon.' The Chancellor added earnestly: 'No: we are leaving him to perish.' The Premier broke up the sitting rather abruptly, but indeed he had no choice, for it was time to go down to the House. But we have settled nothing. . . .

27 July 1884: . . . Sir R. Morier[15] came to dine & sleep. Interesting talk with him on many subjects. He is improved by success: less inclined to make personal grievances & to dwell upon them, & his conversation less egotistic. The Spanish climate suits him – for he is very gouty – & improved health brings a happier state of mind. Lord Granville said of him the other day: 'He is the cleverest man in the diplomatic service, and the greatest bore in it.' I do not think him the latter, but he is fond of hearing his own voice, & rather needlessly copious both in speech & writing.

28 July 1884: . . . My financial position is as follows: invested, £500,000: kept in reserve, £12,000: with Coutts & at home, £20,000. Total £532,000, & £50,000 either in Ward's hands or due from the Trust. . . .

30 July 1884: London early . . . to Coutts, where I bought £10,000 Consols . . . making total investments £510,000: & there I think they must end for the year. . . .

2 Aug. 1884: . . . **Note** that the Manchester [Ship] Canal Bill is thrown out by a committee of the Commons, Sclater-Booth[16] in the chair: they were unanimous. The supposed reason was the danger of injuring the navigation. The decision causes some surprise, & is a heavy blow to the promoters: they must have dropped at least £100,000, some reports say £150,000.

In Cabinet today, Granville announced that the conference is over, no result having been come to. It is not formally broken off, but adjourned with no day fixed for meeting again. It seems that Waddington proposed an ultimatum which we could not agree to, & the other powers, seeing an understanding to be impossible, abstained from expressing any opinion.

Granville announced that he wishes for help in dealing with the Egyptian business, & after some talk it was agreed that Sir E. Baring shall stay in England to look after it. Then came the question, who shall go to Egypt in his place? Granville suggested Malet. Others mentioned Goschen, who was objected to, as being against the policy of withdrawal. The Premier named Dufferin, but this only as a temporary expedient. Childers would prefer to send [J.K.] Cross[17], who can be spared from the India Office & is able: but it was thought he would not have authority enough, & doubted whether he speaks French, which is necessary. Granville then suggested that Northbrook should go out for a time, with power as commissioner. We all seemed to approve, but it was felt that he ought not to be called upon to say yes or no at a minute's notice, & the question was adjourned. Some talk followed as to the probable feeling of parliament, & it was thought that the failure of the conference would at first be popular, but that the feeling would change when it was seen that we did not mean to keep Egypt. Then came a discussion, which led to no result, as to the steps to be taken to meet the financial difficulty in Egypt. Sir E. Baring was called, & much conversation passed as to what would happen if a creditor, not being paid, sued the Egyptian government in its own courts, & got a decision in his favour. The Chancellor said that France, or whatever other country the creditor belonged to, would have a *casus belli* in the event of Egypt refusing to pay. Chamberlain cited some opinion given by Jessel to the effect that no state is bound to pay to its creditors money that may be absolutely required for its own administration. Harcourt thought there were only two alternatives – either to leave Egypt at once, or to make ourselves responsible for the debt. Hartington wanted to guarantee the preference debt. Chamberlain declared that the H. of C. would not look at any such proposal. He suggested a personal appeal to Bismarck to get us out of this trouble: 'Bismarck is a vain man, like most great men, & will be flattered at being asked for assistance.' Harcourt repeated that if we did not get out at once the probable result would be war with France. There the matter dropped, no solution reached.

Hartington got the consent of the Cabinet to a vote for £300,000 to meet the possible event of an expedition to rescue Gordon being required. Chamberlain said he was against it, fearing that the vote would bring on an expedition, but he was ready to give way. Hartington wanted the sum increased to £500,000, but this the Cabinet would not consent to. . . .

4 Aug. 1884: C. Münster said little about the conference, but expressed his conviction that Gladstone was pleased at its failure, & hinted that he (G.) never meant it to come to any result. This is the language which German representatives hold everywhere – evidently by instructions. I did not note that it was mentioned yesterday in Cabinet that Lyons has written to say that Bismarck is advising the French to stand firm against us, and assuring them that they need fear no interference from Germany. Meanwhile he is advising us to take Egypt: so as if possible to stir up a quarrel between the two countries. This is the game he has played ever since the Constantinople conference, & possibly much earlier. . . .

5 Aug. 1884: . . . London by 11.43 train . . . office, & work there till 2.00, when to a Cabinet. We sat till 4.15 . . . I ought to have gone to the Lords, but did not, finding a mass of work in the office: finished in time for the 6.35 train, & back to Holwood.

Our Cabinet today from whatever cause was curiously distracted & confused. We began by a long discussion of the precise conditions on which Northbrook should go out[18]: the Premier dwelling much on what seemed to me the unimportant point of whether a set of instructions should be drawn up for his guidance or not. Precedents were cited *pro* & *con*: in the end we agreed that none was wanted. We were three-quarters of an hour over this. Then followed a desultory conversation on Egyptian affairs: Hartington again pressing for a guarantee of at least the privileged debt. The Premier & Northbrook wished to obtain from the Sultan an express permission to stay on in Egypt: which the Sultan will no doubt grant, but what will he ask in return? Some talk began, I scarcely know how, as to the employment of Turkish troops, which Chamberlain objected to in strong terms, saying the H. of C. would not stand it. Nothing came of any of these suggestions. – Harcourt in a grave & quiet manner asked leave to read a paper, which he did: it was his protest against remaining in Egypt, which he declines to be responsible for, believing that it will involve us in a European war.

Hartington then proposed an increase of the army, by keeping men in the ranks who would in the ordinary course go out into the reserve: & embodying some regiments of militia. He said we had not more than 7,000 troops, other than new recruits, in England & Scotland.

Granville raised the question of Rothschild's loan, part of which is now repayable, & Rothschild could sue the Egyptian government for it, but will not do anything to create embarrassment. Granville also raised the question of what shall be said to Persia as to possible protection of Khorassan against Russia! The Persians naturally want something more than vague promises of support, & yet we cannot trust them, nor are they fit to help themselves[19]. These three subjects also dropped without any conclusion come to. In fact we talked much & settled nothing. I think this is mainly from want of anyone to keep order, & put the question – the Premier does not seem to care to do this, & nobody else can.

6 Aug. 1884: . . . Cabinet at the H. of Commons at 2.00. The room close, & Northbrook being unwell had to leave. We began with some discussion of Egyptian affairs – vague & indefinite as usual: the chief points being whether we should invite the co-operation of the Porte, which we agreed to do: and whether we should ask for Turkish troops to help in keeping order, as to which we said neither yes nor no, but hung up the question for Northbrook to report upon.

The truth is that we do not know our own minds about Egypt: most of us wish to go out as soon as we can, while the English public wishes us to stay: the chief use of Northbrook going out as commissioner is that he possibly may be able to come to some conclusion, & if he does we shall probably accept it.

I raised the question of New Guinea, which has been waiting for some time, explained at some length how it stood, & asked for the establishment of a protectorate. The Chancellor, who was very hostile some weeks ago, yielded to the plea that we should go there not to plunder the natives but to protect them: Childers, Kimberley, Dilke, Chamberlain, were strongly in favour: no one decidedly against it except Harcourt: & he is so much in the habit of opposing everything that his influence is less than from its ability it ought to be. Gladstone said he agreed reluctantly, thinking the Australian pretensions monstrous, but seeing the difficulty of opposing them. This is exactly my own view, & he cannot dislike the thing more than I do, but I believe it to be inevitable, if we do not want to break with Australia[20].

After the Cabinet, Gladstone asked Granville, Kimberley, & me to stay, & discussed the question of Ripon's successor in India. It seems he wishes to leave in the autumn instead of next spring, when his term is up: whether from weariness of the place, in which he has certainly not succeeded, or having received a hint (which I suspect) that in view of the uncertainty of politics it will be well to secure the appointment of the next governor-general while the power is still in our hands. Anyhow, he is coming home: and his successor has to be named. There are two names thought of: Spencer & Dufferin. Both are capable, & both have claims of service: the Premier inclined to choose Spencer: the rest of us preferred Dufferin. My reasons (I cannot answer for the others) were: that Spencer is more likely to be of use at home, officially: that Dufferin notoriously looks to India as the reward of a successful administrative career: that he has done well wherever he has served: that missing his object he will be at home, unemployed, & with a grievance (though no doubt it is possible to give him another embassy instead): that the public expects him to have the place: that his appointment will relieve the block in the diplomatic service: & that he is sure to be popular among Anglo-Indians by his pleasant manners & brilliancy. I think also he is the more cultivated and trained of the two men intellectually. . . .

7 Aug. 1884: Granville tells me that our talk of yesterday has converted the Premier, & that he is now in favour of sending Dufferin to India rather than Spencer. He consulted me as to who should go to Constantinople in Dufferin's place. I said: 'Thornton[21]: he is steady & safe, & will get you into no trouble.'

8 Aug. 1884: . . . **Note** that for a long while, some say 100 years, wheat has never been as low in the market as it is now: 37s. to 38s. If this lasts, it will soon cease to be grown in England.

9 Aug. 1884 (Sat.): . . . Went up by 11.43 train, expecting a Cabinet at 2.00, but found it suddenly put off till 4.00, on account of a sitting of the H. of C. Work at office till 4.00, when to Cabinet. Granville was in the gout, & Spencer away. Others came late, & it was altogether a rather disorderly meeting. But we settled the speech. We settled also, after much discussion, to modify our decision of Wednesday as to New Guinea so far as to exclude from the proposed protectorate the north coast: this in consequence of a representation by Münster as to German claims, which we are not in a position to dispute, having absolutely no settlement in the country, & no more right than anybody else. I could not but feel the reasonableness of the argument, which all admitted, except Childers: he dwelt much & warmly on the disappointment which the Australians will feel, and as to the fact I suppose he is right: but are their expectations reasonable? They wish, in effect, to lay down a Monroe doctrine for Australia, & exclude all foreign powers from the south Pacific: which is not justice nor sense. But the wish to humour & gratify colonists is so strong that they will probably find supporters at home in their wildest pretensions, even apart from the influence of party . . .

10 Aug. 1884 (Sunday): Another very hot day: there has been no summer like this for many years: I think none since 1870. On Friday the temp. in shade, at various places, ranged from 85° to 90°[F].

. . . Report in the *Observer* of a great meeting at Manchester addressed by Salisbury, R. Churchill, & Hicks Beach: the only notable facts about which are the reconciliation of the first two, & the great numbers assembled, near 50,000. The Lords show no sign of yielding so far, & I do not see how the quarrel is to be made up.

We have bought from the D. of Marlborough the most valued picture in his collection, a Raphael, at a cost of £70,000: probably the largest sum ever given for a bit of canvas since the world began. When it was mentioned in Cabinet, Gladstone, though he had assented to the purchase, shook his head & looked very grave. Dilke, & I think also Chamberlain, expressed warm satisfaction. . . .

11 Aug. 1884: Another hot day, in fact it turned out the hottest we have had yet: in London 90° in the shade & upwards.

Rode early, 10.00–11.15, but came home heated & half stupefied by the glare. London . . . Office 2.00–4.20: then to Lords, where not over a dozen peers present . . . At office, saw Herbert & settled the answer to the question about to be put to the Premier about New Guinea[22] . . .

12 Aug. 1884: Holwood. Weather a little cooler, but still sultry. Newspapers full of deaths by sunstroke & bathers drowned.

Sent £10 to the National Cyclists' Union, who ask for help. . . .

14 Aug. 1884: . . . In the papers, two deaths: one that of the D. of Wellington[23], 32 years after his father. He had a good deal of natural ability, but was unambitious, & crushed as it were by the weight of his father's reputation. The old duke hated him with a strange & perverse hatred, nobody knew why: perhaps he did not know it himself: the son deserved, & got, credit for the good sense he showed in the difficult position so made for him: showing no resentment, giving no provocation, & taking much pains after the old man's death to do honour to his memory.

The other deceased peer was Lord Lauderdale[24], killed by lightning while shooting on his own moors: a strange death.

15 Aug. 1884: . . . Wrote to Herbert about Ld Granville's request that Meade should go back for a time to F.O. to look after Egyptian matters there. I can scarcely refuse, but my consent is reluctantly given, for such changes are inconvenient, & unfair to the colleagues of the official thus taken away, whose share of work is increased.

Wrote to Ward to send me £10,000 more, making in all £510,000 drawn from the office since 1870 inclusive, & £270,000 since 1879: I had not intended this, but I note that when a large balance is left Hale is apt to spend more freely on improvements than he need . . .

The Duke of Buccleuch's will is proved, about £900,000, taking England & Scotland together, which is not much for a landowner who had at least £150,000 a year, probably much more, for nearly 60 years. But he was eaten up by the multitude of his houses & places to keep up: & he spent vast sums, whether usefully or not I don't know, on a pier at Granton. . . .

18 Aug. 1884: . . . Letter from Granville, saying that the Queen is pleased with the idea of Lorne[25] going to N.S. Wales, which I had mentioned to G. in conversation as a possibility. It seems, from what G. told me in London, that the Princess has taken a violent dislike to him [Lorne, her husband], & the Queen's object is to arrange some decent pretext for a separation. – I answer that I see no objection to Lorne having the place, but that we had better not pledge ourselves as yet, the vacancy being still in the future. I added something as to the political situation, which looks awkward. It is almost certain that the peers will not in November consent to what they rejected in July. Why should they? There is no change of circumstances, no new reason alleged. If they yield at all, they yield simply to threats, and to an agitation which hitherto has not appeared very formidable.

What can we do on a second rejection of the bill? We can dissolve, which is exactly what the opposition want, & a defeat for us. We can resign, which comes to the same thing, for the opposition will take office, & dissolve at once. We can make peers, if the Queen consents (which very likely she will not) but can we make them in numbers sufficient for the purpose? It is an extreme measure, & the success very doubtful. Lastly, we can offer the bill a third time to the Lords, & so postpone the dispute till January: & merge the comparatively small issue now raised in the much larger one of a general discussion of the position of the H. of Lords. But this is playing a dangerous game, & with no certainty of winning. I do not at present see my way.

19 Aug. 1884: . . . Letter from the Premier, pressing me to find if possible an appointment in the colonies for Clifford Lloyd: which I am not unwilling to do, but it is not easy.

Letter from Granville, asking for the transfer of Meade to the new Egyptian department at F.O. about which I am in correspondence with Meade himself & Herbert. – He, Ld G., mentions also the odd & violent outbreak of feeling in Germany against England, which shows itself in the German press, & is probably inspired by Bismarck: but the origin & meaning of it are equally inexplicable, at least to me. What can he gain by picking a quarrel with us? And what provocation has been given? None, that we know of: & perhaps the best proof that there is none is that the German newspapers are crying out against our retention of Heligoland – which we have held for nearly a century – as an insult to German nationality. But imbecilities of this kind would not be encouraged by Bismarck without an object: & what can his object be? . . .

20 Aug. 1884: . . . Granville writes: (1) About New South Wales, which it appears the Queen is anxious to secure for Lorne . . . I shall not object, for Lorne is likely to do well in the place, but I decline to bind myself by a promise to appoint him, as the vacancy does not yet exist. (2) He answers my question as to the cause or causes of Bismarck's irritation on colonial subjects, & against England generally. He thinks it mainly assumed to catch popular feeling in Germany, before the elections, there being just now a strong demand for colonies. But he [B.] also hates Gladstone, & believes him to be the author of an article in one of the reviews, signed 'G.' which appeared lately, & is decidedly anti-German in tone[26]. (3) As to the franchise bill he agrees with the ideas I have expressed, thinks our position a bad one, & regrets that we did not dissolve at once after the failure of the bill in the Lords. He thinks the opposition will carry their point, & obtain a dissolution on the old constituencies, in which with Parnellite help they will probably win, & be in power for six months. He says our strength lies mainly in Gladstone's popularity, & the distrust which is felt of Salisbury & R. Churchill: the latter motive will continue: but, as to the former, Gladstone is not immortal.

21 Aug. 1884: . . . Wrote to the Premier about Clifford Lloyd, pointing out some difficulties in the way of appointing him to a colony, owing to the number of outsiders whom I have brought in to the service: Lansdowne, Loch, Norman, Blake – the last at Spencer's request. But I add a strong expression of my wish to help him: mainly on the ground that his being shelved would be a triumph to the disaffected party in Ireland, who openly boast that they will ruin any man who has made himself conspicuous, as Lloyd has done, by activity against them. I am not sure that this sentiment will command entire sympathy from Gladstone, who is slow to believe in the depth & reality of Irish disaffection: but its expression may be useful. . . .

23 Aug. 1884: . . . Wrote to Coutts to buy for me £10,000 more Consols: which will make up investments to £520,000, leaving £12,000 in reserve, & nearly £10,000 with Coutts. In all, £540,000: which is more than till of late I ever thought to be worth. . . .

24 Aug. 1884: . . . Settled to see a deputation of sugar planters . . . they pressing for an interview, & crying out loudly that they are being ruined. I believe as a matter of fact that many estates are likely to be abandoned, especially in the smaller islands, where the planters are poor: the price of sugar being lower than ever before, which they ascribe wholly to foreign bounties, whereas I hold that scientific culture, & the superiority of European over negro labour, has more to do with the result. But in any case they are badly off, and I may as well hear them, whether help be possible or no.

. . . Short walk in the morning, but the sun was too much for me, & I came home soon. The heat if anything is increasing.

. . . The drought is growing serious.

25 Aug. 1884: . . . In afternoon the weather changed suddenly to cold, by a more rapid transition than I have almost ever known in this climate.

. . . Received a telegram from Sanderson announcing Ld Ampthill's death: it is a blow to M. who has known him from a boy: and both publicly & socially it is a loss. English diplomacy is not strong in able men: Lyons must soon retire: & when that happens, except Malet & Morier, & perhaps Ford, I know of no one in the future who is at all above mediocrity.

26 Aug. 1884: . . . Day fine but cold: the drought continues.

The papers are full of Odo Russell [Ld Ampthill], whose remarkable ability seems recognised on all sides. He was eminently fit for the life he led, having by nature the easy unimpassioned temper which belongs to a diplomatist: and having been brought up among Germans[27], whose language he spoke as familiarly as his own. Indeed it was his own, for he talked English with a slight, but perceptible, foreign accent, & certainly knew less of English than of continental life. He told stories, & conversed, admirably well: there were few pleasanter companions. His health was never strong, & latterly had failed a good deal, owing to sedentary habits. He never took exercise, & was a heavy eater in German fashion, though temperate in drink. He had an art both in writing & talking, more than any man I have known, of insinuating what he did not think it desirable or prudent to say openly: so that you knew what he thought, yet could hardly assert that he had given an opinion. In conversations of business, he was perhaps over-anxious to avoid any appearance of difference with his interlocutor, & people who did not know his ways accused him of being insincere: but it was seldom difficult to discover whether he really agreed, or was only assenting out of politeness.

In politics he professed the opinions of his family, as far as he could be said to have any politics: professional duty & personal taste combined to keep him as nearly neutral as an Englishman in a prominent position can be. He at one time made no secret of his ambition to be Foreign Secretary: an ambition which might perhaps have been realised had he lived, but I do not think the post would have suited him, nor he it. He was exactly in his place as ambassador at Berlin, & we shall never have a better. . . .

31 Aug. 1884: . . . Four heavy pouches from office, with a great deal in them. Work upon them most of the morning.

Long walk in afternoon for exercise . . . the roads full of hop pickers, men, women, girls, & boys, not all sober, & their language of the kind most used at the east end of London. The picking season has begun, & will last about a fortnight or three weeks.

Odd & disagreeable incident: two donkeys, favourites of Margaret, have been found cut & wounded, evidently out of malice, by some boy or man about the place.

1 Sept. 1884: Wet night & morning, which is well, for the country is still dried up, & the brooks have ceased to run. . . . Incessant rain early, making exercise impossible: so that I had really nothing to do except to read the papers: which does not often happen.

Left at 12.30 . . . Reached Walmer about 6.00, & found there Pauncefote, Meade, a Mr. Tisza, son of the minister, Sir J. Lacaita, & his son. Long & serious talk with Granville before dinner on the situation. After dinner, cards were played, & we sat till near 12.00.

2 Sept. 1884: Up early & about the place. Walmer is an old castle or fort built by Henry VIII, a nearly circular building with a deep dry ditch round it turned into a garden. The walls are immensely thick, except where modern additions have been made: the house is a very bad one, the rooms dark and ill shaped, but there is a platform outside the drawing room windows on which a battery of 32-pounders is mounted, the shot piled between them, and flowers in abundance making an odd contrast. The views over the sea are pleasant (Downs, Goodwin Sands, & the French coast clearly seen). There is a large & very pretty garden, said to have been made by Ly Hester Stanhope[28], where, being protected from sea wind, all kinds of trees & shrubs flourish. The park, or pleasure ground, is small & poor. The beach lies immediately below the walls, but being steep & rough the bathing is not good. The country inland is dreary & bare, good for riding, but that is all that can be said . . .

Granville, who is very hospitable & generally has in the house as many guests as it will hold, has no study of his own, but does his work in the drawing room, Sanderson & he having separate tables, & writing & settling affairs amidst the conversation of anybody who may be there. An odd way of doing business: but the business gets done somehow.

We drove, Ly D., Margaret, Ld G. & I, to the little place called St. Margaret's where Sackville [Cecil] has some land & Ld G. much more, which they are trying to develop into building ground. It is pretty & pleasant but separated from the country inland by a steep hill which must lessen its chances in the future. Ld G. tells me he has about 600 acres of his own near Walmer. The castle of course is held only for life.

In afternoon walk with Pauncefote, Meade, Sanderson, & young Lacaita, to a hilltop about 2 miles off, where Ld G. has amused himself by building a pretty little cottage on a site which commands an exceptionally fine view, & surrounding it with a kind of wild garden or shrubbery. He & Sir J. Lacaita followed us in a fly. There is a bowling green, & some of the party played bowls. We returned by the beach, having had a good walk & an agreeable afternoon.

Before setting out, Ld G., Pauncefote, Sanderson, Meade, & I, had a conference of an hour in a little back room, at which we discussed Angra Pequena, West Indian sugar negociations, & the line to be taken in the Chinese quarrel with France[29]. After dinner, cards, & we sat again till near 12.00.

3 Sept. 1884: . . . I had another conversation with Granville before leaving, on the claims of respective candidates to the vacant Garter: Sefton stands first on his list: Kimberley & Rosebery the other two. He did not name Northbrook, whose claims I should have thought the strongest of the lot. He complained of Sefton being unpopular in Lancashire, where it is said he makes none but Conservative magistrates. This I do not believe, & told Granville so, but Sefton's unpopularity is a fact. It is caused by his loquacity, his somewhat swaggering manner, & occasional fits of temper: added to which he will seldom make speeches on public occasions, though when he does they are very good.

We speculated much on the future: he told me that Harcourt is bent on the reversion of the Chancellorship: in which case he will probably get it, for in the H. of C. he would be a dangerous & unscrupulous enemy, if thwarted, & he could neither lead himself, nor would he suffer anyone else to lead. – Dodson it seems wants a peerage, & would probably get one if he were willing to give up his office: but he hesitates as to this, & we cannot have more Cabinet ministers in the Lords. – I gathered from something that Ld G. said that he had already tried to make room for Rosebery by getting rid of Carlingford, to whom he had offered Constantinople, but he did not expect to succeed.

Reverting to the leadership of the Commons, he did not see his way: did not think Hartington would get on with the radicals, even if he remained where he is, which the

Duke's age makes very doubtful[30]. He thought Chamberlain a stronger man than Dilke, but less popular in the Commons: Dilke rather an amateur politician than one in earnest. Courtney, Fawcett, Lefevre, none of them capable of leading. (Trevelyan he did not mention.)

We discussed the immediate prospect, of which he spoke in the same sense as he had written. Dissolution, offer of resignation, making of peers in sufficient numbers, all are impossible: there remains only the expedient of sending up the bill a third time if rejected in October, which is simply an appeal to continued agitation. Now this agitation may rather weary the public than excite it – for nobody believes the struggle to be about anything except who shall have the settlement of the redistribution question – or, if it increases in violence, it may break up the party by separating Whigs from Radicals. In either case it is a bad look out.

Our earlier conversation turned on Angra Pequena, as to which we settled our course of proceeding: on the attitude to be observed in the quarrel between France & China: the W. Indian sugar question: & other merely departmental affairs.

We both regretted the absence of sufficient discussion in Cabinet: where often some trifling question in the H. of C. takes up most of the time, & leaves none for the most serious questions. For instance, the final decision to send a relief expedition up the Nile, though talked about, was never regularly discussed & decided upon: nor was the sending out of Gordon, which has led to most of our subsequent trouble. It is a bad slovenly way of doing business: due partly, Ld G. thinks, to the Premier's dislike of Cabinets: partly perhaps to the wish to avoid differences, which might easily *grow serious.*

Ld G. talked about Hartington: regretted the society that he (H.) lives in: a fast fashionable set, very Jingo, where he is constantly hearing the action of his colleagues blamed & ridiculed: this makes him, Ld G. thinks, more Tory than he would naturally be: for no man can resist the influence of those who are perpetually about him.

Talk about the Berlin vacancy: Ld G. thinks Malet[31] the best man for it, Dufferin having accepted India, & being out of the question: I thought it well to explain Malet's situation in regard of the Bedford family.

My observation of Ld G. on this visit somewhat lessened the impression of age & infirmity which his manner in the H. of Lds. had created. Though lame from gout, & rather deaf, he seemed full of activity & interest, not a moment unoccupied, & always in conversation, talking & listening even while he worked, in a way which would have been impossible to most people. . . .

5 Sept. 1884: Fine bright day, the country again green & fresh after rain: the brooks running. Two pouches only from office.

. . . It seems that the Duke's[32] consent to Malet's marriage with [his] daughter is likely to be given: but he makes delays & difficulties, & is angry with M. for having as he believes promoted it. The Duchess too, who has high ideas of birth & fashion, thinks the connection a low one: which is foolish, for Malet is a gentleman by birth, & at the head of his profession: & an ambassador is socially the equal of anybody. His only fault is want of money: & that the Duke can remove. . . .

6 Sept. 1884: Two pouches from office . . . Sent £5 to a sailor who has lost his legs on a whaling expedition: a real case of distress for once, which M. has discovered . . . Rain incessant all day. Walked an hour in the wet for exercise.

7 Sept. 1884: . . . News from Westmoreland that my uncle C. Stanley[33] is in a state of health which makes it impossible that he should live many weeks: unable to leave his bed, & often wandering in mind. His family are with him. He is 76, which is a greater age than either my father or H. Stanley reached. In youth & middle age he had remarkable strength, & for many years he walked, I should think, 20 miles a day, shooting or fishing if he had the chance: if not walking for the simple pleasure of exercise. He was always on his legs, & in the air. These active habits, which he kept up till within the last ten years, counteracted the effect of the daily bottle of port which was his *minimum*, & a *minimum* often exceeded. He disliked London, & all sedentary or regular occupation: preferring to lead a life of independence, though with little employment. I do not think his plan of life answered: though kind hearted, he was very irritable, & his temper, especially in early days, was such as to make him difficult to live with. He had little reading or knowledge, but plenty of hard sense, & some power of sarcasm, which he was fond of using at the expense of his company, especially after dinner. . . .

9 Sept. 1884: . . . Day warm & close . . . Letter from Froude about his son, which I enclosed to Sanderson, asking that he may be nominated to F.O. or rather to the diplomatic service[34].

News that Northbrook & Ld Wolseley are arrived in Egypt: the next question is, what will they do?

The agitation about the franchise bill has either lulled, or the papers have ceased to report the speeches: at any rate, we hear little more on the subject. Gladstone is in Scotland where the enthusiasm felt for him seems undiminished. The political world is quiet, taking its holiday.

The chief news is the spread of cholera in Italy, where in Naples alone, if our reports are correct, 300 have died in one day . . .

11 Sept. 1884: Four pouches from office. Disposed of nearly all.

. . . Wrote to Harcourt on the political situation, very much to the same effect as I did to Granville (v. 18 Aug.) last month, not so much with the view of giving him ideas, as of eliciting his. I hear he now says we shall resign before the year is out.

. . . The appointment of Dufferin to India is announced today: well received (as it was sure to be) by the press on all sides. He is lucky in succeeding Ripon, whose enthusiasm for reforms led him into a quarrel with the whole Anglo-Indian population, in which he was worsted, and had to give way. He is a weak well meaning peer, a favourite of Gladstone, who liked him on account of his love for theology & religious cast of mind. Dufferin is popular everywhere, having pleasant manners, ready wit, considerable power as a speaker, and a fair share of Irish 'blarney'. He has succeeded both in Canada and at Constantinople: keeping well with all parties. India is the prize to which he has long looked forward: &, apart from ambition, he needs office, having been through most of a fortune not originally large.

12 Sept. 1884: . . . An uncomfortable telegram from Ld Wolseley to Hartington, asking for large reinforcements, sufficient to raise his army to 5,000 fighting men at or near Khartoum, besides what are wanted to keep up communications. He urges haste if anything is to be done in the present year. Altogether the relief expedition is growing in size, & of course in consequent expense: but I suppose there is no help. It is unlucky that these questions come up for decision just when no Cabinet, or private meeting of ministers to discuss them, is possible.

13 Sept. 1884: G. Duncan came for the day, having travelled from London on a tricycle, which however he broke at the last hill, & had to return by rail. He meant to have done the whole distance, nearly 60 miles, on his pair of wheels. Such long journeys have become usual: I read in the papers of a tricyclist having ridden from London to Edinburgh, 390 miles, in 3 days. These vehicles, whether on two wheels or one, are more & more becoming the poor man's horse.

Wrote to Kimberley on the so-called crisis, much in the same sense as to Granville & Harcourt, but rather with a view to elicit than to express opinion.

Three heavy pouches from office, which kept me at work most of the morning.

Long walk in afternoon . . . I was walking nearly 3 hours, in much heat, & came home drenched with perspiration, but scarcely weary: which I am glad of.

14 Sept. 1884 (Sunday): . . . Four pouches from office, & heavy: disposed of nearly all . . . In afternoon, called on C. Stanley at Coldharbour. Heard from him of his father, the same report that we had a week ago. He, C.S., the same strange being as ever: cheerful & harmless: well content to live on small means – which is not common – but with a more total want of interests & ideas than I ever observed before in a person in full possession of his faculties. Conversation with him is impossible: for he never speaks except in answer, & then in the fewest possible words: I cannot make out that he has any occupation or acquaintance here, though he has been some years settled. His wife has sense, & I suppose manages all.

15 Sept. 1884: Nothing from office . . .

News of Malet's appointment to Berlin . . . It is probably the best choice that could be made. No man in the service has an equal claim: & there is no outsider whom opinion points to as specially fit. If the newspaper report be true, that an offer or overture was made to Carlingford, I think the refusal of it was lucky: though no doubt it is an object to get him replaced in the Cabinet by Rosebery. He had an offer of Constantinople before, as Granville told me at Walmer, & declined it. The Crown Princess is said to have wished for Grant Duff, who is a personal friend of hers: but he is doing at Madras work for which he is qualified, & is the least diplomatic of mankind. Lorne has also been talked about: but foolishly: for without his wife he has no claim to the place, nor any special fitness: and, if she went with him, the two sisters would be sure to quarrel.

16 Sept. 1884: Three heavy pouches from office: but few letters: & of late I have had scarcely any to beg. It shows how the art of begging is systematised, that applications invariably fall off in August & September, when people are taking their holiday, & begin again in October.

. . . Summing up the situation as regards my own department, I think we have fewer troubles than usual to deal with:

In Canada there is nothing going amiss.

In Australia the question of federation hangs fire, & what we are doing about New Guinea, though it will not content the more violent annexationists, ought to prevent any extreme outbreak of popular discontent.

In New Zealand, Hong Kong, Singapore, & Ceylon, nothing.

In Fiji, a vehement dispute between the governor & the chief justice, which must end in one or both being removed: but I do not think it will be taken up at home.

In the West Indies, a good deal of distress & complaining from the low price of sugar: but it does not seem possible to do much beyond endeavouring to open to the planters the American market.

South Africa is as usual the principal source of trouble

Nothing that can be done there is likely to be satisfactory either in itself or to the public: but there seems a probability that both in Zululand & among the Bechuanas matters will settle themselves, not quite as we might have wished, but still so as to put any farther fighting in those parts out of question. On the whole, therefore, I think we stand well. Egypt and the franchise between them monopolise attention, & will continue to do. There is no glory to be got in the colonial department, but there is no immediate prospect of a storm there: though it does not take long for one to get up. – In general politics there is nothing new or specially interesting: for the agitation against the Lords has been so far exhausted that the speeches in connection with it are mere repetitions of what has been said before: &, though there can be no reasonable doubt as to the general drift of opinion, it is a question whether any deep popular interest is felt in the dispute. The other matter of interest is the Egyptian expedition, on whose success or failure the popularity of the government will turn: it is in any case a disagreeable necessity, and a vast expense without any permanent good result.

17 Sept. 1884: Three heavy pouches from the office. Work most of the morning . . . Short walk: the day so unusually close & hot that I would not attempt more. Rather oppressed & depressed: not from business, for of that I have little: perhaps we have been here long enough, & a change is wanted. Yet I look forward with no pleasure to Knowsley: & with still less to the session that is to follow.

There came to tea here Lyons, Sir E. May, Mrs. T. Hankey, & Ly May. Talk with Lyons about French affairs . . . He confirmed my opinion, that Bismarck is incessantly trying to make us quarrel with the French, & the French with us: & believes as I do that his present ill will is mainly due to the knowledge that he has failed in that attempt.

18 Sept. 1884: . . . We went to the high ground which we call Breeze Hill, & took leave of the place, which we shall not see again till next year. It is looking its best, & we leave it with regret: for here we enjoy more rest and quiet than is possible in Lancashire, & our time passes at our own disposal.

19 Sept. 1884: Left Fairhill early, & by 9.45 train to London . . . Busy at home till 1.00, when to office: there saw Herbert & Meade: with them by appointment to see Granville at F.O. to discuss various questions in which both departments are concerned: talk afterwards with Ld G. alone: office again till 4.00: then home: saw the Duchess of Bedford and her two daughters: they talk now of the Malet marriage as a thing settled, though the Duke has not formally consented: congratulated the young lady: the Duchess is pleased, though much disliking the match at first: yet the style of an ambassador has gone far to reconcile her. . . . Reached Knowsley at 10.30, 6 hours exactly.

. . . My conversation with Granville turned on various subjects. He had offered both Berlin & Constantinople to Carlingford, who had refused them saying that he was too old to begin a new life: on which it appears the Premier wrote him a letter – Ld G. says an extremely clever & plausible one – in which he hinted at the expediency of Carlingford vacating his seat in the Cabinet, in order to make room for Rosebery. Carlingford however was naturally hurt, & has so far refused to take the hint. There is no doubt that the change would give us strength: still it is an odd proceeding on the part of Gladstone, as C. is one of his most devoted followers, & perhaps the only peer who thoroughly approved of, & is always ready to defend, the Irish land legislation. But Ld G. says that the Premier has taken amiss his dissent from his, Gladstone's, Egyptian policy: though expressed in very moderate terms, & though the Premier has himself been obliged to modify it. In all our talk on this matter, which was long, I thought that Ld G. meant to indicate plainly, though he did not express in so many words, his distrust of Gladstone's judgment.

He told me, what I was sorry to hear, that Trevelyan is knocked up at last & his nerves shattered, by the hard work & incessant insult & abuse to which he has been exposed: he will not go on with the office: the Irish know it, & shriek with delight: not that they have any quarrel with him personally, but they wish, on system, to make the office untenable by an Englishman. – Lefevre is the probable successor[35].

Talk of the vacant Constantinople embassy – Ld G. distrusts Morier, does not think West quite strong enough, & seems to hesitate between Thornton & Ford. There is a chance yet for Morier: the Spanish mission may be raised to an embassy, which would give him promotion. But it is hard upon him to be twice passed over: though the fault is in great measure his own.

Talk, vaguely, of Dodson resigning & taking a peerage: the latter he himself wishes, but we cannot have more peers in the Cabinet, & it is not certain that he would be willing to pay for his dignity by resigning his office.

Ld G. regretted that the Premier by his speeches in Scotland[36] had made dissolution impossible, which he thinks is the case. He does not see his way, & believes that nobody does.

Talk of the necessity for an early Cabinet: the Egyptian complications are growing thicker, & some early decision is necessary. Two questions especially press: Northbrook has been compelled by the state of the Egyptian exchequer to suspend payment of the sinking fund: which is in violation of international engagements, though justified by sheer necessity. It must be explained to the powers, & possibly they will protest. The other difficulty arises from Gordon's attitude. He has determined to hold the Soudan, contrary to orders, & has made public two wild telegrams in which he asserts this intention, & attacks the government for not supporting him. He is in fact in mutiny – there is no other word for it.

20 Sept. 1884: . . . Talk with Ward . . . He gave me at my request the rentals since 1880 inclusive: they stand, 1880, £198,540: 1881, £206,629: 1882, £211,986: 1883, £218,845: 1884, £226,897. An increase in 4 years of over £28,000, or at the rate of £7,000 a year.

21 Sept. 1884 (Sunday): Knowsley. Two pouches from office . . . Sent Rev. J. Kempe £25 for parish charities. Gave Latter £7 for the charity account.

Note that Hale tells me that the new map & survey of the estate is nearly completed: he expects that the area will prove to be larger than we supposed: 80,000 acres at least, instead of about 70,000 as I have always been told. It is just as well, considering the feeling of these days, that the landowners' return of 1873 puts me down so much below the real amount[37].

. . . Saw Mrs. Hale, returned from 12 months in the south, & apparently cured. Walk on . . . with Hale in the rain, & much talk on estate affairs. . . .

26 Sept. 1884: Wet morning, which stopped intended shooting.

Three pouches from office: disposed of all.

. . . Letter from Childers, warning me of the probability of trouble in Australia, arising out of the New Guinea question, & the expected demand of the colonists for the islands lying beyond New Guinea. I answer at once: & as to New Guinea advise him to speak to Granville, with whom rests any delay that has occurred: for the C.O. has been ready to act for some time[38].

Letter from the Premier about S. Africa, but vague, he as yet knowing nothing about the question. . . .

27 Sept. 1884: Four pouches from office.

Balances from Ward . . . [He] makes out that the trustees have still to receive . . . in all over £30,000 fairly certain . . . & farther sums . . . large but uncertain as to amount & date. There is room therefore for additional purchases of land if I choose.

. . Talk with Lyons, in his room, at some length, on French affairs . . . he thinks as I do that neither royalists nor imperialists have a chance: that the republic is safe from attack: unless in the case of a successful war, carried on by a general who had both ability & ambition . . . he does not believe that French statesmen have any plan of creating a colonial empire, but that they only annex here & there as opportunity offers, because it is popular at the time: they do not think much of the future. He supposes that no French minister, present or future, desires a war: but, if they did, it would probably be a war with us: Germany being too strong to attack: I said, why not Italy? which he admitted as a possible alternative. He does not understand the late outbreak against us in the French press. He is not quite easy about Northbrook's late performance in Egypt, suspending the sinking fund of the debt: saying that the powers have a reasonable cause of complaint, & ought to have been consulted.

Garden party in afternoon, 3.00 to 6.00: about 400 came. Day fine & all went well.

28 Sept. 1884: Two pouches: work at home till 12.00 . . .

. . . Some talk yesterday at the party with Holt[39]: he wants the Premier to come to Liverpool & make a speech: which I deprecate, thinking that he makes too many: he proceeded to talk of the situation: and, to my entire satisfaction, but also rather to my surprise, expressed a strong opinion that if the bill were again lost in the Lords we ought to dissolve: seeing that, if they persist, the Lords can in the end force a dissolution by mere lapse of time: and not believing that their determination so to do will excite any violent anger in the public mind. As to the objection that to dissolve is to give the opposition what they want, he answers justly that if we win at the polls all's well that ends well: if not, we at least know the mind of the country, and the question is settled for a time. – As Holt is certainly the clearest headed & most sensible man among the Liverpool Liberals, his opinion is of value: & I write it to Ld Granville.

. . .

30 Sept. 1884: ... The state of public business is unsatisfactory. In home affairs, the franchise agitation, and the almost certainty that the bill will again be thrown out in the Lords: in foreign relations, the unexpected action of Northbrook in Egypt, which may have been necessary, probably was so, but has disturbed the minds of all foreign states, & is the subject of general protest: in Egypt itself, the costly expedition of Ld Wolseley, & the utter uncertainty as to what can be done if he gets to Khartoum – for to keep that place or to let it go are equally unwelcome alternatives – in the colonies, South Africa in disorder, a fresh war there possible, Australia anxious about French convicts, divided on the question of federation, & likely to explode in anger when the colonists find that they cannot annex all the islands within 1,000 miles of their coasts – these are not agreeable conditions under which to meet parliament, and to them must be added general depression in trade & a stationary if not declining revenue. On the other hand, there is no discontent in general among the working class: food is very cheap: and, though in some trades wages are low, the losses of the employers have not yet told on the employed.

1 Oct. 1884 (Wednesday): Two pouches from office, & little in them.

News from Granville that the Germans are making trouble about our proposed protectorate of New Guinea[40]: which does not surprise me, but it is awkward.

... Telegrams in cypher from Gladstone & Granville: the first I could not read, at least not the whole, but I made out that it relates to a Cabinet proposed for Tuesday. It is quite time we held one. Egypt, South Africa, N. Guinea, all require to be dealt with: the franchise business also it may be well to talk about, though that can wait.

... Saw Hale, & talk about an Irish doctor in Prescot, who is writing abusive letters because his privilege of coming into the park has been withdrawn. It appears that his name has been struck off the medical register, & that he does not deny having been in gaol in Ireland. The police also report of him as a dangerous & disreputable person.

2 Oct. 1884: Nervous & uncomfortable without reason ...

Read to M. ... an article written by Pope-Hennessy[41], intended to show that Ld Beaconsfield was a Home Ruler. What it does show is that being always anxious, as he was, to secure the Irish vote, he coquetted a good deal with Irish patriots: as he would have done with any party which he could utilise. He was no doubt willing to bring into prominence the fact that the Penal Laws in Ireland, & the general system of Orange rule, were established by the Whigs: which is true, & a useful weapon for his purpose. He was also extremely desirous of conciliating the Catholic priests: but he could not give them the one thing they wanted – the disendowment of the Protestant church. This article by Hennessy looks as if he were beginning to bid again for Irish support: intending to take a part, probably, as one of Parnell's followers.

Three pouches (I think) from office.

Received from London Malmesbury's newly published memoirs[42]: they are gossippy, trivial in parts, containing little information as to men or things, but amusing, and as far as I can judge not ill natured. Whether it is altogether delicate to publish gossip about living friends & acquaintance is another matter: but if the thing was to be done at all he has done it in a fairly unobjectionable manner. His two heroes are my father and Louis Napoleon: he has inserted a good many letters from my father, some characteristic. There are also one or two from Disraeli, with whom he was on civil, but never on cordial terms. On the whole the book is harmless, & not foolish: it will give my old friend no fame as an author, but it may put a few hundreds in his pocket, which I am afraid are much wanted[43].

3 Oct. 1884: Woke, & continued all morning, somewhat nervous & depressed, the former to a degree not explained either by the prospect of a not very difficult speech this evening, or by anything in either public or private affairs. The feeling passed off in great degree after a brisk ride, but not wholly. I suspect the time of year, the damp climate, & surroundings less bright than those of Holwood or Fairhill, have much to do with it. Work & conversation do not drive it off, though of course it would be aggravated by absence of occupation.

Two pouches from office, which disposed of early.

Ride, in bright fine weather, which partly relieved the discomfort. Walk afterwards alone.

. . . The dinner was at 7.00, & like all Mayor's dinners: good, but far too long to be pleasant. About 120 were present. . . . The speeches were few & short: mine rather longer than necessary, as I thought, but very well listened to, & it seemed to give pleasure. Home late, but in bed soon after 12.00.

4 Oct. 1884: Woke free from the nervous depression of the last few days, well in health & spirits, as far as feeling goes, but I must take care lest this most detestable complaint should return. . . .

5 Oct. 1884 (Sunday): The meeting of the Cabinet was fixed for Tuesday: but yesterday late I got a sudden telegram putting it on to Monday, in consequence of which I decided to go up today. . . .

6 Oct. 1884: . . . At 3.00 Cabinet, which lasted till 6.30: Northbrook, Spencer, & Chamberlain absent. We discussed the French in China, the question being whether it is necessary or desirable that we should offer good offices. Opinion seemed divided: some of us, Harcourt especially, thought the French in their present mood were sure to give trouble somewhere, & that it was a good thing rather than otherwise that they should have their hands full in China: Granville, I, & some others, replied pointing out the mischief which war would do to our trade, the risk of complications involving neutrals, the probability that Russia would use her opportunity to seize some part of the empire. A third party, for whom the Chancellor [spoke], took a more scrupulous view of the matter, & thought we ought not, by pressing the Chinese to yield, to condone, & apparently sanction the outrages with which they began. In the end it appeared open to doubt whether the time had come for successful mediation: & the subject dropped.

Talk as to Gordon: it is agreed to send him out the G.C.B. & a letter from the Queen to congratulate him on his successful defence: after which we considered a strange proposal by Northbrook, to the effect that he should be allowed, if he chooses, to retire on the equatorial provinces, giving up his command, & acting as a private person. To this the obvious objection is that do what he may, & go where he will, he cannot divest himself of his character as representing England: & we should be held just as much responsible if he were killed on the White Nile or the Congo, as if it had happened at Khartoum. It is clear that Northbrook believes he will not come away of his own accord, & wishes to avoid the scandal of his being compelled to do so.

From these matters we passed to the question of New Guinea & the German claims: as to which a lively discussion came off: Kimberley contesting vehemently these claims, denying that they have any existence, & commenting quite justly on the odd contrast between the high-handed dealing of the Germans themselves (as at Angra Pequena & the Camaroons) and their excessive sensitiveness when any pretension of their own is disputed. In the end we decided not to wait for their assent, nor refer the matter to a commission, which they had proposed, but declare at once our protectorate of the southern coast of New Guinea, leaving the rest open for discussion. Childers took the Australian side in this discussion: Harcourt said truly that neither the Australians nor the Germans, nor we, had any valid claims on the island, & added that we had better settle the matter quietly as our paper annexations would go for nothing in international law if disputed.

We then went on to S. Africa: as to which I obtained the sanction of the Cabinet for protection to be given to Montsiou[44]: we have really no choice in the matter, for it was distinctly promised him: but as the decision may involve a quarrel with the Boers (though I do not think it will) I could not take it on my sole responsibility.

7 Oct. 1884: Saw Mr. Long, Lawrence's partner, about Mrs. H. Stanley's affairs: she has run into debt to the extent of £600, part of which I am willing, or at least ready, to pay: her bills for medical attendance especially: for she is I believe slowly dying with cancer & dropsy. She has so often feigned illness when she wanted money that I did not at first quite believe this: but it seems true[45].

Saw Lawson, who defines the situation fairly enough, saying that he shall continue to write up a compromise, though not expecting it to succeed. . . .

8 Oct. 1884: . . . Cabinet at 12.00: sat till 3.00: then to office for a few minutes: then Travellers' for luncheon or early dinner: left the Square at 4.30 & reached Knowsley at 10.30 exactly. . . . I found in the house Talbot[46], my sister, their daughter, young E.[ddie] Stanley, Ly W. Herbert, Miss Hope, & Sanderson.

The Cabinet occupied itself entirely with considering possible compromises with a view to settle the question between the two Houses. The discussion was long & rather desultory: ending in no conclusion except the quite reasonable, but purely negative, one that no offer can be made from our side. But in truth there is no probability that it will be made by the opposition, for what they want is a dissolution under the present franchise, & that they can secure, if they do not fear the results of the agitation which they will provoke, merely by resisting the passing of any bill until the lapse of time makes dissolution inevitable. They hope for a majority, with Irish help, or, failing that, for a minority strong enough to control the majority, with the aid of all the facilities which our system of parliamentary procedure gives for delay.

The Premier said today among other things that 'it was useless to talk of passing either a redistribution bill, or any other bill of importance, until procedure was radically altered. At present the minority are the masters. They may not be able to carry anything, but they can hinder everything'.

Towards the end of the sitting Spencer detailed to us the last device of the disaffected party in Ireland. They get hold of informers on whose evidence men have been convicted for murder or assaults, & induce them to declare publicly that their information was false. This has been done especially in the Maamtrasna case, where a careful enquiry has proved that the story told at the trial was true. In this case his motive for recalling his statement was disappointment at having got less from the authorities than he expected in the way of reward: & probably also fear of private revenge. It is an effective weapon in the hands of the nationalists, for the effect must be to make juries even less willing than they are now to convict on the evidence of informers.

9 Oct. 1884: Walk early with Sanderson, over 2 hours . . . Four pouches from the office, but nothing special. Ward called after luncheon, & brought the balance sheet of the year, made up as usual to 30 June.

The rents are in all £217,965: miscellaneous receipts £876. Total receipts £218,841. Besides this I have received from the trustees £25,000 advanced for improvements already executed, which is to be repaid in a term of years. Including this, the total receipts are £242,904. The expenditure is classed as follows:

Compulsory deductions	£26,824	- Less than ever before
Estate expenses	£82,550	- High, but less than last year
Household	£27,000	
Benefactions	£11,632	
Miscellaneous	£00,360 [sic]	
Drawn by me	£70,000	
Total	£233,376	Excluding what I have drawn which is not spent, but invested, the total is £163,376

I had fixed on £160,000 as the limit of reasonable expenditure, & it has not been greatly exceeded.

Note: My total receipts being now about £240,000 including interest . . . I ought to be able to divide it into three equal parts: £80,000 to spend on the estate: £80,000 to lay by: and £80,000 for all other purposes.

The yield of the various estates is as follows:

1) E. Lancashire, £72,618: a slight falling off
2) Liverpool estates, £67,513: an increase
3) Home estates, £52,573: an increase
4) Fylde & outlying, £25,259: an increase.

Ward calls attention, reasonably, to the large outlay in Kent & Surrey: & he tells me what I am sorry to hear that about Ormskirk the anti-rent feeling, stimulated by socialist agents, has spread a good deal. One Williams is the leader: he has been resisting payment of tithes (not to me) &, by reason of some irregularity in the proceedings, has gained a suit arising out of them. There is, however, to be an appeal. – I spoke to Hale about this later: he did not seem to think it serious.

10 Oct. 1884: The Talbots left us: my sister as I thought looking very old and careworn: she talks vaguely of her eldest son having 'got into bad hands' but specifies nothing, & it is not easy to make out whether there is any reason for her anxiety.

. . . Much sensation created by the appearance in the *Standard* of a draft scheme for redistribution of seats, framed by a committee for submission to the Cabinet. It was fraudulently secreted & sold by one of the printers employed, & there is some surprise that a paper like the *Standard* should have made use of information obtained in this dishonest way. But the inducement was strong: for the boroughs sentenced to disfranchisement will naturally do what they can to induce their members to vote against reform, or stay away, & thus lessen the majority on the franchise bill. The scheme is in no sense that of the Cabinet, which has not yet seen it: but the opposition will argue with some truth that it represents at least the views of some members of the Cabinet, & those which are thought likely to be accepted by it as a whole.

Lawson told me on Tuesday that he had had the same offer made to him as his brother editor, but had declined, & warned Spottiswoode's firm that they were being betrayed.

11 Oct. 1884: . . . Sanderson understands that the change about which Ld Granville talked to me at Walmer is about to take effect: Trevelyan to be admitted into the Cabinet, & Lefevre to take his place in Ireland. The first of these changes is an act of justice: the second will probably be a failure, but was inevitable. The Irish members are said to boast that no man can remain in the post of Irish secretary for more than two years: however indifferent one may be, or may think oneself, to unpopularity and insult, the constant abuse, in the press, the incessant attacks in parliament, & the sense of everywhere being regarded as an enemy, will tell in the long run. I suspect they are not far wrong.

12 Oct. 1884: . . . Note of governors appointed by me in the last 2 years:

1) Lansdowne to Canada: generally approved.
2) Norman to Jamaica: not objected to in any quarter, & succeeding well.
3) Loch to Victoria: I had great difficulty in finding anyone fit for this place who was willing to go: he is able, but it is impossible yet to judge how he will get on.
4) Gordon to Ceylon: this was practically settled by Gladstone & Kimberley before I came into office. He is very able, though not popular in the other colonies where he has served.
5) Simmons[47] to Malta: chosen by the War Office, & only concurred in by me but I believe is doing well.
6) Glover to Newfoundland: he served there before, & I put him back again, having no one better. This is the most doubtful choice of any I have made.
7) Lees to the Leeward Islands: promotion from the Bahamas, fairly earned.
8) Blake to the Bahamas, at the urgent request of Lord Spencer that I would provide for him: a strong man.
9) Musgrave transferred from Jamaica to Queensland: this is hardly promotion. He was unpopular in Jamaica, but could not have been removed without giving him another appointment.

13 Oct. 1884: E. Stanley[48] left us: I gave him £20: I am pleased with his manner & conversation &, though not seeing any trace of superior abilities, I think there is reason to hope that he will fill his place creditably as head of this family. . . .

16 Oct. 1884: . . . I determined to go up to London tomorrow, in consequence of telegrams from South Africa, which show the situation to be complicated & difficult.

. . . Saw Hale: talk about Mr. Williams of Ormskirk, who has got up a committee which demands a remission of two-thirds the existing rent, fixity of tenure, etc. His followers are few & not important, but any movement of that [kind] wants watching.

More speeches: Randolph Churchill has delivered one in which occurs a violent personal attack on me: Dilke another, in an opposite sense[49]. I never remember an extra-parliamentary campaign so hotly fought. But, when all is said & done, there is not a new idea, hardly a new phrase, to produce on either side: the same old story over & over again.

17 Oct. 1884: Three pouches from office, but not heavy.

Left at 3.00 . . . reached No. 23 at 9.00 exactly, had only tea instead of dinner, & worked till 11.00 on letters & office papers.

. . . M. left Knowsley soon after me, to see her brother in Wales. Neither she nor I are the better for the damp Lancashire climate, which always tends to depress my spirits & make me nervous. She feels it in the same way, with the addition of mischief to her eyes.

18 Oct. 1884: Slept ill, which I seldom do . . . Letter from the Premier saying, after comments on S. African affairs, that Dodson is to be a peer, Trevelyan to take his place, & Campbell-Bannerman to go to Ireland. The first change is decidedly good: Dodson, though sensible & good tempered, is not a strong man: and Trevelyan replaces him to advantage. He, Trevelyan, I hear is entirely knocked up by two years of the Irish office: result of living in an atmosphere of popular hatred . . . He now has an easy post in which he can rest, advise the Cabinet, & help in debate. Campbell-Bannerman I don't know personally: what I hear of him is all favourable: and his speeches confirm it: he seems a hard-headed Scotchman, impervious to bluster & blarney: but two years of that office may break him down too, if he stays in it so long. In answering Gladstone, I expressed satisfaction as to his arrangements, & added that, if only he could manage to take in Rosebery also, his Cabinet would be as strong as it could well be made.

. . . Dined Travellers': sat next Waddington & some interesting talk . . . I said that I had long believed that, if we had had in England a peasant proprietary 40 years ago, the corn laws would have been in existence to this day. Jealousy of aristocracy, & the notion that corn laws added to the wealth of the rich at the expense of the poor, gave strength to the movement against them. There would not have been half so much bitterness had the landowners been poor themselves.

. . . Talk of Chinese in America & Australia: he likened the feeling against them to that against the Jews: in both cases their thrift & moneymaking power lay at the root of their unpopularity.

19 Oct. 1884: An odd nearly solitary day. Worked early on office papers, disposed of all that was to be done in that line. Wrote to Ly Stanhope & others. . . . Walked sharply round Regent's park for exercise: a dismal but necessary occupation. Luncheon on a biscuit or two. Called on the Harcourts, but they were not at home. Called on Granville, & sat with him half an hour or more: I did not think well of his appearance: he seemed sleepy or stupefied, and misplaced names a good deal. He said the Queen had made difficulties about bringing Trevelyan into the Cabinet (on account of army matters, I suppose, the mere discussion of which in Parliament she always resents)[50]: but he assumed that Gladstone would persevere. He wished that Rosebery could be brought in, but that involved turning out Carlingford, who knew that it was desired that he should go, but declined to move: which Granville thought odd. (I am not sure that I do.) He talked freely & not very favourably of Gladstone: thought a late speech of his had been indiscreet, & was sure to be construed as a threat to Germany, which was needless & quite inconsistent with Gladstone's antecedents: disliked his friendship, & public avowal of it, with that 'Russian adventuress' Madame Novikoff: 'a vulgar woman separated from her husband': some other oddity he mentioned too, I forget now what. It is clear to me that there is no great love lost between the leaders of the two Houses.

About the political crisis he was vague, hoped the majority might be greatly reduced: but had no definite ideas as to what ought to follow on our inevitable defeat. He seemed to hint at making peers, if the number required was not very large: but he said nothing definite. The rest of our talk was departmental. . . .

21 Oct. 1884: Received from the Queen a very excited letter about the Bechuana business. Answered it in due form, which was the easier as we are going to do what she wishes, or at least what she professes to wish: but her real, hardly disguised, desire is to fight the Boers again, & get a victory to set against Majuba hill. Wrote to the Premier on the same subject. . . .

22 Oct. 1884: . . . Cabinet at 2.00, which sat till 4.30. All present except Northbrook, though some came an hour late. The chief business discussed was the possibility of using good offices to put an end to the war between France & China. This question was talked about rather than argued, & generally our conversation was desultory The Premier went to sleep, & remained so for a considerable time. The only thing at all notable that I remember is his saying apropos of the alarmist articles that have appeared in the *Pall Mall Gazette*: 'That man of the *Pall Mall* who has not yet taken his proper place in a lunatic asylum . . .'

After the Cabinet we had a meeting of the foreign & colonial committee: Granville, Kimberley, D.[erby], Dilke, Chamberlain, Herbert, Ashley, Courtney, V. Lister, & Fitzmaurice. We sat half an hour, considering chiefly the question of an African company trading on the Niger, which has applied for a Charter giving them territorial powers. These we think it better not to grant, pending the conference which is about to sit. . . .

23 Oct. 1884: . . . At 4.00 to the opening of parliament. As it was known that in our House there would be no business for some time, the attendance was not large, & the galleries were comparatively empty. Ld Belper[51] moved the address & did it well: Ld Lawrence[52] who followed was not a success: he diverged from the appointed subjects, talked about Ld Ripon & Ld Dufferin, the strength of the navy, & a variety of other topics which he handled in a style of independent criticism on which Salisbury reasonably commented as belonging rather to the opposition than to a supporter of government. I do not think he meant to show independence: all was awkwardness & a desire to say something not hackneyed.

Salisbury followed as usual: his speech was light & easy, without much bitterness, but also without seriousness: as though he wished to make as light as possible of the actual state of things. Granville answered him, speaking rather well, but nothing out of the common. Carnarvon discoursed on S. Africa, & I had to follow him, speaking in answer to his questions, on a variety of subjects without notice or preparation: I satisfied myself fairly well as to argument, for in truth I had a good case, & knew it thoroughly: but details of colonial politics are not amusing, & I had a small audience, as indeed had Carnarvon also. All ended by 7.00: coming home to dinner, I found M. arrived, after a six days' separation, the longest this year.

24 Oct. 1884: Lawson called, & talked over the situation: more hopeful of a compromise than I am.

F.A.S. called, & we discussed together the position of the C. Stanley family: they are seven: the four daughters all seem to wish to live separately: they will have from £250 to £300 apiece of income. The two younger brothers have in addition to this, one his living, of perhaps £200 a year: the other his retired pay to nearly the same amount. The eldest has nothing but his share of the family property, & he has children to keep. I settled with F. to allow him (C. Stanley) £200 a year, & each of the daughters £100: which will make them comfortable, & is more than they expect. They are an odd family by his report: all anxious to get away from one another, & very secretive as to their plans.

. . . Write to the Queen to appoint Gen. Scratchley[53] special commissioner for the New Guinea protectorate.

In the H. of C. yesterday, all passed quietly: the Premier made a temperate speech[54]: towards the end of it, when referring to the conduct of the Lords, he drew out a piece of paper, & read from it what he had to say. This is the first time he has ever been known to take a precaution of that kind: as words never fail him, the object must have been to make sure that he did not say more than he had intended: and in fact he was moderate enough.

25 Oct. 1884: In H. of C. last night, a bitter & unscrupulous attack was made by the Irish members on Lord Spencer & Trevelyan: they were charged with having caused the execution of an innocent man (one Joyce) for a murder which he did not commit, obtaining his conviction by inducing an informer to perjure himself[55]. It is almost incredible that they received at least partial support from Gorst & R. Churchill: so far will the spirit of faction go. The Irish Home Rulers are going into strong opposition, either as having got all they can hope to get from the present Cabinet, or thinking to extort fresh concessions.

I am inclined to think that we gain by this: the more evident it becomes that the nationalist party is irreconcilable, the less we can be censured for failing to reconcile it, and the difficulty of taking the necessary steps for the maintenance of order is diminished in proportion. . . .

27 Oct. 1884: Saw Mr. Bruce[56], colonial secretary at Mauritius, who asks for a transfer, ostensibly on the ground that the island is too much out of the way: but really, as I am told, because he finds it impossible to work with Pope-Hennessy[57]. – Hennessy is a clever, intriguing, unscrupulous Irishman, whom Disraeli employed a good deal in negociating with the Catholic bishops of Ireland: & then sent to the West Coast of Africa to get rid of him: perhaps in hope that the climate would bury all secrets. It did not: & Hennessy has held a series of colonial appointments, in all of which he has shown some ability, but more of capacity & disposition to intrigue. In Mauritius he has exerted himself to stimulate the French jealousy of English officials, and will never if he can help it promote or employ any one not of French descent. This may perhaps be excused on the Home Rule principle: but it is not advisable for a governor of a British colony, especially such a colony as Mauritius, to tell everybody that he is Irish, not English, & that he comes from a country which has had more to complain of from England than any other. This language Hennessy is reported to hold: &, though there may be exaggeration in the report, it cannot well be wholly fiction.

. . . The common talk is that the quarrel between the two Houses will end in a compromise: the Redistribution Bill being brought in, & perhaps read a second time: on which the Lords would let the Franchise Bill pass. This is a simple & rational solution: too simple, I fear, to be accepted.

28 Oct. 1884: . . . Office at 2.00, stayed till 5.00. Saw Col. Warren[58], the col. sec. of Cyprus, who reported well of the state of the island, both as to prosperity & contentment: but I found he agreed with me that, when the Cypriotes have got from us all they are likely to get, in the shape of roads, harbours, police, & efficient administration, they will do as the Ionians did, cry out for annexation to Greece: & probably they will get it.

Next came a member of the Cape Parliament, a Mr. Irvine[59], a frequent writer to *The Times*: well informed, strongly prejudiced against the Dutch, not foolish, but tedious from anxiety to pour out all he knew. He was with me an hour. Very anxious that the imperial government should assert its authority: saying that at the Cape it was believed among the English that England meant to abandon South Africa altogether: on this point I was able to reassure him. He said the difficulty between the races would be only for a time: the English increase faster than the Dutch, & are helped by immigration: the natives (black) are all on the side of England, hating the Dutch, & with reason: in a few years, as I understood him, there would be an assured English majority in the Cape colony. He was against giving colonial legislatures any control over dependent native tribes: saying that, where that was done, the natives were sure on one pretext or another to be robbed of their lands: this I believe to be true.

. . . After him came Mr. Esselen[60], the former interpreter to the Transvaal deputation. He talked big about the objections which the Boers felt to imperial interference: the hardship of clearing out from Bechuanaland white settlers who had gone there in the belief that the titles to land which they had bought were valid: he asked so many questions that I enquired of him in turn whom he represented, & on whose behalf he made those enquiries? He said on his own account only, he was a colonist, & interested in S. Africa. I told him, but laughing, that I was willing to be cross-examined in parliament but not by visitors at my office: at which he apologised. There was no intended impertinence, but a good deal of colonial bumptiousness. My belief is that he was put on by some agent of the Transvaal to find out whether we were in earnest. . . .

29 Oct. 1884: . . . The Irish have occupied a second night in discussing the Maamtrasna case, which they did with great violence. They interrupted & insulted Gladstone repeatedly in the course of his speech: & they did not conceal that their chief object in asking for an enquiry was to compel Ld Spencer's resignation. They had some radical and some Conservative support, but divided only 48. As far as I can see, the bitterness of Irish feeling against England is quite undiminished.

30 Oct. 1884: Long debate in the Commons yesterday on South Africa, showing a nearly unanimous opinion that Bechuanaland must be protected[61]: the attack turned entirely on the delay in sending out an expedition. But, as this is now to be done, the mere question whether it should be done a little sooner or a little later excited no strong feeling. The debate dropped at the end of the sitting, & apparently will not be renewed.

Indeed I believe the chief object of raising it was to occupy a day, & so delay the franchise bill.

Five new peers are announced: Lord De Vesci[62] & Lord Herries[63] receive English peerages: neither has a son, so these are life peerages only: Ld Arran[64] is also made an English peer: Dodson & Sir Walter James[65] are the other two. All seem fit persons, if more peers are to be made, and apparently that is a necessity just now.

31 Oct. 1884: The papers are full of last night's attack by R. Churchill on Chamberlain, & of his reply. Churchill accused the President of the B. of Trade of personally instigating the late riot at Birmingham: he did not, however, attempt to prove his charge, but merely dwelt on certain indiscretions of language & violent speeches in which Chamberlain has indulged. The latter retaliated by similar charges against his opponents . . . a waste of time as regards public business. The majority for government was only 36, but in a thin house, 214 to 178. The debate on the address still goes on . . .

Finished correcting a speech for Hansard, which I had almost entirely to rewrite: a tedious & useless occupation.

1 Nov. 1884: . . . Saw Mr. Warr, & talk to him about the City Companies Commission. He tells me that the report is thought fair & moderate by the majority of those whom it concerns: they probably expected that the total abolition of the companies would be recommended, & are glad things are no worse. He believes they would not resist a bill founded on the report, except in details.

. . . The H. of C. was pleased to waste another evening on a theoretical discussion of 'fair trade'. The speeches were not remarkable, & the attendance, I am told, was small. But the object of the speakers was attained: the whole night being taken up. This practice of using the opportunity given by the address for discussion of every subject under the sun, however unconnected with present legislation, is new, & I suppose has been taken up as a method of obstructing which is not easy to repress. The minority say: 'All legislation that is likely to pass in this parliament is unfavourable to our interests – therefore let us have as little of it as we can.' And it is possible that a good many Liberals by profession feel with them, at least so far that they will not interfere until the intention to obstruct becomes too evident. And then they will denounce it, but do as little as they can. . . .

2 Nov. 1884 (Sunday): . . . I have not noted the Cabinet of Friday, & indeed there was little notable in it: except for the look of things, I scarcely know why it was called, for all that we settled might have been dealt with departmentally. Trevelyan sat for the first time. Some talk about the smallness of the majority on Thursday night, which was partly accident, due notice not given: partly abstention of certain Whigs who do not like Chamberlain. A Whig lady said of the two radical members: 'Chamberlain is not a gentleman & does not try to be one: Dilke tries & does not succeed.' Unjust, yet with a certain approach to truth in it. Talk of the commission on merchant shipping, for which it has been difficult to find a chairman: Cairns, Richmond, Argyll, refused: Goschen also: in the end Aberdeen accepted: honest he will be, but rather weak. The shipowners insist that Chamberlain shall not sit, he being their accuser: he fairly answers that they also are parties interested, & should be excluded if he is. In the end we agreed to put on two more members, which it is thought will pacify the more reasonable section of them.

Some discussion followed as to S. African affairs, & it was agreed to stop two regiments, one intended for Egypt, the other returning from India, in case they should be wanted.

Childers raised the question of public payment for passages of royal persons in special steamers, which is costly, & needless: the Queen, however, holds on to it as her right, & we agreed to let the matter stand over, there being more important questions to settle with H.M. As a sample of the jobs that are possible even now, it was mentioned that formerly the royal carriages, horses, etc., were sent by sea to Aberdeen on their way to Balmoral: this practice being found inconvenient is discontinued: but the Queen charges their conveyance by land to the Admiralty, on the plea that she might have sent them by sea if she liked!

Discussion as to civil servants becoming candidates for seats in parliament: general agreement that they ought to resign their offices before beginning a canvas.

Trevelyan related a conversation with the Queen. He says she is now impressed with the danger of a dissolution: understanding that after the agitation of the autumn it would open the whole question of an organic change in the constitution. Richmond has been dealt with, & is anxious for a settlement. – Hartington had seen Hicks Beach, who talked freely, but did not seem to wish for an arrangement. He declared himself in favour of electoral districts, or at least of a much nearer approach to them than is embodied in the scheme laid before the Cabinet & accidentally published.

This, I think, was the chief part of what passed.

3 Nov. 1884: . . . Office: received a deputation on S. African affairs, headed by Sir D. Currie: what they chiefly came to ask was the annexation of Zululand. This I declined, & left them not well pleased. One or two of the speakers were rather violent in their language. . . .

4 Nov. 1884: . . . At 1.30 went to the site of the new National Liberal Club . . . for the laying of the first stone. As chairman of the building company, I was put into the chair: & opened the proceedings with a short speech. Gladstone followed, & spoke nearly half an hour: dwelling much, & strongly, on the waste of time in the Commons, & the necessity of more stringent rules if the House is not to be discredited. Granville, Hartington, Harcourt, & Dilke followed. The speaking was in an immense tent, the audience large & crowded. The whole affair lasted two hours. I had a very cordial reception, & the Premier one which was enthusiastic. Some of the speeches were strong against the Lords, though none exactly to be called violent. The Premier, I think, the most moderate of all. . . .

5 Nov. 1884: Troubled with cold & cough, the latter unusual with me: did not leave the house: but papers came hourly from the office, so that no time was lost.

Wrote to Northbrook to suggest that he should put his Egyptian scheme in the form of a mem. or minute, so that the Cabinet may see, & have leisure to consider it. (He answered that he was doing this, and in fact I got his report next day or Friday.)

. . . Received from Granville an unexpected letter, asking me to lend him £8,000, for a year or less, paying 5% for it: the reason for the demand being that he has failed to receive from his ironworks the sum of £17,000 which he expected, owing, as he says, to legal difficulties. I do not much love loans: but it was not easy to refuse: &, unless Ld G.

is ruined, which there seems no reason to suppose, I presume the money is safe. I therefore wrote at once agreeing: & wrote to Coutts to sell out £8,000 Consols[66].

Busy with office papers: saw Drage, who sent me to bed early: & in fact I was not unwilling, being feverish & full of cold.

6 Nov. 1884: Lay in bed till near 11.00, then dressed, but did not leave the house all day. Much troubled & weakened with heavy cold & frequent coughing . . . Much business from the office: in fact I have seldom had a heavier mass of papers to deal with, but except some instructions for Sir C. Warren they were not specially important.

I dined upstairs, but went very early to bed.

7 Nov. 1884: . . . Sent Granville a cheque for £8,000, leaving it to him to settle what security for repayment he chooses to give. He sent me back two promissory notes.

. . . There being a Cabinet at 2.00, and I unable to attend it, I wrote to the Premier excusing myself: and mentioned two matters which I supposed would be discussed. One was a quarrel between Ld Spencer and the corporation of Limerick, in regard of which I expressed a hope that he would be supported, & the law vindicated: for the proceedings of the Corporation are mere sedition. The Premier answering my note only says that it is a 'very ugly business'. The other subject was the Northbrook report: as to this I said I hoped it would not be rejected summarily, but at least fully considered: that my first impressions had been against it: that I saw all the objections, which were grave: but on the other hand it was clear we could not get out of Egypt at an early date: since the failure of the conference we could not say we were there with the consent of Europe: that we could not afford to have everybody against us: that, if we held Egypt, we must make ourselves responsible for the country being decently administered: and it was awkward on our sole authority to violate the international engagement which secured the bondholders in their rights. If we refused to make sacrifices such as N. suggested, might we not have to spend a great deal more in military preparations? Mr. G. replies that this matter is not urgent: and that it 'oppresses him enormously'.

Late in the evening the Premier called, & talked of what had passed. He said Northbrook's plan had not been even mentioned, being thought unripe. The Limerick affair, as I understood him, had been postponed also, it being thought that payment of the sum due might be obtained without proceedings against the Corporation. The chief subject discussed had been redistribution: and he spoke in a hopeful tone of the prospects of a settlement. He was willing to defer to the ideas of the opposition, in favour of a larger plan of redistributing seats than he had favoured at first: that is, he would do so if agreement could thereby be secured. He had suggested a meeting between Hartington & Dilke on the one side & two opposition leaders on the other, & appeared to think it would lead to some result. – While he talked, his confidence of success communicated itself to me: but reflecting upon it afterwards I can see but little substantial ground for his hopes.

8 Nov. 1884 (Saturday): . . . Cold gradually diminishing . . . Wrote to Dr. Chapman[67], now of Paris, declining to buy the *Westminster Review*, which he offers for sale, but telling him that I will let him know if any probable purchaser occurs . . . Left for Keston early, arriving there with M. about 4.00.

The event of the week has been the sudden & unexpected death of Fawcett, the Postmaster General, at the age of 51 or 52. He had, I imagine, never really recovered from his severe illness of two years ago. He is in many ways a loss: he set an example of steady adhesion to his often peculiar ideas, which inspired respect: and, while on most points not merely a liberal, but a radical, he detested the modern semi-socialistic school, which is constantly trying to increase the power of the state, & to do things for men which economists think they ought to be left to do for themselves. He was in fact a sound economist of the older section. He had the defects of his qualities: dogmatism, angularity, and a tendency to pedantry, which however his good sense kept in order. His infirmity of blindness rather helped than hindered his parliamentary success: for it inclined the House to tolerate much from him that would not have been accepted without some such excuse – a certain dry & professorial manner of speaking which seldom wholly left him: and it created sympathy even among opponents. As an administrator Fawcett was hard working & efficient: the only complaint I ever heard against him was that he chose to ignore the Treasury control & spoke & acted as if head of an independent department. But that the public did not know &, if they had, would have liked him all the better for it. I am not sure that he did not die at the right moment: for his admission to the Cabinet could not have been long delayed: & I doubt if he would have long continued to act with a [word missing] set of colleagues.

9 Nov. 1884: . . . Again examined Northbrook's report with a view to discussion at the next Cabinet. Gave M. £100 to pay for her Swedish doctor, & for her secretaries.

The language of the newspapers on both sides is now favourable to the idea of a compromise or arrangement between the two Houses: but neither side seems inclined to give way, and I am less hopeful than the multitude. The franchise bill passing its second reading in the Commons shows that there is no indifference to it there: and all I hear of the temper of the country points to the probability of violent displays of feeling if the bill is again lost in the Lords. But popular feelings are not durable: a success or a disaster on the Nile may turn them one way or the other, & cause this quarrel to fall into the background.

South Warwickshire is gained by the Conservatives, who lost the second seat by a very small majority at the last elections.

10 Nov. 1884: London . . . See Drage, who reports all going on well, but care & medicine necessary for some days yet.

. . . Letter from Ld A. Loftus[68] asking for an extension of his term, which he will not get. His government has been a failure. He is not only foolish, which might not matter, but pompous & inclined to swagger: which colonists do not like any one to do except themselves. His sons take after him, & are even less appreciated.

I had very little business after 5.00 p.m. & simply rested.

11 Nov. 1884: At 11.00, to Treasury Chambers to meet Childers & Hartington on the subject of expenses to be incurred for the Bechuana expedition. We sat an hour, & settled various details. Thence to Admiralty, where met Northbrook, Hartington, Childers, Morley, Brand[69], Sir A. Clarke[70], & others, on the question of naval defences & coaling stations. We sat 1½ hour. Then to office: at 2.00 a Cabinet, where all present except Spencer. We sat till 4.00. Thence, being weary, & not yet quite well, I went home, & did the rest of my work there.

Childers talks of the state of the country as regards prosperity. He says that, though profits are greatly divided, & so cut down, the working classes are well off in general: there is no falling off in their consuming power: the income tax, too, now brings in £2,000,000 for every penny, which is more than ever before.

Talk with him & others about the altered state of feeling among the opposition about the franchise bill: last week they were all for conciliation, now they are defiant & reject every idea of compromise. The chief cause is the S. Warwickshire election[71]: which they think forebodes further successes: and are more & more eager for a dissolution in consequence. They rest their hopes on two feelings: one the desire for renewed protection among the farmers, which is believed to be strong & general: the other jealousy of the labourers being admitted to the franchise.

Some talk among us about Bannerman's appointment to the Irish Office. It seems to be intensely unpopular in Ireland: he is a Scotchman, & supposed to be a freethinker[72], both qualities disagreeable to the Irish, but where would they have found a secretary to please them? It is understood that the R.C. hierarchy, who used to be suspicious of Parnell, are reconciled to him & accept his political leadership, which if true (& it was spoken of as certain) makes the situation more serious than it has been yet. In Cabinet, the chief business done was to consider the means of paying for the Soudan & S. African expeditions. The total sum required is between £2,500,000 and £2,600,000, of which Childers believes that he can provide £500,000 out of revenue already voted: the remaining £2,000,000 must be met by another penny on the income tax. Some alternative propositions were talked of, as increase of house tax, reimposition of duty on horses, or raising the tax on beer: but it was felt that none of these would do. The necessity for the S. African expenditure was admitted by all except Harcourt, who ranted in his usual style.

We next came to discuss the possibility of coming to terms with the opposition as to redistribution: but all the H. of C. men agreed that a complete change had come over the Conservative mind since last week, & that they would now listen to no terms. Chaplin said to some one, who had referred to Cross's conciliatory speech of last week: 'Poor old Cross – he was drunk as usual – but we will set that all right.' It is clear to me now that no compromise is possible.

12 Nov. 1884: . . . Letter from my sister, in distress about her son, now working at the office. His manner & conduct have been odd, & she ascribes it to drink, of which however neither I nor Antrobus saw any signs in him. He is disposed to throw up his engagement in the office: which is very indifferent to me, but will not be in his own interest.

. . . Weighed myself, 14 st. 12 lbs., which is less by 3 lbs. than last month.

13 Nov. 1884: . . . Saw Drage, who reports well, but forbids me to speak in public, or use my voice much . . . Office 2.30 to 5.00: saw only Herbert & Ashley.

. . . A box was sent round by the Premier, asking leave of the Cabinet to bring in a redistribution bill before the franchise bill goes into committee in the Lords – that is, I presume, supposing he can make terms with the opposition leaders. I gave my consent very willingly.

Reading Croker's memoirs[73], which I have finished: they are full of interest, & raise my opinion of a man whose character has been (I think unjustly) lowered by the anger which his criticisms provoked. Macaulay as a Whig partisan hated him with an undisguised hatred, & did all he could, which was much, to ruin his edition of Boswell by a hostile review: Disraeli from some personal reason which I have never known, probably connected with the *Quarterly*, attacked him in *Coningsby* under the name of Rigby: in that sketch he is represented as a compound of all the meanest vices which a man can display: a parasite, a doer of dirty work for great men, servile & insolent. Now we have the real Croker, & nothing can be less like his portrait. He appears as the friend of the D. of Wellington, of Peel, Canning, Graham, Walter Scott, & many more of the leading men of his day, corresponding with them, & indeed reading them lectures and offering advice unasked, in the style of a teacher. Sycophancy certainly was no fault of his: the tendency of his nature was to domineer: and he indulged it. As an administrator, he was laborious & certainly no jobber: as a politician, a steady Tory of the old school: full of prejudices, but evidently sincere in them: and his freedom from personal ambition was proved by his voluntary retirement after the reform bill passed. As a reviewer he was harsh, dogmatic, and sometimes violent: which was more the fashion of that day than of this. It is easy to understand that he should have made many enemies: which no doubt he did. I remember him in 1847-1850: met him at Wimpole[74] among other places: he was then old, about 70, his brilliancy in conversation had left him, & he was tedious. He talked much, in a slow oracular tone, which grew wearisome when the oracle delivered nothing but commonplaces. Needless to add that he was intensely pessimistic: I remember his saying solemnly that the question before England was not under what form of government we should live, but whether the institution of private property should continue to exist. . . .

15 Nov. 1884: Work at home till 12.00, when to a Cabinet, which sat till near 3.00: but we did not do nor settle much.

. . . In Cabinet, it was mentioned that news is received from Gordon, who was safe on 4 Nov., & could hold out 40 days from that date.

On the franchise question it was agreed that nothing more can be done in the way of negociation with the leaders of opposition: that has been tried & failed: they insist not merely on seeing the redistribution bill, but on its being passed through the Commons before they will pass the franchise bill: which is an extravagant claim, & cannot be agreed to: the only thing that remains to do is to make public the offers which we have made, & so appeal to the rank & file of the party against its leaders. And this will accordingly be done on Monday in both Houses.

Note (20 Nov.): This was a perfectly accurate summary of what passed, though two days later all was changed. Success was despaired of when it was nearest. . . .

17 Nov. 1884: . . . H. of Lords at 4.15: there was a moderately full attendance: Granville made the promised statement, offering to read the Redistribution Bill a second time in the Commons before the Franchise Bill was finally passed through the Lords: this concession, which went, I think, a little beyond what we had settled in the Cabinet of Saturday, evidently took the opposition by surprise: some of them even gave a faint cheer: it was clear that they had not expected so much. Granville tells me that Cairns & Richmond are known to be in favour of a peaceable settlement: Salisbury of course is against: but the bulk of the party are growing alarmed, & would like to see the dispute ended.

I walked home with Spencer: he seemed discouraged as to the state of things in Ireland: especially at the failure to convict a noted Fenian called Fitzgerald[75], the most important capture, he said, that has been made since 1868: the proofs were conclusive, but the jury acquitted him. He was displeased also at the course taken by the Cabinet (at the sitting from which I was absent) about the Limerick magistrates: he thought they ought to have been proceeded against, whereas the proposal to legislate on the question gives them a victory, & causes endless delay at the best: I quite agreed with him. He saw little or no improvement in the feeling of the people: the future he thought very dark.

Harcourt has sent round a box with a minute on the question of Egypt: very able: but quite impracticable: he wants us to give notice to the powers that we shall evacuate the country at the end of 12 months, & in the meanwhile to refuse all financial assistance. The difficulty is immense, & I think increasing, but we cannot cut the knot in that way.

18 Nov. 1884: Lawrence came to talk about Mrs. H. Stanley's affairs: she has borrowed from everybody who would lend at any rate of interest that they chose to ask: & is being threatened with legal proceedings. I gave him full power to negociate with the creditors. Lawson called to talk over the situation.

Eustace Cecil came to luncheon, & told us that the opposition has accepted the terms offered, so that the dispute is settled.

– Office. Saw there the Australian agents, who came to speak about the French convicts bill, and pressed for a fresh representation to be made. I agreed, provided that F.O. think it expedient. They then talked of international arrangements to be made for the S. Pacific islands: a complete reversal of their language of last year, when they would listen to nothing except annexation of them all. One of them said laughingly that I had 'rapped their knuckles' last year, which is true, so far as that I expressed dissent from their ideas of that date: I reminded them civilly of the change, which they did not deny, & we parted with entire agreement.

To the Lords, where found a full house, the galleries & steps of the throne especially crowded. There was, however, little to hear: Kimberley spoke barely five minutes in moving the second reading: Salisbury was about twice as long in reply, accepting the compromise, but asking for fuller explanation on certain points. Granville gave it, & all was over in half an hour[76]. The House then emptied, & the remaining business was unimportant.

Home, quiet evening . . .

19 Nov. 1884: Much business from office, but disposed of all.

. . . The compromise is naturally in everybody's mouth: and I have seldom known any move in politics which was so generally approved. The radicals are angry, having hoped for a crusade against the H. of Lords: but even they are much consoled by having secured the passing of the bill, and by the knowledge that a large redistribution of seats will follow. The Whigs & moderate Liberals are specially pleased, having foreseen a quarrel in which they could not have sided heartily with either party. The Conservatives affect to treat the arrangement as a victory, which it is not: & profess to feel sure that, if the fight had gone on, they should have won: but they do not pretend to regret the result.

– The most remarkable part of the affair is the moderation shown by the leaders on both sides: contrary to their natures & habits of mind: I explain it thus: Gladstone is old, quite fit for fighting when he must, but no longer looking forward to a sharp struggle with the pleasure he might have felt some years ago: he wants to pass these bills & retire with credit: Salisbury, on the other hand, knows well the real weakness of the H. of Lords, & is not the dupe of his own big words. And on both sides it may reasonably have been felt that the quarrel was not one worth pushing to the last extremities.

20 Nov. 1884: . . . Work on office papers, & cleared all.

. . . Cabinet at 2.00: nominally: but we did no business till 2.20, & separated at 3.30. Then office for an hour. . . . Home by 6.00.

. . . The election at Hackney, caused by Fawcett's death, has seated a Liberal by 15,000 votes to 8,000, in round numbers[77]. A close contest had been expected. The chief interest of the affair consists in the fact that the Conservative candidate put forward protection to native industry, or 'fair trade' as its new name is, as the first article in his programme.

Much gossip about an action for breach of promise, brought by Miss Finney, a popular actress, [against] Cairns's eldest son, Lord Garmoyle. The youth, who is not very wise, proposed to her, was accepted, induced his family to consent, & then broke it off, as some say, by their persuasion. She got £10,000 damages, which had been offered in the first instance as an amicable settlement, but refused. I believe the truth to be that the Cairnses gave their consent sincerely, trying to make the best of it, but the young lady's free and easy ways, & unrefined manners, were too much for their tolerance. They are well out of the scrape, even at the cost of £10,000. . . .

22 Nov. 1884: Cabinet at 11.30, which sat only till 12.00, to consider Northbrook's report. A kind of compromise had been arrived at between him & Childers, by which his plan is to be adopted with considerable modifications. So far all was plain sailing: but N. wished his report to be published as it stands, & refused to listen to the obvious objection that we could not possibly carry through parliament the plan of the Cabinet, or recommend it to the powers, if a rival plan were put out at the same time on the authority of our own commissioner in Egypt. N. however said that he had given his opinion: he would acquiesce in ours, seeing all the difficulties of the case, but would not farther it. In this we were compelled to agree that he was only within his right: in the end it was settled that he should publish only that part of his report which consists of a statement of facts: his conclusions being treated as confidential, & meant only for the use of his colleagues. This expedient, which was indeed the fairest that could have been hit upon, satisfied all parties.

(Of the Cabinets of the 19th & 20th I have kept few notes. They were confused & disorderly: & the discussion turned chiefly on small points of detail respecting the terms to be made with the opposition leaders. They, it seems, are in a conciliatory mood & seem really to wish for a settlement. The chief point of difference is that they press for the grouping of small towns, whereby to take the urban voters out of the counties, & divide town & country by a sharp line of separation. This we do not like, & say so.) . . .

24 Nov. 1884: . . . Saw . . . Manners Sutton[78], [Lord] Canterbury's brother, who wants any place, however small, in any climate. I have only a clerkship in Honduras, but he jumped at that. He says it is absolutely impossible to find employment in London: he was in business, but his employers either failed or reduced their staff: there are many others in the like position.

To the Lords, where all was over in an hour: then to office again. Occupied with an enormous bundle of papers concerning one Rapinet, a magistrate at Malta, accused of unnatural offences. He has been suspended, & appeals to the office. There are at least six hours' work in the papers, & they must be read.

25 Nov. 1884: . . . Working on the Rapinet case. Dull foggy day. Finished minute on the R.[apinet] case . . . Office 2.30, stayed till 5.00. Business all routine.

Home, & by 6.20 train to Windsor to dine & sleep, the invitation having reached me only this afternoon. M. was asked also, but declined on the plea of a bad cold. Found there the Gladstones, Sir J. Macdonald, Ld Thurlow, Ly Abercromby, & a few more. The Princesses Louisa & Beatrice came in with the Queen.

H.M. looked older than I have yet seen her, more grey & bent: but was in good spirits & good humour, & accepted with evident pleasure the compliments which I paid her on the part she has taken in settling our domestic differences. She said she had had great trouble: that Cairns & Richmond were easy to deal with, but Salisbury very much otherwise: she had despaired of success. She is proud of having shown her influence, & the enjoyment is one which nobody need grudge her, for it has been usefully exercised. Nothing passed of special interest: only Ponsonby told me that she has talked much to him about the arrangement & says that everything might be settled so easily, if it were not for party.

. . . Talk with Gladstone: he has been reading Malmesbury's book, says it is amusing, not ill-natured, but full of inaccuracies. He (G.) says also that last week was nearly the busiest he has ever gone through – with the conference at Berlin & the franchise & redistribution arrangement: both to be dealt with at the same time.

Some talk with Sir J. Macdonald[79], of which I remember nothing special except that he again expressed his conviction that the imperial federation scheme would not work.

26 Nov. 1884: Left Windsor early . . . reached home by 10.30. Working on office papers all day. Home at 5.30.

Dined at the Empire Club, a dinner given in honour of Sir J. Macdonald . . . The guests may have been from 60 to 80 . . . the whole affair intolerably tedious. Sir John certainly spoke very well, occupying nearly an hour. I did not get home till 1.00.

Settled the Maltese case with Wingfield[80]. . . . I am inclined to believe that he is really innocent, and that the charge is a plot to extort blackmail . . .

27 Nov. 1884: . . . Sent £20 to the Birkbeck Institution . . .

Cabinet at 12.00, but business did not begin till 12.30, & even then the discussion was irregular & confused. Office till 4.30, when came away, there being no business left to do. In Cabinet, we discussed redistribution, as to which the negociations go on pleasantly enough. The Conservatives rather oddly seem more against small boroughs than we are: we had proposed total disfranchisement only up to a line of 10,000 population, which after discussion was raised to 15,000, and possibly may go as high as 20,000. Grouping we object to, but we have agreed to a large number of single-member districts, which in an indirect way give a certain representation of minorities. Boundaries of boroughs we wish to have fixed by a commission of three or four members, to report by February. The least popular part of the scheme, as I expect, will be the addition of 10 or 12 members to the total number, & the retention undiminished of the excessive Irish representation, which will be called with truth a reward given to sedition & disloyalty. The Premier dwelt a good deal on the necessity of settling the matter at once, saying remarkably: 'This negociation is unprecedented: it can be justified only by necessity: & nothing but success can save it from being ridiculous.'

The only member of the Cabinet who stood up strongly for the small boroughs was

Childers: I don't know why. Chamberlain & Dilke acquiesce in, but greatly dislike, the single-member districts: they would have preferred to have several members for each constituency, & the constituencies larger.

I have now sat nearly 2 years in this Cabinet. It has been harmonious, though not very businesslike. The Premier listens with more patience, & speaks less than anywhere else. He is far from being dictatorial, though necessarily his opinion has greater weight than that of anyone else. Granville mostly confines himself to foreign affairs: his deafness prevents his taking much part in general discussion. Harcourt harangues more than anybody, & very cleverly, but is seldom in the same mind two days running. Chamberlain & Dilke both assert themselves a good deal, & the former is apt to threaten resignation, though indirectly. He 'will find it impossible to support' this, that, or the other. He is not much liked: Dilke on the contrary is popular. The Chancellor, Northbrook, Trevelyan, & Childers are generally silent except when specially appealed to. Ld Spencer attends too rarely to know much of what is doing, except on Irish subjects. Kimberley is less loquacious in Cabinet than anywhere else. Hartington's observations are frequent, but generally mere growls of dissent. He does not like his situation, & makes the fact evident. . . .

1 Dec. 1884: London by usual train. Rain falling, some fog, & the roads deep in mud . . . so dark that I wrote & read by lamplight all morning. Saw Antrobus & Sanderson: read, wrote, etc., till 1.30.

. . . Wrote to Hale that I will give £1,000 to the extension of the Bootle hospital . . . The borough has done well for me, & I can afford this.

Office, where as at home obliged to work by lamplight. Stayed there till 4.15, when to Lords. Not many peers were there, though the franchise bill stood for committee, for it was known that there would be no debate. Salisbury asked for an adjournment till Thursday, which after a little talk was agreed to. Redesdale deplored the compromise, & was not consoled by his leader . . . All was over by 5.00 p.m.

Returned to the office, & worked there till late.

In the Commons, Gladstone brought in the redistribution bill: he spoke 50 minutes, studiously avoiding all controversial matter: there was much curiosity, but no excitement (so I am told), it being felt that the matter was settled.

Courtney has resigned from his office at the Treasury in consequence of no provision being made for the representation of minorities.

The scheme is larger than that of 1832 in respect of the number of seats redistributed: 160 in all, besides those added.

2 Dec. 1884: . . . Day cold, raw, & foggy, & having taken medicine I stayed at home till it was time to go to the Cabinet. Lawson called, but had no particular news. Cabinet sat from 12.00 to 2.30: thence office till 4.30: thence to the Lords, till 7.00: when home & quiet evening.

In Cabinet, Granville told us that the Egyptian question is at a standstill, no government seems willing to express any opinion: the Germans wish for a meeting of the ambassadors which would be equivalent to an informal conference. A question arose of sending Blum Pasha to assist Malet, as to whom Childers said he would not trust him farther than he could see him. Northbrook, irritated, answered: 'You have no right to say that', & showed some temper. In the end he was rejected on the plea that his going to Berlin would be generally known, & would give too formal a character to the affair.

Granville said in the course of this discussion that 'the French government is more in Bismarck's pocket than ever'. **Northbrook** then proceeded to explain his naval scheme, which he repeated later to the Lords. He laid stress on the probable importance in the future of torpedoes: dwelt on the probability of future changes in ships, as a reason for not doing too much at once: said he saw no reason to fear Russia as a naval power, & we were still superior to France at sea. **Harcourt** laid stress on the need we have for what he called a police navy, in addition to the fighting navy, having trade & colonies everywhere. **Childers** thought much money had been wasted in patching up ships that were & are of no permanent value. **Granville** said the U.S. attaché had told him that we were stronger at sea than France & Italy together, or than France & Germany together, but not than all three. Some talk followed about Whitworth, his guns, the difficulty of dealing with him, of which Hartington complained loudly. **Chamberlain** made sarcastic remarks as to the *Pall Mall Gazette*, which has got up this naval scare[81] – it was governing the country, not we. – The original proposal was that £10,000,000 should be spent, the outlay spread over 5 years: £3,100,000 on the navy, the rest on guns & fortifications. But at this point the Premier interposed in an unexpected manner.

He had been wholly silent, & ill pleased, to judge by his looks: but now he broke out. He talked of his fixed intention to retire: the time for his withdrawal was near: he felt that he should not be justified in opposing the decision of his colleagues, when he could not expect to be present to defend them: he had therefore acquiesced in this scheme, but he must protest against it. The outlay on the navy he did not object to: the rest he thought useless &, if he had intended to remain in office, nothing would have made him agree to it. One thing he praised: the decision that no part of the charge was to be borne by a loan, but all honestly paid for out of taxes. There was silence when he ended: **Harcourt** broke it by complaining that the Cabinet had not had due notice of this proposal: he objected to forts: and diverged into a criticism of the Portsmouth defences. He would spend more if necessary on ships, less on forts. Earthworks could be raised easily, & at short notice. **Dilke** thought we wanted more information, especially as to the plan of fortifying the coasts. He agreed with Harcourt about earthworks. **Northbrook** said if nothing was done about forts we should require larger naval defences. **Chamberlain** thought the Premier's statement very important. If he in his personal judgment was adverse, the case was altered. **D.[erby]** spoke much in the same sense, agreeing in the naval plan, condemning the rest. In the end we agreed to propose an outlay of £5,500,000, to be spread over 5 years. **Hartington** consenting, reluctantly, & in a manner more than usually surly, to postpone the War Office demands. . . .

4 Dec. 1884: . . . Office till 4.30 when to the Lords. There the Franchise Bill went through committee, after irrelevant speeches from Wemyss, Brabourne, & Fortescue: that poor lunatic, Ld Denman, moved some amendments, which came to nothing: no serious objections were taken. The House was not full, about 50 peers present. . . . Home, & quiet evening, but found a great mass of office papers.

Childers came to see me in the afternoon, about Australian affairs, & in conversation said he was convinced that Gladstone would retire as soon as the two bills were passed. Kimberley, to whom I quoted this opinion, said the same thing, adding a reason which had not occurred to me: 'It will probably be necessary to renew the Irish Crimes Act: to this Gladstone, who was only with great difficulty brought to acquiesce in passing it in the first instance, will never consent: it will seem to him like an acknowledgment of failure: and he will be glad to escape from the difficulty by retiring.'

5 Dec. 1884: Lawrence called . . . He talked of the difficulty of selling land just now, especially in Essex & Lincolnshire, where he says there are thousands of acres unlet, & going out of cultivation.

. . . W.P. Talbot came to luncheon: he said the Conservatives as a body were not well pleased with the passing of the bill, nor with the Seats Bill: some of them doubted whether they should return 100 members to the next parliament.

Forster called to talk about S. Africa: he also discussed the bill: said he approved the single-member clause, as the only practicable method of giving a representation to local minorities: he admitted that it was generally unpopular among the politicians of the towns, but merely, as he thought, because it disturbs the arrangements of the wire pullers, & lessens their influence: if this be true, & I think it likely, it is the best thing I have heard of the plan, & justifies the opposition in the stress they laid upon it.

Office 2.30 to 4.30: thence to the Lords, where business chiefly formal: the Franchise Bill was read a third time, without a word said: a thin House, & only a slight cheer when it passed. Truro asked a question about Egypt, which Salisbury made use of as a peg to hang a speech upon. – Talk with Kimberley about the vacancy at Bombay: he offers it to Ld Reay, but doubts his acceptance[82]. We discussed the fitness of A. Gordon for the place: he is unpleasant & ungracious, but able.

6 Dec. 1884: . . . Ministers are scattered, Gladstone gone to Hawarden, Granville to Bournemouth: few will be left in London. The sudden collapse of the reform bill agitation has left politicians with a bewildered feeling of having a new situation to deal with, yet not knowing how to begin. No person on either side can in the least judge what the new voters will be or do. The Conservatives seem to be taking up protection to native industry under its new name of fair trade. – Sclater Booth who, though without talent, has fair sense, seems to have gone in for that in a late speech. That, and imperialism, which practically means increase of armaments & extension of territory, seem to be just now their leading ideas.

If Churchill speaks in their name, the idea of 'Tory democracy' is to make things pleasant to the working classes by spending money lavishly in giving employment, such money being of course not raised by taxation, which would be disagreeable, but by loan. This system, the same adopted by the last Napoleon in France, is an utterly reckless one as regards the future, but for the moment has advantages. It pleases the workers who are employed, & the capitalists who find an investment, & the taxpayers who are glad to escape without fresh burdens: the only interests that suffer are those of the future. To these, one may expect a democracy to be indifferent: yet it is just to remember that America has set us a good example in the direction of paying off war debt: a better one than we did 50 years ago.

7 Dec. 1884 (Sunday): Keston. Day, fine, mild, & pleasant. Three pouches from office, but nothing special. Read a good deal to M. . . .

. . . Rather depressed & bored, for no particular reason, but that I see few people (M., from the state of her eyes, being unfit to give dinners, even if the house were in a condition for such) & there is nothing exciting in the daily routine of official work.

Of colonial matters on hand, the most important are:

1) The New Guinea protectorate, which has passed out of my hands, & is in a fair way to get settled.

2) The Bechuana business: which is unpleasant & stupid, being forced upon us by opinion here, but will probably succeed, though at more cost than it is worth.
3) The federal Australian bill: about which I do not anticipate trouble.
4) Zululand: a muddle, & likely to remain so.
5) French & German rivalries in various parts of Africa. These may long continue to give trouble: but they concern F.O. more than C.O.

I don't think there is serious trouble ahead in any other part of the world: faction in Malta, riots in Trinidad, & distress in the sugar islands generally, are matters of local importance, but not likely to cause trouble in parliament or even in Downing St.

The chief administrative danger to my thinking lies in the careless, slipshod way in which Cabinet business is done: questions taken up, talked about, dropped with no decision taken, & then after some weeks one finds that they have been settled by the sole authority of some one department, perhaps with, perhaps without, the sanction of the Prime Minister. I trace in his speech & manner no sign of old age: but I can scarcely think that in his best days he would have let things slide as he does now. To this hour I do not know who was responsible for the sending of Gordon to Khartoum: nor when the expedition for his relief was finally settled. This latter proceeding, it is fair to say, had become absolutely inevitable, & we all felt it so: still it was important enough to justify a formal discussion in Cabinet.

8 Dec. 1884: Wet warm morning . . . reached the Square at 10.50. . . . Office at usual time: saw there, besides officials, the Maltese magistrate, Dr. Rapinet, who wished to state his case personally. His manner confirmed my previous impression of his innocence, & I shall do what is possible to enable him to clear his character. . . . My chief business today was another case of a suspended magistrate: one Gibbons, a district judge in Jamaica . . . I kept the papers to consider at leisure.

Walk an hour in the dark for exercise: dull, but useful.

9 Dec. 1884: Wet day . . . disposed of all business: office 2.00 to 5.00: then walk an hour in the dark for exercise.

Münster came to see me late: he laughed at Bismarck's suspicions that we are intriguing against his colonial policy: but was glad to be able to give the requisite assurances: Bismarck's last craze is that the expedition to Bechuanaland is a menace directed against the new German colony of Angra Pequena! I got the map, showed Count M. that 500 miles of nearly waterless desert lay between Bechuanaland and the coast, & had no difficulty in showing him that the apprehension was absurd. It would be serious if these alarms were simulated, since they would then indicate a desire to pick a quarrel: but both Meade & Malet write from Berlin that they are apparently sincere, & that the great minister knows nothing of these colonial questions, & is distrustful owing to ignorance.

10 Dec. 1884: . . . Dined with the Granvilles, meeting . . . C. Villiers[83]. Pleasant enough. C. Villiers now 80 or more, talking as acutely & sarcastically as ever, but dirtier as to hands & linen than I ever saw anyone in a drawing room. He thought no man could form the least guess as to what the new electors would do or be: did not think they would be violent, at least not at first. . . .

12 Dec. 1884: Indoors all day, feeling ill with cough, cold, & some fever. Went to bed at 5.00 p.m. . . .

Papers from the office were brought to me both yesterday & today, so that there has been no interruption to public business.

Promised £1,000 in aid of an extension of the Bootle hospital, which I was glad to have an opportunity of doing, the town having many claims upon me, & I not caring to give very largely in answer to clerical applications, which the majority of those made to me are.

Disposed of the usual routine business from the office . . .

13 Dec. 1884: Indoors again all day, but disposed of the office business as it came.

Letter from Gladstone, asking my concurrence as to giving Meade the C.B. I willingly agreed.

In evening, heard from the Central News of an attempt, real or sham, to blow up London Bridge with dynamite. There seems to have been no mischief done except breaking a good many windows.

The lull in political affairs is complete: neither party has so far got used to the idea of the compromise, though I believe 9 out of 10 think it right & wise: but for the moment it has put an end to discussion. Conservatives cannot describe a measure as revolutionary to which their own leaders have assented: and Liberals cannot complain of a peaceable settlement which leaves them in possession of all they asked for. Meanwhile the work of fixing boundaries is going on steadily, & so far with little local opposition. One would predict that the whole scheme would pass easily through parliament, but that so complete apparent unanimity, like a very bright morning, suggests the probability of a coming storm. I can hardly think that some attempts will not be made at a diversion, either by getting up a foreign quarrel, or a crisis in Ireland: there must be so many among the Conservatives to whom the change is disagreeable & even alarming.

14 Dec. 1884: Mending in health, & came down to breakfast, but still very weak. I am strangely liable to be pulled down, as the phrase is, by a little fever.

Sent £50 to the Fawcett testimonial, and £15 to Col. Vivian[84], the latter with some reluctance, for I cannot think it consistent with the habits of a gentleman for an utter stranger to beg help of me three times in a few months: & he has had some £30 or £40 already. But I have told him this must be the last application.

. . . Singular trial lately ended: two sailors, wrecked & adrift in a boat, after many days of exposure, & nearly starving, killed & ate a boy who was with them, & who was dying when they killed him. They were picked up, recovered, & did not conceal what they had done. Their defence was that they had acted to save their own lives, & had not sacrificed any life, since the lad who was killed could not in any case have lived many hours. They were tried for murder, & after some legal delays found guilty, but respited at once, & only sentenced to a few months' imprisonment without hard labour: the object of the trial being to assert the principle of the law . . . The result is generally accepted as just: but some people, especially the writers in the *Spectator*, are shocked at the notion that any indulgence should have been shown, & would have hanged them in the interests of high morality[85].

15 Dec. 1884: Death of the Duchess of Somerset[86], reputed the most beautiful woman of her day: I remember her well at Achnacarry (1846? or 1853?) when Malmesbury's guest, & she created a good deal of scandal by perpetual tête-à-têtes with her host. The three sisters (Mrs. Norton & Ly Dufferin the other two) were in their day perhaps the best known & most admired beauties of London, & they had in addition the Sheridan wit & cleverness.

Letters asking for everything that can be asked for, from governorships down to a few shillings, in greater numbers than I think I had ever before. Begging is certainly on the increase . . . and just now depression in trade has caused a good deal of real distress.

. . . Ld Reay[87] who has accepted Bombay called to talk over Indian affairs with me. I think he will do: he is anxious to learn, thoughtful, and rather elaborately polite: not brilliant, nor likely to initiate ideas, but capable of appreciating them when suggested.

16 Dec. 1884 (Tuesday): . . . Bismarck has had a defeat on a question which with us would be one of confidence. He appealed for a vote of £1,000 extra for his office, in connection with the new colonial policy which he has adopted: he declared 'on his oath of office' that it was necessary . . . & made a strong personal appeal. But the vote was refused by 141 to 199, not without insulting comments. The smallness of it makes the blow more felt: but nobody can suppose that the amount was grudged: the refusal can only have been a form of protest against the policy adopted. From this point of view it may be important.

. . . Talk with Sanderson about Ld G. who seems to me growing older, his lapses of memory more frequent, etc. S. says this is rather accidental than habitual, but does not believe he would accept the Premiership if vacated by Gladstone (what then is the alternative?). The truth is, the F.O. is overweighted, especially with Egyptian affairs thrown in.

S.[anderson] tells me that Bismarck, in addition to his other causes of complaint, real or imaginary, is 'frantic' at the selection of Morier, whom he considers as a personal enemy, for Petersburg.

17 Dec. 1884: Saw Antrobus, disposed of all business, & with M. to Knowsley . . . arriving 5.30. Our carriage was of a new construction, having a passage along the compartment, & a stove: but we liked it less than the older sort . . . Day cold & some snow. Many letters, chiefly to beg. One from Mr. R.N. Philips asking help for the S.E. Lancs. registration.

I note it as odd that, with a greater outcry about distress than has been heard of late years (and I presume there must be some reason for it), the deposits in savings banks have increased from £86 to £90 millions in the last twelvemonth, being the most rapid rate of growth yet known. Who are the depositors? I presume, in great measure, clerks, servants, artisans of the higher grade, school teachers, & in general people belonging to the lower middle rather than the working class. Still, the fact is remarkable.

Sir W. Forwood, the leading Tory (or Tory Democrat, as he calls himself) of Liverpool, has written a sensible letter to deprecate the renewed protectionist agitation: pointing out that in America, where every trade is protected, & in France, the same depression exists as here: which is true, & answers many foolish criticisms.

I find among many people a growing opinion, or perhaps rather suspicion, that one of the causes at least of the universal wave of depression is the increased value of gold, consequent on diminished production all over the world. They argue that the great prosperity of the years from 1850 to 1875 was mainly due to the Australian & Californian discoveries, cheapening gold everywhere: & that now a contracted supply is causing an opposite result. I do not think this theory unreasonable, but should not accept it without more enquiry.

18 Dec. 1884: . . . Saw Ward, who brought the book of leases for me to verify. The new rental of this year is £5,144, not quite so great an increase as in some preceding years, but still very large, probably larger than on any other estate in England.

Saw Hale, & long talk with him about estate matters. The exchanges at Halewood with Col. Blackburne are now complete, and that estate is now for the first time compact . . . The rest of our business was chiefly small matters – charitable gifts & subscriptions, & the like.

19 Dec. 1884: . . . Occupied some time in hearing the details of a village dispute, one Norbury having been entrusted with and lost the funds of a local Odd Fellows Society. It seems clear however that he has not been dishonest, & I shall help him to pay the debt.

20 Dec. 1884: Three pouches from office.

. . . In the last few weeks, having less press of business than usual, I determined to see whether I had forgotten my Greek, & have read through several plays of Euripides, especially the *Medea, Hippolytus*, & *Alcestis*. I find many words forgotten, so that without a Latin translation I should have been often puzzled: but on the other hand I certainly appreciate & enjoy what I read more than I did in college days. Latin I have no need to keep up, for that has never ceased to be familiar to me.

21 Dec. 1884: . . . Walk early with Sir H. Elliot[88].

Five pouches from office, & heavy. Working on them most of the afternoon.

22 Dec. 1884: . . . Went shooting in the Meadows: 695 head, nearly all pheasants.

. . . Much interesting talk yesterday & today with Sir H. [Elliot]. – He tells me (which I did not know or suspect) that there is a good deal of soreness among our diplomatists because Granville never writes to them privately but communicates only in despatches, so that they do not feel sure that they know his real mind. I gather too, though he did not say it in plain words, that the opinion is growing that Ld G. is past his work. . . .

25 Dec. 1884: Walk early with Sir H. Elliot: later with Sir W. Thomson[89]. Wrote to Granville on the expediency of declaring a protectorate of the S. African coast where it is not yet claimed as ours; i.e. Zululand, Pondoland, etc., over which we exercise a real though not ostensible protectorate. I do not love annexations, but in this case there is no increase of existing responsibilities, & we may have trouble with some German adventurers if we do not secure ourselves.

26 Dec. 1884: . . . Wrote to the Premier much in the same sense as I did to Granville yesterday.

27 Dec. 1884: Sir H. & Ly Elliot and their daughter left us. They were never here before, but are a real addition to our not too large acquaintance. Miss Elliot, especially, made herself agreeable, and Sir Henry's manners are about the best of any that I know . . .

. . . Talk with Hale as to the possible necessity for some reduction of agricultural rents if the depression continues: but at present there is not one farm vacant &, wherever there seems a chance of one, many applicants come forward.

. . . A letter from Lord Latham . . . He is full of a scheme for reclaiming prostitutes, by establishing a home or refuge for them, & wants a site for this: I answered him in a friendly but critical tone, wishing to know more of the plan: suggested Ormskirk as a better neighbourhood than Liverpool, both because of land being cheaper, & inasmuch as a crowded town is hardly the right place for such an institution, if it is to exist at all . . .

. . . Received from the Premier a telegram, approving in general terms my suggestion as to the S. African coast, but asking for a map, which I desired should be sent him from the office.

E. Stanley[90] came to stay . . .

28 Dec. 1884: Frost continues. Skating on the Long Pond, where Arthur, Lionel, and Hope managed to break the ice and fall in, but without damage.

. . . Wrote to Granville again about South Africa[91].

29 Dec. 1884: Shooting . . . We brought in 843 head, mostly pheasants, but a good show of hares. We started at 9.30, & did not reach home till 4.30, a long day at this time of year, but the walking was easy, & I felt no fatigue.

Mrs. –[92] not quite herself, & seems likely to break out again, as such people are sure to do if they cannot keep from liquor altogether. Gorst said the other day that in all his experience he had never known so many women given to drink as now. Is it increased wealth? or greater nervous susceptibility from the more bustling life which most people lead?

30 Dec. 1884: . . . The rest of the party went shooting . . . & brought in 1,119 head [93]. . .

Notes

[1] Sir V. Child-Villiers, 7th E. of Jersey (1845–1915), who succ. his father, 1859: paymaster-gen. 1889–1890, gov. of N.S. Wales 1890–1893.

[2] Sir A.W.B. Cust, 3rd E. Brownlow (b. 1844), who succ. his brother, 1867: lord-lieut. Lincs.: Ecclesiastical Commissioner from 1872, Trustee of the National Gallery, M.P. N. Salop. 1866–1867: minor office 1885–1886, 1887–1889, 1889–1892.

[3] Earl Cairns gave notice (1 July) of his intention to move 'that this House, while prepared to concur in a well considered and complete scheme for the extension of the Franchise, does not think it right to assent to the second reading of a Bill having for its object a fundamental change in the electoral body which is not accompanied by provisions which will insure the full and free representation of the people, by any adequate security that the Bill shall not come into operation except as an entire scheme'.

[4] A piracy and kidnapping case in which the Rajah of Tenom tried to use U.K. nationals to gain leverage in his quarrel with the Dutch who had been blockading his coast. An Anglo-Dutch ultimatum was eventually sent, July 1884, offering money for the release of the captives, and threatening a joint punitive expedition.

[5] *Parl. Deb., 3,* vol. ccxc, cols. 97–112 (7 July 1884).

[6] Cairns carried his amendment to the 2nd Reading of the Franchise Bill, after two nights' debate, by 205 to 146 votes.

[7] George Spencer-Churchill, 8th Duke of Marlborough (1844–1892), who succ. his father July 1883: brother of Lord Randolph: styled Marquess of Blandford 1857–1883: he m. Abercorn's dau. 1869, but marriage dissolved 1883. He m. secondly a New York widow who outlived him.

[8] *Parl. Deb., 3*, vol. ccxc, cols. 389–402 (8 July 1884).

[9] The premier's party meeting at the Foreign Office, 2.30–3.30, was, he wrote, 'well received by Goschen, Bright, & the meeting' (*Diaries*) and was followed by the announcement in parliament of an autumn session to reconsider the Franchise Bill, followed by a normal session to deal with Redistribution.

[10] Lord Wemyss' motion for an autumn sitting on the Redistribution Bill was defeated 17 July (see Note 14).

[11] *Parl. Deb., 3*, vol. ccxc, cols. 872–876 (14 July 1884). Salisbury engaged in a procedural wrangle as to whether Wemyss' proposed compromise was out of order.

[12] On the death of his cousin William Wellesley, 5th Earl of Mornington (1813–1863), the Wiltshire estates of Wellesley's mother, the heiress of the Long family, passed to Earl Cowley by Wellesley's will. These were worth £25,000 p.a.

[13] Wemyss proposed an early autumn session on Redistribution, in return for the House of Lords resuming progress on the Franchise Bill (see Note 14).

[14] *Parl. Deb., 3*, vol. ccxc, cols. 1334–1380 (17 July 1884). Wemyss's motion was defeated 182–132.

[15] Morier was then minister at Madrid (1881–1884) and shortly to become ambassador at St. Petersburg, 1884–1893.

[16] Sclater-Booth was president of the local government board, 1874–1880.

[17] J.K. Cross (1832–1887), cotton spinner: M.P. (Lib.) Bolton 1874–1885 (defeated): undersec. for India January 1883–1885.

[18] Northbrook and Wolseley left London for Egypt, 30 August 1884, the former as British High Commissioner, the latter to arrange for the relief of Khartoum.

[19] Cf Firuz Kazemzadeh, *Russia and Britain in Persia, 1864–1914: A Study in Imperialism* (New Haven, Yale U.P., 1968), pp. 87–92. Russian aggression on the ill defined Khorasan frontier of Persia in May–September 1884 was a minor episode linking the more serious crises over the annexation of Merv (February 1884) and the Russian move against the northern Afghan frontier (spring 1885). Britain did not become involved over Khorasan because Granville asked too high a price in terms of commercial advantages in southern Persia in return for U.K. support.

[20] Gladstone recorded a definite Cabinet decision for a protectorate (rather than annexation) with little detail: 'Agreed to on the basis of Sir R. Herbert's memorandum dated (9 & 18 July) . . .' The decision reached parliament on 11 August (see n. 1466 below).

[21] Sir E. Thornton (1817–1906), at this time ambassador in Russia, shortly became ambassador to Constantinople, 1884.

[22] *Parl. Deb., 3*, vol. ccxcii, cols. 438–439 (11 August 1884). Gladstone explained that the British protectorate did not include the islands N. and E. of New Guinea, but would afford protection to natives against foreigners as well as U.K. subjects.

[23] Arthur Wellesley, 2nd Duke of Wellington (1807–1884), who succ. his father, 1852: M.P. (Cons.) Aldeburgh 1829–1832, Norwich 1837–1852: d.s.p. and was succ. by his nephew: master of the horse 1853–1858, a nominal Derbyite who gave general support to Palmerston, but had radical notions: retired from army, 1863.

[24] Charles Barclay-Maitland, 12th E. of Lauderdale (1822–1884), 2nd cousin of the 11th E., whom he succ. 1878: himself the son of a Wiltshire rector: a Cons. Died unm. having been killed by lightning on the moors near Lauder: formerly for several years a railway porter and later a station master.

[25] Lord Lorne (1845–1914), who succ. his father in 1900 as 9th D. of Argyll, m. Princess

Louise (1848–1939), the Queen's 4th dau., in 1871. Lorne was Gov.-Gen. of Canada, 1878–1883.

[26] 'England's Foreign Policy', by G., *Fortnightly Review*, vol. 41 (June 1884), pp. 705–711. Authorship uncertain, but probably by Escott guided by Dilke, perhaps in the belief that it genuinely represented the premier's views. Gladstone protested at the mischievous signature.

[27] Lord Odo Russell (1829–1884), ambassador at Berlin 1871–1884, was the son of Lord William Russell, ambassador at Berlin 1835–1841.

[28] Lady Hester Stanhope (1776–1839), eldest dau. of 3rd E. Stanhope and housekeeper to Pitt when premier: later withdrew to Syria and lived as a native.

[29] The French assault on Foochow on 23 August 1884, with 3,000 Chinese killed, marked the start of the Sino-French War, which continued until the armistice of March 1885. War was never formally declared by either side, and it was not until late November 1884 that England decided a state of war existed. Port facilities were therefore denied to France. See Lloyd E. Eastman, *Throne and Mandarins: China's Search for a Policy during the Sino-French Controversy, 1880–1885* (Cambridge, Mass., 1967).

[30] The 7th Duke of Devonshire, born in 1808, was now 75, and his demise could obviously be expected before long. This was a large consideration in the Liberal leadership issue. In the event His Grace d. 21 December 1891.

[31] Malet was minister at Brussels 1883–1884 before succeeding Russell at Berlin.

[32] Hastings Russell, 9th Duke of Bedford (1819–1891), who succ. his cousin, 1872.

[33] Lt.-col. Charles James Fox Stanley (1808–13 October 1884), 3rd son of 13th E. of Derby, brother of the premier, and uncle of the diarist: not otherwise mentioned.

[34] J.A. Froude's son Ashley Anthony Froude (1863–1949) secured a position (albeit unpaid) as Private Secretary to the Permanent Under-Secretary in November 1886. He then became secretary to the Royal Commission for the division of Malta into electoral districts in 1888 and was later attached to the Bering Sea Arbitration, receiving a CMG.

[35] In fact Lefevre stayed put and Campbell-Bannerman succeeded Trevelyan.

[36] Cf *Political Speeches in Scotland in 1884* by The Right Hon. W.E. Gladstone, M.P. (Edinburgh, 1884). 144 pp., covering 27 August–26 September 1884.

[37] *The Great Landowners of Great Britain and Ireland* (4th ed., 1883) by John Bateman nevertheless still gives Derby's acreage as 68,942, an understatement repeated in D. Cannadine, *The Decline and Fall of the British Aristocracy*, p. 710.

[38] Though Derby first brought the question of a British protectorate over New Guinea before the Cabinet on 27 June 1884, no decision was taken until 6 August 1884, and was then announced to parliament on 11 August 1884. The proclamation announcing the British Protectorate was delayed until 11 October 1884 and not until 5 November 1884 was the flag actually hoisted at Port Moresby.

[39] R.D. Holt, leader of Liberal party in Liverpool.

[40] News arrived, 22 December 1884, that the German flag had been raised in northern New Guinea and adjacent islands.

[41] J. Pope Hennessy, 'Lord Beaconsfield's Irish Policy', *Nineteenth Century* (October 1884), pp. 663–680. Cf John Pope-Hennessy, 'The Tory Party and the Catholics', *Contemporary Review* (July 1875), pp. 290–310.

[42] *Memoirs of an Ex-Minister: An Autobiography*, by the Right Hon. The Earl of Malmesbury, G.C.B. 2 vols., London, Longmans, 1884.

[43] For Malmesbury's life at this time, see *The Later Derby Diaries*, ed. Vincent (1981 ed.), ch. iv.

[44] Montsioa (or variant spellings), Bechuana chief of the Barolong tribe, whose country, after conquest by Boer freebooters, was annexed to the Transvaal, 16 September 1884, the annexation being subsequently reversed under British pressure. A force of 4,000 British troops under Col. Warren then prepared to restore peace to Bechuanaland.

[45] Mrs. Henry Stanley had claimed to be dying since about 1870, according to Derby, whose contact with her had been through his lawyer Lawrence.

[46] Talbot was the diarist's brother-in-law.

[47] Sir J.L.A. Simmons (1821–1903), distinguished career with Royal Engineers: governor of Malta, 1884–1888: field marshal, 1890.

[48] The future 17th Earl of Derby.

[49] Dilke at Oldham (14 October) threatened a 'moral earthquake' if the Lords rejected the Franchise Bill again, and at Manchester (15 October) said there had been 'far too much compromise already'. Churchill, at Liverpool with Northcote (17 October), was no less defiant in insisting on delaying the Franchise Bill until Redistribution was dealt with.

[50] One should look to 1880 for an explanation of the Queen's hostility (as a minister, he had been entirely inoffensive since). But in 1880 Trevelyan asked three disrespectful questions about the privileges of army top brass, in particular questioning an honour conferred on the Duke of Cambridge's private secretary, who had never seen active service but was much in favour in high circles. See *Parl. Deb., 3*, vol. 254, col. 1353. It was unlikely this had been forgiven.

[51] Henry Strutt, 2nd Baron Belper (b. 1840), M.P. (Lib.) Derbs. E. 1868–1874, Berwick, April–June 1880: succ. his father, June 1880: minor office 1895–1906: a Unionist from 1886: chairman Notts. County Council.

[52] John Lawrence, 2nd Baron Lawrence (1846–1913), barrister: lord-in-waiting 1895–1905: son of the viceroy, whom he succ. 1879.

[53] Sir Peter Henry Scratchley (1835–1885), Royal Engineers officer with responsibilities for Australian defences, 1860–1881: major-gen. 1881: returned to U.K. 1883: high commissioner for south-east New Guinea, 1884.

[54] *Parl. Deb., 3*, vol. ccxciii, cols. 83–100 (23 October 1884), announcing the premier would introduce Franchise Bill again next day.

[55] The Maamtrasna case.

[56] Sir Charles Bruce (1836–13 December 1920), Sanskrit scholar and colonial governor: educ. Harrow, Yale, and Germany: assistant librarian, British Museum, 1863: prof. of Sanskrit, King's Coll., 1865: rector, Royal College, Mauritius, 1868–1878: director of public instruction, Ceylon, 1878–1882: colonial sec., Mauritius, 1882–1885: lt.-gov. Br. Guiana, 1885–1893, gov. Windward Is. 1893–1897, Mauritius 1897–1903 (retired): numerous publications.

[57] Sir John Pope-Hennessy (1834–1891), colonial governor: M.P. King's Co. (Cons.) 1859–1865 (defeated), being the first R.C. Tory M.P.: defeated at co. Wexford November 1866: barrister 1861: gov. of Labuan 1867–1871, Gold Coast 1872–1873, Bahamas 1873–1874, Windward Is. 1875–1876, Hong Kong 1876–1882, Mauritius 1882–1889: M.P. Kilkenny N. (anti-Parnellite home ruler) 1890–7 October 1891 (died).

[58] (Gen.) Sir Charles Warren (1840–1927), Royal Engineers officer and archaeologist: successfully commanded Bechuanaland expedition, 1884–1885: chief commissioner, Metropolitan Police, 1886–1888: commanded at Singapore, 1889–1894.

[59] Not traced, but possibly Thomas W. Irvine, author of *British Basutoland and the Basutos* (priv. pr., 1881).

[60] D.J. Esselen (1851–1919), s. of a Rhenish missionary in the Western Cape: negotiator on behalf of the Boer Nieuwe Republiek 1884–1888, when it merged with Transvaal: Esselen then became a lawyer and translator, and was deeply involved in Swaziland affairs, 1889–1895.

[61] *Parl. Deb., 3*, vol. ccxciii, cols. 441–514 (29 October 1884).

[62] John Vesey, 4th Vt De Vesci (1844–1903), who succ. father, 1875: raised to U.K. peerage, 1884, as baron: Lord-Lieut. Queen's Co. 1883–1900: became a Unionist: owned 15,000 acres.

[63] Marmaduke Francis Constable-Maxwell, 11th Baron Herries (1837–1908), who succ. his father in the Scottish title, 1876: educ. Stonyhurst and m., 1875, a dau. of Lord Howard of Glossop: lord-lieut. of Kirkcudbright and E. Riding: cr. a peer of U.K., 10 November 1884: d.s.p.m., the U.K. barony becoming extinct, and the Scottish title devolving on his dau., the Duchess of Norfolk.

[64] Arthur Gore, 5th E. of Arran (1839–1901), lord-lieut. co. Mayo 1889–1901: succ. his father,

25 June 1884: diplomatist 1859–1864, civil servant 1865–1884: cr. U.K. baron, November 1884, and succ. by his son as 6th E.: a Lib. until 1886.

65   Sir Walter James, 1st Baron Northbourne (1816–1893), M.P. (Cons.) Hull 1837–1847 (retired), director of National Gallery (1871): cr. baron, November 1884: d. 4 February 1893.

66   For more light on Granville's finances, cf *Later Derby Diaries* (1981 ed.), ch. iv.

67   (Dr.) John Chapman (1822–1894), physician and publisher: editor and proprietor of *Westminster Review* from 1851.

68   Governor of New South Wales, 1879–1885.

69   Hon. Henry Robert Brand (1841–1906), surveyor-general of the ordnance from January 1883: M.P. (Lib.) Herts. 1868–1874, Stroud July–December 1874, 1880–1886: succ. as 2nd Vt Hampden, 1892.

70   Inspector-general of fortifications from 1882.

71   S. Warwickshire election, 7 November 1884: Lloyd (Cons.) 3,095, Compton (Lib.) 1,919. Maj. 1,176 (1880 maj. 114).

72   Religion was not a marked feature of C-B's character, but for his very Scottish outlook on such matters see J.A. Spender, *The Life of . . . Campbell-Bannerman*, ii, 57–58.

73   *Memoirs, Diaries, and Correspondence, of the Rt. Hon. John Wilson Croker,* ed. by Louis J. Jennings (3 vols., 1884).

74   Wimpole was Lord Hardwicke's house in Cambridgeshire.

75   Patrick Neville Fitzgerald (d. Dublin, 1907), Fenian: b. Midleton, co. Cork: IRB organiser in co. Cork: member, Supreme Council: acquitted of treason-felony, 1884: involved in organising Gaelic Athletic Association.

76   *Parl. Deb., 3*, vol. ccxciii, cols. 1806–1810 (17 November 1884).

77   Hackney byelection (19 November 1884) on Fawcett's death: Stuart (Lib.) 14,540, McAlister (Cons.) 8,543. Maj. 5,997 (1880 maj. 6,675).

78   Without any success, though understandably: his father had been thrice a colonial governor. Neither Lord Canterbury nor his brother Graham ever worked for the Colonial Office, though Graham Manners-Sutton had a son, Francis, who was there in 1891–1893. Canterbury never became Gov. of St. Helena. The Canterbury estates around Norwich had a gross rental of £8,000 p.a.

79   Sir J.A. Macdonald (1815–1891), premier of Canada 1878–1891.

80   (Sir) Edward Wingfield (1834–1910), colonial assistant under-secretary 1878–1897.

81   The *Pall Mall* had raised the naval issue in late summer. Parliament returned to it in depth in December 1884, extracting government assurances of a large future shipbuilding programme (against a background of deep depression in the shipbuilding and steel industries). The enemy was assumed to be France, fighting without any allies.

82   Reay was governor of Bombay 1885–1890.

83   C.P. Villiers (1802–1898), M.P. (Lib.) Wolverhampton 1835–1898.

84   Col. A.P. Vivian (1834–1885), M.P. (Lib.) W. Cornwall 1868–1885 (defeated): 3rd s. of J.H. Vivian of Singleton, Swansea: a col. in Glamorgan Volunteers: or more probably Col. Sir Robert John Hussey Vivian (1802–1887), natural son of 1st Baron Vivian, a soldier, E. India Co. director, and member of Council of India 1858–1875.

85   See R. v Dudley and Stephens [1881–1885] All England Law Reports 61 (Queens Bench Division): also A.W.B. Simpson, *Cannibalism and the Common Law: The story of the tragic last voyage of the 'Mignonette' and the strange legal proceedings to which it gave rise* (Chicago, Chicago U.P., 1984).

86   Jane, Duchess of Somerset (1809–14 December 1884), one of the three celebrated Sheridan sisters, and Queen of Beauty at the Eglinton tournament, 1839.

87   Donald Mackay, 11th Baron Reay (1839–1921), governor of Bombay 1885–1890: Dutch born and educated: 1st pres. of the British Academy.

88   Sir Henry Elliot (1817–1907), ambassador at Vienna 1877–1884.

89   Sir William Thomson, 1st Baron Kelvin (1824–1907), physicist, Fellow of Peterhouse, professor at Glasgow, Ulsterman, and ardent Unionist.

[90]   The future 17th E. of Derby, the diarist's nephew. His parents never visited Knowsley after 1878.

[91]   Derby was opposed on this issue by a sleepless and irritable premier who detested imperial expansion. Gladstone wrote (21 December) that he would be 'extremely glad' to see the Germans in S. Africa. He repeated this view to Hamilton (2 January 1885) in identical terms (Hamilton Diary, ed. Bahlman, p. 761) and continued to block a Cabinet decision on the subject (Carlingford, *Journal*, 3 January 1885). Though 'heartily' in favour of closing the gap between the Cape and Natal, Gladstone's obstructionism was otherwise largely successful.

[92]   Mrs. Hale, an intermittent alcoholic.

[93]   Not to mention over 800 head on 2 January.

1885

January–June

1 Jan. 1885: . . . I begin the year in good health, except a slight remains of cold & cough, which is not now troublesome: during 1884 I have been well in general, not on any day unfit for business, though kept at home 5 or 6 days by cold in the head & throat. Serious ailments I have had none: and I do not think I have lost anything either in mental or bodily energy. – I have been fortunate in the absence of domestic or other trouble: Ly D.'s health is good, her eyes not worse, and her spirits better than some years ago. Nothing has gone wrong with me in any relation of private life. In regard of material conditions I have been very unusually prosperous. The rental of the estate has increased by £5,500 in 1884: & now exceeds £220,000. Rents have been steadily paid, & there are very few complaints, notwithstanding hard times. I have added to the family estates, since Jan. '84, about 800 acres in Kent, & something over 100 in Lancashire. My private savings fall little short of £600,000, safely invested or kept in hand. (The savings of 1884 are exactly £83,000.)

   . . . In public affairs, the outlook is less cheerful. The reform question is to all appearance virtually settled, & nothing remains except to wait for the verdict of the constituencies a year hence: but in other respects we have been less lucky. Legislation has entirely failed, owing in part to obstruction, & in part, I think, to general apathy on all subjects except Egypt & reform. Ireland is kept quiet only by coercive laws, & desperate efforts will be made to get them repealed, or rather to prevent their being renewed. Trade is bad &, though there is not much severe distress, the situation of the working classes is rather below than above the average. We have been forced into a huge & costly expedition up the Nile, the result of which no man can foretell: & the diplomatic complications surrounding the Egyptian settlement have increased rather than lessened. Bismarck, whether from temper or policy, is very hostile, & is giving us much trouble by his proposed annexations in New Guinea. The Australian colonists are furious at his action, & at us for not stopping it. If parliament were now about to meet, we should have a very stormy opening: but many things may happen in six or seven weeks. . . .

2 Jan. 1885: . . . London by 9.45 train . . . Cabinet at 4.00, which lasted till near 7.00. Lawson called at 7.00 to pick up what he could. Dined with Harcourt, meeting Childers only: much political talk.

   Gladstone at the Cabinet[1] appeared very ill, said he was rheumatic & unable to sleep: he wants rest, & talks of going abroad, but in what state does he leave the Egyptian question? Is it possible for a minister to be absent at such a time for 5 or 6 weeks? especially as there is no agreement about Egypt. Hartington wants to stay there indefinitely, the rest of the Cabinet dissent, but no two are of the same mind, & a break up seems imminent. Gladstone avowedly wishes to retire &, if he does so, the question of who is to succeed will be exceedingly perplexing. Granville is said to be unpopular with the party in the Commons, and is growing visibly infirm: the natural successor would be Hartington: but he is opposed to the bulk of the party on Egypt, which is the question of the moment. Harcourt thinks, & Childers seems to agree, that a new government could not be formed on the present lines, & that the Tories must have an offer – whether they would accept it or no is doubtful.

Our reports from various quarters are unsatisfactory: Wolseley's telegrams show that he has got before him a more serious business than he counted on, & it will be necessary for him probably to run the risk of failure in a dash on Khartoum, or to see Gordon forced to surrender before he can arrive there. Malet writes in strong terms about the hostile feeling against us at Berlin: and Lyons sends a despatch in which he indicates the probability of French resistance to whatever we may propose for Egypt, in which resistance they would be backed up by Germany, Austria, & Russia. That is to say, we may have to face a European combination. In addition there are reports of Russian advance on Herat as imminent: & obviously we are in the worst possible position to resist such an advance, with a large proportion of our army, such as it is, locked up in central Africa.

3 Jan. 1885 (Saturday): Very busy until 12.00, when to Cabinet, calling on Granville on the way, whom I found in a confusion of despatches & telegrams, with two or three people in the room. Gladstone was better, but leaves for a week's entire rest at Hawarden. – Office at 2.30. Saw Sir S. Samuel[2]: left at 4.00. [To] Knowsley by 5.00 p.m.: arriving about 10.30. A cold night, but the carriages were warmed with hot air: which is new.

4 Jan. 1885 (Sunday): . . . Walk early alone, 3 miles on terrace: later with Sir R. M.[orier]. He full of talk: as usual, inclined to be egotistic, brags of his services, complains that they have never been duly recognised – in short, his conversation explains & justifies the prejudice felt against him at F.O. & in the profession. He denounces violently the office, its chiefs, Gladstone, & English statesmen in general, for their ignorance of foreign affairs: in which he is perhaps borne out by various occurrences in his own experience: but his argument all went, as I told him, to prove that diplomacy was impossible under a popular & parliamentary government. When he got away from these subjects he was interesting: he announced that within 4 or 5 months the Russians would be at Herat: which rather startled me to hear, as he said he knew it on the best authority: but his authority turned out to be a newspaper correspondent at Paris. He talked of the king of Spain[3], sketched his character, which seems a curious one: 'He is an admirable speaker: has often said that he would give up his crown to have the power & popularity of a great orator: is very clever, superficially: rapid in picking up knowledge: but not really much interested in anything, nor has studied any subject, thoroughly. He is anxious to be thought *fin*: proud of outwitting people with whom he has to deal: & has in this way gained a character for duplicity. He lives in a debauched set, & is not particular as to their characters: one of his familiars, having forged a signature, had to leave Madrid: the king missed him, settled the matter with the intending prosecutor, & took him back. He is always in distress for money: & is supposed to dabble in speculation: for which, if true, he has the excuse that his mother's[4] incessantly renewed debts, which he has had to pay again & again, keep him poor.'

5 Jan. 1885 (Monday): . . . Walk with Sir R.M., whom I found a little tedious. He lectures well, but does not converse: his talk is a monologue, & he tolerates interruption as little as Macaulay or Carlyle. I can understand now why he is not popular at the courts where he has served. But of his cleverness & knowledge there can be no doubt.

I kept only a brief & rough note of what passed at our two Cabinets. At the first, Gladstone appeared very ill, complained much of pain (rheumatic, I believe) and of want of sleep. On Saturday he was better, but still talking of the necessity of absolute rest. Granville said to me & others that he was not as ill as he thought himself but, being unused to suffer, he believed the case more serious than it was. We discussed Egypt in the first place: the question being as to a draft dealing with the claims of Germany & Russia to be admitted to some control of the Caisse. Granville was for acceding to the demand, provided we got some assurances of the wish of the Powers to bring about a settlement: the Chancellor would have liked a quid pro quo: Kimberley was against concession, saying we must reckon on the deliberate hostility of Germany: Chamberlain did not like the notion of yielding to Bismarck just now: Northbrook thought his professions of intending to support us would be worthless if they were given: D. agreed as to Bismarck's feeling, but thought this would not be a convenient ground of quarrel. We settled a draft: Ld G. mentioned an unsatisfactory discussion between Lyons & Ferry, the latter making difficulties as to everything.

The Premier spoke of his health, of the need for rest, his complaint of two years ago had returned: he wished to go away, & left with us a plan for dealing with France, in the shape of a mem. to be put into the form of a despatch, if agreed to. It was read & discussed. Chamberlain did not like the notion of taxing Egypt more heavily for the sake of French bondholders. Northbrook agreed in the expediency of dealing specially with France, but disliked what he understood to be our financial proposals. He believed the Powers would not agree to a reduction of interest. Harcourt said we had broken up the conference rather than agree that the bondholders should be paid in full, & we could not now go back. Gladstone said significantly that such a solution (which involves our stay in Egypt) might be possible to some other government, but not to his. – The idea seems to me that Ferry is very hostile, & that the French will try to embarrass us by delay. The Cabinet of Saturday was chiefly occupied with New Guinea & S. Africa – I was too actively engaged in the discussion to take a note.

6 Jan. 1885: . . . Four pouches from office: work on them: walk 4 miles on the measured terrace: day very fine.

Sudden summons at 1.30 for a Cabinet early tomorrow, of which there was no expectation, or intention to hold it, when we separated on Saturday. The reason probably is Egypt, but I shall soon know.

Rent day dinner, & speeches as usual . . . The tenants were cordial, but I thought less warm in their cheers than on some former occasions. No doubt they feel the bad times.

Left by 5.10 train, and at No. 23 by 10.30.

7 Jan. 1885: Cabinet at 1.00, which sat till 4.00. All present except the Premier & Ld Spencer. Thence office where busy till near 7.00.

Dined with Harcourt, meeting Carlingford, Northbrook, Trevelyan, & Chamberlain. The latter talked in a rather swaggering style about what the new electors would do: assuming that an enormous majority of them will return candidates of the ultra-democratic type. He was also full of a plan, which I understood very imperfectly, for compulsory purchase of land for labourers' cottages & allotments. He has lately made a speech at Birmingham, sound enough in defence of the policy of his colleagues, but wild in his references to property, & dangerous in the apparent leaning which it shows towards socialist ideas. It is, however, only just to add that his words were exceedingly vague, & really pledged him to nothing.

The Cabinet began with a reference to Samoa, with which the Germans are said to have made a treaty implying almost entire control of the island. We agreed to wait till we see what the treaty is, but to protest strongly against any attack on Samoan independence. Some talk followed as to the possibility of being forced into a war with Germany. Harcourt thought it impossible, in the actual state of Ireland, of our army, etc.: in short that we had not the means. Granville inclined to the same view. Trevelyan thought we had no case in this instance. Kimberley did not agree, & was bellicose in his talk. Chamberlain took the same line, saying that, if we submitted to insolence, we might be driven into a quarrel.

The rest of our discussion, & that for which the Cabinet was called, was on military measures to be taken in Egypt: a diversion to be made at Suakin, etc. The French as we expected refuse to consider our proposals for Egypt, & insist on bringing forward theirs. We agree, though deprecating the consequent delay.

8 Jan. 1885: Left London by 10.10 train: Knowsley at 3.30.

. . . The Egyptian crisis is now practically suspended till the 15th, or a day or two later, when we shall have the counter-proposals of the French government. In the opinion of both Lyons & Malet, it is probable that they will be such as we shall find much difficulty in agreeing to, & that they will be supported more or less by Germany, Austria, & Russia. The question will then be, how to meet them? I do not for my own part see, though Harcourt does, a split of the Cabinet into two hostile parties: the situation is rather that every man has his own ideas, & no two of them are alike. The peculiar position of the Premier, who is always declaring himself to be on the point of retiring, increases the difficulty, for he is very unwilling to do anything that may bind him to stay longer in office, & we cannot act without him.

– The comparatively unimportant colonial troubles are settling themselves. The Australians are angry at the German occupation of New Guinea, but they can do nothing, nor can we, & as time goes on they will discover that their loss is imaginary, & that they have secured three-fourths of all they asked for. The S. African affair is also in a better way of settlement – though I do not believe in any permanent pacification there. . . .

10 Jan. 1885: . . . Saw Hale . . . Talk of getting gradually into my own hands the land immediately adjoining the park, as opportunity offers: so that, in case of any law being passed giving the occupiers fixity of tenure, I shall have land enough in hand for convenience, & to keep off nuisances. I think Hale understood me, & will act on the hint. . . .

11 Jan. 1885: . . . Gave Margaret[5] £20, she having spent more than she has on local charities & help to dependants, in which all her money & much of her time is absorbed. She has done much for the popularity of the family in this neighbourhood.

Politics have calmed down in a sudden and singular fashion. A fortnight ago, German annexations filled every newspaper, & I hardly know which of us was more loudly denounced, Bismarck for making, or Granville & I for allowing, them: now the hubbub is over &, as generally happens, people are beginning to discover that there is much ado about nothing. Party politics are dead: the reform question being settled, & it not being worth while to raise any other in a parliament which is so soon to die. Everybody is thinking of the new constituencies, & the business of fixing boundaries for the districts goes on very smoothly. It is certainly an odd & almost inexplicable thing that a system of electoral districts, or what comes nearly to the same thing, should have been not merely acquiesced in, but pressed on the Cabinet, by the Conservative leaders. In the long run I dare say they are right, & they gain so far that all farther agitation on that subject is impossible: but it is a complete abandonment of their former position. . . .

15 Jan. 1885: Thaw, & the snow nearly gone . . . Three pouches from office, & another from Hamilton to Antrobus, to say that Ld Lorne does not wish for the offer of N.S. Wales, which I had proposed to make. I suspect an intrigue on behalf of Ld Carrington[6], the P. of Wales's friend, who wants the place, and will probably have it, failing Ld Lorne: he is fairly fit for it, & there is a difficulty in finding the right sort of men for there. – I referred the whole matter to Granville, who asked that Ld Lorne should be appointed, & got from me something like a promise that this should be done.

Letter from the Premier, deprecating any attempt to buy the Dutch claims in N. Guinea which Sir H. Loch[7] recommends. He seems to have been in correspondence with Granville on the subject.

. . . News of Ld Sherbrooke, who lost his wife in November, being about to marry again[8]: an odd proceeding at his age of 72: but he is now nearly blind, very helpless & has no near relative or friend who could live with him. . . .

16 Jan. 1885: . . . Three pouches from office. In them come, though not yet officially communicated, the French proposals as to Egypt. These are under six heads: (1) Loan of £9,000,000 under guarantee of all the Powers. (This is the point on which difficulty will arise.) (2) Domain & Daire debts not to be meddled with. (3) Nominally, no reduction of interest, but they qualify this by agreeing to a moderate tax if necessary on the interest of all the loans. (4) Abolition of the exemption of foreigners from taxation. (This is right & just, & ought to have been done long ago.) (5) An international commission of enquiry into Egyptian finance (may mean anything, or nothing, & requires explanation). (6) Some agreement as to the Suez Canal.

It is announced that we must consider these terms in a Cabinet to be held early next week. They will raise the whole question whether Egypt is to be English or European: & on this question it seems probable that the Cabinet, or the majority of them, may be on one side, & the public on the other. We may split among ourselves, which is disagreeable. Or we may agree, & be censured by a vote of the Commons: in which event we should fall in a good cause.

17 Jan. 1885: . . . Wrote to Ld Granville on the French proposals, which seem to me satisfactory, & such as may at least serve very well as a basis for negociation.

The papers are much employed in commenting on a recent speech by Chamberlain, which has given offence, not I think unreasonably. He has not very definitely pledged himself to anything, but the general tone of it is socialistic. He is in effect addressing the new electors, & trying to bribe them by the promise of large slices out of the property of those who have any. . . .

19 Jan. 1885: . . . Left with M. at 3.30. London . . . by 8.40 . . . Supper & bed at 11.00. The press has got hold of the Egyptian proposals, & is not yet quite decided in regard to them, but the general tendency is unfavourable. The English public may not have made up its mind to annex Egypt, but the idea of sharing our power there with any other country is no ways agreeable.

Heard of the death of my cousin, Lord Wilton[9], who has held the title & estates for only 3 years . . . There is not much to be said of him: a quiet, fashionable, gentlemanlike peer, fond of society & hunting: he rode well, dressed well, & had good manners. He sat some years in the H. of C. but took no active part. He is succeeded by his brother[10]: a great scamp, in former years at least, but he may be mended now: he nearly killed himself with drink, & sold the reversion to the estates: but his father bought it back. He is separated from his wife, whom he might have divorced, so far as her conduct was concerned, but his own character would have enabled her to recriminate, & so they remain married, though separated.

20 Jan. 1885: . . . The German oculist . . . Murren[11], came to see M. He reports the general state of her eyes better than it was three years ago: and the cataract little if at all increased. He seems to think it may not grow worse.

Office at 1.00 . . . Cabinet at 3.00, which sat till past 7.00. Chamberlain was absent from illness: & Ld Spencer in Ireland. The Premier seemed well, & said nothing about going away: I suppose he felt it to be impossible while we are in the thick of our Egyptian troubles. Granville was present, but in great distress, having just lost his only sister, Ly G. Fullerton[12]. He fairly broke down & sobbed when Gladstone said a few words of condolence. But business once begun he rallied & took his part with the rest.

We began by agreeing that the Khedive, Tewfik, should be reassured as to our support, which he seems to fear will be withdrawn. Some talk followed about African protectorates, how far their rights extended, etc., etc., not important, nor much to the purpose.

– Then began discussion as to the Egyptian proposals made by France. Germany, Russia, & Austria support them. Italy does not interfere. No power objects to them. We talked of Bismarck's despatch, which is reasonable in substance, but neither friendly nor courteous in tone. Granville says his outbreak of bad feeling against England is owing to domestic causes, not to action taken here. The Crown Princess is his avowed enemy, & controls her husband the future emperor: & he is working to destroy her influence by holding her up as the representative of English ideas, & England as the enemy of Germany. The Premier said he had expected a direct demand for international control & was agreeably surprised at the moderation of these proposals. Hartington objected absolutely to a financial enquiry. Northbrook thought it would make our position untenable. Childers held the same language. Harcourt gave reasons for it: without enquiry there will be no guarantee. Are we prepared to give the necessary guarantee ourselves? – Egypt is practically bankrupt, & a bankrupt must submit to have his affairs examined. Several of us raised the question whether the enquiry might not be confined to revenue, excluding the question of expenditure. Childers said if we had the sole control of Egypt we could make it pay, debt & all. But to do that we must have a finance minister not to advise only, but to govern. The Premier objected to this rather warmly – said it would be single control instead of dual control: we should be governing the country under false pretences. – I said the question was whether we meant to stay in Egypt or no. If we did, it would be right to reject these proposals: as we did not, we must accept them & try to modify what we objected to.

After a very long discussion, the question was put: 'That the French proposals form a reasonable basis of friendly communication, with a view to settlement.' Hartington, Northbrook, Childers, & Carlingford, say no. The rest say yes. As to the enquiry, we accept it in principle, but propose a different mode of choosing the commissioners, some delay, & that it shall be mainly confined to revenue. It was thought best that one member should be chosen by each Power, including Egypt & Turkey. Hartington pressed for the use of words vetoing a multiple control, which we agreed to, though not thinking a verbal protest likely to be of much use.

21 Jan. 1885: . . . Cabinet at 12.00, which sat till 2.30. Early dinner at the club. Left with M. at 4.30, Knowsley by 10.30. The day & night very cold, but we had a carriage warmed after the new fashion, & did not feel it.

We began business today by a discussion as to whether full sovereignty, or protectorate only, should be declared in British New Guinea. I pressed strongly for the former, on the ground that without it, according to the Law Officer's opinion, we could not exercise jurisdiction over foreigners, which is absolutely necessary if we are to keep order at all. Dilke, Kimberley, Harcourt, supported me. The Chancellor wished for a bill giving special powers, which was objected to on the double ground that it would be contrary to international law, & that it would be very difficult to pass through the Commons. The Premier opposed, or rather questioned, the proposal at first, but professed himself satisfied by the argument: & it was settled. We considered, on Granville's suggestion, a question raised by Sir H. Loch, as to whether the Dutch shall be asked to sell their half of N. Guinea: but it was decided to do nothing. They would almost certainly refuse, & the invitation might provoke other Powers to press them in the same sense, who perhaps would not take a refusal.

Talk followed about a charter to an African Company on the Niger, of which Aberdare is chairman. It ended with no conclusion, as well as I could make out, nor was it clear what would be the effect of granting a charter. Another conversation about the relation of the Porte to Egypt led to no definite conclusion.

Then we came back to the subject dealt with yesterday, the French proposals. (I understand that after the Cabinet yesterday Hartington & Northbrook talked seriously of resigning, & that it was decided to revive the discussion in order to see if agreement were possible.) Hartington began by saying that he would declare the French proposal for an enquiry into finance inadmissible, at least for the present, and would tell France that if these negociations failed we would take the whole matter into our own hands. He ended the conversation by saying that he would not now press the point, but could not agree to any enquiry of the kind proposed. He thought we should be defeated in parliament on these proposals. Northbrook & Trevelyan thought the French would give way on this point.

The Premier said that to resist all Europe on the question of refusing an enquiry into finance was choosing our ground to fight on very badly. Childers said the opposition would not quarrel with France, but extend the guarantee much farther. We talked about the possibility of the opposition carrying a vote of censure on the Egyptian policy. I thought they would try, & possibly succeed: but Dilke & Harcourt thought they would not risk it, as success would commit them to the policy of seizing Egypt & holding it against Europe. In the end we compromised so far as to agree to try to induce the French to give up the *enquête* – not however proposing to break off negociations if they refuse. So the secession is averted: but Hartington & Northbrook hang very loose to the Cabinet, & may drop off any day. Carlingford & Childers sympathise, but will probably not go so far as to resign.

22 Jan. 1885: . . . News of a battle[13] in the Soudan, in which Gen. Stewart, with 1,500 men, defeated a large force of Arabs – our reports say 10,000, but probably no one knows. They fought hard, once broke the square, & inflicted on the British troops a loss of about 170 killed & wounded. The victory appears to have been complete, but it is impossible to read the story of it without misgiving as to the future. If the Mahdi has many more men like those just defeated, & if they fight the same way, Lord Wolseley may reach Khartoum, but he will have trouble in coming away & leaving any settlement behind him. We must either stay at enormous cost, or retire with nothing to show for an outlay of several millions. This is the difficulty, & it will increase rather than diminish. The natural solution would be to make terms with the Mahdi after beating him: but it is said that his character as a religious leader, pledged to war against non-mussulmans, makes all negociations with him impossible: he either will not treat, or cannot be trusted if he does. Such is the common talk: I do not judge.

23 Jan. 1885: . . . More details of the fight in the Soudan. Two peers were in it & wounded – Lds Airlie[14] & St. Vincent[15]. Among the killed was Col. Burnaby, a well known figure in London. Almost a giant, an athlete from boyhood, his pleasure was in rough & dangerous adventure with no special object except the excitement & perhaps the consequent notoriety. His journey to Khiva is well known. He went to Spain to see fighting in the last civil war there: served as a volunteer in Gen. Graham's fight on the Red Sea coast: went up 13 times in a balloon, & generally missed no opportunity that offered of getting himself killed. He was only 43, but his friends say that he would not have lived long in any case, having developed heart disease by violent exertion – the common end of an athletic life. He was very popular in the army[16], and will be regretted both there and in the conservative clubs.

24 Jan. 1885: . . . News came by telegraph of three more dynamite explosions in London: one in the Tower, one in Westminster Hall, one in the H. of Commons. A good deal of damage seems to have been done.

. . . Having ascertained that Capt. Hamber's[17] request for assistance was genuine, I sent him £25, to help in paying off his debts. He is now editor of the *Advertiser*, but I knew him when employed on the *Standard*, a good many years ago.

25 Jan. 1885: Trevelyan came . . . Day dark & foggy . . .
. . . Much talk with him about affairs. He thinks that the next H. of C. will not differ so much as is supposed by many: that candidates of a good class socially will come forward nearly everywhere, & have the best chance of being returned: that mere adventurers will have less support under a single member system than they had before: in short, as regards England & Scotland he is entirely optimistic. For Ireland, his previsions are different: he does not see his way, & says so. He thinks Parnell will be master of the situation – is so now – that he will control the selection of candidates, & that his boast of having a nationalist party of 80 members in the next parliament is well founded. He drew a striking picture of the violence, offensive language, & bad manners of the Irish . . . He

said O'Brien, Healy, and one Harrington[18] were the most dangerous of the party: O'Donnell, Callan, & Biggar, the most offensive. Their strongest dislike, Trevelyan says, is to the English radicals . . . His only hope seems to be that governments in future will be stronger than they are now (I don't know why they should) and that if they give trouble they will be dealt with more severely.

We discussed the burning question of the leadership: he thought that the party as a whole would accept the leadership of Hartington, even Chamberlain not objecting: the only risk was that of the D. of Devonshire's death, which would upset the arrangement. He considered Harcourt wise in not aiming at the leadership in the Commons, for which he was not fit, & where he would not be popular. The chancellorship was the place for him. Of Granville there was no mention. Gladstone will no doubt try to obtain the successorship for him, & the Queen would probably agree: but the party has taken a dislike to him, & would rather have their leader in the Commons. It is said by Ld G.'s personal friends that he would not care to hold office long, but that it is his chief wish to be Premier if only for a week: that he may end his public life in the first place. I hope for his sake he may, but the chances seem against it.

26 Jan. 1885: Wet morning: long talk with Trevelyan in the conservatory & library. Walk with him later, both before & after luncheon.

The papers are full of the recent dynamite explosions, which seem more serious than any we have had yet. The inside of the H. of Commons is described as being wrecked. In Westminster Hall & the Tower less damage is done, but still a good deal.

. . . In a speech delivered within the last few days, Parnell has told an Irish audience that the Land Act is a failure, that the tenant is insufficiently protected, & that the movement for reduction of rents must begin afresh. This cannot be agreeable to the Premier, who was till lately, perhaps still is, confident that his policy has pacified Ireland.

27 Jan. 1885: . . . Trevelyan, Arthur, Hale & his son .. went shooting . . . no hares nor hens to be killed. They brought in 164 head, T.[revelyan] at the head of the list, & pleased like a boy.

28 Jan. 1885: Trevelyan left us early. He has made a favourable impression on all the family, and I reckon his acquaintance an acquisition. He began as an ardent radical, but has cooled down a great deal, with time, experience, & probably also the sense of being prospectively a man of large landed property. He evidently distrusts & dislikes Chamberlain, to whose half socialist talk he referred as being dangerous both to the party & the country.

. . . Saw Hale, talk about . . . Mr. Williams, the socialist farmer at Burscough, who has paid no rent for 2 years, & is under notice to quit if he continues to refuse. He is a Catholic, and his connections are mostly Irish, but he seems to be acting under the influence of a certain Democratic Federation whose headquarters are in London.

More news of fighting from the Soudan. Sir H. Stewart[19] has again beaten off the Arabs, & is safely encamped on the Nile near Metemmeh, whence apparently he is able to communicate freely with Khartoum. But he is himself severely wounded & disabled, & his losses have been heavy.

29 Jan. 1885: . . . Called at the new stores established in the village under Margaret's superintendence. Spent there £5 to be given in presents of tea, flannel, etc., to the old women, or sick people. . . .

30 Jan. 1885: . . . Wrote to Hale about (1) a new door in the park wall: (2) removal of certain notices that 'trespassers will be prosecuted' which seem useless & invidious: (3) our decision not to undertake the altering of the house this year, which I rather regret, but do it to satisfy Ly D. with the understanding that, if we are alive in 1886, it shall be undertaken then.

Long speeches made at Birmingham by Bright & Chamberlain: the former retrospective, & on his old subjects: the latter still somewhat in the socialist line, but less offensively so than in his harangue of a fortnight ago. He dwelt a good deal on the excessive taxation paid by the poor: which is scarcely in accordance with fact, since a teetotaller not subject to income tax or house tax pays hardly anything to the State.

But his favourite notion, borrowed from Jesse Collings, is the compulsory purchase of land by local authorities for the benefit of labourers, or very small farmers. This project, not yet worked out into practical shape, is screamed at by conservatives as robbery & confiscation – which it is not, any more than the taking of land compulsorily for any other public use.

Another objection taken, in which there is more reason, is that the unlimited power of expropriation given to small local bodies might lead to jobbery & possibly to blackmail. But to me it seems more likely that, if legislation of the kind proposed were carried, it would remain a dead letter in 90 parishes out of 100. Neither farmers nor shopkeepers would care to pay higher rates for the purpose of creating peasant proprietors half of whom would soon be paupers.

31 Jan. 1885: Day wet & stormy: the glass lower than I have almost ever seen it. But it cleared later . . .

. . . Ly Sefton has seen the Premier, who came to stay at Norris Green for the marriage[20] of his son in Liverpool on Thursday. He seemed ill & anxious, and Mrs. G. spoke with dread of the effect upon him of London: I suspect he is ill pleased (as who in his place would not be?) at the turn affairs have taken in Egypt. All Europe wishes us to go out: all England wishes us to stay, at least for a time, and many would have us stay permanently. How to reconcile these different views? If he retires, he leaves trouble & difficulty behind him: & I believe he is sincere in thinking his strength unequal to much parliamentary work.

1 Feb. 1885 (Sunday): . . . Cleared off all remaining affairs, & walk with Hale in afternoon, to look at some new clumps (they are too small to be called plantations) which I am making . . . I urge upon Hale to enclose, wherever he can, the old pits & pieces of rough land, which abound in these parts, which are of no value to the tenant, & yet would give room for a fringe of trees, alder or sycamore, sheltering the field, & breaking the monotony of a flat surface of ploughed ground.

2 Feb. 1885: . . . [To London.] In the papers, a speech from Goschen, meant as a reply to Chamberlain, & which will be peculiarly acceptable to moderate Liberals, who have no sympathy with socialism. – The cry against Chamberlain from the classes having property is loud & general, & they are certainly right in thinking his manifesto hostile to them, but what he has said has been deliberately uttered, & he evidently thinks it will please the majority of the new electors. The design to set up a radical party distinct from the liberals is clear & indeed undisguised. But it may end in the defeat of both instead of one.

3 Feb. 1885: Sir C. Lampson called to talk over Peabody fund affairs, which he thinks are in a good state, and I believe it is so, and it is his doing. He estimates the income of the fund at £27,000, says we shall be out of debt in 7 or 8 years (but this is sanguine), and the capital will then be worth £1,200,000. Meanwhile we have spent our available capital, & the interest must go in paying off debt, so we can do no more building.

... Office 2.30–5.30: saw there Granville, who came with a draft to talk over, about the north coast of N. Guinea: I found him anxious to give way to Bismarck in everything, & with some trouble induced him to abstain from promising concessions on the question of boundary larger than I think we are bound to make.

Sir S. Samuel came to discuss the expenses of the new annexation: I thought him sensible and friendly, which indeed the government of N.S. Wales has shown itself in these troubles: he showed me a confidential telegram which he has received suggesting that the D. of Manchester[21] would be a popular appointment as governor. The Duke, though a good and harmless man, is so simple minded as to be almost silly: but there was no need to consider the matter, for in the first place the choice would not be approved at home: in the next, the Duchess certainly would not consent to go out, & a governor without a wife, or rather whose wife will not join him, is in a false position. I told him confidentially of my ideas about Lord Lorne, adding that they would probably not lead to any result.

... The papers are full of an attempt to shoot O'Donovan Rossa[22], the leader of the dynamite party, made by a young English woman at New York. She seems to have been in a lunatic asylum, & to have twice attempted her own life, so probably she is mad. But Rossa, who is not severely hurt, will of course describe her as employed by the British government: & the Irish will believe him.

4 Feb. 1885 (Wednesday): Work till 11.00: Sanderson called: received then an immediate summons to meet other ministers at the Admiralty, where found Granville, Northbrook, Trevelyan, & Childers. Dilke came in later. The rest, I suppose, are out of town. The subject was the Congo conference[23], as to which the Portuguese have complicated matters by seizing on the land they claim at the mouth of the river, notwithstanding the outcries of the Association[24], with King Leopold[25] at their head. We settled instructions for Malet[26], & had much talk on the relations with Germany, the conference, & other matters – not on Egypt, which was barely mentioned. We sat till 1.00. Home for luncheon ... office at 3.00: saw there Sir F. Bell[27], who has a plan for inducing some of the Scotch crofters to emigrate to New Zealand. He is of all the agents the most satisfactory to do business with: sensible, well informed, & a gentleman in manners. They vary a good deal. Sir S. Samuel[28] is also sensible & well disposed: less polished in manners, but means to be civil & friendly. Mr. Garrick[29] I scarcely know. Murray Smith[30] is more like a Yankee: clever & shrewd, but inclined to be bumptious. Capt. Mills[31] is a good plain old soldier, whom I like, but he knows little of what his government is about, & I seldom see him. Sir C. Tupper[32] comes seldom, for we have no question unsettled with Canada. Sir A. Blyth[33] has little to do at the office, & I scarcely ever see him.

There was circulated in the afternoon a letter from the Premier, enclosing a cutting from the *Observer* of last Sunday, in which a nearly, but not quite, accurate report was given of the decision of the Cabinets of 20 & 21 Jan., and of the division of opinion which nearly led to a crisis.

He protests against this disclosure as a breach of faith, reasonably enough. We all answer by disclaimers of having anything to do with the *Observer* – which I for one can conscientiously give, for I know no one connected with the paper. I say 'all' but the box reached me before it had quite gone round. I added to my declaration of innocence a suggestion that it would be better to do or say nothing that could attract public attention to the paragraph, which I believe has passed with but little notice, as only one of the many guesses at what is passing in which the small fry of journalism indulge . . .

5 Feb. 1885: . . . Soon after breakfast came from the Central News a report of Khartoum having been surrendered or taken, as is said, by the treachery of some of the garrison. This report was soon confirmed by a long telegram from Ld Wolseley, who asks for instructions. It is not known what has become of Gordon. Sir C. Wilson[34] had advanced with a small force nearly to Khartoum, but was compelled to return.

This event necessarily compels an immediate summons of the Cabinet: and we are to meet early tomorrow, Gladstone & several others being too far away to get back before night. It is too early to speculate on possible consequences.

Granville looked in, & asked himself to dinner. Mary G. [alloway] came also, & young E. [ddie] Stanley. We had some talk later. In reference to the late disclosure of Cabinet secrets, Ld G. has no doubt that the offender is Hartington – not intentionally, but he has no notion of secrecy or reserve, & gossips among his acquaintance about his relations to his colleagues. I know that he said to [Lord] Sefton the other day: 'We shall soon be at it again, hammer & tongs, all quarrelling among ourselves.' Moreover, he tells everything to the Duchess of Manchester & she, like all women of that sort, likes to show that she is acquainted with what is passing, which she can only do by letting out secrets in her turn.

Death of Sir R. Phillimore, whom Gladstone made a baronet, nobody knew why: except that he was very loud & somewhat abject in his devotion to him, Gladstone. He was learned in civil & especially in ecclesiastical law: & fairly able as a judge: in the H. of Commons extremely tedious: a strong High Churchman, not notable in any other respect.

6 Feb. 1885: Very busy till 11.00, when to Cabinet, which sat till past 2.00. Entire agreement in principle as to what we ought to do, & I think we took a less gloomy view of the situation than the majority of men outside. The decision come to is in all the newspapers, to which we sent it. In substance it comes to this: Gordon if alive is to be rescued: the Mahdi's advance on Egypt guarded against: with these objects in view, Ld Wolseley is to have full discretion, & is assured of support. There was much verbal discussion as to the telegram to be sent, & some on details: but no substantial difference. I note it as characteristic of English public life under present conditions that we took nearly twice as long to consider what should be said to the British public as to consider what orders should be given to Lord Wolseley. The Premier wished to insert in the latter a suggestion as to negociating with the Mahdi: but this was universally objected to, as suggesting more admission of defeat than the public in its present mood would endure, & also because Ld W. can negociate on his own account with special directions, if he thinks fit.

Office . . . Left at 4.30 . . . saw Lawson: there dined with us Granville, young E. Stanley, & the Russell young ladies.

The papers are of course full of Khartoum . . . Great exaggeration prevails, one article saying that no such calamity has occurred since the Indian Mutiny, another referring
as a precedent to the destruction of the army in Afghanistan, 40 years ago. It will perhaps
occur to these writers on reflection that in the present case there has been no British
defeat, & that the very fact of the praise bestowed on Gordon for going out to Khartoum
shows that the risk was well known beforehand. And, as our sole object was to prevent
the Mahdi from advancing on Egypt, we have not failed, unless he should prove strong
enough to threaten Wolseley, which is not in the least likely.

7 Feb. 1885: . . . Cabinet at 12.00, which sat till 3.30, & would have sat longer, but that
some of us had to go away. All present except Ld Spencer. Looked in at office, where
luckily there was nothing to do . . . Keston by 4.12 train, & quiet evening. Read to M. &
bed early.

The Cabinet of today was long, & the discussion desultory for the most part, as generally happens when men come together, not to argue in favour of a preconceived opinion,
but to form one by exchange of ideas. Hartington read an answer from Wolseley to our
message of yesterday, dated 6 Feb. at midnight: it is long, deals mainly with military
details, & will be in print. He asks what we mean to do as to an advance on Khartoum,
says we cannot make certain of taking it during the present cold weather & suggests various movements as possible. He will try to discover what has become of Gordon, but
observes truly that no military operation can help him, since if he is a prisoner the Mahdi
can send him away beyond the reach of help. The comments made on this message were
various. **The Premier** said he believed the public cared very much about Gordon, but
very little about the Soudan. **Hartington** thought what the public cared about was the
supposed blow to our military reputation. **Chamberlain** did not understand why the
Mahdi was so anxious to fight us, as he had been told again & again that we had no wish
to stay in his country. **Dilke** would take Berber. **Trevelyan** would negociate, but prepare
to fight at the same time. **Granville** thought Khartoum might still be taken. **D.[erby]**
held that, unless the Mahdi came to terms, we must go to Khartoum next cold season.
Kimberley agreed. **Harcourt** reminded us that we had pledged ourselves to establish a
government of some sort at Khartoum. **Northbrook** said that we could not retreat, we
must check the Mahdi.

A letter was read from Dr. B. – [illegible], advising having recourse to Zebehr. This we all
objected to, the more as it is believed he has been in league with the Mahdi. Some talk
followed as to negociating with the Sultan, as to sending Indian troops, calling out the
reserves, etc. The feeling in general was against Indian troops, Kimberley especially, & I think
Northbrook also, thinking it dangerous that they should be exposed to contact with the
fanatical Arabs, whose enthusiasm might prove catching. In the end we drafted a telegram,
saying that we recognise the necessity of overthrowing the power of the Mahdi, that we leave
it to him to decide on the military measures necessary, & to determine whether he shall
advance now or next season. We ask him to state at once what additional force he will require.

– We had also some talk about an intended visit of the P. of Wales to Ireland. It seems
he wants to go 'in state', whatever that may mean, & hold a levee, but the Queen objects
furiously, and he gives that up, but insists on being paid his expenses. Ld Spencer guarantees his safety, so we cannot object.

Childers said something about Fiji claims, & the question of opening the S.
Kensington museum on Sundays was raised, but not disposed of.

Granville told me that, when the Khartoum news first arrived, the Queen sent off a telegram accusing him, in the violent language she often uses, of having been the cause of all the mischief. But not content with this, she sent this part of her message, not as usual, in cypher, but in plain words – it is difficult not to suppose, with the idea that the newspapers would get hold of it. Ponsonby would not have been guilty of such a piece of ill manners, unless he had had positive orders: & it must have passed through his hands. A strong hint as to H.M.'s feelings, which indeed we knew pretty well before. . . .

9 Feb. 1885: . . . Cabinet at 2.00, which sat till 5.00. Then office. Home to dinner & quiet evening.

The premier announced to us in Cabinet the accession of Rosebery & Shaw-Lefevre. The former is undoubtedly a great gain: being one of the best speakers in the Lords, & having lately shown signs of an inclination to make himself unpleasant if his claims were overlooked: so that we neutralise a probable enemy, as well as secure an ally. Shaw-Lefevre is also brought in, less for his own merits than to keep even the balance of peers & commoners. The Cabinet is certainly not more democratic in consequence of this addition: one of its new members being an earl of old family with a fortune of two millions: the other nephew to a peer, & heir to a considerable landed estate.

In talk, it was observed that among the natives in Egypt there is much doubt whether Khartoum is really taken: the chief reason for doubting is that they think the Mahdi would have proclaimed it abroad if true. The question was discussed whether Italian co-operation should be invited or accepted. The Italians are quite ready to give it. **The Premier** said, & we all agreed, that as the main object was to influence opinion in the east acceptance of foreign help would be a confession of weakness. We agreed that any offers of Canadian assistance, of which there have been several, should be welcomed. **Granville** said the French answer on the financial question was on the whole satisfactory. Some of its details were discussed. – The use of Indian troops was next considered. The Indian authorities dislike the notion of employing them. They say (through Kimberley) that of the whole Indian army only about 25,000 are fit to face Arabs or Europeans. They are Sikhs, Gurkhas, & Mahometans, but the Gurkhas, accustomed to a cold climate, would not bear that of the Soudan, & the Mahometans could not be prudently employed. – It was decided on Ld Wolseley's request to send a force to Suakin to meet Osman Digna, & prevent his helping the Mahdi. The force will be about 6,600 in number, sent from here. Talk as to who shall command it: Wolseley wants a certain Gen. Greaves[35] employed: the D. of Cambridge objects to him as too young (he is about 50). **The Premier** said Ld W. must be allowed to have his way. **Childers** observed that Gen. Greaves was a junior only because the D. of Cambridge would not promote him, arguing as he always does that promotion should in the main go by seniority, that everybody should have their turn. This it seems is an old quarrel between the H.[orse] Guards & the War Office. We agreed to ask Ld W. which he prefers – Greaves or Alison[36]. We ended by a long discussion on the military & naval estimates, **Hartington** contending that works of fortification in various places should be pushed on notwithstanding the war – **the Premier, Chamberlain,** & others of whom I was one, arguing that we had enough to do in Egypt, & that military expenses not absolutely necessary must be put off. **Hartington** had the frankness to own that, if a large outlay on guns, etc., which the War Office strongly pressed in 1877–1878 had been sanctioned, the whole would have been useless by this time, from changes in armament.

10 Feb. 1885: Lawrence called, but with little to say: he tells me that within his knowledge many landowners are, or expect soon to be, unable to pay the interest of their mortgages, & estates cannot be sold.

Lawson came for news: talk about the Russians & Herat: he takes for granted that they will be established there shortly, & we are in no position to object, with our army locked up in Africa. Talk about Bismarck: whose offensive ways he ascribes to pique rather than policy. there is no doubt that he personally dislikes & distrusts Gladstone, & this is mutual: for the two men represent respectively two opposite forms of government: the absolutist-military, & the parliamentary. Talk of our army, its weakness, etc. He seems to think the only remedy is higher pay.

. . . Office at 2.00, committee of Cabinet met in my room at 2.30: Granville, Kimberley, Chamberlain, Childers, Ashley, & Herbert: chiefly on the W. Indian treaty: they sat till 4.00. Office till 5.30: then called in Curzon St. A.D. better, but does not leave the bedroom: describes herself as having been very near death, and I believe it was so.

11 Feb. 1885: . . . Sudden summons to a Cabinet at 11.00, which sat till 12.30. Thence to office, where stayed till near 3.00. Then to meeting of the Literary Fund, where we agreed that the D. of Argyll should be asked to take the chair at the next anniversary dinner &, failing his acceptance, Lord Lytton. . . .

12 Feb. 1885: News of a fresh battle on the Nile at or near a place called Kerbekan, a victory, but dearly paid for. Gen. Earle[37] in command of the English force was killed, & several other officers.

The death of Gordon is apparently confirmed, but some continue to doubt. According to the most probable story, his troops, or some of them, mutinied, the officers having made terms with the Mahdi: they let in the enemy &, as Gordon came out of his room to see what was the matter, they murdered him.

The Cabinet of yesterday was short, & mainly confined to one subject, the choice of the officer who is to command the Suakin expedition. It seems that the War Office on consideration object to Gen. Greaves, as he would supersede many officers who are not only his seniors, but some (as Sir Evelyn Wood) have seen more service. This after discussion was thought reasonable, but some of us were for leaving Lord Wolseley absolutely free to choose, the Premier, Granville, & I, taking that view. We were outvoted, & an arrangement, which Ld W. has partly agreed to, was determined on: Gen. Graham[38] to command, & Greaves to be his chief of staff.

Note: The Italians have taken Massowah, with no reason alleged, & apparently mean to keep it. The French have taken Tajoura[39].

13 Feb. 1885: Office at 2.00, & stayed till 5.00 Saw there Hartington, who came about the Australian proposal to send a force to Suakin: & Gen. Cameron, who is going out to Hong Kong: a good gentlemanlike officer, with nothing remarkable about him . . . There called also Sir F. Napier Broome[40], governor of Western Australia, who rather disappointed me, for I had heard well of him: he seemed awkward & embarrassed (I believe he was very shy) & the greater part of his conversation was a bitter attack on Pope-Hennessy: whom he accuses of opening his letters at the post office! There is a quarrel between them, &I have no doubt that Hennessy has been unscrupulous & tricky: but, as he declined to make any official complaint, I do not see what there is for me to do in the matter.

[Lord] Sefton called, with a sketch of the speech he intends to deliver at Liverpool, where a dinner is to be given to Lord Ripon: he had introduced into it a strong censure of Chamberlain's late speeches, which, however reasonable in itself, & natural in his position, would have certainly provoked a disturbance. I prevailed on him to modify it, & put in its place a few sentences deprecating extreme opinions . . . as tending to frighten away moderates & break up the party.

Granville dined with us.

14 Feb. 1885 (Saturday): . . . The Premier called yesterday (or Thursday?) on M. & talked freely, though other persons were present, about his own habits & tastes. He said he found his great pleasure in reading,- &, when someone suggested that he could not have much time for books, he answered that at his age he found much work impossible. Three hours were his usual limit, in case of necessity he could go up to five hours, but anything more exhausted him. Thus he had of necessity a good deal of leisure. He was very full of the biography[41] of a young lady, a Miss Watson, who had been brought up among men of science, & was like them an agnostic, but who became religious as her health failed. He said it was one of the most interesting works that he had ever read. – He has been much blamed for going to the theatre on the night when the capture of Khartoum, & probable death of Gordon, were announced: one does not see why, for what good could he have done by staying at home? but the public resents any appearance of want of sympathy where it is itself inclined to be sympathetic & is disposed to be angry with Gladstone as being responsible for Gordon's death: which it would not be easy to prove, but popular sentiment does not stop to reason. – It is perhaps more imprudent to talk openly of his diminished power of labour, however natural at 75 that may be. The comment is sure to be: 'Why then remain a minister?' . . .

16 Feb. 1885: . . . Cabinet at 2.00, which sat till 5.30, Rosebery & Shaw-Lefevre present. Thence office, where remained till near 7.00 . . .

In Cabinet, we discussed the rough estimate for our Egyptian campaign, which Hartington puts at £5,000,000, including in this the cost of a railway to Berber. **Chamberlain** objected to the last item, if it was supposed to involve a permanent occupation. **Dilke** also thought it raised the whole question of our future policy. **Chamberlain** said, in a speech of some length, the question was how long we meant to stay. **Kimberley** observed that we had 3 possible alternatives: (1) to stay in the Soudan ourselves: (2) to establish a settled form of government there & come away: (3) to come away at once. **Harcourt** reminded us that we authorised Gordon to stay & form a 'settled government' at Khartoum. **The Premier**: Do you consider that a pledge still binding? **Kimberley**: You must overthrow the Mahdi. **D.[erby]**: We are pledged to the protection of Egypt. **Trevelyan**: There are many natives who have taken our side, & who will be massacred if we retire. – More talk followed, & in the end we agreed to meet again tomorrow. It was settled, not at once to call out the reserves, but to offer inducements to men in the reserve to join.

We discussed a bill, promised by Harcourt, for the relief of the crofters in the Western Highlands, the principle of which is only to give leases for 19 or 30 years, under certain conditions, with rents fixed by arbitration: the rents at the expiration of said leases to be settled by contract, as before. This is so moderate an interference that I could not object to it, especially as it applies only to holdings under £30, & within certain geographical limits: it is in fact what the majority of the landowners themselves are prepared to agree to: **Chamberlain** avowed his dislike of it on that ground, & thought the Irish land bill was the *minimum* of what the crofters would accept. But in fact they ask much more: some claim to hold land without paying rent at all (having been influenced by Henry George and the party of land nationalisation), others do not go this length, but demand as a right that they shall be allowed to hold as much land, taken from the large sheep farms, as their increasing families may require. The latter is not a wholly unreasonable request if asked as a favour, but obviously it is not a kind of claim which the law can support.

The fall of Khartoum has produced its natural effect, & the Cabinet is not at this moment popular: indeed very much the reverse, in London & among the upper classes. It is said by persons who ought to know, but how truly I cannot judge, that this feeling is confined to them, & that the mass of the electors care much more for the franchise & for home questions than for Egypt. But in the London press the general sentiment is hostile. *The Times* attacks us daily: & with unusual violence: so does the *[Morning] Post*: the *Standard* more temperately: the *Telegraph* in the main supports, but only on condition that we do what they want in Egypt: the *Daily News* is friendly: the *St. James's Gazette* never desists from invective: the *Pall Mall Gazette* writes so wildly that it is scarcely intelligible, but its general language is that of a kind of Jingo radicalism. A few debates in parliament will clear the air.

17 Feb. 1885: . . . Cabinet 2.30–4.30: office again till 6.00, when home . . .

The Cabinet of today gives me little to note, for it was almost entirely occupied with a discussion as to the line which we should take in debating the Egyptian question in parliament. This was talked over at length, & with a remarkable (to me unexpected) agreement. The necessity of common action has forced men like Chamberlain & Hartington into union, & this I think not insincerely, for it is not now a question of what anybody might wish to do, but of what we must do.

I raised two questions connected with colonies: one as to the expenses of the N. Guinea protectorate, the other as to the answer to be given to the Canadian offer of troops. Both were settled as I wished them.

While the Cabinet was sitting yesterday, a meeting professedly of unemployed workmen, really a socialist demonstration, came to Downing Street. It was meant to be a display of numbers, but heavy rain made it a failure, & we knew nothing of its existence till all was over. Mr. Hyndman[42], the socialist agitator, was at its head, or at least the leading personage present: & he delivered to the assembled crowd a speech such as has not been heard in an English town in our time. He said the people were being murdered, that they must have life for life, & he advised the forming of a secret society after the Irish model. – Harcourt tells me that he has been seriously considering whether it was possible to avoid prosecuting Hyndman for this speech, which is a direct instigation to violence.

18 Feb. 1885: . . . It seems certain now that the opposition will move a vote of censure in the Commons, probably next week, & this is well, & much better than a series of desultory debates without result: but I greatly doubt whether they wish to carry it. The division will turn on the conduct of disaffected Whigs & Radicals who like Lawson think we ought never to have gone to Egypt. The former have been alarmed by Chamberlain's speeches, & some of them probably will not vote: the latter are doubtful, disliking what has been done, but not seeing that matters will be mended, from their point of view, by bringing about a change of government. The Irish are expected to be hostile: they could no doubt be bought by a promise not to renew the Crimes Act which expires this year, but that is a price which we shall not pay. – On the whole, the thing most to be feared is that we should carry the division by a very small majority, 5 to 10, which would shake us seriously, without justifying resignation.

– The opposition are weak in personal ability: especially in the Commons: Northcote is said to be in failing health, Cross worn out, R. Churchill, who is clever & active enough, too erratic to be trusted, & Hicks Beach is the only effective debater except him.

In the Lords, where their strength lies, they are better off: but even there Cranbrook, Cairns, & Lytton, are all out of health, & none of the three has appeared in the House since the opening.

19 Feb. 1885: . . . Letter from Childers, which I answered, about the New Caledonia question.

. . . To the Lords, where the house very full, especially the galleries, where many had come expecting a debate: but they were disappointed. Granville made a short statement, carefully prepared, & which, for the first time that I ever saw him do so, he had had written out in full. It was entirely a statement of fact, avoiding argument. He seemed nervous, & worried, to which the death only just announced of his brother-in-law may have contributed (Campbell of Islay[43] – they were warm friends). Salisbury answered him, speaking with some bitterness, but avoided any distinct declaration as to a vote of censure. A few words were said by one or two peers, & the conversation ended. In the Commons Northcote announced his vote of censure, which is long, & so qualified in the latter part as to give him an opportunity of backing out of it if he sees a certainty of failure. Gladstone made a short speech in the same sense as Granville, but no debate followed.

Granville, Kimberley, Spencer, Northbrook, & I, met at F.O. after the H. of Lds, Spencer being anxious to re-establish some sort of diplomatic intercourse with the Pope. He said the nationalists had got hold of him, & there was risk of men being appointed to bishoprics who were extreme in opinions, & more or less tainted with socialist ideas. We talked the matter over – Kimberley & I contending that the Pope could not but be a nationalist where Ireland was concerned, since an independent Irish nation would be a great gain to the Catholic cause. In the end we agreed that nothing can be done formally, but it was thought that Ripon might be induced to make a tour in Italy, & pay him a visit . . .

20 Feb. 1885: . . . Cabinet at 2.00, which sat till 4.00. Then to the Lords, where answered a question . . . as to colonial military assistance. Then office, where stayed till near 7.00.

In Cabinet, most of our time was passed in discussing the coming motion. The general opinion was that it is so framed, purposely, that it cannot be carried. The party of whom [John] Morley is the representative, who thinks it a mistake to have interfered in Egypt at all, are precluded from supporting it by the terms of the concluding sentence, & many of them will probably on that ground vote against it. The Irish, much as they hate the government, will not pledge themselves to the destruction of the Mahdi. It is impossible that these results should have been overlooked, & the necessary inference is that nothing more is meant than a demonstration. 'Northcote,' said one member of the Cabinet, I forget who, 'does not want to turn us out – Forster does.' He, Forster, I believe to be one of our most bitter opponents: holding himself to have been ill used in being compelled to resign his Irish post by the pressure of Irish members.

Hartington said that some of the Whigs would support the censure, & many stay away. Trevelyan expressed uneasiness at Morley's amendment, thinking it a more serious danger than Northcote's motion, inasmuch as it will divide the party at the coming elections. Harcourt said also that he could speak against Northcote, but not against Morley. Some talk followed as to the colonial offers of troops . . .

21 Feb. 1885 (Saturday): Notice given that Northcote accepts Monday next as the day for his vote of censure. Nothing is said yet as to a corresponding motion in the Lords.

. . . Office at 2.00: saw there two of the colonial agents, Mr. Garrick & Mr. Murray Smith, about Samoa, etc. They were as reasonable as possible, & a little ashamed of the excitement which lately existed in Australia, & is now cooling down. Saw also Sir J. Swinburne[44], at his request: a north country baronet, who has been high sheriff for his county, a descendant or relative of the traveller of 100 years ago, and of the poet: his business was to tell me about the Boers, who as he says are planning an expedition into the Matabele country due north of the Transvaal, & north of the Limpopo. This country as he believes is full of gold, & he seems to have been speculating in goldfields there. He seemed to think it was our duty to restrain the Boers in that direction: and I did not argue with him: but merely thanked him for his information: but if they must spread out in some quarter, and it is apparently their nature to do so, where can they go with less injury to us, or indeed to anybody? And will not their rough and ready kind of civilisation be an improvement on native savagery? Sir John talked pleasantly enough: I could not make out what had taken him gold hunting into these parts, but he talked of his agents there.

Keston by 4.13 train . . .

22 Feb. 1885: . . . The first excitement produced among politicians by the vote of censure is dying out, since nobody believes it will be carried, & few believe that its movers are in earnest: no expectation therefore remains of an early change of ministry, & it is beginning to be known that the Cabinet is not divided, as was supposed, by irreconcilable differences as regards present action, whatever divergence of tendencies there may be in the future. But there is much speculation as to Gladstone's course & its effect on his colleagues. His sudden decline in popularity is remarkable. Even attached supporters, like Dalhousie, talk of him in language which a year ago they could not have believed that they should ever use. (D. told me the other day that his idol had been broken, & that he had never been so deceived in any man's character before.) They accuse him of refusing to see what does not suit his preconceived ideas, of want of patriotism, obstinacy, intolerance of criticism, etc.: in short he is as unreasonably abused as he has often been immoderately praised. It is thought (and here the public is right) that his extreme dislike to send out an expedition to relieve Gordon caused it to be delayed: and that delay has caused the failure: which is not so. He is blamed for having made either no mention, or very slight mention, of Gordon in his speech on Thursday: which was an odd omission, & the speech was a failure. He also ignored the sending of the Australian troops, which perhaps was not strictly a part of his subject, but it was expected that he should notice it. I have heard that his reception by the House, both when he rose & when he sat down, was absolutely cold: hardly a cheer being heard from any quarter. The substance of all this – that G. is growing old, that, as he says himself, he is not equal to continuous work for long together: and also that the imperialist ideas now dominant, the disregard of economy, & the semi-socialist tendencies of a considerable section of the Liberal party, are distasteful to him. He is out of harmony with the prevailing tendencies of the moment, & probably knows it. I have no doubt that he would willingly withdraw, but at this crisis (as the public calls it, though there is really nothing very alarming abut it) retreat is impossible.

23 Feb. 1885: . . . To the Lords, where sundry questions, leading to irregular & desultory conversations, such as would not be tolerated in a place where there was anything real to do: but among us nobody cares, & perhaps they are right. One was put to me by Ld Belmore[45] about the Australian Federation Bill: whereupon Carnarvon took the opportunity to go off into a panegyric of the public spirit of the Australian colonies in making their offer of troops – a subject which had nothing to do with the question put, even if it had not already been answered . . . This kind of miscellaneous talk lasted till past 6.00: when home, & worked on office papers till dinner, & in the evening.

Northcote moved his vote of censure, in a speech which is not praised by his supporters: they think it too moderate, & even feeble: Gladstone replied: the whole interest of the evening's debate was in these two speeches.

24 Feb. 1885: . . . Dined at The Club . . . talk about George Eliot . . . Sir J. Paget mentioned a curious proof of her accuracy: she had represented some personage as dying with certain symptoms, & being told they were impossible consulted him: he said she was right, & she answered with more gratitude than the occasion seemed to require, saying he had relieved her from great uneasiness.

A meeting of Conservatives at the Carlton today, in which it is said very free comments were made on Northcote's weak handling of his case, as the party consider it: it is generally desired that he should resign the lead, but they have nobody to put in his place. He himself would not be unwilling, being out of health: but nobody likes to be superseded. At the same time they require an efficient chief in the Commons, as Salisbury cannot direct the party from the Lords. – In the H. of C. the debate on Egypt was delayed for two hours by an Irish row, which ended in the suspension of a member, O'Brien. Not the least odd part of the incident is that many Conservatives supported the Irish in their attempt at obstruction: & this although the motion obstructed was their own vote of censure! Goschen & Trevelyan were the chief speakers later.

I find it everywhere assumed that the motion is merely a peg to hang a debate upon, & not a serious offer for power. It is not strange that the opposition leaders should prefer to keep out of office while these troubles continue: in their own interest they are right: and next year will bring an entirely new world, for nobody in the least knows what the new voters will or will not care for.

25 Feb. 1885: Received a half mad, half socialist circular sent round by Mr. Williams of Ormskirk, against payment of tithes or rent[46]. I sent it on to Hale.

Day wet & foggy . . . Office 2.30–4.30 . . . Called on A.D. Dinner to Lord Ripon in St. James's Hall, Kimberley in the chair. Present about 600, as was said. . . . I noticed that every allusion to Gladstone produced great enthusiasm: which a few months ago would have been taken as a matter of course, but just now he is so out of favour with the upper classes that it is something to be assured that the feeling against him does not extend to the more numerous body of his supporters.

Some talk with Carlingford, whom I sat next, & who has always taken a very optimist view of Irish affairs. He now, however, admits that the Irish feeling against England is at least as bitter as it ever was, if not worse.

26 Feb. 1885: ... At 11.00 I am quite clear of work, & free to look over notes for a speech this evening. This I did, with rather more than less than the usual nervous discomfort which I feel on such occasions . . . . . . To the Lords at 4.30. Salisbury rose at once, & spoke for an hour, attacking the whole conduct of the government in regard to Egypt: with much bitterness in substance, but no excessive acrimony of style. Northbrook followed him, somewhat dull & dry, & resting too much on details, but sound in argument, & his style improved towards the close. Then the attendance began to be thin, peers went away to dinner, & the House might as well have adjourned till 10.00, for no one remained on the benches except the half dozen who wanted to deliver speeches for the newspapers. I rose at 10.30, following Ld Waterford, & spoke nearly an hour, to a very attentive though hostile audience. I satisfied myself fairly well, but as always my chief feeling was relief at having got the business over. Ld Harrowby followed me, not very effective: & we adjourned at 12.00.

Walk home with Granville: & talk as to the result of what is passing. There is no doubt that the party wish Gladstone to retire. Ld G. does not think that they would follow him: doubts whether Hartington would take any place but the first. The Cabinet, he says, is full of intrigue: Hartington hates the Premier, & hardly disguises it: Childers has some quarrel with him: Northbrook is sore about his report on Egypt not having been adopted: Dilke & Chamberlain keep aloof, & aim at making a party of their own: in short there is no unity & little mutual confidence. So Ld G. thinks, & I am inclined to agree with him. I do not see what reconstruction is possible, if once we break up. The calculations as to the division in H.C. vary greatly: yesterday opinion gave us a majority of 30 to 50, today 15 to 20 are the favourite numbers, but nobody knows. It is all guesswork.

27 Feb. 1885: . . . Lawson called, & commented on the sudden disappearance of Gladstone's popularity. He said that when in the H. of C. an opposition speaker, I forget who suggested that he ought to retire, not only all the Conservatives cheered violently, but the galleries joined, & many clapped their hands. (But of this feeling there appeared no evidence the other day in St. James's Hall.)

He thought Harcourt, who with Dilke was the chief speaker last night, was 'riding for a fall' – that he wanted to make the support of Goschen and the waverers impossible. It may be so. Harcourt is sick of his present office, thinks that with Hartington as chief he should be right hand man, & that the Chancellor would retire along with Gladstone, & leave him that place, which he has long coveted. A reconstruction would suit him, even at the cost of a few months' exclusion from office. He argued with me that we could not go on with a majority reduced to 10 or 12, as some say it will be.

Office 2.30–4.30: then to the Lords, where yesterday's debate was renewed . . . We divided 68 to 189: the result being known before excited no interest, & in fact it was noticeable that the peers themselves seemed to attach no importance to the whole matter, knowing that it was only a sham fight, & that the real battle was going on elsewhere.

Walked home with Granville, who has been talking to Gladstone, & finds the latter disposed to retire if circumstances make it possible. I have no doubt but that Ld G. will be glad of an escape from the enormous labour & anxiety of his present post. He is growing old, & the work is too much for any but a young & strong man.

28 Feb. 1885: Wrote to Granville, saying (with reasons) that I thought on the whole our best course was to resign, the majority last night having been only 14. He answered entirely agreeing.

Saw Lawson, who seemed to assume that the result of last night was a victory for the government, & seemed surprised when I told him that I did not see it so.

Cabinet at 2.00, which sat till 6.30: one of the longest, & certainly the most interesting, that we have held. When it broke up, there was a short meeting of the colonial committee in my office. Home at 7.30, & dined with the Lord President, the usual official dinner at which sheriffs are pricked for. I came away as early as I could, having an immense mass of work from the office: & worked upon it till 12.00.

In Cabinet, the Premier began by simply asking our opinions on the situation as to what we should do. **Granville** spoke first, & briefly, without reasons, said he thought we ought to retire. **Harcourt** followed in the same sense: saying he did not rest his decision on the vote of last night: that was not much worse than the vote of last May: the party had shown great fidelity: few had voted against us, & those for the most part not important persons. But on the other hand, if we broke up now, we should do so with a party still united. By going on we should grow weaker, we should quarrel with our own followers on the Soudan business, & this while involved in perplexities: Bismarck hostile: Russia moving on Herat: the Irish as bad as ever, etc. The end would only be more ignominious for being deferred. **D.[erby]** concurred with Harcourt, for the same reasons, dwelling mostly on the certainty of disunion in the party. **Trevelyan** thought the division not much worse than that of last year. **Kimberley** was inclined to resign, but disliked the appearance of being turned out by the Irish. **Chamberlain** gave no definite opinion: the majority, though small, justified our staying in, unless we thought retirement best for the party. **Harcourt** observed that last year Forster & Goschen were neutral, now they are hostile. **Northbrook** said the trouble was that 60 of those who had voted for us were opposed to the policy which we must necessarily follow. **Hartington** said the support of many had been given with hesitation & would not be given again. And, when we came to action, divergences of opinion would show themselves. **Granville** said if the troops remained through the summer they would suffer, & there would be a great outcry: 'We are in a false position: we are rather ashamed of our victories than proud of them: we cannot carry our party with us.' **Kimberley**: The difficulties with Russia are becoming serious: feeling is strained here: still more so in India: there is risk of war. Could we leave matters safely in the hands of the opposition? **D.[erby]**: They will be reckless in pushing us on to war: they would be more cautious if themselves responsible. **Granville**: spoke of Bismarck, his hostility to the Crown Princess, & to this government. It will be easier for another party to make terms with him than for us. **Spencer**: doubts whether we are strong enough to face the difficulties before us: but is in doubt, altogether, & gives no opinion. **Chamberlain**: argues in an undecided manner: 'If we go out, we offend the party: they won't understand it: we shall leave matters in a dangerous state. The Tories would readily go to war with Russia. Then they would dissolve on the present constituencies, negociate with the Irish, put off a redistribution bill, & bring in one quite different.' **Dilke**: Hicks Beach is violent against the arrangement as to seats, will upset it if he can, & is likely to be the next leader. **Gladstone**: will abide by the decision of the Cabinet. Leans to the belief that we ought to stay. We are in a false position as to Egypt, carrying out a policy which is not ours &, if that were alone in question, we should be better out. But there is no precedent for resigning while in a majority. He does not fear division among ourselves. We are on better terms with France & Russia than the other party. There would be great difficulty too as to finance, a new government would not be in time to provide for the wants of the year. He lays much stress on this. Agrees that we cannot go on relying on Tory support. Thinks we shall probably be beaten on some financial question. Then we can go out honourably. **Harcourt** will support the Prime Minister if he thinks it right to stay. **Trevelyan, Carlingford, Shaw-Lefevre**, think we ought to stay. **Hartington** does not like to carry on the war against the wishes of the party. **Ld. Chanc.** would decide for staying in, if it were not for the foreign troubles. These make him hesitate. **Rosebery**: talks of divisions in the party. Fears we shall sink lower & lower, & go out in a stink.

Granville: thinks we differ too much among ourselves to carry on a war. Refers to the case of the Crimean war, which he says either Ld Aberdeen or Ld Palmerston would separately have kept out of, if either had had his own way. **Chamberlain**: fears we shall split, & on that ground is in favour of resigning now. **Gladstone**: sees clearly what the opinion of the majority is, & will not set his own against it. (He spoke briefly, & sat silent, evidently much annoyed & disapproving.) **Harcourt** (impulsively): does not like it to be said that our chief was willing to hold on, & that we forced him to run away. **Gladstone**: denies having any strong opinion, admits that the circumstances are most difficult. Sees that we cannot go on long in any case.

Much more conversation took place, but nothing new was added. Those most earnest for resignation were Granville, Chamberlain, & Hartington. – Harcourt avowed that he should go against his opinion in deference to the Prime Minister. On the other side were Kimberley, Trevelyan, & Dilke: but none very strongly. We divided at last 9 to 7: but several of the 9 acknowledged that they were not convinced, & yielded to the evident personal feeling of the chief. – Gladstone's conduct was peculiar. At first he seemed really indifferent but, as the discussion went on, it became evident that he felt very deeply the hostile judgment of his colleagues on his chances of success. Granville says that he was yesterday for resigning, & that the ladies of the family have made him change his mind: but I think the cause lay deeper, & that he felt a certain humiliation at the idea of being obliged to abandon the helm in stormy weather. One expression he used which struck me as singular, but in what part of the conversation I forget: 'You may rely upon it that all this excitement about the Soudan is within a mile of Westminster: it does not affect the country at all.' The final division was: For resigning, Granville, Derby, Hartington, Rosebery, Northbrook, Childers, Chamberlain. – Against resigning, Gladstone, Kimberley, Shaw-Lefevre, Trevelyan, Carlingford, Harcourt, Dilke, Spencer, & the Ld Chancellor. But, as Chamberlain observed, nearly everybody was in two minds, & there was no warmth in the discussion, each side feeling how much the other had to say. . . .

3 Mar. 1885: . . . Hale called, unexpectedly: we talked over many small estate matters . . . Meeting at War Office: Hartington, [Lord] Morley, D. of Cambridge, Sir A. Alison, Sir R. Herbert, & the Australian agents. We sat an hour. The object was to discuss the Australian offers of troops: which for the most part are offers of absolutely raw volunteers, under volunteer officers. – But we must make the best of them for political reasons. Thence office, where worked till near 6.00 . . . Dined at the French embassy . . .

4 Mar. 1885: . . . The decision taken at the Cabinet of Saturday appears to have given general relief, certainly to the opposition, who did not like the prospect of coming in, & in general also to the Liberal party, though with some exceptions. It is felt that a change of hands at a moment of difficulty has many objections, & on the whole I do not regret the result of our discussion, though the risk of disunion in the future, which was the main argument of those who wanted to withdraw, remains undiminished. But the question of the Soudan is already diminishing in importance: the threatening attitude of the Russians near Herat having made many people feel that it may not be advisable to lock up nearly our whole available army in Africa.

The inexplicable quarrel with Bismarck still goes on: I say inexplicable for, though he breaks out almost every day in some new declaration of hostility, or rather perhaps of ill temper, it is impossible to find out what his real grievance is. The pretexts he puts forward are obviously pretexts only: the three reasons commonly supposed to influence him are – dislike of the Crown Princess, who hates him, does not conceal it, & is never tired of holding up English institutions as a model to Germany – personal dislike of Gladstone, which he is said to feel strongly – and fear of the growth in Germany of a parliamentary English system, which he believes would be fatal to the empire. – These three motives are in fact one, though with slight variations in form: for both Gladstone & the Princess represent to him the detested parliamentary system.

5 Mar. 1885: . . . Talk with Granville: Herbert Bismarck has come over with some message from his father, who seems disposed to make up the quarrel: which is not difficult if he wishes it, since there is no real subject of dispute. He, young Bismarck, is staying at Lansdowne House as Rosebery's guest, and R. seems to have had some hand in inducing him to come over. Ld G. told me that he thought as I do that there is an intrigue between Dilke & Rosebery, who want the foreign & colonial offices respectively, and that this move is part of it: they are trying to make the Germans believe that we, Granville & I, are the obstacles to a good understanding. G. told me that he had told Gladstone he was willing to resign, if by so doing he could expedite matters: the Premier of course declined.

6 Mar. 1885: . . . Death of Mrs. H. Stanley[47]: which will be regretted by nobody, for she was drunken, disreputable, & always in debt: altogether a discredit to the family. . . . Her only living son[48] is in New Zealand, where he has led a disgraceful life, more than once in gaol, but now is out of health & incapable of active mischief. Her granddaughter who lived with her was seduced by the man who has since married her, a schoolmaster dismissed from his employment under the local school board, & who has neither means nor character. The other two sons who, though helpless, were decently respectable, are dead: they have left children who are doing fairly well, as far as I can learn. – The real history of my uncle's marriage with this unlucky woman just dead I could never learn: he & other officers of his regiment had lived with her, she had neither very good looks nor cleverness, & I am afraid the object can only have been to vex his family. However, that chapter of family history is closed . . .

7 Mar. 1885 (Saturday): . . . Cabinet at 2.00, which sat till past 5.00 . . . [then] to Keston . . .

In Cabinet, our chief business was to discuss the proposed Suakin-Berber railway. As to this we are in some perplexity. It is about to be proposed in the H. of C. (I believe on Monday) and is certain to be strongly opposed: in part on the ground of expense: in part as tending to make our occupation of the Soudan permanent: which a large section at least of Conservatives & Whigs desire. Our sole reason for agreeing to make it was a military one, Lord Wolseley having declared it necessary for his operations in the autumn. But within the last few days he has sent a telegram saying that he must rely on the Nile route for supplies: that the S.-B. railway can probably not be finished in time, & will be of comparatively little service if it is finished: and he urgently presses for a short line, or series of lines, to be made along the Nile to help the transport. This change of views has taken us by surprise . . . On the other hand, it is fair to remember that, when he [Wolseley] asked for the S.-B. line to be made, circumstances were quite different: the fall of Khartoum, & impossibility of taking Berber, having entirely altered the situation. But, from whatever cause, he has gone round: & the situation as regards parliament is awkward. Our conversation was long & confused: the Premier taking no part, & seeming altogether abstracted in thought, as I observe is apt to happen to him when he dislikes the subject under discussion.

Hartington quoted Fowler the engineer as saying that the line would take two cold seasons to make. **Chamberlain** expressed perplexity: the railway was asked for as a military necessity: he did not see how we could propose it on that ground, keeping back Ld Wolseley's opinion. **Kimberley**: If you give up the railway, you must give up the expedition from Suakin. **Hartington** does not see what objection there is to the railway. **Chamberlain**: Two objections: the cost: and the danger of its being used to keep us longer in the Soudan. **Harcourt**: After beating Osman Digna, are we to advance to Berber? Would ask Ld Wolseley what he really means. **Dilke** doubts if the line proposed by the Nile can be made. And, if the other takes too long, where are we? Doubts if this country will let the war go on during the summer. Believes the undertaking (of smashing the Mahdi) impossible. **Northbrook** thinks Ld Wolseley has miscalculated the chances. Dwells on the strength of the enemy. Would rely chiefly on the S.-B. line. **Dilke** is for stopping the construction of the line at once. **Harcourt** does not believe Ld W. will ever advance beyond Korti. He will tell us it is impossible, & we shall acquiesce. **Ld. Chanc.** would enquire what Ld W. wishes, which he does not understand from the telegrams. **Granville**: We cannot change our plans at once. We must know more. After some further talk, we settle a telegram.

Granville tells us of his two interviews with H. Bismarck. The first was disputatious & unpleasant, the second more friendly. Bismarck had got into his head, among other wild ideas, the notion that we were intriguing against him at the Camaroons through a Polish agent, an adventurer who chances to be out there, & with whom we have had no relations except buying a bit of land from him, or rather a claim to one. I do not believe that the Germans now believe that we are telling them the truth in saying that he is not our agent, but they are satisfied with the disavowal.

Some talk about the Turks holding Suakin, at which, though it is an old proposal, Harcourt was violent, saying he must resign, etc. In the end we settled nothing. . . .

9 Mar. 1885: London by usual train . . . Office, where colonial committee met at 2.30: present, Granville, Kimberley, Childers, Herbert, Meade, Ashley, Pauncefote, Ld E. Fitzmaurice, Anderson. We discussed the charter proposed for the African trading company, & the Niger protectorate.

. . . Dined at home. Went to a party at the German embassy, in consequence of a message received through Ly D. that it was hoped I should show myself there, as I had dined at the French embassy last week. So curious are the susceptibilities of diplomatists.

News that the German officials have hauled down the British flag at Amlas Bay under the Camaroon Mountains: probably a misunderstanding only, but unpleasant. We settled in the committee today to advise the Cabinet to assume a direct protectorate of the Niger, rather than hand it over to a company – the latter course involving just as much responsibility, & giving less power. – I detest these annexations, but they are impossible to avoid when other nations are seizing unoccupied territory everywhere, & then endeavouring to exclude our trade from the districts they have secured.

Granville's statement of Friday is taken by a large part of the foreign press to be an apology, which it certainly was not, but there was an evident expectation that we should quarrel with Germany, & some disappointment, I think, all over the Continent, that we did not.

The real trouble is now at Herat. Will the Russians give way? If they move on Herat it will not be easy to keep the peace.

10 Mar. 1885: Busy, & rather bustled & worried with affairs, though no great mass of work, but one thing came upon another, so that nothing could be properly considered – a growing evil, I suppose inevitable, but when important decisions have to be taken slapdash it is impossible that confusion should not sometimes follow.

Cold disagreeable day with east wind: went to be photographed . . . Office at 2.00 . . . work there till 4.15, when to the Lords. They sat less than an hour . . . Dined at The Club, meeting Rosebery, Reeve, Newton, Maine, & Lecky. Pleasant party, but the wine so abominably bad that we all protested.

In the Commons, the vote for the Suakin-Berber line passed with little opposition, though much talk, but the whole question of expenditure on Egypt will turn up again in various forms. Those who understand the ebb & flow of popular feeling say that the hot fit is already passing off, & the cold fit coming on: and that we shall not be pressed to go to Khartoum. Indeed the chances of a quarrel with Russia have caused the Soudan to be already half forgotten. It is even now possible that we may have to send the troops now in Africa to Afghanistan, leaving only a small force on the Egyptian frontier. The last Russian telegrams that I have seen are polite & friendly, but do not indicate the means of a settlement, & the question is whether the Russian advance into territory claimed by Afghanistan is an unauthorised act of agents who may be disavowed: or whether it is a settled policy to push forward at a moment when we are engaged elsewhere. . . .

12 Mar. 1885: . . . Cabinet, which sat from 12.00 to 3.00, all present except Ld Spencer. Thence office, & to the Lords at 4.30, but no business, only a few questions. Home at 6.00. There dined with us . . . in all, with selves, 20.

In Cabinet we discussed first the question, raised both by Baring & Wolseley, of arresting Zebehr. Baring believes him to be in communication with the Mahdi, though admitting that there is no legal evidence to prove his guilt: 'He may get away at any moment, & the risk is too great of letting him be at large.' **Dilke** objected to acting on so little proof. **Harcourt** remarked that Baring was always in extremes, at one moment ready to trust Zebehr & employ him, at the next wanting him hanged. But he agreed to the arrest. **Kimberley** spoke of the frequency of arrests on suspicion during his government of

Ireland. **Northbrook** believed Zebehr to be the prime mover in a mutiny that broke out in one of our native regiments. **Granville, the Premier**, & **D.[erby]** agreed as to the arrest as a measure of military necessity. It was settled not to deport him, but keep him on board a man of war.

At this stage Granville had to leave for a time, & we filled up the interval with talk about Dover House, which it has often been proposed to reserve for the First Lord of the Treasury. This led to a general discussion on the subject of official residences: Chamberlain, Kimberley, & the Premier, being against them (I also took that side), Dilke, Harcourt, & Hartington inclining to an opposite opinion, on the ground that democracies like their nominees to be well paid. – This is the French view, the Americans take exactly the opposite one. Nothing was settled, nor was there need.

Talk of a proclamation which Wolseley proposes to issue, which is bombastic & to English ideas absurd in the highest degree, outdoing Ld Ellenborough's celebrated manifesto about the gates of Somnauth. **The Premier** wondered why, if he wanted to address the Arabs, he could not tell them what he meant in plain words? **Hartington** answered in his blunt way: 'What is he to tell them? He does not know our policy & it would be odd if he did, since we do not know it ourselves.' This raised a laugh, but Gladstone looked annoyed. It was agreed to warn Ld Wolseley as to the possibility of our being unable to go on with the Soudan campaign if the Russians force us into war, & this was done in a telegram carefully drafted. **Note** that Ld W. is said to be much irritated against us, but I do not know on what ground. The rest of the discussion turned on the Russian action in the country near Herat, but it went too much on details to be reported.

13 Mar. 1885: Early at work, & cleared off all that is to be done in the office, which was less than usual, Herbert being in the gout . . . Office at 2.30. H. of Lords 4.30. Only a few questions. Expected a motion by Wemyss (friendly, not adverse) about colonial troops, but it was the last on the paper &, as W. is talkative & too obviously inclined to thrust himself forward on every possible occasion, the peers did not care to hear him, and only 8 or 10 remained. So he came to me, & said he should put it off. Thence to a Cabinet suddenly summoned in the H. of C. room, to consider: (1) some fresh objections which Bismarck has raised to signing the Egyptian finance settlement, at the last moment, & in violation of his understanding with us: (2) the situation as regards Russia. The first matter admitted of arrangement &, as we hope, is arranged: the second led to a good deal of discussion, but there was general agreement in principle. Harcourt alone took the Russian side, repeated what he had said before: 'You are going to fight for a frontier of which you know nothing.' But he seemed rather to argue for discussion's sake than to be convinced, & in truth there is no room for doubt. The Russians are massing troops on their frontier, which can have no use except to prepare for the seizure of Herat: & no question they expected to be able to seize it while we were engaged in Egypt: probably supposing also that Gladstone would be very unwilling to quarrel with Russia. – In the latter respect they will be deceived, for the Premier, though grave, anxious, & deeply vexed, as his appearance shows, is as little inclined to yield as any of his Cabinet: less than some. For the moment we have an agreement that neither Russian nor Afghan troops are to advance: but the doubt is whether this agreement will be respected by the local commanders. The Russian officers will do all they can, without too open a breach of faith, to bring about a collision, in which the other side shall appear the aggressors: their old game, & one which they play well. In this lies the danger.

14 Mar. 1885 (Saturday): . . . Heard with regret of the death of Sir C. Lampson. He was nearly 80, but still active, & his end seems to have been sudden. He has been throughout the real working head of the Peabody trust – the other trustees only assenting to, or sometimes criticising, what he proposed. Without him it never would have been the success it is. Fortunately our building work is finished for some years to come.

. . . Levee at 2.00: then office till 5.00, where very busy: Keston by 5.17 train. The talk at the levee was in the sense of expecting peace: it is not thought Russia desires a war: and probably this is true: but the ambition or temper of a Russian official, or the blundering of an Afghan, may force on a situation from which there is no retreating.

Engaged among other matters in trying to deal with an awkward dispute which has sprung up between Sir H. Robinson & Sir C. Warren in regard to Bechuana affairs. The former knowing the temper of the Cape colony, & the many dangers, is for a prudent & moderate policy: Warren on the other hand is for a more thoroughgoing course, & has taken on his own authority some rather arbitrary steps. It is probable that as a soldier, remembering Majuba Hill, he rather wishes to drive them into a war than not, & in this feeling, if he has it, he would have the sympathy of all the military party at home. – Sir H. Robinson now proposes to go himself to the scene of action, & take control in civil affairs. I incline to allow him to go, but have referred the matter in a circulation box to the Cabinet.

15 Mar. 1885 (Sunday): . . . Read & wrote: rather nervous & uncomfortable in mind, with no special reason, but the pressure of work upon me in the week has been & will be heavy, & there are many causes of anxiety as regards the public. – Of private troubles, happily, I have none. But I sometimes think my temperament is too nervous for public affairs – that I take them too seriously. I am beginning to have had enough of official life, & doubt whether I shall continue it when the present Cabinet breaks up. . . .

17 Mar. 1885: . . . In evening to a party in Eaton Square, where the bride's presents were displayed – very fine, & the pleasure of the Duchess[49] in their magnificence amusing to witness. The talk in the family is that this is not a love match, that the girl[50] wants to be free, and likes the prospect of a great social position, while not disliking the husband: and he[51] on his side is mainly attracted by the connection, & a little by the fortune, without which the Berlin embassy[52] would have been impossible to a man without private means. Col. Malet the brother holds this language with a quaint simplicity which saves it from being offensive.

. . . The Russian scare has abated, nobody believing in an immediate war, though many may think it is only put off, & I see disappointment among the military party. Even they, however, are aware that this would not be a convenient moment for a quarrel, & probably are not really sorry. The funds have been so far affected as to have fallen from 100 to a little over 96.

The Egyptian financial arrangement is settled at last, to Granville's infinite relief, for its settlement puts an end to Bismarck's power of annoyance, & we are more our own masters than we have been for six months past.

19 Mar. 1885: Walk for exercise: bought some books from Bickers.

At 3.00, with Ly D. . . . to Eaton Square, where we waited till the Bedford party came out, & drove with them to Westminster Abbey. The marriage was duly performed, and I signed among other witnesses, of whom the Premier was one.

20 Mar. 1885: Lawson called, but had no news. He did not seem to think that the parliamentary attack on the Egyptian settlement would be serious. The opposition he thought would scarcely wish to upset it, and so to come into power with the most difficult of all questions unsettled: and with no probability of holding it for more than a few months. They are disorganised to an extraordinary degree: Northcote out of health and unpopular: Hicks Beach preferred by the mass of the party though intellectually inferior: Randolph Churchill despising both, bent on putting himself at the head, reckless, aggressive, & more a radical in opinion than anything else, as far as he can be said to have opinions of his own. The chief election agent, a Mr. Bartley[53], has resigned in disgust: in short, they are all at sixes & sevens. A parliamentary majority in the new constituencies might unite them, but nothing else will, and it does not seem likely that they will get that.

Cabinet at 2.00, which sat till 4.30. It was agreed, after some talk among the members of the Commons, to insist on the Egyptian debate being taken before Easter, on account of the pressing need of money: &, till the H. of C. has sanctioned the arrangement, we cannot raise a loan, nor indeed expect other governments to do their part.

Then came discussion on Bechuanaland business, which I opened, saying that I thought we ought to make one attempt to keep Warren & Robinson together, as a quarrel between them will have a lamentable effect: my first thought had been to allow Sir H.R. to take the control, superseding Warren, & in policy I still believe this course would have been right: but Warren is popular here, he has succeeded so far, & if he resigned we should be thought to have thrown him over. Chamberlain warmly supported me, & there was general agreement, the Premier somewhat dissenting, but giving way.

Granville raised the question of utilising the Turk to help us in Egypt. I did not well understand his plan, which seemed to be to get from the Sultan a confirmation of Tewfik's[54] title as Khedive, and an *iradé*[55] sanctioning the present Egyptian laws. **Harcourt** objected, & all ended in talk. **Childers** explained to us the intended vote of credit. He took as a rough estimate for the whole Egyptian business £7,000,000: said there would be a deficit this year of £2,000,000: and next year one of £9,300,000 to be met. But he did not go into details, & we shall know more exactly when the budget comes on.

Talk about Zebehr: what are we to do with him if no evidence appears in his papers? Some said detain him by way of precaution: the Premier grew indignant, observed 'that these were arguments such as king Bomba might use' & insisted on an early report that we might be able to judge of his guilt or innocence.

Talk about the Gordon diary, part of which the W.O. has printed: **Harcourt** says it contains conclusive proof of Gordon's insanity: few of us had read it: **Northbrook** shook his head, & thought the publication would damage us seriously. Published in some form, apparently, it must be, & the question of property in it is disputed between the brother, Sir H. Gordon, & the War Office. Though called a private diary, it is chiefly an official record of events, meant for possible publication, & oddly interspersed with comments on men & things[56]. Sir E. Baring is the principal object of attack.

Long & serious discussion on the question of Herat & the Russian advance. **Hartington** said sensibly that there was no use in negociating with Russia, we must consider what points we meant to defend, & stick to those. **Chamberlain** did not expect any good to come out of the commission. **Kimberley** said that arbitration (which had been talked of) would have a disastrous effect in India. – He mentioned also the danger of making Herat a strong fortress – that it might very probably get into the hands of some chief who would hold it against the Ameer – possibly might be bought by Russia. **Granville** lamented that Lumsden[57] though honest & zealous was a very stupid man. (Q. if this is so?)

It was admitted that the Russians had a case in one respect – whatever the claims of the Ameer may be, he does not & cannot practically control the Turcoman tribes. The only practical suggestion that I heard was that the force at Quetta should be made up to 25,000 men, which the Gov. Gen. desires, & which we shall agree to. Even there, they are 500 miles from Herat.

21 Mar. 1885: . . . Sent £100 to the Gordon memorial fund . . . It is to build and I suppose endow a hospital in Egypt . . . To Keston by 4.12 train.

The newspapers, having attacked the government unsparingly, are now turning round, & abusing the opposition for having no rival policy to propose. The fact is they have & can have none: for what the imperialist or military party, who are loudest in criticism, would like is that Egypt should be taken & held by us permanently, subject to no European engagements: & this is a proceeding which no responsible statesman will be found to endorse. It is often remarked that, though the difficulties are serious, and likely to continue, especially with Russia, the state of public feeling approaches apathy – and I believe this to be true. My explanation is: (1) that the settlement of the parliamentary reform question has left a void which no other subject of equal interest has yet replaced: (2) that the absolute ignorance in which we are as to the tendencies of the new voters deadens energy, since nobody knows in what sort of a political world he will find himself a year hence: (3) that (Gladstone being out of the way) there is no leader on either side who excites popular enthusiasm – certainly none is felt for either Salisbury, Hartington, or Chamberlain: (4) that foreign questions do not really interest the public, unless something happens abroad to stir up anger or sympathy: a definite & consistent foreign policy is not so much disliked by the masses as inconceivable to them. But the fact is certain – a condition which is full of danger, if not for the present, at least for the near future, finds us as nearly indifferent to politics as a country like ours ever can be. What strong feeling exists on the radical side is more & more tending towards socialism: not socialism in a crude & violent form, but that which calls in the State as an agency to supply all the wants of the poor at the cost of the rich. And of this we shall in the coming years have a good deal. . . .

24 Mar. 1885: . . . Cabinet in the H. of C. room at 5.30, which sat till 7.30. Then home.

. . . In Cabinet we had two questions to discuss, but in that crowded little room I could take no notes, & have only a general recollection of what passed. Our first trouble was the sudden & unexpected refusal of the Sultan to allow Musurus[58] to sign the Egyptian agreement, which he had consented to, so that his turning round is a personal caprice, such as are said to be common with him. We agreed to hold very decided language, to threaten a rupture of diplomatic relations, & to tell him that if that came to pass we should proceed to deal with Egypt independently of any Turkish claims – which among other results would involve the cessation of the tribute. The other question was that of Russia & Herat, which was discussed carefully & at length, with no substantial disagreement. It was decided to take authority to call out the reserves if necessary: to support Ld Dufferin's policy of massing 25,000 men at Quetta: & to assure the Ameer of protection in the event of a move being made on Herat. – I do not think that any of us expect a war, but it is necessary to act as if one were imminent: which will lessen the chance of it. The danger is from some hasty act of either Russian or Afghan officers on the spot, which may put their governments in a position from which it will not be easy to draw back.

25 Mar. 1885: Northcote called about Peabody Trust affairs . . .

. . . The papers are & for two days past have been full of details of a battle near Suakin, or perhaps rather a skirmish on a large scale, in which the Arabs attacked & surprised a part of our force, broke into the zereba, or fortified enclosure, & succeeded in destroying some 500 camels, besides horses & mules. They have thus succeeded in crippling the British transport, and have gained what is really a victory, judging by results, though at a heavy loss to themselves. Sir John Macneill[59], who was in command of the force, is much blamed for not taking precautions, & said to be, though a brave officer, quite incompetent for command. He is in great favour with the court, having been of use to the D. of Connaught, & is thought to have got his appointment so. But we judge by results, & he may be less in fault than he seems.

The desperate fighting of the Arabs is very noticeable – they seem absolutely indifferent to life . . . How we are to get to Berber nobody knows. Possibly the Russian scare may give us an excuse for getting out of this muddle, which now pleases nobody, for those who want England to conquer the Soudan want us also to keep Egypt for ourselves: which is a policy rendered impossible by the present agreement.

Office 2.30–5.00: much discussion with Herbert as to the quarrel between Robinson & Warren, which unluckily is now no secret: we settled nothing definite.

26 Mar. 1885: . . . The D. of Cambridge told me that 1,400 camels had been lost, killed, or disabled, in the Suakin affair: he did not add in express words, but seemed to imply, that the expedition was crippled by the loss of its means of transport, & in fact I find it to be the universal opinion that the Arabs have come off victorious. They were beaten back no doubt, but not until they had done all that they came to do, & made our farther advance extremely difficult.

27 Mar. 1885: Ward . . . expects . . . to send up for investment this year not less than £70,000 . . . This will make at least £75,000 added to savings . . .

. . . Cabinet at 2.00, which sat till 4.15 . . . Dined at Lansdowne House . . . My neighbour was Sir C. Tupper – I told him in the course of talk that I could find no one who believed in the expedition getting to Berber . . .

28 Mar. 1885: Lawson called: talk of the debate & division in H. of C. on the Egyptian convention, which ended last night with a majority of 48 for ministers. No interest is felt outside, & very little in the House itself, for it was well known that the opposition did not wish to win . . . The best speeches are said to have been those of Hicks Beach & Chamberlain.

. . . At the Cabinet yesterday Granville read a draft proposed to be sent to the Russian government requesting an early reply on the Afghan boundary question. This led to much verbal discussion, but without substantial difference, except that **Harcourt** wanted to lay stress on the security of Herat as the one thing important, which others objected to as leaving the hands of Russia free in other quarters: & **Chamberlain** expressed great doubt as to the goodness of the Afghan title to Penjdeh: he was willing to support all necessary preparations, but feared going to war with a divided party, & wished to put Russia more thoroughly in the wrong, if there is to be a quarrel. – There was some talk of Sir P. Lumsden, our agent on the spot, whose telegrams, couched in violent & even offensive language, show something very like a determination to force a quarrel. We agreed to postpone the motion in the Lords for calling out reserves till after the recess.

Harcourt then called in the Lord Advocate, & we discussed the Crofters' Bill. He has guarded its provisions with much care, making it apply only to certain parishes in certain counties, & excluding all leaseholders for however short a term. If it is not altered in the Commons the Scotch landlords will probably not take objection to it: at least so Harcourt, who has been in communication with them, thinks.

Discussion, but vague, and to little purpose, of the prospects of the Soudan campaign. The Premier began it, saying that he noticed the growth in parliament of a strong feeling against continuance of the Soudan operations. Dilke & D.[erby] expressed doubts whether the army would ever get to Berber. **Harc.** said it was a new feature in this war that the English public was as much shocked at the enemy's loss as at our own. The general feeling seemed to be that it was very desirable to withdraw, but impossible, unless the Russian trouble grew more serious.

29 Mar. 1885: . . . In afternoon, called with M. on the Malets at Holwood. Talk with Sir E. [Malet] about German feeling, or rather the feeling of the German government, towards England. He rejects the conclusions come to by Granville & others, which I have noted somewhere in this book: & refers the whole to a personal motive. He says it is no secret in Berlin that Bismarck has done his utmost to get rid of Münster, by describing him to the Emperor as inefficient or indifferent to his duty: that, if he had succeeded, somebody, whom he named, but I have forgotten the name, would have been put into the English embassy to keep the place open, and after a year or two would have resigned to make way for Herbert Bismarck. That to get this place for his son has been the sole inducement to raise the present dispute, and he is the more eager, as he knows that after the Emperor's death he will have no chance. However, the Emperor who, whether from feeling or on system, has a great dislike to parting with old servants, steadily refused to sacrifice Münster, having no cause of complaint against him, & perhaps knowing or suspecting Bismarck's object. Hence the very real & marked indignation which the latter has shown. – Malet talked of the above as being certain, not merely matter of conjecture.

Read much to M. out of [Mark] Pattison's lately published autobiography[60].

30 Mar. 1885: . . . Office, & at 3.00 met the Australian agents to discuss the Federal Council Bill, as to which we agreed on all except one or two points, the chief being that we propose that any colony shall be at liberty to withdraw from the arrangement if it thinks fit: to this Murray Smith as representing Victoria objects, chiefly I think on the ground that it is regarded as a concession to N.S. Wales. The jealousy of these two colonies comes out in a marked way.

Dined Grillions: meeting Northcote, Sir J. Paget, Harrowby, & Fortescue.

31 Mar. 1885: . . .News last night of the sudden downfall of the Ferry Cabinet, consequent on a defeat, or rather check, which the French have sustained in Tonkin. The minister thereon asked for a credit of £8,000,000 to send out fresh troops: but the Chamber, without, as it seems, asking or waiting for explanations, passed a vote which was practically one of censure by a large majority. The average duration of French ministries since 1870 has scarcely, if at all, exceeded 12 months . . . And yet, where is the remedy? And shall we, with a more democratic constitution, escape from the inconvenience, to call it nothing worse, of these incessant fluctuations? . . .

2 Apr. 1885: . . . Answered a letter from the Premier, on various subjects. I said . . . all the world wanted to be out of the Soudan, if we only knew how: that as between Robinson & Warren I was trying to keep the peace, with little hope of success: that I believed Robinson's policy to be the more prudent, but that popular sympathy, both here and on the spot, was with Warren: & that, however little we might sympathise with the contempt of economy, & desire for universal annexation, which are now showing themselves, there was no doubt in my mind as to the reality of these feelings, & as to their tendency to increase: witness America & France.

As to the Russian business, I mentioned that I had heard of Adlerberg[61] saying, what I well remember Schouvaloff used to say 7 years ago: 'Russia does not want to invade India, nor to conquer Afghanistan: but she does wish to establish herself in such a position on the Indian frontier as to be able to prevent England from interfering with her when she next moves on Constantinople.' And I added, I believe this is the truth.

3 Apr. 1885 (Good Friday): . . . Read the Russian answer to our proposals, which is vague, conciliatory in tone but, as I read it, concedes little or nothing in substance. But its language will bear various constructions, & other people may not read it as I do.

Read in the papers, with surprise & regret, of the sudden death of Cairns, at the age of 65. He had been out of health, & only appeared once in the Lords this year, but when I saw him about three weeks or a month ago he seemed quite recovered. He died of congestion of the lungs, caused by a chill. I believe that his health, always delicate, suffered from the folly of his son, who engaged himself to marry an actress, & broke off the marriage without apparent justification: thus committing a double folly. The consequent action for damages last year, ending in a verdict for £10,000, attracted much notice, & Lord Garmoyle thought it wiser to escape cross-examination by going abroad. Cairns himself was blamed – I think quite unjustly – for his conduct in the affair. He did not forbid the marriage, which would certainly have caused it to come off, but allowed the lady to come on a family visit: where, removed from theatrical surroundings, & placed among gentlewomen, her manners soon convinced the foolish lad that he had made a mistake. This was called treachery by enemies of the family: with no reason that I can see. But Cairns through life had many enemies: not least in his own party. He was a man sincerely religious, strict in his morals, & somewhat grave & austere in his demeanour: living little in the world or in general society: which avoidance of itself society always resents. He was moreover a member of the religious party which just now is least popular: the evangelical: and, as he was supposed to have influenced Disraeli in regard to clerical patronage, it is no exaggeration to say that the High Church section loved him less than if he had been a professed atheist. His relations with Salisbury were cold, though not absolutely hostile: to which jealousy on both sides contributed, for they were not ill matched in point of intellect, & of oratory. As a speaker, I preferred Cairns to any one in the H. of Lords: his perfect clearness of thought & expression, his logical habit of mind, & skill in the arrangement of an argument, were eminently suited to convince. He rarely attempted declamation, but succeeded in it when he did. There was nothing artificial about his oratory, though there was much art in it: he argued earnestly & strongly, in plain words, without needless flourishes. He had not much humour, though some power of sarcasm: and did not aim at making phrases. His only failing as a speaker was the lawyer's fault of dwelling too much on details: all were to the purpose, but some might have been spared. He seldom addressed public meetings: & was at his best in the Lords. – In general politics he will be greatly missed, quite as much by Liberals as by his own friends: for he exercised a moderating influence, knew when it was safe to resist and when prudent to give way: thus he has more than once averted a crisis: as in the Irish church debates of 1869, & more lately on the arrears act. I do not believe that but for him the arrangement as to redistribution would ever have been come to. With him it is probable that D. of Richmond will practically disappear from public life: he was guided by Cairns, & they helped one another, the Duke contributing rank & social power, Cairns finding brains. Somebody said of him long ago that he occupied towards the Conservative aristocracy the position of the family solicitor to a great house: not exactly one of themselves, but trusted and followed, as knowing their interest better than they themselves did.

4 Apr. 1885 (Saturday): Left by early train for London . . . Cabinet at 12.00, which sat till 2.00 (Dilke, Childers, & Spencer absent), when Granville went to see the Russian ambassador. We met again at 3.00, & sat a short time. Office till 4.40, when to station, & at Fairhill again by 6.30.

. . . At the Cabinet today there was some casual talk about Cairns, whom Granville & others spoke of with regret, as being more amenable to reason than most of his colleagues, & thought his loss would be felt in the H. of Lords. I noticed that neither the Premier nor Ld Chancellor joined in his praise: the High Church feeling was too strong. When we came to business, we discussed the Russian answer to our despatch. **Kimberley** said it was plain & outspoken, which Russian communications seldom were. **The Premier** did not understand it for, if read in the natural sense which the words would bear, it is a [curt?] refusal, & almost an insult. The question it raised was not one of boundary, but of the footing on which the two governments should treat: whether as equals, or as inferior & superior. **Kimberley** assured him that he had not misread it. **The Chancellor** observed that the Russians must have misled Thornton as to its nature. (He had telegraphed that it was conciliatory in tone.) **Chamberlain** thought Russia had a strong case on the merits, & was ready to advise large concessions, but must admit that it was impossible to make them in answer to this note, which was offensive & insulting. He would not make any counter-proposal, but dwelt on the danger of dividing the party, & especially of alienating the Nonconformists, who had been steady so far, but who would insist that there should be no war until all means had been employed to preserve peace. **Carlingford** wanted to know what were the Ameer's own wishes, which all agreed are important, but nobody could tell him. **Harcourt** dwelt on the advantage to us of having time for preparation. The Russians he said were ready on the spot & we were not. **D.[erby]** thought this was not the last word of Russia: the Russians were only 'trying it on': if we took a decided line they were likely to give way. **The Premier** threw out some hints about arbitration, but did not explain himself fully. **Northbrook**, being appealed to as to the feeling of India, said what would be cared about there was that the Ameer should be satisfied, & that Herat should be safe. **Kimberley** dwelt on the necessity of holding firm language where Russians were concerned. **Granville** had a short draft of what he was to say to Staal[62], which all present assented to, except Harcourt. **Harcourt** called it a declaration of war, & declaimed violently against it: but had no support. Some talk followed as to military preparations.

At 2.00, **Granville** went off to meet Staal: at 3.00 he returned, having seen him & said what he meant to say, but could get no satisfactory answer. 'Russia,' the ambassador said, 'does not require the immediate acceptance of her line, but wishes it to be taken as a basis of negociation.' This is the language of the despatch over again, & equivalent to a refusal. . . .

7 Apr. 1885: . . . Kimberley sends from I.O. a confidential telegram received from Dufferin, reporting the latter's interview with the Ameer: he, the Ameer, attaches little importance to Penjdeh, & would accept the proposed Russian line of boundary, with slight alterations only, if desired by us. He puts himself into our hands as regards the frontier question, so that there seems no fear of alienating him. On the other hand he decidedly objects to our fortifying Herat, or to any English troops going there: he says, on account of the suspicions of his people, but it is probable that he shares them himself, though this in courtesy he of course disclaims.

It is to me evident that, though he fears & distrusts the Russians, he has the same feeling as regards us (and who can wonder?) & does not desire, if he can help it, to break with either. This news greatly lessens the chances of war: since we cannot be more Afghan than the ruler of Afghanistan. . . .

9 Apr. 1885: . . . Luncheon at the club, where met Kimberley & Hartington: the latter just sitting down to his meal as we were going off to the Cabinet, but he was not more than his usual 20 minutes late. We sat till 4.15, meeting at 2.00: I went to the office for half an hour, & returned by 4.55 train to Fairhill . . .

The Cabinet was called, I believe, to discuss Soudan affairs: but these were never mentioned: for early in the morning came news of an attack, to all appearance unprovoked, by the Russian army on the frontier, on the Afghan garrison of Penjdeh. The Afghans, 4,000 strong, were beaten with loss variously reported at 200 to 500, losing also their camp, guns, baggage, etc. This is the collision which diplomatists on both sides have been trying to avert, & which (whether acting under orders or not) the Russian generals have evidently determined to bring on. They do not allege in their official report that they were attacked, or in danger of being so: & from our own officers we hear that they did everything in their power to provoke the Afghans to fire the first shot, which these, acting on English advice, declined to do. This news brings war nearer than it has ever been since 1856: & the gravity of it was fully appreciated. Our discussion was very desultory, consisting chiefly in comparing the various reports which we have received. The first step to be taken was to ask the Russian government for explanations, and this was done before we met: the immediate question we had to settle was what should be said in the H. of C. which meets today. The Premier was very uneasy about his statement, & in the end it was put in writing, partly by Dilke, & he went down with it in his pocket.

10 Apr. 1885: . . . In the papers, general expectations of a Russian war: for once there seems no disposition to find fault: the House yesterday afternoon listened patiently to Gladstone's statement, & put very few questions. All turns on the explanation which the Russian government may be able or willing to give of the action of their general &, if unexplained, on the reparation which they may be willing to make for what seems an unprovoked aggression. Reconciliation is still possible, but it is not easy, for on the one hand we are afraid of parliament & the public, & on the other the Czar is not strong enough to offend his army – the true governing power in Russia.

The money market has been in wild excitement: consols have fallen only to 95 (three months ago they were at par) but in foreign & especially Russian securities the collapse is sudden & heavy, & it is expected that much ruin will follow. Russian securities have fallen 10 per cent: but they are not largely held here.

11 Apr. 1885 (Saturday): Up early, & to London by 8.40 train . . . Busy till near 12.00 on letters . . . At 12.00, Cabinet, which sat till 3.00: Spencer was absent in Ireland: Carlingford with the Queen: the Chancellor was kept away by the death of his wife: & Rosebery by that of his brother in the Soudan[63]. So we were only 12. After the sitting I went across to C.O. & stayed there till time to leave by the 4.55 train: reached Fairhill at 6.30 . . .

Our discussion in Cabinet today was more than usually interesting. Granville said to me as we sat down: 'This will be a historical Cabinet.' We waited 20 minutes for Hartington, as we always do: and began by talking over arrangements for the order of business in H. of C. **Harcourt**: Whatever you do, make your vote of credit big enough. A large vote goes through more easily than a small one. Would ask for ten millions. **Dilke**: Russia will never believe that we are in earnest till she sees our preparations. **Kimberley**: We are preparing in India, on a great scale. **D.[erby]**: does not object to a large vote, but does not suppose any part of it will remain unspent if you vote it. Remember 1878. **The Premier**: strongly objects to asking for more than you want. That is a system fatal to the rights of the H. of C. Some talk followed as to navy expenses, & it was mentioned casually that the vote for the Soudan would be nearer 8 millions than 7. **D.[erby]**: impossible to fix amount of vote till you know your policy: are you going to carry on two wars at once? On this the Premier made us a speech. He said we had not long to consider the question. Some might think the operations in the Soudan not justifiable in themselves – others who did not take that view might consider that they ought to be dropped, on account of the state of the Russian negociations. For his part, he thought military honour was satisfied, Osman Digna was defeated. He could not be followed into the mountains. It was admitted that the railway would be of no use for an expedition to Khartoum. Ld Wolseley's demands were continually increasing: he, Ld W., had said in a letter that this was the largest military operation since 1815.

This led him to denounce Ld W. as a politician: 'He is able in the field, but a weaker brain does not exist in the three kingdoms.' **D.[erby]**: If you abandon the Soudan campaign, rest your change entirely on the altered conditions produced by the Russian crisis. **Chamberlain**: does not agree. Better say that we have found the danger to be feared from the Mahdi less formidable than we expected. **Hartington** (sneeringly): 'Are we sure of that? Shall we be believed if we say so?' **Harcourt**: Better say that the objects to be gained are less, & the price to be paid larger, than we expected. You may fairly bargain for an estate or a house which you think will cost £20,000, & give it up when you find that the price will be £50,000. **Hartington**: The Mahdi may be quiet now, but will he remain so? What will be thought of a complete reversal of policy within 2 months? **Derby**: Would agree in that, but for the quarrel with Russia, which therefore I would give as the sole reason for the change. **Granville**: had been disposed to leave the other side to undertake the evacuation, thinking we could not consistently do it. Feels the excessive difficulty of the position, but thinks we must face the responsibility.

Lefevre: We may settle not to go on to Khartoum, but are we to stay at Dongola?

Chamberlain & **Harcourt**: No. Others dissent.

Hartington: We shall have killed a great many Arabs for nothing. **Northbrook** & **Chamberlain**: would hold on to Suakin.

The subject drops, as not all members of the Cabinet are present. **Kimberley** reads telegrams from Dufferin, to the effect that the Ameer is now thoroughly cordial, promises to explain to his people that we are friends, & quite acquiesces in the suggestion that, if we are to protect him against the Russians, we may have to advance into his country to do it. He accepts some heavy guns for Herat, & a subsidy. He quite approves our moving up to Quetta. The Viceroy on the whole believes in his sincerity, but does not advise that Lumsden should put himself in his, the Ameer's, power. We agreed to meet again on Monday.

12 Apr. 1885 (Sunday): . . . Letter from Childers, written in some uneasiness about a contract for telegraphic communication with the W. coast of Africa, as to which correspondence has passed between F.O., C.O., & Treasury, & he seems to think he has been misled, or that there has been a misunderstanding. I answer him briefly, & send the papers to Meade for a further explanation to follow.

13 Apr. 1885: Lawson calls, says his news is very warlike, & advises strongly the abandonment of the Soudan campaign. Says that is everybody's opinion, & that it will be pressed upon us by the opposition in parliament.

Cabinet at 12.00, which sat till 4.15. Thence straight to the Lords, where Granville & Salisbury each said a few words about Cairns, & Lord Coleridge spoke at greater length, a kind of funeral oration, rather more elaborate than is the English custom, but he did it well. Salisbury appeared to be saying what he did not feel, though his language was warm enough. There was mutual respect, but no liking, between the two. . . . At 5.30, to the office, & there worked till near 7.00. Home: dined Travellers'.

Our Cabinet was long & interesting. Granville read a disagreeable telegram from Lyons, in which Freycinet, the new minister, insists on redress for the action taken at Cairo in suppressing the *Bosphore Egyptien*, a violent & abusive journal which Nubar has put down. Freycinet does not formulate his demands, but insists on full & immediate compliance with them, in a tone not usual in diplomacy. The explanation is that he knows how we are situated in regard to Russia & the Soudan, & that we can resent nothing. – The question of the Soudan was raised again. **Hartington** read a tel. from Wolseley, urging the prosecution of the war, on account of the danger of seeming defeated, & of future danger to Egypt from the Mahdi. **H.** supports this view, dwells on the sums wasted in Egypt, on the impossibility of suspending operations on the Nile, on the certainty of a vote of censure, etc. **Kimberley**: You will have a vote of censure proposed either way. Does not believe that the English people, as they now are, will persevere in any long & difficult enterprise: they are sure to get tired of it. **Harcourt**: You will not be able to carry a vote of credit to take an expedition to Khartoum. **The Premier**: had hoped we should be able to agree – if not – can we go on? We are in difficulties with France as well as Russia. We cannot abandon responsibilities. No other government can deal with the Russians as well as we can. For himself, apart from the trouble with Russia, does not see what right we have in the Soudan. We have no moral title to set up a government there. Repeats what he said before, that the Soudanese are fighting for freedom. **Northbrook**:

does not believe that Ld Wolseley can get to Khartoum anyhow. **Childers**: agrees to the withdrawal from the Soudan, but only on the ground of our Russian embarrassments. **Granville**: does not like to rest the decision on that ground only. Egypt is to us a source of weakness, not of strength, & the Soudan would be worse. The necessity of concentration of force is itself reason sufficient. **Kimberley & Harcourt**: We are now for the first time neighbours to a great military power. That alone alters our whole position. **Hartington**: As war minister had to take a leading part in defending this expedition, & cannot now turn around & defend its abandonment. **Kimberley**: You need only decide now on not advancing to Khartoum. Details must stand over. **Northbrook**: would not give up Dongola in haste. – After more talk, we nearly agreed to a tel. to Wolseley, but Hartington again took objections, & we agreed to meet tomorrow.

There was also much conversation on the Russian affair, but nothing very definite could be settled.

14 Apr. 1885: . . . Office early, about 1.00: thence to Cabinet, which met at 2.00, & sat till 3.30 . . .

At the Cabinet today, **the Premier** declined to raise again the question of leaving the Soudan: ostensibly because farther information is wanted from Ld Wolseley, really, I suppose, because Hartington is half converted, & another day may bring him round. **Granville** mentioned a long letter received from Baring, who is against going to Khartoum, against keeping British soldiers in the Soudan, & in favour of calling in the Turks.

We then discussed Russian affairs. Staal has made indirectly, first through R. Brett, then through Rothschild, a suggestion that the Russian troops should withdraw from the debated ground, the Afghans giving through us a pledge that they will not advance. He only offers this as personally from himself, as what he would suggest to his government if assured that we would accept it. He now seems frightened at his own courage, & inclined to draw back. He says plainly that Comaroff[64] cannot be recalled. The Russians are reinforcing, & they make an odd complaint of one Capt. Wells[65], who is somewhere near the Persian frontier, & who they say is watching their movements. There seems a general feeling in the Cabinet that the quarrel is one that may be settled, if only the Russians wish it: we are not disposed to be unreasonable, the Ameer is anxious for peace, & the boundary line can very well be arranged by a compromise: the danger is lest Russian swaggers should irritate our people, & lest the Russian military men should think the opportunity of striking a blow too good to be lost. The Czar is believed to be in the hands of the military party, but nobody appears to know what his personal wishes are.

15 Apr. 1885: Working till 11.00, when all clear . . . Office early, about 1.00: at 2.30 to a Cabinet, which lasted till 5.00: office again till near 7.00, when home, & dined at the Travellers'. A busy day, but no fatigue.

At the Cabinet, **the Premier** read a rather violent telegram from the Queen against withdrawal from the Soudan: and **Granville** produced a long letter from Baring in favour of it, the same which he had mentioned yesterday.

Granville also produced an unpleasant communication from Berlin (or from Münster, I forget which) to the effect that Bismarck wishes the new Egyptian loan equally divided among the guaranteeing powers, in order that no one of them may have the influence which would be derived from holding all the stock. This is not in itself important, but shows a disagreeable *animus.*

Telegram read from Dufferin to effect that the Ameer, who has all along treated the Penjdeh catastrophe lightly, now breaks out about it unexpectedly, at the last moment, shows it is a stain which he must wipe out, etc., etc. Chamberlain, on this being read, broke out in his turn, objecting to our treaty with the Ameer, on the ground that it enables him to drive us into a quarrel with Russia whenever he likes.

Talk about the suppression of the *Bosphore,* which the French do not object to in itself, but contend that the closing of the office where it was published is illegal, that the French consul was insulted. We send a conciliatory message, denying the illegality, but expressing readiness to discuss it.

Discussion on the Soudan question, vague & confused, at least I could make little of it, but it seems that Hartington is quite reconciled to not going to Khartoum, only makes difficulties as to the language to be held. To satisfy him, **Gladstone** has produced a draft statement, which is studiously ambiguous, & I should think would please nobody. Much conversation as to whether we are to continue to hold Dongola but, as usual, nothing definite is settled. . . .

17 Apr. 1885: . . . The D. of Bedford told me yesterday that he has remitted to his tenants half their rents in the midland counties, and 25 per cent in the west. He gives as his reason that he does not like to have farms on hand, being sure to lose that way, whereas by his concession he hopes to induce his tenants to hold on.

. . . Lawson called: inclined to believe in the prospects of peace, which he considers as only a putting off of the inevitable conflict. The City, and society in general, has suddenly changed its views. Three days ago everybody regarded war as certain: now, three people out of every four are convinced that there will be no war: and there is just as much, or as little, reason for one belief as for the other. . . .

18 Apr. 1885: . . . Lawson called, says (as yesterday) that all the world is now satisfied that we are to have peace, & the same impression prevails abroad: but nothing new has happened to explain the change.

Sanderson called, said the tone of the latest Russian communications is considered at F.O. not to be amicable, but I have not yet seen the paper.

Day very bright, warm, & fine. Being the anniversary of Ld Beaconsfield's death, his followers, according to a custom which they have invented, wore primroses, & the number of persons so decorated was remarkable about the West End. It is made a kind of demonstration, & zealous agents distribute the flowers, & canvass people to wear them. . . .

20 Apr. 1885: . . . Letter from Ld Lansdowne on disturbances in the [Canadian] north-west. He says the half breeds have been dissatisfied ever since the annexation to Canada. . . . Nearly 5,000 troops are being moved, but the difficulties of transport are immense. The Fenians over the border are watching their opportunity to give trouble, but so far the U.S. govt. appears to have been acting honestly.

Cabinet at 2.00, which sat till 4.30: the only subject discussed was the budget and (as part of it) the vote of credit. We differed a good deal, & time failing agreed to adjourn until tomorrow. Thence to the Lords, where Ld Sidmouth put two questions on Maltese affairs . . .

In Cabinet, Childers explained his proposed budget: an increase of income tax, of death duties, of spirit & beer duty. The last two proposals led to warm discussion: **Dilke & Chamberlain** absolutely objecting to any increase of indirect taxes, **Harcourt** siding with them (not, as he said, on any ground of abstract justice, but for fear of alienating the agricultural voters). This annoyed the **Chancellor**, who made some remark about justice, at which Harcourt sneered, saying we had to consider votes, & not justice. He argued farther that all the cry for war came from the upper classes, they should therefore bear the whole burden. **Granville, the Premier**, & I contended that all classes should bear their share of the burden. **Hartington** saw no use in new taxes: why not borrow as much as we wanted? **Dilke** attacked the sinking fund, which the Premier & I defended. The discussion ended without result, for want of time, having shown the existence among us of very wide differences of opinion.

A confidential mem. from the War Office, as to the possible means of attacking Russia, is not pleasant reading. From this paper it seems clear: (1) that blockade is as against Russian commerce an entirely ineffectual expedient, since the trade will only go round through neutral countries: (2) that nothing whatever can be done in the Baltic: (3) that not much is possible on the Pacific coast: (4) that Batoum in the Black Sea is the only vulnerable point, & it is to that the W.O. wish attention directed. But the first requisite for attacking a port in the Black Sea is to [be] able to pass the Dardanelles, & this while Turkey remains neutral we cannot. On the whole it seems as if Russia, though not strong for aggression, were almost invulnerable. Ships can do little against her, & our army is too small for a land invasion on a great scale. The Russians no doubt understand this as well as we do, & will act accordingly.

21 Apr. 1885: . . . Hale called . . . . . . Mr. Williams, the socialist farmer at Ormskirk, who refuses on principle to pay rent, is under notice to quit.

. . . Cabinet at 2.00, which sat till 4.30: then to the Lords, where remained till 7.00. Home, & quiet evening, but a mass of business has accumulated.

In Cabinet, talk about Lumsden's answer to the Russian despatches, which is a flat contradiction. Then about the statement to be made in both Houses today, which Hartington complains is not full enough, & will be misunderstood. Then followed a discussion as to the form of moving the vote of credit – whether in one lump, or separately for the Soudan & the Russian preparations. Strong objection was taken to the separation of the two, on the ground that the Soudan vote standing alone would not be carried. Agreed to put off the budget till after the vote of credit is passed. The discussion as to the new taxes to be put on was continued. **Harcourt** dwelt again on the party view of the case, the danger of an election cry. **Chamberlain** said the incidence of taxation as it stands now was unjust to the poor. **Hartington** preferred borrowing, but would leave the decision in the Premier's hands. **Gladstone**: could not reconcile his judgment to raising the whole sum by exclusive direct taxation. The **Chancellor** pointed out that increase of income tax is felt by the masses, in reduced employment. The question was adjourned again.

– We passed on next to the latest Russian communications, which certainly are not conciliatory in tone. They say nothing more about withdrawal, and refuse any expression of regret for the Afghan conflict. The only favourable indication is that they say they will leave the matter open for discussion, & await further details. **Chamberlain** thought at first that the Russians had a good case: does not think so now: their answer is insulting.

Let us find a solution if we can, but we need not lick their boots. **Harcourt** argues rather angrily on the other side. **Kimberley**, being appealed to as to Indian opinion, dissents strongly from **Harcourt**: who answers him offensively, treating what K. said as an interruption: 'If this incident is disposed of, I suppose I may finish what I was saying', etc. **Kimberley** had the sense & temper to take no notice, but the effect was disagreeable. **Hartington** thought neither India nor the H. of C. would bear much delay in settling the question. **The Premier** thought the contrary, & advised waiting. We broke up with but little settled, having to go to the Houses. . . .

23 Apr. 1885: . . . To the Lords, where moved the second reading of the Australia federal bill, speaking only a quarter of an hour, as no opposition was probable: and in fact Carnarvon & Norton, who both spoke, were in favour, & nobody against it. The Egyptian loan bill was read a second time, Salisbury making a temperate speech, & the D. of Marlborough one which would have been violent but for being feeble. That duke has some cleverness, and may train on, but as yet he is not a success.

Attempt this morning, between 10.00 & 11.00, to blow up a room at the Admiralty, in which Mr. Swainson, the assistant under-secretary, was sitting. The explosion wrecked the room, severely injured Mr. Swainson, & broke a great deal of glass. It caused less excitement than one might have expected: the world is getting used to these unpleasant little incidents. But this one differed from its predecessors in so far that the offender managed to deposit his explosive, whatever it was, inside the room which was to be blown up: which creates a suspicion that he must have been some person, clerk, or servant, employed in the office. . . .

25 Apr. 1885 (Saturday): . . . Bought £10,000 4% N.S. Wales bonds . . . This makes £50,000 invested in N.S. Wales, £80,000 in Australia (including the former sum), & in all £540,000.

Cabinet at 12.00: which sat till past 3.00, all present except Spencer. . . . Dined at Gloucester House, a large party, over 30, pleasant enough, only rather too crowded. Most of the government were there: I sat between D. of Bedford & Ld Cork . . . By 11.15 train to Keston.

In Cabinet, talk of finance. **The Premier** announced that the dissentients on the question of beer & spirit duty had given way, & **Chamberlain** confirmed this, saying frankly that he disliked the arrangement, but that he would acquiesce in it. We had an animated little debate as to whether church property should be taxed as well as corporate property: **the Premier** opposed the proposition warmly: **Kimberley** thought it just, but impolitic: **Harcourt** did not see how the exemption could be justified: **D.[erby]** thought that, for the sake of £160,000 to be obtained from the corporations, it was not worth while to raise this very awkward controversy: **Harcourt** agreed: in the end we left the matter unsettled. Then followed talk about a proposal in H. of C. to split the vote of credit into two: so that the vote for Soudan operations may be taken by itself: **Dilke** & **Chamberlain** both said that we must resist, but that we might not impossibly be beaten.

Next followed a long, discursive, & very tedious discussion of the *Bosphore* case, the law officers being called in: we found that what has been done is beyond law, & a form was devised in which to express regret. **Chamberlain** started the odd notion that we might make this incident an excuse for withdrawing from Egypt, but this suggestion met with general dissent, for it would be, in appearance & in fact, allowing the French to turn

778   LORD DERBY'S DIARIES

us out: which the English public will not stand. Kimberley read us the latest telegrams from India: it seems we could send at once 15,000 men to Quetta & even to Kandahar, if the Ameer wished it: but the difficulty of feeding them at either place would be serious. We ended by much vague talk about the vote of credit to be asked for on Monday: as to which it seems to be thought safer to say as little as possible, I mean about the causes which lead to our demand: Hartington, in his grumbling way, observed that no government till now had ever asked for 11 millions without giving reasons, or saying what they were going to do with it: which is true, & I think our reticence, though it may be diplomatically safe, will do us no good in the H. of Commons.

26 Apr. 1885 (Sunday): Keston. Day fine & pleasant . . . a day of rest.

Papers sent round from the Ld Lieut. of Ireland: they relate in part to the Crimes Act, which he analyses, & recommends that the greater part of it be re-enacted: but he also calls attention to three other questions which he thinks the present parliament can deal with. One is the abolition of the Lord Lieutenancy: one, the entire reform of the system of local government: the third, the plan of land purchase proposed last year, & dropped for want of time. Any one of these three subjects would occupy the greater part of a session, as debates are now managed: & it is inconceivable to me that so able a man as Ld Spencer can believe the present H. of C. capable of handling them[66].

I have not noted that on Friday a meeting was held, Carnarvon in the chair, to get up a company for buying land & selling it in small lots, so as to suit poor purchasers: I was asked to attend, could not, but wrote a letter approving the experiment, which was read. It is the very thing I have for many years past recommended in speeches about land: not as believing that it will succeed generally, or on a large scale, but as a fair method of testing the fact whether the 'industrious working man' really does care to be a freeholder or not: & as a way of stopping the mouths of those who cry out that the law makes small freeholds impossible.

27 Apr. 1885: London by usual train . . . I went across to the Commons to hear the debate on the vote of credit . . . but Gladstone's answers to questions were quite inaudible, which is new. The House very full, eager, but more orderly than I have generally seen it of late. – Ashley tells me that the apathy now shown about public affairs is incredible: M.P.s come for the questions, go away to dinner, & do not return: it is often difficult to keep a house.

After I left, a motion to split the vote of credit in two was rejected by 229 to 186, & Gladstone moved the vote in a fine speech of an hour, cheered from both sides, & not replied to or opposed[67]. The risk of war seems daily greater yet here it is not universally expected: on the continent people consider it virtually begun. The funds have fallen from 100 or 101 . . . to 94-95, but they would fall lower if immediate fighting were anticipated. The situation is this – we have suggested arbitration in some form on the Penjdeh dispute, leaving all details to be settled later: if this proposal is absolutely rejected, we can scarcely avoid breaking off relations, but even then hostilities need not necessarily follow: if however the Russian emperor is (as many believe) in the hands of the military party or, in other words, if he is more afraid of his own army than he is of us, some blow will be struck in Afghanistan which will compel us to resent it on behalf of our ally. The personal character of the Czar will influence the decision: & nobody that I have seen knows what he really is. The general belief is that he has little ability, & a high idea of the necessity of maintaining his authority. If the world is correct in these respects, he will probably desire a military success as the best method of strengthening himself at home: and he will be pushed on to the utmost by the powerful revolutionary party, who count on the suffering & distress caused by war to further their designs.

28 Apr. 1885: . . . Sent money to sundry charities . . .

. . . Cabinet at 2.00, which sat till 4.15. Then to the Lords, where a bill for the protection of girls, already twice discussed in former sessions, occupied us for nearly three hours: useful, I dare say, but deadly dull. . . . Home weary & irritated, not quite reasonably, at the waste of time.

. . . The speech made last night by Gladstone has had an extraordinary effect. It is praised on all sides, and the most practical evidence of its effect is that it killed the debate: Northcote was to have followed, & R. Churchill, Hicks Beach, & others were ready to speak. But nobody liked to rise: & the vote was carried without discussion: which in the actual state of foreign affairs is the best thing that could have happened.

The foreign situation is this: that we have made a proposal to refer the Penjdeh business to arbitration: that we are waiting for the answer: & that all depends on that answer. If our suggestion is met by a different one, negociations go on: if it is accepted, the incident is over: if unconditionally rejected, diplomatic relations can scarcely be continued: but, even so, war, at least immediate war, would not be a necessary consequence. What would bring on war inevitably would be a farther Russian advance towards Herat.

29 Apr. 1885: . . . In Cabinet yesterday, a sort of explanation of the Penjdeh incident was read. It is vague, but so far satisfactory that it does not shut the door against further discussion. But our chief subject was the legislation of the session, as to which very sanguine hopes are held out. First, there is provision to be made for the princess[68] about to be married. That we are pledged to: but the question was argued whether we should promise an enquiry into the whole system of these grants. **Dilke** & **Childers** represented it as urgent: **Harcourt** disliked the subject: **Gladstone** was for promising an enquiry in the new parliament. **D.[erby]** asked how we could pledge the new parliament? **Gladstone**: Only so far as the present ministry is concerned. (This does not look as if he meant to retire.) – We agreed to bring in a crofters' bill. then came the Irish question. **Spencer** wants to announce a land purchase bill, a local government bill, the abolition of the viceroyalty, & the renewal of the Crimes Act. The last is a necessity: the others are intended to make it go down more smoothly. **Chamberlain** said he objected exceedingly to the Crimes Act, but if accompanied by a good local government bill that would make some difference. **Spencer** expressed anxiety for a land purchase bill. **Childers** observed that both parties wished for that, the landlords in order to get paid, the tenants in order to get rid of them, but they all agreed that the Treasury must bear the whole risk. **Granville, Hartington**, & I protest against asking parliament to undertake work which everybody knows it cannot & will not dispose of. **Harcourt** says it does not matter that the bills should pass – the object is to get the credit of bringing them in. – He wished we had brought in a London government bill for the same reason. Gladstone partly inclined to the same view, thinking a declaration of policy important. **R. Grosvenor**, being called in, warned us that Irish obstruction has begun again – & I hear it is regularly organised. The discussion ended with no definite conclusion.

30 Apr. 1885 (Thursday): . . . Chamberlain having made on Tuesday night a speech at the Eighty Club, attacking Goschen & laying down new & socialistic doctrines as to property, I wrote to the Premier to suggest his remonstrating, putting it on the ground of the party being divided, & support lost, by ministers putting forward theories which only the most extreme radicals will approve. Chamberlain's new formula is this – that every owner of property (I suppose he means on a large scale) is by such ownership an offender against society, & must make atonement for his offence by paying ransom – not the ordinary taxation in which all share, but a special fine, of indefinite amount, by way of penalty.

– The Premier asked me to call, which I did, & he immediately began to talk, & continued for an hour with scarcely a pause. What he said was very discursive, & at first seemed to have no reference to the subject which he had asked me to discuss: I cannot attempt to follow his ideas, & indeed the digressions were many: but what it came to was this – that Chamberlain was determined not to allow the Crimes Act for Ireland to be renewed, unless it were accompanied by a measure for local government on the largest scale: his plan includes the creation of a central elected board sitting in Dublin, dealing with administrative affairs generally, & which would be called, & probably would call itself, an Irish parliament: Mr. Gladstone spoke of this scheme not as having absolutely accepted it, but thinking that it deserved consideration, & favourable to it rather than otherwise: he did not ask my opinion, which I was glad of. Talking later to Spencer, Carlingford, & Granville, I found them all very hostile, thinking it would be Home Rule little disguised. But Mr. G. believes that, unless something of this sort is done, Chamberlain will secede, & the Cabinet be broken up. Granville & Carlingford seem to think that Chamberlain wants an excuse for secession, preferring to have his hands & tongue free at the coming election: though as things are the holding of office does not much restrain him.

– Mr. G. showed me also a thing which had surprised him as much as it did me: a telegram from the Queen in a very pacific sense, to the effect that, if the boundary question could be settled, the Penjdeh incident might very well drop. As she has been incessantly screaming for war, anywhere, or with anybody, during the last two years this is a singular & sudden change. Probably her German relations have explained to her that in a Russian war there would be more risk than glory. – Office, where received a deputation on the defences of Singapore. H. of Lords, where passed the Australian bill through committee without trouble . . .

1 May 1885: . . . Office, where saw the Maharajah of Johore[69]: whose object in coming was to assure himself that his status of independence is not to be affected: on that point I was able fully to satisfy him. Sir F. Weld[70] came with the Maharajah . . .

. . . On a private bill, Salisbury made an odd speech desiring that the standing orders should be relaxed in its favour: on the plea [that], if proceeded with at once, the undertaking would give employment which is much required. This novel view of the purpose for which docks or railways should be made created some discussion: & the move was considered as a piece of electioneering – perhaps unjustly.

2 May 1885: . . . To office, & work there till 5.00. I was just leaving for the Academy, when came a sudden summons to a Cabinet. This lasted an hour. Academy at 6.00, for the yearly dinner, & left at 10.40. My neighbours were Granville & Kimberley.

. . . The Cabinet today was short & satisfactory: the news which we were summoned to consider was the virtual acceptance by Russia of our suggestion to have the matter in dispute referred to arbitration: & such discussion as took place turned entirely on details. It seems also that the Afghans gave more provocation than was known to us (no doubt artfully incited so to do): & that their case is in consequence weaker than we had supposed. The arbitration as I understand it is to be only in case we & the Russians cannot agree: & it seems possible that we may be able to come to an agreement without calling in any third party.

3 May 1885 (Sunday): . . . We are now presumably out of our greatest trouble, the risk of a Russian war: & compared with that all other difficulties are from a national point of view unimportant: yet two questions remain, either of which, or both, may give serious trouble, & one of them may break up the Cabinet.

(1) Are we to retire at once from Dongola to Wady Halfa, and to give up the Berber-Suakin railway? If we do not, there is no security against recurrence of all the old difficulties attending a campaign in the Soudan. If we do, what is to happen to the friendly chiefs & tribes, whom we cannot take with us, nor effectually protect on the spot, & who will be exposed to the revenge of a savage enemy? It is a choice of evils, & I see no way out of the trouble that is not in some respects unsatisfactory.

(2) What are we to do about local government in Ireland? This is politically the more urgent question of the two. Chamberlain announces his resignation if the Crimes Act is passed without the acceptance of his plan: &, if we accept it, we virtually comply with the demand for Home Rule, & open a door which can never be closed again. A few days will see us out of the difficulty, for some decision must be announced very shortly.

4 May 1885: The Russian difficulty is now understood to be settled: & the general feeling is one of relief, though on the Conservative side disappointment will be loudly professed. – A Russian war under actual circumstances would probably have been costly, protracted, and indecisive. Europe would no doubt have intervened to prevent Turkey from opening the Dardanelles: so that our points of attack would have been limited by sea to the Baltic, where nothing effective can be done, & to the Pacific coast, which is too distant for any loss there to be seriously felt at Petersburg or Moscow. Russian trade by sea is small, and could have been carried on through Germany with little inconvenience so that our blockade would have served little purpose. The fight would have been practically localised in Afghanistan: where, from the barren & difficult nature of the country, it is not easy to feed & move an army of 50,000 men. Under these conditions neither belligerent could have done the other much harm, except so far as Russian privateers might have injured our trade, for probably the old practice of privateering would have been revived. – I observe as a curious national habit that we always talk of having beaten the Russians in the Crimea, ignoring the fact that we were there four to one – France, Turkey, & Sardinia helping – just as we ignore the Spaniards in the Peninsula, & the Prussians at Waterloo.

5 May 1885: . . . Last night in the Commons was a debate on the vote of credit, noticeable

chiefly as showing that, with the relief of the opposition at war no longer seeming imminent, there was mixed a good deal of disappointment. The only speech above the average
was one by Churchill, the ablest, I think, he has yet made, & which certainly would not
have been possible to Hicks Beach, Cross, or even Northcote. He is gaining continually
in reputation &, if he holds out as regards health & strength, must be leader. But he is
often an invalid, & the family madness[71] has in part appeared in him, though not going
beyond eccentricity.

6 May 1885: . . . Party at No. 23, which went off very well, except that it was a little too
crowded. The invitations sent out were 1,100, & it was supposed that about 600 persons
came. It lasted till 1.30. A wet night increased the difficulty of getting away.

7 May 1885 (Thursday): To a Cabinet, which met at 12.00, but I was not there till
12.20: we sat till about 3.00. All present, including Spencer.

The Cabinet of this morning was the most important & interesting which we have held
for some time. The question discussed was whether we should make a probable defeat on
the registration bill, next Monday, an excuse for resigning? The real reason of this wish
to break up the government is that we cannot agree either on the budget or on Irish
policy: and, if we are to fall, it is better to do so as an ostensibly united body than by
disruption among ourselves & mutual quarrels: – . . . R. Grosvenor was called in, & gave
it as his decided opinion that we should be beaten on registration. **Harcourt** said that
either the opposition would come in & be responsible for Irish policy, or they will refuse,
& then we shall come back stronger for their refusal. He did not see how we could now
alter the budget: we had laid down a principle & were pledged to it. **Chamberlain** saw
no use in getting out of one difficulty, if we were immediately to be involved in another.
It seemed to him clear that we could not go on, & the registration bill was the best excuse
for resignation. **Dilke** agreed, but thought that in fairness to the party they should be told
that we meant to make this bill a question of confidence. If we did, he thought there
would be no defeat. **Kimberley** & **Trevelyan** thought that in taking a pretext to resign
we were doing what was not candid, nor just to our supporters. **The Premier** said, if we
went out, it would not be on this defeat alone, but as a consequence of the general state
of affairs, & of the feeling in the House. **Spencer** hoped that whatever happened we
should not break up ostensibly on the Irish question. That would do great mischief.
Kimberley would rather fall on the vote of credit, but **the Premier** & others said the
attitude of the opposition made that impossible. **D.[erby]** doubted whether we should be
beaten, & thought the consideration of what we should do in that case premature. Did
not much like the making so transparent an excuse for resigning, though it might serve
as well as any other, but would prefer letting [people see] the plain truth: we could not
keep the fact of our differences secret.

After much more talk, we passed to a consideration of the budget: which Gladstone &
Childers strongly defended, the latter saying he would resign rather than consent to
modify it in principle. But Chamberlain & Dilke object to defend it, & the latter declares
it cannot be carried.

8 May 1885: . . . Lawson came: he suspects nothing as to a crisis, & thinks we are sure to
win on the Registration Bill. He knew, however, that there is a good deal of division in
the Cabinet, especially as to Irish affairs. Indeed this is now no secret to anyone. . . .

9 May 1885: Disposed of all office business, except an interminable story of a quarrel between Sir C. Warren & Sir H. Robinson, which I do not yet see my way through. . . .

10 May 1885 (Sunday): . . . At the Cabinet yesterday: we began by talking about the arbitrator to be selected on the Russian question: & agreed to consent to the Russian proposal of the K. of Denmark.

Hartington then explained what his statement was to be on Monday: he would announce final abandonment of the Khartoum expedition, & that we do not leave Dongola at once, but try to set up some kind of a government there. As to Suakin & the railway, he would leave the matter vague for the present.

Kimberley absolutely objected to leave [any] Indian troops at Suakin. Talk followed as to whether the Turks would hold it, or the Italians.

In the course of this conversation **Hartington** accused **Granville** (but in good humour) of not speaking out in parliament. Granville answered: 'How can I speak out while I represent a Cabinet of which one half want one thing done, the other half the contrary?'

Kimberley then explained in some detail the proposed Russo-Afghan frontier. Some talk as to whether an engagement should be exacted from Russia not to advance farther. Some of us wished for this, but others, Northbrook & I especially, thought that the demarcation of the frontier answered this purpose sufficiently, since once laid down it could not be crossed without bringing on war: which, if desired by the Russians, no assurances would guard against.

Next came a conversation on the budget, & we agreed, as the Spanish government repudiates the treaty which we had made, a provision in which included a reduction of the wine duties, to raise these, & thus get rid of the plausible objection that we were lowering taxes on the rich man's luxuries, & raising them on those of the poor. The Premier suggested as much delay as possible, that we might know what savings could be made out of the 11 millions which we proposed to spend. He hoped for 3, or even possibly 4.

The last subject of discussion was Chamberlain's Irish scheme of local government, which he explained very clearly & ably, treating it as the only possible alternative to Home Rule. It consists, briefly, in the creation of a central board elected by municipalities, to deal with all local affairs.

The Premier professed himself favourable to the idea: **Spencer** had the strongest possible objections to it: **Kimberley** thought a simple repeal of the Union would be preferable: **Carlingford** regarded it as impracticable: **Granville**, **Hartington**, & **D.[erby]**, while objecting to the plan in itself, dwelt chiefly on the impossibility of discussing a change which is equivalent to a revolution in the last few weeks of a dying parliament. In the end Chamberlain withdrew his proposal.

11 May 1885: . . . Levee at 2.00: came away 2.30 . . . – Talk at the levee with Spencer: from what he said I gather that the Irish difficulty with Chamberlain is got over &, if we win on registration tomorrow, no difficulty remains except the budget.

12 May 1885: . . . The division about which so much alarm was felt, & which was to have decided the fate of the ministry, came off before dinner, with little excitement, & gave a majority of 22: 280 to 258. . . .

14 May 1885: . . . Called on Granville at F.O. at his request: according to him the Irish dispute is by no means settled: Spencer on one side, Chamberlain & Dilke on the other, are fighting, the one to keep as much of the Crimes Act as he can, the others to reduce it to nothing. Gladstone is trying to mediate, but hitherto has not succeeded. His personal sympathies are on Chamberlain's side: he likes & pities the Irish, does not realise the strength of their anti-English feeling, & believes that good administration will satisfy them without Home Rule. But he will not be driven: & Granville believes that, if forced to choose, he will allow C. & D.[ilke] to resign, & go on without them. . . .

15 May 1885: . . . Went by appointment to a meeting at Devonshire House, where found Spencer, Northbrook, Granville, Kimberley, Hartington, Rosebery. Spencer explained to us at length his negociations with Chamberlain, and we gave our several opinions. Mine was in the sense of advising Spencer to stand firm: that he had already conceded all that could reasonably be asked. It seems that Chamberlain & Dilke will only give their support on an extraordinary condition: viz. that they shall be free to withdraw it if the bill is threatened with serious opposition, seeing that their personal feelings are on the side of the objectors. To this of course we cannot listen. . . .

. . . Thence to Cabinet at 2.00, which sat till 4.15. . . . Our discussion in Cabinet was the least satisfactory that we have had yet. No temper was shown, which is so far good, but the divergences of opinion seemed wider than ever. We began by discussing the bills to be brought in. When land purchase, Ireland, was mentioned, **Chamberlain** objected absolutely to it unless accompanied with a scheme for local government: **Harcourt** thought that both Ulster & the Home Rulers agreed as to land purchase. **Spencer** pressed it, saying that without it nothing was settled: **Carlingford** did not believe that much advantage would be taken of it, the tenants having already got all they wanted: **Kimberley** disliked the notion of buying Irish support: **Dilke** & **Chamberlain** thought it would do more to divide than to unite the two countries: inasmuch as the Irish would see in the British government a creditor whose claims should be got rid of if possible: **Rosebery** would leave the land alone, & abolish the vice-royalty, that being the one thing on which we could agree: **Harcourt** agreed in this: & disliked the land plan, saying that similar demands for state aid to buy their farms would be made by the Scotch tenants: **Childers** took the view explained above, that a land purchase bill would promote separation. **Lefevre** would try it experimentally & on a limited scale: **Gladstone** suggested a trial of the bill for one year, the matter to be then reconsidered. He then said that a bill partially renewing the Crimes Act must be brought in. **Spencer** says he has consented with great reluctance rather than break up, to reduce the bill to what is now proposed,& recapitulates the changes in it. **Dilke, Chamb.** & **Lefevre**, all protest, saying that they allow the bill to be brought in, but reserve their freedom in regard. (This was said by Chamberlain, but the other two assented.) **Granville** dissented from this proposal as unconstitutional. If they agree to bring in the bill they were pledged to it. **Gladstone** made the peace, said all he understood them to mean was that they did not look at the loss of the bill, or the question of its being passed for one year or more, as vital. **Dilke** however would not have this, & wished it understood that he & **Chamberlain** would not consent to fall on the question of this bill, but would exercise their discretion as to retiring if matters came to a crisis in regard to it. Then discussion was renewed on the land purchase bill, & the differences were more marked than before. **Spencer** said he had made no bargain, but without his bill his policy was destroyed. We must go to the Irish constituencies with something in our hands besides coercion. **Dilke** thought we ought not to hold together – we were at the parting of the ways. He & his friends wished to be able at least to state their Irish policy. **Carlingford** & **Hartington** supported **Spencer**, **Kimberley** saw no use in the scheme. **Harcourt** declaimed angrily against all who wished us to break up. **D.[erby]** agreed in principle with Spencer but doubted its being possible to pass a land bill this year. – In the end we seemed to have concluded that this was so, & that the question must be postponed.

16 May 1885: [Saw] a man sent by Prof. Huxley, to beg assistance for some new scientific device, I hardly know what: but in honour of Huxley I put down my name for £100.
. . . Cabinet at 12.00, which sat till 2.00 exactly: then to office, & Keston by 4.12 train.
In the Cabinet of today we chiefly discussed finance. Something was said about a telegram from the Queen, in which she again earnestly deprecates withdrawal from the Soudan: & something of R. Grosvenor's gloomy predictions as to the effect on Ireland of dropping the Land Purchase Bill. Childers then proceeded to explain at length his proposed amendments in the budget. He expects to be able to do with 8 millions instead of 11 of extra burden for the year: making for the total deficit 12 instead of 15. Since his statement was made, the negociations with Spain on the wine duties have broken down: which relieves us of the awkward necessity of having to lower wine duties while raising those on spirits & beer. He now proposes to raise the wine duties, gaining £300,000: to take the extra beer duty for one year only: & lessen the increase of the spirit duty making it 1s. instead of 2s. per gallon. He believes that he can thus conciliate the brewers, partly satisfy the spirit interest, & get rid of the feature most complained of. When he had done, **Harcourt** said sneeringly that this budget must be the end of the government, that it was not worth while to discuss a plan which was sure to be defeated by a large majority: that the House would not bear those taxes now that 3 million less are wanted, that he was prepared to fall, but objected to make this the cause of our falling. He would have no indirect taxes, & a penny less on income tax. **Gladstone** objected to this as an inadequate provision for the wants of the year. **Kimberley** hoped we should not break up till we had settled with Russia, & passed the Seats Bill. **Chamberlain** said he must decline to ruin our prospects at the next election for the sake of our financial virtue. **Lefevre** would settle matters by suspending the sinking fund. **Gladstone** & **Granville** both protested against the assumption as a certainty that we should not want as much money as we did a month ago – the negociations might yet fail. **Gladstone** especially contended that the time had not come when we could settle the budget. **D.[erby]** & **Childers** argued that, whether we wanted less or more, part of it ought to come out of taxes on consumption. **Gladstone** agreed, said he himself leant to that view, but thought the mischief of delay would not be serious. He attached extreme importance to securing the settlement with Russia. **Kimberley** said that, if we were to disagree, it had better be three weeks hence rather than now. **Childers** objected to delay which he said would be fatal, it would give time for agitation, and give an opportunity for evading the new wine duty. The **Chancellor** deprecated his resignation (at which he had plainly hinted) saying that he himself had accepted many things which he did not like, rather than destroy the cohesion of the Cabinet by retiring. **Harcourt**, **Gladstone**, & **Carlingford** all protested against Childers resigning merely because his budget was postponed – it had not been rejected. But Childers did not withdraw his threat, & when we broke up it was understood he would resign. But he may change his mind. – In any case, it seems as if this government

could not last long. Kimberley said to me: 'The Cabinet had more lives than a cat': but Dilke & Chamberlain are as good as out, Childers seems to mean what he said, & Spencer will take any opportunity of leaving, in which he would be justified for, as he says truly, his Irish policy has been entirely negatived, & he is required to govern Ireland without the measures being taken which he has declared to be necessary.

17 May 1885 (Sunday): . . . News of the capture of Riel[72], leader of the Canadian insurgents, which probably ends the affair, so far as fighting is concerned.

18 May 1885: London by usual train . . . See Lawson, who prophecies smooth things for the Cabinet. He has heard of the divisions on Irish affairs, but not of any difficulties on the budget.

. . . Childers has withdrawn, or rather delayed, his resignation: which is reasonable, for he has not yet a fair cause of complaint, though he may have one soon. His proposals have not been rejected, & the delay, though dangerous to them, may not be fatal. But he is in bad health &, though by nature good tempered, is disposed to be irritable when thwarted. I do not think his life a good one.

19 May 1885: . . . We are in an odd situation, as a government. There is no parliamentary opposition to fear, the party outside is united, & the election prospects, though necessarily uncertain, are favourable: yet we have been more than once, & still are, on the verge of disruption, and it is quite possible we may break up before July. Hartington is sick of the whole affair: the Chancellor would gladly retire: Spencer is kept at his post only by a strong sense of duty: the Premier's state of mind is variable, at times wishing to resign, at others bent on holding on: Harcourt wants the Chancellor's place: Dilke & Chamberlain want all the Whigs turned out: Granville has grown indifferent, seeing his chances of the Premiership gone – in short nobody is satisfied, except the new recruits, & they will not be long content. Childers, besides his disappointment about the budget, is I think breaking down in health: yet if we resign, as a consequence of our quarrels, who is to succeed? Salisbury was not much trusted when he stood by himself: but it is now inevitable that Churchill should be his leading colleague, & Churchill with all his remarkable cleverness is thoroughly untrustworthy: scarcely a gentleman, & probably more or less mad.

20 May 1885: . . . Dined with the Gladstones, meeting Ld & Ly Hampden, Ld Acton, Ly Ripon, Col. Farquharson[73], Ld C. Russell[74], etc.

. . . Brief conversation with Gladstone, who tells me of a new trouble. Finding that a land purchase bill with funds limited to one year would not be objected to by the opposition, & that Spencer is very anxious for it, he discussed the matter with Dilke & Chamberlain, & as he thought obtained their consent: on which he gave notice of a bill: but no sooner had he done this than they declared they had been misunderstood, & sent in their resignations. He is trying to set matters straight, but does not know if he shall succeed.

21 May 1885: . . . An informal Cabinet suddenly called, to discuss the Russo-Afghan frontier: about which the Russians are making fresh difficulties, & it is feared that the military party has got the upper hand at Petersburg.

Talk, before this meeting, both with Granville & Gladstone: the latter had passed an hour with the two dissentients, & believes that he has satisfied them: they both attended with the rest of us but, when I expressed to Chamberlain my hope that the catastrophe was averted, he answered rather sulkily: 'It is postponed.' Harcourt says (but he has a loose tongue) that they avow their determination to cut themselves free from the Cabinet, so that they may be able to put forward a purely radical policy at the elections, unhampered by more timid or scrupulous colleagues.

22 May 1885: . . . The trouble with Chamberlain & Dilke is now no secret: in fact they have taken care to publish it, & avow their design to break up the Cabinet, or at least to separate themselves from it in view of the elections. But they have still hope of taking Gladstone with them, and will not quarrel with him if they can help themselves. Whatever the end may be, their inclination to side with the Parnellites will cost many votes to the Liberal party in England, when the elections come on. There never was a time when it was less easy to look forward: Gladstone professes to be bent on leaving office when the new parliament meets: & at his age it is only reasonable that he should: but where is the successor? Granville would have been possible 3 or 4 years ago: but he is now old, very deaf, and the necessity of the leader being in the Commons will be more strongly felt in a new parliament. Hartington, with every wish to think well of him, & with a sincere respect for both his abilities & his character, I cannot hold to be equal to the position especially with reluctant followers, as the radicals would be: & there is the chance that his father may die at any time, compelling a fresh arrangement. It is an utter puzzle to me &, I believe, to many others. . . .

24 May 1885 (Whitsun Day): . . . Talk of the state of F.O. – Fitzmaurice[75] works in it to good purpose, but is not much liked, & is thought to be snappish & pert in his answers to parliamentary questions. This I have myself noticed. When Ld G. retires, it is expected that his place will be disputed between Dilke & Kimberley, the latter having more claims from service, though I should doubt whether he would care to change his present post. . . .

26 May 1885: . . . Gossip in the papers about a visit which Rosebery is paying to Berlin[76]. He is supposed to have some private mission to Bismarck, but I doubt it, for why should he be employed rather than Malet, who is popular at his post, & trusted at home? Sanderson knew nothing, at least he said so, & I believe him. But Granville is undoubtedly fond of working through special & secret agents: to my mind a questionable policy.

27 May 1885: One pouch only, & little in it, except a mem. by Gladstone, which he circulates to the Cabinet, explaining the misunderstanding between himself & Dilke & Chamberlain as to a land purchase bill. It is only an expansion of what he stated verbally to me on the 20th. He admits that they are free after the holidays to do as they think best about the bill. – The newspapers, which have got the story pretty accurately, refuse to believe that they will secede, pointing out quite truly that it is only a question of a year's delay, & that to pass a local government bill for Ireland through the Commons would be useless even if it were possible, since the Lords would certainly throw it out. Everything confirms me in the belief that this question, like that of the budget, is only a pretext for recovering their political independence: which in view of the elections they desire. . . .

29 May 1885: . . . Received in a circulation box a letter from Gladstone to Chamberlain, in which the former remonstrates against the publication, in detail, of all that has passed between them in regard to the crisis. This publication first appeared in a Birmingham paper, & has thence been widely copied. In reply Chamberlain denies all responsibility for the statement in question: which is probably true in the letter: but he admits that he has talked freely in answer to questions, & it is evident that the article was at least inspired by him. . . .

2 June 1885: . . . Mary G. dined in company with Chamberlain, a few days ago, & describes him as talking very wildly. He said that none of us in the upper classes had an idea of what was coming – that it would be a new world, a complete social revolution, the land transferred to the people, all large properties broken up, class distinctions broken down & more to the same effect. She is not given to exaggerate, so I suppose that he really did hold language of this kind, but it does not seem justified by anything that we can yet see of public feeling. He added that parliament must have less control over the ministers – the electors ought virtually to choose a dictator for five or six years. This I suspect is a common idea, & natural enough considered as a reaction from the excessively minute interference of the present H. of Commons, which has for its effect to paralyse or to precipitate action. . . .

5 June 1885: . . . Cabinet at 11.00, which sat till 2.30 . . . The Cabinet of this morning was long (3½ hours) and seemed likely to end in the resignation of Childers. We discussed the budget exclusively. It was understood that the requirements of the year would be less by £2,000,000 than was expected a month ago – the Russian scare being over. Childers proposed a diminished increase of spirit duty (2s. per gallon extra reduced to 1s.): the beer duty to be taken for one year only, which will conciliate the brewers: and to meet these losses he wished to tax wine (which we are free to do, the arrangement with Spain having broken down) by raising the duty, so as to get about £300,000 more. This was discussed at great length, & rather warmly: the argument in favour being that we in this way got rid of the odium of taxing beer & spirits, while leaving wine, the rich man's drink, untaxed: & deprived the opposition of their most plausible ground of objection: Dilke & Chamberlain, as well as the majority of the Cabinet, took the other side, contending that the French would resent taxation of their wines, & retaliate on our trade, which they are well inclined to do: this argument was much pressed, & weighed with most of us: the radical wing, I suspect, wished to retain the least popular feature of the budget, in the hope that it might not pass. Harcourt, backed by Chamberlain, wished to stop the paying off of debt – a policy which he treated with marked contempt. Gladstone was piqued, & retaliated. But Lefevre backed Chamberlain: & I see well that the new democracy do not care to reduce debt: perhaps they think that it may be got rid of in a more summary fashion. The discussion led Gladstone to dilate on the folly of having occupied Egypt as he did in 1882. He said he repented it heartily, it had been the cause of all our subsequent troubles, and he hoped that 'our folly might be a lesson to our children & grandchildren, & great-grandchildren'. In the end the Cabinet decided to stand on the budget as it is, & not to touch the wine duties. Childers, who was ill and more agitated by the discussion than its importance warranted, refused to acquiesce & left the room, thus virtually announcing his resignation. Selborne, Granville, Harcourt, & Gladstone went out to reason with him: he was not disposed to yield at once, but did so in the course of the afternoon, which Gladstone announced by a box sent round. We had, before separating, agreed to accept any compromise on which Childers might insist, provided Gladstone agreed to it: but in the end he (C.) yielded absolutely, & the wine duties are not to be touched. His other alterations are not objected to, though they involve a loss of £300,000 at least, and possibly a deficit at the end of the year. I noted that in the course of our talk Gladstone more than once spoke as if the age of economy were past: nobody asked, he said, or cared for it. This is true, &a bad sign.

Some vague, but important, talk about Irish measures. Chamberlain explained what had passed. He said his & Dilke's resignations were and are in suspense. He would have swallowed coercion, though hating it, if accompanied with a local government bill such as he approved. But the Cabinet was not disposed to agree to this, and now 'we claim to have our hands free. We object to going before the electors tarred with this abominable coercion brush'. He did not believe the new parliament would tolerate coercion: and there were two compromises which he would accept: either the act for one year only, or that it should be brought into operation only by order-in-council, or proclamation (I did not well understand this, & may not be exact) in which case it might be for three years. Dilke & Lefevre supported Chamberlain, Kimberley warned them not to be misled by an apparent cessation of crime, such had often happened before, & never lasted long. But he would accept the act for one year. It was agreed that we must adjourn the discussion to next week. . . .

7 June 1885 (Sunday): . . . **Note** that at yesterday's dinner [Lord] Lorne, who is standing for some London constituency, argued with me the question whether protective duties on articles imported, but which may be made at home, were not advisable. He excluded necessaries & articles of food, but seemed to think that as regards luxuries protection might be re-introduced, & that opinion was tending in that direction. I note this as an indication of the current drift of opinion.

8 June 1885: . . . Office at 1.00, where worked till 2.00. Then Cabinet, which sat till 4.00, all present, including Spencer. Office again till 5.00, when to the Lords, where the Seats Bill, managed by Kimberley, went through committee, with no serious trouble. We divided, I think, three times, but only on questions of names . . . Went to dine with Kimberley at the Travellers'. Home at 10.15, & worked on papers for an hour.

In Cabinet, Spencer addressed us at some length, saying that he had already made larger concessions than he thought right, that intimidation is even now kept down with difficulty, boycotting is still common, no one can buy or sell at a fair without a Land League ticket. He wished that part of the law which deals with intimidation to be maintained intact. He would yield as to other parts, & allow them to be brought into operation only in certain districts, after proclamation. The one year plan he would not consent to. – Gladstone supported Spencer, but in a diffuse & feeble speech. He seemed uncomfortable, & evidently wished to make it clear that he gave his support only because the Lord Lieutenant wished it. Carlingford & Harcourt both spoke strongly as to the state of Ireland, Harcourt saying in his swaggering way that the objections came from those only who knew nothing about Ireland. Chamberlain objected. Dilke said bluntly & frankly that the differences among us are so deep rooted that we ought not to try to keep together. Hartington said that, even if we agreed now on what should be done, we should differ in debate. Granville tried to minimise the differences. I supported Spencer unconditionally. In the end, after 2 hours' discussion, we came to no conclusion, & agreed to adjourn till tomorrow – a disruption seeming nearly certain.

9 June 1885 (Tuesday): News this morning in the papers that we were beaten on the budget by 12 (264 to 252): the smallness of the numbers showing that there must have been many abstentions. This simplifies matters, & puts an end to quarrels among ourselves.

Saw Lawson, & Sanderson: at 12.00 to Cabinet, which had been agreed on yesterday under different circumstances. It was curious to see the changed countenances of the party. Expecting either disruption, or as the only possible alternative some compromise which would be satisfactory to neither party, and having grown weary of perpetual squabbles among ourselves, we were far more pleased with our defeat than our opponents can have been with their victory. Granville was radiant: Harcourt went about slapping his friends on the back and laughing in his obstreperous fashion: the Chancellor for the first time since his wife's death ceased to look miserable: Hartington was absolutely genial: Dilke & Chamberlain showed themselves relieved from anxiety: Spencer the same: Northbrook & Kimberley appeared, & probably were, indifferent: the only exception was Gladstone, who seemed out of temper and out of spirits at first, but soon recovered.

There was no discussion, except on details of how long to adjourn for, what to say to the Queen, & the like: resignation was taken as a matter of course, which indeed it was, for both Dilke & Gladstone, speaking on behalf of the government, expressly declared the vote of last night to be 'a question of life or death': which, had there been no other reason, would have been enough to make the acceptance of defeat impossible.

The Queen, on hearing the news, at once telegraphed to say that under no circumstances must she be asked to leave Balmoral before the day she had fixed (about ten days hence). The scene in the H. of C. when the numbers were announced is said to have been peculiar. Churchill & some others stood up on the seats, shouting & waving hats: the Irish yelled like savages, Healy taking the lead: 'No coercion', 'Buckshot', and 'Down with Foxy Jack' being among the cries uttered: the last is a playful allusion to the red hair & beard of John Ld Spencer, who as the representative of British power in Ireland appears to be hated with an almost insane hatred. More than 40 Liberal members were absent from the division: some from dislike of the new succession duties, more in consequence of pressure from constituents. The whole strength of the publican interest has been thrown into the movement: and it is considerable.

10 June 1885: Newspapers full of the crisis: it seems to be generally understood that the outgoing ministers are not unwilling to retire, & indeed we are generally supposed to have arranged our own defeat, which is certainly not the case for, though considered as possible, it was not expected at the Cabinet on Monday. . . . The disposal of the F.O. will be the greatest difficulty of our successors. Carnarvon & Lytton are both possible, but both weak. . . .

11 June 1885: . . . I called on Granville, who showed me the letters & telegrams that have passed between Gladstone & the Queen. According to Ld G. Gladstone is not at all desirous of resigning, & will require little pressing to induce him to take back his decision. For this he would have some excuse, for the newspapers are full of letters . . . from the 40 Liberal M.P.s who were absent from the late division most of them giving excuses for their abstention, & protesting that, if they had known the existence of the government to be at stake, they would have made a point of attending. So that, if we wished it, the vote of Monday night might easily be reversed. But the risk of breaking up would still remain &, except the Premier, nobody wishes to take back the places we have resigned.

12 June 1885: . . . Office 2.30–4.15: then to Lords, where Granville made his announcement in the fewest & plainest words possible: after which we accepted Commons' amendments in the Seats Bill, & finally passed it. The new constituencies are now created, & the next election may be taken in November. . . .

13 June 1885: . . . Dinner at Trinity House . . . I sat between the new D. of Wellington[77] & Northbrook. The Duke a strange being, enormously fat & heavy, but with a pleasant manner, & I should think had sense, though not what is called talent.

Talk with Northbrook: I asked him 'whether the horse was pulled on Monday?' He said: 'No, he thought not, but certainly the spurs were not used.' It will be impossible, I suspect, to make people believe that Grosvenor could not have secured a majority if it had been desired, & many of the opposition now reproach their leaders with having fallen into a trap. . . .

15 June 1885: London by usual train. Saw Lawson & Antrobus. . . . Called on Granville: negociations are still going on, he says, as to the amount & kind of support which the incoming ministers think themselves entitled to receive. He thought Gladstone inclined to be stiff and reticent: but agreed with me that it would be a mistake to give the Conservatives a fair excuse for backing out: since that would be to play their game, besides looking unpatriotic. . . .

16 June 1885: . . . In parliament last night an odd incident. It was settled between Gladstone & Northcote that some rather urgent business which had come down from the Lords should be dealt with at once. The House in general saw no objection: and in fact there was none, as far as I can judge: but Churchill took the opportunity of objecting, a wrangle followed, & in the ensuing division Hicks Beach & Raikes voted for him, & against their nominal leader. The incident in itself is unimportant, but has some significance as bearing on the personal relations of leading members of the party to one another.

. . . Sent through Antrobus presents of £5 each to the two doorkeepers, & 5 messengers, at Col. Office.

Received a summons to a meeting in Downing St. at 3.00, where most of the late Cabinet were assembled. The object was to consider an application made by Salisbury, or rather an overture, to know what degree of support the incoming ministers might expect. This overture was made to Gladstone in a verbal message from A. Balfour: which the recipient did not much like, thinking the manner of communication unusual & uncourteous. It ought, he said, to be in writing, so as to remain on record, & be liable to publication if necessary. This it seems he had said to Balfour in reply, & awaited a written answer, which however did not come. We talked over matters for upwards of an hour, not, as I thought, to much purpose: I noticed that Harcourt, who had been more demonstrative than anybody in his expressions of satisfaction at getting free, was less disposed than anybody to give a fair chance to our successors. Dilke & I took the opposite line more strongly than any others, contending that it was for our advantage that they should be able to form a government, & we should rather remove obstacles out of their way than put them there. Gladstone seemed restless & eager, but not out of humour. – I learnt that he had just had from the Queen the offer of an earldom, which he had declined. Granville, Hartington, Spencer, Trevelyan, were absent: all the rest came.

Then office, where found a large heap of papers, & worked till near 7.00.

17 June 1885: . . . Papers from office in considerable quantities . . . Called in afternoon on A.D.[78] who is weaker than I have seen her yet. . . .

18 June 1885: News in the papers that the new Cabinet is partly formed. Salisbury takes the F.O. as well as the Premiership, an impossible arrangement for a continuance, but for six months in the recess it may do: Sir H. Giffard, not Brett as was expected, takes the Chancellorship: . . . Churchill is named for India, for which he is about as unfit as a man well can be: but with a strong governor-general, & a council at home, he will be partly kept in check.

. . . Another Cabinet . . . was held in Downing St., attended by most members of the government. Gladstone read us communications which had passed between him & the Queen, the purport of which is that Salisbury, before accepting office, wants assurances of support more definite and particular than we are disposed to give. There was a good deal of splitting of hairs, as it seemed to me: discussions about the exact meaning to be attached to words used on both sides, & so forth. In the end we all agreed that nothing can be conceded beyond a general pledge to abstain from obstruction & factious proceedings. – Chamberlain talked a little violently when some question was raised of a possible delay in taking the new elections, hinting that there would be riots all over the country in that event, but nobody answered him & the matter dropped. Gladstone then went to Windsor.

Office, where much business . . .

19 June 1885: . . . Carnarvon is announced as Lord Lieut. of Ireland, the last place I should have thought of for him, & I do not think it will suit him, or he it.

. . . H. of Lords at 4.30, where Salisbury suggested a farther adjournment till Tuesday, which we agreed to, but wished first to pass the redistribution bill, which has come back to us with some amendments by the Commons. Salisbury, however, objected to this &, dividing on the question whether they should be dealt with now, beat us by two to one. The object of this move is not clear, & it does not seem a wise one: since it tends to strengthen the otherwise incredible report that the incoming government entertain the idea of dissolving on the old constituencies – an act which would be not merely unpopular & impolitic, but almost insane. Yet, if this is not intended, no other explanation can be given . . . While I write, the same subject is probably being debated in the Commons. It is understood that there is a hitch in the arrangements, & that the attempt to form a new government may not improbably fail.

20 June 1885: Cabinet suddenly summoned at 11.00, but only 9 or 10 out of the 16 were present. We sat till 12.30.

Home: saw Lawson, who inclined to think that the Conservatives would be able to go on: I dissented, & we ended by a bet.

Office, where next to no business.

. . . Our meeting this morning was occupied in discussing the answer to be given to Ld Salisbury's demands. He claims all the time of the House required for financial arrangements, which in practice means a veto on all measures which he may object to: and an arrangement about the budget, vague in terms, but which points to the probability that instead of the taxes censured by H. of C. there should be a loan to cover the deficit. These proposals we were unanimous in condemning: & indeed the general impression among us was that he can have put them forward only in order to be refused, & have a fair pretext for throwing up the cards. – Gladstone on his side would not go beyond a disclaimer of any factious proceedings: which means nothing: and even that was not expressed in warm or decided terms. He (Gladstone) is evidently reluctant to go out, even for a few months: Granville's feeling is strong the other way: Harcourt was more violent in favour of resignation than anybody, but now seems not unwilling to go back: Dilke & Chamberlain wish the opposition to come into power, that they may be free to begin an agitation at once, which indeed they have already done. – Churchill takes a very high tone, as I am told: he said to Lawson: 'We are masters of the situation, & we will not come in except upon our own terms.' He has asserted his power, & dethroned Northcote: & it is thought that he would not be sorry to have the matter end there, so that he may leave off a winner. – Northcote, I hear, had a very cordial reception yesterday in the House: cheered by both sides: a genuine expression of personal sympathy, for it is felt that he has been badly used, & that he gives way rather than struggle against men less honourable & scrupulous than himself.

22 June 1885: London by usual train . . . Find no change apparent in the political situation . . . Office at 2.30, but found scarcely anything to do: left again between 4.00 & 5.00. Dined Grillions, meeting Lds Acton, Clinton, Sherbrooke, & Norton: Gladstone, & Mills. A pleasant evening: the Premier told me before dinner that he did not know how we stood 'whether on our heads or our heels'. Ponsonby had been with him six times in the course of the day: he could not make out whether the Conservatives would accept his assurances as sufficient or not.

If the affair goes on, Sir H. Giffard is announced as Chancellor in lieu of Brett, who was first thought of, and as some say has refused the place, but this I do not believe, but think rather that his son's connection with Hartington stood in the way. Sir Hardinge is reputed a good lawyer, & popular with the bar: but not the equal of Cairns or Selborne, & in politics a nonentity. Cross is to return to the Home Office, where he did well during his six years' tenure of power: since that date he has gone down in reputation, having once made an exhibition of himself by speaking in the House when quite drunk, & having to be pulled down by his friends. Churchill goes to the India Office, where Dufferin in India, & the council at home, may possibly keep him in order: but it is a risky appointment. Hicks Beach will be a strong Chancellor of the Exchequer, I should expect: but his manners are disagreeable, & he will not be a popular leader. Northcote will be in a peculiar and very anomalous position as First Lord of the Treasury, without being Prime Minister: either the place is a sinecure of £5,000 a year, or there will be two Chancellors of the Exchequer.

Carnarvon, if he really goes to Dublin, will be as much out of his element as it is possible for a clever & industrious man to be. Smith, who thoroughly understands the Admiralty, is to be transferred to the War Office, of which he knows nothing: & G. Hamilton, who has not kept his early promise of a great success, is named for the Admiralty, no one knows why. These three last appointments are unintelligible. Of the rest there is not much to say: Gibson will be a good Irish Chancellor, & my brother a safe Colonial minister if, as the papers have it, he is my intended successor. The double duty of the Premiership and Foreign Office, which Salisbury has reserved for himself, is more than any man can wisely undertake: but for a few months of the recess the arrangement may answer well enough.

23 June 1885: The papers announce as settled the intention of the Conservatives to take office, but I have heard nothing authentic. Lawson called early: he believed the story, but had no positive evidence.

. . . Office at 3.00, and stayed till 4.15. There Granville called, & told me that all was settled at last: but negociations were going on to the last moment.

To the Lords at 4.30, where the taking of office by our successors was announced. The amendments to the Seats Bill were briefly disposed of, and I came away. It was understood that the statement was to be put off till Thursday, Salisbury being at Windsor.

. . . Disposed of some office business, the last I shall have.

24 June 1885: Received from my brother a letter, written in good taste, announcing his appointment to my late office: I answer, & fix a time to see him this evening.

Saw Lawson, & talk about the various appointments made.

. . . To Windsor by special train, with the rest of the late government, arriving about 1.30. At 3.00 a council was held, at which Sir H. James was sworn in P.C.: we afterwards resigned our offices severally. The Queen, though no doubt well pleased at the change, seemed anxious & weary: she said very little, as far as I could make out, to anybody. We left about 3.40: Kimberley & I walked together through the parks, a very hot afternoon.

At 6.30 F. came, & I explained to him the state of matters in the office, at some length. Our conversation was very friendly, & he keeps on my secretaries, which is to his advantage & that of the office. I advised him to appoint Havelock[79] to Natal, which indeed I had settled to do, & asked him: but my decision is not binding on my successor. I also warned him to support Robinson against Warren in the dispute between them, which I have not been able to settle, as the information on which a decision must be based is still on its way: but, from what I know of the case before, I have no doubt on which side justice and policy lie. . . .

26 June 1885: . . . The Conservatives have promoted Northcote to an earldom[80], for which he is not grateful, since it is only a decently veiled dismissal at the instigation of Churchill: and he is neither desirous of being shelved, nor rich enough to make a peerage suitable. . . .

30 June 1885: . . . The new appointments are not yet complete . . . None is much objected to, as far as I know, except that of Wolff[81] to Egypt. Wolff is a notorious speculator & jobber, not well looked upon in any society, though he has never committed himself so far as to be altogether shut out of it: he is mixed up with a bank which is one of the chief creditors of Egypt, & closely connected with Churchill, whose attacks on the Khedive were so grossly personal as to disgust the H. of Commons.

Gibson[82] is Irish Chancellor, succeeding a Mr. Naish[83]: who held the post less than six weeks, & between them they are entitled to £8,000 a year pension for life. This is all in order, & legitimate, but it may draw notice to the very high rate of judicial pensions. . . .

Notes

[1] For Cabinet meetings in January–June 1885, see also *Lord Carlingford's Journal: Reflections of a Cabinet Minister, 1885*, ed. A.B. Cooke and J.R. Vincent (1971).

² (Sir) Saul Samuel (1820–1900), agent-general in London for New South Wales, 10 August 1880–1897 (retired), K.C.M.G.: 'energetic, shrewd, and efficient': first practising Jew to become a minister of the Crown (1860): a leading figure in Jewish public life.

³ Alfonso XII (1857–1885), king of Spain 1875–1885.

⁴ Isabella II (1830–1904), queen of Spain 1833–1868.

⁵ Lady Margaret Cecil.

⁶ Charles Carington (1843–1928), 3rd Baron and 1st Earl Carrington (cr. 1895): Governor of New South Wales, 1885–1890: cr. Marquess of Lincolnshire, 1912.

⁷ Sir H.B. Loch (1827–1900), governor of Victoria 1884–1889.

⁸ Sherbrooke remarried 3 February 1885.

⁹ Arthur, 3rd E. Wilton (1833–1885): M.P. (Cons.) Weymouth 1859–1865, Bath 1873–1874: cr. Baron Grey de Radcliffe, 1875: styled Viscount Grey de Wilton till 1882: succ. father, 1882.

¹⁰ Seymour, 4th E. Wilton (1839–1888).

¹¹ One of a succession of oculists in whom Lady Derby reposed initially high hopes but without lasting benefit.

¹² His younger sister: died 19 January 1885.

¹³ At Abu Klea, British forces numbering 6,500 under Stewart defeated 9,000 Arabs in desperate combat (17 January 1885).

¹⁴ Incorrect. David Ogilvy, 6th E. of Airlie (1856–1900), was in fact only slightly wounded at Abu Klea. After being thrice wounded in action, he was eventually killed in battle in the Boer War.

¹⁵ Edward Jervis, 4th Vt Saint Vincent of Meaford (1850–1885), educ. Harrow 1864–1867: army career 1871–1885: served in Zulu War, Afghan War, Boer War, Egyptian Campaign, and Soudan Campaign. D. of wounds received at Abu Klea.

¹⁶ I have since heard this denied, & am told that he made many enemies (Diary, 24 Jan.).

¹⁷ Capt. Thomas Hamber, Conservative editor: sometime ed. of *Standard*, then of *Morning Advertiser* (1877): once close to Disraeli and Salisbury, but d. in obscurity.

¹⁸ Timothy Charles Harrington (1851–1910), M.P. Westmeath 1883–1885, Dublin (Harbour) 1885–1910: proprietor of *United Ireland*.

¹⁹ Commander of column marching on Khartoum: died from wounds, 16 February 1885.

²⁰ The marriage was of the premier's son Stephen to Annie Wilson, dau. of a Liverpool physician.

²¹ William Drogo Montagu, 7th Duke of Manchester (1823–1890).

²² J. O'Donovan Rossa (1831–1915), Irish–American extremist.

²³ The Berlin West African Conference, 15 November 1884–26 February 1885. See Sibyl Eyre Crowe, *The Berlin West African Conference, 1884–1885* (1942).

²⁴ The International Association of the Congo, f. November 1879, and recognised as a sovereign entity by Britain on 16 December 1884, Britain being the first European power to do so.

²⁵ Leopold II, King of the Belgians (1835–1909), succ. 1865.

²⁶ Sir Edward Malet, 4th Bt (1837–1908), ambassador at Berlin 14 September 1884–1895.

²⁷ Not traced

²⁸ See n. 1538 above.

²⁹ (Sir) James Francis Garrick (1836–1907), lawyer: moved from Sydney to Brisbane, 1861: Q.C., 1882: Queensland agent-general for immigration in London, June 1884–October 1895 (except for 1888–1890): energetic and enterprising.

³⁰ Robert Murray Smith (1831–1921), educ. Repton and Oriel: migrated to Victoria 1854: Victorian agent-general in London, 1882–1886.

³¹ Not traced

³² Sir Charles Tupper (1821–1915), Canadian conservative leader and high commissioner in London: premier of Nova Scotia, a Founder of the Confederation, ally of Sir J.A. Macdonald, and member of federal cabinet: as minister of railways 1879–1884 largely responsible for Canadian Pacific Railway: bt., 1888, premier of Canada, April–June 1896.

[33] (Sir) Arthur Blyth (1823–1891), premier of S. Australia 1864–1865: minister *c.* 1857–1877: agent-general for S. Australia in London, February 1877–1891: delegate to Colonial Conference, 1887: K.C.M.G., 1877.

[34] Sir Charles William Wilson (1836–1905), soldier: major-gen. R. Engineers: head of ordnance survey, Ireland, 1870–1886: U.K. consul-gen. Anatolia 1879–1882: chief of intelligence, Nile expedition, September 1884: director, U.K. ordnance survey, 1886–1893.

[35] Gen. Sir George Richards Greaves (1831–1922): served in Mutiny, Maori War, Ashanti War, Soudan Campaign: on staff at War Office, 1870–1878: chief sec., Cyprus, 1878: c.-in-c., Bombay, 1890: resigned, 1893.

[36] Sir Archibald Alison, 2nd Bt. (1826–1907): commanded Highland Brigade at Tel-el-Kebir: lt.-gen. 1882: commanded force in Egypt, 1883: commander, Aldershot, 1883–1888.

[37] William Earle (1833–1885), major-gen.: military sec. to Northbrook 1872–1876: commanded Alexandria garrison, 1882–1884: killed in Soudan war, at battle of Kirkbekan, 10 February 1885.

[38] Gen. Sir Gerald Graham (1831–1899), soldier: lt.-gen. R.E.: V.C., 1857: fought 4 battles against Osman Digna around Suakin, 1884–1885.

[39] A port and gulf in what became the French colony of Djibouti, lying opposite Aden.

[40] Sir Frederick Napier Broome (1842–1896), N.Z. sheep farmer 1857–1869, colonial sec. of Natal and Mauritius, governor of W. Australia (1882–1890), and of Barbados and of Trinidad.

[41] A. Buckland, *A Record of Ellen Watson* (1884).

[42] H.M. Hyndman (1842–1921), stockbroker and leading Marxist.

[43] John Francis Campbell of Islay, F.G.S., author of *Tales of the West Highlands*, who d. aged 62, 17 February 1885.

[44] Sir John Swinburne, 7th Bt. (b. 1831), M.P. Lichfield 1885–1892.

[45] Sir Somerset Lowry-Corry, 4th E. Belmore (b. 1835): succ. 1845: under-sec. at home office 1866–1867: governor of New South Wales 1867–1872: m. Gladstone's niece.

[46] See also 28 January 1885 above, and 21 April 1885 below.

[47] Widow of Henry Thomas Stanley (d. 1875), diarist's uncle and brother of the premier.

[48] Edward Henry Stanley (b. 1838), the only surviving child.

[49] Wife of Hastings Russell, 9th D. of Bedford (1819–1891).

[50] Lady Ermyntrude Russell.

[51] Sir E. Malet (1837–1908), fourth bt.

[52] Ambassador at Berlin, 1884–1895: previously at Brussels.

[53] G.C.T. Bartley (1842–1910), M.P. (Cons.) Islington N. 1885–1906: sometime principal agent at Conservative Central Office.

[54] Mohammed Tewfik Pasha (1852–1892), Khedive 1879–1892. Son of Ismail II, whom he succeeded on his abdication.

[55] A decree signed by the Sultan.

[56] Alfred Egmont-Hake ed., *The Journals of Major-Gen. C.G. Gordon, C.B., at Khartoum* (1885), pub. July 1885.

[57] Gen. Sir Peter Lumsden (1829–1918), U.K. commissioner for demarcation of N.E. boundary of Afghanistan, 1884–1885; Chief of Staff, India, 1879: seen by Liberals as a Russophobe.

[58] Musurus Pasha (1807–1891), Ottoman minister in London 1851–1856, and ambassador 1856–1885.

[59] Sir John Carstairs McNeill, V.C. (1831–1904): served in Mutiny, Maori War, Red River expedition: chief of staff, Ashanti War, 1873–1874: major-gen., 1882: commanded brigade in Soudan, 1885: retired, 1890.

[60] Mark Pattison, *Memoirs,* ed. by Mrs. Emilia Pattison (1885).

[61] Diplomatist: not traced.

[62] Baron de Staal (1822–1907), Russian ambassador in London 1884–1902.

[63] Lady Selborne d. 10 April 1885: Rosebery's brother Everard Primrose d. in Egypt, 9 April 1885. Rosebery had pulled strings so that his brother could see active service.

64 Gen. Komarov, commanding Russian forces on the Afghan frontier, attacked and defeated the Afghans at Penjdeh on 30 March 1885.

65 Perhaps Henry Lake Wells (1850–1898), lt.-col. R.E.: in Afghan War, 1878–1879: surveyed telegraphs in Kashmir, 1879–1880, and Persia, 1880: director of Persian telegraph, 1891.

66 Despite this pessimism, the outgoing parliament did succeed in passing a major land purchase act (Ashbourne's Act), much the most ambitious measure of its kind to date.

67 *Parl. Deb., 3*, vol. ccxcvii, cols. 847–866: £11 m. voted for naval and military operations without a division, and with no speeches after that of the premier.

68 Princess Beatrice (1857–1914), Queen Victoria's fifth and youngest dau.: edited Queen's diaries: m., July 1885, Prince Henry of Battenberg (1858–1896).

69 Abu Bakar's visit to London was caused by his suspicions of Weld, Johore being the main independent Malay state remaining. Notwithstanding Derby's assurances, the Colonial Office used the occasion to impose a new treaty on Johore which in some ways restricted its independence. British officials claimed to fear German or French attempts to annex Johore. In other ways the visit went well: he arrived in London a mere Maharajah, but left it promoted to Sultan.

70 Sir F.A. Weld (1823–1891), colonial governor: N. Zealand M.P., explorer, minister, and premier (1864–1865) during Maori War: gov. of W. Australia, of Tasmania, and of Straits Settlements (1880–1887).

71 An allusion to Lord Randolph's mother, Lady Frances Vane (d. 1899), whose half-brother, Frederick, 4th M. of Londonderry (d. 1872), passed many years in mental illness.

72 Louis Riel (1844–1885), Canadian rebel: leader of two risings by half-breeds: executed 1885.

73 Col. James Ross Farquharson (1834–1888), soldier: educ. Eton: army career 1853–1864: severely wounded in Crimea: co-founder of Bachelors Club, Piccadilly: personal friend of P. of Wales: lt.-col. 1859.

74 Perhaps Lord Charles James Fox Russell (1807–1894), 6th s. of John, 6th D. of Bedford: M.P. Beds. 1832–1848: serjeant-at-arms to H. of C. 1848–1875: father of G.W.E. Russell.

75 Lord Edmond Fitzmaurice, 1st Baron Fitzmaurice (1846–1935), under-sec. for foreign affairs 1882–1885.

76 For Rosebery's Berlin visit of 22–26 May 1885 (for which he was indeed briefed by Granville) see Crewe, *Rosebery*, i, 239–241.

77 Henry Wellesley, 3rd D. of Wellington (1846–1900), nephew of the 2nd Duke: M.P. Andover 1874–1880: d.s.p., and was succ. by a grandson of the 1st Duke. His widow m., in 1904, as his 3rd wife, his notorious kinsman, Col. the Hon. Frederick Arthur Wellesley, 3rd s. of the 1st E. Cowley. He d. 9 February 1931: she d. 11 March 1939.

78 Lady Dartrey (*neé* Augusta Stanley of Cross Hall, Lancs., a distant kinswoman) d. 9 August 1887, aged 64.

79 Sir Arthur Elibank Havelock (1844–1908), colonial governor: in army, 1862–1877 (retired): served in W. Indies 1874–1881: gov. of W. African Settlements, 1881: gov. of Natal 1886–1889, of Ceylon 1890–1895, of Madras 1895–1901, and of Tasmania, 1901–1904.

80 Iddesleigh.

81 Sir Henry Drummond Wolff (1830–1908), P.C. 1885: U.K. commissioner to reorganise Egyptian administration, 1885–1886: Rugbeian.

82 Lord Ashbourne.

83 John Naish (1841–1890), lord chancellor of Ireland: Irish bar 1865: Q.C. 1880: Irish law officer 1883–May 1885: Irish lord chancellor May–June 1885 and February–June 1886.

THE LATER DERBY DIARIES

1885–1893

Selected Passages

Contents

Derby: The Last Phase

The diaries of Edward Henry, fifteenth Earl of Derby (1826–93), run without a break from 1861 to within three days of his death on 21 April 1893. They are in large printed Letts's diaries of varying sizes, with a page to each day. It is very rare indeed for a day to be missed by the diarist. The entries were made normally on the day concerned or the following day, though sometimes when ill or too busy Derby fell behind and wrote up several days at once. It is, however, for all practical purposes a contemporaneous record without subsequent afterthoughts or corrections. These diaries were probably written chiefly for purposes of recording business done, but the writer obviously found some relief in communing with himself on paper.

The diaries appear to have been unknown and unused until 1974, when they came to light by chance in the cellars of Knowsley. Since July 1980, they have been deposited with Liverpool Record Office, where they are now readily available. A selection from the diaries up to September 1869, the year in which the diarist succeeded his father in the title, was published in 1978[1]. Because of the very large amount of mainly party and governmental material relating to Derby's period as a senior minister between 1870 and 1885, Derby's years out of office after June 1885 have been treated separately. This is, therefore, the fourth and final volume of extracts from the Derby diaries, though the second in order of publication[2].

The diaries show clearly the three main calls upon the time, energy, and purse of a serious-minded Victorian magnate: begging letters, voluntary committee work and public speaking, and administering the estate. Derby when out of office did not have a secretary, fearing loss of privacy, and he spent much of each morning, almost every day of his life, answering begging letters; and very few, if any, went unanswered. In consequence, their number steadily increased decade by decade, most being from total strangers or the remotest of acquaintances. His charities were on the whole more extensive than useful, for, while only the blackest of black sheep received a peremptory refusal of help, Derby did not on the whole actively seek out good causes. It was the sponger and the ne'er-do-well who did best out of his conscientious approach to charity.

The estate also occupied much of his time. He was, in fact, his own head agent, taking important decisions about property transactions, but also expecting quite small details of estate management to be referred to him by his perfectly capable and honest estate staff. Matters concerning plantations were as important to him as sporting matters had been to his father. The owner of Knowsley, Derby thought, did not need to seek occupation; it came to him. This was particularly true of civic duties. He presided over Kirkdale quarter sessions, of which he was chairman from 1856, with great success and conviction that he was doing something for which he was well fitted, and he was drawn into all major civic occasions in Liverpool. He had a close connection with the young university at Liverpool. He shut the door resolutely, however, against anything connected with the clergy, refusing for instance to support a cathedral on the Isle of Man, saying that he could think of few less pressing needs in the late nineteenth century. He had also considerable contempt for the impracticality and narrow ideas of most would-be philanthropists.

In fact his charities were considerable: on one occasion he wrote: 'Made up private accounts for the month. I have spent £615, but of this nearly £500 is gifts or loans - words in my experience meaning exactly the same thing.'[3] Over the whole period from his father's death in 1869, to 1889, the gross income of the estate was nearly £4,000,000, of which about £670,000 was deducted at source, leaving about £3,200,000 net actually reaching Derby's hands. Of this about £1,600,000 was put back into the estate, £800,000 saved and invested in securities and land purchases; and £800,000 spent on household, charitable, and miscellaneous expenses. The household at Knowsley probably cost about £20,000 to £25,000 a year to run; Derby on inheriting had thought it unduly expensive and tried to make reductions.

The chief pleasure of Derby's last years was his success as a landed proprietor. He had accumulated a very large fortune in quite a short period, had paid off all debt on the estates, and died a millionaire in his own right, having started with nothing but an income and no capital in 1869. He wanted very much to show that he could be a financial success (unlike his father) and when he accomplished this, despite the severe depression of the 1880's, the material achievement did much to counter-balance his relative lack of political success, and the early onset of age. What did he want the money for? There were probably three reasons: first, it gave him a sense of achievement, secondly he liked the sensation of having so much money, and thirdly he had the very definite object of building up a large capital sum under his own control, which he hoped on death, or after twenty-five years' accumulation in trust, to give back to the family estates, perhaps to buy more land. It is one of the paradoxes of Derby that, though he represented that element in the landed class which had most fully come to terms with the reality of an urban industrial England, yet his personal ambitions lay in the direction, not simply of enlarging the Stanley fortunes, but enlarging them in terms of a traditional agricultural estate.

Much of Derby's success, as he admitted, was because he possessed building land in Liverpool and Bootle, and because Lancashire, not being a corn county, came through the agricultural depression exceptionally well. About half of Derby's rental by the mid-1880's came from urban leases. The estates, which were 120 square miles, or about one-thousandth of the land area of the British Isles, were divided as follows:

	acres
Lancashire: E. Fylde	14,651
E. Lancs.	15,408
Knowsley	27,670
Liverpool, Bootle	1,141
Total Lancashire	59,340
Cheshire, Flintshire	9,870
Kent, Surrey	6,056

The rental was as follows (rents actually received being about £5,000-£10,000 lower):

1800	£31,881	1884	£226,897
1820	£48,614	1885	£231,130
1840	£72,616	1886	£235,605
1860	£126,196	1887	£237,686
1880	£198,541	1888	£241,736
1881	£206,629	1889	£244,416
1882	£211,986	1890	£243,716
1883	£218,845		

From his life interest in the income of the estates, which were technically in the hands of trustees, Derby saved the following personal fortune:

1878 (December)	£195,000	1883	£440,000
1879	£220,000	1884	£520,000
1880	£300,000	1885	£600,000
1881	£350,000	1886	£680,000
1882	£390,000		

This was inexorable progress indeed, and a never-failing cure for despondency. By 1888, Derby had saved £1,100,000. Of this, £860,000 had gone into fixed interest securities, which had risen in value since purchase to £980,000: £20,000 was un-invested: and £100,000 had been put into land[4]. When Derby took over from his father the estates were heavily in debt, to the tune of £500,000. Derby in the 1870's had made it his first task to pay this off, before building up his own fortune, so that his own success in accumulation was even bigger than first appears.

How and why did Derby invest his money? Very cautiously and defensively; he sought not so much to make, as to avoid losing money[5]. His most risky holdings were railway debentures. He regarded Indian government stocks as unsafe. In his younger days he had bought industrial shares; now he avoided them completely. He was less restrained when it came to land, where he bought on a falling market, in small amounts, throughout the 1880's and early 1890's, taking the view that prices could not fall much farther, and that if revolution came[6], a possibility which he often pondered, land would at least be no worse than any other investment. He made purchases on grounds of scenic value, as in Kent and Surrey, and in order to round off awkward gaps in the Lancashire estates. On the whole he wished his rural estates to become larger, though he tried to avoid buying land in counties where he was not previously a proprietor, because of the increased social, political, and charitable obligations it would involve. Though the urban land in Liverpool had been the golden goose of the family fortunes, he declined as early as 1884 from deliberate political judgement[7] to acquire any more land within the city. Derby, in managing his estates so frugally and impeccably, considered that he was striking a blow not only for himself and his family, but for the public reputation of the whole system of great landed estates.

In 1888 Derby left a note[8] of the investments in his private estate:

Railway debentures	£400,000
English funds	£170,000
Australian funds	£100,000

Miscellaneous	£745,000	in securities (at cost)
Worth at current prices	£805,000	
In Land	£18,000	
Lent to Lord Granville	£5,000	
	£828,000	

By 1891 Derby was able to value the family estates at six to seven millions, and his own private fortune at a million or so[9]. The following retrospect conveys something of Derby's attitude to the estate:

16 Jan 1887: . . .What have I done for this place and estate since Jan. 1870? To sum up briefly, I have:

1. Paid off nearly £500,000 of debt.
2. Increased the rental from £170,000 to £230,000: the credit of which, however, scarcely belongs to me, for the increase has arisen from the taking up of building land and from renewals of leases.
3. Bought the Hazels, Finch House, Wheethill, and numerous small freeholds in Eccleston, Rainford, Huyton, etc.
4. Bought about 1,000 acres, perhaps more, in the Fylde.
5. Bought three estates in Kent and Surrey, on two of which are houses, and the third, Witley, would make a nearly perfect park if a house were built upon it, and the ground laid out.
6. Rebuilt, I suppose, half the village of Knowsley, and added many cottages else-where.
7. Made some, though not great or costly, improvements in the house[10].
8. Laid by £700,000, of which part at least will go to increase the estate for my successor. This is a satisfactory retrospect: though against the purchases named must be set considerable sales of land. . . I omit here all mention of the Irish estate, as it was left to my brother. . . [These sales] being in towns, have not appreciably lessened the area of the estates: which is nearly 77,000 acres, or as exactly as possible one-thousandth part of the area of the British islands. I have not taken notice in the above of improvements in the park and plantations: though these are in much better order than I found them in. Nor have I taken credit for the enlargement and partial rebuilding of the London houses and also of Holwood and Fairhill.

★ ★ ★

Derby summarised his investment policy thus: 'While circumstances remain as they are, I can afford to put by for investment, or to lay out in land, or to apply to any other purpose, £60,000 a year at least or, if the year be favourable, and no unusual expenses occur, from £70–75,000 . . . And as increased taxation is nearly a certainty, and increase of rents very uncertain, I am bound to provide against a future less favourable than the present time.'[11]

Derby was very much the head of a family, as well as of a great estate. Of his wife, Mary, Lady Derby, who outlived him by seven years, it is hard to glean anything from his diaries. Much more sociable than her husband, she preferred life in London, where she continued to attract a variety of callers, including Gladstone. Her sight had largely failed, from cataract, by the early 1880's, and this must have limited her social horizons. It was probably Derby's main reason for refusing office in May 1882. For all that, she and her husband were rarely apart, whether in or out of office; and much of their leisure was taken by his reading to her from serious periodicals. From the mid-1880's there was always a hope that an operation for cataract could be performed within the coming year, though in fact this was not done until 1892. Making all allowance for Derby's extreme reticence and his evident devotion it seems that by the 1880's Lady Derby had begun to outlive her generation, essentially that of the Sixties, in a way her husband had not. Certainly there was little for her to do at Knowsley, which she disliked, and where she and her husband made few local friends. She did little in the way of entertaining there on her own account, beyond looking after her Cecil children. That intimacy between a few choice metropolitan spirits, not of common clay, in which she excelled, was almost a thing of the past for her. Despite this, the depression which had affected her in the 1870's apparently disappeared, and she no longer gave Derby cause for anxiety about her mental condition.

Derby's only brother and successor, Frederick Stanley, sixteenth Earl of Derby[12] (1841–1908), was never seen at Knowsley in the years between 1878 and 1893. This might seem surprising, for 'Freddy' was not the sort of man it was easy to quarrel with. He was fat, lethargic, honourable, not too bright, uxorious, without high seriousness but absolutely straight. He was subject to occasional fits of serious depression, like his brother and father. He was, like his father, but unlike his brother, interested in racing; and Derby 'hated the idea of racing and would have nothing to do with it in any way whatsoever. He would never forgive my grandfather for having horses to race'.[13] These of course were not causes of quarrel, for until 1878 Derby had been consistently proud of his younger brother. Nor was the breach politically motivated, for when Freddy came into the cabinet in his elder brother's place Derby did not allow it to come between them.

Rather, it was something Freddy's wife had said in 1878 that proved unforgivable. We know not what was said, but that something was said, some unbearable slur on Derby, or perhaps on Lady Derby, is certain. The wound was so deep that thereafter family meetings at Knowsley were impossible, though Derby managed on one occasion to give them both luncheon in London before they set off for Canada. The Stanleys, Freddy and Constance, though living in the same county, and heirs to Knowsley, could not visit it, and Derby never visited them at Witherslack[14]. It is unlikely that there was much bad feeling between the brothers. When they met in the street in London, all passed off well enough; and when Freddy had to take major steps in his career in 1885, 1886, and 1888, he consulted his elder brother first. Derby appreciated the compliment, and was relieved and delighted when his brother, too staunch and non-political to succeed as a cabinet minister, found a post much more suited to his good nature as governor-general of Canada. Freddy, for his part, was pleased that his eldest son was made much of as the future heir of Knowsley, and to learn that most of Derby's private fortune would be left to augment the family estates.

Despite this unseen amiability, the brothers remained publicly separated to the last. The seventeenth Earl, Freddy's son, grew up thinking 'that my Father and his brother .. did not speak', ascribing this 'for the most part to my mother's influence', and claiming that Mary, Lady Derby '. . . and my mother cordially disliked each other, and if there was anything either of them could say against each other they did so'[15]. Derby's sister, Emma, who outlived both her brothers, so rarely appeared in Derby's life that she could hardly act as peacemaker. Her distance from Derby remains something the diaries hardly explain, though she seems to have placidly followed the normal life of the minor gentry. Derby did, however, try to assist her unfortunate eldest son (see below pp. 865–6) with a position in the Colonial Office and, when he heard that his sister's eldest girl was to be married to a Mr. Eastwood, a lawyer, with some private means, the young couple were invited to Knowsley and the husband received official approval. But, such family concerns apart, Derby and his sister had apparently no ties and nothing to say to each other, and Emma rarely visited Knowsley.

There was one last twist to the story of the relations between the Stanleys of Knowsley and the Stanleys of Witherslack. Not the least important object of Derby's life had been substantially to enrich his brother's family, in the interests of dynastic feeling. In a new will made in 1892, he left £700,000 of his own money for the purchase of land to add to the family estates; up till then he had left £500,000 for that purpose. He was of course free to leave the fruits of these savings from his life interest anywhere he pleased. That he left them as he did was more a tribute to the power of the dynastic idea than a sign of deserved confidence in his brother.

15 Sept. 1891: . . . I hear with regret that my brother has borrowed £85,000 from an insurance office, on the security of his charges on the Knowsley estates. This amounts to exactly half the capital of his fortune, and reduces his income from £7,500 to less than £4,000 a year. It is certainly not an encouragement to me to add to the fortune of the family, if it is to be wasted by my successors. I had heard before of the state of things, but less authoritatively. There is no remedy and, if it ends there, the mischief is not great. If it does not end there, at least I shall not see it. But it surprises me, for my brother is careful, and in his family is even thought to be close[16]. It is of course possible that he has used the money borrowed for an investment or speculation of some kind, but I do not think it likely.

When the widowed Lady Salisbury married Lord Derby in 1870 and left Hatfield for Knowsley, she did not arrive alone. She brought with her a brood of five Cecil children, three sons and two daughters, the offspring of her first husband, James, second Marquess of Salisbury. In theory the five Cecils, being in 1870 already in their early twenties or late teens, might soon have gone their separate ways and played little part in the life of Knowsley, but for a variety of reasons they were much about the house until their mother left in 1893 to spend her widowhood in Kent. The Cecils, despite the apparent advantage of having grown up at Hatfield, were not particularly able, aristocratic, politically minded, or successful in their lives, but as the visitor to late Victorian Knowsley would be likely to meet them, and they were part of Derby's daily life, it is perhaps worth attempting to piece together some idea of their lives and characters.

Only one of the five children completely left the nest and made a life for himself. This was Lord Sackville Cecil (1848–98), a man of great technical ability who succeeded in business as manager of the London Underground. He was rarely seen at Knowsley, and the fifteenth Earl in his diaries has little or nothing to say about him, beyond portraying him as irascible and difficult in personal matters. The seventeenth Earl, writing in extreme old age, recalled him briefly as 'a queer half-mad creature, but who was very kind to me' and 'a very able fellow, but a bit of a crank'. Sackville died unmarried.

The two younger brothers, Arthur (1851–1913) and Lionel (1853–1901) were bracketed together as 'the lads'. The fifteenth Earl, rightly but without too much sympathy, saw them as lifelong boys. They seem to have had the same very close relationship that one sometimes finds in twins. They wished to spend their lives together indulging in being enthusiastic high farmers, at a time when even the crudest kind of farming could hardly pay its way. They farmed a large Scottish farm, Orchardmains, in the 1870's and 1880's, until, their capital exhausted, they fell back on being rather restless and penurious pensioners of Lord Derby in the late 1880' s, when they were much about Knowsley[17]. Lionel's personal amiability was beyond dispute. He was good with guests, always in good spirits, and went to great trouble in organising large shooting parties, leaving Derby free to stay indoors with his papers. For this Derby was duly grateful[18]; and the seventeenth Earl, looking back to his youth, recalled the Cecil boys as 'huge fat creatures, but both very good fellows, more especially Lionel', who, he added, 'was quite one of the best fellows I ever came across. He was kindness itself. His size prevented him afterwards from doing much. . .' (Lionel, like his brother Sackville, never married.) Lionel's only defects were that he had no wish to be more than a farmer, and that he was unable to see that money lost on worthy agricultural prospects was, in the end, just money lost.

Lord Arthur Cecil was, by comparison, a complex character. (He became director of an insurance company.) Whereas Lionel was remembered by the seventeenth Earl as 'a very good fellow: the kindest-hearted man in the world', Arthur in contrast 'was always trying to do something rather tricky and everybody disliked him'. There are two stories behind these probably exaggerated expressions. First, Arthur had not only married, but made a mésalliance. Lord and Lady Derby not only opposed the union at the time (in 1874-5) but seemed to have gone to unusual lengths to show their opposition to their daughter-in-law later on. Arthur had married when an agricultural student the daughter of the farmer whose pupil he was. She was extraordinarily fat and, according to the seventeenth Earl of Derby, a frequent visitor to Knowsley in the 1880's, was treated in the most extraordinary way by her relations. 'She was never allowed to dine down if there was a single person in the house, and even if there was nobody she was mostly told to dine upstairs. She did sometimes have luncheon, but as a matter of fact I hardly ever saw her. She had two boys, for neither of whom did I care very much, Jim and Reggie . . .'[19]. Lady Arthur Cecil[20] was not a chorus girl, nor an actress; she was 'quite nice, very harmless, but third-rate to a degree' according to the seventeenth Earl; she produced Lady Derby's only grandchildren; yet, as the seventeenth Earl wrote, 'more brutal treatment of a daughter-in-law I do not think I have ever known'[21]. (Lord Derby in his diaries simply ignored her existence.)

Lord Derby found Arthur 'excellent company, and always ready to assist in whatever wants doing. The prospect of losing all his money in the farm which he has taken does not in the least disturb him: nor affect his spirits, which are exuberant. He enjoys country life and all its pursuits with the keen pleasure of a boy: and in fact he will remain a boy (one of the best sort) all his life'[22]. His nephew Eddy Stanley, the future seventeenth Earl, had more mixed feelings about Arthur, whom he saw as 'kind, but he was an awful tittle-tattle and got me into awful trouble by talking one day about a telegram which I had sent having a bet. He used to go down and look at every telegram that was sent out of the house, in which he was abetted by a man who was a sort of footman and confidential servant to Margaret, Fred Capon, a most mischievous man, who, when my uncle died, I had to turn out of the house'. There is certainly some truth in this. Derby did get to hear of his nephew's fast ways, and for the last years of his life regarded him, without dislike but with anxiety, as a brand to be saved from the burning; in particular Derby welcomed his nephew's early marriage as a useful way of settling him down to steady ways.

His exposure over his betting telegrams, which so justifiably rankled with the seventeenth Lord Derby, concerned others besides Arthur. The artful footman, Capon, used also to show young Eddy Stanley's telegrams to Lady Margaret Cecil, who in turn sometimes spoke to Lord Derby about them. She was religious and somewhat solitary in her ways, and despite her step-father's rather aggressive scepticism she conducted religious services in a chapel in the tower. (Derby rudely always called her chapel 'the howling shop'). She even tried to get Eddy Stanley to join her chapel, but as one of the conditions was a pledge of lifelong teetotalism, 'which did not suit me', she did not get very far. Of all the children, she spent most time at Knowsley, and was probably closest to Derby and Lady Derby; but in the end she decided to live on her own small estate at Burwash in Kent. Lady Margaret leaves little more than an impression of sensitivity; she was no Mary Gladstone or even Gwendolen Cecil, and in the seventeenth Earl's eyes 'she had got rather a bee in the bonnet about religion, and she put her entire faith in a man who was her footman - Fred Capon. People said they were married, which was absolutely untrue'.

Romance had in fact offered itself, if only once, to Lady Margaret Cecil. Derby's private secretary at the Foreign Office, a young man of good but poor gentry family called Thomas Sanderson (1841–1923), became very close to both Lord and Lady Derby and was constantly at Knowsley. The inevitable followed, for Sanderson was young, musical, spirited, and highly intelligent:

25 Dec. 1875: Margaret asked this morning to speak to me, and explained that (as we had long seen) an intimacy had been growing up between Sanderson and her, which had led to his making speeches of which she could not misunderstand the meaning. An explanation between them followed, in which she seems to have spoken her mind with great frankness and even some toughness. What she said was that he was not to entertain the hope that she would marry him either then or at any future time. He is disappointed, and not unreasonably, for she undoubtedly gave him a good deal of encouragement, more than she ought: but she has no experience of the world, and was naturally pleased with his attentions. . . . She repeated to me three times that her mind was made up, and that she should not change it, but on that point I am not so certain. If she did so, want of means need be no obstacle, for I have enough for both: and S. is a man thoroughly to be trusted: but in any event a London life and a moderate income would be hard to bear, for she has always lived in great houses, and likes nothing so well as the country. I am not sure that the matter is ended yet.

28 Dec. 1875: Talk with M. [Lady Derby] about Margaret's business: I pressed her not to throw any obstacles in the way, if her daughter really liked Sanderson: indeed I do not know where she could find a better husband for her, and I am certain that, for a girl of rather passionate and romantic temperament, a marriage of convenience and reason would not be a success, though it has answered well enough in her sister[Mary]'s case.

Nothing ever came of it. Sanderson continued to live almost as one of the family for the rest of Derby's life, and in due course became his executor. He succeeded in his career, becoming the senior official at the Foreign Office and earning a peerage. But he, like Lady Margaret, appears never to have come near to marriage again.

The elder sister, Mary, struck Eddy Stanley as 'very clever, and if she had not been married to that awful fellow Galloway would I think have had a very happy life, but he drank like a fish and was altogether a dreadful creature. I remember him shooting here once. He went out after luncheon very drunk, tumbled into a ditch and lay there in the water. Everybody agreed the best thing to do was to leave him there and let him taste something he had never tasted before, water. Mary was a very delightful and dear creature, but one was never allowed to see much of her . . . She had great ability and never had an opportunity of using it'.

Alan, tenth Earl of Galloway (1835-1901), whom Mary married in rather a conventional way in 1872, appeared to have nothing much wrong with him, even if there was not a great deal that was right. He had been an M.P.; he was commissioner to the Church Assembly in 1876–7, perhaps as a Disraelian compliment to Derby. Everything seemed normal in the first ten years of marriage; though there were never to be any children. But by the mid-1880's he was never sober. His finances became much embarrassed, and to make matters worse his brother faced bankruptcy[23]. The crash came when he was charged with an offence against a young girl (of which he was acquitted) and then some time later was discharged after being arrested for indecent conduct in Glasgow. It is likely that he did not know what he was doing at the time, and that mental illness had as much to do with it as alcoholism; it is also possible that designing persons, seeking to be bought off, made the most of an easy target. These incidents were too much for his wife, who formed a violent dislike for her husband, and forced a separation rather less discreetly than Derby would have liked. Rather surprisingly, Lord Galloway recovered by the late eighties sufficiently to give up whisky, though he had to travel in the care of a doctor, and lived to a relatively ripe age. His wife died two years after him in 1903.

The Cecil children were in an unenviable position. If they married at their own level of fortune and ability, it would constitute a *mésalliance* in their parents' eyes; yet, with their small incomes, they were unattractive propositions in the grander marriage market of London society. They were encouraged to treat Knowsley as theirs; yet young Eddy Stanley was made much of as its ultimate heir, before their very eyes. Dispossessed from Hatfield by a new and hostile régime, they were equally certain to be dispossessed from Knowsley, having lived as the children of both houses. Moreover, they were Cecils, not Stanleys; but Cecils by a second marriage. Their status depended on the continued existence of their mother, which unfortunately prevented them finding occupation[24] or marriage at a lower level of existence.

Derby's activities after leaving office in June 1885 were far from negligible. For a short time, early in 1887, he felt 'low spirits and depression' from a sense of unemployment, but the mood did not recur. He continued to speak, and keep himself before the public, in Lancashire and elsewhere, until his first real illness in spring 1891 made further platform speaking impossible. He served on three important inquiries into social questions: the House of Lords select committee on sweated labour, the Royal Commission on Markets, and the Royal Commission on Labour. He became more of a Lancastrian than perhaps at any previous time, finally moving his correspondence to Knowsley early in 1887 (in 1886 he had spent no more than 87 days there). He carried on till 1888 as chairman of Kirkdale sessions, retiring in November 1888 after thirty-two years. Austere though he was, his knowledge of low life and crime in Liverpool must have been unrivalled.

When in London, he frequented Grillions, the dining club where political enmities were (almost) forgotten: he was a central figure in the financing of the National Liberal Club, taking the chair at its shareholders' meeting in 1888; he supported Smith-Barry's scheme for helping the Irish landlords, whom he thought, however, were a feckless lot whose impecuniosity long antedated Parnellism. Editors, particularly Lawson of *The Daily Telegraph*, consulted Derby during the session, and he kept in touch with foreign politics through Sanderson's very frequent letters from the F.O. French, German, and Russian ambassadors still came to shoot at Knowsley. Over Christmas 1889 his guests killed 3,700 head of game, and sat down 25 to dinner. Attendant intellectuals like Lecky and Froude provided company. Only the major politicians were conspicuously absent; but they had never been frequent visitors to Knowsley. Nor did Derby visit country houses, but he had always valued isolation.

The seventeenth Earl of Derby (1865–1948), known to his family and contemporaries as 'Eddy' Stanley, visited Knowsley quite often from the mid-1880's. His impressions of life there under the fifteenth Earl, written at various times in the 1940's, recall the habits of the household vividly.

To give an idea of our sort of life at that time', he wrote, 'breakfast was at 9.00, to which anybody who liked came down. Luncheon was at 2.00, to which everybody had to come, and dinner at 8.00. It was not a question of being down soon after the gong rang. It was rung twice: at 5 minutes to 8.00 and at 8.00. Everybody was expected to be down by the time it was rung the first time and we went into dinner the second time it rang regardless of anybody not being down. My uncle [the fifteenth Earl] used to sit an inordinate time after dinner. He always had somebody with whom he loved talking. The two I remember best were Froude and Lecky. . .

'There were many other guests who used to come, of course all of them Liberals. Gladstone of course came, and he was really wonderful to younger people. I remember his talking to me once about the Guards Chapel which had just then begun to be beautified by officers of the Brigade. He knew everything about it, and what was intended, and who had given the things for the decoration, etc. How he got to know I haven't the least idea.

'. . .Of course there were lots of shooting parties. . . It was all great fun and my uncle and aunt [Mary, Lady Derby] were very kind to me in asking my friends to shoot.

'The smoking room was what is now the Liverpool Room, and no smoking was allowed under any circumstances anywhere: nor was a dog allowed in the house.

'. . .At 10.00 precisely my uncle and aunt used to go off to bed. Their rooms were off the gallery, what are now the breakfast and morning room.

'. . .There was a custom which lasted right through my father's time and through part of mine, of having markers behind each gun: each one had a marked card and pin, and for each bird shot he put the pin into the card. A list of what everybody had killed was solemnly handed round at dinner time, and my uncle used to make the most caustic remarks about everybody's shooting. He himself was an extraordinary shot. He never missed a rabbit or hare, and if pheasants were coming over he generally killed the first one, but never attempted to fire at a second.

'The head keeper was old Barnes, whose son succeeded him, and whose grandson is now my loader. The park keeper was a man named Silcock, I think he was brother-in-law to Barnes. He was the last man about here to keep the old Derby Fighting Cocks, black-breasted reds: and I have often been up to his place on a Sunday for a cockfight.

'There was a very curious custom here on Sunday. My Uncle never went to Church, but in the morning a message was sent round to ask who was going, and according to the number that went so there were shillings deposited on the table in the hall for everybody to give for offertory, and my uncle would have been very much offended if anybody had refused to take the shilling.

'. . .I do not think I mentioned the curious costume my uncle used to wear when shooting. A soft hat which was then called a Homburg, thin black frock coat, brown trousers and button boots, and on the wettest days he used to put on a very thin overcoat. He had a curious sort of walk, but he would walk nine men out of ten down.

'He was kind in a way to me, but I was very much afraid of him. I always wish now, however, that somebody would write his life. One, a very bad one, was written, but now that people see things in their true perspective he would stand out as a much bigger man than his own generation thought him.

'. . . My uncle was a man of extraordinary habits, doing exactly the same thing on the same day every year. He never missed, if he could help it, going out for a walk in St. James's Square, walking all the way round Regent's Park and back, and when he was at Knowsley all the paths were marked with distances, and he made a point of walking ten miles a day.

'Nine times out of ten he would be very abstemious. He used to drink a bottle of champagne every night, but it was the most extraordinary stuff. It was not real champagne, but a sort of doctored wine in which there was absolutely no strength nor harm. Then sometimes for no reason whatsoever he would drink every other wine, and the result was occasionally a little deplorable. I think I said he went to bed every night at 10.00, it did not matter who was there. He got up very early in the morning, always doing an hour's gymnastic exercises before breakfast, which he sometimes had in his own sitting room, but generally in the breakfast room. He never smoked himself,[25] and had no sympathy with those who did'.

Home Rule

'I am not clear that Gladstone has not destroyed the Union. . .'
Lord Derby, 14 August 1886.

(The later diaries of Lord Derby were only discovered in the same year, 1974, that the most recent study of the Home Rule crisis was published[26]. Had the diaries been available to the authors of that work before they went to press, they would have been able to give a fuller, richer, and in some respects different account of motive and conversation among senior liberals in 1885–86. Some use was made of the diaries in the Raleigh Lecture for 1977[27], but most of the passages relevant to Home Rule are printed here for the first time. The chief exceptions are résumés given in the diary of Derby's letters to Granville, which correspond closely to original letters printed by Granville's biographer.

Between June 1885 and January 1886 Derby moved nearer to the centre of Liberal (or Liberal Unionist) party affairs than he had done before or would do again. Freed from departmental chores, he maintained contact with a wide range of colleagues, was taken into Gladstone's confidence on Irish matters, and took an active part in the general election of autumn 1885. Far from looking for a pretext to withdraw from Liberal politics, he made every effort to keep the party together. One of his arguments against Home Rule was that 'the Liberal party would be nowhere if they supported it'[28]. There were many types of Liberal Unionist. There were those who wanted a split, and those who feared one; those who were mainly interested in Ireland, and those who were not.

Derby was almost free of ulterior motive in approaching the question. He deeply regretted the price that had to be paid in personal and party terms for the disruption. He staked his position on the purely Irish ground, which went back to his days looking after the family estates in Tipperary in the 1860's, that Irish feeling was ultimately irreconcilable and separatist. In maintaining this view he was not taking up a new position to meet the crisis of 1885–86, but only saying what he had often said in private argument in previous decades. In a sense, Derby was recognising Irish nationality as irreducible, where Gladstone denied it.

There is nothing in the diaries to support the statement by Derby's friend Russell, editor of the *Liverpool Daily Post* and a Home Ruler, that 'at one time he [Derby] was pretty firmly of the opinion that Irish Home Rule would come' and that the question was 'only a choice of evils'[29]. Derby may have seen both sides of the case in philosophical discussion over dinner, and perhaps was inclined to defeatism, but in political practice he had no doubt which 'evil' he preferred. His willingness to resist what he took to be the will of the Irish people is remarkable, given his usual tendency to concession, and his first-hand knowledge of the Irish peasantry and their feelings. He may have unwittingly misled Gladstone about his opinions at one point, by saying that if forced he would prefer to have Ireland treated like Canada, rather than given a more limited but less final form of local government[30]. In early August 1885, before his holiday, Gladstone told Granville 'both you and Derby are on the same lines as Parnell . . .' This belief that Derby might potentially be on his side, engendered in July and August, probably explains Gladstone's candour about Ireland when they met at Hawarden on 1 October[31]. What Derby never said was that he would himself be willing to play a part in furthering a wide Irish settlement, a distinction Gladstone overlooked.

Derby's comments on the Home Rule question revolved around Gladstone and the reactions of a limited number of ministerial politicians to him. Gladstone had lain low since the defeat and resignation of his second ministry on 9 June 1885. There was little that needed doing, and he had in any case strained his throat and required rest. By the time of prorogation on 14 August, he was already on a Norwegian holiday (8 August–1 September). He returned to find the Liberals and Irish set on a collision course. Hartington at Waterfoot on 29 August, and Chamberlain at Warrington on 8 September, repeated at Glasgow on 15 September, came out decisively against Irish claims before Gladstone was able to give a lead. Parnell, for his part, encouraged by a secret interview with Carnarvon on 1 August, was pressing his demands more aggressively than previously.

Gladstone's address, issued on 17 September, was principally directed to uniting the quarrelling wings of the party on a programme for the next parliament. It contained no revelations on Irish matters. Not until his speech at Edinburgh on 9 November did he address himself to Irish demands, and then negatively. To public view, he was refusing to bid for Irish votes. Meanwhile, however, he was trying to win round a few colleagues by selective indiscretion to his idea of what was required should the election create an opportunity for action.

19 July 1885: Letter from Gladstone, enclosing three which he has written to other persons on the subject of local government for Ireland; he writes strongly in favour of the plan of a central governing board, and seems to intimate, though in obscure terms, that unless his ideas are agreed to he will not care to go on. I answered briefly, promising deliberate consideration and a fuller reply later: but said that the proposal appeared to me either to go too far or not far enough. The new board meeting in Dublin would be considered by everybody as a local parliament, and would certainly claim to be one: thus laying the ground for innumerable difficulties hereafter: while England would not obtain the one special advantage of Home Rule, the exclusion of Irishmen from the H. of Commons. I shall consult with Granville and others before committing myself to a decision, but as at present advised I do not like the scheme.

22 July 1885: Two bills of some importance have passed through the Lords: one, that for better housing of the working classes in London, which is in fact a confession of failure, for it does scarcely anything except devote the sites of one or two disused prisons to workingmen's dwellings, which is an infinitesimally small gain: and being the sole result of the commission of enquiry, about which so much noise was made, shows that what reasonable people said at the time was true, and that the matter is not one that can be effectually dealt with by legislation. The second is the Irish land purchase bill, taken with variations from that which we proposed last year, but limited to an outlay of £5,000,000, so that it is in the nature of an experimental trial rather than that of a final settlement. It is an act of justice to the Irish landlords, who can find no other market for their estates, but whether the tenants will take advantage of it is much disputed. They have got what they wanted - security of tenure - and they have a better chance of securing further reductions of rent by dealing with weak and impoverished landlords than if they became debtors to the State.

24 July 1885: Received today a letter . . . on the subject of Scottish disestablishment. I could not see them, but offered to read anything they might send me, and expressed my opinion that the question is one which ought to be decided by the Scotch themselves. If there is a majority of Scotch members in favour of disestablishment (I said) I can see no reason why English members should interfere to prevent the Scotch from having their own way: if on the other hand the Scotch are not ready for the change, it is not our business to force it upon them[32].

25 July 1885: Wrote to Gladstone in answer to his letter of the other day, declining to give a final opinion on a matter which I have not heard discussed, but repeating at greater length, and enforcing, the objections which occur to me to the local government scheme of which the principle is the setting up of a central board in Dublin. I object (1) on the ground that in such a board, or council, Ulster will be in a permanent minority - that to Ulster men the idea will be intolerable, and that we shall begin by alienating the only real friends whom we have in Ireland. I say (2) that the new body which it is proposed to call into existence will consider itself, and be considered by the Irish people, as a real parliament: that a constant pressure will be put upon us to enlarge the sphere of its functions and increase its importance: that we shall thus have introduced Home Rule in principle, without either satisfying the Irish people or gaining the advantage of getting rid of the Irish out of the H. of Commons. I could understand that the acceptance of Home Rule might under some circumstances be a necessity: but if we are to have it let us know what we are doing, do it deliberately, and make our terms. It did not seem fair, I added, to leave the Irish members free to meddle in our local affairs while leaving them the exclusive management of their own. And I did not understand that it was proposed to establish any similar system for England or Scotland. All the difficulties which I had suggested would be removed if four local boards were created instead of one, each province having its own. The above was the substance and main argument of my letter, of which I kept no copy.

26 July 1885: Talk with Lady Janetta Manners [wife of Lord John Manners, then in the Cabinet], who in her gossiping way tells me of great disagreements among the new ministers . . . and she expressed doubts whether they would be able to hold together till November.

5 Sept. 1885: . . . Wrote to Kimberley[33], and in my letter expressed a hope that Gladstone would stand firm in the matter of concessions to Parnell.

Wrote to A. Russell[34] expressing similar views. This was in answer to a letter from him to Ly D. in which he relates a conversation between Gladstone and Goschen, as reported by the latter. Goschen believes that he has converted W.E.G. to the necessity of supporting the Union. I doubt!

24 Sept. 1885: Talk with Northbrook[35] in the intervals of shooting. He is doubtful as to elections – thinks the present government have a fair chance of a majority with Parnellite support – is not sure that their being in power for a year or two would be a bad thing – agrees with me that union among Liberals is possible only under Gladstone, and while he lives – does not see the future leader – Hartington may at any time be transferred to the Lords – Harcourt is impossible from unpopularity, and does not wish it – Chamberlain is disliked in the House, and represents only a section. In short, he is very much in the dark, and so am I.

25 Sept. 1885: Northbrook shows me letters concerning Ireland, one from Mr. Jenkinson[36], lately employed on secret police business at Dublin, and at one time secretary to Ld Spencer. This gentleman takes a very gloomy view of the situation, says Home Rule is now inevitable, that the only choice is between a bloody and a bloodless revolution, that even if Parnell tried to restrain the movement he could not, but would only be left behind by it - and more to the same effect.

26 Sept. 1885: Wrote to Gladstone, expressing satisfaction at the tone of his manifesto, as tending to union[37]. I ended by saying that we should keep together as long as he remained leader, but not 24 hours longer: which I believe to be the truth.

1 Oct. 1885 (Thursday): . . . Left at 12.15 with M. for Hawarden where a visit had been promised: reached Chester at 2.00, Hawarden before 3.00: stayed till 4.30, and returned, reaching Knowsley a little after 7.00 and bringing with us the Duchess [of Bedford][38], her daughter, and Margaret [Cecil][39], who had called at Hawarden on their way back from visiting W.S. West[40] at Bangor.

Nearly the whole hour and a half was filled up, so far as I was concerned, by a conversation with Gladstone. He seemed to me in a changed mood: not excited, nor eager, but anxious and feeling the difficulty of the situation. He plunged into the personal part of it at once. He blamed Chamberlain severely, said his language was altogether new and unprecedented, and his demand that the party shall adopt his programme[41] unreasonable (I am not quoting words, but this was the purport): but Chamberlain in correspondence had owned to him that a crisis might occur which would make it his duty to ignore what he had said, and act with the party irrespective of the particular measures to which he is pledged. He, Gladstone, had pressed him to say why he could not be content with a list of measures, quite sufficient to occupy the party for five years, leaving himself free for the future? But he did not tell me what answer if any Chamberlain had made. He spoke of Hartington with slight friendly censure, regretting that he (H.) made himself too exclusively the spokesman of one section of the party, forgetting that he was the destined future leader of the whole. But he thought he (H.) had shown temper and good sense in the long correspondence which had passed. I asked for a general indication of his (G.'s) ideas as to what should be said about land, and was glad to find that they agreed substantially with mine - I told him I put the question in view of a speech to be made next week.

He then turned to Ireland, about which he discoursed for fully half an hour, with scarcely any interruption from me. He said the plan of a central council put forward by Chamberlain would have been accepted by Parnell, who then thought he could do no better for the Irish cause: but R. Churchill by seeking his alliance had induced him to raise his terms, and now he would be content with nothing short of a local parliament, having full powers of legislation. He thought the question of the Irish Union one which must be studied seriously. He had been reading old debates upon it, including Pitt's speech in proposing it to parliament, and he was not satisfied with the argument in its favour. He had come to the conclusion that the Union was a mistake, and that no adequate justification had been shown for taking away the national life of Ireland. (These last words are nearly, if not exactly, those used by him.) He did not agree that a single executive cannot co-exist with two independent legislatures. Norway and Sweden were an example to the contrary: Austria and Hungary another. He did not agree in the assertion that the Irish would not be content with less than absolute legislative independence.

He thought Irish members might still be allowed to vote in the imperial parliament on imperial questions, though having their own parliament for local affairs: the Speaker could decide to which class any particular question belonged. I asked whether he thought the English public would consent to repeal the Union on any terms – whether the majority would not be against it? He shook his head, and said there was a vast amount of prejudice to be reckoned with, and he did not know how that might be. One thing he saw plainly, that parliament could not go on as it had done: the Irish organisation had been perfected during the last ten years, the Irish had never been united as they were now, there was very high ability among them, much higher than among the average of English members, whatever other faults they might have: and it would be impossible to avoid coming to terms with them, if they returned to the next parliament eighty or ninety strong. He mentioned Healy as one who was moderately disposed, as well as able. He spoke of the necessity of taking some security for the protection of the landowners, whom an Irish parliament left to itself would certainly not treat with fairness. – The above was the chief of what he said. He asked no opinion and I gave none, beyond saying that I thought he took a sanguine view of the reasonableness of the Irish party. – I listened with some surprise for, though I knew that he favoured the Irish claims, I was not prepared for what is in fact a declaration in favour of Home Rule[42].

2 Oct. 1885: Wrote to Granville the substance of the conversation mentioned above, but more briefly than I have done here. . . . I expressed my opinion that Gladstone's language constituted 'a new departure with a vengeance' and expressed doubts whether Ireland would not break up both parties.

5 Oct. 1885: . . . I have a letter from Granville, in answer to mine about Gladstone's conversation: he does not indicate any surprise at G.'s language, from which I gather that something of the same kind has been said to him, but under obligations of secrecy. But he observes with truth that talk in this sense does not harmonise well with the speeches made in a different sense by Hartington, and even by Chamberlain[43].

7 Oct. 1885: Sent £10 to a Mr. Pigott[44], an Irishman, who is publishing an anti-Parnellite pamphlet. He was a rebel, and I suspect him to be a rogue, but thought it better not to refuse.

[In mid-October 1885 Derby had a cluster of guests at Knowsley. Lord Arthur Russell and his family were there by 10 October, and left on 14 October. On 12 October Kimberley and the Lowes came, and were joined by the German ambassador Count Münster. Kimberley was still at Knowsley on the 15th, probably leaving on the 16th; the Münsters left on the 17th.]

14 Oct. 1885 (Wednesday): The [Lord] A. Russells left this morning, with their son and daughter. A. Russell[45] does not conceal his regret at going out of parliament, which he does because his brother [the ninth Duke of Bedford] from some unexplained caprice does not choose he should remain there: for he never speaks, nor takes much part in the business, but he is one of those men who find a continual enjoyment in looking on at the game of life, not caring themselves to play, but watching the play of others[46]. He is well acquainted with the politics of the Continent as a professional diplomatist, and is now going on to Hawarden to pick up what he can of Gladstone's views about things in general. The children are well brought up, but whether from natural disposition or parental instruction, the most absolutely silent pair I ever came across. In six days I have not heard either of them speak.

16 Oct. 1885 (Friday): Count Münster went over to Hawarden for the day, leaving his daughter here.

17 Oct. 1885: Count Münster and his daughter left us. The reason of his transfer to Paris is not explained, and he says he does not know it himself. It is a mistake so far as this country is concerned: for no successor will ever identify himself with English life as he has done. I suspect either a job of Bismarck's having for its object to bring on his son, or a piece of spite, for he dislikes Münster, and the transfer to Paris, while very disagreeable to the latter, cannot be resented, since it is rather a promotion than otherwise. Or perhaps it may be thought at Berlin that Münster is too English - too closely connected with England to be able, or willing, to make himself disagreeable. I regret his loss: he is a gentleman, a pleasant companion, and has for years past been a constant visitor at this house.

22 Oct. 1885: [This passage from the diaries[47] of Lewis Harcourt is included without apology for its Gladstone interest.] Hawarden Castle, Chester. Arrived here 1 p.m. Mr. G. at luncheon said he was in a very Conservative mood - had just been reading programme of Church Liberation Society - they want not only to disestablish and disendow but to destroy Church of England as a religious body - says it is of little moment to him as Disestablishment is a subject he could never have to deal with. Miss Mary [Gladstone] said: 'Oh, but you said that about the Irish Church which you disestablished within two years of that time.' He said that was quite different. Irish Church rotten but nobody thought about it; dearth of political energy before Palmerston's death, if P. had lived Irish Ch. might not have been disest. for years.

Talked about reform of the H. of L. He is in favour of a certain number of peers being elected by House of Commons each Parlt. Also of a Peer by inheritance being able to say whether he will sit as a Peer or stand for a constituency. That decision being binding for one Parlt. but being free to choose again before the next Parlt. elected.

. . . Mr. G. thinks that some years' training in the H. of C. would be of great value to Peers who through early succession are not now able to obtain it. He says would have been of great use to Rosebery and in the case of the Duke of Argyll might have changed the whole tenor of his political tendencies. He repeated what he had said before of the love of the English people for a peer. Talked of an association started in the H. of C. in the year [blank] for endeavouring to decrease the number of peers in the Govt. but said it was useless and failed and so strong was the natural instinct of love for a Peer that, when any of the petitions had to be presented by one of their numbers, they always employed Lord John Browne, their only Lord, to do so.

Mr. G. is opposed to the abolition of the H. of Lords and dislikes the idea of only a single Chamber. He says that in other countries the upper Chambers have not been found to override the lower. I quoted America but he said: 'Oh, I do not consider that to be a constitutionally governed country as we understand the term.'

Talked of Bishops, of Ely's illness, and from that of the Bps in the H. of L. I quoted Ld Melbourne: 'Bishops first to forget their maker.' He said he had not found that true of those he had appointed, who had as a rule behaved well. Some of Dizzy's very bad; e.g. Gloucester, who said to the Archbp. of Cant. when Reform Bill came to the H. of L. last year: 'This is an occasion on which I think I might forget that I am a Bp and vote with my party.'

He said: 'I do not think people sufficiently realise the fact that men have ten times more power for doing mischief than they have for doing good. Some men have great powers of attack and none of defence. Lowe is a striking example of that; all through Palmerston's Govt. he was practically useless.'

Forster to some extent the same but had some powers of defence; or, on the other hand, Hartington has great powers of defence and not much strength in attack. Brabourne he says has neither strength in attack or defence.

Mr. G. feels Forster's behaviour bitterly, spoke especially about Forster's behaviour on the night of the introduction of the Reform Bill which he criticised much. Seemed surprised to hear that Forster might be beaten.

The Disestablishment of the Irish Church: he said there was an attempt made in, I think, '66 [sic] in Ld. Palmerston's Govt. to strengthen the Irish Establishment by re-organising it and putting a certain number of Irish Bps on the Judicial Committee of the P.C. but he added: 'When I found out what was going on I went to Johnny Russell and, finding that he was agreed with me in objecting to this, we put our foot down & crushed it.'

I tried to impress on Mrs. and Miss G. the absolute necessity of having fewer peers in the next Cabinet. They agreed that Ld. Ripon must be taken in and that Carlingford and Selborne should go but they could not see that Granville and Derby ought also to be left out. I am afraid this will be a great stumbling block in the future with Chamberlain. I impressed upon them the great popularity of Free Education with audiences in the Country but they have heard what Schnadhorst told Chamberlain about it and do not like the idea. Mr. G. has a great contempt for and distrust of Randolph Churchill. He says he thinks Chamberlain far the most conservative of the two and anticipates more danger from extreme doctrines in the former than the latter. He spoke of the 'Radical Programme', said that he did not thoroughly know Chamberlain's opinions but believed him to be in favour of the monarchy, does not like the tone of the R.P. article on that subject and, with reference to the chapter on the House of Lords, says that the writer seems to have underestimated the amount of real conservatism in the Country.

Miss M[ary] asked if I were not very much struck with the great advance Chamberlain has made in public estimation. She evidently thinks very highly of him.

She said Mr. G. does not even now consider himself bound to take office after the General Election, at which I laughed loudly. I told Mr. G. *re* moderate Liberal defections that perhaps the Grand old umbrella had lost a rib but Adam had done the same with very satisfactory results. He was much amused at this.

31 Oct. 1885: . Dined in Liverpool with the Reform Club: about 150 present . . . The dinner was in honour of Sefton[48], who is president . . . I spoke about twenty minutes discussing the particulars of Chamberlain's new programme, not with approval, but in such a sense as to minimise the differences between us, and ended by urging strongly the necessity of union.

[Derby's activities in Dec.1885 may be readily summarised. He remained in London, or at his nearby house at Keston, until 12 December, when he returned to Knowsley, remaining there until 12 January. From 19 December he had guests in the house, none of them senior parliamentary figures. He shot on 21, 22, 23, 28, 29, 30 December. He chaired meetings of the new-born, but still unbuilt, National Liberal Club, whose finances were in a parlous state, and raised £34,000 in guarantees from the directors, Derby himself going surety for £6,000 (1 and 8 December). He declined to join with some Liverpool academics in a eulogy of Ruskin, not agreeing with his teaching. 'It is in fact simple socialism, so far as it is intelligible at all' (2 December). On 24 December Derby told his wife that he was raising her allowance from £1,500 to £2,000. On Christmas Day, he discussed the origins of the solar system with his guest, the great physicist Sir W. Thomson, later Lord Kelvin; and on the last day of the year he sat as chairman for five hours over 104 Lancashire magistrates at Preston, discussing roads and bridges.

Derby's comments on the election results are given day by day, as the political implications of each day's news are something one needs to have before one in order to read the political correspondence of the period in its correct context.]

1 Dec. 1885 (Tuesday): Election returns from the counties beginning to come in: the figures up to last night stand Liberals 180, Conservatives 162, Parnellites 30.

2 Dec. 1885 (Wednesday): More polling in the counties: the numbers now stand: Liberals 196, Conservatives 180, Parnellites 37. The figures vary in different newspapers, but only to the extent of two or three.

3 Dec. 1885 (Thursday): Polling in the counties continues, and with marked success to the Liberal candidates: the numbers are now, according to 'The Times': Liberals 234, Conservatives 196, Parnellites 48. . . .If this state of things continues, as it probably will, Parnell is master of the situation, and the present government can stand only by his support.

4 Dec. 1885 (Friday): Election returns continue favourable to the Liberals: numbers now stand: Liberals 261: Conservatives 214: Parnellites 53, so that the united forces of the two latter give a majority of only 6 over the former. Gladstone has published a fiery manifesto in the form of a letter to his constituents: and Chamberlain has made a speech, in which he ascribes the failure of the Liberals in borough constituencies to their not having adopted a sufficiently pronounced radical policy. He intimates plainly that the next parliament is to be a short one, and that the question of disestablishment is to be brought to the front.

Began the draft of what may be a magazine article on colonial federation, but probably it will never get itself finished.

Saw Harcourt, who naturally was full of political talk. He thought the present government would act wisely if it resigned at once, but that the party would make that impossible. That its existence depended on Parnell, and the question was, what terms would he insist upon? He understood that the Irish meant to insist on the late Speaker not being reappointed: and, if the Conservatives gave way on that point, a division would be taken, and the Irish alliance be exposed. He thought Gladstone very wild on the Home Rule question, and said Chamberlain was alarmed, and trying to keep him back. On the other hand Hartington was more than ever disgusted with Chamberlain's language and policy, and intends to say so in public. So that we are altogether a happy family.

5 Dec. 1885 (Saturday): Election returns up to last night give: Liberals 282, Conservatives 228: 54 majority: and Irish Parnellites 59. There remain only 100 members to be elected. Oddly enough, one vacancy has already occurred - Sir J. Gorst having accepted a judgeship - and one candidate, Col. Trefusis, has died while the polling was going on.

Count Münster came to luncheon: he talked freely of eastern affairs: thinks badly of them: the risk of collision between Russia and Austria he seemed to think serious: and their agreement equally so: if Austria occupied Servia, Russia would do the same with Bulgaria: and then what was to follow? His first experience of Paris has not been pleasant: the keys of his despatch boxes having been stolen: nothing else was taken, so it was clear, he thought, that the object was to get at his papers and cypher: I could not make out if the thieves had succeeded as to the last.

At the club, met Sir H. Ponsonby: he was full of questions, which I answered to the best of my power: he said the Queen was very uneasy lest Ld Salisbury should think it necessary to resign at once. I said this was unlikely, as he could not know that he would have a majority against him, and at any rate would wish to put his policy on record. He was evidently looking out to hear what is being said, and report to her.

6 Dec. 1885 (Sunday): Election returns now give, as well as I can make out, Liberals 311: Conservatives 245: Parnellites 70. The two latter sections united having thus a majority of 4. The unexpected Conservative tendency of the boroughs has been neutralised by the equally unexpected Liberalism of the counties. How far the latter result may be due to vague and wild promises made to the labourers is a question hotly disputed: and how far those measures shall be made good is another question, which will give trouble in the not distant future. . . . As far as I can see, the personal composition of the new parliament does not promise to be brilliant.

8 Dec. 1885 (Tuesday): Election results today give: Liberals 317, Conservatives 247, Parnellites 73.

Went to Devey the architects to see a model of the house at Knowsley which he has made, with various suggested improvements. . . This is hardly a time for needless outlay, when no man can tell how the new democracy will deal with property.

10 Dec. 1885 (Thursday)[49]: . . . Letter from Granville[50], who writes from Chatsworth. He has seen Hartington, Harcourt, Spencer, and Gladstone[51]: 'The first does not like the present state of things, and is furious with Chamberlain, who seems to have lost his head and his temper.' 'Spencer[52] is absorbed by Ireland: he thinks the prospect very black, much more so than people are aware. If no concession is made to the Irish, the outrages, refusal to pay rent, etc., will be worse than has ever been the case. He sees nothing for it but very strong coercion, or concession, to which he would not object[53], if he could secure the landlords, and satisfy Ulster. But how is this to be done? Gladstone is well and very keen. When I first saw him he was for attacking the government at once whatever might be the case. He told me on going away that, if the Tories and Parnellites are united, and have half or more of the H. of C. there will not be an obligation from the opposition to move. But if they are a minority, or disunited, he believes it to be necessary to vote that it is not constitutional, excepting with the intention of an immediate appeal to the country, that the minority should carry on the government. He believes it will be necessary to deal with Ireland but, if we cannot agree, he is willing to form a government, to deal with the programme set forth in the manifesto. To this I have answered, briefly, that I agree in Spencer's appreciation of the state of Ireland: and that it seems to me useless to talk or think of taking the place of the government, unless we know what we mean to do about that question: that we are masters of the situation, if we know what we want: but not otherwise. I did not add, thinking it needless or invidious, that I am sure we are not agreed, and that if we took office now we should very soon quarrel among ourselves. The state of things I imagine to be this: Gladstone has no time to spare, and wants to get back to Downing St. The Whigs or moderate section incline in that direction, but with less eagerness. On the other hand, the Radicals, Chamberlain and Co., are not in a hurry. They had rather wait to get rid of Gladstone, Granville, and the Whig party in general, thinking themselves strong enough to form a purely Radical cabinet. Dilke, at a late meeting, has expressed himself strongly in favour of delay, though not assigning that reason. (In his case a personal motive may be presumed, since if the divorce suit in which he is a co-respondent goes against him, he will be incapable, practically, of holding office till there has been time for the affair to be forgotten.)

11 Dec. 1885: Northbrook called to talk over affairs, and was with me an hour. . . . I found Northbrook inclined to dwell exclusively on the question: which, as he thinks, and I agree with him, will supersede all others, at least for the moment. He was quite alive, he said, to the importance of the bribe which Parnell could offer: for the withdrawal of the Irish from the H. of Commons would be a quite incalculable gain: on the other hand, he did not see how it was possible to secure joint or friendly action on the part of an Irish parliament. If it were free to deal with its own finances, how could we prevent protective duties being put on to exclude English goods? How could we object to the raising of a volunteer force, say of 100,000 men, which would be in effect a hostile army? How could we save the landlords from plunder? How could we reconcile Ulster[54] to a régime which would be in fact a government of priests and Catholic peasants? These and various other points were discussed, ending in a general agreement between us, that we do not see our way to Home Rule in any form, that we had better not express an opinion upon it till absolutely required, but see what Parnell asks, and what answer the present government will give him. He is going to see Spencer, and promised to let me know what he hears[55].

12 Dec. 1885: . . . Left at 3.30 for Knowsley . . .

13 Dec. 1885 (Sunday): . . . Wrote to Kimberley on the general situation, especially as regards Ireland. My general conclusion was that we could not satisfy the Irish by anything which it was possible to offer: that we had better not displace the present government at once, even if it were in our power to do so: but that we could not altogether avoid showing our hand when Parnell brought forward his scheme, which I assumed that he would do. Should we be united? I had my doubts. I believed Gladstone to be anxious to return to power, Granville probably also, Chamberlain and Dilke to prefer waiting, even for years, in the hope of forming an exclusively radical Cabinet, Hartington to be unwilling to take office again. I asked K. to give me his ideas, as I had given him mine. I have rather regretted, since sending this letter, that I did not keep a copy of it: but it is only in substance what I have often said before, and shall probably often have to say again.

15 Dec. 1885 (Tuesday):. . . . Received from Kimberley a sensible answer to my letter of Sunday. He agrees that it is impossible to satisfy the Nationalists: but dwells on the absolute necessity of coming to some understanding with Parnell if business is to be carried on at all: thinks any such arrangement must be unpopular, and had better therefore be left to the present government to make: that we are not called upon for an opinion at present, and had better offer none. He does not believe the government can go on long, and hopes the change may come in Gladstone's time, else the radicals will, he thinks, certainly break up the party.

16 Dec. 1885 (Wednesday): News in the papers of three more peers created . . . it is scarcely wise to increase the permanent Conservative majority of the peers, which is the chief danger of the peerage, since sooner or later it must bring on a serious collision with the other house.

. . . As well as I can make out, for statements in various newspapers do not exactly agree, the balance of parties is as follows: Liberals 330 at least, some say 2 or 3 more; Conservatives 250 at most, some say 247 or 248; Parnellites 86, and about half a dozen whose pledges are vague, and who are reckoned as independents. 0n the whole I judge it probable that the Conservatives, if all the Parnellites go with them, have a majority of 4 or 5: but this is a precarious reliance [sic] and they have no other.

The story, which Harcourt told me in London, of their intending to run another candidate for the Speakership against Peel, is now formally contradicted: so that if that intention were ever entertained it is abandoned.

It is also announced in a semi-official way that no Irish demand for a separate parliament will be listened to. The report is that Carnarvon and Ld Ashbourne had framed a scheme on this basis, but that the Cabinet would not have it.

Sir C. Dilke has expressed his strong opinion that the government ought not to be ejected: the 'Daily News', probably inspired by Gladstone, and the 'Pall Mall Gazette', writing in the interest of Home Rule, oppose this conclusion: and Gladstone is believed to be eager for immediate action.

17 Dec. 1885 (Thursday):. Wrote to Granville à propos of a report which is in our local papers, to the effect that Gladstone has a plan of Home Rule cut and dry: the 'Standard' repeats it with details, and as if on good authority. It is scarcely credible that the leader of a party should pledge himself and them to such an extent on such a subject, without consultation: yet I know that when he decided on the dissolution of 1874 his then colleagues were completely taken by surprise: and what has been done may be repeated.

18 Dec. 1885 (Friday): In the papers, yesterday's news, ascribing to Gladstone a plan of Home Rule as being prepared and ready for production, with some details as to its nature; it is contradicted on authority but in such a manner scarcely to amount to a denial of the fact. It is, however, so far satisfactory that it negatives the idea of any such plan being sprung upon us as a surprise.

Wrote to Hartington, stating my strong objections to an Irish parliament, my conviction that it would not long remain subject to any limitations that might be imposed upon its power, and that its establishment would only serve as the basis for a fresh agitation. I invited his opinion, and asked him as to Spencer's, saying that much depended on him at this juncture, that I, being in the Lords, could take refuge in silence: he could not: if he thought this concession inevitable, I did not see that resistance was possible, and should probably drop out of the affair altogether. But if he were ready to express himself against it, I should support him. This was the substance of my letter, which was long, and of which I kept no copy. We shall see what he answers. Of his personal opinion I have no doubt, but he has been dragged so far by his colleagues, and by the natural dislike which he must feel to give up his position in the party, that I feel no confidence in his power of resistance.

20 Dec.1885 (Sunday): The elections are now all over, and the most authoritative reports give Liberals 333, Conservatives 251, Parnellites 86. But I think in the above calculation several are included in both sides whose votes cannot be certainly counted on. And half a dozen Parnellite votes secured would give the opposition a victory: a dangerous temptation to the keen partisan.

21 Dec. 1885: Answers both from Granville and Hartington: the former somewhat vague and enigmatic. He says Gladstone admits having 'opinions' and 'ideas' on Home Rule, but denies having any 'intentions'. He will not commit himself, advises others to do the same, and proposes to 'leave space' to the government. To this I answer that there is no use in discussing the incident farther . . . the thing is done. Practically Gladstone has given in his adhesion to Home Rule, which complicates a situation already sufficiently difficult. It may be that the movement will now become irresistible. But I dislike it so much, and think it so dangerous, that I cannot see the circumstances under which I would be responsible for bringing forward a measure in support of it. I fear the party will be split up, and so beaten in detail. I see nothing to do except to wait. We should not be justified in taking power into our hands, unless we were agreed upon and prepared with an Irish measure.

22 Dec. 1885: . . . Hartington's letter, which I answered today, is much longer than Granville's, and more explicit. He does not know, he says, exactly what Gladstone has been doing, but his action 'has put us all in a position of the greatest difficulty'. He does not think that G. has a definite scheme, but that he has been discussing the whole question very freely in conversation and correspondence. He agrees with me 'that the plan of a subordinate legislature in Dublin is inadmissible, and that an independent legislature would be preferable. The first alternative would be certain to lead to the second'. He is not disposed to give way to Parnell without a farther struggle, though 'seeing the most tremendous difficulties in the way of resistance'. He expects a worse state of disorder and outrage to follow on the refusal of Parnell's demands than has yet been known in Ireland: and doubts whether Parliament will give to any government the necessary powers to deal with it. He then refers to a letter of his lately published, which he says is meant to show 'that I am not only committed but am opposed to the scheme': and to prevent the whole party drifting into acquiescence with what he fears are rightly supposed to be Gladstone's opinions. He is afraid that Spencer is likely to give way. I answered briefly, thinking and agreeing, and asking him here[56].

25 Dec. 1885: . . . Wrote to Granville, asking what version he thought it prudent to give of the late disclosure of Gladstone's Irish policy. Was it to be treated as in the main an invention of journalists? or as a disclosure of ideas really entertained, but not meant to be published, due to the indiscretion of someone at Hawarden? or should it be acknowledged as a feeler - as an attempt to test public opinion on the subject? I added that the last view would be that taken by the public, whatever we might say. And I referred to the expression of popular opinion elicited by the manifesto, as proving that the policy embodied in it could not be given effect to without splitting the party, and would be intensely unpopular in England[57].

26 Dec. 1885: Since the elections a great calm has come over the country: no question is being discussed with much interest, except the Irish, and that has come to the front chiefly in consequence of Gladstone's outbreak upon it. Strange to my mind is the slight impression made on the public by events which are nevertheless really important. The conquest, and probable absorption, of the Burmese empire is scarcely noticed: Egypt as much noticed as though it had never existed: the complication in the Balkans serves to talk about, but nobody seems to care how it ends. Irish affairs do get some attention, and the public mind is set strongly against repeal of the Union: but even about this there seems little warmth of feeling, all English politicians, except a small section, being substantially agreed.

[The New Year found Derby at Knowsley, accompanied by Lecky and Froude, whose total agreement about Ireland prevented their clashing as Derby had feared, the French Ambassador and his wife, Mme. Waddington, a lively American, the faithful Sanderson, and Eddie Stanley, now very much recognised as the eventual heir of Knowsley. Derby gave Eddie, a young Guards officer, a tip of £100 towards his expenses.

Indulging in his annual retrospect, Derby looked back on a year 'without one day of illness', and was 'not conscious of any loss of power in body or brain, though grown somewhat more indolent: but this is rather from want of motive than from incapacity for work. . .' His wife's failing eyesight apart, 'there is no circumstance . . . I could wish altered'. Turning to the new parliament, over half of whose members had not sat before, Derby thought Gladstone's 'strange and wild action' made it impossible for him to take office again. More comforting was Derby's view that: 'The extreme party in politics has been weaker and less successful at the elections than its members expected. Chamberlain's programme has not gone down: and, though the present H. of C. represents a somewhat lower grade of society than its predecessors, there is no appearance about it of anything revolutionary. . . . We can only do the best with the means we have, and trust to the habitual good sense of the English people.'

Derby remained at Knowsley until 12 January, when he went to London. He did estate business, chiefly rents: spoke at two tenants' dinners, reminding them that their rents were 20% below the average in Lancashire, that they had not as a rule been raised for forty years or more and that one-third of rent received had gone to repairs or improvements; dismissed a very drunken housekeeper, to his regret, 'but she has exposed herself before the household generally, and cannot stay'; arranged a tenancy, settled a dispute about a school site, and negotiated with the War Office about the sale of land in Bury; and discussed new building and forestry projects at Knowsley. Perhaps because of these occupations, perhaps because nobody was too concerned about his views, Derby took no part in the informal meeting of Liberal leaders on 1 January, and saw no colleagues before he returned to town.]

3 Jan. 1886: . . . Wrote to Granville, again, about the Irish situation, rather with a view to ascertain from him what is going on than because I had anything new to tell. I said incidentally that I heard that Gladstone was supposed to wish to turn out the government, but that I doubted his being able to do it, nor did I see how we could join him in making a cabinet without full knowledge of his intentions in regard to Ireland. I mentioned a remark which Waddington made to me when here, to the effect that foreigners without exception believe us to underrate the danger from Ireland and say that we choose to ignore the determined hostility to us of the Irish people. We ascribe their angry feeling to this or that grievance, whereas it is we ourselves that are the grievance - they want to be quit of us altogether. He said he had never known a diplomatist who did not take this view.

5 Jan. 1886: . . . Received from Granville a letter on Irish matters, which shows the extreme perplexity of his mind. He wants me to come up to town, which I must do soon, but the certainty of disagreement makes me unwilling to enter into oral discussion. He says Gladstone has given up his idea of attacking the government on the address: and they on their side will not ask for a vote of confidence.

6 Jan. 1886: . . . Wrote to Granville[58], in answer to his friendly but perplexed letter, to say that I will come up when wanted, but to do so with no pleasure anticipating only disagreement. That I do not consider the question at issue as one of detail: it is simply the question, shall we have an Irish parliament or not? For myself, I do not see that I can possibly consent to the establishment of one: though quite willing to efface myself and drop out of politics: but what is more important, I do not believe that Gladstone can carry the whole of his party with him, or carry the measure. If it passed the Commons, it would be thrown out in the Lords: a dissolution must follow: and the Conservative party would have the advantage of a cry such as they never had before. We should disappear as Fox and North disappeared in 1784. I ended by saying that I had no wish to see Downing Street again, but that it seemed a pity that we should go down in a storm of our own raising.

7 Jan. 1886: . . . The Irish question continues to be discussed in the papers . . . Sir J. Stephen, the judge, has published two powerful letters upon it in *The Times* – a new thing for a judge to do where a political controversy is concerned . . . I note as a novelty that the parliamentary discussion has been and is being anticipated not only by journalists but by public men members of both houses . . . writing to the papers . . . instead of waiting for the session to open.

8 Jan. 1886: . . . Wrote to Harcourt on the Irish question, pointing out the difficulties, and inviting his opinion. I did not disguise mine, but said in substance what I have said before to Granville and Hartington.

10 Jan. 1886: . . . Harcourt writes me a long letter[59] in answer to mine . . . What he thinks most dangerous is that G. should be known to have a plan, and that it should be thought that his colleagues have suppressed it. This last sentence I do not wholly understand, and it suggests the suspicion that H. is reserving for himself an excuse for supporting a measure which he disapproves. But perhaps this is is an unjust interpretation.

12 Jan. 1886: [Derby left Knowsley at 10.15, reached his London house at 4.15, and about 5.15 called on Granville, whom he found with Hartington and Spencer.] . . . He [Granville] seemed low in spirits and ill at ease: he said more than once that the present crisis was the worst of any in his recollection: he did not see how it was possible for parliamentary business to go on with 85 Irishmen bent on obstruction, and would make almost any sacrifice to get them out of the House. But he fully admitted the impossibility of conceding the demand for Home Rule in the actual temper of the English public. It seemed to me that his objection was chiefly on this ground, and that he would like the thing done if he saw his way to do it. He said Chamberlain was stronger than anyone against coercion, and had quarrelled with his friend Morley for advising it. He, Chamberlain, with Dilke and some others, had sent a joint remonstrance to Gladstone, which the latter was not well pleased with. I gathered that Gladstone had shown much eagerness to attack at once, but found no supporters, and abandoned his intention, or at least postponed it.

I strongly suspect that Chamberlain's attitude is not due solely to dislike of Home Rule, or fear of what the constituencies may say: but that he does not wish to come into office again under circumstances where his section of the party will be, as he thinks, inadequately represented.

Dining at the Travellers', I met Kimberley, and we had a long conversation upstairs. It was in much the same sense as Granville's, only more outspoken against concession to the Irish. He thought it was not our business to speak first – let us see what ministers proposed, and what Parnell said to their proposals – then it would be time enough to make up our own minds. He thought that something must be yielded, but that the concession would be fatal to whatever ministry made it – better therefore let it come from the other side.

13 Jan. 1886: . . . [Lawson] came for news and exchange of ideas. He seemed to understand the situation perfectly. . .

. . . Called on Gladstone, and had with him an interesting conversation which lasted nearly an hour. He spoke the whole time, except a word or two that I put in now and then. He talked of the Union – called it a 'frightful and absurd mistake', thought Pitt had been persuaded into it by the King, who believed it would act as a check on the Catholics, said that every Irishman 'who was worth a farthing' had opposed it, and if he had been an Irishman he should have done so to the utmost. He believed in nationality as a principle – whether Italian, Greek, Slav, or Irish – quoted, as I had heard him do before, a saying of Grattan about 'the Channel forbidding union, the ocean forbidding separation' – which he considered as one of the wisest sayings ever uttered by men – then dwelt on the length of time during which Ireland had possessed an independent, or at least a separate, legislature. All this was in substance what he had said in October, but more forcibly put. There is no doubt now possible about the fact that he is a Home Ruler on conviction and in principle, though using his discretion as to the time and manner of declaring himself. He seemed to think that he could avoid expressing an opinion on the subject early in the session and wait for the Ministerial proposals. He talked of Granville and Spencer as being, he hoped, gained over to his way of thinking, but did not speak very decidedly. He read me a letter from Campbell-Bannerman, which he considered as implying adhesion, but to me it read more like a polite and courteous explanation of reasons why he could not agree. He talked with some bitterness of Chamberlain, who is more strongly opposed to him than any of the others, and saying that he, Chamberlain, belonged to the new school, and construed the 'obligations' of a Cabinet minister differently from men who had not been trained in the earlier traditions. He did not explain himself on this point, but I believe he considers there has been an intrigue against him, of which C. is the head. - He was extremely vague, I suppose on purpose, as to what he meant to do and, though he talked for some minutes on this point, I could make out nothing definite. I put the case of a bill embodying Home Rule being passed in the Commons, and thrown out in the Lords - would not this lead to a dissolution, and should we not be in a very bad position if we had to fight an election on the Home Rule cry? He had his answer at once. Why should the peers reject it? who could tell that they would? and if once, would they do it a second time? What need was there for a dissolution? He then went into an argument as to the right of the peers to force a dissolution, as if he had contemplated the case occurring. He said among other things that he should not give a dinner as head of the opposition at the beginning of the session arguing that this practice was novel and undesirable. He introduced various other topics parenthetically, as it were for the pleasure of discussing them. I left him with the conviction that his mind is made up about Home Rule, and that he will draw us all into the support of it if he can.

. . . Called on Harcourt: who talked freely, in his accustomed style, abusing Home Rule, foreseeing nothing but mischief from the adoption of Gladstone's ideas, saying that, do what we may, civil war is inevitable (much as he wrote to me a few days ago), but ending with the unexpected conclusion that Gladstone must have his own way, since it would be impossible to resist the Irish demands when once it was known that he was favourable to them. He said (which I find hard to believe) that Spencer was more in favour of Gladstone's principles than Gladstone himself. ˙ I left Harcourt disappointed, having hoped that he would hold out, and seeing that he is prepared to side with the strongest[60].

Dined Travellers' with Sanderson, and talk with Kimberley later.

14 Jan. 1886: . . . Ponsonby, no doubt at the Queen's desire, has been suggesting an eccentric way out of the difficulty. He says that Salisbury ought to resign the premiership, retaining the F.O. with Hartington as premier and a Whig contingent. Salisbury was spoken to, and acquiesced in the suggestion: of course knowing that Hartington would have nothing to say to it; and probably willing to widen the existing differences between him and Chamberlain.

[On 15 January Derby returned to Knowsley, where he dealt with estate business and sessions, before returning to London at 4.00 p.m. on 20 January.]

20 Jan. 1886: . . . Hardly settled in my room, when Gladstone called. He seemed excited by a communication received from the cabinet, to the effect that new rules of procedure are to be framed, and that they are to take precedence of all business, except the debate on the address. He thought this a trick, that the government want to be defeated on some question not affecting their Irish policy, and so to resign. He talked about this at some length, contending that they must know the impossibility of dealing with the question of procedure, unless they meant to give the whole session to it. I took him upstairs to tea with Ly D.

Dined with Granville, about 45 peers present, the speech was read as usual after dinner. There is a passage strongly supporting the Union, which is obviously meant as a challenge to the Parnellites, and probably also as a trap for the opposition. If they accept it, they lose the Irish vote: if they protest, they are accused of favouring Home Rule: the most damaging just now of all possible accusations in England.

After the rest had gone Kimberley, Spencer, Northbrook, Rosebery, Granville, Hartington, Harcourt, and I discussed the speech, not separating till 12.00: but I did not see that we settled anything. The fear was general, that Gladstone, compelled to speak early in the debate, will say something that the Irish can represent as favourable to their claims. Harcourt did most of the talking: Hartington said little, and seemed ill-pleased.

21 Jan. 1886: . . . At 11.00, went to Granville's house, where most of the late cabinet was assembled: Granville, Spencer, Kimberley, Northbrook, Rosebery, D., Gladstone, Trevelyan, Dilke, Chamberlain, Hartington, Harcourt. We discussed for $1\frac{1}{2}$ hours the language to be held in debate: with special reference to the possibility of a Parnellite amendment. Gladstone insisted warmly and obstinately that the paragraph about the Union was improper, that it was an attempt to induce the House to commit itself prematurely, and he for one objected to being so bound. He would not vote for Parnell's expected proposal to leave out the corresponding paragraph on the address, but he certainly would not vote against it, believing the opinion embodied in it to be sound. No argument could move him from this position, and so we left the matter.

22 Jan. 1886: Read the debate in the Commons, which was cautious, and has not made matters worse, but the Irish all know him to be on their side, and so do the rest of the House. . . Ministers have published their new intended rules of procedure, some of which seemed very good . . .

23 Jan. 1886: . . .Shaw-Lefevre called, ostensibly to talk about a subscription for Mr. Hill, late editor of the *D. News*, and dismissed from his post for no apparent reason. He went on to speak about Ireland and, though disliking Home Rule, would accept it as inevitable, the only alternative in his mind being coercion, which he felt sure parliament would not tolerate. I asked whether he meant by coercion any legislation, which should substitute special for common juries. 'Yes,' he said, 'any exceptional legislation.' 'But why object to deal specially with a complaint which does not exist in England?' 'Because it would hurt the feelings of the Irish people – it is mainly a matter of sentiment.' I could not agree that innocent people ought to be murdered with impunity.

24 Jan. 1886: . . . My conversation with Hartington yesterday was too long and turned too much on details to be noted in full. He dwelt on the impossibility of any business being done in parliament while the Irishmen sat there: this evil he seemed to think incurable by any regulations or systems of procedure. He thought it absolutely necessary that they should be turned out. 'Then,' I said, 'you must give them full control over their own affairs in a local parliament.' He did not see that, thought it did not follow, was not for making concessions to them, would get rid of them for our own sake, not for theirs, assumed that in any case there must be a power in the English parliament to override a local legislature set up in Dublin – in short, he would restore the Irish parliament as it was before Grattan and 1780. 'Did he suppose that would satisfy the Irish? Would they not be worse off than before?' He could not tell, and did not much care. 'But will

Gladstone agree to a plan quite different from his own?' That he did not know either. 'Would he, Hartington, agree to Gladstone's plan, by which the Irish are to be retained in the House?' 'No, certainly not.' 'Then what is to happen if the government go out?' Much discussion followed. He seemed to think that Gladstone would try to make a government and fail, and that possibly matters might end in the present Cabinet coming back with Whig support. He distinctly assured me that he would not take office on the mere chance of being able to agree on Irish policy afterwards, but would insist on knowing what was proposed[61]. If he stands firm, we are safe: all the pressure put upon him is great, especially from Harcourt, to whom six weeks of office would mean the glory of being [Lord] Chancellor, and the pension for life.

25 Jan. 1886: . . . It seems doubtful whether Gladstone will be able to form a cabinet on the basis of Home Rule.

26 Jan. 1886: [Lawson talked of]. . . Churchill having compromised himself with the Irish, so that he could not turn against them.

27 Jan. 1886: . . .. Ministers beaten last night . . . Saw Hartington early; he doubted whether ministers would resign, but admitted that if they did not the difference would be one only of a few days, since any other question would serve equally well to defeat them, and even with some Whig support they would be in a minority of 100. He thought it likely that the Queen might send for him, but in that case he could only advise her to make Gladstone her minister as he was head of the party. He thought G. would be able to make some sort of a government with the Radicals to help him - though how long it would last was doubtful. He implied, he did not expressly say, that he would have nothing to do with it.

28 Jan. 1886: Walk with Kimberley, who is ready to do anything that the party wishes, but dislikes the whole business. He says the only choice is between three alternatives, all of them bad: 1) coercion, which he thinks impossible; 2) going on as we are; 3) Home Rule in some shape. He is for turning the Irish members out of the H. of C. and thinks no good will be done if this is not a part of the programme. He talked of the government which is to be formed, and thought it would be very weak in the Commons, if Hartington stood aloof, and Harcourt went to the Lords. Except J. Morley, he did not see any of the younger Radicals whom it would be possible to promote to high positions . . .

29 Jan. 1886: . . . Hartington called upon me at 5.30. He said in answer to my question that no great pressure had been put upon him to join the cabinet about to be formed: his opinion was known. He assured me he would not join in any case, and if his opinion altered in consequence of what he heard he would let me know before taking any step. I asked if he thought it possible that Gladstone would give up his plan of Home Rule, seeing the impossibility of passing it? He said no, he thought not; even if it were postponed it would be there in the background, and might be brought forward at any time. For himself, he had no choice. He had been accused of yielding too much, and as he thought with some justice. He had spoken strongly and decidedly about Home Rule, and could not go back from what he had said without discredit. I told him that was my case also. We talked about the future of the H. of C. He thought Goschen might be able to lead the moderate Liberals when he has gone to the Lords. He said exactly what Kimberley had said about the weakness of the new Government in the Commons, and thought it possible that Harcourt might be forced to give up the Chancellorship in order to remain in the Commons. He assumed that Granville would be President of the Council, being too deaf and indolent to go back to F.O. Much more talk passed, but nothing specially worth noting.

30 Jan. 1886: . . . Granville calls while I am out, and leaves a note, in consequence of which I call on Gladstone about 1.00. My visit was short, not more than 15 or 20 minutes. He explained his ideas about Ireland in general terms, and read a mem. or minute which had been evidently drafted with much care, and was meant to be shown. It was to the effect that he (G.) proposed an examination of the question, to see by what means, if any, the wish of Ireland for a local legislative body could be satisfied. Some kind of control was to be left to the Imperial parliament, the precise nature of which the mem. did not state. Gladstone drew a distinction between Home Rule - a phrase which he said he disliked - and the 'local autonomy' which he thought it possible to create.

He referred briefly to former conversations, and asked me if I could agree in the programme indicated above? I answered with all due expressions of regard and regret: that I could not; that I doubted the possibility of creating an Irish parliament which would work with that at Westminster saying that I had fully explained my views to Granville (of this he said he was aware); and that, considering how often and strongly I had spoken against Home Rule, even if I believed it now to have become a necessity, I had rather that someone else should be responsible for introducing it into parliament. I thought nothing except imperative necessity justified a public man in supporting in office a policy which he had denounced, and which he still disapproved. Sir R Peel might have been justified in the repeal of the corn laws but only on the ground that no one else could have carried it through.˙ In the present instance there were plenty of willing hands, and I was not required to make the sacrifice. I added that if matters should come to a dead-lock, as was likely enough if a Home Rule bill ever got into the Lords, I thought I could be of more use in dealing with it as an independent peer than as an official. Gladstone listened gravely and courteously, said he knew what I had said to Granville, he regretted my decision, but had nothing to complain of (he did not use these words, but this was the sense, I forget the precise expression): he did not argue the matter, nor press me for reconsideration: in short, he seemed prepared for what I had said, and received it in a friendly spirit. I went away from this interview glad that it was over, and that he had not made it necessary for me to argue the question: I should note that in the early part of the conversation he drew a distinction which I could not well follow, but to which he seemed to attach some importance - he said he disliked the name of Home Rule and preferred to call it 'local autonomy'. He did not explain the difference.

Meeting my butler in the street soon after, I told him that I had refused office. Secrecy was not enjoined and indeed could not be long maintained.

Hartington came to see me later, and brought me the draft of a letter which he said Gladstone had asked him to write, explaining his reasons for not joining - I suppose with the intention that it should be used in parliament. We went through the letter together, and made a few verbal changes.

2 Feb. 1886: . . . In conversation yesterday, Granville told me that Gladstone had offered him any office which a peer can hold . . . Our conversation was thoroughly friendly. I said at parting, what he thoroughly concurred in, that if we came to a difference on the Irish question we must be careful to do it so as to place no difficulties the way of united action when it was disposed of.

6 Feb. 1886: . . . Lubbock sympathises with Hartington and me, but has a speech to make at a political meeting in a few days, and is much perplexed as to what he shall say. I could only advise him not to assume prematurely that the Government are going to give way to the Home Rulers, to express hope that they will do what is right, but maintain his intention to support the Union.

8 Feb. 1886: . . . Talk with Northbrook: he had never any doubt as to refusing office, but evidently thinks resistance to the Home Rulers impossible, now that Gladstone's conversion to their cause is public . . .

13 Feb. 1886: . . . Sefton called, and chattered away in his boisterous good-natured fashion. He now says he did not want a court place, and thanks me with effusion for warning him against taking one. In fact, he has not had the offer: Cork, who is strong against Home Rule, is also very poor in consequence of non-payment of rents, and has swallowed his scruples.

17 Feb. 1886: . . . I am glad that the theory of Dilke's innocence is held by men who are good judges, for I have never known him otherwise than as a courteous and pleasant colleague: but I am afraid that the general verdict will not be that way. . . . If it [Gladstone's letter to Lord De Vesci, seeking advice on Ireland] means anything, it implies that there is no plan either now ready or in preparation.

18 Feb. 1886: . . . I asked Kimberley what his friends thought should be the line taken in defending it [the letter to De Vesci]: he laughed after his manner and answered: 'The less said the better.'

25 Feb. 1886: . . . A dinner was given last night (or Tuesday ?) to the new working men M.P.'s, at which about 200 were present, when the Queen's health was proposed as usual, a large number of them refused to stand up, and some hissed. This is a new display of feeling . . .and it can be meant only as an expression of republican opinion.

11 Mar. 1886: Lawson called: he had seen Chamberlain the night before, and ascertained that at that date he, Chamberlain, knew nothing of the Irish plan, and had not even seen a draft of it . . .

15 Mar. 1886: . . . Dined Grillions. Talk of the new H. of C. Its ways are peculiar: very few go away to dine: they sit like hens: sit through the whole evening: no chance of a count-out: some live at the House altogether, using it as a club, and having only a bedroom in some lodging house near. Cross described them as very rough: Arch, for instance, goes about in a country coat and round hat, and they are quite unmanageable by the whips (this everybody agrees in): but Cross thinks there is plenty of sense among them, when they get used to the ways of parliament.

19 Mar. 1886: . . . Gladstone's hold on the masses is so strong that it would be unsafe to predict his failure. That his proceedings have been a bid for office merely is a calumny not seriously believed even by those who utter it: but I can well understand that the desire to close his public life by settling the Irish question finally may have influenced him more than he would himself admit.

21 Mar. 1886. Granville called, and talked over the situation in a friendly way. He spoke of Chamberlain as certain to leave, and as having come round to a policy of coercion, though only within the last few days: said he (C.) had not convinced the Caucus, thought he had lost control of that agency, that at the next election it would not count for much. He spoke of C. with some bitterness, contrasting his conduct with that of Hartington, though he did not define exactly in what the contrast consisted. He said frankly that he did not expect to carry the bill through the Lords: but counted a good deal on the support of the Irish vote in the constituencies. He asked me if I knew for certain that Carnarvon had been converted to Home Rule? I said no, that I did not think it unlikely, but had no proof. He thought if the question were not settled that Irish landlords would be in a bad way – no rents would be paid. On the other hand he believed Parnell would show himself very conservative as an Irish statesman: and that the Irish in America would give no farther trouble. I thought all this sanguine, but did not argue. He spoke of Gladstone as quite wonderful in the renewal of his old activity, which had seemed to be diminished: and agreed in my remark that no business wearied him except business which he disliked, and approached unwillingly, as was the case in the Egyptian affair.

Somebody spoke to Chamberlain of Gladstone as an 'advanced Liberal'. 'Say rather "advanced lunatic",' Chamberlain answered. This was told to M. by a man who heard it.

23 Mar. 1886: . . . Called on Hartington, and had with him a conversation which lasted an hour. I cannot note it in detail, but only preserve a few leading points. I advised him not to encourage the talk of a coalition with the Conservatives, I did not suppose it would succeed: coalitions were always unpopular, and seldom lasted long: the respective sections were sure to quarrel: and in this case union with the Conservatives must mean extinction to the Whig party. They would be fewer than 100 probably, the Conservatives 250, and the smaller body would be merged in the larger. Let us support a Conservative cabinet, if we choose: but keep independent of it. He said that Harcourt had been holding nearly the same language to him – and he was inclined to agree – I then urged him to come to an understanding with Chamberlain, assuming as I did that his resignation was certain – and thereupon we went into a long discussion to as to what the conditions of agreement with him might be. He told me that Chamberlain had been speaking to him lately and among other matters expressed uneasiness at the state of feeling among the working class, thinking that they were in a revolutionary mood, and would break out if something were not done to improve their condition. We talked a good deal about a movement among the Whig peers and others, headed by E. Bouverie and the D. of Bedford, who want to hold meetings in favour of the Union, and get up a Whig cave. He is much pressed to join them – I advised caution – we are not to discourage them, but as late colleagues it is not our business to head an attack on Gladstone – for that is what it really comes to.

29 Mar. 1886: . . . The prevailing idea is now that the land purchase will be either abandoned or postponed, or reduced to very small proportions, it being recognised as impracticable in its present form . . . I have seldom seen any man look more miserable than he [Spencer] since the present government was formed.

5 Apr. 1886: . . . Kenmare . . . says that in his part of the country [Kerry] the League is absolute, and no other law is obeyed. He volunteered too to add that the priests were the worst of any, the most violent (strong language for a R.C.) whereas until quite lately they had exerted themselves to repress outrages. Neither he nor I made any allusion to the plan which is to be brought out on Thursday.

7 Apr. 1886: ..Called on Hartington, and talked over with him the language to be held in debate tomorrow[62]. The difficulty . . . is increased by the fact that no one knows what the ministerial scheme in its latest developments is to be. It has been considerably modified in the last day or two (so much seems certain) and may after all be much less extreme than it was when Chamberlain and Trevelyan retired. - Chamberlain has shown some temper and written rather a huffy letter (which Hartington read to me) about the arrangement of the debate: but H. hoped to be able to smooth him down. He is not a pleasant colleague, certainly, either in opposition or office: dictatorial, and apt to take offence where none is meant.

12 Apr. 1886: Met Granville, and some friendly talk. He owned that things looked badly, but would not admit that the bill must fail: in any case some such plan would be carried within the next two or three years. I could not but agree that after Gladstone's proposal, supported by half the liberal party if not more, it would be difficult to set the Union on its legs again.

16 Apr. 1886. . . .Camperdown came early, and helped to arrange for the meeting of [Liberal Unionist] peers, which was fixed for 12.00. They met in the upstairs dining-room, to the number of 48, and 15 more sent excuses, expressing sympathy. I introduced Hartington and opened proceedings in a speech of ten minutes. I then asked him to speak, which he did for about the same length of time. Argyll followed, then some others, in a conversational style. Selborne spoke more rhetorically, and strong against Gladstone, saying that the Liberal party must not sacrifice its principles to the wishes of one man, however distinguished, especially if that man were supporting what until now he had always opposed. My speech was to the effect, that the gathering was private, that nobody was pledged to anything by attending it, though as a fact I suppose we were all of one mind: that attempts would be made to declare us seceders from the Liberal party, which we could not allow, since our opinions were those which all Liberals, save a small section, professed twelve months ago: that our leaders had quitted us, not we them: that we must assert our position, and disclaim all ideas of a coalition: that it was not premature to organise now, and especially to exert ourselves in the country, among the electors, that the Home Rule question had never been before the constituencies: that they had been misled and thrown over by their representatives: and that if the bill came to our house we ought to throw it out, and press for an early dissolution. All this was very well taken. We sat nearly two hours.

23 Apr. 1886 (Good Friday): . . . Found [in London] Camperdown, very hot on the question of getting up an agitation against the Irish bill: but I had not much time to talk it over with him[63].

4 May 1886: . . . Rosebery . . . talked of it [Gladstone's manifesto of 1 May] to me with disapproval; Hartington chaffed Granville about it in my hearing, and G. did not seem to dissent from his criticism. - It is odd that Ld Spencer has just been making a speech at Leeds which shows clearly that he was unaware of this letter and had not been consulted upon it.

5 May 1886: . . .Much to her surprise, Gladstone called on M. this afternoon, and sat talking to her for an hour, as if he had nothing to do: he said he could think of nothing but Ireland: he felt confident that the country was with him: but the difficulties were immense: he had no fear as to trouble in Ulster: and he felt certain that the thing would be done: but when, and whether by him, was doubtful. He said emphatically that he would do nothing to bring about a conflict between the two Houses, but on the contrary use all his efforts to avert one: for he knew what the effect would be: if the Lords won, Home Rule would be postponed for a long while: if they were beaten, the effect on them would be nothing short of a revolution. He talked very earnestly, but not in an excited manner: and ended by giving M. a little book of religious biography, the life of one Baseby, I think, whose name was new to me, but he seemed much interested in it.

6 May 1886: . . . Walk with Carnarvon, who is very friendly: is against the Irish bill, but owns he does not see how we can help giving Ireland some sort of parliament.

11 May 1886: . . .At Croxteth the Queen called me to her and talked about the political crisis eagerly, for five or six minutes, which she has not done for years: but present agreement cancels past differences. I told her I thought the bill was dead, which she liked, but that the question would give infinite trouble in the future. I said farther, which is really my opinion, that even in the Cabinet there is hardly anybody who approves the proposed legislation, though some may accept it as inevitable and others agree rather than break up the party.

29 May 1886: . . . Dined at the Prime Minister's, the birthday dinner, having first ascertained that both Hartington and Chamberlain would be there: we sat down about 30, as I suppose, an odd mixture, and somebody hazarded the joke that a vote of want of confidence might have been carried in the Premier's own dining room. All was friendly and pleasant. I sat next to the old man himself, and nothing could be more varied or agreeable than his conversation. He did not avoid the subject of the moment, though naturally I kept clear of it, and went off into a panegyric of Parnell, whom he described as one of the most remarkable men he had ever known, and in his belief entirely sincere. 'He, Parnell, was in a difficult position: so far he had been able to keep the party of dynamite in the background, but they would not give him unlimited time: a long delay would be fatal to his (Parnell's) influence, and then we should have to reckon with the party who were for violent methods.' He praised the Irish members generally: said, as I remember he did in the autumn, that they were far above the average in the House in point of ability: they were soured by their position, and no wonder, since alone among parliamentary politicians they could have no hope of gratifying personal ambition. I asked whether Mr.

G. did not think that Parnell would be put aside to make way for a Catholic when his work was done? He did not altogether dissent, but seemed to think religion had not much to do with the matter. Our conversation was interrupted at this point by the Prince on Mr. G.'s other hand, saying something, and the rest of dinner time I talked to my other neighbour Lord Acton, who had much to say about the state of France.

. . . Whatever may happen in future, there is as yet no appearance of ill feeling between the different sections of the party. Harcourt and Chamberlain were in confidential talk, as were also Spencer and Hartington. It is understood that between Chamberlain and Gladstone there is no love lost, but that is not new, and has grown out of the refusal of the actual leader to acknowledge the younger man as his successor. Hartington, as far as I can judge, is spoken of with respect by all sections.

10 June 1886: . . . The political prospect is not such as I can see with any pleasure. Either the Conservatives must win, which is not in itself desirable, and will lead to a violent Radical reaction . . . For Whigs and 'Liberal Unionists'[64] there is no outlook.

12 June 1886: . . . That the [Conservative] Cabinet intended to take up Home Rule at one time is nearly certain: though they may not have settled how far they meant to go . . . [Fear] caused them to back out of their half-given pledges.`

13 June 1886: . . . Habits of amusement are not formed in a day, any more than habits of business: and there are few so-called pleasures which give me any pleasure. Yet there is nothing tempting in becoming the servant of a really democratic parliament such as ours now is: and even if I wished it the circumstances of the time make a return to power impossible to me, except at a price which I do not care to pay.

17 June 1886: . . . In the papers, an election address by Hartington, which is remarkably well done, clear and forcible, without a single word that can be objected to as imprudent or in bad taste. It is the best thing he has written yet.

17 June 1886: . . . M. tells me of a visit paid her on Thursday (I think) by Gladstone, Ly Airlie and others present; he seemed to have begun at the Irish subject, and to have declaimed rather than talked upon it with so much vehemence as to alarm his listeners. Her description of his manner reminded me of what I have read in various memoirs of the time about Burke when excited by discussion on the French revolution. He left on their minds no doubt of the sincerity of his convictions, but some doubt as to his sanity. Or, to put it more fairly, he seemed to his hearers to be in a state of morbid excitement. His public utterances have been in the same strain. He has likened the proceedings of the English in 1798 to the massacre of St. Bartholemew: and in a letter which appears today he speaks of the 'baseness and blackguardism' of the means by which the Union was passed.

[Throughout 1886 Derby had seen Liberal Unionism as a way of preventing straight-forward desertions to a Conservative party he did not admire. He had also been through-out against any idea of coalition. When the elections were over, Derby's line remained unchanged. He came up to town to dissuade Hartington from coalition, partly on the ground Salisbury's good faith could not be relied on: 'Salisbury might easily find a pretext for breaking up the concern and coming in with his own men only, when once the break between Hartington and the Liberals was complete.[65]. There was also news from Drage, Derby's doctor, who thought ill of Salisbury's prospects of life. He was said to have kidney trouble as well as eczema[66]. Churchill, 'as uncertain as hereditary madness can make him'[67], was 'too eccentric and crazy to be trusted'[68]. There was also a difficulty about filling the Foreign Office, for 'except Lytton I see no one fit for the place. He is the least incompetent of the lot, but his ways of life are not those of a hard-working minister'[69]. By this Derby meant, among other things, that 'Lytton is said now to have gone heavily into opium-eating or smoking'[70].

On 24 July Derby was summoned by telegram to Devonshire House at 4.00 p.m. where he found Hartington with James. Salisbury had been with him that morning, offering him the premiership, with Salisbury as foreign secretary. ˙ All Hartington's friends were against this offer: but Hartington 'was stricken and uncertain when the moment of decision came'[71]. Derby' s impression was that Hartington cast fond glances in the direction of 'absolute union under himself as premier, but was held back not only by colleagues but by another difficulty: 'He (Hartington) also observed that if he had been disposed to accept the offer there was one difficulty personal to himself: he certainly would not have been again returned by his present constituency, and might not easily find another seat'.[72]

F. Stanley called to consult his brother about his political future, in effect seeking permission from the head of the family to take a peerage. Derby in fact advised him to take the India Office and remain in the Commons, but his brother's preference was clear: 'He said he had been over twenty years in the H. of C., was growing weary of it, felt the work harder than he liked, did not feel sure that he agreed with his intended colleagues on many points, disliked Churchill as a leader, and thought he should be more free in the Lords.' In the end F. Stanley gave up the India Office in response to appeals, despite early hopes or promises of it, and took the Board of Trade, a peerage, and a cabinet place[73]. Derby was not pleased to learn (through Mary Galloway) that Cross's appointment to India had been forced on Salisbury, to his disgust, by the Queen, her motive supposedly being the promotion of the Duke of Connaught in India and then at home, Cross being notoriously a creature of hers.

One more practical question faced the Liberal Unionists: where to sit? Derby and his colleagues agreed to sit with the opposition, only Selborne wanting to sit with the government[74].]

31 Aug. 1886: Death of Lord Henry Lennox, a brother of the present Duke of Richmond, whom in early days I knew familiarly. He was by far the cleverest of the family, and had to a certain extent educated himself, which except the Duke none of the rest have done. He accomplished a fair parliamentary success, and held several minor offices. With his position, and being as he was ambitious, it seemed as if he ought to have gone higher: and perhaps he would, but for an unlucky love of speculation, which caused him to be mixed up in sundry not very creditable affairs, and in the end caused his retirement from office . . . I do not believe he ever did, or connived at, anything dishonest: but no man could be associated with Albert Grant and come away with perfectly clean hands. In addition to this, his manner was affected, and his temper irritable: so that he was never popular in the society of his own class: but he lived much among actors, speculators, and small hangers-on to newspapers; and in this world he was much appreciated. He was always in money difficulties from which marriage with a rich widow did not extricate him: for his debts were once at least paid by his family: and latterly he went through the bankruptcy court.

4 Oct. 1886: . . . He [Churchill] evidently models himself on Disraeli, but with this difference, that the eccentric and outrageous utterances in which he often indulges are with him outbreaks of his real nature, whereas with Disraeli they were carefully calculated for effect. There is in him a certain love of mischief for its own sake, result probably of inherited insane diathesis [predisposition to illness] which may show itself at the most inconvenient time[75].

11 Dec. 1886: . . . The prospect of a reunion of the party seems more distant than ever . . .

19 Dec. 1886: . . . Answered a letter from Mrs. Gladstone in her usual gushing style, the purport of which is to beg £100 for one of the many charities on behalf of which she is always canvassing. It is a mistake in a statesman's wife to beg in this way, for those who are connected by political ties to the husband feel bound to give and often do so unwillingly[76].

24 Dec. 1886: . . . .If I could believe Churchill to be serious and sincere in his wish for economy, my sympathies would be all with him - but I judge him to have acted more from temper than policy. He has been the spoilt child of politics . . . In his curious nature, tinged as it is with madness, the love of mischief for its own sake enters largely. I am sure he is enjoying the confusion he has made, as a monkey might enjoy the breaking of crockery[77].

Liberal Unionism

> I do not think democratic politics will have many attractions for
> cultivated men in the next generation.
> - Lord Derby, 14 January 1887.

[From 1886 to 1891 Derby was leader of the Liberal Unionists in the House of Lords.
This was a stopgap appointment, for Hartington's father was very old, and his death
would necessarily mean that Hartington, as Duke of Devonshire, would succeed to
Derby's post. This he in fact did in or shortly after the death of the old Duke in December
1891. Why Derby, rather than some other Liberal Unionist of ministerial position,
became leader is something which the diaries do not explain, and it may have been simply
a question of seniority, his ministerial career going back much further than that of any of
his colleagues.

Derby was in one sense a good leader, in another a mediocre one and in a third way
little fitted to his post. His chief virtue was that he was uncompromisingly against Home
Rule, and could make out a good case against it which was based on something deeper
than temporary alarmism and prejudice. This was not a question on which Derby sat on
the fence. He even took a certain pride, most unusually for him, in his speeches on the
subject[78]. On the other hand Derby had a very clear perception of the limitations of the
Liberal Unionists. They were a party of one topic, Ireland, on which by 1887 nothing new
could be said. They had no other themes, the public were weary of hearing about
Ireland[79], and so was Derby[80]. In practice this meant that he refused many invitations to
speak on public platforms, simply to avoid tedious repetition. He was in considerable
demand as a speaker, but had no qualms about refusing such invitations.

Derby's chief defect as a party leader was that he had no wish to turn the House of
Lords into a battleground. His motives included indolence, political judgment, and a
preference for Liberal opponents over Conservative allies. Though the diaries are silent
on the subject, he appears not to have exchanged a word with Salisbury[81], and one must
presume, in the absence of contrary evidence, that for five years the leaders of the two
Unionist groups in the House of Lords were not on speaking terms, because of the mortal
insult of 1878.

In some ways he remained very much a Liberal. He was critical of the 1887 coercion
bill, and thought the government might be defeated on its more invidious clauses. He
thought the Parnell Commission a mistake from the first. He publicised his willingness
to see the Welsh Church disestablished. He sympathised with Churchill, believing him to
have resigned at least partly in opposition to jingoism in foreign policy.

Derby's view was that the Home Rule split ought to be viewed as temporary[82], even if
he did not expect it to be healed in the life of the existing parliament. He considered
coalition between Liberal Unionists and Conservatives 'out of the question'[83] except in
the special case of Goschen. He continued to feel a real tie of loyalty to Gladstone. It was
true that it was Gladstone who sought out the company of Derby and Lady Derby, rather
than the reverse, but then that had always been so. 'Under all circumstances,' it was
noted, 'Lord Derby spoke with the highest respect of Mr. Gladstone. He did not praise
him, but always spoke as if Mr. Gladstone were a being of quite a higher sphere, though,

of course, to be criticised as to policy and methods by practical standards.' Derby had 'even a generous admiration for moral enthusiasms which many would think eccentric': he spoke feelingly of Gladstone's rescue work[84]. On the other hand, Derby had little good to say of the Salisbury ministry of 1886-1892, condemning the reshuffle of January 1887 as 'bad for the departments, and {giving} an impression of weakness'[85]. He had no contact, while a Unionist, with either Salisbury or Churchill, and did not think it the business of a Liberal Unionist to admire Conservatives[86] or to secede by stages to that party. For Derby, Liberal Unionism was a device for separating Liberals from Conservatives, rather than Liberals from Liberals.

Derby had no personal motive for exertion, seeing 'no prospect of a return to office, and do not desire it' and even, oddly, rejoicing that 'no quarrel, nor misfortune, nor trouble of any kind[87]' had come his way in 1886. But it was chiefly for political reasons that he deprecated aggressive attacks on former Liberal colleagues. He was neither anti-Liberal nor anti-Gladstonian, and he was pained by those ex-liberals who were. Even if he thought reunion impossible in the existing parliament, he was implicitly calculating on an altered situation once Gladstone's death removed the Home Rule issue from the centre of politics. He therefore wished to let the dust settle in the House of Lords, not pressing former colleagues in debate. In this he was not particularly successful, his more polemically minded supporters being most unwilling to let matters drop.

Among the younger peers, Camperdown deserves special notice. His name recurs in the role of a terrier snapping at Derby's heels, trying to press him into greater eagerness. Camperdown had emerged in spring 1886 as the most chronically eager of the Liberal Unionist peers, if not the most rancorously polemical. He wanted Liberal Unionism to be a movement, rather than a secession, and he wanted, as Derby well knew, to run Derby. Derby was not having this, but evasion was not easy. Camperdown figures in accounts of the Liberal schism, but probably deserves more mention. 'Camperdown, in fact, is less a Unionist than an opponent of Gladstone, for whom he has an antipathy he does not disguise', the origin of which Derby never knew. He added ominously that Camperdown had 'a morose and sour disposition which is growing upon him, and seems morbid' and that his father had put an end to himself[88]. It is puzzling that in 1892 Derby added a codicil to his will leaving £1,000 to Camperdown 'as a mark of friendship'.

The formal tasks of leadership were light. Consultation with Hartington did not take much time, because Hartington did not do much consulting with his co-leader: as Sir H. James's papers show, it was the latter whose advice Hartington chiefly sought. There were few meetings of the Liberal Unionist inner leadership recorded by Derby; nor were larger party meetings held for the rank and file, though in 1888 there was a meeting of 53 Liberal Unionist peers at Derby's house, with 25 apologies[89]. Derby also entertained for the party at the opening of the session when Hartington would or could not do so, as in 1889 and 1890, when he dined peers and M.P.s together contrary to practice. One final point: Derby's financial backing for Liberal Unionism is not clearly recorded after 1886[90].]

7 Jan. 1887: Wrote . . . to Northbrook. . . . Said that I was glad he had not seen his way to join the ministry: Goschen's case was peculiar . . . I added that I did not well understand Hartington's point of view, in advising his friends to do what he would not do himself: if the Cabinet was good enough for them, why not for him? and I was glad that nothing had come of the move[91].

26 Jan. 1887: . . . Hartington called by appointment to talk over the Speech, which he had got in his pocket. He seemed thoroughly depressed and disgusted, did not see what was going to happen, feared the government could not hold its own: if they failed he saw nothing for it except the return of Gladstone to power. 'Why not try on your own account?', I asked: but he answered with some truth, that if the Conservatives could not hold their own with his support, he should be in no better position with theirs. I never saw him so much disposed, as it seemed to me, to throw the whole thing up.

5 Feb. 1887. . . .Met Hartington . . . I complimented him on a speech just delivered at Newcastle, which he pronounced to have been long and dull: as to the session he was utterly despondent: did not see how any plan for what would be called coercion could be made to pass the H. of Commons: then, what would happen? Salisbury must resign, and Gladstone follow with Home Rule, and another dissolution. I did not argue the point, but it seemed to me that what Hartington foresees and fears is the being obliged to form a government on his own account, which would be intolerable to him, but in honour he could scarcely refuse.

5 Mar. 1887: I hear that Gladstone tells his friends he shall be in power again before Easter.

15 Mar. 1887: . . . Some talk with Sir H. James, who is very despondent as to the future of the Liberal Unionists: thinks they will none of them be returned to the next parliament. I answered, it might be long before that was tried: he doubted, saying the present Cabinet is very weak, has no constructive power and little hold on parliament: he seemed to predict its fall at an early date.

20 Mar. 1887: . . . In conversation with Hartington yesterday, he told me that he thought the attempt at reunion of the party had never been serious: Chamberlain expected large concessions from Gladstone, who had no thought of making any: he believed, as H. James does, that our prospects at the next election were bad, but that need not trouble us yet, many things might happen meanwhile: there would be a desperate fight over the so-called coercion bill[92] which all Gladstone's followers would oppose, and if they failed, or seemed likely to fail, in the House, would agitate the country against it: he thought Balfour had made an unlucky beginning, his speech last night being thought flippant and too violent. He complained of the sub-commissioners under the Land Act, who are cutting down the rents quite recklessly: he says, because these appointments expire next year, and they will not be chosen again unless they have satisfied the tenants.

I made the remark that, if we meant to satisfy Irish feeling, Gladstone's plan did not go nearly far enough: there could be no real nationality without an army, a navy, a diplomacy, power to deal with tariffs, etc., all of which G. had reserved to the imperial parliament. I said I could see no medium between maintaining the Union, or giving to Ireland the practical independence of Canada or Australia. He said he had heard Smith, the leader of the House, say much the same thing, except that he, Smith, considered the only alternative to be total independence.

26 Mar. 1887: . . . A Mr. Asquith, a new member, a lawyer, unknown before to me, and to most people, secured a political position by one performance which, judging by the reports, seems to have been remarkable for a beginner.

30 Mar. 1887: . . . The chief subject of my conversation with Kimberley on Monday was the following. Can anything in the nature of an Irish parliament be created, reserving a certain class of questions for the sole consideration of the imperial parliament at Westminster, with the slightest chance of such limitation of its power being agreed to? or will not the parliament in Dublin at once declare itself the sole authority entitled to make laws for Ireland? I found he agreed with me that this result must inevitably follow, a little sooner or later as accident might determine: and thought that nothing would really satisfy the Irish except independence not less than they enjoyed between 1782 and 1800, nor less than that of Canada and Australia now. But he thought the English would be reconciled to even that change, provided it came gradually. - Ulster, he said, was in his mind the only difficulty.

4 Apr. 1887: . . . Salisbury looked very ill [at the colonial conference]: fagged, beat, and his face discoloured by eczema . . . I hear frequent speculations on the possibility of his breaking down . . .

29 July 1887: . . . Met Gladstone, and some friendly talk . . .

10 Oct. 1887: . . . Saw Lubbock: talk with him as to prospects of the Unionists, which he evidently does not think well of. He agrees with me in deprecating a coalition as fatal to the Lib. Unionist party.

10 Oct. 1887: . . . Sent off a mem. to Hartington, which he has asked for, on the present state of the Irish question. It seems that some of the Unionists are anxious that we should bring in or support some plan of Home Rule safeguarded so as to prevent danger to imperial interests: which they suppose to be possible. I write combating this proposal, and say, what I've said again and again, that there is no middle course possible - no alternative except complete union or virtual separation.

. . . In *The Times* of Saturday appears a brief letter of mine on the question of Welsh disestablishment: it is merely to say (I being appealed to) that the question in my judgment ought to be settled in accordance with the wishes of the Welsh people, whenever these are authoritatively declared[93]. It is odd that Gladstone, with whom I have had no communication, has answered the same query in almost identical words.

9 Nov. 1887: . . . Northbrook called: he talked of the prospects of Unionism, which he thought were neither better nor worse: he agreed with me as to the uselessness of attempting a compromise, and thought it fortunate that the so-called conference had fallen through.

27 Dec. 1887: . . . Gladstone is on his way to Italy, having been ordered abroad for his health. Parnell is said to be dying slowly of cancer: and Morley has had a very narrow escape from some internal complaint, of which for some days he was expected to die.

21 Feb. 1888: Walk with Kimberley . . . K. made a remark which struck me: he said he thought the Irish disruption was not an unmixed evil, as interposing an interval for consideration before other questions came on. Without some such check, the radical movement would have been too rapid. Probably there are many who think as he does.

25 Apr. 1888: . . . Ld Stalbridge called by appointment, and asked me to join with a few others in buying up the Central News press agency, so as to get it out of the hands of Home Rulers - the chief proprietor is a Mr. Saunders, nearly if not quite a socialist. He says the D. of Bedford has taken shares to the value of £5,000 in it: expected they would pay well, but of course the thing is a risk. I asked a little time to consider.

7 May 1888: . . . Lawson called . . . He did not see the prospects of the Liberal Unionist party as regards office: nor do I.

5 Nov. 1888: .. Lawson talked of the personal weakness of ministers - said there were at least three who ought to resign - D. of Rutland, Cross, and Matthews. . . He thought old Toryism was dead and buried, and there ought to be a coalition on the basis of resistance to the new radical or semi- socialist party.

6 Dec. 1888: . . . Great anger against R. Churchill among Conservatives caused by his having yesterday suddenly moved the adjournment of the House to discuss the question of Suakin. He gave no notice to ministers whom be meant to attack, but summoned the Home Rule party. The move was intended as a surprise, and nearly succeeded, for the majority was not in the House, no party debate being expected, and a defeat was narrowly escaped. Tricks of this kind are contrary to parliamentary traditions, and held discreditable: but Churchill is as mischievous as a monkey, and is too mad to have any sense of honourable obligation.

12 Dec. 1888: . . . Granville called . . . He said to M. in a marked way, 'We don't want to have Churchill among us' as though C. were expected to leave his party. Certainly if he is anything he is a radical . . .

27 Jan. 1889: . . .Letter from Camperdown, who likes my late speech and hopes I shall deliver many more! The invitation does not tempt me. I will speak as often as I have anything to say that is at all new, and to the purpose: but I will not repeat the same ideas again and again, whatever party managers may desire.

14 Apr. 1889: . . .I have not noted that two or three days ago I met Hartington and had some talk with him. He was despondent as to Unionist prospects: said that in Ireland people were losing confidence, and some beginning to talk about a moderate Home Rule bill being desirable, as an alternative to one of a more violent kind. He did not, however, accept this view of the situation for himself: and I think he is constitutionally apt to be despondent.

25 Apr. 1889: [Talk with Jesse Collings, whom Derby saw as] an enthusiast for peasant proprietors, but not an enemy to the rich as such. Indeed he praised the country gentlemen effusively for their willingness to serve in the new county councils[94].

10 May 1889: . . . I do not rate my own speeches highly, but those I have delivered on the Irish question during the last three years have, I think, been the least bad of any that I have made.

17 Dec. 1889: . . . R. Churchill has given in his adhesion to the [Eight Hours] movement, as a good piece of electioneering: it would be absurd to credit him with a serious conviction on that or any subject.

5 Mar. 1890: . . . Some talk with Hicks Beach . . . He thinks the next parliament will be very radical, and will give Irish Home Rule in principle, but that the difficulty of fixing on any plan will be extreme.

12 Mar. 1890: Much talk in society, and in the papers generally, about a speech delivered last night by R. Churchill: it was directed against the government, the language exceedingly and unusually violent, and the supposed intention is to break up the existing party, bring in Gladstone for a time, and so clear the way for a new combination, of which Churchill shall be head.

20 May 1890: . . . Ld Rothschild asked me what I would contribute to the L.U. fund for the general election, about which it seems Hartington is beginning to be anxious. The whole sum wanted is £60,000. I said I had not thought about it, and enquired what he (Ld R.) would give. He said £5,000, and pressed me to name a sum. I named £2,000, saying perhaps it might be more[95].

15 Oct. 1890: . . . Reeve put into my hands the forthcoming number of the *Edinburgh*, calling special attention to an article by A. Elliot . . . recommending a coalition between Lib. Unionists and Conservatives, though not till after the next elections. It seemed to me premature . . . In fact, I do not consider it a thing either possible or desirable. Chamberlain could not act permanently with the Conservatives, nor they with him.

3 Dec. 1890: .. .Dined Grillions, with a large party of 17 or 18, including Gladstone, Ld Jersey, Knutsford, and Norton, Boehm, R. Herbert, Meade, A. Russell, Lecky, etc. I was in the chair, and Gladstone sat next me, with whom I had a curious and interesting conversation. He talked freely of Northcote, whom he liked, but did not seem to think highly of as a public man, complaining that he used to give pledges in regard to the conduct of public business, which his party would not allow him to keep, and he could not control. Then he spoke of R. Churchill, whose character was a puzzle to him but, when I hinted at an eccentricity arising from hereditary tendencies, he seemed surprised, as if the idea had not occurred to him. By what transition I forget, he began to speak of Parnell, saying with a kind of grim humour: 'A large chapter has been added to my experiences of human nature in the last few weeks.' And he went on to express his astonishment at the breach of confidence, saying that in all their previous communications Parnell had shown himself entirely and even scrupulously truthful. (I remember the exact words used.) I asked if he had not heard a good deal of the O'Shea business before? He said yes, but only reports, and he made it a rule to attach no importance to these, as anybody might be accused.

20 Feb. 1891: . . . Northbrook called. . . He thought the growth of socialism formidable. The next elections ought to be put off as long as possible: if Gladstone were still alive and active when they came on, the prestige of his name would carry all before it: whereas, if he were out of the way, none of his successors would have any hold on the public mind. We talked about the troubles on the Clanricarde estates, which he says were originally caused not by high rents or distress, but by the personal unpopularity of the owner.

22 Nov. 1891: . . .Saw Camperdown in afternoon: he was full as usual of Unionist politics, and eager about them: he thought the Home Rulers were losing ground in Scotland. He talked much of the necessity of a reform of the H. of Lords, which I agreed in, but I suspect he does not allow for the two great obstacles [i.e. of traditionalism, and of radical dislike of a strengthened upper house][96].

Two Foreign Secretaries: Malmesbury and Granville

21 July 1880: . . . London is busy with a singular story. Old Ld Malmesbury[97] aged 73 has within the last three months committed the folly of engaging himself to marry a young widow, more 'fast' than respectable, who had been separated from her husband before his death in South Africa. His family naturally were disgusted, and a coolness has followed. The marriage was on the point of coming off, when it was discovered that the lady had already a husband living, one of the Kingscote family, whom she had married immediately after the death of the first husband and before her engagement to Malmesbury. Why she should have amused herself with practising a deception which must necessarily be detected no one seems to know, but as matters stand she has extracted many valuable presents from the old man, and left him in a ridiculous position. I believe the story, chiefly because it is too improbable to have been invented, and feel some regret for Ld M. . . . But he was always under female influence of some kind: and as a minister was induced by such influence to perpetuate not a few jobs[98].

9 May 1881: . . . An address was moved to the Crown for a public monument to Ld Beaconsfield . . . [After Granville and Salisbury] Malmesbury followed, no one knew why, and talked wretched twaddle, not even made endurable by sincerity: for he was no friend to Ld B., at whom he used to sneer (rather vulgarly) on the ground of his Jew origin and inferior social position.

13 June 1884: Letter from old Ld Malmesbury, now 77, who intends to publish his memoirs, and sends me letters of my father and some of my own to know if I object to their being published. I answer in a friendly way, and ask a few days to look at the letters.

2 Oct. 1884: Received from London Malmesbury's newly published memoirs: they are gossipy, trivial in parts, containing little information as to men or things, but amusing, and as far as I can judge not ill-natured. Whether it is altogether delicate to publish gossip about living friends and acquaintances is another matter: but if the thing was to be done at all he has done it in a fairly unobjectionable manner. His two heroes are my father and Louis Napoleon: he has inserted a good many letters from my father, some characteristic. There are also one or two from Disraeli with whom he was on civil, but never on cordial, terms. On the whole the book is harmless, and not foolish: it will give my old friend no fame as an author, but it may put a few hundreds in his pocket[99], which I am afraid are much wanted.

18 May 1889: In his office he [Lord Malmesbury, just dead] was laborious, and would have been more successful than he was but for an unfounded suspicion which had been instilled into his mind, I believe by Disraeli, that Hammond was a strong Whig partisan, and his personal enemy. Consequently, he set Hammond on one side, and consulted instead of him a very inferior subordinate, one James Murray, who, being weak and prejudiced, gave him bad advice.

 . . . In society Ld M. was always popular, being of a kindly nature, a good story-teller, and knowing the world well. He courted women, respectable and disrespectable:

succeeded in the pursuit: and was somewhat promiscuous in his love affairs, which continued till late in life. He leaves no children[100].

Granville

[Granville and Derby had always been on friendly terms, and during and after the Home Rule crisis they became if anything even more so. Their friendship was political, not personal or social. Derby in fact thought that it was impossible to penetrate Granville's façade of ease and charm and find out what lay behind. Nevertheless, in 1885-1886 it was chiefly to Granville that Derby unburdened himself on Home Rule, and after 1886 Derby was on closer terms with Granville than with any Liberal Unionist colleague[101]. Granville came to stay at Knowsley: no other Liberal Unionist of standing, still less any senior Conservative, entered those gates. Hartington and Derby never exchanged visits, except in London. It was not that Granville expected Liberal reunion in the existing parliament[102]: but he, like Derby, agreed in not wishing to widen the Liberal breach. Derby's policy of inactivity in the House of Lords no doubt owed something to Olympian indolence, but its avowed object was to prevent men like Granville and Spencer being forced, out of loyalty, to say more in support of Gladstone than was necessary.

Derby sympathised with Granville on another level. Granville's finances had for some years been in disorder. He faced the prospect of leaving a young family ill provided for. The problem lay in his dependence on an ironworks at Stoke-on-Trent, at a time when the iron trade was severely depressed. His friends, including Derby, Spencer, and Rosebery, became involved in a prolonged attempt to rescue him from public scandal. In this, at least, they were successful, but at a price. The ironworks was sold off as a company, on terms unfavourable to Granville. 'They have squeezed me,' he said. Momentarily things improved, at least on paper. Granville was able to offer to pay Derby £3,000 out of the £4,700 owing him in the form of shares[103]. However, the Barings crisis shortly afterwards shook business confidence, and Granville asked to defer even the share payment[104]. When he died early in 1891, the position could not have been worse.

The story of Granville's insolvency is both extraordinary and pathetic. For many years he depended on colleagues who were either political opponents, like Derby, senior colleagues, like Spencer, or younger men like Rosebery whose chief ambition was to step into his shoes. How early in the eighties his difficulties began, how many were involved in helping him, and how much money was involved cannot be told here. His biography is understandably entirely silent on the subject. As an exercise in Whig honour and solidarity it is remarkable; politically his debts must be borne in mind as at least a minor factor in his relations with colleagues, and in his political standing.]

2 Sep. 1884: [At Walmer Castle, home of Lord Granville in his capacity as Warden of the Cinque Ports.]. . .Granville, who is very hospitable, and generally has in the house as many guests as it will hold, has no study of his own, but does his work in the drawing room, Sanderson [now Granville's private secretary] and he having separate tables, and writing and settling affairs amidst the conversation of anybody who may be there. An odd way of doing business: but the business gets done somehow.

We drove . . . to the little place called St. Margaret's, where Sackville has some land and Ld G. much more, which they are trying to develop into building ground. . . . I doubt its success as a speculation. Ld G. tells me he has about 600 acres of his own near Walmer. The castle of course is held only for life.

In afternoon walk with Pauncefote, Meade, Sanderson, and young Lacaita to a hill top about two miles off, where Ld G. has amused himself by building a pretty little cottage on a site which commands an exceptionally fine view, and surrounding it with a kind of wild garden or shrubbery.

5 Nov. 1884: . . . Received from Granville an unexpected letter, asking me to lend him £8,000, for a year or less, paying five per cent for it: the reason for the demand being that he has failed to receive from his ironworks the sum of £17,000 which he expected, owing, as he says, to legal difficulties. I do not much love loans: but it was not easy to refuse: and unless Ld G. is ruined, which there seems no reason to suppose, I presume the money is safe. I therefore wrote at once agreeing: and wrote to Coutts to sell out £8,000 consols[105].

[In autumn 1885 over a hundred Whig peers subscribed £10 each for a presentation to Granville, in what was to be the last collective act of a united Whig peerage. The collection, alas, went on two portraits[106], which were not Granville's most pressing necessity.]

10 Dec. 1885: . . . I do not feel equally secure about the £6,350 which Granville owes me, he said he would write about it in a few days, and it is now a month since he hinted at a continuance of the loan, in which I acquiesced.

2 Feb. 1886: [Granville told Derby that he had rejected the Presidency of the Council for the Colonial Office as being too evidently put on the shelf: Derby however suspected] . . . that the difference of salary had much to do with his choice.

On 14 May 1886 Derby offered to defer repayment of the loan, and to make it free of interest, but Granville declined at the time. When the autumn came, however, Granville, now without the prop of an official salary, was unable to pay the interest, which Derby agreed to defer, commenting: 'He evidently has not got the money.' While staying at Knowsley for family festivities in October 1886, Granville asked if he could continue the loan for another year, Derby again agreeing.]

28 Oct. 1887: [At Knowsley] before saying goodbye to Granville, I offered him the continuance for another year of the loan of £4,700 for which I hold his cheque. He accepted with an eagerness which does not bode well for his solvency: and indeed he told me that the iron industry is in a bad way. I have perhaps done what was imprudent, but the loss at worst is not heavy: and I have both a respect and a liking for Ld G. He is much aged, gone very deaf, and has lost much of his spirits.

23 Apr. 1888. [Pender] gave a lamentable account of Ld Granville's financial position, which he seemed to know: saying that he, Ld G., had sold all the best of his pictures privately, and was disposing of whatever else he could sell. Lawson, whom I met later, told me the same.

9 Nov. 1888: Received from Ld Granville a letter asking to continue the loan for another year. There is still unpaid £4,700, with interest £235. I answer saying that it shall be as he likes, but hinting that he may prefer to pay off the odd £700.

12 Nov. 1888. Received from Granville a letter, very grateful for my consent to renew the loan: which I am willing enough to do, but in fact I have no choice, for I am sure he cannot pay. He sends me three cheques, but the sums are all wrong, and I am obliged to send them back.

27 May 1891: Talk of Ld Granville's affairs, which seem to have been left in utter confusion. His lawyer says the liabilities are £280,000, and the assets consist largely of shares in a coal and iron co. which at present are unsaleable. It is doubtful whether the debts can be paid, leaving nothing for the family.

9 Nov. 1891: Ld Granville's will is in the papers: £32,000 gross, and only £900 net. In fact he died insolvent: for he left debts which will neither be claimed nor paid. It is strange that in this state of finances he can have gone on living as he did.

22 Sep. 1892: . . . Letter from the D. of Devonshire, a circular confidentially printed, on the affairs of the late Ld. Granville. It seems from this document that he put his whole fortune into a coal and iron company, in which he held shares to the value of more than £250,000. The shares are only three-fourths paid up, and a new call about to be made will require £10,000 now and £20,000 more in a few months. This demand will pretty nearly swallow up what is left of the Granville estate, and the Duke in his circular promises help, and asks it from others. I answered at once, expressing sympathy, but saying I had already cancelled nearly £5,000 of debt owing to me by Ld G. and thought that sufficient contribution on my part.

Some Peers

[The misfortunes of peers became almost an obsession with Derby. His vision of a frugal and hard-working aristocracy spending their lives answering letters by return and attending public meetings was not one which all of his class found acceptable. Even within his own family circle there were lapses. His wife's relations, the Russells and the Sackvilles, had an erratic history; the Cecil stepchildren, though amiable and upright, could be distinctly difficult. The worst case was that of Lord Galloway, the husband of Lady Derby's daughter Mary Cecil, who found himself before the courts on two occasions.

Throughout the period Derby seems to have felt that drink, going on the turf, and the ever-present pressures on sanity were greater risks to the political and economic future of the aristocracy and especially to its prestige, than socialism, taxation, and pressure from without. Any study of the late Victorian aristocracy which is narrowly economic and political, and does not take into account what they were like as people, must inevitably be unrealistic, especially as little or nothing is known of the great majority of non-political peers, and as the reference books, like G.E. Cokayne's *Complete Peerage*, showed a certain caution in discussing near-contemporaries.]

26 July 1883: . . . Gossip about the D. and Dss of Teck selling off their furniture etc. They are £50,000 in debt, having chosen to keep up royal state, which cannot be done on £6,000 a year. Neither the Queen nor the Duchess of Cambridge will help them, except on condition of their living in Germany: which they do not choose to do. The sale has created a good deal of talk, though an excuse is ostensibly put forward that they are going to move into a smaller house at Richmond, and therefore do not want the property they are disposing of[107].

29 July 1883: Talk of an odd event in Lord Cairns's family: his eldest son[108], a rather fast youth, is engaged to marry a Miss Fortescue, an actress, who will find herself in very uncongenial surroundings. Cairns, with his usual good sense, has taken the affair well: and finding it could not be stopped has given his approval. So at least the talk ran today.

28 Sep. 1883: . . . Walk with Camperdown. He talks of Dalhousie: likes him as I do: but says nothing can be more reckless or silly than his dealings with his tenants. He has taken without enquiry or verification every complaint they make as well grounded, has given them all they wanted without even consulting his agent, and is consequently a good deal embarrassed, his estate though large being heavily encumbered, and his reductions having hugely diminished the available margin of income[109].

12 Apr. 1884: . . . Received back from Sir T. Martin the Lyndhurst letters, which I had sent him, with a civil note. He has made little use of them, nor could he. Lord Lyndhurst[110] wrote like an indolent man and a man of business, so far as the two are compatible: that is, briefly, without ornament or attempt at style, saying what he had to say in the fewest words, and often in such a way as not to be intelligible without the letter which he was answering. He had also the peculiarity of never, or seldom, dating his notes. I think it likely that his objection to have his correspondence published was due to the fact that he felt it could not enhance his immense reputation, founded on the personal impression which he made on his contemporaries. Nor was it in his nature to care for posthumous fame. Martin' s life of him[111] is a dull book, not by the fault of the author, but in part from the want of adequate material: in part from its controversial character. It was written as a reply to the attacks in Ld Campbell's biographical sketch . . . The truth I take to be that he was neither better nor worse than the average of lawyer-politicians: that like most clever men he may have talked radicalism in his youth: that he was never a Tory in the sense of feeling any great veneration for existing institutions, but probably had a thorough contempt for the intolerant zeal of half-educated reformers . . . That he was a great orator and a delightful companion his worst enemies never denied. He was socially damaged by the conduct of his first wife, a handsome fashionable woman whose extravagance was great, and was certainly not paid for by her husband: but paid for it was, and, the scandal of the day asserted, with his knowledge and connivance. - He was Voltairean in religion during most of his life, but is said to have become a believer in old age. I knew him in his latest years: when though nearly blind and very infirm his spirits were generally high, never depressed. He was kept informed of the latest news and gossip of the clubs, which he would discuss eagerly: I noted as a peculiarity that he seldom cared to talk of the past, indeed it was not easy to lead him to do so: contrary to the nature of old men in general.

16 Apr. 1884: In the papers, death of the Duke of Buccleuch[112], aged 78: he had reigned (for his estate was a small sovereignty) just 65 years, probably the longest tenure of a title and territory of any now in existence. He had the good fortune to be universally respected: in politics a very moderate Conservative: in estate affairs a good and careful landlord: active, but not fussy, in local concerns, and not desirous of being more before the public than his position made inevitable. I scarcely know any one of whom it can be said that he filled an important position with so quiet and consistent dignity. His estates are supposed to give a rental of £250,000[113]: but the number of large country houses which he had inherited - seven or eight, I think - reduced his real income: and, as he made it a point of duty to live part of the year in each of them, his existence was as nomadic as that of a gypsy. The only foolish thing which I know of his doing was building that huge palace at Whitehall[114]: a mistake for any one who does not care about taking a lead in fashionable society. He had a singularly fortunate life, with few troubles, of which perhaps the chief was his wife turning papist. He concerned himself more directly and closely with the management of his estates than most large proprietors do: being in fact, like the D. of Bedford, his own head agent. He was not a man of superior ability: if he had been he would probably have created more antagonism: and received less general respect: for the public does not as a rule like to see unusual ability combined with great wealth and high rank: whether from jealousy or the influence of these things combined, or from thinking that so many advantages are too much for one man, or simply because they are irritated by what they do not understand.

He represented fairly the average opinion of the conservative part of the upper class: and so bore himself that those who opposed him had little personal fault to find. His son, Dalkeith[115], will not fill his shoes: being a kindly, well-meaning, amiable, but very indolent gentleman who will not take trouble as his father did, nor care to assume the same position in local administration. But he will act respectably, and keep up the family credit, though not increase it.

26 July 1884: . . . Much excitement in the family. Sir E. Malet[116], the diplomatist, having proposed to Ly Ermyntrude Russell [daughter of the ninth Duke of Bedford, and niece of Lady Derby], who half accepted, but referred him to the Duke. It is a good match, he being quite the most rising of the younger diplomatists, and sure of an embassy: while his manners are remarkably pleasing. On the other side, he gains high rank, and some fortune, for each of the Russell daughters have £100,000 of their own.

26 Aug. 1884: The papers are full of Odo Russell[117] [just dead] whose remarkable ability seems recognised on all sides. He was eminently fit for the life he led, having by nature the easy unimpassioned temper which belongs to a diplomatist: and having been brought up among Germans, whose language he spoke as familiarly as his own. Indeed it was his own, for he talked English with a slight, but perceptible, foreign accent, and certainly knew less of English than of continental life. He told stories, and conversed, admirably well: there were few pleasanter companions. His health was never strong, and latterly had failed a good deal owing to sedentary habits. He never took exercise, and was a heavy eater in the German fashion, though temperate in drink. He had an art both in writing and talking, more than any man I have known, of insinuating what he did not think it desirable or prudent to say openly: so that you knew what he thought, yet could hardly assert that he had given an opinion. In conversations of business he was perhaps over-anxious to avoid any appearance of difference with his interlocutor, and people who did not know his ways accused him of being insincere: but it was seldom difficult to discover whether he really agreed, or was only assenting out of politeness. In politics he professed the opinions of his family, as far as he could be said to have any politics: professional duty and personal taste combined to keep him as nearly neutral as an Englishman in a prominent position can be. He at one time made no secret of his ambition to be Foreign Secretary: an ambition which might perhaps have been realised if he had lived, but I do not think the post would have suited him, nor he it. He was exactly in his place as ambassador at Berlin, and we shall never have a better.

20 Nov. 1884: Much gossip about an action for breach of promise, brought by a Miss Finney, a popular actress, against Cairns' eldest son, Lord Garmoyle. The youth, who is not very wise, proposed to her, was accepted, induced his family to consent, and then broke it off, as some say by their persuasion. She got £10,000 damages, which had been offered in the first instance as an amicable settlement, but refused. I believe the truth to be that the Cairns gave their consent sincerely, trying to make the best of it, but the young lady's free and easy ways, and unrefined manners, were too much for their tolerance. They are well out of the scrape, even at a cost of £10,000.

14 Jan. 1885: Death of Lord Aylesford[118], in Texas, aged 36. He had run through his whole fortune by gaming, racing, and extravagance generally: and was one of the very worst examples of the English peerage. Naturally, he belonged to the Marlborough House set. There will probably be a lawsuit as to the title: his son, so-called, being notoriously the son of the D. of Marlborough, who lived openly with Ly Aylesford . . .

19 Jan. 1885: Heard of the death of my cousin, Lord Wilton[119], who has held the title and estates for only three years. He had been slowly dying of cancer for months past. There is not much to be said of him: a quiet, fashionable, gentlemanlike peer, fond of society and of hunting; he rode well, dressed well, and had good manners. He sat some years in the H. of C. but took no active part. He is succeeded by his brother[120]: a great scamp, in former years at least, but he may be mended now; he nearly killed himself with drink, and sold the reversion to the estates; but his father bought it back. He is separated from his wife, whom he might have divorced, so far as her conduct was concerned, but his own character would have enabled her to recriminate, and so they remain married, but separated.

31 July 1885: In the papers, will of Lord Dudley, who has left £1,026,000, thus solving the problem which has long puzzled his acquaintance. Some thought him enormously rich, others believed that he was often in difficulties for money: the foundation for the latter belief being probably an insane reluctance to pay any debt on a bill until compelled, for which he was notorious. He was a large proprietor of iron mines, some of which he worked himself: I know (having been chairman of a railway committee before which the fact came out) that his profits were in one year £300,000; but probably they were balanced by corresponding losses in other years, for no business is more speculative.

Lord Selkirk also leaves over £500,000 personally.

23 Aug.1885: This day is the 400th anniversary of Bosworth - the foundation of our family greatness. It has been well maintained so far, through many vicissitudes: indeed, we never played a more considerable part than in the last generation, and are still fairly prominent in public affairs. As to wealth, we have more of it than at any former time; but that is the result of chance rather than our work. Will either last?[121]

18 Oct. 1885: In the papers yesterday, the death of Ld Strathnairn[122] is announced. He was 82 or 83, and of late had become so infirm that longer life could not be desired for him by his friends. Yet, as sometimes happens to old men, he was desirous of marrying, and I understand that a marriage was nearly arranged between him and the Countess Olga Münster when he died. Of his military abilities there can be no question: they are proved by what he did. And his bodily endurance and energy were equally tested by the Indian campaign in the hot weather of 1858, when he was several times struck down by sunstroke. Yet to a casual observer he would have seemed singularly unfit to bear hardship. His manner was languid, almost effeminate: he spoke with a drawl, as if speaking were an effort: and his marked courtesy was unmixed with the slightest vivacity. In later years, when alone I knew him, he was apt to be tedious, developing his ideas at great length, and not very clearly. He spoke, or tried to speak, often in the Lords, but was quite inaudible[123]. In short, he gained nothing, but rather the reverse, by being seen or heard: a stranger meeting him casually in a drawing room would have taken him for a survival from the days of George IV - a dandy of the old school, with all the acquired peculiarities of that character. But he did his work well: his great reputation as a soldier has been fairly earned, and will survive him.

31 Oct. 1885: All our party left . . . This is the largest gathering that has been held in the house since the visit of the Queen of Holland: 28 to 30 sleeping in the house, which is as much as it can hold. . . . The shooting was good . . . and they danced every night. I have no pleasure personally in these gaieties, but they are part of the necessary business of a house like this, and Lionel, Mary, and Margaret [Cecil] have taken nearly all the trouble off my hands. Lionel especially has made himself very useful[124].

1 Nov. 1885: . . . Gave E. Stanley £25 for the quarter. He leaves for London this evening. . . . Strange talk about E.S. and his mother[125]: who it appears is jealous of the attention paid to her son, as to the future heir of the family, and does not conceal her dislike of his being so much here. But I do not think my brother shares in this feeling, which is peculiar to, and strongly marked in, the Villiers family.

2 Nov. 1885: . . . Death of the Duke of Abercorn[126] . . . at 74. He was known in his younger days chiefly as a fop, being remarkably handsome, and as vain of his looks as any woman . . . But, contrary to general expectation, he made an excellent and popular Lord-Lieutenant: and his dukedom, though a rare honour, and perhaps scarcely earned, was not reckoned a job. He was respected, latterly, in society: and had the good fortune to see one of his sons[127] in high political place before his death.

Death also of Ld Buckinghamshire[128], a parson, remarkable only as being the father of the H. of Lords. He was 92 within a few days . . . seldom seen, and chiefly known as the father of the late Lord Hobart[129], an able though crotchetty man, and of the Anglo-Turkish admiral, Hobart Pasha[130].

30 Nov. 1885: . . . Death of the Duke of Somerset[131], aged 80. He was a typical Whig aristocrat: haughty and sarcastic in manner, able as an administrator, unusually well read, and with some scientific knowledge, a free-thinker in religion, as to which he cared neither to conceal nor to propagate his opinions. He disliked Gladstone, whose ecclesiastical sympathies and somewhat gushing oratory were equally objectionable to him. He had no sympathy for radicals, but accepted them as necessary allies. The Conservatives he stood aloof from, even when in opinion he agreed with their conclusions. He spoke always shortly, but very much to the point, and spared neither friend nor enemy when in a critical mood. He had few intimates, Ld Sherbrooke had as much of his confidence as anyone. To his wife[132], said to be in her youth the most beautiful woman in England, he was devoted to the last. He had two sons, but lost both: and is succeeded by a brother whom no one has ever seen or heard of.

16 Feb. 1886: . . . The death of Lord Cardwell[133]. He had for several years suffered from softening of the brain . . . He was devoted to the memory of Sir R. Peel: in later years a follower of Gladstone, but by no means a warm admirer, if I may judge by the language which I have often heard him use.

9 June 1887: . . . News in papers of the death of Ld Winchilsea[134] (1815–1887): a man now long obscure and nearly a pauper, but in his early days known to everybody in London, both as a rising politician and a member of fashionable society. The latter was his ruin, for racing and love of display soon exhausted his means, never considerable and, though not without wit, and having some literary aptitude, he was incapable of the sustained effort required for distinction in public life. To me he always seemed a poor creature: but I always have been, and am, perhaps unduly prejudiced against that kind of character. He is succeeded by a half-brother, reputed to have both means and sense: so that the family is not destroyed.

12 Sep. 1887: . . . Talk with M. about family affairs. The D. of Bedford[135]in a very odd state: he had a slight seizure, or fit, some weeks ago, from which he entirely recovered, in fact he was not ill more than a few hours: but since that date he has talked much of his approaching death . . . though to other eyes he seems in good health enough. He quarrelled violently with his younger son, Herbrand Russell[136], a year or two ago, the young man never knew why, except that the Duke complained of his manners, and accused him of disrespect: he has since gone out to India, chiefly in order to be out of the way. Now the quarrel is with Tavistock[137], who is equally ignorant of the cause of offence. The tendency seems hereditary, for the Duke's mother, Ly W. Russell, a woman of great cleverness and socially popular, used to go on in just the same way with her children.

25 Sep. 1887: Herbrand Russell wrote to M. wanting to marry a parson's daughter at Simla, but expecting the Duke to object and himself to give way.

28 Sep. 1887: To the surprise of all, we learn that the Duke has assented without asking a single question to H. Russell's proposed marriage[138]: which would be odd in anyone, but is especially so in him, for he treated his son with no kind of consideration or indulgence: in fact, drove him to India by constant fault-finding without intelligible reason. The most likely explanation of his conduct is that he foresees that his son, as a married man, will be more absolutely in his power than before. Perhaps also he thinks that the youth does not really desire the marriage, but has been entangled as happens to young men: and has a malicious satisfaction in refusing to extricate him by putting a veto on the match. If these motives do not operate, his action is hard to understand: for affection is out of the question. Yet I believe the Duke is really interested in the welfare of his family: but whether from temper or from an excessive idea of his rights as a father . . . he has made them all dread and dislike him.

4 Oct. 1887: . . . An unpleasant story about the young Ld Ailesbury[139] (he is only 24) who has been warned off all race courses under the control of the Jockey Club, by a vote of that body. His offence is having arranged fraudulently to lose a race: and there appears no doubt as to the fact. He is a disreputable youth married to a woman of bad character, and unfit for decent society: from which he will now be excluded. But the awkward fact remains that, though he will probably be voted out of every club of which he is a member, he cannot be voted out of the House of Lords, .and the scandal of his possible presence there will remain the same, whether he attends or not. In this matter a practical reform is desired by all parties . . .[140]

9 Oct. 1887: [With Lord and Lady Sefton] . . . Talked of the ruin of so many peers and squires: he thought Lathom[141] in a very bad way, Ld Ellesmere[142] is on the turf, Gerard[143] half-ruined, and likely to be so altogether, Wilton[144] the same: it is a worse prospect for the rural aristocracy than has ever been yet in my time.

23 Jan. 1888: . . . [The news of Lady Sackville's death at Knole was unexpected because of] Ld Sackville[145] having broken off all intercourse with the rest of the family. There is no cause of quarrel, and in fact there is no quarrel, but his state of mind borders on insanity, which shows itself in suspicion of all about him. On one occasion he turned off most of his servants, saying that they were in a plot to poison him. He lives in absolute seclusion, and I can see that M. is uneasy lest his morbid condition, increased by this misfortune, should drive him to do what his elder brother[146] did in 1873.

19 Nov. 1888: Death of Ld Devon[147], aged 81: he was a respectable conservative of the old sort, and strong high churchman: he is succeeded by a son[148] who has squandered all that was in his power, and is said to be thoroughly disreputable.

23 Jan. 1889: All I hear of the Duchess of Manchester[149] . . . is unsatisfactory. She plays high at whist: is always in debt: and, her living being far in excess of her known means, it is believed that the difference is paid by Hartington, her liaison with whom is paraded more openly than is either decorous or prudent.

16 Mar. 1889: Ld Mandeville[150], the D. of Manchester's son, has just gone through the bankruptcy court, owing £100,000, and his debts being due to betting and gambling. An additional reason for keeping clear of the whole lot[151].

28 Mar. 1889: . . . Death of the Duke of Buckingham[152], aged 65 or 66. He seemed in good health, and was busy as usual up to last week: but I hear that he had been suffering from diabetes, and was not expected by his family and intimate friends to live long. His dukedom dies with him, and with it ends the direct line of the great parliamentary family of Temple, though the title passes to female relatives. The Duke gained much credit in early life by his strenuous and uncomplaining exertions to retrieve the family fortunes, ruined by the extravagance of three successive generations. In this he partly succeeded, and in his later years was well off, though poorer probably than most dukes, and far poorer than his predecessors. He was a fairly good business speaker and, though brusque in manner, not unpopular among the Lords. As an administrator he was painstakingly honest and fairly shrewd, a little too much given to lose himself in details, and to undertake duties which his subordinates could have performed better. He was probably more at home in his last appointment (chairman of committees) than in any of the others which he had filled. The least successful part of his public life was his administration of Madras, which by Indian officials was reckoned a failure. As a politician he was moderate, cautious, and not much of a partisan. A certain ill-luck attended him through life. . .

5 Oct. 1892: . . . The talk of the moment is about the D. of Sutherland's[153] will, an extraordinary and discreditable one. He left everything that he could to his second wife, a woman of no character, with whom he had long lived as his mistress before marriage. Her acquisitions are said to be not less than a million. The new duke will be crippled for means: for the estate, immense in area, is not valuable, and can probably never be made so[154]. How is it possible to keep up an aristocracy in England if the leading members of it are ready to sacrifice the permanent interests of their families to personal likes and dislikes? It is said the will is to be disputed, and dark rumours are going about as to the manner of the late Duke's death. The will is said to have been executed only a few days before he died.

Faits Divers

[Though Derby did not set out to compile a record of the gossip of the day, inevitably much found its way into his diary, and some is worth putting into print, even where no pattern exists. Derby had an eye for the quaint, especially where money was concerned, as in the case of Lord Dudley, who died in 1885 leaving £1,026,000 and a reputation for refusing to pay any bill until compelled. He was less interested in the major scandals, dismissing the O'Shea-Parnell liaison as a 'matter of common talk for years past' and merely sympathising with Dilke in his predicament. Glimpses of historic figures interested him, as in the case of Lady Russell, a warm Home Ruler, 'living very poorly' in a 'dirty and ill-kept house' contrasting strangely with the Pembroke Lodge of thirty years before.

Expressions of admiration are rare, though Iddesleigh's death drew the comment 'no man in public life . . . whom I liked better'. More typical was the story told by Derby's doctor, Drage, that the German emperor's disease was venereal in origin. (There is much evidence in the diaries that London society doctors were major sources of indiscreet and unreliable gossip, often about their own patients.) Victorian emotionalism is revealed in the meeting held to support the widow of Matthew Arnold (the poet had left only £10,000), with Lord Coleridge in the chair weeping copiously. Another author, Wilkie Collins, died aged 'only about 65, but a confirmed opium-eater'.

Though economics rarely intrudes, Derby found his Bury agent presciently worrying about cheap Asian competition: 'a friend of his was setting up a mill in Japan which would be one of the largest in the world'. In the conflict between political economy and romantic conservatism, Derby as always knew where he stood, dissuading Carnarvon from a project for building artisan housing on the sites of disused London prisons. As for subversion, Pilkington of St Helens, the glass magnate, said that emissaries of the American Knights of Labor were busy in Lancashire, but that Scotland Yard was watching them.

The great millowners, though still less wealthy than the landlords, left appreciable amounts. Hugh Mason, the arch-puritan tyrant of Ashton, and an old friend of Derby's, left £290,000, while Philips, father-in-law of Sir G.O. Trevelyan, left landed estates and £428,000 to his children, of which all but £200,000 went to the family of the radical baronet. Their lives did not much interest Derby, perhaps because they were free from disasters. Among the few middle class casualties mentioned were Gurney, once Derby's fellow-member for King's Lynn, who had lived in obscurity since the Overend and Gurney crash of 1866, and whose wife had run away with a servant: Col. Maude, former consul-general at Warsaw, now an applicant for help, 'a good officer, and not a bad consul: but an incurable gambler, and consequently always in money troubles': J.K. Cross, a promising junior minister, who hanged himself at 54: and Lord Cross, the Disraelian social reformer, who lost his eldest son from typhoid in 1892, this being the second loss of the kind suffered by him. There is much comment on the breakdown and death of Lord Dalhousie, Gladstone's Scottish secretary in 1886, who never really recovered from the strain, and during the year before his death made over the whole management of his estates to his relative and political opponent Camperdown. More cheerfully, Malmesbury had made £3,000 from his indiscreet memoirs, published four years after his second marriage in 1880, while Lord Winmarleigh, the Nestor of Lancashire conservatism, recalled in 1887, the jubilee of 1810, celebrated in his village by the baiting of a bull and two bears.

Two curiosities of parentage in which Derby seems to have believed concerned diplomatists. Sir W. White, ambassador at Constantinople, was allegedly a Pole and a natural son of the Czartoryski family, and therefore anti-Russian: while Sir A. Malet, a 'dull official' who died in 1886, owed his success to his wife, widely believed to be Brougham's natural daughter. Straws in the wind the above no doubt are; in many cases they are almost certainly false, their sole significance lying in the fact that they were being said, and considered worth noting by Derby.]

29 Jan. 1884: Saw Mr. Escott, editor of the *Fortnightly Review*, who wanted a place in Mauritius for his brother[155].

24 May 1884: Bought from the Duchess of Marlborough the star and other garter decorations of the late Duke, for £882, the price which he had given. They have been valued and the price declared not excessive.

27 Aug. 1885: A Mr. McNeil writes to ask me to be a director of the Manchester ship canal co. - this I shall decline in the plainest terms. It is a doubtful speculation at best, and intensely unpopular in Liverpool. Besides, great peers and men engaged in public affairs ought to keep out of directorates.

Odd letter from a Mrs. Ford who lives at the East End, and applies to me in distress, having as she says given away all she had, and pledged her furniture in order to assist the working people of her neighbourhood. I know her, and do not doubt the story. I sent her help.

4 Nov. 1885: A labourer was charged with an unnatural offence against a cow. The case was not absolutely clear, and I persuaded the jury to acquit him.

2 Dec. 1885 (Wednesday): . . . Read a life of Fawcett, by Leslie Stephen: it is not well done, perhaps could hardly be; for even in these days, when reticence is not our habit, Fawcett's very freespoken opinions on men and things could not decently be published within a year or two of his death. And apart from these his biography has only one interest, the history of his blindness and of his struggle against it. To me looking back it is clear that his infirmity was a political advantage to him rather than the reverse: it excited sympathy, and the courage with which he fought against it created a certain admiration: and the existence of these feelings made the H. of C. tolerant of much which in any one else they would have disliked: the hard, uncompromising, and somewhat dictatorial style of speaking which was natural to him: and of which he never got rid entirely. I am inclined to think that he died at the right time for his fame: having reached as high a position as he was likely to attain to: and having escaped the disappointment of continued exclusion from the cabinet: to which the latter-day Liberals would have been ill disposed to admit him.

26 Dec. 1885: Among my letters this morning was one from a lady now keeping a school, which contained the modest request that I will make good to her the loss of £900 odd, which she has been persuaded to invest in South American securities and has thus parted with. She has never seen me, has no claim of any sort, but thinks I cannot refuse her so small a favour. I wish I now I had kept all the eccentric and wildly unreasonable applications which I receive: they would contribute to the history of human oddities.

[The unemployed riots in the West End in February 1886 gave Derby no cause for alarm. He saw 'no trace of method and design' in 'the mischief done' and did not believe 'either destruction or plunder were intended by the leaders . . . They could not do enough in that line to intimidate: and mere irritation of the upper and middle classes could not help them'[156]. He promised £100 to the Mansion House relief fund[157], but noted that, contrary to common opinion, the riots had checked gifts, which had reached only £27,000. 'But for the alarm and anger produced in the middle class, it would have been £100,000 before now.'[158] The average temperature in February 1886, he noted, had been 'the lowest known in this generation'[159]. When agitation broke out in Liverpool for a 25% cut in Derby's ground rents, he wrote without anxiety 'but to this I shall make no concession'[160], being much too absorbed by parliament to concern himself about revolutionary symptoms.]

3 Apr. 1886: The main cause of our present difficulties is the increase of population, 300,000 a year, for which we have not employment: unless we could find means of dealing with that, all other expedients are only temporary. This is true and sound - the old Malthusian doctrine . . . No politician ventures to say as much in public, and if any did so, they would probably get a rough reception.

19 Jan. 1887: . . . Letter from Ly S.[161], who tells me among other matters that R. Churchill is taking steps to get rid of his wife, whom he accuses of playing tricks with four men! A pleasant disclosure of manners in that set.

20 Jan. 1887: Looked over a mem. relating to the action of F.O. in 1875, when a fresh war between France & Germany was expected, & we intervened to make up the quarrel. Waddington while here asked me for a record of what we had done, he having been minister at the time. Sanderson arranged to have the papers looked over, and a mem. made from them by one of the clerks in the Librarian's department, I paying for the extra work. – I sent £10, & suggested corrections in the M.S. which I am to revise with Sanderson.

18 Mar. 1887: . . . [Talking with Granville about Spencer Walpole's projected biography of Lord John Russell] I discovered from his talk that he had no great respect or liking for his former chief: for, when I said something about Lord John having been always a strong party man, he answered: 'Scarcely that: he was always a strong Russellite': and went on to comment on his factious proceedings about the time of the Crimean War. He accused Ly Russell of being the instigator of these, saying that she always, and purposely, kept him out of the way of his old friends, that her influence might not be shaken.

25 Jan. 1887: . . . Read, with much interest, a volume just published called *The Service of Man* by Cotter Morrison, whom I knew as a writer, but was not aware that he was one of the leading lights of the Positivist sect. It is neither more nor less than the plan of a new religion without prospect of future rewards or punishments, but in which service rendered to humanity is regarded as the sole end of existence. The weak point of his case in my judgment is that he can give no reason why anyone should adopt this religion . . . But he seems to rely on the power of habit and certainly it is conceivable that in two or three generations a race of men might be developed in whom devotion to the community of which they are members should be the strongest feeling, having in fact become something like an instinct. The best part of his essay is an attack on the orthodox doctrine of repentance, by which a man who has led a disreputable and mischievous life, by a momentary change of feeling perhaps dictated by fear, is placed on the same footing as one who has laboured all his life for what he thought right and true. The author contends, I think truly, that this theory, if really accepted, would be destructive to all morality. This to me is no new speculation, for it used to puzzle me when little more than a boy.

10 Apr. 1887: Ly Abercromby[162] tells me that the Queen has established a new way of doing business: Ponsonby is employed as before in public matters, but whenever her personal wishes are concerned, and when she thinks that Ponsonby might not approve, or be zealous in the cause, Ly Ely[163] is employed to communicate with ministers: family matters are generally dealt with in this way, and negotiations affecting the D. of Connaught's position have been so carried on with Cross. It was with a view to these that Cross was retained by the Queen's strongly expressed wish at the India Office: Salisbury meant to get rid of him, but would not press for his removal at the risk of giving offence.

9 Aug. 1887: . . . Letter from E.L. Long, in which she describes her sister as dying. . . . It is the breaking of a very old tie. My cousin Augusta Dartrey and I became acquainted in 1844, when I was her guest at Dartrey: she 21, I 18: from that date a friendship and correspondence[164] began, which has never been intermitted, though of late years we had seen less of one another. There is no other person living with whom I have been for so long on terms of intimacy. . . . Her beauty in early life was remarkable, and traces of it remained to the last. Her kindness and warmth of heart made her popular everywhere . . . indeed I believe the war of classes in Ireland . . . aggravated her disease by weighing constantly on her mind.

9 Sep. 1887: The Trades Unions held their annual Congress, and passed some curious resolutions . . . But the Trades Unions do not have the influence they had a generation ago, and indeed many of them are said to be nearly or quite insolvent.

22 Sep. 1887: . . . In afternoon, a dinner was given to the labourers on the estate, as last year: about 130 came . . . I made them a short speech of welcome.

1 Dec. 1887: . . . Saw Sheffield, the secretary and intimate friend of Lord Lyons, who thinks him dying, and believes that he has been much troubled by the persistent efforts of the Norfolk family to convert him. They did not succeed while he was well - though it is admitted that he was more than once in a hesitating state of mind - but in his nearly unconscious condition it has been easy for them to call in a priest and have him 'received': which has been done.

5 Dec. 1887: . . . Death of Ld Lyons, which was not unexpected, and is so far well, that his recovery could never have been more than partial. Indeed had his health been restored to some extent, he had little to live for. No home, nor wife nor child, no sport or amusement nor, as far as I know, much taste for reading. Diplomatic business was both his work and pleasure and I remember that in the autumn he said to Ly D.: 'I know I shall be unhappy when I retire, but it is better for me.' He had held the French embassy longer than any of his predecessors, as far as I am aware: and no man ever filled a diplomatic post more ably. Having no political passions or prejudices, his naturally sound judgment was quite unbiased: he was on equally good terms with imperialists and republicans, and I never traced in his letters a preference for either over the other. He could not be angry or impatient: it was not in his nature. Neither his conversation nor his writing were brilliant: he never tried at saying a good thing: but what he said was always worth hearing, and remembering, and his letters, though colourless, and avoiding detail, left a clear impression of general results. His official correspondence, if ever published, will be useful as material for history: and we shall never have a representative who can be more thoroughly relied on as safe.

31 Dec. 1887: Morier left us . . . He has not been a social success here: his interminable monologue wearies everybody and, though he has much to say, and is really worth hearing, he is so long in saying it, and so apt to mix egotistical comments with remarks on public affairs, that he becomes a bore. He is best when alone with one interlocutor, for if you listen patiently you are sure to carry away something worth remembering. Nothing less than his remarkable industry, energy, and acquired knowledge would have given him diplomatic distinction in spite of his absolute want of tact. I respect, and in some ways admire him; but I am never sorry when he goes away: nor as far as I have seen, is anyone[165].

15 February 1888: . . . Mr. Malcolm MacColl, who has made himself conspicuous as a hot defender of the eastern Christians, was put up for the Athenaeum, and had 57 blackballs, a number supposed never to have been reached before[166].

11 Apr. 1888: . . . Mr. Lushington, the intimate friend and executor of Lear the artist, sent me a few days ago a large parcel of drawings which he had reason to believe, from some letter or memorandum left by him, that Lear intended to bequeath to me[167].

30 Apr. 1888: Some talk with Chamberlain about his American mission. He has no hope that his treaty will pass the Senate, but is sanguine of its being only postponed, not rejected. He told an amusing story of how he was pestered by the interviewers, who in America are apt to report purely imaginary conversations and, if you refuse to see them, ascribe to you every possible absurdity: to avoid being made author of speeches which he never delivered, he arranged to see all who applied, but jointly, and in another's presence: thus they were made to be a check on each other: an ingenious device which amused the American public.

3 May 1888: . . . Dined with Froude, meeting Chamberlain and Sir H. de Villiers from the Cape. Much interesting discussion. Chamberlain has been in communication with the missionary agent, Mackenzie, and seems to have adopted his views, which are imperial and anti-Dutch. At least he argued in that sense, admitting that he had till now taken the other side. Froude and De Villiers opposed him, and the former seemed ill pleased, for no doubt when he asked C. to meet the Dutchman he expected entire agreement.

However, the conversation was friendly throughout, and C. may not have meant all that he said, or seemed to imply, in the course of an argument.

16 May 1888: . . . Borthwick gave me an amusing account of the Primrose League, of which he is one of the founders: his way of talking would have astonished the believers in it and him, but would not be fair to set down.

6 Nov. 1888: . . . [Gladstone's speech at Birmingham] laid great stress on the principle of one man, one vote - as to which I think he must have forgotten that it was he more than anyone else who objected to its introduction into the Reform Bill of 1884.

23 Nov. 1888: . . . Count Münster[168] produced a curious object, brought from Paris: a common copper coin . . . with the outer edge removed, and replaced by a new one, bearing the superscription, 'Boulanger, Empereur'. The head in the centre . . . had in some way been retouched to produce a likeness of Boulanger. He declares that these coins are largely circulated in Paris, with a view to familiarise the public mind with the notion of an imperial candidature.

21 Dec. 1888: . . . Speech by Salisbury at Scarborough, but nothing in it specially new except that he again announces his adhesion to the principle of giving women votes - the policy of the clerical party, and for the purposes of that party a sound one.

14 Feb. 1889: . . . I notice it as a special and unexpected piece of good luck that, whereas a few years ago we fully expected to be driven out of our old home by the increase of chemical vapours, the nuisance caused by these has almost entirely ceased[169].

6 Mar. 1889: [Lawson of the *Daily Telegraph*] talked of R. Churchill, who has lately allied himself with one North, a speculator enormously rich, but with few respectable acquaintances: the bargain between them apparently being that he should give North a social position, and North help him with money: for he is ruined. He [Lawson] did not think Churchill would ever come to the top again.

17 Mar. 1889: . . . My trouble will be, to induce me to interest myself in the preservation of my own life sufficiently to induce me to take precautions. I can feel no anxiety, and scarcely no concern on the subject: and what I do feel is [more] from an abstract dislike of failure and mismanagement than because continued existence seems desirable.

23 Mar. 1889: Hear with regret of the death of Schouvaloff, Russian ambassador here in 1876-78, of whom I saw much during that disturbed and anxious time. He was, I think, as truthful as his instructions allowed him to be: sincerely desirous of peace, which he helped to maintain at the cost of his own popularity in Russia, and a pleasant talker, though rather more given to wine than is approved in our sober time, and sometimes showing the effects of it. For M. he had a real attachment, which did not cease when he left England.

5 May 1889: . . .Called on Ly Abercromby: pleasant talk and sat long. She tells me of a journal regularly kept during her life at court, and which she sometimes wishes to destroy, lest it should fall into bad hands. I deprecated the destruction, and advised her to go over it again, selecting what is likely to be of interest, and putting the extracts in a shape for possible future publication[170]. The advice is good, but I could not but feel while giving it that I should be far too indolent to act upon it myself. She talked a good deal of the Queen, whom she had known intimately for many years: said that Ponsonby is now her adviser in everything and that she acts on his advice: spoke of the extraordinary influence that her servant Brown had over her for several years, and of her enjoyment of his conversation, though he was an illiterate, and at the utmost only a half-educated man. She had become thoroughly afraid of him towards the end of his life: for he did not care what he said, especially towards the last when he had taken much to whisky: his death shocked her, but was felt on the whole as a relief. It was a strange friendship, for she confided in him entirely.

15 May 1889: Talk with Ld Rothschild about Randolph Churchill, who is an intimate friend of his, and whom he declares to be the best debater in the H. of C. He thinks C.'s resignation of office was a freak of temper: but C. himself always defends it as a simple miscalculation, saying that he did not know that Salisbury had 'the king up his sleeve', in other words that he was ready to fill up the vacancy by appointing Goschen.

17 May 1889: . . . Dined with the Gladstones, a very small party, the only guests being Ld Lyttelton, Sir J. Millais, Ld De Vesci, and Ly F. Cavendish. The old man full of spirits and animation, showing no sign of age except a slight increase of deafness. His conversation was varied, and very discursive: of course no reference was made to current politics. The house where he now lives is a small one, looking over the parade ground of the Wellington barracks. Mrs. G. is much aged, and both have felt the illness of their eldest son, which is serious, though not immediately dangerous. It seems to be of a paralytic nature, though he is little more than fifty years of age, if so much.

27 May 1889: . . . I see no sign of agitation, nor any cause for it: the country being fairly prosperous, trade reviving, and the Irish question having become a mere weariness to all parties.

6 June 1889: . . . I have not noted my interview with Sir Hercules Robinson on Monday. The state of things which he describes is peculiar. He has been eight years at the Cape, is popular with all parties., and professes to be willing to go on serving there if he can obtain from the Col. Off. a promise of support in his policy. This it appears he cannot induce the Cabinet to give him: although (which is the odd part of the story) both Ld Knutsford and Herbert say that they entirely agree with him. His enemies are a body calling itself the South African committee, to which Chamberlain seems to have given his name and support: and probably it is fear of offending Chamberlain that has caused the difficulty. Sir H. has resigned: and the post has been offered unsuccessfully to eight or ten persons.

10 June 1889: . . . Talk yesterday with Sanderson about Sir H. Robinson, whom he thinks wrong, and says that opinion in Downing St. is against him, not on account of the policy which he supports, but because he had no right to lay down a programme of his own, and announce that if it were not accepted at home he would not continue to serve. Technically and in point of form, Downing Street is right: but I take the truth to be that Sir H. does not care to serve any longer: had in fact rather retire than not, if he can do it honourably and with a certain *éclat*: and he might himself add that he is so far and has been so long committed to the line of policy which he supports that it would be difficult for him to act on any other as he would be notoriously doing so against his own judgment.

26 June 1889: . . . There came in together at 5.00 p.m. to tea, Mr. Gladstone, Ly Jersey, Mary G. and Galloway separately, and the D. of Argyll (I mean that they were all in the room at the one time: they came not expecting to meet one another). As the Duke and Mr. Gladstone were at one moment on cool political terms, from political reasons, M. was uneasy at the meeting: but they seemed friendly enough. Gladstone was full of a new invention in printing - a kind of typewriter - which he said would revolutionise literature by cheapening books, to an extent which we could not now foresee: he talked about this in a vehement excited tone, which rather startled his audience.

8 Sep. 1889: . . . [Sanderson] told me a story of Ld Granville, how that, in a doubtful case, three alternative drafts had been prepared and sent up for his approval. They came down again with his initial affixed to all three . . . Sir Henry Elliot talked of his brother-in-law Lord Russell doing business in a strange unmethodical fashion - announcing important decisions in private letters of which he would keep no copy . . .

20 Oct. 1889: Balfour left us for London. I had some talk with him on Irish affairs. He is anxious to bring in and pass a land purchase bill on a scheme of his own, which he has not yet explained to his colleagues. He is reasonably anxious to do this before anything important is done in the way of local self-government, on the ground that when once the tenants are possessed of the soil there will be no inducement to job and waste the money raised by rates, which there must be so long as the rates are paid by landowners who are often Englishmen, and often unpopular. He tells me that one of the chief difficulties in the way of land sales arises from the number of owners who, if they were to sell, would receive absolutely nothing. All the price would go to pay off mortgages or other charges, and they would be left with nothing, whereas now they have at least a house over their heads, and game and garden produce to live upon.

29 Oct. 1889: . . . Granville talked about Gladstone: we touched on the burning question: he assured me that G. had not formed any plan of yielding to the Irish demand till just before he announced it: he had been uneasy on the subject for 13 or 14 years, but that was all: only at the moment he felt the impossibility of going on as before. This is no doubt the truth: but is it the whole truth?

1 Dec. 1889: . . . Froude had yesterday a singular conversation with M. [Lady Derby]. He is engaged in collecting materials for a biographical sketch of Ld Beaconsfield[171], and in so doing consulted Ld Rothschild, who promised him information, and wished to guarantee the financial success of the book, or at least the absence of loss upon it, if Froude would write in accordance with his (Ld R.'s) views. This Froude declined, saying that he had always had a free hand in dealing with his subjects, and would not write on any other terms. They then talked of the eastern question of 1877–78: and Ld R. assured Froude that he had known thoroughly well the intentions of Ld Beaconsfield during the crisis: that he (Ld B.) had determined in favour of war: that it was necessary to his policy: that the Queen pressed him on (this I know to be true): and that he was checked only by the opposition which he met with both in and out of the Cabinet. This revelation is curious, and valuable: but I wish I could get it more directly from Ld Rothschild.

3 Dec. 1889: . . . Gladstone has delivered a long and rather discursive speech at Manchester: in the course of which he hinted at a new anti-Turkish agitation, but in vague terms: condemned, with some justice, the union of the foreign office and premiership in one hand: censured the sugar convention, of which he spoke very much as I did, as not likely to come to any result: went into electoral statistics and indulged in promises of early victory: and then plunged into a long catalogue of social reforms, the leading idea in which seemed to be that the power of county councils should be almost indefinitely extended: that they should have enlarged powers of taxation, the control of schools, liquor laws, etc. He avoided giving pledges of an embarrassing kind, but spoke so as to create an impression that he is personally in favour of all the changes he alludes to. He kept clear, however, of the eight hours bill and of all schemes for the legislative regulation of labour.

10 Dec. 1889: . . . Froude called . . . He told M. and me that he was inclined to abandon his original plan of writing a sketch of Disraeli's entire political life, and instead to undertake the editing of D.'s correspondence with Mrs. Willyams, which is in the possession of Ld Rothschild, and which Ld R. is willing to place in his hands. . . . This project seemed to both of us far preferable to his original design, and we encouraged it warmly[172].

22 Dec. 1889: . . . With Lecky . . . Some conversation about Ireland . . . he admits that the 'English garrison' had disqualified themselves for that position by reckless extravagance, being in fact three-quarters ruined before bad times came . . . He holds that Mitchel's Irish history has had more effect on the popular mind than any other work - it is circulated everywhere at a low price and is to be found in most farmhouses and cottages. It is of course written in the most bitter anti-English spirit.

10 Mar. 1890: . . . Dined Grillions, the first time this year: meeting Gladstone, Kimberley, Boehm [the sculptor],Fortescue, Norton, A. Russell, Col. Saunderson, etc. I was in the chair: Gladstone sat next me. He talked very freely on many subjects, though in a hoarse voice: when condoled with on having a cold, he said: 'It is not that: the cause lies deeper: but happily I can always find my voice again when I have occasion for it.' Talking to me he entered on the Irish question, which I should have left alone: praised a speech just made by Sexton as a wonderful performance: told me that the Irish members intended to prove that the government had a hand in getting up the *Times*'s case, and that the subject would be enquired into: and said that if the next parliament gave him a majority the present proceedings would be expunged. I ventured to answer that in that event he would have enough to do with the present and the future, without going back on the past: to which he said that what he proposed would give an impetus to the movement. He earnestly hoped the Lords would have nothing to do with the proceedings of the Commission. In general conversation he talked about the age of trees, English words, the preservation of books, and many other matters: speaking with great animation, though his voice was weak and husky.

5 May 1890: . . . A great meeting was held yesterday in Hyde Park, perhaps one of the largest ever known: the ostensible object being to demonstrate in favour of a limitation of the hours of labour to eight . . . The number was variously estimated from 100,000 to 300,000, including lookers-on. This is the first time a movement in favour of the working class has displayed itself all over Europe simultaneously, and it is an important sign of the times, good in so far as it tends to international peace, dangerous if taken as an indication of social revolt . . .

1 June 1890: . . . Dinners and gatherings in honour of Stanley Africanus continue, and the public mind is more excited on African subjects than at any time in my recollection. The idea of the people seems to be that there are in Africa mines of wealth to be had for the trouble of opening them: and a vast population eager to trade with Europe if it only gets the chance. I doubt the reality of these visions: I doubt whether central Africa will be civilised, or pay the expense of opening it up: but it is good that the popular imagination should have something to amuse itself with, and this subject is at least a safe and harmless one to play with[173].

7 June 1890: . . . Talk with Chamberlain last night: he tells me that government has in contemplation a scheme for carrying on bills from one session to another, so that they may be taken up after a prorogation at the stage they have reached, instead of having, as now, to bring them in again as if they were new. This is a change desirable in itself, and which will act as a check on merely obstructive criticism: it will not, however, be popular in all quarters: for many M.P.s are glad to see many bills lost for want of time which they are afraid to vote against. I remember that nearly thirty years ago my father proposed this very change, but found parliamentary feeling strong against it.

14 July 1890: . . . The chief public interest of last week has been created by strikes - the police and the postmen both offering to come out. The new head of the police, Sir E. Bradford, showed firmness and sense, dismissing at once the men who refused to obey orders, and in two days the trouble was over. The postmen never had a chance, for their work can be done by any able-bodied man with little training. There can be no doubt but that the simultaneous movement was the result of an organised socialist movement, which was expected and intended to spread more widely. The exhibition of discontent (it scarcely reached the importance of a mutiny) by some of the Guards was soon over, and the men are generally admitted to have good grounds of complaint.

21 July 1890: . . . In youth I never expected to reach old age: partly from the weak constitutions of both my father and mother - which was a reasonable inference - partly from a certain want of elasticity and physical energy in myself, and frequent illnesses when young. Now, I scarcely know what to think, and indeed am more indifferent on the subject than I should have once thought possible. My one strong wish is not to outlive either my intellect or my wife.

14 Sep. 1890: . . . My sister writes to Ly D. that her eldest son Charles[174] cannot live more than a few weeks. He was always weak in health, and has destroyed his chances of life, which were never good, by drinking and perhaps other unwise pursuits. I tried to make something of him by employing him as an extra private secretary, but he was absolutely useless and unteachable. He is not to be regretted but I cannot forget the strange fascination which as a child he exercised over my father[175] in the years 1865-70. I thought then, and have thought since, that there was something not quite right about his head.

13 Oct. 1890: Received this morning a very odd application: it is from a lady who gives an assumed name, and the local post office for an address: she states that she is of an old county family, is not in want or distress, but has never any money to spare: will I give her £50 that she may for once know the pleasure of being able to spend it as she likes, without reproaching herself for not having saved it instead?

31 Oct. 1890: . . . [Granville] talks of Gladstone's innumerable articles in magazines from a point of view which was new to me: saying that Mr G. makes £1,500 a year by his pen, and that the money is much needed. I knew that editors were ready to pay fancy prices for all that he writes, but had not thought of him as writing for money . . .

27 Nov. 1890: . . . Biddulph called, and talked of the [Baring] crisis, which he said had not affected the west-end banks. . . . He said that Northbrook had put £250,000 into the new company for the honour of the family. He said Ld Revelstoke had put by nothing and settled nothing in trust: his share of the profits used to be about £75,000 a year.

28 Nov. 1890: In the papers, Ld Connemara[176] has just had a sentence of divorce pronounced against him, and in favour of his wife, on the ground of cruelty and adultery. The cruelty was in communicating to her a certain complaint caught in loose company, a good many years ago, but she declares that till lately she did not know the cause of her illness. Bourke was a real Irishman – good-natured, careless, and muddle-headed, not an efficient subordinate, nor a good speaker: at Madras he was popular, genial, and plausible. I know no man whom I should have less suspected of a cruel disposition: and probably there were faults on both sides, for his wife[177] thought much of herself as a daughter of Ld Dalhousie, and an heiress, and the marriage was notoriously one of interest on his side more than of liking.

6 Dec. 1890: Went at 12.00 to Devonshire House: met there Hartington, Chamberlain, H. James, Ld Stalbridge, and two or three more: we talked for an hour, and Chamberlain, backed by James, expressed a strong wish for a manifesto to be issued dealing with the present [Parnell divorce] crisis. I did not absolutely object, but thought we had better first see how the negociations ended, adding that our present position seemed to me so good that we could hardly improve, and might run some risk of spoiling it. Hartington was rather of the same mind, but yielded to the others. Chamberlain surprised me by talking as if Home Rule were already dead, and the only question to his mind was what move Gladstone would make, and what programme he would take up with instead. I thought Home Rule would take a good deal more killing, and said so, but did not persist, as it is useless and invidious to discourage sanguine people. We agreed to meet again on Monday.

12 Dec. 1890: I went to Abingdon St., happily for the last time, to attend the Markets Commission. We have sat ever since July '87, and collected, I suppose, as large a mass of evidence as ever was brought together on any subject. The report is not unanimous, but that matters little, for parliament will have before it the argument on both sides, and can judge for itself. Lord Balfour said a few civil words as to my conduct of the enquiry, which were very cordially received. For my part, I am weary of the subject, and glad to have done it, though my colleagues have been civil and friendly., and we have had no unpleasantness.

3 Feb. 1891: Heard a good deal about the high play of the P. of Wales and his friends at country houses, at one of which he came away a winner of £1,300, and at another of £1,700: how he tries to induce young men to play, and is angry when they will not: all probably exaggerated by report but there is enough in it to destroy his popularity if it came to be generally known, and of course it must be. It is added, which if true is worst of all, that he resents refusals to play when, as often happens, they tell him they cannot afford it[178].

14 Mar. 1891: Talk with Hartington, who has accepted the chairmanship of the Labour Commission. I agreed to serve upon it[179]. We discussed the composition, which is not finally settled, and its general scope[180]. Hartington plainly sees, as I do, that one main object in appointing this commission is to gain time, and avoid the necessity of acting on the dangerous eight hours question until after the general election. But he also thinks, and I agree, that there is an advantage in compelling the agitators to formulate their demands, and to give reasons for them. On an enquiry such as this there is no room for declamation in which their strength lies: they must define what they want, and deal with the obvious objections in their way: which is less easy than haranguing on platforms.

1 July 1891: . . . Corrected for Hansard my speech of Friday last. Since a reporter was put on the floor of the House, as he is now, this correcting of proofs has ceased to be a trouble. Formerly I had to rewrite half my speeches, under penalty of having nonsense ascribed to me in the permanent record.

11 Oct. 1891: . . . Much talk with Pender . . . about Baron Hirsch, whose influence over the P. of Wales was a puzzle to society, since he is neither a gentleman, nor reputed altogether honest. It seems one Mackenzie, a Scotch capitalist, had lent the Prince £250,000, first and last, which the latter did not expect to be called upon to pay: but, Mackenzie dying, his trustees were obliged to call in the debt. This caused confusion at Marlborough House, and Hirsch seized the opportunity to pay off the debt, make the Prince his debtor, and so secure for himself a social position.

23 Apr. 1892: . . . Received from London a pamphlet[181] written by Gladstone against female suffrage: it is temperate in style, as it had to be, since most of its opponents are among his supporters: and forcible, as it seems to me, in argument. His strongest point is that the right to elect carries with it the corresponding right to be elected: or at least that where one is granted the other must follow: that if women vote for M.P.s they must sit in parliament: and farther that, if they do so, they cannot be put under the special disqualification of being excluded from executive office: which at present nobody desires they should hold. The plea is ingenious and, though not absolutely new, I have never before seen it so clearly and strongly urged. Gladstone's motive, of course, is fear of dividing the party: but he does not often express his meaning with so little ambiguity.

17 May 1892: . . . At teatime Sir R. Morier, Sir H. Pender, and last, Gladstone came to call on Ly D. The other two went away, and Gladstone sat with her: after a little while I left them together. The great man is certainly much aged: he is partly deaf, and his voice in conversation is that of an old man: he moved too with some difficulty. But there was no diminution of energy in his talk. He seemed quite excited about the famine in Russia, and disappointed that the English subscription for its relief had not been larger. Something led him to talk about agricultural depression in Wales, and he threw out an ominous hint that there, as in Ireland, the sympathy between landlord and tenant was imperfect. Does this foretell a Welsh land bill?

28 June 1892: . . . While at Chester, somebody, an old woman as is supposed, threw a gingerbread nut at Gladstone, and hit him in the eye, causing some pain and temporary injury. At first great attempts were made to pass this off as a deliberate outrage on an elder statesman: but the nature of the missile, and position of the thrower, made the pretence of indignation impossible to maintain. If the aggressor had been a man, and the weapon used a stone, twenty elections might have been turned in favour of the Home Rule party. (Later enquiry showed that the woman was an enthusiastic Home Ruler, and a drunkard well known to the police: which destroyed her value for political purposes.)

1 July 1892: . . . It is a sign of the division which began long ago between the social and political world that, although the elections are on, and all concerned in them are engaged in canvassing, balls and parties in London are as much frequented as ever. Formerly 'the season' would have closed with the session. Now they seem to have nothing to do with one another.

7 Jan. 1893: I have from Sanderson a grateful letter in which he recapitulates all I have done for him in enabling him to support his family through a time of trouble. What he says is true, but there is a good deal to say on the other side. With a less energetic and devoted secretary my life at F.O. would have been less successful than on the whole it was.

18 Jan. 1893: . . . A singular circumstance happened to me this morning early. Being asleep between 5.00 and 7.00, I dreamt that a friend had come to me (I suppose at Cambridge) and asked help to finish a copy of English verses which he had to send in, and with which as he had written them, he was not satisfied. This I did for him, composing eight lines which since waking I have set down. They are not good, but correct both as to sense and metre. . . . The whole composition must have taken place during sleep.

28 Feb. 1893: . . . Having received from the bookseller a copy of a new translation of Rabelais, I tried for the first time to read a little of that famous satire, but soon gave it up, disgusted with the dirty buffoonery, and shall never open the book again[182].

A View of Anthony Trollope

Anthony Trollope was a preacher as well as a story teller. He preached the practical virtues: common sense, balance, sanity, manliness, steady work in the daily tasks of life. How far this laureate of normality practised what he preached has never been easy to see, for Trollope made himself invisible with some success. His surviving published *Letters* are as dull and unrevealing as they are thin; he left no arrangement for a *Life and Times* on the standard Victorian model; and the picture he gives of himself in his *Autobiography*, by stressing certain sides of his character so skilfully, may fail to alert us to others. Any crumbs of evidence are welcome which support with hard fact Escott's impression that 'Throughout life it was Trollope's tendency to ponder a petty vexation or trivial crossing of his own will till it became a grievance'[183]. It is a theme of Escott's sympathetic and well informed study that Trollope was a difficult, even an irascible, person, with a taste for working up a conflict, and a low point of combustion.

Edward Henry Stanley, fifteenth Earl of Derby (1826–1893), whose comments on Trollope are cited below, had little social contact with Trollope. They were brought together by their common membership of the committee of the Royal Literary Fund, a working body which met quite frequently to decide on distributions to needy writers and their families. Derby was president of the Fund from 1875, and took a full part in its work even when in office, almost up to his death. It is hard to say that Trollope had Derby in mind when he wrote of Plantagenet Palliser. It is equally hard to think of a leading politician of the period when the Palliser novels were being written, more resembling Palliser than the fifteenth Earl of Derby: studious, not a party man, with an ambitious wife, the rising hope of moderate opinion, driven by a sense of responsibility quite alien to his father's generation, all of a piece in his personal and public character, yet not aiming at the democratic appeal of a Gladstone. Hence the irony of Derby's strictures on Trollope's middle class bumptiousness: they represent the views if not of Palliser at least of a man uncommonly like him.

Derby won some of his large fund of credit among studious men by his work on the Literary Fund Committee. Lecky, a fellow-member of the Committee for many years, observed how far Derby was from treating his presidential position as a sinecure: 'The regularity of his attendance, the constant attention he paid to every detail of the charity, the infinite pains which he would bestow upon obscure cases of distress, marked him out as a model president, and many of those whom our rules did not allow us to help were assisted by his bounty. He contributed with a large but discriminating generosity to many causes that were conspicuous in the eyes of the world, but his special bias was towards unostentatious and unobserved benevolence, and crowds of obscure men in obscure positions were assisted by him.[184]

11 Jan. 1879: . . . Letter from Dr. Smith[185], received yesterday afternoon, and answered at once, saying that the Lit.[erary] Fund Committee propose to select as chairman for their dinner in May the young Prince Imperial[186]! I express my objection to the choice, on the grounds (1) That it is not advisable, if it can be helped, to select a foreign prince to take the chair at the dinner of an English charity, (2) That the young Prince has no personal distinction, no literary connection, and no claim of any kind on literary men, (3) that his selection is quite sure to be made use of by the anti-republican party in France, backed by a large section of English 'society', as a demonstration in favour of Imperialism, which is exactly what we wish to avoid. - I don't know whether my letter will have any effect, but I put the matter plainly and strongly.

20 Jan. 1879: . . . Received a letter[187] from Trollope the novelist, saying that in consequence of something that has passed at the last two meetings of the Lit. Fund he feels himself obliged to resign his place in the committee. Not knowing what the grievance is, nor having heard of any dispute, I write in general terms, deprecating haste, and asking Mr. T. to tell me what was the matter, so that we might see whether explanations would not set all straight. Wrote also to Dr. Smith to ask what has passed.

22 Jan. 1879: . . . Letter from Dr. Smith, surprised to hear of Trollope's intended resignation, saying that there had been no unpleasantness, though some difference of opinion, at the two meetings: so that I am at a loss to conjecture the cause.

23 Jan. 1879: . . . Received from Trollope a letter explaining what he had objected to in the proceedings of the Lit. Fund: which his explanation does not make very clear: nor do I understand why he wishes my letter to Dr. Smith entered on the minutes. It seems that this letter convinced the committee that their proposed application to the French Prince was a mistake: and among those convinced is Trollope himself, for he says so: yet he dislikes the reversal of a decision come to by the committee, and seems to fear lest the president should be claiming too much authority. His letter, however, is that of a gentleman, and shows no sign of temper. I have told him in my reply that my letter may be put in the minutes as far as I am concerned, but that the committee alone are empowered to decide that point: as to the rest I have written him a long explanation which I think will put an end to the dispute. I suspect that he and Dr. Smith are not on the most comfortable terms, at least not mutually congenial: and that the Dr. who, though a worthy man, is a little pompous in his ways, has made a fuss about my communications which irritated his brother author. I am the less vexed with Trollope, because I think that in similar circumstances I should have felt as he does.

27 Jan. 1879: . . . Received by second post a letter from Trollope, in answer to mine, civil, and apparently not disposed to make his grievance personal to me, but not quite satisfied, nor can I make out what is at the bottom of it. But, as he means to raise a discussion at the next meeting, we shall know more.

12 Feb. 1879: . . . At 3.00, meeting of the Lit. Fund Committee: present, Ld Carlingford[188], Ld J. Manners[189], Dr. Smith, Dr. Richardson[190], Trollope, Ouvry[191], Godwin[192], the secretary and some others. We voted away about £230 in grants, several applicants were refused. Trollope brought on a motion in the sense of his letter to me . . . for which he found scarcely any support. He recited what had passed at the last two meetings, was very civil to me, did not complain of my letters, either as to the form or substance of them: but did complain that Dr. Smith had only read them, and that they had not been treated as official. He spoke with temper, but evidently felt strongly. Our difficulty in dealing with his grievance was that we could none of us understand where it lay: nor why he attached importance to the matter. In the end I induced him to adjourn the discussion for a fortnight, on the plea that several members present had not expected the matter to be discussed, and wanted time to consider it. He told us plainly he would retire if he did not carry his motion. His manner was that of a gentleman throughout, but he seemed to have a fixed idea, which no discussion would shake. Jealousy of someone on the committee - I think of Dr. Smith - is evidently at the bottom of the business.

25 Feb. 1879: . . . Letter from A. Trollope, enclosing one which is to be read to the meeting tomorrow, which he does not mean to attend. He writes with abundant courtesy, and I think has really no feeling against me, though he may have against Dr. Smith: but his grievance is scarcely more intelligible than before.

26 Feb. 1879: . . . In the afternoon to meeting of the Lit. Fund Committee, about 9 were present: Carlingford, Smith, Ouvry, Richardson, the secretary, Mr. Godwin, etc. We negatived Trollope's resolution, but passed one suggested by Dr. Richardson, which it is thought he will accept instead and, as it only represents our actual practice, it can do no harm. None of those present understood Trollope's cause of complaint any more than I do: and the question was treated simply as one of humouring his fancies, rather than lose a well known literary name. From remarks made I gather that his bouncing, dictatorial way of talking has made him unpopular with his colleagues.

9 July 1879: . . . Lit. Fund meeting at 3.00: 14 present, including the secretary and myself: Trollope, Ouvry, Ld O'Hagan[193], Dr. Richardson, Mr. R. Sturgis[194], etc. We gave away £400, in six gifts. There remained above £1,000 of which it was proposed to invest half[195], but this proposal Trollope objected to talking in a noisy blustering way[196] for which there was no reason or provocation but I find this is his habitual style, and he is disliked by his colleagues in the trust accordingly, though for his name as a writer it is not desirable that he should leave us. He talks as if any dissent from his opinions was a personal affront. We adjourned the question, to avoid needless quarrelling.

23 Feb. 1881: . . . Lit. Fund meeting at 3.00: no grants were made: but a plan of saving expense by curtailing the yearly report was considered: Trollope being its chief author. He was noisy and violent in discussion, as his way is but, being outvoted by three to one, took defeat in good humour. We agreed to shorten the introduction, or history of the Fund, a long, wordy, and pompous document, but to make no other change.

9 Mar. 1881: . . . To the yearly meeting of the Lit. Fund, where took the chair. The meeting was small, few except the members of committee or council present. All passed off smoothly. There was some discussion as to the possibility of inducing the Guild of Literature to unite with us. That society was set up by Dickens and Forster as a rival to the Lit. Fund, the management of which they disapproved. They took great trouble in starting their scheme, and were helped by the late Ld Lytton[197]: but it gained no support, and is now a complete failure, having left out of its capital some £2 or £3,000 which can find no application. A Mr. Rae[198] declared that the managers were willing now to unite with the Lit. Fund, and we passed a resolution expressing willingness to consider the matter. The L.F. itself is remarkably prosperous: over £50,000 of realised property, and a larger yearly revenue from gifts than ever before.

7 Dec. 1882: . . . News in the papers of the death of Trollope, which was expected: he was only 67 or 69, but had worked double tides all his life. A more prolific novelist has never existed: in bulk of publications he far surpasses Walter Scott: some are good, some indifferent, but all entertaining: and as pictures of the manners of the time they may have an interest beyond the moment. A strong family likeness runs through them all, producing, to those who know them well, a certain sameness. They are not works of original genius, but better than any writer now living can produce in the same kind. - Trollope personally was not agreeable [sic] as a casual acquaintance, and still less to do business with: he had a blustering manner which was not conciliatory, and which I believe did injustice to his real character. But it is possible that my judgment may be prejudiced: I saw him only at the Literary Fund, in regard to which he was jealous of interference and I fancy that my appointment to the Presidency was disagreeable [sic] to him - though I don't know why.

17 Oct. 1883: . . . Read with interest an autobiography of the late A. Trollope, which contains some curious details. . . . He describes himself as having been incessantly bullied and ill used in youth, and miserable until he reached the age of 25. Possibly this is the explanation of the singularly arrogant and swaggering manner which he assumed in later life, though, as I believe, a kind and good-natured man when not opposed. Or possibly the same intolerance of contradiction belonged to him from the first, and caused his early troubles.

Appendix I

Harcourt on Home Rule, Jan. 1886

Harcourt's antipathy to Home Rule, which he considered 'insane folly'[199], was notorious in contemporary political circles[200], if fairly well hidden from the public. What is less obvious is why, feeling as he did, he ended up on the Gladstonian side, and why he took a leading part in putting Gladstone into office in 1886. The letter of 9 January 1886 cited below displays the curious process of thought that led Harcourt into the Home Rule camp.

7, Grafton St.,
London
[Saturday] 9 January 1886[201]

My dear Derby,
    I have very little difficulty in answering your question as to my own opinion on the question of Home Rule in Ireland – meaning by Home Rule a separate Irish Parliament. I regard it as wholly impracticable. I do not think it could be carried if we were all agreed upon it and I am certain that if it were carried it would result in Civil War. We are quite in the dark at present as to Mr G.'s real views on the subject. Beyond some obscure letters to Hartington and the imperfect denials of Herbert G.'s revelations we know nothing[202]. He [i.e. Mr G.] is coming to town on Monday [11 January] and then I suppose we shall receive more information[203]. All we have been able to get up to this time is that he has 'opinions but no intentions or plans'. I don't believe that he has the support of any one of his former colleagues in what are supposed to be his views unless it be Rosebery[204].
    I have seen a good deal of Chamberlain lately[205]. He and Dilke are quite as adverse to separate Parliament[206] as the Hartingtonian section. Till quite lately Mr G. was vehemently anxious to storm the Treasury bench and take the Govt. by assault counting on the Parnellite vote but the warning as to the temper of the troops I think has cooled his ardour.
    I don't expect now that he will himself move anything on the Address as he had originally intended, but we are not masters of the situation and either Parnell or the Govt. may force our hand.
    I think everybody feels that our policy if possible is to keep the Govt. in at present but that may be very difficult if the Parnellites are determined to put them out. It is not easy to make a sack stand upright.
    As to Home Rule, to my mind it is not a question of more or less. It is idle to patch up constitutions for people who are inspired with inveterate hostility towards us. *Quid leges sine moribus?* But with all this there is the other side of the picture which must also be looked at.

If Home Rule is refused, as it will be, you will stand face to face with a resistance better organised and more strongly supported than any we have yet had to encounter. We shall have a strike against rent, against taxes, against law in every shape. We shall have outrage and dynamite all about the place both in England and Ireland. How is this to be met? You will require a Coercion such as has not been seen since '98 so *quacunque via data* you come round to the same issue of Civil War. Is there stability and strength of mind enough in the Commons to 'put it through' as the Americans say? This is what makes the gravity of Mr G.'s attitude. Can the Coercion which will become necessary on the rejection of Home Rule be maintained by any Govt. however constituted with Mr G. outstanding with a policy which he declares would obviate such a necessity?

I am very clearly of opinion that the question at issue like that between the Northern and the Southern states in America will only be finally settled by fighting, but is it possible to fight as we shall have to do with a divided opinion? i.e. until all conceivable remedies have been exhausted. Of course the present Govt. have infinitely weakened their own hands and that of others for maintaining peace in Ireland by their profligate conduct last June. It is impossible now to get back to the Spencer *status quo ante*. The unsatisfactory conclusion which all this leads to is that it is equally impossible to make a Govt. for Home Rule or one which shall be able to take the necessary measures against Home Rule. For the moment the best thing seems to me to be to get Gladstone's plan (if he has one) developed, so that it should be adopted if it were feasible, but if not that all the world should know that it was impracticable. The worst thing that could happen would be that he should retire with a mysterious plan in his pocket and that we should be supposed to have strangled it in its birth. The mere idea that such an alternative existed would fatally paralyse the hands of any Govt. which should attempt to carry out the measures which I foresee which will become indispensable very soon in Ireland.

You will have observed that I have held my tongue in public on these subjects not knowing what to say. I agree with you that if the Liberal Party is sent to the country on Home Rule it had better have the nether millstone round its neck.

Appendix II

Derby's Speeches and Public Letters, 1885–1893

Note: Speeches which are marked with an asterisk appear, normally abbreviated and with some editorial revisions, in the collected speeches edited by Sanderson and Roscoe. Speeches are dated either according to their date of appearance in *The Times*, in which case the page and column are shown, or according to the date when they were delivered as stated in the collected speeches.

1885	Blackburn*; in support of Liberal candidate; 4,500 present;very warm reception	12 Oct., 13a	Attacks Parnellism and Tory Democracy, the latter for Jingoism and profligacy. Calls for elective local government as central feature of Liberal programme. Against compulsory purchase for allotments. 'If a thing will pay, then private enterprise can do it.' In England, 'disestablishment, and at least partial disendowment must, in my mind, ultimately come' but not at present; would accept it for Scottish and Welsh if they wanted.
	Liverpool; dinner at Reform Club in celebration of honours conferred on local worthies	2 Nov., 12a	Argues party split is needless. All are agreed to postpone disestablishment and the Lords as questions of the future. All agree on local government, law reform, and procedure. Why borrow trouble? No problem about Unauthorised Programme. No worry about free education leading to socialism; state already pays two-thirds, so why not one-third more? Land purchase not alarming either; powers already existed but ratepayers never used them. Graduated income tax also made light of. 'Do not let us magnify differences. We have plenty to do on which we are all heartily agreed . . .'

1886	Liverpool* ; great Unionist meeting at Hengler's Circus	30 June, 12a	Ireland. Not a single homogeneous nation; Ulster would have to be coerced; no country in Europe had made such material progress in the last generation.
1886	Manchester	[October - not traced]	hospitals
	Liverpool; University College opening	4 Oct., 6c	progress of university
	Liverpool; town hall banquet for Derby; 50 guests	21 Oct., 10c	economic depression misleading – consumption, savings and production increasing
	London*; banquet at Hotel Metropole under Hartington; 400 present	8 Dec., 7a	Ireland and Liberal Unionism; essential 'to keep up our separate organisation'; land as much as nationality the key; Liberal Unionists were 'Liberals minus Home Rule'.
1887	Preston*	27 Apr., 9f	the training of the blind; 'all human life is, or ought to be, a struggle'.
	Liverpool*	4 June, 9e	Ireland
	Manchester*	3 Sept., 3c	agricultural depression
	Liverpool*	31 Oct., 8c	hospitals
	Liverpool	2 Nov., 8c	public affairs
	Crewe*	given 7 Nov.	technical education
	Letter	3 Dec., 13f	evening schools; 'school teaching alone will never civilise the masses. How should it when teaching ends at the age of 13 or 14 and is never taken up again'.
	London*	given 8 Dec.	Ireland
	Preston; chairman of annual session of Lancs. Justices	30 Dec., 10c	county government; rate-payers entitled to a say in local affairs, but will never get a cheaper, more effective and less corrupt system than the present one
1888	?	30 Jan., 4e	first sod of St. Helens-Wigan railway cut by Derby; better to invest at home than abroad; limited liability companies dangerous; colonies can only absorb limited capital
1888	Letter	1 Mar., 8a	on Liberal split; in answer to a Bolton Liberal, does not think differences can be made up at a general election. Regrets this state of affairs, but there can be no compromise on home rule

	Liverpool; banquet in Derby's honour by Mayor	8 Nov., 7e	public affairs; dangers of cheap Asian competition; cannot now return to agrarian simplicity; must go on or collapse; approves ministerial reduction of debt and local government bill; sanguine as to peace; the young German Emperor might enjoy a war, but what for?; other powers cautiously led
1889	Liverpool*	[given 21 Jan.]	the value of emigration as a social remedy
	Ashton-under-Lyne*	[given 23 Jan.]	Ireland
	Preston*	[given 31 Jan.]	technical education
	London*	[given 12 Apr.]	the House of Lords
	Birmingham*	[given 24 Apr.]	Ireland
	London*	[given 27 June]	Ireland
	Manchester*	[given 9 Oct.]	continuation schools; evening occupations for young persons
	Ormskirk*	[given 28 Oct.]	secondary education
	Rochdale*	14 Nov., 13d	economic questions
	Manchester; Town Hall; annual meeting of Lancs. and Ches. Mechanics' Institutes	20 Dec., 12a	on the institutes; extols Cobden, and extension of education
1890	Liverpool; Reform Club: Unionist banquet for T.W. Russell; Derby presided over 200	17 Jan., 10b	anti-Irish tirade; Irish misconduct not related to grievances; condition of Ireland greatly improved
1890	London; hospital fund-raising dinner	8 May, 13b	hospitals; against free treatment; poor should make some contribution
	London*	given 22 May	mitigation of the smoke nuisance
	Bury; with Sir H. James	1 Sept., 6b	?
	Liverpool*	27 Sept., 7d	technical education; in praise of science
	Liverpool, St. George's Hall	6 Oct., 4d	Liverpool University College; non-political
	Liverpool; St. John's Ambulance	17 Oct., 5e	St. John's had the men but not the money; non-political
	Liverpool*	30 Dec., 10a	in support of emigration of homeless children

1891	Manchester	16 Jan., 4b	home rule
	Bury	given 28 Jan.	education; supports continuation schools
	reply to enquiry about Goschen's budget giving free education	29 Apr., 9f	in view of surplus, and buoyant revenue, free education 'quite defensible. It removes popular grievance, while it imposes no fresh burden on any class'
	Manchester*	given 18 Oct.	on unveiling of Bright's statue
1892	letter	19 Feb., 9f	pauper immigration; exclusion the right of every state, but no evidence for present necessity. Jewish immigrants hardly ever become paupers. Addition to London population 'absolutely insignificant, compared with that due to natural increase'. No case for legislative interference
	London University	12 May, 12a	university affairs
	Letter	9 Dec., 6b	funeral reform; declines to take sides over cremation
1893	letter	30 Mar., 6b	has not commented on new home rule bill because of illness; thinks it as bad as 1886 one, and worse in detail. Irish M.P.s at Westminster unworkable; bill if passed would make Irish relations much worse
	letter	15 Apr., 11e	on Gladstone's famous speech at Knowsley in 1881 attacking Parnell; pointing out that it was given at a very small meeting in his own dining room and that therefore the reporters must have heard Gladstone's words correctly. This was in reply to a letter alleging that the press had been so inconveniently placed that they were unable to take notes

Appendix III

A Conversation with Gladstone, 1855[207]

Heads of conversation with Gladstone, Dec. 1855

Generally favourable to entire abandonment of colonies, when able to stand alone. Thinks all the Ionian islands, except Corfu, should be given up. Costly - useless - the people hate us - government almost impossible.

Objects to income tax: it must be inquisitorial: the powers of Commissioners are greater than any Parlt. would now grant: thinks the tax can be done away when it expires.
  Substitutes:
  1) House tax augmented, extended, perhaps graduated.
  2) Annuities about to fall in.
  3) Increase of yield of indirect taxation.
Fears economy will now be utterly neglected - since war makes profusion, and Hume is gone.

Full of plans and contrivances:
  a) Underground railroads, London.
  b) Line under Mersey, a tunnel to connect the two shores.
  c) Telegraphs: greatly cheapened and extended.
  d) Atmospheric tubes (principle of the atm. railway) through which letters may be shot with the speed of a cannon-ball.
  e) Railroads: would have them bought by Govt.: leased in short lengths, not too long for efficient private superintendence: would lower fares, improve 2nd-class carriages.

Strong for military reform: against purchase: no more commissions should be sold: seniority also bad: did not seem to fear jobbing.

Attaches great importance to C. Service reform: would reduce number of clerks, appoint by examinations, promote by merit, not seniority: separate the mechanical from the mental work, and establish a separate copying department.

Fixed property in Gt. Britain, he said, was 3,500 millions: moveable property immense in amount, no estimate. Computed that since 1846 50 millions yearly were laid by, till the war came.

English peasantry: he thought their good qualities many: love of order: sense of justice:

respect for superiors: industry: their faults, gross ignorance, drinking, and sexual vice. On the dairy-farms of Cheshire the intercourse between boys & girls is almost promiscuous: virginity at marriage is unknown.

Mr. T. Grenville, the octogenarian, once said to G.: 'The greatest change in my time is that wh. has taken place in the Eng. clergy - formerly, the majority were worldly, self-seeking, careless: now, the reverse.' G. much struck by the quantity of wealth brought into the Church: by men of small private fortune entering it for sake of a profession.

G. said that, if the temperance movement were to have a considerable success, it would lead to a financial revolution: you would save something in increased consumption of tea and sugar, something in diminished crime, but the loss wd. be immense.

Expressed annoyance, almost alarm, at the vast power of *The Times*. Lowe ought to be saddled with the responsibility of it in the H. of C.

The happiest time of his life, he said, had been while holding office under Lord Aberdeen. Thinks a system of organised parties desirable - the morality of such parties, though not the highest, being higher than that of average M.P.s.

On marriage laws - the proposal to enable a Court of justice to divorce *a vinculo*, he spoke with great warmth. The State did not make marriage, and cannot unmake it: he did not believe that any power existed by which the tie could be dissolved before God. He seemed to doubt the propriety of divorces even by a legislative act. He could not, he said, reconcile it to his conscience to sue for one under any circumstances. The question really was: whether the voice of the Church should be heard on that subject at all?

He dwelt much on relations of Church and State: seemed to think that under a popular Govt. separation must become inevitable: the subjection of the Church to the State must lead to immorality in the former. The State can never have the right, though it may have the power, to make laws for the Church.

He spoke of the King of Sardinia with great contempt - thought his character insignificant, and his motives interested: doubted the wisdom of his course in ecclesiastical matters.

He believed in the judgment of character by handwriting: and also, partially, in the application of the electrical test to the brain. [This every electrician knows to be absurd.] Mesmerism was a fact, not to be discredited: and perhaps clairvoyance also. He seemed unwilling to laugh at spirit-tapping: thought there was more in it than we understood, however ridiculous the explanations given of its phenomena.[208]

Notes

[1]   John Vincent (ed.), *Disraeli, Derby, and the Conservative Party: Journals and Memoirs of Edward Henry, Lord Stanley, 1849–1869* (Hassocks, Sussex: The Harvester Press, 1978). Stanley' s 'diaries'

for the period 1849–1855 are not strictly speaking true diaries because, though in the form of daily entries, they were revised in 1855 by Stanley from originals which probably no longer exist.

  [2] Preceded by *The Derby Diaries 1869–1878* (1994)

  [3] 30 January 1887

  [4] 13 October 1888.

  [5] At one time in the 1880s he owned one-thousandth of the national debt.

  [6] 3 February 1884.

  [7] Derby had read quite widely and unemotionally in the English socialist literature of the 1880s. He thought the Jubilee of 1887 proved 'the absence of any strong revolutionary feeling among the lower classes' (25 July 1887) and he was unruffled by the riots of February 1886. Later his qualms returned; but he read Hyndman (i.e. Marx in plagiarised form) aloud to his wife without undue emotion.

  [8] 1888 diary, fly-leaf.

  [9] 1892 diary, fly-leaf. His rents lost their buoyancy in the early 1890s but he was able to save larger sums than usual in those years, so his pleasure in his frugality was not diminished.

  [10] In 1892 he put electricity into the house at Knowsley.

  [11] January 1889. Derby at that date did not think it likely he would reach the age of 73 (i.e. live to 1899).

  [12] Col. F. Stanley, colonial secretary 1885–6, president of the board of trade 1886–8, governor-general of Canada 1886–93; created Baron Stanley of Preston 1886; while in Canada hoped for promotion to India, in Derby's view unwisely; cf. also *The Governing Passion*, pp. 257–8.

  [13] Memorandum by Edward, 17th Earl of Derby, eldest son of the 16th Earl. Freddy Stanley had the singular good fortune to have in his butler the local bookmaker, who sometimes let fall red hot tips for Eddy Stanley's benefit, with such effect that he was in due course able to introduce his father to owning horses.

  [14] The house in the north of the county which Freddy built on a whim following a happy picnic under two thorn trees there. His son recorded wonder at his father's courage with a limited income, 'in building what even now seems to me a very big house'. Witherslack being far from the station, Freddy tried to build a road straight there from the station, but after completing half the distance found some of the land did not belong to him at all and had to abandon the project.

  [15] In another passage the seventeenth Earl remarks of Mary, Lady Derby: 'I was very fond of her, but she hated my father and still more my mother and would do anything against them she could'.

  [16] Freddy's house at Witherslack was not cheap; he was a keen yachtsman; and his expenses in Canada would have been not easy to meet. But, taking an average between Freddy's good nature and Constance's animosity, is it possible that they were running down family capital with some pleasure in contravening Derby's plans?

  [17] It was characteristic, both of 'the lads' and of Derby, that when they looked after his horses, they never made any attempts to get a matching pair for his carriage, as convention required; they were bought absolutely indiscriminately, as if appearance meant nothing.

  [18] In 1885 Lionel Cecil was offered a post as agent on the Derby estates, but held himself pledged to his brother to go on with the Scotch farm, 'in which they are both sinking their fortunes, as far as I can see, with no prospect of getting anything back' (Derby's diary, 1 November 1885).

  [19] Born 1875 and 1878 respectively.

  [20] *Née* Elizabeth Wilson, daughter of Joseph Wilson of Woodhorn Manor, a leading farmer. Her brother (Sir) Jacob Wilson (1836–1905), was a well known national figure in the agricultural world (see *D.N.B.*) whose son was a godchild of Edward VII. He was 22, she was 30 when they decided to marry. Lady Derby was 'naturally much disturbed in mind' by the news, and the boy was sent to see Salisbury as head of the family, who reported that nothing could be done, especially as 'unluckily he is master of his own property, which though not large is enough to marry on' (Diaries, 17, 23, 24 July).

²¹ Derby may not have intended to be unkind. On her belated first visit to Knowsley he described her (28 December 1875) as 'large and plain, but not vulgar, at least not more than many women in society, and has a look of good sense. Her husband is as young, as boyish, and as well satisfied with himself as ever'.

²² Diaries, 12 January 1883.

²³ 30 March 1888. Somewhat later Lady Margaret artfully evaded a proposal from the future Lord Esher, whose interests lay elsewhere.

²⁴ When there was talk of Lionel standing for a Scotch constituency - for which party is not clear – Derby thought 'it would be inconvenient in various ways' and got Lady Derby to discourage the idea (4 May 1884).

²⁵ In fact Derby liked cigarettes, and therefore liked denying himself them, except on very rare occasions.

²⁶ A.B. Cooke and John Vincent, *The Governing Passion: Cabinet Government and Party Politics in Britain, 1885–86* (Brighton, 1974).

²⁷ John Vincent, 'Gladstone and Ireland', *Proceedings of the British Academy*, volume lxiii (London, 1977).

²⁸ Fitzmaurice, *Granville*, ii, 469.

²⁹ Sir Edward Russell, *That Reminds Me-*, pp. 279, 287. Russell's interesting chapter on Derby is otherwise remarkably accurate where it can be tested against the diaries, except that Russell appears not to have been on such close terms with Derby as he implies.

³⁰ Morley, *Gladstone*, ii, 215–16, referring to Derby's letter of 19 July.

³¹ Derby's movements after the ministerial crisis of June 1885 were as follows. On 26 June he left London for Knowsley, returning on 30 June. On 13 July he went back to Knowsley for the sessions. From 18 July to 19 September he was either in London or at his house in Kent, doing nothing in particular. From 19 September to 7 November he was at Knowsley. From 7 November to 12 December he was in or near London. He made no significant visits during the period, though he had important guests at Knowsley. His only direct conversation with Gladstone was on 1 October.

³² For similar views on Welsh disestablishment, cf. below, Ch. iii, 10 October 1887.

³³ John Wodehouse, first Earl of Kimberley (1826–1902), member of all Gladstone's cabinets; colonial secretary 1880–82, India secretary 1882–85; had worked closely with Derby on colonial matters, and had acted with him in cabinet in vigorous defence of the landed interest, 1882–85. Even when politically opposed to Kimberley, Derby was able to write to him as Indian secretary pressing the claims of a kinsman to a senior judgeship in India (8 March 1886).

³⁴ Lord Arthur Russell (1825–92), M.P. (Lib.) Tavistock 1857–85. His elder brother, the ninth Duke of Bedford, was Lady Derby's brother-in-law.

³⁵ Thomas George Baring, first Earl of Northbrook (1826–1904), viceroy of India 1872–6, first lord of the admiralty 1880–85. Northbrook's support for Gladstone is the more significant because of strained relations between the two men over the failure of Northbrook's Egyptian mission in autumn 1884. For Northbrook's position in 1885, see A.B. Cooke and J.R. Vincent, ed., *Lord Carlingford's Journal: Reflections of a Cabinet Minister, 1885* (Oxford, 1971), passim. On 2 November 1885 Carlingford talked to Northbrook about 'Mr. G. (whom Northbrook does not love)' (loc.cit., p. 140).

³⁶ Edward George Jenkinson (1836–1919), under-secretary at Dublin Castle responsible for police and crime, 1884–6; a kinsman of Northbrook; his letters widely circulated among Liberal leaders in the winter of 1885–86; see *Carlingford's Journal*, p.31 (31 October 1885) reporting Jenkinson's view that 'Home Rule . . . must be given'.

³⁷ Cf. Carlingford's reaction, 20 September 1885: 'It is very skilful, and must have a great effect in keeping the party together - What power he has! What influence over public opinion and action! – generally well used' *(Lord Carlingford's Journal*, p.134). Cf. also Sir W. Harcourt to his wife, 'Gladstone's manifesto has put me in high spirits about politics', and Harcourt to Gladstone, 21

September, saying 'without you . . ."the bottom of the tub would come out"' (Both printed in Gardiner, *Harcourt*, i, 540).

38 Lady Derby's sister.

39 Lady Derby's daughter by her first marriage.

40 Col. W. Sackville-West (1830–1905), brother of Lady Derby.

41 Made in Chamberlain's speech at the Victoria Theatre, Lambeth, reported in *The Times*, 25 September 1885, p. 7. For analysis, cf. *Lord Carlingford's Journal*, pp. 134–5.

42 Cf. Derby to Granville, 2 October 1885, printed in Fitzmaurice, *Granville*, ii, 465, summarising much of above, and describing Gladstone's statement as 'a new departure with a vengeance, and I had rather express no opinion upon it as yet'. Derby thought Ireland might break up both parties: 'It will certainly break up the Conservatives if Churchill gets his way' (loc. cit.). Part of Derby's letter also appears in Garvin, *Chamberlain*, ii, 111.

43 By Hartington at Waterfoot on 29 August, and by Chamberlain at Warrington on 8 September and at Glasgow on 15 September. Chamberlain visited Hawarden on 7–8 October, a week after Derby, but was given little indication of Gladstone's Irish views (Garvin, *Chamberlain*, ii, 105–110).

44 Richard Pigott (1829?–89), nationalist, journalist, and forger. The Derby Papers at Liverpool Record Office contain three long wheedling letters from him (September–October 1885), containing only occasional spelling mistakes; e.g. expince, tranquility.

45 Lord Arthur Russell (1825–92), M.P. (Lib.) Tavistock 1857–85. His elder brother, the ninth Duke of Bedford, was Lady Derby's brother-in-law. Lord Ampthill (Odo Russell, the diplomatist) was the youngest of the brothers.

46 A letter from Lord A. Russell to Goschen records a conversation between Kimberley, Derby and Russell about Gladstone and Ireland. The letter probably refers to a conversation on 13 October (possibly 12 October). It is printed in P. Colson., ed., *Lord Goschen and his Friends*, pp. 71–2: 'At Knowsley Lord Derby said to me after a long silence: "The longer I live the odder I find the English people!"' I did not answer "And the odder they find you" - but I thought it. Lord Kimberley asked: "How did you find the great Chief when you were at Hawarden?" "Well, I found him leaning towards Home Rule," answered Lord D. "What he calls a National Council: I confess I don't see my way to it, as I explained at Blackburn." When I saw him last," said Kimberley, "he was much troubled by the immoral means which we've used to bring about the Union; he felt that a great national sin had been committed and his conscience was troubled." "Oh! damn his conscience," answered Lord Derby.' What passed between Russell and Gladstone, and Münster and Gladstone, on their respective visits to Hawarden, seems not to have been known to Derby. Of Kimberley's conversation on Ireland with Gladstone, not even the time and place are known, but he must be added to the list of Gladstone's ministerial confidants in autumn 1885.

47 M.S. Harcourt (Bodleian Library), dep. 372, ff. 54–64.

48 William Molyneux, fourth Earl of Sefton (1835–97), succeeded his father, 1855: the figurehead of Liverpool Liberalism.

49 I am deeply indebted to Dr. Peter Gordon of the University of London Institute of Education for guidance on the movements of Liberal leaders in early Dec.1885, and for information about Spencer's activities.

50 Granville arrived at Hawarden on Saturday, 5 December, leaving for Chatsworth on Monday, 7 December, by the 8.10 a.m. train. He stayed there for some days. He was ready to return to Hawarden on Wednesday, 9 December, but was not required. Granville thus left Hawarden a day before Rosebery and Spencer arrived on the Tuesday. Granville had, however, been on the Monday evening and Tuesday morning at Chatsworth. As Spencer reported to his wife on Tuesday evening from Hawarden, he (Spencer) had arrived at Chatsworth at 7.30 p.m.: 'The Granvilles, etc., and a heap of relatives made up 26 to dinner. I had long talks with Granville and Hartington last night and this morning.'

51 Gladstone professed uncertainty about the election result to the last. At the time of

Granville's visit, Gladstone still hoped for an overall majority, and indeed a letter of his to a candidate appeared in *The Times*, urging voters in the last few seats to create a ministry not dependent on Irish support. Granville, at Chatsworth, wrote to Spencer, at Hawarden, on Tuesday, 8 December: 'The situation is most extraordinary. G. will not abandon the hope (which appears to me to be lost) of being in a majority over Tories and Parnellites. He is very bilious, and all for revolution anyhow'.

52   Spencer had been rather inactive since the fall of the ministry in June. He had made two election speeches (28 October, 3 November). He visited Rosebery, the Duke of Grafton, and Wolverton, but was mostly at Althorp. He was at Sandringham 9 –16 November, but spent late November and early December at home. He was invited to Hawarden in a letter of Sunday, 6 December, for the following Wednesday, as Rosebery was also asked for that day 'and there is so much difficulty for me (physical as well as otherwise) in proceeding by single threads of conversation'. Spencer left Althorp on Monday, 7 December, staying that night at Chatsworth, where he was able to discuss matters with Hartington and Granville. Spencer then travelled on to Hawarden on Tuesday, 8 December, arriving at 5.30 p.m., and leaving early on Thursday, 10 December.

Rosebery was in Edinburgh on 6 December, travelled to London that night, leaving on Tuesday, 8 December, on the midday train for Chester, arriving at Hawarden before Spencer. He left shortly after noon on Wednesday, 9 December, for The Durdans.

Spencer, Rosebery and Gladstone discussed Ireland freely; as Spencer wrote later in the month to Rosebery: 'You and I, and I know not whether you still hold the views you held at Hawarden . . . will stand alone among Mr. G.'s colleagues'. (*The Governing Passion*, 319). On Tuesday evening, Spencer wrote to his wife: 'We have already a long talk, not to great purpose, but Mr. G. is really hot on Ireland but I am glad to say sees the difficulties.' On Wednesday, after a walk with a very hoarse Gladstone, Spencer wrote: 'Rosebery has gone [i.e. earlier that day] and we have had tremendous talks. I dread the political prospects more than ever.' A hint of Spencer's restraining role appears in Gladstone's letter of 17 December to Hartington, where he refers to protection of the minority as a difficulty 'on which I have talked much with Spencer'. On Sunday, 13 December, Spencer, back at Althorp, had 'very thorough discussion' with Northbrook, who seemed to Spencer to admit the force of 'my plea for a large measure, but he was very strong on the necessity for the greatest caution in procedure' (Mallet, *Northbrook*, 224). At Chatsworth the following week, those present spoke of Spencer's 'sine qua non, that the landlord should have some guarantee'.

53   Spencer made no secret of his views. Spencer' s discussion with Northbrook at Althorp on Sunday, 13 December, was followed by two letters from Northbrook, on 16 and 18 December, the latter running to sixteen sides on home rule. There was no party division between unionists and Gladstonians at this stage. On Tuesday, 15 December, Spencer told Goschen that he leaned to some understanding with the Tories, followed if possible by negotiation with Parnell. Spencer wrote to Granville of his talk with Goschen: 'I perhaps put the case for a big measure more strongly than I ought. At least I argued that way and did not perhaps show how difficult I thought all the guarantees were. What I carried away from 1½ hours' conversation was that Goschen admitted a good deal but felt tremendously the difficulty of yielding to a Pack of people like Parnell and his crew.' Spencer remained at Althorp for the rest of the year. On Christmas Day, he drew up a memorandum on home rule. On 30 December, Hartington arrived at Althorp, and on the same day Spencer wrote in pessimism and disgust to Rosebery about the harm done by the Hawarden Kite, but still hoping the Tories 'may take the thing up'. 'I will hold to the necessity of guarantees, but I think they could be got. Underlying all this how odious (and maybe wicked) it is to think that Parnell and his crew are to govern Ireland . . . I expect that unless the Tories act, all will end in smoke' (Crewe, *Rosebery*, i, 356).

54   Cf. 10 July 1885, on the Central Board scheme: 'Granville does not like the scheme, saying that it will be resisted in Ulster, even to the length of civil war': and 22 July 1885, when Derby wrote to Gladstone putting objections to a Central Board, the first objection being 'that to Ulster men the idea will be intolerable'. . . (Derby diaries).

[55] Northbrook discussed Irish matters with Derby (see above, 24–25 September), with Carlingford (31 October–3 November), with Spencer at Althorp on 13 December, with Hartington and Harcourt at Chatsworth on 14 December and with Trevelyan and Campbell-Bannerman on 5–8 January 1886 (*The Governing Passion*, p. 322). Northbrook 'had refused all invitations to speak' in the 1885 election (*Lord Carlingford's Journal*, p. 139).

[56] Hartington did not accept this invitation.

[57] For part of text, see Fitzmaurice, *Granville*, ii 469. Derby objected particularly to the notion of a local parliament subject to a Westminster veto. Granville replied from Walmer 27 December (loc.cit., 469–470), saying that the true explanation of the 'Hawarden Kite' was anybody's guess, suggesting a waiting policy till Parnell and Salisbury showed their hands, and rejecting the idea of Chamberlain and Harcourt, backed reluctantly by Hartington, that Gladstone should be called to account at an immediate meeting of the ex-cabinet.

[58] Letter printed in Fitzmaurice, *Granville*, ii 478–9, with minor changes of emphasis from above version.

[59] For full text, see below, appendix i.

[60] Lewis Harcourt's journal reported this afternoon call as showing that Derby 'was in a confused state' and had 'no appreciation of the gravity of the situation'. Derby had said that Gladstone considered the elder Harcourt a convert to Home Rule. Derby thought Gladstone more strongly in favour of Home Rule than on 1 October, but also 'frantically anxious to come into office on any terms' (M.S. Harcourt dep. 375).

[61] Entry of 24 January up to this point was printed in Vincent, 'Gladstone and Ireland', *Proc. Brit. Acad.* (1977), 237–8, with list of other sources for Hartington's apparent momentary leaning towards a punitive form of home rule.

[62] Derby's immediate reaction (8 April) to Gladstone's bill was: 'I do not yet see my way clearly enough through the scheme to give any opinion . . .' He also reported Lawson's news that Davitt 'treated the plan as a mere trick to extort money from Ireland' (9 April). Iddesleigh thought the bill would never reach the Lords, but thought its introduction would make the future maintenance of the Union 'extremely difficult' and, like Derby, did not see what was to follow the fall of Gladstone's ministry (10 April).

[63] Derby had been at Knowsley for quarter sessions, 19–23 April. He had also had Camperdown to lunch on 17 April to talk over the same topic. Camperdown had taken the lead in asking Derby to let the Liberal Unionist peers meet at his house (13 April).

[64] Prompted by Hartington and Albert Grey, Derby had written giving his name as a member of the Liberal Unionist committee (28 April). On 22 May he said a few words at a meeting of 'over 200' Liberal Unionists at the Westminster Palace Hotel. On 10 June he wrote to Biddulph, the banker who was Liberal Unionist treasurer, giving £2,000 towards the elections, that being the amount contributed by the Dukes of Bedford and Westminster and by Lord Cowper.

[65] 12 July 1886.

[66] 21 July 1886.

[67] ibid.

[68] 23 July 1886.

[69] 23 July 1886.

[70] 28 July 1886.

[71] 24 July 1886.

[72] 24 July 1886.

[73] 29 July 1886.

[74] 9 August 1886.

[75] Cf. 19 May 1885: '. . . Churchill, with all his remarkable cleverness, is thoroughly untrustworthy: scarcely a gentleman, and probably more or less mad.' Cf. also 18 June 1885: '. . . Churchill is named for India, for which he is about as unfit as a man well can be.' Derby had in mind the streak of insanity in the Londonderry family, from which Churchill's mother came. On Churchill's

resignation, Derby 'doubted Lord Randolph would be taken from public life either by sudden death or failure of health. He added, or failure of mind' (Sir E. Russell, *That Reminds Me* -, 284.)

[76]   A reminder letter from Mrs. Gladstone three days later, asking for £100 at once, did not improve matters, Derby sending the money 'with no great good will . . . I have no confidence in her judgment, while her gushing style irritates my taste'.

[77]   Derby's reaction to Churchill's resignation was to oppose coalition more strongly than ever, fearing a jingo war over Bulgaria urged on by the Queen.

[78]   Described by an opponent as the best on the Unionist side (Sir E. Russell, *That Reminds Me* -, 287).

[79]   13 March 1887, also below, 10 May 1889.

[80]   On the tedium of speaking on Ireland for Derby, see Russell, loc. cit., confirmed by many remarks in the diaries.

[81]   When Salisbury spoke at Liverpool, at a time when Derby was at Knowsley, the two 'allies' did not meet (13 January 1888). Mr. J. France of Christ's College, Cambridge, kindly informs me that of 99 letters from Derby in the Salisbury Papers at Hatfield, only one, dealing with the chancellorship of London University, is later than 1877. Derby had virtually no contact with other Conservative ministers in the House of Lords.

[82]   He stopped one political subscription early in 1887 'till the feud in the Liberal party is ended', and another 'saying however that I shall be glad to renew it whenever the question of Home Rule is settled, and the party reunited'. In 1888 Derby refused to entertain the party on the grounds 'nor have we so far constituted ourselves a distinct party: nor I think ought we'.

[83]   2 January 1887.

[84]   Sir E. Russell, op.cit. (1899), 286.

[85]   9 January 1887.

[86]   For his low opinion of Smith and Beach, see Russell, op.cit., 285, confirmed by remarks in the diaries.

[87]   2 January 1887.

[88]   12 January 1887. Cf. below, 27 Jan. 1889, 22 Nov. 1891.

[89]   4 July 1888.

[90]   But see below, 25Apr. 1888; 20 May 1890 & f.n.

[91]   In the ministerial crisis of January 1887 Derby was reported as saying that he 'could not understand . . . why Lord Hartington should be expected to join the government' (Sir E. Russell, op.cit., 284.).

[92]   When Camperdown tried to make Derby speak publicly in support of coercion, Derby, disliking aspects of the bill, put him off (2 April 1887).

[93]   Derby had written earlier in the year (19 January 1887) saying 'that I am quite content that the Welsh electors should decide the question of disestablishment'. Cf. above, 24 July 1885, for Derby's similar opinion on Scottish disestablishment.

[94]   Cf. an earlier discussion with Collings on allotments, 12 March 1889: 'I say little but, as I have always done, treat the proposal as in the nature of an experiment, to be tested first on a small scale, and the result carefully watched.'

[95]   In an earlier note on Liberal Unionist finances (4 April 1889), Derby records being approached by Wolmer, who had secured contributions of £1,000 from the Duke of Bedford, £1,000 p.a. from Lord Rothschild, and £500 p.a. till the next election from the Duke of Westminster.

[96]   Cf. 4 March 1888, on Camperdown and Lords reform: 'His chief object seemed to be to get the subject out of the hands of Rosebery. . . I think there is a strong personal feeling of jealousy.'

[97]   James Howard Harris, third Earl of Malmesbury (1807–1889), foreign secretary 1852, 1858–1859, lord privy seal 1866–1868, 1874 – August 1876.

[98]   Cf. 6 November 1880: '. . . My poor old friend, Ld Malmesbury, aged 73, and too infirm to walk steadily across a room, has committed the folly which he threatened in the spring and, having

been thrown over by one woman who concealed the fact that she was actually married when he proposed to her, has now married her sister. He will probably not have long to repent his mistake.'

99 Malmesbury made £3,000, according to a later diary entry by Derby.

100 For a similar sketch of Malmesbury, written by the 15th Lord Derby in 1856, see *The Stanley Diaries*, p.351. Malmesbury told Stanley, 5 January 1853, that he expected Derby to retire either in the event of Disraeli embracing the radicals or if there were a large falling off in Derbyite support; both events he considered probable. 'I could not help suspecting from his manner of talking on this subject that he looks for the succession to the vacant post of leader: which is absurd . . .' wrote Stanley.

101 Derby also took to Rosebery, another opponent, in the late 1880s: 'The more I see of Rosebery the better I like him' (6 June 1888).

102 22 February 1887.

103 13 December 1890.

104 27 December 1890.

105 'Sent Granville a cheque for £8,000, leaving it to him to settle what security for repayment he chooses to give. He sent me back two promissory notes' (7 November 1884).

106 Fitzmaurice, *Granville*, ii, 475–476.

107 Cf. 12 August 1883: '. . . Ly Abercromby talks of the Teck sale: it has brought very little in money directly, but has accomplished its object, which was to compel the princess's family to give help by an ostentatious display of poverty. The Queen, the old Duchess of Cambridge and others have contributed and their immediate wants are relieved.'

108 Arthur William Cairns, second Earl Cairns (1861–1890): succeeded his father, 1885: at this time styled Lord Garmoyle. In fact he married in 1887, and not to a Miss Fortescue; but there was much talk of an actress at this time. The matter was of some importance, as the Cairns peerage had been created on the understanding that it would in due course be endowed by the enormous McCalmont business fortune of several millions. But with Lord Chancellor Cairns predeceasing McCalmont, and the second Earl being a scamp, McCalmont changed his mind and left his money to a different branch of the family. See below, 20 November 1884.

109 Cf. Sir E. Russell, op.cit., p.290: '[Derby] said Lord Dalhousie's main characteristic was that he believed everything anybody told him. "When you are dealing with politicians and Scotch tenants," Lord Derby said, "that won't do".'

110 John Singleton Copley, first and only Lord Lyndhurst (1772–1863), Lord Chancellor 1827–1830, 1834–1835, 1841–1846.

111 *A life of Lord Lyndhurst, from letters and papers in the possession of his family*, by Sir Theodore Martin (1833).

112 Walter Francis Montagu-Douglas-Scott, fifth Duke of Buccleuch and seventh Duke of Queensberry (1806–1884): succeeded his father 1819: cabinet minister 1842–1846.

113 Bateman's *Great Landowners* gives £217,000 p.a. rental.

114 Montagu House, Whitehall, London.

115 William Henry Walter Montagu-Douglas-Scott, sixth Duke of Buccleuch and seventh Duke of Queensberry (1831–1914): contested Midlothian against Gladstone, 1880.

116 Sir E.B. Malet (1837–1908), envoy at Berlin 1884–1895: married Lady E. Russell, March 1885. The Duke of Bedford obtained from Derby a written testimonial to Malet's private character (3 August 1884). The Duke made difficulties, and was angry with Lady Derby for having as he believed promoted the marriage. The Duchess 'who has high ideas of birth and fashion' thought the connection a low one (5 September 1884).

117 Odo, first Baron Ampthill (1829–1884), son of Lord George William Russell (1790–1846), general, and ambassador at Berlin 1835–1841; nephew of seventh Duke of Bedford (d. 1861) and of Lord John Russell; married Clarendon's daughter, 1868; ambassador at Berlin from 1871; baron, 1861. For a comparative view, see diary, 25 August 1884: 'Except Lyons, we have no better diplomatist . . . English diplomacy is not strong in able men; Lyons must soon retire; and when that

happens, except Malet and Morier, and perhaps Ford, I know of no one in the future who is at all above mediocrity'.

[118] Heneage Finch, seventh Earl of Aylesford (1849–1885): according to Burke 'died leaving no male issue' and was succeeded by his brother: succeeded his father 1871. At his divorce hearing in 1878, it emerged that he used to take a house at Bognor and fill it with negro minstrels and ladies who 'danced around the room in smoking caps' (R.F. Foster, *Lord Randolph Churchill: A Political Life*, p.31).

[119] Arthur, third Earl of Wilton (1833–1885) of Heaton Park, near Manchester; eldest son of the second Earl, whom he succeeded in 1892, and who had married a daughter of the twelfth Lord Derby.

[120] Seymour, fourth Earl of Wilton(1839–98), second son of the second Earl; married the daughter of [Lord?] William Russell.

[121] A sense of insecurity was already leading Derby, in 1886, to consider enlarging his home park, in case English tenants demanded Irish land legislation.

[122] Sir Hugh Rose, first Baron Strathnairn (1801–1885), C.-in-C. Ireland 1865–1870; a hero of the Indian Mutiny, created Baron 1866 and Field-Marshal 1877.

[123] Cf. diary, 27 March 1884: '. . . old Lord Strathnairn made a pitiable exhibition, rambling into all sorts of subjects, and talking to the House of Lords in a confidential whisper'.

[124] The next day Derby offered Lionel a post as agent on the Derby estates, but he declined out of loyalty to his brother.

[125] Edward ('Eddy') George Villiers Stanley, seventeenth Earl of Derby (1865–1948). His mother Constance, née Villiers, was a daughter of Lord Clarendon, the foreign secretary.

[126] James, second Marquess and first Duke of Abercorn (1811–1885), Lord-Lieutenant of Ireland 1866–1868 and 1874–1876: created duke 1868: the original of the Duke in Disraeli's *Lothair*.

[127] His son Lord George Hamilton entered Salisbury's cabinet in June 1885.

[128] Augustus, sixth Earl of Buckinghamshire (1793–1885), rector of Wolverhampton.

[129] Vere Henry Hobart, Lord Hobart (1818–1875), governor of Madras 1872–1875: financial authority and essayist.

[130] Augustus Charles Hobart-Hampden (1822–1886), admiral in the Turkish service 1867–1885, commanding Turkish Black Sea fleet 1877–1878.

[131] Edward Adolphus Seymour, twelfth Duke of Somerset (1804–1885): succeeded to title 1855: first lord of admiralty 1859–1866.

[132] When a guest of Malmesbury at Achnacarry, 'she created a good deal of scandal by perpetual tête-a-têtes with her host'(15 December 1884).

[133] Edward Cardwell, first Viscount Cardwell (1813–1886): cabinet minister 1859–1866, 1868–74.

[134] George James Finch-Hatton, eleventh Earl of Winchilsea (1815–1887): succeeded his father 1858. According to Derby (20 April 1884) he had nothing to live on except the rent from his house at Eastwell, which was let to a Duke. 'His only son, a great scamp, died of drink at the age of 26: the successor is a cousin [in fact a half-brother], who inherited half the estates at the father's death, and will have all: said to be a sensible man into the bargain.'

[135] Francis Charles Hastings Russell, ninth Duke (1819–1891), who married Lady Derby's sister Elizabeth Sackville-West. He succeeded his cousin in 1872. He shot himself, the family increasing the sensation by at first trying to conceal his suicide. Though a Whig M.P. 1847–1872, he 'never seemed much interested until the break-up of the party in 1885–1886. He used to enjoy dilating to his friends on the certain victory of the socialist Movement, and the ruin in consequence of both aristocracy and plutocracy' (18 January 1891).

[136] Herbrand, eleventh Duke of Bedford (1858–1940); succeeded his brother 1893.

[137] George, tenth Duke of Bedford (1852–1893): succeeded his father 1891.

[138] As the elder brother, Lord Tavistock, was childless, 'and likely to remain so', the permission

for the younger brother to marry Miss Tribe of Simla made her a probable Duchess some day. 'Both brothers are eccentric,' Derby noted, 'in a quiet way: both cultivated and not wanting in brains: neither, I think, will take any public part.' Miss Tribe, in fact the daughter of the Archdeacon of Lahore, became a Duchess within six years, and survived to die in an air crash in 1937.

[139] George, fourth Marquess of Ailesbury (1863–1893): succeeded his grandfather 1886.

[140] Derby promised Rosebery general support for his House of Lords reform plan, but was not surprised when it was defeated 97–50 (12 March 1888).

[141] Edward Bootle-Wilbraham, first Earl of Lathom (1837–1898): succeeded as baron 1853: created earl 1880: had lost £20,000 in Canadian land (Derby's diary, 5 April 1888).

[142] Francis Egerton, third Earl of Ellesmere (1847–1914): succeeded his father 1862.

[143] William Gerard, second Baron Gerard (1851–1902): succeeded his father March 1887.

[144] Seymour Egerton, fourth Earl of Wilton (1839–1898): succeeded his brother 1885: according to Derby 'a dipsomaniac . . . his only son is in the same line'.

[145] Mortimer, first Baron Sackville (1820–1888), a brother of Lady Derby, duly died later in the year, under the delusion that he had committed high treason. He left all he could away from his own family (diary, 20 August 1885, 5 October 1888). The title passed to his brother, Lionel Sackville, second Baron Sackville (1827–1908), a career diplomatist. The latter, then U.K. minister at Washington, soon after compromised himself and was forced to resign his post, by appearing to interfere in the U.S. elections (October–November 1888), thus completing the family misfortunes.

[146] Charles Richard, sixth Earl De La Warr (1815–1873), another brother of Lady Derby, had walked out of his hotel at Cambridge and drowned himself. The title passed to his brother, Reginald Windsor, seventh Earl (1817–1896).

[147] William, eleventh Earl of Devon (1807–1888): succeeded to title 1859: Chancellor of Duchy of Lancaster 1867–1868.

[148] Edward Baldwin, twelfth Earl of Devon (1836–1891): M.P. 1864–1868, 1868–1870: died unmarried.

[149] Countess Louise d'Alten (died 1911 at Sandown watching racing): married firstly (1852–1890) the seventh Duke of Manchester, and secondly (1892–1908) the eighth Duke of Devonshire: hence sobriquet of 'Double Duchess'; enthusiastic card-player (hence 'Ponte Vecchio'). Cf. M.S. Harcourt dep 370, f.76 (26 June 1885), where Harcourt *fils* wrote in his diary: 'There have been some very ugly stories about lately of her [the Duchess of Manchester] having had some rather too successful speculations on the Stock Exchange and it is intimated that she has her information from Hartington . . .'. Dilke had also picked up rumours, relating to spring 1885, of a storm 'which never burst but threatened greatly for some time, as to stock jobbing . . . one great lady (the Duchess of Manchester) was perhaps guilty . . .' *(The Governing Passion*, 187). The case remains not proven.

[150] George, eighth Duke of Manchester (1853–1892); succeeded his father, 1890. [151]
Derby's concern arose from Eddy Stanley's marriage to Alice, youngest daughter of the seventh Duke of Manchester, on 5 January 1889.

[152] Richard Temple-Nugent-Brydges-Chandos-Grenville, third and last Duke of Buckingham (1823–1889); succeeded his father, 1861; chairman of L.N.W.R. 1853–1861; cabinet minister 1866–1868; governor of Madras 1875–1880; chairman of committees in House of Lords 1886–1889.

[153] George, third Duke of Sutherland (1828–1892); succeeded his father, 1861; widowed in November 1888, he married his second wife in March 1889.

[154] Cf. diaries, 11 October 1879: [Sir W. Harcourt] . . . 'talked of the Duke of Sutherland, who seems to have embarrassed his property by speculations of various kinds, and to be in some trouble: he (the Duke) blames Pender for leading him into the trouble, and they are not now friends'.

[155] T.H.S. Escott, an outstanding contributor to late Victorian higher journalism. Cf. diary, 17 February 1885: 'Saw . . . Escott: the latter wants promotion for his brother in Mauritius, and makes

it a matter personal to himself, which is inconvenient, since I shall probably not be able to do what he wishes.' Escott began to cultivate Derby in 1882, sending him a copy of his book on *England*, pointing out that he had written a favourable leader in the *Standard* on a speech by Derby - 'so deeply impressed by its statesmanship' - and adding 'you may have heard of my name through my friend and relative Lord Carnarvon' (31 January 1882). In August 1882 he asked for a further interview, expressing great annoyance that the *Standard* was taking a line contrary to Derby. On 19 September 1882 he asked Derby to write for the *Fortnightly*, perhaps on Egypt. There is nothing further of consequence in their scanty correspondence.

[156]   9 February 1886.

[157]   11 February 1886.

[158]   15 February 1886.

[159]   7 March 1886.

[160]   8 March 1886.

[161]   Probably Lady Sefton.

[162]   Julia, Lady Abercromby, wife of fourth Baron (1837–1917), whom she married in 1858; a Lady in Waiting to Queen Victoria.

[163]   Cf. diary, 11 June 1890 '. . . In the papers, death of Ly Ely: who for many years occupied a peculiar position at court. She was much in the Queen's confidence, and was employed to carry private messages, and hint at wishes without committing her employer by too distinct expressions of opinion. For this kind of work she was well fitted, having a good deal of finesse and cunning: while her silliness in the ordinary affairs of the world prevented her from being suspected of intrigue. She was good-natured, and I believe did little or no mischief.'

[164]   On 28 August 1887 Lord Dartrey returned Derby's letters to his wife. These Derby later described (9 November 1887) as 'a vast bundle of letters written by me to A.D. some of them 25 years old'. These have not been traced, but there is no record of their destruction.

[165]   Cf. diary, 17 August 1888, where Morier is called 'certainly the ablest man we have in diplomacy' though his monologues 'make him socially an object of terror'.

[166]   Chamberlain had just received several blackballs at the elections to Grillions (diary, 11 February 1888).

[167]   Derby, after making enquiry to find whether Lear had any relations, accepted the bequest.

[168]   Derby had in 1887 drawn up a memorandum of the political situation for his guest Countess Münster, who probably sent it to the Empress. 'I have done this several times before,' he noted, '. . . whether it goes farther I do not know.'

[169]   The reason suggested by Derby was that the depression had driven the smaller St. Helens chemical works out of business, leaving only the more modern and less noxious plants.

[170]   If it exists, the journal will not be easy to trace. The writer was childless, and her brother-in-law, John, fifth and last Baron Abercromby, had only one child, a daughter, who married M. Nasos, Director of the Athens Conservatoire, in 1906. Mme. Nasos (b. 1897) was still living at 4, rue Heracliou, as late as 1959, but nobody of that name now lives there.

[171]   Derby did not expect Beaconsfield to have left much of interest for a biographer, partly because when he knew him he did not even take copies of his letters (Sir E. Russell, *That Reminds Me–*, 284).

[172]   Froude eventually produced a biography on conventional lines. Froude's Disraeli, with his Carlylean overtones, was very different from the Disraeli that Derby recalled. Another biography in which Derby had some hand was Kebbel's life of the fourteenth Lord Derby, which Derby read in proof at the author's request.

[173]   Cf. diary, 13 June 1889: '. . . I doubt whether Central Africa will not defeat the European attempt to civilise it, as it has done in all times up to the present . . .'

[174]   Charles Stanley Chetwynd-Talbot (1862–October 1890); died of consumption; son of Derby's only sister, Emma. Cf. diary, 10 December 1883: 'My sister came . . . Suggested what I have for some time thought of, that her eldest son, who is hanging about London doing nothing, should come into the C. office as an unpaid assistant private secretary, to give him something to do, and in order that

he may learn how business is done. She liked the idea . . .' But by 24 July 1884 Derby was having to talk to the boy's father, W.P. Talbot, about his son 'concerning whom there seems to be some mystery: the young man is constantly away from the office, on the plea of illness: and I believe it is true, for he looks much out of health: but for some domestic reason which I do not understand the father ignores this, and says that he has been regularly in attendance'. On 10 October 1884 Derby's sister was talking vaguely of her eldest son 'having got into bad hands'.

[175] Cf. the seventeenth Earl's memories of his grandfather, the premier, who died when he was four: ' . . . we used to sail cork boats in the gutter outside the Old Hall Door. . . . By blocking one end and turning on the tap we got a stream. They were cork boats with coloured paper sails. I can just remember my grandfather's excitement over it.'

[176] Robert Bourke, first Baron Connemara (1827–1902), younger brother of Lord Mayo, viceroy of India; under-secretary at the Foreign Office 1874–80, 1885–86, governor of Madras 1886–90; cr. peer, 1887, Derby commenting (21 Apr.) 'an odd selection . . . a good-natured pleasant member of society, he has done nothing: as an under-secretary, he was not very successful'. In office Derby complimented Bourke on being 'more catechised than any under-secretary in my recollection. He has got through his questions well (to be sure they have always been answered for him in the office, the answers drawn out on paper, and sent to me for approval): as a speaker he has not absolutely failed, but in the department I have not found him of much use. He is, however, willing enough, and popular in parliament'(10 Aug. 1877). When the ministry was formed, Bourke was 'thought of as Irish Secretary' by the leaders (17 Feb. 1874) but then sent to junior office at the India Office, whence he was retrieved to take Lord G. Hamilton's place when it emerged that the latter 'cannot speak a word of French' (21 Feb.). Bourke was Derby's 'original choice for the place, and I am thoroughly satisfied with the appointment' (23 Feb.). Cf. diaries, 12 Aug. 1886, on Bourke's appointment as governor of Madras 'it being necessary to provide for him, and no post that he would accept available at home. He was not a success either in the office or in parliament, being a clumsy speaker, and utterly without method or order in doing business. But he has pleasant manners, good sense, and some Irish humour: is likely to be popular, and may do as well as another. I am glad he has got something, for he is well-meaning and needy; and for high office at home he would certainly have been unfit'.

[177] Lady Connemara rather spoilt her case by writing to Derby (6 Jan. 1893) denying that she was insane, but adding that her food was being poisoned.

[178] This was written shortly before the baccarat scandal.

[179] Derby had been invited to serve by W.H. Smith.

[180] Cf. Thomas Spyers, *The Labour Question. An Epitome of the Evidence and the Report of the Royal Commission on Labour*, London, 1894.

[181] *Female Suffrage: A letter from the Right Hon. W.E. Gladstone, M.P., to Samuel Smith, M.P.,* London: J. Murray, 1892. 8p. Gladstone wrote: '. . . a permanent and vast difference of type has been impressed upon women and men respectively by the Maker of both. Their differences of social office rest mainly upon causes, not flexible and elastic like most mental qualities, but physical and in their nature unchangeable . . . The fear I have is, lest we should invite her unwillingly to trespass upon the delicacy, the purity, the refinement, the elevation of her own nature, which are the present sources of its power'. The bill, which excluded married women, would probably have worked electorally against the Liberals.

[182] Though Derby liked Sir R. Burton, 'whom I made consul at Damascus', he deplored his *Arabian Nights*, 'so full of indecency of the filthiest kind' that 'the volumes cannot be left about in any decent house'.

[183] T.H.S. Escott, *Anthony Trollope: His Public Services, Private Friends, and Literary Originals.* (1913: reissued in 1967 by Kennikat Press, Port Washington.)

[184] W.E.H. Lecky, p. xli,'Prefatory Memoir' to *Speeches and Addresses of Edward Henry XVth Earl of Derby K.G.,* Selected and Edited by Sir T.H. Sanderson K.C.B. and E.S. Roscoe, 2 Vols., London, Longmans, 1894, p.xli.

¹⁸⁵ (Sir) William Smith (1813–1893), classical scholar and lexicographer: registrar of the Royal Literary Fund, 1869: knight, 1892.

¹⁸⁶ Louis Napoleon, Prince Imperial (1856–1879), only son of Napoleon III: left England to take part in the Zulu War, Feb. 1879: killed in a Zulu ambush, 1 June 1879.

¹⁸⁷ The relevant letters, which are formal in character, are in the general correspondence of the fifteenth Earl of Derby in Liverpool Record Office. Trollope wrote to Derby, resigning, on 20 Jan.; Derby deprecated his resignation in a formal letter on the 23rd, and also wrote a private letter on the same day which almost went on bended knee to Trollope. Trollope replied to Derby, also on the 23rd, saying he thought that Derby was right in considering the Prince Imperial unsuitable, but '. . .I do not care to be one of a body which is governed by private letters, brought by one member from another.' Trollope, however, conditionally agreed to remain if Derby's letter were read as addressed to the committee, instead of to Dr. Smith. On the 26th Trollope wrote to Derby that he would propose at the next meeting on 12 Feb. that letters should be read by the secretary. No conclusion being reached on the 12th, Trollope wrote again to Derby on 24 Feb., ahead of the meeting on the compromise put in its place. In this final letter Trollope wrote of the committee having been 'altogether against me' on 12 Feb.. Seeing himself as 'a member thoroughly discordant', he proclaimed that 'a man can some-times accomplish by dying that which he cannot do by living. If by my dissolution I can achieve any such victory - which may not be impossible - I shall, I think, have made the sacrifice to good purpose.' No other correspondence between Derby and Trollope has been found in the Derby Papers, and none is specially noted in Derby's diaries.

¹⁸⁸ Chichester Fortescue, first and only Baron Carlingford (1823–1898), cabinet minister and husband of Lady Waldegrave.

¹⁸⁹ Lord John Manners, later seventh Duke of Rutland (1818–1906), minister in all Conservative cabinets 1852–1892.

¹⁹⁰ (Sir) Benjamin Ward Richardson (1828–1896), physician, anaesthetist, and first user of amyl nitrite: physician to the Royal Literary Fund.

¹⁹¹ Frederic Ouvry (1814–1881), antiquary, one of the treasurers of the Fund.

¹⁹² George Godwin (1815–1888), architect, sanitary reformer, and editor of *The Builder*: a trea-surer of the Royal Literary Fund: member of the royal commission on working class housing: a collec-tor of the chairs used by famous authors, he bought Trollope's chair.

¹⁹³ Thomas O'Hagan, first Baron O'Hagan (1812–1885), Irish lawyer and Liberal politician: Lord Chancellor of Ireland 1868–1874, 1880–1881.

¹⁹⁴ J.R. Sturgis (1848–1904).

¹⁹⁵ By 1882 the Fund had £50,000 invested, giving £1,800 p.a., leading Derby to remark: 'If the present state of things continues, we shall hardly know how to spend it' (Derby's diary, 8 Mar. 1882).

¹⁹⁶ Cf. the comment on a meeting of the Fund in 1882: '. . .Trollope absent, which made business easier and quieter' (ibid., 12 July 1882). Occasionally there was an outbreak of peace; e.g. after one meeting Derby '. . .walked home with Dr. Smith and Trollope, who talk of the necessity of finding a new secretary before long, Blewitt being old and no longer very competent'.

¹⁹⁷ (Sir) Edward Bulwer-Lytton, previously Lytton Bulwer, first Baron Lytton (1803–1873), novel-ist and Conservative cabinet minister.

¹⁹⁸ Probably William Fraser Rae (1835–1905), *Daily News* journalist and authority on Junius and Sheridan: the *D.N.B.* makes no reference to any connection with the Guild.

¹⁹⁹ Crewe, *Rosebery*, i 25, i 254.

²⁰⁰ Cf. above, ch ii, entries for 8, 10, 13 Jan. 1886.

²⁰¹ Written just before leaving for Mentmore, where Harcourt spent the weekend with Rosebery in apparently relaxed contemplation of an impending Gladstone ministry in which they would figure prominently. Cf. *The Governing Passion*, pp. 322–323. The original is in the Derby Papers in Liverpool Record Office

²⁰² Cf. Gladstone to Harcourt, 3 Jan. 1886, in Gardiner, *op.cit.*, p. 557, discouraging premature discussion.

[203] Harcourt went to see Gladstone at noon on Tuesday, 12 Jan., and took part in a meeting with Granville, Spencer and Chamberlain. Cf. Gardiner, *op.cit.*, p. 559, giving a fuller account than in *The Governing Passion*, p. 325, which omits Harcourt's visit. This was Harcourt's first conversation with Gladstone since the latter went to Norway on 8 August 1885.

[204] Spencer's support for Home Rule must have been known or assumed. Hartington had been at Althorp before the Devonshire House meeting on 1 Jan., and probably declared Spencer's views on that occasion (Gardiner, *op.cit.*, i 556–557).

[205] The only two letters from Sir W. Harcourt in the Chamberlain MSS between New Year 1886 and Chamberlain's resignation are dated 4 and 7 Jan., and concern a common front to stop, or at least control, Gladstone. Cf. *The Governing Passion*, p. 483, n. 27.

[206] Chamberlain's proposal for a 'protected State' with its own Houses of Assembly made little apparent impact when proposed on 1 Jan. to Harcourt, Hartington and Dilke. Derby did not know of it. Dilke at this stage was sitting on the fence, partly because of his weak personal position.

[207] Derby MSS, Liverpool Record Office, uncatalogued. Cf. memorandum on future measures, 16 Feb. 1856, in *The Gladstone Diaries*, ed. H.C.G. Matthew, vol. v, and editor's comments, *op.cit.*, p. iv.

[208] For Stanley's visit to Hawarden, 8–12 (Sat.–Wed.) Dec. 1855, see *Gladstone Diaries*, v, 91. The relevant passages are: 8th, 'Lord Stanley came: we had much conversation.' 9th, 'Walks and much conv. with Ld S. on Church and other matters.' 10th, 'Long walk with Ld S. and most of the morning too.' 11th, 'Walk with L. [Lyttelton, another peace man] and Lord Stanley.' 12th, 'Exhibited my room, etc., to Stanley before (to our regret) he left us. He will if spared write his name on the page of Engl. History.' During the visit, Gladstone wrote to Aberdeen, 10 Dec. 1855, Add. MSS. 43071 f. 275: 'I am very greatly struck, and scarcely less pleased with him. The force and vigour of his mind, combined with the adaptation of its general construction to the demands of the nineteenth century as it moves towards its close, mark him out, especially when his lineage and social position are taken into view, for a high but perhaps agitated destiny.'

Postscript

Dark speculation has long hung over Derby's name. There can be two distinct reasons for this: human frailty on his part; or, on the contrary, bitter enemies seeking to blacken his name. Regard to truth and to justice compels one to examine both possibilities. One may as well start with the question of the biography. Why was one never commissioned?

★ ★ ★

Lady Derby, his widow, certainly wanted a conventional tombstone biography. She approached a reputable man of letters, Sir Herbert Eustace Maxwell (1845–1937), biographer of WH Smith, Clarendon, and Wellington, and editor of Creevey, who accordingly went down to luncheon with her at Holwood. Maxwell's memoirs[1] then take up the tale:

'. . . Said I,

"Before we go further into the question, Lady Derby, I must ask whether you are prepared to give me a free hand."

"What do you mean by a free hand?" she asked.

"Why this, that you entrust me with *all* papers and correspondence, and allow me to form and express an independent opinion on them."

"I am afraid I cannot do that" said she, "I will give you such papers as will enable you to prepare a full account of his career."

"Then," I replied, "you must excuse me if I decline the undertaking. I cannot work to my own satisfaction upon a selection."

And that was the end of our negotiation. I learnt some years later [when writing the *Life of Clarendon*[2]], that her ladyship had very good reasons for not giving me a free run among the late Earl's letters.'

It may be noted that no mention was made of Derby's wholly innocuous diaries, the perfect foundation for an inoffensive "tombstone" biography. One should perhaps add that there is no positive evidence that Lady Derby knew of the existence of the diaries during Derby's lifetime – or indeed subsequently.

Why Lady Derby should have been willing to risk a biography and yet also been nervous about giving a biographer full access is not at all clear. Where Derby's letters were concerned, one would expect her to have known how much he had destroyed, since his regular bonfires cannot have gone unnoticed. His official letters were hardly going to set the Thames on fire. Ministerial biographies, as written in 1893, were very discreet affairs: Lady Derby had little to fear. As for Maxwell, what seems to have shocked him in Clarendon's papers was the free-and-easy exchange of confidential matters between leading men of different parties. Here Maxwell made the mistake of applying the standards of the bitterly partisan 1890s to the sweetly corrupt 1860s.

The evidence of Maxwell, then, would probably be scant cause for concern, were it not supported. Rather more significantly, however, Derby's executor (Lord) Sanderson virtually vetoed the idea of any biography by anyone, in the process bullying his co-executor Lady Derby into accepting the formula of a *Speeches and Addresses* in two volumes. Their correspondence, which became quite strained, has survived,[3] and Sanderson's anxiety about what might come out, can be sensed. What other lives of Victorian statesmen, one has to ask, were forced into this leaden coffin of a collection of speeches and addresses? The various anxieties of Maxwell, Lady Derby, and Lord Sanderson do not enable us to draw any definite conclusion, though they hint at an atmosphere of suspicion and doubt.

We turn next to a piece of evidence only recently made known. The American scholar Richard Milman cites a letter of July 1878 in which an army officer told Lytton, then Viceroy of India, "There is a report today that at the time of the Bulgarian atrocities he [Derby] was at Manchester and raped a little factory girl of 15, to hush up which he has to make the mayor a knight." Subsequent confusion of identity cannot be ruled out here. Later, in a notorious case, Derby's stepson-in-law and frequent guest Lord Galloway was indeed tried and acquitted on a related charge, involving an encounter with a young girl in a wood.[4] This is the only allegation of its kind which has come to light, but the knowledge that such things were alleged may explain the extreme caution of biographer and executor.

The allegations, of course, come from political enemies, at a time of exceptional political tension. There are further questions. Was any mayor of Manchester made a knight about this time? Was Derby, a busy foreign secretary, even in Manchester in May 1876, the actual month of the Atrocities?[5] Did Derby press Disraeli to honour any Mancunians at this time?

The next piece of evidence concerns a bitter family rift. Relations with his brother Freddy and Freddy's wife Constance were normal in an unthinking way from their marriage in 1864 to 1878:

27 Jan 1878 Dined with F. and C. Pleasant evening

There was no hint here of growing tension or of future estrangement, nor did Disraeli's artful promotion of Freddy in Derby's place, in the cabinet reshuffle of April 1878, lead to coldness. Then the heavens fell in overnight, apparently as a result of some rash remark by Constance about Derby, the nature of which we shall never know but which was so utterly hateful as to prevent any further contact.

5 Apr 1878 Heard with some pain, of language held by [Constance Stanley] which I think I will not more specially note, as this mem. is sufficient for my recollection.

15 May 1878 Talk with M. as to whether any overture shall be made to C.S. of whose unfriendly language & conduct we have more evidence than enough. The problem is how to mark our sense of it without an actual rupture & without awkward explanations. On the whole we agree to leave matters where they are, to keep aloof, & to let any demand for explanations come from the other side.

Freddy and his wife never entered Knowsley, or any family home, again, though the brothers continued to meet amicably in the park and in the street, and Freddy's elder offspring were much at Knowsley.

What Constance said about Derby (or possibly Lady Derby and her friendship with Schouvaloff) could have been almost anything. It was unlikely to have been a particularly political onslaught since there is no sign that she was politically inclined, and Derby's fracture with the Tories was nowhere near as deep in April and May 1878 as it later became. One can only suppose that Constance alluded unforgivably to some private wound. One should perhaps remember here that Constance was her father's daughter, and that her father was that greatest gossip of his day, Lord Clarendon, creator of the "Mrs Brown" rumours about Queen Victoria.

This brings us to the question of Derby's alleged kleptomania. For this there is no direct evidence, or none on which one would hang a dog. There is no hint at all of any incident of the kind in his adult life; there may or may not have been one in extreme youth. Such allegations as there are seem to come mostly, perhaps entirely, from bitter opponents at times of bitter political controversy who had little means of knowing an Eton incident of three decades before, and who had waited thirty years before making their charges. None the less, historians, perhaps to their discredit, have come to accept the idea of kleptomania as fact, because it has been asserted.

My most substantial witness is my colleague Emeritus Professor M.R.D. Foot, who writes to me:

". . . I got the story about the future 15th Earl of Derby, then a schoolboy, being paraded on the terrace at Knowsley,[6] by his father, in front of the whole staff – over a hundred people – and denounced as a thief, from J.L. Hammond, by word of mouth, *ca.* 1948. Hammond, the most honest and least gossipy of men, told me he had got it from Rosebery's son-in-law and biographer Crewe.

That at any rate is what I now remember, over fifty years on; and Crewe also must have been relying on memory, about as ancient. Sometimes tales like this do carry historical weight."

One will at once recall that Knowsley was not at his father's disposal until the death of his grandfather in 1851. Besides, it is almost unthinkable that the future heir to the title and estates would have been disgraced in front of the servants.

Crewe was born in 1858, a generation after Derby's schooldays; his most likely informant was his father Lord Houghton, born 1809, an avid source of gossip; but privately educated, and at Trinity in 1827–30, and thus of an earlier academic generation than Derby, and not a contemporary authority upon the events of Derby's youth.

The printed records of Derby's schooling tell us little. Derby was born on 21 July 1826. He was admitted to Cotton House, Rugby, on 21 July 1840, his birthday, aged 13/14. In his will he left a handsome scholarship to the school, where he thrived.

The Eton Lists from 1791 to 1850 (every third year after 1793) (London 1863) are oddly arranged on the basis of triennial snapshots. "Those names which would have dropped out between these triennial periods, have been collected from the Headmaster's Books and placed in 'Intermediate Lists' in order of their admission to the School." Derby appears in the printed 'Intermediate Lists' of boys admitted in 1838–41 but leaving before 1841. He signed the entrance book in September 1838, his tutor being Charles Abraham. The removal of a boy is usually recorded in the entrance book only if it happens very early on. The absence of such an entry in Stanley's case is not of itself any use in resolving the fine point whether his change of school was caused by psychological frailty or illness. Family letters show he received an Eton school report in January 1840.

The question of illness may indeed be relevant. Derby in later life always feared the recurrence of a potentially fatal disease he had suffered in early youth. On 3 April 1879 the diaries note 'a possible return of the complaint I had in 1843. In that case *"bonsoir la compagnie."'* Family letters of the time confirm a sudden medical emergency at Rugby in

1843. His change from Eton (then considered an 'unhealthy' school) to Rugby in 1839–40 might have been a disappearance caused by sudden illness and interpreted by schoolboy flights of fancy. The Eton Archivist is at pains to underline that their ignorance is just that and not the result of anxiety to conceal matters better not known.

There is other evidence which bears albeit indirectly on the question of kleptomania. There is perhaps most directly the correspondence from both parents to him as a schoolboy, not large in amount but suggestive in tone, surviving in his papers. There is the willingness of his father to see him brought into the public eye at a precocious age. There is the complete lack of embarrassment at working with senior Knowsley staff, whose company he rather sought out. This suggests that fear of exposure was not a consideration, for instance when he stood for election in March 1848 at Lancaster, very nearly winning, or when he became chairman of the Lancashire magistrates in 1854, holding the office for nearly thirty years, or on his appointment by his father as Foreign Under-Secretary in 1852. These were not the actions of one seeking to evade critical scrutiny, or of one who wished to wait till a youthful lapse had been forgotten.

Derby was a fanatical pedestrian, believing that in exercise lay his only hope of defeating congenital disease, an anxiety which never really left him. The circuit of Regent's Park especially had claims upon him. This may have been misinterpreted by some, at a time when men of his rank rode rather than walked. He was also something of a compulsive shopper, his walks in central London taking him to the curiosity shops, art dealers, and antiquarian booksellers. This failure to conform may have been blown up by malicious rumour. Prim to a degree, a compulsive saver for no very obvious object, anxiously exact about small sums and petty details, averse to most forms of enjoyment, appalled by debt wherever it occurred, not happy unless kept supplied with work, always speculating anxiously about the future, and prone to inexplicable serious depression, Derby was probably a recognizable personality stereotype. His oddities may or may not go back to events which may or may not have taken place in early youth: we are unlikely ever to know for certain. Fortunately, however, not everyone who is psychologically odd indulges in odd conduct. Derby, though the sort of person who might perhaps have indulged, remains innocent of adult kleptomania till proven rather more guilty than is the case at present.

Having said what little can be said about the allegations, one has to examine the other possibilities; namely, that Derby may have had enemies who for various reasons, or even for none, made it their business to blacken his name. This suspicion – it is perhaps no more – falls under various headings, which may have had nothing to do with each other. There is the question of the antagonisms within the Cecil family arising from Derby's relationship with Lord Salisbury's stepmother. There was the belief within the Jingo camp that Derby stood in the way of war with Russia. There was the belief among the Bulgarian Atrocities campaigners that Derby did not stand for the liberation of the Christian from the Turk. And there was the obsession in the Disraeli camp between 1865 and 1878 that Derby might be his supplanter in the leadership.

Any or all of these four unrelated situations might engender the abnormal intensity needed to justify a serious attempt to discredit Derby and/or Lady Derby. The Jingoes and the Atrocitarians, though fervent, and though in the latter case (through Freeman) indeed alleging kleptomania in private discussion, did not remain at fever pitch long enough to make a deep and lasting mark. Those in each group who believed their cause demanded that they stop at nothing, were only part of wider and more moderate groupings of opinion, not inclined to acts of passion. In the end, only the Russian Ambassador's visit to Lady Derby at Knowsley when Derby was absent, was seized upon as an act of apparent complicity with an enemy power. The point at issue here is not the relatively tangled one of Anglo-Russian collusion, but simply that of the alacrity with which Hughenden turned a trivial news item towards discrediting Derby.

Derby, despite his wealth and prominence, largely succeeded in avoiding radical attacks from the Left until Chamberlain's social radicalism of the mid-1880s. Such attacks respected his private character. Not so the attacks deriving from Tory factionalism. My reason for pursuing this train of thought is that by chance I came into possession of a scandal sheet of the late 1860s entitled the *Queen's Messenger*. Such titles were rare in the 1860s and became common in the 1870s. The *Owl* was the best-known forerunner, *Truth* the fully developed example. The *Queen's Messenger* purported to be based on inside knowledge of the Foreign Office and foreign policy during Derby's first foreign secretaryship of 1866–68. Its stock-in-trade was rancorous vilification of Stanley (as he then was), his foreign policy, and his alleged attempts to supplant Disraeli. Its bitterness was unrestrained, at a time when the outward surface of politics was apparently calm. It is the raw hatred of Stanley, shown by Disraeli's partisans, presumably at much trouble and expense, that makes one ask whether Stanley's enemies sat beside him. Unfortunately the journalism of slime and character assassination is today almost inaccessible, and the question of who was framing whom remains unexplored. But one should not be unsuspicious.

The negative testimony of established scholars who have worked on the private correspondence of the period cannot constitute proof, for one can never quite prove a negative. It is however weighty circumstantial evidence. No modern scholar has located any reference, even by his enemies, to Derby's supposed frailties, before the foreign policy crisis of 1876. In particular, those who have studied the private letters of the Fifties and Sixties have found plentiful references of all kinds to Derby, but none to his alleged weakness. The biographer of the elder Derby, Dr Angus Hawkins, having thought long on the issue, and finding it unsupported by any evidence from the correspondence of the Fifties, has come to see it as a "canard".[7] Mr Maurice Cowling, in the course of his work on politics in the mid-1860s, found no mention of it in the political correspondence of that era. Dr Hawkins further points out that the leading diarist and gossip of the Mid-Victorian period, Greville, who was notoriously no friend to the Stanleys and who includes some unflattering stories about both Derbys, makes no mention of an allegation which, if current, would have been grist to his mill. The argument from this silence in the evidence, while it does not show that the charges of kleptomania were necessarily unfounded, probably does show that they were not current in the period 1850–70 when Derby first attracted national attention. And surely, one may add, had they been true, or even plausible, they would have emerged from the rumour mill of London society.

Chronological résumé

None of the above publications brings forward any new evidence in support of its allegations – and mere repetition of a rumour, no matter how frequent, should never by itself be mistaken for proof of its truth.

The evidence of family letters strongly supports the above argument. The papers of the 15th Earl (here referred to as Derby) in Liverpool Record Office include a handful of letters from his parents for the period of his boyhood and youth. It must be admitted of course that the letters are infrequent and that Derby decided which letters survived. That objection apart, these letters from his parents lend no support to the idea that anything in his conduct may have given his parents cause for concern, or that any dreadful family crisis occurred in his youth. On the contrary, there is a letter from his father recording "a glow of pleasure" on receiving from Derby's housemaster "an expression of entire satisfaction with your conduct in every respect."

This was at the late date of 31 January 1840, virtually on the eve of Derby's move to Rugby, a move on which the family letters throw no direct light whatever, save in the general sense that anxieties about Derby's health were much in his parents' minds.

Derby grew up in a close-knit, warm, and loving home, where he was made much of as "little emperor", not only by his parents but also a much younger brother and sister. We hear of his letters being passed eagerly round the family circle, and of their being fondly read and re-read by the parents side by side. His father painstakingly commented on his translations and took his schoolboy hoaxes in good part, and by 1846 was making him his political confidant. We see no hint of the bad relations reported in the colourful stories from the 1850s, stories which for all their fame perhaps call for more critical examination.

What is clear enough is that between about 1837 and 1842 Derby, for reasons unknown, was threatened with loss of sight (a difficulty which recurred about 1856–58) and that about 1843 he had a sudden attack of life-threatening illness, involving swelling legs (possibly kidney trouble), the recurrence of which he feared throughout adult life. These were the documented crises of his youth.

Notes

[1]   Rt Hon. Sir Herbert Eustace Maxwell, *Evening Memories* (London:Maclehose, 1932), p 271.

[2]   The Right Hon. Sir Herbert Maxwell Bart., *The Life and Letters of George William Frederick, fourth Earl of Clarendon KG., GCB.* (London: Edward Arnold, 1913) 2 vols. Clarendon 'always hated Derby' (*Kimberley Journal*, ed. Powell, 490), which reduces the value of any allegations made by Clarendon's daughter against Derby's son.

[3]   Derby MSS, Liverpool Record Office.

[4]   R. Milman, *Britain and the Eastern Question 1875–1878* (Oxford, 1979) , p 476

[5]   The date of the Bulgarian atrocities is vague and can be interpreted variously. It is however remarkable that Derby was not at Knowsley between 2 May and 23 September 1876, spending the summer in London and Kent. He was at Knowsley, and nowhere else, 23–29 September, then returned south. On 30 April–2 May 1876 he was at Knowsley for his mother's funeral. There are no visits to Manchester.

[6]   i.e *circa* 1840

[7]   Dr Hawkins's exact words, quoted by permission, are as follows: "As the evidence stands at the moment, I think the accusation of kleptomania should be considered as a rather vicious canard instigated by Freeman – until solid evidence to the contrary comes to light."

[8]   R.S. Churchill, *Lord Derby, King of Lancashire* (NY 1960), p9

[9]   Blake, *Disraeli*, p623

[10]   D.M. Schreuder, *Gladstone and Kruger* (Toronto 1969), p308

[11]   A. Ramm, *Sir Robert Morier* (Oxford 1973), pp 141–2

[12]   The question of Derby's alleged alcoholic excess is discussed in Millman, *op. cit.,* pp 9–10, 477 n. 23, citing a number of allegations relating to the late 1870s, but tending to dismiss them as a myth. The memorandum by the 17th Earl on his youth refers to Derby drinking "a bottle of champagne every night, but it was the most extraordinary stuff. It was not real champagne, but a sort of doctored wine in which there was absolutely no strength nor harm." The 17th Earl also mentions that Derby got up very early in the morning and did an hour's gymnastic exercises before breakfast – hardly a mark of over-indulgence. The diaries show Derby paying strict attention to medical advice on restricting his use of alcohol. The alleged alcoholism seems likely to be a spiteful charge put about by opponents of his foreign policy, including Salisbury, as a way of putting the worst possible construction on his illness of spring 1878. The evidence for alcoholism being so dubious, it need not be discussed in detail here. The greater the number of serious allegations against Derby and his wife – kleptomania, rape, alcoholism, adultery, treason – the greater the likelihood that he was the victim of a campaign of vilification.

Index

ABEL, Sir F.A. (1827–1902), chemist, 565n

Abercorn, 1st Duke of (1811–85), 853, 888n.

Abercromby, Lady, *née* Duncan, Lady Julia, 381n, 526, 859, 861

Aberdare, Henry Austin Bruce, 1st Lord (1815–95), 410, 439n, 661, 681n, 743

Aberdeen, Lord, premier, 533

Academy Dinner (1879), 133

Acton, Lord (1834–1902), 73n, 835

Adair, Sir Robert, *see* Waveney, Lord

Adam, W.P., Liberal whip, (1823–81), 199n.

Adams, Sir Francis (1826–89) diplomatist, 181, 198n.

Adderley, C.B., 1st Baron Norton (1814–1905), 68n., 238, 242, 681n., 777

Afghan affairs, Derby's speech on (1878), 63

Afghan War of 1841, 193

Afghan War (1878–), 39, 41, 43–4, 51, 58, 60, 191–3, 211; defeat near Kandahar (Maiwand), 259; sortie from Kandahar fails, 265; our forces besieged there, 266; ultimate British victory, Sept. 1880, 268

Afghanistan, alleged Russian proposals for partition of (1876), 306

Africa, 488, 513, 541, 549, 593, 605, 613, 671, 743, 761

Agricultural depression 121, 125, 130, 132, 141, 149, 169, 171, 173, 182, 187, 395, 399, 775

Ailesbury, 4th Marquess of (1863–93), 854, 889n.

Airlie, Lady, 360, 385

Airlie, Lord, 360, 744

Aitchison, Sir C.V. (1832–96), Indian official, 381n.

Albany, 1st Duke of, see Leopold, Prince

Albany, 2nd Duke of (succ. posthumously 19 July 1884), 680n.

Alcester, F. Paget, 1st Baron (1821–95), 'Swell of the Ocean', 566n., 639

'Abd Al–Hamid II (1842–1918), sultan, 156n.

Alcock, Sir R. (1809–97), diplomatist, 563n.

Alexander II murdered, 312

Alexander, Prince of Orange (1851–84), 197n.

Alexander, Mr, owner of Holwood (d. Aug. 1882), 455

Alexandretta, 63, 78n.

Alice, Princess (1843–78), 63, 92n.

Alfonso XII of Spain (king 1875–85), 592, 738

Alison, Sir A. (1826–1907), 796n.

Amlas Bay (Cameroons), 762

Ampthill, Lord (1829–84), 85n.

Amsinck, local historian, 188, 198n.

Andrassy, Count (1823–90), Austrian foreign minister, 55, 89n., 188

Anglo–Russian agreement published in *Globe*, 80n.

Anglo–Turkish convention (1878), 80n.

Angra Pequena, 660, 669, 671–2, 680n., 683, 699, 700, 708, 727

Antrobus, (Sir) R.L. (1853–1942), 562n.

Arabian Nights, indecent nature of, 891n.

Arch, Joseph (1826–1919), trade union leader, 85n., 831

Archer, Thomas (1823–1905), Queensland pioneer, 565n.

Argyll, 8th Duke of (1823–1900), 91n., 138, 185, 210–11, 214, 231, 256, 297, 306–7, 324, 328, 330, 350, 410, 443 533, 643, 685, 751, 817, 833

Armenia, 151

Army, 98

Arnold, A. (1833–1902), pseud., 465, 490n., 526, 565n.

Arnold, Matthew, poet, 365–6, 465, 856

Arnold–Forster, H.O. (1855–1909), 441n.

Arran, 5th Earl of (1839–1901), 715, 734n.

Artisans Dwellings Act (1875), 158n.

Artisans Dwellings Act (1885), 813

Ashantee, 303

Ashbourne, Edward Gibson, 1st Baron (1837–1913), 565n., 822

Ashburnham purchase, 548, 559

Ashburton, Lady, patroness of Carlyle, 472

Ashley, Hon. Evelyn (1836–1907), colonial junior minister, 562n., 679n.

Ashmead–Bartlett, (Sir) Ellis (1849–1902), 645, 679n.

Asquith, H.H., premier, 840

Aspden, author, 400, 438n.

Aspinall, C., coroner of Liverpool, 64, 92n.

Auckland, 4th Baron (1829–90), 645, 679n.

Australian Federal Council Bill, 768, 777, 780

Australian imperialism, 561, 611–2, 721

Australian tariffs, 227

Australian volunteers, 759

Aylesford, 7th Earl of (1849–85), 851, 888n.

Ayrton, A.S., radical (1816–86), 437n.